THE GLORY AND THE DREAM

A Narrative History
of America

1932-1972

BOOKS BY WILLIAM MANCHESTER

HISTORY

THE DEATH OF A PRESIDENT
November 20–November 25, 1963

THE ARMS OF KRUPP 1587–1968

THE GLORY AND THE DREAM
A Narrative History of America, 1932–1972

BIOGRAPHY

DISTURBER OF THE PEACE
The Life of H. L. Mencken

A ROCKEFELLER FAMILY PORTRAIT
From John D. to Nelson

PORTRAIT OF A PRESIDENT
John F. Kennedy in Profile

FICTION

THE CITY OF ANGER

SHADOW OF THE MONSOON

THE LONG GAINER

DIVERSION

BEARD THE LION

# WILLIAM MANCHESTER

THE GLORY AND THE DREAM

A Narrative History
of America

1932–1972

VOLUME ONE

LITTLE, BROWN AND COMPANY
BOSTON — TORONTO

COPYRIGHT © 1973, 1974 BY WILLIAM MANCHESTER

ALL RIGHTS RESERVED. NO PART OF THIS BOOK MAY BE REPRODUCED IN ANY FORM OR BY ANY ELECTRONIC OR MECHANICAL MEANS INCLUDING INFORMATION STORAGE AND RETRIEVAL SYSTEMS WITHOUT PERMISSION IN WRITING FROM THE PUBLISHER, EXCEPT BY A REVIEWER WHO MAY QUOTE BRIEF PASSAGES IN A REVIEW.

Acknowledgments of permission to reprint excerpted material appear on pages 1641–1644.

Portions of this book were first published in slightly altered form in the *New York Times Magazine* and *New York* magazine.

Published simultaneously in Canada by Little, Brown & Company (Canada) Limited

PRINTED IN THE UNITED STATES OF AMERICA

To
Laurie Manchester
and to
her future

Whither is fled the visionary gleam?
Where is it now, the glory and the dream?
—WORDSWORTH

Contents

PROLOGUE: Rock Bottom ... 1

VOLUME ONE

PART I
Rendezvous with Destiny
1932–1941

1 The Cruelest Year ... 35
   Depression Montage ... 83
2 Roosevelt! ... 84
   Portrait of an American: ELEANOR ... 109
3 Stirrings ... 112
   Mid-Thirties Montage ... 148
4 The Roosevelt Referendum ... 149
   Portrait of an American: STOCKBROKER RICHARD WHITNEY ... 175

5	The Conservative Phoenix	179
	Late Thirties Montage	208
6	A Shadow of Primitive Terror	209
	Portrait of an American: NORMAN THOMAS	250
7	Through the Night with a Light from Above	254
	Montage: The Last of Prewar America	288
8	America on the Brink	289

PART II
Sacrifice and Transformation
1941-1950

9	Counterattack	321
	Pacific Montage	352
10	The Home Front	353
	Home Front Montage	401
11	Lilacs in the Dooryard	402
	ETO Montage	444
12	A New World, Under a New Sun	445
	Portrait of an American: THE REDHEAD	475
13	The Fraying Flags of Triumph	480
	Postwar Montage	510
14	Life with Harry	511
15	A Little Touch of Harry in the Night	530
	Late Forties Montage	578
16	The Age of Suspicion	579
	Portrait of an American: EDWARD ROSCOE MURROW	628
17	Into the Abyss	633
	Early Fifties Montage	675

PART III
Sowing the Wind
1951-1960

18	A House Divided	679
19	Right Turn	733
	Montage: The Early Eisenhower Years	785
20	What Was Good for General Motors	786
	Portrait of an American: NORMA JEAN BAKER	841

VOLUME TWO

21	Mr. Chairman, Mr. Chairman	847
	Montage: The Mid-Fifties	894
22	With All Deliberate Speed	895
23	The Pursuit of Happiness	945
	Montage: Eisenhower at Flood Tide	962
24	Beep Beep	963
	Portrait of an American: THE EDSEL	997
25	The Crusade Falters	1001
	Late Fifties Montage	1035
26	Tattoo for the General	1036

PART IV
Reaping the Whirlwind
1961-1968

27	A New Generation of Americans	1089
	Montage: The Early Sixties	1132
28	Now the Trumpet Summoned Us Again	1133
	Portrait of an American: PETER CARL GOLDMARK	1190

29	Don't Let It Be Forgot	1195
	Montage: JFK/LBJ	1236
30	The Long Arm	1237
31	A Dream of Greatness—and Disenchantment	1275
	Montage: The Johnson Years	1326
32	Up Against the Wall	1327
	Portrait of an American: KARL HESS III	1370
33	The Year Everything Went Wrong	1375
	Montage: The Late Sixties	1411

PART V
Nixon, After All
1969-1972

34	The Rise of the Silent Majority	1415
	Portrait of an American: BENJAMIN MCLANE SPOCK, M.D.	1454
35	Nattering Nabobs	1458
	Early Seventies Montage	1498
36	The Divided States of America	1499
	Portrait of an American: RALPH NADER	1538
37	Pride Goeth	1542
	EPILOGUE: Echoes	1589
	Acknowledgments	1595
	Chapter Notes	1597
	Bibliography	1631
	Copyright Acknowledgments	1641
	Index	1645

THE GLORY AND THE DREAM

A Narrative History
of America

1932-1972

Prologue

ROCK BOTTOM

IN THE DESPERATE SUMMER of 1932, Washington, D.C., resembled the besieged capital of an obscure European state. Since May some twenty-five thousand penniless World War veterans had been encamped with their wives and children in District parks, dumps, abandoned warehouses, and empty stores. The men drilled, sang war songs, and once, led by a Medal of Honor winner and watched by a hundred thousand silent Washingtonians, they marched up Pennsylvania Avenue bearing American flags of faded cotton. Most of the time, however, they waited and brooded. The vets had come to ask their government for relief from the Great Depression, then approaching the end of its third year; specifically, they wanted immediate payment of the soldiers' "bonus" authorized by the Adjusted Compensation Act of 1924 but not due until 1945. If they could get cash now, the men would receive about $500 each. Headline writers had christened them "the Bonus Army," "the bonus marchers." They called themselves the Bonus Expeditionary Force.

BEF members had hoped in vain for congressional action. Now they appealed to President Hoover, begging him to receive a delegation of their leaders. Instead he sent word that he was too busy and then proceeded to isolate himself from the city. Presidential plans to visit the Senate were canceled; policemen patrolled the White House grounds day and night. For the first time since the Armistice, the Executive Mansion gates were chained shut. HOOVER LOCKS SELF IN WHITE HOUSE, read a *New York Daily News* headline. He went even further. Barricades were erected; traffic was shut down for a distance of one block on all sides of the Mansion. A one-armed veteran, bent upon picketing, tried to penetrate the screen of guards. He was soundly beaten and carried off to jail.

In retrospect this panoply appears to have been the overreaction of a frightened, frustrated administration. The bonus marchers were unarmed, had expelled radicals from their ranks, and—despite their evident hunger—weren't even panhandling openly. They seemed too weak to be a menace. Drew Pearson, a thirty-four-year-old *Baltimore Sun* reporter, described them as "ragged, weary, and apathetic," with "no hope on their faces." Increasingly, the BEF vigil had become an exercise in endurance. A health department inspector described the camps' sanitary conditions as "extremely bad." Makeshift commissaries depended largely upon charity. Truckloads of food arrived from friends in Des Moines and Camden, New Jersey; a hundred loaves of bread were being shipped each day from one sympathetic baker; a thousand pies came from another; the Veterans of Foreign Wars sent $500, and the bonus marchers raised another $2,500 by staging boxing bouts among themselves in Griffith Stadium. It was all very haphazard. The administration was doing virtually nothing—Washington police had aroused Hoover's wrath by feeding the District's uninvited guests bread, coffee, and stew at six cents a day—and by mid-August brutal temperatures were approaching their annual height, diminishing water reserves and multiplying misery.

In those years Washington was officially classified by the British Foreign Office as a "sub-tropical climate." Diplomats loathed its wilting heat and dense humidity; with the exception of a few downtown theaters which advertised themselves as "refrigerated," there was no air-conditioning. In summer the capital was a city of awnings, screened porches, ice wagons, summer furniture and summer rugs, and in the words of an official guidebook it was also "a peculiarly interesting place for the study of insects." Lacking shade or screens, the BEF was exposed to the full fury of the season. When the vets' vanguard had entered the District, gardens were flowering in their springtime glory. By July the blossoms of magnolia and azalea were long gone, and the cherry trees were bare. Even the earth, it seemed, was pitiless. The vets had taken on the appearance of desert creatures; downtown merchants complained that "the sight of so many down-at-the-heel men has a depressing effect on business." That, really, was the true extent of their threat to the country.

But if the BEF danger was illusion, Washington's obscurity on the international scene in that era, and its dependency upon Europe, were more substantive. Among the sixty-five independent countries then in the world, there was but one superpower: Great Britain. The Union Jack flew serenely over one-fourth of the earth's arable surface—in Europe, Asia, and Africa; North, Central, and South America; Australia, Oceania, and the West Indies. The sun literally never sank upon it. Britain's Empire commanded the allegiance of 485 million people, and if you wanted to suggest stability you said "solid as the Rock of Gibraltar," or "safe as the Bank of England," which with the pound sterling at $4.86 seemed the ultimate in fiscal security. Air power was the dream of a few little-known pilots and a cashiered American general named Mitchell; what counted then was ships, and virtually no significant world waterway was free of London's dominion. Gibraltar, Suez, the Gulf of Aden, the Strait of Singapore, and the Cape of Good Hope were controlled directly by the Admiralty. The Strait of Magellan was at the mercy of the British naval station in the Falkland Islands, and even the Panama Canal lay under the watchful eye of H.M.'s Caribbean squadron. As a consequence of all this, the United States was shielded by the Royal Navy as surely as any crown colony. Lloyd's of London offered 500-to-1 against any invasion of the U.S. And when *Fortune* assured its readers that the Atlantic and Pacific were "still a protection and will forever remain so, no matter how fast ships may sail or airplanes may fly," the magazine was assuming that the British fleet, which had ruled the waves throughout American history, would go right on ruling them.

Washington made the same assumption; the country lacked the status, the pretensions, and most of the apparatus of a great power. The capital was a slumbering village in summer, largely forgotten the rest of the year. In size it ranked fourteenth among American cities. Most big national problems were decided in New York, where the money was; when federal action was required, Manhattan's big corporation lawyers—men like Charles Evans Hughes, Henry L. Stimson, and Elihu Root—came down to guide their Republican protégés. President Coolidge had usually finished his official day by lunchtime. Hoover created a stir by becoming the first Chief Executive to have a telephone on his desk. He also employed five secretaries—no previous President had required more than one—and summoned them by an elaborate buzzer system.

Foggy Bottom, the site of the present State Department Building, was a Negro slum. The land now occupied by the Pentagon was an agricultural experimental station and thus typical of Washington's outskirts; "large areas close to the very heart of the nation's lawmaking," the *Saturday Evening Post* observed, "are still in farm hands." The government employed fewer than two thousand foreign service officers. It is an astonishing fact that the Secretaries of State, War, and Navy were all under one mansard roof, across the street from the White House in that ugly, smug mass of balusters, cupolas, and pillared porticoes known today as the Executive Office Building. Indeed, after a fire gutted the President's oval office in 1929, he and his staff had moved in with them and no one had felt crowded. There was little pomp. The East Wing of the White House, which would later house military attachés and social secretaries, hadn't been built. The Secret Service had not yet closed West Executive Avenue to the public; it was just another city street, and on a normal day you could park there within an easy stone's throw of the oval office. If you called on the Secretary of State, he sometimes met you at the door. Army Chief of Staff Douglas MacArthur, on the same floor of the Executive Office Building, was separated from his sole aide by a single slatted door. When the general wanted help he called "Major Eisenhower," and Ike came scurrying.

It was a *Fortune* writer, fortunately anonymous, who described the general as "shy and genuinely unsympathetic to publicity." That was nonsense. MacArthur, even then, spoke of himself in the third person, flourished a long cigarette holder as he talked, and had heightened his image by installing a fifteen-foot-high mahogany mirror behind him. As Eisenhower later recalled, when MacArthur felt slighted he was capable of expressing himself in "an explosive denunciation of politics, bad manners, bad judgment, broken promises, arrogance, unconstitutionality, insensitivity, and the way the world had gone to hell." He can hardly be blamed. Those were dog days for professional soldiers. Up through the rank of colonel, promotion was by seniority only, and by the early Thirties it took twenty-two years to climb from captain to major. There wasn't much to do except watch the calendar. Sheer boredom nearly drove Eisenhower to the point of resigning his commission, and it was in these years that he developed the habit of reading Street & Smith pulps: *Two-Gun Western, Western Story, Thrilling Western,* and *Cowboy Short Stories.* Across the Potomac at Fort Myer, George S.

Patton Jr.—who had been a major since 1919—could be observed playing polo Wednesdays and Saturdays at 4 P.M. Riding his own horses he had collected four hundred ribbons and two hundred cups; already known for his pearl-handled revolvers, he also pursued steeplechasing, fox hunting, skeet shooting, and flying. But Major Patton, unlike Major Eisenhower, was rich.

Perhaps nothing is more illustrative of American provincialism four decades ago than a brief glance at the military establishment; it requires no more. The U.S. had the sixteenth largest army in the world, putting it behind, among others, Czechoslovakia, Turkey, Spain, Romania, and Poland. When every $17.85-a-month private had suited up, there were 132,069 Americans in uniform. On paper they could have put up a stiff fight against Yugoslavia (138,934), but in reality they would have been torn to pieces, because most of MacArthur's men were committed to desk work, patrolling the Mexican border, and protecting U.S. possessions overseas. The chief of staff was left with 30,000 troops—fewer than the force King George sent to tame his rebellious American colonies in 1776.

Moreover, the quality of the Army was appalling. It cost roughly a quarter of one percent of today's military juggernaut, and looked it. *Fortune* called it the "worst equipped" of the world's armed forces; no one disputed the judgment. In a crisis MacArthur could have fielded 1,000 tanks, all obsolete; 1,509 aircraft, the fastest of which could fly 234 mph; and a single mechanized regiment, which had been organized at Fort Knox that spring, and which was led by cavalrymen on horses which wore mustard-gas-proof boots. The United States Army, one writer reported, "forever walks the wide land in the image of a gaping-mouthed private with an ill-fitting uniform carrying an obsolete rifle at an ungraceful angle."

MacArthur was the only four-star general in the country—and there were no three-star generals. As chief of staff he received $10,400 a year, a home at Fort Myer, and the exclusive use of the Army's only limousine. To his aide he seemed to occupy a distant pinnacle. Major Eisenhower's annual salary was $3,000. Because he doubled as the military's congressional lobbyist, he frequently went up to Capitol Hill. But his employer never loaned him the limousine. Nor was the major given taxi fare; in all of official Washington, there was no such thing as a petty cash fund. Instead, as he liked to recall in later life, Eisenhower would walk down the hall and fill out a form, in exchange for which he received two streetcar tokens. Then he would stand outside on Pennsylvania Avenue and wait for a Mt. Pleasant trolley car.

It wasn't a long wait. Washington was laced with trolley tracks; there were nearly seven hundred streetcars in service. Except in winter, when they were vulnerable to short-circuits, the cars were efficient, and traffic jams lay a generation away. If you drove to work (observing the 22 mph speed limit), you parked in front of your office. There was almost always room at the curb. There was also an extraordinary variety among the square-shouldered Packards, Studebakers, Grahams, Pierce Arrows, Terraplanes, and Stutzes, for the automobile business, by later corporate standards, was practically a cottage industry.

Men of all classes, including civil servants, worked Saturday mornings. In summer they wore a seasonal wardrobe: white linen ("Palm Beach") or cotton suits; straw boaters or Panama hats; shirts with "soft" collars; and light underwear, which was restricted to the warm months because central heating was recent and far from universal. The District's five daily papers were crowded with news of social unrest in 1932, but none of it was about Negroes. Although 26 percent of Washington was black (the highest ratio in any American city), Negroes accepted their appalling lot with remarkable unanimity. "Dark-skinned children of the South," a government guide explained, were confined to domestic service and "manual work." Department stores, movies, and government cafeterias were closed to them. Black workmen digging the foundations of the new Justice Department building on Pennsylvania Avenue either brought their lunches or went hungry; even if they wanted a glass of water they had to walk two miles out Seventh Street to find a restaurant which would serve them. The president of Howard University, the Negro college, was a white man. When President Hoover sent Gold Star mothers to France, black mothers were assigned to a second (and second-class) ship. And the most popular radio program in the country, *Amos 'n' Andy*, was a nightly racial slur, with its Negro parts played by two white men affecting minstrel show accents ("I'se regusted"; "Dat's de propolition").

Blacks occupied Foggy Bottom, southwest Washington, and all of Georgetown, which had not yet been discovered by lovers of the quaint, possibly because the rest of the city was so picturesque. The District was greener then; there were six shade trees for every inhabitant. The most exotic neighborhoods were Kalorama Heights and upper Massachusetts Avenue. As every Jew knew, the lovely mansions there were "restricted," but anti-Semitism was no more unfashionable than white racism; it didn't even trouble the diplomatic community, since there was no such nation as Israel. Embassy Row, now on Massachusetts Avenue, was then on Sixteenth Street, within walking distance of the White House, and the ambassadors wore striped pants and frock coats. They had to step carefully if they roamed the downtown area, for much of it was cobblestone. Supermarkets were still a California phenomenon; District food shopping was done in small groceries, in red-fronted outlets of the Great Atlantic & Pacific Tea Company, in open markets, or on pavements. Organ grinders and pushcart peddlers could be heard in the streets, together with the shouts of men wheeling grindstones and inviting housewives to bring them scissors and knives for sharpening. Downtown, flower and fruit stands provided vivid splashes of color on street corners. Oyster markets flourished down by the wharves. The Washington District Market was on Pennsylvania Avenue where the National Archives now stands. The Farmers Market was on K Street—a swarming spectacular celebrated for the cries of its fish hawkers and racks of dead rabbits. There was even a saddlery with a life-size wooden horse in front; there were still several thousand workhorses in the District in 1932. The K Street cobbles were dotted with their mementos, the scent of which, mingled with fragrances from the great markets and the corner stands, would soon vanish in deference to the great god macadam.

Even during the Depression Washington was visited by swarms of tourists, but they did not land at Washington National Airport, through which would pass in 1970 a total of 24,000 passengers a day. Those frantic acres then lay silent under the waters of the Potomac. Air travel was rare. The labor market being what it was, airlines could require that every stewardess be a registered nurse, but passenger planes, usually trimotor Fords, never flew at night or in bad weather. There were no coast-to-coast flights. The average airliner speed was 155 mph. By changing planes, one man crossed the country in eighteen hours; his picture was in all the papers. Although Washington had a field—Hoover Airport, on the Virginia side of what is now the Fourteenth Street Bridge (then called Highway Bridge)—it was used by only 250 passengers a day. The vast majority of travelers, eleven million of them each year, arrived at

Union Station. The glorious reign of the steam engine was at the height of its Indian summer. There were 20,000 locomotives snuffling across the countryside (as compared to fewer than 300 in 1970), and the long, plaintive wail of the steam whistle stirred restless young men all over America. Fifteen-year-old John F. Kennedy heard it at the Choate School in Wallingford, Connecticut; Lyndon Johnson, then a teacher of public speaking, heard it in Houston; and in Whittier, California, a college student named Richard M. Nixon listened in the night, wondering what lay across the eastern horizon and what Washington, D.C., was like.

What did those who came see? To begin with, they looked at the train station. Union Station had become the first mass of masonry erected under the plan for a metropolis of classical buildings, and its imperial facade together with the Capitol dominated the city. The Capitol itself stood much as it does now, facing eastward, a tribute to one architect's belief in which direction the city would grow. Because the long expansion of presidential power had not begun, Congress was Washington's focal point, and tourists, like the BEF, made the Hill their first stop. For some it was also the last; the White House discouraged visitors, and there weren't many other attractions. There were the Lincoln Memorial and the Washington Monument, with its new elevator (though youngsters still felt challenged by the 898 steps up). The Botanical Gardens were open; so was the Folger Shakespeare Library. The Smithsonian Institution was popular in these months after the successful landing of Juan de la Cierva's Autogiro, a prototype of the helicopter, on the museum's lawn. If you liked drawbridges, there was the Arlington Memorial Bridge, which had been dedicated by President Hoover in January. Finally, there were a few—a very few—government office buildings: the Department of Agriculture on C Street, the old Interior Building on Eighteenth Street, the Civil Service Building on Seventh Street, and, bordering the Ellipse, the titanic Commerce Department Building, all of it under an eight-acre roof, erected in the 1920s by Secretary of Commerce Hoover as a shrine to American business.

What is most striking about 1932 Washington is the absence of so many landmarks which have since become familiar. There was no Jefferson Memorial, no Marine Corps Memorial, and no Supreme Court Building; the judges sat in the Capitol between the Senate and the House, almost directly under the Rotunda. The Tomb of the Unknown Soldier and the Washington Cathedral were under construction, the Shrine of the Immaculate Conception in the planning stage. Constitution Avenue, as we know it, did not exist. It was merely an extension of B Street. The long, clear mall could be found only in blueprints; the ground that summer was just another Washington Park, thick with trees, crisscrossed by streets, and marred here and there by temporary World War buildings which had never been removed. Except for the Commerce Building, the Federal Triangle was unbuilt. Secretary Andrew Mellon and Senator Reed Smoot were especially interested, the *National Geographic* reported, in a four-billion-dollar program to line "the entire south side of Pennsylvania Avenue" with "monumental structures," and in September Hoover was scheduled to lay the cornerstone for a new Post Office Building. Meanwhile that great edifice and its neighbors—the Department of Labor, Interstate Commerce Commission, Department of Justice, National Archives, Federal Trade Commission, and National Gallery of Art—awaited the future. There were no FBI tours, no viewing of the Constitution and the Declaration of Independence. Until recently, most of the land had been in commercial use. Some of it still was, but here and there land had been broken, and some buildings to which the Treasury Department had taken title were scheduled for razing.

Of these, the most interesting were on a Pennsylvania Avenue tract now occupied by the National Gallery, the Federal Trade Commission, and the District tennis courts. There, on the morning of July 28, 1932, stood a row of ugly old red brick buildings which had once contained warehouses, a cheap hotel, automobile show rooms, a Chinese restaurant, and an undertaking parlor. Many of the walls had been knocked out, and the buildings would have been leveled weeks ago, but on the night of June 17 members of the Bonus Expeditionary Force had quietly occupied them. The District police superintendent, a retired brigadier named Pelham D. Glassford, was reluctant to deprive the veterans of shelter, especially since so many were accompanied by their wives and children. By midsummer, however, Glassford was under a cloud; Congress had rebuked him for allowing the vets to enter the city, and the White House let it be known that Hoover had reached the end of his patience. The President was determined to evict the ragged squatters even if he had to call out the Army—which, as things turned out, is exactly what he did.

That Pennsylvania Avenue camp was not BEF headquarters. The veterans' main force lay on the far side of the Anacostia River in southeast Washington, just across the Eleventh Street Bridge. But the Pennsylvania Avenue vets, living within three blocks of the Capitol, were the most conspicuous. To the administration they were an eyesore and a humiliation, and its determination to exorcise them reflected a general hardening throughout the land of the attitude of the well-fed toward the ill-fed. This was not true of those who moved among them. General Glassford liked them; so did General Billy Mitchell and Marine Corps General Smedley Butler, twice winner of the Medal of Honor. Drew Pearson wrote that the men "did not know what it was all about. They had no work, they were hungry, their families were hungry, they wanted to be paid. That was all they knew." Will Rogers said the BEF held "the record for being the best behaved" of any "hungry men assembled anywhere in the world."

But in the days before television newscasts it was possible to deny the obvious. Attorney General William D. Mitchell declared that the Bonus Army had been guilty of "begging and other acts." Vice President Charles Curtis had called out two companies of marines; bristling with fixed bayonets and steel helmets, they arrived on the faithful trolley cars, whereupon Glassford, pointing out that the Vice President of the United States lacks any authority over troops, ordered them back to barracks. Still, the appeal of force grew, here and elsewhere in the country. On March 7 three thousand hungry men and women had tried to demonstrate outside Henry Ford's plant in Dearborn, Michigan. The police had fired into their ranks, killing four and wounding a hundred others—who were then handcuffed to their hospital beds, charged with rioting. "Responsibility is not hard to fix," the *Detroit Free Press* thundered. "The inciters were William Z. Foster and the other Red agitators." Now other newspapers were egging on the President. The *Washington Evening Star* wondered editorially why no District policeman had "put into a healthy sock on the nose of a bonus marcher all the strength of healthy emotions," and the *New York Times* reported that the marchers were veterans who were "not content with their pensions, although seven or eight times those of other countries." Except for the disabled, there were no pensions at all, but sound men were beginning to make even more peculiar statements. One of Major Eisenhower's friends was Brigadier General George Moseley, whom

Eisenhower later described as "a brilliant" and "dynamic" officer "always delving into new ideas." Among Moseley's new ideas that summer was a proposal to arrest the bonus marchers and others "of inferior blood," and then put them in concentration camps on "one of the sparsely inhabited islands of the Hawaiian group not suitable for growing sugar." There, he suggested, "they could stew in their own filth." He added darkly, "We would not worry about the delays in the process of law in the settlement of their individual cases."

Night and fog didn't worry the Pennsylvania Avenue vets; MacArthur had promised one of their leaders that if dispossession became necessary, he would permit them to retire with dignity, and as good soldiers they accepted the word of a four-star general. Reports had reached them that the Army might be on its way; they thought it a good rumor, thought that if men in khaki appeared they would fall into one another's arms. In their camp faded flags hung everywhere, and to them it was inconceivable that doughboys would attack the colors. Their greatest concern on that morning of Thursday, July 28, was the weather. By 9 A.M. they knew they were in for a day of extraordinary discomfort, and they talked wistfully of the new refrigerated theaters, whose current talkies featured Janet Gaynor and Charles Farrell in *The First Year*, William Powell and Kay Francis in *Jewel Robbery*, and Jackie Cooper and Chic Sale in *When a Feller Needs a Friend*. Compared to their present quarters, the thought of air-conditioning was an idyllic dream. Railroads had shipped them here free, to clear the yards; one bill of lading had read, "Livestock—Destination: Washington D.C.—55 vets," and they had almost begun to think of themselves as livestock. The partially demolished buildings were largely reserved for women and young children, for whom straw mattresses had been provided by General Glassford. The men lay in what one reporter called a "conglomeration of tented huts made of tattered cloth fixed up on old boards with packing boxes serving as props." Here and there handmade signs read, "God Bless Our Home." They weren't meant to be witty. Men with their backgrounds didn't joke about God, home, or, if it came to that, about patriotism.

They were from the American yeomanry; if the term had been in use then, they would have been called members of the lower middle class. Five who would be in the direct line of any attack across Pennsylvania Avenue were typical. Only one, J. A. Bingham of Harlan County, Kentucky, had been an officer in the American

Expeditionary Force to France, and Bingham could hardly have been thought a member of the leisure class; his most recent employment had been as a strikebreaker, making life uncomfortable for Theodore Dreiser, Sherwood Anderson, John Dos Passos, and the crusade of Ivy League students who had come to Kentucky last March to protest violations of miners' civil rights. John Olson of Sacramento, and Charles P. Ruby, whose DSC had led to his selection as the first man to wish the President Happy New Year in 1931, had both been decorated for bravery in France. Eric Carlson of Oakland had been gassed and, as they said then, "shell-shocked." William Hrushka, whose life was to become a subject of considerable interest, had served as a private first class in the 41st Infantry. All were unemployed. Hrushka, a butcher, had been living in his brother-in-law's windowless basement flat on Chicago's southwest side.

Disaster wears many masks, and for these men, at 10 A.M. that oppressive morning, it was represented by two Treasury Department agents, who stood perspiring on the sidewalk and told them to leave. The veterans declined; the agents vanished. An hour passed and nothing happened except the relentless rise of the temperature. Then, shortly after eleven o'clock, General Glassford arrived on his blue motorcycle, drew up at Third and Pennsylvania, and announced that he had orders to clear the area. His men moved in, nightsticks at the ready.

It was a slow business, but there was little resistance at first, and by noon the first building was cleared. Meantime, however, word of what was happening had reached the main camp on Anacostia Flats. Belatedly, and rather desperately, the police tried to raise the Eleventh Street Bridge. It was too late; BEF reinforcements were on the way; arriving, they hurled brick fragments at the policemen there. Glassford himself was struck on the side of his face, and as he staggered backward he was horrified to see one of his own men, also dazed, pointing a pistol at him. The superintendent jumped behind a pillar. He heard a hoarse voice shout, "Let's get him!" Reappearing, Glassford saw a policeman who, in his words, had "gone wild-eyed" and was firing at a veteran. The vet—Hrushka—fell dead, a bullet in his heart. Other officers were also firing; in a moment three more vets fell, one—Carlson—mortally wounded. Glassford shouted, "Stop the shooting!" They did, but word of the incident was on its way to the White House. Attorney General Mitchell had already ordered the evacuation of all veterans from government property. Hoover learned of the shooting at lunch. After an interval, while everything was put into writing, the President told Secretary of War Patrick J. Hurley to use troops, and Hurley passed the word to the chief of staff.

Now came another, embarrassing lull. The chief wasn't in uniform. His aide didn't think he should be. "This is political, political," Eisenhower said again and again, arguing that it was highly inappropriate for a general to become involved in a street-corner brawl. The general disagreed. "MacArthur has decided to go into active command in the field," MacArthur declared. "There is incipient revolution in the air." So the soldiers, who were arriving from Fort Myer, milled around on the Ellipse, watched by Hoover from his oval office while an orderly dashed across the river to fetch the chief's tunic, service stripes, sharpshooter medal, and English whipcord breeches. The general also ordered Eisenhower into uniform. "We're going to break the back of the BEF," he said, and led his staff to the limousine. At Sixth and Pennsylvania (which later became the site of Washington's largest cut-rate liquor store) the car pulled over and began still another wait. "What's holding us up?" someone asked. "The tanks," MacArthur replied. He was going to use tanks. Everyone sat back and sweated—everyone, that is, except MacArthur. This is the first recorded instance of the general's remarkable inability to perspire. He remained cool, poised, and starched. It gave him an immense psychological advantage, and there were those who bitterly resented it.

Meanwhile the White House was issuing communiqués. President Hoover announced that the troops would "put an end to rioting and defiance of civil authority." A few minutes later the White House revealed that the men who had clashed with the police were "entirely of the Communist element." Reporters, finding MacArthur in his car, asked him what he was going to do. "Watch me," he replied. "Just watch me." Instead they were watching the astonishing display of force which was arriving, at last, down Pennsylvania Avenue. Troopers of the 3rd Cavalry, led by Major Patton, pranced along brandishing naked sabers. Behind the horses marched a machine gun detachment and men from the 12th Infantry, the 13th Engineers, and the 34th Infantry, the sun glinting on their bayonets. Behind these units rolled the six tanks, the caterpillar treads methodically chewing up the soft asphalt. It was now 4:45 P.M. The operation had become the worst-timed in MacArthur's career. Fifteen minutes earlier, the District's civil service workers had begun pouring into the streets, their day's work done; twenty thousand of them were massed on the sidewalks across from the bewildered, disorganized veterans. Someone was going to get hurt if the cavalry commander didn't watch out, and Major Patton was not celebrated for his solicitude toward civilians.

The veterans, assuming that this display was a dress parade for their benefit, applauded. The spectators clapped, too, though they were the first to be disillusioned. Abruptly Patton's troopers wheeled and charged into the crowd. "At first," wrote J. F. Essary, veteran Washington bureau chief of the *Baltimore Sun*, "it seemed that this attack upon the civilian observers was merely the act of a few of the armed horsemen. But later it appeared that it was a part of a concerted movement by the cavalry officers." Essary reported that the troopers charged "without the slightest warning" into "thousands of unoffending people"; that men and women were "ridden down indiscriminately"; and that one man who refused to move from the front of a telegraph office was beaten back into the doorway by two cavalrymen who flailed him with the flat side of their blades. Among those trampled was Senator Hiram Bingham of Connecticut—Panama hat, Palm Beach suit, and all.

"Clear out!" the mounted men yelled, and the spectators shouted back, "Shame! Shame!" The veterans, meanwhile, had hurriedly formed a solid line across the street. Their leaders were waving flags at rallying points, and it was these colors which became the troopers' second objective. Re-forming in extended order, they bounded across Pennsylvania Avenue, converging on the faded standards. The vets were stunned, then furious. Some dared the soldiers to dismount and fight. "Jesus!" cried a graying man—"If we only had guns!"; and others demanded of cavalrymen, "Where were you in the Argonne, buddy?" By now all the bonus marchers were hooting and booing. One soldier in his late teens wrested a banner from the hands of a former AEF sergeant. "You crummy old bum!" the boy spat. A man near MacArthur called out, "The American flag means nothing to me after this." The general snapped, "Put that man under arrest if he opens his mouth again."

MacArthur's written instructions from the Secretary of War specified that "any women and children who may be in the affected area" must be "accorded every consideration and kindness." Given the chief of staff's plan, it is hard to see how such distinctions could have been drawn. In anticipation of this assignment, he had requisitioned three thousand gas grenades from the Aberdeen Proving Ground and Edgewood Arsenal, and gas could not discriminate between sexes and ages. The only participants with real protection would be the general's troops, who were now donning masks. Policemen tied handkerchiefs over their faces, storekeepers who had been warned slammed their doors and transoms, and those veterans who saw the masks spread the alarm, for they knew what was coming. But there wasn't time to do much. The infantry came running on the heels of the horsemen, pulling the blue tear gas bombs from their belts and throwing them ahead. Suddenly the air was sharply tainted; the spectators broke and fled. A sickly-sweet haze hung over Pennsylvania Avenue, and beneath it the BEF women, blinded and choking, stumbled from the occupied buildings clutching pots, pans, and children. "It was like a scene out of the 1918 no-man's land," reported the Associated Press. It wasn't quite. Washington was the capital of a nation at peace. The uneven struggle was being waged in the very shadow of Congress. Most of those present were noncombatants, and some were professionally neutral, though armed authority regarded newspapermen with suspicion. One reporter darted into a phone booth outside a filling station to call his office; a soldier tossed a bomb inside and drove him out.

Resistance vanished. Driven by sabers, bayonets, and a rising wind—which blew the vile gas southward—the stricken BEF retreated toward the Anacostia River. It was a clumsy withdrawal. The women were carrying infants and their husbands shabby suitcases, and the retirement was harried by the puffs of fresh gas bombs. Gallinger Hospital was beginning to fill up with casualties. The evening noises were frightening: ambulance sirens, fire engines, galloping horses, tramping soldiers, newsboys hawking extras, and the clanking of the tanks, whose role was, and would continue to be, quite vague; "so far as I can recall," Eisenhower wrote toward the end of his life, "they took no part whatever in the movements to evacuate the veterans," although there was plenty of time for them, because the retirement "proceeded slowly." Nevertheless, by 9 P.M. the refugees had crossed the Eleventh Street Bridge and joined the main BEF camp on the far shore. MacArthur's force had cleared out other camps on C Street, on Maryland and Maine Avenues, along the wharves, and near the Congressional Library. Stacking arms near a gas works at about eight o'clock, the troops messed at a field kitchen while their leader contemplated his next move.

To him the decision was obvious. His mission was the destruction of the BEF. There was no substitute for victory. His job wouldn't be complete until he had crossed the river, invaded the vets' sanctuary, and leveled their headquarters. General Glassford vehemently disagreed; he begged the chief of staff to abandon plans for a night attack, calling it "the height of stupidity." MacArthur was adamant, and the outranked police superintendent turned away. A direct order from the President of the United States was something else. Commander in Chief Hoover had his own ideas about how his army should be used, and they stopped at the water's edge. To make certain his instructions reached the general, he sent duplicate orders through General Moseley and Colonel Clement B. Wright, secretary of the General Staff. According to Eisenhower, the President "forbade any troops to cross the bridge into the largest encampment of the veterans, on open ground beyond the bridge." That was clear enough, and another general would have submitted instantly. Not MacArthur. He was choleric at this civilian meddling. He told the astonished Moseley that his plans had to go forward; he would not brook interference. To Eisenhower the chief of staff declared emphatically that he was "too busy and did not want either himself or his staff bothered by people coming down and pretending to bring orders." For the first but not the last time, the general decided to disobey a President.

Mounting heavy machine guns on the bridge to meet any counterattack, MacArthur led a column of infantry across, with Major Eisenhower at his side. They debouched on the other side in files of two—and marched into chaos. The Anacostia camp was a jumble of packing crates, fruit crates, chicken coops, burlap-and-tarpaper shacks, tents, lean-tos, wrecked touring cars, and dun-colored, tepee-like shelters. It didn't seem possible that anyone could have become attached to so preposterous an array of junk, but it was the only home the BEF families had. They were huddled here in the dark, praying for deliverance. What they got was another fusillade of tear gas bombs. Some fled screaming, some hid; one large group of about five hundred gathered on the edge of the camp and mocked the troops with the chant, "Yellow! Yellow! Yellow!" Veterans who had planted vegetable gardens pleaded with the infantrymen to spare their crops. The green rows were trampled anyhow. At 10:14, the Associated Press reported, soldiers put the torch to the hodgepodge of buildings. Flames leaped fifty feet in the air and spread to a nearby woods; six companies of firemen had to be summoned. From his White House window the President saw the glow in the eastern sky and demanded to know what had happened. To Eisenhower "the whole scene was pitiful. The veterans, whether or not they were mistaken in marching on Washington, were ragged, ill-fed, and felt themselves badly abused. To suddenly see the whole encampment going up in flames just added to the pity one had to feel for them."

The major's compassion wasn't universal. Seven-year-old Eugene King, a vet's son, tried to rescue his pet rabbit from the family tent. "Get out of here, you little son-of-a-bitch," said an infantryman, and before the boy could move, the soldier ran a bayonet through his leg. Again ambulances raced the two miles from Gallinger Hospital. There were over a hundred casualties. Two babies were dead of gas, and the angry editor of the BEF newspaper suggested the epitaph for one: "Here lies Bernard Myers, aged three months, gassed to death by order of President Hoover." That was unfair, but the veterans were bitter. They had seen soldiers pouring gasoline on their huts while well-to-do Washingtonians in yachts cruised close to look at the show. And at 11:15 P.M. they had watched Major George S. Patton Jr. lead his cavalrymen in a final destructive charge. Among the ragged bonus marchers routed by their sabers was Joseph T. Angelino, who, on September 26, 1918, had won the Distinguished Service Cross in the Argonne Forest for saving the life of a young officer named George S. Patton Jr.

Major Eisenhower advised his chief to avoid newspaper reporters; this operation had been more political than military, he continued to argue, and the politicians should do the talking. MacArthur shook his head. He enjoyed talking to the press. Furthermore, whether he liked it or not—it seems quite clear that he relished it—his decision to cross the Anacostia had put him squarely in the middle of presidential politics. At fifteen minutes past midnight he appeared before reporters with Secretary of War Hurley. From the outset his strategy was obvious: he disclaimed responsibility and praised Hoover for shouldering it. "Had the President not acted within twenty-four hours, he would have been faced with a very grave situation, which would have caused a real battle," the general said. "Had he waited another week, I believe the institutions of our government would have been severely threatened." Secretary Hurley added, "It was a great victory. Mac did a great job; he's the man of the hour." He paused thoughtfully and added, "But I must not make any heroes just now."

The real problem was the making of martyrs. Hounding men who fought for their country was not a political master stroke. Already sympathizers were offering the BEF farmland in Maryland and Virginia. Senators Hugo Black of Alabama, William Borah of Idaho, and Hiram Johnson of California were deeply shocked by the Army's behavior, and Representative Fiorello La Guardia of New York wired the President, "Soup is cheaper than tear gas bombs and bread is better than bullets in maintaining law and order in these times of Depression, unemployment, and hunger." General MacArthur dealt with this problem in an aside. The BEF were "insurrectionists," not ex-soldiers, he said. "If there was one man in ten in that group who is a veteran it would surprise me."

At the White House, which had announced that the President was staying up "until a late hour getting bulletins from the Bonus Army front," discrediting the BEF became the official line. Later Hoover would have private words of reproach for his insubordinate general, but now he declared that the bonus marchers were "not veterans," that they were "Communists and persons with criminal records." The percentage of nonveterans varied from spokesman to spokesman. MacArthur had put it at 90 percent. Hurley thought it was about 33 percent. Then Hoover wrote an American Legion post in Boston that it was his "impression" that "less than half of them ever served under the American flag." General Glassford protested that this was untrue, thereby assuring his early retirement in October. Some of the dirt was bound to stick. In an extraordinary charge to a Washington grand jury the day after the rioting, a member of the District Court said, "It is reported that the mob guilty of actual violence included few ex-service men and was made up mainly of Communists and other disorderly elements. I hope you will find that it is so and that few men who have worn the nation's uniform engaged in this violent attack upon law and order."

Unfortunately for the Hoover administration's place in history, no one thought to check with the Veterans Administration. Before the BEF attacked law and order by becoming the targets of a gas attack, the VA had completed an exhaustive survey of its membership. According to the VA figures, 94 percent of the bonus marchers had Army or Navy records, 67 percent had served overseas, and 20 percent had been disabled. Glassford and the ragged men he had championed were vindicated. It cannot be said that it did them much good. Remarkably few newspapers reprinted the survey, and most of those that did ignored it on their editorial pages. The *New York Times* described the veterans as "ordinary trespassers" whose "insubordination" had "led to a violent outbreak, almost amounting to insurrection." The *Boston Herald* declared: "The people . . . have had enough of holdups by the undeserving." The *New York Herald Tribune* ventured that the BEF cause now found "not a shred of sympathy left anywhere." To the Cleveland *Plain Dealer*, "camping on the Capitol grounds" was "cheap heroics," and although *Time* was critical of the administration, *Fortune* concluded that MacArthur, by realizing that "bayonets and an overwhelming show of strength were the only means of preventing fatalities" (the fact that there *were* fatalities was overlooked) had earned the nation's gratitude for having "skillfully executed" a difficult task.

On the morning after the disorders, the general feeling in comfortable American homes was that the government had thwarted men bent upon violent revolution. There were exceptions. Noting that during the BEF's period of greatest frustration the chief executive had received a heavyweight wrestling champion, members of the Eta Upsilon Gamma sorority, and the winners of a high school essay contest, Walter Lippmann wrote, "Mr. Hoover does not shrink from holding conferences and issuing statements. How can he justify the fact that he never took the trouble to confer with the Bonus marchers?"

At the executive mansion in Albany, New York, the atmosphere was funereal. Eleanor Roosevelt read the papers with what she later called "a feeling of horror." Her husband seemed even more deeply affected. Professor Rexford Tugwell of Columbia, a house guest, was summoned to the master bedroom, where his host lay surrounded by clouds of newsprint. As Tugwell entered, Governor Roosevelt covered photographs of the rioting with his hands, as though in shame for his country. The governor recalled that in 1920 he had proposed Hoover as a presidential candidate. He apologized for that now. "There is nothing inside the man but jelly," Roosevelt said angrily. "Maybe there never was anything else. Why didn't

Hoover offer the men coffee and sandwiches, instead of turning Pat Hurley and Doug MacArthur loose?" It was characteristic of Franklin Roosevelt that he saw the incident not in terms of principles or high policy, but as a human calamity. He might feel sorry for the President, he told Tugwell, if he weren't moved by a greater sorrow for the veterans and their families. "They're probably camping on the roads leading out of Washington," he said in anguish. "They must be in terrible shape."

They were in terrible shape, but they weren't bivouacked on those roads. The Democratic governors of Virginia and Maryland had seen to that. About two hundred veterans slipped into Arlington County before Sheriff Howard Fields blocked off the Potomac bridges; he told them that unless they left Virginia soil within twenty-four hours, Governor Pollard would call out the militia. Governor Ritchie's orders to the Maryland State Police were: "Make them go by the main highway toward Baltimore or don't let them enter Maryland." It was impossible to keep them out altogether, so motorcycle policemen met the exhausted bonus marchers at the District line and escorted them through sleeping Baltimore to the Pennsylvania line. In Pennsylvania a few found temporary sanctuary in Johnstown's Ideal Park. Most, however, were herded by the state police there to the Ohio line, where another uniformed escort waited. And so it went. Some, finding sympathy along the way, turned to begging. One railroad put together a special train to carry those bound for the plains states; Kansas City civic leaders raised $1,500 to keep it from stopping there, and the boxcars hurtled onward like Lenin's sealed car. There is no record of its eventual destination. All that is known is that by autumn most of the BEF had merged into the enormous transient population which roamed the land in 1932.

Roughly two million Americans—over a quarter-million of them between the ages of sixteen and twenty-one—were on the road that year. *Fortune* called them the Depression's "wandering population." In convoying the veterans from border to border, state policemen were following a ritual which had been established early in the Depression by county sheriffs. Every local government had more welfare cases than it could handle; impoverished strangers were charged with vagrancy and dumped across the nearest county line. A few cities, like East St. Louis, were famous for their compassionate

Salvation Army stations. Most communities cultivated inhospitable reputations. California first set up forced labor camps and then posted guards on highways entering the state, to turn back the poor. In Atlanta shabby outsiders were sentenced to thirty days on the Fulton County chain gang. Eric Sevareid, who was one of the twenty-year-old wanderers in the early 1930s, later recalled that "cities were judged and rated on the basis of their citizens' generosity with handouts and the temperament of the railway 'deeks' who guard the freight yards. You did not, for example, attempt to travel through Cheyenne, Wyoming, if you had any alternative. You were apt to be chased from the yards there not only with clubs, which was fairly common, but with revolver shots. and it was a long walk to the next station."

Who were the vagabonds? There was a hard core of seasoned hoboes, whose "jungles" provided squalid havens for the others, but most Americans on the road were new to it. They were dispossessed sharecroppers, foreclosed farmers abandoning farmland parched by three summers of drought, ragged bands of youths who had graduated from school and could not find jobs—members of what was called the "locked-out" generation. Sevareid was a bankers' son, and the percentage with middle-class backgrounds was very high. Mobility was in the American tradition; "'Scuse our dust," they had been fond of saying, and "You've got to be a go-getter if you want to get ahead," and "I'm on my way," and "Your Uncle Dudley's going places." Often an unemployed man would pile his family into the old car, head off in any direction optimistically looking for work, and wind up destitute and far from home.

"They are the people whom our post offices label 'address unknown,' and whom we call transients," Newton D. Baker wrote in the *New York Times* that year. "Every group in society is represented in their ranks, from the college graduate to the child who has never seen the inside of the schoolhouse. Expectant mothers, sick babies, young childless couples, grim-faced middle-aged dislodged from lifetime jobs—on they go, an index of insecurity in a country used to the unexpected. We think of nomads of the desert —now we have nomads of the Depression." It was true; in every city breadline there were sprinklings of chesterfields and homburgs, and magistrates never knew who would appear before them on vagrancy charges. One Brooklyn defendant, who pleaded guilty to sleeping in a vacant lot for forty-six days, was an alumnus of the

University of Colorado and had served the governments of Panama, China, Chile, and Venezuela as a civil engineer. Another was one of the most famous chefs of the Twenties; he had been living in a condemned attic and tormenting himself reading his old menus.

The descent from the middle class was rapid and sickening. Among the unskilled laborers building a California reservoir were farmers, ministers, engineers, a school principal, and the former president of a Missouri bank. In Chicago two hundred women were sleeping nightly in Grant and Lincoln parks. They had no shelter, no blankets, no protection of any kind; when night fell they lay on the cold ground and shivered until dawn. In Babylon, New York, Long Island policemen found a registered nurse starving in a maple grove on a private estate where for two weeks she had slept in a bundle of old rags and papers. In Oskaloosa, Iowa, an unemployed teacher and her two children were preparing to spend their second winter in a tented hole in the ground. As Cabell Phillips of the *New York Times* observed, the man who knocked on your door at night "might be the same fellow who a few months or a year ago had cheerfully O.K.'d your loan at the bank or had written the editorials in your newspaper or had been the vice president of a leading real estate company."

Eminent writers were among the very poor in 1932, and some have left a record of what transient life was like. John Steinbeck washed his clothes with soap made from pork fat, wood ashes, and salt. He couldn't even afford postage on his manuscripts; his agent paid it, although none of them sold then. The prospect of illness, he later recalled, frightened the nomads most of all: "You had to have money to be sick then. Dentistry was out of the question, with the result that my teeth went badly to pieces." Steinbeck was in the country. City caravansaries were more foul. Thomas Wolfe regularly visited the public latrine in front of the New York City Hall, watching men quarrel over the possession of stools while foraging in their tattered overcoat pockets for crusts of bread or old bones with rancid shreds of meat still clinging to them. The nomads there, he wrote:

> . . . were just flotsam of the general ruin of the time—honest, decent, middle-aged men with faces seamed by toil and want, and young men, many of them boys in their teens, with thick, unkempt hair. These were the wanderers from town to town, the riders of freight trains, the thumbers of rides on highways, the uprooted, un-

wanted male population of America. They drifted across the land and gathered in the big cities when winter came, hungry, defeated, empty, hopeless, restless, driven by they knew not what, always on the move, looking everywhere for work, for the bare crumbs to support their miserable lives, and finding neither work nor crumbs. Here in New York, to this obscene meeting place, these derelicts came, drawn into a common stew of rest and warmth and a little surcease from their desperation. . . . The sight was revolting, disgusting, enough to render a man forever speechless with very pity.

Years later Mrs. Lyndon Johnson would remember her husband's excited shout when he managed to get boys "out of boxcars and into jobs." That was the essence of the transients' problem. To workers in the U.S. Children's Bureau and the National Association of Travelers' Aid Societies it sometimes seemed that the youth of a nation was being destroyed on the rails. Paying Pullman passengers would find only one or two berths in a car occupied in 1932, but on the rods beneath them, and in the freight cars, humanity was dense. An average of seven hundred train hoppers a day passed through Kansas City. In twelve months, the Southern Pacific Railroad reported, its guards had thrown 683,000 people off freights. Riding the rods was dangerous. Testifying before a subcommittee of the Seventy-second Congress, R. S. Mitchell, chief special agent of the Missouri Pacific Railway, mentioned that he had taken "official notice" of 387,313 Depression nomads, of whom 335 had become casualties. He was asked for details.

> SENATOR COSTIGAN: Have you observed any ill effects on the health of people traveling under these conditions?
> MR. MITCHELL: The health conditions in the winter . . . is a very serious thing. It is a very serious thing for a tender individual not properly clothed, to ride outside in winter weather. I do not see how they can escape pneumonia.
> SENATOR COSTIGAN: There is considerable exposure?
> MR. MITCHELL: Yes, sir.

There were other kinds of exposure. Forty years ago the line between the sexes was sharply drawn, and girls, joining nomad caravans for the first time, frequently disguised themselves as boys. But they were soon unmasked; among other things, they lacked the strength and dash of boys who could hide in culverts at daybreak and raid passing produce trucks. To earn their keep, they offered themselves to fellow travelers. But the going rate for nomad prostitutes was only ten cents, and for a dime the girl was risking not only pregnancy—with the unlikelihood that a physician could be found nine months later—but also eventual venereal infection.

In the South there was an additional hazard. Both races were riding the freights. Intercourse between them was a crime, and a white girl under suspicion of working what was called "the black market" was strongly tempted to cry rape—with fatal consequences for her customer. In fact, this had happened the previous year on a slow gondola car between Chattanooga and Scottsboro, Alabama, giving rise to one of the great liberal causes of the decade. Nine illiterate Negro youths were sentenced to death on testimony from two white southern mill girls with police records, one of whom gave evidence in language so foul that reporters could not use any of it. The case went through countless appeals and two Supreme Court reversals of conviction until, twenty years later, the last of the Negro prisoners died of cancer. The Communist party made "the Scottsboro boys" known around the world, and their persecution provided incalculable fuel for black despair and, later, militancy.

But in 1932 you didn't have to be black to suffer on the road. Prison was often regarded as a godsend; as Agent Mitchell told Senator Costigan, when nomads were threatened with arrest, "they would laugh at the officers and say, 'That is what we want. That will give us a place to sleep and eat.'" To find out why they preferred jail fare, Thomas Minehan, a graduate student at the University of Minnesota, dressed in rags and joined a gang of young transients. Nourishment, he found, was acquired at breadlines, which might be in missions, churches, hospitals, Salvation Army flophouses, or municipal welfare stations. The lines should more accurately have been called soup kitchens: "the soup is invariably—I write from experience—thin, watery, lukewarm, tasteless, and served without even stale bread, and never with soda crackers. A portion equals about a small cupful." No second bowl was ever given, and eviction after the first or second day was inevitable.

Everywhere Minehan saw signs of malnutrition—prominent ribs, concave abdomens, arms and legs on which the skin was loose and baggy, hungry eyes, and nervous mannerisms. Newton D. Baker asked, "Can we afford to permit permanent injury to this generation of youth?" Baker was dismissed as a windy politician. Yet eight years later, when the children of the Depression were called to the draft, he was vindicated. National Physical Fitness Director John B.

Kelly (father of Grace Kelly) found that 40 percent of the young men examined were unfit. Most rejections were for bad teeth. Other defects, in the order of prevalence, were poor eyesight, diseases of the heart and circulation, deformities of arms and legs, and mental disorders. To those were added the invisible scars inflicted in hobo jungles by thieves, drug addicts, and hardened inverts—men like the strapping homosexual who tried to seduce young Sevareid for a quarter.

Henry Ford said, "Why, it's the best education in the world for those boys, that traveling around! They get more experience in a few months than they would in years at school." If President Hoover believed otherwise, he never said so. Certainly nothing in his personal experience contradicted it. Because he couldn't bear to watch suffering, he never visited a breadline or a relief station, despite the pleas of William Allen White. He never turned his head when his limousine swept past apple salesmen on street corners. Not until that autumn did his train leave Washington to cross states he had never visited since taking his oath of office on March 4, 1929. It was then, staring out of his guarded car at night, that he saw the campfires of hundreds of thousands of his people, mostly boys and girls who, Gene Smith wrote, "were aimlessly traveling the highways by day and sleeping near them at night."

Hoover had considered economy in the White House kitchen, then decided that would be bad for the country's morale. Each evening he entered the dining room wearing black tie—he was the last President who unfailingly dressed for dinner—and addressed himself to seven complete courses. The reporter who had coined the 1928 Republican campaign slogan ("A chicken in every pot and two cars in every garage") was broke and pleading for loans to support his three children, but the chief executive believed that America would despair if its first family lost faith in the return of prosperity.

Usually some of the courses were out of season; so were the cut flowers on the table. A custom-built humidor held long thick cigars handmade in Havana to the President's specifications; he smoked twenty a day. As the Hoovers ate, a remarkable number of men stood around and watched. The butler and footmen—all had to be the same height—stood at attention, absolutely silent, forbidden to move unbidden. In the doorways were duty officers from the company of marines who stood by wearing dress blues, to provide ceremonial trappings, and there were buglers in Ruritanian uniforms whose glittering trumpets announced the President's arrival and departure from the nightly feast, even when the only other diner was his wife Lou. Hoover was proud of Lou. She spoke five languages fluently, was president of the Girl Scouts of America, and set what was conceded to be the finest table in White House history. Sometimes she wondered whether the President really appreciated the food. He wolfed it down with such incredible speed.

By the fourth year of his administration, Herbert Clark Hoover had become a national riddle. A sardonic Texan had written a bonus marcher, "Of course, you won't have to worry about chow, being so close to the world's greatest food administrator." Yet that is precisely what Hoover had been; his feat in rescuing starving Belgium is still one of the brightest chapters in the long history of American humanitarianism. Maxim Gorki had written him, "You have saved from death 3,500,000 children, 5,500,000 adults." Finland added a verb to its language; to "hoover" meant to help.

Now it was all turned round. As the nation's anger deepened and darkened, stories were spread that he had made a fortune in Belgium, that dogs instinctively disliked him, that he was the mastermind behind the kidnapping and murder of Charles Lindbergh's son in March 1932. Junky shantytowns of tin, cardboard and burlap were Hoovervilles—Manhattan had two big ones, below Riverside Drive and near the obelisk in Central Park. The unemployed (an adjective which had become a noun in these years) carried sacks of frayed belongings called "Hoover bags." In North Carolina the rural poor sawed the fronts off broken-down flivvers, attached scrawny mules, and called the result "Hoovercarts." (The government tried to change the name to "Depression chariots," but no one bought it.) "Hoover blankets" were old newspapers which park bench tenants wrapped around themselves for warmth. "Hoover flags" were empty pockets turned inside out. "Hoover hogs" were the jackrabbits hungry farmers caught for food. Vaudeville comedians called out, "What? You say business is better? You mean Hoover died?" or reported that Hoover asked Secretary of the Treasury Mellon for a nickel to telephone a friend and was told, "Here's a dime, phone both of them."

There was a fine irony in Hoover's plight, for by the standards of the Twenties he had been considered a liberal politician. President Coolidge had scorned his brisk Secretary of Commerce as "the miracle worker" and "the wonder boy." Republican conservatives had not been grateful to Hoover for regulating radio and making airwaves public property. His great dream, on the day of his inauguration, had been to become a mighty social engineer, manipulating industrial forces for the common good. That was not quite what the Grand Old Party stood for; when the first few paragraphs of his inaugural address reached the *Chicago Tribune,* Colonel McCormick had wired his Washington bureau, "This man Hoover won't do." Hoover had been sharply critical of Coolidge-Mellon easy money. He had predicted an economic downturn because of it, and one of his first acts as President had been to persuade the Federal Reserve Board to tighten credit in the hope that the blow might be softened.

When time came to sail near the wind, however, it developed that he wasn't so heretical after all. By manipulation he had meant that the government should act as a supervisor and coordinator. Its function was to bring about "a condition of affairs favorable to the beneficial development of private enterprise," he explained, and he added that the only "moral" way out of the Depression was self-help: the people should find inspiration in the devotion of "great manufacturers, our railways, utilities, business houses and public officials." Since by 1932 the people in large numbers had become convinced that the great manufacturers and their colleagues were a bunch of crooks, a credibility gap appeared and widened.

The President professed to ignore it. He was an apostle of what John Kenneth Galbraith later called the conventional wisdom. He believed the gold standard to be sacred—even though eighteen nations, led by Great Britain, had abandoned it. He was convinced that a balanced budget was "indispensable," an "absolute necessity," "the most essential factor to economic recovery," "the first necessity of the nation," and "the foundation of all public and private financial stability"—all this despite the fact that in 1932 he was running the federal budget four billion dollars into the red. When he became convinced at last that the government must do something, he created the Reconstruction Finance Corporation to prop up sagging banks, and agreed to spend twenty-five million dollars on feed for farm animals on the condition that a bill authorizing $120,000 for hungry people be tabled.

This sounds absurd today, but in those days sound men accepted it as the revealed word. "Federal feeding would set a dangerous precedent," argued the *Schenectady Star;* it would be too dangerously like the dole, which paralyzed British labor. "If this country ever votes a dole," said Silas Strawn, president of the United States Chamber of Commerce, "we've hit the toboggan as a nation." Everyone knew how England's moral fiber had been sapped; the *American Magazine* reported that pubs were crowded with topers on the dole. Henry Ford declared that unemployment insurance would only guarantee increased unemployment, and his logic was accepted as flawless. The enlightened editors of *Fortune* explained that business should reject the very concept of social responsibility, on the ground that the introduction of any noneconomic factor would destroy the benign workings of a free market. Even Walter Lippmann, while taking the position that action was necessary, insisted that money be raised by state legislatures, not Congress.

It was a business country, Calvin Coolidge had said, and it wanted a business government. Coolidge went further. "The man who builds a factory," he wrote, "builds a temple," and "the man who works there worships there." During the Republican Twenties business had become much more than the accumulation of cash; it had come to be the guiding light in schools, press, even in churches. True believers continued reading Bruce Barton's best seller about Jesus Christ, *The Man Nobody Knows,* in which Barton claimed, among other things, that if Jesus were alive he would be an account executive in an advertising agency—a startling thought for those who had been taught that the Saviour had been a member of the building trades.

The harder times became, the greater Hoover's faith in business became. He reduced individual and corporate income taxes, thereby narrowing the government's tax base at a time when it desperately needed every source of revenue. To preside over the Reconstruction Finance Corporation he appointed Chicago banker Charles G. Dawes, who then loaned ninety million dollars to his own bank. As the impasse continued, the President turned to Mellon for counsel, and that social Darwinist replied, "Liquidate labor, liquidate stocks, liquidate the farmers, liquidate real estate." It almost seemed, as Galbraith later wrote, that everyone called upon for advice "was impelled by the conventional wisdom to offer proposals designed to make things worse."

Years later Richard Nixon came to believe that "Hoover had the misfortune to hold office at the wrong time." Certainly Hoover was trying desperately to find solutions. He worked eighteen hours a day, proclaimed a statesmanlike moratorium on war debts, and even cut his own salary. And he was hopeful. In the end, he felt, what he called "rugged individualism" would win.

Over and over the President explained that help for the poor must come from private charities and local or state governments. To be sure, no state had had a department of public welfare until Franklin Roosevelt opened New York's, but others would have to follow the governor's example. Meanwhile, the President said firmly, there would be no irresponsible experiments performed simply to "do something." The United States, he wrote a public works advocate on May 20, 1932, couldn't "squander itself into prosperity." When the Democratic Congress passed a two-billion-dollar relief bill, he vetoed it and issued a scathing message calling the measure "an unexampled raid on the public treasury." He added, "Our nation was not founded on the pork barrel, and it has not become great by political log-rolling!"

At about this time men in power began to discover "outside agitators." It was always strangers, never "the deserving poor," who whipped mobs into a frenzy of irrational behavior. Hoover's contempt for mobs had been set down ten years earlier. In a little book entitled *American Individualism* he had written, "Above all, beware the crowd! The crowd only feels; it has no mind of its own which can plan. The crowd is credulous, it destroys, it consumes, it hates, and it dreams—but it never builds." Conceivably, he concluded, this "destructive criticism" could lead to revolution. Destructive critics were blamed for the hunger march on Ford's Dearborn plant, for the bonus riot, and especially for the unrest in Harlan County, Kentucky. Rugged individualists in both parties regarded the college students who had gone into Kentucky as fair game. They were beaten, jailed, and denounced by the county attorney as a "godless, self-appointed, nondescript, iconoclastic minority of grandiloquent egotists."

Riffling through Hoover's papers, one sometimes has the strange feeling that the President looked upon the Depression as a public relations problem—that he believed the nightmare would go away if only the image of American business could be polished up and set in the right light. Faith was an end in itself; "lack of business confidence" was a cardinal sin. Hoover's first reaction to the slump which followed the Crash had been to treat it as a psychological phenomenon. He himself had chosen the word "Depression" because it sounded less frightening than "panic" or "crisis." In December 1929 he declared that "conditions are fundamentally sound." Three months later he said the worst would be over in sixty days; at the end of May he predicted that the economy would be back to normal in the autumn; in June the market broke sharply, yet he told a delegation which called to plead for a public works project, "Gentlemen, you have come sixty days too late. The Depression is over."

Already his forecasts were being flung back at him by critics, but in his December 2, 1930, message to Congress—a lame duck Republican Congress; the Democrats had just swept the off-year elections—he said that "the fundamental strength of the economy is unimpaired." At about the same time the International Apple Shippers Association, faced with a surplus of apples, decided to sell them on credit to jobless men for resale at a nickel each. Overnight there were shivering apple sellers everywhere. Asked about them, Hoover replied, "Many people have left their jobs for the more profitable one of selling apples." Reporters were caustic, and the President was stung. By now he was beginning to show signs of the most ominous trait of embattled Presidents; as his secretary Theodore Joslin was to note in his memoirs, Hoover was beginning to regard some criticism "as unpatriotic." Nevertheless he persevered, pondering new ways of waging psychological warfare. "What this country needs," he told Christopher Morley, "is a great poem." To Rudy Vallee he said in the spring of 1932, "If you can sing a song that would make people forget the Depression, I'll give you a medal." Vallee didn't get the medal. Instead he sang:

> *They used to tell me I was building a dream*
> *And so I followed the mob.*
> *When there was earth to plough or guns to bear*
> *I was always there right on the job.*
>
> *Once I built a railroad, made it run*
> *Made it race against time.*
> *Once I built a railroad, now it's done.*
> *Brother, can you spare a dime?*

But not everyone let Hoover down. A presidential commission reported that the country's number one problem was "law and order," which in those days meant prohibition gangsters. Hoover endorsed the report, and a spokesman for the National Association of Manufacturers endorsed the President's endorsement, observing that "Many of the bad effects of the so-called Depression are based on calamity howling." Catching the presidential mood, industrialists put up a brave front. One source of embarrassment to the administration was the stretch of Pennsylvania Railroad track between Washington and New York. It was lined with thousands of billboards. Half were blank, which raised awkward questions in the minds of passengers until admirers of the President began renting them to spread the slogan WASN'T THE DEPRESSION TERRIBLE? Agreeing that it had been, but that it was past, the International Association of Lions Clubs celebrated Business Confidence Week.

"Leaping lizards!" cried Little Orphan Annie, the President's favorite comic strip character. "Who said business is bad?" Not Nicholas Murray Butler, president of Columbia University; Dr. Butler assured Columbia men that "Courage will end the slump." Not the president of U.S. Steel; he said the "peak" of the Depression had passed. Not Owen D. Young, board chairman of General Electric; he announced that the "dead center of the Depression" had come and gone. Not Secretary of Commerce Thomas Lamont; he reported that "The banks of this country generally are in a strong position." And certainly not the *New York Times*, which had argued as early as New Year's Day 1931 that conditions were so dreadful that they had to better—that people would have to start spending all that money they must have saved and begin to replace their "worn-out private belongings."

There were, indeed, few alarmist voices in the press. Youngstown's mayor was chastised by its newspaper for "borrowing trouble"; the Depression would be over, the editor maintained, before relief would be needed. On July 28, 1932—the day World War veterans and their wives and children were being driven through the streets of Washington like animals—the lead story of the International News Service began: "That the sun of a new prosperity is beginning to rise above the clouds of economic distress was indicated by developments in many parts of the country"; and that same week these headlines appeared on American newsstands:

BUSINESS PULSE
BEATING FASTER
FACTORIES REOPENING ALL OVER COUNTRY

BOOM AWAKENS TEXTILE PLANTS IN NEW ENGLAND
CAPACITY PRODUCTION REPORTED IN SOME CITIES, IDLE EMPLOYEES FIND JOBS

REVIVAL IN TRADE GAINS MOMENTUM THROUGHOUT EAST

ROAD IS CLEAR TO PROSPERITY CAPITAL FEELS

MARK SULLIVAN NOTES A CALM CONFIDENCE; OBSTACLES TO RECOVERY ARE GONE

SHOWING BEST IN WEEKS FOR RESERVE BANKS

TRADE UPTURN WITHIN 90 DAYS NOW EXPECTED

BRIGHT SPOTS GROW ON U.S. BUSINESS MAP
CURTIS SEES BETTER TIMES

Nowhere in any of these newspapers was there mention of the remarkable fact that in the United States of America, the richest country in the world, more than 15 million men were looking for jobs that did not exist.

I

RENDEZVOUS WITH DESTINY
1932–1941

One

THE CRUELEST YEAR

THAT AUGUST a writer for the *Saturday Evening Post* asked John Maynard Keynes, the great British economist, whether there had ever been anything like the Depression before. "Yes," he replied. "It was called the Dark Ages, and it lasted four hundred years." This was calamity howling on a cosmic scale, but on at least one point the resemblance seems valid. In each case the people were victims of forces they could not understand.

Some vaguely blamed "conditions," Hoover's euphemism. Others confused the Depression with the stock market Crash of 1929—"We haven't been to the city since the Depression," they would say, or "I used to, but that was before the Depression." A remarkable number of sufferers stoically accepted the implicit charge of malingering made by President John E. Edgerton of the National Association of Manufacturers: "Many of those who are most boisterous now in clamor for work have either struck on the jobs they had or don't want to work at all, and are utilizing the occasion to swell the communistic chorus." An explanation lies in the strength of the Protestant ethic forty years ago in America. Although millions were trapped in a great tragedy for which there could plainly be no individual responsibility, social workers repeatedly observed that the jobless were suffering from feelings of guilt. "I haven't had a steady job in more than two years," a man facing eviction told a *New York Daily News* reporter in February 1932. "Sometimes I feel like a murderer. What's wrong with me, that I can't protect my children?"

Such men had been raised to believe that if you worked diligently, you would succeed. Now failure was dragging down the diligent and the shiftless alike. Men were demoralized, and "a demoralized people," as Walter Lippmann wrote then, "is one in which the individual has become isolated. He trusts nobody and nothing, not even himself." Seventeen years later, in *The Lonely Crowd*, Riesman explained the plight of the inner-directed man caught in such a crisis: "If repeated failures destroy his hope of future accomplishment, then it is likely that his internal strengths can no longer hold the fort against the external evidence. Overwhelmed with guilt, he will despise himself for his failures and inadequacies." Newspapers of that period are crowded with accounts of men who took their own lives rather than go on relief. Emile Durkheim had created a special category, "altruistic suicides," for men who killed themselves rather than become a burden to the community.

The real blame lay in the false underpinnings of the Coolidge-Hoover "New Era" prosperity. Seen in perspective, the Depression appears to have been the last convulsion of the industrial revolution, creating a hiatus before the technological revolution. In the aftermath of the World War, the techniques of mass production combined to increase the efficiency per man-hour by over 40 percent. This enormous output of goods clearly required a corresponding increase of consumer buying power—that is, higher wages. But the worker's income in the 1920s didn't rise with his productivity. In the golden year of 1929, Brookings economists calculated that to supply the barest necessities a family would need an income of $2,000 a year—more than 60 percent of American families were earning. In short, the ability to buy did not keep abreast of the volume of goods being turned out. It was part of the foolishness of the time to argue that the surge in production was no problem, that "a good salesman can sell anything." In practice this meant that while the rich (and many who weren't rich) were speculating in stocks, zealous salesmen were encouraging a kind of mass speculation. Customers of limited means were being persuaded to take products anyhow, the exchange being accomplished by an overextension of credit.

The stock market, honeycombed with credit in the form of brokers' loans, crashed of its own weight, calling to account the millions of little deals consummated by commercial travelers who had sold anything and everything to people lacking the means to pay for it. Thus ended the New Era prosperity. The panic followed, and the country couldn't cope with it. The last extended economic crisis had been in 1893; since then America had become so industrialized that a massive return to the farm was impossible. There was a certain rough justice in Herbert Hoover's ascent to the Presidency on the eve of the catastrophe, for as Secretary of Commerce he had been fascinated with productivity and indifferent to the dangerous lack of buying power. Long after he left the White House, he realized what had happened and wrote: "A margin of some thousands . . . got too much of the productive pie for the services they performed. . . . Another margin of some 20 percent got too little."

Between the Crash and 1932, the cruelest year of the Depression, the economy's downward spiral was accelerated by measures which, according to all accepted canons, ought to have brought recovery, and which in practice did the opposite. To protect investments, prices had to be maintained. Sales ebbed, so costs were cut by laying off men. The unemployed could not buy the goods of other industries. Therefore sales dropped further, leading to more layoffs and a general shrinkage of purchasing power, until farmers were pauperized by the poverty of industrial workers, who in turn were pauperized by the poverty of farmers. "Neither has the money to buy the product of the other," an Oklahoma witness testified before a congressional subcommittee, explaining the vicious circle. "Hence we have overproduction and underconsumption at the same time and in the same country."

In June 1932, Ivy League seniors joined 21,974 other alumni hunting for jobs. By then New York department stores were requiring bachelor degrees for all elevator operators, and that was the best many of them could do, but twenty-year-old Sylvia Field Porter, Hunter '32, was an exception. She switched her major from English to economics because of what she later called "an overwhelming curiosity to know why everything was crashing around me and why people were losing their jobs" and talked her way into an investment counsel firm. At the same time she began a systematic study of the financial world, with the thought that one day she might write a column about it.* She then discovered that she was in the middle of a crisis without historical precedent.

* Sylvia Porter began writing for the *New York Post* in 1935.

Ever since the fiasco of England's South Sea Company in 1720, the phrase "South Sea bubble" had been used to describe a doomed business venture. The bubble had certainly burst; South Sea stock had plunged to 13.5 percent of its highest quotation. Yet it subsequently rallied, and the firm continued to do business for eighty years. By the time of Miss Porter's commencement, however, United States Steel and General Motors had dropped to 8 percent of their pre-Crash prices. Overall, stocks listed on the Big Board were worth 11 percent of their 1929 value. Investors had lost 74 billion dollars, three times the cost of the World War. More than 5,000 American banks had failed—in Iowa City, just across the county line from Hoover's native West Branch, all five banks were shut—and 86,000 businesses had closed their doors. The country's Gross National Product had fallen from 104 billion dollars to 41 billion (in 1973 it would be 2,177 billion). In 1932, 273,000 families were evicted from their homes, and the average weekly wage of those who had jobs was $16.21.

Some enterprises flourished. The contraceptive business was netting a quarter-billion dollars a year, a fact which the youth of that day conveniently forgot after they had become parents. Over half the population was going to the movies once a week (admission was a quarter for adults, a dime for children), and each year saw an increase in the number of cigarette smokers, none of them aware that the habit might be harmful. Kelvinator refrigerators and Atwater Kent radios were moving briskly. Miniature golf courses and circulation libraries were booming. Alfred C. Fuller was doing very nicely with his corps of door-to-door brush salesmen; in the grim month of August 1932 his sales leaped from $15,000 to $50,000 and grew thereafter at the rate of a million dollars a year. A prodigy named J. Paul Getty was quietly picking up cheap petroleum wells; that February he gained control of 520,000 of the Pacific Oil Corporation's one million shares. Here and there a venture was lucky. In Quincy, Massachusetts, the owner of a curious restaurant with a bright orange roof and pseudo Colonial architecture was almost bankrupt when a stock company opened across the street. Its first play was Eugene O'Neill's nine-act *Strange Interlude*. Every evening there was an 8:30 intermission for supper, and the restaurateur, Howard Johnson, survived.

But these were exceptions. U.S. Steel, the key to heavy industry, was operating at 19.1 percent of capacity. The American Locomotive Company didn't need much steel. During the 1920s it had sold an average of 600 locomotives a year; in 1932 it sold one. Nor was the automotive industry the big steel customer it had been. Month by month its fine names were vanishing: the Stutz Motor Company, the Auburn, the Cord, the Edward Peerless, the Pierce Arrow, the Duesenberg, the Franklin, the Durant, the Locomobile. One rash man decided to challenge Ford with another low-priced car. He called it the Rockne, lost 21 million dollars, and killed himself. In January an inventive bacteriologist named Arthur G. Sherman had become the sensation of the Detroit Auto Show by exhibiting the first crude, hand-carpentered, wooden trailer. In 1932 he sold just eighty of them. Air transport nose-dived. Airliners then had twelve seats, of which, the Department of Commerce reported, an average of seven were flying empty. And with the exception of the new talkies, most entertainers were foundering. In four years the jazz musician Eddie Condon landed four recording sessions; the phonograph recording industry had dwindled from 50 million dollars a year to a quarter-million. Sally Rand was making a precarious living with her celebrated fans; to a reporter who asked why she did it, she replied, "I never made any money till I took off my pants."

Because poverty was considered shameful, people tried to conceal destitution from neighbors, often with considerable success. One could never be sure about the family across the street. The smartly dressed young lawyer who always left home at the same time each morning may have been off to sell cheap neckties, magazines, vacuum cleaners, pressure cookers, or Two-in-One shoe polish door-to-door in a remote neighborhood. He may have changed his clothes and gone to another part of the city to beg. Or he may have been one of the millions who looked for work day after day, year after year, watching his children grow thinner and fighting despair in the night. There were certain skills developed by men who spent their days in the streets. You learned to pay for a nickel cup of coffee, to ask for another cup of hot water free, and, by mixing the hot water with the ketchup on the counter, to make a kind of tomato soup. In winter you stuffed newspapers under your shirt to ward off the cold; if you knew you would be standing for hours outside an employment office, you wrapped burlap bags around your legs and tied them in place. Shoes were a special problem. Pasteboard could be used for inner soles, and some favored cotton in the heels to absorb the pounding of the concrete. But if a shoe was really gone, nothing worked. The pavement destroyed the cardboard and then the patch of sock next to it, snow leaked in and accumulated around your toes, and shoe nails stabbed your heels until you leaned to walk with a peculiar gait.

It was remarkable how ingenious an impoverished, thrift-minded family could be. Men resharpened and reused old razor blades, rolled their own cigarettes or smoked Wings (ten cents a pack), and used twenty-five-watt light bulbs to save electricity. Children returned pop bottles for two cents or stood in line for day-old bread at the bakery. Women cut sheets lengthwise and resewed them to equalize wear, retailored their clothes for their daughters, and kept up a brave front with the wife next door—who may have been doing the same thing on the same meager budget. Families sorted Christmas cards so they could be sent to different friends next year. Sometimes a man would disappear for weeks. All the neighborhood knew was that he had gone on a "business trip." It was a considerate husband who withheld the details of such trips from his wife, for they were often more terrible than anything she could imagine.

He was, of course, looking for work. The legends of job hunting had become folklore by 1932, and some of the unbelievable stories were true. Men *did* wait all night outside Detroit employment offices so they would be first in line next morning. An Arkansas man *did* walk nine hundred miles looking for work. People *did* buy jobs. In Manhattan a Sixth Avenue employment agency *did* have five thousand applicants for three hundred jobs. It is a matter of record that a labor subcommittee of the 72nd Congress heard testimony about men setting forest fires in the state of Washington so they would be hired to put them out. *Business Week* verified the fact that a great many people who no longer loved America either left it or attempted to. Throughout the early Thirties the country's emigration exceeded its immigration. Amtorg, the Russian trading agency in New York, was getting 350 applications a day from Americans who wanted to settle in Russia. On one memorable occasion Amtorg advertised for six thousand skilled workers and a hundred thousand showed up, including plumbers, painters, mechanics, cooks, engineers, carpenters, electricians, salesmen, printers, chemists, shoemakers, librarians, teachers, dentists, a cleaner and dyer, an aviator, and an undertaker.

New York drew countless job seekers from surrounding states, though the city had a million jobless men of its own. A few strangers joined Manhattan's seven thousand nickel shoeshine "boys" or found furtive roles in the bootleg coal racket—10 percent of the city's coal was being sneaked in by unemployed Pennsylvania miners—but most outsiders wound up on one of New York's eighty-two breadlines. If a man had a dime he could sleep in a flophouse reeking of sweat and Lysol. If he was broke he salvaged some newspapers and headed for Central Park, or the steps of a subway entrance, or the municipal incinerator. The incinerator's warmth drew hundreds of men on winter nights, even though they had to sleep on great dunes of garbage.

Returning from such an expedition in or under an empty freight car, a husband would review family assets with his wife and estimate how long they could keep going. Wedding rings would be sold, furniture pawned, life insurance borrowed upon, money begged from relatives. Often the next step was an attempt at a home business, with its implicit confession to the neighborhood that the pretense of solvency had been a hoax. The yard might be converted to a Tom Thumb miniature golf course. The husband might open a "parlor grocery." The wife might offer other wives a wash, set, and manicure for a dollar. In Massachusetts, idle textile workers erected looms in their living rooms; in Connecticut, households strung safety pins on wires, toiling long hours and earning a total of five dollars a week for an entire family.

These last-ditch efforts rarely succeeded; there were so few potential customers with money. Finally hope was abandoned. The father went to the city hall, declared himself penniless, and became a statistic. Because those figures were poorly kept, the precise extent of poverty is unknown. Somewhere between 15 million and 17 million men were unemployed, with most of them representing a family in want. *Fortune*, in September 1932, estimated that 34 million men, women, and children were without any income whatever. That was nearly 28 percent of the population, and like all other studies it omitted America's 11 million farm families, who were suffering in a rural gethsemane of their own.

During the Nixon Presidency, when America's farm population had shrunk to 5.2 percent of the population, it was hard to realize that only forty years earlier 25.1 percent had been living, or trying to live, on the land. They had not shared in New Era prosperity; the Crash merely worsened a situation which had already become a national scandal. By 1932 U.S. farmers had come to remind one reporter of Mongolian peasants seen in the rotogravure sections of Sunday newspapers, and the shadow of imminent famine fell across the plains. Agricultural prices hadn't been so low since the reign of Queen Elizabeth. Farmers were getting less than twenty-five cents for a bushel of wheat, seven cents for a bushel of corn, a dime for a bushel of oats, a nickel for a pound of cotton or wool. Sugar was bringing three cents a pound, hogs and beef two and a half cents a pound, and apples—provided they were flawless—forty cents for a box of two hundred.

Translated into the bitter sweat of rural life, this meant that a wagon of oats wouldn't buy a pair of four-dollar Thom McAn shoes. A wagon of wheat would just do it, but with mortgage interest running at $3.60 an acre, plus another $1.90 in taxes, the wheat farmer was losing $1.50 on every acre he reaped. In cotton fields the strongest and most agile man would toil from "can see" to "can't see"—fourteen hours of daylight—and receive sixty cents for the 300 pounds he had picked. It was cheaper to burn corn than sell it and buy coal. With meat bringing such ruinous prices, a man would spend $1.10 to ship a sheep to market, where it would return him less than $1.00. In Montana a rancher bought bullets on credit, spent two hours slaughtering a herd of livestock, and left it rotting in a canyon. It wasn't worth its feed. Turning away, he muttered to a reporter, "One way to beat the Depression, huh?"

As farm prices caved in, tens of thousands of mortgage foreclosure notices went up on gateposts and county courthouses. It has been estimated that one-fourth of the state of Mississippi was auctioned off. William Allen White, the Republican country editor who had pleaded with Hoover to come and see what was happening to the Middle West, wrote, "Every farmer, whether his farm is under mortgage or not, knows that with farm products priced as they are today, sooner or later he must go down." When the farmer did fail, unable even to pay the small costs of binder twine, tool repair, and seed, the bank would take title as absentee landlord, and he would rent from it the land his family had owned for generations. Meantime, while ranchers fed mutton to buzzards and warmed their hands over corn fires, millions in the cities could not afford the low prices which were destroying farmers (butter at 39 cents a pound, prime rib roast at 21 cents, two dozen eggs for 41 cents) because so many were idle and those who had jobs were often earning what could only be called starvation wages.

There was no one to protect them. The President disapproved of wage cuts and said so, but he was equally opposed to wage-hour legislation, so that when U.S. Steel made its second big wage slash in the spring of 1932, the workers were helpless. The labor movement was almost extinct; AFL membership had dwindled from 4.1 million in 1920 to 2.2 million, about 6 percent of the work force. There were strikes of desperation in 1932. All were lost. Miners were paid $10.88 a month, were at the mercy of checkweight men, and were required to buy groceries at inflated prices in the company store; when they rebelled the protest was bloodily suppressed by armed strikebreakers backed by the National Guard. The United Mine Workers were too weak to offer the victims anything but sympathy.

In such New England mill towns as Lynn and Lowell, where only one worker in three was employed, men were treated like serfs; one of them left Manchester, New Hampshire, to apply for a job in New Haven, was arrested, brought before a judge on a charge of vagrancy, and ordered back to his Manchester mill. The immense pool of job seekers tempted employers to slash their wage bills again and again. Department stores paid clerks as little as five dollars a week. An investigation in Chicago disclosed that the majority of working girls were getting less than twenty-five cents an hour; for a fourth of them, it was less than a dime. In 1932 hourly rates had shrunk to ten cents in lumbering, seven-and-a-half cents in general contracting, six cents in brick and tile manufacturing, and five cents in sawmills. Before the Depression, Massachusetts textile mills rarely required skilled operators to be responsible for more than twenty looms eight hours a day. Then the mills introduced speedups and stretch-outs, and Louis Adamic saw teen-aged girls running thirty wide looms from before dawn until after sunset.

In the sweatshops of Brooklyn fifteen-year-olds were paid $2.78 a week. Women received as little as $2.39 for a fifty-hour week. In the summer of 1932 the Connecticut Commissioner of Labor reported that there were over a hundred shops in the state paying as little as sixty cents for a fifty-five-hour week. New York City was the worst sweat spot in that state, and its garment industry, employing fifty thousand women, was the most sweated trade. "Unscrupulous employers," *Time* reported, had "battered wages down to the

Chinese coolie level." Hat makers crocheted hats for forty cents a dozen; in a week a worker could make two dozen. Apron girls were paid two-and-a-half cents an apron; they earned twenty cents a day. A slipper liner received twenty-one cents for lining seventy-two pairs; if she completed one slipper every forty-five seconds, she took home $1.05 after a nine-hour day. Girl cleaners in a pants factory were paid a half-cent for each garment they threaded and sponged. It was a five-minute operation; their income was six cents an hour. Honest employers could not survive that kind of competition. Welfare rolls grew longer and longer, the President continued to withhold federal help, and as the fourth Depression winter loomed the relief structure began to disintegrate.

When a senator declared the workers simply could not survive on one or two days' wages a week, President J. E. Edgerton of the National Association of Manufacturers said, "Why, I've never thought of paying men on the basis of what they need. I pay for efficiency. Personally, I attend to all those other things, social welfare stuff, in my church work." Doubtless he thought he did. As *Fortune* explained it, the theory was that now, as in the past, private charity and semipublic welfare groups could care for the old, the sick, and the indigent.

It wasn't working. The Depression, while multiplying the demands upon charities, had dried up their sources of contributions. By 1932, private help had dwindled to 6 percent of the money spent upon the needy, leaving some thirty million people to public welfare. Unfortunately, local governments couldn't handle the burden. State and city budgets had been in the red since 1930. About nine-tenths of municipal income came from taxation on real estate, which in terms of the Depression dollar was ludicrously overappraised. Landlords were liable to taxation if they held title to buildings; their inability to realize income from their houses was legally irrelevant, even when their tenants were on municipal relief, which never paid rentals. The landlords tried desperately to get their money. At first, in exasperation, they turned penniless occupants out. In New York there was hardly a block without a daily dispossession, and in Philadelphia so many families were put on the street that little girls invented a doll game called Eviction.

But empty tenements solved nothing; they merely contributed to the unpopularity of men of property while leaving tax bills unpaid.

Eventually, as Professor Sumner H. Slichter of the Harvard Business School explained to the Senate Committee on Manufactures, there was "a more or less national moratorium on rents, insofar as the unemployed are concerned." Delinquent tax ratios hovered between 20 and 30 percent in metropolitan areas, and the cities, lacking this revenue, cut services. Roads were unpaved, sidewalks crumbled, streets blocked by winter snow were left unplowed. Chicago, deprived of two years' receipts by a taxpayers' strike, borrowed from the banks—and agonized over its unemployed population of 600,000.

Given the bankruptcy of public treasuries, and the widespread feeling that the poor were somehow responsible for their fate, it was inevitable that admittance to relief rolls would be made extremely difficult. Before applications were even considered, homes and possessions had to be sold, insurance canceled, credit exhausted, and evidence produced that all known relatives were broke. Even then, in many cities no assistance was granted to unmarried people or people without young children. Every possible stigma was attached to aid. In September 1932 Lewiston, Maine, voted to bar all welfare recipients from the polls, a goal already achieved by property requirements in the constitutions of ten states from Massachusetts to Oregon. West Virginia hospitals refused to admit patients unless payment for services was guaranteed; a referring physician suggested to one surgeon that he delay operating upon a child until the parents promised to pay $1,000. Two doctors in Royce City, Texas, put the following advertisement in the local paper:

> TO WHOM IT MAY CONCERN: If you are expecting the stork to visit your home this year and he has to come by way of Royce City, he will have to bring a checkbook to pay his bill before delivery.

In some communities taxpayer associations tried to prevent welfare children from attending schools, and families receiving public assistance were known to have been excluded from churches.

Even those who surmounted all barriers found that the approval of a welfare application was exceptional. In mill towns, mining communities, and on sharecropper farms, *Fortune* reported, "relief is merely a name." In the cities only 25 percent of qualified families were getting some form of help. The mayor of Toledo said in 1932: "I have seen thousands of these defeated, discouraged, hopeless men and women, cringing and fawning as they come to ask for public aid. It is a spectacle of national degradation." Admittance to the rolls did not end the defeat, discouragement, and hopelessness. In Philadelphia a family of four was given $5.50 a week, which hardly encouraged the debauchery predicted by those who objected to the dole, and Philadelphia was munificent compared to New York ($2.39), Mississippi ($1.50) and Detroit ($0.60). At the most, assistance covered only food and fuel. Since welfare families had often been inadequately clothed before the Crash, their rags three winters later sometimes defied description. It was not uncommon to see the head of a family dressed like a vaudeville tramp, wearing a buttonless suit coat out at one elbow, a pair of trousers out at the knee and in the seat, an old summer cap that had hung for years in some furnace room, worn tennis shoes covered by patched rubbers, a pair of mismatched canvas gloves; the whole covered by a filthy old sheepskin.

Frequently public employees were almost indistinguishable from public wards, since money for both came from the same sources. As a rule community elders found a way to provide their policemen with decent uniforms, for it was a time of anxiety about public safety. This concern did not cover schoolteachers, who more than any other group were victims of local governments' inadequate tax base. At the beginning of the Depression they had been assessed part of their pay to finance soup kitchens. With the school population increasing by over two hundred thousand each year, further economies were inevitable. Desks were set up in corridors, in coal-heated portables, in tin shacks; courses in art and music were stricken from the curriculum; the same textbooks were handed down semester after semester, until they had become dog-eared, dirty, with pages defaced or missing. Classrooms became more and more crowded. Finally, the money to pay the teachers began to disappear.

By 1932, a third of a million children were out of school because of lack of funds. Teachers in Mississippi, northern Minnesota, Idaho, South Dakota, and Alabama managed to eat only by "boarding around" at the homes of parents. In Dayton, Ohio, schools were open only three days a week; in Arkansas over three hundred schools were closed ten months or more. In Kansas, twenty-five-cent wheat meant rural teachers were being paid $35 a month for an eight-month year—$280 a year. In Iowa they were receiving $40 a month, half the income Washington had said was necessary for industrial workers to exist. Akron owed its teachers $300,000, Youngstown $500,000, Detroit $800,000, and Chicago's debts to its teachers were more than 20 million dollars.

The story of the Chicago schools was a great Depression epic. Rather than see 500,000 children remain on the streets, the teachers hitchhiked to work, endured "payless paydays"—by 1932 they had received checks in only five of the last thirteen months—and accepted city scrip to be redeemed after the Depression, even though Chicago bankers would not accept it. Somehow the city found money to invest in its forthcoming World's Fair of 1933, when Sally Rand would gross $6,000 a week, but it turned a deaf ear to the Board of Education. A thousand teachers were dismissed outright. Those who remained taught on at immense personal sacrifice. Collectively the 1,400 teachers lost 759 homes. They borrowed $1,128,000 on their insurance policies and another $232,000 from loan sharks at annual interest rates of 42 percent, and although hungry themselves, they fed 11,000 pupils out of their thin pocketbooks.

Teachers, welfare workers, and policemen saw hardship at close range. Nobody called cops pigs in the early 1930s. Even when they were used to break strikes, it was widely acknowledged that they were as exploited as the workers.* In New York, men on the beat had been distributing food in the most stricken neighborhoods since 1930. The money came from city employees, including themselves, who contributed 1 percent of their salaries; as Caroline Bird pointed out, this was "the first public confession of official responsibility for plain poverty, and it came, not from the top, but from the lowest civil servants, who worked down where the poor people were."

Once more the teachers bore witness to the worst, for the most heartbreaking Depression martyrs were in the classrooms. In October of that terrible year, a month before the presidential election, the New York City Health Department reported that over 20 percent of the pupils in the public schools were suffering from malnutrition. In the mining counties of Ohio, West Virginia, Illinois, Kentucky, and Pennsylvania, the secretary of the American Friends Service Committee told a congressional committee, the ratio was sometimes over 90 percent, with deprived children afflicted by "drowsiness, lethargy, and sleepiness," and "mental retardation." A teacher suggested that one little girl go home and eat something;

* The day after the bloody suppression of hungry marchers at the Ford plant on March 7, Detroit's police commissioner laid off 162 policemen.

the child replied, "I can't. This is my sister's day to eat." A little boy exhibited his pet rabbit to a visitor and the boy's older sister whispered, "He thinks we aren't going to eat it, but we are." Lillian Wald, a social worker, asked in anguish, "Have you ever seen the uncontrolled trembling of parents who have starved themselves for weeks so that their children might not go hungry?" A bitter father said, "A worker's got no right to have kids any more," and a Massachusetts priest said, "One family I know has lived on lentils, nothing but lentils, all this year. They can't afford to buy bread. What is going to happen to our children?"

"Nobody is actually starving," President Hoover told reporters. "The hoboes, for example, are better fed than they have ever been. One hobo in New York got ten meals in one day." In September 1932 *Fortune* flatly called the President a liar and suggested that "twenty-five millions in want" might be a fairer description of the nation's economic health. Cases of starvation were being chronicled by *Fortune*, the *San Francisco Chronicle*, the *Atlantic*, the *New York Times*, and in congressional testimony. The New York City Welfare Council reported 29 victims of starvation and 110, mostly children, dead of malnutrition. Hoover simply hadn't seen the suffering, though he was not to be spared after his departure from the White House; on a fishing trip in the Rocky Mountains he was led by a native to a hut where one child had succumbed and seven others were dying of hunger.

Millions stayed alive by living like animals. In the Pennsylvania countryside they were eating wild weed-roots and dandelions; in Kentucky they chewed violet tops, wild onions, forget-me-nots, wild lettuce, and weeds which heretofore had been left to grazing cattle. City mothers hung around docks, waiting for spoiled produce to be discarded and then fighting homeless dogs for possession of it. After the vegetables had been loaded on trucks they would run alongside, ready to snatch up anything that fell off. A cook in a midwestern hotel put a pail of leftovers in the alley outside the kitchen; immediately a dozen men loomed out of the darkness to fight over it. In Long Beach, California, a sixty-six-year-old physician named Francis Everett Townsend glanced out his window while shaving and saw, among a group of refuse barrels, "three haggard very old women," as he later called them, "stooped with great age, bending over the barrels, clawing into the contents." Whole families were seen plunging into refuse dumps, gnawing at bones and watermelon rinds; a Chicago widow always removed her glasses so she wouldn't see the maggots. At night in New York Thomas Wolfe observed "the homeless men who prowled in the vicinity of restaurants, lifting the lids of garbage cans and searching around inside for morsels of rotten food." He saw them "everywhere, and noticed how their numbers increased during the hard and desperate days of 1932."

It was considered benevolent by well-to-do Americans that year to give your garbage to fellow countrymen who were famished. The Elks of Mount Kisco, New York, and the eating clubs of Princeton University instructed their servants to see that their leftovers reached the needy. The *Brooklyn Eagle* proposed a central depot where edible swill could be sent by charitable citizens and where the poor might apply for portions of it. In Oklahoma City John B. Nichlos, a gas company executive, worked out a plan under which restaurants, civic clubs, and hotel chefs would pack swill in "sanitary containers of five (5) gallons each," to be "labeled 'MEAT, BEANS, POTATOES, BREAD AND OTHER ITEMS.'" The Salvation Army would pick up the cans, the contents of which would then be distributed to jobless men who would first chop wood donated by—of all people—the farmers. "We expect a little trouble now and then from those who are not worthy of the support of the citizens," the gas man wrote Secretary of the Army Hurley, "but we must contend with such cases in order to take care of those who are worthy." Hurley thought it a marvelous idea, and urged the administration to adopt it. It was vetoed by the director of Hoover's Emergency Committee for Employment on the ground that the gesture might be misunderstood.

It never seems to have occurred to Nichlos, the *Eagle*, the Princetonians and the Elks that more dramatic solutions might lie ahead. But already there were those who pondered the contrast between the well-fed rich and the starving multitude, and who thought they saw the dark shadow of things to come. Thomas Wolfe would talk to the tragic men in New York's public toilets until he could not stand their anguish any more. Then he would mount the steps to the pavement twenty feet above and gaze out upon "the giant hackles of Manhattan shining coldly in the cruel brightness of the winter night. The Woolworth Building was not fifty yards away, and a little farther down were the silvery spires and needles of Wall Street, great fortresses of stone and steel that housed enormous banks. The blind injustice of this . . . seemed the most brutal part of the whole experience, for there . . . in the cold moonlight, only a few blocks away from this abyss of human wretchedness and misery, blazed the pinnacles of power where a large section of the entire world's wealth was locked in mighty vaults."

In adversity Americans have always looked for scapegoats, and by early 1932 other hunters, like Wolfe, were closing in on lower Manhattan. The prey there was fat and vulnerable. In the Twenties American financiers and industrialists had become national folk heroes. In vain had William Z. Ripley of Harvard warned President Coolidge that "prestidigitation, double-shuffling, honeyfugling, hornswoggling and skulduggery" were threatening the economy; Coolidge refused to be daunted by prophets of gloom and doom. For nine years, as Arthur Schlesinger Jr. later wrote, the government had treated business as though it had "discovered the philosopher's stone which would transmute the uncertainties of the capitalist system into permanent prosperity." Mellon had become known as "the greatest Secretary of the Treasury since Alexander Hamilton," and *Nation's Business* had reported that the American businessman was "the most influential person in the nation." But now, three years after the Crash, children were singing:

> *Mellon pulled the whistle,*
> *Hoover rang the bell,*
> *Wall Street gave the signal,*
> *And the country went to hell.*

The high priests of finance weren't listening. Their world remained insular, arrogant, and out of touch. In the *Literary Digest* they read of the Depression's blessings: "People are growing more courteous in business, and often more reasonable at home, thoughtless women especially. Unappreciative wives who were indifferent to their husbands and neglected their homes have become tame and cautious." A Republican candidate for governor of New Jersey had good news for the voters: "There is something about too much prosperity that ruins the moral fiber of the people." A member of the Du Pont family was reported to have rejected a suggestion that he sponsor a Sunday afternoon program on the ground that "at three o'clock on Sunday afternoons everybody is playing polo," and J. P. Morgan observed that if "you destroy the leisure class, you destroy civilization. By the leisure class, I mean the families who employ one servant—twenty-five or thirty million families." He seemed startled when told that census figures showed there were fewer than two million servants in the entire country. The people were not surprised by his misinformation; by then, Walter Lippmann wrote, industrial and financial leaders had fallen "from one of the highest positions of influence and power that they have ever occupied in our history to one of the lowest."

In 1932, 65 percent of American industry belonged to 600 corporations; 1 percent of the population owned 59 percent of the wealth. One man, Samuel Insull of Chicago, held 85 directorships, 65 board chairmanships, and 11 company presidencies. His utilities empire was a conglomerate of 150 companies, with 50,000 employees serving 3,250,000 customers. On New Year's Day its securities were valued at over three billion dollars, and unemployed men warming themselves over scrap wood fires on the lower level of Wacker Drive looked up at the Insull offices far above and wondered aloud to reporters why the old man couldn't help them.

He couldn't because he had problems of his own. His pyramid of holding companies was collapsing, and thousands of Chicagoans— including a great many schoolteachers—were about to learn in horror that their Insull stock had dropped to 4 percent of its 1931 value. Insull scurried about trying to salvage something, protected day and night by thirty-six bodyguards, but in April his two investment trusts went into receivership. By June he had fled to Europe, sixty million dollars in debt; a Cook County grand jury indicted him. In Paris he craftily scheduled a press conference, sneaked out the back door to board a midnight express for Rome, and flew on to Athens. His lawyers had told him he would be safe there, because there were no extradition treaties between Greece and the United States. It was true then, but by early November the diplomats had signed one. Disguised as a woman, the fugitive chartered a boat for Turkey. The Turks turned him over to American authorities; he was brought back, tried—and found not guilty, because holding companies were not subject to regulation. "A holding company," Will Rogers said dryly, "is a thing where you hand an accomplice the goods while the policeman searches you."

Rogers also said, "There's a lot of things these old boys have done that are within the law, but it's so near the edge you couldn't slip a razor blade between their acts and a prosecution." Looking for evidence, the Democratic Congress was turning over stones up and down Wall Street, and some remarkable specimens were crawling out. Banker Albert H. Wiggin had sold the stock of his own bank (the Chase) short and then lied about it. Because of the depressed economy, Charles E. Mitchell of the National City Bank had broken an agreement to merge with the Corn Exchange Bank; at the same time he was tormenting his own clerks and tellers by demanding that they keep up their installment payments on National City stock bought at pre-Crash prices ($200 a share, now down to $40)—and loaning $2,400,000 of the stockholders' money to bank officers, with neither collateral nor interest, for market speculation. Mitchell had avoided federal income tax by selling securities to a member of his family at a loss and later buying them back. Through similar loopholes J. P. Morgan had paid no income tax in 1929, 1930, or 1931. Colonel Robert R. McCormick of the *Chicago Tribune*, sent the government a token $1,500 a year while writing long editorials urging his subscribers to pay their taxes in full.

As Secretary of the Treasury, Andrew Mellon had also hounded people who were reluctant to meet their tax obligations—and had similarly applied a different standard to himself. The country was astonished to learn that at Mellon's request his commissioner of internal revenue had prepared a memorandum for him describing twelve ways to evade federal taxes. A Treasury Department tax expert had then been assigned to work on Mellon's personal returns. Five of the commissioner's suggestions had been followed, including the recording of fictitious gifts and losses to reduce tax liability. These disclosures aroused Representative Wright Patman of Texas, who on January 25, 1932, asked the House to impeach Secretary Mellon "for high crimes and misdemeanors," but there were those who still regarded Mellon with reverence. To them the publication of these singular facts was a form of *lèse majesté;* one admirer, Mellon's lawyer, sharply rebuked a *New York Times* reporter for "providing ammunition for radicals."

Like the Insull machinations, tax dodges were legal. But despite the tax legislation of the time, some men had crossed into criminal territory. Ivar Kreuger, "the Swedish Match King," was a Grand Officer of the French Legion of Honor, an adviser to President Hoover on European aspects of the Depression, and a man of such probity that in 1928, when the Boston firm of Lee, Higginson prepared to issue millions on Kreuger securities, its officers had agreed with the Match King that an audit of his books was unnecessary. On March 12, 1932, he bought a large pistol, locked the door of his luxury apartment in Paris, and killed himself. After all the moving eulogies had been delivered, it turned out that the king had been a common thief, guilty of swindling, fraud, and forging Italian government bonds. Among other things he had stolen over three hundred million dollars from trusting investors.

Every week brought fresh shocks. Joseph Wright Harriman, a banker (or "bankster," as *Time* had it) and a cousin of Averell Harriman, left his failing bank and took refuge in a Manhattan nursing home. As the law closed in, he escaped to a Long Island inn, registering under an alias. The Nassau County police found him anyhow. Harriman tried to drive a butcher's knife between his ribs, failed at that, too, and served two years in prison for falsifying his bank's books and misapplying its funds. Saul Singer, executive vice president of the Bank of the United States—the largest American bank ever to fail—went to the penitentiary on the same charges, and later Howard Hopson, president of the Associated Gas and Electric Company and responsible to 188,576 investors, was captured in Washington after a wild taxicab chase and found guilty on seventeen counts of mail fraud. "Confidence in the erstwhile leadership of this country is gone," George Sokolsky wrote. Representative Fiorello La Guardia said of a stock manipulation case, "Sordid as these facts may seem, I believe the same sort of story could be told regarding every stock in which there was a pool," and Joseph P. Kennedy, himself a market tycoon, concluded, "The belief that those in control of the corporate life of America were motivated by honesty and ideals of honorable conduct" had been "completely shattered."

Viewed in this light, the conduct of Hoover's Reconstruction Finance Corporation can only be called a major political blunder. In 1932 the congressional leadership finally pushed through an act authorizing the RFC to advance the states 300 million dollars for unemployment relief. By the end of the year only 30 million had actually reached the states, one-third of the amount Dawes had loaned to his Central Republic Bank and Trust Company of Chicago. It was perhaps symbolic that when the President telephoned former Senator Atlee Pomerene of Ohio to appoint him Dawes's successor, Pomerene had exactly ninety-eight cents in his pocket, and that on his way to be sworn in, a dozen panhandlers approached him. As public policy the RFC was broke. Millions were calling it "a breadline for big business," which was exactly what it had become.

But such phrases, like the demand for Mellon's head, provoked violent reactions from men like General MacArthur, who believed that the national security was endangered. The well-to-do were becoming genuinely afraid of the hungry, and that fear does much to explain a sudden attack upon one Democratic leader by a former friend in the spring of 1932. Alfred E. Smith, born in an East Side tenement, had become a checker in the Fulton Fish Market at the age of fifteen and had risen through Tammany's ranks to become governor of New York. In 1928, during Al Smith's unsuccessful campaign against Hoover, Franklin D. Roosevelt had been elected to succeed him in Albany. "After I left Albany," Smith said later, "after living in a mansion for six years, I couldn't see First Avenue very well, so I went over to Fifth Avenue. I signed a lease for $10,000 a year." Smith had been riding around Manhattan in a chauffeured limousine since the Crash, a director of banks and insurance companies, a crony of tycoons, the president of the Empire State Building. He had found a new level, a higher level, and he liked it.

Then, on Thursday, April 7, 1932, the nation heard a new voice over a nationwide hookup—the warm, vibrant, confident voice of Franklin Roosevelt. The governor denounced the Hoover administration for relieving the big banks and corporations. He mocked "shallow thinkers" who knew no way to help the farmer. "These unhappy times," he said, "call for the building of plans that put their faith once more in the forgotten man at the bottom of the economic pyramid."

Smith exploded at a Jefferson Day dinner. Flushed and hoarse, he said, "This country is sick and tired of listening to political campaign orators who tell us what is the matter with us," and that "this is no time for demagogues. I will take off my coat and vest and fight to the end any man who persists in any demagogic appeal to the masses of the working people of this country to destroy themselves by setting class against class and rich against poor!"

In retrospect Smith's outburst appears extraordinary both in its virulence and in the mildness of the sentiment which had triggered it. The governor had, after all, merely suggested that something be done for the starving poor.

The Roosevelt for President campaign was then being waged from an inconspicuous office at 331 Madison Avenue in New York City, and it was not going well. Since his smashing gubernatorial victory FDR had been the Democratic front runner, but as the convention approached he was losing ground rapidly. His most devoted subordinate was sixty-one-year-old Louis McHenry Howe, an uncomely little ex-newspaperman who liked to answer the telephone by saying, "This is the medieval gnome speaking." Many out-of-state politicians were repelled by him. But then, there wasn't much about the Roosevelt candidacy that critics found attractive. On the right, Bernard Baruch called the governor "wish-washy," Boss Frank Hague of Jersey City said he had "no chance of winning in November," and the Scripps-Howard newspapers, coming out for Al Smith, said, "In Franklin Roosevelt we have another Hoover."

He was the only leader in either party who had suggested progressive solutions for the national dilemma, yet the liberal abuse of him was even harsher. Heywood Broun, Elmer Davis, and Walter Lippmann scorned him. The *New Republic* dismissed him as "not a man of great intellectual force or supreme moral stamina." In an open letter to Roosevelt on May 11, editor Oswald Garrison Villard of the *Nation* wrote: "You have deeply stabbed the faith that is within Americans that an emergency brings a leader, that our institutions are to survive." Riffling through preconvention issues of the *Nation* one finds such anti-Roosevelt comments as ". . . there is small hope for better things in his candidacy" . . . "his candidacy arouses so little real enthusiasm" . . . "no evidence whatever that people are turning to him as a leader" . . . "weakness and readiness to compromise" . . . "To put into the Presidency at this hour another weak man in the place of Herbert Hoover would be all the more disastrous because of the mistaken idea that Franklin D. Roosevelt is really a liberal," and, picking up the Scripps-Howard refrain, "A Hoover, perhaps, by any other name is still a Hoover."

To win the Democratic nomination under the convention rules of 1932, a candidate needed two-thirds of the votes. Smith quickly became the leader of the coalition opposing FDR; both men entered the Massachusetts primary late in April, and Smith gave Roosevelt a beating, capturing all of the state's thirty-six convention votes. The popular margin was three to one. The following month red-baiting John Nance Garner, Speaker of the House and Hearst's candidate, carried the California primary by 60,000 votes, with FDR second and Smith a strong third. There was only one way Roosevelt could win the convention now, and that was by dealing with the bosses. Late in June the Democrats gathered in Chicago—where two weeks earlier the Republicans had renominated Hoover, after a delegate who wanted to nominate Coolidge had been muscled from the hall by Chicago policemen—and Howe began spinning his web from suite 1502 in the Congress Hotel. "What's your price?" he asked former Governor Harry Byrd of Virginia. Byrd said he wanted to be a U.S. Senator. "Is that your price?" the medieval gnome demanded. Byrd said that was it. Virginia already had two Democratic senators, but Howe said, "Very well. We'll put either Glass or Swanson in Franklin's cabinet." Politicians in those days were very direct.

Down at the podium of the Chicago Stadium John E. Mack was about to deliver a lackluster speech putting Roosevelt's name in nomination. Already the party had adopted an appalling platform promising a 25 percent reduction in federal spending, a balanced budget, loyalty to the gold standard, laissez-faire economics, and, its saving grace, repeal of Prohibition. The Roosevelt supporters didn't even have a theme song. Smith had preempted "The Sidewalks of New York." Since the governor's home town of Hyde Park didn't have sidewalks anyhow, Howe had decided to use "Anchors Aweigh" as a tribute to his man's naval service. While the judge approached the podium, Howe's secretary burst in on him and said "Anchors Aweigh" wouldn't do at all; it was being used in a radio commercial for a cigarette company. Instead she suggested a song written the year of the Crash for the MGM film *Chasing Rainbows*. She skipped up and down the bedroom of suite 1502, humming and snapping her fingers. Wearily agreeing, Howe picked up the phone and said, "Tell them to play 'Happy Days Are Here Again,'" thus giving a generation of Democrats its anthem. The judge finished, the demonstration began, and from the cheap pipe organ came:

> *Happy days are here again!*
> *The skies above are clear again!*
> *Let's all sing a song of cheer again—*
> *Happy days—are—here—a—gain!*

Although rousing, it wasn't enough; after three ballots the convention was still deadlocked. Some Roosevelt delegates were wavering.

Under the unit rule the switch of a single vote in the Mississippi caucus would mean the loss of the entire state. The Roosevelt floor managers, led by a Long Island politician named Jim Farley, promised Garner the Vice Presidency. Hearst was afraid that disintegration of FDR strength would bring in a dark horse advocate of the League of Nations, and on his advice Garner accepted the deal. From Washington, Garner phoned Sam Rayburn, his man on the floor. California switched—and the galleries, packed with Smith men, erupted in rage. Smith's delegates refused to make the party's choice unanimous; instead they ran around tearing up Roosevelt posters. Will Rogers said, "Ah! They was Democrats today. They fought, they fit, they split and adjourned in a dandy wave of dissension. That's the old Democratic spirit." Others were less kind. Heywood Broun jeered that Roosevelt was the "corkscrew candidate of a convoluting convention." H. L. Mencken wrote in the *Baltimore Sun* that the Democrats had picked their weakest candidate. The *San Francisco Chronicle* concurred, and so, during his daily medicine-ball workout with friends next morning, did President Hoover. They nodded; one assured him that the country was still conservative. Another said it was inconceivable that voters would elect a hopeless cripple. Already that whispering campaign had begun.

Roosevelt flew to Chicago in a trimotor Ford, writing his acceptance speech on the two-stop, turbulent, nine-hour flight from Albany. No one had ever accepted a presidential nomination with such alacrity, but this nominee believed that the Depression called for all sorts of unprecedented action; standing before the convention, his leg braces locked in place, he said he hoped the Democratic party would make it its business to break "absurd traditions." He cried, "I pledge you, I pledge myself, to a New Deal for the American people." Some delegates thought the phrase a brilliant combination of Theodore Roosevelt's Square Deal and Woodrow Wilson's New Freedom. Reporters, however, were discovering that FDR was a great borrower. "The forgotten man" had come from a speech delivered by William Graham Sumner in 1883, and Stuart Chase had just published a book entitled *A New Deal*. Roosevelt didn't much care about the genesis of a word, an idea, or a program. His statecraft was summed up in a speech at Oglethorpe University, when he said, "The country needs and, unless I mistake its temper, the country demands bold, persistent experimentation.

... Above all, try something." He had already begun recruiting college professors to generate suggestions. James Kieran of the *New York Times* called them "the brains trust"; then everyone else, Roosevelt included, borrowed *that* and shortened it to "brain trust."

If one definition of genius is an infinite capacity to make use of everyone and everything, the Democratic nominee certainly qualified. He reminded John Gunther of "a kind of universal joint, or rather a switchboard, a transformer," through which the energy and intelligence of other people flowed. Within a year he would become obscured by the mists of legend, but as a candidate he was still seen as mortal—a big, broad-shouldered man of fifty whose paralyzed legs were partially offset by his long arms and huge, hairy, freckled hands. His hair was gray and thin, and he had a small paunch, deep blue eyes set close together over permanent brown shadows, and two long wrinkles that formed parenthetical curves around his mouth. Undoubtedly his breeding as a country gentleman, guided by the old-fashioned morality of Groton headmaster Endicott Peabody, contributed immeasurably to his inner strength; he was perhaps the only politician in the country who thought of economics as a *moral* problem. Rooseveltian confidence was striking—someone said "he must have been psychoanalyzed by God"— and so was his memory. He remembered Italian streets and buildings he hadn't seen since his youth. Once in wartime a ship sank off Scotland; either it had been torpedoed or it had struck a rock. FDR said it was probably the rock, and then proceeded to reel off the height of the tide at that season on that coast and the extent to which that particular rock would be submerged. One of his favorite performances (and he was always a showman) was to ask a visitor to draw a line in any direction across an outline map of the United States; he would then name, in order, every county the line crossed. He was an apostle of progress; as soon as he saw the Sahara he wanted to irrigate it. Now in a world bereft of progressive action he was already a world figure. In Brussels *Demain* was investigating his horoscope. Among other things, the astrologers found excessive idealism, zeal for too rapid reformation, and "great good judgment." After 1941 he would be in danger of accidents.

He was telling the country that "to accomplish anything worthwhile . . . there must be a compromise between the ideal and the practical." That wasn't at all what the ideologues wanted to hear. Roosevelt, Harold Laski sneered, was "a pill to cure an earthquake."

Lippmann called him too soft, too eager to please and be all things to all men. The country yearned for a Messiah, Ernest K. Lindley reported, and Mr. Roosevelt did not "look or sound like a Messiah." John Dewey felt the argument that Governor Roosevelt was the lesser of two evils was "suicidal." Organized labor, such as it was, refused to endorse any candidate.

Disenchantment with the two major parties ran high. Will Rogers concluded, "The way most people feel, they would like to vote against all of them if it was possible." In Kansas, Republican gubernatorial candidate Alfred M. Landon was threatened by a third-party adventurer named Dr. John "Goat Glands" Brinkley; in California, District Attorney Earl Warren of Alameda County, running for reelection, was threatened by a half-dozen crank candidates. In FDR's own party he had the dubious honor of receiving support from Huey Long, the pasha of Louisiana, who packed a gun and who, in Roosevelt's private opinion, was one of the two most dangerous men in the country. (The other was General MacArthur.)

Lippmann saw "no issue of fundamental principle" between Roosevelt and Hoover, and defections on the left were particularly heavy. "If I vote at all," said Lewis Mumford, "it will be for the Communists. It is Communism which desires to save civilization." Professor Paul H. Douglas of the University of Chicago, later to become a brilliant ornament of the Democratic party, declared then that its destruction would be "one of the best things that could happen in our political life." John Chamberlain wrote in September that progressivism "must mean either Norman Thomas or William Z. Foster, ineffectual though one or both may be." Thomas supporters included Stephen Vincent Benét, Reinhold Niebuhr, Stuart Chase, Elmer Davis, Morris Ernst, and the editors of both the *New Republic* and the *Nation*. Villard continued his litany of the left; of Roosevelt he wrote: "He has spoken of the 'forgotten man,' but nowhere is there a real, passionate, ringing exposition of just what it is that the forgotten man has been deprived of or what should be done for him. . . . we can see in him no leader, and no evidence anywhere that he can rise to the needs of this extraordinary hour."

This was overstated, but when TRB wrote in the *New Republic* of "the pussyfooting policy of Roosevelt's campaign," and *Time* said the governor "emerged from the campaign fog as a vigorous well-intentioned gentleman of good birth and breeding" who "lacked crusading convictions," they were reading the record correctly. The candidate delivered only one really radical speech, to the Commonwealth Club of San Francisco on September 23. It was not repeated. His own convictions at this time were largely conservative; he believed in the gold standard, a balanced budget, and unregulated business competition. Moreover, he had to hold his party together. For every Huey Long on the left there were ten men like Al Smith, who said, "We should stop talking about the Forgotten Man and about class distinctions" and Garner, who sent word to Roosevelt that if he went too far with "wild-eyed ideas" they would have "the shit kicked out of us." FDR didn't go too far. His speeches were laced with ambiguities and contradictions. Many passages seem to reflect a shallow optimism, and one address, delivered in Pittsburgh, was a dreadful blunder. Among the new members of his brain trust was General Hugh S. "Ironpants" Johnson, a friend of Baruch's who had been Douglas MacArthur's classmate at West Point and had later shared a tent with George Patton on the Mexican border. As a child he had chanted, "Everybody's a rink-stink but Hughie Johnson and he's all right." That was still his attitude; to him the other brain-trusters were rink-stinks, and during their absence from the campaign train he persuaded the Democratic standard-bearer to embrace the platform plank calling for a 25 percent slash in the federal budget. FDR would hear about that four years later.

But his audiences were less interested in his stand on tariffs and the power business than in taking the measure of the man, and what they saw was a magnificent leader—his leonine head thrown back, his eye flashing, his cigarette holder tilted at the sky, his navy boat cloak falling gracefully from his great shoulders. He was the image of zest, warmth, and dignity; he was always smiling; he always called people "my friends." If his speeches were inadequate as statements of public policy, politically they were brilliant. Editors read, "The only real capital of the nation is its natural resources and its human beings," and they groaned. Voters felt the governor's obvious sincerity and were moved. To them his messages were lucid, specific, and illumined by homely metaphors. He cared about people. They could feel that. And the campaign was as much of an education for him as for them. Heading westward across the plains, he realized for the first time just how desperate the country's economic situation had become. "I have looked into the faces of thousands of Americans," he told a friend. ". . . They have the frightened look of lost children."

Meanwhile, back at the White House, Herbert Hoover had come alive. Roosevelt's speeches hadn't done it. The *Literary Digest* poll predicting a Roosevelt victory may have helped; so may the gambling odds, which were running seven to one against the President. The real shock, however, came from Maine. Maine still voted in September then, and when the ballots were counted it turned out that the state had elected a Democratic governor and two Democratic Congressmen—the first such slippage from the GOP since the Civil War. Hoover had carried forty states in 1928; he was bewildered. He told his secretary that this meant "we have got to fight to the limit." Earlier he had said that in four months of campaigning Roosevelt would lose the confidence of business, which in some mysterious way would, he thought, decide the election. Such firms as the Ford Motor Company had in fact notified their employees that "To prevent times from getting worse and to help them get better, President Hoover must be elected." But apparently workers weren't listening to their employers. Furthermore, there had been several startling desertions from Republican ranks, notably Senators Borah of Idaho and Hiram Johnson of California.

So Hoover put on his high-button shoes and celluloid collar and went to the people. He was lucky to come back alive. He deliberately chose the low road; to a member of his cabinet he confided that there was "hatred" for him in the country, and that the only way to win was to incite "a fear of what Roosevelt will do." In Des Moines he said of his tariff, "The grass will grow in the streets of a hundred cities, a thousand towns; the weeds will overrun the fields of millions of farms if that protection is taken away." They jeered and paraded Hoovercarts bearing signs that read, WE'LL GET THERE REGARDLESS OF HOOVER, AND THIS AIN'T NO BULL. In Indianapolis he told listeners that Roosevelt was peddling "nonsense . . . misstatements . . . prattle . . . untruths . . . defamation . . . ignorance . . . calumnies," and they hissed. In Cleveland he promised that no "deserving" citizen would starve, and they hooted. In St. Paul, referring to the rout of the bonus marchers, he said, "Thank God we still have a government in Washington that still knows how to deal with a mob," and the crowd replied with one vast snarl. Detroit was the worst. The city was carrying a quarter-million people on its relief rolls. At the station he was greeted with boos and catcalls.

Mounted police, swinging batons, scattered the throng, but all along his limousine route tens of thousands more shouted "Hang Hoover!" and shook their fists. Signs read, DOWN WITH HOOVER, SLAYER OF VETERANS!; BILLIONS FOR BANKERS, BULLETS FOR VETS. Afterward a Secret Serviceman told a reporter, "I've been traveling with Presidents since Teddy Roosevelt's time, and never before have I seen one actually booed, with men running out into the streets to thumb their noses at him. It's not a pretty sight." Chief Agent Sterling looked at Hoover and saw a man stricken. The President could hardly talk. By now people were throwing eggs and tomatoes at his train as it moved across the stricken land. He didn't know what else to do, so he phoned Calvin Coolidge.

Coolidge said his throat was bothering him and, what's more, "I find it terribly hard to know what to say." His difficulty was understandable. In Northampton, Massachusetts, his own bank was collapsing. Finally he agreed to speak in Madison Square Garden. Republicans thought the magic of his name would pack the Garden. Instead fewer than a third of the seats were filled, and frantic ushers ran outside begging passersby to come hear the country's only living ex-President. Inside, the party faithful gave him a two-minute ovation which he throttled by holding out his watch, showing that the cheers had wasted $340 of radio time. "That's Cal!" someone shouted. But it wasn't the Cal of old, nor was this the kind of audience he had known. He said, "The Republican party believes in encouraging business in order that the benefits from such business may minister to the welfare of the ordinary run of people." He waited for applause. There was silence. He began another sentence, "When I was in Washington—" and they roared with laughter. Baffled, he shook his head. No one had ever laughed at a Coolidge speech before. He stumbled through the text and went home declaring himself "burned-out"; in fifteen weeks he would be dead.

Now the party in power was really desperate. The Secretary of Agriculture maligned the New York governor as "a common garden variety of liar"; the Secretary of the Navy predicted, "If Roosevelt is elected, the homes and lives of a hundred million Americans might be in danger." Hoover cried, "My countrymen! The fundamental issue that will fix the national direction for one hundred years to come is whether we shall go in fidelity to American traditions or whether we shall turn to innovations." His shoulders sagged, the crow's-feet about his eyes deepened, the lines around his mouth grew harder. In his final radio plea to the electorate he premonished against "false gods arrayed in the rainbow colors of promises," and William Allen White noted "how infinitely tired" his voice was and "how hollow and how sad in disillusion" his words had become.

The contrast with Governor Roosevelt could not have been greater. "You may not have universally agreed with me, but you have universally been kind to me," FDR said to his radio audience; ". . . Out of this unity that I have seen we may build the strongest strand to lift ourselves out of this Depression." He was magnanimous and sure of himself, and no presidential challenger ever had better reason. Sitting in Democratic headquarters in New York on election night at the Hotel Biltmore, his Phi Beta Kappa key gleaming on his dark blue vest, he listened to reports of the growing avalanche until, at 12:17 A.M., Hoover conceded. The President-elect had carried 42 of the 48 states—all but Connecticut, Maine, Vermont, New Hampshire, Delaware, and Pennsylvania—and had won 472 electoral votes; the "President-reject," as *Time* cruelly called him, had but 59. It was the greatest victory in a two-party presidential race since Lincoln beat McClellan 212 to 21, though there were those who noted that the popular vote for Norman Thomas had jumped from 267,240 to 728,860. Louis Howe broke out a twenty-year-old bottle of sherry. Three babies born that night at Brooklyn's Beth-El Hospital were named Franklin Delano Mayblum, Franklin Delano Finkelstein, and Franklin Delano Ragin.

Franklin Delano Roosevelt retired to his town house at 49 East Sixty-fifth Street, where his mother embraced him and said elatedly, "This is the greatest moment of my life." Her son, however, seemed to have lost some of his campaign assurance. Upstairs his twenty-five-year-old son lifted him into bed, leaned over, and kissed him goodnight. Looking up, the President-elect said, "You know, Jimmy, all my life I have been afraid of only one thing—fire. Tonight I think I'm afraid of something else." The young man asked, "Afraid of what, Pa?" and his father replied, "I'm just afraid that I may not have the strength to do this job."

Next morning, propped in bed, he was heartened by the nation's editorial comment. Even the *Chicago Tribune* said that his "personality and his ideas pleased the people. They were impressed by his good will and good faith." Those qualities were there, but they could not be traded upon. He had not won the Presidency without a shrewd eye for hidden motives, and he needed it that morning.

Hoover's congratulatory telegram had arrived; it must be answered. At first he wrote on the back of it that he was prepared "to cooperate with you" in the months ahead. Then he paused and struck that out. In its place he scrawled that he was "ready to further in every way the common purpose to help our country." In 1932 Presidents were not inaugurated until March 4. A four-month interregnum lay ahead. He had a hunch that Hoover would try to tie him to the discredited policies of the outgoing administration, and he was right.

On December 5 the lame-duck 72nd Congress limped back to Capitol Hill, and those of its members who were under the impression that the rout of the BEF had frightened jobless families away from Washington were in for a shock. Over 2,500 men, women, and children greeted them at the Capitol steps, chanting, "Feed the hungry, tax the rich! Feed the hungry, tax the rich!" The District's new police commissioner had orders not to humor such wraiths, and he followed them scrupulously. Policemen with gas guns and riot guns defended the Hill, then rounded up the throng and herded it down New Jersey Avenue to Camp Meigs, a wartime cantonment on New York Avenue. The commissioner told the press he had concentrated his wards in a "detention camp." Their guards ridiculed them and denied them water, food, medical attention or even the right to dig toilets; a Wisconsin congressman reported to his constituents that he had seen policemen deliberately provoking people. After huddling on the frozen ground for forty-eight hours, the prisoners were released. Leaving, they sang the newly learned words:

> *Arise, ye prisoners of starvation*
> *Arise, ye wretched of the earth*
> *For justice thunders condemnation*
> *A better world's in birth. . . .*

Throughout the early Thirties, and especially in the months bracketing the last session of the 72nd Congress, the sound of famished men on the march was heard from coast to coast. In New York thirty-five thousand men and women packed Union Square to hear Communist party orators. Crowds in Oklahoma City, Minneapolis, and St. Paul broke into groceries and meat markets to rifle shelves. Feelings of desperation were still internalized in most men (the suicide rate tripled that winter) but more and more mobs were beginning to coalesce. In Lincoln, Nebraska, four thousand men occupied the statehouse, another five thousand took over Seattle's ten-story County-City Building, and five thousand Chicago teachers, tormented beyond endurance, stormed the city's banks. The strains of "L'Internationale" were becoming increasingly familiar to the jobless; a forty-two-year-old radical named Louis Budenz led the Ohio Unemployed League mass march on the Columbus statehouse. His slogan was: "We must take control of the government and establish a workers' and farmers' republic."

The sense of institutions, authority, and private property—the intuitive discipline which Daniel Patrick Moynihan would later call "the glue that holds societies together"—was showing signs of disintegration. The tax strikes and the bootleg mining of company coal seams were ominous; so was the frequency with which empty lots were being gardened without their owners' consent, and the scattered, aimless rioting in Detroit, where relief had simply stopped. Some communities quit. Key West, Florida, was going into bankruptcy; there was no money to pay the sanitation department, and whole streets were filling up with rubbish and garbage. Here and there the starving were muttering violence. The mayor of a Massachusetts town, watching two thousand idle men milling around his city hall, wrote that "a spark might change them into a mob." Governor O. Max Gardner of North Carolina warned of the danger of "violent social and political revolution." Mayor Anton Cermak of Chicago, faced with the state's reluctance to appropriate funds for the city's six hundred thousand out-of-work men, told the legislature, "Call out the troops before you close the relief stations."

The well-fed were edgy. Company men in employment offices became curt, bank tellers nervous, elected officials quicker to call the police, policemen faster with the nightstick. Henry Ford had always been a pacifist. Now he carried a gun. In Richmond, Virginia, a delegation from the local Unemployed Council called on Mayor J. Fulmer Bright a few days after Thanksgiving; the mayor told his police chief, "Take these men by the scruff of the neck and the seat of the pants and throw them out." Jittery company guards killed four miners in Pennsylvania's Fayette County. New York ordered the apple sellers off its sidewalks, and John P. O'Brien, the new occupant of Gracie Mansion, promised his city, "You're going to have a mayor with a chin and fight in him. I'll preserve the metropolis from the Red Army." Plainclothesmen swinging truncheons waded into a Union Square rally; the *New York Times* reported "screams of women and cries of men with bloody heads and faces." Oklahoma City police used tear gas to break up meetings. Seattle police evicted the squatters from its County-City Building with fire hoses. Chicago law enforcement officers clubbed the unpaid teachers with billies, two of them holding one middle-aged woman while a third smashed her face.

Testifying before a Senate committee about the "sporadic uprisings in a number of our industrial cities," an AFL spokesman said that "the great bulk of those people know nothing about Communism. They wanted bread." To the propertied classes, the distinction was irrelevant. As Robert Sherwood wrote, the way ahead seemed to be clouded by "black doubt, punctured by brief flashes of ominous light, whose revelations are not comforting." If the government could not keep order, each man must look to his own. Businessmen in a number of cities formed committees to cope with nameless terrors should railroad and telephone lines be cut and surrounding highways blocked. Candles and canned goods were stockpiled; a Hollywood director carried with him a wardrobe of old clothes so that he could "disappear into the crowd" on a moment's notice. In New York, hotels discovered that wealthy guests who usually leased suites for the winter were holing up in their country homes. Some had mounted machine guns on their roofs.

They weren't paranoid. The evidence strongly suggests that had Roosevelt in fact been another Hoover, the United States would have followed seven Latin American countries whose governments had been overthrown by Depression victims. Charles M. Schwab was one of many tycoons who believed revolution was just around the corner. The dean of the Harvard Business School said, "Capitalism is on trial and on the issue of this trial may depend the whole future of Western civilization." Articles debating the imminence of revolt appeared in the *Yale Review, Scribner's, Harper's,* the *American Mercury,* and the *Atlantic.* Norman Thomas later said of the period "between the popular election and the inauguration" that "never before or since have I heard so much open and bitter cynicism about democracy and the American system."

There was a great deal of disagreement about which form of government the United States should adopt. Most intellectuals had turned leftward. Socialism to them was the middle of the road; John Dos Passos scornfully compared it to drinking near beer. Those who openly espoused Communism included Dos Passos, Sherwood Anderson, Erskine Caldwell, Malcolm Cowley, Lincoln Steffens, Granville Hicks, Clifton Fadiman, Upton Sinclair, and Edmund Wilson, who urged taking "Communism away from the Communists," and subsequently added that Russia was "the moral top of the world where the light really never goes out." William Allen White called the Soviet Union "the most interesting place on the planet." *New Russia's Primer* was a Book-of-the-Month Club choice; it compared American chaos with Russian order. "Those rascals in Russia," said Will Rogers, ". . . have got mighty good ideas. . . . Just think of everybody in a country going to work." Elmer Davis said the profit system was dead. Even Scott Fitzgerald was reading Marx and writing, "To bring on the revolution, it may be necessary to work inside the Communist Party." Stuart Chase asked in *A New Deal*, "Why should Russians have all the fun of remaking a world?" More than one man in office flirted with the left. Governor Theodore G. Bilbo of Mississippi confessed, "I'm getting a little pink myself," and Governor Floyd B. Olson of Minnesota, more forthright, told a Washingtonian to go back "and tell 'em Olson is taking recruits for the Minnesota National Guard, and he isn't taking anybody who doesn't carry a Red Card." To be sure he wasn't misunderstood he added, "Minnesota is a left-wing state."

But the greater danger lay at the other end of the political spectrum. Intellectuals lacked power, and Bilbo and Olson were political eccentrics. The money, the influence, and Secretary of the Army Hurley were on the right. As early as 1931 the administration had resisted attempts to reduce troop levels because the cut would "lessen our means of maintaining domestic peace and order," and that September the American Legion had passed a resolution asserting that the economic crisis could not be "promptly and efficiently met by existing political methods." The "American Facist [*sic*] Association and Order of Black Shirts" had been founded in Atlanta, and although its name was unpopular—asked if fascism would come to America, Huey Long said, "Sure, but here it will be called antifascism"—the Black Shirts had been joined by Silver Shirts, White Shirts, Khaki Shirts, the Minute Men, and the American Nationalists. A secret clique of reserve army officers was reported ready to act if the new President proved ineffective. General Smedley D. Butler testified that a New York bond salesman had attempted to recruit him for the right with an offer of $18,000 in cash. Nicholas Murray Butler told his students that totalitarian regimes brought forth "men of far greater intelligence, far stronger character, and far more courage than the system of elections," and if anyone represented the American establishment then it was Dr. Butler, with his Nobel Prize, his thirty-four honorary degrees, and his thirty-year tenure as president of Columbia University.

Who else was prepared to sacrifice constitutional government for this vision of expanded intelligence, character, and virility? Apart from the president of Columbia and General Butler's bond salesman, few came out for totalitarianism as such, but plenty advocated the principle. Governor Landon of Kansas declared, "Even the iron hand of a national dictator is in preference to a paralytic stroke." Congressman Hamilton Fish Jr. of New York said in 1932, "If we don't give it [dictatorship] under the existing system, the people will change the system." In February 1933 he wrote the President-elect that he and his fellow Republicans were ready to "give you any power you may need." Al Smith thought the Constitution ought to be wrapped up and laid "on the shelf" until the crisis was over. *Vanity Fair*, whose associate editors included Clare Boothe Brokaw (later Luce), demanded, "Appoint a dictator!" Walter Lippmann wanted to give the President full power at the expense of Congress; "the danger," he said, "is not that we shall lose our liberties, but that we shall not be able to act with the necessary speed and comprehensiveness," and Republican Senator David A. Reed said outright, "If this country ever needed a Mussolini, it needs one now."

In a *New Yorker* cartoon a girl at a Greenwich Village party told a limp young man, "Oh, it's all very simple. Our little group simply seizes the powerhouses and the radio station." That was where the danger lay, most people thought; in the cities. Secretary Hurley was believed to be concentrating the few troops he had near metropolitan areas, but rebellious populations have a way of outfoxing authority, and the opening revolt came where it was least expected. Farmers had always been considered the most conservative of Americans, yet it was in Republican Iowa—Hoover's home state—that sunburned men of native stock first reached for their pitchforks and shotguns. They were finally taking up arms against a system which paid them two cents a quart for milk that distributors sold for eight cents in Sioux City.

Under the leadership of Milo Reno, a sixty-four-year-old former president of the Iowa Farmers Union, they blocked all ten highways leading into the city. Spiked telegraph poles and logs were laid across the roads. Only milk for hospitals was allowed to pass. Other trucks were stopped and the milk cans emptied into ditches or taken into town and distributed free. Sympathetic telephone operators warned the insurgent farmers of approaching convoys an hour in advance; sheriffs were disarmed and their pistols and badges thrown into cornfields. Route 20 became known as Bunker Hill 20. Peering at Mary Heaton Vorse of *Harper's* from under the brim of a ten-cent straw hat, an old man said, "They say blockading the highway's illegal. I says, 'Seems to me there was a tea party in Boston that was illegal too.'"

The movement spread until Des Moines, Council Bluffs, and Omaha were isolated. In Wisconsin, embattled farmers invaded a dairy three times in one day, dumped 34,000 pounds of milk on the ground, and poured gasoline in the vats. A congressional subcommittee heard Oscar Ameringer of Oklahoma City describe a conversation with a rancher whom he had known to be conservative. The man had said, "We've got to have a revolution here like they had in Russia." Ameringer had asked him how he proposed to do it, and the man had replied, "We will have four hundred machine guns . . . batteries of artillery, tractors and munitions and rifles and everything else needed to supply a pretty good army. . . . If there are enough fellows with guts in this country to do like us, we will march eastward and we will cut the East off. We will cut the East off from the West. We have got the granaries; we have the hogs, the cattle, the corn, and the East has nothing but mortgages on our places. We will show them what we can do." Ameringer told the House Labor Committee, "I have heard much of this talk from serious-minded prosperous men of other days."

Will Rogers said, "Paul Revere just woke up Concord. These birds woke up America." And on Route 20 the Iowans sang:

> *Let's call a farmers' holiday*
> *A holiday let's hold;*
> *We'll eat our wheat and ham and eggs*
> *And let them eat their gold.*

The Sioux City siege was lifted shortly after a mysterious shotgun attack on the camp of some Milo Reno followers near the town of Cherokee, forty-eight miles east of the city. He quit, and farmers surrounding the other invested cities quit with him. But Reno said, "You can no more stop this movement than you could stop the revolution. I mean the revolution of 1776." Both in their violence and their uprising they were being faithful to American tradition. And they went unpunished. At Council Bluffs sixty had been arrested, but when a thousand of their fellow insurgents marched on the jail, they were hastily released. Deciding that direct action paid, the farmers now decided to do something about mortgage foreclosures.

On the outskirts of a Kansas village police found the murdered body of a lawyer who had just foreclosed on a five-hundred-acre farm. In Cheyenne County, Nebraska, the leaders of two hundred thousand debt-ridden farmers announced that if they didn't get help from the legislature they would converge on the statehouse and raze it, brick by brick. Throughout Hoover's last winter as President there were foreclosure riots in Iowa at Storm Lake, at Primghar, in Van Buren County, and at Le Mars. The Le Mars incident was particularly ugly. Black-shirted vigilantes invaded the courtroom of Judge Charles C. Bradley, dragged him from the bench, blindfolded him, and drove him to a lonely crossroads. Their leader demanded, "Will you swear you won't sign no more mortgage foreclosures?" The judge said no. Again and again the demand was repeated, and the answer was the same. He was slapped, kicked, and knocked to the ground. A rope was tied around his neck; the other end was thrown over a roadside sign. A greasy hubcap was clapped down on his head—"That's his crown," one of the men shouted. The judge never did give his word, but though he was stripped and beaten, he declined to press prosecution afterward.

When papers had been signed, hundreds of farmers would appear at the auction shouting, "No sale!" Prospective bidders would be shoved aside; then neighbors would buy the land for a few dollars and return it to its original owner. At one sheriff's sale a horse brought five cents, a Holstein bull five cents, three hogs another nickel, two calves four cents, and so on, until the entire property had changed hands for $1.18. It was deeded back to the householder for ninety-nine years. Lawyers representing insurance companies in the East were kidnapped and threatened with the noose until the home office relented and agreed to a mortgage moratorium. By the end of January 1933, John A. Simpson, president of the National Farmers Union, told the Senate Committee on Agriculture, "The biggest and finest crop of revolutions you ever saw is sprouting all over this country right now." Edward A. O'Neal III, president of the American Farm Bureau Federation, added, "Unless something is done for the American farmer we'll have revolution in the countryside in less than twelve months."

Here and there that troubled winter were sensitive boys now reaching the age of awareness who would, a generation later, become American leaders. Although their reactions to the world around them varied, none would ever forget the Great Depression. American history in their lifetimes would be a succession of crises, but for them this first crisis was formative.

A glance at some names is useful. In 1932 Robert F. Kennedy became seven years old; Frank Church and James Baldwin were eight; Mark Hatfield and Norman Mailer nine; John Lindsay, Nicholas Katzenbach, and Floyd McKissick ten; Whitney Young and John Glenn eleven; James Farmer, Stewart Udall, and Charles Percy twelve; Edward Brooke, George Wallace, McGeorge Bundy, and Russell Long thirteen; Billy Graham, Orville Freeman, and Arthur M. Schlesinger Jr. fourteen; John F. Kennedy, Robert Taft Jr., John Connally, and Lawrence F. O'Brien fifteen; Arthur Miller, Robert McNamara, Eugene McCarthy, and John Tower sixteen; David Rockefeller, Peter Dominick, Herman Wouk, Saul Bellow, Walter Heller and Theodore H. White seventeen; William Westmoreland, Tennessee Williams, Jonas Salk, and Stewart Alsop eighteen; and Gerald Ford and Richard M. Nixon nineteen.

Nixon had entered his junior year at Whittier College that autumn, majoring in history and running the fresh vegetable counter at Nixon's Market, the family store; each morning before dawn he drove to the Los Angeles Public Market to haggle with produce growers over prices. The family had enough to eat, which put Nixon in the great silent majority of eighty million Americans who were neither starving nor on relief. His collegiate status set him apart, however; fewer than one youth in eight between eighteen and twenty-two was in college, and only half had gone to high school. For millions, formal education was still confined to the one-teacher elementary school, of which there were 143,391 in the country.

If it were possible to be transported back in time to the typical middle-class neighborhood of that year, it would probably be in a city; suburban areas had begun to form, but only 18 percent of the population lived there. It was still feasible for a man and his family to live decently within walking distance of his office. Arriving on a street in the neighborhood, a visitor from the 1970s would first notice superficial differences—stop signs were yellow, mailboxes green; milk bottles thick and heavy—and then the seedy appearance of the houses. Few had been painted since 1929; often those which had been under construction had been left unfinished. On Detroit's East Jefferson Street, for example, the Elks suspended work on an eleven-story building, and its naked beams stood silhouetted against the sky for thirty-four years.

Appliances, gadgets, and creature comforts of the 1970s were rare. There were no power mowers, home air-conditioning units, automatic dishwashers, clothes driers, electric blankets, clock-radios, thermopane windows, nylons, drip-dry clothes, frozen foods, automatic coffee makers, cordless shavers, filter cigarettes, electric toothbrushes, vinyl floors, ball-point pens, electric typewriters, Dictaphones, Xerox machines, Styrofoam, hi-fi stereo sets, Scotch tape, home freezers, cassette recorders, color or Polaroid film, Fiberglas fishing rods, garbage disposal units, tape recorders, snow blowers, electric knives, home hair driers, electric can openers, or Muzak, and although Gilbert Seldes was predicting in *Harper's* that soon "we shall probably have the simple and comparatively inexpensive mechanisms, now being perfected, which will throw on a small screen set up beside the home radio set a moving picture projected from a central broadcasting station," there was no television, not even plain black-and-white. Somehow the middle class survived the Depression—the entire decade of the Thirties—with none of these. O Pioneers!

Most American homes were heated by hand-stoked hot air furnaces, which had to be tended twice daily. The country needed nearly 400 million tons of coal to get through a winter, and it was brought to a house by a grimy man who would back his truck to a cellar window and empty the coal down a chute into a bin near the furnace. "Refrigerator" didn't mean an *electric* refrigerator; it was an icebox, kept filled by an iceman who knew how many pounds a housewife wanted because she notified him by placing in her kitchen window a card with the figure 100, 75, 50, or 25 turned up. It was an affluent husband who bought his wife a toaster that would scorch both sides of a piece of bread simultaneously ("Our SUPREME toaster!" cried the Sears, Roebuck catalogue that year), for in most homes bread was singed in a gas oven or a coal or wood-burning "kitchen range." The stove might also be used to heat heavy sadirons for pressing clothing that had come back from the laundry rough-dried, or, in a home without hot water, for heating bucketfuls before a bath.

Phonographs had to be wound by hand; they might be called Victrolas or Gramophones, but never record players. A housewife began her heavy cleaning by donning a dustcap, and as a rule her only mechanical help was a carpet sweeper; in December 1932, in all the houses served by the Alabama Power Company, there were exactly 185 vacuum cleaners. Most farms depended upon kerosene lamps for illumination. Electricity was available to one American farmer in every ten—in Mississippi the ratio was one in a hundred—and 90 percent of all rural families were without either bathtubs or showers. Seventy-five percent lacked indoor plumbing. Half carried their water from wells or brooks and did their laundry—and washed their children—outdoors. (For that matter, millions of urban housewives also had only a washboard to cope with the family laundry, which was usually hung out on Mondays.) Insects were always a summer problem. There was no DDT. Both on farms and in cities the only preventives were spray guns ("Quick, Henry, the Flit!") and flypaper. A mother who wanted fruit juice for her children had to work at it. She bought Sunkist oranges and laboriously squeezed them, one by one, on an aluminum juice extractor.

Before a girl learned how to handle bobby pins—at about the same age that boys were acquiring their first long pants—her mother had explained the difference between a lady and a woman. Being a lady had certain advantages. Men opened doors for her, stood up to give her a seat on buses and streetcars, and removed their hats when she entered elevators; butchers cut her meat to order, grocers took orders over the telephone and delivered to her door, and when she had a baby she was expected to stay in bed ten days (at a total cost, including the doctor's fee, of $25). On the other hand, she was expected to defer to her husband; at the altar she had sworn "to love, honor, and *obey* him." Her activities in public were circumscribed by convention. A middle-class lady could neither smoke on the street nor appear with hair curlers. In her purse she carried cosmetics in a small disc called a compact, but this, too, could be produced only in private or a ladies' room. She never swore or told dirty jokes. (Sometimes she wondered what a lesbian was. But whom could she ask?) Advertising copywriters saw to it that she had enough worries anyway: halitosis, B.O., undie odor, office hips, paralyzed pores, pink toothbrush, ashtray breath, colon collapse, pendulosis, and athlete's foot. Her skirts came to mid-calf. (Any woman whose hem did not cover the knee was assumed to be a prostitute.) A lady would no more leave the house without her cloche than her husband would without his snap-brim felt hat. She might squirt Ipana (for the smile-of-beauty) on her Dr. West toothbrush, and even use Tangee lipstick, but fingernail paint and hair dye were highly dubious. Hairdressers didn't know how to use dye. Respectable women didn't even talk about it; a clever young NYU chemistry major, who sold his homemade Clairol dye from door to door, discovered that to make ends meet he had to talk about hair "coloring."

As a mother, the middle-class wife often had to double as a nurse. Illnesses were long and painful then. Even a visit to the dentist meant an hour of agony; Procaine, a primitive form of Novocaine, was widely used, but it had to be mixed at the chair and was accompanied by disagreeable side effects. Thousands of patients still had to take the big burring drill straight, and since fast drills hadn't been invented, not much could be accomplished in one visit. In many hospitals, anesthesiologists were limited to chloroform; ether would soon succeed it, though the improvement was questionable. There were no sulfa drugs and no antibiotics. Meningitis killed 95 percent of its victims; pneumonia was often fatal. Even viral infections (called "the grippe" then) were a serious business. Though hospitals were comparatively inexpensive, practically no one had hospital insurance—the American Medical Association didn't approve Blue Cross until 1933—so most patients remained at home, which meant with mother. She seldom had the help of medication. Ethical drugs were largely limited to a few barbiturates, notably phenobarbital. So remote was the drug nightmare of the next generation that 3,512 drug firms failed between 1932 and 1934, leaving liabilities of over 59 million dollars.

If motherhood was more difficult, it was also a greater challenge. Parents had a tremendous influence upon their children. The teenage subculture did not exist; indeed "teenage," as defined by Merriam-Webster, meant "brushwood used for fences and hedges." Young people were called youngsters, and youngsters were loyal to their homes. Since the brooding omnipresence of the peer group had not yet arrived, children rarely felt any conflict between their friends and their families. No youngster would dream of discussing parental conflicts with other youngsters. If a middle-class family was going to take a drive in the country on Sunday afternoon, as it usually was, children quit the baseball or hopscotch game and hopped in the back seat. The Depression increased all family activities; a study of over a hundred white-collar and professional families in Pittsburgh discovered that a majority had increased family recreation—ping-pong, jigsaw puzzles, checkers, parlor games, bridge, and most of all listening to the radio.

As often as not, the radio was the most prominent piece of furniture in the living room. Whether an Atwater Kent, Philco, Silvertone, or Majestic set, it was likely to be a rococo console in high Grand Rapids style. Network programs were scheduled with the family in mind. Mother's serials came during the day; news, comedians, and variety programs in the evening. Between the two was sandwiched the children's hour, part of which might be listed in the local newspaper as:

5:15	WTIC	1040	Tom Mix
	WEAF	660	Story Man
5:30	WTIC	1040	Jack Armstrong
	WJZ	760	Singing Lady
5:45	WJZ	760	Little Orphan Annie
6:00	WOR	710	Uncle Don

In the winter of 1932-33 a young middle-class boy wore, almost as a uniform, a sheepskin-lined tan cloth coat, a knitted hat, corduroy knickers, and high-cut lace-up boots with a small pocket on the side of one of them for a jackknife. (In summertime he wore short pants and Keds.) If he was lucky, he owned a Ranger 28-inch-wheel bike with a coaster brake and cushion tires, the tires protected by Neverleak and the whole locked, when not in use, by a $1.50 slip-shackle padlock. The times being what they were, he was very much aware of money and what it bought. A nickel would bring a three-flavored cake of brick ice cream, a Horton's Dixie Cup, a candy bar, a loaf of bread, a local telephone call, a cup of coffee, or a copy of the *Saturday Evening Post*, *Collier's*, or *Liberty*. For a penny you could get candy, a pencil, a postcard, a pad of paper, a glass marble, or your best friend's thoughts.

If you had an allowance (a Sunday nickel, say) or had earned some money shoveling snow or mowing lawns at a quarter apiece, the quickest place to spend it was at the corner drugstore, drinking a Coke at one of the marble-topped, wire-legged tables, though in

Youngstown, Ohio, children bought ice-cream-on-a-stick from a confectioner who drove slowly through the suburbs in a white truck, ringing a bell, and who called himself the Good Humor man. A boy who accumulated as much as fifty cents could get the latest in the Tom Swift series. As David Riesman has pointed out, the heroes of boys' literature were "ambitious. They had goals. And the reader identified with them and tried to emulate them. . . . The virtue which brought victory was frequently an ability to control the self, for instance, to be brave." Significantly, the most widely read book in middle-class homes was Charles Lindbergh's *We*.

Inner-direction (or, as Paul Elmer More then called it, "the inner check") provided children with a built-in need to achieve, though the Depression discouraged them from reaching for anything beyond their grasp. In 1931 the *Literary Digest* had conducted a survey of vocation preference among children. Boys of eight wanted to be cowboys, aviators, or army officers when they grew up; girls wanted to be movie stars. At eighteen the boys were looking forward to being lawyers, electrical engineers, or architects; eighteen-year-old girls were taking stenographic and secretarial training. Adolescence was a sobering experience. But then, it wasn't supposed to be much fun. "Childhood is so short and the balance of life so long," Dorothy Dix explained. "At best, a mother can satin-pad the world for her children for a few years. Then they are bound to face realities, and it is a bitter price they must pay for her folly in turning them into weaklings, instead of strong men and women, and making them unable to cope with the difficulties that they are inevitably destined to encounter."

One of the first lessons a child learned—because it would be a future asset when he applied for a job—was the importance of personal appearance. "Sit up *straight!*" he was told, and "Here's fifteen cents, go get a haircut." He might prefer a Flexible Flyer sled or a Simplex typewriter, but what he got first was an $8.95 blue serge suit comprising a coat, vest, and knickers, and a pair of black $2.98 Gold Bond shoes. He wore them Sundays and on the first day of each semester, when every mother examined her son like a first sergeant going over his men before a white-glove inspection. (Somehow he always forgot his white handkerchief.) She wanted his new teachers to have a nice impression. It is not recorded that any child ever asked why.

To school he also brought a Masterpiece tablet, bearing on its cover a blurry reproduction of a great painting; in it he laboriously copied assignments with a big, circular Palmer Penmanship script. Seats in the classroom were frequently arranged alphabetically. The walls of at least one room would be decorated with the ruins of Pompeii or a bust of Caesar, etchings and statues which, as Riesman noted, would "signify the irrelevance of the school to the emotional needs of the child." Some of his lessons make interesting reading today. Young Lyndon Johnson had read in his geography book:

> French Indo-China resembles Siam both in climate and the character of people. Its forest-covered hills yield valuable teak and ironwood, and in its valleys are extensive fields of rice and millet. Silk, cotton, tea and spices are other products and there are also extensive coal beds.

A civics textbook explained:

> The child who has not learned obedience is handicapped for life. If he does not obey at home, he is not likely to observe the laws of the state, even though he helps elect the men who make them. Boys and girls who study our Government will quickly discover that obedience to authority is as necessary in a government by the people as in a monarchy.

And this paragraph appeared in Professor Thomas Marshall's widely used *American History,* published by Macmillan in 1930:

> *The slaves.* Although he was in a state of slavery, the Negro of plantation days was usually happy. He was fond of the company of others and liked to sing, dance, crack jokes, and laugh; he admired bright colors and was proud to wear a red or yellow bandana. He wanted to be praised, and he was loyal to a kind master or overseer. He was never in a hurry, and was always ready to let things go until the morrow. Most of the planters learned that not the whip, but loyalty, based upon pride, kindness, and rewards, brought the best returns.

Nor did unreality stop there. In schools of the Thirties—including, for several years, Washington, D.C.—teachers were forbidden to so much as mention the Soviet Union. On maps the area occupied by Russia was left blank, like the many "unexplored" tracts in Africa. School days usually opened with both the pledge of allegiance to the flag and a Protestant prayer, in which Jewish and Catholic children were expected to share. God was very much alive in 1932, and he was something of a prig. There is a great deal of social comment in *Time*'s prissy review of Earl Carroll's *Vanities* that October. Like Erskine Caldwell, Carroll sorely tested the Luce tolerance: "Mr. Carroll's shows have long held the record for borderline humor. In Comedian Milton Berle is to be found the acme of hysterical vulgarity. While one part of the audience blushes and the other part guffaws, Comedian Berle proceeds to imitate a person of uncertain gender, quip about the show girls' fundaments, shout depraved announcements into a loudspeaker. He seems to get a great deal of fun out of it." What especially entertained Berle—and infuriated *Time*—was that some of the chorines appeared with their brassieres clearly visible.

Mae West appeared that year with George Raft in *Night After Night*, and there were gasps in middle-class America when, in reply to a friend's remark, "Goodness, what beautiful diamonds," Mae replied, "Goodness has nothing to do with it, dearie." Will H. Hays, then czar of all the rushes, also overlooked an exchange in Busby Berkeley's first musical, *Forty-Second Street;* one chorus girl said, "I'm afraid I gotta run," the second said, "First door on your left," and the first said, "In my stocking." Such outrageous lewdness didn't get by often. For adolescents, sex was the most forbidden of all subjects. Like the myths about bogeymen and truant officers and the lists of New Year's resolutions which were faithfully made out each January 1 and broken within a week, the treatment of sex information virtually assured massive guilt feelings. Every growing boy knew masturbation led to brain damage and, in time, to the growth of hair on the palms of his hands.

Girls similarly worried over who had the reputation for being the "hottest" or "dirtiest" girl in school. Their difficulties were increased by the fact that the world of adolescence was largely male chauvinist. Girls were rarely invited to go bike riding, swap steelies or gum cards, discuss the Cleveland National Air Races, or play mumblety-peg, king-of-the-mountain, capture-the-flag, or (unless they were sisters or tomboys) ringolevio. A boy and girl might hold a strained conversation about the relative merits of the Ipana Troubadors, the Cliquot Club Eskimos, and the A & P Gypsies, but girls were largely spectators who emitted squeals during the great annual festival of July 4, when the anniversary of independence was celebrated by firing Bangsite cannon, hurling torpedoes at the sidewalk, and blowing up tin cans with two-inchers and cherry bombs.

Middle-class parents who could afford it—and at eight dollars a week the cost was not prohibitive—sent their children away for at least part of the summer, if only because of the annual polio terror. When an epidemic of infantile paralysis struck, people stayed home from movies and meetings; some wouldn't even appear outdoors without gauze masks. Thus many a middle-class city child learned to swim at a Scout or YMCA camp, came to love the scent of honeysuckle and the flight of fireflies and June bugs around a campfire, and was told the sound of katydids in August meant frost in six weeks.

Sometimes the whole family would strap suitcases on the running boards of the new Chevrolet ($445, F.O.B. Detroit) and go "touring." Touring was an adventure, with real hazards. The spare tire mounted on the back of a roadster or a sedan was frequently needed, and with the tires of that era a blowup was a real explosion. Automobiles were uncomfortable. Meals in "roadhouses" were of uncertain quality. Overnight rest was difficult; rooms were hard to find. According to the American Automobile Association, the average American on tour spent a week getting to where he was going and a week coming back, which seems like a lot of touring until you realize that on the roads of that day he could average only 234 miles a day. Route 1 went right through the center of Washington, Philadelphia, New York and Boston; you had to use ferries at the Delaware River and the Hudson (the George Washington Bridge was still under construction); and in Maine, Depression winters had left the roads high-crowned and weak-shouldered. Speed traps were everywhere. There were no interstate highways. The only way you could drive coast to coast from the east was to take route 30 (the Lincoln Highway) into the center of Chicago, where you picked up route 66. Both were two-lane roads, both had stretches of unpaved dirt, and 66 traversed the Rockies with ungraded hairpin curves.

If all this sounds a trifle primitive, it must be added that, as Caroline Bird had pointed out, certain aspects of American society then could be quite pleasant. To be sure, you needed money, but not a great deal; an income of $5,000 or $6,000, or even less, brought comforts unknown today. The middle-class world was much quieter. There were no sonic booms, pneumatic paving breakers, high-impact rock drills, air compressors, chain saws, hi-fi sets, tape recorders, playback units or 125-decibel rock groups, and very few riveters. It was more private. The FBI had fewer than three million fingerprints, and the digital society of social security numbers, zip codes, direct distance dialing, and credit card memory banks was unknown. Getting into college was relatively easy. Only thirty-five thousand applicants took college boards in 1932. If you preferred to fly the scheduling was primitive, but passengers received first-class service—the labor market being what it was, airlines could require extra effort from their R.N. stewardesses.

You never needed reservations at hotels, fine restaurants, hairdressing emporia, or hospitals. Nobody worried about pollution; factory chimneys were cold. Tutors, barbers, dressmakers, music teachers, and even physicians came to your house. If you worked in an office, secretaries arrived on time in the morning. They didn't disappear for coffee breaks, didn't make personal telephone calls from the office, and didn't object to working overtime. "The best guarantee of efficiency is a long line at the factory gate," was the way Samuel Insull put it (he would), but John Kenneth Galbraith stated the principle less cruelly. The more retrograde an economy becomes, he said, the more service improves.

Apart from amenities, the most cheerful feature of life then, as seen from the 1970s, lay abroad. Not only was America untroubled by foreign crises; as far as the vast majority of Americans were concerned, there were no foreign affairs at all. The Japanese were behaving badly in China, but who had time for that? In the German presidential elections eighty-four-year-old Paul von Hindenburg defeated forty-three-year-old Adolf Hitler. Americans were bored by both. In London the Prince of Wales made a date with a Mrs. Wallis Simpson, who had just been presented at court, but of course nothing could come of it because she already had a husband. Saigon was so remote that Hollywood used it as the background for *Red Dust*, an escapist film starring Clark Gable. The Middle East was quieter than the Middle West; as *Time* reported on April 4, the Jewish population of Palestine was "a minority (16.9 percent) without political power, save for the advisory powers conferred on the Jewish Agency by the mandate allotted to Great Britain ten years ago."

Although the decade was two years old, many figures who would later be identified with the 1930s were still relatively obscure. The name of Winston Churchill appeared in print as the author of *Amid These Storms*, an anti-Communist tract. (Other authors of 1932 were William Faulkner, Christopher Morley, Aldous Huxley, John Dos Passos, Robinson Jeffers, T. S. Stribling, Hendrik Willem van Loon, James M. Barrie, and Charles Nordhoff and James Norman Hall.) The men whose birthdays were matters of public note—e.g., George Bernard Shaw, Rudyard Kipling, George M. Cohan, and John Galsworthy—belong in memory to an earlier age. This was particularly true in the world of entertainment. The five top box office stars were Marie Dressler, Janet Gaynor, Joan Crawford, Charles Farrell, and Greta Garbo. Irene Dunne had just made her film debut; so had Claudette Colbert (with Maurice Chevalier). Ginger Rogers was simply another tap dancer in Busby Berkeley's chorus line. Nelson Eddy and Fred Astaire wouldn't arrive in Hollywood for another year. Four-year-old Shirley Temple was appearing on the nation's standard (eighteen feet high, twenty-four feet wide) screens in a series of one-reel shorts called *Baby Burlesks*. Benny Goodman was rooming with Tommy Dorsey, working in New York pit bands and playing clarinet cadenzas on radio for the Hoffman Ginger Ale Hour. In Beaumont, Texas, sixteen-year-old Harry Haag James approached a traveling band leader named Lawrence Welk and asked, "You don't happen to be looking for a trumpet player, do you?" The leader asked for a demonstration, James blasted away, and Welk shook his head. He said, "You play too loud for my band, son."

In retrospect, America seems to have been singularly blind to the future. When Professor Auguste Piccard penetrated the stratosphere in a balloon and wrote in his log, "We have attained an altitude of 54,120 ft. All human records broken!" there was no way of knowing that time would make the entry seem quaint. People were impressed by Dr. William Beebe's bathysphere and its brief dive to 2,200 feet off Bermuda; they wouldn't have believed that aquanauts a generation later would live at that depth for a month. It was in the naval maneuvers of 1932 that an American aircraft carrier, slipping past picket destroyers northeast of Oahu, attacked Pearl Harbor in a dawn "raid" and "sank" the warships anchored there. Nobody noticed the watchful Japanese in Honolulu, or knew that Tokyo was filing a long memorandum on the paper victory.

Most striking of all, newspaper readers were unaware that at Cambridge University Sir James Chadwick had discovered the neutron, the key to atomic fission. Its significance was unappreciated. According to physics doctrine at the time, only projectiles with fantastic penetrating power could split the nucleus of an atom. The very notion of such a split was highly theoretical, and certainly it couldn't be achieved by the neutron, which carried no electrical charge whatever. Lord Rutherford told a meeting that people who foresaw large-scale release of atomic energy were "talking moonshine." Albert Einstein, then en route to asylum at Cal Tech, agreed that the idea was "fantastic." The only practical use for uranium worth mentioning was to paint luminous figures on clock dials. Here it served as a substitute for radium, abandoned in the spring of 1932 when the owners of a New Jersey clock factory discovered that their dial painters were dying. Imbibed radium, they were shocked to learn, accumulated in the bones and led to certain death. The clockmakers turned in relief to uranium. It was so safe, so benign; no one could possibly associate it with death or even illness.

Depression Montage

FATHER OF TEN DROWNS SELF
Jumps from Bridge, Starts to Swim
Gives Up, Out of Work Two Years

THE BEARDED LADY
TRIED A JAR
SHE'S NOW
A FAMOUS
MOVIE STAR —
BURMA SHAVE!

REPEAL THE EIGHTEENTH AMENDMENT

Work-is-what-I-want-and-not-charity-Who-will-help-me-get-a-job-7-years-in-Detroit-No-money-sent-away-furnish-best-of-references-Phone Randolph 8381: Room #59

COPS TRAIL LINDY BABY
KIDNAP CAR TO NEWARK

RIN TIN TIN DEAD AT 14

WHOLE INDUSTRIAL REGIONS IDLE

WARNER BAXTER & BEBE DANIELS
in
FORTY-SECOND STREET
with
Guy Kibbee, Ruby Keeler, Dick Powell,
Una Merkel, George E. Stone,
Ned Sparks & Al Jenkins

A Scout is trustworthy loyal helpful friendly courteous kind obedient cheerful thrifty brave clean and reverent.

INTERNATIONAL CORRESPONDENCE SCHOOLS

DIRIGIBLE AKRON CRASHES IN LIGHTNING STORM AT SEA

BABE DIDRIKSON STARS IN Xth OLYMPIAD IN L.A.

ANNOUNCER: Olly-olly-in-free!
Wheaties, breakfast of champions, bring you the thrilling adventures of Jack Armstrong, the aaaaaaaaallAmurrican boy. Jack Armstrong is climbing up the dangerous mountain trail to the cave of the glacier. High above him the towering peaks of the Andes press their eternal snows against the South American sky. And far below lies the valley with its hotel, "Winter Sports." Jack and his friends are seeking Hungster, whom enemy agent Lucano captured and brought to the cave of the glacier. Right now Uncle Jim leads the way ...

I can't give you anything but love, baby
That's the only thing I've plenty of, baby

Tastyeast is tempting
To your appetite
Creamy, wholesome candy
Try a luscious bite.

DENTIST, WIFE, TAKE LIVES
RATHER THAN GO ON RELIEF

— *Now the Miracle of Vitaphone* —
Brings Broadway to Walla Walla!

Gee, I'd like to see you looking swell, baby
Wearing bracelets Woolworth's doesn't sell, baby
But until that day you know darned well, baby
I can't give you anything but love.

We understand that Mr. Gandhi has stated as part of his creed that civil disobedience is an effective substitute for violence or armed rebellion. In the opinion of this newspaper experience has proven time and time again that in India civil disobedience cannot be carried on without violence. Of course it would be another matter altogether in this country.

Two

ROOSEVELT!

Shortly after the presidential election a band of Communists had arrived unheralded at 49 East Sixty-fifth Street. The President-elect received them, but when one said, "We want you to tell President Hoover that the federal government must—" Roosevelt broke in sharply. "I can't tell the President to do anything," he said. "I'm simply a private citizen as far as the federal government is concerned." He meant it. Until he had the power to act, he would not intervene. Meantime he went fishing on Vincent Astor's yacht, picked an unimpressive cabinet, and appeared to agree with everyone who saw him. Huey Long, battling the conservative influence of Arkansas's Senator Joseph Robinson, said of the President-elect, "When I talk to him he says, 'Fine! Fine! Fine!' But Joe Robinson goes to see him the next day and again he says, 'Fine! Fine! Fine!' Maybe he says 'Fine!' to everybody." So rapid had the processes of social disintegration become (even Eleanor Roosevelt wondered whether anyone could "do anything to save America now") that FDR's genial, vague, not-my-problem attitude seemed irresponsible. People thought that he ought to do *something*—and no one felt this more keenly than the outgoing President.

In November the President telegraphed the President-elect, suggesting that they confer. Roosevelt called at the White House on the way to Georgia, but although the meeting lasted the better part of an afternoon, it settled nothing. Word had reached Roosevelt that a member of the Hoover cabinet had said, "We now have the fellow in a hole that he is not going to be able to get out of." The hole had yet to be dug that FDR could not get out of; hour after hour he parried invitations to board the administration's sinking ship. After his visit he felt strengthened in his conviction not to commit himself, the wisdom of which grew upon him as he read the newspapers in Warm Springs. Hoover had sent the Hill his farewell State of the Union message, a recital of all his shibboleths. More taxes were needed. Europe should pay its war debts. "We have built a system of individualism. The background of our American system is that we should allow free play of social and economic forces." The country must have "confidence in the future."

America's patience was running out. So was its cash. On St. Valentine's Day 1933—Hoover was singing his swan song at ten o'clock that evening before the Republican National Committee—the nation's banking system began its final collapse. That afternoon Governor William A. Comstock of Michigan had received an urgent telephone request to join a conference of bankers in downtown Detroit, and he had been there ever since. Detroit's Union Guardian Trust Company was in straits. If it failed it would probably take every other bank in the city with it, and the financiers were asking Comstock to declare a banking moratorium throughout Michigan. At midnight he agreed, drove to the state capitol at Lansing, and issued a proclamation closing the state's 550 banks for eight days. He called it a holiday.

In Washington, Hoover scribbled a letter to FDR; he was so distraught that he misspelled his successor's name on the envelope. The President-elect was becoming accustomed to jolts (the week before, an unemployed bricklayer had shot at him and fatally wounded Mayor Cermak of Chicago), and this communication was among the more outrageous. He read it carefully and then called it "cheeky." It was certainly that. Hoover said flatly that the country was afraid of what the new administration might do. In the name of patriotism (and of "confidence") he demanded that Roosevelt publicly promise not to change government programs. The outgoing President was fully aware of what he was asking; to Senator David A. Reed of Pennsylvania he wrote, "I realize that if these declarations are made by the President-elect, he will have ratified the whole major program of the Republican administration; that is, it means the abandonment of 90 percent of the so-called new deal." He had already told friends he thought FDR an amiable lightweight. Now he was treating him as a fool. When the declarations were not forthcoming, he changed his mind again; to Henry Stimson he said that Roosevelt was "a madman."

The President-elect would certainly have been of doubtful sanity had he associated himself with Hoover's policy, for by then it was clear that under that policy the entire country was going stone broke.

Michigan's plight had been especially aggravated by plunging real estate values, but the problem was nationwide. Since the Crash more than 5,500 banks had failed, and the public, understandably, was nervous. It responded by hoarding. Gold was vanishing from vaults at the rate of 20 million dollars a day, and depositors who couldn't get metal were taking paper, so that the Treasury was called upon to expand its currency at the very time the gold upon which it was based was disappearing.

Bank panics are always suicidal. In this crisis, however, the situation had been complicated by the three years of deflation. Even the soundest institutions held mortgages and securities which had fallen to a fraction of their former value. America's 18,569 banks had about six billion dollars in cash to meet 41 billion in deposits, and bankers forced to liquidate mortgages and securities to raise cash would suffer heavy losses.

Now that Michigan's banks had fallen, the daily outflow of gold from the rest of the country's banks abruptly jumped to 37 million; currency withdrawals to 122 million. Banks everywhere were swarming with breathless depositors taking out cash—in the Bronx a young mother rented her baby, at twenty-five cents a trip, to women who used it to claim preference at the head of withdrawal lines. During the week of February 20, while both houses of Congress were whooping through Prohibition repeal, the Baltimore Trust Company paid out 13 million dollars, nearly half of it on Friday. Late Friday night Governor Albert C. Ritchie declared a holiday for Maryland's two hundred banks. The second state had gone under.

Rallying to the standard of confidence, responsible men made painfully self-conscious efforts to keep their heads. The *Detroit News* commented, "It is an experience we shall have to look back upon, and no doubt grin over," and the *Baltimore Sun* said cheerily, "Life . . . will be filled with pleasant and unpleasant things as it was before. And it will have the additional advantage that everybody will have something to talk about." The president of the Baltimore Association of Commerce saw no reason why business should not continue as usual; the Bureau of Internal Revenue issued a stern reminder that income taxes were due in two weeks.

Nothing from Hyde Park dispelled the illusion of unreality. Roosevelt, as Robert Sherwood put it, knew that he had the advantage of "a good act to follow." Already a master of timing, he realized that the poorer Hoover's exit, the better his own entrance would be. If his refusal to cross bridges before he reached them was irresponsible—it is hard to see what he could have done—it was also in keeping with an old tradition in American politics. As Charles A. Beard pointed out, until Lincoln's hand was forced he "never adopted the system of unconditional emancipation. He understood it, but did not commit himself to it." All the same, there was an almost pixie quality about FDR's selection for Secretary of the Treasury—a puckish little railway equipment manufacturer who wore a gray toupee, loved puns, collected five-dollar gold pieces, and spent his leisure time composing on a guitar. A week later, when the new administration took office, the country was to know William H. Woodin as hard-driving and ingenious, but on the eve of office he was celebrated only as the composer of a song for children:

> *Let us be like bluebirds,*
> *Happy all day long,*
> *Forgetting all our troubles*
> *In a sunny song.*

In Indianapolis and Akron that Sunday, February 26, banks announced that withdrawals would be limited to 5 percent of balances. During the night institutions in a dozen other Ohio cities fell into line, and on Monday—as flames gutted the German Reichstag and Japanese troops marched into a Manchurian blizzard—the number grew to one hundred. Across the river from Cincinnati, five Covington, Kentucky, banks adopted similar restrictions. Monday evening Governor Gifford Pinchot of Pennsylvania signed a bill permitting individual institutions to close at will, and Thomas W. Lamont sent word to Hyde Park that in the view of J. P. Morgan, "the emergency could not be greater."

It could be, and soon was. By Wednesday, March 1, frantic governors had declared bank holidays in seventeen states. Pinchot acted so hurriedly he had to watch the inaugural five days later with 95 cents in his pocket. Governor Oscar K. Allen of Louisiana, on the other hand, withdrew his expense money for Washington and then entrained, leaving behind his dictated proclamation closing all banks. It was on Wednesday that the President-elect—who, Arthur Krock reported in the *New York Times*, was being asked by responsible men to seize power *now*—drove to his East Sixty-fifth Street town house and went into conference with Woodin. They did not emerge until Thursday afternoon, when, preceded by the screaming sirens of twenty motorcycles, they raced down Fifth Avenue and turned west toward the Hudson River ferry. During the morning a light snow had sifted over the city. New Yorkers stood silently in it, staring at the cavalcade. Outside Radio City Music Hall a cardboard King Kong, erected to dramatize his first Manhattan run, leered toothily. In the river the French Line steamer *Paris* lay quietly at berth, her cargo space reserved—though no one in the President-elect's party knew it yet—for nine million dollars in fleeing gold. On the other side of the ferry a special B & O train was waiting, and that afternoon, talking now with Woodin of banks, now with Farley of religion, Franklin Roosevelt thundered southward through a cold fog, toward Washington.

It was sleeting when they reached Union Station. In the presidential suite of the Mayflower Hotel a sheaf of telegrams awaited Roosevelt: banks were closed, or closing, in twenty-one states and the District of Columbia, and Federal Reserve figures showed the week's gold loss to be 226 million dollars. There wasn't enough money in the Treasury to meet the federal payroll, not to mention the 700 million dollars in short-term certificates which would fall due March 15. The President-elect had scarcely unpacked when Woodin drew him aside. Secretary of the Treasury Ogden Mills and Eugene Meyer of the Federal Reserve Board had telephoned to suggest a national proclamation closing all banks. President Hoover felt less drastic action would do. FDR's opinion was solicited. He shook his head; he still refused to advise anyone. Fair skies had been forecast for Saturday's inauguration, but now the barometer was falling.

The last page of the *New York Times* of Friday, March 3, carried an advertisement showing "John Doe" and "Jane Doe" acclaiming the "Good Work" of the Bowery Savings Bank. Presumably its purpose was to reassure depositors. It failed. By noon long lines of

New Yorkers had formed opposite Grand Central Station and were filing into the world's largest private savings bank, demanding cash. At 3 P.M. the Bowery closed its doors with a huge crowd still unpaid. At the same hour Governor Henry Horner of Illinois sat in the Federal Reserve Bank of Chicago plucking nervously at his moustache, reading figures which showed that Chicago banks had paid out 350 million dollars in two weeks. After seventeen days in the hinterland, the storm was hammering at the nation's two financial strongholds.

That morning Miss Catherine Shea, a messenger for the Treasury Department, had brought Herbert Hoover his last $500 pay check. He received it with a semblance of cheer; reports reaching him before noon suggested that the panic might be lessening. After lunch it was clear that this was only an illusion. Minnesota and Kansas were gone, North Carolina and Virginia were going. Hoover, too exhausted and too embittered for the traditional inauguration eve dinner with the President-elect, formally received the Roosevelt family for tea at 4 P.M. By his lights, he had every right to be angry. In his words, the country was "on the verge of financial panic and chaos"—and all because this fellow from New York lacked confidence. At tea he reviewed his figures and asked Roosevelt to join him in bipartisan action. Once more FDR said he would wait; tomorrow he would be President. Preparing to go, he adjusted his leg braces. "Mr. President," he said, "I know it is customary to do so, but you don't have to return our call if you don't want to."

Hoover strode across the room and loomed above him menacingly. In his most cutting voice he said, "Mr. Roosevelt, when you have been in Washington as long as I have, you will learn that the President of the United States calls on nobody!" He turned his back to leave the room.

Jimmy Roosevelt glanced at his father; he had never seen him so angry. Before FDR could speak, Eleanor Roosevelt jumped up and said quickly, "It's been very pleasant, but we must go now."

In fact a complete break between the two men was impossible. Illinois and New York were on the brink; their governors, Horner and Herbert Lehman, had given up all hope of attending the inauguration. Back at the Mayflower, Roosevelt kept in touch with Hoover by telephone until 1 A.M., when he suggested that they both get some sleep. They did, and as they slept their advisers huddled at the Treasury Building and decided everything for them. Before them lay the latest bleak Federal Reserve report. During the last two days 500 million dollars had been drained from the nation's banking system. They were convinced that the New York bankers did not understand the enormity of the disaster and must be protected. Mills and Woodin agreed that Lehman must be persuaded to close the New York banks and that Horner must also declare a moratorium for Illinois. Horner proclaimed his holiday at 2 A.M.; Lehman's decision came at 4:20 A.M. Hoover was told at 6 A.M. "We are at the end of our string," he said. "There is nothing more we can do."

The financial heart of the country had stopped beating. Banking in every state was wholly or partly suspended. Flags flew in Wall Street honoring the inauguration, but the Stock Exchange was officially closed, and so, for the first time in eighty-five years, was the Chicago Board of Trade. On Manhattan's Fifth Avenue, Norman Vincent Peale was writing a sermon for delivery the following morning demanding that bankers and corporation heads get down on their knees before God and confess their sins. In Kansas, Governor Landon was calling industrialists "racketeers." Arthur Krock compared the atmosphere in Washington to "that which might be found in a beleaguered capital in wartime." The sky was the color of slate. Over a hundred thousand people blackened the forty acres of park and pavement in front of the Capitol's east facade, awaiting the inaugural. General MacArthur was in command of the inauguration parade, and he anticipated trouble. (It says something about the departing administration that Walter F. Brown, the outgoing Postmaster General, had requisitioned a new limousine for the occasion because he could not sit erect in the old one while wearing his tall silk hat.) Army machine guns had been mounted at strategic points. In many ways the occasion had the marks of an impromptu affair. John Nance Garner wore a borrowed muffler against the chill wind. Woodin, unable to reach his seat, perched on a railing with a cameraman.

The Capitol clocks struck twelve noon. Franklin Delano Roosevelt had at last become the thirty-second President of the United States.

Hatless and coatless, he threw back his great shoulders and repeated the oath after Chief Justice Charles Evans Hughes. The new President's hand lay on the three-hundred-year-old Roosevelt family Bible, open at the thirteenth chapter of Paul's First Epistle to the Corinthians:

Though I speak with the tongues of men and of angels, and have not charity, I am become as sounding brass, or a tinkling cymbal.

And though I have the gift of prophecy and understand all mysteries, and all knowledge; and though I have faith, so that I could remove mountains, and have not charity, I am nothing.

He turned to the podium. Ignoring applause, he drew from his pocket a longhand manuscript which he had written in his Hyde Park study the Sunday before. No phrase was borrowed; it was pure Roosevelt:

"Let me first assert my firm belief that the only thing we have to fear is fear itself—nameless, unreasoning, unjustified terror which paralyzes needed efforts to convert retreat into advance."

The radio networks carried his ringing voice out across the suffering land, over the sweatshops and flophouses, the Hoovervilles and hobo jungles, the rocky soil tilled by tenant farmers, the ragged men shivering in the iron cold outside factory gates.

"I shall ask the Congress for the one remaining instrument to meet the crisis—broad Executive power to wage a war against the emergency, as great as the power that would be given me if we were in fact invaded by a foreign foe."

Herbert Hoover slumped and stared at his feet, but in the three-decker tenements with radios the hungry children looked up; in county courthouses the embattled farmers looked up; housewives patching threadbare clothes looked up; there was a kind of magic in the air; and in Santa Monica Will Rogers pecked out on his typewriter: "If he burned down the Capitol, we would cheer and say, 'Well, we at least got a fire started somehow.'"

"The people of the United States have not failed. In their need they have registered a mandate that they want direct, vigorous action. They have asked for discipline and direction under leadership. They have made me the present instrument of their wishes. In the spirit of the gift I take it."

In Walt Whitman's phrase, the new President had made a "tremendous entrance"; Roosevelt's face was "so grim," wrote Arthur Krock, "as to seem unfamiliar to those who have long known him." Henry L. Stimson confided to his diary, "I was thoroughly scared." The new First Lady thought the inaugural "very, very solemn and a little terrifying" because "when Franklin got to that part of his speech when it might become necessary for him to assume powers ordinarily granted to a President in wartime, he received his biggest demonstration." Edmund Wilson, in Washington to cover the ceremonies for the *New Republic*, scorned "the old unctuousness, the old pulpit vagueness." At the same time he wrote, "The thing that emerges most clearly is the warning of a dictatorship." The intellectuals still didn't understand FDR; some of them never would. Indeed, the man was mysterious even to those closest to him. It is a remarkable fact that he had not told his own wife of his decision to run for the Presidency; she had learned it from Louis Howe. Perhaps she came closest to the mood of thoughtful people in those first hours of his first administration when she said, "One has the feeling of going it blindly, because we're in a tremendous stream, and none of us know where we're going to land." Yet the people, on the whole, did not share her uncertainty. To them the speech had been a triumph; that weekend 450,000 wrote Roosevelt to tell him so.

Eleanor went to the inaugural ball while her husband stayed in the Executive Mansion to work with Howe. Sunday morning after breakfast the President had himself wheeled down newly installed ramps and into the empty oval office. Alone, he contemplated the room. The desk was empty. Hoover had taken everything movable except the flag and the great seal. There was no pad, no pencil, no telephone, not even a buzzer to summon help. Slowly it came to him that he could do nothing by himself here. He gave a great shout, and his secretary and an aide came running. The incident was notable because it was the last time he would feel utterly helpless as President. By that evening he was ready to act. His cigarette holder atilt, he invoked the World War's half forgotten Trading with the Enemy Act to declare a four-day holiday for all banks. The 73rd Congress was being called into special session Thursday, when emergency legislation would be ready. Meantime the country would have to manage without moneychangers.

It was a challenge to American ingenuity, and it was met by improvised combinations of scrip, credit, barter, stamps, streetcar tokens, Canadian dollars, and Mexican pesos. The Dow Chemical Company was coining magnesium into "Dow-metal Money," with an arbitrary value of twenty cents. A Wisconsin wrestler signed a contract to perform for a can of tomatoes and a peck of potatoes; an Ashtabula, Ohio, newspaper offered free ads in exchange for produce. A New York state senator arrived in Albany with twelve dozen eggs and a side of pork to see him through the week. The most spectacular transactions were conducted by the *New York Daily News,* which was sponsoring the semifinals of the Golden Gloves tournament in Madison Square Garden. The seat price was fifty cents, but any article worth that amount was accepted as admission provided the five-cent amusement tax was paid. An appraiser was engaged who during the evening inspected frankfurters, mattresses, hats, shoes, overcoats, fish, noodles, nightgowns, steaks, spark plugs, box cameras, jigsaw puzzles, sweaters, canned goods, sacks of potatoes, golf knickers, mechanics' tools, foot balm, copies of the New Testament, and what girls of that day called step-ins.

Nearly everyone assumed the holiday would end with the formal adoption of scrip—local currencies, managed by states, cities, and individual firms. Atlanta, Richmond, Mattituck, and Knoxville, of all places, were already on the stuff; before the week of March 6 was out Nashville would have a million dollars of it in circulation and Philadelphia eight million. In Nutley, New Jersey, a paper company which had been working three days a week went on three shifts, turning out six tons of scrip for Wisconsin and Tennessee. To Secretary of the Treasury Woodin, however, the thought of state and municipal currencies and company certificates floating around the country was appalling, and at breakfast on Tuesday, March 7, he told Ray Moley that he had decided scrip wasn't needed. "We can issue currency against the sound assets of the banks," he said. "It won't frighten people. It won't look like stage money. It'll be money that looks like money." There was nothing to lose. After all, he said publicly, "We're on the bottom. We're not going any lower."

Working around the clock in his Carlton Hotel suite with Senator Carter Glass, Woodin met Thursday's legislative deadline. As congressmen filed into the special session the finished bill was handed to the clerk—"My name's Bill, and I'm finished, too," Woodin muttered—and was read aloud. Few representatives heard it above the hubbub. They had no copies of their own; there had been no time to print them. Even the copy given to the clerk bore last-minute changes scribbled in pencil. In thirty-eight minutes they whooped it through while Mrs. Roosevelt sat knitting in the gallery like a benign Madame Defarge, counting votes. Then they crowded into the Senate chamber to hear Glass explain just what it was they had done.

The little Virginian backed it, though he acknowledged there were parts which shocked him. It was, in fact, a shocking measure, ratifying all acts "heretofore *or hereinafter* taken" by the President and the Secretary of the Treasury. It provided prison terms for hoarders, appointed "conservators" (receivers) for weak banks, and authorized the issue of two billion dollars in new currency based on bank assets. At 8:36 P.M. a rumpled Roosevelt signed it in the White House, surrounded by unpacked books and pictures from Hyde Park. That evening the Bureau of Engraving and Printing recruited 375 new workers. The official printing presses of the United States were going into action.

All that night and the next the lights of the Bureau twinkled across the tidal basin. There was no time to engrave new dies, so plates bearing the imprint "Series of 1929" were used. There wasn't even an opportunity to acquire facsimile signatures from each of the twelve Federal Reserve banks; signatures were taken from government files and sent by messenger to the American Type Foundry in Jersey City, where logotypes were cut. Early Saturday morning planes began taking off from Washington bearing bales of cash. The first were received in the New York Federal Reserve bank shortly before noon. Transfer to member banks began immediately.

The real trick was prying open the rigid fists of hoarders, who in one week had taken 15 percent of the nation's currency out of circulation. Even a bewitched Congress couldn't make the penal clauses apply to hoarding that had already taken place. Instead, the government turned to the spur of publicity. On Wednesday, March 8, the Federal Reserve Board announced that its banks would prepare lists of persons who had withdrawn gold since February 1 and who failed to bring it back by the following Monday. Newspapers had scarcely appeared with this announcement before bank switchboards were jammed. Callers were told only that if they had gold and wanted to return it, the banks would open for them and newspapermen would be kept out of the lobbies. In the next few hours thousands of mattresses were torn open, cans dug up, hidden boxes brought forth. Banks everywhere reported long queues, reminiscent of the preceding week's panic but comprised this time of men and women carrying Gladstones and briefcases. Encouraged, the board extended its order on Friday, asking for reports covering withdrawals of the past two years. The widened hunt brought bigger game; by Saturday night the Federal Reserve banks had recovered 300 million dollars in gold and gold certificates—enough to support 750 million dollars in additional circulation. And even before the planes flew out from Hoover Airport with new bank notes, Woodin had permitted individual savings banks to release ten dollars to each depositor. Business began to stir. Within a week 13,500—75 percent —of the country's banks were back in business, and gongs were heard again in stock exchanges. In New York, where stocks jumped 15 percent, the Dow Jones ticker clicked off the message "Happy Days Are Here Again."

They weren't really. But the panic had ended without currency chaos or nationalization of the banks. Undoubtedly the medicine had been strong; the inflationary movement, once started, would prove irresistible in the long run. Yet Roosevelt had had very few options. A friend told him that if he succeeded he would go down in history as the greatest American President and that if he failed he would be known as the worst. FDR replied, "If I fail I shall be the last one." But he had no intention of failing. His Hundred Days had begun.

In the eye of the Hundred Days hurricane—from March 9, when the Emergency Banking Act was cheered into law, to the passage of the National Industrial Recovery Act (NIRA) on June 16—the new Chief Executive was continually revealing fresh reservoirs of imagination and energy. Before Congress adjourned in exhaustion he would have delivered ten major speeches, given birth to a new foreign policy, presided over press conferences and cabinet meetings twice a week, taken the country off the gold standard, sent fifteen messages to the Capitol, and shepherded through its chambers thirteen major pieces of legislation, including insurance for all bank deposits, refinancing of home mortgages, Wall Street reforms, authorization for nearly four billion dollars in federal relief, legalization of beer, and laws creating the Civilian Conservation Corps (CCC), the Agricultural Adjustment Administration (AAA), and Tennessee Valley Authority (TVA). "Occasionally," he remarked at one point, "I think I am a bit shell-shocked."

It was all improvised. "Take a method and try it," he told his New Dealers. "If it fails, try another. But above all, try something." He interpreted his landslide victory as a mandate for change, almost any change, as long as it was quick. At first he had planned to put through Woodin's save-the-banks law, send Congress home, and work with the powers of the Presidency. Such a step would have been supported by the national consensus. The hour demanded "dictatorial authority," the conservative *Boston Evening Transcript* editorialized. "This is unprecedented in its implications, but such is the desperate temper of the people that it is welcome." Senator Burton K. Wheeler said congressmen would "jump through a hoop" for the new President, and their constituents, said Charles Michelson, were ready to believe FDR could "see in the dark." Later, John Gunther was to suggest that the President could easily have become a dictator: "We are apt to forget nowadays the immense, unprecedented, overwhelming authority conferred on FDR by an enthusiastically willing Congress during the first hundred days of his first administration. The Reichstag did not give Hitler much more."

Roosevelt preferred to work within the Constitution. He said he wanted to become a "preaching President," like his cousin Theodore Roosevelt, and the tremendous volume of White House mail suggested to him that his legislative revolution—for it amounted to that —might well be accompanied by a campaign to educate the people about the New Deal goals. He had no U.S. Information Agency, no Voice of America. He didn't need one; with him as teacher, the country became one vast classroom.

The first lesson came on his fifth day in power, when he assembled the White House correspondents around his desk. It was the first of what would become an unequaled number of press conferences (998), and it was an instant success. Will Rogers commented that Roosevelt could take a complicated subject like banking and explain it so that everyone could understand it, even the bankers; subsequently Charles A. Beard, no Roosevelt admirer, wrote that FDR discussed "more fundamental problems of American life and society than all the other Presidents combined." At the end the correspondents burst into applause. In one stroke the President had shifted the news capital of the country from New York to Washington. The United Press tripled its Washington staff; 25 percent of all Associated Press news was coming from the capital. Metropolitan newspapers sent men to cover the White House, and smaller papers began running syndicated Washington columnists, who were joined, in time, by the President's own wife.

On Sunday, March 12, Roosevelt preached his second lesson directly to the people. Microphones of the National, Columbia, and Mutual broadcasting systems were installed on the ground floor of the Executive Mansion in front of the fireplace in the Diplomatic Reception Room. The President said he wanted to catch the spirit of a man in his own home talking informally to his neighbors in their living rooms. In that case, said Harry C. Butcher, manager of the CBS Washington office, the talk might be called a "fireside chat," and so it was christened. His cigarette burning down in its long ivory holder, FDR spoke to the nation about the bank moratorium: "My friends, I want to tell you what has been done in the last few days, why it was done, and what the next steps are going to be. First of all, let me state the simple fact that when you deposit money in a bank the bank does not put the money into a safe-deposit vault. It invests your money in many different forms of credit—bonds, mortgages. In other words, the bank puts your money to work to keep the wheels turning around. . . ."

Somehow he did it without condescension, translating the complexities of an industrial economy into phrases and metaphors almost anyone could comprehend. His language was plain and functional—and so was the decor he was introducing into the White House. The elegant trappings of the previous administration were being chucked out. There were no footmen, no buglers, no trooping of the colors, no changing of the guard, and above all, no seven-course meals. Roosevelt's cuisine was perhaps the least distinguished in official Washington. He couldn't become a gourmet; he hadn't the time. Guests who spent any amount of time in the mansion compared the monotonous fare to that of a boardinghouse. One woman was served the same dessert three evenings in a row: a single slice of pineapple with two cherries and a walnut lying in a pool of watery whipped cream. Even so, she was getting something of a treat; the President's lunches—hash with one poached egg—cost nineteen cents.

In a sense all this was deceptive. He didn't need the accouterments of power because he had the real thing. In Arthur M. Schlesinger Jr.'s felicitous phrase, FDR was a "natural President." Few men in history have dominated their times as he did. He ran his administration as a one-man show, and loved to exercise authority. "Wouldn't you be President if you could?" he jovially asked one visitor. "Wouldn't anybody?" After meeting him, Dr. Carl Gustav Jung said, "Make no mistake, he is a force—a man of superior but impenetrable mind, but perfectly ruthless, a highly versatile mind which you cannot foresee." W. M. Kiplinger had never known any President "as omnipotent as this Roosevelt." Ed Flynn observed that FDR's aides and cabinet members were little more than messenger boys, that "he really made his own decisions." Arthur Krock reported that he was "the boss, the dynamo, the works." At no time, wrote Henry Morgenthau, was Roosevelt "anything else but a ruler." Morgenthau liked to argue with FDR. FDR enjoyed it, too—up to a point. Then the big freckled fist would bang down on the desk, then he would stop saying "I think" and start saying "The *President* thinks." The argument was over, and there was no doubt about who had won it.

The President opened a typical fourteen-hour day by breakfasting in bed while skimming through diplomatic cables and clouds of newspaper. The bedroom walls were decorated with pictures of ships, the mantel with family photographs and Victorian bric-a-brac. During the Hundred Days favored advisers would come in for bedside conferences, but usually he had this time to himself. Sometime after nine o'clock he would shave and then dress with the help of his valet, Irvin McDuffie, who would push him to his office in the small, armless presidential wheelchair. The day's appointments would begin at ten o'clock. If Congress was in session he would spend a full quarter of his time on the telephone. He always used first names. In the first week of his administration, before Washington had become accustomed to Secretary of Labor Frances Perkins's brown tricorne hat or she to Washington, one of her assistants picked up a phone and heard a voice say, "This is Frank. May I talk to Miss Perkins?" The assistant relayed the message. The secretary said, "Frank? I don't know any Frank. Ask him whom he's with." Questioned, the caller chuckled and said, "With the United States. This is the President."

He would accept calls at almost any time, even in the middle of a cabinet meeting. His availability was astonishing; about one hundred people could get through to him without first stating their business to a secretary.* It was hard to remember he was crippled; his sources of information seemed unlimited. In cabinet meetings he would quote people from all over the country, including Mrs. Roosevelt—"My Missus," he would remark, "says there's typhoid fever in that district." One of his first orders as President was that people in distress who telephoned the White House for help should never be shut off; someone in the administration must be

---

* By contrast Robert S. McNamara, the most available high official thirty years later, could be so reached by only twenty-five people.

found to talk to them. This brought him the most remarkable correspondence in presidential history. One note ran:

> Dear Mr. President:
> This is just to tell you that everything is all right now. The man you sent found our house all right, and we went down to the bank with him and the mortgage can go on for a while longer. You remember I wrote you about losing the furniture too. Well, your man got it back for us. I never heard of a President like you.

Nor had anyone else. His daily mail was running between 5,000 and 8,000 letters, ten times Hoover's. One congressman compared him to Jesus Christ, and in a poll among New York schoolchildren God ran a poor second to FDR. Americans really felt that they *were* his friends. Forty-one popular songs were written about him. And when he locked his braces and appeared in public, people literally reached out to touch the hem of his cape. In New York, the cast for *Strike Me Pink* responded to curtain calls by singing, to the tune of "Wintergreen for President," "Roosevelt is President!"—and never failed to bring the crowd to its feet in a roaring ovation. Anne O'Hare McCormick observed in the *New York Times* that "no President in so short a time has inspired so much hope." Even Pierre Du Pont and William Randolph Hearst were delighted; a tycoon told John T. Flynn that he considered Roosevelt the greatest leader since Jesus Christ, and he just hoped God would forgive him his vote for Hoover. Walter Lippmann, revising his earlier estimate, wrote, "In one week, the nation, which had lost confidence in everything and everybody, has regained confidence in the government and in itself."

Roosevelt's magnetism lured swarms of bright young men from campuses and offices. Suddenly the most flourishing business in the capital was the boardinghouse industry; the huge old brownstone mansions lining G Street, R Street, New Hampshire Avenue, and Twenty-first Street were converted to housing for New Deal bachelors. Traditionalists in the capital were appalled; Arthur M. Schlesinger Jr. later talked to one who said, "A plague of young lawyers settled on Washington. . . . They floated airily into offices, took desks, asked for papers and found no end of things to be busy about. I never found out why they came, what they did or why they left."

Some never left, or left to come back in other roles. Among those rallying to the New Deal banner were Dean Acheson, Undersecretary of the Treasury; J. W. Fulbright, a young lawyer in the Department of Justice; Hubert H. Humphrey, who quit studying pharmacy to become a relief administrator; and Henry Fowler, a TVA lawyer. One of the most efficient newcomers was Lyndon B. Johnson, administrative assistant to Congressman Richard Kleberg of Texas. Johnson contrived to step briefly into the public eye by persuading the White House that the first farmer to plow under a part of his cotton crop as part of the AAA war on agricultural surpluses should be one of Kleberg's constituents.

Minor deities in the New Deal constellation were Sam Rosenman, Rexford Tugwell, Adolf Berle, "Ironpants" Johnson; Harold Ickes, who secretly liked his public nickname, "the old curmudgeon" (and was unaware that Roosevelt privately called him "Donald Duck"), and Ray Moley, the lordly occupant of a Washington hotel suite and the brightest of the lot, of whom more obscure men sang:

Moley! Moley! Moley!
Lord God Almighty!

Morale was particularly high in the Department of Agriculture. The new general counsel there, Jerome N. Frank, had recruited a dazzling group of young attorneys: Thurmond Arnold, Abe Fortas, Adlai Stevenson, Nathaniel Weyl, John Abt, Nathan Witt, Lee Pressman, and Pressman's Harvard Law School classmate Alger Hiss. Admirers in other departments agreed that one day fame would come to most of them, especially Hiss.

Hiss, Pressman, Witt, Abt, and Weyl were members of a Communist party cell which met secretly in a Connecticut Avenue music studio. They were studying the new administration, and they were confused, which is not surprising; Moley was then regarded as a passionate liberal, while Secretary of Agriculture Henry A. Wallace was vehemently opposed to the diplomatic recognition of Russia. Communism set class against class, he argued, sounding like Al Smith. Most puzzling of all was the President. On inauguration day Roosevelt was empirical but still conservative, and his early measures strengthened his right-of-center support. It is curious to note that his first measure, once he had rescued the banks, was a bill cutting veterans' pensions and government salaries, including those of congressmen.

His Civilian Conservation Corps (CCC), which put slum youths to work on conservation projects, was also popular with conservatives. A Communist spokesman called it "forced labor" and William Green of the AFL said it smacked "of fascism, of Hitlerism, of a form of Sovietism." But the CCC was Roosevelt's pet project, and thanks to Army help it was an instant success. Organized by MacArthur, it brought to the President's attention a colonel named George C. Marshall, who made his reputation by his efficient administration of seventeen CCC camps in the South. (Major Eisenhower ran into trouble in Pennsylvania by appointing Republicans to all key posts; it hadn't occurred to him to consider their politics.) Eventually over two and a half million boys wore the forest-green CCC uniform, planting two hundred million trees in a shelterbelt conceived by FDR and stretching from Texas to Canada.

The President's departure from the gold standard on April 19 was less popular with the right, for reasons which now seem rooted in superstition. For centuries Europeans and Americans had clung to gold in the belief that it was the hallmark of Western culture; during the Victorian age gold had become identified with great powers, silver with backward countries. Some Republicans called devaluation a "rubber dollar program," Al Smith said that he was "for gold dollars as against baloney dollars," and Roosevelt's own budget director said the executive action meant "the end of Western civilization." However, an 88.5-cent dollar—by summer it had leveled off at 83 cents—meant America could once more compete in world markets with European nations which had already turned to inflation. If Main Street didn't understand this, Wall Street did. Charles G. Dawes applauded; so did the Republican leadership. Russell Leffingwell, a Morgan partner, wrote Roosevelt, "Your action in going off gold saved the country from complete collapse," and J. P. Morgan himself stifled criticism by declaring in a rare public statement that "I welcome the reported action of the President. . . . It seems to be clear that the way out of the Depression is to combat and overcome the deflationary forces."

Any move welcomed at 23 Wall Street could scarcely be called revolutionary or even liberal. Roosevelt's turn to the left didn't come until late March, when he asked Congress for the Agricultural Adjustment Act and the Federal Emergency Relief Act, and he signed both on May 12, the sixty-fifth of the Hundred Days. Triple-A was a direct response to the Iowa insurrectionists; it raised prices by creating scarcity. The idea of paying a farmer *not* to farm was a flagrant violation of the conventional wisdom. Henry Wallace spoke for millions when he said, "I hope we shall never have to resort to it again. To destroy a standing crop goes against the soundest instincts of human nature." Four months later he had to authorize the slaughter of six million little pigs. He hated to do it, and blamed Coolidge-Hoover policies for making it necessary. (FDR casually suggested birth control for hogs.)

Federal relief was more controversial in the long run, but as Harry Hopkins tartly observed at a congressional hearing, "People don't eat in the long run, Senator, they eat every day." Lanky, tousled, sardonic Hopkins, whose relationship with the President was to outlast the New Deal, had been fighting the Depression as a New York social worker. He had entered the administration underneath a staircase. He couldn't reach the President, so he buttonholed Frances Perkins at a crowded New York function, led her to a nook under the stairs—in the hubbub it was the only place he could make himself heard—and explained the urgent need for national relief. Miss Perkins recommended him to FDR, and FDR recommended his program to Congress. Republicans were shocked. Representative Robert Luce of Massachusetts called it "socialism"; Representative Carroll L. Beedy of Maine cried, "God save the people of the United States!"

But their God had failed; it was Roosevelt's turn, and on May 22 he brought Hopkins to Washington. Under changing leadership (Hopkins, Ickes, and back to Hopkins) and various titles—Civil Works Administration (CWA), Works Progress Administration (WPA), Public Works Administration (PWA)—federal relief was to continue until 1942. "I'm here to see that people don't starve," Hopkins said bluntly. Fiorello La Guardia said, "I can go down to the market here and buy a parrot for two dollars, and in one day I can teach it to say, 'Dole, dole, dole.' But that parrot would never understand an economic problem." Opponents of relief were unimpressed, and the words they used were far less polite than dole. Sweatshop owners in the North and southern planters were furious because their sources of cheap labor were depleted. To upper-middle-class critics, the symbol of the reliefer would forever be a man leaning on a shovel or a rake, and their greatest triumph was the distortion of an obscure word. Testifying before a New York aldermanic inquiry, a handicraft teacher named Robert Marshall explained that he taught unemployed men how to make boondoggles—a word coined in 1925 by an upstate scoutmaster to describe such useful pioneer handiwork as weaving belts from rope. Presently newspaper editorials all over the country were ridiculing "boondoggling," and they were so successful that millions of subscribers believed (and still believe) that make-work was all Hopkins and Ickes achieved.

In point of fact, both administrators despised idleness. Hopkins in particular felt that relief without jobs would destroy individual pride. He liked to hear women say, "We're not on relief any more. My husband works for the government." And for the most part it *was* work, and hard work at that. CWA, WPA, and PWA funds went into over thirty thousand New Deal projects, paying teachers and building waterworks, post offices, bridges, jails, airports, sewers, culverts, public swimming pools, athletic fields, playgrounds, power plants, and railroad stations. During Hopkins's years in Washington he was responsible for 10 percent of all new roads in America, 35 percent of all new hospitals, 65 percent of new city halls, courthouses, and health facilities, and 70 percent of new schools. Denver was given a water supply system; Ohio's Muskingum Valley a flood control system; Brownsville, Texas, a port; and Key West roads and bridges connecting it with the Florida mainland.

Investing in projects beyond the scope of private enterprise, the WPA, with its forerunners and derivatives, transformed America. It built the Lincoln Tunnel, connecting New York and New Jersey under the Hudson, and the Triborough Bridge, linking Manhattan and Long Island. It electrified the Pennsylvania Railroad. It underwrote the first diesel engines. The District of Columbia owes its zoo, its mall, and the Federal Trade Commission its building to the WPA. Without WPA workers California would lack the Camarillo Mental Hospital, Kentucky the Fort Knox gold depository, San Francisco its fairgrounds, Dallas its Dealey Plaza, St. Louis its floral conservatory, the Columbia River its Bonneville Dam, and the Colorado its Boulder Dam. Nearly two hundred WPA men lost their lives building Boulder Dam, which the Republicans liked so much that when they regained control of Congress in 1946 they renamed it Hoover Dam. And all the relief projects combined cost less than twenty billion dollars—one-fourth of the Pentagon's annual budget in the first Nixon administration.

The *Army and Navy Register* later reported that in these years, "when the regular appropriations for the armed services were so meager, it was the WPA worker who saved many army posts and naval stations from literal obsolescence." Without WPA undertakings the wartime and postwar expansion of American business would have been impossible, and without TVA, another inspiration of the Hundred Days, the two atomic bombs which ended World War II could never have been constructed—a mixed blessing, to be sure, but one which must be set against the dead certainty that the Soviet Union would have mastered the challenges of nuclear weapon production by the mid-1950s anyhow. Of course, that was not TVA's primary goal. It began with a series of Tennessee River dams, providing and selling electrical power to the people that lived in the valley. In the end it saved three million acres from erosion, multiplied the average income in the valley tenfold, and repaid its original investment in federal taxes. TVA had long been the dream of Senator George Norris; it came true because Franklin Roosevelt, while still unpacking in the White House, sent Norris a note saying that "as soon as this rush of emergency legislation is over" he hoped Norris would come and talk to him about "the Tennessee Basin development." Under such a President, people began to feel that anything was possible.

Some things were impossible. Banks could be saved, farmers rescued, the hungry fed, and the mighty Tennessee tamed, but the United States was an industrial nation, and no law could solve industry's problems. Roosevelt tried. The National Recovery Administration (NRA) was the New Deal's greatest effort. It cannot be dismissed as a total failure. The NRA lifted men's hearts, and it is arguable that by strengthening organized labor it contributed enormously to eventual recovery. If it did not fulfill Roosevelt's hopes for it—and clearly it did not—it did give the country a kind of temporary wartime unity. The NRA was like a spectacularly successful football rally followed by a lost game, or, as General Hugh Johnson predicted at the outset in a splendid mix of metaphors, "It will be red fire at first and dead cats afterwards. This is just like mounting the guillotine on the infinitesimal gamble that the ax won't work."

Johnson, the most colorful of the New Dealers, was chosen to administer the NRA. Possibly his everybody's-a-rink-stink-but-Hughie attitude injured its chances. He denounced people who obstructed him as men "in whose veins there must flow something more than a trace of rodent blood," or "perfumed guys from the State Department," or "merchants of bunk, guff, and hooey," and he hurt Herbert Hoover's feelings by comparing offices in the Commerce Building to pay toilets in Union Station. But NRA's problems were visible when the idea first surfaced in FDR's second fireside chat, on May 7. The President said he wanted "a partnership in planning" between business and government, with the government having the right to "prevent, with the assistance of the overwhelming majority in that industry, unfair practices and to enforce this agreement by the authority of government."

His purpose, which every decent businessman could endorse, was the elimination of cutthroat competition and the sweating of women and children. But the industry-by-industry codes inevitably meant the end of trust-busting and the return of price-fixing. Labor was jittery, so Donald R. Richberg, counsel for the Railway Brotherhoods, persuaded Johnson to write NRA's historic section 7(a), legitimizing collective bargaining and thus providing impetus to the labor movement of the 1930s. Big business saw it coming. In Senate hearings the National Association of Manufacturers and the Chamber of Commerce protested bitterly. Roosevelt summoned disputants and advocates of the bill to a White House conference, which lasted until they reached an agreement on wording. They emerged with 7(a) intact, but it was an inauspicious beginning. The industrialists and their legislative spokesmen had gone along only because some of them believed in abolishing all free enterprise. As Ralph Flanders, then president of the Jones & Lamson Machine Company, put it, they were "thoroughly sold on the idea that recovery and prosperity depended on the restraint of competition."

Ironpants Johnson was such a superb showman that these prickly issues were undiscovered through most of 1933. Henry Wallace had told him about thunderbirds, and the general drew a blue eagle based on the old Indian ideogram. Under it he lettered the legend *We Do Our Part*. To the press he growled, "May God have mercy on the man or group of men who attempt to trifle with this bird." Firms which complied with his codes were entitled to display blue eagles. Consumers affixed eagle decals on their windshields, *Time* printed the symbol on its covers each week. Four girls had it tattooed on their backs. In a San Francisco baseball park eight thousand children stood in formation to form a gigantic NRA eagle, and

Busby Berkeley, not to be outdone, rewrote the finale of *Footlight Parade* so that Ruby Keeler, Dick Powell, Joan Blondell, and every extra in Hollywood formed (1) the American flag, (2) the profile of FDR, and (3) Johnson's eagle. It was dazzling, it was exhilarating, and with the general racing around the country getting his codes signed, it looked real.

Much of it was. By midsummer some nine million workers were under NRA work and wage codes signed by one million employers. But most of these were small businessmen. Of the ten largest industries—textiles, coal, petroleum, steel, automobiles, lumber, garments, wholesale trade, retail trade and construction—only textiles had signed up, and that had taken six weeks of furious campaigning. There were mutinous sounds in New Deal ranks; "Hugh," said Hopkins, "your codes stink." Indifferent to the blue thunderbird, coal mine guards were shooting miners, and Henry Ford refused to do his part. Johnson traded in his Lincoln for a Cadillac. The President ordered government departments and bureaus to do business only with NRA firms. A newspaperman asked Johnson what would happen to objectors who wouldn't go along with the codes. Wiping beer suds from his lips, he snapped, "They'll get a sock right on the nose."

Then the general changed his strategy. He launched a nationwide campaign to pledge all employers to a twelve-dollar, forty-hour week; formal codification would come later. The President made it the subject of his third fireside chat, on July 24, 1933: "In war, in the gloom of night attack, soldiers wear a bright badge on their shoulders to be sure that comrades do not fire on comrades. On that principle, those who cooperate in this program must know each other at a glance." The implication was plain—do your part or lie low. The NRA now took on an evangelical air. Mayor James Michael Curley assembled a hundred thousand children on Boston Common and led them in the pledge: "I promise as a good American citizen to do my part for the NRA. I will buy only where the Blue Eagle flies. I will ask my family to buy in September and buy American-made goods. I will help President Roosevelt bring back good times."

Every community with any civic pride held an NRA parade, with floats and bands playing "Happy Days Are Here Again." New York's eclipsed all the rest. For ten hours two million New Yorkers watched a quarter-million marchers. Symphony conductor Walter

Damrosch led the radio workers, Charles Winninger the actors, Al Jolson the motion picture employees. There were a thousand barbers; ten thousand bankers, brokers, and stock exchange clerks; and twenty thousand garment workers. At the reviewing stand, fifty carrier pigeons were released, carrying good wishes to FDR. Night fell, the Fifth Avenue lights went on, and still the delegations came tramping out of Washington Square—grocers, jewelers, pawnbrokers, butchers, firemen, policemen, librarians, druggists, book publishers, and bartenders. But you didn't have to be in New York to feel the enthusiasm. In Tulsa, Hugh Johnson's seventy-seven-year-old mother led the parade, warning, "People had better obey the NRA, because my son will enforce it like lightning, and you can never tell where lightning will strike." Everywhere, wrote Heywood Broun, marchers felt hope and confidence: "When a line forms and your shoulder touches that of a fellow and a comrade, solidarity is about to be born." Suddenly General Johnson was flooded with draft codes, two million of them. Every major industry endorsed the NRA except automobiles and coal; then the car makers joined (Ford remained an exception) and, finally, coal. In the general enthusiasm, even Herbert Hoover signed an NRA pledge.

Then came the reaction. Hoover changed his mind and decided that the NRA was totalitarian. Businessmen denounced it as "creeping socialism" and union leaders as "business fascism." William Randolph Hearst charged that NRA stood for No Recovery Allowed. A writer for *Harper's Magazine* toured four states and found that firms displaying blue eagles were guilty of monstrous NRA violations. Of the more than 700 codes, 568 had price-fixing clauses, which is presumably what Hopkins had had in mind. Walter Lippmann wrote of the NRA that "The excessive centralization and the dictatorial spirit are producing a revulsion of feeling against bureaucratic control of American economic life."

What had happened? Earlier in the year columnists and industrialists had been begging the President to become a dictator. The difference now was that he had turned the country around; he was paying the price of success. During his first four months in the White House, the Federal Reserve Board's adjusted index for industrial production had risen from 59 to 100. Brokers spoke of "the Roosevelt market." Men who would have been too weak or too frightened to oppose Johnson in March were now dealing from strength. "We have had our revolution," said *Collier's*, "and we like it." "Up go the prices of stocks and bonds, adding millions of value," cheered the *Literary Digest*. "Up go the prices of wheat, corn and other commodities, putting millions into the pockets of Depression-harried farmers." The *Digest* didn't mention the AAA, which was directly responsible for farm price rises, but the *New York Times* declared that Roosevelt had turned an unprecedented crisis into a personal triumph: "That was because he seemed to the American people to be riding the whirlwind and directing the storm. The country was ready and even anxious to accept any leadership. From President Roosevelt it got a rapid succession of courageous speeches and achievements which inclined millions of his fellow citizens to acclaim him as the heaven-sent man of the hour." Roosevelt, said Ray Moley, had saved capitalism.

The institution of the Presidency had been transformed. When Roosevelt rode up Capitol Hill bystanders clapped loudly; and Secret Service agent Richard Jervis, who had guarded Hoover for four years, said, "It sounds good to hear that again." In August the President jauntily greeted a press conference with the announcement, "I have some rather grand news for you." A year earlier it would have been incredible: a government 500-million-dollar issue of 3.25 percent bonds—the first long-term Treasury issue since September 1931—had been oversubscribed *six times*. Despite Hearst, there could have been no more decisive proof of business confidence in the New Deal. For the first time since 1929 businessmen were discounting the future. And why not? Nothing, it seemed, could blunt Roosevelt's attack on the Depression. The Congress was his, and Thomas Reed Powell, professor of constitutional law at Harvard, declared that "In my judgment, there are sufficient doctrines of constitutional law to enable the Supreme Court to sustain any exercises of legislative or executive power that its practical judgment would move it to do." If Professor Powell didn't know, who did? The answer was Chief Justice Charles Evans Hughes. Unfortunately, no one had thought to ask him.

Portrait of an American

ELEANOR

Her father was T.R.'s brother, her mother a famous beauty, and she was born Anna Eleanor Roosevelt in 1884. So sad, everyone said. Such an *ugly* child.

When visitors called she would hide and suck her fingers till her mother called, "Come in, Granny," explaining to the guest, "She's such a funny child, so old-fashioned that we call her Granny." And the little girl would want to sink through the floor.

Her mother died of diphtheria when she was eight, her father died of alcoholism when she was nine. She was sent to live with her maternal grandmother, a strict disciplinarian. Until she was fifteen she had no friends her own age.

At eighteen she was presented to Society. Society shuddered. The girl was nearly six feet tall. Her voice was loud and scratchy. Her front teeth protruded. She wouldn't use cosmetics. She giggled at odd times. Sometimes she burst into tears for no apparent reason. Her mind was going, the family said, and when Cousin Franklin proposed to her, his mother Sara fought the marriage for three years.

At the wedding, on March 17, 1905, Teddy gave the bride away. She had inherited his fantastic energy. Not proper in a woman, everyone clucked, and they disapproved of the way she spent it. Someone asked whether housekeeping bothered her. She said, "I rarely devote more than fifteen minutes a day to it." Instead she worked among the poor. And while she was out of the house in 1913, her young husband fell in love with her part-time social secretary, Lucy Mercer.

Lucy married a rich old man named Rutherfurd in 1920 and next year polio crippled Franklin. Sara wanted him to give up public life, to retire to Hyde Park as a cripple, but the doctor told Eleanor that he should return to politics; she could serve as his eyes and ears. The two women struggled. Eleanor joined the Women's Trade Union League, worked till she dropped for the Democratic party, and told Franklin that he must be governor. Sara's benevolent dictatorship grew weaker. She wrote her brother, "Eleanor is in the lead."

He was elected governor, then President.

And at the inaugural he arranged for a front-row seat and a private limousine for lovely Lucy Mercer Rutherfurd.

After the inauguration Eleanor visited the second encampment of the bonus marchers. She sang songs with them, and afterward they said, "Hoover sent the army, but Roosevelt sent his wife."

The President could seldom tour the country, so his First Lady covered forty thousand miles every year, delivering lectures and visiting slums, nursery schools, playgrounds, sharecroppers. Franklin always questioned her closely when she returned; he jocularly gave her the Secret Service code name Rover.

"For gosh sakes," said one goggle-eyed miner to another in a *New Yorker* cartoon, "here comes Mrs. Roosevelt!"

While she was away, Lucy called on the President.

In Washington, Eleanor held a press conference once a week for women reporters in the Treaty Room on the second floor of the White House. Her column, *My Day*, appeared in 135 newspapers. She wrote a question-and-answer page for each issue of the *Woman's Home Companion*. As a radio personality she was second only to Franklin. Her twice-a-week broadcasts were sponsored by Sweetheart toilet soap, Simmons mattresses, Johns-Manville building materials, Selby shoes, and Pond's cold cream; she gave all the money to the American Friends Service Committee. Once she kept two White House receptions going at once, moving back and forth between the connecting door.

The President would meet Lucy on roads beyond Georgetown and Arlington. Once his Washington to Hyde Park train detoured to a little-used siding at Allamuchy, New Jersey, so he could visit her at her estate.

Eleanor by now knew that she could have neither romance nor a close relationship with Franklin.

"Back of tranquillity lies always conquered unhappiness," was her favorite quotation.

To her admirers she was mother, wife, politician, stateswoman, journalist, and First Lady—all at once, and often all at the same time. She broke more precedents than her husband, had a greater passion for the underdog, and was always a little farther to the left. Once at Hyde Park she debated with Winston Churchill the best way to keep peace in the postwar world. By an Anglo-American alliance, said he; by improving living standards throughout the world, said she.

Her critics, led by Westbrook Pegler, called her a busybody, a do-gooder, a bleeding heart. Cartoonists drew savage caricatures of her. Anti-Eleanor jokes were cruel: "Eleanor can bite an apple through a picket fence." In London, Ambassador Joseph P. Kennedy said she was the greatest cross he bore—"She's always sending me a note to have some little Susie Glotz to tea at the embassy."

Once she wondered whether her outspokenness might be a liability to Franklin. (At the time she was defending the right of Americans to be Communists.) He chuckled and said, "Lady, it's a free country."

She was at a meeting of Washington clubwomen when word came that he had died in Warm Springs.

In the White House she learned that Lucy had been with him at the end. She wept briefly; then, as always, she steadied herself.

Wounded by her mother, her father, her mother-in-law, and her husband, she now embraced all humanity. She continued her column, wrote fifteen books, reformed Tammany Hall, and represented the United States at the United Nations. Year after year in the Truman and Eisenhower administrations, American women voted her the woman they most admired. Gallup reported she was the most popular woman in any part of the world.

Aged seventy-four, she wrote, "We must regain a vision of ourselves as leaders of the world. We must join in an effort to use all knowledge for the good of all human beings. When we do that, we shall have nothing to fear."

Four years later she was dead. "Her glow," said Adlai Stevenson, had "warmed the world." The U.N. stood in silence in her honor. The three Presidents who had succeeded her husband bowed their heads as her coffin joined his in the Hyde Park garden. Over both stood a stone with an inscription she had chosen: "The only thing we have to fear is fear itself."

Lucy was absent. She had died in a New York City hospital fourteen years earlier.

Three

STIRRINGS

In May 1934 the first comics magazine, *Famous Funnies*, appeared on American newsstands. Its readers did not include J. Edgar Hoover, director of the Federal Bureau of Investigation. The nation's top cop enjoyed comics—his favorites were Dick Tracy and Secret Agent X-9—but he had little time for them that spring. Hoover had his hands full getting ready to move the Justice Department into its new building on Pennsylvania Avenue, carrying out a presidential order to keep an eye on Fascist organizations, studying the new crime control acts just passed by Congress, and absorbing into his FBI agents from the now defunct Prohibition Bureau. The director wanted all the help he could get. "The criminal in America is on the march," he had told the public, and the public could only agree. It had hoped that prohibition repeal would wipe the dark stain of violence from the American national character. Instead, the bootleggers turned to holding up banks. The reputation of bankers being what it was, the thieves were widely regarded as Robin Hoods; an Indianapolis admirer of the FBIs Public Enemy Number One wrote, "Dillinger does not rob poor people. He robs those who became rich by robbing poor people. I am for Johnnie."

Johnnie's record of ten murders, four bank stickups, and three jailbreaks ended when he lost a confrontation with the fastest guns in the FBI, led by Melvin Purvis. The lesson should have been obvious, but as a national commission was to find thirty-five years later —amid what could hardly be called a serene era—public tolerance of violence during the 1930s was the highest in American history. Dillinger was more dangerous dead than alive. He became a kind of folk hero, and people who had never even seen a pistol spoke casually of the rod, the roscoe, the equalizer, or the heat. Farmers had demonstrated that direct action worked; now all sorts of people were advocating it, including the governor of California, who congratulated a lynch mob for doing "a good job." Chester Gould, Dick Tracy's creator and therefore presumably a man after J. Edgar Hoover's heart, said, "Big gangsters were running wild but going to court and getting off scot-free. I thought: why not have a guy who doesn't take the gangsters to court but shoots 'em?" If it came to that, why not shoot anybody big who angered you? An alarming number of letters threatened Eleanor Roosevelt; on the advice of the Secret Service, she never left White House grounds without a roscoe of her own in her purse.

It was symbolic that Dillinger had been equalized while leaving a theater featuring a gangster movie. Hollywood was churning out fifty such films each year, many of them casting crime in a romantic light. Opinions about the director's other gifts have varied, but no one ever doubted his genius for public relations. In 1934 the bureau's files were opened for the producers of *G-Men*, a new kind of movie with the part of an FBI man played by an appealing young actor named James Cagney. Then the director turned to radio. Melvin Purvis was dispatched to appear on the Fleischmann Yeast Hour. This was a near disaster; Purvis horrified Hoover and inflamed ulcers at the J. Walter Thompson advertising agency by belching into the microphone. On the other hand, a program called *Gangbusters* proved to be immensely popular. Dick Tracy himself could be heard during the children's hour; millions of children sent in Quaker Oats box tops for detective badges. But the country's flesh-and-blood supersleuth was still Hoover himself. He was constantly running around the country, drawing up public enemy lists, and pursuing such outlaws as "Pretty Boy" Floyd, "Baby Face" Nelson, "Ma" Barker, "Machine Gun" Kelly, and—last and least in those days—Bonnie Parker and Clyde Barrow.

The most distinguished guest to call at 1600 Pennsylvania Avenue that May was John Maynard Keynes. Bearing a letter of introduction from Felix Frankfurter, the economist came to recommend deficit spending: "Nothing else counts in comparison with this."

Afterward Roosevelt wrote that he and Keynes had had "a grand talk." In fact it had been rather chilly. The Keynesian manner was reserved, even arrogant, and FDR still had difficulty accepting the idea that a country could spend its way to prosperity. Still, he permitted Tugwell to introduce Keynes to key figures in his administration. Despite New Deal pyrotechnics, more than eighteen million Americans were reliefers. Some states—for example, Arkansas, Mississippi, and South Carolina—received 90 percent of their relief money from the federal government. Beyond doubt Roosevelt had saved the country from anarchy, but the Depression continued to be intractable, and Keynes's contention that complete recovery could be achieved only by annual deficits of 300 million dollars would be remembered in the capital long after he had left.

These were hard days for the New Deal. The NRA was collapsing under its own weight. In despair, General Johnson turned to the bottle and his secretary; he justified her salary to the press by saying she was "more than a stenographer," and when they printed that, he protested, "Boys, you're hitting below the belt"—an unhappy metaphor. The business community had begun to turn against Roosevelt two months earlier when he proposed legislation to regulate the stock market. George M. Humphrey, Sewell Avery, and Tom Girdler had led the fight against a Securities and Exchange Commission. A Republican congressman charged that it was part of a plot to "Russianize everything worthwhile." President Richard Whitney said of his New York Stock Exchange that it was "a perfect institution"; it was after Whitney's testimony that Will Rogers drawled, "Those Wall Street boys are putting up an awful fight to keep the government from putting a cop on their corner." They lost the fight, and their disappointment turned to fury when FDR appointed Joseph P. Kennedy, a notorious speculator, to head the commission. The President had acted on Moley's advice; since Kennedy knew all the loopholes, Moley argued, he could plug them. Wall Street was unappeased. When Whitney took Kennedy on a formal tour of the exchange floor, he surrounded him with bodyguards; otherwise, he explained coldly, the brokers might attack the new SEC chairman. Some tycoons were calling Kennedy "a traitor to his class." They weren't saying that about FDR yet, but that time was approaching, for the President had coupled insult to injury by firing Dean Acheson because he refused to sign the devaluation order. Already Acheson was toying with the idea of becoming a charter member of the nascent Liberty League.

A much greater storm lay over the horizon. Over a thousand cases involving New Deal legislation were in litigation. Individual judges could issue injunctions against federal laws in 1934, and as Attorney General Homer Cummings had warned Roosevelt, only 28 percent of the federal judiciary was Democratic. Eventually all cases would reach the Supreme Court, but that was small comfort. The high court judges were on the average seventy-eight years old and conservative. Eventually almost every strong President had come into conflict with the Court. Roosevelt was the strongest since Lincoln, and the battle, if it came, could be shattering.

One cabinet member, at least, had good news for the country. Secretary of State Cordell Hull pored over cables from Berlin and announced that "Mistreatment of Jews in Germany may be considered virtually terminated."

In a Pennsylvania Avenue cafeteria that same spring, Alger Hiss met Whittaker Chambers for the first time, though not under that name. The introductions were made by J. Peters, a Soviet agent, and Harold Ware of the American Communist party. They merely told Hiss that this was "Carl," to whom he would be answerable in party matters. The cafeteria was just a few doors away from the *Washington Post*, yet even if the city desk had known of the meeting, it seems highly unlikely that an account of it would have been published. Communists were not yet regarded as horrid. John W. McCormack of Massachusetts, chairman of the eight-week-old House Un-American Activities Committee, was preoccupied with the American right. It would be three years before J. Edgar Hoover would receive presidential instructions to put Communist organizations under surveillance, and even then the sole concern was espionage.

The United States had extended formal recognition to the Soviet Union the previous Thanksgiving. Russia's new ambassador had just been the guest of honor at a Waldorf-Astoria banquet; among the younger guests was an ex-president of the National Student Federation, Edward R. Murrow, who angrily wrote his future wife about America's economic system, which "damns some of us before we are born." (Murrow was indignant about the price of the banquet tickets, an unheard-of six dollars a plate.) In May 1934 the Popular

Front was only six months away. Earl Browder would soon stand under banners proclaiming *Communism Is Twentieth-Century Americanism.* Westbrook Pegler would call him "more Kansan than Landon," and Browder became the author of an unemployment insurance bill introduced by Congressman Lundeen of Minnesota. Before the decade was out he would achieve the acme of acceptability, an invitation to share a Cleveland platform with Robert A. Taft, who wanted all the votes from the left he could get.

On May 14, 1934, a Missouri relief administrator named Harry S. Truman filed for the Democratic statewide primary. He wrote a note to himself early that morning:

> It is 4 a.m. I am about to make the most momentous announcement of my life. I have come to the place where all men strive to be at my age . . . now I am a candidate for the United States Senate. If the Almighty God decides that I go there I am going to pray as King Solomon did, for wisdom to do the job.

The event went unnoticed in Washington. The only man in high office even to have met Truman was Harry Hopkins, and their acquaintance was confined to a single conference, in Hopkins's Pullman drawing room between Chicago and Kansas City the previous October. Had the New Dealers known more, they would have been unimpressed. The candidate wasn't even solvent; since the failure of his haberdashery he had been saddled with an unsatisfied judgment of $8,944.

The capital *was* intrigued by the formation of La Follette's Wisconsin Progressive party and Upton Sinclair's stunning primary triumph in California; Sinclair had received more votes than all eight of his Democratic opponents combined. But most of Washington was taking a political breather. The spectacles of the past year had exhausted them, and on the eve of the off-year elections they talked of other things. Hervey Allen's 1,224-page *Anthony Adverse* was leading all best-seller lists, though it was being challenged by James Joyce's *Ulysses,* which had just been cleared by a Manhattan judge. Ernest Hemingway had caught a record 468-pound Marlin without harness, Max Baer had outpunched Max Schmeling, Glenn Cunningham had run a 4:06.7 mile; Sir Malcolm Campbell had driven his *Blue Bird* 272.1 mph—faster than airliners. St. Louis was afflicted by sleeping sickness, New England elms by the Dutch elm disease.

Moviegoers marveled at the eclipsing of Dolores Del Rio and Gene Raymond, the stars of *Flying Down to Rio*, by two "feature players," Fred Astaire and Ginger Rogers. The brightest comedian on adult radio was Jack Benny. During the past two years he had failed to catch the public ear with three sponsors, Canada Dry, Chevrolet, and General Tires. Now he was finally making it for Jell-O. Children preferred *The Lone Ranger*, who with his horse Silver had been thundering past microphones since New Year's Day.

In short, there was time for trivia. The despair of 1932 had fled. There was a feeling that almost anything could happen. In Canada, on May 28, Mr. and Mrs. Oliva Dionne had become the parents of quintuplets. Last fall the Washington Senators had actually been in the World Series. It might happen again sometime.* Most Washingtonians were enjoying the dry, pleasant spring and the flowering cherry blossoms, though Henry Wallace wished to God the country would get some rain.

Among the most unpleasant aspects of the mid-1930s, once the fear of chaos had subsided, was the weather. At one time or another the Mississippi, Ohio, Potomac, Tennessee, Delaware, Connecticut, Missouri, Susquehanna, Columbia, Allegheny, and Merrimack rivers —streams draining virtually every major basin in America—rose over their banks and roared through the streets of cities. One flood, that of the Ohio River in 1937, was the worst in the nation's history; it destroyed the homes of a half-million people. Flood and windstorms in these years took 3,678 lives. Winters were uncommonly bitter, and in a single summer, 1936, while one of her inhabitants was trying to win the Presidency, Kansas recorded almost sixty days of 100 degree heat, but in the early Roosevelt years the most urgent problem was a combination of drought and high gales, bringing what were known as "black blizzards." That was Henry Wallace's nightmare. Before his Triple-A and CCC conservation could alter the country's agriculture, the topsoil of the Middle West was blowing away.

For years conservationists had warned that ecological catastrophe hovered over the Great Plains. The so-called short-grass country west of the hundredth meridian was favored by fewer than twenty

* It never did.

inches of rain a year. Early explorers had labeled the frontier beyond the Missouri "the great American desert," and then it was relatively stable, hammered flat by millions of bison and untilled by the Indians. Then the settlers arrived with their John Deere plows. Before the Depression they were blessed by extraordinarily heavy rains, but as they pushed their luck by overgrazing and overplowing, the ineludible drew nearer. Even in the 1920s a hundred counties in Colorado, Kansas, New Mexico, Texas, and Oklahoma had been called the "dust bowl." Now in 1934 the National Resources Board estimated that 35 million acres of arable land had been completely destroyed, the soil of another 125 million acres had been nearly or entirely removed, and another 100 million acres were doomed. Abruptly the bowl grew to 756 counties in nineteen states. Like Ireland and the Ukraine in the nineteenth century, the Plains were threatened with famine.

The first of the great storms had blustered out of the sky on Armistice Day 1933, in the ninth month of the new administration. In South Dakota the farms began blowing away that morning. By noon the sky was darker than night. Men were literally vomiting dirt, and when the sun reappeared, fields had been replaced by sand, while roads, trees, sheds, fences, and machinery had disappeared beneath great hanging dunes of soil. By then the wind was headed for Texas. A towering pall darkened Chicago, and was visible as far east as Albany.

That was only the beginning. The drought continued through 1934 and 1935, accompanied by fantastic windstorms howling down from such remote Dakota towns as Chugwater, Niobe, Wounded Knee, and Spotted Horse. "In 1934," wrote Tugwell, then Undersecretary of Agriculture, "rainfall had been so short that severe damage had been done." Actually that year's farm calamity could be traced back to the previous winter; light snows had left the land too hard to absorb what rain there was. The earth could be seen through the thin grass, and the wheat was so thin that Tugwell compared it to the stubble on an old man's chin. In the same month that Keynes visited Roosevelt and Truman filed for the Missouri primary, the first storms of 1934 struck the Texas Panhandle. Whole counties were transformed into shifting Saharas. Wives packed every windowsill, door frame, and keyhole with oiled cloth and gummed paper, yet the fine silt found its way in and lay in beach-like ripples on their floors.

A Texas schoolboy described the storms as "rolling black smoke." In Oklahoma Nathan Asch found that even food tasted gritty. He wrote that the dust "blew into the eyes, underneath the collar; undressing, there were specks of dust inside the buttonholes; in the morning it had gathered like fine snow along the window ledge; it penetrated even more; it seeped along the wiring of the house; and along the edges of the door . . . there was a rusty brown stain." For three weeks Oklahoma streetlights were on day and night. People wore dust masks, and to compound misery, the temperature seemed stuck at 108 degrees.

Lorena Hickok, on a field trip for Hopkins, reported from Huron, South Dakota:

> We started out about 8:30 in the morning intending to drive into the northern part of the county to see some farmers. We had gone less than ten miles when we had to turn back. It kept getting worse. You couldn't see a foot ahead of the car. It was truly a terrifying experience. Like driving in a fog, only worse because of the wind that seemed as if it would blow the car right off the road. It was as though we were picked up in a vast, impenetrable black cloud which was hurling us right off the earth.

"Speaking nationally," Tugwell wrote, "that drought had been an ironic blessing—it had helped reduce embarrassing surpluses of wheat—but for the individuals and families involved it was disastrous." In fact, the Department of Agriculture inadvertently increased the human disaster; under the AAA acreage reduction programs, wealthy farmers were discovering that they needed less help. Their tenants, turned out, took to the road in rattletrap 1925 Dodges, 1927 La Salles, and 1923 Model Ts, looking for a greener land. They were joined by small farmers whose "For Sale" signs marked the start of the dust-bowlers' migrations. Drought had destroyed the wheatlands of Eric Sevareid's father and broken his bank; he moved on. In Hall County, Texas, the population abruptly dropped from 40,000 to less than 1,000. Most picturesque of all were Oklahoma's ragtag "Okies," to be immortalized five years later in John Steinbeck's *The Grapes of Wrath*. In the interim Steinbeck would conduct a dog census in California's Monterey County—one of the few idiotic Hopkins projects—and he was destined to see the migrants because California was their destination. It beckoned as a land of milk and honey: "I like to think how nice it's gonna be, maybe, in California," Ma Joad said. "Never cold. An' fruit ever' place, and people just bein' in the nicest places, little white houses in among the orange trees." In reality it would bring the Joads the drudgery and want which were the fruit pickers' lot. Simultaneously, the Okies' pilgrimage would help ruin the promising gubernatorial campaign of Upton Sinclair.

Those people in little white houses among the orange trees were appalled by the advancing army of dust-blown, indigent farmers who, as Arthur M. Schlesinger Jr. wrote, seemed to represent "the threat of social revolution by a rabble of crazed bankrupts and paupers—a horrid upheaval from below, led by a Peter the Hermit, which could only end in driving all wealth and respectability from the State." It was Louis B. Mayer, the motion picture tycoon, who cast Sinclair in the role of Peter the Hermit, thus sowing a seed in media manipulation which would bear weird fruit a generation later.

Sinclair was vulnerable. In a state celebrated for its eccentrics, the fifty-four-year-old author had emerged as one of the oddest. His candidacy had been launched in a pamphlet entitled *I, Governor of California, and How I Ended Poverty: A True Story of the Future*. He proposed to set up a statewide net of socialist communes toiling under the symbol of a wide-winged honeybee and the slogan "I Produce, I Defend." Roosevelt liked Sinclair, and the writer's program was endorsed by Theodore Dreiser, Archibald MacLeish, Dorothy Canfield Fisher, Stuart Chase, Morris Ernst, Clarence Darrow, and, curiously, Father Charles E. Coughlin of Royal Oak, Michigan. But Norman Thomas said it was "economically and politically absurd." Sister Aimee Semple McPherson, the shopworn Los Angeles evangelist, called Sinclair "a red devil." The California Boy Scouts were mobilized against the accused, who was then repudiated by the regular Democratic organization.

The Republican candidate, Frank Merriam, came out for the Townsend Plan—$200 a month for everyone over sixty—which had been launched in Long Beach on January 1, 1934, and presently legions of white-haired Californians were marching for the GOP, singing:

> *Onward, Townsend soldiers,*
> *Marching as to war,*
> *With the Townsend banner*
> *Going on before.*

Sinclair's slogan, "End Poverty in California" (EPIC), was twisted to mean "Empty Promises in California." The three big Los Angeles newspapers, *Time* noted, "simply quit reporting news of EPIC and its sponsor." Metro-Goldwyn-Mayer taxed its employees to underwrite the anti-Sinclair campaign, and though some stars revolted (Cagney and Jean Harlow among others), most not only went along but permitted their talents to be exploited in fake newsreels. Mayer, the state Republican chairman, had hired the big advertising firm of Lord & Thomas and put MGM studios at its disposal. Gangs of extras dressed as hoodlums and hookers tumbled off freight trains while MGM cameras ground and commentators explained that their audiences were witnessing actual Okie invasions. One elderly bit actress, dressed as a kindly grandmother, declared that she could never vote for Sinclair because he believed in free love, while elderly male actors appeared with fake beards and stage accents shouting aggressively that they were supporting the author ("Vell, his system vorked vell in Russia, vy can't it vork here?"). In October FDR thought Sinclair would win, but nothing could withstand the MGM offensive. California went Republican by a quarter-million votes, and the defeated writer returned to his typewriter to hammer out a new book, *I, Candidate for Governor: And How I Got Licked.**

Not everyone on the left was licked. In the state of Washington radicals rallying under an almost identical banner ("End Poverty in Washington") elected a senator, half the legislature, and, as prosecutor of King County, young Warren Magnuson. The La Follettes were triumphant in Wisconsin, winning the senatorial and gubernatorial races and taking seven of the ten congressional seats. Strapping Floyd B. Olson sat in the Minnesota statehouse, growling at interviewers, "You bet your life I'm a radical. You might say I'm radical as hell!" And the incomparable Fiorello La Guardia was now mayor of New York City.

"Too often, life in New York is merely a squalid succession of days," La Guardia said, "whereas in fact it can be a great, living, thrilling adventure." Under the swashbuckling five-foot-two-inch mayor, it became an adventure in light opera. He wore a black sombrero, shouted his commands in an incongruously shrill voice, and carried out his duties with piratical dash. One minute after he

---

* Among the interested California observers of the campaign were Jerry Voorhis, a Sinclair supporter who was later elected to Congress, and the man who would later unseat Voorhis, Richard M. Nixon, Whittier '34.

was sworn in he ordered the arrest of Lucky Luciano, the eminent hood. He used the city's building, fire, and health departments to help striking waiters. When laundry owners begged him to be neutral in a dispute over their sweatshop wages, he blandly picked up his telephone and ordered his water commissioner to show the city's impartiality by turning off the water in all laundries. (The owners settled immediately.) He ruled Manhattan like a laird, leading police raids in person, showing up without notice to preside over night court sessions, reading comic strips over the radio to children, and hanging on the back of a racing fire engine, an outsize helmet on his head. La Guardia's hymn was "Who's Afraid of the Big Bad Wolf?" His flair for the dramatic, even the preposterous, sometimes camouflaged his advocacy of socialism, yet none who worked with him ever doubted his views or his effectiveness.

The elected radicals allied themselves with the New Deal; the doctrinaire left kept its distance. Contemplating Marxism and FDR's experimentation, the *New Republic* stated flatly, "There is no middle course." When Tugwell boasted of the administration's aversion to "blind doctrine," James Wechsler, then the Marxist editor of Columbia's student daily, wrote that doctrine was precisely what the New Deal needed, and I. F. Stone and Max Lerner enthusiastically agreed. More than thirty years before Herbert Marcuse roused the New Left with his call for "selective tolerance," Lincoln Steffens said, "Get the notion of liberty out of your heads. . . . We want liberty for us, but not for Hitler and Mussolini." The *New Masses* used even more Marcusian language: "We would deny democratic rights to Fascists, to lynchers, to all those who wish to use them as a means of winning mass support for reaction."

Tom Wolfe, who was three years old at the time, would one day write a brilliant article for the *New York Magazine* about "radical chic." Wolfe had Leonard Bernstein and the Black Panthers in mind, but the concept was equally valid in the mid-Thirties. Hede Massing, a Soviet agent, was startled and amused when one of her earnest socialite protégés in the State Department sang "The International" to her in Russian from the steps of the Lincoln Memorial. As Budd Schulberg was to note in *The Disenchanted*, face styles had even changed among intellectuals since the Twenties; F. Scott Fitzgerald's "sleek, shiny, Arrow Collar perfection, finely etched, sharp-featured, a pretty-boy face drawn with the symmetry of second-rate art, pear-shaped, with a straight nose, cleft chin, dark hair parted smartly down the middle, combed back and plastered down with Vaseline or Sta-comb," had been replaced by the heavy bone structure, unruly hair, and Slavic features of the proletarian image. Indeed, wrote Frederick Lewis Allen, if you listened carefully at certain cocktail parties "you might have heard a literary critic who had been gently nurtured in the politest of environments referring to *himself* as a proletarian, so belligerently did he identify himself with the masses." At dinner parties in New York's elegant upper Eighties the most recent caller at the Communist party's headquarters at 35 East Twelfth Street would be the cynosure of all artistic eyes, and if in his cups he could always find comradely voices to join him in the rousing refrain:

> *To make it Soviet*
> *One more S in the USA*
> *Oh, we'll live to see it yet.*
> *When the land belongs to the farmers*
> *And the factories to the working men—*
> *The USA when we take control*
> *Will be USSA then.*

The threat from the left was absurd, if colorful; the rightist threat was inchoate, if greater in potential. As the 1934 off-year elections approached, the most persistent criticisms of the New Deal came from businessmen. During the Hundred Days, most of them had approved of Joseph Medill Patterson's moratorium on harassment of the administration; in his *New York Daily News* he had promised, "Whatever President Roosevelt does or doesn't do, we're going to be for him. We're going to withhold hostile criticism for one year at least." Now over a year had passed, and on reflection they decided they didn't much like FDR's paraphrase, in his inaugural, of Matthew 21:12—"The moneychangers have fled from their high seats in the temple of our civilization." The first to speak out had been Al Smith. In a December 1933 editorial in his *New Outlook* Smith scorned the New Deal's proliferation of acronyms: "It looks as if one of the absent-minded professors had played anagrams with the alphabet soup." He had added, "Some of my readers may ask why others have not pointed out the dangers in the CWA program. The answer is very simple. No sane official who has hung up an empty stocking over the municipal fireplace is going to shoot Santa Claus just before a hard Christmas."

"The hell they won't," Hopkins said dryly. "Santa Claus really needs a bullet-proof vest." Roosevelt himself wrote to one of his ambassadors, "The inevitable sniping has commenced, led by what you and I would refer to as the Mellon-Mills influence in banking and certain controlled industries." Congress approved increased relief spending in 1934, but the SEC battle thickened the ranks of snipers. On June 8 the President was sufficiently concerned to postpone his request for social security and its payroll tax until the following winter. It didn't matter; no truce was possible now; two months later the American Liberty League convened in Miami and declared formal war. "All the big guns have started shooting," Roosevelt wrote William C. Bullitt in Moscow. "Their organization has been labeled the I CAN'T TAKE IT CLUB."

Sometimes he asked them to take a lot. Jesse Jones of his revitalized RFC castigated a meeting of financiers in Chicago, telling them that they were failures on their own terms, reminding them that half the audience represented institutions that had failed, and demanding that they "Be smart for once" and "take government into partnership with you." Perhaps the point of no return in Roosevelt's break with Wall Street was reached on October 24, 1934, when four thousand members of the American Bankers Association met in the DAR's Constitution Hall to hear FDR himself. Jackson E. Reynolds, president of the First National Bank of New York, delivered an introduction which can only be described as obsequious. He told the President that the financial community was in a "chastened and understanding mood" and actually thanked him for everything the New Deal had done to "rescue and rehabilitate our shattered banking structure." Roosevelt's reply was one of his more unfortunate lapses into Endicott Peabodyism, asking for an alliance of all economic forces in the nation, including business, banking, labor, capital, and government. "What an all-America team that would be!" he exulted—as though Ironpants Johnson had not just led precisely such a team to a dismal string of defeats. The applause was polite, though the bankers felt Reynolds's surrender had gone too far. Then, back in their hotels, they learned that they had been sold out. The White House had insisted upon censoring Reynolds's speech in advance, deleting such wry asides as his recollection of the days when he had been a Columbia law professor and Franklin Roosevelt his less than perfect student. Neither for the first nor the last time, FDR had been too clever for his own good.

Business baiting of the President mounted in the last days of the 1934 election campaign, but the great middle class was largely unaware of it. In a masterly fireside chat he said, "I am not for a return to that definition of liberty under which for so many years a free people were being gradually regimented into the service of the privileged few." At the same time he praised "the driving power of individual initiative and the incentive of fair private profit." Republicans were rediscovering that it was impossible to come to grips with such an opponent, and a note of ugliness began to creep into some of their speeches; in Wisconsin a Republican nominee bitterly referred to Roosevelt as "a man who can't stand on his own two feet without crutches." FDR, knowing that such tactics could boomerang, thought Democrats would do well at the polls, though even he was surprised by the results. On the morning of November 7 the country awoke to find that the party in power had actually increased its congressional margins to 229 seats in the House and 44 in the Senate; the Republicans were left with only seven governorships. Among the thirteen freshman senators, all Democrats, was Harry S. Truman of Missouri.

In his preelection fireside chat Roosevelt had questioned the price-fixing aspects of the NRA. Johnson then resigned—he assembled his employees in the Commerce Department auditorium and tearfully quoted, in Italian, the dying words of Madame Butterfly before she committed hara-kiri—and was replaced by Averell Harriman. The departure of old Ironpants made little difference. The NRA was due to expire in June 1935 anyway, and before it could die with dignity the Supreme Court declared it unconstitutional. Implications of that decision were ominous only insofar as they affected other New Deal legislative achievements. The execution of the blue eagle—which left as its only legacy trade-in allowances for buyers of new cars—was in many ways a relief. By then it had been superseded by the acts of the Second Hundred (actually a hundred and seventy-seven) Days of 1935.

Planning for those days was begun by Roosevelt and Hopkins in the wake of the election returns, which could only be interpreted as a mandate. The general goals of the new laws were to be a more sensible use of national resources, security against unemployment and old age, and slum clearance and better housing. The chief beneficiaries would be labor and the small farmer. Roosevelt sketched its broad outlines in his State of the Union message to the new, heavily Democratic Congress on January 4, 1935. Then he and his aides began drafting the bills. They were not the same aides who had dazzled the capital two years earlier. Moley, Tugwell, Acheson, Richberg, Berle, Douglas, and Johnson were gone or going. The new New Deal required different talents, which the President found in, among others, Felix Frankfurter, James M. Landis, Marriner S. Eccles, Tom Corcoran, and Ben Cohen. Cohen and Corcoran lived together in what soon became famous as "the little red house on R Street." They reminded *Fortune* of "those minor state counselors in Shakesperian comedies who serve the Duke, make astute comments, and are always perturbed at developments."

There was plenty of perturbation, but it lay elsewhere, notably in the Washington offices of the Liberty League and other conservative strongholds. The Holding Company Act provided a good example of how far big business would now go in fighting Roosevelt. It applied to public utilities and included a five-year "death sentence" clause which provided that any holding company not able to prove its usefulness to its community within that time would be dissolved. Opposition appeared on several different levels. On the most dignified plane there was Wendell L. Willkie, then a utilities attorney, with a counterplan for state regulation. Several notches down was the utilities lobby, which, the Scripps-Howard Washington bureau reported, employed more agents than there were senators and congressmen. Finally, at the very bottom, were the forgers of fake messages from voters. This extraordinary campaign almost killed the bill. It cost the utilities nearly two million dollars; they sent out 250,000 telegrams and five million letters demanding rejection of the death sentence. Senator Truman alone received 30,000 such appeals. He burned them and remained loyal to Roosevelt. The House at first rejected the death sentence, however, and changed its mind only after a congressional committee headed by Hugo Black proved that the mail response was a fraud.

Social security was the most emotional issue that session. Republicans protested that if the administration bill were passed, children would no longer support their parents, the payroll tax would discourage workmen so much that they would quit their jobs, and that, taken all in all, the measure would remove the "romance of life." Throughout the rest of his life Roosevelt was especially proud of his battle for social security, and in retrospect it seems the greatest of his legislative achievements. But it was a battle hard won. Every conceivable argument was raised against it, including militant interruption of hearings; Frances Perkins was testifying in its behalf before a congressional committee when a woman leaped up and shouted that the bill had been copied, word for word, from "page eighteen of the Communist Manifesto, which I have right here in my hand, Mr. Chairman."

Coolidge-Hoover prosperity had identified the Republican party with big business, and as 1935 advanced into spring and then summer, antagonism toward FDR welded the two together. Utility lobbyists were so successful in their whispering campaign charging the President with insanity that by July the Washington press corps was being badgered by hometown offices inquiring whether Roosevelt had in fact lost his mind. The handful of Republicans in the Capitol took turns excoriating the New Deal's plan to "sovietize America." When Roosevelt proposed to raise income taxes in the higher brackets and introduce an inheritance tax, Hearst branded the program "essentially Communism," a "bastard" measure attributable to "a composite personality" which might be labeled "Stalin Delano Roosevelt."

The Senate struck out the inheritance tax and reduced assessments in the top brackets, but FDR got most of what he wanted that session. Among the fruits of the Second Hundred Days were the Soil Conservation Act, a National Resources Board; a strengthened Federal Reserve Board; the Rural Electrification Act, which eventually brought electricity to a million farm families; the Guffey-Snyder Coal Act, which superseded the NRA in the mining industry; the Wagner-Connery Act, replacing section 7(a) and establishing a National Labor Relations Board; and the National Youth Administration, providing employment for youths from relief families and part-time jobs for needy students. Lyndon B. Johnson, who had just moved his young wife Lady Bird into a two-room apartment with a rollaway bed at 1910 Kalorama Road N.W., was appointed NYA administrator for the state of Texas, where he would soon meet and hire, at 17 cents an hour, a sharecropper's son named John B. Connally Jr. (The North Carolina administrator was more openhanded with Richard Nixon, who had moved from Whittier to Duke Law School; Nixon's NYA job paid 35 cents an hour.)

"Boys, this is our hour," a grinning Hopkins had told his staff after the off-year triumph. "We've got to get everything we want—a works program, social security, wages and hours, everything now or never. Get your minds to work on developing a complete ticket to provide security for all the folks of this country up and down and across the board." Despite charges that Hopkins used relief money to buy votes—Republicans insisted he had said, "We will tax, tax, spend, spend, and elect, elect"—he went to great lengths to keep the WPA above politics. Nevertheless, those who had been saved from want could hardly fail to be grateful, and it was in these early months of 1935 that Roosevelt turned the Democrats into the country's majority party by forging his grand coalition of labor, the South, women, ethnic minorities, city bosses, and Negroes.

Viewed from the 1970s, FDR's appeal to blacks may seem baffling. They were barred from TVA construction work, evicted from farms under the AAA crop reduction policies, and subject to new forms of discrimination by southern Democrats administering New Deal programs in Dixie. At its inception in June 1934, the Federal Housing Administration introduced restrictive clauses into its housing contracts. At the Warm Springs railroad depot there were separate toilets, waiting rooms, and even baggage rooms for "colored." New Dealers were lukewarm about anti-lynching bills; in 1934 Louis Howe buried one in his files with the note: "Not favored at this time—may create hostility to other crime bills."

Roosevelt benefited largely from comparison with Hoover, whom Walter White of the NAACP had called "the man in the lily-White House." (During his four years in the Executive Mansion Hoover had declined to speak to the two Negro porters there.) The Republicans continually promised to protect the Negro's economic status, which, as Jonathan Daniels observed, "was exactly what he wanted to escape." Championing of black causes by Eleanor Roosevelt, Frances Perkins, and Harold Ickes helped; Ickes desegregated the Interior Building cafeteria and brought Robert Weaver into the administration. Negroes were accepted by the CCC and WPA, social security was color-blind, Howard University received a three-million-dollar government grant, relief projects built schools for blacks, and three hundred thousand Negro adults learned to read under a New Deal emergency education program. It was all tokenism, perhaps, but blacks hadn't been able to get even tokens in the past.

The formation of every presidential cult is met by its opposite, and so it is with coalitions. By the end of the Second Hundred Days the first anti-Roosevelt bloc had emerged. It was a loose alliance of the Liberty League, Townsendites, William Dudley Pelley's anti-Semitic Silver Shirts, the Hearst press, admirers of red-baiting Elizabeth Dilling, Huey Long's Share Our Wealth movement; the Reverend Gerald L. K. Smith, Long's chief lieutenant; and Father Charles E. Coughlin's National Union for Social Justice, formed on November 11, 1934. The Liberty League supplied much of the money. Followers were recruited from the lower middle class—often from the same neighborhoods which were to support Senator Joseph R. McCarthy in the early 1950s, Governor George Wallace in the late 1960s, and Spiro Agnew in the early 1970s.

During the Second Hundred Days the anti-Rooseveltians scored twice—both times in the name of isolationism, then at the height of its appeal. Defying the President's reluctance to have his hands tied in foreign affairs, they lobbied through the Neutrality Act of 1935, which required him to prohibit arms traffic with nations at war and to forbid American citizens to travel on belligerent vessels, except at their own risk. The measure was immediately applied to the Ethiopian War. In the second instance, they turned back an FDR appeal to Congress asking American adherence to the World Court. On the Senate floor Long enlisted the support of Hiram Johnson and Borah; in the nationwide mail campaign Will Rogers joined Hearst and Father Coughlin. The Radio Priest claimed rejection of the Court as a personal victory, and since his audience at the time was estimated at 45 million listeners, his claim was undisputed.

The building of Father Coughlin's empire had been a brilliant one-man accomplishment in media manipulation, exploiting aspects of the national character which were then but little understood: American innocence, the nation's yearning for simplest solutions, its joiner complex, and the carnival instinct for collecting shiny junk. Had the priest been born a generation later, he would have made a superb host on a television talk show or a Madison Avenue account executive, for he was a born salesman. He could have merchandised almost anything. He chose to peddle hate.

Now in his forty-fifth year, he was a big, sleek, well-groomed, bespectacled Canadian with a voice like an organ. Detroit had first heard that marvelous voice in 1926, when the Ku Klux Klan—toward which he would later display a peculiar tolerance—burned down his church in Royal Oak, a Detroit suburb. The shocked director of the local radio station WJR suggested that he deliver a series of sermons over the air asking contributions for a new church. By the end of 1930 Coughlin had organized the Golden Hour of the Little Flower, broadcast over seventeen CBS stations, plus occasional local cut-ins, from 6 to 7 P.M. CST Sundays. Members of his vast unseen audience could not only hear the radio priest's florid metaphors and rolling tirades; they could also acquire a Sacred Relic by sending him money. In return they received a tiny chrome-plated cross stamped "Radio League of the Little Flower," and with it this letter:

> My dear Friend:
> With this letter it is my privilege to send you a souvenir crucifix. As I announced over the air, it has touched a relic of the True Cross. . . .
>
> Devotedly yours in Christ,
> CHAS. E. COUGHLIN
>
> P.S. If some friend wants a crucifix, let me know.
> C.E.C.

Three months after he joined CBS, he was getting an average of 80,000 letters a week enclosing more than $20,000. Eventually, after especially popular broadcasts, the number of envelopes would pass a million and require 150 clerks to sort out the bills and stock the change. In 1934 he was getting more mail than anybody in the country, including President Roosevelt. His church had been rebuilt long ago (with nonunion labor). The marble and granite tower of its seven-story Shrine could be seen all over Royal Oak; at night dazzling spotlights played across a gigantic bas-relief figure of Christ spread across it. Beneath the Saviour was carved the single word, "Charity." On the stones of the church were various inscriptions, some from the Scriptures and some just good service club slogans. *Time* claimed that "Charity Crucifixion Tower reminds many Detroiters of a silo" and christened its architect "Silo Charlie." In riposte Coughlin cried that the news magazine "is not forgiven for indirectly insulting the crucified Christ whose monument is described by *Time* as a 'silo.' By inference, are we Catholics and Protestants who receive our spiritual food and drink from the Victim of the cross—are we cattle, content to fill ourselves with silage? By printing such classical billingsgate *Time* has stubbed its toes against eternity."

From the side of Charity Crucifixion Tower, Christ's agonized expression looked out upon a bizarre scene—a gasoline station beneath a gigantic sign reading "Shrine Super-Service," a "Shrine Inn," and a Little Flower hot dog stand. Inside the church itself other vendors spread their wares: picture postcards of Silo Charlie, crucifixes "personally blessed" by him, Bibles, anti-Semitic pamphlets, copies of the Brooklyn *Tablet*, and, after 1934, stacks of the Father's *Social Justice* magazine. (At the height of its popularity, *Social Justice* was on sale in two thousand American churches.) Tourists were asked to make as little noise as possible—not, as one might suppose, because they were in a place of worship, but because at the very top of the tower, accessible only by a circular staircase, the radio priest sat chain-smoking, stroking his Great Dane, and composing his weekly sermon. The enormity of this task was well-known to the visitors. After CBS dropped him because he had become controversial, the priest organized his own network of over sixty stations, supported by contributions from the faithful. His flock had become the largest in the history of Christianity. *Fortune* called him "just about the biggest thing that ever happened to radio"; he outdrew *Amos 'n' Andy*, *Dr. Fu Manchu*, and Ed Wynn. So great was his weekly harvest of currency that he had become the country's principal speculator in silver, which he described on his Sunday programs as "the Gentile metal." Like a Pope, he granted audiences; occasionally he would graciously consent to receive the President's personal emissary, Joseph P. Kennedy, who was frantically trying to find some common ground between them.

It was impossible. No such ground existed. Father Coughlin had supported FDR in the beginning; his war cry in 1932 had been "Roosevelt or ruin," and as late as April 1934 he assured a rally in New York's Hippodrome Theater, "I will never change my philosophy that the New Deal is Christ's deal." It was a rash promise. For one thing, he now had 500,000 ounces of silver, and the President wasn't being very cooperative with the silver bloc. The radio priest was mortified when the Secretary of the Treasury gave the press a list of silver speculators, headed by Coughlin's private secretary. He could have survived that—after all, Woodin's successor at the Treasury was Henry Morgenthau, who as a Jew could be depicted as a born enemy of the Gentile metal—but in his need to create new sensations or lose his audience, the radio priest was being driven to excesses which, in the long run, could only lead to hostility toward a President who had preempted the political center.

The hostility grew as Coughlin's power grew. His National Union for Social Justice claimed a signed-up membership of 7,500,000, the most militant of whom took to the streets in what *Social Justice* called "platoons" of twenty-five each, looking for Jews. The preferred method for creating an incident was to offer copies of the magazine for sale to passersby who were known to be or just looked Semitic, and jump them when they declined; it was employed several times in front of Nedick's orange juice stand on Times Square, where Irish policemen were admirers of the radio priest. Meanwhile he was opening fire on Roosevelt's new allies in the labor movement. He denounced the American Federation of Labor, recommending that the government, following the example of Italy and Germany, settle industrial disputes by decree. What he wanted, Raymond Gram Swing pointed out, was "a fascist solution of the labor problem."

Supported by Bishop Michael Gallagher of Detroit, Coughlin insisted that he also had the backing of Pius XI. It was true that the Pontiff had said "every minister of the holy religion must throw himself, heart and mind, into the conflict for social justice," but the *Osservatore Romano,* speaking for the Holy Father, took pains to point out that he hadn't meant the kind of Social Justice advocated by the priest of Royal Oak, and William Cardinal O'Connell of Boston accused Coughlin of disseminating "demagogic stuff to the poor." By this time the radio priest was beginning to display the arrogance of power; he informed his ecclesiastical betters that his magazine was a private venture and therefore none of their business. Anyone who crossed him now was going to have his knuckles rapped. La Guardia was awarded the Shrine's "ill will" prize for criticizing Adolf Hitler and thus "breeding international bad feeling." Liberals were called Communists. Organized labor, the flock was told, was being masterminded in Moscow. The faithful must "think Christian, act Christian, buy Christian" and beware of world Jewry: "Call this inflammatory if you will. It is inflammatory. But rest assured we will fight and we will win."

Early in 1935 Coughlin published the totalitarian program of his National Union for Social Justice. Point One set the tone: he demanded "Liberty of conscience and education," but no freedom of speech, which would have meant the end of his Radio League—unless he was running the country, which presumably was what he had in mind. At the same time he broke with Roosevelt. The New Deal became the "Jew Deal." The President was "a liar," an "anti-God"; in a Cincinnati speech Coughlin advocated the elimination of FDR by "the use of bullets." This was too much for Westbrook Pegler, a Catholic layman and admirer of European strong men; in his column he wrote that federal investigators of subversion should have treated Coughlin just as they were treating Earl Browder, instead of tiptoeing "around him for fear he would cry up a holy war."

It wasn't too much for Mrs. Dilling, whose list of powerful Communists included Senator Borah, Chiang Kai-shek, Eleanor Roosevelt, H. L. Mencken, and Mahatma Gandhi. It didn't offend James True, inventor of the "kike-killer" (Pat. No. 2,026,077), a short rounded club made in two sizes (one for ladies). It didn't offend Joe McWilliams, the soapbox Führer, or Lawrence Dennis, the intellectual of the radical right. Most interesting of all, no reproaches were found in the Hearst press. "Whenever you hear a prominent American called a 'Fascist,'" Hearst declared, "you can usually make up your mind that the man is simply a LOYAL CITIZEN WHO STANDS UP FOR AMERICANISM." Beginning in November 1934, Hearst sent reporters disguised as students into college classrooms, to trap teachers in unconventional comments. Nobody wanted to change the American economic system, he said, except for "a few incurable malcontents, a few sapheaded college boys, and a few unbalanced college professors."

Considering the tens of millions who were reading and listening to incendiary remarks, it is not surprising that some of them reacted violently. Between June 1934 and June 1935 the American Civil Liberties Union noted "a greater variety and number of serious violations of civil liberties" than in any year since the World War, and the ACLU records were incomplete, owing to the suspension of all constitutional guarantees in the state of Louisiana.

If Father Coughlin was the propaganda minister of Depression extremism, Senator Huey Pierce Long Jr. was universally acknowledged as its leader. The radio priest had the audience, but he preached nihilism. Dr. Townsend, who had become their ally, could count ten million followers, but he didn't know how to get things done. Huey Long, the consummate politician, had everything: constituents, a program, and an intuitive sense of when and how to seize power. He was the only antagonist who genuinely frightened Franklin Roosevelt.

The legend of Huey Long has been set down in two memorable novels, by John Dos Passos in *Number One* and Robert Penn Warren in *All the King's Men*. The truth is at least as compelling. Huey was born in a log cabin, in the bitter poverty of Winn Parish, and he was distinguishable from other wool-hats only by his genius. He began by selling a shortening called Cottolene to the gallused men and calicoed women who would trust him to the grave and beyond. In eight months he completed the Tulane University three-year law course and, by special dispensation from the Louisiana Supreme Court, became a lawyer at the age of twenty-one, an achievement that no Tulane student, before or since, has ever matched. Later he displayed his virtuosity before the United States Supreme Court, establishing the constitutionality of a school book law which had been rejected in the lower courts. He presented his argument without legal assistance, without a lawbook, with only a one-page brief; and he won the admiration of Chief Justice William Howard Taft.

Huey could never have been elected governor without back-room deals with Standard Oil lawyers. He took it the way he could get it. But Huey, unlike the corrupt politicians of New Orleans, saw what had to be done. Louisiana was held in thrall by out-of-state corporations. There were only thirty miles of paved roads in the entire state, hospitals were virtually closed to the poor, the major rivers were unspanned by bridges, there was no schooling for half the children. As Secretary of Commerce, Herbert Hoover came to visit Louisiana. It amused him. He even smirked at the state's treasured Evangeline myth. Very little was known about her, he said; even her name was questionable; she might have been called Gwendoline. It was an unforgivable thrust, and in the autumn of 1928 Huey, now thirty-five and a candidate for governor, parried it for the wide-eyed rednecks and Cajuns. Standing on a cotton bale beneath flickering torches at Martinville, he delivered one of the most moving perorations in American politics:

"And it was here that Evangeline waited for her lover Gabriel who never came. This oak is an immortal spot, made so by Longfellow's poem. But Evangeline is not the only one who has waited here in disappointment. Where are the schools that you have waited for your children to have that have never come? Where are the roads and highways that you spent your money to build, that are no nearer now than ever before? Where are the institutions to care for the sick and disabled? Evangeline wept bitter tears in her disappointment. But they lasted through only one lifetime. Your tears in this country, around this oak, have lasted for generations. Give me the chance to dry the tears of those who still weep here."

Elected, he broke the power of the corporations. Louisiana's poll taxes were abolished, new taxes were levied on business, a debt moratorium was declared, the poor were exempted from the general property tax, textbooks were free, children rode in school buses. In three years he gave the state 2,500 miles of paved roads, 6,000 miles of gravel roads. Twelve bridges went up. Property assessments were reduced 20 percent, and at his new night schools 175,000 illiterate adults were taught to read and write. He was the only southern governor to treat blacks as equals; when the head of the Ku Klux Klan threatened to come into the state and campaign against him, Huey told reporters, "Quote me as saying that that Imperial bastard will never set foot in Louisiana, and that when I call him a son of a bitch I am not using profanity, but am referring to the circumstances of his birth."

He had been elected on the slogan "Every man a king, but no man wears a crown." One man did. Huey did. He called himself Kingfish after the head of Amos 'n' Andy's lodge, the Mystic Knights of the Sea, and "by the spring of 1935," Hodding Carter wrote, "Huey Long owned Louisiana." Newspaper critics like Carter went armed day and night. Some were beaten, kidnapped, and jailed. When his secretary's husband threatened to sue him for alienation of affections on the eve of his election to the Senate, Huey had him put in an airplane and flown through the skies all over the state until votes were in; then he was brought down. Every state judge was in his pocket, including the entire state supreme court. All policemen, state and municipal, reported directly to him. He alone held power over the schoolteachers, tax collectors, the state government, the banks, and the governor. Finally his legislature outlawed democracy. Huey, not voters, would decide who had been elected to what. When New Orleans rumbled with discontent, he called out the militia and entered the city at the head of his troops, like Caesar. He said he had tried to reason with his opponents: "That didn't work and now I'm a dynamiter. I dynamite 'em out of my path."

Early in 1935, after his legislature had shouted through forty-four bills in twenty-two minutes, one of the few honest men left in it rose to say, "I am not gifted with second sight. Nor did I see a spot of blood on the moon last night. But I can see blood on the polished floor of this capitol. For if you ride this thing through, you will travel with the white horse of death." He was hooted down. If any blood was spilled, it wouldn't be Huey's; he was surrounded by bodyguards carrying revolvers and submachine guns. And soon, his henchmen prophesied, he would be protected by the U.S. Secret Service, because it was clear to them—and to many of his enemies—that Huey's next address would be 1600 Pennsylvania Avenue in Washington.

Already he was a national figure, second only to FDR. He was the most widely discussed politician in the country. Clearly he was preparing to move beyond the borders of Louisiana. He was deeply involved in Texas politics, and he was planning to purge Joe Robinson of Arkansas, Senate majority leader, and Pat Harrison of Mississippi, chairman of the Senate finance committee. His outrageous clowning was the subject of editorials and cartoons in every metropolitan newspaper. At a Long Island party he drank too much, sauntered into the men's room, and ordered a tall young man standing at the urinal to "Step aside for the Kingfish of Louisiana." When the youth wouldn't, Huey, unconventional as always, attempted to direct the trajectory of his stream between the other's legs. He missed, and left the party with a black eye. That was low comedy, but there was little laughter in a Senate cloakroom when he told his colleagues, "Men, it will not be long until there will be a mob assembling here to hang Senators from the rafters of the Senate. I have to determine whether I will stay and be hung with you, or go out and lead the mob."

The President wrote his ambassador to Italy that Americans "are going through a bad case of Huey Long and Father Coughlin influenza—the whole country is aching in every body." That included Roosevelt. Like the radio priest, Huey had supported Roosevelt in 1932. (Unlike Coughlin, the Kingfish could rightly claim that FDR couldn't have been nominated without him.) Now he was angry at the entire New Deal. His income tax returns were being questioned, Farley was withholding federal patronage from him, and WPA projects in Louisiana had been suspended because of irregularities in local administration. The Kingfish's chief grievance, however, was that he wasn't President, and he felt he ought to be. He wrote a book, *My First Days in the White House*. (Roosevelt, he wrote, would be his Secretary of the Navy.) Asked if there would be a Long-for-President movement in 1936, he snapped, "Sure to be. And I think we will sweep the country." One of the few men on Capitol Hill to stare Huey down was Harry S. Truman. The obscure Missourian was carrying out one of the traditional chores of freshman senators, presiding over the Senate, when Long delivered one of his more venomous speeches. Afterward the Kingfish asked him what he thought of it. Truman answered sharply, "I had to listen to you because I was in the chair and couldn't walk out." But as the New Deal approached its second anniversary there were fewer and fewer Trumans. Huey was openly ridiculing the President on the Senate floor as "a liar and a faker," and it is a measure of Roosevelt's desperation that he was driven to solicit support from Theodore Bilbo of Mississippi, the most noisome racist in the South. Bilbo scorched "that madman Huey Long," but all he achieved was to attract a tornado of angry mail from his own constituents.

On February 5, 1935, the Louisiana peril cropped up in a discussion of federal appointments. The proceedings of the National Emergency Council recorded this exchange:

THE PRESIDENT: Don't put anybody in and don't keep anybody that is working for Huey Long or his crowd! That is a hundred percent!

VICE-PRESIDENT GARNER: That goes for everybody!

THE PRESIDENT: Everybody and every agency. Anybody working for Huey Long is not working for it.

SECRETARY OF STATE HULL: It can't be corrected too soon.

THE PRESIDENT: You will get a definite ruling any time you want it.

It made little difference. As Hodding Carter later noted, "On our side we had only the federal patronage. In a vote-getting sense, this consisted mainly of WPA work orders which were distributed by the thousands to the anti-Long organizations. They didn't help much. The poor jobless devils took the work orders readily enough, but they didn't vote WPA. Few among us could have won even an honestly conducted election."

On March 5, the second anniversary of Roosevelt's inaugural, the administration formally conceded that the country had something to fear besides fear itself. Speaking at a Waldorf-Astoria banquet, Ironpants Johnson, now the WPA administrator for New York, attacked the right-wing alliance "between the great Louisiana demagogue and this political padre." The Kingfish and the radio priest replied over the networks. Johnson returned to the attack—"If you put quotations from Hitler and Father Coughlin in parallel columns, you can't tell them apart, including anti-Semitism"—and the New Deal's heavy artillery joined him. Harold Ickes permitted himself to be quoted as saying, "The trouble with Senator Long is that he is suffering from halitosis of the intellect. That's presuming Emperor Long has an intellect."

Huey's intellect was greater than the old curmudgeon's; he seized equal time to lay his Share Our Wealth program before a nationwide radio audience. Fortunes would be limited to five million dollars. No one's annual income could be greater than $1,800,000 or less than $2,000. Provisions would be made for old-age pensions, bonuses for veterans, and cheap food through AAA surpluses. Children would receive a free education from kindergarten through college. Every family would be entitled to a $6,000 homestead grant and a radio, an automobile, and a washing machine. In their one foray outside Louisiana, members of Huey's Share Our Wealth clubs (there were no dues) had elected Mrs. Hattie W. Caraway to fill out her dead husband's Arkansas Senate seat. Now Huey's catchy ditty could be heard in slums all over the country:

> *Every man a king, every man a king,*
> *For you can be a millionaire*
> *But there's something belongs to others.*
> *There's enough for all people to share.*
> *When it's sunny June and December too*
> *Or in the wintertime or spring*
> *There'll be peace without end*
> *Every neighbor a friend*
> *With every man a king.*

To Forrest Davis, author of *Huey Long: A Candid Biography*, the Kingfish confided that he intended to outlaw the Democratic and Republican parties and serve four terms "as the dictator of this country." Throughout that spring and summer his popularity snowballed to frightening size. Turner Catledge of the *New York Times* felt that the administration had blundered in striking back at him; its replies had "probably transformed Huey Long from a clown into a real political menace." The Democratic National Committee conducted a secret poll showing that Huey, running for the Presidency on a third-party ticket, might take four million votes away from Roosevelt and capture enough key states to throw the 1936 election into the House. Jim Farley, the country's most skillful political fortuneteller, told Ickes in September that the Kingfish's vote would exceed six million. Already Huey and his allies were a visible influence in the Second New Deal; social security had acquired much of its momentum from the Townsend Plan, which Long backed, and the raising of taxes in the upper brackets and the Holding Company Act owed much to Huey's charge that FDR was a prisoner of the rich and the utilities. Huey knew it. In July he charged that Roosevelt was "copying my share-the-wealth speeches that I was writing when I was fourteen years old. So he's just now getting as smart as I was when I was in knee breeches."

Late in August, when Congress adjourned, the Kingfish was still skipping up and down Senate aisles, mocking "Prince Franklin," "Lord Corn" Wallace, "Sitting Bull" Johnson, and Ickes, "the Chicago Chinch Bug." Yet Huey, like his lonely scold in Baton Rouge, was visited by premonitions. A month earlier he accused his enemies of plotting his assassination with "one man, one gun, and one bullet" and a presidential pardon for the assassin. Now he said that in the next session he expected Congress to obey his orders, "provided I am back here—I may not be back here. This may be my swan song, for all I know."

It was. On September 8 he was in the Baton Rouge statehouse, cracking the whip over his legislature. Meanwhile one man with one gun was hiding behind a marble pillar in the capitol, ready to fire the one bullet. His name was Carl Austin Weiss; he was an idealistic young physician whose father-in-law, a district judge, had crossed foils with the Kingfish. Huey had retaliated by gerrymandering the judge out of his district and circulating rumors about his ancestry. At 9:20 P.M. Huey strutted across the capitol rotunda. Dr. Weiss stepped out and shot him in the stomach. In the next instant the Kingfish's bodyguards riddled the doctor's body with sixty-one bullets, but their chief was fatally wounded. "I wonder why he shot me?" he asked before he lapsed into a coma. Others wondered, too, and their speculation grew during the two days the body lay in state, dressed in white tie and tails. Floral tributes covered three acres; some 250,000 came to watch their leader's burial on the capitol's front lawn. "He was the Stradivarius, whose notes rose in competition with jealous drums, envious tomtoms," the Reverend Gerald L. K. Smith cried in his eulogy. "His was the unfinished symphony." Afterward Smith blamed the crime on the news media and Bilbo. Bilbo answered by describing Smith as "a contemptible, dirty, vicious, pusillanimous, with-malice-aforethought, damnable, self-made liar." Still, the speculation continued. In the bayous, Louisiana's poor, who owed the Kingfish everything, sang:

> *Oh they say he was a crook*
> *But he gave us free school book*
> *Tell me why is it that they kill Huey Long?*
>
> *Now he's dead and in his grave*
> *But we riding on his pave'*
> *Tell me why is it that they kill Huey Long?*

Over thirty years later Smith told students at the University of Illinois, "It cannot be proved that President Roosevelt ordered the assassination of Huey Long, but it can be proved that those who discussed his assassination were positively of the opinion that it would please the President." The President's first reaction to the murder—he was lunching with Father Coughlin and Joseph P. Kennedy at the time—was one of horror. No humane man could find pleasure in such a violent death. In the long run, however, the disappearance of the Kingfish from the national scene certainly brought FDR relief from a serpentine threat. Huey Long was one of the very few men of whom it can be said that, had he lived, American history would have been dramatically different.

Roosevelt knew he must face a third-party challenge from the right anyhow. Smith, Coughlin, and Townsend were determined to see Huey's symphony finished. Nine months after the funeral the radio priest announced to his vast audience—his hookup had grown to thirty-five stations—that a new party, the Union Party, had been formed. Its convention was held in Cleveland, where Coughlin ripped off his clerical collar, linked arms with Smith and Townsend, and brought admirers to their feet in a standing ovation. If they had come for a show, they got one. His oration was one long slander of the President. Every slur was greeted by waves of frantic applause, and the speech reached its climax in the most dramatic of all rabble-rousing techniques; Coughlin's great voice wavered and he staggered away from the lectern, collapsing into the arms of his guards as thousands screamed. That had never happened to him on radio. But he was more than a radio personality now, more than a priest; and it had been years since he had delivered anything remotely resembling a sermon.

In the spring of 1935 the President's closest advisers concluded that he was slipping in his role as a public educator. When they told him so, he replied, "People tire of seeing the same name day after day in the important headlines of the papers, and the same voice night after night over the radio. . . . Individual psychology cannot, because of human weakness, be attuned for long periods of time to constant repetition of the highest note in the scale."

Here the public wisdom may be deeper than it seems. There is more to history than politics. In the trivia of one decade the life style of another may lie, awaiting nothing but competent management and a change in the economy. This is not true of all minutiae; one searches in vain for any note of significance in the chain-letter craze that swept the country in May 1935. On the other hand, the excitement in Enrico Fermi's quaint little Roman laboratory appears in retrospect to be a study in understatement; it is clear from the humorous account by Fermi's wife Laura that by systematically bombarding all the elements with neutrons, Fermi and his students, though they didn't know it at the time, had just become the first physicists to split the uranium atom—establishing nothing less than a chain reaction.

Between the trifles and the stupefying are curious developments, some of them far more memorable than any congressional battle that year, which made 1935 a kind of technological watershed. Tiring of Father Coughlin and spinning the radio dial, for example, Sunday listeners might pick up twenty-year-old Orson Welles, playing The Shadow, alias Lamont Cranston:

MARGOT: Oh, Lamont, look! When that waiter started for the kitchen, the door opened without his touching it!

SHADOW (*casually*): Yes. Works by photoelectric ray.

MARGOT: Oh, what's that?

SHADOW: Look at each side of the door, Margot. See those chromium fixtures sticking out of the floor? Lights hidden at the top of them? There's a beam of light between those two bulbs. When anybody approaches the door, his body breaks that ray. Whenever the beam is broken the door opens without touching it.

MARGOT: How clever!

It *was* clever in 1935, and it was also the crude beginning of the electronics industry, which would eventually eliminate not only doormen but elevator operators, bowling alley pinboys, letter sorters, billing clerks, matchers of textile hues, counters of passing objects, guards at prison gates, insurance actuaries, accountants, magazine distributors, and a thousand other skilled and unskilled occupations. Automation, in a word, had begun.

So had the communications revolution, the displacement of privacy and the written word by Marshall McLuhan's global village. In June 1935 George Gallup conducted his first poll, for the advertising firm of Young & Rubicam. "Public relations" offices were opened by John Hill, Earl Newsom, and Carl Byoir. In 1935 *Becky Sharp*, starring Miriam Hopkins, began appearing in downtown theaters. Though many screens were not equipped to handle the process, it was the first feature-length Technicolor motion picture. To color film should be added certain allied developments. Nobel Laureate Gugliemo Marconi had discovered short waves that could be "bent" around the earth's surface—the microwaves which would first be used in World War II radar and, later, in television broadcasting. The Associated Press introduced its wirephoto service in 1935, to be followed by *Life* in 1936 and *Look* in 1937; the country was becoming accustomed to the concept of image. Combine all these with two other 1935 innovations—the first night baseball game, in Cincinnati, and the invention of the beer can—and the future middle-aged recreation of boys then in their teens begins to assume a familiar form.

Arthur Sherman's trailer industry had turned the corner during 1933's Hundred Days and was rapidly becoming America's fastest-growing business; within a year two thousand trailers and house cars would convene in Sarasota, Florida. American youth was still expected to be mechanically minded then, and the hottest thing in *Mechanics Illustrated* was the General Motors independent front-wheel suspension, as described by G.M. President Alfred P. Sloan Jr.: "The simplest way to explain it is to say that we have put knees on our automobiles. Each front wheel will be attached individually to the chassis by its own soft spring. When it encounters a bump or a hole, it will rise or fall independently, as your leg is lifted or straightened by its knee without affecting your other leg or the equilibrium of your body. The result will be that the wheel, not the passenger, will get the jar." Knee action! But not even Alfred

Sloan (or Arthur Sherman) foresaw the growth in American mobility and the interstate highway net.

In 1935 the sound of the Thirties—swing music—was heard for the first time. Benny Goodman, a forty-dollar-a-week clarinetist the year before, was trying to improve his situation by leading his own band. He wasn't having much luck; on the evening of August 21 the band was about to wind up an engagement at the Palomar Ballroom in Los Angeles, and no one had offered to pick up its option. The musicians were as bored by the saccharine, bland fox-trot music as the dancers. Goodman decided to go down in style to the swinging rhythm his sidemen preferred in after-hour sessions, using a Fletcher Henderson arrangement (Henderson, a Negro, was unacceptable to white ballroom managers). Suddenly the audience was aware of vibrant brasses, strong drums, singing saxophones smashing away at full speed, and wild improvisations as hot soloists, including Benny, rose in turn under the spotlight to embroider the theme. The result was electrifying; the room came to life, and in the eyes of the entertainment business the twenty-five-year-old Goodman overnight became king—King of Swing.

Not everyone was enthusiastic; a psychologist told the *New York Times* that swing was "dangerously hypnotic" because it was "cunningly devised to a faster tempo . . . than the human pulse" and would tend to "break down conventions." Yet it was characteristic of the decade that there was some form of swing for every age group. Goodman, Artie Shaw, Glenn Miller, and Tommy Dorsey—who was about to make his own memorable debut with "Marie" in Nixon's Grand Theater in Philadelphia—were idols of the tulle-and-white-buck Palomar, Roseland, Savoy, Hollywood Palladium, Glen Island Casino dancing youth. But there was also swing for children (Spike Jones), sweet swing for the middle-aged (Kay Kyser), sticky swing for the geriatric set (Guy Lombardo, Wayne King, Vincent Lopez), and even intellectual swing at Carnegie Hall, where one could hear subtle, intricate patterns for the most sophisticated ear. Through the reborn phonograph industry, every form of swing was available on 35-cent Bluebird and Decca or 50-cent Columbia records. The diversity, or, as some would have it, the balkanization of taste lay thirty years in the future.

This ecumenicalism was true of all lively arts. The concept of X, R, and GP films would have been inconceivable. Everything had to be GP, because 85 million Americans went to the movies once a week, a large part of them as families; the average family annual movie budget was $25, astonishing in the light of Depression admittance prices. There were 17,000 theaters in the country, more than there were banks, twice as many as there were hotels and three times as many as department stores. Each theater owner showed between a hundred and four hundred films a year. He didn't have time to screen them all. Fortunately for him (and unfortunately for cinema art) the Hays Office, later the Breen Office, did it for him. The Catholic League of Decency, which began its vigil in 1934, saw to it that Hollywood avoided long kisses, adultery, nude babies, or married couples sleeping in anything except twin beds. Language on the silver screen was, as they said then, Rinso White; when Dennis King sang "to *Hell* with Burgundy," a thrill ran through audiences, as though a naked woman had run among them. Even titles went through the washing machine. *Infidelity* mysteriously became *Fidelity,* and *Good Girls Go to Paris Too* was transmogrified into *Good Girls Go to Paris.* In part this censorship is attributable to the values of the time. As Mae West said later, "We weren't even allowed to wiggle when we sang." Mae's films were picketed after her reply to Cary Grant's "Darling, you need a rest—let me take you away somewhere" slipped past Breen. (Stroking her coiffure and running her tongue over her teeth, she answered, "Would you call that a rest?") *Life* had to go to court for the right to distribute its issue on "Birth of a Baby," and *Time*'s thin-lipped comment on Erskine Caldwell's *God's Little Acre* was that it "underlines a recent tendency of U.S. publishers: to go as near the limits of censorship as possible."

In equal part, censorship reflected the needs of a depressed population seeking not realism but an escape into celluloid. Hollywood, John Dos Passos wrote, offered a "great bargain sale of five and ten cent lusts and dreams." Even in the Depression a dime didn't buy much lust, if only because blue movies, then as now, appealed to a selected audience. Everyone dreams, on the other hand, so escapism reached the largest possible audience. Americans of all ages and persuasions could enjoy *Mutiny on the Bounty, Little Miss Marker, Captain January,* Busby Berkeley, and the thrillers of Alfred Hitchcock, which began appearing in the United States in 1935.

Moviegoing in this period attained its own ambiance, only part of which was seen on the Magnascope screen or heard over the Fox sound-track-on-film which replaced Vitaphone recordings.

Everything that came out of the projector became part of the aura. The double feature was important; so was the Saturday serial and selected short subjects—a Terrytoon cartoon, say, with a Pathé newsreel, a Thelma Todd–Patsy Kelley comedy, and a Fitzgerald Traveltalk (". . . and so we say *Auf Wiedersehen* to picturesque, peace-loving Germany"). There were also bank nights, dish nights, bingo, Fleer's Dubble Bubble Gum, Assorted Charm wrappers, slug-like Tootsie Rolls, a carpet of cold popcorn underfoot, and a great deal of amorous foreplay in the back rows. Most important was the dreaming in the darkness inspired by The Face, The Look, or The Body on screen. The movie mystique began to dissolve with the advent of television, but while it lasted, its power was immense; Gore Vidal was probably right when he put into Myra Breckinridge's mouth his own conviction that the movies of 1931 to 1945 were the most formative influence upon those who came of age in that "post-Gutenberg and pre-Apocalypse" era.

Or rather, he was *half* right. The other great familial activity in the Thirties was listening to radio. Like the cinema, it was tightly controlled; seven hundred of the country's nine hundred stations were organized into four networks, NBC-Red, NBC-Blue, CBS, and Mutual. Radio, too, was more innocuous than television today. Television hosts are permitted a certain amount of room for maneuver, but the announcer for a child's program in the Thirties who, thinking he was off the air, muttered, "I guess that'll hold the little bastards for a while," was all through. The entire family was concerned with what the shiny wagon-wheel microphones of the time picked up. Symbolically, perhaps, one of the most durable programs was NBC-Red's *One Man's Family*, a Norman Rockwell myth heard in 28 million homes on Wednesdays at 8 P.M. The announcer always began by declaring that the play was "dedicated to the Mothers and Fathers of the Younger Generation and to their Bewildering Offspring."

For millions, twisting the dial was a kind of tribal ritual. It was a rare household that could not identify Kate Smith with "When the Moon Comes Over the Mountain," Ruth Etting with "Shine On, Harvest Moon," Amos 'n' Andy with "The Perfect Song," Rudy Vallee with "My Time Is Your Time," Morton Downey with "Carolina Moon," and Ray Noble with "The Very Thought of You." MUrray Hill 8-9933 was the best-known telephone number in the country; you called it to register your opinion of performers on the

Major Bowes Amateur Hour. The national audience couldn't imagine Christmas without Lionel Barrymore's presentation of *A Christmas Carol*. It is improbable that many Americans lost sleep over the question "Can this girl from a mining town in the West find happiness as the wife of a wealthy and titled Englishman?" but if they thought it foolish, they kept it to themselves. Because every scene had to be staged in the imagination, and because imagination is more colorful than any twenty-one-inch screen, the best of radio can never be matched by television. Charlie McCarthy, Edgar Bergen's whittled imp, was so real that Louis B. Mayer, the king of Sweden, and Winston Churchill extended their hands upon being introduced to him.

The ultimate significance of radio's appeal is that through it the first steps were taken toward a manipulated consumer society. Advertising's pioneer then was George Washington Hill, president of the American Tobacco Company. Thanks to Hill, American became the first firm to buy testimonials (including one from Madame Schumann Heink, the opera singer, who didn't even smoke). The concept of product identification began with the comedians "Jones and Hare, the Interwoven Pair"; when you laughed at them, you were supposed to think about socks. *Gangbusters* meant Cue, the liquid dentifrice; Bergen and McCarthy, Chase & Sanborn coffee; *Your Hit Parade*, with its obnoxious tobacco auctioneer's chant, reminded you of Lucky Strikes. The chant was Hill's idea; explaining its usefulness, he once spat on a polished board of directors' table. The act was disgusting, he said, wiping up the bubbly spittle with his silk handkerchief, but for that very reason you would never forget it. "LS/MFT" was another Hillism. Announcers repeated, "Lucky Strike means fine tobacco. Yes, Lucky Strike means fine tobacco," until listeners thought they would lose their minds, and a grateful nation should not have forgotten the local news commentator who was handed a flash in mid-program on September 13, 1946, and said to the mike, "Ladies and gentlemen, George Washington Hill died today. Yes, George Washington Hill died today."

At the time, "Not a cough in a carload" (Old Golds), "Ask the man who owns one" (Packard), "First he whispers, then he shouts!" (Big Ben), "Banish tattletale gray" (Fels Naphtha soap), and "Reach for a Lucky instead of a sweet" were regarded as nothing more than minor irritants. The idea that the mass-production-consumption society was, in George E. Mowry's words, tying together "big business and the masses in a symbiotic relationship so close that the health of one was the health of the other" had not yet emerged. Few would have understood it, anyhow. Had they been told that a later college generation would deprecate consumer orientation and scorn society's preoccupation with security, they would have been baffled. Mechanical servants were just becoming available in large numbers. A surfeit of labor-saving gadgets was unimaginable. Security, moreover, was the impossible dream of the Depression. Nobody could have enough of it, and the viability of President Roosevelt's limited concept of social security—the act of 1935 covered only wage earners, not their families—was to be displayed in the presidential election of 1936, which loomed ever larger in the American consciousness and which, everyone agreed, would be a referendum on the New Deal.

Mid-Thirties Montage

Hello, Mr. and Mrs. America and all the ships at sea! Flash!

Oh, you push the first valve down
And the music goes round and round
Whoa, ho ho, ho ho ho
And it comes out here!

Barbasol! Barbasol!
The brushless shaving cream supreme!
Leaves your face so smooth and clean!

John Barrymore, Lionel Barrymore, Marie Dressler, Jean Harlow, Wallace Beery, Lee Tracy, Billie Burke, Edmund Lowe, Jean Hersholt and Madge Evans

in

DINNER AT EIGHT

Mon. Tues. Wed.

FOX-POLI   Continuous Performances

Margaret Mitchell's "Gone With the Wind" (Macmillan, $3) is an outstanding novel of Civil War and Reconstruction in Georgia. It is, in all probability, the biggest book of the year: 1,087 pages... Scarlett O'Hara is growing up on the family plantation, a magnificent place. In April, 1861, she and her sisters wear hooped skirts, their scores of Negro slaves are lovable and happy....

WILL ROGERS, WILEY POST KILLED IN PLANE CRASH

And now — The Romance of Helen Trent! The Romance of Helen Trent: the real-life drama of Helen Trent, who, when life mocks her, breaks her hopes, dashes her against the rocks of despair, fights back bravely, successfully, to prove what so many women long to prove in their own lives — that because a women is 35 — or more — romance in life need not be over — that romance can begin at 35!

ADVANCE TO GO (COLLECT $200)

EDWARD VIII RENOUNCES BRITISH CROWN

CANDID CAMERA SALES UP FIVEFOLD

FIBBER: Gosh darn it, I'll fix it myself. Where's my hammer? Oh, it's in the closet.

MOLLY (in alarm): Don't open that door, McGee!

I'm putting all my eggs in one basket
I'm betting everything I've got on you

NRA

Here in Lakehurst it's starting to rain again, the rain had slackened up a bit. The back motors of the Hindenburg are just holding it, just enough to keep it from — It's bursting into flames! Get that shot! Get that shot! It's cra-crashing, crashing, terrible, oh, my, get out of the way please, it's burning, bursting into flames, and is falling on the mooring paths and all the people agree this is one of the terrible, worst tragedies in the world! Oh, flames four or five hundred feet into the sky, it's a terrific crash ladies and gentlemen, the smoke and the flames now and the crashing to the ground, not quite to the mooring, oh the humanity, and I told you, I can't even talk, mass of smoking wreckage, I can, I can hardly breathe, ohh, ohhh, ohhhh

LINDBERGH RANSOM RECEIVER SEIZED, $13,759 FOUND AT HIS EAST BRONX HOME

Knock, knock.
Who's there?
Eskimo, Christian, and Italian.
Eskimo, Christian, and Italian who?
Eskimo Christian and Italian no lies.

Me Tarzan, you Jane

The trumpets blow so low, so um-pah-pah
While everybody's shouting "Hotchacha!"

Four

THE ROOSEVELT REFERENDUM

BEFORE REPEAL* Benito Mussolini had declared, "I can sum up the United States in two words: Prohibition and Lindbergh!" That was totalitarian dogma; America was a land of gangsters and kidnappers. Then he was asked his opinion of American foreign policy. He replied, "America has no policy." This time Il Duce came painfully close to the truth. There was no mention of events abroad in Roosevelt's first inaugural address. He silenced all official advocacy of American participation in the League of Nations, and in his first appearance on the world scene he torpedoed the International Monetary and Economic Conference of 1933, an attempt to knit together the gold bloc nations. Alone among economists, John Maynard Keynes was delighted; Keynes preferred managed currencies to the gold standard, and he pronounced Roosevelt "magnificently right." But the President had not been swayed by Keynesian theory. He was deliberately sacrificing international good will to domestic priorities, putting the American house in order before turning to threats overseas.

All this was to change five years later, after Hitler showed his fist at Munich. Yet the danger to peace became evident much earlier. Before Roosevelt's second presidential campaign, Mussolini had seized Ethiopia; Spain had burst into flame; Germany had rearmed, occupied the Rhineland, and, Hull's soporifics to the contrary, made life wretched for Jews, 80,000 of whom had arrived in the United

---
* Of the Eighteenth Amendment. Repeal meant virtually nothing else in the early 1930s.

States by 1935. In Tokyo militant young officers drove Hirohito's government toward expansionism and imperialism; when a Japanese soldier slipped across the Marco Polo Bridge to patronize a Chinese brothel, his officers accused the Chinese of kidnapping him and then attacked Peking and Tientsin. Amelia Earhart, America's most celebrated aviatrix, is believed to have caught a glimpse of Japanese fortifications in the mandated Marianas. She was almost certainly forced down and murdered. Her fate was unknown at the time, but repeated provocations by the Japanese, all of them front-page news, seemed designed to determine whether or not America was chickenhearted.

America was. State Department spokesmen protested and talked vaguely of "moral embargoes." Roosevelt and Hull expressed confidence in something mysteriously called "world opinion"—as though there were such a thing, and as though dictators could be intimidated by it. Congress passed new neutrality acts and resolutions, which the President reluctantly signed. He hesitated largely because he disliked any curb on presidential power; there was then little difference between the administration's conduct of foreign affairs and opinion on Capitol Hill. The New Deal had no designs on other countries. In signing a neutrality pact with twenty-one Latin American countries, Hull made it quite clear that America wanted nothing so much as to be left alone, and one of the few Hoover decisions endorsed by FDR was a refusal to join Great Britain in a condemnation of Japanese aggression in Manchuria.

In the Depression most of this was sensible; the home front demanded every resource the government could summon. But there was no sense in the Johnson Debt Default Act of 1934, barring loans to countries which had failed to repay their World War debts, or the Pittman Neutrality Resolution of 1935, which notified the world that under no circumstances would the United States help victims of aggression. Such measures merely encouraged dictators and tied the President's hands. Yet the fact that he said so, together with his support of the World Court, angered the high priests of isolationism. "Believing that he is under moral obligation to help decide the agelong quarrels of Europe and Asia," Charles A. Beard wrote, "President Roosevelt has resisted every effort of Congress and the country to impose limits on his powers of intervention abroad. In case of a major war in Europe or Asia, there is ground for believing that he will speedily get the United States into the fray. But with what outcome? That Americans will be euchred at the peace conference, whether they lose or win the war, is fairly certain."

In reality, speedy intervention would have been impossible. The country's military establishment continued to shrink during Roosevelt's first term, until America had fewer soldiers than Henry Ford had auto workers. The Army's real enemy, as Eisenhower later noted, was "money, or its lack." In 1934, when the President visited Oahu, the commanding officer decided to stage an exercise in his honor. The spectacle turned into a travesty; half the trucks and seven of the twelve World War tanks broke down in front of the startled commander in chief. The following year *Fortune* reported that although the M-1 Garand rifle had been adopted by the infantry, there weren't enough of them to equip a single regiment. "At the present rate of purchase," the magazine calculated, "it will take about thirty years to equip just the Regular Army with the new Garand, by which time it might well be obsolete." The title of the article was "Who's in the Army Now?" Among those in uniform, it reported, were a forty-seven-year-old first lieutenant and a sixty-five-year-old sergeant. The average captain was forty-three.

A great many Americans believed that *nobody* should be in the Army. Scholars generally held that the country had been tricked into the World War by wicked Europeans, and for once the people —71 percent of them, Gallup found—agreed with the professors. The Depression had started in Europe, they believed; Europeans didn't pay their debts. From *Three Soldiers* and *A Farewell to Arms* to *What Price Glory?* intellectuals had argued that peace was worth almost any price. Had the story of Amelia Earhart's death been known, it wouldn't have been accepted; Allied propaganda about Belgians had immunized Americans to atrocity stories. Richard H. Rovere was but one of millions of schoolchildren who would later recall an idealistic civics teacher fond of saying, "We have a War Department. Wouldn't it be a splendid thing, boys and girls, if we had a Peace Department, too?" In 1934 the Convention of Episcopal Bishops resolved that "The Christian Church . . . refuses to respond to that form of cheap patriotism that has as its slogan, 'In time of peace prepare for war.'" Their congregations approved. (So did Adolf Hitler. "Those who support the pacifist ideal," he observed, "inevitably support efforts to conquer the world to its fullest.") Scarcely anyone in America was paying attention to Germany's new

Führer; even the Veterans of Foreign Wars were campaigning for 25 million signatures to convince Congress that more neutrality legislation was needed. Among those who needed no persuasion was Senator Gerald P. Nye of North Dakota. Nye was chairman of the Senate Munitions Investigating Subcommittee—his chief assistant legal counsel was Alger Hiss—and he achieved the ultimate in scapegoatism by uniting villainous Wall Street financiers with foreign warmongers. "We didn't win a thing we set out for in the last war," he cried from podiums across the land. "We merely succeeded, with tremendous loss of life, to make secure the loans of private bankers to the Allies."

Among college students wealthy enough to defy tradition, militant pacifism was something of a cult. Their poorer classmates, although usually silent, agreed with them. In a national poll, 39 percent of undergraduates said they would not participate in any war, and another 33 percent said they would do so only if the United States were invaded. At Columbia and Berkeley, strongholds of pacifism, only 8 percent were willing to fight under any circumstances. In 1935 over 150,000 students demonstrated in a nationwide Student Strike for Peace, despite attempts to intimidate them at Harvard, Johns Hopkins, and CCNY. Subsequently a half-million undergraduates signed a pledge that if Congress declared war they would refuse to serve. Their concept of what they called "the system" was not far removed from "the establishment" their children would later learn to loathe. They were opposed to compulsory ROTC, violations of academic freedom and student rights, and Fascist activities; they wanted reform of college administrations. Radicals were members of the Student League for Industrial Democracy (SLID), a forerunner of the Students for a Democratic Society. Their bible was SLID's *Blueprint for Action: A Handbook for Student Revolutionists.* Among the more memorable undergraduate pests were James Wechsler of Columbia, Eric Sevareid of the University of Minnesota, and Clark Kerr, Swarthmore '32.

The character of "the movement" (it was called that, too) varied from one campus to another. At Minnesota "We didn't like the leaders we observed in political life, and we didn't like the university authorities, who we thought were merely serving the system and not the cause of truth," Sevareid recalled. "Of all the instruments designed to uphold the existing order, I think we most hated the military establishment. . . . We began to detest the very word 'patriotism,' which we considered to be debased, to be a synonym for chauvinism." ROTC was the target of the demonstrations in which Sevareid participated, and on his campus they abolished it.

Princetonians treated the military as a sick joke, advertising themselves as members of a new VFW—Veterans of Future Wars. Vassar played hostess to a national convention of the supermilitant American Student Union. When the president of the College of the City of New York received a delegation of Italian Fascist students, his own undergraduates hissed; he called them "guttersnipes," and next day CCNY blossomed with lapel buttons reading, "I am a guttersnipe." The president broke up one meeting of militants by swatting them with his umbrella. Such retaliation was rare, but not unknown. A less primitive reaction occurred at the University of Pittsburgh, which invited General MacArthur to speak at commencement. The leaders of a protest demonstration were arrested and fined. A higher court reversed the conviction, but the following week matriculating Pitt students were required to swear allegiance to the U.S. Constitution, the Pennsylvania laws, and the university regulations. The university business manager explained to the press, "We want right-minded students here."

The vast majority of undergraduates were, if not right-minded, at least well-behaved. Then, as now, the militants were a tiny minority—1 percent at CCNY; three-tenths of 1 percent nationally. By demonstrating, marching for the rights of labor, raising money for the Scottsboro Boys, and picketing Hearst newsreels they created a lot of noise, as later in the decade a quite different group made front pages by swallowing goldfish. Generalizing from a small sample is a peculiarly American failing. In 1970 a national advertiser taunted middle-aged Americans by running a photograph of a 1930s marathon dance and asking pawkily, "Now What Were You Saying About Today's Youth?" He was under the impression that marathon dance contestants had been exhibitionists. Quite the contrary; they were submitting themselves to an appalling torture in hope of winning a little desperately needed cash.

As members of the locked-out generation, most college students of the 1930s were preoccupied with acquiring marketable skills. The Depression hit their age group hardest; in January 1935 there were still several million youths between the ages of sixteen and twenty-four who were on relief, and a college president told his seniors that the 150,000 students being awarded degrees that June were emerging into a society which did not want them. *Fortune* polled twenty-five universities and concluded that undergraduates wanted a haven in a "job that is guaranteed to be safe and permanent." Wryly they chanted:

> *I sing in praise of college,*
> *Of M.A.s and Ph.D.s*
> *But in pursuit of knowledge*
> *We are starving by degrees.*

It was a poor joke. With tuition out of reach for 80 percent of American parents, a diploma often represented a four-year fight for survival. It was not unknown for undergraduates to work forty hours a week when school was in session and eighty-four hours a week during vacations. A study at Duquesne University found students employed as filling station attendants, undertakers' helpers, railroad firemen, steel mill laborers, and tombstone cutters; one Duquesne boy held 27 odd jobs on campus and in adjacent Pittsburgh. At the University of Michigan, Arthur Miller washed dishes for board and earned $15 a month from the NYA by feeding a building full of mice. He lived on that. At Minnesota, Hubert Humphrey couldn't afford textbooks, so he used those in the university library.

Working one's way through college has never been easy, and considering the rigors of a depressed economy it is something of a marvel that anyone made it. For ambitious youth, the challenges of the depression continued right down to Pearl Harbor. That was not true of the rest of middle-class America, however. By the third year of the Roosevelt administration the country had drawn back from the abyss, and Jonathan Mitchell could write in the *New Republic,* "It feels good to have money again. . . . Happy days are here again. Of course, things aren't so good. . . . A man can be fired, and next morning there are ten men in line waiting for his job. But the unemployed have been around a long time. No one can expect us to sit home and be sympathetic indefinitely." There was even enough change around to provide allowances for adolescent children. Not much, to be sure; not enough to support a Woodstock Nation; but sufficient to finance a few fads and some bizarre badges of juvenile distinction.

The music came first. The great thing was to see a big band in person, but you could often hear good live music on college campuses—from the University of North Carolina's student band, led by Hal Kemp, or from Les Brown's Blue Devils of Duke. In obscure halls and bars were unknown entertainers whose time would one day come: Alvino Rey, who played (an omen) an electric guitar, the first amplified instrument most Americans had ever heard, or young Frankie Sinatra. Between 1933 and 1937 Sinatra was one of the worst-paid entertainers in the country. He entered amateur contests, filled in on local radio stations, and sang at lodge meetings for carfare, seventy cents. The great Sinatra constituency was still too young to support him in the manner to which he would become accustomed, still distracted by Big Little Books, Shirley Temple hairdos, G-Man underwear, Yale-bred Flash Gordon, bike foxtails, and scooters fashioned from orange crates and roller skates.

Meanwhile their older brothers and sisters were evolving the first youthful life-style since the jazzy Twenties. It had its own language (such as "keen," "gas," "copacetic"), its arcane humor ("Confucius say," "Knock, knock"), its virility symbols (jalopies), and its special uniforms. Both sexes wore rubber-soled brown-and-white saddle shoes, beer jackets autographed by their friends, and reversible raincoats, preferably dirty. Girls' daytime wear also prescribed twin-sweater sets (cashmere or angora cardigans for the affluent), mid-calf plaid dirndl skirts, ankle socks (later to be known as bobby sox), and babushkas. Sport coats and slacks were essential for boys; saddle shoes could be replaced by heavy brogues shod with V cleats of steel, so that the wearer could click as he walked; and it was rather a good thing to have an argyle sweater knitted by a heavy steady. At formal dances—one a year in high school, at least four a year in college—all this changed. Under a gym ceiling transformed by crepe paper, girls glided across the waxed floor in long swirling tulle gowns, an orchid or gardenia corsage pinned on the left shoulder strap, with boys wearing rented tuxedos or dark suits and white bucks.

If the dancers limited themselves to fox-trot shuffles or the sedate Carioca, it could all be incredibly dull, but if the band was swinging the steps became much more athletic. By the mid-Thirties the jitterbug was known all over the country. The legitimate descendant of the Charleston, the Lindy Hop, and a dance called the Texas Tommy—which went all the way back to the Darktown Follies of 1913—jitterbugging became as diversified as events in a track meet, which it sometimes resembled. There was the Charleston Swing,

Truckin', Peckin', the Shag, the Suzy-Q, the Circle Swing, the Praise Allah, and Kickin' the Mule, in which boys and girls leapfrogged one another. Because of its suggestiveness, and because spirited girls sometimes revealed their pants, jitterbugging was unpopular among chaperones; as late as 1942 it was banned at all Duke dances.

The continuing repression of sex may be seen as a reflection of apprehension that all customs might vanish in what was, by any standard, a turbulent decade. Pregnancy was treated as a disgrace, often even among married women; maternity clothes were advertised as designed to "keep your secret." Everything about sex was secretive. The closest thing to a girlie magazine was *The Stocking Parade*, which published photographs of fully clothed young women whose skirts were hoisted five or six inches above the knee. Pornographers were midgets in those days. A puritanical society held them in check for the same reason that it recoiled from the jitterbugging coeds—or, to turn to another face of the prism, with the same motivation as the radio station manager who cut Tommy Dorsey off the air for swinging "Loch Lomond." The manager felt that too many traditions were being challenged as it was. Conventions honored for generations were vanishing. Most conspicuously, the nation's workmen, too weak to protest in Hoover's last months, were now on the march. The thunder of their boots frightened white-collar, middle-class America, but Labor's time had come. The unions were organizing, there was fighting on the barricades, blood was being spilled on the streets outside the mines and mills, and the worst was yet to come.

In many ways John Llewellyn Lewis was a preposterous figure. A barrel-chested, beetle-browed, six-foot three-inch goliath of a man, he relaxed by reading Shakespeare, the Bible, the *Iliad*, the *Odyssey*, Oswald Spengler, and the *Panchatantra*, an Oriental book of fables. The son of a blacklisted Welsh miner, he had become president of the United Mine Workers at the age of forty, but under his leadership the UMW had dwindled to half its pre-Lewis size; in 1930 a miners' group said of him, "He killed more than the leaders of our union. He killed its very soul." During the 1930s he was to become loved and despised as the symbol of militant unionism. Yet he had entered the decade as a Hoover Republican, an apostle of free enterprise, and the sworn enemy of progressive union policies.

In private John L. Lewis was a brilliant and engaging conversationalist, the grand strategist and champion of oppressed working men. To the public he seemed to be a peculiar combination of evangelist, thespian, and hamfatter. He said incredible things. Of his own propensity for self-aggrandizement he observed, "He who tooteth not his own horn, the same shall not be tooted." At the opening of a labor convention he said, "Heed this cry from Macedonia that comes from the hearts of men! Methinks that upon this decision of this convention may rest the future of the American Federation of Labor." Of his opponent William Green, president of the AFL, he cried, "Alas, poor Green! I knew him well. He wishes to join in fluttering procrastination, the while intoning, 'O tempora, O mores!'" And after he had split organized labor in half he crowed, "They smote me hip and thigh, and right merrily did I return their blows."

Few laughed; liberals saw him as a man of vision, while to his critics he was evil incarnate. In certain circles he had a capacity for arousing hatred matched only by President Roosevelt. Once former Secretary of War Patrick J. Hurley, appearing at a hearing as a coal owners' attorney, boasted that while a young man he had belonged to the UMW. Lewis gathered his million muscles, rose, and said sonorously, "It is a matter of pride to a member of the United Mine Workers to see a man of that organization go out into the highways and byways of national politics and make a name for himself that is recognized throughout the country." He paused heavily. "But it is a matter of sorrow and regret to see a man betray the union of his youth"—he paused again—"for thirty lousy pieces of silver." Hurley flew at him and had to be restrained. Lewis said carelessly, "Strike out 'thirty pieces of silver.' Let it stand 'betray the union of his youth.'"

That was pure ham. It was also courageous. When the President's Commission on Violence reported in 1969 that the United States "has had the bloodiest and most violent labor history of any industrial nation in the world," it alluded specifically to the 1930s. Organizers of industrial unions were being murdered. Governors were calling out the National Guard to suppress unruly workers. In Georgia, Eugene Talmadge built a concentration camp for pickets. Mine owners in Duquesne, Pennsylvania, a typical coal town, invested $17,000 in munitions during one year, bombed miners' homes, and burned crosses on hillsides. In Johnstown, Pennsylvania, the mayor of a company town told reporters that "A world without policemen"—he made it clear that he meant company policemen—"would be like a world without music." His district attorney added, "Give me two hundred good, tough armed men and I'll clean up them sons-of-bitches on the picket line." When unrest spread among women in the textile sweatshops, the trade journal *Fibre and Fabric* declared editorially, "A few hundred funerals will have a quieting influence."

The wonder is that the unions survived the onslaughts against them. When Roosevelt entered the White House they had been very weak. Lewis's UMW membership had fallen to less than 100,000 members. The American Federation of Labor as a whole had dropped to 6 percent of the work force; it was losing seven thousand dues-paying members each week, and was so servile to management that in 1932 it had opposed unemployment insurance. Aggressive industrialists were convinced that in confronting organizers they were battling the devil himself. They didn't mean to lose. As the La Follette Civil Liberties Committee was to discover in December 1934, over 2,500 American employers employed strikebreaking companies, the largest of which were Pearl Bergoff Services and the Pinkerton National Detective Agency. Bergoff was a multimillion-dollar heavy; the Pinkertons, favored by Detroit's automobile industry, earned nearly two million dollars between 1933 and 1936. Each of them maintained a small standing army which was ready to move into struck jobs carrying machine pistols, gas guns, and clubs. Both also infiltrated workmen's ranks as undercover agents. When a senator asked Herman L. Weckler, vice president of the Chrysler Corporation, why he hired spies, he replied, "We must do it to obtain the information we need in dealing with our employees." Thousands of men were literally working at gunpoint; the Pittsburgh Coal Company, for example, kept machine guns trained on employees in its coal pits. A congressional committee asked why. Chairman Richard B. Mellon answered, "You cannot run the mines without them."

Under these circumstances, the eagerness of workers to organize was really a measure of their desperation. The frightened miners, the sweated garment workers in Manhattan, the dime-an-hour laborers at Briggs Manufacturing in Detroit, and the nickel-an-hour clerks in Detroit knew that nothing else worked. State laws had been tried. In Pennsylvania employers systematically checked off

33 cents a week from the pay of each child to indemnify themselves for $100 fines imposed upon them for working the children ninety hours a week. The average steelworker's clothes caught fire at least once each week. Rather than invest in safety devices, the Pittsburgh mills lost over 20,000 workers a year maimed by industrial accidents. Girls working in five-and-ten-cent stores at five-and-ten wages read of the various aristocratic marriages contracted in Europe by Babs Hutton, the Woolworth heiress, and sang bitterly:

> *Barbara Hutton has the dough, parlez-vous*
> *Where she gets it sure we know, parlez-vous*
> *We slave at Woolworth's five and dime*
> *The pay we get is sure a crime*
> *Hinkey-dinkey parlez-vous.*

Potbellied Bill Green—"Sitting Bill," Lewis called him—had been indirectly responsible for the National Recovery Act's section 7(a). He had been among those nervous labor men who had complained to Hugh Johnson that NRA's industrywide agreements might be used to throttle unions, so the impulsive cavalryman had scribbled in the collective bargaining guarantee. But Green didn't see the possibilities in the clause. It was, in fact, quite vague; employers were not obliged to recognize unions, they could deal with company unions if they wished, and the method by which workers might choose their bargainers was not spelled out. Lewis, however, realized that details could wait. What was important was 7(a)'s propaganda value. It was a declaration of intention by the federal government. He compared it with Lincoln's emancipation of slaves and sent his brawny lieutenants into the coal fields with sound trucks and leaflets: "The President wants you to unionize. It is unpatriotic to refuse to unionize. Here is your union. Never mind about the dues now. Just join up!"

The alacrity with which the miners responded startled even Lewis. The NRA, which was supposed to revive business, was stimulating industrial unions instead. Within three weeks after FDR's signing of the act, 135,000 former UMW workers had taken up their cards again; by early 1934 Lewis had nearly 400,000 men on its books. Then Sidney Hillman and David Dubinsky brought the sound trucks and leaflets into New York. In less than a year their International Ladies Garment Workers Union had tripled its membership, to 200,000; by the end of the decade it would stand at over 400,000.

Franklin Roosevelt missed few political cues, but he was slow picking up this one. Nothing in the President's background had prepared him for a role as confederate of organized labor. He regarded himself as a succorer, a Good Samaritan to exploited workmen, which was not the same thing as a trade union ally. While he wanted higher wages, shorter hours, and better safety precautions, he was not at all sure that Lewis's way was the best, or even the right, way to do it. If labor became a powerful new economic force, the President might be unable to stand aloof, as he wished, from industrial conflict. Therefore in these first years he hesitated. "Labor's public enemy number one is Franklin D. Roosevelt!" Heywood Broun cried at a mass meeting. That was absurd. Nevertheless, the President did believe that Frances Perkins and Francis Biddle were too prolabor, and the only labor advocate on the Hill whom FDR admired was Senator Robert Wagner of New York. Wagner, pressing for fresh labor legislation, was slowly bringing the President around. Unfortunately the situation was too volatile. There was no time for persuasion.

As Lewis signed up more and more workmen—watched uneasily by Green, who kept warning, "Now John, take it easy"—the inevitability of crippling strikes drew nearer. Industry was preparing to man the barricades, and sometimes even preparing the barricades. The domestic market for munitions had never been so great. During eight weeks in the summer of 1933, policemen in the tiny Kentucky town of Lynch bought 41 rifles, 21 revolvers, 500 cartridges, and a supply of tear gas canisters. When federal marshals pointed out that instigators of violence might face federal charges, the company towns hotly replied that they were private property; Washington had no power over them. In Muncie, Indiana, the research team of Robert and Helen Lynd found that General Motors was subsidizing an expanded police force to jail suspected organizers. The A & P shut down its Cleveland stores for several days and docked its bewildered employees for the lost time—just to show them what they might expect if they joined a union. When Lewis opened the labor wars of the Thirties by taking out 70,000 Pennsylvania miners in 1934, and the strike spread across the Allegheny valley, the mayor of Duquesne talked as though the strikers were

Indians he intended to head off at the pass: "We're going to meet 'em at the bridge and break their goddam heads."

In all, there were 1,856 strikes in 1934, most of them for union recognition. It was a time of martyrdom; terrorism colored that year of labor history like one vast bloodstain. Outside the Frick mines hired guns shot union miners emerging from the shafts. In the company town of Kohler, Wisconsin, strikebreakers opened fire on an AFL picket line, killing two men and wounding thirty-five. At Toledo's Electric Auto-Lite Company, where the newly organized United Auto Workers were trying to bargain with an intransigent management, National Guardsmen shot twenty-seven workmen. Striking longshoremen were murdered in San Francisco, striking teamsters in Minneapolis, and striking textile workers—fifteen of them—in New England and the South. In Minneapolis two special deputies were also killed, one a businessman. Eric Sevareid covered that strike for the *Minneapolis Star*. He watched, horrified, as vengeful policemen delivered a fusillade of shotgun fire into an unarmed, unwarned crowd, shooting sixty-seven people, two of them fatally. "Suddenly I knew," he wrote afterward; "I understood deep in my bones and blood what Fascism was." John L. Lewis said, "Labor, like Israel, has many sorrows. Its women keep their fallen and lament for the future of the race."

Labor's sorrows were deeper, and the laments greater, because so many seemed to have died in vain. Local unions won recognition in Toledo, San Francisco, and Minneapolis, but in the big industries —steel, textiles, automobiles, rubber—anti-union employers were triumphant. When Congress established a National Labor Relations Board, the National Association of Manufacturers pressed its members to ignore it, and in a test case one firm did; what happened was that the company's right to fly the blue eagle was withdrawn. The administration was still vacillating. Late in February 1935 a federal district court found NRA section 7(a) unconstitutional. Immediately Senator Wagner and Congressman William P. Connery Jr. of Massachusetts introduced legislation creating a National Labor Relations Board, establishing the right of workers to bargain collectively with management through unions chosen in federally supervised elections, and defining unfair labor practices. Roosevelt signed it on July 5, won over by Wagner's argument that the Depression could not end until workmen's wages were high enough to make them consumers of the goods they produced. Businessmen were unswayed. The Liberty League circulated a statement signed by fifty-eight eminent members of the bar declaring that the Wagner Act was just as unconstitutional as 7(a). Clearly the labor movement still had far to go. Employer resistance remained high; thirty-two more strikers and strike sympathizers were killed in 1935, and National Guardsmen were called out in South Dakota, Illinois, Nebraska, Kentucky, Georgia, and Ohio. Progress was still measured in inches, with miles of assembly lines unorganized, underpaid, and sweated.

For all anyone could tell, Bill Green had never read the Wagner Act. But John L. Lewis had. He had studied it while it was in committee, and realized that under its canopy of government protection a new House of Labor could be built. The defects in the old house were obvious. The American Federation of Labor was a loose alliance of jealous little barons, mostly descended from early immigrants to America. Except for miners and textile workers, its members were divided into craft unions: boilermakers, carpenters, machinists, upholsterers, punch machine operators, painters, etc. Ohio rubber workers, attempting to organize themselves, were visited by an AFL representative who quickly separated them out into nineteen locals because that many skills were required to make rubber. To Green the United Auto Workers was a temporary abomination; in time its members would be sundered into a hundred craft chapters.

It was at the October 1935 AFL convention in Atlantic City that Lewis voiced his cry from Macedonia. It was a call for industrial unionism, in which mass production workers would be bound together by the nature of their products. Steelworkers would have one union, for example; the building trades another. It was, he argued, the only way big business could be successfully struck. The cry went unheeded. The convention voted him down. In the parliamentary maneuvering which followed, Big Bill Hutcheson, the rajah of the carpenters, called Lewis a "bastard." It was a mistake; in full view of Green and the thousands of delegates, Lewis slugged his tormentor so hard that the carpenter, streaming blood, had to be carried off the stage. Lewis adjusted his clothes, lit a cigar and sauntered out of the hall and, as it developed, out of the AFL. He wrote a one-line resignation to Green and told the press, "The American Federation of Labor is standing still, with its face toward the dead past." Then he announced the formation of a rival union complex, the Committee for Industrial Organization (CIO), later reorganized as the Congress of Industrial Organizations.

Belting Hutcheson had been a bit crude, perhaps, but it made Lewis more of a hero than ever to the millions of unskilled and semi-skilled workers awaiting deliverance from economic servitude. There was a kind of fire in the strapping tragedian's eye now, and it lit up a whole movement. CIO meetings became singing meetings. The men joined in the ballad of Joe Hill, who died at the hands of the goons. To the tune of "The Battle Hymn of the Republic" they sang:

> *It is we who plowed the prairies, built the cities where they trade,*
> *Dug the mines and built the workshops, endless miles of railroad laid;*
> *Now we stand outcast and starving mid the wonders we have made*
> *But the union makes us strong!*
>
> *Solidarity forever!*
> *Solidarity forever!*
> *Solidarity forever!*
> *For the union makes us strong!*

If the CIO represented the non-Communist left in 1936, a great many New Dealers were coming to believe that the non-Fascist right was located not far from the new temple of the United States Supreme Court, which opened for the fall session of 1935. Facing the Capitol across Second Street N.E., it bore the inscription, sculptured in its marble facade, "Equal Justice Under Law." From the White House—and from much of the rest of America, including the dust bowl and John L. Lewis's bastion in the coal-laced hills—it appeared that the "nine old men," as Drew Pearson and Robert S. Allen called them, were committed to strange notions of justice. To be sure, interpretation was the very purpose of the Court. "We are under a Constitution," Chief Justice Charles Evans Hughes had said nearly thirty years earlier, "but the Constitution is what the judges say it is." The difficulty, according to *Time*, was that "the pure white flame of Liberalism has burned out, in Hughes, to a saltry ash of conservatism." In this the Chief Justice typified both the bench and the bar of his time. Franklin Roosevelt's legislative program was the closest thing to a revolution the country had seen since the War of Independence. The lower courts, which had been sitting in judgment upon it, represented the old order. Most of the federal district judges had made their reputations under Republican leadership or in corporate law. They were stockholders, trustees, members of exclusive clubs; men of industrial power were their friends, and like them they looked upon the New Deal upheaval as an atrocity. By the end of FDR's first thousand days in the Presidency, over a hundred of them had issued some 1,600 injunctions against federal laws. In addition, blue-chip attorneys were writing what amounted to private rulings discrediting unwelcome laws. The Liberty League's refutation of the Wagner Act was typical of the technique. The National Association of Manufacturers distributed it among its members, encouraging defiance of legislation passed by Congress and signed by the President on the ground that it was illegal.

The eminence of Supreme Court justices should have freed them from any sense of alliance with the past, and in fact the Court was more divided than many had realized. Seated at the Court bench in their black robes they looked monolithic, but in chambers they split three ways. Willis Van Devanter, James C. McReynolds, George Sutherland, and Pierce Butler were more zealous in their homage to Adam Smith than Herbert Hoover had ever been; they believed it was downright criminal to interfere with the fundamental "laws" of laissez-faire economics. Hughes and Owen J. Roberts were right of center and usually voted that way, but because they held their convictions less deeply they were regarded as swing men. Only Benjamin N. Cardozo, Harlan Fiske Stone, and Louis D. Brandeis belonged wholly to the twentieth century.

The conflict between Roosevelt and the Court had begun in the early spring of 1935, when the President, learning that 389 fresh challenges of new legislation were on federal dockets and realizing that he could not postpone the issue of constitutionality much longer, approved an immediate appeal to the Supreme Court of a district judge's ruling that the NRA was unconstitutional. Choosing the NRA was unfortunate; all nine justices agreed that it was invalid (though their reasons varied), and May 27, thereafter known to New Dealers as Black Monday, Hughes read the majority decision. What made it so black was not the rejection of the NRA, which had become excess baggage, but the extraordinary vehemence of Hughes's opinion. He all but branded Roosevelt an outlaw, and he took the unprecedented step of warning the President and Congress not to base broad federal statutes on their constitutional right to regulate interstate commerce.

FDR was the last man in the country to be intimidated by a conservative fiat *de haut en bas*. He was pretty good at taking stands himself, and on Wednesday he called a press conference to do just that. While Eleanor sat beside him, knitting as furiously as she had during the First Hundred Days, he called Monday's ruling "more important than any decision probably since the Dred Scott case." He reviewed Hughes's opinion that business is essentially local and thus lying within the jurisdiction of the states—that even though it might have an impact on the country as a whole, intervention by the federal government was illegal. By rejecting the concept that the forty-eight states were members of one interdependent community, the Chief Justice seemed to be suggesting that no matter how great a national economic crisis might be, Washington could do nothing about it. This, said the President, was a "horse and buggy definition of interstate commerce." He, too, was issuing a warning.

Attorney General Cummings believed that prospects of a reconciliation were gloomy. "I tell you, Mr. President, they mean to destroy us," he said vehemently, adding, "We will have to find a way to get rid of the present membership of the Supreme Court." For a while Roosevelt was more optimistic. As late as December 1935 he wrote the chief U.S. delegate at a London naval conference, "Things are going well in spite of Supreme Court majority opinion and Hearst and an 85 percent newspaper opposition." The new year changed his mind. On January 6, 1936, by a 6 to 3 vote, the Court declared the AAA unconstitutional. Agriculture, Roberts argued for the majority, was not a national activity. The attempt to picture it as one was an invasion of states' rights, raising the specter of "a central government exercising uncontrolled police power in every state of the union." Near Ames, Iowa, farmers hanged in effigy the six justices who had joined in this staggering interpretation. The tories, undaunted, proceeded to strike down the Securities and Exchange Act (6 to 3); Sutherland compared the investigation of Wall Street to the "intolerable abuses of the Star Chamber." Next to fall was the Guffey-Snyder Coal Act (5 to 4), on the ground that mining was purely local, even though the coal might be shipped all over the country. Then the Municipal Bankruptcy Act was thrown out (5 to 4), on arguments so tenuous that the entire New Deal, including social security and the Wagner Act, seemed doomed. All the voided law had done was to permit state-federal cooperation in the readjustment of public debts, the initiative lying with the states. To the conservative justices, apparently, any federal participation in local problems was forbidden.

In the first 140 years of its history, the Court had invalidated only sixty laws. Now, in little more than one year, the Hughes Court had nullified eleven Roosevelt measures. Its last victory of the session came on the eve of the national conventions, and it was the most shocking. Having already dismissed federal wages and hours legislation, it proceeded, in Morehead v. Tipaldo, to consider a New York state law on minimum wages for women. The vote was against it, 5 to 4. Butler, for the majority, wrote that "The right to make contracts about one's affairs is a part of the liberty protected by the due process clause," and "In making contracts of employment, generally speaking, the parties have equal rights to obtain from each other the best terms they can by private bargaining." In other words, he held sacred the right of a fifteen-year-old girl in one of Manhattan's sweatshops to reach an agreement with a textile millionaire under which she would be allowed to earn $2.39 a week. Neither Washington nor the states could interfere. *Nobody* had the right to put a floor under wages or a ceiling over hours.

There was merrymaking that night in the stately mansions overlooking the mill towns of New England and North Carolina, but conservatives in public life were dismayed. Here, clearly, was too much of a good thing. Herbert Hoover said, "Something should be done to give back to the states the powers they thought they already had." Sixty newspapers called for a congressional amendment; Governor Landon agreed with them. The Republican platform that year offered a nebulous promise to do something to protect women and children, without saying how, and the Democrats called for a "clarifying amendment." Only the President was silent. He was weighing courses of action, but first he must be reelected, and as he told Ray Moley, "There's one issue in this campaign. It's myself, and people must be either for me or against me." He expected them to be for him. He also anticipated more 5 to 4 or 6 to 3 decisions, and in a sense he would welcome them. As Ickes noted, he could use them "as a background for an appeal to the people over the heads of the Court."

In 1936 the United States lacked the political sophistication which would later transform national elections. There were no computer consoles then, no studies of key precincts, and only the barest beginnings of scientific polling. Returns were a mystery until election day evening; meantime partisans could speculate and assemble supporting data. Afterward, of course, everything was clear (political scientists have always had superb hindsight) but few had predicted a Roosevelt landslide that year, and a great many had written him off as a one-term President.

Their arguments were not all tortured. Here was a President who had promised to balance the budget four years earlier, and was instead running an annual deficit of six or seven billions. Seven million Americans were still looking for work; the programs designed to rescue them were turning out to be unconstitutional and hence useless. For most of the past eighty years the party now in power had been a minority party. The election of one of its members to the Presidency was interpreted by many as a freak of circumstance, and support for this one was being diminished by the defection of such distinguished Democrats as Newton D. Baker, Dean Acheson, and John J. Rascob; former Democratic presidential candidates Al Smith and John W. Davis; and Democratic governors Joseph B. Ely of Massachusetts, Albert Ritchie of Maryland, and Eugene D. Talmadge of Georgia. The vast majority of the big newspapers were anti-Roosevelt. Hearst wrote front-page editorials denouncing the "Raw Deal." Switchboard operators at the *Chicago Tribune* answered calls by saying, "Good morning. Do you know you have only [number] days left to save your country?" *Tribune* headlines (ROOSEVELT AREA IN WISCONSIN IS HOTBED OF VICE) and stories ("Governor Alfred M. Landon tonight brought his great crusade for the preservation of the American form of government into Los Angeles") strongly implied that its subscribers might be turned away from the President.

Walter Lippmann was against Roosevelt; so was Dorothy Thompson. Mark Sullivan, another distinguished political writer, had forecast an FDR defeat as early as 1935, and that same year Charles A. Beard had written that "Roosevelt's spell of leadership is definitely broken." Bankers and brokers, whose contributions had accounted for 25 percent of FDR's war chest in 1932, were giving only 4 percent of this one. Indeed, the Democrats' perennial shortage of money, which was to continue into the 1970s, began in 1936. The

Republicans were to spend $9,000,000 on Landon; Roosevelt's candidacy attracted little more than half that.

There was irony here. Republicans could afford to splurge because the economy had turned round since the last campaign. In 1933 Roosevelt's role had been that of a receiver in bankruptcy, and the intervening years had been far more prosperous than anyone had then thought possible. Unemployment was less than half of that in 1932. The Federal Reserve Board's Adjusted Index of Industrial Production had climbed from 58 to 101 in 1935 and would reach 121 in 1936. (It had been 125 in 1929.) Insurance assets had increased by three billion since inauguration day. The banks had been rescued. The national income and company profits had risen by over 50 percent; the Dow Jones industrial average by 80 percent. For the first time since the Crash, Wall Street was nervous about inflation —the sure sign of a bull market—and investors who had papered the walls of one room in the Union League Club with worthless securities four years ago were steaming them off and cashing them in. Nevertheless, a huge electric sign attached to the front of the club read, LANDON AND KNOX 1936. LOVE OF COUNTRY LEADS.

Earlier in the year the Republican nomination had been worth more. FDR's popularity, according to the few yardsticks then available, had touched bottom; a Gallup report had given the opposition an even chance to unseat him. As late as July the Democratic National Committee was writing off New York and Illinois and clinging to only the faintest hope in Minnesota, Indiana, and Ohio. By then, however, the President had assumed personal command of the campaign. In February he told Secretary Wallace, "Henry, through July, August, September, October and up to the fifth of November, I want cotton to sell at twelve cents. I do not care how you do it. That is your problem. It can't go below twelve cents. Is that clear?" Like paving roads during a campaign, that was traditional politics. What was new was his coalition theory. He believed that the Democratic coalition would smash Republican strongholds and establish his party as the majority party—provided the Democrats were blessed with that greatest of political assets, luck.

They were so blessed. The first piece of luck came on January 25, 1936, when two thousand men in full dress and women wearing ermine assembled in Washington's Mayflower Hotel for a Liberty League banquet to launch its campaign against Roosevelt's reelection. It was perhaps the most ostentatious meeting in the history of

American politics; the *New York Times* said that it represented, "either through principals or attorneys, a large portion of the capitalistic wealth of the country." The chief speaker was Al Smith, now busy fighting legislation which would prohibit child labor. He arrived wearing a high silk hat and delivered a hysteroid, anti-New Deal polemic ("The New Deal smells of the stench of Communistic Russia") which thrilled everyone with an annual income of $100,000. Pierre S. Du Pont called it "perfect." John Nance Garner agreed. The Democrats didn't have to spend a cent or deliver a speech, the Vice President said; their return to power had been assured by tycoons who had completely misjudged the American temper.

On June 11 the Republicans nominated Alfred M. Landon, thereafter to be known as Alf, in Cleveland. He was a good governor, and his platform was to the left of the one Roosevelt had run on in 1932. Unfortunately for Landon's chances, his essential liberalism was obscured by the men around him. Republican chairman Henry P. Fletcher defined the campaign issue as "constitutional government." Henry Ford said he hadn't voted in twenty years, but he would this time because "Landon is like Coolidge." Landon was christened "the Kansas Coolidge"; his symbol was to be the Kansas sunflower, of which FDR dryly noted that it was yellow, had a black heart, was useful only as parrot food, and always died before November.

For Landon there was the further embarrassment of Herbert Hoover. The thirty-first President arrived in Cleveland with an uninstructed California delegation—chaired by Earl Warren—and quietly let it be known that he could be prevailed upon once more to honor the ticket with his name. Republicans weren't that unbalanced, at least not in June, but they did greet him with a fifteen-minute ovation. Roosevelt's acronyms had almost exhausted the alphabet, he said slyly, "but of course the new Russian alphabet has thirty-four letters." For the next four months he bombarded Landon with advice. The Kansas Coolidge escaped his blandishments, if not the stigma of his endorsement, and Hoover was reduced to listening to Roosevelt's speeches over the radio and booing the loudspeaker whenever the President paused for breath.

On adjournment the GOP delegates had sung, to the tune of "Oh, Susanna":

The alphabet we'll always have but one thing sure is true,
With Landon in, the New Deal's out and that means PDQ.

*Alf Landon's learned a thing or two, he knows the right solution,
And in the White House he will stay within the Constitution.*

*Oh, Alf Landon!
He's the man for me!
'Cause he comes from prairie Kansas
His country for to free!*

Somehow one feels that Pierre Du Pont could have afforded something better. Certainly the gentle governor had deserved a more dignified scenario. For a few days political reporters thought they had witnessed the year's record in convention slapstick, and then Father Coughlin and his colleagues preempted the lunatic fringe, presenting for the voters' consideration their new Union Party. The Union candidate for President was Congressman William Lemke of North Dakota, a strange individual with a pocked face, a glass eye, and a shrill voice; to the radio priest's dismay he insisted upon wearing a gray cloth cap and an outsize suit. Coughlin baptized him "Liberty Bill," and Gerald L. K. Smith drew up plans to guard the November polls with a hundred thousand Townsendite youths. The radio priest promised to quit the air forever if he didn't deliver nine million votes for the Union ticket. That seemed extravagant, but in June both major parties were taking Lemke seriously. Unlike the song "Oh, Alf Landon!" the sobriquet "Liberty Bill" was catching on. Father Coughlin rather liked the alliterative resemblance to "Liberty Bell." Then, too late, he remembered something: the Liberty Bell was cracked.

The following week the Democrats descended upon Philadelphia, gleefully driving McCormick reapers up and down the streets to remind everyone of Hoover's prediction that grass would grow there if Roosevelt moved into the White House. They were euphoric; except for the shadows cast by the Hughes Court, they had just about everything they had wanted four years earlier. Even the soldiers' bonus had passed that spring; Roosevelt's veto had been halfhearted and easily overridden. Being Democrats, they had to have at least one fight; Senator "Cotton Ed" Smith of South Carolina walked out when a Negro minister delivered a convention prayer. But even that fitted the coalition plan. In that year the black vote was still to be had for a prayer.

Roosevelt had passed the word; he was going to run against the Liberty League, not Landon. Accordingly, Alben Barkley's keynote address brought the convention to its feet with his scorn for Wall Street's anguish over the AAA: "My friends, their bitter tears are not shed for the little pigs. Their real grief comes from the fact of the slaughter of the fat hogs of Republican plunder which they had fed on the substance of the American people." That was powerful political medicine, but the President himself was going to excoriate big business in his acceptance speech as the "enemy within the gates."

His address was delivered at Franklin Field on June 27 before over a hundred thousand, who according to Marquis Childs "cheered wildly at each pause, as though the roar out of the warm, sticky night came from a single throat." It was not a flawless performance. The President was awaiting his introduction, and Robert Trout was describing the scene to his CBS radio audience, when, to Trout's horror, "the braces of his legs gave way and he fell. The pages of his manuscript were scattered. They were picked up by willing hands. He put the pages together as best he could in the few minutes before he was introduced. The manuscript was damp, crumpled, and spattered with mud." Afterward Roosevelt said, "It was the most frightful five minutes of my life," and, in a phrase which would have lost him the black vote in the 1970s, "I was the damnedest, maddest white man at that moment you ever saw."

Once under way he was magnificent. That was the night he said, "Better the occasional faults of a government that lives in a spirit of charity than the consistent omissions of a government frozen in the ice of its own indifference," and the prophetic, "There is a mysterious cycle in human events. To some generations much is given. Of other generations much is expected. This generation has a rendezvous with destiny." Afterward the vast crowd joined him in two choruses of "Auld Lang Syne" and then stood to give him a long, mighty ovation as he circled the stadium track in an open car, beaming up at them and waving his battered campaign fedora.

He planned to remain detached until five weeks before the election, when, his sense of timing told him, the electorate would be ready for him. In the meantime he would do his job and hope his rivals made mistakes. They obliged him. Before the end of the summer the Union Party was dissolving in its own excesses. Gerald L. K. Smith permitted himself to be quoted as saying of the electorate, "I'll teach 'em to hate." Father Coughlin declared, "I take the road of Fascism." Coughlin was beginning to fear Smith, who said, "The blood memory of Huey Long is still hot in my eyes," and, astonishingly, "Dr. Townsend and I stood under the historic arch at Valley Forge and vowed to take over the government." Presently Dr. Townsend was in no position to take over anything; he was in a District of Columbia jail cell, sentenced for contempt after he had refused to testify at a congressional hearing. Roosevelt pardoned him, and then Smith was jailed for disturbing the peace and using obscene language in New Orleans.*

Had Governor Landon been a more forceful man, he might have salvaged something, if only his dignity. Unhappily he came across to the public as a colorless, bespectacled little man with a flat, raspy voice. He read his speeches badly, and they were bad speeches; opening his first campaign trip in Pennsylvania, he declared for the ages: "Wherever I have gone in this country, I have found Americans." Moreover, like all men who ran against FDR, he became increasingly maddened by the elusiveness of his opponent. He told amazed Baltimoreans that if the President remained in power, he would erect a guillotine and decapitate his critics. He tacitly accepted endorsement by Fritz Kuhn's German-American Alliance (later Bund), let the Republican National Committee identify FDR as the candidate of the Jews, and insinuated that the President was a Communist.

It was in this campaign, the first to schedule nationwide broadcasts, that the concept of selling a presidential candidate was introduced. The GOP had set aside over a million dollars for radio, and Robert Choate of the *Boston Herald* wrote Landon that he felt "the handling of Republican publicity should be on the same basis as the handling of any other article that wants to be merchandised to the public." On the networks, issues were shelved; the people were to be manipulated, not convinced. Front-page Hearst editorials charged that the Democratic campaign was being masterminded by Moscow; the GOP national chairman, John D. M. Hamilton, cried that Roosevelt's hands were stained with the blood of murdered Spanish priests; and such firms as Johnson & Johnson and Ingersoll Rand stuffed workmen's pay envelopes with caveats that they would be fired if Landon didn't win.

Beginning in October, other employers put in slips implying that

---

* At this point the political evangelist disappears from this narrative. In the late 1960s the Reverend Mr. Smith was discovered in Los Angeles, where he described himself as "for all practical purposes, the senior adviser and liaison contact for something over 1,700 right-wing organizations."

social security contributions would come only from workers' pay: "Effective January 1937 we are compelled by a Roosevelt 'New Deal' law to make a 1 percent deduction from your wages and turn it over to the government. . . . You might get your money back, but only if Congress decides to make the appropriation. . . . Decide before November 3—election day—whether or not you wish to take these chances." This was part of the Republican game plan. Landon's strategists actually expected a ground-swell of hostility against retirement pay for sixty-five-year-old workmen. On radio spots, actors hired by the Republican National Committee revealed in shocked tones that each man would be given a number—as though there were any other way to keep track of social security accounts—and perpetrated the hoax that people would be fingerprinted. On October 20 mammoth signs in factories put readers on notice: "You're sentenced to a weekly tax reduction for all your working life. You'll have to serve the sentence unless you help reverse it November 3." Finally, Hamilton went on the air to disclose that every man and woman who worked for wages would be required to wear around his neck a steel dog tag ("like the one I'm now holding") stamped with his social security number.

Until then Roosevelt had been campaigning in low key; his speeches, Marquis Childs wrote, were "more like the friendly sermons of a bishop come to make his quadrennial call." But when the Republicans mounted their attack on social security, his proudest achievement, it lit a bonfire in him.

On the evening of October 31, 1936, before a capacity crowd in Madison Square Garden, the flame blazed high in one of his greatest fighting speeches. He identified his enemies: "business and financial monopoly, speculation, reckless banking . . . organized money." The audience, on its feet throughout, waving cowbells and horns, howled its approval. In an edged voice he said, "Never before in all our history have these forces been so united against one candidate as they stand today. They are unanimous in their hate for me—and I welcome their hatred." The *New York Times* compared the applause to "roars which rose and fell like the sound of waves pounding in the surf." The President said, "I should like to have it said of my first administration that in it the forces of selfishness and of lust for power met their match." Now his voice rose: "I should like to have it said—" He had to pause, the ovation had begun; then, as the din abated slightly: "I should like to have it said of my second administration that *in it these forces met their master.*" Like a mighty storm, the cheering rose and continued long after his departure.

A few blocks from the Garden, nine-year-old Daniel Patrick Moynihan chanted, "Roosevelt's in the White House, waiting to be elected, Landon's in the garbage, waiting to be collected." The Republican candidate wouldn't have agreed. He and Chairman Hamilton were confident. The *Literary Digest*, basing its straw vote on telephone listings and automobile registrations, predicted a large Republican victory—32 states with 370 electoral votes against 16 states with 161 votes for the President. A Harvard professor of statistics foresaw an electoral vote of 241 for Landon, 99 for Roosevelt, and 91 uncertain. Congressman Connery, cosponsor of the Wagner Act, had written Farley that "it looks like 60-40 in favor of Landon." In September Arthur Krock had told readers of the *New York Times* that "the Republican party will poll a far larger popular and electoral vote than in 1932. . . . Roosevelt's big majorities are over." Later he called this a "conservative" estimate. The President himself thought in June that he would win in the electoral college 340 to 191; at the end of the campaign he revised this, giving himself 360 to 171. Farley told reporters that Roosevelt would carry every state but Maine and Vermont. Most political writers agreed with Frederick Lewis Allen: "Whoever believes a campaign manager's prophecies?"

On the night of November 3 they discovered that a great many people who lacked telephones and automobiles knew the way to the nearest voting booth. Roosevelt had won the greatest victory in the history of American politics. His plurality was eleven million votes, which meant that since the 1932 election over five million Republicans had turned Democratic. Farley had been absolutely right; Landon had won only Maine and Vermont. The electoral vote was 523 to 8. Even Joseph Schechter of Brooklyn, the plaintiff in the Supreme Court case which doomed the NRA, had voted for Roosevelt. So had the other fifteen members of his family. So, for that matter, had Huey Long's father. Lemke had fewer than a million votes, and Father Coughlin announced that he was quitting radio. Later he changed his mind, but his influential days were over. The *Literary Digest*, similarly ill-starred, sold out to *Time*.

FDR, it seemed, could have almost any legislation he wanted, for more than 75 percent of both houses of Congress were now

Democratic. The Republicans were reduced to tiny minorities—17 senators and 103 representatives. There was grave doubt that the GOP could survive. And Europe was more than ever aware of the new world statesman. Winston Churchill and the French Chamber of Deputies congratulated the President. "Henceforth," wrote *Paris-Soir*, "democracy has its chief!" The chief himself was indulging in one of his favorite recreations, enjoying the cut and thrust of fencing with the White House press corps. "I knew I should have gone to Maine and Vermont," he said quizzically, "but Jim wouldn't let me." He showed reporters his election eve electoral college guess. One of them asked why he had given himself only 360 votes. His eyes danced. He said, "Oh, just my well-known conservative tendencies."

Portrait of an American

STOCKBROKER RICHARD WHITNEY

HE WAS KNOWN as the patrician's patrician, the White Knight, the hero of Wall Street. With his background he could afford to cut Franklin Roosevelt, which he did whenever possible.

He was descended from a family which landed at Salem in 1630; he had been captain of the Groton baseball team, had rowed varsity for Harvard, and made the Porcellian Club.

When he married, his father-in-law was an ex-president of the Union League Club. When he took a mistress, she was a rich, red-headed, fox-hunting widow from Wilmington. When he opened his own brokerage firm in 1916, he became J. P. Morgan's man on the floor—his brother George was a Morgan partner.

Richard Whitney was a big, strapping man, proud of his membership in the ruling class; he owned an elegant house at 115 East Seventy-third Street in Manhattan and a 495-acre New Jersey estate, where he stabled his eighteen thoroughbred horses, raised champion Ayrshire cattle, and reigned as Master of Fox Hounds for the Essex Hunt. His two daughters made magnificent debuts. His wife was an organizer of the Butlers' Ball. The Whitneys contributed to all the proper charities. They were Society.

On Black Thursday, October 24, 1929, at 1:30 P.M., the first big day of the Crash, Richard Whitney kept his head while all about him were losing theirs. As the representative of a bankers' pool, he waded through the chaos on the floor, reached Post No. 2 and offered to buy 10,000 of U.S. Steel at $205. Although his quieting of the panic was only temporary, it made him a national figure.

Post No. 2 was permanently retired and placed on display in the lobby of Richard Whitney & Company.

For five years he was president of the New York Stock Exchange.

In Philadelphia he delivered a widely quoted speech before the Chamber of Commerce on "Business Honesty."

On Capitol Hill he was called "the most arrogant, supercilious witness in the history of congressional hearings." Jovially he agreed.

But the White Knight had problems with, of all things, money. The presidency of the stock exchange was unaccompanied by salary —it was considered honor enough in itself—and M.F.H. Whitney had expensive tastes. Between giving balls, serving on boards, supporting Republican candidates, breeding horses and cattle, chasing foxes, and fornicating with the well-born Mrs. Margery Pyle Montgomery in Delaware, he couldn't make both ends meet.

When Repeal came, he enviously watched Joseph P. Kennedy multiply his already considerable fortune by winning the right to import Haig & Haig and Gordon's gin. Kennedy was an upstart and a New Dealer. Whitney was sure he could do better. The coming drink, he believed, was applejack, and during Prohibition distilleries near his country estate had turned out a highly profitable brand called Jersey Lightning. Whitney took over, organized the Distilled Liquors Corporation, and issued 148,750 shares of stock on the Curb Exchange. The price shot up to over $45 a share and Whitney was elated; Distilled Liquors was going to drive Joe Kennedy's Somerset Importers up against the wall.

Suddenly—almost overnight—it was Richard Whitney who was at the wall. Nobody was buying Jersey Lightning. To recoup, he bought 106,000 gallons of Canadian rye, paying for it with Distilled Liquors stock and warrants. The rye didn't move either. Distilled Liquors dropped to $13 a share, and the Canadians demanded more collateral.

He mortgaged his estate for $300,000 and desperately plunged into get-rich-quick schemes: a patented air-pressure bearing, a process for spraying metal to repair rust. They were even more unpopular than Jersey Lightning, and after borrowing from everyone in sight he began to steal.

As one of the most trusted men in New York, with Morgan power behind him and a gilt-edged office address of his own at 15 Broad Street, he was in a position to steal quite a lot. His first theft was $150,200 in bonds belonging to the New Yacht Club, which had been placed in his care for safekeeping. This was criminal embezzlement, but no one knew of it; indeed, New York University conferred upon him the honorary degree of Doctor of Commercial Science ("Your career in the world of finance has now become of nationwide significance"). And of course he intended to pay everything, once Distilled Liquors stock went up.

It went down. Trying to peg it at $9 a share, he borrowed from everyone he knew—and all his friends were millionaires. It wasn't enough, so he filched bonds belonging to Harvard, St. Paul's School, and his wife's and then his sister-in-law's trust funds. In a stroke of luck, he was named a trustee of the Stock Exchange Gratuity Fund, set up for the widows and families of deceased brokers. He rifled it for $667,000.

Then, at a routine meeting of the Gratuity Fund trustees—which Whitney was too busy to attend—a clerk blurted out that over a half-million dollars was missing, that Whitney had taken it and hadn't put any back. At the same time William O. Douglas, representing federal regulation, threatened to audit the books of all brokers. The exchange decided to beat him to it. Accountants looked at the books of Richard Whitney & Company and recoiled.

By now Jersey Lightning was a national joke. Whitney had bought up every share of Distilled Liquors to come on the market, 139,400 of them, now down to $3.50 a share. Over the past four months he had borrowed $27,361,500, five million of it with no collateral, and a million taken in outright theft.

J. P. Morgan, Thomas W. Lamont, and George Whitney were told but kept quiet. They considered it the gentlemanly thing to do.

Confronted by Charles R. Gay, Whitney's successor as president of the stock exchange, the tarnished White Knight asked that the charges be dropped. "After all, I'm Richard Whitney," he said. "I mean the stock exchange to millions of people."

It was a point. All the haters of Wall Street would gloat. The New Dealers would celebrate. That grinning traitor-to-his-class in the White House would be triumphant.

Gay thought it over. Then he rang the exchange gong, announced that Richard Whitney & Company had been suspended for insolvency, and pressed charges.

New York County District Attorney Thomas E. Dewey drew up the indictment.

At the St. Elizabeth Street police station, awed Bowery derelicts stood aside while he was booked for grand larceny. The lieutenant at the desk said, "Mr. Whitney, I'm sorry to see you in all this trouble, and I wish you luck." The prisoner thanked him icily.

Whitney was released on bail, but at the trial he was sentenced to five to ten years in Sing Sing. His butler bowed double when he left his town house to serve time. A crowd of five thousand gathered at the train station to see him off, and all that day limousines drew up at his town house, delivering flowers to Mrs. Whitney. She remained true to him.

Harvard announced with regret his resignation from the Board of Overseers' Visiting Committee to the Department of Economics.

At Sing Sing other convicts took off their caps when he approached them, and in prison yard baseball games they always let him get a hit. People respected an important man in those days.

But when Post No. 2 was auctioned off for five dollars, William O. Douglas just laughed.

Five

THE CONSERVATIVE PHOENIX

To put the aftermath of the New Deal's great referendum in perspective: the year 1937 lay midway between FDR's entry into the White House and Pearl Harbor—at dead center, that is, of the prewar Rooseveltian experience. The inconveniences and economies of the Depression had been institutionalized; 98 percent of American families now lived on less than $5,000 a year. Excluding reliefers, the average was $1,348. Typically, that income supported a mother, a father, and one or two children who lived in a four-or-five-room apartment or a six-room house. The house was almost always rented; after the great shakedown of 1929–33, few white middle-class Americans owned their own homes. Taxes, on the other hand, were inconsequential. Most people paid no income tax, and the top earners of 1937—Louis B. Mayer of MGM, $1,161,753; Major Edward Bowes, $427,817; and Thomas J. Watson of IBM, $419,398; and George Washington Hill, $380,976—spent or kept most of what they made.

Between May or June of 1937 and April of 1938, Alger Hiss's Woodstock typewriter was clattering most of the time on Thirtieth Street N.W., though in August he, his wife, and Whittaker Chambers took a break and drove to New Hampshire to see *She Stoops to Conquer*. Richard M. Nixon was then being investigated by the FBI. He wasn't suspected of anything. He wanted to be an agent, had taken the bureau's examination, and, as he wrote his law school dean, "They have been investigating my character since that time." The FBI rejected him. For others of his generation, however, 1937 was the year of making it. Joe Louis knocked out James Braddock and became heavyweight champion of the world. A Colorado halfback named Byron "Whizzer" White became an all-American. Lana Turner, who had something called oomph, was discovered on a drugstore stool and replaced Jean Harlow, who had just died, as Hollywood's sex bomb. Mary Martin was about to make her Broadway debut singing "My Heart Belongs to Daddy," supported by a chorus which included Gene Kelly and Van Johnson. It was, in short, a marvelous year for entertainers, and America's sweetheart was twenty-five-year-old Ginger Rogers. Housewives envious of her narrow waist shopped tirelessly in girdle departments, to the immense satisfaction of rubber planters in what was then called the Dutch East Indies.

Du Pont chemists had developed a synthetic rubber called Duprene, but its significance would be overlooked until the Japanese seized the Indies plantations five years later. Although all sorts of exciting discoveries were being made in laboratories—the sulfanilamides, insulin shock treatment for schizophrenics, and a polyamide fiber made from coal, air, and water named Nylon—the country was largely unaware of them. Business was wary of new products. In searching for prosperity it clung instead to its 1920s faith in salesmanship, and 1937 was preeminently the year of the hard sell. George Washington Hill was still the trail blazer. To compete with him, full-page advertisements announced that "By speeding up the flow of digestive fluids and increasing alkalinity, Camels give digestion a helping hand"; a midget bellboy called Johnny Roventini made America's ears ring with his howling, "Call for Philip Morris"; and Old Golds were tested for British thermal units in something called an oxygen bomb calorimeter.

But pioneer manipulators could be found in almost all industries. It is perhaps symbolic that John D. Rockefeller—the symbol of traditional capitalism, who had defiantly listed himself as "capitalist" in *Who's Who in America*—died in 1937. Replacing him were management executives, with their newfound manipulation techniques and their reliance on A. C. Nielsen's "Advertising Effectiveness" reports. Listerine reduced germs "up to 86.7 percent." Women got the Monday Blues while worrying about Flour Face, Dated Skin, and Housework Hands. Men were fired because of Five O'Clock Shadow, owed their inability to get a date to the fact that they were Ninety-Eight-Pound Weaklings, and became social bankrupts because they lacked Talon zipper flies. (Most trousers were still equipped with buttons. In mixed company one man would tell another that a button was unfastened by saying cryptically, "It's one o'clock." That watchword held no terrors for the Talon man, but the other poor slobs would have to feel around furtively to make sure they were Gap-Free.)

Increased leisure, with all its implications for family life, was becoming widespread in 1937. By introducing part-time employment in the bad years, industry had assured the five-day work week. In recreation, radio and the movies held their supremacy—that year audiences first saw *Snow White and the Seven Dwarfs*, and heard Nelson Eddy and Jeannette MacDonald bellowing at one another in *Maytime*—but with more free time there were also more choices: amateur photography, stamp collecting, Chinese checkers, bingo, golf, bicycling, skiing, bowling, and the softball craze. The National Football League was in the fourth year of its east-west championship play-offs, though professional football's great moments awaited television.

Taking the oath of office for the second time on January 20, 1937, Franklin Roosevelt saw "one-third of a nation ill-housed, ill-clad, ill-nourished." Social protest continued to be the overriding theme among intellectuals, and would be until the world crisis preempted their attention. But the well-housed, well-clothed, well-fed two-thirds was less given to vicarious suffering. For the first time since the Crash, youth was speaking in tongues. Girls spoke of boys as smooth; a boy called a girl neat, though he knew she might give him the shaft. The ultimate accolades were "in the groove" and "terrific." Among the terrific hit songs of 1937 were several whose lyrics were as obscure as the most esoteric rock: "The Dipsy Doodle," "Tutti Frutti," "Three Itty Fishes in a Itty Bitty Brook," and "Flat Foot Floogie with a Floy Floy." It was that kind of year.

It was a strange year in Washington, too. The President's extraordinary victory, combined with his political skill and an overwhelmingly Democratic Congress, should have given him an even freer hand than in the First Hundred Days. It didn't. Indeed, very little went his way. At times he appeared to have lost control, both of the country and, even more dismaying, of the party which owed him so much. Part of the difficulty could be traced to errors of presidential judgment, though his miscalculations were not so obvious at the time. Certainly he was entitled to interpret his lopsided victory over Landon as approval of Rooseveltian leadership, and the most powerful force thwarting that leadership—and the will of the people—was the Supreme Court.

His "horse and buggy" press conference hadn't been well received, and for over a year after that he had said nothing on the record about the Court. Even then, his objection to the ruling that no one could regulate wages and hours was no stronger than Hoover's; he merely observed that that opinion created a "no-man's-land" into which neither Congress nor the legislatures could trespass. Meanwhile, however, he was scheming. The Court's challenge had been on his mind even before it had arisen; during the 1932 campaign he remarked that at the time of the Crash Republicans had been in charge of all branches of the federal government— the White House, the Capitol, "and, I might add for good measure, the Supreme Court as well." Thus he viewed the issue as partisan. He may have been right, but the American people, including the men on the Hill, believed the Court and the Constitution were above politics. That strategic blunder was compounded by a tactical error. The struggle brought out what John Gunther called Roosevelt's "worst quality," a "deviousness," a "lack of candor" that "verged on deceit." He gave the impression of sneaking up on the Nine Old Men; as John Randolph said of Martin Van Buren, he "rowed to his object with muffled oars."

Those oars first became audible, for those with highly sensitive ears, on that rainy January day when he took the oath of office for the second time. Afterward he told friends that when the Chief Justice "came to the words 'Support the Constitution of the United States,' I felt like saying, 'Yes, but it's the Constitution as I understand it—flexible enough to meet any new problem of democracy. . . .'" Actually he had said something very like that in the speech that followed, and Hughes had heard him. The American people were determined to go forward, the President declared, and they "will insist that every agency of popular government use effective instruments to carry out their will." One New Dealer who was watching Hughes's face noted, "There was no doubt that the Chief Justice understood."

Two weeks later the President and the Chief Justice came face to face again. This year the Court had agreed to attend the annual judiciary dinner, and everyone present left with the impression that both men had been in high good humor. The reason for the jurist's jollity is unknown. FDR, on the other hand, was enjoying a private joke, soon to become public. Digging back in Justice Department records, Attorney General Cummings had found a proposal to invigorate the federal judiciary by appointing a new judge for every judge who had reached the age of seventy and had failed to retire. The document was dated 1913, and its author had been Attorney General James C. McReynolds—now the most vehement of the Court's Four Horsemen. If the principle were applied to the Hughes Court, Cummings pointed out, the President could name enough liberal justices to reverse the reactionary tide of 6–3 and 5–4 decisions. Hence the origins of what was to become famous (and infamous) as the "Court pack."

"That's the one, Homer!" Roosevelt had cried. He had then flown off to a conference in Rio de Janeiro, leaving his attorney general to draft the legislation. Cummings thought the plan sound, though at the judiciary reception he was uneasy, whispering to a colleague, "I feel too much like a conspirator." Roosevelt felt conspirational, too. That was why he was enjoying himself. The occasion appealed to his love of irony and secret deals. On February 4, 1937, Roosevelt and Cummings unveiled the bill, S.1392, to the assembled cabinet and Democratic congressional leaders. Ickes was delighted, but he didn't have to carry the ball on the Hill. The congressional leadership, which did, said little. Riding back down Pennsylvania Avenue, Representative Hatton Sumners of Texas, chairman of the House Judiciary Committee, abruptly said to the others, "Boys, here's where I cash in." No one knew it at the time, but Vice President Garner had reached the same decision.

Predictably, the Liberty League came back to life and joined the fight against Court reform. Arrayed with it were the U.S. Chamber of Commerce, the National Association of Manufacturers, the Daughters of the American Revolution, and something called the Constitutional Government Committee, led by Frank Gannett, a right-wing newspaper publisher. All this had been predictable. But there was also a spontaneous surge of protest on the community level, from American Legion posts, Kiwanians, and women's clubs. Most dismaying of all, the independent Senate liberals—Borah, Hiram Johnson, and Burton K. Wheeler—came down hard on the Court's side. Roosevelt took off his gloves; in a fireside chat he accused the justices of usurping power and vetoing a reform program which had just been endorsed by the electorate. At a $100-a-plate Democratic dinner at the Mayflower he appealed to party loyalty and demanded passage of S.1392. Wheeler struck back, crying that "a liberal cause was never won by stacking a deck of cards, by stuffing a ballot box, or by packing a court," and Senator Edward R. Burke, in the unkindest cut of all, told a New York rally that constitutional government faced "a rendezvous with death."

Meanwhile the Supreme Court, for the first time in its history, was preparing to emerge from its cloister. The Chief Justice had been telling friends lightly, "If they want me to preside over a convention, I can do it." Inwardly he was splenetic, however, and when the President argued that an overaged, undermanned Court was unable to deal with a logjam of appeals, Hughes decided to challenge him. According to Burton K. Wheeler's recollection, Hughes telephoned him and invited him to his home. As the Senator entered, the Chief Justice said solemnly, "The baby is born," and handed him a letter. Rapidly scanning it, Wheeler saw that it was everything he had hoped for. The Court was abreast of its calendar, it declared; no one was overburdened, and even if the President's charge were true, the adding of justices would slow, not hasten, the administration of its business. Furthermore, the Court had closed ranks; Brandeis and Van Devanter had endorsed the letter. As the senator left, Hughes said, "I hope you'll see that this gets wide publicity." Wheeler did; next morning he read it to the Senate Judiciary Committee, and, as he recalled long afterward, "You could have heard a pin drop in the caucus room."

That crippled Court reform. Even more interesting, the tory justices discovered liberal sympathies hitherto concealed. On March 29—which was immediately christened White Monday by New Dealers—the Court reversed itself on minimum wages for women and children. Next the Wagner Act was upheld, and then, to the immense relief of the administration, social security. When Van Devanter announced his decision to retire, S.1392 seemed pointless; with the President's appointment of Hugo Black to succeed him, the New Deal had a clear majority on the bench. But Roosevelt had committed his prestige to the bill. He refused to withdraw. Instead he turned patronage screws harder and harder, and drove Joe Robinson, his Senate majority leader, mercilessly. The result was catastrophe. On July 14 Robinson fell dead of a heart attack, the *Congressional Record* gripped in his hand.

Now the insurrection spread among regular Democrats. Alben Barkley of Kentucky, Roosevelt's choice to succeed Robinson, won by just a single vote, 38 to 37, over Pat Harrison of Mississippi, and the Vice President plotted S.1392's defeat on Robinson's funeral train, defiantly telling the President, "You are beat. You haven't got the votes." Garner was right, though his insurrection meant that he would never again run on a Roosevelt ticket. Meeting in executive session, the Judiciary Committee reported the bill unfavorably. Next the full Senate voted it down, 70 to 20, and while still in a mutinous mood it overrode the President's veto of a farm loan act. For the first time in over five years, FDR had sustained a major legislative defeat in the Senate. In the bedlam which followed, most of his other big measures—wages-and-hours legislation, executive reorganization, a comprehensive farm program, and the creation of small regional TVAs—were lost for that session. Challenging the White House, which would have been inconceivable for any Democrat in 1936, was now acceptable.

The long-term effects of the failure of his Court reform plan are difficult to assess. The President had won his immediate objective. Interpretation of the interstate commerce clause had been immensely broadened, and because the nine old men really were old, death and retirement would shortly permit Roosevelt to choose a Chief Justice and his eight associate justices. The price was extremely high, however, and was correctly gauged by young Congressman Lyndon Johnson, who took his seat that year. FDR's miscalculation, Johnson reasoned, was responsible for the formation of the Southern Democratic and Republican coalition—a cross which would be borne by all subsequent Democratic Presidents, including Johnson himself.

On February 4, 1937, the day before he sent his Supreme Court plan to Congress, the President had put through a person-to-person call to John L. Lewis in Detroit. Like millions of middle-class Americans, Roosevelt had been exasperated by reports that General Motors workers were sitting down on the job, tying up plants and costing GM a million dollars a day. Every twentieth-century President, including Roosevelt, had endorsed collective bargaining, but no President could approve of trespass. Moreover, Roosevelt told Lewis, strikes threatened the rising prosperity, of which the administration was so proud. In March 1934 he had successfully used that argument with the AFL, which was then organizing the auto workers. The AFL had obligingly canceled a strike date, provoking 75,000 men into turning in or tearing up their cards. Now the rank and file were at it again. The President sympathized with them, but the timing was inconvenient. Lewis could hardly have agreed more. For him the workmen's rebellion was a personal humiliation. Having organized the coal mines, his CIO was devoting its energy and money to the steel industry. He wasn't prepared for a new confrontation elsewhere, and had mustered all his rich eloquence to persuade auto workers that for the time being their assembly lines must be kept moving.

It wasn't enough. Labor's leaders had misjudged the temper of their followers. Even Sidney Hillman, the radical Lithuanian, had not sensed the significance of the Court's 9–0 vote against the NRA. He had been downcast by Brandeis's vote. The justice had once devoted himself to closing sweatshops, Hillman protested; now he had "cleared the way for their reopening." What the junking of the NRA had really done was to open the way for revolt. The men had taken all they could. They were literally prepared to die rather than take more, and before the uproar was over some of them would do just that. It was not a popular strike. General Motors was well regarded by the general public. Its cars were popular, and somehow it had acquired the reputation of being a benevolent employer. That was unjustified. GM paid its twenty top executives an average of $200,000 a year; its workmen scarcely $1,000. Its spy system was one of the most vicious in the country. Complainers were dismissed on trumped-up charges, and foremen controlling the tempo of the assembly lines—the great moving belts carrying frames to which men would fasten and tighten bolts, rims, fenders, engine blocks, doors, and axles, hour after relentless hour—were merciless. "So I'm a Red?" a malcontent told a reporter. "I suppose it makes me a Red because I don't like making time so hard on these goddamned machines. When I get home I'm so tired I can't sleep with my wife." Another said, "It takes your guts out, that line. The speedup, that's the trouble."

Late in 1936 the United Auto Workers had written William S. Knudsen, GM's executive vice president, requesting a conference on the general subject of collective bargaining. Knudsen replied that the UAW should seek adjustment of grievances with local plant managers—as though GM policy weren't determined at the top.

UAW leaders were debating their next step when the men decided it for them. The origins of the sit-down were European. Two years earlier, groups of Welsh and Hungarian miners had refused to come to the top until their wages were raised. It was in America, however, that the all-night sit-down, the affirmation that the worker has a vested interest in his job, became famous. It began on December 28, 1936, when workmen in Cleveland's Fisher Body Plant No. 1 spontaneously sat down and ignored the steel skeletons on the belt. Quick as fever the movement spread to Fisher Body Plant No. 2 in Flint, Michigan, and then to Pontiac, Atlanta, Kansas City, and Detroit itself, until 484,711 men employed by sixty plants in fourteen states were involved. To some it seemed almost miraculous. In Akron, for example, the men struck Firestone Plant No. 1 at 2 A.M. January 29. A puzzled foreman watched as a tire builder at the end of the belt moved three paces to the master safety switch. At this signal, with the perfect synchronized rhythm mass production had taught them, all the other tire builders stepped back. The switch was pulled, and a great hush fell over the plant. Into this silence a man cried, "We done it! We stopped the belt! By God, we done it!" The worker beside him burst into tears.

Some small firms capitulated to the early sit-ins, but the bigger plants, notably those of General Motors, didn't budge. Machine guns were being brought into Flint. In Dearborn, Harry Bennett, the former Navy boxer who had won the affection of Henry Ford, was recruiting a private army of three thousand, and blackjacks were stockpiled in the union camp. Inside each factory a cadre of tough young workers converted shops into fortresses. Armed with clubs and brake parts, they took turns guarding barricaded gates while those off duty played cards or made beds on the floor beside incomplete car chassis. Company property was carefully protected, but company men weren't allowed inside. When Fisher Body executives turned off the heat, the men roller-skated, sang, and danced. Periodically UAW men ran food in past the police.

To the management mentality of 1937, the sit-down was the ultimate outrage. Private property was held to be as sacred as human life, perhaps more so. White-collar executives had always suspected that the union leaders were Communists. Now they knew it. If subversives could prevent an owner from using his shop by draping their bodies across its doors, erecting flesh and blood blockades to keep him out, General Motors might as well turn the country back to the Indians. Their lawyers counseled patience. Obviously this tactic was unlawful. Why not turn it over to the forces of law and order? General Motors did, and instantly acquired an injunction ordering evacuation of the plants. Front offices were elated. But the moral force of the injunction collapsed when reporters discovered that the judge was a major GM stockholder.

Enter John L. Lewis. By now he had realized that if he didn't lead the auto workers he would lose them; therefore he went on the air to declare, "The CIO stands squarely behind these sit-downs." Father Coughlin called Lewis "a Communist stooge." Hermann Schwinn, Nazi leader on the West Coast, and General Nicholas Rodríguez, head of the Mexican Gold Shirts, offered their services to GM management. The NAM erected antilabor billboards all over the country. William Green, speaking for the AFL, denounced the strikers, and in the President's oval office Roosevelt, Garner, and Secretary Perkins debated the wisdom of issuing a statement.

Garner left the meeting under the impression that Roosevelt would take a stand. He didn't, and his silence meant that the man under the gun was Governor Frank Murphy of Michigan. GM lawyers had appealed to another judge, not a stockholder, and this time the evacuation order threatened the strikers with prison sentences and a fine of fifteen million dollars if they didn't quit the shops by 3 P.M. on February 3. By this time the workers were vowing that they were ready to die on their barricades. GM had selected the battleground: its Chevrolet plant in Flint. Murphy had called out the National Guard, and the plant was surrounded by soldiers, the Flint police force, and strikebreakers armed with pokers, clubs, and crowbars. Milling around in between were UAW sympathizers from Detroit, Akron, and Toledo. Over the mail gate hung a strikers' placard: THEY SHALL NOT PASS.

Murphy was ready to send Guard bayonets against the workers. Then, at the last moment, he called John L. Lewis and uneasily asked him what he would do. "You want my answer, sir?" roared Lewis. "I shall personally enter General Motors Chevrolet Plant Number Four. I shall order the men to disregard your order, to stand fast. I shall walk up to the largest window in the plant, open it, divest myself of my outer raiment, remove my shirt and bare my bosom. Then, when you order your troops to fire, mine will be the first breast that those bullets will strike. And as my body falls from the window to the ground, you will listen to the voice of your grandfather as he whispers in your ear, 'Frank, are you sure you are doing the right thing?'"

Murphy hesitated; his grandfather had been hanged after an Irish uprising. And the threat of blood was no Lewisian metaphor. Already it had begun to flow in Flint. During night skirmishes fourteen strikers had been wounded. The police had retreated, and the strikers were derisively describing the "Battle of the Running Bulls" to newspapers, a taunt which was almost certain to trigger police brutality. Wearily the governor tore up his orders. Then he forbade General Motors to impede delivery of food to the sit-downers. Embittered conservatives afterward claimed that Murphy had broken GM's morale. He had helped. So had Lewis. So, by remaining silent, had the President. The crushing blow, however, had been the UAW's technique. Under it the union had immobilized General Motors while making only token demonstrations at Chrysler, Ford, Nash and Packard. In theory—Liberty League theory—the others should have stood with GM in antilabor solidarity. In practice they had been carving up the GM market for their own cars. On February 7 GM directors had to cut its dividend in half. This cost Pierre Du Pont an estimated $2,500,000. From Wilmington came word that principles were all right, in their place, but management should not lose its head, not to mention Du Pont cash. At that General Motors capitulated. After forty-four days of crisis, Knudsen agreed to a conference. When the sit-downers heard about it they square-danced wildly in the frozen yards outside the plants.

Chrysler fell in line, and by summer every firm except Ford—who held out until 1941—had signed a contract recognizing the UAW, seniority, grievance committees, surveys of speedup evils, the forty-hour week, and time and a half for overtime. It was nothing less than total victory. For a while perching on the job, any job, was the rage. New Jersey barbers sat in a nonunion shop, chefs in Washington's Willard Hotel sat on cold stoves, striking seamen sat in deck chairs, Woolworth clerks sat on their counters, striking waitresses persuaded their friends to occupy all seats and then order coffee, Chicago wet nurses sat until they were paid a higher rate per ounce, and a New York motion picture projection operator stopped the show to tell the infuriated audience that he was underpaid.

Now John L. Lewis's CIO had eclipsed the AFL. Industrial labor had put a very large foot in Detroit's very large door. The fact that Lewis had contributed a quarter-million dollars to Roosevelt's reelection campaign came to light, and a chill fell over the Union League Club. The *New York Sun* warned of THE CALLOUS SELFISHNESS OF JOHN L. LEWIS. The man's agents seemed to be everywhere. He learned that the Vice President had opposed him and thundered, "All labor asks is twenty-five lousy cents an hour. The genesis of the campaign against labor is a labor-baiting, poker-playing, whiskey-drinking, evil old man whose name is Garner. Garner's knife is searching for the quivering, pulsating heart of labor. I am against him officially, individually and personally, concretely and in the abstract." It was suggested that the CIO "explore" the possibility of a reunion with the AFL. Lewis snorted, "Explore the mind of Bill Green? I give you my word there is nothing there."

Everyone in industry knew his next target was U.S. Steel. He admitted it. "If we can organize here," he said, "the rest will follow. If the crouching lion can be routed, it's a safe bet that the hyenas in the adjacent bush may be scattered along the plain." The prospect of a conflict between the CIO and Big Steel was appalling. Huge as General Motors was, it was dwarfed by U.S. Steel, or "the Corporation," as it was more simply known to its officers. In 1934, despite the Depression, the Corporation earned $35,218,359. Its by-products alone—from ammonia to cement—came to more than a quarter-million tons a year. It owned mills and mines from Canada to Brazil, a fleet of ships rivaling the U.S. Navy, and thousands of miles of railroad track. It was the largest thing in American industry. Yet the average steelworker, working in constant danger, earned $369 a year and had to support six people with it. If anyone in America was ready for revolution, he was. By comparison, the auto worker was affluent, and now, with the heavily publicized settlements in Detroit, the steelworker knew it. It was noted that when *Modern Times* was shown in Pittsburgh, blue-collar audiences did not laugh at Charlie Chaplin's parody of a workman's five-minute break, in which his hands continued to mime the machine at first and then slowed down just long enough to allow him to grab a glass of water. The pantomime was too close to their real routines, the lockstep lives they meant to change.

But how? The right to organize, it seemed, could only be bought with blood. And then came a surprise. There would be more bloodshed in 1937, but none of it at Big Steel. On the lazy Saturday of January 9, when the GM sit-downs were entering the third week, Lewis had been in Washington, lunching at the Hotel Mayflower with Senator Guffey. There was a stirring around the maître d'hôtel's post and in walked bespectacled Myron Charles Taylor, the patrician chairman of U.S. Steel's board of directors and chief executive of the Corporation. Taylor bowed to the two men; then, after escorting Mrs. Taylor to another table, he strolled across the room to chat with Guffey and Lewis. The senator left, and the president of the CIO joined the Taylors for a pleasant twenty-minute talk. It was one of the more sensational moments in the history of the Mayflower, but no reporter was there to record it, and the lobby was empty next day when Lewis, at Taylor's invitation, arrived at the industrialist's hotel suite for another conversation.

At first they discussed Gothic tapestries, medieval manuscripts, and Elizabethan drama. Taylor, finding his guest captivating, suggested the two of them begin conferring at his New York home, in secret, to resolve differences between Big Steel management and the CIO Steel Workers Organizing Committee (SWOC). Lewis brought more than charm to these meetings. He had figures showing that SWOC had signed up enough U.S. Steel workers to cripple it just as orders were piling up. For fifty years the Corporation had fought its own employees with guns and strikebreakers; surely, he suggested, it was time for a truce, formal talks, and a contract. Taylor reflected awhile and consented. Eight weeks later he initialed a pact agreeing to an eight-hour five-dollar day and a forty-hour week for steelworkers, and to paid vacations and seniority rights. Then they called in the press. When an organizer stumbled into Philip Murray's SWOC office and said he had just heard on the radio that U.S. Steel had been meeting with the CIO, Murray told him he was crazy and threw him out. Taylor's subordinates were equally shocked, though when the contract was signed March 7 Benjamin Fairless, president of U.S. Steel, came over to Murray and told him that he was the son of a miner. "Call me Ben," he asked. Murray answered, "Yes, Mr. Fairless."

Lewis had reached the peak of his glory. In the afterglow of the GM and Big Steel triumphs, firm after firm came round until the CIO had 30,000 contracts and three million members. Organized labor had become a significant American constituency, with partisans far beyond working-class wards. Thirty New York clergymen qualified for AFL admission as Ministers Union of America, Local 1; college students began singing labor's new anthems, and altered meanings of liberal (pro-union) and conservative (anti-union) came into general use. The CIO had won two famous victories. However, the routing of the crouching lion did not mean the scattering of the hyenas, by which Lewis had meant Little Steel—Republic, National, Inland, Bethlehem, and Youngstown Sheet and Tube. None of them would speak to CIO organizers. Tom M. Girdler of Republic, the tycoon who became the leader of Little Steel's intransigents, said he would quit his $130,000-a-year presidency and go back to hoeing potatoes before he would meet workers' demands.

On May 26 Lewis took the men out—70,000 workers in 27 plants. Little Steel company police, and hired guns wearing local police uniforms but paid by management, expanded by 7,000 men. A Senate investigation subsequently reported, "Over $4,000,000 was expended directly attributable to the strike. A total of $141,000 worth of industrial munitions was assembled for use." Strikebreakers inside the mills were fed by parcel post and parachute drops, and local newspapers cooperated in back-to-work campaigns. Girdler paid strikers who played informer $25 a week while accusing union leaders of "interference in a man's private affairs." He added, "An ominous fact was repeated in the sketchy facts we had about some of these fellows: they were Communists." He refused to permit "intimidation" of "loyal workers" by "outside agitators." And he pledged: "I won't have a contract, verbal or written, with an irresponsible, racketeering, violent, communistic body like the CIO, and until they pass a law making me, I am not going to do it." The fact that the Wagner Act was such a law, and that it had been signed by the President and upheld a few days earlier by the Supreme Court, was unmentioned.

Violence came on Memorial Day, outside Republic Steel's South Chicago plant. Several thousand strikers and their families had gathered on a stretch of flat, sparsely inhabited prairie east of the factory. They were planning a protest parade. From the beginning of the strike, the police had interfered with token picketing; this time, however, Mayor Edward Kelly had announced that a peaceful demonstration would be permitted. It was hot and humid. Vendors with refrigerated pushcarts bearing nickel-a-cake brick ice cream were mobbed. On a signal the marchers formed ranks quickly, displaying their hand-lettered signs: REPUBLIC STEEL VIOLATES LABOR DISPUTES

ACT, REPUBLIC STEEL SHALL SIGN A UNION CONTRACT, and WIN WITH THE CIO. Two men carrying American flags led the procession. Reporters and photographers swarmed around, and there was a camera crew from Paramount News. Like a long crocodile, the marchers crossed the fields singing "Solidarity Forever."

Just ahead, between them and the mill, the singers saw a line of five hundred heavily armed Chicago policemen. They hadn't expected this. It was, in fact, in direct contravention of the mayor's orders. The cops were there, it later developed, because an "anonymous source" had informed them that the pickets planned to march into the mill and seize it—that defenseless families, in other words, would try to overpower the professional strikebreakers manning Browning 30-caliber heavy machine guns at the gate. Anyhow, the bluecoats believed it, or said they did. To the approaching pickets a police captain shouted, "You dirty sons of bitches, this is as far as you go."

The parade slowed, but doggedly it edged toward the factory. There was no further warning. About 250 yards from the mill a wedge of bluecoats attacked a band of workers' wives, nightsticks thrusting into breasts. Other cops were aiming gas guns or yanking revolvers free. The men with flags shouted, "Stand fast! Stand fast! We got our rights! We got our legal rights to picket!" But police shouted back, "You got no legal rights!" and "You Red bastards, you got no rights!" In that instant the provocations later cited by Chicago police spokesmen took place; a few empty soda pop bottles were thrown, and workers called out taunts. At that, police grenades began to fly, a pall of nauseous tear gas settled over the procession, children screamed in terror, and the line buckled and broke. Then the murdering began.

At first the shots were scattered. As the general flight began, however, the bluecoats fired volleys. Some policemen pursued individuals. A woman tripped and fell; four cops held her down, smashing in her face with the butts of their pistols. Pickets lay on the grass or crawled about aimlessly on all fours, vomiting blood, and officers stood over them and fired into their backs. It was all there on the Paramount newsreels. Ten were dead, over ninety were wounded. The reporters called it the Memorial Day Massacre, but Tom Girdler said, "There can be no pity for a mob. As that artistic brawler, Benvenuto Cellini said, 'Blows are not dealt by measure.' Some of the mob were clubbed after they had started to run from the wrath they had aroused. Some women were knocked down. The policemen were there performing a hazardous and harsh duty. What were women doing there?"

The Paramount newsreel was suppressed on the fatuous ground that movies audiences—though conditioned by years of gangster films—might be incited to riot. The *St. Louis Post-Dispatch* exposed the suppression, but the *Chicago Tribune* described members of the unarmed procession as "lusting for blood." Both the McCormick and the Hearst press branded the CIO (and, by implication, the wives and children of CIO men) as communistic. No one was ever prosecuted, though eight more workers were killed, one of them a crippled veteran who was selling tickets to a CIO dance, before the strike was over. It ended when the men returned to work without a contract. Girdler's tactics had been too much for them.

They were not, however, too much for Robert M. La Follette Jr. The Wisconsin senator launched one of the most exhaustive and memorable investigations of the decade. His committee found that:

> . . . provocation for the police assault did not go beyond abusing language and the throwing of isolated missiles from the rear ranks of the marchers. . . . From all the evidence we think it plain that the force employed by the police was far in excess of that which the occasion required. Its use must be ascribed either to gross inefficiency in the performance of the police duty, or a deliberate attempt to intimidate the strikers.

Photographs had been enlarged and distributed, testimony from participants and witnesses published, and the story unfolded bit by bit for a public which, until then, had assumed that all strikers were suspect. When the casualty list first appeared, President Roosevelt had probably spoken for the middle class when he quoted Shakespeare: "A plague on both your houses." Lewis had replied, "It ill behooves one who has supped at labor's table and who has been sheltered in labor's house to curse with equal fervor and fine impartiality both labor and its adversaries when they become locked in deadly embrace." Roosevelt explained that he meant the extremists on both sides. It was not often that the President felt it necessary to explain anything, and when it developed that all the extremists in South Chicago that day had been anti-union, he moved to labor's side. Public opinion moved with him, and the National Labor Relations Board brought Girdler to his knees. Thus the Little

Steel strike was won after all, with union shops in all its plants except Bethlehem Steel.

The killings and beatings of CIO men continued throughout the year, and when all incidents had been reported to Secretary Perkins, she remarked that 1937 had been the most savage in the history of twentieth-century labor. It was in fact the high-water mark of the decade's spectacular picket line confrontations. Of the 4,720 strikes in 1937, the Department of Labor estimated that 82 percent had ended in settlements favorable to unions. By the year's end, nearly eight million workers were carrying union cards. "For the past four and one-half years," *Fortune* observed late in 1937, "the United States has been in the throes of a major labor upheaval which can fairly be described as one of the greatest mass movements in our history."

In 1941, when Ford and Bethlehem Steel were swept up in the tidal wave, there would be ten million union men; late in the 1940s the figure reached fifteen million. Lewis fell into public disfavor during the war, when he seemed to be blackmailing the President by threatening to withhold coal from war industries. The CIO, embarrassed to find that there really were some Communists in its ranks (Lee Pressman was for a time the CIO general counsel) was obliged to purge itself of them. Nevertheless, the original goal had been reached and was never again in jeopardy; American workmen had gained security and dignity, and with a new surge of prosperity they themselves would move to suburbs and join the expanding middle class.

Hardly anyone noticed when, on February 27, 1939, the U.S. Supreme Court declared the sit-down strikes illegal. The circumstances at the time had seemed to render that point irrelevant. If labor had sometimes stepped outside the law in its great struggle, liberals could argue, then surely it had been provoked. Any suggestion that the sit-downs had been a form of collective violence was denied or shrugged off; any mention of other incidents in which labor was at least as guilty as management—such as the bloody strike against the Aluminum Company of America in Alcoa, Tennessee, or of jurisdictional disputes between AFL and CIO pickets—brought hostile stares.

But a people cannot escape its past so easily. Certain precedents had been established, and would be remembered. Nor were those precedents to be altered by the fact that union men had been acting in concert with American history. They were, but that would merely strengthen the resolve of the rebels of the future. Violence had brought the United States independence, freed the slaves, and first conquered the West and then tamed it. Now it had raised working men up from the industrial cellar. Labor might forget that and turn conservative, but for liberals to deny other oppressed groups the right to revolt would prove impossible. Thus were the seeds of later anguish planted in innocence, even in idealism.

By late summer of 1937 the President felt he had to get out of Washington for what he called a "look-see" trip. In September his air-conditioned ten-car train nosed out of Union Station and rolled westward, pausing at selected stations long enough for him to deliver his simple little discourses from the back platform, remind constituents of what the administration had done ("How do you like your new high school?"), and enjoy the warmth of their affection. At Boise he told his audience that he felt like Antaeus: "I regain strength just by meeting the American people." Their enthusiasm seemed even greater than in the last campaign, and reporters, noting it, saw something else. Invitations to the presidential car were following an interesting pattern. Senators Burke of Nebraska, Wheeler of Montana, and O'Mahoney of Wyoming—Democrats who had fought FDR's Supreme Court bill—were being deliberately overlooked. At Casper, Wyoming, the President told the crowd that voters didn't have much use for politicians who gave lip service to ideals and then did nothing to put their ideals to work.

This was correctly interpreted as a threat to mutinous Democrats, though he didn't follow it up immediately. As usual, Roosevelt's mind was exploring several channels at once. He was pondering new legislation, looking toward the coming off-year elections, sifting the alternatives in foreign policy, watching the strikes, and brooding over his budget, which he had promised to balance in his first campaign. Until now that had been impossible, but he still wanted to do it if he could. This looked like the year. In its first months *Time* had reported: "Last week, with Depression lapsing into memory, the portents of Boom drummed excitingly throughout the land," and now, in report after report, Morgenthau was noting a small but accumulating surplus in the Treasury. To be sure Leon Henderson, the WPA economist, was worrying about rising prices; he had written a troubled memorandum expressing fear of a business collapse. Roosevelt had seen it, but he didn't want to renege again on the commitment to balance. During the Court fight he had assured Garner, "I have said fifty times that the budget will be balanced for the fiscal year 1938. If you want me to say it again, I will say it either once or fifty times more."

The prescription was as wrong for Roosevelt as it had been for Hoover. Stocks slumped. The President was tempted to say that conditions were "fundamentally sound"—he really believed that they were—but then, remembering his predecessor, he held his tongue. It made no difference. On October 19, "Black Tuesday," wave after wave of selling orders hit the market, the tape was twenty-five minutes behind the trading, and the backup of new selling orders indicated that bottom had not yet been touched. The following winter brought painful memories of 1929–30.

The New York Stock Exchange blamed the Securities and Exchange Commission, the SEC blamed the exchange, businessmen blamed a loss of confidence in the administration, New Dealers muttered darkly of a "capital strike." Certainly the year's real strikes, affecting 1,950,000 workers, had scarred the economy. In any event, the recession, as it was called, deepened the gloom in what was already a dark year for the President and the country. The skid downward was actually steeper than in the first months after the Crash. By the spring of 1938 five million people who had found jobs since 1933 were out of work again, and nearly 14 percent of the population was on relief.

It was hard for the President to abandon hope in a balanced budget, but Roosevelt was not Hoover; the spectacle of millions in want moved him more than Manchester economics ever could. And this was not 1930. A growing number of Democrats, including Henderson and the President's son James, had become Keynesian advocates. FDR hadn't read Keynes—he rarely opened a book when he could pick up the same information in conversation—and he was unimpressed by a long letter from England dated February 1, 1938 ("You received me so kindly when I visited you some three years ago that I make bold to send you some bird's-eye impressions"), in which Keynes recommended massive deficit spending. It couldn't be massive. In politics some goals, no matter how enchanting to the academy, are unattainable. Still, limited deficits had already passed Roosevelt's supreme test: they worked. In 1934 and 1935 they had fueled better times, increasing the money supply and pushing indices up. With his advisers recommending a Keynesian solution, and with the recession deepening as 1938 grew older, the President capitulated. On April 2, lunching on the train between Warm Springs and Washington, he told Harry Hopkins and Andrew Williams, director of NYA, that he was going to quit trying to balance the budget. Twelve days later, in a fireside chat, he explained to the country that he planned to ask Congress for three billion dollars to increase public works, relief, flood control, and housing. In June the stock market came to life, and in eight months the Dow index spurted from 99 to 158. Happier days, if not happy days, lay ahead.

His critics were unimpressed. Long ago the most vociferous of them had turned aside from any serious inquiry into current affairs and abandoned themselves to orgies of presidential vilification. When he floated one of his little valentines for them the week after the April fireside chat—he attacked big business's control over "other people's money, other people's labor, other people's lives"—they salivated as predictably as a Pavlovian kennel. Keynes thought that very naughty of Roosevelt. In that February 1 letter he had attempted to advise the President on the management mentality. Businessmen were not snarling beasts, he wrote. It was best to treat them as "domestic animals by nature, even though they have been badly brought up and not trained as you would wish."

This was one Keynesian recommendation that Roosevelt didn't even acknowledge. Let the Englishman stick to his last; FDR was the reigning expert on public opinion, and he wasn't going to dangle olive branches before his sworn enemies. Anyway, by then it was too late to reconcile the quarrels between the President and the American business community. Too much had been said, too many slights inflicted, too many ritualistic needles rammed into waxen images, too many stakes driven into imaginary hearts.

Willard M. Kiplinger, whose weekly newsletter circulated in business offices, later dated the reaction against the administration among the well-to-do from March 1, 1934. By that September *Time* had noted that "Private fulminations and carpings against the New Deal have become almost a routine of the business day," but the President himself was still too popular for open attacks upon him, let alone his family.

A stronger reaction was inevitable once the propertied classes had convalesced from their terror of early 1933 and discovered that by "recovery" FDR did not mean a return to New Era prosperity.

He wanted changes, and those changes would benefit not the rich, to whose schools he had gone and in whose circles he had moved, but the oppressed. Talk of the Forgotten Man, businessmen agreed among themselves, merely fomented unrest. Anti-New Deal columns began appearing under the bylines of David Lawrence in *U.S. News*, Mark Sullivan in the *New York Herald Tribune,* and Frank R. Kent in the *Baltimore Sun.* The *Saturday Evening Post* was a particular haven for mourners of the past. One of its editorial writers declared indignantly, "We might just as well say the world failed as that American business leadership failed." The *Post* published a spirited defense of child labor, insisting that "the surest prescription for starting an American boy toward understanding success is to let him go to work before he is fully grown," and when Carter Glass said of New Dealers, "Why, Thomas Jefferson wouldn't even speak to these people," it was clear that opposition to Roosevelt was along class lines, not party lines.

The 1936 election returns indicated that excoriation of Roosevelt was counterproductive. It did not disappear, though. Instead it turned more virulent and went underground: to Westchester County and Orange County, Grosse Pointe and Miami Beach, Brookline and Longmeadow; Greenwich, Shaker Heights, Scottsdale, Kenilworth, and Winnetka; Wall Street, State Street, Chestnut Street, and La Salle Street. In lighter forms it could be amusing. There were the stories of the psychiatrist who went to heaven and was immediately sent to God "because He has delusions of grandeur; He thinks He's Franklin D. Roosevelt," and "Why is a WPA worker like King Solomon? Because he takes his pick and goes to bed." When FDR saw the celebrated Peter Arno cartoon of the overdressed rich on their way "to hiss Roosevelt" at the Trans-Lux Theater, he scribbled "Grand!" across it.

But there was nothing grand about the anti-Roosevelt sewage being circulated in upper-class and upper-middle-class clubs and homes in the late 1930s. Of course, they told one another knowingly, everyone in Washington knew That Fellow had caught gonorrhea from "El-ea-nor." (A Negro had infected her.) Franklin D. was dying of VD, and that was the reason El-ea-nor was gallivanting around the country; after he was dead she was going to turn the country over to the Russians. Then she was going to Moscow and learn unspeakable sexual practices, taught only in the Kremlin.

"Jimmee" Roosevelt would probably stay; his protection racket, selling "insurance" to honest businessmen, was battening.

"One is apt to forget nowadays," John Gunther wrote in 1950, "the furtive vindictiveness of the whispering campaign against Roosevelt, the sheer defamatory wickedness of the calumny that descended on him. . . . One forgets the atmosphere of the 'better' country clubs in the late 1930s, the ghoulish talk at the bankers' lunches, the burble of poisonous gossip at fashionable dinners." There were the Army officers who, even in uniform, refused to toast the President of the United States. There were the old men in mahogany-walled city clubs repeating the incantation, "Just another Stalin—only worse," or "We might just as well be living in Russia right now." There was even the Boston bookstore which informed Bennett Cerf, the President's publisher, that it would sell FDR's collected speeches "only if bound in that man's skin."

And over and over there were the clichés: That Man, That Fellow, trying to destroy the American way of life, you can't spend your way out of a Depression, our children's children will be paying, half the people on relief are foreigners anyhow, cut the relief rolls and enlarge the police and let trouble come, John L. Lewis has a key to the back door of the White House, That Man's smile has been grafted on his face by plastic surgeons, he has never earned a nickel in his life and just lives off his mother's income, and he's only a Jew anyway, descended from Dutch sheenies who changed their names, nothing but a New York kike. (An elaborate genealogy was worked out for this last, going back to a fictitious Colonel van Rosenfeld.)

In two striking magazine articles ("They Hate Roosevelt," *Harper's*, May 1936, and "They Still Hate Roosevelt," *New Republic*, September 14, 1938) Marquis W. Childs analyzed the haters. His first study cited "a phenomenon which social historians of the future will very likely record with perplexity if not with astonishment: the fanatical hatred of the President which today obsesses thousands of men and women of the American upper class. No other word than hatred will do," he went on. "It is a passion, a fury, that is wholly unreasoning." Childs suggested that "It permeates, in greater or less degree, the whole upper stratum of American society. It has become with them an *idée fixe*."

What especially baffled him was that the majority of those who railed against the President had to a large extent "had their incomes restored and their bank balances replenished since the low point of March 1933." The value of some stocks had doubled, tripled, or quadrupled—"and indeed has multiplied some of them by ten." Corporate dividends were up over 40 percent. Thus far the incomes of the wealthy had not been heavily taxed. (A man who made $16,000 a year was taxed $1,000.) Much of the burden in Roosevelt's tax programs had been passed along to the mass of consumers through processing or excise taxes.

Nevertheless the rich—Childs called them "the 2 percent"—regarded the administration of Washington as though it were an alien government. Indeed, in repeating the "Rosenfeld" myth they were quoting a Goebbels tract word for word. Some of them said outright that they would prefer Hitler to Roosevelt. While this was nonsense, it does suggest the depth of their feeling. Atwater Kent retired in June 1936 because he refused to do business while Roosevelt was President; a Du Pont vice president was honestly indignant when his servants left him because they could get more money from the WPA; a Bethlehem Steel executive had a heart attack when FDR was quoted—accurately for once—as saying of Bethlehem's president, "Go tell Eugene Grace he'll never make a million dollars a year again!" As Childs discovered, the fury of the rich was passed along to the middle-class white-collar workers who still believed in them, who had retained their faith in the shibboleths of the 1920s. Reviling Roosevelt became a status symbol among men who, unlike their "betters" (as the 2 percent were still called), were unthreatened by the labor unions and the transfer of power from financiers and big businessmen to Washington.

The President's reaction to this was puzzling. In Madison Square Garden he had said that he welcomed their hatred, but he was not the kind of man to relish widespread detestation of anyone, let alone himself and his family. Childs wrote, "He doesn't seem to mind." There is some evidence that he did. Raymond Moley has left an account of how Roosevelt, planning a conciliatory address on the role of American industry, would listen to New Dealers repeat the stories going the rounds of Forsyte homes until his face stiffened and it became clear that the speech would be "more like a thistle than an olive branch." The President told Norman Thomas that he was saving capitalism and resented the criticism of the capitalists. At one of his press conferences he quietly handed around, with minimal comment, a "confidential backgrounder" from a national news service to subscribing editors hinting at proof that FDR had syphilis.

As long as he lived, the 2 percent and their admirers would be ready to spring on his most innocuous move. When in 1939 he proposed that Thanksgiving be celebrated a week early to extend the Christmas shopping season—a boon to small businesses—the country split wide open; twenty-five governors agreed, twenty-three revolted (including the governor of Maine, who ate a symbolic can of sardines), and the issue had to be solved by a joint resolution of Congress. Even in death there were those who reviled him. One of them was Harold Gray, creator of *Little Orphan Annie*. Shortly before the President was stricken in 1945, Daddy Warbucks, unable to stand the thought of another term under Roosevelt, threw himself to his death. After the President's funeral, Gray brought Daddy back on the ground that "since the climate is different around here recently," it would be possible for a man of property and decency to breathe freely again.

Daddy Warbucks and the man behind him belonged to what Teddy Roosevelt once called the lunatic fringe. Pearl Harbor thinned the ranks of the haters, who had reached their crest during the late 1930s. In the opinion of Frederick Lewis Allen, their rage "flared higher and higher during 1934 and 1935 and continued at a high temperature until about 1938, when it appeared to weaken somewhat, if only through exhaustion." Meantime they had enjoyed FDR's 1937 reverses as much as if they were reading Defoe's *Journal of the Plague Year*, and though they were disappointed by the swiftness with which his 1938 recession faded, they were to feast joyously on a Roosevelt defeat once again in the fall.

Clearly the New Deal was on its last legs. The two Hundred Days periods had just about exhausted the administration's legislative creativity; the few presidential measures which hadn't passed contravened the growing conservatism in the country. Reforming zeal was nearly dead on the Hill. Only a man with Roosevelt's extraordinary gift for leadership could have held his huge, amorphous coalition together in November 1936. Next time only a war would keep it intact. The South was its weak link, and the conservative bloc fused in the Court reform fight was developing stronger ties each month.

Congressman Martin Dies of Texas, chairman of the House Un-

American Activities Committee, explained that it would be incorrect to identify the bloc as southern, because it had "the support of nearly all small-town and rural congressmen." Its enemies, he continued, were "the men from the big cities which . . . are politically controlled by foreigners and transplanted Negroes," whose "representatives have introduced insidious influences into the New Deal."

The influences had been there all along; it was the congressmen who had changed. As one embittered New Dealer put it, "The farmers have forgotten that they were just as hungry and desperate as the people in city slums before the President bailed both out." It was true, but irrelevant. The anti-urbanism which Dies expressed was a powerful new force in the country, and in its hostility to the ways and ideas of city slickers, it was essentially conservative. Opinion polls in 1938 reported that while the President retained his popularity, his methods and his power were being questioned. Furthermore, the quality of his support had changed. According to a *Fortune* survey, about 62 percent of the voters were still for him, but those who felt he was essential—as against those who believed merely that the good in his administration outweighed the bad— had dropped from 34.9 to 17.7 percent. There had been little faith in pollsters since the *Literary Digest* debacle, but the coming off-year campaigns would confirm the trend, and congressmen who read their mail could sense it.

The last New Deal reform measure was the Fair Labor Standards Act, introduced early in 1937. It had a dreadful time. It provided for a forty-cent hourly minimum, a maximum work week of forty hours, with time and a half for overtime and no labor for children under sixteen. Employers were to be given eight years to meet the standards, starting with twenty-five cents an hour. In retrospect it does not seem Draconian. All the same, it was first forgotten in the battle over the Court plan, and then pigeonholed by southerners from low-wage states. FDR called Congress back into special session after his "look-see" trip convinced him that the country was behind him. The wages-and-hours law came up in the House and was trounced. It came up again, and lost again. Finally, in late June of 1938, it was sent to the White House for Roosevelt's signature.

By then he had decided he must do something about the Hill. Good Democrats up for reelection must win; the others should leave Washington. In the spring he had written a "Dear Alben" letter to Barkley, who faced a popular primary candidate in Kentucky's Governor A. B. "Happy" Chandler. Alben's opponent, Roosevelt wrote, was "a dangerous person . . . of the Huey Long type, but with less ability." Next he invited John L. Lewis to the White House and persuaded him to put his men and his money behind Barkley. Finally—or it should have been final—FDR announced that he would personally stump Kentucky to campaign for Alben. Unhappily local WPA administrators, eager to please the chief, also showed favoritism toward Barkley, and this blunder was documented in the Scripps-Howard press. It was an ugly overture.*

The entire country learned firsthand of the President's determination to intervene in local primaries through a fireside chat late in June 1938. Democrats in the 75th Congress, he reminded the electorate, had been elected by running on an "uncompromisingly liberal" platform. Citing the year-long battle over wages and hours, he said, "Never before have we had so many Copperheads." Copperhead was not a flattering term; it meant people in northern states who sympathized with the South during the Civil War. He explained liberal principles and then said that "as head of the Democratic party" he felt that he had "every right to speak in those few instances where there may be a clear issue between candidates for a Democratic nomination involving these principles, or involving a clear misuse of my own name."

That was all. Yet newspaper editorial writers, who had popularized the phrase "Court pack" so successfully that most readers did not know it had been introduced as a measure for Court reform, promptly christened this new venture a "purge"—thus inviting dark comparisons with the bloody events in Moscow a year earlier. To read some papers one would have thought that the President intended to bound back and forth across the land with a sickle, lopping off the heads of inoffensive men who had been audacious enough to disagree courteously with him once in a while.

And yet—one wonders precisely what FDR *did* have in mind. Jim Farley, who knew when to leave a ship, fled to Alaska, groaning, "It's a bust." By any gauge of conventional politics, it was. Here was the leader of a national party—generally regarded as the most skillful politician ever to occupy the White House—deliberately inviting reverses. In off-year campaigns local personalities are usually far more important than national policy. Issues also tend to be local,

---

* It led directly to the Hatch Act (1939), forbidding political participation by federal employees below the policy-making level.

and in 1938 there was a bewildering array of them: corruption in Pennsylvania, a state pension plan in California, the sit-downs in Michigan, a Rhode Island race track scandal, bribery in Massachusetts, bossism in New Jersey, strikes everywhere, and, in Connecticut, an uproar over a revolutionary proposal to build a four-lane, fifteen-million-dollar landscaped highway through the townships of Greenwich, Stamford, New Canaan, Norwalk, Westport, Fairfield, and Trumbull. As James MacGregor Burns has noted, "Putting out campaign brush fires all over the country was no way to leave the President in a commanding position."

But to Roosevelt this was no ordinary campaign. Ever since the Court fight he had been planning a realignment of the parties. Most conservatives were Republicans; let that party be their home. He saw the Democratic party as the instrument of liberalism. As the first national hero of peace, he was ready to spend his popularity in a gigantic political reform, and the first stage of his crusade was encouraging. His appeal to the people was undiminished. Everywhere crowds were unprecedented. In Marietta, Ohio, an elderly woman knelt to pat the dust where he had stepped; in Idaho, where the railroad tracks ran beside a quiet lake, a man had erected two American flags on a tiny homemade pier, and as the presidential car passed he stood at attention between them, his hand raised in a military salute.

FDR gave Happy Chandler the back of his hand. Chandler was so thick-skinned, and so determined to seize a piece of the President's coattails, that he had to be all but kicked and dragged from the platform. It was done, and Roosevelt leveled him with such magnificent scorn that Kentuckians could have no doubt about the presidential choice. In Texas the hallowed hands fell on the brows of Congressmen Lyndon B. Johnson and Maury Maverick; Senator Tom Connally, who had voted against the Court plan, was almost incoherent with rage when he heard Roosevelt announce—and from the train's rear platform at that—the appointment to the federal bench of a Texan the senator loathed. In Oklahoma, Colorado, Nevada, and California blessings were bestowed more discreetly, and one marked man, Senator Pat McCarran of Nevada, demonstrated that he was a better athlete than Chandler by actually fighting his way to FDR's side. On the whole the President's surgical job had been well done, however, and boarding the warship *Houston* the commander in chief wore a triumphant glow. In the big races, including Kentucky, his men had won. McCarran had barely slipped in, and in lesser contests little presidential prestige had been committed.

Now he was prepared to commit a lot. In Barnesville, Georgia, he cast the evil eye on Senator Walter George while George sat on the same platform. When FDR finished reading him out of the party, the senator said, "Mr. President, I regret that you have taken this occasion to question my democracy and to attack my public record. I want you to know that I accept the challenge." "Let's always be friends," FDR replied fatuously. The rest of the Georgia politicians present were jittery; they were trying to think how on earth they could survive such a feud. Traveling north, Roosevelt hexed "Cotton Ed" Smith of South Carolina and Millard Tydings of Maryland. In early September he spent two days speaking against Tydings, a man who, he charged, wanted to campaign "with the Roosevelt prestige and the money of his conservative Republican friends both on his side." His New York scourge was Congressman John J. O'Connor, who, although he was the brother of the President's former law partner, had used his position as chairman of the House Rules Committee to bottle up New Deal legislation.

Then the people voted. The result, for FDR, was calamity and humiliation—the only election in which it can be said that the President was crushed. Of the ten principals marked for the political void, only O'Connor fell, brought down by an attractive candidate backed by La Guardia, Hopkins, Corcoran, and boss Edward J. Flynn. All the rest, including Tydings, George, and the medieval Smith, coasted in on landslides or sweeps. The southern Democratic party, with an identity all its own, was a mighty force now. Of it, President Kennedy was to observe ruefully in 1962, "Some Democrats have voted with Republicans for twenty-five years, really since 1938 . . . so that we have a very difficult time, on a controversial piece of legislation, securing a working majority."

In November surviving Democrats collided with rejuvenated Republicans. Conservatives beat George Earle in Pennsylvania, Philip La Follette in Wisconsin, and Frank Murphy in Michigan.* Among the new Republican faces were Robert A. Taft and John Bricker of Ohio, Leverett Saltonstall of Massachusetts, and Thomas E. Dewey, who ran Governor Lehman of New York such a close race that he was already being spoken of as a presidential possibility

* But labor took care of its own. Murphy was appointed to the Supreme Court.

in 1940. Although Democrats retained control of both congressional houses, liberal strength in the House had been cut in half (Lyndon Johnson made it, but Maverick didn't). Overall, the GOP, which only two years earlier had seemed to be on its way to joining the extinct Whigs, had picked up a dozen governorships, eighty-two House seats, and eight new Senate seats. Republican incumbents had not lost a single race.

At his first post-election press conference the President was asked, "Will you not encounter coalition opposition?" FDR replied that he didn't think so. The reporter said, "I do!" and his colleagues laughed. Cryptically the President commented, "The trees are too close to the forest."

And so they were. The challenges to freedom's leaders no longer lay within the United States; they were on the other side of the world's two greatest oceans, in Germany and Japan. As early as Christmas 1935 Roosevelt had written Baruch, "I still worry about world affairs more than domestic problems which include the election." Now, two elections later, his worries had multiplied. The country was still overwhelmingly isolationist; alerting it to the distant threats was a challenging task, so vast that it beggared description. But this much seemed certain: coalition politics on Capitol Hill would be irrelevant for some time. Even the hard-core Roosevelt haters would swing in line if the nation faced an outside enemy. Childs had conceded that; in 1936 he had written, "A major war would serve, of course, as it did for Wilson, to dissolve the fury," and, in 1938, "One thing, and one thing alone, could bring about a shift in the attitude of the hating class, and that, of course, is a war. . . . It is no accident that those who rail most violently against the Roosevelt domestic policies speak with grudging approval of the President's foreign policy."

What made this phenomenon remarkable was that his critics were endorsing something which did not exist. At this time he still had no foreign policy. He needed one; he knew that. He had begun looking for it during his first administration, and the search, still unfulfilled, had been pressed in earnest since a December day, nearly eleven months before the 1938 off-year election, when the United States gunboat *Panay*, lying at anchor on the Yangtze River above Nanking, had been deliberately bombed and sunk by aircraft from the Empire of Japan.

Late Thirties Montage

KARPIS CAPTURED IN NEW ORLEANS BY HOOVER

There's a small hotel
By a wishing well
I wish that we were there
Together

Miss Otis regrets she's unable to lunch today, madam.

=== Feed it to me Gene ===

MAN: They found Lefty!
AGATE: Where?
MAN: Behind the carbarns with a bullet in his head!
AGATE: (crying): Hear it, boys hear it? Hell, listen to me! Coast to coast! HELLO, AMERICA! HELLO. WE'RE STORMTROOPERS OF THE WORKING CLASS. WORKERS OF THE WORLD... OUR BONES AND BLOOD! And when we die they'll know what we did to make a new world! Christ, cut us in little pieces. We'll die for what is right! Put fruit trees where our ashes are!

Bei mir bist du schön
Please let me explain,
Bei mir bist du schön
Means that you're grand

"Isn't this Los Angeles?" inquired Flier Corrigan. "Los Angeles! This is Dublin!" he was told. Flying a $900 plane which authorities had described as "not airworthy," traveling without official permission, passport, visa, parachute, or radio, he made the trip on $62.26 for gas and oil and has been dubbed "Wrongway" Corrigan.

Spank the skin

Rush, says the boss, work like a hoss;
I'll take the profits and you take the loss,
I've got the brains, I've got the dough,
The Lord Himself decreed it so

NAZIS SEIZE AUSTRIA AFTER HITLER ULTIMATUM GERMAN TROOPS ENTER, INVITED BY VIENNA

Who's afraid of the big bad wolf!
The big bad wolf! The big bad wolf!

Mamma's little baby
loves a union shop

Any evening, any day
If you come down Lambeth way
You'll find us all
Doin' the Lambeth Walk — oy!

FORD BRINGS OUT MERCURY, FIRST NEW CAR SINCE CRASH

HUMPHREY BOGART
and
LESLIE HOWARD
in
THE PETRIFIED FOREST

A fine romance!
With no kiss-es!
A fine romance!
My friend, this is!

BRENDA FRAZIER CATCHES COLD ON DEBUT EVE

Six

A SHADOW OF PRIMITIVE TERROR

Like another bright Sunday four years later, December 12, 1937, was a day of rest for the ships of the U.S. Navy. The officers and men of the U.S.S. *Panay* felt they deserved it. Although the 450-ton, shoal-draft gunboat had been designed merely to protect American shipping and American citizens from irresponsible guerrilla bands roaming the shores of the Yangtze, her crew had worked around the clock for the past two nights. Nanking was about to fall to the Japanese army. Chiang Kai-shek's foreign office advised Americans in the city to leave. All that Saturday the gunboat had been taking aboard staff from the U.S. embassy, foreign correspondents, photographers, and American businessmen. Fully loaded, and with shellfire uncomfortably close, the *Panay* weighed anchor. Pursued by Japanese artillery, she sailed twenty-seven miles upstream and anchored in quieter waters beside three Standard Oil tankers. Afterward, American isolationists charged that the *Panay* was "convoying" the tankers and deserved her fate. But this was ridiculous. By treaty the Yangtze was an international waterway. It was spangled with the flags of all trading nations. Nobody was convoying anybody.

Indeed, the *Panay*'s commanding officer, Lieutenant Commander J. J. Hughes, had special reason to be tranquil. Twelve days earlier the American ambassador in Tokyo had informed the Japanese government of the gunboat's position and its probable mission. Hughes was flying the Stars and Stripes prominently. Japanese officers storming Nanking knew precisely where he was—which, as it turned out, was unfortunate for him, his ship, and Standard Oil's vessels. At 1:30 P.M. two flights of Mitsubishi warplanes with the rising sun on their wings dive-bombed and strafed the gunboat and the tankers until they all sank. Then, as lifeboats carried the survivors shoreward, they, too, were machine-gunned. Two American bluejackets and one civilian were killed; eleven sailors were gravely wounded. Ambassador Joseph C. Grew, remembering the *Maine*, expected the United States to declare war.

Nothing of the sort happened. In Washington Tokyo's explanations and apologies were eagerly accepted. The State Department agreed that the attack had been a "mistake." It wasn't. A court of inquiry in Shanghai later brought out incontrovertible evidence that the sinking was ordered by responsible Japanese officers. The likeliest explanation was that it had been a test of American nerve. If so, the attackers had reason to be pleased. In Tokyo Grew was told that the Open Door policy was no longer applicable in China—although if the Chinese door was really shut, the biggest intruder was the Imperial Japanese Army. This inherent contradiction didn't trouble the aggressors. They knew now that America was a paper tiger. Gallup had polled voters with an opinion about the *Panay* incident and found that 70 percent favored complete withdrawal of U.S. citizens from the Far East, including clergymen and medical missions. "Apparently no American except Mr. Grew," Samuel Eliot Morison wrote acidly, "remembered the *Maine*."

Those who did might have pointed out that the *Maine* had blown up ninety-two miles from the continental United States; the *Panay* had sunk seven thousand miles away. In the 1930s distances meant more than in the Seventies. A courier couldn't take off on the next international flight. There weren't any. It would be another eighteen months before Pan American would inaugurate the first regular transatlantic passenger service. Even coast-to-coast flights still took a day and a night, and the China Clipper, flying mail only, flew from San Francisco to Manila in 59 hours 48 minutes.* Most Americans who went abroad (they were few) sailed on ocean liners. A superb steamer took New Yorkers to Rome in ten days; Californians could reach Tokyo in fifteen days if the captain was deft and the

---

* Of course, in the summer of 1938 Howard Hughes *did* encircle the world in less than four days, but he was a daredevil. A lot of people thought he did it for the publicity.

weather right. Only when this enormity of prewar oceans is borne in mind does the isolationism of the Depression become comprehensible.

But there were other factors. To pacifists a repetition of the last war's insensate horrors was unthinkable. America's European allies of 1918 were despised as people who welshed on their debts. England was a special demon; only along the eastern seaboard and in the South could anglophiles be found in great number. Inevitably antagonism toward the Old World found political expression. As Richard H. Rovere and Arthur M. Schlesinger Jr. have pointed out, "Among oceans, the Pacific has always been the favorite of American isolationists: this is true for the simple reason that the Pacific is not the Atlantic. . . . Isolationism is opposed to the introduction of 'European ideas' in American politics; it has never had to oppose the introduction of 'Asian ideas' because scarcely anyone has tried to introduce them. Among the more virulent isolationists, indeed, one detects almost a hatred of Europe." And, one might add, an even deeper hatred of those rich, overeducated Easterners who still doted on Europe.

In 1937 these feelings were compounded by ignorance. The Depression had obscured foreign affairs by turning the country inward. Americans simply hadn't had time for the troubles of others. At each deepening of the international crisis, their attention had been diverted by developments at home. The following parallels are suggestive:

Hitler becomes dictator	March 1933	Roosevelt becomes President
Germany rearms	March 1935	Second Hundred Days
Italy invades Ethiopia	October 1935	Assassination of Huey Long
Germany reoccupies Rhineland	March 1936	Supreme Court challenge to New Deal reaches peak
Formation of Rome-Berlin Axis	October 1936	Reelection campaign
Sino-Japanese War begins	July 1937	Labor strife
Austrian Anschluss	March 1938	Recession

The men who went down with the *Panay* were not forgotten, but the time to speak for them had not arrived, as the President had discovered two months before the incident. On the way back from his "look-see" trip he had stopped in Chicago to dedicate the Outer Link Bridge, a PWA project. He stayed overnight in the home of George William, Cardinal Mundelein, the first prelate to speak against totalitarianism. (It was Mundelein who had called Hitler "an Austrian paperhanger, and a poor one at that.") Next day, in his dedication speech, Roosevelt floated a trial balloon: "The epidemic of world lawlessness is spreading. When an epidemic of physical disease starts to spread, the community approves and joins in a quarantine of the patients in order to protect the health of the community against the spread of the disease." Peace-loving nations, he said, must act in concert with other nations of the world community. The colorful homily was typical of him. It caught the country's attention, as he had hoped, but the howls of protest were deafening. Editorials and his personal mail charged him with warmongering. Quarantine aggressors? It sounded like Woodrow Wilson. A typical wire to the White House read, IF YOU "HATE" WAR DO NOT TRY TO INCITE IT BY SUCH APPEALS. He had touched one of the country's most sensitive nerves. Overnight he was driven to the defensive. Later he confided to a friend, "It is a terrible thing to look over your shoulder when you are trying to lead and to find no one there."

Some of his constituents were there. Cardinal Mundelein was; so were Rabbi Stephen S. Wise of New York and Henry L. Stimson, who had been Hoover's Secretary of State. After the quarantine proposal was shot down, Stimson wrote, "Mr. Roosevelt seemed to conclude that the country was not ready for strong political medicine." Certainly the President was warier. Although the League of Nations condemned Japanese aggression, the State Department blandly joined Japanese diplomats in a conference on the situation in the Far East, which could hardly be construed as an act of quarantine. Ickes thought the President had "the appearance of a man who had more or less given up."

It was deceptive. The quality of FDR's leadership was complex, and consistency was not his strong suit. He was no Winston Churchill, a lone voice in the darkness. He had to remain in the cockpit of action, and therein lay his genius: he rarely let the distance between himself and the American consensus grow too wide. But he never retracted the quarantine speech. On the contrary, he quietly hewed to the same line. On December 21 he said American isolation from the twentieth century was impossible—he wouldn't want peace at any price—and in Kingston, Ontario, he promised that the United States would not "stand idly by" if Canada were attacked.

Every now and then he reaffirmed his hatred of war, or even claimed credit for neutrality legislation which he detested. He was the first President since Wilson to assert American presence in world affairs, and he was making his historic pivot when isolationist enthusiasm stood at flood tide. Any presidential move abroad, in any direction, provoked outcries. Liberal senators of both parties—Wheeler, Hiram Johnson, Pittman, Borah—were united in their stand for Fortress America. To Borah diplomacy was "power politics." *Time*, then staunchly isolationist, expressed anxiety over "Roosevelt's bent for international power politics," admired Borah, and for a time carried all foreign news under the standing head "Power Politics." Americans who had fought Franco in Spain lost their passports. American firms continued to provide half of Japan's oil and scrap iron needs—without which the war with China would have been impossible—and the National Council for the Prevention of War even tried to ban newsreels of the sinking *Panay* because they had "the unquestioned effect of arousing the American temper."

These were the months when the Dies committee discovered that the New Deal was Communistic while ignoring Father Coughlin, who gave a Nazi salute at a rally in the Bronx and shouted, "When we get through with the Jews in America, they'll think the treatment they received in Germany was nothing." Dies seemed to be blind to the activities of the Coughlin "Crusaders," the Citizen's Protective League, the Christian Front, American Patriots, Inc., and the German-American Bund. Right-wing organizations were trying to intimidate Congress, and sometimes they succeeded; the House rejected Roosevelt's request for funds to defend Guam because Tokyo might interpret it as a provocative gesture. At the final vote, 205 to 168, Congressman-adman Bruce Barton merrily cried out, "Guam, Guam with the wind!" Guam was gone, all right; the Japanese were to seize it the week after Pearl Harbor, and its recapture in August 1944 would cost the Marine Corps nearly eight thousand casualties.

Late in April 1937, when Congress extended the Neutrality Act, the *New York Times* observed editorially, "The passage of this misnamed neutrality bill may mark the high tide of isolationist sentiment in this country." The *Times* was too optimistic. The crest came nine months later, in a piece of legislative inanity introduced by Representative Louis Ludlow of Indiana. The Ludlow resolution stated that the authority of Congress to declare war could not become effective until confirmed by a majority vote in a nationwide referendum. President Roosevelt wrote Speaker William B. Bankhead that such an amendment would make the conduct of foreign affairs impossible. Nevertheless, a national poll reported that 73 percent of the people favored the idea, and only a second poll, showing support had dropped to 68 percent, sent the resolution back to the committee. At that, the House vote was 209 for the Ludlow resolution and 188 against it. A two-thirds majority being required, the country was saved from a situation in which, as Roosevelt had told Bankhead, other nations could have mistreated the United States with impunity.

"Democracy is sand driven by the wind," Mussolini said that year. At times it certainly looked that way. Shackled by neutrality legislation, the State Department watched helplessly while a Japanese general seized Kwangsi province, reached the border of Indochina, and shook hands with a French officer in Lang Son—Lang Son, the mountain pass through which munitions would pour into Vietnam for the next third of a century. Isolationists, always hypersensitive, sometimes seemed paranoid. The President's simplest moves were misinterpreted. When the king and queen of England decided to visit America (to heal the scars of which was known in polite society as *l'affaire Simpson*"), Congressman Hamilton Fish predicted that America would revert to its status as a British colony, Congressman George Holden Tinkham of Boston said that "a sinister secret diplomacy is now directing American foreign policy," and Senator Borah suggested that the President wait until there was a lull in the conversation and then ask casually when it would be convenient for Their Majesties to repay the $21,385,000,000 borrowed from Americans in 1914–18.

It is important to remember the character of this opposition. Because of it, and because the President knew America to be in jeopardy, he was caught in a historic dilemma. In the coming months he would be driven to set new precedents—extensions of executive authority which would later be abused by other chief executives who forgot that the power to declare war is vested in Congress. Yet had Roosevelt acted otherwise he would have been false to his oath, in Samuel Eliot Morison's opinion, and would have deserved impeachment. Unlike critics on the Hill, Roosevelt and Hull had access to European diplomatic cables. In 1938 they saw the Czechoslovakian crisis coming, saw through Hitler, and saw little fiber or imagination in the British and French governments. The fear of another war had infected Whitehall and the Quai d'Orsay. Certainly Roosevelt's Washington was not without its defeatists; in the last fiscal year the Army's plans for new equipment had been limited to 1,870 more Garand rifles. Perhaps the generals were only being realistic; they would have had a difficult time getting much more on the Hill. But Roosevelt saw an alternative. The most resolute hard-core isolationist, believing only in Fortress America, conceded the need for a strong Navy. Therefore the President rode down Pennsylvania Avenue on January 28, 1938, and asked for a billion-dollar "two-ocean" Navy.

He got it, in the Vinson Naval Act. At the same time he sent Hopkins to the Pacific coast for a survey; he wanted to know how quickly aircraft factories could convert to the production of warplanes. As Hopkins later noted, the President felt certain that war was coming to America "and he believed that air power would win it." His statement in 1938 that the United States needed 8,000 planes distressed almost everyone, including generals and admirals. An exception was Air Corps General Arnold. Briefing the commander in chief, Arnold had estimated that Germany then had 8,000 bombers and fighters. America had 1,650 pilots, a few hundred obsolete planes, and thirteen B-17s on order, to be delivered at the end of 1938. The general added pointedly that the lead time for modern weapons was very long. Roosevelt gave him the green light for expansion. Without that sanction, Arnold declared after the war, the sky over Normandy could not have been cleared of the Luftwaffe in 1944, and D-Day could not have been scheduled for June 6.

Lacking a military establishment in those years of the locust, Roosevelt was left with the power of persuasion, which had never been conspicuously successful in increasing the comity of nations. Still, he could try. His attempts to replace aggression with international understanding had failed in Spain and China. Undaunted, he wrote Prime Minister Neville Chamberlain proposing a great conference at which treaties would be altered without resorting to force and all nations assured access to raw materials. Chamberlain declined. He had his own plan. Roosevelt's conference, he replied, would merely undermine Great Britain's new policy to grant "a measure of appeasement" to the dictators.

He didn't say how large the measure would be, but the world was about to find out. In the spring of 1938 the German Führer screamed that Germans living in the Sudetenland—mountainous, heavily fortified Czech territory along the German frontier—were being mistreated. Goebbels further accused Prague of harboring Soviet warplanes and permitting the Russians to build airdromes on Czechoslovakian soil. Despite Czech protests, these accusations were repeated, and at the height of the Nazi campaign of denunciation, former President Thomas Masaryk died. Prague police suppressed Sudeten demonstrations during the funeral, Sudeten deputies boycotted the Czech parliament, and Hitler rattled his saber. Suddenly Europe was in the middle of a desperate crisis—and the American public, thanks to radio, had a ringside seat.

There had been few precedents for the transatlantic radio coverage of contemporary history. NBC and CBS had sent home short-wave summaries of the London Naval Conference of 1930; six BBC announcers had described the coronation of George VI; early in 1938 London and Chicago had exchanged signals; and that same year Americans heard their first coast-to-coast broadcast, between Al Goodman's orchestra in New York and W. C. Fields in Hollywood. Regularly scheduled commentators such as Lowell Thomas and rapid-fire Floyd Gibbons (he delivered a fantastic 217 words a minute) took their material right off the wire service tickers. CBS didn't even have a regular Washington correspondent; when one was needed, Senator Lewis B. Schwellenbach filled in. There had been nothing approaching serious radio coverage of a big European story until the Nazis lunged into Austria six months before the Czech crisis. With all Europe in an uproar, Paul White, a CBS executive in New York, called William L. Shirer in London and asked for a half-hour Paris-Rome-Berlin-Vienna-London "roundup." He asked, "Can you do it?"

There was every reason to say no. Ed Murrow was six hundred miles away in Vienna, and with the German armies marching, vital lines could be cut at any time. Shirer and Murrow would have to recruit inexperienced commentators in five great capitals, hire engineers, lease transmitters, and coordinate a live broadcast down to the second. Furthermore, there was almost no time. New York wanted the roundup that evening—and the day was a Sunday; offices were closed, technicians were on holiday, and responsibility for communications was in the hands of caretakers who had no authority and could scarcely understand sophisticated radio jargon in their own language, let alone in English. Technically the challenge was almost insurmountable. The very idea was madness. Shirer said they would try.

He got through to Murrow, who was watching gangs of Seyss-

Inquart thugs racing between the chestnut trees and shouting, *"Ein Reich, ein Volk, ein Führer!"* Bit by bit the two young Americans put a skeletal framework together: Frank Gervasi of INS in Rome, Edgar Ansel Mowrer of the *Chicago Daily News* in Paris, a newspaper friend of Shirer's in Berlin, and a lady M.P. who agreed to leave her weekend in the country and speak from a BBC studio. All transmitting problems were solved except Rome's—the Italians couldn't figure out a way to "landline" Gervasi's voice across the Swiss border to a big transmitter in Geneva. They *could* put him through to London via radiophone, however, so he read his account from a booth, and Shirer reread it to New York. Such were the humble beginnings of the world news "roundup," with all its implications for the future and American public opinion.

In July 1914 Karl von Wiegand of the United Press had cabled 138 words on Austria-Hungary's ultimatum to Serbia which set off World War I, and he had been reprimanded for wasting money. Now, despite the strength of isolationism, Americans wanted to know what was happening overseas. There was a lull in late spring; the Czechs stood firm and Hitler backed down, agreeing to negotiations. His absorption of Austria, however, had altered the strategic complexion of central Europe; the expanded Reich now threatened Czechoslovakia from three sides. Prague continued to be refractory, and thus an embarrassment to England and France, who were committed to the Czechs by treaty and were beginning to wish they weren't. But the talks dragged on all summer. Apparently nothing was going to happen.

Then came the German chancellor's September 12 address to the annual Nazi rally in Nuremberg. As *Variety* explained, America's two big networks were handling the event differently. NBC would carry the speech live, but had adopted a policy of "playing down the current agitation and tension in Europe." CBS decided it was history and built it up. On that Monday morning CBS announcers reminded listeners that "the entire civilized world is anxiously awaiting the speech of Adolf Hitler, whose single word may plunge all of Europe into another world war." At 2:15 P.M. an announcer cut into the net to say, "We interrupt the program of Enoch Light in order to bring our listeners the world-awaited talk on Germany's foreign policy to be delivered by Adolf Hitler to the Nazi Congress at Nuremberg. . . . We take you now to Nuremberg, Germany."

The address, relayed by a shortwave station in Berlin, came through clearly. Next day *Variety* was to comment: "A dynamic, spellbinding speaker, the broadcast was most impressive when he worked up the thousands of Nazis in attendance to frenzied cheers, 'Heil Hitlers' and 'Sieg Heils' ('Hail Victory')."

Kurt Heiman of CBS's New York staff translated passages of the address as it ran along, with some help from Kurt von Forstmeyer in Nuremberg. *Variety* complained that NBC's man "appeared to be soft-pedaling" and that he refrained from editorial comment. CBS's commentary came from an obscure, sixty-year-old Harvard graduate of German descent named Hans von Kaltenborn. At 3:36 P.M., after Hitler had finished speaking, Kaltenborn came on with a thorough analysis: "Adolf Hitler has spoken and the world has listened. . . . There was in it, and through it all, a very definite declaration that Germany would no longer tolerate the oppression, as he called it, of the Sudeten Germans in Czechoslovakia, and that Czechoslovakia would have to reach a settlement with the Sudeten Germans or the Germans would see to it that a settlement was reached." Kaltenborn didn't miss a detail, noting all such new information as Hitler's revelation that 280,000 Germans were working around the clock on the Siegfried Line.

American newspapers, which had not yet come to terms with radio journalism, published special editions when a big story broke. These were hurriedly printed and newsboys were sent into the streets calling, "Extra! Extra! Read all about it!" Suddenly they were on every corner shouting about mobilization in Germany, Italy, Czechoslovakia, France, and England. Great troop movements were under way. Fleets were at sea. Aircraft had been sent to camouflage fields. Smudged newsprint photographs showed Chamberlain, always carrying an umbrella, scooting back and forth between Godesberg, Berchtesgaden, and London. English children carrying tiny gas masks were being taken into the country, Frenchmen were digging trenches in public parks, and Europe was expected to burst into flame at any moment.

Millions of Americans, hearing Hitler for the first time over shortwave, were shaken by the depth of his hatred; on his lips the Teutonic language sounded cruel, dripping with venom. Those fluent in German—Franklin Roosevelt was one—could take it straight. The rest depended upon translators, and especially on CBS's chief analyst, who, *Variety* reported, was drawing "the greatest and most profoundly interested listening audience in radio history, next to the English king's abdication address." It was an exhausting ordeal for a man of Kaltenborn's age. During eighteen days starting that Monday he delivered eighty-five extemporaneous broadcasts from Studio Nine on the seventeenth floor of the CBS Building in New York, dozing on a deskside cot whenever the tension eased. On the nineteenth day he emerged, rumpled, haggard, and with a slight alteration in his name which had been made earlier because of the public animosity toward Germany. He was now plain H. V. Kaltenborn, and at that moment he was one of the most famous men in the United States.

At 7:30 that Monday evening, when the Czechoslovakian countdown began, Robert Trout had taken over the CBS network:

> TROUT: Tonight, as nations of the world digest the long-anticipated talk of Chancellor Adolf Hitler at Nuremberg, we will hear in rapid succession from London, Berlin, Prague, and Paris. . . . The four speakers are to be: Edward R. Murrow, chief of Columbia's European staff, speaking from London; Melvin Whiteleather of the Associated Press, speaking from Berlin; William L. Shirer, Columbia's Central European representative, speaking from Prague; and John T. Whitaker, of the Chicago *Daily News* Syndicate, speaking from Paris. Mr. Murrow will speak to you from London, England. . . .
>
> MURROW: There is little optimism in London tonight. . . .

It sounded very professional. Only a veteran journalist could have sensed how thin CBS coverage was. Despite their elaborate titles, thirty-year-old Murrow and thirty-four-year-old Shirer were still the sole CBS analysts on the program—were, for that matter, the network's only two men in Europe. They had been scurrying around the continent talking to one another from phone booths. It was a zany, patchwork quilt they were putting together, a kind of Rube Goldberg approach to broadcasting, and one explanation for its success—which was enormous—was European ignorance of what was going on. Finding out took a while; when Eric Sevareid arrived in the Netherlands a few months later as a CBS reinforcement, the Dutch were bewildered when they learned that he intended to send back news of the day. All previous broadcasts from Holland to America had been about tulips and windmills. To Europeans broadcasting was entertainment—as indeed it had been for most Americans.

To the astonishment of conservatives in the news media, radio coverage of European turmoil not only held its own, it became increasingly efficient. Kaltenborn, installed in Studio Nine with his sandwiches and black coffee, was fed streams of accurate information from the jerry-built Murrow-Shirer structure across the ocean. Because censorship was gagging native journalists there, while American speech remained free, people in the United States knew more about the September crisis than European listeners. The BBC wouldn't even allow Winston Churchill to speak; there was suspicion (well founded) that he might try to sabotage the peace. One British magazine editor suggested that readers who really wanted to know what was going on in the Czechoslovakian crisis ought to tune to shortwave broadcasts from the United States.

Murrow was rapidly becoming almost as famous as Kaltenborn. He made thirty-five broadcasts himself that September and set up another 116 from eighteen European cities. As the European chief he was Studio Nine's link with the continent; when communications became difficult or fadeouts frequent, the fascinated country would hear Kaltenborn say in a querulous hush, "Calling Ed Murrow! Calling Ed Murrow!" In the first days of the crisis this sort of thing was infrequent. European staffs had improved enormously since spring; one Czech switchboard girl was keeping track of a hundred placed calls. The weather was so clear that two-way conversations were possible. It was actually possible to hold "round table" discussions with correspondents overseas. The listening audience, holding "crisis maps" which the networks mailed on request, could listen to Murrow or Shirer talking to Kaltenborn or Trout, and follow reported movements of troops toward the Maginot Line, say, or in Silesia. It was almost like Monopoly, if you didn't think about it too much.

Then, on September 15, the fourth day, something went wrong. With armies in place, diplomatic confrontations reported hourly, and Hitler and Chamberlain eyeball to eyeball—no one then knew how quickly the prime minister's eyes would become shifty—the weather went bad. Shortwave transmissions, unlike those over ordinary frequencies, are highly vulnerable to atmospheric conditions. Day after day CBS frequencies remained inaudible; Kaltenborn called Murrow in vain, and was left to rely on cabled news. Suddenly, to the horror of CBS, NBC men in Europe began coming through loud and clear. The other network had found a fantastic solution, relaying shortwave over a Capetown to Buenos Aires to New York circuit. Broadcasts originating from Europe were traveling three times the distance on this circuit, but the delay was only a few seconds. And they were clear. CBS caught on, though direct broadcasts were still preferred.

The weather over the Atlantic was still unspeakable (what *was* going on out there?) when events in Prague reached a climax. The Czechs, as punishment for standing firm, were being treated shabbily by their two great allies. At 2:15 A.M. on September 21, the British and French ministers to Czechoslovakia routed President Eduard Benes out of bed and bluntly told him that their governments intended to break their covenants. In spite of their pledged word, they would not march; either the Czechs would capitulate to the Nazi dictator or they would be left to fight alone. All through the day Benes, staggering from fatigue, consulted with his cabinet, party leaders, and generals. At about five o'clock that afternoon of September 21 his government submitted. A Czech communiqué explained to the world: "We had no choice, because we were left alone." Benes said, "We have been basely betrayed."

At 5 P.M. it was still only 11 A.M. in New York and New England. Radio engineers were still complaining of the weather at sea, and merchant sailors were muttering about the strange copper-colored sky at last evening's sunset, but no one else worried about it. The forecast in that morning's paper wouldn't have panicked anyone. It read: "Rain and cooler."

It actually said just that.

In 1938 the United States Weather Bureau was but a shadow of its future self. It lacked the superb instruments of the next generation: radarscopes, jet-propelled aerial surveillance, and weather-reporting satellites equipped with television cameras. Its chief devices then were the sixteenth-century thermometer, the seventeenth-century mercurial barometer, and the medieval weathervane. The greatest need was oceanographic information. Outposts on land could exchange reports with one another, but the seas were mysterious. Meteorologists relied entirely upon voluntary observations from merchant ships and aircraft. In the Depression the government wasn't going to let weathermen fly around in expensive planes of their own, observing conditions there. So the meteorologists wondered, or guessed. They had long known that one of their guesses might be tragically wrong, and now the law of probability was closing in.

Yet it would be wrong to limn them as helpless scapegoats. Not to put too fine a point on it, the Weather Bureau was a slack outfit. *Some* new skills were known, to others if not to them. Estimating the approach of a big storm by studying wind velocity and barometric readings, a proficiency required of all licensed navigators, baffled many veteran forecasters. And when one remembers their great need for data, it is an astonishing fact that key meteorologists did not even attempt to phone one another that day until the blow had already fallen, carrying the telephone lines with it. Ironically, the *New York Times* ran an editorial praising the bureau on September 21. The humdrum forecast was published on the lower left corner of page 27. Nowhere was there any suggestion that the most destructive hurricane in American history—and the first to hit Long Island and New England since September 23, 1815—was on its way.

It is possible to trace the progress of the storm with some confidence. Atlantic hurricanes, known to seamen as tropical cyclones, begin as small disturbances in the doldrums, west of the Sahara Desert and east of the Cape Verde Islands, a calm area between the trade winds that blow from the northeast and southeast. The first stage of a tropical cyclone occurs when a column of hot moist air starts to rise. Cooler air moves in below it, the cycle accelerates, and the eastward rotation of the earth sends it spiraling off counterclockwise toward the western hemisphere. The longer the cyclone is over the water, the more powerful it becomes. This one was first sighted at 9:30 P.M. on September 16 by the captain of a Brazilian freighter, the S.S. *Alegrete*. It was 350 miles northeast of Puerto Rico, and the captain radioed that he could find nothing good to say about it.

The closest U.S. weather station was in Jacksonville, Florida. It was also the one most experienced in judging hurricanes. But the storm lay in the area most dreaded by American meteorologists—the triangle of sea between Long Island, Bermuda, and Georgia. Weather there was notoriously unstable, yet they had no idea what was happening. They kept listening for signals from afflicted ships. None came; if any merchantmen were there, they were either lacking in public spirit or already in Davy Jones's locker. Despite its ignorance, Jacksonville made the right moves. Warnings went out on

Sunday, September 18, and Monday, September 19. Floridians, accustomed to this sort of thing, bought candles and boarded up windows. Many from New England, anxious to miss the winds, took the train home. At that point trains were moving faster than the cyclonic winds. They weren't going to miss anything after all.

Monday night the hurricane turned away from Miami. Jacksonville dutifully reported that the storm was "moving rapidly north" and only possibly "east of north." The eye was then estimated to be 275 miles south of Cape Hatteras; that is, just off North Carolina. At Hatteras it automatically passed from Jacksonville's jurisdiction to Washington's, and here an incompetence bordering on the criminal began to creep into forecasts. To grasp what was happening one should bear in mind that a fully developed hurricane, blowing 75 mph, is as powerful as 500 Nagasaki-type atomic bombs and contains more electricity than the entire United States uses in six months. That is an *ordinary* hurricane. *This* cyclone was churning around at over 200 mph. How far over is a matter of speculation, but on Wednesday the Harvard University observatory at Blue Hill, ninety miles from the vortex, was measuring a steady 121 mph, with 186 mph gusts, and New York City, far west of the storm center, noted 120 mph on top of the Empire State Building. Washington didn't know that, but it had a report from the skipper of the Cunard White Star liner *Carinthia*. His barometer measured its pressure at 27.85, one of the lowest barometric readings ever taken off the Atlantic coast. Nevertheless, the Washington station, staffed by the most seasoned meteorologists in the country, dropped the word "hurricane" from its forecast. As late as 2 P.M. September 21, when the storm had torn up Atlantic City's boardwalk and was transporting entire houses across Long Island Sound, Washington reported that the "tropical storm" was rapidly blowing out to sea.

New York and Boston went along with the Washington brass. Every meteorologist knew there was a lot of commotion just offshore, but it had been 123 years since a tropical cyclone had turned inward, and they just couldn't believe it would happen now. As it passed along the Carolinas, Virginia, Delaware, and New Jersey, the forecasters, snug inland, watched their barometers dip and rise again as the eye moved on. They sighed; *that* was over. Yet their instruments were warning them that it was far from over. Since 8:30 A.M. the hurricane's isobars—lines of equal barometric pressure—had been lengthening into ovals, all pointing north. Nevertheless, the forecasters kept talking about "shifting gales," as though this were a good day to fly heavy kites. Their folly was compounded by a cruel coincidence. The hurricane was coming when the moon was nearest the earth, and the sun and moon, pulling together in phase, caused tides a foot higher than usual. And the storm wave was going to hit precisely at high tide.

The weathermen hadn't thought of that; implicit in their logs was the assumption that once Miami was saved, it was all over. What they had failed to see (apart from their own instruments) was that just when the storm seemed about to swing northeastward at Cape Hatteras, its path had been blocked by an unusually broad high-pressure plateau covering almost the entire North Atlantic. Caught between that and another high pressure area just inland, the cyclone was unable to spread out and dissipate its power. On the contrary, the winds doubled and redoubled in force.

Long Island and New England had been lashed by rain for four straight days and nights. The air there was unnaturally warm and muggy. Ears felt queer, because atmospheric pressure was decreasing. In Vermont people noticed the smell of the seashore in the air. Hurricanes love nothing so much as warmth and dampness, and this one lurched toward the broad moist carpet six hundred miles long. Moreover, at the instant it crossed the shore, another dreadful principle would come to bear upon it. Usually hurricanes weaken over land, but the soggy ground, extending all the way to Canada, meant the storm would continue to blow as hard as though it had been in the Caribbean—picking up speed from the sticky air until the eye was moving at 60 mph, as fast as a tornado, fast enough to reach Montreal that same night.

The 1 P.M. news broadcast from New York brought the first sign that some forecasters were belatedly coming to terms with reality. The announcer said the storm had changed course and would "probably hit Long Island." That was something, more warning than New England was going to get, but it was too late for effective precautions. Besides, the vast majority of people missed the broadcast, and the Coast Guard had not been alerted. The richest seaboard in the world, from Cape May to Maine, was completely unprotected. Among the striking stories which later came to light was the experience of a Long Islander who had bought a barometer a few days earlier in a New York store. It arrived in the morning post September 21, and to his annoyance the needle pointed below 29, where the dial read "Hurricanes and Tornadoes." He shook it and banged it against a wall; the needle wouldn't budge. Indignant, he repacked it, drove to the post office, and mailed it back. While he was gone, his house blew away.

It happened that quickly. One moment the barometer read 27.95 inches. A moment later the winds struck, and people on the south shore saw what one of them described as "a thick and high bank of fog rolling in fast from the ocean." He added, "When it came closer we saw that it wasn't fog. It was water." With gusts already bellowing and the wind raving at every door jamb, the great wall of brine struck the beach between Babylon and Patchogue at 2:30 P.M. So mighty was the power of that first storm wave that its impact registered on a seismograph in Sitka, Alaska, while the spray, carried northward at well over a hundred miles an hour, whitened windows in Montpelier, Vermont. As the torrential forty-foot wave approached, some Long Islanders jumped into cars and raced inland. No one knows precisely how many lost that race for their lives, but the winners later estimated that they had to keep the speedometer over 50 mph all the way. Manicured lawns a mile inland at Quogue were under breakers two feet high, and a cottage near there floated away with ten people on its roof.

J. P. Morgan's multimillion-dollar estate at Glen Cove was blown to flinders. Thirty-room mansions at Westhampton were swept away, and owners couldn't rebuild because the land had gone with them. Seventeen people were huddled chest-deep in brine on the second floor of one of these châteaux; then the walls collapsed. The 190-foot Mackay radio tower, out toward Montauk Point, was gone. The Bridgehampton freight station had been moved to the wrong side of the tracks. Pullman cars weighing sixty-seven tons were rocking. Fishing craft were split apart, fishermen's shacks were sailing into Connecticut. The entire coastline had been altered, and obviously this was only a beginning; thirteen million people lay in the storm's path, which could now be projected through New Haven, Hartford, Springfield, Northampton, Vermont, and Montreal. Had the hurricane come three weeks earlier, six thousand dead could have been expected. Even as it was, Long Island Sound, beaten into one solid mass of foam, was hurling corpses at the wreckage of what had been comfortable cottages only that morning.

At 3:40 P.M., when the forward edge of the doughnut-shaped storm was uprooting Yale's famous old elms, the eye of the storm reached Long Island. The survivors assumed that they had been saved. The sun came out, the sky was blue, zephyrs whispered in the wreckage. Then the distant roaring drew near again, and they knew they were in for it again. Actually, the worst was to come; the mightiest force in a hurricane lies in the swifter, titanic winds behind the eye. The most remarkable accounts of this phase will never be told, for the participants were dead before evening. We know that the second storm wave destroyed the Westhampton section of the outer barrier beach, blew the dunes away, leveled most of the houses left standing, flooded the Maidstone Club golf course, and swamped the Montauk Highway and the Long Island Railroad tracks at Napeague Beach, temporarily cutting Long Island in two. At the height of it, one couple actually swam across Moriches Bay with two dogs and a Coastguardsman. Arriving, the drenched woman dismayed bystanders by announcing that Long Island was sinking. That part of it nearly did. Of 179 Westhampton houses, 153 had completely vanished, and most of the others were too battered ever to be inhabited again. In and around them were twenty-nine corpses.

In effect, Long Island was serving as a breakwater for the seventy-mile stretch of Connecticut shore across the sound, including New Haven and Bridgeport (which were having other problems). The exposed Connecticut and Rhode Island shores east of Montauk Point were being belted by even stronger seas, and the city struck hardest was Providence, at the mouth of Narragansett Bay. One huge wave, a hundred feet high, swept up the bay, crushed the docks into kindling, and broke near City Hall, drowning pedestrians outside. The sea pulled people from automobiles, sometimes from behind the wheel, thereby saving their lives. When it subsided, downtown Providence was under thirteen feet of water. Policemen in motorboats patrolled the Mall and Exchange Place. The headlights of thousands of automobiles shone under water, and short-circuited car horns blew steadily, like a traffic jam in a nightmare.

Meanwhile, the hurricane had been thundering through Connecticut and Massachusetts. There was a grayness around everything that afternoon, as though the storm were veiling its atrocities. Wesleyan University's hundred-year-old stone chapel steeple had been blown down. New London was burning. In Hartford and Springfield men were toiling with sandbags, holding back the Connecticut River, already at flood. Among the waiting mobs of refugees—no one had time for them now—was Katharine Hepburn; she had waded to safety from her parents' summer cottage an hour before it was carried away.

By nine o'clock that evening Dartmouth College, in New Hampshire, was as embattled as Yale had been at 4 P.M., with the wind building and the rain slanting vertically, but by the next morning the sky, as the Weather Bureau cheerfully reported, was clear. Conditions were hardly normal, though. The New Haven Railroad estimated that 1,200 trees and 700 telephone poles lay across its tracks. The Shore Line of the New York, New Haven and Hartford was trying to find a missing train and wondering what to do with a 300-foot steamship that lay across its tracks in New London. American Airlines was searching for an empty plane that had blown away from Logan Field in Boston. Not one Connecticut highway was open. The *Hartford Courant* described September 21 as the "most calamitous day" in the history of the state. "As near as the crippled communications can indicate," the editorial said, "no community of any size escaped damage. New Haven is still dark and battered. The heart of New London is in smoking ruins."

The Red Cross reported 700 people killed and 1,754 injured, and that 63,000 had lost their homes. President Roosevelt sent Hopkins north with 100,000 men from the Army, the Coast Guard, and the WPA. Before long they had the current running again, but much that had been lost in the storm could never be brought back. New England mourned its trees; 16,000 were down in Springfield alone, and someone calculated that the hurricane had toppled enough wood to build 200,000 houses. The season's apple crop was a total loss. Maimed shore cottages that had lost their beaches were being auctioned off for pittances. And because only 5 percent of the losses had been insured, many factories which had been in trouble since the Crash went out of business.

For a while an imaginative beggar roamed Boston Common wearing a placard which read, "For 25¢ I will listen to your story of the hurricane." One of the best tales was about the American flag on New York's Whitehall Building. It had been torn to shreds. Inside, a few feet away, was the regional office of the U.S. Weather Bureau.

Long Islanders and New Englanders traveling to other parts of the country that fall were startled by the number of well-informed men and women who knew nothing of the hurricane. In part this reflected the magnitude of the disaster. For the first twenty-four hours the *New York Times* hadn't been able to get any reliable news at all. Even the *Boston Globe*'s editors, who could see overturned freighters in their own harbor, didn't publish an interview with a survivor until Friday, two days after the big wind. That same morning the *Times,* piecing together scattered reports, realized that the country had suffered a greater disaster than the Chicago fire, the San Francisco earthquake, or any Mississippi flood. Then the paper ran eight-column headlines about the hurricane. Surprisingly, few readers read them or retained what they read; within a week they had forgotten it, and the story has been one of the forgotten fragments of American history.

The big reason for this mnemonic failure was that the country's attention was still riveted on Czechoslovakia. The crisis in Europe had become the first of those mass communications phenomena which might be called the shared simultaneous experience. Unlike those which followed—the Army-McCarthy hearings of 1954, for example, or the Kennedy funeral of 1963—Czech developments were not televised. Yet the impact was immense. Listeners became helpless spectators following events which they knew might alter their own lives. After the Munich Pact was signed on September 29, CBS hailed the arrival of radio "not merely as a disseminator of the news, but as a social power."

This was true, but it was not all good. Over radio, fear had fed on fear; everyone had wanted a happy ending, and when eventually it did end, the best possible construction was put upon the agreement. Chamberlain was the hero of the hour, as much in America as in Britain. It took a while for people to realize that he was a weak old man who had sold out a resolute and embattled ally for a worthless Hitler promise. Churchill knew it, and said, "Britain and France had to choose between war and dishonor. They chose dishonor. They will have war." Roosevelt knew it; to his ambassador in Portugal he wrote, "The dictator threat from Europe is a good deal closer to the United States." Murrow and Shirer knew it. Meeting in Paris, they agreed that war was likely after next year's harvest. And H. V. Kaltenborn knew it; even before Chamberlain's visit to Berchtesgaden he said, "My own feeling is that it will be little more than a truce. There is grave doubt as to whether or not the visit will bring peace."

The people were beginning to understand. A *Fortune* survey showed that only 11.6 percent of the American people thought the Munich agreement commendable, and 76.2 percent believed that the United States would participate in a general European war. The percentage held in every part of the country. "This is news," the editors commented. "Eighteen months ago only about 22 percent of the population thought that we would be drawn into a foreign war in the next two or three years. Now more than three times that many believed that we actually would have been embroiled in the war that was so narrowly averted. . . . Thus has been shattered our sense of secure alliance upon the sentiment: 'Thank God for two wide oceans!'"

In short, the Czech crisis had awakened America from a long slumber, and the country was anxious, biting its nails, drumming its fingers. Bombs, invasions, war—all that had been unthinkable as recently as last summer—were suddenly very real. Radio had transformed the country into one vast theater crowded with skittish spectators, and four weeks after the Munich Pact a brilliant twenty-three-year-old producer shouted, "Fire!"

The journalistic hoax has a long, picaresque, and not entirely dishonorable history. Edgar Allan Poe became famous on the strength of his "Unparalleled Adventure of One Hans Pfall"; H. L. Mencken's spurious account of how the first bathtub was invented became a national joke and found its way into some encyclopedias. The most successful of all, Richard Adams Locke's Moon Hoax of 1835, told wide-eyed readers of the *New York Sun* that one "Sir John Herschel," using "an immense telescope based on an entirely new principle," had identified bat-man inhabitants of the moon. Poe, Mencken, and Locke were quickly forgiven, for newspapers, being what Marshall McLuhan calls a "cool medium," are not likely to incite a riot. The mass media are "hot," and radio has never been hotter than the night before Halloween in 1938.

The recipient of that heat was then the most versatile and successful young man on Broadway. Actor-director, producer, at the age of twenty Orson Welles had been radio's "Lamont Cranston" (*The Shadow*). He had dressed Julius Caesar in a business suit, put on a Negro *Macbeth* with Haiti as the background—and made money with both. When his WPA production of *The Cradle Will Rock* was ordered canceled on opening night by Washington—on political grounds—Welles defied the government. He and his theatrical company led the customers through the streets to an empty theater. The play became an enormous success, and CBS invited the prodigy of show business to broadcast a one-hour drama from the network's Studio One each Sunday evening at 8 P.M. There were no sponsors; the program was what was called "sustaining." CBS wasn't making much of a gesture. It couldn't sell the time, because its NBC competitor, the Chase and Sanborn Hour, was the most popular program of the week. Don Ameche was the master of ceremonies there, Dorothy Lamour the singer, and high comedy was provided by ventriloquist Edgar Bergen and his redheaded dummy Charlie McCarthy. Carved by a Chicago bartender for $35, and based on a Bergen sketch of a Chicago newsboy, Charlie had been No. 1 for eighteen months. His witty, insolent personality dominated Sunday prime time.

When it came to a choice between great theater and listening to Bergen talk to himself, most Americans preferred Bergen. Both the Crosley and Hooper radio censuses conducted the week before that Halloween gave the Chase and Sanborn Hour 34.7 percent of the total possible audience and Welles's Mercury Theater 3.6 percent. (There was a hidden factor here, withheld from advertisers because it would damage their morale; we shall enounter it presently. Still, the figures doubtless held up on an average Sunday.) Of the 32 million families then living in the United States, about 27.5 million owned radios. Thus when CBS played the opening strains of the Tchaikovsky Piano Concerto in B Flat Minor—the Mercury's opening theme each week—Welles could assume that about a million people were tuned to him. On October 30 that figure would grow.

Roosevelt had sent a personal message to Hitler on September 26 asking him to stop issuing ultimatums and proposing instead a conference of "nations directly interested in the present controversy" as an alternative to the battlefield. He suggested it be held immediately in some "neutral spot in Europe." It never came off—other conferences were being arranged—but on that same day Orson Welles had an inspiration. Why not dramatize H. G. Wells's *War of the Worlds?* His agent thought the idea silly, and Howard Koch, his writer, believed it was impossible. The young producer insisted. Being a strong personality, he won, and Koch went off to translate Wells into Welles. On Tuesday, October 25, five days before the show, he phoned John Houseman, the Mercury's editor. He was throwing in the towel, he said; science fantasy couldn't be turned into radio drama. The Mercury's secretary agreed. "You can't do it!" she cried. "Those old Martians are just a lot of nonsense! We're going to make fools of ourselves! Absolute fools!" Houseman thought of substituting *Lorna Doone,* but Orson wouldn't discuss it, so writing the Wells script became a team effort. By Thursday they had a show—a dull show, everyone agreed.

Then someone—later no one remembered who—made a suggestion. Wouldn't it be a good idea to make the whole thing a simulated news broadcast? As realistic as possible? Even a voice like Roosevelt's? It was all possible, including the voice; Kenneth Delmar, whom Fred Allen would later make famous as Senator Claghorn, could summon commanding tones. The actor who would play Carl Phillips, the first network "announcer," dug into the CBS record library and listened, over and over, to the semihysterical radio commentator's description of the *Hindenburg* exploding at Lakehurst. Welles himself would appear as a Princeton scientist. They were to open with a weather report, dance music, and then the special bulletins. The cast thought Welles dragged this part much too long. He shook his head; that, he explained, was what gave it authenticity.

It certainly did. The public had become accustomed to sudden interruptions during the Czech crisis; each had provided a significant development later confirmed in the newspapers. Radio, indeed, had become the accepted vehicle for important announcements. And there were other circumstances which would increase authenticity. Since the 1936 election, *Fortune* had found, people had more faith in commentators than in newspapers. Indeed, for many the line between reality (news) and fantasy (drama) had become hopelessly blurred. In one of the more penetrating postmortems of the performance, *Variety* doubted that "any explanation would have prevented some people taking the whole thing in deadly earnest," because "evidence of the seriousness with which many listeners take radio dramas is the concerned letters numerous dialers write in about the characters and happenings in the daily serial shows."

It was, furthermore, an era in which people still respected authority, and Kenneth Delmar would be identified as "the Secretary of the Interior." For audiences in New York and New Jersey, real streets were to be named: the Pulaski Skyway, South Street, route 23. Added to all these, a Princeton University study later found, were intellectual and emotional immaturity, Depression insecurity ("Things have happened so thick and fast since my grandfather's day that we can't hope to know what might happen now," one respondent said afterward) and, outweighing everything else, the "recent war scare in Europe."

Welles seems to have had some apprehension. The script opened and closed with explanations that this was only a play, and four CBS station breaks were to interrupt the actors and say the same thing. All that was fine, given their assumption that listeners would join them at eight o'clock and stay till the end. But the assumption was unsound. Here the rating surveys' little secret assumed tremendous significance. Their discovery, which would have discouraged sponsors, was that when a commercial or an unpopular entertainer came on, people reached over and twisted their radio dials. Everyone enjoyed Edgar Bergen and Charlie McCarthy, but they were only part of a variety show.

The Mercury's relatively small but faithful audience heard the Tchaikovsky theme, the introduction, an authentic weather report, and "We now take you to the Meridian Room in the Hotel Park Plaza in downtown New York, where you will be entertained by the music of Ramón Raquello and his orchestra." Periodic bulletins traced the progress of Carl Phillips and Professor Pierson to the New Jersey town of Grovers Mill. There were sirens and crowd noises in the background. At that moment, 8:12 P.M., Charlie McCarthy finished his first skit and a soothing voice began to recommend the rich flavor of Chase and Sanborn coffee.

Nearly six million people spun dials to CBS. This is what they heard:

ANNOUNCER: . . . I'll move the microphone nearer. Here. (*Pause*) Now we're not more than twenty-five feet away. Can you hear it now? Oh, Professor Pierson!

PIERSON: Yes, Mr. Phillips?

ANNOUNCER: Can you tell us the meaning of that scraping noise inside the thing?

PIERSON: Possibly the unequal cooling of its surface.

ANNOUNCER: Do you still think it's a meteor, Professor?

PIERSON: I don't know what to think. The metal casing is definitely extraterrestrial . . . not found on this earth. Friction with the earth's atmosphere usually tears holes in a meteorite. The thing is smooth and, as you can see, of cylindrical shape.

PHILLIPS: Just a minute! Something's happening! Ladies and gentlemen, this is terrific. The end of the thing is beginning to flake off! The top is beginning to rotate like a screw! The thing must be metal!

Excited crowd voices were heard; then back to the microphone.

ANNOUNCER: Ladies and gentlemen, this is the most terrifying thing I have ever witnessed! . . . Wait a minute! Someone's *crawling out of the hollow top.* Someone or . . . something. I can see peering out of that black hole two luminous discs . . . are they eyes? It might be a face. It might be . . .

(*Shout of awe from the crowd*)

ANNOUNCER (*sobbing and retching*): Good heavens, something's wriggling out of the shadow like a gray snake. Now it's another one, and another! They look like tentacles to me. There, I can see the thing's body. It's large as a bear and it glistens like wet leather. But that face. It . . . it's indescribable. I can hardly force myself to keep looking at it. The eyes are black and gleam like a serpent. The mouth is V-shaped with saliva dripping from its rimless lips that seem to quiver and pulsate. . . .

The announcer temporarily loses control. Silence. A few bars of "Clair de Lune." A second announcer, cool and professional, says, "We are bringing you an eyewitness account of what's happening on the Wilmuth farm, Grovers Mill, New Jersey." A few more bars of Debussy, then the cool announcer again: "We now return you to Carl Phillips at Grovers Mill." Policemen, it develops, are advancing on the thing, but the Martians turn a sheet of flame upon them. Screams are heard, and unearthly shrieks. A barn blows up; then the mike goes dead. In comes the second announcer, saying quietly, "Ladies and gentlemen, due to circumstances beyond our control, we are unable to continue the broadcast from Grovers Mill. Evidently there's some difficulty with our field transmission. However, we will return you to that point at the earliest opportunity." Now the action escalates. The state police have been burned to cinders. "Brigadier General Montgomery Smith, commander of the State Militia in Trenton," makes an official statement, in behalf of the governor of New Jersey, placing the counties of Mercer and Middlesex, as far west as Princeton and east to Jamesburg (all real places), under martial law. New spaceships are landing, and Pierson, who has made a miraculous escape, says the invaders are armed with something which "for want of a better term, I shall refer to . . . as a heat-ray."

Now the second announcer is upset:

> ANNOUNCER: Ladies and gentlemen, I have a grave announcement to make. Incredible as it may seem, both the observations of science and the evidence of our eyes lead to the inescapable conclusion that those strange beings who landed in the Jersey farmlands tonight are the vanguard of an invading army from the planet Mars.

In shocked tones he reveals that Martians have annihilated the New Jersey National Guard. Martial law is declared throughout New Jersey and eastern Pennsylvania. The President has declared a national emergency. The Secretary of the Interior, sounding like FDR and even using his phrases, begs the country to do its duty and pray God for help. The Army Air Corps is wiped out. An operator comes on jerkily:

> OPERATOR: This is Newark, New Jersey. . . . This is Newark, New Jersey! . . . Warning! Poisonous black smoke pouring in from Jersey marshes. Reaches South Street. Gas masks useless. Urge population to move into open spaces . . . automobiles use routes 7, 23, 24. . . . Avoid congested areas. Smoke now spreading over Raymond Boulevard. . . .

In the last sequence before the middle break, Ray Collins, the only surviving announcer, is standing on a New York rooftop. Bells are ringing in the background warning New Yorkers that it's time to evacuate the city; the Martians are coming. "Hutchinson River Parkway is still kept open for motor traffic. Avoid bridges to Long Island . . . hopelessly jammed." Voices in the background are singing a hymn; you can just hear them as Collins, his voice choking, reads a bulletin announcing that "Martian cylinders are falling all over the country. One outside Buffalo, one in Chicago, St. Louis. . . ."

Toward the end of Collins's speech (8:32 P.M.) Davidson Taylor, a CBS program supervisor, was asked to leave the Studio One control panel; an urgent phone call awaited him. He left and returned, his face a white knot. Already 60 percent of local stations had broken into the broadcast to reassure listeners that all this was make-believe, and New York policemen were surrounding the CBS Building. None of the performers or technicians would be allowed to leave after the show; some urgent questions needed answering. When Taylor came back to the control booth, Collins was describing the Martians, tall as skyscrapers, astride the Pulaski Skyway, preparing to wade through the Hudson River. It was seconds before the break, so Taylor decided to let Collins end, which he did in a voice ravaged by gas:

> COLLINS: . . . Now they're lifting their metal hands. This is the end now. Smoke comes out . . . black smoke, drifting over the city. People in the streets see it now. They're running toward the East River . . . thousands of them, dropping like rats. Now the smoke's spreading faster. It's reached Times Square. People are trying to run away from it, but it's no use. They're falling like flies. Now the smoke's crossing Sixth Avenue . . . Fifth Avenue . . . 100 yards away . . . it's 50 feet . . .
>
> OPERATOR FOUR: 2X2L calling CQ . . . 2X2L calling CQ . . . 2X2L calling CQ . . . New York. Isn't there anyone on the air? Isn't there anyone . . . 2X2L . . .

Now came the break; now a regular CBS announcer told them that they were listening to a CBS presentation of Orson Welles and his Mercury Theater. The second half of the program followed. It was sensitively written, with no hysterics, but that didn't matter any more. Before the break hundreds of thousands of screaming Americans had taken to the streets, governors were begging their constituents to believe that martial law had *not* been declared, and the churches were jammed with weeping families asking for absolution of their sins before the Martians came to *their* town. Altogether, the Princeton study discovered, approximately 1,700,000 believed the program to be a news broadcast, and about 1,200,000 were sufficiently distressed to do something about it. "For a few horrible hours," the study concluded, "people from Maine to California thought that hideous monsters armed with death rays were destroying all armed resistance sent against them; that there was simply no escape from disaster; that the end of the world was near."

In every state, telephone operators were overwhelmed. Local stations reported a 500 percent increase in incoming calls. In New York CBS and police switchboards were jammed. Riverside Drive became impassable; it was packed with mobs of sobbing people. Conditions were worse in northern New Jersey, where the first Things had been "discovered." Weeping families clung to one another, terrified men ran blindly across fields, and drivers raced about in all directions, all hoping to escape asphyxiation and flaming death. Train terminals and bus stations were filled with wild-eyed people demanding tickets to anywhere; one New York woman phoning the Dixie Bus Terminal for information gasped, "Hurry, please, the world is coming to an end and I have a lot to do."

When Dorothy Thompson wrote, "Nothing about the broadcast was in the least credible," there was a tendency among those who had not heard the program to dismiss the stricken mobs as ignorant. It was untrue. Miss Thompson to the contrary, *War of the Worlds* was a magnificent technical achievement; even today a transcription of it is chilling. And while there was some correlation between fear, education, and economic status—the most vulnerable were listeners who had not completed grammar school and had been on relief for more than three years—the well-to-do could not be let off so easily. Princeton found that 28 percent of the college graduates who were tuned to the program, and 35 percent of those with high incomes, believed they were hearing straight news. On a southern university campus, sorority girls wept in each other's arms and took turns telephoning their parents for a last goodbye, and an Ivy League senior, driving back from a Vassar check-in, was convinced when he flipped on the car radio that "Princeton was wiped out and gas was spreading over New Jersey and fire."

In Studio One, Welles signed off jovially: "Goodbye everybody, and remember, please, for the next day or two the terrible lesson you learned tonight . . . and if your doorbell rings and nobody's there, that was no Martian! It's Halloween." The red light went out; the Mercury Theater was off the air. But it was Studio One's doorbell that was ringing, and somebody was out there—not Martians but New York's finest, determined to teach Orson Welles a lesson he would never forget. Before opening the door, Welles and Houseman answered a shrill telephone in the control room. As Houseman later remembered it, the call came from "the mayor of some Midwestern city, one of the big ones. He is screaming for Welles. Choking with fury, he reports mobs in the streets of his city, women and children huddled in the churches, violence and looting. If, as he now learns, the whole thing is nothing but a crummy joke—then he, personally, is coming up to New York to punch the author of it on the nose!"

They hung up, the door burst open, the studio was suddenly

crowded with dark blue uniforms, and what Houseman called "the nightmare" began—interrogations hinting darkly at countless suicides, traffic deaths, and a "fatal stampede in a Jersey hall." At the moment the police could think of no law that had been broken, so the two men were released to a more terrible fate: the press. It seemed to Houseman that the press was being vindictive because radio had eclipsed newspaper coverage of the Czech crisis. Reporters countered that the broadcast was a big story, which it certainly was. Next morning scare headlines read:

RADIO WAR TERRORIZES U.S.

PANIC GRIPS NATION
AS RADIO ANNOUNCES
"MARS ATTACKS WORLD"

TIDAL WAVE OF TERRORISM SWEEPS NATION

PHONE CALLS SWAMP POLICE
AT BROADCAST OF FANTASY

"The show came off," Houseman said wryly. There was no doubt about that. For two days it drove Hitler off front pages, while CBS put to rest the fears of those still distressed by following its hourly time signal ("9 P.M. B-u-l-o-v-a, Bulova Watch Time") with an explanation that "the entire story and all of its incidents were fictitious." The Federal Communications Commission issued a statement describing the program as "regrettable" and proposing a new radio code. For a while there was talk of criminal action, but it died away. By then Orson Welles had rocketed to national fame, and his Mercury Theater, no longer CBS's poor relation, had acquired a lavish sponsor in Campbell Soups. Eventually Welles was invited to a White House function. The President took him off to one side and said, "You know, Orson, you and I are the two best actors in America." He seemed serious, but Welles wasn't sure how to take it, so he merely bowed.

The *War of the Worlds* broadcast revealed, as clearly as any mass convulsion can, that American nerves were being stretched ever tauter. In a popular phrase of the time, the country was "all balled up." *Fortune* noted a mood of fatalism among people. It did not, however, report despair. Though men might feel that they had little control over their individual futures, there was a kind of momentum to the decade, a feeling that America had touched bottom at the start of it and was moving inexorably toward some grand historic climax. Radio was part of it; the European tempo mounted month by month, and ignoring its crises was impossible. There was also the immense vitality of the time; looking back on it Frank Brookhouser wrote, "It was, granted, a grim and heartbreaking period in many ways. But the people triumphed over the loss and the disappointment and the suffering and the heartache. And never was the nation's heartbeat so loud and clear." Finally, Roosevelt discouraged any sense of mindlessness. He believed in generational destiny, and as long as he was the conductor, beaming and flourishing his baton, it was almost impossible to doubt that eventually it would all make sense.

Sometimes, when the fire is low and the bourbon just right, the images and lost notes may drift down from the past, evoking memories for those who were then alive of what 1939 was like for a quite ordinary American in that year. If his morning newspaper was the *Chicago Tribune*, he was relieved to learn that Colonel Robert R. McCormick had just abandoned his crusade for simplified spelling ("agast," "staf," "lether," "jaz," "fantom"). The *Tribune* was elated by the new congressional coalition against a Roosevelt spending bill ("Mutiny on the bounty!") but wrathful about a Court of Appeals ruling that schoolchildren needn't salute the flag. *Tribune* editors expressed dismay that New York children thought habeas corpus was a kind of disease, approval of Senator Taft's maiden speech on governmental economy, sadness over Lou Gehrig's farewell to baseball, awe over the twenty-three-stitch gash Joe Louis inflicted on Two-Ton Tony Galento, resentment of those enemies of tradition who had changed the Boston Braves to the Boston Bees, and pleasure that the new Pope, Pius XII, had appointed conservative Francis Joseph Spellman an archbishop. Colonel McCormick would have given a great deal to know that an apostate Communist named Whittaker Chambers was visiting Adolf Berle at Berle's Washington home on Woodley Road and telling him of subversion in the government—which Berle then disregarded. It remained a secret—then. But the colonel's time would come.

J. Edgar Hoover was wrapped in combat with, of all people, District Attorney Thomas E. Dewey. Dewey thought the FBI wiretappings were invasions of privacy, and one high police official in Manhattan accused Hoover of being a "publicity hound," a "David

Belasco in the squad car." Fighting back, the FBI director issued a blast: "Communists at a meeting yesterday in New York have instructed two of their best writers to portray me as a Broadway glamour-boy." At the American Legion's national convention he said, "Intellectual license and debauchery is un-American. In righteous indignation it is time to drive the debauchers of America out in the open." Dewey announced for the Presidency, which may not have been what Hoover had in mind.

The fastest-selling record was Hildegarde's "Deep Purple." Frankie Sinatra was still plugging along at $25 a week, but one night in a hotel Harry James's wife turned up the volume on her radio and said, "Honey, listen to this boy sing." Harry drove to Englewood, New Jersey, found Sinatra in a roadhouse called the Rustic Cabin, and signed him up. Their first record, "All or Nothing at All," sold only eight thousand copies, but the Sinatras were eating regularly now. The Lone Ranger was being heard three times a week by twenty million people on 140 stations . . . Bette Davis, Spencer Tracy, and Frank Capra won Oscars . . . Alfred Hitchcock was making a lady vanish . . . Bobby Breen had to retire at the age of twelve because his voice was changing.

Otherwise—or moneywise, as they were already saying in the motion picture industry—Hollywood was at the crest of its supercolossal glory. Shirley Temple was only ten. At box offices the top three were Mickey Rooney, Tyrone Power, and Spencer Tracy. Every movie was marvelous, amazing, spellbinding, sensational, and the reigning genies were entitled to leave their imprints in the wet cement slabs of Grauman's Chinese Theatre on Hollywood Boulevard. On the prewar silver screen, stars demonstrated incredible, magnificent deeds. Judy Garland persuaded a humbug Frank Morgan to confer courage upon cowardly Bert Lahr. Laurence Olivier, David Niven, and Merle Oberon recklessly pursued one another across the foggy moors ("Heathcliff! Heathcliff!") of *Wuthering Heights*. Gene Autry sang of the West. Watching Robert Donat as *Mr. Chips*, you knew the Empire would last forever. Clark Gable was something of a cutup. He took his shirt off right in front of Claudette Colbert,* and to the consternation of cotton mill owners

---

* One of the more entertaining aspects of showbiz was its ethnic deodorization. A generation later this practice would be challenged, but in the 1930s the lively arts were—apparently—wholly Anglo-Saxon. Though debatable, the custom endures. Thus we have or have had Doris Day (her real name, Doris Kapplehoff), Judy Garland (Frances Gumm), Claudette Colbert (Claudette Chauchoin),

he turned out to be topless; textile stocks dropped 8¼ in one week. Gable got that raffish "damn" into GWTW, though when the world premiere was held in Atlanta, the president of the United Daughters of the Confederacy was reported to have succumbed to the vapors. Even worse, Gable led a mutiny against Charles Laughton, who had kept calling him "Mr. Christian."

George Arliss was a man of such dignity, such sang froid, that he became typecast as a historical figure, and a school superintendent expressed anxiety that a whole generation of schoolchildren might grow up believing that all great men of the past looked like George Arliss. He outmaneuvered Gladstone, outwitted D'Artagnan and the Three Musketeers, and outspent the rest of the Rothschild brothers. Arliss left audiences feeling euphoric; the French Revolution always left them sobbing. In *Marie Antoinette* Norma Shearer rode bravely to the guillotine in a tumbril. Ronald Colman rolled right behind her in *A Tale of Two Cities*, and as he laid his handsome neck under the blade you knew then, before his head even dropped into the basket, that it was a far, far better thing that he did than he had ever done; it was a far, far better rest that he went to than he had ever known.

Both Europe and America had suffered through one of the coldest winters on record. There were a million dead in Spain. Heinrich Himmler banned *Time* from Germany, to the delight of Henry Luce, and Hitler posed before the $396 Volkswagen he had designed himself. (Later the price would go up, but the little auto would look the same.) There were *two* world's fairs in America in 1939, and if you could swing it, an excursion train would take you to both at a cut rate. Not many took advantage of the bargain. For most fairgoers one was enough, and that one was usually New York's. San Francisco's Golden Gate Exposition was designed with taste; its aeronautic display took your breath away, and its color floodlighting revealed a genuine flair. But the Golden Gate Exposition had no gimmicks, no camp, no corn, no sideshows—and, most important, no Grover Whalen.

At fifty-three Grover Aloysius Whalen, who had never been seen

---

Karl Malden (Malden Sekulovich), Laurence Harvey (Larry Skikne), Tony Curtis (Bernie Schwartz), Tab Hunter (Arthur Gelien), Mitzi Gaynor (Mitzi Gerber), Ethel Merman (Ethel Zimmerman), Vic Damone (Vito Farinola), Judy Holliday (Judy Tuvim), Rita Hayworth (Margarita Carmen Cansino), Jane Wyman (Sarah Fulks), Kirk Douglas (Issur Danielovitch), Danny Kaye (David Kaminsky), and Jack Benny (Benjamin Kubelsky).

in public without a gardenia in his lapel, was New York's official "greeter." Visiting dignitaries who were not met by Whalen and presented with a key to the city felt insulted, and rightly so; it was like breaking diplomatic relations. The New York fair—he called it "The World of Tomorrow"—was conceived as his masterpiece. He intended to greet all guests by offering them anything they could possibly want, from great art to skin shows, from a robot called Elektro that could talk and smoke a cigarette to the Lord's Prayer in three hundred languages. "It was the paradox of all paradoxes," Sidney M. Shalett wrote of the fair in *Harper's* the year it closed. "It was good, it was bad; it was the acme of all crazy vulgarity, it was the pinnacle of all inspiration." Meyer Berger of the *New York Times* called it "Mad Meadow." But there was a method in its madness, and in retrospect that motive seems more significant than its lapses of taste, even more important than the snub from Nazi Germany, the only major power that stayed away. In a word, the fair was a triumph of technology, the force that would do so much to shape postwar American society.

The hit of the fair was GM's Futurama, which drew 28,000 paying customers a day, each of whom sat on a conveyor belt armchair for fifteen minutes, listening to a recorded explanation while he observed Norman Bel Geddes's notion of what the American landscape would be like in 1960. Bel Geddes's prescience was less than twenty-twenty. He predicted tall, tanned, vigorous people spending most of their time having fun. (There was no mention of black people; blacks, apparently, would have ceased to exist.) Possessions would bore Americans in his 1960, so there weren't many in the Futurama. The countryside was crisscrossed by fat highways. Cars were air-conditioned and cost $200. Most of the land was forested. The luckiest Americans dwelt in one-factory villages producing a single industrial item and growing their own food.

Inventors and engineers would use a little atomic energy, but their chief source of power would be liquid air. Tremendous telescopes permitted men to see the moon a hundred times more clearly. Cancer would be cured; the average life span was seventy-five years. Houses were light and disposable; when you tired of one you just threw it away. (Where you threw it was unmentioned.) Most people had high school educations. Every village had an airport, with elevators taking aircraft to and from underground hangars. Office buildings and apartment condominiums were 1,500 feet high and were bordered by fourteen-lane turnpikes.

John Brooks has pointed out Bel Geddes's most conspicuous Futurama flaw. He had no grasp whatever of the urban problems which would produce the crisis of America's next generation. Cities were to be divided by the superhighways, and neighborhoods were to be zoned residential, commercial, or industrial. The dreamland was built to bring more automobiles into cities faster, yet there was no provision for parking. That was Bel Geddes's most accurate forecast. It is precisely what has happened—to our despair. As Brooks observes of the Futurama, "many of its prophecies of Heaven have become facts; the only trouble is that now that they are here they look more like the lineaments of Hell."

Among the foreign visitors to arrive at Mad Meadow's gate in mid-June of 1939 was an Englishman with an awkward stutter and the name George the Sixth, by the Grace of God, of Great Britain and Northern Ireland and of his other Realms and Territories, King; Emperor of India; Head of the Commonwealth; Defender of the Faith. He was accompanied by his queen, the former Elizabeth Angela Marguerite Bowes-Lyon, and a host of protocol officers, secretaries, and aides. It was probably the biggest moment in the greeter's life. His smile benevolent above a flowing white stock, he gave them his blue-ribbon personal tour and then saw them off to Hyde Park.

FDR was very much the squire that day. He drove his royal guests around the county in his custom-built Ford with manual brakes and served them hot dogs and—at the request of the Defender of the Faith—Ruppert's beer. In Washington, 600,000 people lined the parade route, John Nance Garner cackled "Here come the British!" and Kate Smith, again by royal request, sang "When the Moon Comes Over the Mountain." It was all very low-key, but its political significance was prodigious. Three months earlier Hitler had seized the rump Czech state. War was now imminent, and the President was letting the world know that he could do more than send pious messages to the Wilhelmstrasse. America had been a slumbering giant, he said, but now she was awakening; the aggressors had better watch out. The Führer displayed his customary charm by describing the President as a "pettifogging Jew" and adding that "the completely negroid appearance of his wife" showed that she was "half-caste."

Hitler had an adoring Reichstag; Roosevelt faced a coalition Congress, and for the White House the difference was painful. The President asked the Führer for assurance that weak nations would not be attacked; William L. Shirer noted how "the paunchy deputies rocked with raucous laughter" when their leader solemnly promised not to invade the United States. Senator Nye, speaking for the isolationist bloc, said Roosevelt had "asked for it." The strong wind FDR had sowed in the off-year primaries reaped a whirlwind in the Senate Foreign Relations Committee; after the shock of Munich the committee had been expected to recommend repeal of the neutrality laws, but the vote was 12–11 against it, and the majority included Walter George and Guy Gillette, two of the senators Roosevelt had tried to retire.

Second only to the President among public figures, Charles A. Lindbergh could command the largest radio audience. "We must not be misguided by this foreign propaganda that our frontiers lie in Europe," he said. "What more could we ask than the Atlantic Ocean on the east, the Pacific on the west? An ocean is a formidable barrier, even for modern aircraft." Later he would put his case more strongly. Senator Arthur H. Vandenberg swore never to send American boys to war under any circumstances. Earl Browder, speaking at the summer Institute of Politics at the University of Virginia, was asked whether Stalin might form an alliance with Hitler; as Browder later recalled, "I replied that I could easier imagine myself being elected president of the U.S. Chamber of Commerce." Fritz Kuhn was convicted of forgery and theft; his German-American Bund called him Roosevelt's first political prisoner. Hitler issued his first demand for Danzig on August 20, and when Berlin and Moscow jointly announced their nonaggression pact on August 21 the Poles were doomed. Yet military analysts kept talking about Poland's bad roads and "General Mud," as though World War II might be called off because of bad weather.

America's yearning for simplism prevented any rational debate over foreign policy and the threat to national security. Chamberlain hadn't understood why British lives depended upon Czech fortifications in the Sudetenland, and U.S. public opinion couldn't see beyond the fastness of its seascapes. But Roosevelt and Hull realized that the British Empire was no longer the world's great stabilizing force; Munich had exposed its flabby muscle. H.M.'s fleet remained intact, but if France fell and the English were cornered on their island, the center of geopolitical gravity would inevitably move westward. Hitler had declared that his ultimate goal was *"die ganze Welt"* (the whole world), and already German agents were active in Argentina. Roosevelt believed that he could buy peace for his generation, but he knew the price; the next generation of Americans would have to fight alone, against overwhelming odds. Lincoln had said that you could do anything with public opinion, and nothing without it. What was the public's opinion now? Dr. Gallup reported that 65 percent of his pollees favored boycotting Germany, 57 percent wanted neutrality legislation revised, 51 percent expected war in Europe in 1939, 58 percent believed the United States would be drawn into it, 90 percent said they would fight if America were invaded, and 10 percent said they would fight if America were not invaded.

Anything approaching a declaration of war, then, would be an invitation to insurrection. The President had to cut his cloth to fit the public mood. That boxed him in. But he could make two important moves now: keep the congressional leadership informed and strengthen the armed forces, which were, that summer, weaker than Poland's. The President did not know—or could not prove— that Hitler had decided in May to destroy Poland and then move on England and France. His intelligence services were quite good, however; a mountain of data could admit of but one conclusion: that the Wehrmacht was preparing to rupture the borders of the Reich.

In the last week of July the President invited the leaders of Capitol Hill to his second-floor oval study. With Hull at his elbow, he reviewed the evidence of Hitler's intentions, estimated that the Allies had only a fifty-fifty chance of surviving, and asked for neutrality revision. Hitler had acknowledged to Roosevelt that the one American force which impressed him was "the vastness of your nation and the immense wealth of your nation." Why not intimidate him with it? Under the neutrality law's present working, the United States was required to withhold sales of arms to aggressors and victims alike. Revision now might deter the Nazi dictator and so save the peace. To his guests the President said, "I've fired my last shot. I think I ought to have another round in my belt."

He was really talking to one man, Borah, who could carry the Senate if he would. He wouldn't. "There's not going to be any war this year," he said. "All this hysteria is manufactured and artificial."

In despair Hull said, "I wish the senator would come down to my office and read the cables."

Borah said impassively, "I have sources of information in Europe that I regard as more reliable than those of the State Department." He explained what he meant: foreign newspapers.

With Hull near tears, Garner polled the room on embargo repeal. To the President he said, "Well, Captain, we may as well face the facts. You haven't got the votes, and that's all there is to it."

Roosevelt remarked quietly to the leadership that the responsibility was theirs and bade them good evening.

There remained for him the state of national defense. For the first time in five years the U.S. Navy was maneuvering in the Atlantic—the excuse was a ceremonial visit to Mad Meadow—but that was about all that could be said for American naval might; the most memorable naval event of 1939 was the inexplicable sinking of the submarine *Squalus* off Portsmouth in 240 feet of water. The House had authorized $499,857,936 for the Army, including $50,000,000 to increase the Air Corps from 5,500 to 6,000 planes. "Bluff and jitterism," snorted Borah, and this time he was right. None of the aircraft belonged in the same sky with the British Spitfire, the French Nieuport, or the German ME-109. Even the new P-40s which were beginning to appear on American bases carried only machine guns synchronized to fire through the propellers—as in 1918—and these planes had just reached the experimental stage.

In May the President had once more demonstrated his skill in picking men by choosing as his new chief of staff Brigadier General George C. Marshall (who was to be sworn in the same day that Germany invaded Poland). Marshall had 227,000 soldiers but equipment for only 75,000: Garand and Springfield rifles, twenty-year-old machine guns, and a few French 75s brought home after the Armistice in 1918. In August Lieutenant General Hugh Drum assembled his First Army for maneuvers and reported with a straight face that he was short of combat strength by 246,000 men, 3,063 machine guns, 348 howitzers, and 180 field guns. In European terms, *Time* wrote, "the U.S. Army looked like a few nice boys with BB guns." Dean Acheson quoted the old chestnut about America's lack of military preparedness: "God looks after children, drunkards, and the United States." J. P. Morgan capsulated the country's myopia when, upon sailing for Scotland to shoot grouse, he said, "If they start war, my shooting will be interrupted."

They started it at 5:20 A.M. Polish time, September 1, when a German warplane bombed Puck, a fishing village and air base on the northwest coast of the Gulf of Danzig. At 5:45 A.M. the German ship *Schleswig-Holstein* fired the opening shell, a direct hit on a Polish ammunition dump at Westerplatte. Then the first Wehrmacht infantry attack went in through a gentle rain, under gray skies. Four hours later, at 2:30 A.M. Washington time, the telephone beside the President's bed rang. It was his ambassador in Paris. "This is Bill Bullitt, Mr. President."

"Yes, Bill."

"Tony Biddle has just got through from Warsaw, Mr. President. Several German divisions are deep in Polish territory, and fighting is heavy. Tony said there were reports of bombers over the city. Then he was cut off...."

"Well, Bill, it's come at last. God help us all."

In the beginning the war went swiftly. The German General Staff had calculated that it needed a month to conquer Poland. After eleven days essentially all was over but the screaming in Himmler's new concentration camps. In its September 25 issue *Time* introduced its readers to a new word: "This was no war of occupation, but a war of quick penetration and obliteration—*Blitzkrieg*, lightning war." Every thirty seconds Americans tuned to shortwave could hear eleven stirring notes—the opening of a Chopin polonaise—a sign that although the rest of the country had been overrun, Radio Warsaw was still free. Then, at 4 A.M. on September 17, the Russians burst into Poland through the back door. Radio Warsaw fell silent. When next heard from it burst into a triumphant "Deutschland über Alles."

Kenneth Crawford rhetorically inquired for the *Nation*, "Is the Roosevelt Administration neutral? Certainly not. Is there any chance for the United States to stay out of another world war? Practically none." That was not the line the White House was taking, however. "This nation will remain a neutral nation," Roosevelt announced in a fireside chat on September 3, "but I cannot ask that every American remain neutral in thought as well." At the President's first wartime press conference, Phelps Adams of the *New York Sun* asked, "Can we stay out of it?" After a pause FDR answered slowly, "I not only sincerely hope so, but I believe we can, and every effort will be made by this administration to do so." Shoring up Latin America, he suggested that the Inter-American Conference warn warships to avoid naval action in the western hemisphere south of Canada, and in a declaration from Panama it did so. At a second press conference he was asked how far U.S. territorial waters extended toward Europe. He said evasively, "As far as U.S. interests require them to go." The reporter inquired, "Does that reach the Rhine, Mr. President?" The President laughed. He was, he explained "talking only about salt water."

He was thinking about it, too. The only place Americans might encounter Germans in force was on the high seas. Already a U-boat had sunk the S.S. *Athenia*, and in England furious U.S. survivors had been interviewed by Ambassador Kennedy's twenty-two-year-old son Jack. Young Kennedy's words to them—"We are still neutral and the Neutrality Act still holds"—had satisfied few. That viewpoint didn't satisfy Roosevelt, either. Now that war had begun, his policy was changing. Neutrality, in his rather unusual definition, was now defined as meaning no American soldiers shooting at German soldiers. It did not preclude helping the Allies exploit their command of the sea. He therefore closed U.S. waters to "belligerent submarines" (subs, of course, were Nazi vessels) and called Congress into special session, asking that foreign powers be permitted to buy American munitions on a "cash-and-carry" basis. In her column Mrs. Roosevelt had concluded that "much as we may dislike to do it, it may be necessary to use the forces of this world in the hope of keeping civilization going until spiritual forces gain sufficient strength everywhere to make an acceptance of disarmament possible." That is what her husband really meant by neutrality.

But it wasn't what Lindbergh meant, or Borah, or Vandenberg, or Wheeler, or even—at first—a majority of newspaper editors. Thus cash-and-carry became America's first wartime issue. It marked the emergence of a new Lindbergh. In a radio speech on September 15 he said, "This is not a question of banding together to defend the white race against foreign invasion"; this was "a quarrel arising from the errors of the last war." His wife Anne had just finished a book, *The Wave of the Future*, which seemed to argue that a worldwide Nazi victory was inevitable. But Anne's mother was working on a William Allen White committee supporting cash-and-carry. It was a time of divided families, divided loyalties, and hard words. Harold

Ickes asked publicly, "How can any American accept a decoration at the hand of a brutal dictator who, with that same hand, is robbing and torturing thousands of fellow human beings? Perhaps Henry Ford and Colonel Charles A. Lindbergh"—both decorated by Hitler in 1938—"will be willing to answer."

The German chargé d'affaires protested Ickes's remarks, Sumner Welles coldly rejected the protest, and suddenly the issue wasn't just neutrality revision; it had become one of patriotism. Roosevelt proclaimed an unprecedented "limited national emergency." Lawyers and scholars asked one another what a limited national emergency was. It wasn't anything; it was just FDR's way of showing the flag. The only people in the country who tried to honor the vague proclamation were the managers of movie theaters, where "The Star-Spangled Banner" was played at the end of each evening's performance (a practice which was to continue for nearly six years). In the sharp exchange with the isolationist bloc, the President won. The captain had the votes now. Both houses passed the cash-and-carry amendment, and arriving British merchantmen began picking up harbor pilots on November 3.

In the subsequent legislative lull, Americans noticed something, or, to be more precise, the absence of something. Wasn't there supposed to be a war in Europe? There was, but the only bellicose sounds came from London's music halls, where Cockney harpies were breaking up audiences with a dreadful ballad called "We'll Hang Our Washing on the Siegfried Line." There was some action at sea, where the British held the initiative. On the Western front, however, Hitler was playing a waiting game, letting French morale drop ever lower. On the Maginot Line the cooped-up French Army squatted and grew flabby—"the strongest army in the world," as a British general would put it, "facing no more than twenty-six divisions, sitting still and sheltering behind steel and concrete." German civilians were calling it Sitzkrieg, "sit-down war." "This so-called war," said Senator Vandenberg, "is nothing but about twenty-five people and propaganda." Senator Borah called it the "phony war," and the epithet stuck.

Thus the 1930s, which had begun with a cry for bread, ended with a yawn. There was no Battle of the Marne this time, nor even a sizable border skirmish. It was a period in American history when international challenges were about to replace domestic problems, but it was marked in little ways. Granville Hicks resigned from the Communist party because of the Hitler-Stalin pact; hardly anyone noticed. Tyrone Power and his wife Annabella flew home from Lisbon. Rhodes Scholars were recalled—Byron White entered Yale Law School—and then they all felt rather foolish; they had run away from nothing but a silent confrontation. In the first days of the war grocers were selling sugar in hundred-pound sacks, canned goods by the case, flour in fifty-pound bags. Presently the squirrelers too felt silly; there were no food shortages.

For a while there *was* a shortage of pins with colored heads for armchair strategists, and Rand McNally & Company was briefly sold out of large-scale European maps. New York's Transportation Board announced that subways would make excellent bomb shelters. A Standard Oil subsidiary at Bayonne, New Jersey, replaced German natives on its tanker crews with American-born seamen, and a rug manufacturer changed the name of his most popular line, Dictator Carpets, to Liberty Carpets. But when boredom set in, the early, impulsive gestures were regretted. By Christmas, European maps were a glut on the seasonal market. Elmo Roper found that 67.4 percent of the people wanted no part of the war. And by New Year's Day 1940, the country was much more interested in whether a scrappy, lightweight Tennessee team could dance its way around Southern California's musclemen in the Rose Bowl. (They couldn't; USC won, 14-0.) Jukeboxes were announcing that "Annie Doesn't Live Here Any More," and Bonnie Baker's Lolita lisp was describing the assets of her steady with "Oh, Johnny!" At the University of Illinois a member of the Pi Kappa Phi house wrapped five baby white mice in lettuce and swallowed the lot. People were lining up under marquees to see Bette Davis in *Dark Victory* and James Stewart in *Mr. Smith Goes to Washington.* President Roosevelt sent a final conciliatory message to Hitler and was informed that the Führer was asleep. He did not, however, sleep long.

Portrait of an American

NORMAN THOMAS

HE WAS THE AMERICAN ISAIAH,
    the nation's conscience,
    the voice of the mute,
    the advocate of the dispossessed,
    the patrician rebel,
    the prophet who spoke out when others fled into silence.
He ran for the Presidency six times and never came close to a single electoral vote. Yet he refused to yield his idealism to despair, declined to quit the system, and in the end he found he had won as much as the winners—and without the loss of integrity.

Norman Thomas was an evangelist. It was in his blood, in the bone of his bone. His father and both his grandfathers had been Presbyterian ministers, and as a boy in Ohio, delivering copies of the Marion *Star*, owned by Warren G. Harding, he practiced intonation alone until he had developed the spellbinding delivery of a Bryan, a Debs, a Theodore Roosevelt.

He had the style. What he needed now was something to say. A trip around the world after leaving Princeton—he was class valedictorian—persuaded him that colonialism was evil. Back in New York, he became a social worker in Manhattan's blighted Spring Street neighborhood. The misery and want there tore at him, he looked for answers, and found some from Walter Rauschenbusch at the Union Theological Seminary. Later he said: "Life and work in a wretchedly poor district in New York City drove me steadily toward Socialism, and the coming of the war completed the process. In it there was a large element of ethical compulsion."

That war came in 1917. He campaigned against it, was stoned, and founded with Roger N. Baldwin the American Civil Liberties Bureau, later League. In 1918 he wrote Gene Debs:

I am sending you an application for membership in the Socialist party. I am doing this because I think these are the days when radicals ought to stand up and be counted. I believe in the necessity of establishing a cooperative commonwealth and the abolition of our present unjust economic institutions and class distinctions based thereon.

He was moved by:

. . . grotesque inequalities, conspicuous waste, gross exploitation and unnecessary poverty all around me.

Debs died in 1926; Thomas became the party's new leader. He was now forty-two, six-foot-two, 185 pounds, with merry blue eyes —a gentle moralist, a good-humored Puritan. His health was oddly affected by the human condition. If the world was peaceful and prosperous, he glowed with vitality; if world conditions deteriorated, so did he. But he never let illnesses stop him.

In 1932 he knew he could not be elected, and warned his young followers to prepare for defeat. But, "Vote your hopes and not your fears," he told them, and, "Don't vote for what you don't want and get it."

The planks in his presidential platform were public works, unemployment insurance, minimum wage laws, low-cost housing, slum clearance, the five-day week, abolition of child labor, health insurance for the aged, anti-Communism, civil liberties, civil rights for Negroes, and old age pensions. Nearly every one of these proposals was then considered radical.

The program was approved by 728,860 voters and by the man from New York who won the election.

In 1936 Thomas's vote dwindled to 187,342, and he knew why: ". . . the Socialists watched with some eagerness as Democrats adopted policies they had long recommended in such fields as tariffs and trade barriers, labor legislation, social legislation, social security, and . . . farm policy, such as the Resettlement Administration."

He would join almost any picket line, mount any stump, whatever the danger. In March 1935, in a Mississippi county called Birdsong, he spoke out for black sharecroppers, and a drunken mob of whites dragged him from the platform, beat him bloody, and threw him across the county line. One said, "We don't need no goddam Yankee bastard to tell us what to do with our niggers."

Three years later he went into Jersey City to speak against Mayor

Frank ("I am the law") Hague. Hague forbade the rally and warned Thomas to stay away. Thomas came. Hague's police slugged him, drove him across the Hudson, and ordered him never to enter Jersey again. He returned to it an hour later. The cops mauled him again and again threw him, hemorrhaging, on a Manhattan sidewalk. This time he went to a federal court. A judge issued an injunction against the mayor and his heavies, and Thomas, bandaged but upright, denounced "Hagueism" to an enormous throng in Jersey City's Journal Square.

Communists hated him. He visited Moscow during the purge trials and later declared:

> For the believer in the dignity of the individual, there is only one standard by which to judge a given society and that is the degree to which it approaches the ideal of a fellowship of free men. Unless one can believe in the practicability of some sort of anarchy, or find evidence there exists a superior and recognizable governing caste to which men should by nature cheerfully submit, there is no approach to a good society save by democracy. The alternative is tyranny.

Leon Trotsky hooted, "Norman Thomas called himself a Socialist as the result of a misunderstanding." But Thomas was firm: one must work within the system. He believed the New Deal should have nationalized the steel industry, but he became convinced that Roosevelt's election had brought "the salvation of America . . . the welfare state and almost a revolution."

In World War II he battled against the internment of Japanese-Americans and Roosevelt's demand for unconditional surrender. He believed "the lowest circle of hell" would be a Nazi victory, but thought a call for a statement of democratic peace terms would be more reasonable.

Almost alone in 1945 he condemned America's use of atomic bombs: "We shall pay for this in a horrible hatred of millions of people which goes deeper and farther than we think."

His last campaign was in 1948; he entered only because he saw how the Communist party was manipulating Henry Wallace. The day after the election an eminent New York Democrat said, "The wrong man lost." "Dewey?" asked a friend. "No," said the Democrat, "Thomas."

In later years he spoke not as a candidate, but as the evangelist he had always been. In 1960 he anticipated the ecological crisis and the need for disarmament. He was convinced that ultimate disaster lay in military aid to other nations, and he believed in the wisdom of the Marshall Plan.

Along the way he wrote twenty books. His energy was unbelievable. In his eighties, crippled by arthritis, this old man deformed by sickness crisscrossed the country by auto or in trains—sleeping in upper berths to save money—speaking out against the Vietnam War. And college students, who had sworn to distrust everyone else of his generation, crowded halls to hear his indictment of the war. But he never counseled them to violence:

"The secret of a good life is to have the right loyalties and to hold them in the right scale of values. The value of dissent and dissenters is to make us reappraise those values with supreme concern for truth. Rebellion per se is not a virtue. If it were, we should have some heroes on very low levels."

A reporter once asked him what he considered to be his achievements over the years. He replied in part:

"I suppose it is an achievement to live to my years and feel that one has kept the faith, or tried to . . . to be able to sleep at night with reasonable satisfaction . . . to have had a part . . . in some of the things that have been accomplished in the field of civil liberties, in the field of better race relations, and the rest of it. It is something of an achievement, I think, to keep the idea of socialism before a rather indifferent or even hostile American public."

When he died in his sleep in December 1968, President Johnson, Vice President Humphrey, Governor Nelson Rockefeller, United Nations ambassador Arthur Goldberg, and New York Mayor John Lindsay issued shining tributes to him. Everyone agreed he had kept the faith.

They omitted the end of Norman Thomas's answer to the reporter's question: "That's the kind of achievement that I have to my credit. As the world counts achievement, I have not got much."

Not much. Only a beam of immortality.

Seven

THROUGH THE NIGHT WITH A LIGHT FROM ABOVE

IN HITLER'S THIRD REICH the science of fundamental physics did not exist. There was Jewish physics, which was against the law, and German physics, the responsibility for which was vested in the Ministerium für Wissenschaft, Erziehung und Volksbildung (Ministry of Science, Education and National Culture) at No. 69 Unter den Linden. Actually a Jewish woman was, until March 1938, one of the ministry's brightest stars. Working with Otto Hahn and Fritz Strassmann, Lise Meitner had been bombarding uranium with neutrons in the laboratories of Berlin's Kaiser Wilhelm Institut, and logging unbelievable results. Dr. Meitner was an exception to anti-Semitic legislation because she wasn't a German. She was Viennese.

After the Anschluss all Austrians were transformed into citizens of the Reich, however, and as a non-Aryan, Lise Meitner found herself locked out of her own laboratory. The shadow of the concentration camp lay across her path. Her eminent colleagues went to the Führer himself. Race had nothing to do with science, they argued. Physics was either true or false, and because Germany had been guided by truth, the fatherland led the world in Nobel laureates—three times as many as the Americans. Hitler angrily dismissed them as "white Jews." A warrant for Lise Meitner's arrest was issued. She slipped over the Dutch border disguised as a tourist and made her way to the small Swedish seaside town of Kungälv, near Göteborg. Two great physicists, Niels Bohr in Copenhagen and Hahn, now in Stockholm, were hospitable and kind, but to her it seemed that her career was over, her life in ruins.

In point of fact all of them, and their colleagues in the United States, stood on the threshold of science's Elizabethan Age. Astonishing discoveries were being made simultaneously in a half-dozen countries. Enrico Fermi had won a Nobel Prize for his work with neutrons. Hahn, Strassmann, Bohr, Chadwick at Cambridge, and the Joliot-Curies in Paris were at the frontier of investigation and driving hard. Over thirty years earlier Albert Einstein measured atomic energy in the abstract from his theory of relativity. Einstein observed that a body in motion has a greater mass than a body at rest, the difference being defined by the velocity of light. Now real neutrons were splitting real nuclei, new elements were being discovered, three isotopes (types) of uranium were under investigation, and formulae had been committed to paper which, under conceivable circumstances, might translate Einstein's theory into a stupendous reality. The nuclear physicists didn't expect the world to understand. They could hardly credit their own work. When Hahn posted a report on his atom splitting to *Naturwissenschaften* on December 22, 1938, he felt that somehow he must be wrong: "After the manuscript had been mailed, the whole thing once more seemed so improbable to me that I wished I could get the document back out of the mailbox." But when Bohr read it, he struck himself on the forehead and cried, "How could we have overlooked that so long?"

They were fascinated, awestricken, frightened, and at odds with one another over what it all meant. Einstein told William L. Laurence of the *New York Times* that fission could not produce an explosion. Bohr, arguing with a colleague, ticked off ten persuasive reasons why such a device could never be built, and Hahn said of it, "That would surely be contrary to God's will!" But across the Atlantic there was disagreement. On February 2, 1939, Leo Szilard wrote Joliot-Curie from America:

> When Hahn's paper reached this country about a fortnight ago, a few of us at once got interested in the question whether neutrons are liberated in the disintegration of uranium. Obviously, if more than one neutron were liberated, a sort of chain reaction would be possible. In certain circumstances this might then lead to the construction of bombs which would be extremely dangerous in general and particularly in the hands of certain governments.

He did not identify "certain governments." Everyone knew; it was on all their minds: with such bombs, Hitler could rule or destroy the world.

Haunted by this specter, the giants of European physics joined Lise Meitner in a general migration. Leaving Fascist Italy to receive his prize in Stockholm, Fermi canceled his return ticket in Sweden and headed for New York and the laboratories of Columbia University. Young Edward Teller went to George Washington University. Victor F. Weisskopf joined the Rochester faculty, and Bohr was packing to join Einstein in Princeton. He suggested that Lise Meitner and her nephew Dr. O. R. Frisch remain in Copenhagen long enough to conduct a confirming experiment. On January 16, 1939, Bohr reached New York. Awaiting him was a cable from Meitner and Frisch. The experiment had been affirmative—staggeringly so; the atom they split had freed 200 million volts of electricity. If uranium could be harnessed, theoretically it would be twenty million times as powerful as TNT.

Had the man on the street grasped this, he would have been as astonished by the source as by the fact. Popular notions of the scientist were of wildly impractical eccentrics—Dr. Frankensteins, giggling madly as they juggled retorts and vials and threw enormous switches. It is worth noting that when General Leslie R. Groves later recruited a staff to work with the nuclear scientists, he said: "Your job won't be easy. At great expense we have gathered here the largest collection of crackpots ever seen." The scientists were aware of their reputation and were indifferent toward it. There was about prewar nuclear physicists an informality, a casual air which would vanish in a terrible cloud six years later. In 1939 the very word "physicist" was uncommon; many Americans couldn't even pronounce it. Universities paid men with Ph.D.s in science $1,500 to $1,800 a year. They accepted because they had little choice. Industry didn't want them. In one year, 1937, there were only four research openings for them in the whole country, and the mite set aside for government research was largely confined to the Department of Agriculture.

In return, science was left alone. Genuinely international, scientists had no secrets from one another. Even in the Soviet Union, A. I. Brodsky could publish an article on the separation of uranium isotopes in 1939, and two of his colleagues carried out fission experiments in a shaft of the Moscow subway. (The Kremlin then ordered the work discontinued on the ground that it had no practical value.) Even when the concept of security crept in, scientific investigators didn't worry about it. They could talk shop with confidence that no layman could understand them. Indeed, only a handful of their own colleagues knew of fission in its new context. Before leaving Denmark, Bohr had been well aware that the Wehrmacht might invade his little country, and he was concerned about his precious hoard of heavy water—water in which the hydrogen has an atomic mass of two, invaluable for slowing down neutrons. But how many Nazis had heard of it? Very few, so he solved his problem by pouring it into a large beer bottle and putting it in his refrigerator, where it sat through five years of alien rule.

It was in America, perhaps, that dedication to academic freedom was greatest, and it was here that the first moves on the atomic chessboard were made in full view of an incurious public. The Meitner-Frisch cable had been sent in clear. The idea of coding information would have been considered absurd. Similarly, the experiment was reconfirmed by the simple expedient of reserving a Columbia laboratory for the night of January 25, calling in Fermi as an adviser, staging the uranium test, setting up an oscilloscope to measure energy, and pushing a button. The needle registered precisely 200 million volts; duplication was that exact. To discuss interpretations, everyone moved into lecture room 301 of Columbia's Pupin Physics Laboratory at Broadway and 119th Street. The door wasn't even closed, let alone locked. Anyone could have walked in from the pavement and learned of the latest developments in nuclear science—provided, of course, he could understand the jargon and the graphs, charts, formulae, and chalk scribbles on the blackboard.

Even a Washington conference was free in 1939. Fermi and Bohr were among those attending the spring meeting of the American Physical Society there, and Bohr went to the lectern to report on their work. He stated flatly that a projectile armed with a tiny fragment of U-235 under bombardment from slow neutrons could blow up most of the District of Columbia. As he lectured, delegates slipped in and out of the hall, placing long-distance calls to their campuses, and one young American, Robert Oppenheimer, was scrawling furiously away on a yellow pad, roughly calculating what the critical mass would be. There was a *New York Times* reporter at that meeting, but either he or his editors failed to grasp the full weight of what had happened. The *Times* did carry a brief account on the achievement of uranium fission. The next morning Dr. Luiz W. Alvarez was getting a haircut at the University of California when the story caught his eye. He leaped right out of the barber's chair, swirled the sheet around him like a toga, and dashed into the Radiation Laboratory to spread the news.

Aside from the moral issue—which was being raised even then—a thousand questions needed answering. Ahead lay the discovery that uranium was not only rare; 99.6 percent of it was U-238, too stable for fission. U-235 had to be separated from the masses of U-238 and refined until the metal had reached a degree of purity unknown in America. Any bomb would have to be designed, a task which in the event would be entrusted to a German refugee named Klaus Fuchs with interesting political opinions. Most important, the move from theoretical physics to an actual device would be so expensive that private sponsorship would be inadequate. Thousands of millions of dollars would be needed, and only one man in the country commanded resources that great. Probably they would have gone to Roosevelt in any event. Moral checks were not strong yet, and scientific curiosity was. But debate became pointless, because a single argument swept all before it. The scientists were now absolutely convinced that Hitler was building his own bombs—was, on the evidence, far ahead of them.

The Nazis knew about nuclear fission, of course; Hahn had told them in his *Naturwissenschaften* article. Early in 1939 two German physicists called at No. 69 Unter den Linden and suggested the possibility of constructing a "uranium machine." In April the Reich's six most distinguished atomic scientists met twice in Berlin; they agreed to join in such an undertaking and keep quiet about it. Then Dr. S. Flügge, an anti-Nazi physicist, learned the details. Nobody had sworn Flügge to secrecy, and he thought the world's scientific community ought to know what was going on. He published an extensive report on uranium chain reaction for the July 1939 number of *Naturwissenschaften* and then gave a simplified version to an interviewer from the *Deutsche Allgemeine Zeitung*, a conservative newspaper Goebbels hadn't yet suppressed. The inevitable copies found their way out through Zurich, slipping past the censors because the material was as incomprehensible to ordinary Nazis as it was to ordinary Americans. But the scientists in America didn't know the where or the why. They thought Flügge was showing them only the tip of the iceberg, and if the tip was that large, the world was in trouble. Then, that summer of 1939, came the most alarming development of all. Suddenly, without explanation, the Germans forbade the export of uranium ore from Czechoslovakia and ordered a blackout of all news about uranium. Since the known uses of uranium were confined to pottery and the painting of luminous dials on clocks, there could be only one interpretation of the embargo. The gentlemen at No. 69 Unter den Linden must be on their way. And in truth, they were. Being Germans, they had naturally tricked out their project with lines of authority, word of which also drifted through Zurich. It was Operation U, directed by appointed members of the Uranium Verein (Uranium Society) and responsible to the Heereswaffenamt (Army Weapons Department) in Berlin.

Roosevelt must be warned. But how? Most of the nuclear physicists in the United States who knew about fission were newly arrived expatriates. They had no friends in power; some were still learning the language. Szilard and Teller went to Washington and were met with blank stares. Even Fermi, with his Nobel Prize, was received coldly. The Army and Navy needed all their energies to acquire conventional weapons; they had no time for Buck Rogers games. The State Department saw no reason for urgency. According to their files, uranium was a rare and rather useless metal which was found, among other places, in Czechoslovakia and Belgium. Europe was in the last days of peace, armies were mobilizing, the crisis was desperate, and foreign service officers had no time for disheveled men who talked like organ grinders about splitting atoms.

But there was one tousled scientist, the sloppiest of them all, who could not be ignored. Albert Einstein was so famous that when he decided to wear his hair long he added a phrase to the American idiom. By July, after bureaucratic Washington's last turndown of Fermi, Einstein left Princeton for his summer holiday on Long Island. When Szilard and Eugene Wigner sent word that they must see him, however, he consented. Their plans were vague. They doubted that even Einstein could get through to the President; it seemed more practical to warn Brussels through Einstein's friendship with the Belgian queen mother. First, of course, they had to find Einstein on Long Island, and that turned into quite an expedition. On the hottest day of the year they set out for an address which had been given to them over the telephone. It had sounded like "Patchogue" but was really Peconic. Even after reaching Peconic they were bewildered. Szilard was arguing that they ought to quit, that they ought to go home and think it over, when a small boy volunteered to lead them to Einstein's house.

The great man shuffled out in slippers and led them to his study. According to Szilard, "the possibility of a chain reaction in uranium had not occurred" to Einstein. "But almost as soon as I began to tell him about it he realized what the consequences might be and immediately signified his readiness to help us and if necessary 'stick his neck out,' as the saying goes." They proposed the Belgian solution—which might have altered the outcome of the whole war, since Hitler would be in Brussels by spring—with Einstein writing the queen. Unsure of the protocol, they decided after leaving him that a copy should go to the State Department; the original would be held for two weeks, to give the State Department a chance to protest. But during the following week, as they discussed the mission with friends, the question of another approach was raised. Gustav Stolper, former editor of *Der deutsche Volksvirt* (*The German Economist*), was acquainted with Alexander Sachs, a financier and adviser to President Roosevelt. Why not go straight to the White House? Sachs thought the idea excellent, and on August 2 Szilard returned to Long Island with Teller. Einstein dictated a letter to the President in German; Teller translated it. Hitler's embargo on Czech uranium was cited, and the work in Berlin. The key passage explained the possible implications of a nuclear chain reaction: ". . . extremely powerful bombs of a new type may thus be constructed. A single bomb of this type, carried by boat and exploded in a port, might very well destroy the whole port, together with some of the surrounding territory."

Sachs handed the letter to Roosevelt on October 11, and to make certain that it wasn't lost in a shuffle of other papers, he read it to him aloud. That was a mistake. The letter was too long. Roosevelt became bored and said at the end that he thought government intervention might be premature at this stage. Sachs begged for another meeting, at breakfast the following day, and the President nodded. The financier couldn't sleep that night. Repeatedly he left his room at the Carlton Hotel and walked the two blocks to Lafayette Park, directly across Pennsylvania Avenue from the White House. He was trying to think of a way to dramatize the issue. The way he chose at breakfast was to remind FDR that Robert Fulton had taken his steamship invention to Napoleon, who had dismissed it as impractical, thus losing the vessel which might have permitted an invasion of England and victory. The President thought a moment, then produced a bottle of Napoleon brandy and two glasses.

Filling them and lifting his to Sachs, he said, "Alex, what you are after is to see that the Nazis don't blow us up."

"Precisely."

Roosevelt summoned his military aide, General Edwin "Pa" Watson, and handed him Einstein's letter, together with supporting documents Sachs had brought. The President said, "Pa, this requires action!"

So began the secret war, or S-1, as it was known to a few selected Americans—a very few, not even including the Vice President. Like the other war, this one had its triumphs and heroes, not all of them in laboratories. Seven months after Roosevelt and Sachs toasted their new understanding, France's nuclear physicists carried out a daring plan to thwart the Nazi scientists at No. 69 Unter den Linden. The Germans knew that the French owned virtually all the heavy water in Europe—185 kilograms in twelve sealed aluminum containers, bought in March 1940 from a Norwegian firm, Norsk Hydro. Led by Frédéric Joliot-Curie, and with enemy troops all around them, the French scientists concealed their cache in the death cell of the Riom prison. Although the Nazis knew it was nearby and were looking for it, the French smuggled it out of Bordeaux aboard a British collier while Joliot-Curie duped his German interrogators into believing the heavy water was on another ship.

Senator Borah died in January 1940, and his phony war died three months later when the Wehrmacht invaded Denmark and Norway, but the seismic shock of 1940 was Hitler's campaign in the west. It was like a seven-week Halloween broadcast by Orson Welles. Daily, hourly, the armchair strategists moved their colored pins while commentators described panzer thrusts far behind the Allied lines, the slaughter of refugees by Stuka dive bombers, and endless lines of blond Aryan youths who hurtled into the Lowlands and France shouting, "Heil Hitler!" Apart from the relentless advance of the field-gray columns, it was hard to tell exactly what was happening. Europe was obscured by a haze of conflicting reports. In this mist men like Joliot-Curie and Pierre Laval forged their separate destinies, while other figures, new leaders, tried to rally the demoralized Allied troops. Premier Paul Reynaud replaced Premier Edouard Daladier, Generalissimo Maxime Weygand succeeded Generalissimo Maurice Gamelin, and in London Chamberlain stepped down for Churchill, whose magnificent prose began to roll across the Atlantic.

Every American now knew what blitzkriegs were, and this was the greatest of them all. The German offensive opened on May 10. Four days later Holland surrendered. On the sixteenth day Belgium quit, and over the following weekend the British Army conducted its desperate, heroic evacuation from the beaches of Dunkerque. That left the French Army. It had been accounted the best in the world, but now in this seventh and last week of the Nazi *coup de main*, shortwave sets in Washington were picking up an impassioned but vain plea for Roosevelt to intervene, delivered by Reynaud himself.

On June 22 France capitulated. Paris was German, and a new fascistic government was established in the resort city of Vichy under Marshal Henri Philippe Pétain and Laval.[*] One of its first acts was to try *in absentia* a French tank general who had flown to England, sentencing him to death. Scornful of the men of Vichy, Charles de Gaulle sat in a Chelsea flat writing his first broadcasts to the people with whom he felt a mystical union, and whose destiny he would share. Like Reynaud, he was counting on the United States. So was Churchill, though he was too adroit a politician to beg. Instead he made grand references to the time when "the New World, with all its power and might," would step forth "to the rescue and the liberation of the Old."

Now came the Battle of Britain, the RAF struggling with the Luftwaffe for mastery of the skies over England. The city of Coventry was destroyed and thousands of Londoners were slain in the streets as a lesson to British stubbornness. The lesson did not take. The people huddled in bomb shelters and subway tubes—in one of them, four-year-old Julie Andrews was learning to sing—while their prime minister told Hitler that England would rather die than submit: ". . . we shall not flag or fail. We shall go on to the end. We shall fight in France, we shall fight on the seas and oceans, we shall fight with growing confidence and growing strength in the air, we shall defend our island, whatever the cost may be, we shall fight on the beaches, we shall fight on the landing grounds, we shall fight in the fields and in the streets, we shall fight in the hills; we shall never surrender."

---

[*] As the ministers, deputies, and civil servants left Paris for Vichy, the two American films playing at the Champs Elysées were *Going Places*, and *You Can't Take It with You.*

Now the mass media began to show their real power. In retrospect the Martian broadcast appeared to have been a kind of shakedown cruise, to steady the nerves of the high-strung. But this war was real, it was happening in Europe as listeners heard about it, and there was no way to avoid emotional alliances. Not many Americans favored the Nazis. The Germans were displaying a genius for bad public relations. They not only committed atrocities; they advertised them. They had been shooting hostages from the outset, and there was hardly an ethnic group in the United States whom they had not alienated. And there was worse to come. Nazi offenses against Italy, their present ally, lay in the future; so did conquest of Greece, with that unforgettable moment when a Wehrmacht officer ordered a Greek soldier to lower the blue-and-white colors of Greece from the Acropolis. The soldier did it. Then he wrapped the flag around him and stepped off the edge of the Acropolis parapet, falling silently to his death three hundred feet below.

You didn't have to be an American of Greek descent to be moved by that, and those who were praying for England in 1940 weren't all anglophiles. Just before the French collapse, Edna St. Vincent Millay had written in the *New York Times*:

> *Oh, build, assemble, transport, give,*
> *That England, France and we may live*
> *Lest we be left to fight alone.*

Now night had fallen over France, and about all that England had left that summer were RAF courage, Churchill's voice, and the legacy of Shakespeare: *This England never did, nor ever shall/ Lie at the proud feet of a conqueror.* But since Shakespeare's language was also America's, it could rouse some Americans to extraordinary pitches of emotion. In the late summer of 1940 the American writer Alice Duer Miller published from England a slim volume of verse—that least popular of art forms. It was entitled *The White Cliffs*, and in three months it went through eleven printings. There were people who could recite long passages from it, including the closing quatrain, which so eloquently expressed the anglophilia of the author—and millions of her readers:

> *I am American bred,*
> *I have seen much to hate here—much to forgive,*
> *But in a world where England is finished and dead,*
> *I do not wish to live.*

The destiny of Britain had become a national obsession for the multitudes of interventionists; now, for the first time, many realized how much they owed England, and how closely they were bound to England's fate. Radio addicts—and there were those who hardly ventured more than a few feet from a loudspeaker that summer—could hear the tramp of jackboots as German soldiers marched into the Channel ports, could hear the troops singing "Wir Fahren Gegen England" (We're Sailing Against England). It sounded hopeless. There was no way of knowing then that the Spitfires and Hurricanes were winning their dogfights over the Channel. On one September night a Luftwaffe air fleet of 1,500 planes dropped 4,400,000 pounds of high explosives on London. It was the city's greatest catastrophe since the Great Fire of 1666. The priceless windows of St. Mary le Bow were lost; the House of Lords was hit by one bomb; Buckingham Palace by five. In her tube little Julie Andrews joined the other children in chanting:

> *Now come the incendiaries to light you to bed,*
> *Bring out the sandbags and kill them all dead.*

Over 32,000 British children had been evacuated to the United States. In the way of things that year, the children had to have a song. The fall of France had inspired "The Last Time I Saw Paris," the Battle of Britain "A Nightingale Sang in Berkeley Square," and so, in honor of America's young guests, Tin Pan Alley turned out a haunting tune for the lyrics:

> *My sister and I recall the day*
> *We left our friends and we sailed away*
> *And we think of the ones who had to stay—*
> *But we don't talk about that.*

This went on until men were willing to leave perfectly good drinks in bars not to hear the voices not talking about that. But there really was no escape. Kate Smith seemed to be singing "God Bless America" everywhere. The movies needed a longer lead time; it would be many months before the premiere of *Mrs. Miniver*, with Walter Pidgeon sailing out in his little boat to do his bit in picking up the Tommies at Dunkerque, but already Edward G. Robinson was the FBI man in *Confessions of a Nazi Spy*, listening to such hissed threats as, "I vill get efen mit you for zis zometime, Mister G-Mann!" It made you squirm but was ineluctable; every great moment in history has its sleazy exploiters and souvenir salesmen. This propaganda campaign turned out some classic films—including *Casablanca*, which some regard as the greatest movie of all time—and one immortal stratagem, which was so successful that it has been used by political movements ever since.

It was invented by a Belgian refugee named Victor de Laveleye. Like Charles de Gaulle, de Laveleye made daily shortwave broadcasts to his countrymen telling them to keep stiff upper lips. One evening late in 1940 he suggested that they chalk the letter V (for *victoire*) in public places to show their confidence in an ultimate Allied triumph and create a nuisance for the Nazis. It became the most popular symbol since the introduction of the crucifix. V was an astonishingly versatile letter. In Serbian it stood for *vitestvo* (heroism), in Czech *vitzstvi* (victory), and in Dutch *vrÿheid* (freedom). The BBC began introducing its programs beamed to the continent with the first four notes of Beethoven's Fifth Symphony, three dots and a dash—the Morse code symbol for V. In the occupied countries the did-dit-dit-dah was used to knock on doors, blow train whistles, honk car horns, and fetch waiters. People waved to one another with two stretched fingers of the hand. In restaurants, cutlery was arranged in Vs. Stopped clocks were set at five minutes past eleven, and crayoned Vs were everywhere, even in the private toilets of German officers. Goebbels tried to steal the thunder by insisting the symbols all represented *Viktoria*, complete triumph for Hitler, but no one, not even Germans, believed him. Then the craze leaped the Atlantic. Rhinestone V brooches were on sale in department stores, and at Tiffany's you could get a quite good one, set in diamonds, for $5,000.

"Don't think you will win the war by making silly noises in restaurants," jeered one of Quisling's Norwegian henchmen. He was right, of course. Hitler's empire was now larger than Napoleon's, and his power was as absolute. On land he was strong enough to launch offensives in four directions simultaneously; at sea his three hundred U-boats were strangling Britain's lifelines. Only the consecration of embattled Britain stood between him and absolute mastery of Europe—unless the United States intervened.

In the United States nearly everyone was now either an isolationist or an interventionist, and while there were degrees to both, all interventionists believed that *something* ought to be done. In the dazed aftermath of the French armistice, their gestures, like their V brooches, were rather ineffectual. In Jeannette, Pennsylvania, a gun club practiced marksmanship so they would be ready to pick off descending Nazi parachutists. A coffee shop in Kirkland, Washington, changed "hamburger" on its menu to "liberty steak." The American Legion, hot for war, booed from its platform Senator Bennett Champ Clark and Congressman Fish, who had come to state the case for isolationism. There was a lot of nonsense about America's "going soft," as though the country's youth had lain around eating banana splits during the Depression; even Ed Murrow wrote his parents, "The price for soft living must be paid, and we may soon be paying that price." For all interventionists the arch villain was Charles A. Lindbergh. Charlotte, North Carolina, changed the name of Lindbergh Drive to Avon Terrace, the *New York Times* said he was "a blind young man," liberal columnists referred to him as "Herr von Lindbergh," and President Roosevelt mildly insulted him (he called him "a Copperhead")—whereupon Lindbergh angrily resigned his reserve commission as an Air Corps colonel.

A surprising number of people believed Lindy was a traitor. It seems fair to suggest that they felt betrayed because they had adored him when he flew the Atlantic alone, and now his feet had turned to clay. In the beginning, at least, he was one of the less abrasive isolationists. "Let us not delude ourselves," he said in the first month of the war. "If we enter the quarrels of Europe during war, we must stay in them in peace as well," and "This war is the climax of all political failure." As Nazi spearheads were knifing through France in May 1940, he said, "We are in danger of war today not because European people have attempted to interfere in America, but because we American people have attempted to interfere with the internal affairs of Europe. Our danger in America is an internal danger. We need not fear a foreign invasion unless American people bring it on through their own quarreling and meddling with affairs abroad." He saw interventionists as men seizing "every opportunity to push us closer to the edge."

That was above the belt; some interventionists could accept the charge and even exult in it. But Lindbergh was being driven to excesses by some of his supporters, who unlike him were pro-German, and by his briery relationship with the press. He was neither the first nor the last public figure to become persuaded that the news media hated him. On several counts one must sympathize with him; their behavior during the kidnapping and death of his child had been shocking. All the same, he was fighting a war of words—at a New York rally he addressed himself to "that silent majority of Americans who have no newspaper, or newsreel, or radio station at their command," but who believed in isolation—and he was beginning to choose the wrong words. In Des Moines, with Senator Nye beside him, he all but destroyed the America First movement. He actually warned American Jews to shut up—or else. Because of Jewish "ownership and influence in our motion pictures, our press, our radio and our government," he said, if war came "they will be blamed for it." In a stroke he lost all Jewish support and, among others, Thomas E. Dewey, who called the speech "inexcusable."

But then, all isolationist rhetoric had become scorching. The favorite adjective of the season was "tantamount"; every Roosevelt order was "tantamount to a declaration of war." Key Pittman, chairman of the Senate Foreign Relations Committee, proposed that the British give up their home islands and retreat to Canada; that, he thought, would satisfy Hitler. Pittman was even agreeable to letting the Nazis control the Atlantic. Senator Ernest Lundeen of Minnesota recommended American seizure of all British and French possessions in the western hemisphere. Senator Vandenberg thought cash-and-carry was "like the first drink of whiskey." Joseph P. Kennedy, back from London, said talk that Britain was fighting for democracy was "bunk." Ironpants Johnson accused his old chief in the White House of "a reckless shooting craps with destiny." John Foster Dulles, who would be contributing to America First groups as late as November 1941, said, "Only hysteria entertains the idea that Germany, Italy, or Japan contemplates war upon us." Burton K. Wheeler told the Senate that Roosevelt's "new triple-A plan" was "to plow under every fourth American boy." ("Dastardly," said the President, and Wheeler took it back.) Perhaps the most interesting remark in the Senate came from Robert A. Taft. He noted White House displeasure over a growing Japanese presence in Vietnam. Taft said no American mother was ready to have her son die "for some place with an unpronounceable name in Indochina."

KEEP THE U.S. OUT OF WAR! read a telegram to the President signed by a thousand Dartmouth students. Having been schooled by isolationist and pacifist teachers since they were children, it was not surprising that undergraduates found it impossible to shift gears on such short notice. Here they split with their faculties. College teachers saw the issues much as Roosevelt did—they were, if anything, impatient with him for not going faster. A few idealistic students crossed into Canada and enlisted; Charles G. "Chuck" Bolte, whose interventionist editorials in the Dartmouth newspaper had offended his classmates, joined the British Army and lost a leg at El Alamein. But most students wanted only to be left alone, as British ambassador Lord Lothian discovered when he spoke at Yale's commencement in June 1940. The most extreme isolationists saw Hitler satisfied with conquest of the United Kingdom, while the British fleet cheerfully steamed westward to put itself at the disposal of Washington. Lothian tried to confront his audience with reality. Isolation, he declared, was completely impossible. The world would force itself on America as it had on Britain. American wealth and strength would become a magnet to other powers; it would be an irresistible challenge to Hitler or anyone who dreamed of international power. The Yale faculty was enthusiastic. Most of the seniors sat on their hands.

Roosevelt's thoughts were along Lothian's lines, and he carried the analogy with Britain a step farther. The keystone in the arch of Whitehall's foreign policy had always been the principle that no one nation must ever control the continent. That was why Marlborough and Wellington had crossed the Channel, why the Kaiser's crushing of Belgium had been intolerable in 1914, why England was at war now. In the long cycles of history, Roosevelt believed, the United States must take the same position in the Atlantic community.

The President's quandary was intensified by the fact that 1940 was an election year, and no President had served more than two terms. Running for a third term wasn't unconstitutional, but the two-term Presidency was a powerful tradition. He hadn't planned to flout it. He had expected to retire in January 1941, but he didn't see how he could now. The country might elect an isolationist President, and that would be a disaster whose limits were beyond imagining. Just helping Britain and at the same time winning the election was going to be quite a trick. To carry it off, he felt—and Hull agreed with him—they would have to drop their policy of being frank with the American people.

A certain deviousness had marked administration conduct from the first days of the war. One of the new top-secret Douglas A-20 bombers had crashed in a test flight, and the Associated Press reported that among the men injured was a M. Chmedelin of the French Air Ministry. The Senate Military Affairs Committee had hit the roof. Again, on FDR's instructions, the State Department had reached an agreement with the British under which freedom of the seas would be restricted by H.M.'s vessels. Any German goods —made there or destined for there—could be seized at sea, and this policy applied even if a ship was sailing between two neutral countries. The neutrals protested, but Whitehall said that was hard cheese; there was a war on. And after Dunkerque the British Army was not only soaking wet but, worse, disarmed; therefore Roosevelt sent the whole surplus store of new American arms by fast freighters to England.

America at this time was still not even a third-rate military power. The basic machine tool industry had almost vanished since the Crash. The biggest forges in the country could hold only bathtubs and auto frames; howitzers were being turned out on machines made for streetcar axles. On the day the Wehrmacht invaded Holland, Hull told the President he should go before Congress and ask for 50,000 planes a year. Roosevelt gasped, but he did it, and since even the isolationists believed in the Fortress America concept, they voted him the money. "Unbelievable!" Hermann Göring said, but eventually the United States would be turning out 60,000 planes a year.

The President repeatedly spoke out as an enemy of the Axis— when Italy declared war on France, then in her extremity, he said, "On this tenth day of June, 1940, the hand that held the dagger has struck it into the back of its neighbor"—and in the middle of the presidential campaign he gave the British fifty overage U.S. destroyers in exchange for ninety-nine-year leases on British naval and air bases in the western hemisphere. The swap wasn't even legal, and it made the United States a nonbelligerent ally of Britain. But General Pershing and George Fielding Eliot spoke up for it. *Time* agreed with the President that it was the most important event in American defense since the Louisiana Purchase, and an isolationist senator said, "Listen, you can't attack a deal like that. . . . Roosevelt outsmarted all of us when he tied up the two deals."

Two days after the destroyer swap papers were signed, the largest, richest, and most influential antiwar organization was founded by a Yale law student, R. Douglas Stuart Jr., a son of the first vice president of Quaker Oats. This was the Committee to Defend America First. Its argument was that the country should prepare to fight for the United States, not Britain—thus sacrificing a valuable ally, though America Firsters never put it that way—and its leader became General Robert A. Wood, chairman of the Sears, Roebuck board of directors.

In less than six months they had 60,000 members. Every isolationist on Capitol Hill was enrolled. Novelist Kathleen Norris became the movement's chief propagandist, Charles Lindbergh its most popular speaker, and Wood, Henry Ford, Robert Young, Sterling Morton, Edward Ryerson Jr., and Lessing Rosenwald its financial sponsors. America First's war chest seemed inexhaustible. At one point it ran full-page advertisements attacking Roosevelt's foreign policy in sixty newspapers and then repeated the ad in another seventy-nine. Joseph P. Kennedy, Alice Longworth, and John Foster Dulles made it respectable. Rally after rally was held in Madison Square Garden and in Chicago, where the audience, to Lindbergh's embarrassment, repeatedly booed Churchill's name.

William Allen White countered by forming the Committee to Defend America by Aiding the Allies, which formed its own chapters across the country—its greatest support, significantly, came from the eastern seaboard—and which gathered signatures, mailed pamphlets, and distributed handbills taking the other side. The White committee's spokesmen included John J. McCloy; writer Elizabeth Morrow Cutter, Lindbergh's mother-in-law; and the intellectual community, led by Robert Sherwood. The committee was strongly backed by most big newspapers, except the *Chicago Tribune* and the *Washington Times-Herald*.

The depth of feeling became apparent in the debate over the country's first peacetime draft, perhaps the most controversial issue ever raised by a President campaigning for reelection. Not even George Washington had ever persuaded a Congress at peace to approve conscription. In 1940 only Canada, Cuba, and a few South American countries shared with the United States the lack of compulsory military training. Millions of Americans wanted it to continue that way; to them a draft represented the Europe they had fled. But General Marshall needed the men, and if the nation was to have an effective defense, he needed them at once. Roosevelt first raised the issue in his June 10 speech; he pledged that America would have "the equipment and training equal to the task of every emergency defense." The operative word was "training," and legislation to translate it into action went into the House hopper as the Selective Training and Service Bill.

John L. Lewis testified that conscription smacked of "dictatorship and fascism." Norman Thomas, Oswald Garrison Villard, and the Reverend Harry Emerson Fosdick said it was immoral—one clergyman predicted it would reduce American youth to "syphilis and slavery"—and Bill Green of the AFL, whose testimony was less than lucid, seemed to be arguing that the draft would be acceptable to him only when an invading army stood on American soil. To the embarrassment of Eleanor Roosevelt, the American Youth Congress, one of her pet projects, vowed that its members would refuse induction. More than a score of Union Theological Seminary students announced they would refuse to register despite the fact that they would be automatically deferred. The Mohawk Indians argued with more persuasive eloquence that they wouldn't fight because they had never been treated as U.S. citizens.

The peace lobby was luckless. The bill came out of the committee in September, when pictures of Nazi bombers and burning London were on every front page. On June 1 Gallup had reported the public feeling on conscription was running fifty-fifty. After the fall of France conscription had been favored by 67 percent, and now 71 percent were for it. Congress approved a one-year draft requiring registration of all men between twenty-one and thirty-five. Overnight New York's J. R. Wood & Sons, one of the country's largest manufacturers of wedding rings, reported a 250 percent increase in business; America was being swept by a wave of beat-the-draft marriages, on the theory that married men would receive permanent deferments. Little did they know their antagonist. As director of the draft Roosevelt appointed an Army officer who had been studying conscription plans since 1926 and knew all the loopholes. His name was Lewis B. Hershey.

Senator Wheeler had been muttering that rather than submit to such slave labor legislation American youth would rise in revolution. They did nothing of the sort. On October 16 over sixteen million men registered. There were no incidents; spirits seemed high. The Secretary of War drew the first numbers on October 29, and presently thousands of mailmen were carrying form letters which began:

> Greeting:
> Having submitted yourself to a local board composed of your neighbors for the purpose of determining your availability for training and service in the land or naval forces of the United States, you are hereby notified that you have been selected . . .

Living in new pine barracks, the draftees or selectees—it was considered impolite to call them "soldiers"—were soon maneuvering with wooden rifles and cardboard boxes marked "tank." After a while that became dull. It wasn't as though the United States were at war. Furthermore, they were dealing with the American peacetime military establishment, always an awkward and uninspiring institution. As the months passed, bored draftees took to studying the calendar. By summertime chalked inscriptions in the camps read OHIO—over the hill in October. Over the hill, in Army cant, means being absent without leave, and when the conscription law expired in October, they would be free. By then it was impossible to release them. War was very near. Yet the House vote on extending the draft eighteen months was 203 to 202—a margin of one vote, an indication of the thinness of the ice on which Roosevelt was skating.

Hitler would have preferred another American President, and after the war it was discovered that the German government had, in fact, spent a lot of money on the 1940 election, most of it in vain. The man with the bag was one Hans Thomsen, an attaché in the German embassy. Thomsen repeatedly placed full-page advertisements in the *New York Times* backing isolationists in both parties, and in his report to the Wilhelmstrasse he took credit for a plank in the Republican platform stressing "Americanism, preparedness, and peace." He added slyly: "Nothing has leaked out about the assistance we rendered in this."

It was a doubtful claim; the Democrats had a similar plank, pledging that American troops would not be sent overseas "except in case of attack." The key to the campaign was the Republican candidate, and friends of Britain could hardly have picked a better man. Racketbuster Thomas E. Dewey of New York had won all the primaries, and Taft had set up headquarters with the confident phone number ME-1940, but this was one convention in which the politicians lost control. The delegates desperately wanted a winner; they were angered by Roosevelt's deft appointment, on the eve of the convention, of Republicans Henry Stimson and Frank Knox as Secretaries of War and Navy. The galleries kept chanting "We want Willkie! We want Willkie!" until on the sixth ballot the convention gave them Wendell L. Willkie.

Willkie was a better man than his campaign. He was plagued by small disasters. His larynx wasn't strong enough for leather-lunged oratory. After two days of speeches in September, his voice literally disappeared. In Rock Island County, Illinois, he croaked gamely, "The spirit is—*squawk*—but the voice is—*squawk*." The rest of it was weird, like a silent movie; the lips moved, but no sound issued from them. Specialists told him to shut up, that was the only cure, but it is one thing no presidential candidate can do. Despite ointments and gargling, his voice cracked and scratched and never did return to normal until after the election.

Some party regulars rejected him on the ground that until recently he had been a registered Democrat. Willkie asked Senator James E. Watson for support, and the old man snorted, "If a whore repented and wanted to join the church, I'd personally welcome her and lead her up the aisle to a pew, but by the Eternal, I'd not ask her to lead the choir the first night." Blue-collar toughs booed him, and an egg hit his wife. More seriously, he was weakened by some of the gut-fighters in his own party who had learned nothing in 1936. A Philadelphia lawyer was quoted as saying that Roosevelt's support was confined to "paupers, those who earn less than $1,200 a year and aren't worth that, and the Roosevelt family." The Republican National Committee's antiwar radio spots were so rough they created sympathy for the President: "When your boy is dying on some battlefield in Europe . . . and he's crying out, 'Mother! Mother!—don't blame Franklin D. Roosevelt because he sent your boy to war—blame YOURSELF because YOU sent Franklin D. Roosevelt back to the White House!"

Willkie was blameless in this. The war was the one issue which might have been turned against the President, but Willkie was too good a man, and too gallant an American, to stoop to use it. He encouraged Roosevelt to send arms to England, supported a peacetime draft and the destroyer deal, and though he faulted the President for bypassing Congress in the swap, the criticism was fair.

He didn't deserve the charge of the Old Guard that he was a "me-too" candidate. He could hardly have taken any other stand when the national security was threatened. Above all, he should never have been subjected to the accusation from Henry Wallace, FDR's new vice-presidential candidate, that Willkie was the Nazis' choice.

During all this, the President went smilingly about his business, giving no indication that he had ever heard of a man named Wendell Willkie. His renomination was masterminded by Harry Hopkins, sitting in a tan-walled bedroom in Chicago's Blackstone Hotel with a direct line to the White House in the bathroom. The names of Farley, Garner, and Tydings were placed in nomination —a sign that since their last quadrennial meeting the Democrats had become a divided party. But the convention was plainly rigged. Chicago's Mayor Edward J. Kelly had hooked a microphone in the basement of the Chicago Stadium to the public address system. At the key moment a Chicago official triggered the demonstration by shouting "We want Roosevelt!" into the mike. Republicans thought it significant that the official was Chicago's Superintendent of Sewers.

The only really controversial moment in Roosevelt's campaign came in Boston five days before the election. Local politicians kept urging him to repeat his promise that American boys would not have to fight abroad. He was weary of this, he told them; he had done it so many times. But he finally consented to say: "And while I am talking to you mothers and fathers, I give you one more assurance. I have said this before, but I shall say it again and again and again: Your boys are not going to be sent into any foreign wars."

Sam Rosenman protested; that wasn't the language of the platform. The President should add the proviso "except in case of attack." Roosevelt shook his head. It was too obvious, he replied: "Of course we'll fight if we're attacked. If somebody attacks us, then it isn't a foreign war, is it? Or do they want me to guarantee that our troops will be sent into battle only in the event of another Civil War?" John Gunther afterward suggested that this was "disingenuous." Robert Sherwood, who had argued for the passage, said afterward that he burned inwardly whenever he thought of those words "again—and again," and other Roosevelt admirers still cringe whenever those lines are repeated. Until this year Roosevelt had always leveled with the American people. That was one of the reasons he was about to be returned to the White House.

The morning after the election John L. Lewis found a huge sign draped across the facade of his United Mine Workers Building: RESIGNATION ACCEPTED. The popular vote was the closest of FDR's career—27 million to 22 million—but the indisputable fact was that he still was, as Willkie had called him: "the Champ." Two days after the election the Champ returned to Union Station and rode triumphantly down Pennsylvania Avenue to the White House, beaming and doffing his old fedora as the 200,000 people lining the curbs cheered. The Roosevelt lovers were still legion. Their opposites were around, too. It is entertaining to find that the election results were buried on page six of that day's *Wall Street Journal.*

In the interval between the conventions and the campaign, Roosevelt visited the 94,000 officers and men of the First Army. He sent word that he wanted no gun salutes, no brass band, no reviewing of troops, and no saluting—the Army, being the Army, gave him all of them—but he did want to see what their equipment was like. There still wasn't much to see. The commanding general told him, "We are using broomsticks for machine guns and rain pipes for mortars." The President laughed and said everyone seemed to be in the same boat.

Not quite everybody; not the British. Roosevelt had not only sent them everything he could lay his hands on after Dunkerque; he was now assigning current production of P-40 fighter planes to Britain. It was a sensible decision; the stronger the British became, the longer America would have to get ready. Explaining its wisdom to the American public would probably have been impossible, however, and as he entered his third term, with events escalating at home and abroad, the secrecy surrounding his moves increased. Except when he needed money from Congress, he tended to act independently, sending personal emissaries like Harry Hopkins to London instead of following regular diplomatic channels. Not until the congressional investigation of Pearl Harbor in 1946 did Congress know that the British military staffs flew to Washington for secret conversations with the Combined Chiefs from January 29 to March 27, 1941. Although the two countries were not yet allies, they were, in T. R. Fehrenbach's phrase, "associated powers" with a common goal.

Clare Boothe Luce, who thought the President should be tougher with Hitler, accused him of waging a "soft war." Every leader has his symbolic gesture, she said: Churchill's fingered V, Hitler's stiff arm, Mussolini's strut. When she was asked about Roosevelt, she moistened her finger and held it up to test the wind. It was clever, it was true, and it was absolutely necessary. The President had to know how Americans felt. Divided countries do not win great wars. He could be a step ahead of the people, perhaps even two steps. But if he ever lost them he would fail them and his oath of office. "To serve the public faithfully and at the same time please it entirely," Benjamin Franklin wrote, "is impossible."

The polling business was among the booming new industries. Some of the pollsters' findings were predictable. New York City was more interventionist in spirit than the rest of the country. Yet Texas was more belligerent toward Hitler; anglophilia was rare in Texas, but nationalism was intense. The only section of the country with genuine war fever was Dixie. (No America First rally was ever held in Georgia.) White Anglo-Saxon Protestant southerners were six times as ready to fight Nazis as their countrymen—perhaps, as Dean Acheson has suggested, because so many southern heroes are soldiers. Taking the country as a whole, 62 percent of America had approved the destroyer swap. Ethnic groups whose homelands had been overrun were passionately hostile to Germans, with the exception of Scandinavians. The upper classes tended to be interventionist; by the early summer of 1940 better than two-thirds of America's business and intellectual leadership favored increased shipments to Britain, and almost half the men and women listed in *Who's Who in America* wanted Congress to declare war at once. By then virtually everyone in the nation (93.6 percent) favored building up the armed forces.

But many of the straw votes defied understanding. In the fall of 1939, 40 percent of all Americans believed the United States would be drawn into the European war. After the fall of France, when the danger was much greater, only 7.7 percent believed it. Late in 1940 60 percent believed Britain was fighting for American interests, but only 13 percent approved American participation. And by 1941 a *Fortune* survey reported that 67 percent of the American people were ready to follow President Roosevelt into a war that 70 percent did not want. "The fact is," Lincoln had said in 1862, "that the people have not yet made up their minds that we are at war."

The *New York Times* concluded in late 1940 that the country was suffering from "a form of schizophrenia." But one set of figures was consistent and indicated a trend. To the Gallup question "Do you think the United States should keep out of war or do everything possible to help England, even at the risk of getting into war ourselves?" the response was:

	STAY OUT	HELP ENGLAND
May 1940	64	36
November	50	50
December	40	60

The President was under immense pressure from extremists at both ends of the spectrum; it came from congressional leaders, aides, cabinet members; even from his wife. In retrospect, his policy seems clearer than it did then. He was giving Britain everything he could lay his hands on. He was mobilizing American industry and arming the country to the teeth. And by drifting ever closer to Hitler's periscopes in the Atlantic, he was hoping for an incident which would weld the entire nation into a single aggressive instrument. He gave little thought to the Pacific, nor, so far as is known, was he shown one poll which in some respects was the most interesting of all. On the West Coast Americans weren't much interested in Germany, but they were ready to take on the Japanese any time.

It was the first aspect of his policy which was weakest in late 1940. The United Kingdom was taking terrible punishment, British arms had been defeated on all fronts, and the pound was disappearing. Roosevelt was brooding about all this while basking in the Caribbean sun aboard the cruiser *Tuscaloosa,* recovering from his third presidential campaign and a subsequent sinus attack, when a seaplane arrived alongside to deliver a personal letter from Winston Churchill—"perhaps the most important letter of his [Churchill's] life," James MacGregor Burns has called it. England was running out of supplies and money to buy more; the exchequer was down to its last two billion dollars. The United States was the greatest industrial nation on earth. Indeed, two days after this last election Hitler himself had declared publicly, "As far as American production figures are concerned, they cannot even be formulated in astronomical figures. In this field, therefore, I do not want to be a competitor."[*] But this, Churchill felt, was the very ground upon which Hitler should be *required* to compete. Was there some way

[*] In 1940 the slowly wakening United States forged 66,993,000 tons of steel while the German Reich, running full tilt, produced only 28,000,000.

that the President, working within the American Constitution, could prevent the British from being "stripped to the bone"?

Hopkins was aboard the *Tuscaloosa* when the letter arrived. He saw no immediate sign that Roosevelt had been impressed by it. It took a while for Hopkins to realize that the President was thinking hard—"refueling," Hopkins put it, "the way he so often does when he seems to be resting and carefree." According to Churchill's memoirs, Hopkins later told him that the President read and reread the letter as he sat alone in his deck chair. For two days he appeared to be undecided; he was deep in thought, reflecting silently. Knowing his moods, Hopkins asked no questions. "Then," according to Hopkins, "one evening, he suddenly came out with it—the whole program. . . . there wasn't much doubt that he'd find a way to do it." The program, the answer to Churchill's dilemma and the weapon Hitler could not match, was to be fortuitously numbered House Bill 1776 and known around the world as lend-lease.

Roosevelt returned to Washington December 16. Next morning he called a press conference, and after saying, "I don't think there is any particular news, except possibly one thing," he proceeded to give them one of the biggest stories in American history, explaining the lend-lease concept for forty-five minutes. "Suppose my neighbor's house catches fire, and I have a length of garden hose," he began. "If he can take my garden hose and connect it up with his hydrant, I may help him put out the fire. Now what do I do? I don't say to him before that operation, 'Neighbor, my garden hose cost me fifteen dollars; you have to pay me fifteen dollars for it.' What is the transaction that goes on? I don't want fifteen dollars—I want my garden hose back after the fire is over. All right. If it goes through the fire all right, intact, without damage to it, he gives it back to me and thanks me very much for the use of it." If the hose were destroyed, the neighbor replaced it "in kind."

As reasoning, the parable was both brilliant and specious. He proposed to loan the British, not hoses, but tanks, warplanes, and ships. How could they be returned "in kind" after the war? Moreover, to accept his own metaphor, the hose was the smallest part of lend-lease. With it he would also be signing over to his "neighbor" the hydrant and a great deal of expensive plumbing. Finally, the President alone would decide what to lend, when to lend it, and to whom. H.R. 1776, entitled "A Bill to Further Promote the Defense of the United States, and for Other Purposes," would give him powers no other President had ever requested. It provided for aid to "any country whose defense the President deems vital to the defense of the United States."

As a precedent, the measure would reach far into the future, eventually penetrating the jungles of Southeast Asia, but at the time the debate over it was seen merely as an epic struggle between isolationists and interventionists. The President described the proposal to the country on December 29—the night of one of London's worst fire-bombings—in a fireside chat. The intent of the program, he said, was confined to lending, leasing, and selling war goods. He named the enemy—the Berlin-Rome-Tokyo Tripartite Axis—and he renewed his pledge to keep out of war. "We must," he said, "be the great arsenal of democracy." It was an exceptionally effective speech; letters and telegrams to the President supported him a hundred to one. The polls reported that 71 percent of the people agreed with him, and 54 percent wanted lend-lease to start now.

It couldn't start now, because the isolationists on Capitol Hill realized that this was their Little Bighorn. Hamilton Fish cried that 1776 would leave Congress "with no more authority than the German Reichstag." Ironpants Johnson testified that lend-lease meant "humanitarian lollipopping all over the world." Senator Nye alone spoke for twelve hours; Clark of Missouri called it a "war bill." But their power to intimidate was gone. Alexis de Tocqueville had observed that "Time, events, or the unaided individual action of the mind will sometimes undermine or destroy an opinion, without any outward sign of the change," and this is what had happened to isolationism. The pendulum of history had swung away from it. Its loyalists were little people in the way. A group called the Mother's Crusade Against Bill 1776 staged a sit-down strike before the office door of Senator Carter Glass of Virginia. Glass called the FBI and then told the press: "It would be pertinent to inquire whether they are mothers. For the sake of the race, I devoutly hope not."

Roosevelt's floor managers had signed up the Republican moderates, every one of them. When Homer Bone of Washington asked the question which had cornered interventionists in the past—"What is worse than war?"—Warren Austin of Vermont replied, "I say that a world enslaved to Hitler is worse than war, and worse than death." The galleries cheered. Bone disappeared into a cloakroom. On February 11, 1941, Willkie testified for lend-lease, assuring its passage. He said, "It is the history of democracy that under such dire circumstances, extraordinary powers must be granted to the elected executive." The bill became law in March, and FDR asked Congress to give him nine billion dollars for starters—which raised the money going to arms at home and abroad to twenty-six billion. American flags flew all over London. Hitler said that despite lend-lease, "England will fall." In Italy Mussolini's press said ominously, "Roosevelt's gesture may cause some unpleasant surprises to England and the United States in the Pacific." But who listened to the Duce any more?

Now developments began to gather momentum. Heavy industry, retooling for war production, hired three million new workers. Red, white, and blue banners over assembly lines warned, TIME IS SHORT. Government regulatory agencies were established, and Washington saw the first influx of top-notch managerial talent since the President and big buisness had crossed swords. Civilians began to encounter shortages; Harold Ickes had turned 150 tankers over to the British, cutting America's tanker fleet by 40 percent and creating the East Coast's first gasoline famine.

In February Mussolini had ordered United States consulates in Palermo and Naples closed. Roosevelt retaliated by shutting down Italian consulates in Detroit and New York; then he declared an "unlimited national emergency," freezing German and Italian assets in the United States. Axis ships, and ships from countries which had been overrun by Axis troops, including Vichy France's *Normandie*, were seized "to prevent their sabotage." The Army Air Corps announced that it would train eight thousand fledgling RAF pilots. Roosevelt transferred ten Coast Guard cutters—old rumrunner chasers, relics of Prohibition—to the British and, in sublime defiance of *de facto* hostilities, he opened up the Red Sea to American freighters by declaring Egypt neutral and therefore not in a war zone. On April 9 the United States and Greenland signed a treaty under which Washington, in exchange for the right to establish U.S. weather stations and other bases there, pledged itself to defend Greenland from invasion. A terse announcement said German weathermen already on the island had been "cleaned out." The defense of Greenland, the President declared, was essential to the security of the western hemisphere.

But how far did the western hemisphere extend? That was what Senator Taft kept asking, and responses from the White House were nebulous. The hottest issue that spring, at both ends of Pennsylvania Avenue, was convoying. Gallup first reported that the public attitude was almost entirely negative. A private poll of the Senate disclosed that forty-five senators would approve of U.S. warships escorting freighters halfway across the Atlantic. But forty were against even that, and appalling figures from the British Admiralty left no doubt that the U-boats were winning the Battle of the Atlantic. If the President wanted his lend-lease supplies to reach England he would have to be very clever out on the deep, and far more daring than the Tafts of the Senate would approve.

In February and March, German raiders and submarines operating in what they called "wolf packs" sank or captured twenty-two ships (115,000 tons). The opening of American shipyards to damaged British ships helped, but not enough; the Atlantic was fast becoming a German sea. The President announced that the United States "safety belt"—reporters called it "the chastity belt"—now reached a thousand miles into the Atlantic. At the same time he disclosed that American warships were "cooperating" with the British fleet. He cabled Churchill on April 11: "The United States will extend its 'security zone' to about west longitude 26 degrees." He requested the prime minister to see to it that the Admiralty notify American naval units in "great secrecy" of its convoy dates, plans and destinations, "so that our patrol units can seek out any ships or planes of aggressor nations operating west of the new line." As Fehrenbach has pointed out, "It was under this policy, and these conditions—unannounced military orders—that America entered the North Atlantic war."

In June popular support for U.S. convoys was up to 52 percent, with 75 percent approving if it appeared that Britain would lose the war without convoys. But Roosevelt remained elusive. Knox and Stimson were publicly arguing for convoying; the President told reporters he was against it, and against Americans being sent overseas. That was duplicity, as we now know. Walter Lippmann saw the credibility gap and wrote a bitter column accusing FDR of treating the American people "cleverly, indirectly, even condescendingly and nervously." It was Roosevelt who had to lead a united country, however, and he knew unity would be strengthened if the flag were attacked on the high seas, which, under his policy, was inevitable.

The first incident occurred on April 10. There wasn't much to it.

The U.S.S. *Niblack*, a destroyer picking up survivors from a torpedoed Dutch freighter, made sound contact with a U-boat and drove it away with depth charges. Not even Roosevelt could make much out of that. Still, with the British continuing to lose 400,000 tons of shipping every month, he felt he had to make *some* move. As he told the press, "It would be suicide to wait until they are in our front yard." Therefore he extended the western hemisphere some more. Now, apparently, it would almost reach the North Sea. The spark plug behind the new move was the Chief of Naval Operations, who on June 17 sent Hopkins a memorandum proposing that the 1st Brigade, U.S. Marine Corps, relieve the British troops in Iceland and ready themselves for "operations." Back came the memo, initialed: OK FDR.

On July 7 the marines landed at Reykjavik, Iceland's capital, backed by a presidential statement noting that the Icelandic government had invited the troops and that Roosevelt agreed to prevent the use of Iceland "for use as a naval or air base against the Western Hemisphere." That was absurd. As the bomber flew, Reykjavik was 3,900 miles from New York but only 2,800 miles from Berlin. Iceland was being "protected" from other powers. Confronted with a variation of the very stratagem they used so often and so effectively, the Nazis were indignant. The German Navy wanted to turn loose its U-boats against American shipping, but Hitler, sensing that Roosevelt was looking for just that sort of trouble, refused to be baited. He ordered Admiral Erich Raeder to take every possible precautionary step to see that no American vessel was attacked. Of course, he added, he understood the possibility of an honest U-boat error. So did Roosevelt. The American presence in Iceland put U.S. troops and ships squarely into the Battle of the Atlantic. "If ever there was a point when Roosevelt knowingly crossed some threshold between aiding Britain in order to stay out of war and aiding Britain by joining in the war," Burns wrote, "July 1941 was probably the time."

It was also a time when the Führer had to exercise self-control. Two weeks earlier, on Sunday, June 22, he had taken the boldest gamble of all, invading the Soviet Union on a two-thousand-mile front from the Arctic to the Ukraine. If there was one thing he didn't need right now, it was another enemy. In any event, he suspected that this new invasion would not be entirely unpopular in the United States. It wasn't. *Time* probably expressed the average

American's lack of commitment when it commented, "Like two vast prehistoric monsters lifting themselves out of the swamp, half-blind and savage, the two great totalitarian powers of the world now tore at each other's throats." Senator Harry Truman—in a remark Stalin would never forgive—said he hoped "the Nazis will kill lots of Russians and vice versa." Washington's generals and admirals thought Russia a lost cause and recommended that no supplies be sent there. Roosevelt and Hopkins disagreed. On October 1 a billion-dollar lend-lease protocol was signed with Soviet diplomats, and Russian freighters began making the long, dangerous Murmansk run.

Hopkins and Averell Harriman, lend-lease coordinator, were working with their staffs in seventeen hastily cleared rooms of the Federal Reserve Building. Mobilization was changing the face of Washington. Both the Pentagon and the new State Department Building were finished that autumn. Temporary buildings were rising on the Mall—though the "temporaries" of World War I were still in use. Here and there a name suggestive of the future appeared. Aboard the U.S.S. *Augusta* a young Knox assistant briefly conferred with the President over a labor problem; the ship log noted the call by "Adelai" Stevenson. In the Louisiana Army maneuvers Robert Sherrod told Eric Sevareid, "Be sure you see Colonel Eisenhower—he makes more sense than the rest of them." Eisenhower himself was amused to see his photograph accompanied by the caption *Lt. Col. D. D. Ersenbeing*. ("At least the initials were right," he said wryly.)

Hopkins was now the second most powerful man in the country. He occupied a suite of rooms on the southeast corner of the White House second floor, right in the family's private living quarters. Because Churchill admired him and respected him—he called him "Lord Root of the Matter"—he was trusted in London, too. Late in July 1941, sitting with his host in the garden behind 10 Downing Street, he remarked that the President would like to meet Churchill "in some lonely bay or another." The prime minister was delighted. He very much wanted to see his chief ally in the flesh, and the trip would also provide first-rate propaganda. They chose one of the most desolate places in the world, Placentia Bay in southeast Newfoundland. On August 9 the *Augusta* and its escort of cruisers steamed into position beside the British battleship *Prince of Wales* and its escorts; between them they formed a fleet large enough to fight a major naval engagement, which was perhaps the idea. All meetings were held aboard the *Augusta* except on Sunday, when Roosevelt crossed a short gangplank to attend a religious service. After the British and American crews had sung "Oh God, Our Help in Ages Past," Churchill told the President, "I'm not a religious man, but I thank God that such a man as you is the head of your government at a time like this." For over three days the two leaders conferred with their staffs, were photographed together, and drew up a joint statement of principles called the Atlantic Charter.

After they had returned to London and Washington, the photographs were released to the press and the charter was issued in the form of a communiqué. It endorsed the rights of free peoples to choose their own leaders, regain lands wrested from them by force, trade freely with one another, have access to raw materials on equal terms, improve the lot of backward countries, disarm aggressors, and enjoy freedom of the seas, freedom from want, and freedom from fear. Largely based on FDR's most recent State of the Union address—he had also included freedom of speech and of worship—the Atlantic Charter was endorsed by fifteen anti-Axis nations, including (ironically) the Soviet Union, in September. The curious thing is that the charter, in the tactile sense at least, did not exist. A reporter asked FDR about it. The President replied, "There isn't any copy . . . so far as I know. I haven't got one. The British haven't got one. The nearest thing you will get is the [message of the] radio operator on the *Augusta* or *Prince of Wales*. . . . There was no formal document."

There was an understanding, though, and it wasn't confined to strategies of peace. Back in the White House, the President announced that the convoy question was settled; he had settled it by executive order. American warships would convoy merchant vessels west of Iceland. U.S. ships were to darken their lights at sea and be ready for combat, and although the freighters being convoyed were presumed to be American, the operation plan for the Navy stipulated that "shipping of any nationality" could attach itself to the convoys.

The next incident was likely to involve an exchange of fire, and it did. On September 4, in the waters off Iceland, the commander of the German sub U-652, finding himself under bombardment by depth charges and noting that a destroyer was cruising in the water overhead, drew the obvious conclusion: those were Englishmen in that ship, trying to make him *kaputt*. He was in error. The depth charges were coming from a British plane; the destroyer, the *Greer*, was American. When its captain saw two torpedoes churning toward him, he took evasive action and fired his own depth charges in self-defense. Neither the sub nor the *Greer* was damaged, but the fact of the matter was that Germans had fired the first shot. Roosevelt called it "piracy" and changed his naval orders from "search and patrol" to "search and destroy"—in other words, to shoot on sight. The Nazis and the United States were now in an undeclared naval war, and two out of every three Americans told the pollsters that they approved.

On October 17 a sub wolf pack attacked a British convoy about four hundred miles south of Iceland. The convoy commander radioed for help, and steaming to the rescue came five American warships, led by the U.S.S. *Kearny*, a crack destroyer, barely a year old. She took a torpedo in the side, and though she didn't sink, Americans read their first casualty list of World War II: two men wounded and eleven missing, presumed dead. The President declared that this was no random encounter; the Nazis were carrying out a long-range plan to drive American shipping off the seas. History had recorded which side fired the first shot. He said, "We Americans have cleared our decks and taken our battle stations. We stand ready in the defense of our nation."

Less than two weeks later another destroyer, the *Reuben James*, also on escort duty in Icelandic waters, came within torpedo range of a U-boat commander. This time the American ship went down; with her went over a hundred U.S. bluejackets. The sinking created a sensation in the U.S. press. Woody Guthrie wrote a ballad about it:

What were their names, tell me, what were their names?
Did you have a friend on the good Reuben James?

There was real war fever now, all over the country, but the isolationists on the Hill were unimpressed. The President argued that under present circumstances, some clauses in neutrality legislation were obsolete. One of them forbade American merchant ships to carry any weapon larger than a captain's pistol or a harpooner's gun. It should be repealed, he said, and replaced by a measure arming the freighters and permitting them to carry cargoes to belligerent ports. The intensity of the battle in Congress was almost on the lend-lease level, and the administration margin much thinner: 13 votes in the Senate and 18 in the House. Barring dramatic developments, no declaration of war would get past this Congress. Roosevelt wasn't at all sure he even wanted such a declaration. Under the Tripartite Pact of September 27, 1940, all-out war between the United States and any one of the signing powers—Germany, Italy, and Japan—meant war declarations against the U.S. from the other two. Roosevelt didn't believe the United States was strong enough to take on Japan, too.

The more he and his advisers thought about it, the more dismayed they became. For seventeen months FDR had been more or less making up policy as he went along, improvising affronts to Hitler which would have brought Teutonic wrath down upon anyone else's head. But the Führer never lost his temper; he merely knew how to use it. Twice Admiral Raeder had begged him to strike back. The flow of supplies into Britain worried the admiral. He goaded his leader by drawing up a list of twenty bellicose actions by the American Navy. Unperturbed, Hitler counseled patience; once Russia was defeated he would deal "severely" with Roosevelt. After the President's shoot-on-sight order Raeder pleaded again; either let him attack U.S. warships, he asked, or withdraw all U-boats from the Atlantic. Hitler shook his head. Soon "the great decision in the Russian campaign" would have been reached. Then the wolf packs could be turned loose on the American Navy.

The President had hoped that by putting the United States on a collision course with Germany, events would take over and lead to outright hostilities. But Hitler was still the master manipulator of events, and he kept turning his cheek. On the other side of the world the Japanese, who had been similarly provoked, had given every sign that they, too, would refuse to be drawn. They were here in Washington now, negotiating. As the talks dragged on, the Axis powers drew ever closer to world conquest. Roosevelt felt impotent. "He had no more tricks left," Sherwood said afterward. "The bag from which he had pulled so many rabbits was empty." Sherwood, sharing the gloom in Washington, thought he might run up to New York before Christmas and see what was new in the theater.

Late in November the producing firm of José Ferrer and Ruth Wilk announced the imminent arrival on Broadway of *The Admiral Had a Wife*, a new comedy by Lowell Barrington. Those who had seen out of town tryouts described it as a light piece, the haps and mishaps of an ambitious Navy wife in Hawaii and her attempts to win promotion for her husband by using an uncle in Washington. In its exposure of service nepotism it was also called "a good-natured spoof on the Navy." It was scheduled to open at the Playhouse on Wednesday, December 10, 1941.

Montage: The Last of Prewar America

MAN WITH PICKAX ASSASSINATES TROTSKY IN MEXICO

And now—"Gangbusters!" The only national program to bring you authentic police histories! Gangbusters, America's crusade against crime!

A man without a woman Is like a ship without a sail

WONDER DRUG SCIENTISTS FIND "BLOOD PLASMA"

ANNOUNCER: *The Lone Ranger!* (Bugle) *Heigh-ho Silver!* (Salvo of pistol shots) *A fiery horse with the speed of light; a cloud of dust and a hearty "Heigh-ho Silver!" The Lone Ranger! With his faithful Indian companion Tonto, the daring and resourceful masked rider of the plains led the fight for law and order in the early western United States! Nowhere in the pages of history can one find a greater champion of justice! Return with us now to thrilling days of yesteryear, when out of the past come the thundering hoofbeats of the great horse Silver! THE LONE RANGER RIDES AGAIN!*

LONE RANGER: *Come, Silver! Let's go, big fella! Heigh-ho Silver! Away!*

HITLER BEGINS WAR ON RUSSIA, WITH ARMIES ON MARCH FROM ARCTIC TO THE BLACK SEA

*Thanks for the memory
Of sentimental verse, nothing in my purse
And chuckles when the preacher said
"For better or for worse."
How lovely it was!*

What's cookin', good-lookin'?

FDR BUDGET HITS 8.8 BILLION

CLAGHORN: *Claghorn's the name, Senator Claghorn. I'm from the South.*
ALLEN: *Yes, I know. You're from the South . . .*
CLAGHORN: *When I'm in New York I never go near the Yankee Stadium.*
ALLEN: *Now wait a minute . . .*
CLAGHORN: *I won't even go to see the Giants unless a southpaw is pitchin'.*
ALLEN: *Well, look, now . . .*
CLAGHORN: *And I refuse to watch the Dodgers unless Dixie Walker's playin'.*
ALLEN: *Now wait a minute . . .*
CLAGHORN: *Stop interruptin', where's your manners?*
ALLEN: *Manners! I have . . .*
CLAGHORN: *Stop interruptin'. You might learn something.*
ALLEN: *Listen, if I ever learn . . .*
CLAGHORN: *Your tongue's waggin' like a blind dog in a meat market.*

DRIVES FROM CHI TO INDIANAPOLIS IN SIX HOURS

Last week in Wilmington, Del., Du Pont's sheeny, much-publicized hosiery went on sale, sold quickly when salesgirls claimed that one pair of them would outwear four of silk, that they would dry in ten minutes when washed

POPE'S AIR RAID SHELTER IN VATICAN NEARLY READY

*And strictly entre nous
Darling, how are you
And how are all the little dreams
That never did come true? . . .
And thank you so much*

BEARS, LED BY LUCKMAN, WHIP REDSKINS 73-0

$2 complete with 20 blades Schick injector razor

Eight

AMERICA ON THE BRINK

THE AMERICA KATE SMITH kept asking God to bless in the blitzkrieg spring of 1940 had changed mightily since the pit of the Depression, but it was still a very different country from the superpower of the early 1970s. The war boom wouldn't bring real prosperity until the nation went to war. The morning after Roosevelt's third inaugural, in 1941, *PM*—Marshall Field's seven-month-old adless New York newspaper—covered its front page with a picture of ragged, jobless men. There were still such tableaux to be seen in the United States. Nearly nine million men were unemployed, nearly three million were on WPA rolls, and 30 percent of all Negroes were on relief. And this was more than eleven years after the Crash. Millions in their late teens or early twenties had no memories of a healthy economy. Their fathers had come to manhood in World War I, but before World War II could touch the sons they had been tempered and toughened by a struggle for sheer survival.

Since the country needed a lot of soldiers in a hurry, Roosevelt convened a National Nutrition Conference in the spring of 1941 to find out why Army doctors were turning back nearly half of the men called up by Selective Service. They discovered what any welfare caseworker could have told them; the largest single cause was malnutrition during the previous decade. According to the 1940 census, over half of the nation's children were in families with an annual income of less than $1,500 a year. A quarter of the population still lived on farms; the typical farmer made $1,000. As late as the autumn of 1939, Toledo schools were closed two months because of lack of funds. In Manhattan, the unskilled workers who were using the ruins of bombed-out Bristol, England, to build a foundation for the East River Drive were being paid $832 a year.

Even then, visiting Europeans were scornful of American materialism, but young Europeans today would not have thought prewar America cosseted. Though rural electrification was making steady progress, three farms out of every four were still lit by kerosene lamps. Taking the country as a whole, there was one telephone for every seven Americans, one car for every five. One-fourth of all homes lacked running water, one-third were without flush toilets. The average American had left school after the eighth grade. In Washington, lobbyists for the American Medical Association had just defeated Senator Wagner's health insurance plan, and the biggest killer of children between the ages of five and fifteen was rheumatic heart disease.

The country's population was 132,000,000. Demographers agreed that it wouldn't get much larger. Only 17 percent of married women were working—although the number of women working had crept up, almost unnoticed, by a half-million during the 1930s. Doing housework, wives listened to soap operas, the most popular of which was *Vic and Sade,* and to the new singing commercials. One ditty, "Chiquita Banana" was being sung 2,700 times a week.

The Gross National Product was 90 billion dollars a year; the Dow Jones industrial average drifted back and forth over the 150 mark. America's economy, in short, was still depressed. Sylvia Porter, who then constituted the entire financial staff of the *New York Post,* has provided a vivid picture of what deflation was like then. Renters of bachelor apartments paid $25 a month. Hot dogs were a nickel. Prewar movie admission was twenty cents, most magazines were a dime, a dinner was forty-five cents, the average wristwatch repair ten cents, a fifth of scotch $1.25, and the typical bet with a friend five cents.

Business continued to blame its problems on government interference, labor unions, federal spending, lazy workers, and Roosevelt's refusal to accept Hoover's policy of permitting a "healthy readjustment" of wages and prices. Caroline Bird has offered another solution; the businessmen of the 1930s, she thinks, were not really very good businessmen. They thought prosperity depended upon Wall Street financiers and the so-called basic industries—steel, for example. The real key, which eluded them, was the consumer and the inexpensive goods and services he required. "Demand for shoes, drugs, foods, soap, cigarettes, clothes and gas for the jalopy grew directly with the population," Miss Bird points out. "Buses, trucks, gas, electricity, stores, laundries, beauty parlors stayed in business." In the last months of the prewar era, *Fortune* reported in amazement that one industry which had boomed since the Crash was the manufacture of disposable goods: paper napkins, cups and plates; bottles which could not be returned; and sanitary napkins. Men spent more on condoms than haircuts.

To some degree, products seem to have been withheld because entrepreneurs vaguely felt that they wouldn't be good for people. A woman was supposed to wash dishes; it wasn't right to let her throw them away. Drive-in services were wrong because they made everything too easy. For these and other reasons, among them simple failures of imagination, men of property refused to invest in supermarkets, postage meters, air-conditioning, ski resorts, neon lights, transistors, plywood, and motels. Except for the rich, consumer credit was almost unknown. Most people paid small bills with cash; banks discouraged checking accounts by requiring large minimum balances. The suggestion that a bank should give wigs to depositors, or finance "go now, pay later" vacations, would have been attended by as much shock as if the community's leading citizen had committed a public nuisance in the lobby.

Many of the discoveries which were to alter the postwar landscape had been made before Pearl Harbor. Not only radar but even television was receiving finishing touches from engineers. NBC had beamed an experimental telecast from Grover Whalen's Mad Meadow on April 30, 1939, and receivers on Manhattan had picked it up, though the picture on those early DuMont sets was tiny. Professor Charles L. Dawes of Harvard didn't think television would ever achieve popularity, because "it must take place in a semidarkened room, and it demands continuous attention." Fluorescent lighting was coming in, too, and just as nylon and dacron foretold a revolution in fabrics, so were plastics about to replace steel, aluminum, zinc, and nickel in everything from steering wheels to fountain pens (and, later, ballpoint pens). In the spring of 1940 Igor Sikorsky made his first ascent at the Bridgeport, Connecticut, airport in what one reporter described as "a strange, spindle-shanked machine." A news magazine speculated that Sikorsky's helicopters might be useful on a battlefield.

The American automobile had not yet become what one social critic would call an "insolent chariot," but it was on its way. Oldsmobile advertised a $57 extra called its "hydraulic clutch," which in time would dispense with the need for shifting gears, and the Lincoln Zephyr convertible actually had a magic button the mere touching of which would raise or lower the top. Conservative Detroit shrugged at such gimmicks, just as the publishing business, in those last months of peace, scorned the plans of Pocket Books, Inc. Its first paperback volume, James Hilton's *Lost Horizon*, was on sale at selected drugstores. It cost a quarter.

Advance information on the fate of any of these developments would have made a man's fortune. But sometimes it is just as well that we cannot hold the mirror up to the future. As Hitler blazed his way back and forth across Europe, Washington was completing plans to extend the withholding tax principle from social security to federal income taxes, and a brief story on page 20 of the September 2, 1939, *New York Times* reported that a researcher named A. H. Roffo, addressing the International Cancer Congress, described how he had produced cancer in mice by painting them with tobacco tars.

If you were visiting a distant community in the autumn of 1941, you would almost certainly have traveled by train. The new crack diesels were at the peak of their efficiency and popularity. There were always plenty of redcaps at the station. Roadbeds were maintained so that sleepers in Pullmans—in lower berths, at least—could really rest. The porter shined your shoes, carried your bags, and tugged gently at the green curtain when it was time to wake up. If you gave him a half-dollar as you left he said, "Thank *you*, sir," and meant it. Meals on the train were a pleasure. The tables were covered by immaculate linen, the menu offered a genuine choice, and everyone was courteous.

Your reasons for not flying may have been poor food, inaccessible airports, or fear. To be sure, service and schedules were improving, and now Pan American's Yankee Clipper could take you from Long Island to Lisbon in twenty-six and a half hours, but most people weren't in that much of a hurry. You might drive, though it would be an ordeal. The Merritt Parkway and the Pennsylvania Turnpike had just opened; the rest of the roads were still two-lane and three-lane highways, and every town along the way had its speed traps, fines from which paid the local constable's salary. Tourist cabins were little known and rather disreputable; the campaign against them was being led by J. Edgar Hoover. Writing in the *American Magazine*, Hoover called the precursors of motels "a new home of disease, bribery, corruption, crookedness, rape, white slavery, thievery, and murder." What's more, he warned, husbands and wives might occupy mattresses previously sullied by people who had engaged in "illicit relations."

As the train passed through settled areas, you would see no signs advertising discount houses or roadside food franchises. Like the superhighways that would carry customers to them, they lay over a far horizon. People didn't need cars as much then. They could go to work, shop, or reach schools via public transportation. The number of local bus lines which have been discontinued since then is beyond calculation, but we know something about streetcars. In 1940 there were 19,600 miles of electric railway track in the United States. By the late 1960s the figure had dwindled to 2,049—most of them no longer used.

Near the train station stood at least one Victorian hotel with a mansard roof, alert bellboys, and clean beds for a dollar a night. The bellboy always had liquor available; the town hooker hired herself out for three dollars or, if you were a soldier, two. The hotel dining room would be quiet and inexpensive, though if you wanted something livelier, you might look around for a diner, with its inevitable jukebox and local gossip. Some of the slang might baffle youth in the 1970s. A party was a bash. People didn't split; they scrammed. A Casanova was a wolf. If you wanted a wolf to scram, you told him to get lost, drop dead, or just to dry up and blow away. If a girl approved of him, she would call him nobby, cute, nifty, or snazzy. Alone with him, she might find that he was a sap, but if he was pretty sharp, a smooch could end in her going all the way.

The hotel, the diner, movies, and the hooker were diversions for the traveling salesmen. If you were visiting friends or relatives, they met you at the depot, and if you were male and from a well-to-do family, like as not you would be wearing a double-breasted glen plaid suit. Their home might be in what later would be called "the inner city." But for every Beacon Hill there was a Brookline, a suburb, and here one must come to a full stop. The suburb and suburban life of Greenwich or Winnetka were very different from the

Levittowns and Park Forests of the 1970s. Prewar suburbia was rich, exclusive, prep school- and college-educated, and an immense status symbol—an extension not of the shopping center but of the country club. It was inhabited by John P. Marquand characters, by the people John O'Hara envied and James Gould Cozzens knew: the Republican white Protestant upper middle class. Joseph P. Kennedy had to battle as only a Kennedy could to establish his enclave in Hyannisport, and if a Catholic could barely make it, a Jew didn't have a chance. Neighborhoods for him, like his summer camps and winter cruises, would advertise "dietary rules strictly enforced." If his son went to college, bigotry would be translated into separate fraternities.

Unless you objected to this insularity, life in a prewar suburb could be very pleasant. The old houses were roomy and the new mansions elegant. Ten to twenty thousand dollars bought a lot of house in the Depression; the preferred styles were Tudor or Colonial, though here and there spectacular structures of modern design were rising. Handy-andies mowed the grass and cut the wood. Fathers golfed, mothers gardened, and the young "set" or "crowd" danced Saturday evenings at the club. Nobody complained about the rat race. Gray flannel was an acceptable cloth, and anyone who misbehaved might be expelled from the club. Summer evenings a family sat in the yard; the lawn furniture included a rocking couch called a glider, restful for the elderly (but absolutely impossible for young sex). No date would have been caught wearing blue jeans, a fabric spun for cowboys and manual laborers. Despite juvenile fads, youth wanted what age had achieved: dignity and respectability. Nothing then visible could stop them. Even if war came, everyone assumed that boys with this background would be officers. Inasmuch as the armed forces were making the same assumption, the perpetuation of a privileged caste in uniform, with all its implications, was inevitable.

The future for young American blacks was quite different. Jim Crow was practically a member of the military establishment. In 1940 there were two Negro officers in the Army and none in the Navy. Black soldiers were usually assembled in the "port" battalions that loaded and unloaded ships; only three regiments accepted Negro recruits. Black sailors were confined to the mess; if they were lucky they could wear short white jackets, wait upon officers, and bow deeply when spoken to. Early in 1942 Eisenhower rounded up reports on what was called "the colored troop problem" (no one suggested that it was anyone else's problem). He found it virtually intractable, but he took a step forward by removing racial incidents from the war correspondents' censorship list. Some correspondents argued with him; they were afraid "troublemakers" at home would exaggerate their stories. The general refused and asked them, in effect, why America was fighting this war.

They had no answer, but if one had been from South Carolina, he could have pointed out that the legislature there had passed a resolution declaring that American troops were "fighting for white supremacy." Bigotry openly stalked the countryside in those last weeks of peace. It was bad enough for the Jews, who were barred from prestigious law firms, admitted to medical schools on a quota basis, and excluded from employment by the phrase "Christian only"; none of his peers censured Mississippi Congressman John Rankin when he stood in the well of the House and described a newspaperman as "a little kike." But anti-Semitism never achieved the depths of anti-Negro racism. Senator Theodore G. "The Man" Bilbo, Rankin's fellow Mississippian, enlivened official proceedings from time to time with such Bilboisms as "We people of the South must draw the color line tighter and tighter," "The white man is the custodian of the gospel of Jesus Christ," and "We will tell our nigger-loving Yankee friends to go straight to hell."

It was outside a Mississippi fence that a sign read, "Easter egg hunt. White children 9:30 A.M.—colored children 3:30 P.M." But white racism flourished north of the Mason and Dixon line, too. Congress refused to go on record against lynching. The *Baltimore Sun*, which regarded itself as an enlightened newspaper, reported as a scandal the fact that in a federal work relief camp "colored women live in screened-in cabins." In the celebrated Rhinelander divorce suit, the husband claimed that he hadn't known that his wife was part Negro, and Alice Rhinelander had to strip to the waist to prove he must have known it. Amos 'n' Andy's devoted fans included J. Edgar Hoover, who reported to President Roosevelt that "a good proportion of unrest as regards race relationships results from Communist activities." Chicago's great Negro newspaper the *Defender* warned its southern readers to shed their illusions; they weren't wanted in the North.

But remaining in the South meant more than suffering indignities from such thugs as T. Eugene "Bull" Connor, who even then was Birmingham's head of public safety. Staying home meant trying to live on $634 a year in southern cities, or $566 a year in the rural South. That could be doubled in New York or Detroit, and so the migration of a million blacks began, northward to a living wage, but north to ghettos, too. In exchange for food, clothing, and a better education, they paid a terrible price in social disintegration and mass frustration. It was in these years, in northern slums, that many of the militant blacks of the 1960s were born.

Their early heroes were black musicians, and great black athletes like Jesse Owens and Joe Louis. Sportswriters were acclaiming Louis as the greatest prizefighter in history—he had just defended his title successfully for the ninth time—and he was aware of his social role. "I want to fight honest," he said, "so that the next colored boy can get the same break I got. If I cut the fool, I'll let them down." Among his adoring audience was Malcolm X, who wrote in his autobiography that "Every Negro boy old enough to walk wanted to be the next Brown Bomber."

Some of the greatest music ever heard in America was recorded in these years, and the treatment black musicians received from white Americans was a national disgrace. Benny Goodman broke the color line by adding Teddy Wilson to his band, but even then hotel managers refused to let Wilson play with the band on dance floors. In New York, the magnificent Duke Ellington band was allowed to play at Loew's State Theater on Broadway but was barred from the Paramount and the Strand. Road trips were worse. Finding a place to eat and a bed were daily humiliations. On one of Goodman's southern swings two policemen were hustling Lionel Hampton to jail when their chief appeared; he turned out to be a jazz fan and Hampton was saved. Billie Holiday had to enter and leave hotels by the back door, and in Detroit, where a theater manager thought she looked too light-skinned to appear with blacks, she had to apply dark makeup. Once she made a southern tour with Artie Shaw's band. Of it she said, "It got to the point where I hardly ever ate, slept, or went to the bathroom without having a major NAACP-type production."

Now and then they got a little of their own back. Pearl Bailey recalls a confrontation in one of Chicago's Chinese restaurants. A Chinese waiter came over and, she remembers, "started with a language I couldn't understand, but . . . kept ending with 'Me no serve.'

That did it. I told him in a slow, Oriental drawl, 'You think I came to America to pick cotton. I was told you came to do laundry. So, brother, serve.' And you know what? He did." Lena Horne made a magnificent gesture of defiance in one of the first prisoner of war camps. The camp commander had filled the front rows with German soldiers. Their black guards had been seated in back. Lena slowly stepped down from the stage, walked down the aisle, and with her back turned to the Germans, sang to her own people.

President Roosevelt was inclined to postpone a civil rights program until after the war, but now and then his hand was forced. Black leaders, watching federal money pouring into defense plants, saw Negro job applicants being turned away. In the spring of 1941 A. Philip Randolph, head of the Brotherhood of Sleeping Car Porters, told the President that the government was, in effect, subsidizing discrimination, and if it didn't stop he was going to lead a massive protest march on Washington. The President hesitated. Randolph mobilized his men and set the date: July 4. Roosevelt, dismayed at the prospect of a spectacle which would damage the illusion of national unity, yielded on June 25 and issued Executive Order 8802, establishing a Committee on Fair Employment Practices. Employers and unions were required "to provide for the full and equitable participation of all workers in defense industries, without discrimination because of race, creed, color, or national origin." The policing power was weak, and Negro leaders, who had wanted an order with real teeth, felt defeated. Nevertheless the moment was historic; the great movement which eventually emerged from it would challenge all subsequent American Presidents.

Within the administration, Eleanor Roosevelt and Harold Ickes were those most sensitive to the injustices inflicted upon American blacks, and they joined to give prewar America's civil rights record one shining moment of glory. Marian Anderson was widely regarded as the finest singer in the world; "a voice like yours," Toscanini had told her, "comes but once in a century." But she was also Negro, and when a peppy, redheaded newspaperwoman named Mary Johnson heard of plans for an Anderson concert in Constitution Hall, she played a hunch. Constitution Hall, Miss Johnson knew, belonged to the Daughters of the American Revolution. Calling upon the DAR president, Mrs. Henry M. Robert Jr., she asked her where the Daughters' position was in all this. Right in the driver's seat, Mrs. Robert snapped, and the plans could stop right where they were. Neither Marian Anderson nor any other Negro artist would ever be heard in Constitution Hall.

The next move was made by Walter White of the NAACP. He suggested that one way to draw attention to DAR prejudice would be for Miss Anderson to sing in an open-air, free concert in Washington. She consented, and the universal feeling in the NAACP was that the Lincoln Memorial would be appropriate. That was where Ickes came in; the concert could not be staged without permission from the Secretary of the Interior. Told of the DAR's stand, he phoned the White House. The President was just about to leave for Warm Springs. Ickes asked him to wait until he could get over there. When Roosevelt heard the details, he ordered Ickes to stage the greatest outdoor concert possible.

Eleanor Roosevelt resigned from the DAR, and at White's suggestion she and Ickes recruited a blue-ribbon sponsoring committee of cabinet members, Supreme Court justices, senators, congressmen, and other distinguished men and women. What the president of the Daughters had done was to provide the concert with a massive surge of publicity, literally beyond price. A few prospective sponsors weaseled out with the excuse that their positions prohibited them from participation in controversial issues, but the overwhelming majority came, including the diplomatic corps. The audience was seventy-five thousand. From the opening bars of "America" to the last notes of "Nobody Knows the Trouble I've Seen," they sat spellbound. Then there was a convulsive rush toward the singer which for a moment or two threatened to become a stampede. Among those thrusting their hands toward Miss Anderson, White noticed, was a slender black child dressed in Easter finery. Her cheeks were wet with tears, and despite her youth, her fingers bore the marks of manual labor. White said afterward, "If Marian Anderson could do it, the girl's eyes seemed to say, then I can, too."

Such an event briefly attracted the attention of millions, but it would be misleading to suggest that on the eve of Pearl Harbor Americans were preoccupied with great issues or, indeed, with any issues. Most of them were absorbed in personal problems, trivia, shoptalk. Even in Detroit, where engineers were studying the vulnerability of Italy's light Fiat tank, the most popular topic of conversation was sales. This was turning into Detroit's best year. Dealers had sold five million cars, and executives were tingling with pleasure—to the horror of British officers who had come over for consultations. British shock deepened when Henry Ford first threatened to close his factories rather than accept defense contracts and then stipulated that under no circumstances would he make planes for Canada. Pratt and Whitney, in Hartford, was having trouble producing engines for pursuit planes, as fighter aircraft were then called. Glenn L. Martin had signed a $131,000,000 contract for a thousand B-26s, but at last report only twenty were on the assembly line.

In Hollywood, Louella Parsons and Hedda Hopper exulted over Dorothy Lamour's generosity; the actress had just donated the sarong she wore in *Her Jungle Love* to the Los Angeles Museum of History, Science and Art, which, being in Los Angeles, had accepted it. Elsewhere in the same city the body of F. Scott Fitzgerald had been laid out in a cheap funeral parlor; Dorothy Parker stood over it for a long moment and then said quietly, "The poor son of a bitch." It was a season for mourning authors: within six months of one another came the deaths of Fitzgerald, James Joyce, Sherwood Anderson, and Virginia Woolf.

In 1941 the *Boston Evening Transcript* expired after one hundred and eleven years of continuous publication. That was an omen: the long, slow attrition of American newspapers was gathering momentum; within the next two decades one in every four morning dailies would go. Harvard, alma mater of *Transcript* editors, lamented its passing. The university wanted straight news, now of all times, for like all campuses in periods of great change, it was seething with ideas. In 1941 W. H. Auden published his poem "The Age of Anxiety," William Barrett brought out *What Is Existentialism?*, Henry Luce appalled nonchauvinists with *The American Century*, and the *Kenyon Review* carried John Peale Bishop's optimistic appraisal of "The Arts." Bishop saw the crisis of the West as a great cultural opportunity for America; he welcomed Europe's refugee intellectuals and artists, and he thought they would stay. "The future of the arts is in America," he wrote, "for only here can the intelligence pursue its inquiries without hindrance from the state and publish its discoveries unmolested by authority."

As subscribers pored over Bishop's hopeful essay, a former chicken farmer named Joseph R. McCarthy, who had put himself through law school by working as a gasoline station attendant, a dishwasher, a pie baker, and a pick-and-shovel man on a road construction gang, was presiding as circuit judge, an elective office, in Wisconsin's District 10. Spiro T. Agnew was a claims adjuster for the Lumbermen's Mutual Casualty Company in Baltimore. Whittaker Chambers, now a fat, sad-looking man who wore baggy blue suits, was the third-string book reviewer for *Time*. Alger Hiss, still living at 3210 P Street, in Washington, was a rising man in the State Department. It is startling to reflect that if the Xerox duplicating machine had been invented by the mid-Thirties, Hiss wouldn't have needed to copy documents on his Woodstock typewriter, Chambers couldn't have proved his case, and it is highly doubtful that Richard Nixon, Chambers's champion, would have ever reached a national audience and the White House.

Sportswriters had a dull time in 1941. There was Seabiscuit, of course. Bob Feller threw a no-hitter, and Joe DiMaggio hit safely in fifty-six consecutive games. But Lou Gehrig died in June, the University of Chicago quit intercollegiate football, and the war canceled all Davis Cup, Wightman Cup, and Wimbledon matches. The Olympics were out, too; they were to have been held in Helsinki. The editors of sports pages covered professional football but not with much enthusiasm; it hadn't yet caught on. Its fans included Ensign John F. Kennedy, who had a ticket to the Washington Redskins home game on December 7, 1941.

It had been a fine, golden autumn, a lovely farewell to those who would lose their youth, and some of them their lives, before the leaves turned again in a peacetime fall. The girls, who would be women before the troopships came home, would never again be so willowy. It is startling to learn that the average American girl was five feet five inches tall (less than now) and weighed 120 pounds (more than now). Perhaps nostalgia blurs hindsight, though changes in fashion doubtless play a part. The prevailing hair style in the fall of 1941 was a shoulder-length pageboy or curled bob. Tossing their hair behind them, they crossed campuses like young goddesses, and as Frederick Lewis Allen said, "every girl appeared good-looking from behind."

College girls wore knee socks, came to dances in strapless organdy dresses, and if they were Smithies their daily uniform included a sweater, or sweater set, and a single strand of pearls. (Vassar girls preferred three strands.) Their shoes were broad and low.

Girls not living on campuses wore snoods around their hair, or bare-midriff dresses, but any public nudity would have been an anomaly; it would have destroyed the charm. Boys were less appealing. Their lapels were too broad, and their pants were so wide at the cuff that in old photographs they are almost embarrassing. White shirts (two dollars apiece in department stores in 1941) were standard. With their steadies in mind, early shoppers after Thanksgiving were inclined to take the copywriter's advice and say "Merry Christmas with fragrant whimsies from Coty."

"God Bless America" was number three on the Lucky Strike Hit Parade, and older people choked up whenever Hildegarde sang "The White Cliffs of Dover," but the swing generation remained loyal to its own. In five years they had increased the sales of phonograph records a hundredfold. They argued over who was the best canary—Martha Tilton, Helen O'Connell, and Marion Hutton were much favored—and whenever possible they went to hear live jive. New York's West Fifty-second Street was known as the Street of Swing: at spots like the Famous Door, the Onyx Club, and Kelly's Stables you could, within a single evening, hear Count Basie, Bunny Berigan, and Bud Freeman. T. Dorsey was playing at the Terrace Room of the New Yorker Hotel, Goodman in the Manhattan Room of the Pennsylvania Hotel. And if you really wanted to swing out and shine, you and your date headed for such gymnasiums as the Roseland Dance Hall on Broadway, with its mirrored walls, its ceiling studded with electric stars, and its sharp hostesses.

Those who suspect that there was more than a little hanky-panky amid all this innocence are quite right. Sex went with swing, was even a part of it. The girl whose 1-A date kept playing "Please Give Me Something to Remember You By" knew exactly which something he wanted. The Lynds found that seven of every ten interviewees admitted having premarital sexual relations. While the figure was doubtless lower in the college population, the percentage of "technical virgins" was certainly high. Marriage was out of the question for most. Until long after the war, middle-class Americans regarded early marriage as a lower-class phenomenon, so campus pregnancies were avoided by recourse to what Dr. Kinsey would later call substitute "outlets."

Predictably, the older generation expressed displeasure at the customs of the young. Professor William H. Kilpatrick, formerly of Columbia Teachers College, deplored the breakup of "old authoritarian morals," which was pretty nervy, considering the job he had been doing to traditional values in the classroom. The Pope appealed to Catholic girls urging them to abandon their "immodest fashions," which made little sense, because most of the time everything was covered except the shins, hands, and face. Maybe he meant bathing suits. The *New York Times* did, and protested against the "almost naked people on beaches."

In Alhambra, a Los Angeles suburb, high school girls moving into a new building discovered that they would have to undress and shower in a common shower room. Sixteen-year-old Joan Aveline Lawrence refused. She would rather flunk gym than have other girls see her in all her nakedness, and her father, an engineer, backed her modesty 100 percent. Joan filed suit for an injunction on the grounds that requiring her to show her birthday suit was immoral, violated a California statute about disrobing in public, and encroached upon her constitutional right to life, liberty, and the pursuit of happiness. It was a popular stand, even within her peer group; 275 of Joan's classmates signed a petition demanding private showers.

The judge was on a spot. He leaned on Solomon: since the school had already been built, the girls had to choose between having their parts examined and going dirty. No injunction was issued. The New York judiciary was of sterner stuff, however, and perhaps nothing is more illustrative of prewar Grundyism and the permissiveness of the 1970s than the case of the third Earl Russell—Bertrand Arthur William Russell. Everybody in academia knew Bertrand Russell was a caution, with unusual ideas above love and marriage. Nevertheless, he was at the height of his mathematical and philosophic powers, he wrote the clearest prose on either side of the Atlantic, and he had taught at Berkeley and the University of Chicago. The College of the City of New York rejoiced when he agreed to become a CCNY professor and chairman of its philosophy department. New York reporters, descending upon him, described the philosopher as an elderly man with very blue eyes, an outsize nose, and a receding chin. One wrote: "The British upper classes believe that he is mad."

The Right Reverend William T. Manning, Episcopal Bishop of New York and himself a Briton, thought his lordship was just a dirty old man, and in a letter to newspaper editors he said so. Quoting Russell's books ("Outside human desires there is no moral standard,

... In the absence of children, sexual relations are a purely private matter which does not concern either the state or the neighbors") the bishop demanded to know whether this was the sort of man to hold up before youth as an example. CCNY's acting president answered, "Mr. Russell has been invited to teach courses in mathematics and logic and not to discourse on his personal ethical and moral views."

Round one to his lordship. But by now indignation was spreading in all the places one might expect it to spread: the Hearst papers, the Ancient Order of Hibernians, the Catholic Daughters of America, the Lutheran Society, the Baptist Ministers Conference, and the American Legion. All of them passed resolutions, wrote to newspapers, held rallies, and staged protest marches. The city's Board of Higher Education went into executive session. It voted to stand by the philosopher. He had won round two.

Today that would have been the end of it—assuming that any modern bishop would launch such a crusade, which seems improbable. In the early 1940s, however, parents would go to great lengths to save their children from wickedness. Mrs. Jean Kay, the wife of a Brooklyn dentist, was such a mother. Suppose, she reflected, that her little daughter grew up, went to CCNY, and fell into the clutches of this fiend? Mrs. Kay consulted Joseph Goldstein, an attorney, who filed a taxpayer's suit in her behalf. They appeared before New York Supreme Court Judge John E. McGeehan with four of Lord Russell's books, which Goldstein described as "lecherous, salacious, libidinous, lustful, venereous, erotomaniac, aphrodisiac, atheistic, irreverent, untruthful, bereft of moral fiber," and "narrow-minded."

Judge McGeehan was a Tammany appointee. He knew a good issue when he saw one. In press clippings he found rumors that Russell had run an English nudist colony, tolerated homosexuality, and enjoyed obscene limericks. Then he dashed off a sizzling seventeen-page decision. McGeehan said that in making this appointment the Board of Higher Education had, in effect, established a "Chair of Indecency" at CCNY. Academic freedom, he ruled, could not permit a teacher to teach that sexual intercourse between students was proper. Besides, Lord Russell was an alien. The judge revoked CCNY's appointment and cast the offender into outer darkness, which, in his case, was a full professorship at Harvard—and Harvard couldn't have been happier about it.

Bertrand Russell had at first been stunned. When a reporter told him the judge's verdict, he gasped. "It strikes me between the eyes," he said. "I don't know what to think or say. I want it understood that I am not as interested in sex as Bishop Manning." He authorized the American Civil Liberties Union to act in his behalf. After a while he began to brood. Three years later he returned to England to become one of the most caustic and bitter critics of the United States.

In the spring of 1940 Pat Ryan and Dick Nixon became engaged, and after a June wedding they rented an apartment over a Whittier garage. On the weekend of December 6–7, 1941, he was thinking of applying for a government job. Twelve miles northwest of Whittier, Norma Jean Baker, a fifteen-year-old, sexually precocious girl, was spending less time in her tenth-grade classes than in movie theaters. Dean Acheson left a California Street mortuary in Washington, where he had bowed his head over the body of Justice Louis Brandeis. On the morning of December 7 he had visitors on his Maryland farm; Archibald MacLeish and his wife had driven out to help clear fallen timber in the woods and share a picnic lunch. President Roosevelt was in his oval study, wearing an old pullover sweater and going through his stamp collection. Hamilton Fish was celebrating his fifty-third birthday. Senator Harry S. Truman was writing letters, trying to get more defense contracts for small Missouri businessmen. Richard Whitney, who had been paroled four months earlier, was resting at the home of a friend. At Fort Sam Houston in Texas, Brigadier General Dwight D. Eisenhower, exhausted by his staff work during the recent maneuvers, was taking a nap. Donald Nelson, one of the able executives who had come to the capital to help mobilize the economy, was enjoying a Sunday luncheon at the Maryland farm of Harold Ickes and redheaded young Mrs. Ickes. Senator Nye was enroute to an isolationist rally in Pittsburgh. Myron Taylor had just praised the peace efforts of the Pope and the President at a communion breakfast of the Notre Dame Club of New York. Three days earlier the *Chicago Tribune*, attempting to prove Roosevelt a warmonger, had published top-secret plans—the hypothetical kind that all war offices prepare, to meet any emergency—showing an invasion of Germany by five million Americans in 1943, and at weekend parties Justice Department lawyers were seriously debating the wisdom of charging Colonel McCormick with treason. Norman Mailer was playing scrub football on a Harvard lot. Edward R. Murrow was shaving with particular care; he was to be the President's dinner guest that evening. Seventy-year-old Cordell Hull was on his way to the old State, War and Navy Building, beside the White House. He had just scheduled a meeting with two Japanese diplomats at their urgent, inexplicable request.

Two of the best sellers that weekend were *Reveille in Washington* by Margaret Leach and *The Sun Is My Undoing* by Marguerite Steen.

The Sunday papers advertised Matson Line cruises to Hawaii.

The rising sun, Japan's ensign, appeared over Pearl Harbor on the wings of hostile aircraft that morning, and bombing with devastating precision, the enemy proceeded to cripple the U.S. battle fleet, damage the base, and kill 2,403 Americans.

The attack can never be adequately explained, because it was an irrational response to a miscalculated provocation—or, more accurately, a series of provocations. The first step in the long minuet which ended that disastrous Sunday had been taken nearly two years earlier, when Congress, at the urging of Senator Vandenberg, ended the U.S.-Japanese trade agreements of 1911. Hull then informed Tokyo that future trade between the two nations would be on a day-to-day basis. At the time Walter Lippmann had strongly condemned the move as a step toward war. It put the United States, Lippmann wrote, "in the position of challenging a great power." It did more. It opened the way to a chain of diplomatic moves which made the Japanese jittery, cost them face, and deprived them of vital imports, including, toward the end, the lifeblood of their armed forces—oil.

All that is clear now. It was not so obvious at the time. The administration was too busy following developments on the Atlantic to give the Pacific more than an occasional glance. To the President, the issue in Asia was a moral one. The Japanese were aggressors; they should go home. But he regarded Hitler as the prime disturber of the international peace and dreaded a two-front war. He was always ready to negotiate, and as late as December 6 he sent a message to Emperor Hirohito urging Japanese withdrawal from Indochina. Had it arrived in time, the course of events would almost certainly have been altered. Grew, his ambassador in Tokyo, wanted a softer line from Washington. But Hull and his senior advisers at

State were hard-liners, and they could be steely because Congress, including most of the isolationist bloc—even Senator Wheeler—was vehemently anti-Japanese.

The fall of France, Holland, and Belgium had wholly altered the strategic picture in Asia. Their colonies there were now almost defenseless, and Washington felt avuncular. Hull warned Tokyo on September 4, 1940, to leave Vietnam alone. Later in the month the President proclaimed an embargo on scrap iron and steel to all nations outside the western hemisphere, Great Britain excepted. The following day the Japanese, goaded by what they called this "unfriendly act," signed the Tripartite Pact with Germany and Italy.

The point of no return was reached in the summer of 1941. On July 24 Japanese troops formally occupied Indochina, including Vietnam. Two days later President Roosevelt froze all Japanese credits in the United States, which meant no more oil from America. Great Britain took the same action. This was serious but not desperate; Japan's chief source of petroleum was the Netherlands East Indies, which sold her 1,800,000 tons a year. Then came the real shock. The Dutch colonial governor in Djakarta froze Japanese assets there—and immediately suspended its current oil contract with Tokyo. For Prince Fumimaro Konoye, Hirohito's premier, this was a real crisis. Virtually every drum of gas and oil fueling the army's tanks and planes had to be imported. Worse, the navy, which until now had counseled patience, joined the army in calling for war. Civilian petroleum was rationed immediately; when Ambassador Kichisaburo Nomura arrived in Washington in September he sadly told the press, "All over Tokyo are no taxicab."

His country could hold out for a few weeks; no more. Until Christmas they could count on a trickle of petroleum from private sources, Anglo-American companies with storage tanks on neutral soil. But every day counted now. Konoye submitted his government's demands to Grew: if the United States would stop arming Chiang Kai-shek, stop building new fortifications in the Pacific, and help the emperor's search for raw materials and markets, Konoye promised not to use Indochina as a base, to withdraw from China after the incident there had been "settled," and to "guarantee" the neutrality of the Philippines. Grew warned Washington that there were worse men around the throne than Konoye; humble him, and one of them would replace him. Unimpressed, Hull sent back an ultimatum: Japan must withdraw all troops from China and Indochina, denounce the Tripartite Pact, and sign a nonaggression pact with neighboring countries.

Hull seemed to feel that the United States could treat the Japanese in any way it chose. As far as politics was concerned, he could. If such an ultimatum had been sent to Berlin, there would have been America First rallies all over the country and impeachment proceedings on the Hill. But Grew had been right; Konoye stepped down on October 16 and was succeeded by General Hideki Tojo, the fiercest hawk in the Orient.

The embargoed Japanese now believed that they had no choice. They had to go to war, unless they left China, which was unthinkable. They began sharpening samurai swords. American intelligence, in possession of the Japanese code, could follow almost every development. On November 22 a message from Tokyo to Nomura and Saburo Kurusu, who were still negotiating in Washington, warned that in a week "things are automatically going to happen." On November 27 the Signal Corps transcribed a conversation between Kurusu in Washington and Isoroku Yamamoto in Tokyo. They were using a voice code in which "Miss Umeko" referred to Hull and "Miss Kimiko" meant President Roosevelt. The term "matrimonial question" meant the negotiations in Washington. Yamamoto asked, "How did the matrimonial question go today?" Kurusu replied, "There wasn't much that was different from what Miss Umeko said yesterday." Then he asked, "Does it seem as if a child will be born?" Yamamoto answered in a very definite tone, "Yes, the birth of the child seems imminent. It seems as if it will be a strong, healthy boy." Finally, on November 29, a conversation was monitored in which an embassy functionary asked, "Tell me what zero hour is. Otherwise I can't carry on diplomacy." The voice from Tokyo said softly, "Well, then, I will tell you. Zero hour is December 8"—that is, December 7—"at Pearl Harbor."

Washington now knew that the negotiations were a meaningless minuet, a stall for time; that an attack was coming, and when it would come. The objective of the assault was unknown, so commanders in Hawaii and the Philippines received this message:

THIS DISPATCH IS TO BE CONSIDERED A WAR WARNING. NEGOTIATIONS WITH JAPAN LOOKING TOWARD STABILIZATION OF CONDITIONS IN THE PACIFIC HAVE CEASED. AN AGGRESSIVE MOVE BY JAPAN IS EXPECTED WITHIN THE NEXT FEW DAYS. EXECUTE AN

APPROPRIATE DEFENSIVE DEPLOYMENT PREPARATORY TO CARRYING OUT THE TASKS ASSIGNED IN WPL-46.

WPL-46 was the war plan. On December 6 General Walter Short, the Army commander in Hawaii, was handed another message, from Army intelligence:

JAPANESE NEGOTIATIONS HAVE COME TO PRACTICAL STALEMATE. HOSTILITIES MAY ENSUE. SUBVERSIVE ACTIVITIES MAY BE EXPECTED.

Short concluded that this was a reference to Japanese civilians on Oahu. Therefore he ordered all aircraft lined up in the middle of their fields, wing tip to wing tip—where they could be instantly destroyed by hostile warplanes. He and Admiral Husband E. Kimmel, Hawaii's naval commander, decided not to execute the war plan. Put on constant alert, they felt, the men would become exhausted. In fact, officers and men were given their customary Saturday evening liberty. No special guards were mounted on the United States Pacific Fleet—94 ships, including eight battleships and nine cruisers—the only force-in-being which could prevent further Japanese invasions.

All this is baffling. Short and Kimmel later testified that neither had considered an attack on Pearl Harbor a possibility. Yet it is difficult to think of many moves in military history which had been predicted more often. Confronting one another across the Pacific, each nation had long pondered the strategy of a surprise raid on the base. The U.S. naval maneuvers around Pearl in 1932 have been noted. Japan's interest in them arose from the fact that beginning in 1931, every member of each graduating class in Japan's naval academy had been required to answer one question: "How would you execute a surprise assault on Pearl Harbor?" In January 1941 Ambassador Grew alerted Washington to the possibilities of a sneak raid on Pearl. (In his diary he wrote, "There is a lot of talk around town to the effect that the Japanese, in case of a break with the United States, are planning to go all out in a surprise mass attack on Pearl Harbor. I rather guess the boys in Hawaii are not precisely asleep.") The Peruvian ambassador in Tokyo heard the same talk, and obligingly sent it to Washington via Grew. The American military establishment was not perturbed. Men in striped pants! Peruvians! What would they know about war?

But other Americans had seen the future clearly. In July 1941 Richmond Kelly Turner, then chief of the Navy War Plans Division, had named Hawaii as the "probable" target of any Japanese offensive, and he also predicted that the attack would be made by aircraft. Navy Secretary Knox had written Stimson, "Hostilities would be initiated by a surprise attack on Pearl Harbor." There were warning flags everywhere. An intercepted Tokyo message on December 3, four days before the raid, had inquired whether there were "any observation balloons above Pearl Harbor," and on December 5 FBI agents in Honolulu had told the high command at Pearl that the Japanese consulate there was burning its confidential papers. Rear Admiral Kimmel himself—his memory to the contrary—had warned his staff that "Declaration of war might be preceded by a surprise attack on Pearl Harbor."

What happened? Four years later, with the war won and Congress investigating the catastrophe over which Kimmel and Short had presided, the question was still unanswered. That the commanding officers had failed was evident enough, but why? Part of the answer may lie in the fact that Americans, for complex reasons that included racial chauvinism, had never taken the Japanese people seriously. They were such funny little men, with their thick spectacles, buck teeth, and bowlegs. Everyone knew America might go to war with them, but no one believed it. It was both inevitable and out of the question. On August 11 *Time* reported that "the Navy is fairly well off with its . . . own defenses"; on November 24 it declared that official Washington felt the chances "were nine-to-ten that Japan and the U.S. would go to war"; and in its December 8 issue, which was on the presses when the base on Oahu was going up in flames, *Time* reflected the general confidence: "From Rangoon to Honolulu, every man was at battle stations."

Every *Japanese* was at battle stations, and troop formations were poised to strike at Manila, Hong Kong, Malaya. Months of planning and rehearsal had gone into this coordinated effort. Secrecy had been perfect; no word of the offensive, not even a rumor, had reached foreign agents. And yet, in the end, the Japs bungled it. They had outfoxed themselves. The crux of their diplomatic maneuver had been to declare war on the United States and *then* bomb Pearl Harbor, before the dazed Americans could respond. In the 1970s, after a quarter-century of undeclared hostilities, this may seem too fine a point, but in 1941 most great powers did not make war until the declaration had been made. To do otherwise was considered treacherous.

The schedule drawn up in Tokyo required the two Japanese envoys in Washington to telephone Hull at 10:20 A.M. on December 7 and ask for a 1 P.M. appointment. Tokyo was cabling a fourteen-point message to its Washington embassy, the last part of which contained a carefully worded end of diplomatic relations—in effect a war declaration. Twenty minutes after Hull had the document, the carrier-borne warplanes would swarm over Pearl Harbor. At 10:20 A.M. Nomura obediently arranged the appointment—and then made a dreadful discovery. Yesterday, when he left his embassy, his decoders had been working on the long document. Now, to his horror, he learned that the decoders had quit work early Saturday and would need two or three hours to finish. It was nearly 11 A.M. They were fighting the clock, and they couldn't beat it.

At 12:32 P.M. Eastern Standard Time (7:02 A.M. in Hawaii) a radar operator on Oahu reported the imminent arrival of a large force of aircraft. His superior officer told him to forget it, that the blips were probably U.S. planes coming from the mainland. At 1:20 P.M. Washington time the attack on Pearl Harbor began. At 1:48 P.M. the Navy's traffic chief was called to the Washington-Honolulu circuit by an alert to stand by for an urgent message from the Honolulu operator. At 1:50 it came in:

NPM 1516
Z OF$_2$ 1830 OF3 OF4 O$_2$FO O

FROM: CINCPAC

ACTION: CINCLANT CINCAF OPNAV

AIR RAID ON PEARL HARBOR THIS IS NOT A DRILL

Nomura and Kurusu reached the old State, War and Navy Building at 2:05 P.M., and they were a sorry sight. For three hours they had been struggling with codes and hunting and pecking on typewriters. The message was marred by typographical errors, but they hadn't had time for another draft. As they entered the building, Hull's phone rang. It was the President. He quickly gave his Secretary of State the few scraps of information which had come in, confirming what they already knew from Signal Corps decoding. Meet

Nomura and Kurusu, Roosevelt ordered Hull; don't mention Pearl Harbor, and then icily bow them out.

The Japanese envoys were ushered into his office at 2:21 P.M. Nomura held out the translation and said apologetically, "I was instructed to hand this reply to you at 1 P.M."

His voice trembling with anger, Hull said, "Why should it be handed to me at 1 P.M.?"

"I do not know why," said Nomura.*

Glancing at the translation, Hull said bitterly, "I must say that in all my conversations with you during the last nine months I have never uttered one word of untruth. . . . In all my fifty years of public service I have never seen a document that was more crowded with infamous falsehoods and distortions—infamous falsehoods and distortions on a scale so huge that I never imagined until today that any government on this planet was capable of uttering them."

Nomura moved to speak; Hull dismissed him with a curt nod toward the door.

Moments later Associated Press tickers chimed in the country's newsrooms:

FLASH
WASHINGTON—WHITE HOUSE SAYS JAPS ATTACK PEARL HARBOR
222PES

Curiously, only one network interrupted a program for the start of the war. Len Sterling, staff announcer for the Mutual Broadcasting System, broke into a professional football game between the Dodgers and the Giants at the Polo Grounds. NBC and CBS continued with a Sammy Kaye serenade and a program of studio music; both networks had scheduled news broadcasts at 2:30, and they decided to let their listeners wait until then. Meanwhile, more was coming in:

BULLETIN
WASHINGTON, DEC. 7 (AP) PRESIDENT ROOSEVELT SAID IN A STATEMENT TODAY THAT THE JAPANESE HAD ATTACKED PEARL HARBOR, HAWAII, FROM THE AIR.
THE ATTACK OF THE JAPANESE ALSO WAS MADE ON ALL NAVAL AND MILITARY "ACTIVITIES" ON THE ISLAND OF OAHU.

---

* How much the Japanese ambassadors knew has never been established. It is thought that they—like Hull—had known everything except the target.

THE PRESIDENT'S BRIEF STATEMENT WAS READ TO REPORTERS BY STEPHEN EARLY, PRESIDENTIAL SECRETARY. NO FURTHER DETAILS WERE GIVEN IMMEDIATELY.

AT THE TIME OF THE WHITE HOUSE ANNOUNCEMENT, THE JAPANESE AMBASSADORS KICHISABURO NOMURA AND SABURO KURUSU, WERE AT THE STATE DEPARTMENT.

FLASH

WASHINGTON—SECOND AIR ATTACK REPORTED ON ARMY AND NAVY BASES IN MANILA.

The second flash was a rumor; the Philippines were to have a day's grace—though when the Jap Zeros did arrive, they found that MacArthur, like Short, had huddled his planes together, and in the middle of Clark Field they were gutted just as easily. The radio networks, having canceled all scheduled programs, were now putting everything they could get on the air, including some canards.

Millions of Americans first learned of the attack when they turned on their radios to hear the CBS broadcast of the New York Philharmonic concert at 3 P.M., and one of them was Rear Admiral Chester Nimitz. He was waiting for his set to warm up; at the announcer's first phrase ("Japanese attack on Pearl Harbor today"), Nimitz was up and away—to replace, it subsequently developed, Pearl's unfortunate Admiral Kimmel. Simultaneously a telephone rang at Fort Sam Houston, arousing Brigadier General Eisenhower. His wife heard him say, "Yes? When? I'll be right down," and then he was running for the door, dressing as he went and calling over his shoulder to her that he was on his way to headquarters and didn't know when he would be back.

Inevitably, some reactions were odd. Len Sterling, who had interrupted WHN's account of the football game at the Polo Grounds, was being hounded by calls from infuriated fans who wanted to know what was happening on the field. The same was true in Phoenix, where people were phoning the *Arizona Republic* to say irritably, "Have you got any score on the game between the Chicago Bears and the Cardinals? Aren't you getting anything besides that war stuff?" In Denver a KFEL religious program was canceled; a caller wanted to know whether the station considered war news more important than the gospel. A girl in Palm Springs said, "Everybody knew it was going to happen, so why spoil a perfectly good Sunday afternoon worrying about it?" In New Jersey an elderly man cackled, "Ha! You got me on that Martian stunt; I had a hunch you'd try it again." A reporter asked Senator Nye his reaction. The senator, who perhaps could hear the bell of political oblivion tolling in the distance, growled, "Sounds terribly fishy to me."

But Senator Wheeler caught the national mood: "The only thing to do now is to lick hell out of them." So divided had the country been before this Sunday that President Roosevelt, at a White House lunch the week before, said he doubted he could get a declaration of war out of Congress if the Japs invaded the Philippines. Now the country was united as it had never been. The sneak attack, the presence of two Japanese ambassadors in Washington pretending to negotiate peace, and an old distrust of what some still called the Yellow Peril combined to transform the war into a crusade against treacherous Orientals.

"No!" the President had gasped when the Secretary of the Navy telephoned him the news. Like Knox, Roosevelt had thought that the first blow would fall on the Philippines. No American officer, including General Marshall, had expected a carrier strike on Hawaii now, because Hirohito's crack divisions were in Indochina, ready to jump off for Malaya, Singapore, and the oil fields of the Netherlands East Indies. Pearl Harbor wasn't anywhere near this corridor of advance. Pearl was a logical target in war games, but in the context of the December 1941 strategic picture it seemed almost irrelevant. Now they saw the bitter truth. The enemy had decided to win in a stroke by sinking the Navy. Except for the American aircraft carriers, which had been at sea, Tokyo had made a good job of it. All eight battleships had been knocked out, with the nine cruisers and many destroyers. The United States no longer had a Pacific Fleet.

After calling Hull, the President of the United States did nothing for eighteen minutes. He may have been praying, or planning, or merely adjusting to the new situation. He sat perfectly still. Then he looked up and personally dictated the first news bulletin. He was composed, and so, to a remarkable degree, was the capital. There were exceptions; some zealous superpatriot chopped down one of the Japanese cherry trees around the tidal basin, Civil Defense Director Fiorello La Guardia was racing around in a sirening police cruiser yelling "Calm! Calm! Calm!"—and announcing over the radio, "We are not out of the danger zone by any means"—while a crowd gathered across the street from the Japanese embassy watching the smoke of burning diplomatic papers rise from the chimney and looking, as one woman said, like "a lynch mob I once saw in Valdosta, Georgia."

There was no necktie party at the embassy, La Guardia collected himself, the rest of the cherry trees remained intact, and the President was working swiftly and efficiently. He called in the cabinet, talked to Churchill on the transatlantic phone, briefed the congressional leadership, ordered guards around defense plants, advised Hull to keep South American governments informed, and reviewed the Army's troop dispositions with Marshall. Ed Murrow, who had heard the news while golfing on the Burning Tree course, had assumed their dinner engagement would be canceled, but Mrs. Roosevelt called Janet Murrow and said, "We all have to eat. Come anyway."

They ate, though the President's chair was empty. The Executive Mansion's lovely oval study had abruptly become the commander in chief's general headquarters. While Sumner Welles stood by, Roosevelt dictated tomorrow's war message, and from time to time, when a door was opened, his resonant voice could be heard in the hall: "Yesterday comma December seventh comma nineteen forty-one dash a date which will live in infamy dash the United States of America was suddenly and deliberately attacked by naval and air forces of the Empire of Japan period. Paragraph The United States was at peace with that nation and comma at the solicitation of Japan comma was still in conversation with that government and its Emperor looking toward the maintenance of peace. . . ."

Murrow thought he ought to go, but several times the First Lady left the table, and she always returned with a message from the President: he wanted Murrow to stay. At 11 P.M. Janet went home. It was a half-hour after midnight when Roosevelt, obviously exhausted, invited the commentator to share a tray of sandwiches and beer. He took Murrow into his confidence, described the damage at Pearl, and told him that every member of the administration responsible for defense—himself, Knox, Stimson—was incredulous. They just couldn't understand how a major military base could have been so vulnerable, could have suffered such losses. He was still stunned, still angry.

"Our planes were destroyed *on the ground!*" he said again and again, pounding his fist on the table. "On the *ground!*"

Across Pennsylvania Avenue, in Lafayette Park, anonymous Washingtonians stood in a dense mass that evening. Some were singing "God Bless America," but most of them stared up at the White House in silence. There wasn't much to see. The Executive Mansion was dark; the great light over the north portico was unlit for the first time in memory. Already Henrietta Nesbitt, the mansion's housekeeper, was taking measurements for blackout curtains. West Executive Avenue had been closed to traffic; it passed too near the President's office. In the White House basement engineers were chalking off the entry for a tunnel which would pass beneath East Executive Avenue and enter the old vaults under the Treasury Building—the safest shelter in Washington if the capital should be bombed.

Secretary Morgenthau had ordered the White House guard doubled. On the roof of the old State, War and Navy Building, over the room where Hull had confronted the wretched Japanese envoys, soldiers worked in the dark siting antiaircraft guns, and the fifth floor of the old structure was being transformed into a barracks for the troops who would man the guns. At the time none of these precautions seemed extravagant.

Downstairs Marshall was leaving. A presidential adviser asked him about conflicting rumors from Hawaii. Every war has its rumors, the general said, and sometimes it was impossible for anyone to distinguish between myth and reality. He explained: "We're now in the fog of battle."

In Chicago a newsstand was mobbed by people trying to buy *Tribune* extras. In passing, a stocky woman said to a stranger, "What's this?" He replied, "We're at war, lady, for crying out loud." She said, "Well, what do you know. Who with?" The anecdote enjoyed a brief vogue during the next few days, and was usually worth a chuckle. Actually the question was highly relevant. The President was committed to an Atlantic first strategy. When Churchill phoned him that afternoon and asked "Mr. President, what's this about Japan?" Roosevelt replied that yes, it was true: "They have attacked us at Pearl Harbor. We are all in the same boat now." But were they? The nation's shock and anger were directed at the Japanese. The outrage at Pearl couldn't be blamed on Nazis. Emotional as the Congress was, it would probably balk at involvement in a two-front war. Even if it went along with war declarations against the European Axis, the country would be divided again, and morale, now so high, would dive.

Luckily for the Allied cause, Adolf Hitler was no longer entirely rational. He had begun to crack under the strain of the Russian campaign. Increasingly he was given to uncontrollable rages and decisions guided by intuition—by what he called his "artistic" side. On December 8 he left his Wolfsschanze headquarters in East Prussia and hurried back to Berlin by train; the Japanese were invoking the Tripartite Pact. Hitler could have ignored Tokyo. It wouldn't be the first solemn pledge he had made and then broken, and the nature of the Pearl attack could have been called an extenuating circumstance; the text of the treaty bound Germany and Italy to assist Japan only in case of an attack on Japan itself. If the Führer turned his back on Tokyo he could scarcely have been punished. Japan and Germany were on opposite sides of the globe, with the Soviet Union between them.

So his advisers argued. With the exception of Ribbentrop, who vacillated, the men around Hitler begged him not to add the United States to his long list of anti-Nazi belligerents while he chose this, of all times, to recall a verbal commitment he had made to Hirohito's foreign minister: "If Japan should go to war with the United States, Germany, for her part, would immediately take the necessary steps at once." He argued, "if we don't stand on the side of Japan, the pact is politically dead." The Nazi leadership was unconvinced. The debate raged day and night between December 8 and December 11—an anxious time in Tokyo—and then Hitler conceded that his true motive was vengeance. Frustrated by the endless steppes of Russia, he had been seething more and more over the behavior of American destroyers in the Atlantic. In short, Roosevelt's accelerating provocations had driven the Führer to the end of his tether after all. According to the Nuremberg documents, Hitler said that the "chief reason" for opening formal hostilities "is that the United States is already shooting against our ships. They have been a forceful factor in this war and through their actions have already created a situation of war." Thereupon he proclaimed a state of war against America. Mussolini followed suit—by now he was entirely the Führer's creature—and suddenly Roosevelt's problem was solved. Congress had no choice; it reciprocated later that same Thursday. Dean Acheson, who thought Hitler was acting with "colossal folly," later wrote, "At last our enemies, with unparalleled stupidity, resolved our dilemmas, clarified our doubts and uncertainties, and united our people for the long, hard course that the national interest required."

II

SACRIFICE AND TRANS-FORMATION

1941-1950

Nine

COUNTERATTACK

"THE JAP," as MacArthur called the enemy—nearly everyone else called Japanese "Nips," short for "Dai Nippon," the Japanese word for their homeland—may have been the most underrated infantry weapon in history. On parade he resembled a poorly wrapped parcel of brown paper—soiled, crumpled, and threatening to come apart. His leggings were sloppy, his blouse bulged, his trousers were baggy, and his bandy legs were ridiculously short. The image was deceptive, but illusions die hard; even after the ax fell at Pearl, Admiral William F. Halsey Jr. predicted Japan would be crushed by 1943, and at home jukeboxes rasped, "Goodbye, Mama, I'm off to Yokohama," and "I'm gonna slap a dirty little Jap." Any barhop could tell you: America had been winning battles since 1775, and had never lost a war.

But the *Japanese* hadn't lost a war since 1598. The men in the badly wrapped brown uniforms were anything but inept in combat. As sharpshooters they were accurate up to a thousand yards. Each carried 400 rounds of ammunition (twice as many as an American infantryman) and five days' rations of fish and rice. They were absolutely fearless; since childhood they had been taught that there could be no greater glory than dying for the emperor. Moreover, the hardware backing them up was awesome. At Pearl they had sunk America's battlewagons, and presently Washington was learning that Nips' ships were faster, their guns bigger, their torpedoes better, and their air power matchless in number and quality. Over Hawaii they had flown four warplanes, the Kawasaki, the Mitsubishi Zero, the Nakajima B5N1, and the Mitsubishi G4M1, each of them superior to anything comparable the United States could put in the sky then.

Secretary Stimson warned the country in the fourth week of the war: "We'll defeat the Japanese in the end, but we shouldn't look at the war with them through rose-colored glasses. There have been reports that the Japanese . . . are badly trained troops, ill equipped. The cold truth is that the Japanese are veterans and they are well equipped. The Japanese soldier is short, wiry and tough. He is well disciplined." By then the fiction that any red-blooded American could lick ten Orientals had yielded, in Washington at least, to a shocked realization that the capital had entered its grimmest period since the Civil War. U.S. military intelligence—it was called intelligence—had ruled out an air strike at Pearl because, among other things, the enemy was known to be massing troops in Saigon, and everyone knew that Tojo couldn't mount more than one offensive at once.

Everyone was wrong. By New Year's Day the troops of Dai Nippon had not only thrust southward from Saigon; they had also made landings on Guam, Hong Kong, Borneo, Wake, and the Philippines. Tojo was outblitzing Hitler. He was carving out an enormous salient —a tenth of the globe—into the direct route between the West Coast and Tokyo, and he was receiving invaluable assistance from Admiral Raeder's unleashed U-boats. Shipping had been short from the outset. Raeder was determined to break the Anglo-American alliance, making the supply of overseas garrisons impossible by sinking every vessel flying the Stars and Stripes or Union Jack. In early 1942 it looked as though he would succeed. Merchantmen were being torpedoed almost nightly within view of Americans living on the East Coast. Within a few hours of each other that January, Nazi submarines dispatched the 6,768-ton British tanker *Coimbra* and the freighter *Norness* off Long Island and the U.S. merchantman *Allan Jackson* and tanker *Malay* off North Carolina. That year U-boats blew up 1,160 ships, better than three a day, including the destroyer *Jacob Jones*, which, when it went down off Cape May, New Jersey, became the first American warship to be torpedoed in her own coastal waters.

It was in these desperate months, with defeat following defeat, that the Axis powers seemed invincible. The Nazis were taking Stalingrad and reforming for their final leap on Moscow. Rommel was approaching Cairo—British diplomats there were burning their papers—and it seemed only a question of time before the Germans would be at the gates of India, where they would greet their Nipponese allies sweeping in from the east. Like Hitler, Tojo seemed unstoppable. General Joseph Stilwell limped out of Burma muttering, "We got a hell of a beating. We got run out of Burma and it is as humiliating as hell." In Washington there were strategists who thought it might take ten years to beat Japan. The two protective oceans appeared to have shrunk; not only were American seamen being killed within sight of the eastern seaboard, but the Pacific Coast heard gunfire, too. Jap submarines shelled Seattle, and fifteen carrier-borne Zeros bombed Los Angeles in early March. Militarily the attacks were only of nuisance value, but as psychological thrusts they were brilliant. The President decided to calm the nation. He scheduled a fireside chat and asked the newspapers to publish world maps so listeners could follow him. But the Japanese had access to American radio, and while Roosevelt was quietly assuring the public that there was no reason for defeatism, another flotilla of Jap U-boats strafed Santa Barbara. Antiaircraft guns began to rise around Los Angeles and San Francisco.

Apart from Pearl, the first movement in the concert of offensive Tojo had prepared for December 7 was Malaya. A few foreign service officers in Washington, proud of their ability to read the Oriental mind, had hazarded a guess that the Japanese might trespass in Thailand. In a way they were right—as right, say, as forecasters who had predicted that New England might get a little rain that memorable September day three years earlier. Having taken advantage of Vichy weakness to convert Indochina into a staging area, General Tomoyuki Yamashita had entered into secret negotiations with the Thai government. As a consequence, the Thais surrendered to him after four hours of sham fighting on December 7. Now he was ready for his first big show: Malaya.

Surging through Thailand, three bristling columns invaded the peninsula under an umbrella of planes from Vietnam, driving the British back and back. The Japs didn't really need so large a force, but they hoped to divert the RAF and lure the British Navy into a trap. It worked. Admiral Sir Tom Phillips went for the bait with the pride of H.M.'s Navy—the *Prince of Wales,* Britain's newest battleship, and the heavy battle cruiser *Repulse.* His one carrier ran aground, depriving him of his eyes, and on the third day of the war Mitsubishi torpedo bombers sank the only two Allied capital ships then off Hawaii. Nothing could save Malaya now. The enemy advance accelerated—wild stories were circulated of Jap "monkey men" who swung from tree to tree, like Tarzan (in fact they were using bicycles), and Winston Churchill learned to his horror that the great guns of Singapore pointed only at sea and couldn't be turned.

Those were Hirohito's crack troops. While they had lunged southward, Lieutenant General Masaharu Homma had been landing regular divisions on Luzon since December 10, the day Tom Phillips drowned and unfortified Guam fell into the Jap bag. In less than three weeks Homma was ashore at nine points. MacArthur declared Manila an open city (it was immediately bombed) and American soldiers and Filipino scouts were retreating into Bataan peninsula. Roosevelt wanted to save MacArthur. He knew how difficult the general could be, but respected his military judgment. He ordered him to Australia, and in the darkness of a February night MacArthur boarded a PT boat with his wife, his son, and the son's governess. The men left behind sang bitterly:

> *We're the battling bastards of Bataan:*
> *No momma, no poppa, no Uncle Sam,*
> *No aunts, no uncles, no nephews, no nieces*
> *No rifles, no guns or artillery pieces*
> *And nobody gives a damn.*

Their complaint about the lack of weapons was painfully close to the truth. The defense was disintegrating; the only U.S. regiment on the peninsula, the 31st Infantry, was down to 636 men, so they withdrew into the tadpole-shaped island fortress of Corregidor, supported by ten obsolete planes and a few PT boats. The ranking naval officer, Admiral Tom Hart, had left the day after Christmas flying his four-star flag from the biggest warship he had, the submarine *Shark*. For a while the men in Corregidor's underground chambers hung around the Signal Corps radio, but then they quit; the news broadcasts were too depressing. Hong Kong had fallen, its nurses raped in the streets by Jap soldiers. Wake was gone too, after a valiant two-week stand by five hundred marines under Major James Devereux, who beat off an attempted landing and then waited, in vain, for relief. By New Year's Day, when Vice Admiral Hart surfaced off Java and joined Field Marshal Wavell's Allied command, Nips in defeated Singapore were taking dead aim on Java and Sumatra. Wavell studied his war map and flew off to India, leaving the Indies, as the angry Dutch said, to their fate.

It was a terrible fate. Led by a Dutch admiral whose orders had to be translated to Allied captains, seventeen Allied warships without air power sailed out to stop the invasion of Java. They were hopelessly outmatched. The largest among them were two cruisers, and looming over the horizon were the pagoda-like forecastles of seventy-four Jap ships, including four battlewagons and five carriers. In the seven-hour Battle of the Java Sea half the Dutchman's ships went down with him; Jap planes proceeded to polish off most of the rest. The last two surviving vessels, the American *Houston* and the Australian *Perth*, tried to escape through Sunda Strait. The enemy had closed it, and in the night of March 1 they went down fighting, the *Houston* encircled by enemy steel, all her guns blazing defiantly and a bluejacket bugler standing on the sloping fantail sounding Abandon Ship.

It was difficult for people at home to understand what was happening in the Pacific. Pearl Harbor, like the Alamo and the *Maine*, is better remembered than the war that followed. One reason is that except for the West Coast, America was preoccupied with Hitler. Another is geography. Men on Iwo Jima got V-mail from relatives who thought they were still fighting in the "South Pacific." Names from the European theater were a familiar echo from school days, but who had heard of Yap? Where was Ioribaiwa? And what was the difference between New Britain, New Caledonia, New Guinea, New Ireland, and the New Hebrides?

American teachers, unfortunately, hadn't gone into that. They couldn't be blamed. Until the air age, islands like Wake, Midway, and Iwo had been almost worthless, and as late as 1941 entire archipelagoes were of interest only to Standard Oil or Lever Brothers. The U.S. Navy started the war with obsolete eighteenth-century charts; sea battles were actually broken off because no one knew where the bottom was. The Marine Corps had to survey King Solomon's Isles as they went along. Their first engagement there was fought on the wrong river—they thought it was the Tenaru, and discovered afterward it was the Ilu.

Most of what the public did know about the Pacific had been invented by B movie scriptwriters. The South Seas were pictured as exotic isles where lazy winds whispered in palm fronds, and Sadie Thompson diddled with missionaries, and native girls dove for pearls in fitted sarongs, like Dorothy Lamour. It was an appealing myth, and there was a flicker of truth in it. The girls looked more like Lister bags than Lamour, but most veterans of the Greater East Asia War, as the enemy called it, can recollect scenes of great natural beauty—the white orchids and screaming cockatoos in Guadalcanal's dense rain forests, for example, or the smoking volcano in Bougainville's Empress Augusta Bay, or Saipan's lovely flame trees.

But American men hadn't come as tourists. They were fighting a savage war, and the more breathtaking the jungle looked, the more ferocious the combat turned out to be. Some islands were literally uninhabitable—Army engineers sent to survey the Santa Cruz group for airstrips were wiped out by cerebral malaria—and the battles were fought under fantastic conditions. Guadalcanal was rocked by an earthquake. Volcanic steam hissed through the rocks of Iwo. On Bougainville, bulldozers vanished in the spongy, bottomless swamps, and at the height of the fighting on Peleliu the temperature was 115 degrees in the shade. Sometimes the weather was worse than the enemy. At Cape Gloucester sixteen inches of rain fell in one day. The great sea battle of Leyte Gulf was halted by a double monsoon, and a month later a typhoon sank three American destroyers.

Like any war, this one had its special sights and sounds, to be remembered in later years as a kind of blurred kaleidoscope or a random selection of old film clips, enough to jog quiescent memories later, and sometimes even to stir the dark recesses of the mind where the terror of those days still lurked. There were the Quonseted troops on sandy outposts ringed by the brasslike sea—castaways on cartoon islands, vindicating Justice Holmes's definition of war as an "organized bore." There was scratchy monotony on the ship PA systems, the smell of sweat, the sickening heft of an empty canteen. Temporary airstrips were paved with slabs of perforated metal like pieces from a gigantic Erector set. There were the blossoms of artillery crumps in the banyan jungles, the meatballs on Zero wings flashing under the equatorial sun, the way phosphorescent organisms in the water would light up when a zigzagging prow taking evasive action creamed through them, and the image of carrier pilots scrambling across a flattop deck, helmets flapping and chart boards clutched under their arms.

To former marines and GIs, however, the most poignant memory is likely to be of that almost unbearable tension in the small hours of Z-day or A-day or L-day of a new operation, when they stumbled down from their hard transport bunks, toyed with a 3 A.M. breakfast, watched the warships sock the shore with their fourteen-inch salvos and then crawled down in the swinging cargo nets to rocking Higgins boats, those unbelievably small landing craft, with their packs tugging hard on their already aching backs. Peering nervously toward the purply land mass ahead, they would highball in toward Red Beach One, say, or Green Beach Two, hoping there would be no reefs this time to hold them in Jap machine gunners' sights, wondering what the terrain would be like, and knowing it would be another miserable blast furnace—torture for the foot soldier, yet touched, as all the islands were, with a wild, unearthly splendor.

Lurid settings produced bizarre casualties. Twenty-five marines were killed during the Battle of Cape Gloucester by huge falling trees. Shipwrecked sailors were eaten by sharks. Japanese swimming ashore after the Battle of the Bismarck Sea were carved up by New Guinea headhunters, and others, on Guadalcanal, were eaten by their own comrades. The jungle was cruel to defeated soldiers, who, as America's growing sea power cut off lines of escape, were usually Nips. If they were surrounded, only cannibalism and ferns were left to them, and they had to share the bush with snakes and crocodiles. Even when they had an escape route the odds were against survival. Just one man in five was able to bear arms after Admiral Mori's retreat across New Guinea's Huon Peninsula, and during General Horii's disastrous flight across the Owen Stanley Mountains, the general actually drowned.

Japanese surrenders were proscribed until the Son of Heaven ordered it, and even after Hirohito had done so, diehards sulked in caves until well into the 1950s and even afterward. Japs considered it disgraceful to be taken alive. Some carried suicide pistols with a single bullet in the magazine. When defeat loomed in the middle years of the war, officers would round everybody up for a traditional *banzai* (hurrah) suicide charge. Men without rifles were issued clubs, men unable to walk were given hand grenades or land mines and told to blow themselves up. No one was exempt. The

Saipan commander was too senile to kill himself, so an aide shot him, and it was on Saipan that five-year-old Japanese children formed circles and tossed grenades back and forth until they exploded.

Hara-kiri had always been highly regarded in Japan, but to the samurai warlords last-ditch resistance also made military sense. Having captured more of Oceania than they needed in half the time they had allowed, they were maneuvering for a negotiated peace. "We are prepared to lose ten million men in our war with America," General Homma had warned in 1939. "We will build a barricade across the Pacific with our bodies," said a crudely lettered sign over the Jap dead on Peleliu. Their propaganda never mentioned anything except total victory over the Yankees, though in their inner councils they were more realistic. If the U.S. regained the initiative, the admirals and generals planned a war of attrition. The closer Americans came to their homeland, the more determined the Japanese would become. Tokyo would mobilize suicide boats, human torpedoes, and great clouds of kamikaze planes. Faced with landings on Japan itself, the national slogan would be: "One hundred million people die proudly!" They knew MacArthur expected fifty thousand U.S. casualties the first day of an invasion of Japan, followed by a campaign which might last years. The American people, they reasoned, would not pay such a sacrifice for unconditional surrender. Therefore they prepared posters to be put up in Tokyo toward the end: "The sooner they [the Americans] come, the better."

What made Pacific combat so ferocious, and turned it into a conflict in which few prisoners were taken, was that Japs thought it shameful for their enemies to surrender, too. Their captives were not treated gently. Corregidor's survivors were led on a "death march" after their capitulation—that is, the weak and the wounded were literally marched to death. Nips beheaded marine raiders captured on Makin Island, and at Milne Bay they left behind bayoneted Australian prisoners whose penises had been lopped off and the foreskins sewn to their lips. Above hung a taunting sign: "It took them a long time to die."

Such behavior brought swift retaliation; not since the French and Indian War had American troops been so brutal. Women and children were excluded; there were none of the atrocities against civilians which were to stain the Army's honor a quarter-century later in Vietnam. But in combat there were no truces, no chivalric gestures. The U.S. Navy waged unrestricted submarine warfare. Nips in the Admiralty Islands who preferred starvation to surrender were left in the bush and used for target practice. It was a hard war. Generals and flag officers could be as bloodthirsty as riflemen. Lieutenant General Lesley J. McNair told his troops, "We must hate with every fiber of our being. We must lust for battle; our object in life must be to kill." Admiral William F. Halsey ordered the erection of a huge billboard on a Tulagi hillside, visible to passing ships:

> KILL JAPS. KILL JAPS.
> KILL MORE JAPS.
> You will help to kill the yellow
> bastards if you do your job well.

In the same mood, MacArthur told General Robert L. Eichelberger that if he didn't take Buna he needn't come back alive, and in 1943, when spies reported where Japan's great Admiral Yamamoto was, American commanders deliberately sought him out with P-38 fighter planes and killed him.

Yamamoto was a genius, an Oriental Nelson. He had masterminded the multipronged naval offensive which had seized 3,000 square miles of Oceania in six months. Had he known that the U.S. Signal Corps had broken his Purple Code, the war would have taken a very different turn. As it was, he came so close to annihilating American power that he became a perennial Pentagon argument for staggering defense budgets long after he was dead.

After his total victory in the Battle of the Java Sea, the rising sun was blinding. Singapore had capitulated on February 17 ("All I want from you," Lieutenant General Yamashita told Britain's Lieutenant General A. E. Percival, "is *yes* or *no*"), and fourteen of her huge Vickers naval guns were moved to an atoll in the Gilbert Islands exotically named Tarawa. Burma followed swiftly. By the second week in March 1941 the Nips were on the Road to Mandalay, which they took on May Day, sealing off China.

Singapore had been a big name; its loss was shocking. Less familiar, but more vital, was Rabaul, an Australian outpost in New Britain captured by the enemy in January. He moved in 100,000 troops, paved five airfields, and built Rabaul into an impregnable fortress, the key to a chain of outposts in New Ireland, the Solomons, and New Guinea. Jap pilots were now within range of

Australia; after heavy air raids, Darwin, on the north coast, had to be abandoned. In New Zealand every man under sixty-five was called up, and the country's pursuit planes were readied for combat —all nine of them. The prime minister of Australia warned his people to expect invasion hourly. In Washington Ernest J. King, the new Admiral of the Fleet or COMINCH (the abbreviation had been hastily changed from CINCUS), was arguing against the abandonment of both dominions. "The Pacific situation is now very grave," Roosevelt cabled Churchill, and Tokyo Rose jeered, "Where are the United States Marines hiding?"

Apart from the southern Solomon Islands, Port Moresby (the tail of birdshaped New Guinea) and dying Corregidor, the Japanese controlled the entire Pacific west of Midway and north of the Coral Sea. They had expected 20 percent casualties in their blitz, and they had been scarcely touched—one of their fleets had sunk five Allied battleships, a carrier, two cruisers, and seven destroyers without receiving a scratch. MacArthur spoke brave words in Australia; King ordered Admiral Nimitz, who had been hastily sent out in mufti as the Pacific's new commander, to hold the Midway-Samoa-Fijis-Brisbane line "at all costs." Yet this seemed like whistling in the dark. After the Java Sea disaster America was fielding scratch teams. U.S. forces in the Pacific were beset by every conceivable calamity, including subversion. U.S. headquarters at French Nouméa were infested with Vichyite colonials, who sent the enemy bulletins on U.S. ship and troop movements.

At home, American morale was being braced with cheerful lies: that an Air Corps flier named Colin Kelly had sunk the battleship *Haruna* (he didn't); that a naval brush in Macassar Strait, off Borneo, was a great victory for the U.S. (it wasn't); and that the marines on Wake had radioed "Send us more Japs" (they certainly hadn't). Tojo and Yamamoto, undeceived, confidently reviewed the Japanese war plan of 1938. Guadalcanal and nearby Tulagi in the Solomons were next on the timetable, and were easily taken May 3. On May 6 Corregidor surrendered. The Philippine tragedy was now complete. In Australia MacArthur wrote, "Corregidor needs no comment from me. But through the bloody haze of its last reverberating shot I shall always seem to see the vision of its grim, gaunt and ghostly men, still unafraid."

The following day a Japanese amphibious force steamed into the Coral Sea, east of Australia, intent upon capturing Port Moresby.

They were heartened by the conquest of the Philippines and flushed with what Admiral Hara, the carrier commander, later called a "victory disease." The battle which followed was the first carrier versus carrier action in history, and it was a curious engagement. The Americans were desperate. To save Australia they had to save Moresby, and two of the five surviving U.S. flattops had been sent to block the way. For the enemy, this was a sideshow. Yamamoto was saving his strength for the great Battle of Midway. Even so, Japanese airmen inflicted heavy losses in the Coral Sea; among others they sank the *Lexington* and crippled the *Yorktown*. U.S. Navy fliers picked off seven ships, including a light carrier—"Scratch one flattop," the pilot radioed. A draw, at best. Yet Moresby and Australia had been reprieved. The pagoda forecastles turned back. And at Pearl 1,400 mechanics, working around the clock, took less than two weeks to repair the *Yorktown* in time for Midway.

Now came the first great crisis in the Pacific war. The Allies were running out of islands. Japanese troops had seized the islands of Attu and Kiska in the Aleutians, and Roosevelt, like the Australians, had to contemplate the incredible possibility of an invasion of his own homeland. Hirohito's navy had never been more confident. It had three times as many warships as the decimated U.S. fleet. May 27, 1942, was the thirty-seventh anniversary of Japan's great victory over the Russian Navy, in which Yamamoto had fought as a junior officer, and he chose that day to make his historic move on Midway. Steaming seaward, his force was led by a screen of sixty-five destroyers. Then came twenty-two heavy cruisers and eleven battleships, headed by the admiral's flagship, the superdreadnought *Yamato*. Twenty-one submarines ringed this armada, four fast fleet carriers kept seven hundred planes overhead, and eighty transports bulged with troops. Bulling through the water, the men gaily sang war songs, and the Jap marines, who were to land in the first wave, were issued beer. "It looks, at this moment," Roosevelt told MacArthur on June 2, "as if the Japanese fleet is heading toward the Aleutian Islands or Midway and Hawaii, with a remote possibility it may attack Southern California or Seattle by air."

That was precisely what Yamamoto wanted—confusion over where the blow would fall. He had sent a second task force (Japan at this point had more ships than the admiral knew what to do with) in a feint toward Alaska, hoping to humbug the Americans into splitting their forces. Here the admiral overreached himself.

He wasn't as invincible as he thought. "Magic," the Signal Corps cover name for the broken Purple Code, was deciphering his messages almost as fast as he was sending them and passing them along to Admiral Nimitz, who was organizing Midway's defense. Every foot of the island was crammed with troops; every warship that could be spared was at sea: seven heavy cruisers, a light cruiser, fourteen destroyers, twelve submarines, and the four carriers, *Hornet, Lexington, Enterprise,* and the patched-up *Yorktown.*

In the beginning the battle went badly for the Americans. The first Jap air strike, a hundred seagoing bombers, softened up Midway for the invasion, and the U.S. pursuit planes were pitifully inadequate. Nimitz had two new advantages, however. Not only was Magic telling him where the enemy was; Yamamoto hadn't the foggiest notion where the U.S. fleet was. And then the Jap carrier commander committed a grave tactical error. He cleared his decks to recover his planes from the Midway strike—leaving himself almost defenseless when U.S. aircraft arrived overhead first.

American torpedo bombers went in first that morning of June 4, 1942—and they were massacred by flak. Of forty-one, only six survived, and none scored a hit. The pilots of those obsolete planes sacrificed themselves as surely as any kamikaze, and they died believing it was in vain. In fact they had provided the thin edge of victory. The Jap carriers, frantically wagging their fantails to dodge torpedoes, hadn't been able to get any planes off, and the few Zeros that were in the air were down low, intercepting the martyred American pilots. At that decisive moment Lieutenant Commander Clarence McClusky's two squadrons of Dauntless bombers from the *Enterprise* arrived high overhead and swooped down in 70-degree dives. They blew three carriers apart, then jumped another that afternoon and sent her down, too. Since four carriers were all Yamamoto had brought with him, he had to retire; he had lost his umbrella. He sat slumped on his bridge, listlessly sipping rice broth.

Eight weeks later the U.S. Marines whom Tokyo Rose had twitted were in the Fijis, rehearsing the first American offensive of World War II. It was to be a shoestring operation, first to last. With every modern weapon headed for Europe, the 1st Marine Division was armed with 1903 bolt-action, single-shot Springfield rifles. Their leggings dated from 1918; their Browning machine guns and their mortars had been cosmolined since the Argonne.

The only first-class part of the push was the quality of the troops.

The Marine Corps was an elite force, and these were its picked regiments. On August 7, 1942, they waded ashore at Guadalcanal and immediately wished they hadn't. The 'Canal, as it was known evermore, had been accurately described by a former British colonial resident as a "bloody, stinking hole." Taking it would have been difficult any time, and in the summer of 1942 it presented a special difficulty. In capturing Java, the Japanese had acquired the Allies' source of quinine, the only known cure for malaria. In the 1930s German chemists had discovered a substitute called atabrine, and American firms were working feverishly to synthesize it. But none was available yet. The order was: no man could leave the line unless his temperature rose to 102 degrees. Even so, two thousand were hospitalized by October.

On the first day the marines had been lucky. The landing had been unopposed; a handful of Nips fled into the jungle, leaving a 3,600-foot airstrip they had been building. But the second night was disastrous. Yamamoto still had lots of ships and skilled seamen, and after dark he sent a Rabaul task force down the Slot, the channel between the Solomon Islands. The volcanic cone of Savo Island obscured its approach, and the Battle of Savo Island, as that night's engagement was to be called, was one of the most crushing defeats in the history of the U.S. Navy or, for that matter, any navy. Four precious cruisers were sunk; a thousand bluejackets drowned. Next morning the remaining American warships withdrew southward, and the transports, only partially unloaded, followed. As the marine general put it, his troops had been left "bare-arse." They had to go on half rations at once and defend themselves with only a four-day supply of ammunition. Meantime transports of what the marines called the Tokyo Express began landing Jap soldiers from Rabaul on the far shore of the 'Canal—nine hundred a night, forty-five hundred one night.

Supplied via their crude airstrip, the marines hung on in their muddy foxholes, shelled by enemy artillery, attacked by mass formations of charging Jap troops, swept by tropical rains, and weakened not only by malaria but by dysentery and fungus infections ("jungle rot") as well. Then, slowly, the world began to grasp the significance of the struggle for Guadalcanal. Now they were there, withdrawing them was unthinkable. By mid-October MacArthur was warning Roosevelt, "If we are defeated in the Solomons . . . the entire Southwest Pacific will be in gravest danger." Roosevelt wrote Churchill that he was praying that the men could hold their beachhead. Both sides were making the 'Canal a test of strength. In Tokyo Emperor Hirohito announced that Guadalcanal was "a decisive battle." Like Stalingrad and El Alamein, which were reaching their peaks at the same time, the jungle island became a powerful magnet, attracting forces far out of proportion to its strategic importance because each side had decided to commit all, in confidence that it could win all.

MacArthur's plea for Guadalcanal reinforcements contained a sharp barb, as MacArthur communiqués often did. He asked that America's "entire resources" be diverted to the Southwest Pacific. This would have meant stopping all shipments to Britain and Russia and diverting every U.S. troopship bound for Europe to Australia. In his opinion the Japanese threat was that great. But the President was bound to see things differently. Unlike theater commanders, he had to take a global view of the war. That meant risks, and the greater risk would lie in throwing everything at the Japanese. What would he gain if he succeeded there, only to turn and find he had to face Hitler alone? Needing the Anglo-Russian alliance, he was committed to the Atlantic first strategy. Nazi Germany could not be defeated until the Wehrmacht had been destroyed. The Russians were appealing for a second front, and he and Churchill would have to provide it, or something like it, very soon. He knew the peril in the Solomons; he even intervened to send Guadalcanal reinforcements. Beyond that, the embattled Americans and Australians down under would have to manage.

It is improbable that MacArthur could even have imagined what had happened to Washington. Outwardly the capital looked like a city at peace: the cars were shiny, they became entangled in traffic jams, there was plenty of food in the stores, there were almost as many parties as ever. In high places, however, men were driving themselves furiously, trying to deal with high-priority crises. Winston Churchill's visit and his speech before a joint session of Congress had been a matter of very high priority. Even more pressing was the continuing Battle of the Atlantic. The first step had been to turn off a lot of light switches; the glare of cities like Miami, whose six miles of neon shone far out to sea, had been silhouetting merchantmen for U-boat captains. Starting in May 1942 dimouts (or "Byrne-outs," after Economic Mobilizer Jimmy Byrnes) had deprived the subs of that advantage, although another year passed before improved radar, air surveillance, and new destroyer tactics turned back the U-boat challenge.

Building a twelve-million-man Army was expensive, and Roosevelt was sending Congress a $108,903,047,923 military budget, then the greatest in world history. The production challenge was tremendous. Boeing was responsible for the B-17 Flying Fortress (and later for the B-29 Superfortress). Consolidated was making B-24 Liberators, North American P-51 Mustangs, Vought F4U Corsairs. The names of Hughes, Kaiser, and Frazer were becoming familiar. Factories with good records were awarded Army-Navy E (for Excellent) pennants to fly over their shops, and the largest shop of all would soon be Ford's Willow Run. On Pearl Harbor Sunday a lazy creek had meandered over untilled land there, where now stood the biggest room in the world, with a half-mile assembly line. In it Ford expected to turn out a thirty-ton Consolidated bomber every hour. They would be coming off the line so fast that he wouldn't even try to store them; they would be taxied to an adjacent airfield, make their test flights there, and then fly off to combat.

The Willow Run contracts, like everything else, wound up on some Washington desk. In mid-June 1942 Nazi submarines landed six English-speaking spies on Long Island and the Florida shore. Two turned themselves in; the others were captured and their dynamite caches seized. Someone in Washington had to arrange the trial and, later, the execution of the defiant six. Yale wanted to protect its ivy walls with sandbags; somebody in Washington approved it. Sometimes the orders, decisions, and colloquies were ludicrous. In early summer members of the Women's Army Corps (WACs) began to don their new uniforms, designed by Lord & Taylor. *Women's Wear Daily* exulted: "Adoption of girdles and brassieres as part of the women's Army wardrobe will add to the prestige of the corset and brassiere industry." Then the *Brooklyn Tablet* started an arble-garble by revealing that the WAC concept was subversive, cunningly designed "to break down the traditional American and Christian opposition to removing woman from the home and to degrade her by bringing back the pagan female goddess of de-sexed, lustful sterility." Even the liberal Catholic *Commonweal* opposed the recruiting of women. Girls joined up anyhow. Everyone wanted to serve, including dog lovers. The Army gamely organized a K-9 Corps of useful pets and gave it the nickname "Wags." Arthur Roland, dog editor of the *New York Sun*, even wrote a K-9 marching song:

> From the kennels of the country,
> From the homes and firesides too,
> We have joined the canine army,
> Our nation's work to do.

America, Philip Wylie observed at about this time, bestows its affection in peculiar ways; it was, for example, the only World War II army which formed an entire division on a parade ground to spell out MOM. But trivia helped mask the significant and the top secret, some of which needed all the camouflage they could get. In Oak Ridge, Tennessee, eighteen miles northwest of Knoxville, workers were clearing a hillside and putting down footings for a series of buildings. No one there had the slightest notion of what it was all about. Asked what he was making, a worker replied, "A dollar thirty-five an hour." Two thousand miles westward, in the lazy New Mexico town of Santa Fe, tourists, many with foreign accents, were strolling up to a house at 109 East Palace Street and then being ferried thirty-five miles away to a camp they knew only as Site Y which the world would later come to know as Los Alamos.

Huge industrial complexes were rising in the Pacific northwest, and employees who asked the boss what they were doing were told they were turning out "the front part of horses, to be shipped to Washington," or "wheels for miscarriages." The boss himself didn't know. The secret was confined to a few scientists, a major general, and a handful of civilians personally chosen by President Roosevelt. The two billion dollars being spent was hidden in various categories of the federal budget, and when Senator Harry Truman came nosing around to be sure the taxpayers' money wasn't being misspent, the White House warned him off.

The scientists believed they were working against time. British intelligence reported that Berlin had ordered Norway's Norsk Hydro plant to produce 3,000 pounds of heavy water, and then increased the order to 10,000 pounds. Czech uranium was moving steadily into the Reich. On the night of October 15, 1942, a party of commandos parachuted into Norway and destroyed part of the Hydro works. That provided a respite, but no one doubted that the Nazis would rebuild it.

In this instance Senator Truman's time had been wasted. In most cases it was well spent. Roosevelt's introduction of rationing and controls brought expected howls from civilians, and Bumbledom being what it was, some howling was justified. That spring saw the creation of what may have been the longest and least successful acronym attempt in history, the PWPGSJSISIACWPB (Pipe, Wire Product and Galvanized Steel Jobbers Subcommittee of the Iron and Steel Industry Advisory Committee of the War Production Board). There was also something called the Biscuit, Cracker and Pretzel Subcommittee of the Baking Industry of the Division of Industry Operation, War Production Board, and in the first week of December the Office of Price Administration (OPA) decreed that "Bona fide Santa Clauses shall be construed to be such persons as wearing a red robe, white whiskers, and other well-recognized accouterments befitting their station of life, and provided that they have a kindly and jovial disposition and use their high office of juvenile trust to spread the Christmas spirit they shall be exempt from the wage-freezing Executive Order of October 3."

This was the Washington Richard Nixon first knew. As a Quaker he wasn't at all sure he should fight, so after Pearl Harbor he took Pat east and joined the OPA at $61 a week. Nixon had left college a liberal, but, as he later recalled, he became "more conservative" after watching the men administering rationing. Although he was making $90 a week by August, his feelings about how "political appointees at the top feathered their nests with all kinds of overlapping and empire building" led him, one is told, to resign, overcome his Quaker scruples, and join the Navy. Since he had become subject to the draft, the point is irrelevant. As an attorney he was entitled to a commission as lieutenant (j.g.), and he was sent to the South Pacific, where another Navy lieutenant (j.g.) named John F. Kennedy commanded a PT boat. Unlike Kennedy, Nixon spent most of his time in the backwash of the war with an air transport organization (SCAT), playing marathon poker and becoming so adept at scrounging delicacies and even bourbon from visiting ships that his billet became known as Nixon's Hamburger Stand. One day he was on Bougainville when a plane carrying Harold Stassen, then a member of Halsey's staff, touched down. Nixon knew Stassen was a political comer, a man whose presidential chances were ranked high, and he managed to be at the bottom of the ramp in time to greet the visitor. He was greatly impressed by Stassen's firm handshake, though when he mentioned the meeting to him after the war, Stassen couldn't remember it.

In his suite on the second floor of the White House, always within hailing distance of the chief, Harry Hopkins was briefing another future President on the coming strategy in the European Theater of Operations, known henceforth to the swing generation as the ETO. Eisenhower was still a relatively obscure figure. He had made his Army reputation in the Louisiana maneuvers of 1941. Roosevelt, reading reports of it and consulting General Marshall, had decided this was precisely the sort of man to wage that most difficult of conflicts, the coalition war.

Everyone in high office knew that Lieutenant General Eisenhower was a comer, but few resented it. He was the typical American's concept of what the typical man should be, a Norman Rockwell general taken right off a cover of the *Saturday Evening Post*. He was canny, openhanded, brisk, candid, and modest; he enjoyed dialect jokes and singing "Abdul Abulbul Amir" to the thirty-eighth verse. Born in Texas, he had grown up in a small town in Kansas, the American heartland. Most men liked him, and he liked most of them. He must be one of the few Republicans of consequence to have put in a kind word for Hopkins: "He had a grasp of the broad factors in military problems that was almost phenomenal and he was selflessly devoted to the purpose of expediting victory. He never spared himself, even during those periods when his health was so bad that his doctors ordered him to bed."

It was June 1942, and high time the President named an ETO commander. Roosevelt had rashly promised Molotov that Stalin could expect a second front "this year." American troops had sent a token body of troops to Ireland after Pearl Harbor—inspiring one of Tin Pan Alley's more unfortunate wartime ballads—"Johnny Doughboy Found a Rose in Ireland"—and now GIs were crossing to Britain itself. They were being thrust into odd corners, and the British had begun to complain that the trouble with Yanks was that they were "overpaid, oversexed, and over here." Clearly a sense of direction was needed. With Eisenhower installed in Mayfair's Grosvenor Square, renamed "Eisenhowerplatz," the Yanks and Tommies were ready to move.

But where? The Americans wanted a cross-Channel stroke from England; the British preferred what Churchill called "the soft underbelly of Europe." They weren't strong enough to take on either, so they compromised on French North Africa. Timed to match a Montgomery offensive from Egypt, it could knock the Germans out of Africa. The code name for the operation was Torch.

It began, bizarrely, with an American attack not upon Germany, her sworn enemy, but on France, her oldest ally. The invaders lay in eight hundred ships off the coast of Algeria and Morocco on the night of Saturday, November 7, 1942, exactly eleven months after Pearl Harbor. Hiding so large a force was impossible; Berlin and Rome knew of it, tried to guess the convoy's destination, and decided it would be either Malta or Egypt. When the landing craft began putting infantry on French African soil at 3 A.M., Europe was dumbfounded, no one more than Marshal Pétain. The trespass of ninety thousand Yankees offended him deeply. FDR's shortwave broadcast to the people of French Africa (*"Mes amis . . . We have come to help you repulse the invaders . . . Vive la France éternelle!"*) distressed him so deeply that he wrote the President, "It is with stupor and sadness that I learned tonight of the aggression of your troops. You have taken such a cruel initiative."

The American commander in chief was naturally in a very different mood. He was spending the weekend with Hopkins and a few other friends at Shangri-La, his Catoctin Mountain hideaway sixty miles north of Washington. It was still Saturday evening there when the invasion began. The President's phone rang. Grace Tully answered it. It was Stimson. Roosevelt's hand trembled as he lifted the receiver. He listened a moment and then said, "Thank God, thank God. Congratulations. Casualties are comparatively light —much below your predictions. Thank God." He replaced the receiver and turned to his friends. "We have landed in North Africa," he said. "We are striking back."

Eisenhower had directed the landings from a command post deep in the damp tunnels of Gibraltar. On November 23 he transferred his headquarters to the white, hilly city of Algiers; his presence ashore was essential, even if only to boost morale. Americans were beginning to learn how the Wehrmacht had won its reputation. Although caught off balance by Torch, the Germans had moved swiftly and effectively. Before the unblooded American troops could advance, Axis troops had occupied Tunisia and fortified it with men and arms from Sicily. While the GIs trudged through the winter rains and the mud, Stuka dive bombers and Krupp 88 artillery pieces pounded them, their tanks, and the Allied air cover. Then, in February 1943, counterattacking Germans hurled the Americans back through Kasserine Pass.

At the time, the pass seemed an Allied disaster. It turned out to be disastrous for the Axis. Patton replaced the corps commander there, recaptured the pass, and teamed up with Montgomery, who had arrived after chasing Rommel's Afrika Korps all the way from El Alamein. The Germans in Africa were doomed; Rommel flew off to tell Mussolini and Hitler that his men must be evacuated. To survive, the Korps needed at least 140,000 tons of supplies every month, and the Allied navies' command of the Mediterranean was reducing the German trickle from 29,000 to 23,000 to 2,000 tons. Mussolini and Hitler told Rommel he was a Cassandra. Look at Kasserine Pass, they said triumphantly; that was what happened when Aryan troops met mongrelized Americans. To Rommel's horror, they were shipping men *into* the beachhead. Thus, when the Allies snapped their trap shut in early May, they bagged nearly a quarter-million POWs. This, combined with battlefield losses, meant the Axis had lost 349,206 in French Africa. The Americans, in their first campaign, had sustained just 18,500 casualties.

Patton wasn't there at the finish; Eisenhower had sent him off to plan the invasion of Sicily. Here, again, Montgomery and Patton were to work in tandem under Eisenhower. The troops for Husky, the operation's cipher, included a French corps. Despite Anglo-American snubs, Charles de Gaulle had been working behind the lines, dominating the freed French by political maneuvering and sheer force of will, and inspiring them to enlist. Of the Gaullist troops Mark Clark would later say, "A more gallant fighting organization never existed," but all Allied troops looked fearsome now. Europe had turned a psychological corner. The Germans had lost Stalingrad—and another 330,000 men there—and now that they had been thrown out of Africa, the Wehrmacht no longer looked invincible. By this summer of 1943 it was the Allies who terrified their enemies, particularly such half-hearted Axis partners as the Italians and Sicilians.

Sicily was a political battle, fought to knock Italy out of the war, and on those terms it was successful. It was also a military victory; the Allies conquered a barren, mountainous island defended by 255,000 troops, and did the job in little more than a month. In

Rome, King Victor Emmanuel bluntly told the dazed Mussolini that he was no longer head of the government: "The soldiers don't want to fight any more. At this moment you are probably the most hated man in Italy." Mussolini was arrested, and a new government under Marshal Pietro Badoglio began furtive peace talks with Eisenhower's representatives. The upshot was that Badoglio agreed to announce the Italian capitulation over the radio on September 8. That same night, the Allies would be landing troops at Salerno, in the Italian shin. The code name was Avalanche. Its purpose was to capture the startled Germans and clear the entire Italian peninsula of Axis troops.

How they thought they could bring it off is inexplicable. Keeping so big a secret was impossible; talky Italians had given the whole thing away to the Gestapo and Nazi intelligence. Badoglio surrendered unconditionally on September 8, as promised, but by then elite German divisions had poured into Italy and disarmed their former ally. Mark Clark's Fifth Army was pinned down at Salerno, and the GIs, who had been told of Italy's surrender and expected an easy time of it, were angry and confused. Now enemy tank and artillery fire confined them to a beachhead less than five miles deep. Every night loudspeakers, commanded by a bilingual German who evidently admired Hollywood Westerns, roared at the hemmed-in infantry, "O.K., you guys. Come in and give yourself up. We got you covered." This sort of thing went on for four months. In Berlin "Lord Haw-Haw," the renegade Englishman who broadcast propaganda for Goebbels, was predicting "another Dunkerque."

This was the beginning of the Italian tragedy, of useless battles, needless suffering, and endless siege warfare. On the east coast of Italy, Montgomery's Eighth Army had moved swiftly, joining the 1st British Airborne Division—which had taken the naval base of Taranto—and then racing on to the Adriatic port of Bari. The British accelerated their advance to take the pressure off the American infantry. American airmen bombed the hills overlooking Salerno. The beachhead was jammed with artillery until, on September 5, the Germans at last began to withdraw slowly toward Naples.

Company commanders knew what was wrong with the Italian war, even if generals didn't. The Fifth Army was fighting geography. It took them three weeks and nearly 12,000 casualties to reach Naples. The spine of the country was traversed by the Apennines.

Since this mountain chain was the source of Italy's rivers, infantry had to cross an endless succession of valleys, beyond each of which would rise a ridge held by entrenched Germans. The most famous crest was Monte Cassino, the site of a fourteen-hundred-year-old monastery and the western anchor of Kesselring's Gustav Line. Dug in along the heights around the monastery, the enemy decimated American infantrymen with mortars and *nebelwerfers*—"screaming meemies," GIs called them—while U.S. tanks were destroyed by 88s. The Allies believed the monastery was being used as an observation point and bombed it to rubble. Nothing had been solved. Enemy fire was as accurate and pitiless as ever.

To compound the foot soldiers' misery, Eisenhower, recalled to England for planning the cross-Channel invasion of France, took with him his best generals: Patton, Montgomery, and Omar Bradley. In Italy icy winds and heavy snow lashed the jagged ridges. The mud was waist-deep in the daytime and frozen solid at night. Bill Mauldin thought there was something almost supernatural about the muck: "I'm sure Europe never got this muddy during peacetime. I'm equally sure that no mud in the world is so deep or sticky or wet as European mud. It doesn't even have an honest color like ordinary mud." Day after day the war of attrition went on; dead bodies were wrapped in bloody bed sacks or ponchos and stacked like cordwood, bound together by Signal Corps wire. Scavenging dogs ate the throats of the dead. Frostbite and trench foot were epidemic. Sentries shivered at their posts. It was one of the worst Italian winters in memory.

After V-E Day and V-J Day the Army informed American newspapers and magazines that they should stop calling infantrymen GIs, on the ground that GI meant General Issue and was therefore "dehumanizing, demeaning, and disrespectful." In the spirit of victory, editors and publishers quickly submitted. It seemed absurd at the time, but in the long run it turned out to be a good thing, for just as "doughboys" meant the foot soldiers of 1918, and "grunts" those of Vietnam, the GI belongs almost exclusively to World War II. He is the symbol of the swing generation's youth, or the erosion of it: the fresh-faced adolescent who left home in ill-fitting khaki and returned much quieter at twenty-three with dull, resigned eyes and a way of tensing up when the old Third Avenue El or anything else approached overhead with a whir, a whoosh, a whiz, a whistle, or a sound like rapidly ripped canvas.

The sad part is that hardly anyone remembers GIs as they were. Actors pretending to be in the armed forces of those days appear in television situation comedies on TV so often that children are seduced into believing that the war was all thrills and high good humor. Every dogface in the ETO assumed that if he grew old enough to father children at home, one of them would ask one day, "Daddy, what did you do in the big war?" He never imagined that the question would be rhetorical, to be followed by the child's observation that doubtless it was great to have been one of Hogan's Heroes or in McHale's Navy or—cruelest of all—"What fun it must have been to fight with Patton!" There are other dogface images around, but they are just as irrelevant. The harpies of the DAR, the VFW and the Legionnaires see the doggie as a clean-shaven, well-barbered, selfless hero, and college students of the 1970s wonder whether once upon a time it was really possible to wear the country's uniform with pride, shoulder a rifle, and righteously shoot to kill.

There was such a time, and these were its men. By the winter of 1943–44 the ETO foot soldier had become a veteran of war, a skilled foot soldier who would have been valued by Alexander the Great or Napoleon Bonaparte. He was more subdued than they were (or than we have been told they were; combat makes a man suspicious of all warrior legends), and if he had rank he didn't wear it on the line; up front the Krauts, as everyone called them, enjoyed sniping at leaders. GIs didn't shave or get their hair cut while in combat, not because they wanted to become flower children but because they lacked razors, shaving cream, mirrors, hot water, and time.

After two weeks of Italy's driving rain, lying in a muddy foxhole while the enemy tried to hit him with bombs, tanks, grenades, bullets, flamethrowers, booby traps, and HE (high explosive) and phosphorescent shells, a man looked like a tramp. His behavior was often uncivilized. He moved his bowels in full view of his peers, many of whom took a critical interest in his performance. He was foul-mouthed, and especially insulting to men who hadn't been up front ("rear echelon bastards"). The dogface had been wet so long that his combat jacket was disintegrating, and sometimes he smelled vile. Most of all he was tired. Some men took years to recover from that weariness. Some never did.

When it was all over, and the generals had finished decorating and congratulating each other—that sounds cynical, but the GI would have put it that way; you can never understand the dogface until you have grasped the extent of his cynicism—a civilian employee of the Quartermaster Corps did a little historical research and disclosed that the average American infantryman in World War II had carried 84.3 pounds each day. That made him the most heavily laden foot soldier in the history of warfare. The figure startled some people, including, inexcusably, generals. It didn't surprise the former GI. He knew he had been a beast of burden. Moving into the line, he had worn or carried his uniform, his steel chamberpot helmet and helmet liner, an M-1 rifle, a knife, his canteen, an entrenching tool (a combination pick and shovel), his bayonet, his first-aid pouch, a web belt with cartridge magazines in each pocket, two bandoliers of extra ammo, hand grenades hung by their handles from his belt and the suspender harness supporting his pack, and the contents of the pack: a poncho, Primacord fuses, mess kit, cigarettes, a Zippo lighter, writing paper, letters from home, and various rations—C, K, or canned ham and eggs from H. J. Heinz Co., winners of the Army-Navy E pennant. In addition, the GI had to carry part of the outfit's communal weapons: a Browning automatic rifle or its tripod, or Browning light or heavy machine gun or its tripod, or a 60- or 81-millimeter mortar or its base.

These were essentials. He was supposed to carry a gas mask, too, but he had discarded that before he left North Africa; he couldn't bear another ounce on his back. The Army wished he could shoulder more, not because it was sadistic but because he needed more. He ought to have had a blanket at night. He should have had a shelter half, so he and the man beside him could ward off the rain at night. Most of all he needed extra socks. Without a change of socks, GIs accumulated wet mud around their feet and, eventually, trench foot. The pain became excruciating, and when they crawled to the battalion aid station (nobody with trench foot has ever walked), and the medics cut off their shoes, their feet swelled to the size of footballs. Sometimes they had to be amputated. That happened with frostbite, too. Late in the war privileged divisions were issued "shoe packs," which helped keep feet dry, but there was no real substitute for the warmth of socks.

To the strange mud-caked creatures who fought battles, however, the greatest source of anxiety was German artillery. "That artillery did things to you," said a corporal quoted in *Yank*, the GI weekly. "We'd been told not to duck when we heard the screaming of shells; it would be too late. But we ducked anyway. Even the almost silent pop of the mortars was frightening. We got to know exactly where they would land." Of all the Nazi big guns, the most feared was the Krupp 88. Sometimes it almost seemed that it could shoot around corners. At the time, doggies believed that nothing could be as bad as their "incoming mail" (German shells), but the men with iron crosses on the other side of the hill wouldn't have agreed. By 1944 American "outgoing mail" included radar-guided rockets, proximity-fused shells, and a flamethrower fuel invented by Harvard chemists in partnership with Standard Oil technicians, a wicked brew of soap powder and gasoline called napalm.

In a revealing moment President Roosevelt lamented that no one had thought of a fitting title for the war (he rather liked "The Tyrants' War") and that there were no stirring songs like "Tipperary" and "Over There." It tipped his hand because that was the kind of thoughts commanders in chief and five-star generals had. GIs would have hooted. To them giving the war a number was fine; if calling them GIs dehumanized them, and numbering wars deglorified them, they approved; it was justice. Walter Johnson has pointed out that despite the title of Eisenhower's *Crusade in Europe*, the ETO war lacked a crusading spirit. Disillusion with World War I had discredited in advance any slogans or parades, and "the Depression had left its mark, as those unsure of their future in hard times now had war added to their doubts about the future. An adolescent thirst for glory was replaced by a grim determination to defeat the enemy. The justness of the cause was not doubted, but the nation fought with a deadpan face."

Significantly, the two most famous GI cartoon characters in the ETO were anything but comic. War can be preposterous at times, and when the ETO was ridiculous, Willie and Joe noted it with a wry, throwaway wit. But most of the time they were melancholy. Their creator, writing at the time, explained: "We don't have to be indoctrinated or told there is a war on. We know there is a war on because we see it. We don't like it a darned bit, but you don't see many soldiers quitting, so fancy propaganda would be a little superfluous."

And yet, ironically, they were perhaps the best-prepared generation ever to go to war willingly—willingly only because they knew the job had to be done. And that was how they looked at it: it was a job. A dirty, nauseating job, but what else could you do if you were a young, ruddy, well-nourished male with the right reflexes? To be sure, there were those who refused to go. Robert Lowell was a conscientious objector. In his imagination he could see the mutilated victims of air bombings, and he wanted no part of that. But few had his vision, and most of those who did were unwilling to turn the world over to Hitler.

Most of the swing generation, including those who loathed violence, approved of Dr. Henry Sloane Coffin, president of the Union Theological Seminary and uncle of a future Yale chaplain, when he warned that the seminary would not become "a haven for draft dodgers." Doubtless he would have taken another position on the Vietnam War, for the two conflicts are very different. To a shocking degree the American casualties in Vietnam were to be children of the poor; until 1972 college students were exempt and knew loopholes in the draft law by the time they graduated. In World War II everybody who was fit went. Lieutenant Colonel Henry Cabot Lodge Jr. commanded tanks in the African desert. William Fife Knowland was a major in France. Hank Greenberg, the great Detroit slugger, was a shavetail. Jimmy Stewart and Clark Gable were Air Corps officers, Walter Winchell and John Ford naval officers. John Huston became a major, Darryl Zanuck and Frank Capra lieutenant colonels. Jackie Coogan was a glider pilot. Paul Douglas, aged forty, enlisted in the Marine Corps as a private, and other volunteers included Joe DiMaggio, Red Skelton, Robert Montgomery, Douglas Fairbanks Jr., Henry Fonda, Louis Hayward, Tyrone Power and David Niven.

In January 1942 Joe Louis knocked out Buddy Baer in exactly two minutes and fifty-six seconds, then turned his purse over to the New York Auxiliary of the Navy Relief Society and went into the Army—this despite the appalling fact that throughout World War II the Red Cross kept "white blood" and "Negro blood" in segregated containers. Joe might have hesitated if the color line had been drawn in combat, with the rich and the privileged in safe zones. But they weren't. Among those cited for bravery in the naval battle off Casablanca was Lieutenant Franklin D. Roosevelt Jr., a gunnery officer on a destroyer. Major Glenn Miller went down with his plane, and the men killed in action included Lieutenant Wells Lewis, son of Sinclair Lewis; Lieutenant Peter G. Lehman, son of

New York's Herbert Lehman; Marine Sergeant Peter B. Saltonstall, son of the Massachusetts senator; Joseph P. Kennedy Jr., son of the ambassador; and eighteen-year-old Stephen P. Hopkins, Harry Hopkins's youngest boy.

The guys up front read about all this in the *Stars and Stripes, Yank,* or the "pony editions" (small and adless) of *Time* and the *New Yorker.* They were proud of America's democratic Army, just as they were proud of their engineers, who could erect Bailey bridges overnight, and the Seabees, who leveled the mountains of Ascension Island and built a mile-long airstrip there after the British engineers had said it couldn't be done. But they rarely bragged about their country, even among themselves. They got through what they had to go through by adopting a tough, sardonic facade. They griped about rear echelon pleasures that never reached the front—movies, Bob Hope shows, Red Cross girls—though if a gripe turned into a whine they came down on the whiner: "See the chaplain," they would taunt, or "Tough shit," or "Hell, you found a *home* in the Army."

Subjects that could be used for communal grousing were greeted with relish. The K-9 Corps was fair game. So were members of the women's services, who, they told one another, were all sleeping with officers—"Hey! You hear what happened to Halsey? He got sucked under a bridge by a Wave!" (Marines, lacking an acronym, called women marines BAMs—broad-assed marines; the girls struck back by calling them HAMs—hairy-assed marines.) But the greatest source for the mass gripe and the best guffaws was probably advertising from home. That was their one complaint about pony editions. They *wanted* to see the ads, and wrote home asking for them, and they could hardly wait to see what Madison Avenue would do next.

What Madison Avenue was doing, if you believed every word, was winning the war. THE GREAT GIFT TO THE MOTHERS OF MEN! one classic began. The gift, the first two paragraphs of the copy explained, was sulfa drugs, but the advertiser, you learned in the third paragraph, was the air-conditioning company which kept comfortable the scientists who discovered sulfa. Challenged by this creative stroke, a competitor claimed an assist for the torpedoing of a Jap freighter—"air-conditioning made possible the hit itself" because the periscope used by the American sub had been ground and polished in an air-conditioned workshop.

FERTILIZER CAN WIN THE WAR! another plug began, and the guys agreed that if that was true, Madison Avenue was doing the job. A maker of ball bearings assured the home front that GIs would have "a safe highway home" because the soldier's bearings "still ride with him." Sugar was a Nazi-killer. Castor beans had left the medicine chest for Anzio. Lucky Strike green had gone to war. Gillette razor blade steel was going into bayonets. Alarm clocks kept generals on time. The guys read that "cotton cloth can help win an air fight," that "back of every attack is wire rope," that heavy equipment was "playing its part in the clearing away of the rubble of destruction and in the building of a better world," that a manufacturer of metal fasteners—a soldier was shown lying in a hammock—had made certain that "*his* cradle won't drop, because it's furnished with clamps 30 percent stronger than specified." As a rule, the fruitier the prose, the more soldiers enjoyed it, though some pitches were adjudged to be foul. One New York cemetery deliberately timed its commercials to be broadcast after bulletins about heavy fighting overseas; after the guys had heard about it the commercials were hastily withdrawn. In another unbelievable campaign, parents were warned that they should have the right brand of spectacles so they could recognize their returning sons. Again, a blizzard of angry V-mail arrived on the advertiser's desk. And when a copywriter for an aircraft company asked in print, "Who's afraid of the big Focke-Wulf?" the fliers at an Air Corps base wrote, "*We* are," followed it with the signatures of every airman there, including the commanding officer, and mailed it to the sponsoring firm.

The most famous ad of the war was "The Kid in Upper 4," a description of a young soldier lying awake in a Pullman berth remembering "the taste of hamburgers and pop . . . the feel of driving a roadster . . . a dog named Shucks, or Spot, or Barnacle Bill." It continued: "There's a lump in his throat, and maybe a tear fills his eye. It doesn't matter, Kid. Nobody will see . . . it's too dark. . . ." GIs thought that was a lot of fertilizer, too, but at least it was in a good cause (making room for traveling soldiers), like the appeals to buy war bonds, avoid the black market, collect scrap iron, and, if readers learned about troop movements, to "Keep it under your Stetson." The doggies passed over them in silence. What really doubled them up were the flagrant attempts to exploit the war for private gain—the assertion that war production would be increased if everyone chewed a few more sticks of Wrigley's every day, for example, or advertising Munsingwear's foundation garments with a picture of a WAC saying, "Don't tell me bulges are patriotic!" or Sergeant's flea powder advertisement showing "Old Sarge" reporting, "Sighted flea—killed same."

One such plug, "Angel in Muddy Boots," was in a class by itself. A nurse was shown leaning over a wounded GI. The huckster read the soldier's mind: "I remember you . . . you are the girl with flying feet who led the way to laughter . . . you are all the girls I ever liked who brightened a fellow's life. . . . You didn't always wear muddy boots. Once you raced over summer lawns, in bright, skylarking shoes. . . ." This sent the adman to dreaming: "Yes, she grew up. . . . Her muddy boots are an example of that. The men and women—skilled craftsmen all . . . that first gave her the delight of casual shoes in color, turned their hand to meeting the need for a sturdy boot that would carry a nurse through mud and rain. . . . When the war came, these same bootmakers . . . created the Nurses' Arctic, the Soldiers' Arctic, the Jungle Boot, the War Pilots' Boot, the deck-gripping Sea Boot, the Arctic Mukluk. . . . Someday there will be girls again who . . . fly over sun-flecked lawns with the lilt of summer in their hearts and rainbows on their feet." Only the copywriter didn't want them to wear the rainbows. "Playshoes would be back," he promised, "and everyone should remember the brand name. . . ." Somehow one has forgotten it.

What made the Angel in Muddy Boots particularly tasteless was that it was trading on something very precious to infantrymen: their secret dream of love and postwar peace. The dreams of different soldiers were remarkably alike. Loping through fields sown with Teller mines, their legs swinging in the awkward gait of the eternal foot soldier, they had come to resemble one another. Willie and Joe might have been twins; Willie had the big nose and Joe the little one, but sometimes even their creator confused them, and in their propinquity, in their shared agony, they had formed a common vision of paradise. It had nothing to do with headlines, salients, or pincer movements; that was the generals' war. The other war, as John Steinbeck explained it, was "the war of homesick, weary, funny, violent, common men who wash their socks in their helmets, complain about the food, whistle at Arab girls, or at any girls for that matter, and lug themselves through as dirty a business as the world has ever seen and do it with humor and dignity and courage." That was Bill Mauldin's war, it was Ernie Pyle's war, and Sad Sack's war, it was the war of men who cherished their Betty Grable and Rita Hayworth pinups in *Yank*, the war which was completely misunderstood by Postmaster General Frank Walker, who banned *Esquire* from the mails because he thought the magazine appealed to GI prurience.

It appealed to their yearning for tenderness and passion, for beauty and warmth, for real girls to replace the pinups; for a home that was not in the Army. Betty Friedan, then fresh from Smith, later recalled that "women as well as men sought the comforting reality of home and children. . . . We were all vulnerable, homesick, lonely, frightened." Fannie Hurst wrote that American girls "are retrogressing into . . . that thing known as The Home." In Europe GIs moodily listened to the strains of "Lili Marlene," the greatest song of the war, broadcast from behind German lines but universal in its appeal—

> *Vor der Kaserne, vor dem grossen Tor,*
> *Steht 'ne Laterne und steht sie noch davor.*
> *Dort wollen wir uns mal wiederseh'n,*
> *Bei der Laterne wollen wir steh'n*
> *Wie einst, Lilli Marlene*
> *Wie einst, Lilli Marlene.*

—while at home girls, standing on tiptoe for the postwar world, heard:

> *I'll walk alone*
> *Because, to tell you the truth, I'll be lonely*
> *I don't mind being lonely*
> *When my heart tells me you*
> *Are lonely too.*

Or:

> *I'll be with you in apple blossom time*
> *I'll be with you to change your name to mine*
> *Some day in May*
> *I'll come and say*
> *"Happy the bride that the sun shines on today."*

Possibly because there was so much correspondence between the front and home, the girls and the men in the ETO and the Pacific not only longed for the same future; they often agreed about its most minute details. The house would have a white picket fence. It would be within walking distance of a school. The girl would have a chest of silverware, the ex-GI a den. They would garden together. He would probably commute to work, because they lived in a quiet suburb. Naturally they would have children who would be adorable as babies, cute as grade school pupils, and striking as they entered their teens. After high school they would attend the best colleges and universities in the country, where their parents would be very, very proud of them.

Pacific Montage

always the rain and the mud, torrid heat and teeming insect life, the stink of rotten jungle and rotting dead; malaria burning the body and fungus infection eating away

Now hear this! Now hear this!
Sweepers, man your brooms!
A clean sweep-down, fore and aft!

In like Flynn

Oh, Captain Colin Kelly
Put a bomb in her belly
And sent the ship *Haruna*
To the bottom of the sea

Corregidor here   Corregidor here   0200 5 May 42   They are not here yet   We are waiting for God only knows what   How about a chocolate soda   Lots of heavy fighting going on   We may have to give up by noon   We don't know yet   They are throwing men and shells at us and I feel sick at my stomach   They bring in the wounded every minute   We will be waiting for you guys to help   The jig is up   Everyone is bawling like a baby   They are piling dead and wounded in our tunnel   I know now how a mouse feels   Caught in a trap waiting for guys to come along and finish it up   Got a treat   Canned pineapple   My name is Irving Strobing   Get this to my mother Mrs. Minnie Strobing 605 Barbey Street Brooklyn New Yo

In the film version the charm is heightened by the innocence and utter lack of guile on the part of twelve-year-old Elizabeth Taylor, making her screen debut

Mammoth new Pentagon Building in Washington, D.C. Souwespac will be glad to know the fabulous new building has eight cafeterias and two big chow halls serving 40,000 meals a day

Bell-bottomed trousers, coat of navy blue,
He'll climb the riggin' like his daddy used to do!

WCTU OBJECTS TO NATIVES GIVING GI'S WINE

Mairzy doats and dozy doats and liddle lamzy divey
A kiddley divey too, wouldn't you?

Oh, we sent for MacArthur to come to Tarawa, but General MacArthur said no.
He gave as the reason, it wasn't the season, besides there was no USO.

Dear John,

This is the hardest letter I'se ever had to write. But I've been thinking it over and I now see that it wasn't wise for us to be married. I don't want to hurt you but

My mama done tol' me...
A woman's a two-face
A worrisome thing who'll leave ya t' sing
The blues in the night

I'll be seeing you
In all the old familiar places
That this heart of mine embraces
All night long

ITALY QUITS!
One Down, Two to Go!

Say a prayer for your pal
On Guadalcanal
He needs God's help it's true

AMBASSADOR KENNEDY'S SON DECORATED FOR "EXTREME HEROIC CONDUCT"

Pardon me, boy. Is this the Chattanooga Choo-choo?
Track twenty-nine. And I can give you a shine.
Can you afford to board the Chattanooga Choo-choo?
I've got my fare — and just a trifle to spare

As we go marching
And the band begins to p-l-a-y
You can hear the people shouting,
"The raggedy-ass Marines are on parade!"

KILROY WAS HERE

Ten

THE HOME FRONT

During March 1942, according to an anecdote then sweeping the country, a woman on a bus was reported to have said loudly, "Well, my husband has a better job than he ever had and he's making more money, so I hope the war lasts a long time." At that, another woman rose and slapped her face, blurting out, "That's for my boy who was killed at Pearl Harbor. And this"—a second slap—"is for my boy on Bataan."

The story has an air of apocrypha (what mother had sons on Oahu *and* Luzon?), but its widespread acceptance suggests that it told wartime America something about itself. For tens of millions the war boom was in fact a bonanza, a Depression dream come true, and they felt guilty about it. Not so guilty that they declined the money, to be sure—that would have been asking too much of human nature and wouldn't have helped combat troops a bit—but contrite enough to make them join scrap drives, buy war bonds, serve in Civil Defense units, and once in a while buy a lonely soldier a drink.

Every great war is accompanied by social revolution, and the very dimensions of this war were bound to alter America greatly. Few realized that then. The *New York Daily News* really believed that GIs were fighting "to get back to the ball game and the full tank of gas," and GIs themselves sometimes thought they were in there battling for Mom and apple pie. But history does not let those who make it get off that easily. No country could have survived America's convulsive transformation of 1941–45 without altering its essence and its view of itself. The home front was in reality a battleground of ideas, customs, economic theory, foreign policy, and relationships between the sexes and social classes. Rosie the Riveter, like Kilroy, was everywhere, and she would never be the same again.

The most obvious source of change was the immense transfusion of cash into what had been an austere economy. In 1942 Washington was pumping three hundred million dollars a day into U.S. wallets and purses. After the windup in 1945 the total cost of the war was reckoned at 245 billion dollars—more than the merged annual budgets of the United States from 1789 to 1940, which included the financing of five wars. In 1939 the Gross National Product, the total value of the goods and services produced by the American people, had been 91 billion dollars. In 1945 it was 215 billion, a jump without precedent in the history of the world. The stubborn tumor of jobless men—there had been eight million as late as 1940—had disappeared. The number of working Americans had grown from 45 million to 66 million, over five million of them women. Paul Bunyan was back. The country's old, pre-Crash confidence in itself had returned. Corporate profits in 1943 exceeded those of 1929.

Joseph Paul Goebbels cried, "The Americans are so helpless that they must fall back again and again upon boasting about their matériel. Their loud mouths produce a thousand airplanes and tanks almost daily, but when they need them they haven't got them and are therefore taking one beating after another!" This was mindless, even antic, but there was something disconcerting about a country which could field an Army of twelve million men, fight two awesome empires at the same time, build a Navy larger than the combined fleets of its enemies and its allies—and still record a 20 percent increase in civilian spending over 1939. The phenomenon troubled some commentators. "We live in the light, in relative comfort and complete security," said Edward R. Murrow. "We are the only nation in this war which has raised its standard of living since the war began. We are not tired, as all Europe is tired." Eric Sevareid, observing that most people at home were better off because of the war, warned that "if hardships do things to the mind, so do comforts."

Time trumpeted that America was "getting suddenly rich—everywhere, all at once," but not many Americans were accumulating fortunes. It was true that big, efficient corporations were crowding many small businesses off the stage. However, tax returns testify that the real beneficiary of the war boom was the small family which had saved little or nothing during the Depression. It was all unplanned, but part of the explanation lay deep in the American national character. D. W. Brogan, the Tocqueville of the twentieth century, explained to his fellow Europeans that their new ally took a different view of the conflict: "To the Americans war is a business, not an art; they are not interested in moral victories, but in victory. . . . the United States is a great, a very great corporation whose stockholders expect (with all their history to justify the expectation) that it will be in the black."

Even farmers flourished in the boom, and for a significant reason. At first, wary of the surpluses which had been their undoing in the past, they had held back. By the fall of 1942 their leaders had convinced them that they must become the breadbasket of the world, and when they returned to their fields their crops were 25 percent more bountiful than ever before. Therein lies the significance: during the Depression inventors, chemists, engineers, and horticulturalists had developed new fertilizers, high-yielding seeds, insecticides, and new machinery. Technology had emerged to alter the face of the land. It was the same elsewhere. Forced by the war to work together, scientists, military officers, economists, corporate executives, and public officials were pooling their talents and finding immediate solutions not only to wartime problems but to the challenges of the postwar world. Inventions which had been gathering dust throughout the 1930s were helping win the war. Young men with a managerial bent, like Robert S. McNamara, assistant professor of business administration at Harvard, saw no reason why radar, prefabricated housing, frozen foods, diesel power, and catalytic cracking of crude oil should not contribute to an abundant life in years of peace. The war boom had created the nucleus of a mass market; it seemed clear that a greater mass market would lie beyond victory. "Certainly there took place during the war a cross-fertilization of thinking that was stimulating to all concerned," Frederick Lewis Allen wrote. "All in all, during the war American technology underwent a hothouse growth."

Thirty years later, when the production miracle had long since been taken for granted, its long-range implications began to emerge. World War II gave tremendous impetus to egalitarianism. Traditional criteria vanished; wealth, social class, age, race, sex, and family identity no longer commanded instinctive deference. What James

MacGregor Burns has called the war's "equality of bodies" destroyed the tradition that men were entitled to respect because of "background." Sing Sing would no longer treat men like Richard Whitney as honored guests. Even position based upon achievement would mean little. The scientists and engineers who had helped unlock America's productive capacities, making the new world of technology possible, would soon be dismissed as "eggheads."

All this was not the work of World War II. The social revolution had been gathering momentum for more than a half-century. World War I, Prohibition, the Depression, and, later, the cold war and the impotence of all leaders in the shadow of nuclear warheads, helped discredit all symbols of authority, from the flag to the cross, from Presidents in the White House to each father in his home. Nevertheless, the years between Pearl Harbor and V-J Day were decisive, partly because national mobilization blurred the lines between the classes by putting everyone shoulder to shoulder. Even more important, the war led to the transfer of economic power to the disfranchised. Before the boom America had been a country in which people sought products. With the postwar arrival of the consumer society, products would seek people, and the origin of lower-class affluence would lie in the accumulated pay envelopes of the early 1940s. At the time, big spending was considered unpatriotic, and scarcities and anti-inflation controls discouraged buying sprees anyhow. Still, bankrolls were thickening, and economists worried. By the summer of 1943 the Treasury Department estimated that Americans on the home front had saved some seventy billion dollars in cash, checking accounts, and redeemable war bonds. Randolph Paul, the department's general counsel, called it "liquid dynamite," which, considering what it would eventually do to the character and quality of American life, hardly seems an overstatement.

Until victory had been assured, such considerations yielded to expediency. It would have been presumptuous, and even dangerous, to brood over the challenges of peace until the Axis had been defeated. In 1942 the administration did propose a study of postwar issues by the National Resources Planning Board, but Congress killed that by abolishing the board. At times the President himself seemed to have difficulty focusing on domestic issues. To a correspondent who lingered after his December 28, 1943, press conference he confessed that he was weary of the phrase "New Deal." Ten years earlier, he said, "Dr. New Deal," an internist, had treated the country for an acute internal illness. After recovery, however, the patient had suffered "a very bad accident" on December 7, 1941. Dr. New Deal, knowing nothing about curing such afflictions, had referred his patient to "an orthopedic surgeon, Dr. Win-the-War."

Editorial writers rejoiced. Wrote *Time:* "DEATH REVEALED: The New Deal, 10, after long illness; of malnutrition and desuetude. Child of the 1932 election campaign, the New Deal had four healthy years, began to suffer from spots before the eyes in 1937, and never fully recovered from the shock of war. Last week its father, Franklin Roosevelt, pronounced it dead." But had he? Reform by any other name was still appealing to FDR, and he was preparing two major pieces of legislation for the Hill: the GI Bill of Rights, providing educational and other rights for veterans of the war, and a proposal that men in uniform be permitted to vote.

He had to move warily with Congress these days. The years when he was received there as a constitutional monarch were past. The conservative coalition had picked up strength in the new 78th Congress. Yes it is notable that isolationism had become a dead issue. Senator Arthur Vandenberg was in the middle of his long, historic swing toward advocacy of a world community. Only Hiram Johnson of California, dying with his cause, continued to argue that America should "go it alone." In the autumn of 1943 Johnson delivered the last major isolationist speech. Then, on the question "Should the Senate resolve its willingness to join in establishing international authority to preserve peace?" the vote was 85 yes, 5 no, 6 absent. The House had already passed a similar resolution—introduced by young Representative J. William Fulbright of Arkansas—360 to 29. The way was then clear for the Dumbarton Oaks Conference in Washington, which drew up a preliminary draft for American participation in the U.N. The Senate ratified it, 89 to 2, and in Bretton Woods, New Hampshire, diplomats hammered out agreements providing for an international bank and a world fund for stabilizing currencies and rebuilding war-torn countries. It seemed that Wendell Willkie had chosen precisely the right title for his 1943 book: *One World.*

Meanwhile the great assembly lines were moving round the clock, preparing the armies of Russia, Britain, the Commonwealth, the Free French, and America's own servicemen for the decisive assaults of 1944. Typewriter factories were making machine guns; auto plants, bombers. In Connecticut Igor Sikorsky had opened the world's first helicopter assembly line. Another Connecticut plant, in Stratford, was making more than 6,000 Corsair fighter planes. Chrysler was turning 25,507 tanks over to the Army.

Because of the complexity of sophisticated machines, there was no way to predict what next week's civilian shortage might be. Only a professional hoarder, with a large staff and unlimited funds, could even have attempted to stay a jump ahead of the quirky market. Sugar, butter, alcohol, meat, cigarettes—scarcities of these made sense; they were needed for the troops or war industry. But why was it that in the very week that cigarettes came back, every store was out of book matches? How did it happen that tire-rationed motorists, deciding to ride bicycles, hurried downtown to find that bicycle rationing had begun only yesterday? And why on earth did the war effort absorb hair curlers, wigs, kitchen utensils, lawn mowers, paper, girdles, tea, diapers, bronze caskets, electric toasters, waffle irons, egg-beaters, tin soldiers, electric trains, asparagus tongs, beer mugs, spittoons, birdcages, cameras, cocktail shakers, corn poppers, exotic leather goods, and lobster forks? The invariable answer to every plaintive question was the snarl, "Don't you know there's a war on?" Well, yes, one knew, but still . . .

It still didn't make much sense, a fact well known to Jimmy Byrnes, who ran his Office of War Mobilization in the cramped East Wing of the White House, which was still being built. (Byrnes's news ticker was in the men's room.) In many cases the makers of the missing oddments were now producing cams and cogs for the war machine, of course; like civilian pleasure boats, waffle irons and lobster forks weren't going to be manufactured for the duration. But that was no excuse for not unloading backlogs of stock. The only real answer was that a nationwide mobilization of this size was bound to be marred by kinks and foibles. You couldn't expect to issue sugar ration cards to an estimated 122,604,000 Americans—91 percent of the population—without something going awry. There were blunders, some of them incredible. The Philadelphia ration office had to close down temporarily because it had neglected to ration fuel for itself. Everyone plagued by the housing shortage had heard the story of the Los Angeles murder. A local reporter named Chick Felton arrived at the scene, verified that the corpse was dead, and headed for the victim's address at a run. "Can I rent his apartment," he panted. The landlady shook her head and said, "I already rented it to that police sergeant over there."

Apart from black marketeers, or strategically placed civilians—like the Detroiters who slipped across the Canadian border and stripped bare the shelves of prosperous Windsor—most home-front civilians had to resign themselves to involuntary asceticism, and did so cheerfully. It did, after all, take some gall to gripe while standing beneath a war bond poster showing a dying GI and the legend: "He gives his life—you only loan your money." Naturally some wants were easier to bear than others. Except for the inhabitants of skid rows, few Americans felt frantic about the War Production Board's whiskey drought, which lasted from the autumn of 1942 to the summer of 1944. (Incorrigible drinkers put up with unappealing substitutes like Olde Spud, bearing spirits distilled from waste potatoes and skins, just as incorrigible smokers puffed desperately away at such obscure cigarette brands as Fleetwoods.)

Transportation was another matter. On February 1, 1942, when the last auto assembly line was converted to war production, Detroit had 500,000 precious new cars in stock. The OPA took title to all of them, stored them in government warehouses, and doled them out to applicants with airtight priorities, such as country physicians. By July 1944 only 30,000 autos were left—a three-day peacetime supply for the country's car salesmen, even in the shabby 1930s—and the monthly OPA quota was arbitrarily cut by 22 percent.

If you already had a car, you had to face the gasoline shortage. An ordinary citizen without a defense job received a black "A" stamp on his windshield entitling him to three gallons a week. This was death for racetracks and roadhouses; they had to fold. Trolley cars were popular in cities. When distances were short, walking seemed a sensible solution, but even this posed special problems; civilians were rationed two pairs of shoes a year, and J. Edgar Hoover reported that shoes were third on hijackers' lists, behind liquor and rayon. In the last year of the war remarkable varieties of vehicles were to be seen in America: horses and buggies, resurrected bicycles built for two, elegant Baker Electrics, and puffing Stanley Steamers, the most recent of them made in 1925, when the Stanley company went out of business.

People were fed up with red tape and bureaucratic arrogance; here young Richard Nixon had correctly diagnosed a national mood. Men didn't mind wearing pants without cuffs or coats without lapels, women didn't object to painting "bottled" stockings on their legs and drawing seams down them with mascara pencils, children became accustomed to little butter, less beef, and no bacon; but the tokens and ration stamps in those little OPA books remained a mystery to millions, including the grocers, who almost lost their minds when meats, fats, and cheeses were added to the point system. What made this particularly insufferable was that everyone had heard, from a friend of a friend, of how well captured Nazis were eating in their plush POW camps.

Now and then the government felt it must resort to stern measures. Roosevelt seized the railroads and put their executives in colonels' uniforms; it was the only way he could get the engineers back in their cabs. Sewell Avery, the board chairman of Montgomery Ward, was carried from his office by soldiers because he refused to obey a directive from the War Labor Board. (The boff that week was, "Know what's going to be on the cover of Montgomery Ward's new catalogue? 'We take orders from everybody.'") And War Manpower Commissioner Paul McNutt did "freeze" in their jobs 600,000 Detroit craftsmen, 110,000 merchant seamen, and 1,500,000 aircraft workers on the West Coast.

In 1942, the war's darkest year, the Axis destroyed 1,664 ships—over 7,790,000 tons. Admiral Dönitz had calculated—and he was dead right—that if his wolf packs could average 700,000 sunken tons a month, Britain would starve. Elated by his successes, he wanted to send every U-boat he had to the American seaboard. It would have changed the whole complexion of the war, with unfathomable (and chilling) consequences, but Hitler restrained his admiral. He had just had one of his attacks of intuition. Norway, he said emphatically, would be "the zone of destiny." Norway? Dönitz was incredulous. He spread out a chart. Only a dozen German submarines were lying off the American shore, and in a few weeks they had sunk nearly a half-million tons of shipping, 57 percent of it in tankers. Hitler rolled his eyes toward Scandinavia. "Norway," he repeated, and there the sub reserves went, right where the Allied admirals wanted them.

The Allies were unaware of the maneuver then, of course. The Atlantic threat was far from over; the Germans were building new U-boats every week, and the figures for sunken tonnage continued to rise. The British were grim. The Americans told them to take heart. If there was no other way to win the Battle of the Atlantic, they would simply have to outbuild the U-boats. It was at this moment that Henry J. Kaiser, an aggressive, sixty-year-old industrialist, entered American history. Kaiser had played key roles in the building of Boulder Dam, Grand Coulee Dam, Bonneville Dam, Grand Shasta Dam, and the Oakland–San Francisco Bay Bridge. In March 1942 he had just acquired shipyards in California and Oregon, and there he was introducing revolutionary techniques of prefabrication and assembly which would lead to the mass production of shipping without loss of quality.

From the outset Kaiser's industrial triumphs became legend. Beginning with an initial keel-to-delivery time of over two hundred days, he cut the average work time on a Liberty ship to forty days, and that September, in the tenth month of the war, he established a world record by launching the 10,000-ton Liberty ship *John Fitch* just twenty-four days after laying the keel. By then he had a hundred ships in the Atlantic. And that was only the beginning. In 1944 he was launching a new escort aircraft carrier every week—and he and his fellow shipbuilders were turning out entire cargo ships in seventeen days. During the first 212 days of 1945 they completed 247 of these, better than one a day, but long before then Kaiser had cast an eye elsewhere. If he could make Liberty ships, he argued in Washington, why couldn't he build cargo planes, too? Immediately he was surrounded by government designers and engineers telling him his plans were impossible. But mastering the impossible had been the story of his life, and this time he acquired a partner, Howard Hughes, who had done almost everything Kaiser had done and established a few flying records besides. In late 1942 they struck a bargain: each would invest 50 percent of the capital and harvest 50 percent of the profits.

Kaiser and Hughes were charismatic; they became celebrities. Yet they are best remembered as representatives of their time. The production miracle was accomplished by thousands of hard-driving executives and millions of workers, some skilled veterans and some young women fresh from the kitchen or the bargain counter. American resources and American freedom had united them in a joint effort that Nipponese emperor worship, Mussolini's rhetoric, and Albert Speer's productive genius could not match. To a generation which has grown up under the sound of supersonic booms, some miracles doubtless seem unimpressive. Aerospace designers of the 1970s, for example, are inclined to regard the B-17 Flying Fortress as merely quaint, like a World War I Spad or a De Havilland Tiger Moth. But in the early 1940s the B-17 was a technical triumph, just right for its time. If the passage of a quarter-century has rendered obsolete the weapons which came off World War II assembly lines, it cannot touch the exploits of those who toiled there, competing with equally determined workers in Krupp, Fiat, and Mitsubishi factories and overwhelming them.

To put U.S. military production in perspective, it may be useful to note that on May 10, 1940, when the Wehrmacht burst through the Lowlands and the Ardennes, its historic blitzkrieg was supported by 3,034 aircraft, 2,580 tanks, 10,000 artillery pieces, and 4,000 trucks. In the five years following the French collapse, America turned out:

Warplanes	296,429
Tanks (including self-propelled guns)	102,351
Artillery pieces	372,431
Trucks	2,455,964
Warships	87,620
Cargo ships	5,425
Aircraft bombs (tons)	5,822,000
Small arms	20,086,061
Small arms ammunition (rounds)	44,000,000,000

At Teheran, late in 1943, Marshal Stalin proposed a toast: "To American production, without which this war would have been lost." Twelve years earlier, the U.S. government had doled out streetcar tokens to its commanding general's chief (and sole) aide, Major Eisenhower. In 1938 General George C. Marshall had testified that American armed forces were too weak to repel an invasion of the country. In August 1941 Hitler told Mussolini that the United States was a soft country "whose conceptions of life are inspired by the most grasping commercialism." He should have read the papers of his World War I predecessor. After the Armistice in 1918 Paul von Hindenburg had summed up American war production in one sentence: *"They understood war."*

They did not understand Japanese-Americans, though, and their treatment of California's Issei and Nisei constituted what can only be set down as a national disgrace. Those who like to stamp labels on public figures should find it instructive, for the racist repression did not come from the right, where according to liberal dogma it always lurks; it was advocated and administered by men celebrated for their freedom from bigotry—Earl Warren, Walter Lippmann,

Henry L. Stimson, Abe Fortas, Milton Eisenhower, Hugo Black, and John J. McCloy. One man in the cabinet pleaded for compassion: Attorney General Francis Biddle—and he was supported by J. Edgar Hoover. One senator took the floor to protest—and he was Republican Robert A. Taft. The persecution of 125,000 immigrants, the majority of them naturalized citizens (all would have been except for discriminatory immigration laws), and many with sons in the Army, was a violation of their rights, a shirking of the government's responsibilities, and an abrogation of the very principles for which—if the Roosevelt-Churchill Atlantic Charter meant anything—the country was fighting.

The air strike at Pearl Harbor started the harassment, and the long string of Japanese victories in 1942 stirred a blind yearning for vengeance among American Caucasians—so runs the justification. It might be more persuasive had the judges at Nuremberg not ruled that the fever of war is not an extenuating circumstance. If Germans punished civilians on a racial pretext, so did Americans. To be sure, Japanese-Americans were not tortured, gassed, cremated, or used in sadistic medical experiments. Nevertheless, American authorities took steps down the dark road toward atrocities. Their contemporaries did not judge them; history must.

Why intolerance should have been particularly intense on the West Coast is something of a mystery. In Hawaii, which had a much higher proportion of Oriental aliens, the Army moved quickly and sensibly; leaders of the Japanese cooperated closely with G2 and the FBI, and a few suspects were questioned. There were no charges, or even rumors, of discrimination. But in California, where only 1 percent of the population were Issei (first-generation Japanese-Americans) or Nisei (children of Issei), the trouble began the morning after Pearl Harbor. Governor Culbert L. Olson and Attorney General Earl Warren, working with sheriffs and district attorneys, set a ghastly example. Issei-Nisei were dismissed from civil service jobs; their licenses to practice law and medicine were revoked; in some communities they were forbidden to do business of any sort, and those who made their living as commercial fishermen were barred from their boats. Attorney General Warren, using the same sort of convoluted reasoning which would later be turned against him when he became Chief Justice, said that the absence of any domestic sabotage by Japanese showed just how devious their plotting was. "Opinion among law enforcement officers in this state," he further informed Washington, "is that there is more potential danger among the group of Japanese who were born in this country than from the alien Japanese."

Launched thus by men in public office, and whipped up by the press, the hate campaign against the Yellow Peril became progressively more ugly. On January 29, 1942, a syndicated West Coast columnist wrote, "Why treat the Japs well here? They take the parking positions. They get ahead of you in the stamp line at the post office. They have their share of seats on bus and streetcar lines. Let 'em be pinched, hurt, hungry, and dead up against it. Personally I hate the Japanese, and that goes for all of them." He advocated expulsion to the interior of Americans with Japanese ancestry—all of them, including infants and the infirm—and added: "I don't mean a nice part of the interior, either. Herd 'em up, pack 'em off, and give 'em the inside room in the badlands." Westbrook Pegler declared that every Japanese in California should be under guard "and to hell with *habeas corpus* until the danger is over," and columnists Damon Runyon and Henry McLemore concurred.

The sheep followed the shepherds. Insurance companies canceled Issei-Nisei policies. Milkmen refused to deliver their milk. Grocers wouldn't sell them food. Warren had frozen their funds, and banks declined to honor their checks. Throughout early 1942 white Californians became increasingly fearful and suspicious. The state suggested to the Japanese-Americans that they might prefer to move inland, and it is a sign of their plight that eight thousand took the hint during the next three weeks.

That didn't solve the problem; it merely moved part of it. The germ of racism was spreading. The Nevada Bar Association resolved, "We feel that if Japs are dangerous in Berkeley, California, they are likewise dangerous in the State of Nevada," and Governor Chase Clark of Idaho told the press that "Japs live like rats, breed like rats, and act like rats." Governor Homer M. Adkins of Arkansas followed by announcing, "Our people are not familiar with the customs or peculiarities of the Japanese, and I doubt the wisdom of placing any in Arkansas." Governor Payne Ratner ordered his state police to forbid their cars on state highways, explaining, "Japs are not wanted and not welcome in Kansas."

Life became terrifying for the eight thousand on the run. They found signs in barbershop windows reading JAPS SHAVED. NOT RESPONSIBLE FOR ACCIDENTS, or in restaurant windows, THIS MANAGE-

MENT POISONS BOTH RATS AND JAPS. Gas stations refused them gas. They couldn't get water, or even the use of public toilets. Five Nisei reached New Jersey and were hired by a farmer; a vigilante committee put the farmer's barn to the torch and threatened to kill his youngest child. In Denver, where a Nisei girl found a job, she tried to attend church. The minister himself blocked the way. He asked, "Wouldn't you feel more at home in your own church?" Lieutenant General John L. De Witt, commanding general of the Western Defense Command and an old Philippine hand, thought that letting Japanese-Americans roam the countryside was folly anyhow. "A Jap's a Jap!" he said. "It makes no difference whether he's an American or not."

California was pressing for federal action. Roosevelt, weary of the issue and preoccupied with theaters of war, told Stimson and McCloy, then Assistant Secretary of War, to handle it; he asked only that they be as reasonable and humane as possible. Stimson was busy with his own maps and pins, so the initiative passed to McCloy, who became the administration's prime mover for resettlement, *con brio*. On instructions from General De Witt, Major Karl R. Bendetsen, head of the War Department Aliens Division, had already drawn up an evacuation plan. He was in San Francisco putting the final touches on it when McCloy telephoned him on February 8 to say, "We have carte blanche to do what we want as far as the President is concerned." De Witt, who had already endorsed the Bendetsen draft, promptly mailed it to Washington.

Six days later Attorney General Biddle urged caution, advising FDR that "the Army has not yet advised me of its conclusions in the matter." But at this point he was crossing foils with Stimson, the strong man of the cabinet, who felt that he must support McCloy and De Witt. As Biddle recalled twenty years later, "If Stimson had insisted, had stood firm, as he apparently suspected that this wholesale evacuation was needless, the President would have followed his advice. And if . . . I had urged the Secretary to resist the pressure of his subordinates, the result might have been different. But I was new to the Cabinet, and disinclined to insist on my view to an elder statesman."

Something else happened that Saturday; Walter Lippmann weighed in with what Biddle's staff later called the decisive opinion. "It is a fact that the Japanese have been reconnoitering the Pacific Coast for a considerable period of time, testing and feeling out the

American defenses," Lippmann wrote in his column of February 14. He understood Washington's reluctance to adopt "a policy of mass evacuation and mass internment," but "The Pacific Coast is officially a combat zone: some part of it may at any moment be a battlefield. Nobody's constitutional rights include the right to reside and do business on a battlefield." General De Witt could hardly have put it more forcefully. The offices of Undersecretary of the Interior Fortas and Director Milton Eisenhower of the War Relocation Authority were alerted for supporting roles, and on February 19 the President signed Executive Order 9066 authorizing the War Department to establish "military areas" and to exclude from them "any or all persons."

It was not Roosevelt's finest hour. With a stroke of his pen he had consigned to De Witt's mercies an innocent and bewildered people who, like most first- and second-generation immigrants, were more loyal to their new country than old settlers. The middle-aged Issei had been producing more than half California's fruits and vegetables before Pearl Harbor; by traditional American standards they had made good. The Nisei were in their teens or early twenties. Native-born, conditioned in California's public schools, they talked, dressed, behaved, and danced like their Caucasian peers.

Under Executive Order 9066, as interpreted by De Witt, voluntary migration ended on March 27. People of Japanese descent were given forty-eight hours to dispose of their homes, businesses, and furniture; during their period of resettlement they would be permitted to carry only personal belongings, in hand luggage. All razors and liquor would be confiscated. Investments and bank accounts were forfeited. Denied the right to appeal, or even protest, the Issei thus lost seventy million dollars in farm acreage and equipment, thirty-five million in fruits and vegetables, nearly a half-billion in annual income, and savings, stocks and bonds beyond reckoning.

Beginning at dawn on Monday, March 30, copies of General De Witt's Civilian Exclusion Order No. 20 affecting persons "of Japanese Ancestry" were nailed to doors, like quarantine notices. It was a brisk Army operation; toddlers too young to speak were issued tags, like luggage, and presently truck convoys drew up. From the sidewalks soldiers shouted, "Out, Japs!"—an order chillingly like the "*'Raus, Juden, 'Raus!*" which Anne Frank was hearing from German soldiers on Dutch pavements. The trucks took the internees to fifteen assembly areas, among them a Yakima, Washington, brewery, Pasadena's Rose Bowl, and racetracks in Santa Anita and Tanforan. The tracks were the worst; there families were housed in horse stalls.

These areas, as reports from Milton Eisenhower and Fortas make clear, were only temporary quarters. The prisoners (for that is what they now were) received identity cards and periodic inspections of their belongings and their persons. Although no one told them, they were awaiting the construction of eleven huge "relocation centers." Because state governors felt as they did, all the centers were to be on federal land—the most desolate such land in the country.

The President never visited these bleak garrisons, but he once referred to them as "concentration camps." That is precisely what they were. The average family of six or seven members was allowed an "apartment" measuring twenty by twenty-five feet. None had a stove or running water. Each block of barracks shared a community laundry, mess hall, latrines, and open shower stalls, where women had to bathe in full view of the sentries. Modesty was one characteristic both Issei and Nisei women had in common with their ancestors, but when they raised the point, their guards told them to forget it; weren't they Americans now?

They were to spend three years on dreary tracts east of the Sierra Nevadas, in California's desolate Owens Valley, and at Tule Lake, in northern California's remote Siskiyou County. Surrounded by barbed wire, with powerful searchlights in watchtowers sweeping their windows each night, they struggled to recapture something of the life they had known before Pearl Harbor, teaching the children, holding church services, and attending what eventually turned out to be 2,120 marriages, 5,981 christenings, and 1,862 funerals.

Their cause should have been the cause of everyone who believed in freedom; the American Civil Liberties Union would call it "the worst single wholesale violation of civil rights of American citizens in our history." But that was not a popular view at the time. If the federal government intended to wait upon public opinion in California, the barracks might as well have been made permanent. Racists there had no intention of putting up with free Japs, despite what others said, and the Supreme Court could go hang.

But even the Supreme Court was tepid in its support of liberty. On Monday, December 18, 1944, the Court handed down findings which would have been inconceivable in peacetime. Justice Douglas dodged the issue of constitutionality; Justice Black, in what is now remembered by students of the law as a bad decision, wrote that California had been theatened with invasion, the authority of the military was paramount, and the Japanese hadn't been excluded because of racial prejudice anyhow. (Roberts, Murphy, and Jackson dissented.) In two cases the Court offered divided advice. It upheld the mass evacuation as a proper exercise of the power to wage war and ruled that there was no justification for continuing to detain American citizens whose loyalty was unquestioned. The Army began moving Japanese-Americans back to the coast on December 19—and was confronted by fifty-seven separate acts of violence by anti-Japanese vigilantes. To crown this tragicomedy, the Hearst press raged over reports of a prisoner riot at Camp Tule, citing it as evidence that the interned families were "disloyal."

There had been no riot at Tule. At no time during the detentions were there any disturbances in the camps. The staggering irony is that the patriotism of the Japanese-Americans had been almost wholly unaffected by their mistreatment. With incredible stoicism they had accepted a double standard under which—to cite one instance—a white intern was paid $500 for a schedule of examinations and minor operations while an experienced Issei physician beside him, completing identical tasks, received $19. Others had planted trees, carried out experiments in developing artificial rubber, and painted Army recruiting posters, knowing that they would be paid nothing. To the confusion of their guards, they assembled each morning to raise the Stars and Stripes and salute it while their Boy Scout drum and bugle corps (every camp had one) played the national anthem. At Camp Topaz 3,250 adults were enrolled in camp courses; the two most popular were the English language and American history. Saturday evenings they sang "America the Beautiful," and after January 28, 1943, the men of military age did a lot more than sing.

On that Thursday Stimson announced that the Army would accept Nisei volunteers. Immediately more than 1,200 signed up, and before the war's end 17,600 Japanese had joined the Army, taking the recruit's oath of allegiance while still behind barbed wire. In Italy they served with great distinction in the 100th Infantry and the 442nd Infantry. No Nisei ever deserted. During the Italian campaign the 442nd alone suffered the loss of three times its original strength while winning 3,000 Purple Hearts with 500 oak leaf clusters, 810 Bronze Stars, 342 Silver Stars, 47 Distinguished Service

Crosses, and 17 Legion of Merit awards. In Europe these units were a legend. Bill Mauldin wrote that "to my knowledge and the knowledge of numerous others who had the opportunity of watching a lot of different outfits overseas, no combat unit in the Army could exceed them in loyalty, hard work, courage, and sacrifice. Hardly a man of them hadn't been decorated at least twice, and their casualty rates were appalling."

Those who fought beside the Nisei knew what drove them. They were trusting that when word of their war records reached California, attitudes toward their families would improve, and that the Issei's prewar possessions would be returned to them. It was a vain hope. Japanese-American homes, farms, and businesses had been taken over by white Californians, most of whom, with Hearst's aggressive support, kept their loot. The Nisei themselves, returning in uniform, were rejected by barbershops and restaurants. After the *San Francisco Examiner* had run the headline SOLDIERS OF NIP ANCESTRY ALLOWED TO ROAM ON COAST, a Nisei who had lost a leg in the ETO was publicly beaten. That was too much even for bigots, and overt outrages subsided.

To imply that everyone in the state was a xenophobe would be to compound injustice. But a great many people sat on their hands and looked the other way. The War Department became concerned about Nisei incidents; white officers who had served with them were sent on West Coast lecture tours to describe their gallantry to farmers and businessmen. One first lieutenant was asked by a lanky farmer, "How many of them Japs in your company got killed?" The lieutenant replied, "All but two of the men who started in my platoon were killed by the end of the war." The farmer said, "Too goddam bad they didn't get the last two." People stared at the ceiling, at the floor, at their laps. No one said a word.

Pressing demands of the Western Defense Command kept Lieutenant General John L. De Witt at his desk throughout the war, far from the excitement and challenge of combat. His fidelity did not go unnoticed, however. The Army awarded him the Distinguished Service Medal with two oak leaf clusters, the Navy honored him with its Distinguished Service Medal, France made him an officer in its Legion of Honor, and Mexico decorated him with its Order of the Aztec Eagle. In 1947 he retired with full honors, whereupon, in a remarkable display of Occidental inscrutability, he became an ardent member of the Japan-America Society.

Three weeks after Pearl Harbor, Secretary of Agriculture Claude R. Wickard casually offered Americans a tip. Farmers were going to be busy feeding the Army, he said, so civilians who liked fresh vegetables might like to plant home gardens—he called them victory gardens. Millions of urbanites who didn't know a harrow from a spade and thought a rake was what Errol Flynn was put down peas, carrots, spinach, tomatoes, radishes, beets, lettuce, and cabbages in every open place they could find—backyards, parking lots emptied by gas rationing, playgrounds, Chicago's Arlington Racetrack, the Portland (Oregon) zoo, Ellis Island, and Alcatraz. Guided by advice from the Department of Agriculture and seed firms, victory garden farmers surprised and delighted the country. By 1943 a third of America's fresh vegetables were coming from twenty million victory gardens.

The U.S. wasn't that fond of greens, but it was something to do. In wartime the nation had become one huge transient station inhabited by people saying goodbye, people on the move, or people just waiting, if only for an end to the Kleenex and hairpin shortages. Middle-aged men painted their World War I helmets white and joined Civil Defense, testing sirens, filling boxes with sand and pails with water, practicing first aid and standing watches night after night, scanning the skies for a glimpse of an Axis plane. In government drives women and small children collected scrap rubber, wastepaper, aluminum, tin cans, and toothpaste tubes. Housewives salvaged cooking grease and rolled Red Cross bandages—two and a half billion of them, from Pearl Harbor to V-J Day. A Seattle shoemaker gave six tons of rubber heels. "Cotton Ed" Smith contributed the rubber mat that supported his favorite spittoon. In Boston, Beacon Hill held a black-tie scrap rally, donations to which included an eighty-year-old Gatling gun, a buggy, and Governor Leverett Saltonstall's rowing machine.

Hollywood helped kill time during the long wait. It was primarily addressing itself to GIs; during the war 982 movies were filmed and 34,232 prints sent overseas. The pictures were also available to civilians, and theaters were jammed nightly. These were the years of *H. M. Pulham, Esq.* (Robert Young), *The Man Who Came to Dinner* (Monty Woolley), *Woman of the Year* (Katharine Hepburn, Spencer Tracy), *My Gal Sal* (Victor Mature), *This Above All* (Tyrone Power, Joan Fontaine), *The Song of Bernadette* (Jennifer Jones), *Going My Way* (Bing Crosby, Barry Fitzgerald), *Double

Indemnity (Fred MacMurray, Barbara Stanwyck, Edward G. Robinson), *The Outlaw* (Jane Russell), *For Whom the Bell Tolls* (Gary Cooper and Ingrid Bergman), *Saratoga Trunk* (Cooper and Bergman again), *The Lost Weekend* (Ray Milland), *Casablanca* (all the immortals), Hitchcock's *Shadow of a Doubt,* and *Bambi.* As usual, show business had some bad moments, including one when press agents joyfully announced that Lassie had given birth to a litter of puppies—whereupon a veterinarian revealed that Lassie was male. Still, the level of screen quality remained high, an exceptional achievement when it is remembered that many reviewers were testing not only excellence but patriotism as well. Dorothy Thompson faulted *Lifeboat* because she thought Hitchcock made the Nazi more competent than his fellow passengers, and Bosley Crowther of the *New York Times* agreed that it was "a strangely undemocratic film, excusable on no basis, even in our enlightened society." Hitchcock protested that he had been producing a thriller, not a message; his demurrer was filed in wastebaskets. Even so professional and detached a critic as the *New Yorker*'s Wolcott Gibbs wrote that John Steinbeck's *The Moon Is Down* evinced "a curious tenderness toward the Germans." Audiences were more tolerant; they had come for other reasons. More than ever, with so many people so far from home and family, movies offered brief asylum and tranquillity.

In these years the mass media were also a bond between those who were separated, continents apart, for years. The media gave the lonely something in common when they had little else. Some of it was cloying; "White Christmas," America's first hit tune of the war, was a bleat of self-pity, and "I'll Be Home for Christmas" was even worse. Some was just obnoxious. There were times—as when Jimmy Savo and the rest of the country were singing, "You gets no bread with ONE meatball"—which were almost unbearable for people with sensitive eardrums. "Makes No Difference Now" and "You Are My Sunshine" fell in the same category, and it is a depressing fact that throughout the war Nelson Eddy was the highest-paid singer in the United States. But Broadway promised a brighter tomorrow. *Bloomer Girl, I Remember Mama, The Voice of the Turtle,* and *Harvey* were entering their lusty youth. In the summer of 1942 two men down on their luck, Richard Rodgers and Oscar Hammerstein II, had begun experimenting with a dog-eared script called *Green Grow the Lilacs.* As a play, it had closed in 1931 after only sixty-four performances. "The RH factor," as *Life* later called it, transformed the turkey into *Oklahoma!* It opened at the St. James on March 31, 1944, and before it closed in 1948 it had played 2,248 performances —then a record for musicals. Meanwhile a twenty-six-year-old musician named Leonard Bernstein had composed *On the Town*, another rollicking musical. For the first time in fifteen years ticket scavengers were lurking in Broadway alleys.

Americans on the home front were reading more. The Crosley and Hooper raters reported that radio was still the country's prime source of entertainment, with *Fibber McGee and Molly* and *Town Meeting of the Air* leading the pack, but the biggest audiences gathered at news time. In radio, as in bookstores and libraries, the great swing from fiction to nonfiction had begun. The Pentagon was the world's biggest publisher; in 1945 alone it distributed over sixty million copies of its armed services editions, covering every conceivable topic, and while their double-column format was irritating, they were read hungrily and often sent home. New titles were: Marion Hargrove *See Here, Private Hargrove*, Major Alexander de Seversky *Victory Through Air Power*, Ilka Chase *Past Imperfect*, Elliot Paul *The Last Time I Saw Paris*, William L. White *They Were Expendable*, Richard Tregaskis *Guadalcanal Diary*, John Hersey *A Bell for Adano*, Willkie *One World*, and Ernie Pyle *Here Is Your War* and *Brave Men*. Two clues to a major postwar issue, Richard Wright's *Black Boy* and Lillian Smith's *Strange Fruit*, were hardly noticed by social scientists, though they sold well.

The biggest sellers were magazines. Every popular periodical in the United States increased its sales during the war; in 1944 advertisers invested a hundred million dollars more in them than in 1942. Here again, as Eric Hopkins observed at the time, "Their percentage of nonfiction has . . . been steadily rising; for one thing, facts since 1939 have been outrunning fantasy." (They would continue to do so; by the 1970s serious fiction would be nearly obsolescent.) Magazines for women were of special interest. To countless numbers of their subscribers the war was a four-year bore. Of the 16 million volunteers and draftees who wore a uniform between 1941 and 1945, only a quarter-million were female. At any given time the size of the military establishment was 12 million males—the fittest 12 million—withdrawn from a population of 131 million. So great an imbalance inevitably meant masses of frustrated women.

On blind dates with servicemen, girls had about them an air of enterprise if not of aggression; they weren't wholly jesting when they called their cosmetics "war paint." Older women were more subtle. Lacking counsel from the high priests of Paris, Manhattan's couturiers copied military uniforms—a giveaway to where feminine thoughts were. One popular evening gown was adorned with a huge swooping Air Corps wing of gold lamé, beginning at one hip and curving upward across the bosom to the opposite shoulder. Eisenhower jackets were models for evening wraps or blouses with drawstring waists. Imitations of British commando berets made very dashing hats for daytime wear, and girls who had no intention of joining the Women's Army Corps wore copies of WAC hats decked out with sequins. Even the cloth shortages were exploited; the "Dido," a sort of outsize romper suit, became a playsuit by day and pajamas at night.

Putting horns on overseas GIs was just about the most unpopular thing a soldier's wife could do, and she wasn't often tempted anyhow; as a popular song of the day put it, "They're Either Too Young or Too Old." Doomed to purdah, married women in large numbers took to wearing slacks. The home front wasn't much of a life for them. The younger wives were prey to secret misgivings. Many weddings had been held just before the troop transports left, and the lonely brides wondered whether lasting marriages could be built upon impulse. The tough ones turned to booze; by 1943 the ratio of male to female alcoholics had jumped from 1-to-5 to 1-to-2. Others buried themselves in Emily Post or Dorothy Dix, or lived vicariously with Oona O'Neill, who, to the disgust of her playwriting father, had been named debutante of the year by the Stork Club. Once again, however, the multitude turned to magazines—in particular to three of them created during the war with a feminine mystique in mind: Street & Smith's *Mademoiselle,* Condé Nast's *Glamour,* and Walter Annenberg's *Seventeen.*

Here another wartime phenomenon appears: the emerging adolescent. The end of the Depression had restored interest in nubility. At the same time, high school students whose mothers were working for Lockheed or Boeing came home to a key beneath the doormat, and with so much cash around they either received allowances or earned money themselves. Lester Markel, editor of the *New York Times Magazine,* began trying to work the word "teen-ager" into articles, but the country wasn't quite ready for it yet. High school boys, intent upon military service, seemed more grim than carefree. The girls were gayer and more spirited, and because they all wore short socks they were called bobby-soxers.

The fashions of the swing generation were dead or dying; saddle shoes had been replaced by flat-soled loafers, cardigan sweater sets by Sloppy Joe sweaters, and convertible raincoats by the steady's parka, worn with—another omen—blue jeans. For a while jeans were accompanied by a vogue for men's white shirts (with the shirttails always flapping loose); after V-J Day fathers and older brothers would return to find the closets empty. Beer jackets were still around, but scarcely recognizable to aging jitterbugs; bobby-soxers had decorated them with the divisional insignia of boyfriends, real or imagined, in the service. Another rage was the wearing of rings of black jet symbolizing absent GI friends, and bobby-soxers congregating after school for a bull session (not yet a rap), if asked what they were doing, would reply, "Just messing around."

Yo-Yos, slumber parties, mismatched shoes and socks, striped football stockings—their capacity for fads was no more tasteless or greater than that of middle-class youth of the 1930s. But there was a difference. The country had changed. Older Americans were more inclined to watch them, listen to them, and indulge them. On some issues the generations were united. One was organized labor. They were against it. Looking at labor's wartime record, one wonders why. General Brehon Somervell, the Army's chief of supply, told a Senate committee, "Make no mistake about it, no one has suffered from a lack of supplies. The boys at the front have had everything that could possibly be moved to the front." But the United Mine Workers' ill-timed demands for overtime and extra pay seemed almost designed to wreck labor's reputation, and James C. Petrillo, czar of the musicians' union, was just as inept. Petrillo was a special bogey for bobby-soxers. He demanded royalties for bands and orchestras whose records were played over radio stations, and for twenty-seven months he kept most popular music from the public. Youth seemed to feel that a strike was directed at it, though the real victims were the big swing bands. Between Petrillo's ban, rationing, the cost of road trips, and changes in public taste—bobby-soxers preferred sentimental ballads—the great bands broke up, and the swing era that the GIs had loved quietly died.

Parents beamed. They had favored ballads all along. They were proud of their children's participation in the rubber and paper drives and delighted by much in the new youth culture. In 1944 the country's top song hit was a novelty song for bobby-soxers, "Swinging on a Star." With almost no male college students, there were hardly any college athletes (an exception was West Point, which built its great point-a-minute team around Doc Blanchard and Junior Davis). Attention was thus diverted to high school teams, and revisions of rules made basketball for the first time an exciting spectator sport. Dads and sons could go together, just as moms and daughters could pore over the same features in *Glamour*. Youth is always excited by innovation, and in the summer of 1944 adolescents were among the first to adopt the invention of a Hungarian refugee in Argentina, a pen which used a ball bearing instead of a point. It was imported under the brand name Strato-pen, but users simply called them ball-point pens. Approving adults began buying them, too. On everything from politics to writing instruments, it seemed, the generations on the home front were at peace.

Then a huge gap yawned. The guilty party was a frail, pallid, bow-tied, hundred-and-thirty-five-pound crooner with jug-handle ears and a starved look. He was Francis Albert Sinatra, last seen in this narrative tagging along behind the Harry James band. To his worshippers he looked vulnerable, innocent, and in his teens. Actually he wasn't any of them. Born in a cold-water Hoboken tenement, the son of a Sicilian bantamweight prizefighter, he was a tough, profane loner who believed his patent-leather lungs would carry him to stardom; of any rival he would snarl, "I can sing that son of a bitch off the stage any day of the week." Far from being in high school, he was in his mid-twenties. His explanation for the illusion was, "I'm twenty-five. I look maybe nineteen. Most kids feel I'm one of them—the pal next door, say. So maybe they feel they know me. And that's the way I want it to be. What the hell, they're nice kids."

Sinatra wasn't healthy enough for the Army—he had an occupational handicap, a punctured eardrum—so he overcompensated with fierce drive. His real appetite was for fame. Swing sidemen were often adept at sabotaging crooners, but when Buddy Rich taunted Sinatra by playing little drum riffs during tender moments in his songs, Rich wound up with a mouse and a fat lip. Frankie's obsession with success meant that he couldn't remain in any bandleader's shadow very long. After six months with James he switched to Tommy Dorsey. He attracted some attention with his versions of "Fools Rush In," "Night and Day," and "White Christmas"; then he bought out his Dorsey contract and hired a press agent. He was ready to make it alone. On the night of December 30, 1942, he was singing with all he had on the stage of New York's Paramount Theater when something happened in the audience. A girl in the twelfth row who hadn't eaten lunch fainted—or "swooned." Another girl, startled, stood up and screamed. No one knows exactly what happened in the next few seconds, but Sinatra continued to sing—nobody was going to scream *him* down—and by the time he had finished the theater was a charivari, with every girl in the theater on her feet, shrieking.

The screeching spread like the plague. He became known as the Voice. Wherever the Voice appeared, pandemonium followed. His weekly mail rose to five thousand letters, and two thousand Frankie fan clubs were organized across the country. Autograph hunters chased him through drugstores, restaurants, department stores, and his home. They climbed his roof to peer into his bedroom. If he walked in mud, they dug up the earth and dried it to preserve his footprints. They weren't all kids and they weren't all nice. Twice he was almost strangled by hoydens tugging for possession of his bow tie. They tried to tear his clothes off, with considerable success, and one harpy in her forties cornered him in the Waldorf, ripped open her blouse, and insisted that he autograph her brassiere. By 1944 his reappearance at the Paramount for a three-week engagement was greeted by thirty thousand wailing adolescents; controlling them required 421 riot policemen, twenty policewomen, and over twenty squad cars.

In less time than the GIs needed to capture Sicily, the Voice—alias Frank Swoonatra, alias the King of Swoon—was rich. He had signed contracts guaranteeing him a weekly appearance on the Lucky Strike Hit Parade, an annual RKO movie, and unprecedented royalties from Columbia Records. His annual income was over a million dollars. Despite wartime controls, he seemed to be spending most of it. In Hollywood he built a pink house with every known convenience and some that had previously been unknown; to spare himself the trouble of rising to close the drapes on one wall he installed a gadget which cost $7,000. His tailored clothes were gaudy and enormous in every dimension, from the floppy bow ties and high-waisted slacks to the bulging padded shoulders. His friends, and by now he had accumulated a lot of them, gathered around him like barons doting on a king. They felt privileged just to be in his company, but he made them happy in other ways; among his idiosyncrasies was handing out 150-dollar gold cigarette lighters as casually as Major Bowes distributed Mars Bars. His feminine confidantes were changing, too. Before the war he had married his childhood sweetheart, Nancy Barbate, and early in his celebrity he answered all matrimonial questions with "Nobody comes before my wife Nancy. That goes for now and all time." Then he stopped answering the questions. Ahead lay Ava Gardner and, much later, Mia Farrow.

Frankie's talent, or lack of it, had become a burning issue, like General Patton's slapping of a soldier. "Sinatra's voice," *Time* said, "has become a national feature comparable to Yosemite Valley," but *Life*, *Time*'s sister publication, thought that the "swooner-crooner" made "every song sound like every other song" because he knew only one rhythm: *large alla marcia funebre*. The *New York Herald Tribune* quoted a congressman as saying, "The Lone Ranger and Frank Sinatra are the prime instigators of juvenile delinquency in America." Elsa Maxwell accused the Voice of "musical illiteracy" and suggested his fans be given "Sinatraceptives." Even his old boss Harry James conceded that Frankie's new wardrobe made him look "like a wet rag." Someone told Bing Crosby that "A voice like Sinatra's comes only once in a lifetime." Bing replied, "Sure, but why does it have to be in *my* lifetime?"

Parents were angry and confused. The hero of the hour was supposed to be a strapping, steel-helmeted GI in full battle array, leaping through surf to storm an enemy shore. Frankie, in the idiom of the time, looked as though he had been strained through a condom. Adolescent refugees from Europe thought him a noisome freak. A fugitive from a German concentration camp, herself seventeen, inquired, "Is there no way to make those kids come to their senses? The time they are wasting outside the Paramount Theater could be used for other purposes—for instance, to help win this war." Her American peers went right on shrieking, and speculation over the source of his magic grew. "As a visible object of female adulation," *Newsweek* observed, "Sinatra is baffling."

Psychiatrists and psychologists denied being baffled. They recalled the medieval dance craze and spoke of "mammary hyperesthesia," a "maternal urge to feed the hungry," "mass frustrated love," and "mass hypnosis." Some of Frankie's flip critics said the same thing more pointedly: "It's as if he had musk glands instead of vocal cords," and, "Let's face it—Sinatra's just about the only male left around." The last seems the likeliest. Girls might sing of boys absent in the New Guinea bush—"He's 1-A in the Army and he's A-1 in my heart"—but a male in hand was worth two of them. Besides, it wasn't like dating a 4-F. That would have been treacherous. This was merely a bobby-soxer rite.

If older civilians didn't understand that, the GIs he was replacing did. It is not too much to say that by the end of the war Sinatra had become the most hated man in the Army, Navy, Air Corps, and Marine Corps. Like the bobby-soxers, Frankiephobes in uniform saw in the Voice a symbol; to them he stood for all available civilians. Frankie made just one USO tour in Italy, and that was after V-E Day, when the Axis guns had been spiked. Then he flew off sneering that the USO was strictly for cheap hacks. The *Stars and Stripes* commented that "Mice make women faint, too," and Marlene Dietrich, who had performed near the front, observed that, after all, "you could hardly expect the European Theater to be like the Paramount."

Exactly five weeks before Frankie's first hungry girl fainted in that twelfth row, John J. McCloy ordered the acquisition of the Los Alamos Ranch School for Boys, where Robert Oppenheimer had been educated as a child, for a special war project. Oppenheimer had recommended Los Alamos because it was isolated, and the other Allied scientists agreed that they must have privacy if they were to stand any chance of building a bomb before the Nazis—a possibility most of them felt was exceedingly remote at the time. By now, late in 1942, the Americans and their refugee colleagues were desperate. They had made little progress on the bomb, despite Roosevelt's commitment. Allen Dulles was reporting from Switzerland that large consignments of uranium and heavy water were entering the Reich every week. Germany's atomic physicists were the finest in the world. Moreover, the scientists in America suspected that their own project had been compromised. That autumn two German agents had been picked up in the wild hills near Oak Ridge, Tennessee. How they got there, and what became of them, are questions Washington still prefers to leave unanswered. But coupled with other evidence, it added one more touch of authenticity to the nightmare the physicists then thought they saw in the future: Hitler with an arsenal of atomic weapons and the Allies with nothing.

Of this much they were now certain: such a bomb was practical. The hypothesis had been sound from the outset, but there had been a hitch in its application. In theory, a chain reaction should have developed when neutrons were introduced into a U-235 pile. The neutrons would split the U-235 atoms, each of which would liberate from one to three neutrons—which, in turn, would split more atoms, and so on, until the critical mass was reached. Obviously they couldn't permit that mass to form in a laboratory; that was why they used graphite, to slow neutrons down while they observed the process. In practice, they found, some neutrons went astray and some were "cannibalized" by the pile. A chain reaction was possible only if successive "generations" of neutrons became larger and larger. This was christened the K factor, otherwise known as "the great god K." It was reached under the following conditions. If 100 neutrons which had caused fission in 100 U-235 atoms gave birth to a generation of new neutrons, 105 of which were left to cause fission, the ratio would be 105 to 100, and the K factor would have a value of 1.05. The third generation would be 105 multiplied by 1.05, and so on, until the mass was formed. As William L. Laurence put it, "When the K factor is greater than one, the pile will be chain-reacting, as the birth rate will be greater than the death rate." Conversely, if 100 neutrons produced only 99, the K factor, 0.99, would be inadequate. By purifying the graphite in early experiments, the best they could get in those early months was a birth rate of .87 per 100. Their greatest problem lay in the impurity of the uranium. Dr. Arthur H. Compton called the Westinghouse director of research and—at a time when the world's total hoard of pure uranium metal did not exceed a few grams—asked him, "How soon can Westinghouse supply three tons of pure uranium?" He heard a gagging sound at the other end of the line, but the firm's response was an illustration of American industry's versatility in World War II. Uranium fabrication was stepped up from eight ounces a day to over five hundred pounds, and by November 1942 Westinghouse had delivered the three tons.

The delivery address could hardly have aroused less interest. On Ellis Avenue in Chicago, between Fifty-sixth and Fifty-seventh streets, the ivied Gothic walls of University of Chicago buildings parted to reveal a recess and, within, a door. Beyond that door was a large squash court which had been unused since the outbreak of war. The court lay directly beneath the west stands of Stagg Field, and scarcely anyone had come this way since the university had abandoned intercollegiate football. It was there, that November, that a pile of unprecedented size was being assembled with materials of unique purity. Two carbon companies, working with the National Bureau of Standards, had turned out a graphite highly resistant to neutrons. Other bureau scientists had joined Professor Frank H. Spedding of Iowa State College in further improving the Westinghouse uranium; in the new method the metal was transformed into lumps called "Spedding's eggs." Lastly, engineers were prepared to create a vacuum in the pile—by enclosing it in an enormous square balloon and pumping the air out—to prevent neutron absorption by nitrogen. Dr. Compton predicted that the new mass would yield a K factor "somewhere between 1.04 and 1.05"; others believed it might reach 1.07.

So great a prospect of success raised new questions. Atoms had been split before, but no one in history had ever created a viable chain reaction, and it was impossible to gauge the efficiency of decelerating techniques. The great god K might defy their checks and restraints, might break loose and take all Chicago, or even Illinois, with it. To reduce the risk, seven strips of cadmium and three rods of boron steel—cadmium and boron being gluttonous consumers of neutrons—were passed completely through the pile; sliding them in and out was expected to give the Frankensteins control over the monster they were creating. No one could be sure that would be successful, however, so two young physicists volunteered to form what was called the "suicide squad." The two would stand on scaffolding overlooking the pile with buckets of cadmium solution in their hands. If all other controls failed and the apparatus started to go, they would hurl the liquid at it.

Layer after layer was added, and the speed of neutron counters grew with the pile, until, during the bitterly cold night of December 1–2, 1942, the twelfth layer was in place. The contrivance now weighed 12,400 pounds, and the rapid clicking of the counters was unmistakable. "We knew then," W. H. Zinn later told William L. Laurence, "that if we pulled out the control rods, the thing would pop." At 3:30 the following afternoon, with Fermi present and the suicide squad in position overhead, all the controls except one cadmium strip were removed; then that was partly withdrawn. The counter clicking was so intense that it reminded one of the witnesses of a burring drill. The K factor mounted to 0.98, 0.99, 1.00—and then 1.01, 1.02, 1.03, 1.04, 1.05, 1.06, 1.07, 1.08, 1.09, and 1.10. They had done it: each successive generation of neutrons would now exceed the last. Pure science had gone as far as it could. The chain was now self-perpetuating; transforming it into a deliverable bomb had become a technological problem.

On that same December 2, the technological issue was being discussed only three blocks away, in room 209 of the university's Eckhert Hall. Neither group was aware of the other's presence in the city. Security was very tight; Roosevelt wanted it that way. The President's attitude toward the Manhattan Project was ambivalent, and, like so many of FDR's traits, a reflection of the American national character. Instinctively he trusted people, enjoyed sharing knowledge, and wanted the United States to contribute toward the world's store of learning. But while he spoke of brotherhood—and meant it—he also liked secrets. As James MacGregor Burns has noted, "If Roosevelt was both realist and idealist, both fixer and preacher, both a prince and a soldier, the reason lay not only in his own mind and background, but also in his society and its traditions. Americans have long had both moralistic and realistic traditions."

In Chicago the President was being realistic; the squash court and Eckhert Hall might as well have been separated by a continent. Nevertheless, they were part of the same design, destined to merge in a B-29 bomb bay thirty-one months later. General Groves had called them here to review the Chicago Metallurgical Project. They were America's technological elite—captains of heavy industry, professors from Cal Tech and MIT—and the general was asking them to take a lot on faith. They were being asked to produce material they had never seen for a purpose unknown to them. Their only assurances were that the project was vital to the war effort and that Washington would pay the bills.

They agreed, and beginning that month, contracts were signed with clauses which must surely rank among the vaguest in industrial law. Groves pledged four hundred million dollars for a down payment; the ultimate cost would exceed two billion. Beyond that the contractors knew very little, and the few who had to be told certain secrets were forbidden to mention them even to their wives. They couldn't talk to the scientists because the scientists had, in effect, been removed from society; all their families knew of them was an address: U.S. Army, Post Office Box 1663.

The secrecy seemed excessive to the physicists working at Los Alamos. Certainly some aspects of it seem to have been absurd. The man most closely watched was J. Robert Oppenheimer, and the man watching him was one Boris Pash, an overweight former football coach at Hollywood High School whom the Army's G2 had transmogrified into a specialist in "Communist infiltration." Pash fixed his professional eye on Oppenheimer when he heard that the scientist had contributed generously to liberal causes before the war and had twice been on the verge of marrying Dr. Jean Tatlock, a San Francisco psychiatrist who was also a Communist. In 1943 Oppenheimer picked Jean up at her Telegraph Hill home and took her to the Top of the Mark for a drink. He told her that he would be unable to see her again for months, perhaps years, and that because his work was classified he couldn't tell her what it was or where he would be doing it. Then he disappeared. Seven months later, despairing of ever seeing him again, she committed suicide. Pash, meantime, had shadowed them in San Francisco and had completely misinterpreted their meeting; he thought Oppenheimer had been slipping secrets to a fellow Commie. Telling his superiors that he was on to Oppenheimer's little game, he demanded that the physicist be fired. Groves replied that this was impossible: "Irrespective of the information you have concerning Mr. Oppenheimer, he is absolutely essential to the project."

All this might be dismissed as low comedy were it not for the uncomfortable fact that real Communist spies, following instructions from Moscow, were casting a highly professional espionage net around Los Alamos. The control was a certain Anatoli A. Yakovlev, who operated out of New York's Soviet consulate. Yakovlev worked through Harry Gold, a Philadelphian and a former industrial spy. Another thread in Yakovlev's web led from Julius and Ethel Rosenberg in New York to David Greenglass, Ethel's brother, who as a privileged Army enlisted man at Los Alamos had access to almost every blueprint, sketch, or valuable document and was bright enough to know which would be most valuable to Russians interested in building a bomb of their own. Greenglass wasn't Yakovlev's prize, though. The real treasure was Klaus Emil Fuchs. Fuchs, like Oppenheimer, Compton, and Fermi, was a highly gifted atomic physicist—a member of the Los Alamos inner circle. A native German, he had fled to England when the Nazis started rounding up their enemies. His hatred of Hitler and his loyalty to the Allied war effort were never questioned, and as a naturalized subject of the United Kingdom he had been granted top clearance. Nobody had asked why the Nazis had been after a theoretical physicist; such questions weren't raised then. Only after the war, when the Soviet apparatus came apart, would Fuchs's friends learn that he was a whole-souled Communist.

Usually Harry Gold let other carriers pick up data from Greenglass, but he often met Fuchs, and on one trip he saw both of them. His call on David Greenglass and David's pregnant young wife Ruth has been memorialized by the top of a raspberry Jell-O box, just as the Hiss-Chambers case would be remembered for a pumpkin. Julius Rosenberg had torn the Jell-O top in half and given one piece to his brother-in-law, David. When a man bearing the other half appeared, Julius had said, David should tell the man everything he knew, in the interest of "sharing information for scientific purposes." Gold was therefore welcomed to the Greenglass flat upstairs at 209 North High Street, Albuquerque, when he said, "Julius sent me," and produced his half of the box top. David dutifully produced a sheaf of paper upon which he had set down the best information he could get. It was very good: working in the smallest of the top-secret technical shops at Los Alamos, he had copied several schematic drawings of flat-type lens mold experiments for detonating an atomic bomb. This device bore little relationship to lenses as laymen know them. It was a mix of high explosives which would focus detonation waves as a glass lens focuses light waves, thus triggering the bomb. In Russian hands it would permit Soviet scientists to skip an expensive and time-consuming experimental stage. When David Greenglass put those sketches in Harry Gold's hands, he was making history. He was also opening his wife's eyes. Until that moment he had persuaded Ruth that in some obscure way they really were sharing information for the good of all mankind. But when Gold handed David an envelope bearing $500 in cash, her illusions vanished. After their visitor had left she cried, "Now I see how it is: you turn over the information and you get paid. Why, it's just—it's just like C.O.D.!" The weakest link in the Los Alamos to Moscow chain had just been formed.

Gold had brought no money for Klaus Fuchs. He had offered him $1,500 last time, and Fuchs had politely declined it. He wasn't a man to be bought; he was betraying the bomb project on principle. In Santa Fe Fuchs picked Gold up on Alameda Street, as arranged, and took him on a country ride in his battered Chevrolet coupe. When they parted, Gold was carrying a thick packet of typed notes on the application of theoretical fission to the building of a bomb. It was highly technical, way over Gold's head, but Moscow was elated. The information from both sources, Yakovlev was instructed to tell Gold, was "particularly excellent and very valuable." Six years later a production chief of the Atomic Energy Commission was shown duplicates of the Greenglass sketches. He said, "Why, they show the atomic bomb, substantially as perfected!"

How much this apparatus helped the Soviet Union when it was supplemented by data from Morton Sobell and Alan Nunn May, two other spies, is a matter of conjecture, even among scientists. It was all a question of time. The Russians had the theoretical knowledge and the technologists; sooner or later they would have found the great god K. Greenglass may, in fact, have given them nothing at all. There was really only one way to build the bomb. Edward Teller described its most intimate mechanism—two hemispheres brought into contact until the mass reaches the critical point and detonates—in an early Los Alamos seminar. Beyond that lay a farrago of details: the amount of U-235 needed, the size of the two halves, the speed with which they must collide, the scattering angle, the range of the neutrons to be projected by the chain reaction, and so on. It seemed endless. It was certainly dangerous. Dr. O. R. Frisch, Lise Meitner's nephew and the supervisor of this task, nearly lost his life in one experiment, and two other physicists were in fact killed.

Luckily for those working near Harry Dagnian, the first of them, he was holding only a small amount of fissionable material when he accidentally set off a chain reaction. It lasted only a fraction of a second and he was instantly hospitalized, but his right hand had been saturated with radiation. Within an hour he had lost his sense of touch. Gamma rays had penetrated his skin; his viscera were deteriorating. He became delirious, his hair fell out, the white corpuscles in his blood increased, and he died in agony. After that the tensions in Frisch's labs increased perceptibly. Indeed, the entire settlement was on edge, especially when a carefree young Canadian named Louis Slotkin was looking for "the crit." Slotkin was literally playing with cosmic fire—he called it "twisting the dragon's tail"—

and if he had been guilty of a really big blunder, no one would have survived to tell of it. Los Alamos would have been annihilated, Hiroshima and Nagasaki spared, and history greatly altered.

Slotkin was an adventurer and a follower of causes. He had fought with the Loyalists in Spain and with the RAF during the Battle of Britain. Grounded for nearsightedness, he had drifted into the Manhattan Project because he had the right scientific training. Under Frisch he found his métier, though many of his associates ardently wished he were back in a Spitfire. He would tinker away with two live hemispheres, using screwdrivers to slide them toward one another on a rod while he watched, engrossed. It was like Russian roulette. Sooner or later the law of probability would claim its own and he would neglect to separate the halves in time. It happened. One day a screwdriver slipped. The hemispheres came too close to one another; the lab was filled with a blinding blue glare. He tore the halves apart, breaking the chain and saving the community. He knew that in the process he had forfeited his own life. On the way to the hospital with a friend who had been working near him, he said, "You'll come through all right. But I haven't the faintest chance myself." After nine days of suffering he died. The man assigned to study the incident and ascertain what, if anything, could be learned from it, was Klaus Fuchs.

Most other physicists grumbled about security arrangements— Niels Bohr never became accustomed to his code name "Nicholas Butler" and kept forgetting it—but Fuchs, who knew the real joke, said little. Or rather, Fuchs knew *half* the joke. The Germans remained an enigma. Hitler kept talking about secret weapons, and early in 1944 he unleashed three of them: jet aircraft, snorkel submarines, and his V-1s, the first buzz bombs. None of the intelligence coming from the Reich undercut the original hypothesis of the scientific community in America. Either Hitler had a bomb, they reasoned, or he was about to get one. He might have an arsenal of them deployed as his last line of defense. The man was capable of anything. Today it is impossible to re-create the terror, hatred, and awe that the German Führer roused; yet without a semblance of it, the motivation of the atomic scientists in the New Mexico desert remains obscure.

The issue was discussed on the highest levels in Washington and London (though not in Moscow; Roosevelt and Churchill rightly suspected that Stalin would not share the discoveries of Soviet laboratories). In the autumn of 1943 a special intelligence unit, to be landed in Normandy on D-Day, was formed under the code name Alsos, the Greek word for Groves. Its members, though dressed as soldiers, would wear on their battle dress a recognition badge bearing the alpha sign in white and a jagged line of red forked lightning. Their mission was to collect data about the extent of the Reich's atomic research. Such documents would be translated and appraised on the spot by the team's senior scientist, Dr. Samuel A. Goudsmit of Holland, a distinguished experimental physicist whose hobby was the study of new developments in criminal investigation.

On Thursday, January 7, 1943, the President of the United States delivered his tenth annual State of the Union address to a joint session of Congress—"The Axis powers knew that they must win the war in 1942 or eventually lose everything," he said; "I do not need to tell you that our enemies did not win the war in 1942"—and late Saturday evening, when the capital was quiet, a small cavalcade of limousines glided away from the south portico of the White House, turned right on Fifteenth Street, and parked at a little-known train siding near the Bureau of Engraving and Printing. The President's train was waiting. Following him into the "Ferdinand Magellan," his private car, were Harry Hopkins, Dr. Ross T. McIntire, and a glittering staff of generals and flag officers. In Miami a Pan American Clipper waited to fly the presidential party across the Atlantic, to Casablanca and Winston Churchill.

This was to be a year of Allied summit meetings. After Casablanca —where he sized up Eisenhower and announced his controversial demand for "unconditional surrender" from the enemy coalition—the commander in chief would confer in Quebec (Churchill again), Washington (Churchill and joint military staffs), Cairo (Churchill and Chiang Kai-shek), Hawaii (Nimitz and MacArthur), Teheran (Churchill and Stalin), and then back to Cairo (Churchill once more). During that year the torch of leadership passed from the British prime minister to the American President, and both men knew it. The shift had nothing to do with personalities. America was putting more men and matériel into the conflict, and American generals, notably Eisenhower, would be commanding combined forces in the great battles ahead.

Roosevelt's performance as commander in chief was not without critics; nothing in his life was. Stalin believed FDR's insistence on unconditional surrender would merely prolong the war by uniting the German people, and most historians agree with him. In the Pacific the President may have given MacArthur too strong a hand in what was essentially a war for sea power and was to be won by Admiral Nimitz. But no one doubted that Roosevelt, from 1943 on, was the commander of Allied armies and navies. As early as November 1942 William D. Hassett, a special assistant to Roosevelt, observed in his diary, "The President becomes more and more the central figure in the global war, the source of initiative and authority in action, and, of course, of responsibility." Louis Johnson cabled from New Delhi, "The magic name over here is Roosevelt," and most professional soldiers admired his leadership. Eisenhower wrote, "With some of Mr. Roosevelt's political acts I could never possibly agree. But I knew him solely in his capacity as leader in a nation at war—and in that capacity he seemed to me to fulfill all that could possibly be expected of him." Stimson said that "the Army never had a finer commander in chief," and Major George Fielding Eliot wrote that FDR's grasp of total and global strategy made him "one of the greatest war presidents." American casualties were proportionately lighter than those of any other World War II power, yet on Navy Day 1944 the President could say that during the past year Americans in uniform had participated in twenty-seven landings on enemy beachheads and "every one of those twenty-seven D-days has been a triumphant success."

He certainly didn't look like a military genius. In his flannel shirt, old hat, and carelessly knotted bow tie—his invariable costume when visiting troops—he looked more like a hearty grandfather casually dressed for a weekend of trout fishing. But then, the troops he commanded were casual, too. The United States was not a European country; it was a different kind of nation, and no one represented it better than the American in the White House. David Lilienthal might write that FDR had "the handsomest fighting face in the world," and General Eisenhower might be dazzled by the President's gift for terrain, for grasping and remembering all the features of a countryside; to GIs and bluejackets, however, his greatest gift was his warmth, his concern, his appearance on the world scene as a shirt-sleeved President in a shirt-sleeved America. "As no other man in his time," Jonathan Daniels wrote, "he could speak to the American confidence always underlying American fears. And because he believed in the dignity of the American, he was never afraid to ask or expect America's courage." Nothing is more illustrative of the Roosevelt touch, of his sensitivity to the needs of people, than his visit to a military hospital in Hawaii. He had come to talk to five-star generals and admirals, to plan the great offensives which would bring Japan to its knees. But before he left, he asked to be wheeled through the ward for combat victims whose arms and legs had been amputated. He smiled and waved; he said nothing; his presence said everything. Here was a man who had lost the use of both legs. He knew their bitterness; he had shared it. Yet he had overcome it to become President, and there was no reason for them to despair of their prewar dreams.

Roosevelt was tired now, and he looked it. The White House press corps was convinced he didn't want to run for President again in 1944, and he himself wrote Robert Hannegan, chairman of the Democratic National Committee, "All that is within me cries out to go back to my home on the Hudson River." But there were pressures to stay in office, too. Like any President, he was thinking of history's judgment. He had plans for postwar America; he was as committed to the United Nations as Wilson had been to the League of Nations. And then there were the letters: "Please President Roosevelt don't let us down now in this world of sorrow and trouble," one man wrote. "If we ever needed you it's now. I believe within my heart God put you here in this world to be our guiding star." There were petitions, one signed by over six thousand steelworkers: "We know you are weary—yet we cannot afford to permit you to step down." And from the Third Reich came the voice of Douglas Chandler, a former Hearst man who had turned traitor to broadcast from Berlin under the name Paul Revere: "Get that man out of the house that was once white!"

Roosevelt was politician enough to be swayed, if ever so slightly, by such voices. He eyed Wendell Willkie wistfully. Both men saw things alike, and each secretly admired the other. The President called Sam Rosenman to his office and asked him to serve as an emissary to Willkie. "We ought to have two parties—one liberal and the other conservative," FDR said. "As it is now, each party is split by dissenters." He thought the parties should be realigned after the election, and asked Rosenman to sound out Willkie. "You tell the President that I'm ready to devote almost full time to this," Willkie told Rosenman. In 1940 they might have worked something out—though it is hard to see how—but this was four years later. Willkie had just been discredited in the Wisconsin Republican primary, running behind Dewey, MacArthur, and Stassen. He too was tired; he was angry at the Republican Old Guard, and disillusioned with the political process. He was also sick; on October 8 he died after three heart attacks.

The passing of the Republicans' most impressive presidential candidate since Hughes in 1916 brought out a vindictive streak in the GOP anti-Willkie Old Guard. "One-worlder" became their pet sneer. Spokesmen for the extreme right, silenced since Pearl Harbor, reappeared in 1944—Lawrence Dennis; Mrs. Elizabeth Dilling; and Joseph E. McWilliams, who alluded to FDR as the "Jew King." Congressman Fish's secretary was convicted of perjury for testifying that certain congressmen hadn't used their franking privileges to mail Nazi propaganda as late as November 1941. Newspapers like the *Chicago Tribune*, the *New York Daily News*, Eleanor ("Cissy") Patterson's *Washington Times-Herald*, and the Hearst chain refused to keep military secrets—one *Tribune* correspondent actually gave away American knowledge of the Purple Code, but the Japanese missed his story—and the President thought the Justice Department should crack down on them. The government did have a strong sedition case, but Attorney General Biddle didn't think jailing conservative publishers in an election year would sit well with the electorate, so he sidetracked Roosevelt. Still, the issue was very much on the President's mind. Isolationists remained entrenched in the press and on Capitol Hill, and after victory they might drum up enough support in the country to sabotage American foreign policy. That threat appears to have been decisive. A week before the Democratic National Convention met the President wrote Hannegan:

> If the people command me to continue in this office and in this war I have as little right to withdraw as a soldier has to leave his post in the line.
> For myself I do not want to run. By next spring, I shall have been President and Commander in Chief of the Armed Forces for twelve years. . . .
> Reluctantly, but as a good soldier, I repeat that I will accept and serve in this office, if I am so ordered by the Commander in Chief of us all—the sovereign people of the United States.

On July 20, while the convention was nominating him in Chicago, Roosevelt was perched on a towering California cliff, watching hingeprowed Higgins boats land ten thousand marines in an amphibious rehearsal. As he saw it, he was doing his job while the politicians went through their routine. But the quadrennial meeting of the Democrats has never been routine. United on Roosevelt's candidacy, united on the platform, they were in turmoil over the Vice Presidency. Either the President had overlooked the matter or couldn't make up his mind; the evidence suggests indecision. He thought Henry Wallace had done a poor job, neglecting his duties and needlessly bruising the congressional leadership, but he refused to disown him. Wallace believed he would stay on the ticket, and with reason; Roosevelt had written of him, in a letter to the convention chairman, "I like him and I respect him and he is my personal friend. For these reasons I personally would vote for his renomination if I were a delegate to the convention."

Yet William O. Douglas and Alben Barkley were just as sure that FDR preferred them, and Jimmy Byrnes thought he already had the President's endorsement. Harry Truman was equally certain that Byrnes had the inside track, and had agreed to nominate him. But with Roosevelt indifferent, the National Committee had been looking for the man who would hurt the President least. They decided upon Truman. He was a loyal Democrat, had gone down the line for administration bills on the Hill, came from a midwestern border state, and had led his committee investigating the war effort —a difficult task—with tact and skill. The President didn't know him, scarcely knew his name. When Hannegan raised it, FDR murmured, "Yes . . . yes . . . I put him in charge of that war investigating committee, didn't I?" Roosevelt had not had anything to do with it, of course, but Hannegan's reasoning made political sense. Roosevelt agreed; it would be Truman.

"My God!" the Missouri senator said when told. He was flabbergasted. Truman hadn't even considered running. Convinced only when he heard FDR's voice over the phone—characteristically he asked friends, "Why the hell didn't he tell me in the first place?"—he went off to square things with Byrnes. Even so, the convention took two ballots to nominate him. Then Roosevelt accepted the nomination in a radio address from the Marine Corps San Diego base while Americans were asking one another who Truman was. "The second Missouri compromise," the *New York Times* called him. "A triumph of the bosses," wrote James A. Hagerty. His opposite number, Republican vice presidential candidate John Bricker, said "Truman—

that's his name, isn't it?" He scratched his head and murmured, "I never can remember that name." In its July 31 issue *Time* patronizingly referred to Roosevelt's running mate as "the gray little junior Senator from Missouri."

Thomas E. Dewey, who led the Republican ticket, was a man of wisdom and courage, and there is every reason to believe he would have made an able President. But the Democratic challenge was too great. Prosperity had returned, the people still identified the GOP with Hoover, the armed forces were chalking up victories every day, and FDR was by now the most experienced politician in U.S. history. "There is nothing I love so much as a good fight," he had once told the *Times,* and time had increased his enjoyment of it. His idea of fighting was to shadowbox with Old Guard Republicans and ignore his opponent. These tactics had crushed Hoover, Landon, and Willkie; and in a celebrated speech he displayed a new and even deadlier weapon—derision. Singling out a congressional trio celebrated for obstructionist tactics—Joe Martin, Bruce Barton, and Hamilton Fish—he defended his achievements and said everyone approved except "Martin . . . Barton . . . and Fish." By the third time he used the phrase his audience had caught its cadence and was chanting with him, "Martin . . . Barton . . . and Fish." It was funny, and it was powerful political medicine. Even more effectively, he seized upon a GOP whispering campaign that he had left his Scottie behind on the Aleutian Islands and dispatched a destroyer to bring the dog back. In a voice edged with sarcasm he told the Teamsters Union—and the country, by radio—that "These Republican leaders have not been content with attacks on me, or my wife, or my sons. No, not content with that, they now include my little dog Fala. . . . I think I have a right to resent, to object to libelous statements about my dog."

Dewey was burning. The President's sardonic tone had reached him, and from then on, as someone remarked, the campaign was between "Roosevelt's dog and Dewey's goat." It seemed that each Roosevelt campaign became rougher than the last, as though presidential politics were powered by some invisible but malevolent engine. This one turned increasingly bitter. One GOP target was Sidney Hillman, whose CIO Political Action Committee (PAC) was organizing to bring out the working-class vote for FDR. The story went round that when Truman's name was suggested for the Democratic ticket, Roosevelt had said, "Clear it with Sidney." CLEAR IT

WITH SIDNEY, read billboards across the country. SIDNEY HILLMAN AND EARL BROWDER'S COMMUNISTS HAVE REGISTERED. HAVE YOU? In the last weeks of the campaign Dewey returned again and again to the issue of Communism. Within a decade such charges would make politicians tremble, but in 1944, with Russia a welcome ally against Hitler, their value was doubtful.

Fortune favored the Republicans when Lewis B. Hershey, still director of the draft and now a major general, remarked in public that enlisted men could be kept in the Army as cheaply as discharging them and creating an agency to take care of them. General Hershey's name will reappear in this volume; his gaucheries were to enliven the administrations of other Presidents. In this instance, however, Roosevelt stopped him cold. Stimson was ordered to gag him and clarify the government's plans for rapid demobilization. But a general with foot-in-mouth disease wasn't to put Dewey in the White House anyhow. Neither were attacks on Fala or Sidney Hillman. Dewey needed an issue. Roosevelt was murdering him.

Speaking from his car on Chicago's Soldier Field, with a hundred thousand people in the amphitheater and another hundred thousand standing outside, the President said this was the strangest campaign in his career. The Republicans were calling the Democratic party incompetent and praising the legislation it had passed. They were saying that "Quarrelsome, tired old men" had built the greatest Army and Navy in the history of the world, that none of this would be changed, and "therefore it is time for a change. They also say in effect," said FDR, "'Those inefficient and worn-out crackpots have really begun to lay the foundations of a lasting world peace. If you elect us, we will not change any of that, either. But,' they whisper, 'we'll do it in such a way that we won't lose the support even of Gerald Nye or Gerald Smith—we won't lose the support of any isolationist campaign contributor. Why, we will be able to satisfy even the *Chicago Tribune!*'"

His adversaries had one sound issue: Roosevelt's health. Had this been debated responsibly, with all medical evidence before the electorate, the outcome might have been different. But this was impossible. No one really knew the true state of the President's health, including the President and his physicians, and there was no way to raise the question in public without inviting charges of bad taste. The rabidly anti-Roosevelt press damned the torpedoes and went full speed ahead anyway. "Let's not be squeamish . . ." began a front-page editorial in the *New York Sun* that October. "It is convention, not the Constitution, which forbids open comment on the possibility that a President may be succeeded by his Vice President. Six Presidents have died in office." The *New York Daily News* mentioned in each edition, as a matter of policy, that Franklin D. Roosevelt was sixty-two years old and Thomas E. Dewey forty-two. *Time* said: "Franklin Roosevelt at sixty-two is an old man."

The White House reply came from Dr. McIntire, and he bears heavy responsibility for it. Like most presidential physicians, he bore a military rank—vice admiral—and was a qualified ophthalmologist (eye doctor) and otolaryngologist (ear, nose and throat doctor). He was a wizard at clearing Roosevelt's sinuses. To the press Dr. McIntire announced that his patient was:

> . . . eight or nine pounds under his best weight. Frankly, I wish he'd put on a few pounds. He hasn't been in the pool since before going to Quebec. But he's going to start in the pool again now. He is a powerful swimmer and that gives him a good workout. The buoyancy of the water enables him to walk and he gets exercise there that he can't get any other way. Nothing wrong organically with him at all. He's perfectly O.K. He does a terrific day's work. But he stands up under it amazingly. The stories that he is in bad health are understandable enough around election time, but they are not true.

The doctor thought that should satisfy anyone. It didn't suit Roosevelt. Perhaps because of his paralysis, the President was hypersensitive to rumors about his physical capacities, and he resolved to prove the doctor right by submitting himself to a physical ordeal. The first opportunity arose in New York. He was to lead a four-hour, fifty-mile motorcade from Ebbets Field in Brooklyn through Queens to the Bronx, then to Harlem and mid-Manhattan and down Broadway to the Battery. It was raining that day—a hard, steady, drenching, cold autumn rain which saturated clothes and inflicted misery on everyone not sheltered. The cavalcade was madness. Yet FDR refused to consider ending or even shortening it. Twice he paused for rubdowns and a quick change of clothes, at a Coast Guard motor pool in Brooklyn and in his wife's Washington Square apartment. The rest of the time he stood—smiling, waving his fedora, utterly wretched.

Eleanor, in the Secret Service follow-up car, felt desperate. She had a roof, and she thought that at the very least Franklin should order the canvas top raised over his presidential Packard. La Guardia and Wagner, occupying the jump seats in front of Roosevelt and soaked to the skin, were also worried about him. The downpour grew heavier and heavier, silvering his boat cloak. The President's hair—thinner and whiter than in the last campaign—was plastered down. He could see little through his pince-nez. But hundreds of thousands of Americans were shivering under umbrellas and sodden newspapers for a glimpse of the country's most famous smile, and he was determined to give it to them if he had to grit his teeth all the way. Six days later he repeated the performance in Philadelphia, riding around for hours in the open car, wrapped in sheets of freezing rain. After it the press corps, including reporters from Rooseveltphobic papers, wrote that he appeared to be the very image of vitality.

On November 7 he appeared as usual at the Hyde Park village polling place with Eleanor, told officials his occupation was "tree grower," was solemnly identified as voter number 251, and was introduced for the first time to a polling machine. He failed to master it. After some muttering and bouncing about, his matchless voice came through the curtain: "The goddamned thing won't work." Advice was offered through the curtain, and with it he overcame what was to be his only difficulty of the day. Even before the ballots from absentee servicemen had been counted (they were heavily pro-Roosevelt) he had won 54 percent of the vote. In the electoral college his margin over Dewey was 432 to 99. His coattails had brought Fulbright of Arkansas and McMahon of Connecticut to the Senate; Helen Gahagan Douglas and Adam Clayton Powell would be in the new House; Ham Fish and Gerald Nye had been defeated; and despite John L. Lewis's endorsement of Dewey in mining precincts, the Democratic ticket had swept them. Roosevelt was elated. Repeatedly during the campaign he had told voters that the election was also a referendum on United States participation in the United Nations, and now the ghost that had haunted Woodrow Wilson to his grave had been forever laid.

In triumph the President was also vindictive. Dewey's red-baiting, he had said, deserved "unvarnished contempt." Now, wheeling himself toward his New York bedroom after the Republican's 3 A.M. concession, he told Hassett, "I still think he's a son of a bitch." He never said that in public, of course. By all outward signs, the country had survived a wartime election with no scars.

And yet . . .

If the Fala speech had got Dewey's goat, the implications that Roosevelt was physically unfit had not only touched Roosevelt to the quick; the hurt lingered afterward. In public appearances he now made a point of being brisk and hearty. Returning to Washington like a victorious Caesar, he found the capital engulfed in rain. It was eerie; this was happening to him every time he moved from one city to another. Ten years ago farmers had cheered the downpours that had accompanied his visits, and his staff had called it Roosevelt luck. Now it was unlucky, and could become dangerous to a man his age. The President calmed their fears—and then ordered the Packard top down. In Union Plaza thirty thousand soggy people awaited him. Flanked by Truman and Wallace, he made a joke about the weather. Then the limousine drove slowly down Pennsylvania Avenue past three hundred thousand cheering Washingtonians. FDR (and Truman and Wallace) were deluged. Nevertheless, when they reached the White House Roosevelt was radiant, even euphoric. He had never seemed so robust.

And yet, and yet . . .

Among those close to him Franklin Roosevelt's well-being had been a matter of concern for some time. That October *Time* had reported that sinus trouble was "Franklin Roosevelt's most nagging health problem." The situation was graver than that. His entire cardiovascular system—a branch of medicine in which Dr. McIntire had no special training—was afflicted. As early as 1937 systolic hypertension had been diagnosed in the President, and four years later diastolic hypertension, much more serious, had joined it. McIntire remained cheerful; although his patient was exercising less and worrying more, he remained jovial. But Roosevelt was not as healthy as his physician led the public to believe. Early in 1943 he had been afflicted by two serious illnesses, influenza and an unexplained fever which he blamed on his North African trip, and after returning from Teheran he caught flu again. He complained of evening headaches. By mid-morning, after a good night's rest, he would be exhausted. Sometimes he fell asleep in the middle of a conversation, and once he dropped off while signing his name; the pen just dribbled off the paper. Frightened, his daughter Anna and his secretary Grace Tully confided in Dr. McIntire. He said he shared their anxiety and wanted a hospital checkup, but he seemed intimidated at the very thought of confronting his imperious patient with anything so drastic. Finally Anna spoke to her mother. Eleanor simply told the President that he was going to be bundled off to Bethesda Naval Hospital for an examination, and on March 27, 1944, he meekly went. This time he would be observed not by a single physician, but by a whole battery of specialists.

Among them was a Lieutenant Commander Howard G. Bruenn, a consultant in cardiology and chief of Bethesda's electrocardiograph department. Bruenn was shocked at Roosevelt's condition. The President was worn out, feverish, and suffering from bronchitis. Worse: his heart was enlarged, the vessels around it were swollen, and his blood pressure was alarming. Dr. Bruenn reported hypertension, hypertensive heart disease, and cardiac failure. His colleagues agreed. They recommended rest, and the President, a good patient, went off to lie in the sun at Hobcaw, Bernard Baruch's South Carolina plantation. He cut his predinner drinking to one and a half cocktails (with no nightcap later) and his smoking from twenty or thirty Camels a day to five or six. He wrote Hopkins that he was having a splendid vacation sleeping twelve hours a night, basking in the sun, controlling his temper, and letting "the rest of the world go hang." Lucy Rutherfurd was a frequent visitor.

He was an incurious patient and never asked about the small green pills he was taking. They were digitalis. Commander Bruenn or any of the other Bethesda physicians could have explained his condition to him, but no one in medical school had told them how to inform a President of the United States that he is gravely ill. Besides, they lacked rank, which in wartime was important. All the charts and diagrams were turned over to Admiral McIntire. The Bethesda staff assumed McIntire would tell Roosevelt. There is no evidence that he ever did, and the President's working hours after leaving South Carolina certainly weren't those of an invalid. He traveled fifty thouand miles that year, leading two wars and campaigning for reelection. At the same time he had to supervise the home front and dispose of all the trivia Americans dump on their President's desk. In 1944 his domestic agenda included the seizure of Montgomery Ward in Chicago, drafting the GI Bill of Rights, persuading Alben Barkley to withdraw his resignation as Senate floor leader, approving plans for a Missouri authority patterned after TVA, talking Secretary Stimson out of retiring, submitting the biggest budget in the history of the world, stumping New York in a mayoralty election, studying a proposed moratorium for insurance companies, endorsing a program of postwar scientific research, carrying out secret negotiations with both labor and management in the secret atomic fission plants, and reviewing the court-martial sentence for a young marine who had shot a wounded calf. It was up to him to decide whether Marshall or Eisenhower would lead the invasion of Europe, which was fair enough; what was grossly unfair was that only the President could convince the Navy that it should share the Pentagon with the Army—the admirals wanted their *own* Pentagon—and he alone could decide whether or not to call off the Army-Navy game. "One man simply could not do it all," Stimson said afterward, "and Franklin Roosevelt killed himself trying."

Visitors to the White House were remarking to one another how "wasted" the President's face looked. In July James Roosevelt had his first augury of what lay ahead. They were in the "Ferdinand Magellan" just before the Marine Corps maneuvers off the California coast. Suddenly Roosevelt's face was drained of color. Writhing, with his eyes closed, he gasped, "Jimmy, I don't know if I can make it—I have horrible pains." His son wanted to cancel the appearance, but Roosevelt, recovering after several minutes, overruled him. There is no way of knowing what the attack was since it wasn't reported to Dr. Bruenn. The next incident, however, occurred in public. Leaving his son in California, he met a speaking engagement in Seattle. The Secret Service had suggested that he address the civilian audience from the deck of a moored destroyer, with its guns as a background. The President liked the idea. Everything was in place, and he was in the first paragraph of his address, when he was stricken. Although no one knew it, he was in the grip of an agonizing angina pectoris attack. For fifteen minutes shooting waves of pain crossed and recrossed his chest, lacing his rib cage and both shoulders with excruciating pangs. The wonder is that he could keep his feet at all—his braces were insecure on the slanting deck —let alone deliver a speech.

But only he knew of the pain; Bruenn, standing directly behind him, didn't suspect anything wrong and couldn't find evidence of it until much later. The President's dismayed audience was aware only of the worst speech they had ever heard. His delivery was slurred, uninspired, and at times inaudible. The content rambled wildly, making little sense. He didn't even sound like Roosevelt. Sam Rosenman, listening to a radio, wrung his hands. Rumors that the President was dying were everywhere now, supported by a cruel news photograph showing him with a slack, gaping mouth, a skeletal face, and poached eyes. Mike Reilly of the Secret Service told FDR that some reporters insisted the President had been in a hospital, not South Carolina. Roosevelt said tightly, "Mike, those newspapermen are a bunch of goddamned ghouls."

His response was both understandable and unreasonable. Sometimes it becomes the duty of the press to keep a deathwatch, and this was one of them. Out of their long affection for him they had been writing little about his appearance; the photographer who had taken the ghastly picture of him was ostracized by his colleagues. Members of the President's official family and old acquaintances were far more outspoken. Years of accumulated strain seemed to be taking their toll all at once; within a single week, an observer wrote, the President appeared to have passed "from the prime of life to old age." Frances Perkins was immune to gossip about him (and herself), and she had dismissed all the stories about his decline. But at a cabinet meeting the day before his fourth inaugural, she was stunned. His eyes were glazed and looked as though they had been blackened, his complexion was gray, his face gaunt, and his clothes a size too large for him. His hands trembled. His lips were blue. He had to prop up his head with a hand. "We were all shocked by the President's appearance," Dean Acheson wrote in his memoirs. "Thin, gaunt, with sunken and darkly circled eyes, only the jaunty cigarette holder and his lighthearted brushing aside of difficulties recalled the FDR of former days." John Gunther, seeing him the next day, wrote, "I was terrified when I saw his face. I felt certain that he was going to die. All the light had gone out underneath the skin. It was like a parchment shade on a bulb that had been dimmed. I could not get over the ravaged expression on his face. It was gray, gaunt, and sagging, and the muscles controlling the lips seemed to have lost part of their function." At times, Gunther wrote, his exhaustion was so great that "he could not answer simple questions and talked what was close to nonsense."

Two weeks later, at the Yalta Conference in the Crimea, Anthony Eden thought the President hazy and confused on their first evening together; Lord Moran, Churchill's physician, took one look at the President and decided that he was a dying man. Their impressions, coupled with those formed in Washington, later contributed to the theory that FDR, "the sick man of Yalta," was outfoxed by the Russians at Yalta, and that in letting him run for a fourth term his family and friends had betrayed not only him but also his country. Yalta, in a Republican phrase of the 1950s, had been "a sellout."

There are certain difficulties here. The first is the assumption that anyone could have talked Roosevelt out of running. Eleanor had tried very hard in 1940; he had been unmoved. The second problem was that his ailment was maddeningly inconsistent. One day Dr. Bruenn's indices would warn that the President's condition was about to enter a critical phase; the next day his vitality would be superb. Bruenn found little correlation between his findings and the condition of his patient. Clearly his campaigning in the rain fatigued him; after it he lost color and appetite. Yet his blood pressure had dropped (to 210/112), his lungs were clear, and his heart showed every sign of being in excellent shape. Leaving the destroyer deck in Seattle, he had told Bruenn of his pain. Blood counts and electrocardiograph tracings were made within an hour; both were normal.

His ability to rally when needed was astonishing. Allen Drury, then a UP reporter, watched the President being wheeled in for the annual White House correspondents' dinner and thought how scrawny-necked, elderly, and senescent he seemed; yet before the President left he acknowledged the reporters' cheers "with the old, familiar gesture, so that the last we saw of Franklin Roosevelt was the head going up with a toss, the smile breaking out, the hand uplifted and waving in the old, familiar way." On September 25, 1944, he spoke to union leaders and party professionals in Washington's new Hotel Statler. Rosenman and the President's daughter arrived early, both tense; FDR's condition earlier in the day had been shocking. Anna whispered to Rosenman, "Do you think Pa will put it over? . . . If the delivery isn't just right, it'll be an awful flop." The audience was also nervous. They had all heard the rumors, seen the news photograph from California, and heard the dreadful destroyer speech. Roosevelt spoke sitting down, and his first words sounded odd, "as though," Burns wrote, "the President were mouthing them." He then recovered and delivered a fine fighting speech, as crisp and resonant as his first inaugural.

At Yalta his American staff—Harriman, Byrnes, Admiral William D. Leahy, Edward R. Stettinius—believed he was representing the

United States effectively and with skill. In the early sessions he had a nocturnal cough, but Bruenn found his lungs clear and his heart and blood pressure unchanged. On February 8 (after a row with Stalin over Poland) Roosevelt's blood pressure bothered the doctor, who altered his regimen and his schedule for two days. By then the trouble had disappeared. At the same time Eden had changed his mind. His first impression had to be wrong, he felt. In spite of his poor color and loss of weight FDR was, in Eden's opinion, negotiating with rare good judgment. Not only was he keeping abreast of Churchill's agenda; he was finding time to carry on a conference-within-a-conference with Stalin over Soviet-American roles in Asia.

Unquestionably the Crimean conference hastened the President's death. The same was true of his 1944 campaign against a hard-hitting Republican challenger and his role as an energetic, participating commander in chief. Yalta will be recalled because the President sacrificed much of himself there. He sacrificed little else.*

* See below, pages 425–426.

Home Front Montage

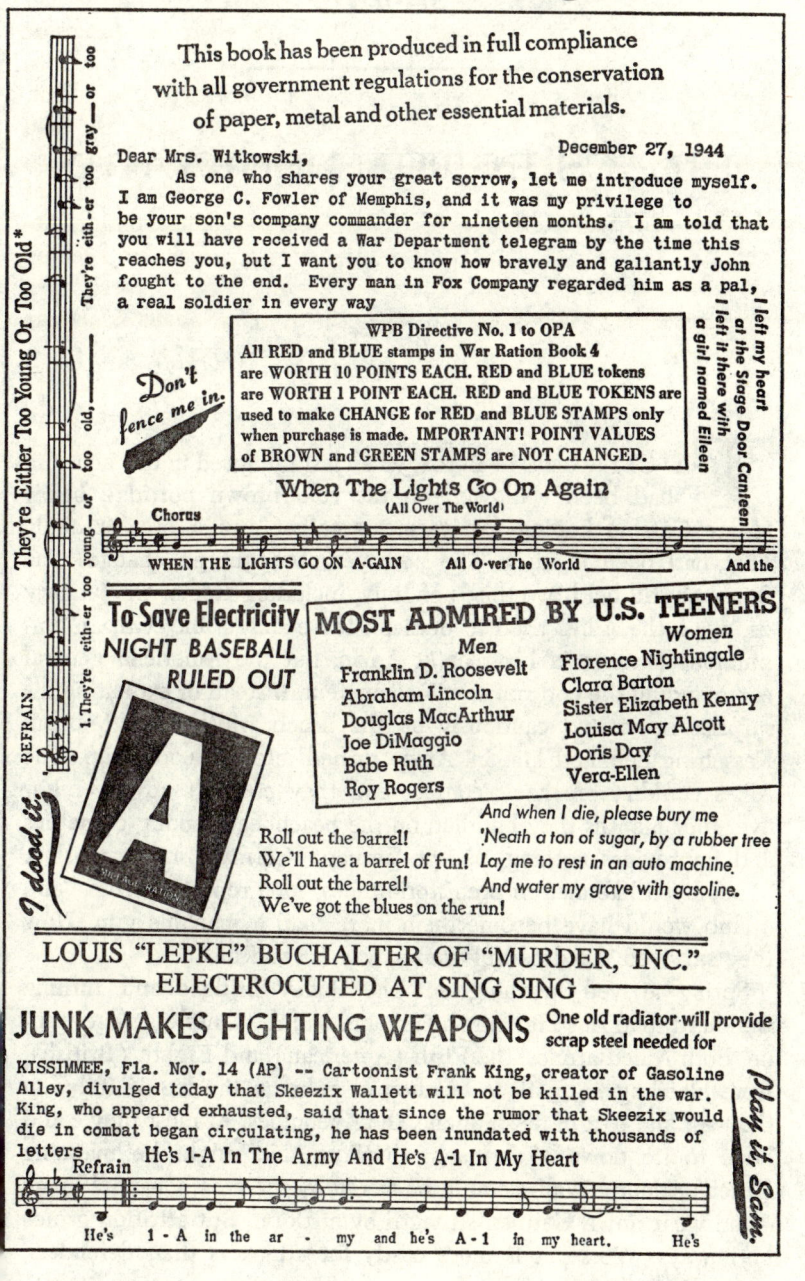

*They're Either Too Young Or Too Old** — They're eith-er too gray — or too old, They're eith-er too young — or too old,

I left my heart at the Stage Door Canteen / *I left it there with a girl named Eileen*

This book has been produced in full compliance with all government regulations for the conservation of paper, metal and other essential materials.

December 27, 1944

Dear Mrs. Witkowski,

As one who shares your great sorrow, let me introduce myself. I am George C. Fowler of Memphis, and it was my privilege to be your son's company commander for nineteen months. I am told that you will have received a War Department telegram by the time this reaches you, but I want you to know how bravely and gallantly John fought to the end. Every man in Fox Company regarded him as a pal, a real soldier in every way

Don't fence me in.

> **WPB Directive No. 1 to OPA**
> All RED and BLUE stamps in War Ration Book 4 are WORTH 10 POINTS EACH. RED and BLUE tokens are WORTH 1 POINT EACH. RED and BLUE TOKENS are used to make CHANGE for RED and BLUE STAMPS only when purchase is made. IMPORTANT! POINT VALUES of BROWN and GREEN STAMPS are NOT CHANGED.

When The Lights Go On Again
(All Over The World)

Chorus — WHEN THE LIGHTS GO ON A-GAIN All O-ver The World And the

I dood it. REFRAIN 1. They're eith-er too young-er too

To Save Electricity
NIGHT BASEBALL RULED OUT

MOST ADMIRED BY U.S. TEENERS

Men	Women
Franklin D. Roosevelt	Florence Nightingale
Abraham Lincoln	Clara Barton
Douglas MacArthur	Sister Elizabeth Kenny
Joe DiMaggio	Louisa May Alcott
Babe Ruth	Doris Day
Roy Rogers	Vera-Ellen

Roll out the barrel!
We'll have a barrel of fun!
Roll out the barrel!
We've got the blues on the run!

And when I die, please bury me
'Neath a ton of sugar, by a rubber tree
Lay me to rest in an auto machine
And water my grave with gasoline.

LOUIS "LEPKE" BUCHALTER OF "MURDER, INC." ELECTROCUTED AT SING SING

JUNK MAKES FIGHTING WEAPONS — One old radiator will provide scrap steel needed for

KISSIMMEE, Fla. Nov. 14 (AP) -- Cartoonist Frank King, creator of Gasoline Alley, divulged today that Skeezix Wallett will not be killed in the war. King, who appeared exhausted, said that since the rumor that Skeezix would die in combat began circulating, he has been inundated with thousands of letters

Play it, Sam.

He's 1-A In The Army And He's A-1 In My Heart

Refrain — He's 1-A in the ar-my and he's A-1 in my heart. He's

Eleven

LILACS IN THE DOORYARD

THE GI INVADERS OF ITALY, when last glimpsed in this account, had been wallowing in the cold brown porridge below Monte Cassino hoping for warmer weather and a breakthrough. That had been in 1943. The new year brought no change. The Germans still held two-thirds of Italy, including Rome. On January 22, 1944, the Allies tried to outflank the enemy's line with an amphibious landing in his rear at Anzio, but the American general commanding the end run was incompetent. Instead of exploiting his surprise he waited cautiously on the beach while Field Marshal Kesselring hemmed him in. Anzio turned into a bloody trap. The Allies couldn't break off contact and they couldn't advance. For over four months they huddled on the beachhead, taking casualties and improving nothing except perhaps German marksmanship. "They lived like men in prehistoric times," one reporter wrote, "and a club would have become them more than a machine gun. How they survived the dreadful winter was beyond us."

Spring arrived, washing out the Bailey bridges and turning iron-hard road ruts into mire again; and still the senseless siege went on. Both Allied armies, the Fifth (American) and Eighth (British), were bleeding to death in head-on assaults up the leg of Italy, on the west and east of its shinbone, the Apennines. At most they could hope to tie down Wehrmacht divisions that might be manning Hitler's Atlantic Wall—soon to be tested by the cross-Channel lunge —and wear down German strength by attrition. But attrition grinds both ways. Worse, it is more costly for attackers than defenders.

Allied casualties rose and morale dropped. Friction between Allies, always a danger sign, was growing. Next to Mussolini, now under house arrest by non-Fascist Italians, Lieutenant General Mark Clark was the most unpopular man in the Italian peninsula. His attempt to blame the bombing of Monte Cassino on General Freyberg, the New Zealand hero, was, to put the best face on it, an ungracious attempt to evade responsibility for what seemed at the time to be a necessary act of war.

Anzio *had* to be relieved. The Allied high command saw but one solution: a big push toward Rome. On June 4, 1944, at 7:30 P.M., elements of the U.S. Fifth Army, with Clark in the vanguard, marched up the Piazza Venezia, the heart of the Eternal City. The conqueror was greeted by flowers, cheers, kisses, and more chianti than he could carry. It was a moment any soldier might savor, but Clark didn't know when to stop. Next morning he called for a meeting of his corps commanders, and when they arrived they discovered they were to be used as foils in a press conference. Clark was striking martial poses at the request of photographers. His subordinate generals, American and Allied, reddened with embarrassment. Even some war correspondents colored. Clark didn't notice their uneasiness. In fact, he decided to say a few words. "This," he began, "is a great day for the Fifth Army."

The press stared. For the *Fifth Army!* How about the Eighth Army, the angry British correspondents muttered to one another? The Eighth, that had come all the way from Cairo fighting every step of the way? And what of the Poles, and all the others? But beyond that, Eric Sevareid wondered, wasn't every victory over Hitler a victory for Europe's enslaved civilians, for the Jews on the beltlines of Nazi slaughter, for people all over the world who had sacrificed so much and were still suffering in the mincing machine of war? Not to Mark Clark, it wasn't. He saw to it that photographers and correspondents were given everything they needed, and cleared cable traffic to make sure everything would be on editors' desks next morning. It arrived. But unhappily for Clark, the next day was June 6, 1944—D-Day in Normandy.

Due north of Portsmouth dockyard, in a thicket of hazel trees near Southwick House, one of the stately homes of England, stood a shabby trailer whose unusual furnishings included a red telephone for scrambled conversations with Washington and a green phone, a direct line to No. 10 Downing Street. In it, sometime during that blustery week preceding the greatest amphibious assault in history, Dwight Eisenhower, now wearing four stars, scribbled two messages. The first, now long famous ("You are about to embark upon the Great Crusade"), would congratulate his troops if they established a foothold on Normandy's shores. The other would be handed to the press if Dunkerque was repeated:

> Our landings in the Cherbourg-Havre area have failed to gain a satisfactory foothold and I have withdrawn the troops. My decision to attack at this time and place was based upon the best information available. The troops, the air, and the Navy did all that bravery and devotion to duty could do. If any blame or fault attaches to the attempt it is mine alone.

Long after they happen, historic events take on an air of inevitability. In thinking of D-Day, we assume that the Germans in France never had a chance—that with Eisenhower's huge armies and unlimited supplies, protected by Anglo-American armadas in the Channel and the air overhead, his crusade was as good as won. Even men who knew better at the time fall under the spell of myth: Montgomery later wrote that "the battle was fought exactly as planned before the invasion." It wasn't.

Much has been made of the rough weather, and how it hampered landing operations. It was really a blessing. Because the weather was poor, key German officers were absent from their headquarters when the blow fell—Rommel, the most gifted of Hitler's field marshals, had taken the day off to celebrate his wife's birthday with her in Ulm. Ten highly mobile panzer divisions were available to throw the invaders back into the Channel. On D-Day only one of them saw combat. Even so, it broke the British line at Caen and drove through to the beach. That force was too small, but if only three of the ten panzer divisions had been thrown into Normandy, wrote B. H. Liddell Hart, the eminent military strategist, "the Allied footholds could have been dislodged before they were joined up and consolidated."

Had Rommel not been so faithful a husband he would have remained in France, and the Allies might have been liquidated. To be sure, the field marshal would first have been obliged to phone Hitler. But the Führer was already convinced that a cross-Channel thrust must be stopped at the waterline; that, he believed, would prevent the reelection of Roosevelt, who, "with luck," would "finish up somewhere in jail." Curiously, Hitler's intuition had told him from the first that the landings would come in Normandy. Then he listened to his advisers and changed his mind. Calais, he said: their main force will land near Calais; Normandy is just a feint. This was the best possible piece of luck for Eisenhower. His troops had enough on their hands as it was. For the past year the Germans had been mining coastal waters, driving great antitank tripods of steel rails into the ground, erecting six-foot-thick concrete pillboxes, fortifying cement tunnels, and weaving military obstacles into natural defenses, using their vast stock of slave labor for the work. From the first, the British were on timetable on their beaches (Juno and Sword), but the American beaches (Omaha and Utah) were taken at great cost. Then the soldiers moved inland and encountered Normandy's hedgerows, ideal for stubborn defenders.

On the other side of the Atlantic a hundred million Americans hovered near radios, awaiting the latest word from France. Franklin Roosevelt was one of them. The President had followed every detail of the massive preparations. He knew how the landing ships built on Lake Michigan had been floated down the Illinois and Mississippi rivers, to sail eastward and then be packed beam to beam with GIs in British ports. Daily reports had briefed him on the construction of fleets of LSTs (Landing Ship, Tank) in California, and the trial runs of the tanks, bulldozers, and trucks they would carry. He had kept abreast of Ike's postponement of D-Day and the nerve-racking, inconclusive predictions of Army meteorologists. He had been told how the general paced the crunching cinder path outside his trailer, rubbing lucky coins from the invasions of North Africa and Sicily. And he had heard from SHAEF how the general had said in a strangled voice, "I'm quite positive we must give the order. . . . I don't like it, but there it is. . . ." Then, slamming his right fist into his left palm: "O.K. We'll go."

With those words, the great bound into Hitler's Europe began. Ed Murrow, a man not given to fantasy, stood beneath the roaring bombers headed for France, and thought he heard the strains of "The Battle Hymn of the Republic." The commander in chief, not that close, could only pray, and that is what he did. Over the weekend, at the Charlottesville home of "Pa" Watson, his military aide, he had reread the Book of Common Prayer, looking for D-Day invocations. On the evening of that Tuesday, June 6, he went on the radio to lead the nation in asking benediction for "our sons, the pride of our nation . . . lead them straight and true," he beseeched, "give strength to their arms, stoutness to their hearts, steadfastness in their faith. They will need Thy blessings. Their road will be long and hard. For the enemy is strong. He may hurl back our forces. Success may not come with rushing speed. But we shall return again and again." Then he asked guidance for those, like himself, who must watch from home: "Give us faith in Thee; faith in our sons; faith in each other; faith in our united crusade. . . ."

Meanwhile the issue was being decided amid the hedges and poppies of Normandy. After eleven days of fighting, Bradley announced his first casualties: 3,283 dead and 12,600 wounded. He had little to show for it, and London had a fresh reason for demanding results; on June 14 Dr. Wernher von Braun had begun the massacre of British civilians with his V-1 rockets, launched from Nazi sites in France and Belgium.* The Allies needed a victory, the generals needed a major port, and everyone wanted an end to the Battle of the Bridgehead. Cherbourg didn't fall until Tuesday, and the Germans had done everything they could think of to spoil the spoils. Breakwaters were smashed, cranes destroyed, piers sown with mines and boobytraps. It would be August before Army engineers could clean up the mess. For the present the expedition had to rely on Mulberry, the artificial harbor they had brought with them and sunk off Arromanches.

Nevertheless, the buildup continued. On July 4 Eisenhower reported to Washington that the millionth man had been landed in France, and 566,648 tons of supplies and 171,532 vehicles were ashore. Furthermore, the Battle of the Bridgehead was turning out to be a disguised blessing. The very ferocity of the fighting had drawn the bulk of Germany's western forces into the Cotentin Peninsula. Panzer divisions were thrown in piecemeal to plug holes in the German line and were methodically chewed up—thus depriving the Nazis of future mobility when they would need it most, behind the peninsula, in the open country of France's heartland. At the same time, Hitler's order not to retreat an inch shackled his field commanders and made tactical retreats impossible. Caen fell to the British on July 9, and Saint Lô—the road junction linking Normandy

---

* In 1955 Dr. von Braun became a naturalized citizen of the United States. He has been among the leaders in the aerospace program. Fifteen American colleges and universities have conferred honorary degrees upon him.

with Brittany—to U.S. troops on July 25. Now Patton was in the cockpit, driving hard. On July 25 he broke out in a powerful armored thrust toward Avranches and into Brittany, and by August 10 he had overrun Brittany and cut it off. Lord Beaverbrook's London *Express* said, "Americans have proved themselves to be a race of great fighters, in the very front rank of men at arms."

On Friday, August 25, General Leclerc's Free French jeeps entered the suburbs, and on Saturday de Gaulle made his triumphant march while across the Atlantic Lily Pons, wearing her USO uniform, sang "The Marseillaise" in Manhattan's Rockefeller Plaza. It was an electric moment, although observers in Paris found the aftermath of the city's liberation to be more complex than they had expected. The Gaullists and their comrades in the underground French Forces of the Interior had a blacklist of seven hundred thousand collaborators, and French girls who had slept with Germans were forced to submit while their heads were shorn and then shaved. But many collaborators escaped humiliation or bought their way to freedom. Paris disturbed some Americans. It didn't look at all like an enslaved capital. Compared to London, it was prospering. Ed Murrow was surprised by the number of well-dressed women on the streets. Not only had the French textile industry flourished throughout the war; the French had developed the first practical television transmitters and sets. All the famous couturiers were in business—Molyneux, Lanvin, Schiaparelli—and their French customers were wearing full skirts and mutton-legged sleeves, which had long been out of the question for American and British women limited by clothes rationing. Discussing the liberation with an American reporter, one Parisian designer sighed and spread his hands in a Gallic gesture. "What shall I do with all this nonsense going on?" he asked. "All my best customers are in concentration camps, because of course they were working for Vichy."

London was still in greater danger than Paris. On September 8 the British capital's lights were turned up after 1,843 dark nights, and for the first time in memory, eight-year-old Julie Andrews saw a lighted city. It didn't stay lit long. That same night von Braun began hurling his V-2 missiles at Britain—Englishmen called them "Bob Hopes" ("Bob down and hope for the best")—and a return to blackouts seemed sensible. For a few weeks the troops in France and the civilians in England had persuaded one another that the war was all but over. The broken Wehrmacht seemed finished; even Hitler, one thought, must realize that he had lost the war. On September 12 GIs crossed the border and entered Germany near Eupen and Trier and probed the outer defenses of the Siegfried Line; western Germany had been invaded. In rapid succession that autumn the Canadians cleared the Scheldt estuary, the U.S. First Army took Aachen and penetrated the Siegfried Line itself in the process, Patton's U.S. Third Army captured Metz and Strasbourg, and other American troops reached the Roer River. That was on December 3. Less than two weeks later, Hitler caught the Allies with a major counterattack. Crack troops flung themselves at the Americans with Field Marshal Gerd von Rundstedt's battle cry ringing in their ears: "Your great hour has struck. Strong attacking Armies are advancing today against the Anglo-Americans. I do not need to say more to you. You all feel it. Everything is at stake. You bear the holy duty to achieve the superhuman for our Fatherland and Führer!"

This was the overture to the Battle of the Bulge. The havoc wrought by English-speaking Germans in GI uniforms; the 101st Airborne's gallant stand at Bastogne; the German ultimatum and Brigadier General McAuliffe's reply of "Nuts!"; Patton's classic maneuver in wheeling to relieve Bastogne, with his lead tank commanded by a thirty-year-old lieutenant colonel in the 4th Armored named Creighton Abrams—all this belongs to American military lore. It was the GIs finest hour in the ETO. Asked what had turned the tide, Montgomery replied, "The good fighting qualities of the American soldier. I take my hat off to such men. I salute the brave fighting men of America—I never want to fight alongside better soldiers. I have tried to feel that I am also an American soldier myself."

The Bulge was Hitler's last mad gamble, and was followed by disintegration. The Russians opened their final offensive in January 1945. Beginning in early February the Allies cleared Holland, took the Saar, captured an unblown bridge at Remagen, and then threw nine more bridges across the Rhine than the Germans had at the beginning of the war, enveloped the Ruhr, captured 325,000 prisoners there, and then seized Mannheim and Frankfurt-am-Main. The end was approaching; everyone in Europe could sense it. Though London was to remain blacked out for another month, Paris became France's city of light once more in the first week of April. Berlin, Hamburg, Dresden, Essen, Düsseldorf, Nuremberg, and Frankfurt had been bombed to rubble; Hitler's fifty-sixth birthday was two weeks away, but there were no plans to celebrate it.

At noon on April 11, 1945, the U.S. Ninth Army reached the Elbe. In Warm Springs at 6 A.M. on April 12, President Roosevelt lay asleep in his corner bedroom. He had retired expecting to read of new developments in the morning, but the mail had been delayed. Instead of his usual newspapers—the *New York Times, New York Herald Tribune, Baltimore Sun,* and *Washington Post*—he would be limited to the *Atlanta Constitution.* Its headlines were:

> 9TH 57 MILES FROM BERLIN
> 50-MILE GAIN IN DAY
> SETS STAGE FOR EARLY
> U.S.-RUSS JUNCTURE

And, from the Pacific:

> MARINES GAIN
> ON OKINAWA;
> FIGHTING HEAVY
> 150 SUPERFORTS HAMMER TOKYO
> IN TWO-HOUR DAYLIGHT RAID

Here in Georgia it was unseasonably warm for early April; the dogwood and wild violets were out, and a neighbor was planning an outdoor barbecue for FDR, with a chair under an old oak tree, where he could enjoy a breathtaking view of the valley. Since the mail had also held up his daily bale of paperwork, there was nothing for the President to do except sit for his portrait. Two years ago Lucy Rutherfurd had commissioned a painter to paint a watercolor of him; now he himself had asked the same artist to do another, as a gift from him to Lucy's daughter.

With the President down here, Bill Hassett and Dr. Bruenn breathed more easily, though they were beginning to despair of recovery. They had heard the gasps in the crowd at Warm Springs station on March 30 when he had been carried from his train to the platform; he had sagged in his wheelchair as he was pushed toward his car, his head bobbing out of control. He had rallied long enough to drive the car here, but they had learned to distrust these brief upturns. In the evening, after the President had retired, they had faced each other in anguish. Hassett had said that Roosevelt was just drifting toward death. His dashing, flamboyant signatures had faded out; they didn't even look like good forgeries. He was the President of the United States and he couldn't write his own name. Bruenn had given his professional opinion: Roosevelt's case was hopeless unless he could be protected from pressure. Hassett said that was out of the question; no President could be so isolated. The two men had been at the point of tears. Hassett confided to his diary:

> Shocked at his appearance—worn, weary, exhausted. He seemed all right when I saw him in the morning. He is steadily losing weight —told me he has lost twenty-five pounds—no strength, no appetite, tires easily—all too apparent whenever you see him after midday. Again observed this to Dr. Bruenn. He admits cause for alarm.

This morning, however, they agreed that his color was much better. The news was good; that helped. And the absence of mail was a godsend. Once more, as so often in these last few weeks, they persuaded one another—against all evidence—that he might, just might, make it.

Among the papers awaiting action on the President's Washington desk were an urgent note from Albert Einstein and an attached memorandum from Leo Szilard, both begging him to order an immediate suspension of all work on an atom bomb. The world situation had changed, they explained; much which they had taken for granted was either untrue or no longer relevant. Any brief military advantage the United States might gain with nuclear weapons would be offset by political and psychological losses and damage to American prestige. The United States, Einstein argued, might even touch off a worldwide atom armaments race.

Obviously something had happened—or not happened—in Hitler's Reich. The blunt truth was that the Nazis had no atomic weapons. This seemed so beyond comprehension that Allied scientists at first suspected an attempt to humbug them. Samuel A. Goudsmit, the senior member of the Alsos intelligence team which landed in Normandy, believed (and continued to believe in the 1970s) that Carl von Weizsäcker, and Nobel laureates Max von Laue and Werner Heisenberg, the three most brilliant German physicists, could have built bombs between them with support from the state. They asked German scientists: what about it?

In those days Germans were blaming Hitler for everything, but in this instance their account was plausible. The Führer's anti-Semitism had driven their most promising colleagues out of the country, the Nazi bureaucracy was indifferent toward long-term research, technical equipment was unavailable, and—a typical example of inept rivalry within the Nazi hierarchy—uncoordinated atomic research was being carried out by the Ministry of Education, the War Office, and even the Post Office Department. The turning point for the Germans had come on June 6, 1942, just as the American scientists were approaching their breakthrough. That Saturday Heisenberg briefed Albert Speer, Hitler's Minister of Supply, on progress in the Reich's uranium research. There was definite proof, he said, that Germany had the technical knowledge to build a uranium pile and acquire atomic energy from it, and theoretically an explosive for atom bombs could be produced from such a source. The next step would be to investigate technical problems—the critical size, for example, and the possibility of a chain reaction. At that point he and von Weizsäcker were talking about a pile not only as a weapon in itself but as a prime mover in weapon production. Speer gave them tentative approval. The work would continue, but on a smaller scale, and their target should be a pile usable as a generation of power. Speer was only echoing Hitler. The Führer, certain of imminent triumph, had just ordered the termination of all new weapon projects except those which would be ready for use in the field within six weeks.

According to Speer—he was convicted at Nuremberg and served twenty years as a war criminal—Hitler had sometimes mentioned to him the possibility of an atomic bomb. Speaking with the Führer on May 6, 1942, Speer raised the question of an all-out program to make one. He suggested that Göring be placed at the head of the Reich Research Council to emphasize its importance, and this was done.

On June 23, 1942, Speer reported to Hitler. The Führer was still interested, but he had no grasp of theoretical physics, and the project was shunted aside. German physicists were now talking to Speer of a three- or four-year project for bomb production. Instead, he recalls, "I authorized the development of an energy-producing uranium motor for propelling machinery. The Navy was interested in that for its submarines." Speer leaves no doubt that had he dreamed of the Manhattan Project, he would have moved heaven and earth to catch up with the Americans. He continued to make periodic inquiries, but now Hitler was discouraging him. The Führer's old party cronies were ridiculing America's reputation for efficiency, and he had taken to describing all physics as Jewish physics (*jüdische Physik*). But if the German dictator had given his own scientists the blank check Roosevelt had given their colleagues in the United States, the maps of Europe and even of the western hemisphere might have been sharply changed.

None of this was known outside the Reich until November 23, 1944, when Patton took Strasbourg. The Alsos detachment headed straight for the university and its new laboratories. Sam Goudsmit was looking for Weizsäcker, Strasbourg professor of theoretical physics, but his quarry had flown three weeks ago, and while Goudsmit debated the propriety of questioning other Strasbourg physicists, the German scientists solved his problem by refusing to have commerce with the enemy.

Strasbourg looked like a debacle until the Alsos team stumbled upon Weizsäcker's private papers. Translating them by candlelight, with GIs playing cards in the same room and the rumble of artillery from the right bank of the Rhine distinctly audible, Goudsmit and his assistant looked for this clue, that hint, for scholarly citations and casual references, until they leaped up with such triumphant cries that the edgy GIs reached for their M-1s and grenades. The scientists had just turned up a thick batch of closely typed pages—the full record of the Reich's U project and the Uranium Verein. There were a few pieces missing, of course, and no entries had been made during the past three months, but this, by all evidence, was the most complete file in Europe on Nazi uranium research.

Until that night Allied scientists had assumed that German physicists led them by a wide margin. To Goudsmit, squinting at Weizsäcker's manuscript in the flickering light, it was clear that the Nazis were two years behind the men at Los Alamos. The Reich lacked plants for the manufacture of PU-239 (Plutonium) and U-235. Apparently they didn't even have any uranium burners worth mentioning. When he cabled Washington reporting his findings, he was reminded that Weizsäcker's papers might be a hoax. He replied that the internal evidence was genuine; this was serious work. The Army suggested that other Germans, elsewhere in the Reich, might be manufacturing atom bombs. Goudsmit replied tartly, "A paperhanger may perhaps imagine that he has turned into a military genius overnight, and a traveler in champagne may be able to disguise himself as a diplomat. But laymen of that sort could never have acquired sufficient scientific knowledge to construct an atom bomb."

Nevertheless, the hunt had to continue. Heisenberg had been an enthusiastic advocate of nuclear weapons; it was conceivable that he and other equally ardent scientists had been at work in secret laboratories, defying official indifference to the possibilities in fissionable materials. In fact, something very like that had happened. During the winter of 1943-44, working through air raids, Heisenberg and his staff had built a small reactor in the Dahlem Institute with three tons of uranium and heavy water. To elude the bombers they had then transferred their laboratory to a tall warehouse, owned by a Stuttgart brewery, in the foothills of the Swabian Alps. Moving out beer vats, they had papered the inside of the warehouse with silver foil, equipped it with a powerful electric plant, and built workshops in the wing of a textile mill.

Once Hitler's Festung Europa began to break up, even this refuge wasn't inaccessible enough for them. Like the Allies, Heisenberg and his colleagues were harried by worries about security, and they moved again, to a great cave hollowed out of rock near Tübingen. It was in this cavern, in February 1945, that the construction of a large pile—roughly comparable to the one Allied scientists had built on the abandoned squash court under Stagg Field—began in earnest. By spring there was an atomic burner comprising heavy water, cubes of uranium, and a graphite jacket. The Germans were moving swiftly toward the accumulation of a critical mass. Shipments of uranium cubes arrived daily from the Thuringian Forest, where a second uranium burner had been built by Dr. Karl Diebner. The gap between Oppenheimer and Heisenberg was still wide, but it was rapidly closing. To the intense annoyance of Goudsmit, who believed in the preservation of all experimental data, the U.S. Army colonel who served as nominal commander of Alsos sent a small unit of Rangers to the grotto with orders to destroy the German apparatus. Sending troops had been a good idea, though. Members of Heisenberg's staff were thwarted in a hasty attempt to smuggle the uranium cubes out under a hay load on an oxcart, and other cubes which had been filched by Hechingen peasants—the peasants didn't know what they were, but had guessed that they were valuable and might be sold to the French—were recovered. Presently all Nazi physicists were in Allied custody, including the elusive Heisenberg. Goudsmit was ecstatic. To a regular Army major who had been detached to serve as a liaison officer with the Alsos group he said,

"Isn't it wonderful that the Germans have no atom bomb? Now we don't have to use ours."

The major looked surprised. He replied, "Of course you understand, Sam, that if we have such a weapon we are going to use it."

From that moment, the officers and scientists who had worked on the Manhattan Project were divided into those who meant to use the bomb if it turned out to be practical, and those who were shocked at the thought. The split wasn't always between soldiers and civilians—Edward Teller was a hard-liner from the beginning—but the first ban-the-bomb advocates were nuclear physicists. Even before the myth of a Nazi bomb had been dispelled, some of them had become convinced that the United States should share its discoveries with the world's scientific community. At their urging Niels Bohr had called on the President at 4 P.M., August 26, 1944, to discuss that very issue. Bohr was an unwise choice. He was garrulous; he took a half-hour to come to the point, and the President's time was precious. In any event, Roosevelt disagreed with Bohr and bade him good day. Bohr then tried Churchill. After listening to his guest for thirty minutes the prime minister turned to Lord Cherwell, who had introduced him, and inquired testily, "What is he really talking about—politics or physics?"

He was talking about both. Many—perhaps a majority—of the scientists believed that in building the bomb they had acquired a moral obligation to all mankind. To confront a Hitler in possession of atomic bombs was one thing, but the Japanese in 1945 were not that advanced in theoretical physics or technology. They were unable to build such weapons themselves, and so, the argument went, using one against them was unthinkable. To introduce such a question raised politics and physics to a level of scientific statesmanship. There were no precedents for it, and wartime was not the best time to think it through, especially when the enemy in the Pacific had opened the war with an unprovoked, devastating air attack. Alexander Sachs was a better emissary than Bohr. He was a close friend of the President, and five years earlier he had persuaded him to launch this two-billion-dollar search. Sachs shared Bohr's convictions, and in December 1944 he called at the White House. It is known that he had a long talk with the President, but that is about all that is known. After FDR's death Sachs said that Roosevelt had agreed that if any test succeeded a second rehearsal should be held, attended by Allied and neutral scientists; that a detailed report on the weapon's implications should be circulated among Allied and neutral scientists; that the enemy should agree to evacuate a given area; and that after a demonstration of the weapon's power the enemy should be given an ultimatum to surrender or be annihilated.

Sachs's minute, submitted to Secretary of War Robert P. Patterson a year later, is an extraordinary document. Roosevelt had signed nothing. The conversation had been unwitnessed. The President had not mentioned it to Stimson, then the Secretary of War and FDR's liaison with X, as Stimson always called the Manhattan Project. Obviously a man of Sachs's integrity would not invent such a tale. But the President had a genius for telling people what they wanted to hear and then hedging it—by hypothetical statements, say, or by skillful use of the subjunctive—so that he stopped just short of commitment. In this case he may have been undecided. That would have been like him; he rarely made up his mind until he had to. The Sachs minute seems less convincing than Stimson's entry in his diary on March 15, 1945. That was the last time FDR and his war secretary talked of X. Stimson wrote: "I went over with him the two schools of thought that exist in respect to the future control after the war of this project, in case it is useful, one of them being the secret close-in attempted control of the project by those who control it now, and the other being international control based upon freedom of science. I told him that those things must be settled before the project is used and that he must be ready with a statement to come out to the people on it just as soon as that is done. He agreed to that."

Like Stalingrad, which had been raging at the same time, the issue at Guadalcanal had remained in doubt for six months—from mid-August 1942 to early February 1943. The valor of the outnumbered marines captured the public imagination, but the decisive struggle was between the two navies. In six separate engagements—"fire-away Flanagans," as nineteenth-century seamen would have called them—the admirals battled for command of the sea. Losses on both sides were shocking. Each lost an even dozen warships. To sailors the waters between the 'Canal, Tulagi, and Savo Island were "Iron-bottom Sound"; to marines, "Sleepless Lagoon." If reckoned by tonnage lost, the naval struggle would be called a draw. It wasn't, because at the end of it the marines still held Guadalcanal and its airstrip, and the Japanese troops were being evacuated, leaving behind twenty-five thousand of their dead. They still felt invincible. On New Georgia they reinforced their Munda base, a whistle-stop for Zeros and Zekes flying down the Slot to bomb the marines. But a corner had been turned. For the first time in the war the Jap had gone over to the defensive.

Nor was that all. Guadalcanal was one of two successful Pacific campaigns, waged at the same time and to the same end: the defense of Australia. The other was in MacArthur's theater, New Guinea. The Coral Sea battle hadn't discouraged the enemy there. In July 1942 he had seized a string of villages along the north shore of Papua, the New Guinea tail, and he was planning to envelop Port Moresby, on the south shore, in a land-and-sea pincer. Coast watchers—British colonial officials hiding in the jungle with radios—warned Americans that the sea assault was headed for Milne Bay, at the tip of the peninsula tail. U.S. warships arrived first and beat off that threat. The Japanese land drive took off from a village called Buna. It was only a hundred miles from there to Moresby as the crow flies, but the Nips had to cross the awesome 13,000-foot Owen Stanley Range on foot. Twenty miles from Moresby the Australians held them and, with the U.S. 32nd Division, began a counteroffensive.

This ordeal, costlier in lives than Guadalcanal, ended when the enemy was pushed all the way back across the mountains and General Eichelberger entered Buna on January 2, 1943. The Australians captured nearby Sanananda two weeks later, but the Japanese collected reinforcements and tried to land a counterattacking force with eight transports. On March 3, skip-bombing B-25s caught the convoy in the Bismarck Sea and sank all eight, together with their four escorts. In the grisly aftermath seven thousand Japanese were drowned or, if they reached land, beheaded by island natives, according to a local custom. Tokyo solemnly announced that Moresby had no military significance.

Rabaul did. The enemy wanted to keep Rabaul; had to, in fact, to hold the South Pacific. Rabaul itself was too strong to be assaulted, so the Americans neutralized it. GIs and marines began by moving into New Georgia in the summer of 1943 and pouncing at Munda. They had to attack through thickets and over flooded rivers, against pillboxed Nips in steel vests. Still, the airstrip fell in August, and American troops had a leg up the Slot. Vaulting to Vella

Lavella and Kolombangara, they mopped up the central Solomons, and on Columbus Day the 3rd Marine Division steamed into Bougainville's Empress Augusta Bay and landed under a three-day-old moon. This was a big step, as steps were measured that year in the Pacific. If Seabees and Army engineers could somehow build a large airfield in this green slime, U.S. fliers would be within fighter range of Rabaul.

The enemy thought it unlikely. He buffeted the invaders by air and sea but held back his best troops, thinking the Americans would use the bay to stage a push elsewhere. On Christmas Day U.S. engineers finished their big strip, Piva Uncle, above the forks of the Piva River. The Americal* and 37th divisions ringed it with a perimeter of steel, and when the Japanese finally came howling down on it with their elite 6th Division they were stopped cold. By then Rabaul was just about surrounded. Emirau and the Green Islands had been occupied; the 112th Cavalry was in Arawe; the 1st Marine Division had taken Cape Gloucester in New Britain; and troopers of the 5th Cavalry, General Robert E. Lee's old outfit, and the 7th Cavalry, General Custer's, were ashore in the Admiralty Islands. Massive U.S. sorties from Piva Uncle were making Rabaul unlivable. The Japanese had no choice; they had to write Rabaul off. They evacuated what they called their "consolation units"—Korean whores —and left the garrison to suffer as U.S. bombers, unescorted and unchallenged, flew in daily and unloaded overhead.

Meanwhile, the character of the war was changing. It had to change; so far Americans had been only nibbling at the outer edges of the expanded Japanese Empire. They had spent nine months moving 250 miles in the central Solomons, and Tokyo was still five thousand miles away. But new equipment was arriving from home. Makeshift World War I weapons—which had been sent here because of ETO priorities—were now being replaced by rockets, amphibious tractors, boats with wheels—DUKWs ("ducks")—and flamethrowers that could lick around corners. The Navy had more of everything: fifty carriers led by the fast *Essex* class, converted from cruiser hulls. If Nimitz could somehow get closer to Japan, his submarines, which had already sunk a million tons of enemy supplies, could destroy the Japanese merchant marine, and since Japan, like England, was surrounded by water, this would have the

---

* So named because it was formed on New Caledonia. Twenty-five years later its junior officers would include one William Calley Jr.

same impact as U-boat triumph in the Battle of the Atlantic. With closer bases Tokyo could also be reached by air; the first B-29 Superfortresses, with a range of 1,500 nautical miles, would soon be on their way. The solution to all this was to open up a new theater of war, the Central Pacific, and on November 20, 1943, the 2nd Marine Division did that. It wasn't supposed to be easy. Everyone knew the Gilbert Islands bristled with Japanese defenders. But no one anticipated a Tarawa.

Tarawa was the battle America almost lost. The enemy commander had boasted that Betio, the key island in the atoll, couldn't be taken by a million men in a hundred years. "Corregidor," said Samuel Eliot Morison, "was an open town by comparison." The marines going in had other problems: the naval bombardment had been too light, the tides betrayed them, they missed H-hour, and at the end of the first day their beachhead was exactly twenty feet wide. Officers stood waist-deep in the water, directing the battle by radio and praying against a counterattack. Only the breakdown of Japanese communications prevented one. The next day the marines drove through and split the defenses, but the attackers had lost three thousand men. The following month Kwajalein and Eniwetok, in the Marshall Islands, were taken more cheaply. Nevertheless, from the very first, battles in the Central Pacific were short and terrible—the 4th Marine Division, blooded on Kwajalein, was in action only sixty-one days during the entire war, yet it suffered 75 percent casualties.

There were several reasons for this sudden lengthening of casualty lists. On Guadalcanal the enemy had been taken by surprise. He would never be caught unprepared again. Furthermore, in storming the Marshalls and the Marianas, U.S. troops were attacking islands which had been mandated to Japan after World War I; the Japanese had been digging in for nearly a quarter-century. The greatest reason for greater bloodshed in the Pacific, however, was a dramatic change in Jap tactics. The Oriental masters of amphibious offense had gone over to an iron defense. Dai Honei, Imperial headquarters, radioed reminders to every outpost that they must prepare a last-man resistance. One of them did more than that. On Biak, an island near the tail of the New Guinea bird, the enemy had ten thousand men. Their commander, Colonel Naoyuki Kuzume, decided that while dying on the beach was all very fine, dying inland would be better; by skillful use of caves and cliffs, his men could prolong the slaughter of what one Japanese diary keeper contemptuously called "those blue-eyed Americans."

Kuzume had made the most murderous discovery of the island war. Tokyo might never have heard of it had Biak not lain directly in the path of MacArthur's drive on the Philippines. Having mopped up the bird's tail, the general was skipping up its back in the spring of 1944, using a new U.S. tactic, "leapfrogging." Americans had stumbled upon this course while retaking Attu and Kiska, the Alaskan isles with which Yamamoto had tried to mislead Nimitz during the Battle of Midway. Lacking strength to attack both, operations officers bypassed Kiska—and discovered, after Attu had been retaken, that the Japanese had quietly evacuated it. MacArthur caught on. Late in April he leaped into Hollandia, and a month later the 41st Division hit Biak. Until now the cost of the offensive had been relatively light, but Kuzume's cliff-and-cave defenders exacted a terrible toll; before the island was secured casualty lists were approaching Tarawa's.

They might have been worse. The Japanese Navy, in hiding for a year, was preparing to emerge and reinforce the garrison. The ships were already at sea when, in mid-June, word reached Admiral Jisaburo Ozawa that Nimitz's Central Pacific drive was about to pounce on the Marianas' key islands—Saipan, Tinian, and Guam. This was the greater threat, and prows were turned that way. The resulting Battle of the Philippine Sea was another of those long-distance aircraft duels that disappointed old line-of-battle salts. It was, nonetheless, a stunning American victory. Hellcats knocked out the enemy's land-based air power on Guam and, in eight hours of continuous fighting in the sky, beat off four massive attacks on the U.S. fleet. It was the most spectacular carrier battle of the war; by the end of the following day Ozawa's air arm had been reduced from 430 operational warplanes to 35. After this Great Marianas Turkey Shoot, as Navy pilots called it, Ozawa withdrew—and Japanese soldiers on Saipan were cut off.

The Nips swore that they would make the Americans pay the highest possible price for Saipan. There were twice as many defenders as intelligence had predicted, and U.S. casualties dismayed Washington. After three thousand Japs had staged the war's biggest *banzai* attack, driving GIs into the surf, surviving soldiers and marines wiped out the rest of the enemy or waited while the suicides saved them the trouble. Two weeks later other marines were fanning out across Guam's reefs. Guam was only half as expensive as Saipan, partly because the *banzai* was less effective. U.S. casualties on Tinian, where the Japanese hadn't thought a north shore landing possible, were even lighter. Even so, the Marianas Islands had cost twenty-five thousand Americans killed or wounded. Yet they were priceless. They gave the B-29s their first base within flying range of the Japanese home islands. Marine Lieutenant General Holland M. "Howlin' Mad" Smith, the commanding officer in the U.S. struggle for Saipan, called it the decisive battle of the Pacific war. Tokyo agreed; the German naval attaché there had reported to Berlin that the island was "understood to be a matter of life or death." The Tojo cabinet fell, and for the first time Americans saw a way to victory in the Pacific, and were heartened.

At the outset MacArthur had opposed the marines' invasion of Guadalcanal, and these thrusts in the Central Pacific so far from his own theater in the Southwest Pacific, suited him even less. "Island hopping," as he now called it scornfully, seemed to him a waste of time—though it was indistinguishable from his own "leapfrogging." By the summer of 1944 he was beside himself. Admiral King was suggesting that U.S. forces bypass the Philippines. America had to keep faith with the Filipinos, MacArthur insisted; it was a matter of honor. A matter of sentiment, King replied, and both appealed to Roosevelt.

The President, whose political advisers wanted him in Chicago at the Democratic national convention, went to Hawaii instead. He had to settle the military issue. On July 26, as the battle for Guam raged, the presidential aircraft touched down at Hickam Field. Nimitz and MacArthur, up from Australia, stated their cases. In a private session MacArthur actually threatened Roosevelt with political reprisals if his strategic plan was set aside; should the general's promise to return to the Philippines be unredeemed, he said, "I dare say that the American people would be so aroused that they would register most complete resentment against you at the polls this fall." This was insolent and probably untrue, but FDR had seen it coming and had made his choice before leaving the White House. He answered, "We will not bypass the Philippines. Carry on your existing plans. And may God protect you."

The Combined Chiefs of Staff weren't satisfied. In Washington they argued for two months before agreeing that MacArthur should return to the Philippines. In the meantime Halsey had made a startling suggestion. The Philippine timetable called for early landings on Peleliu, Yap, and Mindanao. Air strikes convinced Halsey that the enemy's air force was a broken lance. He proposed skipping the preliminaries and charging right into Leyte. His motion was carried, though the Peleliu operation, too far advanced to be canceled, went ahead as scheduled. The consequences were tragic. Biak had become a magic word in Tokyo. Kuzume's lesson had been passed on to the commanding officer on Peleliu, who had made his men moles. Burrowed in natural limestone caves linked by underground tunnels and protected by layers of coral sand and concrete, they cut the 1st Marine Division to pieces, giving all American regiments a bitter taste of what was to come.

By the time the jagged ridges north of Peleliu airfield had been cleared, four American divisions were swarming over the beach at Leyte Gulf. Less than an hour after the main landings on October 20, 1944, the 382nd Infantry had the Stars and Stripes up; four days later General Walter Krueger's Sixth Army command post was ashore and Yamashita's Thirty-fifth Japanese Army was marching against it. Krueger seemed stuck in the mud, and in Leyte Gulf the stage had been set for the greatest naval battle of all time.

Yamamoto was dead, but the Japanese Navy still cherished his dream of a decisive action at sea, preferably while U.S. ships were busy covering a landing. Now, if ever, was the time for it. Four separate Japanese task forces sailed against Halsey's main fleet, which was protecting the Leyte operation, and Admiral Thomas Kinkaid's weaker group of old battleships and small carriers. The enemy admirals knew they couldn't match America's new power—the U.S. had 218 warships, the Japanese had 64—so they hatched a brilliant plan. Leyte Gulf could be reached through two straits, San Bernardino to the north and Surigao to the south. Their center force, led by Admiral Takeo Kurita, was to head for San Bernardino while two southern forces entered Surigao. At the same time the fourth force, Ozawa's, was to lure Halsey away to the north. Kinkaid would then be helpless. *Banzai.*

The southern prongs had no luck. Admiral Jesse Oldendorf had Surigao Strait corked. Torpedoes and gunfire exterminated the first Jap column; the second turned back after firing at radar pictures which later turned out to be islands. In the beginning Kurita's luck seemed bad, too. On the way to San Bernardino, American submarines destroyed two of his heavy cruisers, and his largest battleship was sunk by U.S. aircraft. Actually these losses were a stroke of fortune for Kurita. Halsey, learning of them, thought him finished, and when Ozawa's decoy was sighted Halsey took off after the bait —leaving San Bernardino Strait unguarded. In the darkness of October 24 Kurita slipped through. The following morning he sprang on Kinkaid's exposed carriers in the first moments of daylight.

The carriers' only protection was their screen—destroyers (DDs) and destroyer escorts (DEs), vulnerable vessels ordinarily used for antisubmarine work and manned mostly by married draftees. The destroyers counterattacked Kurita's battleships, and then their gallant little escorts, who hadn't even been taught to form a line of battle, steamed toward the huge Japanese guns. Kurita's goliaths milled around in confusion as the DEs, some already sinking, made dense smoke. The U.S. carriers sent up everything that could fly, and Kurita, with the mightiest Japanese fleet since Midway, turned tail. The rout was complete, for Halsey was thorough in his error; he chewed up Ozawa's bait, and in the final Leyte Gulf reckoning the enemy lost three battleships, four carriers, and twenty other warships. The emperor's sea power was finished.

On Leyte the Sixth and Eighth Armies were now pulling a drawstring around the enemy bag. Yamashita, in Manila, privately wrote off the island at Christmas, though it wasn't freed until the following St. Patrick's Day. By then Yamashita could have done nothing about it anyway. GIs had hit the island of Mindoro on December 12; three weeks later four divisions made an almost unopposed landing at Luzon's Lingayen Gulf. Bypassing the northern defenses of the Yamashita Line, they jumped Bataan, then Corregidor, and finally, in early March, Manila.

On Bataan and Corregidor, as an Army officer wryly remarked at the time, the United States was "right back where we started." B-29s had begun to scar the Japanese homeland, but it was still a remote fortress. Bringing it closer was the task of the other American pincer—the Central Pacific thrust that had driven from Tarawa through the Marshalls to Saipan. Its next target was the volcanic pile of Iwo Jima, "on the ladder of the Bonins," as Admiral King put it. Saipan was within B-29 range of the Japanese capital, but only just. Superfort bomb loads were limited to two tons; those damaged in raids couldn't get back. But if the Americans held Iwo, they would be 660 miles from Japan. The B-29s could carry seven tons of bombs and Tokyo would miss warnings of coming raids now radioed to the capital by Japs on Iwo.

The enemy thought a lot of Iwo's eight square miles. The Navy's seventy-four days of preinvasion bombardment scarcely jarred the defenders, because they had no barracks aboveground. Most of their caves were shielded by at least thirty-five feet of overhead cover. Nearly every Jap weapon could reach the beaches. The first two hours ashore were comparatively tranquil. Then the beachhead was blanketed with mortar fire. Despite this, Mount Suribachi and Motoyama Airfield No. 1 were taken in the early days of the battle, which, in the first year of the war, would have been it. Everyone waited for the Nips to form a *banzai* charge and come in to be slaughtered. They didn't. Enemy soldiers had been thoroughly trained in Biak tactics. They stuck to their pillboxes and ravines, and when the end came in March the grim abacus showed 19,000 marine casualties.

The abacus was grimmer for the enemy. The Japanese equivalent of "It never rains but it pours" is "When crying, stung by bee in the face." Stinging Superforts were swarming low over his homeland, beginning the methodical destruction of eighty Jap cities, killing one hundred thousand people in a single day in the great Tokyo raid of March 9, 1945. Halsey's carriers had broken into the South China Sea, cutting the enemy's oil and rice lines. Hirohito's merchant navy was a skeleton; soon the American submarine score would be over a thousand ships. Shantytowns were rising in Yokohama and Osaka. Jap civilians were racked by tuberculosis and malaria. There was no food for their ration cards. Menacing reports from Japanese commanders in Manchuria reported that Russian troops were mobilizing on their frontier. When crying, stung by bee in the face.

Yet the Japanese morale showed no signs of cracking. Old men and women were being armed with bamboo spears. "Come and get us," Tokyo Rose dared. To oblige, the Americans needed one more invasion base: Okinawa. General Mitsuri Ushijima, Okinawa's commanding officer, had guessed in March that he would be receiving hostile visitors near Yontan Airfield on April 1. He was right. And he had a surprise for them. April 1 was Easter Sunday, but it still looked like April Fools' Day to the GIs and marines wading ashore. There didn't seem to be any enemy soldiers around. No one then guessed that it would take nearly three months to conquer the island, or that Okinawa would be the bloodiest battle of the Pacific war. Actually Ushijima had a hundred thousand soldiers concentrated in the southern third of the island. By April 12 it was clear that this would be another Iwo. Okinawa's burial vaults had been converted to pillboxes; caves masked heavy artillery that could be rolled in and out on railroad tracks. Ushijima expected to win, too. The Japanese strategy was to wait until all American troops were ashore, knock out the U.S. fleet with suicidal kamikaze bombers, and slaughter marines and GIs at leisure.

In Warm Springs, Georgia, where President Roosevelt had dressed and settled in his leather armchair, the global situation was more promising. Chatting with Lucy Rutherfurd and two visiting cousins, Miss Margaret Suckley and Miss Laura Delano, the President was all smiles and optimism. Strategically, American arms were victorious on all fronts. Germany had been cut in half. Apart from a few obstinate pockets the Wehrmacht was disintegrating, surrendering by the tens of thousands. Japan would be more difficult, of course. Iwo Jima had fallen, in time Okinawa would, too; there could be no doubt about the eventual outcome. Yet as of this April 12, the war against the Axis had cost the lives of 196,669 Americans; total U.S. casualties were 899,669 Americans—6,481 of them in the past week. There could be no glossing that over. After so great a sacrifice, he had told those around him, world peace would be absolutely secure.

Shortly before noon Bill Hassett appeared, dragging a leather pouch from Washington. The mail had arrived. Hassett suggested that the President postpone his paper work until after lunch, but FDR said he would do it right now. Hassett put before him a State Department paper requiring his approval. Roosevelt brightened. "A typical State Department letter," he cheerily told the ladies. "It says nothing at all." He worked through the rest of the papers, affixing his weakened signature to a batch of postmaster appointments, routine correspondence, and Legion of Merit awards to eminent Allied statesmen. The White House still regarded ballpoint pens as a passing fad. Fountain pen ink could easily be smeared, blemishing a document, so as the President worked, Hassett laid out the signed papers on a divan, empty chairs, and the rug. When he came to Senate Bill 298, extending the Commodity Credit Corporation, he winked at Lucy Rutherfurd and said, "Here's where I made a law." Just then there was a sound in the outer hall. Madame Elizabeth Shoumatoff, the portrait painter, had arrived. She glanced in, puzzled by the sheets of paper everywhere. "Oh, come right ahead," Roosevelt called. "Bill is waiting for his laundry to dry."

Hassett went about it quickly, and with averted eyes. He did not approve of Madame Shoumatoff. She distracted the President too much, he thought, with her measurements of his nose and requests to turn this way or that, and she even dictated his apparel; this morning, for example, he was wearing a Harvard tie and a vest, neither of which he liked. To Hassett all this was "unnecessary hounding of a sick man." He didn't even think she was much of an artist, but Lucy liked her, and so did FDR. As Hassett left, handing Roosevelt a batch of State Department reports, Madame erected her easel and slipped his boat cloak over his shoulders. Instantly he became engrossed in the state documents.

Because the papers were diplomatic, and because FDR had been troubled all week by Russian duplicity (less than two hours ago he had cabled Churchill, "We must be firm"), it is not too fanciful to suggest that in the last moments of his life the President may have been reflecting upon the Yalta Conference in the Crimea, two months earlier. He had gone there because his military advisers had told him that it was necessary. General MacArthur, General Albert Wedemeyer, and the Joint Chiefs had spoken with one voice: they wanted the Soviet Union to declare war on Japan, and they believed it worth almost any price. At that time—six months before atomic weapons were to alter permanently the nature of war and geopolitics—none of those who knew of the Manhattan Project thought it worth mentioning. "The bomb will never go off," wrote Admiral Leahy, Roosevelt's chief of staff, "and I speak as an expert in explosives."

At Yalta, Roosevelt and Churchill got more from Stalin than they had expected. In the past they had found the Soviet dictator a hard bargainer. He liked to sit impassively behind the impenetrable screen of the Slavic language—his stock of English phrases was confined to "So what?" "You said it," "The toilet is over there!" and "What the hell goes on here?"—and in his present position he could afford to gloat. For nearly three years he had been the weakest of the three, begging the Anglo-Americans to open a second front in Europe and unable to offer them anything in exchange. Now they had to come to him. Nevertheless he was mellow. He secretly agreed to enter the anti-Japanese coalition. In return the Soviet Union would be given certain privileges in Manchuria (notably a half-interest in the eastern end of the Trans-Siberian Railway), the Kurile Islands, half of Sakhalin (another island north of Japan), an occupation zone in Korea, a U.N. veto for major powers, and, in another secret agreement which would later cause domestic difficulties in the United States, U.N. seats for the Ukraine and Belorussia. The Anglo-Americans further agreed to recognize the autonomy of Outer Mongolia.

Poland's borders were to be redrawn, adding lands that had been German. Stalin solemnly joined his allies in guaranteeing all eastern European countries, including Poland, the right to choose their leaders and governments in free elections. Long afterward the American President and the British prime minister were assailed as naive; how, it was asked, could they have trusted pledges from so implacable an enemy of democracy? The fact is that they had very little choice. They were at war with Japan; Russia wasn't; the Red Army could do as it pleased, promises or no promises. At the time it appeared the Russian dictator, flushed from the European victory, was in a generous mood. The greatest beneficiary of the conference seemed to be Chiang Kai-shek. Stalin signed a treaty with Chiang recognizing him as the ruler of all China and promising to persuade Mao Tse-tung's Chinese to cooperate with him.

Pat Hurley and Henry Luce praised the Yalta agreements; so did the American and British press. Averell Harriman and George Kennan, both veteran Kremlinologists, were skeptical. But that was not a popular view in early 1945. Winston Churchill had urged Eisenhower to "shake hands with the Russians as far east of the Elbe as possible." Ike disagreed. He countermanded an order which would have sent Patton into Prague and withdrew his GIs west of the Elbe, permitting the Russians to free Czechoslovakia, eastern Germany, and Berlin. After visiting Moscow Eisenhower declared: "Nothing guides Russian policy so much as desire for friendship with the United States."

In Warm Springs Roosevelt stirred and glanced at his watch. It was 1 P.M. To Madame Shoumatoff he said, "We've got just fifteen minutes more."

She wasn't doing much now. He had become so engrossed in his papers that she hadn't dared ask him to resume his pose. She was occupying her time filling in colors.

Lizzie McDuffie, an elderly black servant, paused at the door and glanced into the living room. She saw Lucy Rutherfurd facing the President. He had just said something witty; she was smiling. "That is the last picture I have in my mind of Mr. Roosevelt," she said afterward. "The last I remember he was looking into the smiling face of a beautiful woman."

FDR slipped a cigarette into his holder and lit it. He had now fallen so far from his pose that the painter despaired of regaining his attention. Watching, she saw him raise his left hand to his temple and press it. He appeared to be squeezing his forehead. The hand fell, the fingers twitched; it was as though he were fumbling for something. Miss Suckley put down her crocheting and stepped over, asking, "Did you drop something?" He pressed his left hand behind his neck, closed his eyes, and said softly—so softly only she heard him—"I have a terrific headache." His arm fell. His head drooped to the left. His chest slumped. It was 1:15 P.M.

Daisy Suckley phoned for Dr. Bruenn and asked Madame Shoumatoff to find the nearest Secret Service agent. The painter did, and then headed toward her car. Flying after her was Lucy Rutherfurd; Eleanor Roosevelt must never know of her presence here. Of course he would recover. As the word spread through the household, everyone felt that way. The thought of an America without Franklin Roosevelt in the White House was insupportable; the young men fighting overseas could hardly remember a time when he had not been President. This was a passing thing. The doctors would fix it, everyone assured everyone else, and all were convinced of it except the doctors.

On orders from Dr. McIntire, Dr. Bruenn had become virtually a member of the presidential staff; he was always just around the corner. At 9:30, just before the President's breakfast, Bruenn had examined his patient. There had been nothing wrong with Roosevelt's heart. His blood pressure was high—180 systolic over 110 to 120 diastolic—but not alarming. It had been running at those levels for some time now. He hadn't been tense. In conversations with the doctor during the past week he had commented bitterly on Stalin's behavior since Yalta, but he hadn't mentioned that this morning. Now Bruenn, racing into the cottage, saw Roosevelt sagging against, and held up by, the arms of his chair. FDR's cousins sat petrified on the couch.

Momentarily the President stopped breathing. Then his breath became harsh. His tongue was blocking his throat. His neck was rigid, his systolic blood pressure over 300, and his left eye was dilating wildly. What had happened was that an artery in Roosevelt's brain had developed a tiny puncture, probably because it was old, fragile, and easily ruptured. Blood from this perforation had seeped into cavities around the brain, and the brain, sensitive to the slightest change, was sending frantic distress signals. The victim's eyes were distorted; he suffered from vertigo; his breathing became more audible; he sounded as though he were snoring. To a physician those signals had but one meaning. The patient was suffering from a massive cerebral hemorrhage. At this point Bruenn could not gauge the severity of the stroke, but he could provide emergency relief. Swiftly scissoring away Roosevelt's clothes, he injected doses of papaverine and amyl nitrite into the President's arm, re-dressed him in striped blue pajamas, and, with the help of a male servant and a Navy physiotherapist who had arrived to give FDR his daily rubdown, gently carried him to his maple bed. The only sound those outside the room could hear were the great gasping, anguished snores.

Bruenn called McIntire in Washington, who endorsed Bruenn's diagnosis and the treatment. Physicians today would hesitate to administer amyl nitrite, which depresses blood pressure and decreases the vital flow of blood to the brain, but the President was beyond help anyway. He had now been unconscious for fifty minutes. Bruenn reported intense narrowing of the blood vessels (vasoconstriction) and partial paralysis. McIntire phoned an eminent Atlanta specialist, Dr. James E. Paullin, and begged him to reach Warm Springs as quickly as possible. Speeding down back roads and shortcuts and expecting, as he later put it, "to be picked up any moment," Paullin made Warm Springs in less than an hour and a half. As he explained in his report to McIntire, "The President was *in extremis* when I reached him. He was in a cold sweat, ash gray and breathing with difficulty. Numerous rhonchi in the chest. . . . Within five minutes of my entrance into the room, all evidence of life passed away. The time was 3:35 o'clock."

Until that moment Fala had been sitting quietly in the bedroom. Now he seemed to sense the change. Abruptly the dog leaped from his corner, brushed the screen door open, and raced, frantically yelping, to the top of the nearest hill. There he stopped barking and stood immobile, as though on vigil.

Inside the bedroom, the first mourner was Grace Tully: "Without a word or glance toward the others present, I walked into the bedroom, leaned over and kissed the President lightly on the forehead." Good taste and form required that the First Lady and the Vice President, the new President, be informed before the press learned what had happened. Hassett and Bruenn asked McIntire to put them through to Steve Early, the President's press secretary. Stifling his own grief, Early told them to say nothing until he could reach Eleanor Roosevelt.

The President's widow was at that moment preparing to speak at the annual tea of the Sulgrave Club at 1801 Massachusetts Avenue N.W. in Washington. Shortly after 3 P.M., when the President had been unconscious for forty-five minutes, Laura Delano called from Warm Springs and guardedly told her that the President had "fainted." A few minutes later McIntire phoned the First Lady. He saw no reason for panic, he said, but he had requisitioned a Navy plane to carry her and him to Georgia. She inquired: should she cancel her speech? Not at all, he said; it might lead to rumors. On that advice she spoke on the United Nations. Afterward Evalyn Tyner, a pianist, began to play selections. Again Mrs. Roosevelt was called to the phone; this time it was Steve Early, "very much upset," in her words, asking her "to come home at once." She had a sinking feeling "that something dreadful had happened. Nevertheless the amenities had to be observed, so I went back to the party." She listened to Miss Tyner complete a piece and then excused herself, saying, "Now I'm called back to the White House and I want to excuse myself for leaving before this delightful concert is finished."

Outside, a presidential limousine awaited her. She "got into the car and sat with clenched hands all the way to the White House. In my heart I knew what had happened, but one does not actually formulate these terrible thoughts until they are spoken." Back in the sitting room on the second floor of the Executive Mansion, she sent for Early. Afterward he quoted her to the press as saying, "I am more sorry for the people of this country and of the world than I am for ourselves." It would have been appropriate, but the truth is that she never said it. The thought was Early's. What Eleanor really did tell him was that she wanted to see Harry Truman at once.

Framed dramatically against a background of red Levanto marble pilasters and heavy blue velvet embellished with a gold embroidered border, the sixty-year-old thirty-fourth Vice President was ostensibly presiding over the United States Senate. In reality he was scrawling:

> Dear Mama & Mary: I am trying to write you a letter today from the desk of the President of the Senate while a windy Senator . . . is making a speech on a subject with which he is in no way familiar. The Jr. Sen. from Arizona made a speech on the subject, and knew what he was talking about. . . .

He hoped they were having nice weather, said it was "raining and misty" in Washington, and told them he would be flying to Providence Sunday morning. He added:

> Turn on your radio tomorrow night at 9:30 your time and you'll hear Harry make a Jefferson Day address to the nation. I think I'll be on all the networks, so it ought not to be hard to get me. I will be followed by the President, whom I'll introduce.
> Hope you are both well and stay that way.
> Love to you both.
> Write when you can.

Senator Alexander Wiley surrendered the floor, Alben Barkley moved for a recess until the following day, and at 4:56, his official day over, the Vice President—ignorant of the fact that he had been America's thirty-third President for over an hour—dropped in on Speaker Sam Rayburn for a drink. He was there, sipping bourbon and water, when the White House switchboard located him. Early told him, "Please come right over and come in through the main Pennsylvania Avenue entrance." Puzzled, Truman thought Roosevelt had returned from Warm Springs early and wanted a word with him on some minor matter. Upstairs, one glance at Eleanor Roosevelt's face told him this was nothing slight. She put her hand on his shoulder gently and said quietly, "Harry, the President is dead." Dazed, he asked if there was anything he could do for her. She said, "Is there anything *we* can do for *you?* You are the one in trouble now."

Seventeen minutes later, at 5:47 P.M., the White House switchboard alerted the Associated Press, the United Press, and the International News Service* to an imminent conference call. News-

---
* The last two later merged and became United Press International (UPI).

papermen for the three wire services were plugged in. They heard: "This is Steve Early. I have a flash for you. The President died suddenly this afternoon at . . ."

That was enough for Hearst's INS; it was first on the wire with:

>   FLASH
> WASHN—FDR DEAD
>   INS WASHN 4/12/547 PPH36.

UP followed thirty seconds later with:

> FLASH. WASHINGTON. PRESIDENT ROOSEVELT DIED THIS AFTERNOON.

Two minutes later, at 5:49 P.M., AP sent:

> FLASH—WASHINGTON—PRESIDENT ROOSEVELT DIED SUDDENLY THIS AFTERNOON AT WARM SPRINGS, GA.

At the United Press Washington Bureau a rewrite man was taking down Early's dictation in reportorial shorthand:

> at Warm Springs, Ga. deth resulted from cerebal hemorrhage— V-P Truman has been notified. Called to W hse & informed By Mrs. R. Secy of State has been advised. Cab meeting has been called. 4 boys in service have been sent message by their mother which sed —(no quote) that the president slipped away this afternoon. he did his job to the end as he wud want you to do. Bless you and all our love. Mrs. R. signed the message "mother."*
>
> Mrs. R. Adm. McIntyre & Steve Early will leave WA by air t aft for warm Springs. We expect (Steve talking) to leave Warm S tmro a.m. by train for Wa. funeral services will be held Sat. aft. east room of W hse. Interment will be at Hyde Park Sunday aft. Detailed No detailed aranns or exact times have been decided on as yet.
>
> for details hv get from man at Warm Springs.

In the office of radio station WRC at New York Avenue and Fourteenth Street N.W., the deskman was twenty-four-year-old David Brinkley. He heard the INS machine ring four bells, ripped off the flash, and took it to his boss. On radio this was the children's hour; NBC was broadcasting the juvenile serial *Front Page Farrell*, CBS *Wilderness Road*, ABC *Captain Midnight*, and Mutual *Tom Mix*. By 5:49, however, commentators were beginning to come through on every network and local station. Radio commercials had been canceled for the next four days; there was nothing else to talk

---

* The actual text: DARLINGS: PA SLEPT AWAY THIS AFTERNOON. HE DID HIS JOB TO THE END AS HE WOULD WANT YOU TO DO. BLESS YOU. ALL OUR LOVE. MOTHER.

about. A Bronx housewife was asked if she had heard the radio bulletins. "For what do I need a radio?" she cried. "It's on everybody's face." People told strangers, who phoned their friends, who put through long distance calls to relatives. The flashes were broadcast in London and Moscow, even in Tokyo and Berlin, before most people in Warm Springs knew what had happened. In Germany, where darkness had fallen, Eisenhower was conferring with Patton and Bradley. They had retired for the night when Patton, realizing that he had forgotten to wind his watch, turned his radio to get the right time. He heard a BBC commentator, his voice breaking with emotion, say, "We regret to announce that the President of the United States has died." Patton woke Bradley, and together they roused Ike. At almost the same time, on a highway near Macon, Georgia, Lucy Rutherfurd asked Madame Shoumatoff if she might turn on the car radio. The painter nodded. They heard soft music, then the break: "We interrupt this program to bring you a special bulletin. . . ." Lucy gasped and covered her face with her hands.

In telegraphing her sons that their father had done his job to the end as he would "want you to do," Eleanor Roosevelt had meant just that. The Victorian sense of duty was strong in her. In leaving the Sulgrave Club she had been careful not to interrupt the proceedings or embarrass anyone. She believed in propriety, and her sons understood her. In the waters off Okinawa, Lieutenant John Roosevelt, USNR, was standing watch on the flag bridge of the carrier *Hornet* when he received a voice contact from the destroyer *Ulvert L. Moore,* under the command of Lieutenant Commander Franklin D. Roosevelt, USNR. In enemy waters identification was impossible but unnecessary; Groton-Harvard accents were rare. "Are you making it home, old man?" inquired the voice from the destroyer. "No," said the man on the *Hornet*'s bridge. "Are you?" Young FDR Jr. said, "Nope. Let's clean it up out here first. So long, old man—over." John Roosevelt: "So long—out."

Americans were incredulous, shocked, and above all, afraid. He had been leading them so long. Who would lead now? Cabell Phillips of the *New York Times* recalls that when the implications of what had happened sank in, the White House press corps was aghast: "'Good God,' we said, 'Truman will be President!'" But at the moment it was unnecessary, and indeed impossible, to think of Truman. The long shadow of Roosevelt's passing lay dark across the land. Only then, Eleanor later conceded, did she realize how direct FDR's dialogue with the American people had been. Anne O'Hare McCormick wrote in the *New York Times* that he had "occupied a role so fused with his own personality after twelve years that people in other countries spoke of him simply as 'The President,' as if he were President of the World. He did not stoop and he did not climb. He was one of those completely poised persons who felt no need to play up or play down to anybody. In his death this is the element of his greatness that comes out most clearly."

Some responses were surprising. His voice trembling with unexpected emotion, Robert A. Taft said, "He dies a hero of the war, for he literally worked himself to death in the service of the American people." The author of the *New York Times* obituary editorial appeared to be almost overwhelmed with grief: "Men will thank God on their knees a hundred years from now that Franklin Roosevelt was in the White House when a powerful and ruthless barbarism threatened to overrun the civilization of the Western World." For the first time since Abraham Lincoln's death in 1865, the New York Philharmonic canceled a Carnegie Hall concert. In London, Churchill was told while entering his study at No. 10 Downing Street. He said he "felt as if I had been struck a physical blow." Buckingham Palace's Court Circular broke precedent by reporting the death of a head of state who was not a member of the royal family. Black-bordered Moscow flags flew at half-mast, and a *Times* correspondent cabled that people there said over and over, "We have lost a friend."

In Washington vast crowds gathered around the White House while Dean Acheson looked down on them from his window next door in the Executive Office Building. "There was nothing to see," he would write in his memoirs, "and I am sure they did not expect to see anything. They merely stood in a lost sort of way." In Berlin, where Russian artillery shells were falling outside the Führerbunker, Goebbels babbled, "My Führer! I congratulate you! Roosevelt is dead! It is written in the stars that the second half of April will be the turning point for us. This is Friday 13 April. It *is* the turning point!" Hitler was impressed. Radio Tokyo, on the other hand, amazed the world by quoting Premier Admiral Kantaro Suzuki as saying, "I must admit that Roosevelt's leadership has been very effective and has been responsible for the Americans' advantageous position today. For that reason I can easily understand the great loss his passing means to the American people and my profound sympathy goes to them." An announcer added, "We now introduce a few minutes of special music in honor of the passing of the great man."

Obscure mourners offered special eulogies. In San Diego, Petros Protopapadakis petitioned a court to change his name to Petros FDR Protopapadakis. The alarm system of the New York Fire Department sounded "four fives" to all fire stations—the signal that a fireman had died on duty. A little boy in Chicago picked a bouquet in his backyard and sent it with a note, saying he was sorry he couldn't come to the funeral. Other boys at Groton were told just before supper that the President, a member of the class of 1900, had just died. Leaving their meal untouched, they followed the headmaster into the chapel for prayer. In the village of Hyde Park, the bells of St. James Episcopal Church were tolling for its senior warden. And the *New York Post*, in a gesture which would have moved the President, simply headed its daily casualty list:

> Washington, Apr. 16—Following are the latest casualties in the military services, including the next of kin.
>
> ARMY-NAVY DEAD
>
> ROOSEVELT, Franklin D., Commander-in-Chief, wife, Mrs. Anna Eleanor Roosevelt, the White House.

A *Yank* editor wrote, "We made cracks about Roosevelt and told Roosevelt jokes. . . . But he was still Roosevelt, the man we had grown up under. . . . He was the Commander-in-Chief, not only of the Armed Forces, but of our generation." An elderly black Georgian said, "He made a way for folks when there wasn't no way." Again and again, strangers told John Gunther, "I never met him, but I feel as if I had lost my best friend." Gunther himself could not, at first, comprehend the tragedy: "He was gone, and it seemed impossible to believe it. FDR's belief in the basic goodness of man, his work to better the lot of humble people everywhere, his idealism and resourcefulness, his faith in human decency, his unrivaled capacity to stir great masses and bring out the best of them—to realize that all this was now a matter of memory was hard to absorb." On Capitol Hill Congressman Lyndon B. Johnson said brokenly, "He was just like a daddy to me always. He was the one person I ever knew, anywhere, who was never afraid. God, God—how he could take it for us all!"

There were a great many Americans, of course, who did not think of him as a war hero, did not feel that they had lost their best friend, and certainly had not regarded him as a daddy. Often their feelings were mixed. One who had fought him bitterly said sadly, "Now we are on our own." Some were delighted to be on their own. In a Park Avenue hotel elevator, when news of the first flash was being whispered about, the wife of a prominent Wall Street lawyer nervously clutched a glove. She couldn't wait to get to a radio. Suddenly, directly behind her, a man said aloud, "So he's finally dead. Isn't it about time?" The woman turned and lashed her glove across the man's cheek.

Of all the eulogies, one by Samuel Grafton may have come closest to the feelings of those who would always think of Franklin D. Roosevelt as *the* President: "One remembers him as a kind of smiling bus driver, with that cigarette holder pointed upward, listening to the uproar from behind as he took the sharp turns. They used to tell him that he had not loaded his vehicle right for all eternity. But he knew he had stacked it well enough to round the next corner, and he knew when the yells were false and when they were real, and he loved the passengers. He is dead now, and the bus is stalled, far from the gates of heaven, while the riders hold each other in deadlock over how to make the next curve."

At 4701 Connecticut Avenue, in a second-floor five-room apartment, twenty-year-old Margaret Truman was dressing for a dinner date when the telephone rang. She remembered afterward that her father's voice sounded "tight and funny," but she, with her mind on the exciting evening ahead, said gaily, "Hi, Dad."

"Let me speak to your mother."

"Are you coming home for dinner?"

"Let me speak to your mother."

"I only asked a civil question!"

"*Margaret, will you let me speak to your mother?*"

Hurt, her eyes damp, the girl returned to her makeup table. Seconds later she glanced up and saw her mother standing in the doorway looking at her—or, as it seemed to Margaret, *through* her.

"Mother, what's the matter? What is it?"

Bess Truman answered slowly, "President Roosevelt is dead."

"*Dead!*"

Bess was phoning a friend when the doorbell rang. Margaret answered it. A strange woman was standing on the threshold.

"Miss Truman?"

"Yes?"

"I'm from the Associated Press. I would like a—"

Horrified, Margaret realized that she had come to the door in her slip. She slammed the door, and at that instant she comprehended that her days of privacy were over. Looking down from a window, she saw a crowd gathering—newspapermen, photographers, friends, curious onlookers, and, as the apartment manager was discovering, a crowd of applicants for a large, conveniently located $120 a month rent-controlled apartment which was about to be vacated.

The widowed First Lady was circling over Fort Benning's landing strip waiting for her plane to land, and in Atlanta Bill Hassett was buying a coffin at the undertaking firm of H. M. Patterson & Co. Hassett wanted a solid mahogany casket with copper lining, but there were none; all copper was going into the war effort. He then specified that the coffin must be six feet four inches long; Franklin Roosevelt had been a big man. Even that seemed unattainable. The undertaker *did* have a long mahogany casket, but he had promised it to a New Jersey funeral home. They haggled and bargained until Hassett, a shrewd Vermonter backed by the prestige of the Presidency, got the best coffin in the house. It arrived in Warm Springs at 10:45, accompanied by two hearses. Forty minutes later Eleanor Roosevelt, Dr. McIntire, and Steve Early drew up.

Mrs. Roosevelt had long talks with Grace Tully and each of her cousins. Who told her about Lucy Rutherfurd is not known; nevertheless she learned of it then, at the worst possible time. She shook visibly, then composed herself and went into the bedroom. Five minutes later she emerged, grave and solemn but dry-eyed. The time had come to plan the funeral, map its route, choose the service, name the clergymen, select the hymns, and decide who, under protocol, would be entitled to occupy the two hundred seats in the East Room of the White House, where the rites would be held. There were no precedents. Warren G. Harding had been the last chief executive to die in office, and the State Department had just discovered that Harding's funeral files were missing. Everything would have to be improvised, with the President's widow as chief improviser.*

A stout bier of thick Georgia pine was installed in the last car of the presidential train and draped with dark green Marine Corps blankets. In the coffin, the lower part of the President's body was covered by his boat cloak. Mrs. Roosevelt nodded her approval, and a flag was draped over the casket. They had worked through the night, in bright starlight, the air around them thick with the fragrance of honeysuckle. It was 9:25 on the morning of Friday the 13th before the procession moved down the red clay road to the train depot, led by the casket on its caisson and Fort Benning musicians beating muffled drums. Helmeted paratroopers lined both sides of the winding road. Many were white-faced, some faces were tear-stained, and one soldier wobbled as the caisson passed and then collapsed and rolled into a ditch. Graham Jackson, a black accordionist and the President's favorite musician, played "Going Home." Military pallbearers carried the coffin into the waiting car, and then, taking advantage of the one-degree grade, the engineer let the train glide silently away. This was to be the four-hundredth and final trip of Roosevelt's special train. The last two cars had been reversed. Mrs. Roosevelt rode in the "Ferdinand Magellan," now next to the last. Behind it, in the car FDR had used as an office, lay the coffin on its crude catafalque. Servicemen stood at attention on either side. Elsewhere on the train most blinds were drawn; here they remained up, and the lights over the flag-draped casket were to be left on all night, to permit outsiders to view it.

No one attempted to estimate the number of anonymous mourners camping by the tracks waiting for a glimpse of that casket. In Atlanta they weren't allowed near it; as the train slowly chugged down the station's track 9 it passed through an aisle of white-gloved soldiers holding bayoneted rifles at present arms. Nevertheless, the faithful had come; traffic was at a standstill for blocks around, and men and women could be seen on the roofs of garages, warehouses, factories, and tenements, peering down from vast distances while private planes circled overhead. Beyond Atlanta that afternoon silent crowds stood at every grade crossing, and as they were ap-

---

* One copy of the Roosevelt funeral plans was deposited in the archives of the State Department, and was used by Jacqueline Bouvier Kennedy for President Kennedy's funeral arrangements eighteen years afterward, in late November 1963.

proaching Gainesville, Merriman Smith, in the press car, cried "Look!" and pointed. In the middle of a cotton field a group of black sharecropper women wearing bandannas were kneeling and holding out clasped hands.

At Greenville, South Carolina, the train paused to refuel, change crews, and acquire another American flag, this one fastened across the front of the locomotive by the new engineer. For at least five blocks on either side of the track, packed masses stood wide-eyed. Then a Boy Scout troop started singing "Onward, Christian Soldiers." It was "ragged at first," Merriman Smith later recalled, "but then it spread and swelled. Soon eight or ten thousand voices were singing like an organ." Heading north in the gathering darkness, Eleanor Roosevelt "lay in my berth all night with the window shade up, looking out at the countryside he had loved and watching the faces of the people at stations, and even at the crossroads, who had come to pay their last tribute all through the night. . . . I was truly surprised by the people along the way; not only at the stops but at every crossing. I didn't expect that because I hadn't thought a thing about it." She had always liked Millard Lampell's poem about Lincoln's death, and now, peering into the night, with Fala at her feet, one quatrain kept running through her mind:

> *A lonesome train on a lonesome track*
> *Seven coaches painted black*
> *A slow train, a quiet train,*
> *Carrying Lincoln home again.* . . .

At 6:20 A.M. on Saturday the train passed through Charlottesville, Virginia. Dawn promised a lovely spring day; over the forests dogwood spread like a pink mist, and everywhere azaleas and lilacs were in full bloom. Less than four hours later President Truman met the train and the funeral procession began, down Delaware Avenue and turning west on Constitution. Franklin Roosevelt had come this way many times, beaming and waving his campaign fedora to the cheering thousands. They were here again today, more of them than ever, but the stillness was unnatural, broken only when twenty-four Air Corps Liberators passed overhead.

The capital had never seen such panoply before. Helmeted soldiers lined the sidewalks. A squadron of policemen on gleaming motorcycles paced the slow procession. The Navy and Marine bands played Chopin's "Funeral March," "Onward, Christian Soldiers," and the "Death March" from *Saul*. A battalion of midshipmen marched. There were tanks, troop carriers, infantry in trucks, detachments of WACs, WAVEs, SPARs (the Coast Guard women), the Liberators overhead again—and then the little black-draped caisson bearing the casket suddenly appeared, led by six white horses and a seventh outrider: eyes hooded, stirrups reversed, sword and boots turned upside down and hanging from the stirrups: the mark of a fallen warrior since the days of Genghis Khan. Arthur Godfrey was describing the event to the nation over live radio; when he saw the caisson his voice broke and he sobbed. "It was so sudden," Bernard Asbell wrote. "It came so quietly. It seemed so peculiarly small. Just a big-wheeled wagon, dragged slowly, bearing the flag-covered oblong box. It was not a huge thing at all, as somehow everyone expected it to be. It was small, as though it might be any man's."

A right turn into Fifteenth Street, a left on Pennsylvania past weeping women—"Oh, he's gone. He's gone forever. I loved him so. He's never coming back"; "Oh Lord, he's gone, forever and forever and forever"—then through the White House northwest gate and up to the north portico. The Navy Band began to play "The Star-Spangled Banner," and a spry figure edged away and hurried toward the presidential office—Harry Truman, already on the job. Scarcely anyone noticed him. All eyes were on the doorway as the honor guard carried the coffin inside to the East Room, followed by the President's widow.

That Saturday afternoon was probably the quietest of the war. Across the country department stores were draped in black. The Ringling Brothers Barnum & Bailey circus had canceled its matinee. Movie theaters—seven hundred in New York alone—were closed. Newspapers had finished their runs early, for they were carrying no advertisements this day. Even grocery stores were locked up from two o'clock to five, and at four o'clock, when services began in the East Room, America simply stopped. AP, UP, and INS teletypes slowly tapped out: SILENCE. Buses and automobiles pulled over to curbstones. Trolley cars were motionless. Airplanes in the sky just circled overhead; those that had landed parked on their runways and did not approach terminals. Radios went dead. There was no phone service, not even a dial tone. In New York's subway tunnels, 505 trains halted where they were, and everywhere you saw men taking off their hats and women sinking to their knees.

In that long moment the United States was as still as the two hundred worshippers gathered in the East Room of the Executive Mansion.

The walls in the room were almost obscured by ten-foot banks of lilies, whose cloying scent was overpowering. The congregation forgot to rise when President Truman entered, but almost no one noticed the lapse, not even Truman, and in every other respect the service went well. Roosevelt's empty wheelchair stood apart from the improvised altar, a mute reminder of the handicap he had overcome. At the widow's request the guests sang the Navy Hymn ("Eternal Father, strong to save . . .") and heard FDR's favorite passage from his own speeches, "The only thing we have to fear is fear itself," quoted by Episcopal Bishop Angus Dun in his eulogy. The benediction was said at 4:23 P.M. Mrs. Roosevelt left first, and it was upstairs, in the private apartment of the First Family, that she exchanged bitter words with Anna. Her daughter had served as official hostess when the First Lady was out of town, and when the President had asked Anna whether she felt dinner invitations to "an old friend"—Lucy Rutherfurd—would be proper, Anna had hesitated, knowing the implications, and then assented. Eleanor felt doubly betrayed. Then she rallied. Drying her tears, she descended to the East Room for a last goodbye. An officer opened the coffin for her. She laid a bouquet within, and the coffin was then sealed forever.

At Union Station two trains awaited passengers to Hyde Park: the first for the Roosevelts, the Trumans, the Supreme Court, the cabinet and close friends, the second for congressmen, diplomats, and the press. At 9:30 P.M. the funeral cortege retraced its morning route, past the stiffly erect soldiers and the hushed public mourners on the pavements. Men in public life being what they are, politics was under discussion the moment the train left Washington. In the "Ferdinand Magellan," Harry Truman was talking earnestly to Jimmy Byrnes and sizing him up as a future Secretary of State, because Byrnes had been at Yalta and had an exact knowledge of the agreements reached there. Harold Ickes was the loudest man in his car, ridiculing Truman and bickering with his own wife. Henry Wallace sat alone, dour and glum. Morgenthau had seen FDR in Warm Springs on Wednesday evening, and he said that although the President's hand had trembled a trifle more than usual when he poured drinks, he had been as alert and well-informed as ever. Harry Hopkins was telling everyone who would listen that the new President's name had definitely not been "picked out of a hat" five months ago, that Roosevelt had been watching Truman's performance for some time and had put him on the ticket because he had led his committee well, was popular, and enjoyed prestige in the Senate, where the peace treaties would be sent for ratification.

In the Bronx they paused again. When they left the Mott Haven yards the second train was leading the President's, and word of the switch was swiftly telegraphed up the Hudson shore to sorrowing New Yorkers waiting there. At daybreak a writer for the *New Yorker*'s "Talk of the Town" drew up at the depot in Garrison, New York, a village directly across the river from West Point. He asked the railroad crossing watchman when the President's car would pass. "Be here between seven-thirty and eight," the man said. "First there'll be the train with the congressmen and then, maybe a quarter of an hour later, the President will go through." A crowd had begun to gather. Among the spectators was a man with a shivering little boy. "You've got to remember everything you see today," the father said. "It's awfully cold," said his son.

Presently two or three dozen cars arrived, from Model A Fords to 1942 Cadillacs. The occupants seemed more excited than stricken, and it struck the writer that maybe this was proper, that "Franklin Roosevelt would have preferred to have left his world with more of a bang than a whimper." As they waited, they gossiped. ("I couldn't tell old Mrs. Beldon on Friday. The shock would have been too much for her." "I wish to God he'd managed to hang on until Germany was licked." "I wish the people would all stand in one place on the platform. It would make a bigger tribute.") A party of bearded brothers from Glenclyffe Monastery appeared in brown cassocks and sandals; they stood in a line, almost with military precision. A nervous woman said, "It will be just terrible if I don't see him." A man assured her, "They'll slow up when they see us."

They did. The first train passed, and then the second locomotive crawled past the station, trailing a plume of white smoke. Men took off their hats, as they had eighty years ago when Lincoln's casket passed here. First a Garrison youth in a red-and-blue-striped mackinaw gave a shout, and then for an instant they all had a clear view of the flag-covered coffin with its military guard of honor.

"I saw him!" a little girl cried. "I saw him real plain!"

"You couldn't have seen him," her embarrassed mother said. "He was sleeping under the American flag." But the child repeated, "I saw him."

The crowd dissolved slowly, as though uncertain what to do next. As the father and his shivering son left, the boy said, "I saw everything." The man said, "That's good. Now make sure you remember it."

Mahopac, Cold Spring, Hopewell Junction, Wappinger's Falls, Poughkeepsie, Arlington, Pleasant Valley—names which would have been increasingly familiar to FDR—passed in succession, and at 8:40 A.M. that Sunday morning the locomotive veered off to a private Hyde Park siding on the edge of the Roosevelt estate. The moment it stopped, a cannon roared. Fifteen seconds later it roared again, and then again and again until the twenty-one-gun salute had been delivered. The West Point Band led the caisson and horses up the steep, wriggling, unpaved road that James Roosevelt had cleared in 1870, a wide trail that James's son Franklin had always called "the river road." Along this shore the boy had learned to swim, to row a boat, and, on the sunlit uplands, to ride a horse. Now one horse scrambled up the bank with an empty saddle and reversed harness.

The family estate was at the top of the hill. There, behind a ten-foot hedge in the rose garden, the fresh grave had been dug. The plan was for the brief ceremony here; every relative, dignitary, friend, and neighbor was escorted to his place. As the cadet escort presented arms, six servicemen bore the casket into the rose garden. Eleanor Roosevelt walked behind it. A crucifix appeared through a trellis green with woven leaves; the Hyde Park Episcopal vicar led the prayers in a ceremony which, Margaret Truman wrote in her diary that evening, "was simple and very impressive." Raising his hand as the pallbearers slowly lowered the coffin into the ground, the rector ended:

> *Now the laborer's task is o'er;*
> *Now the battle day is past;*
> *Now upon the farther shore*
> *Lands the voyager at last.*

> *Father, in Thy gracious keeping*
> *Leave we now Thy servant sleeping.*

A lone plane circled overhead. Advancing with precision, a squad of cadets fired three rounds in the air, terrifying Fala. The little dog yelped, rolled over, and cringed. He was still trembling, looking frightened and lost, when the bugler blew taps.

Eleanor Roosevelt left slowly. In New York, wearing on her black dress the pearl fleur-de-lis Franklin had given her as a wedding present, she dismissed a gathering of reporters with four words. "The story," she said quietly, "is over."

ETO Montage

I've got sixpence, jolly, jolly sixpence
I've got sixpence to last me all my life
I've got tuppence to spend
And tuppence to lend
And tuppence to send home to my wife
Poor wife

*I'm dreaming of a white Christmas
Just like the ones I used to know*

PATTON SLAPS GI FUROR AT HOME

She Copies Nearly Everything with COPYFLEX

"Just gimme a coupla aspirin. I already got a Purple Heart."

O.K., you guys. Reveille. Drop your cocks and grab your socks. *I'm a sa-a-ad sack!*

Out of Wartime Needs Has Come Startling Progress in Dry Batteries

"You'll get over it, Joe. Oncet I wuz gonna write a book exposin' the army after the war myself."*

*Unattributed quotations in this montage are captions from Bill Mauldin cartoons and appear in his *Up Front* (Holt, New York, 1945).

"Oh, I likes officers. They make me want to live till the war's over."

VICTORY and a BURBERRY

Radio Warsaw, this is Radio Warsaw. We lack food and medical supplies. Warsaw is lying in ruins. The Germans are murdering the wounded in the hospitals. They are driving women and children before their tanks as screens. Our sons are dying. Hear us, Holy Father, Vicar of Christ.

To many a truly discriminating man, not the least of the fruits of Victory will be the privilege of buying a Burberry topcoat...

cornball

and then Hope said, "Were the soldiers at the last camp happy to see me! They actually got down on their knees! What a spectacle! What a tribute! What a crap game!"

"This is Fragrant Flower Advance. Gimme yer goddam number."

While on pass you will be observed by civilians who will judge the United States Army by your appearance and conduct as an individual. Failure on your part to conform to regulations with respect to wearing your uniform and to live up to the highest traditions of the service will result in unfavorable criticism of the Army, your organization, and yourself.

I have read and understand the above statement and am familiar with the provisions of paragraphs 1 to 59 of the Soldier's Handbook.

Situation Normal All Fucked-Up

I wouldn't give a bean To be a fancy-pantsed Marine I'd rather be a dog-faced soldier boy.

Man Going on Leave

So what? I'm free, white, and twenty-one.

"Th' hell this ain't th' most important hole in th' world, I'm in it."

"This damn tree leaks."

PARIS LIBERATED!

Picasso Well, Busy In Rue Saint Augustin Studio

"Th' krauts ain't followin' ya so good on 'Lili Marlene' tonight, Joe. Ya think maybe somethin' happened to their tenor?"

flaking out

It's almost over and I'm almost home and I'm scared that maybe just a lucky shot will get me. And I don't want to die now, not when it's almost over. I just don't want to die now. Do you know what I mean?

shackup-job

"Beautiful view. Is there one for the enlisted men?"

I'm just a dog-faced soldier with a rifle on my shoulder
And I eat a kraut for breakfast every day
So feed me ammunition — keep me in the Third Division
Your dog-faced soldier boy's oh-kaaay!

"Ever notice the funny sound these zippers make, Willie!"

Twelve

A NEW WORLD, UNDER A NEW SUN

AT 6:30 ON THE WARM MORNING of April 13, 1945—the Friday that *My Day*'s author submitted no column—Harry Truman stirred on his pillow at 1701 Connecticut Avenue N.W., roused by the dreamy feeling that some extraordinary urgency was awakening him. Then it hit him: *he was President of the United States.* He bounded out of bed in one motion and dove for his clothes as though ready for instant action, because, as he later wrote in his memoirs, watching Roosevelt had convinced him that "being a President is like riding a tiger. A man has to keep on riding or be swallowed. . . . I never felt that I could let up for a single moment."

Truman was a hard rider, an up-with-the-sun Missouri farm boy with the mulish strength of the Middle Border, an incisive mind, and a deeper understanding of world history than most Presidents, including Franklin Roosevelt. Little of this was visible at the time. With "almost complete unanimity," *Time* wrote, his friends "agreed last week that he 'would not be a great President.'" Speaker Sam Rayburn saw Truman as a man "right on all the big things, wrong on most of the little ones." Nothing big surfaced in the first hours of his Presidency, and the country was inclined to take the word of the *Kansas City Star*'s Roy Roberts for it that "Harry Truman is no man to rock the boat." To Roberts and other conservatives the new President was a good-natured but poor politician, a dapper ex-haberdasher who delivered tepid speeches with singsong rhetoric and a flatter Midwest accent than Alf Landon's. He would sit out

Franklin Roosevelt's fourth term, they told one another, and then return to obscurity.

That was how they typecast the new President, and that, in the beginning, was how he looked. Washington believed that he had landed on the 1944 ticket as a compromise candidate. Roosevelt never denied it. If memoirs are to be believed, he scarcely mentioned Truman to anyone after their joint victory. The consequence was that Truman came into office as the worst-prepared President in history.

All transitions have their awkward moments, and no one could be expected to match Roosevelt's flamboyance, but his successor somehow gave the impression of a country cousin who had just arrived in Washington for a quick tour and was stunned by the thought of his own insignificance. As Truman himself recalled it, Secret Service agents arrived at his apartment that first morning and led him down the back stairs, yet despite their presence he kept forgetting that he was the chief executive. A newspaperman addressed him as "Mr. President," and he winced; "I wish you didn't have to call me that," he said. In his first public statement after his hurried oath taking at the White House he had said, "It will be my effort to carry on as I believe the President would have done." To him, as to most of his constituents, the man who had died in Warm Springs remained "the President."

Arriving on the sidewalk that first Friday morning, he hailed an AP correspondent: "Hey, Tony, if you're going down to the White House, you may as well hop in with me." The Secret Service agents looked pained, and their displeasure turned to alarm when, downtown, he insisted upon walking to his bank. They were unaccustomed to a President who walked anywhere. News that the new chief executive was a pedestrian swept adjacent blocks, creating the greatest traffic jam in memory, and Truman ruefully conceded that his bodyguards were right—Presidents couldn't go to banks; it had to be the other way round. He enjoyed the deference, but whenever his new duties were mentioned, he paled. "Boys, if newspapermen pray," he told the White House press corps, "pray for me now."

In perspective his behavior seems natural. The death of the great leader had unnerved everyone; yesterday Truman had been sworn in—after a frantic search for a Bible—by a confused Chief Justice who thought the new President's middle name was Shippe, when in fact the S stood for nothing. Afterward Truman had impulsively kissed the Bible. At that time he knew no more about prosecution of the war than the average reader of the *Washington Post*—which, in fact, had been his principal source of information. Roosevelt had told him nothing. Truman had never been in the White House war room. It is astonishing to reflect that during his first day in office he had never heard of an atomic bomb, while Joseph Stalin knew almost everything about the Manhattan Project. Stimson had tried to take the new President aside for a quick briefing, but there wasn't time then. On the second day, as Truman tells it, "Jimmy Byrnes came to see me, and even he told me few details, though with great solemnity he said that we were perfecting an explosive great enough to destroy the whole world." Truman, from Missouri, just stared. Nearly two weeks were to pass before he would be properly briefed on the developments at Los Alamos, and then Admiral Leahy, speaking once more as an explosions expert, would snort that the project was a complete waste of taxpayers' money, "the biggest fool thing we have ever done."

Washington sophisticates were diverted by anecdotes of Truman's artlessness, though the stories lacked the malice of anti-Roosevelt lore and were sometimes funny. After attending a Paderewski concert, the new President was invited backstage to meet the virtuoso. Vice President Truman had been photographed playing a grand piano with Lauren Bacall, looking very leggy, perched on top of it, and Paderewski murmured politely, "I understand that you, too, play the piano, Mr. President." The President replied modestly, "Oh, no, not like you, maestro." The true significance of such stories is that President Truman could laugh at them, too. Ridicule couldn't touch him. He knew what he was, a rare trait in Washington, and was proud of his lack of ostentation, an even rarer one.

To be sure, he *did* lack grace, tact, brilliance, charisma. But millions who had been daunted by FDR's remote grandeur were delighted by HST's earthiness and unpretentiousness. Roosevelt hadn't told his own wife that he was going to run against Hoover, but after taking the oath Truman phoned his ninety-one-year-old mother in Grandview, Missouri. After that first flash from Warm Springs, the family home in Grandview had been under siege by reporters and photographers who phoned, rang the doorbell, and peered in windows. The elder Mrs. Truman ignored them. She did come to the phone for her son. "Mama, I'm terribly busy," he said. He assured her everything would be all right, but said, "You probably won't hear from me for some time." Reaching home, laden with documents, he followed Bess and Margaret to the apartment of a hospitable family next door. In his words: "They had a turkey and then gave us something to eat. I had not had anything to eat since noon. Went to bed, went to sleep, and did not worry any more that day." The Trumans wouldn't have dreamed of troubling the White House kitchen, or sending out to a restaurant. As in most Depression families, caution with money had become ingrained in their lives. In his faithful weekly letter to Missouri he described how he had learned of FDR's death with humility—"When I arrived at the Pennsylvania [sic] entrance to the most famous house in America, a couple of ushers met me"—and told of problems with the Connecticut Avenue apartment: "Our furniture is still there and will be for some time. . . . But I've paid the rent for this month and will pay for another month if they don't get the old White House redecorated by that time." He ended:

> I have had a most strenuous time for the last six days. I was sworn in at 7:09 p.m. Eastern War Time Apr. 12 and it is now 9 p.m. April 18th. Six days President of the United States! It is hardly believable. This day has been a dinger, too. I'm about to go to bed, but I thought I had better write you a note. Soon as we get settled in the White House you'll both be here to visit us. Lots of love from your very much worried son and bro.
>
> HARRY

Awaiting Eleanor Roosevelt's departure, the new First Family was living out of suitcases in Blair House, diagonally across Pennsylvania Avenue from the Executive Mansion. In her diary, Margaret was breathless: "It is perfectly beautiful. All old and priceless. Visiting dignitaries stay here. Dad is the first President to do so." But then, she was always euphoric these days—"Mother, Dad and I went to the Walter Reed chapel today," reads her entry for April 22. "Then we called on General Pershing! Such *excitement!*" The pejoratives "campy" and "square" were unknown in 1945, but "corny" was, and jaded Washingtonians applied it to Margaret and her natty father, who wore double-breasted gray suits with two-toned wingtip shoes, and opened his first coast-to-coast address by forgetting Sam Rayburn, so that the Speaker had to interrupt him with a hoarse, "Wait, Harry, until I introduce you." "To err," Washington said wittily, "is Truman." Very little was known about Bess Truman until a reporter found a county employee in Independence,

Missouri, who had grown up with her. "She was a great girl," Henry P. Chiles said enthusiastically. "She was the first girl I ever knew who could whistle through her teeth."

Harry Truman was usually indifferent to criticism. Slurs on his wife and daughter were another matter. The most celebrated incident followed Margaret's debut as a professional singer in Constitution Hall. Paul Hume, the *Washington Post* music critic, wrote that the President's daughter "cannot sing very well," was "flat a good deal of the time," and "communicates almost nothing of the music she presents." Minutes after that day's copy of the *Post* reached the White House this holograph was dispatched to Hume:

> I have just seen your lousy review of Margaret's concert.... It seems to me that you are a frustrated old man.... Some day I hope to meet you. When that happens you'll need a new nose, a lot of beefsteak for black eyes, and perhaps a supporter below.
> H.S.T.

Margaret was humiliated. She told the press, "I am absolutely positive that my father wouldn't use language like that," and then ran upstairs in tears. HST humbly acknowledged that "Sometimes the frailties of the human get the better of me" (Hume opened his next recital review with "If I may venture to express an opinion"), and the episode was written off by everyone except those Republicans, Congressman Richard M. Nixon among them, who said they thought Presidents should conduct themselves with greater dignity.

To Truman's critics he was a joke, and a poor one at that. Roosevelt had at least behaved like a chief of state. He could never have forgotten himself long enough to excoriate a music critic or, as in another ill-tempered Truman missive, say that the Marine Corps had "a propaganda machine that is almost equal to Stalin's." Outside Washington, HST behaved like a Legionnaire at a national convention. In Florida he wore a white cap, crazy-colored Hawaiian shirts, and carried an outsize cane. En route to Fulton, Missouri, with Winston Churchill, he donned an engineer's cap and gaily drove the locomotive. In Kansas City he hopped into Frank Spina's barbershop and reminded Frank, "None of that fancy stuff. I don't want anything that smells." The press recorded it all, including his farewell kiss to his mother before boarding the *Sacred Cow* and her last words: "You be good, but be game, too."

In the days and weeks after FDR had been lowered into the earth at Hyde Park, no one expected much of the new President, and only a handful slowly reached the conclusion that by any standards HST was both good and game. In the White House war room, Marshall and Leahy found that they never had to tell him anything twice. Troop units, names of warships, battle plans, enemy dispositions, logistics data—he retained it all and cited it in his own concise appraisals. Before his first week had ended, he had tackled the prickly Palestine problem, was preparing for the first U.N. conference in San Francisco, had shaken up Washington's bureaucracy, and made three cabinet changes. He almost countermanded Eisenhower and sent GIs into Berlin and Prague; it was one of the few times in his life he didn't play a hunch, and the postwar history of Europe would have been far different if he had. In Moscow, Ambassador Averell Harriman, knowing almost nothing of his new boss, had boarded an embassy plane and flown across Asia, Europe, and the Atlantic—a record at the time—to be sure Truman wasn't beguiled by Stalin's deceit. On Monday, April 23, Harriman was admitted to the oval office and met the new President:

> I had talked to Mr. Truman for only a few minutes when I began to realize that this man had a real grasp of the situation. What a surprise and relief this was! He had read all the cables and reports that had passed between me and the State Department, going back for months. He knew the facts and the sequence of events, and he had a keen understanding of what they meant.

Roosevelt had tried to charm the Russians. Truman was blunt. When V. M. Molotov entered the oval office with Andrei Gromyko, the President said briskly that the United States and the United Kingdom had observed every Yalta covenant, but that honoring vows wasn't a one-way street. Molotov replied that the Soviet Union had been equally faithful to its word. Not in Poland, it hadn't, Truman shot back, and he wanted Molotov to know here and now that as long as Red puppets sat in eastern Europe, Poland would not be admitted to the U.N. Moreover, he hoped that sentiment would be conveyed to Stalin in exactly those words. Molotov answered indignantly, "I have never been talked to in my life like this." Truman said dryly, "Carry out your agreements and you won't get talked to like this." Afterward Harriman, who had lurked in the background, recalled, "He got quite rough with Molotov, so much so, in fact, that I was becoming a little concerned. But I must say I was quite proud of the new President."

Back from Hyde Park, Truman had invited Byrnes to join the new cabinet as Secretary of State, and Byrnes, in the President's words, "almost jumped down my throat taking me up on it." Dean Acheson, the new Undersecretary of State, wrote his son on April 30, "The new President has done an excellent job." By chance, he went on, he and Truman had spoken at length just two days before Roosevelt's death, and Acheson had "for the first time got a definite impression of him. He is straightforward, decisive, simple, entirely honest. . . . I think he will learn fast and will inspire confidence. It seems to me a blessing that he is the President and not Henry Wallace."

Marshall, Leahy, Harriman, and Acheson were among the early converts. Others took longer, and some had to be all but struck on the head with a blunt instrument, a skill at which HST was proficient. He had decided to appoint an old Missouri friend, John W. Snyder, as Federal Loan Administrator, and he called in Jesse Jones, the former head of the agency, to tell him the news. Jones was startled. He had expected to be consulted. He asked, "Did the President make the appointment before he died?"

"No," replied Truman. "He made it just now."

In late April the *Geneva Tribune* ran a headline: EVENTS SEEM TO BE SUCCEEDING ONE ANOTHER WITH GREAT RAPIDITY. They certainly were. The Führer's death was announced May 1, and that evening Julie Andrews saw London alight after dark for the second time. Berlin fell May 2. Later in the day the Germans in Italy surrendered. Two days later Wehrmacht commanders capitulated in Holland, Denmark, and northwest Germany. Then, on May 7, General Alfred Jodl and his staff signed unconditional surrender documents at Reims while Field Marshal Wilhelm Keitel was going through the same painful ceremonies under the eye of Soviet Marshal Georgi Zhukov in Berlin. It was a half-hour before midnight. For the first time in modern history the entire armed forces of a nation, officers and enlisted men alike, on land, at sea, and in the air, had become prisoners of war. During the following week all commanders in all armies moved troops, had orders cut, and synchronized watches for a common cease-fire, and suddenly it was V-E Day—May 8, 1945, Harry Truman's sixty-first birthday. The President was on the air at 9 A.M. (Churchill in London and Stalin in Moscow were giving their people the news at the same instant). His first words were, "The Allied Armies, through sacrifice and devotion and with God's help . . ." Hardly anyone remembered what he said after that. They were in the streets, in Times Square, hurling bales of ticker tape out Wall Street windows, dancing in the Chicago Loop, on Boston Common, at Hollywood and Vine, around Indianapolis's war monument and on Washington's Mall, on campuses and in war plants, wherever there was room to dance and sometimes where there was none: department store windows, telephone booths, elevators. Men wanted to kiss, women wanted to be kissed, and for one long moment they felt entitled to forget that other, more complicated war with an empire larger than Germany's and even more determined to fight on until every member of its race was extinct—taking with them the largest possible number of Japan's enemies. V-E Day hadn't dampened Tokyo's morale. The emperor was still divine; sacrificing your life in his name continued to be a guarantee of immortality. To all peace feelers Tokyo made the same reply; capitulation was and always would be out of the question.

History had been moving at breakneck speed since the relief of Bastogne on December 26, and since the momentum was to continue through September, survivors of that time are understandably hazy about the sequence of events. Many had no time for news anyhow. Fighting men were still in replacement centers, canteens, hospitals, cockpits, or on warships. They were mourning their dead, convalescing from military surgery, rereading mail from home, collecting autographs for short snorters, fighting boredom. At home their wives and mothers welcomed home crippled GIs or pored anxiously over casualty lists. In these circumstances, commentators often spoke to deaf audiences, piles of newspapers were thrown out unread, and months merged into a bewildering kaleidoscope.

Earthshaking events had passed in a blur. The United Nations Charter had been signed in San Francisco. Winston Churchill, in American eyes the very embodiment of indomitable Britain, was swept out of office in a Labour party landslide. MacArthur reconquered the Philippine archipelago. Fantastic drugs (drug was a benign word then) were emerging from war laboratories. For the first time in eleven years Fiorello La Guardia was no longer mayor of New York, and the familiar old Bond sign was coming down in

Times Square. Americans scarcely had time to comprehend the pilotless V-2 buzz bombs when they were confronted by reports of the slaughter of six million Jews in Nazi killing centers, of Japan's kamikaze ("divine wind") pilots, who loaded their warplanes and then dove into U.S. ships, and finally—this time at American hands—of the annihilation of two Japanese cities, the first of them the size of Denver and the second larger than Newark.

V-E Day had aroused hope west of Hawaii, but little elation. The ETO had been somebody else's war; in the islands its chief significance lay in the promise of early reinforcement from Europe. Pacific veterans recited doggerel: "Home alive in '45," "Back in the sticks in '46," "Back to heaven in '47," "Golden Gate in '48." Barring a million-dollar wound (serious enough to make a soldier unfit for combat but fit for anything else), the men facing Japan were reconciled to the hard fact that expectations of returning home in '45, '46, or even in '47 were unrealistic. Most of them would have settled for '48; the chances of falling with an unlucky, mortal wound were growing with each battle. In Washington the Joint Chiefs agreed. The capture of Iwo Jima, less than eight square miles of volcanic ash, had cost 25,849 marines, a third of the landing force. Okinawa's price had been 49,151; kamikazes diving from the skies over Okinawa had sunk 34 U.S. warships and damaged another 368. If the Japanese could draw that much blood in the outer islands of their defense perimeter, how formidable would they be on the 142,007 square miles of their five home islands, where they would be joined —as they had been on Saipan—by every member of the civilian population old enough to carry a hand grenade?*

The Joint Chiefs had made an educated guess, based on the Yalta guarantee that Anglo-American forces would receive full support from the Red Army. Assuming a November 1 landing on Kyushu and a midwinter invasion of Honshu, the number of battle deaths, it was anticipated, would eclipse all other U.S. casualty lists, ETO and Pacific, combined. In the February 1947 *Harper's,* Stimson wrote: "I was informed that such operations might be expected to cost over a million casualties to American forces alone." (Total U.S.

---

* Japan comprises four main islands, Kyushu, Honshu, Shikoku, and Hokkaido. Tokyo is in southeastern Honshu. In 1945 the population of these four was 72,598,077. When Radio Tokyo spoke of "one hundred million" Japanese, they were including such settled colonies as Saipan, mandated to the emperor by the Treaty of Versailles.

Pacific losses in World War II in breaching Japan's outer perimeter of defense were 170,596.) General MacArthur was less optimistic. So far, he pointed out, GIs and marines had been fighting isolated island garrisons, cut off from reinforcements. The vast mass of the Imperial Japanese Army, between five and six million troops with thousands of tons of ammunition stowed in underground caves, had never been defeated in battle. They were being brought home from China to defend the sacred soil of Dai Nippon, and were digging in. Unless the Japanese islands were to be blockaded and the people left to starve—the least humane of all solutions—that force must be met and defeated. MacArthur predicted the greatest bloodletting in history. He expected to take 50,000 casualties just in establishing that November 1 beachhead. Before an assault on Honshu could be contemplated, Allied navies must devise some way of protecting themselves against the 5,350 kamikazes known to be waiting in underground hangars, prepared to take that many vessels down with them. Finally, MacArthur warned Washington, all contact with an organized enemy might disappear. The Japs might fade into the mountains to fight as guerrillas. If they made that choice in Japan he predicted a ten-year war with no ceiling on Allied losses.

It was with this prospect that President Truman prepared for the coming conference in the Brandenburg city of Potsdam, seventeen miles southwest of Berlin. He *had* to have the Red Army. When Patton declared to a British audience that the U.K. and the U.S. must weld bonds of postwar friendship "because undoubtedly it is our destiny to rule the world," Stimson quickly told the press that the general spoke only for himself. U.S. newspaper editorials urged Patton to confine his public remarks to "Forward, men," "Fix bayonets," and "Open fire." Had Russia not been America's ally, General Marshall told the press, twice as many GIs would have been needed in the ETO, and General Eisenhower flew to the Kremlin to further cement bonds between Moscow and Washington. The marshals admired him, the commissars liked him, and Joseph Stalin beamed on his distinguished guest. The Soviet dictator presented Ike with a photograph of himself and saw to it that the American general was invested with the Order of Suvorov and Order of Victory. The second of these was a magnificent ornament. With the possible exception of a gold sword trimmed with pearls from Queen Wilhelmina of Holland, it was the most expensive award Eisenhower ever received. Star-shaped and platinum, the medal was three inches in diameter and was set with ninety-one matched sixteen-carat diamonds. It is a historic irony that the holder of this decoration would later preside over an America in which men who had been favored in any way by the Soviet Union would lose their jobs, be browbeaten by congressional committees, and hounded in the streets by their neighbors. But in 1945 all that lay in the future. This was an era of good feeling between the world's two new superpowers. In pleasing Stalin, Eisenhower served his country well, and if two columns of cosmic fire had not intervened that summer, his service might have been even greater.

Stalin was a busy man then, entertaining the Allied supreme commander at the Kremlin, taking the new President's measure in Potsdam, and studying intelligence reports on the untried American super weapon known to the British as "tube alloys," to Stimson as X, to the Joint Chiefs as S-1, to a select few at Oak Ridge as S-Y, and among an even smaller number of scientists in the Los Alamos Tech Area—where the thing existed—as "the gadget."

The crowning achievement of scientific wisdom, the most expensive piece of hardware ever built, it had been designed to become the most efficient instrument of mass murder in history—if, of course, it worked; no one could be sure in advance. Meanwhile military security, unaware of the Fuchs-Gold-Rosenberg-Greenglass leaks, was keeping a tight lid not only on details, but also on the gadget's very existence. Early that spring seventy-five picked fliers had been ordered to Wendover Field in Utah, where they formed the 509th Composite Group of the 313th Wing of the 21st Bombing Command of the 20th Air Force. None of them knew the 509th's mission. All were volunteers, but when they asked just what it was they had volunteered for, they were told that they belonged to an organization which was "going to do something different."

They already knew that. Their flight maneuvers were highly unusual. One B-29 would simulate a high-level raid alone while two others watched for unusual weather, especially electrical storms. The lone raider would carry no blockbusters, the huge high-explosive demolition bombs dropped by normal B-29s. Instead it would be loaded with a large, oddly shaped missile armed with ordinary explosives. In point of fact, the missile was a precise reproduction of the shell of the Los Alamos device, constructed from blueprints while the first bomb was being perfected. The 509th didn't know what to make of it, and remained ignorant when sent overseas to Tinian, within easy bombing range of Japan. Here maneuvers were resumed while Dr. Philip Morrison, a young nuclear physicist, supervised the building of an advance laboratory on the island. The fliers weren't introduced to Morrison; for all they knew, he might have been the planner of a new PX. To add to their frustration, they were receiving warnings against hazards which, to their knowledge, didn't exist. Apparently someone in Washington thought they were all in danger of going blind; they were instructed to wear welders' goggles when airborne and never to look in the direction of a target after the bombardier had emptied the bomb bay.

Each evening at dusk other B-29s took off for Japan, and Dr. Morrison later told a Senate Committee: "We came often to sit on top of the coral ridge and watch the combat strike of the 313th Wing in real awe. Most of the planes would return the next morning, standing in a long single line, like beads on a chain, from just overhead to the horizon. You could see ten or twelve planes at a time, spaced a couple of miles apart. As fast as the next plane would land, another would appear at the edge of the sky. There were always the same number of planes in sight. The empty field would fill up, and in an hour or two all the planes would have come in."

To Morrison it was a majestic sight; to the 509th Composite Group it was a daily humiliation. They were all crack airmen, and leisure was eroding their morale. Tokyo Rose had greeted their unit by name when it arrived on Tinian; maybe *she* knew. Worst of all were the taunts from other fliers in the 313th who nightly dodged flak over the Empire, as B-29 crews called Japan. Some never came back, some returned wounded, while all the 509th did was cruise over tracts of the Empire so barren and strategically useless that the airmen never encountered antiaircraft fire. Now and then they would be told to drop a bomb—one lonely little bomb. It was demeaning, it was bewildering, and to compound their indignity a bombardier from another group mocked them in verse:

> *Into the air the secret rose,*
> *Where they're going, nobody knows.*
> *Tomorrow they'll return again,*
> *But we'll never know where they've been.*
> *Don't ask us about results or such,*

Unless you want to get in Dutch.
But take it from one who knows the score,
The 509th is winning the war.

Tokyo Rose, with her omnipresent sources, picked up the satire. Take it from one who knew the score, she laughed, the 509th was winning the war.

Late in May the pariahs of Tinian were joined by a towering civilian named Luis W. Alvarez. Although no one on the island knew it or would have believed it, Alvarez had risked his life more often than any of them; working in remote canyons far from the mesa where the living quarters and Tech Area of Los Alamos stood, he had perfected the complex release mechanism of the gadget. He called it a "gun-type" contrivance—that is, a bomb in which one hemisphere of U-235 would be shot as a bullet into the second U-235 hemisphere. The Alvarez device, now accurate to one millionth of a second, completed technology's answer to the challenge posed a year and a half earlier under the empty stands of Alonzo Stagg stadium in Chicago.

This is what the bomb looked like in the spring of 1945, and these were its secrets:

Black, whale-shaped, and exquisitely machined, it was 28 inches in diameter and ten feet long. The entire assembly weighed 9,000 pounds; most of it was ballast. Its uranium core weighed only 22 pounds. (If 100 percent efficiency had been achieved, only 2.2 pounds would have been required, but in those primitive days even 10 percent effectiveness was an impressive achievement.) Not only were the 22 pounds, or 10 kilograms, separated to make a premature buildup of the critical mass impossible; it was also important that they be unequal. The "bullet" part was perhaps five pounds, the "target" about seventeen. Obviously the shield dividing the two was crucial. The prime requisite of this shield, or envelope, was that it deflect the fast neutrons which would split U-235 atoms. If the shield failed, the 509th wouldn't win anything, because it would be blown into oblivion—together with its hecklers and the entire island of Tinian. In the Chicago pile purified graphite had served the neutron-resistant function. But building a bomb was far more difficult than a pile. When Germany's nuclear physicists first heard that America had exploded a nuclear weapon, Goudsmit reported, they "believed that what we had dropped on Hiroshima was a complete uranium pile." Because graphite was impractical in a portable missile, the Allied scientists in New Mexico had spent months searching for some other neutron-resistant substance to serve as what was called in the Los Alamos Tech Area the "tamper." The tamper had to be a metal of high density. Gold was a possibility, and at one point Oppenheimer had seriously considered asking for some. An alloy proved to be just as useful, and so twin wombs were woven around the two U-235 eggs, with layer after layer of shrapnel outside, until the completed device would occupy most of the space in a B-29 bomb bay. Contrary to widespread belief later, the bomb was not to be parachuted to its target. B-29s flew high enough and fast enough to permit pilots and crews to escape, so the missile was to be dropped free. It would never reach the ground, however. To achieve maximum effect, the Alvarez mechanism would trigger the explosion in the air above the target area, or, as the target was called in Los Alamos jargon, "Zero." The actual fuse was the lens David Greenglass had sketched for Harry Gold on papers now in Moscow. At that fantastic micromoment when it was touched off by remote control, the neutrons would build up so rapidly that the explosion would take place in one-tenth of a millionth of a second.

Whatever his private misgivings, General Groves had to assume that the gadget wouldn't misfire. He was a soldier and a committed man; after the expenditure of two billion dollars which had been hidden from Congress in countless appropriation bills, he had no intention of writing the project off on any grounds. As early as December 30, 1944, when Bastogne was still on half-rations and flags of the rising sun flapped confidently over Iwo Jima and Okinawa, Groves had written General Marshall that he felt "reasonably certain" a gun-type bomb would be operational at some point during the coming year. At that time Groves thought preliminary testing would be unnecessary. He estimated that the first bomb would be ready about August 1, 1945, the second by January 1, 1946, and the third at some later date, as yet undetermined.

On April 24 President Truman received his first complete briefing on the Manhattan Project from Stimson and Groves in the oval office. The President received them standing, and then, after he had heard it all, he abruptly sat down. The scenario had been changed somewhat, Stimson told him. A test would be held in the uninhabited desert near Los Alamos around the middle of July. If it succeeded, Stimson said, the test device would yield the equivalent of 500 tons of TNT, while the first "operational" bomb would be twice as powerful, yielding the equivalent of 1,000 tons. If anything were needed to show how little these men understood the evil jinni waiting to be born, these figures should suffice, for the test would reveal that the real force locked in that first missile would exceed 20,000 TNT tons. Even so, Truman was wary of it. His first decision on the bomb, reached toward the end of that April 24 briefing, was to order a search for other choices. The hunt would be conducted by two teams, an interim committee of soldiers and civilians and a scientific panel. On May 31 and June 1 the two met together—and discovered that each group while working independently had reached the same conclusions.

Moral implications were not ignored. The interim committee (whose members included Stimson, General Marshall, James F. Byrnes, Vannevar Bush, Karl T. Compton, and President James Bryant Conant of Harvard) was sensitive to the fact that atomic energy could not be "considered simply in terms of military weapons" but must also be viewed "in terms of a new relationship to the universe." At the same time, the investigators were aware that every industrialized nation had its community of atomic physicists; nuclear arms were on the way, whatever the United States decided. Both the interim committee and the scientific committee (Oppenheimer, Fermi, E. O. Lawrence, and Arthur H. Compton) had studied the likeliest alternatives to operational use—a detailed advance warning or a demonstration in some uninhabited area. Both were rejected as infeasible. The nature of atomic explosions was still unfamiliar. Even the forthcoming Los Alamos test, if successful, would not guarantee that a missile would detonate when dropped from a B-29. The desert test would be static. It would tell the technicians nothing about the problem of exploding a bomb at a predetermined height by a complex, untried mechanism. Operational failure was a very real possibility, and if the Americans warned the Japanese and then dropped a dud, enemy morale would stiffen, intensifying last-ditch resistance. Finally, the Americans had no bombs to waste. Apart from the static apparatus to be exploded in the desert, there were just two, bearing the names "The Thin Man" and "The Fat Man."

On June 1, therefore, the President's advisers recommended that the bomb "should be used against Japan as soon as possible," that it be directed at a dual target—a military installation near other buildings more susceptible to damage—and that it should be dropped "without prior warning." The four scientists submitted a unanimous opinion: "We can promise no technical demonstration likely to bring an end to the war; we see no acceptable alternative to direct military use." In a subsequent memorandum to the President, Stimson wrote: "Once started in actual invasion"—preparations for which would have begun instantly if Truman vetoed use of the bomb—"we shall in my opinion have to go through with an even more bitter finish fight than in Germany. I think that the attempt . . . will tend to produce a fusion of race solidarity and antipathy which has no analogy in the case of Germany." Writing a year later in the Atlantic, Karl Compton said of the bomb, "I believe that no man could have failed to use it and afterwards looked his countrymen in the face." Compton was not blind to the horror of Hiroshima's 80,000 dead. He did suggest, however, that critics should remember the fire storms of Dresden and Hamburg and the two B-29 incendiary raids over Tokyo, one of which killed 125,000 Japanese and the other nearly 100,000. If morality was to be judged by statistics, he implied, the men who decided to use nuclear weapons against Japan were far from being the war's greatest war criminals.

On Friday, July 13, exactly three months after Franklin Roosevelt's death in Warm Springs, the U-235 hemispheres, the tamper, and the detonator for the test device left Los Alamos from the Tech Area's "back door," a secret road leading to Site S, a stretch of semidesert fifty miles from Alamogordo, New Mexico. The nearest village was called Obscuro—Spanish for "dark"—and natives knew the site itself as Jornada del Muerto—"Death Tract." The coincidence evoked no gallows humor from the nuclear physicists. They knew they were taking a giant step into the unknown. The warnings to the 509th about lightning had not been fanciful. It was the one imponderable in equations. A stray bolt from an electrical storm could atomize all of them, and since the outer limits of a chain reaction were unknown, conceivably the entire planet might be destroyed. The weight of scientific opinion was against it, but no one could be sure. They drove past Obscuro in the dark, and no one said much.

In the middle of the Jornada del Muerto a 100-foot frame of iron scaffolding had been built against the facade of an old farmhouse. The bomb core would be fitted inside the house, but only at the last moment. The fear of lightning had increased. July was a bad month for thunderstorms in this barren wasteland, and a few days earlier, after a conventional bomb had been strung up here during a rehearsal, a bolt of forked light had struck and exploded it. The scaffolding and farmhouse were absolute Zero. Dr. Robert F. Bacher, head of the Los Alamos Bomb Physics Division, was inside putting the real thing together when, at about dusk, he had a bad moment. Every component had been machine-tooled to the finest measurement, and one of them got stuck in another. He waited, tried again, waited again, tried once more, and in it went, perfecting the mesh.

Oppenheimer and the rest of the scientific command waited, watches in hand, in a bunker ten miles to the southwest, while two B-29s cruising overhead radioed weather conditions. The Oppenheimer bunker, S-10, was the control center and general headquarters. Three other forts of reinforced concrete had been built at other points of the compass, each 10,000 yards from Zero. Preliminary plans had called for a 4 A.M. shot, but the weather was playing hob with the schedule; every time the skies cleared, the B-29s reported new flashes on the horizon. The shot was postponed until 5:30 A.M. That held; the storms vanished. At 5:29:15 on July 16—forty-five seconds before the dawn of the Atomic Age—a University of California physicist flipped a switch activating a master transmitter, which set off second- and third-generation transmitters as each prearranged cumulation of electrons moved into position at exactly the right microsecond.

5:29:50.

A voice rang out, "Zero minus ten seconds!" It was the first countdown. Wordlessly lips formed in the new ritual—5:29:51, 5:29:52, 5:29:53, 5:29:54, 5:29:55, 5:29:56, 5:29:57, 5:29:58, 5:29:59—

At 5:30 everything happened at once. Human beings cannot distinguish between millionths of a second, so no one saw the first flash of atomic fire. They did see its dazzling reflection on far hills. All of them went into mild shock—Oppenheimer was clinging to an upright in his bunker—and thirty seconds later they were jarred again as a wind of hurricane force, followed by a deafening roar, swept the desert. Meanwhile the rising emanation in the sky over

Zero stunned and silenced its creators. It was, wrote William L. Laurence:

> ... a sunrise such as the world had never seen, a great green supersun climbing in a fraction of a second to a height of more than eight thousand feet, rising ever higher until it touched the clouds, lighting up earth and sky all around with a dazzling luminosity. Up it went, a great ball of fire about a mile in diameter, changing colors as it kept shooting upward, from deep purple to orange, expanding, growing bigger, rising as it expanded, an elemental force freed from its bonds after being chained for billions of years. For a fleeting instant the color was unearthly green, such as one sees only in the corona of the sun during a total eclipse. It was as though the earth had opened and the skies had split. One felt as though one were present at the moment of creation when God said: "Let there be light."

Up and up it went, a giant column whose internal pressures found relief in a supramundane mushroom, then up, then another mushroom, finally disappearing into the night sky at an altitude of 41,000 feet, higher than Mount Everest. Oppenheimer was reminded of two passages from the Bhagavad-Gita: "If the radiance of a thousand suns were to burst into the sky, that would be the splendor of the Mighty One" and "I am become Death, the shatterer of worlds." Others groped for words. "Good God!" a senior officer croaked. "I believe those long-haired boys have lost control!" One jubilant physicist shouted, "The sun can't hold a candle to it!" It was literally true: at 5:30 the temperature at Zero had been one hundred million degrees Fahrenheit, three times the temperature in the interior of the sun and ten thousand times the heat on its surface. Sleeping Americans in New Mexico and western Texas had been wakened by the mysterious flash and then frightened as the storm wind blew angrily against their windowpanes.

At Zero nothing could be seen. Fermi, advancing toward it in a Sherman tank lined with lead, gathered earth samples with a mechanical scoop for laboratory examination, but a thorough study had to be postponed; the radiation was too great. When the scientists could enter safely, they found that all life, plant and animal, including rattlesnakes, cacti and desert grass, had been destroyed within a mile of Zero. An antelope herd which the B-29s had spotted miles from the blast had vanished, and the skin of cattle in other parts of New Mexico had developed gray spots. A thirty-two-ton steel tower eight hundred yards from Zero was now a snarled wreck. Around Zero itself sand had been hammered into the desert like a white-hot saucer eight hundred yards in diameter. It wasn't even sand any more. The heat had turned it into a jade-green substance unknown to man but resembling a heavy, unbreakable plastic. The farmhouse and the scaffolding were gone, just gone. They had been transformed into gas and blown away.

General Groves, the first to regain his composure, said to his deputy, "The war's over. One or two of those things and Japan will be finished." The scientists standing around them said little, but one of them crossed his fingers, since "One or two" was all they had. The code name for the Los Alamos test had been Trinity, an allusion to the three gadgets-in-being. If Tokyo guessed the truth (and one of the emperor's warlords was later to suspect it) America's position would be difficult. The better part of a year would pass before any other missile could be readied. Two blasts now, however, just might bring instant peace.

Only one man could make the next decision. Preparation for the test had been in final stages when President Truman sailed for Potsdam. As he later noted in his memoirs, he had been "anxiously awaiting word on the results" because "no one was certain of the outcome of this full-scale atomic explosion." On the morning of July 16 two messages in improvised code reached Potsdam by courier plane. The first was from General Groves to the presidential party: "Operated on this morning. Diagnosis not yet complete but results seem satisfactory and already exceed expectations." The second was addressed to Churchill on the personal stationery of the Secretary of War. Stimson had written, "Babies satisfactorily born." The prime minister muttered, "This is the Second Coming, in wrath." According to Truman's recollection, he "casually mentioned" to Marshal Stalin that the United States had developed "a new weapon of unusual destructive force." The Russian, who might have filled him in on a few details, evinced little interest. He merely replied that he was glad to hear it and hoped the Americans would make "good use of it against the Japanese."

On his desk top in the oval office Truman had put a small sign: "The buck stops here." This buck was now his; he could pass it to no one. His *ad hoc* committee of advisers had just cabled its final conclusion: WE CAN PROPOSE NO TECHNICAL DEMONSTRATION LIKELY

TO BRING AN END TO THE WAR. WE CAN SEE NO ACCEPTABLE ALTERNATIVE TO DIRECT MILITARY USE. As Truman saw it, he had no options. His military advisers were already urging him to let them press forward with what he called "the existing plans for the invasion of the Japanese home islands."

On July 24, eight days later, the President tentatively approved atomic strikes: "The 509th Composite Group, 20th Air Force, will deliver its first special bomb as soon as weather will permit visual bombing after about 3 August 1945, on one of the targets: Hiroshima, Kokura, Niigata and Nagasaki. . . ." In print it looked cold-blooded to Truman. Stimson agreed. As early as June 19 the Secretary of War had written in his diary that a "last-chance warning" must be given to Tokyo. On the President's initiative, he, Churchill and Chiang Kai-shek broadcast to the Japanese what subsequently became known as the Potsdam Declaration. Its first seven points gave detailed assurances of humane treatment, no recriminations, a Japanese "new order of peace, security and justice," freedom of speech, religion, and thought; new industry, "participation in world trade relations," and a limited occupation of strategic points in the home islands—an occupation which would swiftly end once stability had been achieved. The eighth and last point called upon Tokyo to proclaim unconditional surrender of all its armed forces. The alternative, the declaration warned, was "prompt and utter destruction."

In Tokyo the broadcast aroused mixed feelings. There were those who read in it a promise to let the Japanese determine their own form of government after American troops were withdrawn, and they were right; that was precisely what Truman was trying to tell them. But the samurai influence was too strong. Foreign Minister Shigenori Togo favored a waiting game, arguing that no answer at all would be preferable to the flat rejection which the military men in the cabinet could force. Then the premier, Admiral Baron K. Suzuki, blundered. During a July 28 press conference he called the Potsdam Declaration a rehash of old proposals, beneath Japanese contempt. Byrnes told correspondents that this was "disheartening." Truman, hoping against hope that the enemy would reconsider, delayed giving the green light to Tinian until August 2, when he was back on the U.S.S. *Augusta* and sailing home. Then the orders were coded and radioed more than halfway round the world. The point of no return had been passed.

The Thin Man had been flown to Tinian in three Superforts, and on the afternoon of Sunday, August 5, it hung, partially assembled, in the bomb bay of the B-29 *Enola Gay*, flagship of Colonel Paul W. Tibbetts Jr., commanding officer of the 509th Composite Group, who had named the plane for his mother long ago. In less than twenty-four hours, he was told, he and his plane would enter history. By now his men had guessed that their days of ennui were over. Jeeps raced back and forth, bearing brass. Brigadier General T. F. Farrell, Groves's deputy, had just arrived from Los Alamos and was explaining the gadget to Captain William S. Parsons, a naval ordnance expert who would ride to the Empire tomorrow aboard the *Enola Gay*. The more Parsons heard, the more he frowned. Since reaching the island he had seen several B-29s crack up in taking off. If that happened to a Superfort with an assembled bomb aboard it would become the most spectacular accident of all time. Farrell said they would just have to pray that there would be no crash. "Well," Parsons persisted, "if I made the final assembly of the bomb after we left the island, that couldn't happen." Farrell asked, "Have you ever assembled a bomb like this before?" Parsons said no, but he had all day to learn. His decision meant he would be the only man on the *Enola Gay* who knew all the gadget's secrets. Through a fluke he might wind up in enemy hands. As insurance against that, he borrowed a pistol from a young intelligence officer.

That evening the 509th was ordered to meet in its assembly hall, and there, for the first time, Colonel Tibbetts told them their purpose: "We are going on a mission to drop a bomb different from any you have ever seen or heard about. The bomb contains a destructive force of twenty thousand tons of TNT."

He paused, awaiting questions. There were none. The fliers looked stricken.

An extraordinary weapon, he went on, called for extraordinary tactics. That was why their maneuvers had been so peculiar. In a few hours, at 1:45 A.M., three Superforts would take off for the Empire. They would relay weather reports over targets and alternate targets. At 2:45 the second three B-29s would take off. He would be driving the *Enola Gay*, the strike plane, and his two escorts would rendezvous with him over Iwo Jima fifteen minutes after dawn. Then they would go in together. There was a final briefing at midnight, reviewing reports from Los Alamos and explaining why a naval ordnance captain would be aboard the lead bomber. Then the men lay sleepless, most of them wondering whether Captain Parsons could really put the bomb together in the air, Parsons wondering more than any of them.

It was almost a milk run. Dodging large cumulus clouds south of the Bonins, they sailed under starlight until dawn, picked up their escorts at the Iwo tryst, and then soared northwest in the big left-hand turn toward Japan. Apart from a high thin cirrus, the overarching sky was cloudless, cerulean—and free of enemy aircraft. The crew had become restless; there was little conversation and no banter.

Something of their mood is preserved in a Dear-Mom-and-Dad letter written during the flight by Captain Robert A. Lewis, Tibbetts's copilot. "At 4:30," he wrote on the plane, "we saw signs of a late moon in the east. I think everyone will feel relieved when we have left our bomb with the Japs and get half way home. Or, better still, all the way home." The first sign of daybreak came at five o'clock. Nearly an hour later Lewis wrote, "It looks at this time (5:51) that we will have clear sailing for a long spell. Tom Ferebee" —the bombardier—"has been very quiet and methinks he is mentally back in the midwest part of the old U.S.A." A minute later: "It is 5:52 and we are only a few miles from Iwo Jima. We are beginning to climb to a new altitude, at which we will remain until we are about one hour away from the Empire."

Over Honshu Parsons silently set about arming the device. Copilot Lewis's handwriting became jagged and cramped: ". . . Captain Parsons has put the final touches on his assembly job. We are now loaded. The bomb is alive. It is a funny feeling knowing it is right in back of you. Knock wood." Then: "We have set the automatic. We have reached proper altitude. . . . Not long now, folks. . . ."

They had a clear, straight, four-mile run over the target. Ferebee's eye was concentrated on the sight's cross hairs. At 9:15 he pressed his toggle, releasing the single missile. It descended in less than sixty seconds—timepieces below, some of them wristwatches later found on severed arms, confirmed the time—and as it fell its delicately adjusted cams and mechanisms moved faultlessly toward ignition. Captain Lewis had just written his parents: "There will be a short intermission while we bomb our target." Then he scrawled wildly: *"My God!"*

Through their welder's goggles they first saw a tiny point of purplish-red fire, which within a millisecond expanded to a purple fireball a half-mile wide. The whole monstrous seething mass of red and purple fire rose, accompanied by vast gray smoke rings encircling the column of flames until, at ten thousand feet, the seething mass roiled outward to form the first mushroom. The base of the column was now three miles; it was sucking what was left of the city toward Zero and cremating everything combustible. At 50,000 feet the cloud's second mushroom appeared. Taking evasive action from time to time, the *Enola Gay* and its two escorting Superforts snapped photographs and fled. Even after they had put 270 miles between them and Hiroshima they could still see the mushroom cloud entering the stratosphere and flashing every color in the spectrum.

At 9:20 Tibbetts had radioed Tinian: "Mission successful." Successful hardly seemed the right word, but no word was right. Suddenly Tibbetts realized that the 509th fliers would be kings of Tinian. Nobody back at field would mock them any more, and in America millions would believe they had won, or soon would win, the war. But something had been lost too. Hiroshima, a thriving city of 344,000 people at 9:14 A.M., had by 9:16 A.M. lost 60,175 in dead and missing. Four square miles of civilization had been vaporized. In Washington President Truman was soon announcing, "Sixteen hours ago an American airplane dropped one bomb on Hiroshima. . . . It is a harnessing of the basic power of the universe. The force from which the sun draws its power has been loosed against those who brought war to the Far East." That was correct, but when he added that America had "spent two billion dollars on the biggest scientific gamble in history—and won," it was wrong. To speak of such slaughter as a winning bet was tasteless. In savage irony, imprisoned Hermann Göring put it better. "A mighty accomplishment," he said. "I don't want anything to do with it."

Much indelicacy and outright vulgarity of those first days of the Atomic Age can be set down to incomprehension. The concept was too big, it couldn't be grasped at once. It was one thing to say that under the Einstein formula a single gram of matter, four-tenths the weight of a dime, would lift a million-ton load to the crest of a mountain six miles high, or that a breath of air could fuel a powerful airplane, flying day and night, for a year. Accepting the facts was something else. Burlesque queens who advertised themselves as "anatomic bombs," and Sam Goldwyn's unfortunate quip, "That A-bomb, that's dynamite!" betrayed as much ignorance of nuclear fission as the farmer in Newport, Arkansas, who wrote the nonexistent "Atomic Bomb Co." at Oak Ridge, "I have some stumps in my field that I should like to blow out. Have you any atomic bombs the right size for the job? If you have, let me know by return mail, and let me know how much they cost. I think I should like them better than dynamite." Thousands who laughed at the Arkansas rube knew as little about a chain reaction as he did, and many more couldn't, or wouldn't, credit it. William L. Laurence of the *New York Times*, preparing to accompany the second atomic bomb to Nagasaki, eyed the Fat Man with wonder. He thought it "so exquisitely shaped that any sculptor would have been proud to have created it," and although he had witnessed the Alamogordo desert test he asked himself, "Could it be that this innocent-looking object, so beautifully designed, so safe to handle, would in much less time than it takes to wink an eye annihilate an entire city and its population?" It could, it had, and on August 9 it did it again, destroying 35,000 lives in the second target city. Even then there were doubters. On Tinian Lieutenant General Carl Spaatz, commander of the Pacific Strategic Air Command, examined the dimensions of the case in which the U-235 destined for Nagasaki had been brought from New Mexico. "Of course," he said to Dr. Charles P. Baker of Cornell, "the atoms in the material carried in here served as a fuse that set off the atoms of the air over Nagasaki." "Oh no, General!" said Baker. "The explosion came entirely from the material in this case." General Spaatz stared at him. "Young man," he said, "you may believe it. I don't."

Returning from Nagasaki, the second crew of atomic bombers learned that Russia was invading Manchuria. B-29s were ranging over the Japanese homeland, sowing the air with millions of pamphlets:

TO THE JAPANESE PEOPLE

America asks that you take immediate heed of what we say on this leaflet.

We are in possession of the most destructive force ever devised by man . . .

The message warned, "We have just begun to use this weapon against your homeland"; advised readers to cease resistance before they were all exterminated; and urged them to "petition the Emperor to end the war." It made Occidental sense but bewildered Orientals. Hirohito was a god, not a politician. Gods are not swayed by appeals and referendums. Besides, propaganda was unnecessary now. Confronted by declarations of war from every other major power on earth, the Japanese government was past the point of reason. Various emotional tides were tugging it in different directions. The great struggle was between those who wanted to live and those who wanted to die, and only much later did American scholars discover how close to fulfillment the national death wish had come.

Hirohito, like Hitler, had an air-raid shelter in the ground beneath his palace, and it was there, amid scenes of passion and acrimony, that many of the most crucial meetings were held in that second week of August. In the beginning the government had very little information about the pulverization of Hiroshima. Throughout August 6 Tokyo had been unable to establish routine communications with the city, and no one knew why. At dawn next day Lieutenant General T. Kawabe, deputy chief of the army general staff, received a single-sentence report that made no sense to him: "The whole city of Hiroshima was destroyed instantly by a single bomb." Subsequent details sounded to Kawabe like ravings. Later accounts to the contrary, Hiroshima had not been without military significance; the Japanese Second Army had been quartered there. At 9:15 August 6 the entire army had been doing calisthenics on a huge parade ground. The Thin Man had exploded almost directly overhead, wiping it out. That was one of the messages which reached Kawabe. It was as though the Pentagon had been informed that the United States Marine Corps had been annihilated in less than a second while turning somersaults.

Although unable to build nuclear weapons themselves, the Japanese did have one nuclear physicist of international distinction, Yoshio Nishina. Nishina was summoned before the Japanese general staff at nine o'clock that morning and provided with a summary of the situation in Hiroshima. While out of touch with his colleagues abroad since Pearl Harbor, he had been worried about the possibility of a nuclear weapon and had even written out rough estimates of the damage such a weapon could do. It corresponded with everything he was told now, and he said so. This offered the generals little solace, and they dismissed him. Later, a reporter from Domei, the official Nippon news agency, called at Nishina's laboratory. The Americans were circulating stories that they had atomic bombs, said the newspaperman; it was impossible, wasn't it? The scientist turned away. He was almost certain now. The government then flew him over the desolate city, and as Nishina later told American officers who questioned him, "As I surveyed the damage from the air, I decided at a glance that nothing but an atomic bomb could have created such devastation."

On Thursday, August 9, word of Stalin's declaration of war against Japan reached Tokyo just before sunrise, proverbially the darkest hour of the day, but at 11:01 A.M. an even darker word reached the Supreme Council for the Direction of the War, then in session: a second nuclear device had just exploded over Nagasaki. The SCDW promptly moved in a body to the Imperial Palace, from which Hirohito had just sent a covert message to Premier Suzuki urging immediate acceptance of the Potsdam Declaration. The emperor, his premier, and their civilian advisers were in unanimous agreement, and in any other part of the world that would have guaranteed instant capitulation. Not here; the country was going down in flaming ruin, but Japanese custom required that great care be taken to save face, Hirohito's above all. That could be accomplished if the armed forces joined everyone else. The emperor could then vanish into his palace and behave as though the war had been none of his doing.

There was an obstacle, however. The armed forces weren't going along. In the palace they rose one by one, holding their jeweled samurai swords stiffly, and stated their terms. War Minister General S. Anami, General Y. Umezu, army chief of staff; and Admiral S. Toyoda, navy chief of staff, insisted that Washington accept three conditions: Japanese officers were to disarm their own troops, war criminals would be tried in Japanese courts, and enemy occupation must be limited in advance. In a less savage conflict these stipulations might have been acceptable, but from the outset this had been a war without quarter, and the Americans were in no mood to bargain. Foreign Minister Togo said as much. Japan was defeated, he reminded them; immediate peace was mandatory. Anami, Umezu, and Toyoda looked grim and folded their arms. It was a stalemate.

Next a cabinet meeting raged for over seven hours, interrupted only by shocking dispatches from Hiroshima, Nagasaki, and the Manchurian front. At 9:30 on the evening of that August 9, Suzuki and Togo called upon the emperor to report that both the SCDW and the cabinet were deadlocked. They suggested that the SCDW meet as an Imperial Conference in the air-raid shelter with the emperor in the background. Hirohito agreed, and the session began at 11:30 P.M. Hour after hour the wrangling went on, with the two generals and the admiral holding the civilians in check. They were asked for their solution, and their response reveals how well MacArthur had read the enemy's mind. Thus far, they stubbornly insisted, the war had been confined to indecisive skirmishes. Now was the time for Japan's finest hour—to "lure" the Americans ashore and then "annihilate" them, as the original kamikaze "divine wind" had wiped out Kublai Khan in 1281. It sounded very much like Goebbels's words of encouragement to Hitler when Roosevelt died. Reminded that this had been their strategy in defense of Iwo and Okinawa, they answered sullenly that whatever happened, "national honor" required "one last battle on Japanese soil." Suzuki finally appealed to the emperor for an "Imperial Decision." This was unprecedented; the Son of Heaven traditionally limited himself to hovering around, blessing them by his presence. Nevertheless, Hirohito replied at once. He rose, said their only choice was to end the war immediately, and left the room. As the council broke up Suzuki declared that "His Majesty's decision should be the decision of this conference as well."

The military, it appeared, had been defeated. But nobody dies harder than a warlord. Outwardly, the finer points of protocol were carefully observed. The cabinet went into session as the council broke up—it was now 3 A.M., Friday, August 10—and unanimously approved identical messages to Washington, London, Moscow and Chungking accepting Truman's Potsdam Declaration with the understanding that the emperor would remain sovereign. The cables went out at 7 A.M. The momentous news was kept from the Japanese public—still under the impression that Nippon was winning the war—for fear of a coup. The fear was justified. That same morning General Anami, the highest-ranking officer in the Empire, summoned all Tokyo officers down to the rank of lieutenant colonel and told them what had happened. Here, if anywhere, the seeds of incipient revolt would find rich earth. Many did take root; by evening growing restlessness was reported at the War Ministry and in the fleet. All the conspirators needed now was time, and in Washington the Americans were unwittingly giving it to them. Truman, Byrnes, Stimson, Forrestal, and Leahy were pondering the possibility of political repercussions when the American people knew that Hirohito would remain on his throne. Once more the buck stopped with Truman. He decided to let the Japanese keep their emperor, and so advised Suzuki via Switzerland. That was on Saturday, August 11. Now, maddeningly, Hirohito seemed to stall. For the next three days Radio Tokyo was silent, a silence so ominous that the President contemplated a resumption of mass bombing. At one point over a thousand B-29s were actually winging toward the Empire before he changed his mind and countermanded the order.

Insofar as it is possible to interpret Hirohito's thoughts, the emperor seems to have been determined to bring the militant Anami, Umezu, and Toyoda into line. For three days and three nights the struggle of wills went on in the palace air-raid shelter. At least one of those present, General Anami, knew officers elsewhere in the capital were plotting to seize power, though he stopped short of permitting them to use his name. Shortly after noon on Tuesday, August 14, in Tokyo—still August 13 in Washington—Hirohito invoked his imperial powers. He taped a broadcast to his subjects, who had never before been allowed even to hear his voice, telling them to bow their heads to the coming conqueror and ending, "We charge you, Our loyal subjects, to carry out faithfully Our will." The tape was to be played over Radio Tokyo at noon next day, after the United States had agreed to the formalities of capitulation.

Truman learned that Japan had quit at ten minutes before four on that Tuesday afternoon. At 7 P.M. he announced it to the country and declared a two-day holiday of jubilation.

Yet the danger in Tokyo remained. During the night of August 14–15—after the emperor had made his decision but before the people had been told—firebrands were still planning to overthrow the government. They approached the general commanding Hirohito's Imperial Guards Division demanding that he order his troops to disobey the imminent order to surrender. When he refused, they murdered him. Two of his subordinates joined the insurgents and prepared forgeries of imperial orders that would permit them to isolate the emperor and impound the tape of his surrender message. At 8 A.M. the fake orders were ready, and clever counterfeits of Hirohito's seal were being affixed to them, when another Guards general arrived and put them under arrest.

Throughout Wednesday morning Radio Tokyo alerted the nation to the "most important broadcast" coming at noon. These were violent hours in the capital. Hotheads tried to assassinate Suzuki and two members of his cabinet. General Anami, in despair at the loss of national honor, committed hara-kiri. Four of the leading conspirators followed his example. Inexplicably, to the western mind, the general who had suppressed their coup at eight o'clock that morning also knelt and buried a hara-kiri knife in his abdomen. More fittingly, Admiral Takijishi, father of the Kamikaze Corps, followed his example.

Americans were amazed by the docility with which the Japanese accepted defeat. It was a closer shave than they knew. Generals were reconciled to ceremonial suicide, but among younger officers the plotting and counterplotting continued right down to August 28, when the U.S.S. *Missouri* sailed into Tokyo Bay to accept the Japanese surrender while armed bluejackets and the 4th Marines landed at Yokosuka. Last-ditch insurgents had sworn to massacre the landing party, and kamikaze bombers were taxiing into position at the Atsugi airfield, their cockpits occupied by airmen who had sworn upon the honor of their ancestors that they would dive-bomb the *Missouri* and sink her. As she went down, fighter pilots, who were also warming up, intended to strafe the bay until all on the *Missouri*, including Admiral Nimitz and General MacArthur, were dead. Had they succeeded, the vengeance of the American people, confronted with what they would certainly have regarded as a final example of treachery, is terrible to contemplate. Yet it almost happened. In the last frantic hours before the surrender Hirohito was sending members of his family to every stronghold demanding assurances that the imperial promise would be kept. His younger brother, Prince Takamatsu, reached the Atsugi strip just in time to coax the fire-eaters into grounding their planes. It was touch and go right up to the end. To those who later asked whether the bombing of Hiroshima and Nagasaki had been necessary, Samuel Eliot Morison replied that in the light of all the facts, "the atomic bomb was the keystone of a very fragile arch."

The surrender ceremonies aboard the *Missouri* on September 2 marked the official end of World War II. For the first time since September 1, 1939, the *New York Times* observed, no war communiqué had been issued anywhere in the world, and a London headline read, THIS IS THE FIRST UNCENSORED DAILY EXPRESS IN EXACTLY SIX YEARS. But people do not find peace when governments do. For civilian soldiers the war would be over only when they were on their way home. The Army had worked out a sensible demobilization plan in 1944, and ten days before V-E Day it had begun returning the bravest and weariest GIs to the United States.

The plan became famous as "the point system." Each month in the Army counted a point; each month overseas another one. Presence in a battle was worth five points, and combat wounds and decorations for valor brought five each. Thus a soldier who had been drafted forty months earlier, had been overseas thirty-two months, had come under fire in six separate engagements and had been wounded twice, was on his way home with 112 points. So was every other GI who had at least 85 points, or any WAC with 44. Special provisions were made for fathers, WACs married to men being discharged, and other WACs who had been found PWOP (pregnant without permission).

The system was as fair as any could be, and it enraged sailors and marines, whose services had no arrangements at all. By summer the Navy Department got around to announcing its plans for point counting. The minimum was so high that few qualified, and six marines who wrote their congressmen in protest were put in the brig. Meanwhile Stimson was making more friends by lowering soldiers' minimum counts. By July 1945 enough red tape had passed through enough hands to launch a great transatlantic passenger movement. On one day seven transports docked in New York with 31,445 GIs. The *Queen Elizabeth* brought one division; the *Queen Mary* another. In one 72-hour period the Army Transport Service flew in 125,370 veterans from the European and Mediterranean theaters. By summer over a half-million men were home, even though the federal budget continued to anticipate a long war against Japan.

The Bomb changed that. Before it, fresh divisions were being dispatched to the Pacific on attack transports while high-point veterans waited in Brest or Le Havre for one of the *Queens* or an empty C-54. Now vessels bound for the international date line were rerouted. One of them was the transport *General Henry Taylor*, sailing under Captain Leonard B. Jaudon. A few days after the V-J celebrations the transport passed through the Panama Canal, east to west, and headed for the Hawaiian Islands. Abruptly the fo'c'sle bullhorn blared, "Now hear this! This is the captain. Watch the shadow of this ship"—he paused—"as it turns toward New York." The three thousand men from the ETO cheered. Now they believed it. The war was really over. And they were going home—although home, in 1945, was very different from home as they remembered it. The world had changed, America had changed, and so, though they were unaware of it, had the men on the *General Henry Taylor*.

Portrait of an American

THE REDHEAD

APPROPRIATELY, WALTER REUTHER was born on Labor Day eve, 1907. Walter's grandfather Jacob, a Social Democrat, had emigrated from a German farm in 1892 to flee Prussianism. Jacob's son Valentine became an American Socialist and a fiery leader of the Brewery Workers Union. Valentine, in turn, raised his boys to admire Eugene Debs, Big Bill Haywood, and social justice, and when redheaded Walter and his brother Victor arrived in Detroit from Wheeling, West Virginia, they were already on a collision course with the overlords of the automobile industry.

Working in the factories by day, they finished high school by night and enrolled at Wayne University, where they led a successful student protest against ROTC. In 1932, when Norman Thomas was running for President, Walter made a speech for him and was fired by Ford, whereupon the two brothers pooled their savings and bought steerage tickets for Europe. They defied Nazis in Germany, worked in a Russian plant for two years, crossed Asia on the Trans-Siberian Railway, worked their way across the Pacific in the crew of the *President Hoover*—and arrived back in Detroit just in time for the sit-down strikes.

Walter led one of the first of them. He had been elected president of Local 174 of the United Automobile Workers (UAW-CIO). Borrowing three hundred dollars, he hired a sound truck, rented an office, and waited by the telephone while Victor got a job working a punch press for 36.5 cents an hour at the Kelsey-Hayes factory. At Victor's urging the brake assembly line sat down. A bewildered personnel man begged him to get the men back on the job. "Only Walter Reuther can do that," said Victor, and the man, innocent of the future, asked, "Who's Walter Reuther?" Summoned by phone, Walter mounted a packing case and exhorted the men to join Local 174. The anxious personnel man said, "You're supposed to get them back to work, not organize them," and Walter, his eyes sparkling, replied, "How can I get them back to work if they aren't organized?"

In the end an agreement was signed establishing a 75-cent minimum. In six months the local's membership jumped from 78 to 2,400. Suddenly the redhead was everywhere, signing up auto workers all over town and directing strike strategy. He became a marked man. On May 26, 1947, company goons armed with rubber hoses and blackjacks attacked him while he was distributing UAW leaflets on an overpass outside Ford's Rouge plant in Dearborn, beating him and another union organizer to a pulp. A year later Ford gunmen invaded the Reuthers' La Salle Boulevard apartment and threatened his life.

The only result was to increase the redhead's popularity among Detroit's workmen. He became director of the UAW's General Motors department in 1939 and president of the union in 1946. Two years later, on a cool April evening, he was in his kitchen talking to his wife May when a hired killer standing a few feet away fired both barrels of a ten-gauge shotgun loaded with "oo" buckshot. Walter collapsed on the floor, his right arm almost gone and his condition critical. While he was still in the hospital an assassin shot out Victor's right eye and dynamiters tried to blow up UAW headquarters.

The thugs were never caught, but they weren't necessarily hirelings of management. Walter made plenty of other enemies. He drove Communists out of the union and numbers operators out of the shops, and his campaigns against every form of racial segregation in UAW social life alienated bigots. His name attracted lightning like a Franklin rod. To Jimmy Hoffa he was a prig; to John L. Lewis "a pseudo-intellectual nitwit"; to Henry Wallace "the greatest single obstacle" to his Progressive Party. At the same time, his leadership in the ADA, the NAACP, and the United World Federalists had won him many liberal admirers. After he became president of the CIO in 1952, British Labour intellectuals regarded him as the most exciting man in America. Reuther votaries included Chester Bowles, Jawaharlal Nehru, and Eleanor Roosevelt, who thought he might even be qualified for the White House.

While other labor leaders tended to become voluptuaries, Walter was recognized as a true ascetic—a man who shrank from pleasures, sometimes from normal conviviality, and always from ostentation. After his narrow brushes with death he recognized the need for bodyguards, but when the union had Packard build an elegant $12,000 armored car to convoy him around, he protested, "I can't be seen in a limousine." And he wasn't. If he went downtown to the movies, he dismayed his lookouts by insisting that he disembark in an alley, violating the most elementary security precautions. Finally, when the wheels locked in Canada and the car smashed another auto, he sprang out and snapped, "That does it. I'm not going another inch in that." He finished the trip by bus and never entered the limousine again.

Providing the Reuthers with a safe house proved more successful. An isolated, easily defensible one-room summer cottage was found in the country. Walter, being Walter, began wondering how he could improve it. His doctors told him that constant exercise of his injured hand was necessary if he wanted to avoid having a claw hand. For four years he worked at making the cottage livable. He started surrounding it with other rooms, attaching a kitchen here, a bedroom and study there, adding a second story, screening in a porch. He even built the furniture, including an elaborate hi-fi set. At the end his hand was well and his home was complete. Of the original building only the hand-hewn beams in the living room and the rainspouts (which were on the inside) could be seen.

His energy became legendary. So did the creative ferment of his mind. In ideas he found the exhilaration others got from cronies, liquor, or tobacco, none of which appealed to him. He could talk endlessly, on anything; Murray Kempton called him the only man he knew who could reminisce about the future. "Ask Walter the time," said Spencer McCulloch of the *St. Louis Post-Dispatch*, "and he tells you how to make a watch." Sometimes in the torrent wildly confused metaphors would tumble out. Once Walter charged that Hoffa, Dave Beck, and Joe McCarthy were "in bed together, hand in glove," and another time he described a company negotiator as "a man with a calculating machine for a heart, pumping ice water."

The negotiator was not amused. In bargaining sessions the redhead's verbosity was a powerful weapon. The union negotiated with Ford, General Motors, and Chrysler simultaneously, in different parts of town. This was part of Walter's "one-at-a-time" stratagem. It was based on the belief that competition among auto's big three was stronger than their distrust of the UAW. Separate one from the group, he argued; none wanted to be strikebound while the other two seized its share of the market. The whipsaw worked— the tip-off that Walter had picked his prey came when he stowed his briefcase and toothbrush under one table—and one reason for its success was his multiloquence. Flexing his powerful jaw muscles hour after hour, he suggested this, suggested that, expatiated, rebutted, lost his temper, was contrite, turned accusing, and expostulated in a dry monotone until the others were numb.

Sometimes they were numb with fury. The Hoffas and Becks of labor held that it was the union's job to win money and management's to decide whether the stockholders or the public paid the bill. Walter disagreed. He contended that another nickel in the pay envelope wouldn't help a worker if the corporation charged more for its cars, stoking the fires of inflation and raising the cost of living, and he asked the big three to pay higher wages without raising their prices. In corporate boardrooms this was seen as an outright attempt to usurp the traditional prerogatives of the boss. To make matters worse he demanded to look at the companies' books so he could prove his claims were sound. (This came out of the Reuther euphonium as "democracy in the economic sphere.") He didn't get it, but he altered the concept of labor-management relations all the same.

For while his rivals in the union were mocking him as an "egghead" pursuing "pie in the sky," and management spokesmen scorned his "Alice-in-Wonderland things," the redhead from Wheeling was successfully demonstrating that there was more to the job than what Detroit workmen call Cadillac money. After his guaranteed annual wage, after the escalator clauses—after the blue-collar proletariat had been lifted into the middle class—Walter turned his Solidarity House staff loose on broader matters: slum clearance, recreation for the elderly, UAW radio programs, a union newspaper, interracial bowling leagues. And the working stiffs followed their leader. Often puzzled, sometimes even resentful, they nevertheless moved toward what his father had called the brotherhood of man.

On May 9, 1970, Walter and May Reuther were killed in the crash of a chartered plane near Pellston, Michigan. Walter's coffin was draped in the UAW banner, a white gear wheel on a blue background. Mrs. Martin Luther King delivered the eulogy. At the end the mourners sang that most moving of union ballads:

> *From San Diego up to Maine*
> *In every mine and mill*
> *Where working men defend their rights,*
> *It's there you'll find Joe Hill.*

And one redhead.

Thirteen

THE FRAYING FLAGS OF TRIUMPH

INDIAN SUMMER, 1945.
Up before 6 A.M. for his daily predawn raid on a well-stocked White House refrigerator—installed for his convenience near the presidential bedroom—Harry Truman showers, shaves, and dresses with haberdasher nattiness in a white shirt, bow tie, and double-breasted suit. He is alone; the presidential tradition of retaining a valet educes from him a scornful snort. Riffling through the morning papers, he dashes off several memos to his staff while sitting erect at his desk in the stiff, no-nonsense, Palmer penmanship posture he learned as a schoolboy. At seven o'clock sharp he is out of the mansion, hitting the pavement on his prebreakfast constitutional. Accompanied by Secret Service bodyguards and a few panting reporters, he steps off at his brisk, 120-paces-a-minute clip—cutting across Lafayette Square, up Connecticut Avenue to K Street, east to Fifteenth Street, south to New York Avenue, and then down past the Treasury Building and the future office of John W. Snyder, Truman's choice for Secretary of the Treasury after Fred Vinson is elevated to the Supreme Court. His advisers are telling the President that Snyder is too conservative to become a cabinet member in a Democratic administration. Truman shakes his head and reminds them that Snyder, like his military aide General Harry Vaughan, is an old friend. The new President believes in relying on old friends, in trusting them.

The First Family's breakfast is served at eight o'clock: fruit, toast, bacon, milk, coffee, and a little conversational pepper from the head of the household, who tells Bess and Margaret that he wishes Jimmy Byrnes would stop treating him like a freshman senator, that Henry Wallace were less gullible about the Russians, that MacArthur would stop acting like ceremonial viceroy in Tokyo, and that the damned admirals, especially the s.o.b. Radford, would suppress the Navy's mutiny against the administration's plan to unify the armed forces.

Among the issues not discussed by the President are militant students, Black Power, Women's Lib, presidential income tax returns, airplane hijacking, wife swapping, heroin epidemics, heart transplants, SDS trashing, spacecraft modules, racial integration, domestic riots, hard-core pornography, economic game plans, the bombing of office buildings, the CIA, the Middle East, Red China, Indochina, Krebiozen, law and order, the sound barrier, foul-mouthed college girls, ungovernable cities, the Symbionese Liberation Army, the Pill, ecology and charisma—two words then found only in *Saturday Review* puzzles—and the John Birch Society.

The mutilated body of twenty-seven-year-old Captain John Birch, Mercer '39, lay that morning in a fresh grave on a wooded hillside overlooking the Chinese town of Suchow. A Baptist fundamentalist and a brave OSS officer, Birch had met a fate which struck many who had known him as almost predestined. Before it, Major Gustav Krause, his commanding officer, had written in his diary: "Birch is a good officer, but I'm afraid is too brash and may run into trouble." On August 25, 1945, the zealous captain had encountered a Chinese Communist patrol and quarreled violently with its leader, whose men then fell upon him. "In the confusing situation," Krause later said, "my instructions were to act with diplomacy. Birch made the Communist lieutenant lose face before his own men. Militarily, John Birch brought about his own death."

By that autumn Betty Goldstein, *summa cum laude* Smith '42—in college she demanded that her first name be spelled Bettye and was so independent that she stamped on a boy's foot if he tried to open a door for her—had become disillusioned with her Berkeley psychology fellowship. Returning to the East Coast she married a summer stock producer named Carl Friedan. He entered the advertising business, acquired a lovely mansion overlooking the Hudson, staffed it with servants, and came to share with his wife a joint pride in their three handsome children. To neighbors' eyes it would seem that as suburban wives and mothers go, Betty—no longer Bettye—was thriving. In her spare time Betty Friedan began to write short stories about feminine heroines for women's magazines.

Allen Ginsberg had begun working his way through Columbia as a spot-welder in the Brooklyn Navy Yard. He was studying to be a market research consultant. He rarely swore, and he shaved every day.

In the new State Department Building on Virginia Avenue, Alger Hiss, director of the Office of Special Political Affairs, was moving into a larger office. He had just completed his tenure as secretary general of the United Nations Conference in San Francisco and was now principal adviser to the United States delegation to the U.N. General Assembly.

While winning an E certificate as a war worker, Norma Jean Baker had also been photographed for *Yank*. The picture had caught the eye of the Blue Book Model Agency, and by V-J Day Norma Jean was taking the agency's modeling course. Her husband was still overseas; he knew nothing about it. She earned the modeling course's hundred-dollar fee by keeping her war job, calling in sick, and doing a ten-day stint as a hostess.

Joe McCarthy, late of the Marine Corps, was reelected circuit judge in 1945. He immediately began laying plans to stump his state the following year under the slogan "Wisconsin Needs a Tail Gunner in the Senate," telling voters of the hell he had gone through in the Pacific. In reality McCarthy's war had been chairborne. As intelligence officer for Scout Bombing Squadron 235, he had sat at a desk interviewing fliers who had returned from missions. His only wartime injury, a broken leg, was incurred when he got drunk during a party on a seaplane tender and fell down a ladder. Home now, he was telling crowds of harrowing nights in trenches and dugouts writing letters to the families of boys who had been slain in battle under his leadership, vowing that he would keep faith with the fallen martyrs by cleaning up the political mess at home—the mess that had made "my boys" feel "sick at heart."

Sometimes he limped on the leg he broke. Sometimes he forgot and limped on the other leg.

In Boston a skinny, twenty-eight-year-old former naval lieutenant (j.g.) returned home after covering the U.N. opening in San Francisco and the British elections in London as an INS reporter. Newspaper work had an uncertain future, he lacked a graduate degree for college teaching, and the thought of becoming a businessman was unappealing. So John F. Kennedy decided to file for congressman in the Eleventh Massachusetts District, his chief qualifications being his father's money and boyhood memories of his grandfather as mayor of Boston. Meanwhile he established a legal address by renting apartment 36 at 122 Bowdoin Street, just around the corner from the gold-domed capitol. An astonishing number of well-bred young women found their way there.

Republicans in California's Twelfth Congressional District were desperately in need of a presentable candidate to run against incumbent Jerry Voorhis, a liberal protégé of Upton Sinclair's. In the late spring of 1945 a committee of GOP "citizen fact-finders" had advertised in the newspapers for a qualified candidate. None had replied. Then the president of Whittier College mentioned one of his alumni, Richard M. Nixon. After a talk with Nixon's parents, two members of the Republican fact-finders reported that the young man was still in uniform, negotiating naval contracts in Baltimore while awaiting release from the service. A third committeeman, a banker named Herman Perry, then put through a historic long-distance call to Maryland. Perry was uneasy; further inquiries had revealed that Nixon, though a lawyer, hadn't voted until he was twenty-five years old. Even his party affiliation was a mystery. Over the phone he said sure, he'd be glad to run. Perry asked, "Are you a Republican?" There was a pause. Then Nixon replied, "I guess so. I voted for Dewey last time." That would be good enough, Perry said, and he asked Nixon to fly west as soon as possible. At last the citizen fact-finders had a candidate, though his skills needed some honing. His own instinct, as first revealed, was to appear in dress blues outside factory gates where former enlisted men would be leaving work, look them squarely in the eye, hold out his hand, and say sternly, "I am Lieutenant Commander Richard M. Nixon."

In Washington another former lieutenant commander, Lyndon B. Johnson, was once more representing Texas's Tenth Congressional District. Congressman Johnson deplored speedy demobilization in the wake of peace. "We must keep strong!" he cried from the well of the House. "We must have military strength to fulfill our moral obligations to the world. Our supreme duty today is to underwrite the future. We must have a strong police force to protect us from criminals, an Army and Navy strong enough to carry out our pledge to help the United Nations police the world."

A fourth naval officer, Lieutenant Commander Benjamin M. Spock, a former instructor in pediatrics at the Cornell Medical College and now a naval physician, was putting the final touches on his first book, *The Common Sense Book of Baby and Child Care*.

In distant Hanoi, French colonial soldiers had returned on the heels of the withdrawing Japanese army. Ho Chi Minh, a native politician with a mixed background but most recently known as a Chiang Kai-shek protégé, had applied week after week for official recognition of his popular Viet Minh (Viet Nam Independence League), but Admiral Thierry D'Argenlieu, General de Gaulle's representative, had refused to see him. Still independent and still a peaceful advocate, Ho carried his cause to Paris. If thwarted there, he resolved, he would order his followers to blow up the Hanoi reservoir and wage guerrilla warfare from the hills.

A few blocks from Ho's room in Paris, thirty-seven-year-old Major William F. Knowland, presiding over an Army historical section, was notified that he had just become the youngest member of the United States Senate. Governor Earl Warren of California had chosen him to succeed the late Hiram Johnson, confident that he was the most qualified man available. Among Knowland's merits were his youth, his military service, six years in the state legislature, a fine record as a charity-drive organizer, a wife and three children, and his father, Joseph Russell Knowland, a millionaire and the chief contributor to Warren's political war chests.

In May 1945 a strong-minded widow named Marguerite Oswald had remarried, but by fall it had become clear that the marriage was a mistake. The bride insisted upon taking her five-year-old son Lee with them wherever they went, and Marguerite's husband and child found themselves competing for her attention. To Lee, who seemed fond of his new stepfather, the parental quarrels were baffling. He was becoming moody and withdrawn.

The press that autumn was unfamiliar with the public personalities of Jane Alpert, Mark Rudd, Stokely Carmichael, Angela Davis, Diana Oughton, Bernadine Dohrn, H. Rap Brown, Kathy Boudin, the Soledad Brothers, Bill Ayres, Huey Newton, Jerry Rubin, Linda Fitzgerald, William L. Calley Jr., Tom Hayden, Cathlyn Wilkinson, and Patricia Campbell Hearst, because none of them had any.

Descending from the presidential apartment in a small elevator shortly before nine o'clock each morning, the thirty-third President of the United States strode smartly to his oval office in the West Wing of the White House and plunged into work. His zest was genuine and his manner direct. Roosevelt had enjoyed intrigue and sleight of hand; Truman liked clear-cut decisions, the harder the better. To prevent misunderstandings, all of them were put into writing. He never regretted one, never lost sleep over consequences, never glanced over his shoulder. Procrastination was a sin to him, and he despised it. His customary air was that of an alert shopkeeper, all business, and in fact visitors on his daily appointment schedule, from Anthony Eden to advocates of National Poultry Week, were always referred to by the President as "the customers." Each was welcomed with a manly two-pump handshake and escorted to the presidential desk, where, in those first months of peace, Truman liked to call attention to the tiny plow which had replaced his model gun on V-J Day. "It's the little things that count," he would say sententiously. "I like the feeling of having the new little fellow there."

His optimistic air disquieted informed callers, who wondered among themselves when he would face the inevitable reappearance of the Depression. "A war boom?" Frederick Lewis Allen had written in *Since Yesterday* (1940). "No gain thus made could be lasting." In *Harper's* Bernard De Voto warned his readers to be prepared for the return of all of it: labor-baiting, Father Coughlin, and hand-to-hand fighting on the barricades as "the waves of reaction" gathered strength "in the years immediately ahead of the United States." Leo Cherne peered into the future and saw a "cold breeze" sweeping through America. Hungry veterans would roam the streets in packs, he predicted: "Occasionally you will see them in strikes and riots . . . The newly set up employment offices, particularly at first, will grind slowly . . . an occasional soldier will be found on a street corner selling a Welcome Home sign. Others will start house-to-house canvassing in their uniforms." Some economists foresaw another 1932, with 15 million jobless men. Political scientists spoke of revolution, and from his deathbed H. G. Wells concluded in 1945 that since faith in scientific progress had plummeted, man, already "at the end of his tether," was doomed to rapid extinction.

The harder they looked, the more convinced employers were that there was no way to turn industry's juggernaut of superproductivity toward peaceful pursuits without stumbling into disaster. Preoccupied as they were by the Crash and all that had followed, they overlooked one massive difference between Herbert Hoover's America and Harry Truman's. In 1932 people couldn't enter stores, because they were broke. If hard times had taught them nothing else, the importance of saving had been drilled into them. Since Pearl Harbor average weekly earnings in the United States had almost doubled, rising from $24.20 to $44.39 for the 48-hour week—soon to be the 40-hour week, with no loss in pay, after Truman set the example with federal employees. Partly because the Depression had made them frugal and partly because there had been so little on store shelves, the American people had spent the four war years accumulating Liberty Bonds and queuing up at bank deposit windows. There were 85 million bondholders alone. With the shooting over, the public had socked away 136.4 billions in savings institutions and liquid securities. It was burning a hole in their pockets, and the administration's real quandary—one which could never be solved to everyone's satisfaction—was how to prevent a national buying spree in the black market.

Thus the nightmare of factory gates being stormed by jobless GIs was the last bitter legacy of the shabby 1930s. Those terrible years were dead at last; 52-20 unemployment compensation was evidence of it, and so was the GI Bill. Finding jobs for all discharged soldiers would take time, but meanwhile they could learn trades, start small businesses of their own, or move to college campuses. And jobs weren't all that tight anyhow. Women war workers were quitting beltlines by the million to go home and have babies.

A *New York Daily News* headline read:

> PRICES SOAR, BUYERS SORE,
> STEERS JUMP OVER THE MOON

In Kansas City the President of the United States strutted through downtown streets at the head of an American Legion parade. From a curb Eddie Jacobson, his old partner in haberdashery, called, "Harry, what about inflation?"

"I've got my eye on it," Truman called back.

He needed a quick eye. The economy was shifting daily as it hurtled ahead, trying to catch up with black marketeers peddling five-dollar nylons, fifteen-dollar shirts, and twenty-dollar recapped tires. The war had receded into history and the convulsions of readjustment were at their height. Affluence lay in the certain future, but reaching it was an agonizing struggle. When Vinson had prophesied "the pleasant predicament of having to learn to live 50 percent better," he had failed to mention that first the people must face shortages, riots, labor strikes, and the skyrocketing prices of postwar inflation.

Yet controls were exasperating. By the war's end the Office of Price Administration had become a government-within-a-government, with 73,000 full-time employees, 200,000 volunteers, and an office in every community down to the town level. It was an intolerable tyranny, a mockery of freedom, and all that could be said for it was that there was no alternative. Somehow it had managed to hold price rises to 30 percent over their 1939 levels. Not to put too fine a point on it, in 1946 the economy was virtually glued together by the gum on the back of red and green stamps. Even so, it was near chaos. There were a thousand ways to circumvent OPA regulations, and sharpers found them all. You could tip the head waiter twenty dollars and a choice roast would appear. You might barter an automobile for an apartment, say, or a car battery for scotch whisky. The scotch might have been acquired by also agreeing to buy a case of wine or beer. That ruse was called the "tie-in" sale, and its possibilities were unlimited. In Oklahoma City, for example, a car dealer would sell you an automobile if you also bought his dog for $400; afterward the dog would find his way back. Other dealers offered new cars if you would trade your old one in for a two-dollar bill, and in Cincinnati an imaginative customer greeted an auto salesman by saying: "I'll bet you seven hundred dollars I can hold my breath for three minutes." In addition there were endless "bonuses"—a $150 bonus for the landlady who would rent an $80-a-month cold-water flat, or three dollars to the butcher who found a thick steak in his refrigerator.

It was impractical to wipe out the black market with stiff fines and heavy prison sentences, and infeasible, now that the war was won, to retain bipartisan support for controls. The Republicans were feeling truculent once more. In August 1945 they reluctantly decided not to challenge Truman's "hold-the-line" executive order, which envisaged a gradual reduction of wage and price controls, but in September party lines were drawn tight on this issue for the first time since Pearl Harbor. Calling Congress back into special session, the President demanded broad domestic powers. He wanted rationing to continue—some controls were due to expire automatically six months after the war's end—and in addition he asked for congressional approval of a social and economic program whose most notable measures were a 65¢-an-hour minimum wage, nationalization of the housing industry, expansion of natural resources development, federal control of all unemployment compensation, and a fair employment practices bill with teeth. Republican congressmen gagged. Minority leader Joe Martin accused the President of "out-dealing the New Deal," and Charlie Halleck said, "This is the kick-off. This begins the campaign of 1946."

On January 14, 1946, Congress reassembled to hear Truman's first State of the Union message. The heart of it was a request for another year of OPA, with controls being relinquished, commodity by commodity, as the supply and demand of each reached their natural level. But he had telegraphed his punch in September, and now he confronted a formidable alliance: the National Association of Manufacturers, the U.S. Chamber of Commerce, and the Republican leadership. They had prepared intricate charts and graphs to persuade committees that free enterprise was doomed unless Congress struck "the shackles from American business." Outside the Senate's marbled caucus room, corporation public relations men fought for a sellers' market by marshaling parades of clerks, junior executives, ministers, physicians, Legionnaires, Rotarians, and newspaper boys, all of whom testified to the virtues of John Stuart Mill and the wickedness of Karl Marx, who, they insisted, was their true adversary. There was even a sad troupe of bankrupt businessmen, who told of their former prosperity in a free market and how mischievous OPA officials had ruined them.

Lobbying was intense on both sides. OPA's Chester Bowles fielded his own tream of expert witnesses, Truman's congressional liaison men swarmed through the Capitol buttonholing congressmen, and the unions, consumer groups, and women's clubs paraded in the plaza outside, holding pro-OPA signs aloft. On April 19 they staged what the following morning's *New York Times* called "the climax" of the consumers' "crusade." Over a thousand housewives, representing every state, marched up the Hill demanding a twelve-month extension of controls without crippling amendments. According to the *Times*, the demonstration

> . . . served to emphasize that the fight over OPA, in and out of Congress, has reached proportions of bitterness, stridency, and obfuscation which have not been matched in years. . . . The NAM has spearheaded the fight over OPA with the . . . enthusiastic assistance of associations representing the meat industry, retail trade, real estate and others. . . . As the battle has grown each side has become progressively more voluble, they have started to call each other names, and a few blows have been struck below the belt.

Congress's reflex reaction to so savage a struggle was to compromise, and as Bowles had pointed out, wage and price controls were all or nothing. OPA's death rattle followed. So did inflation. Within a month food prices had doubled, angry consumers formed The Militant Marketers to picket stores, livestock men kept cattle in the stockyards until beef would bring over a dollar a pound, and the overall cost of living rose 33 percent and then 75 percent. In August worried congressmen reconvened to pass new controls, dropping Taft's amendment, but it was too late. OPA had lost its grip on the economy. There was no way to turn the spiral back upon itself, and in October Truman bowed to the irresistible force; the lifting of all controls began. Two years later, when the electorate's memory of OPA had mellowed, he would remind voters that he had been battling for price regulation while Republicans had fought on the NAM's side. By then he would be moving in stride with events. At the time, however, the first Taft-Truman confrontation could only be called a draw at most. Presidential popularity dipped in the polls.

Luckily Truman seldom worried about polls. In general he was suited by temperament for the hard choice. This was true even when his decisions hurt those who had supported his political fortunes, which, in the unsettled years after the war, it often did. Taking on the NAM and the U.S. Chamber of Commerce was relatively easy for a Democratic chief executive. Disciplining organized labor was something else. Not only was labor essential to the coalition Franklin Roosevelt had forged; its leaders had been among those who had urged Truman's vice-presidential candidacy upon FDR in 1944. Without labor he would have remained a senator, and another man, either Jimmy Byrnes or Henry Wallace, would be in the White House. Nevertheless, nagging management about prices was pointless unless the administration was ready to take an equally strong stand on wages. And there was no point in that if the workers were always on strike, which at times in 1946 they seemed to be. During that first full year after the war, nearly five million men struck at one time or another and 107,476,000 man-days of work were lost to strikes. Coming when they did, these disruptions deepened middle-class antagonism toward labor. Young couples awaiting their first car were infuriated by photographs of an idle automotive worker. They were applying a double standard, judging the unions more harshly than employers, but that had always been the posture of the middle class. Even Truman, so representative of the American center, was more respectful of white collars than blue.

Blue-collar contributions to the 1941–45 production miracle deserved more recognition than they were getting. Army-Navy E pennants had been earned because employees, sharing their employers' vision of peace and triumph, had sweated themselves for long hours on the line, agreed to speed-ups, volunteered for swing shifts, and put their money in war bonds. In the week after the Japanese attack on Hawaii, President Roosevelt had asked the unions for no-strike pledges, to be honored until the fighting was over. Every labor leader had agreed, and with the exception of two coal miners' strikes and a threatened walkout by railroad workers —all in 1943—the pledges were kept. Even when the few wildcat strikes were counted, less than .0006 of 1 percent of total production time had been lost. By V-J Day, however, the pressure of accumulated grievances was intolerable.

The first sign of trouble came in September 1945; Ford was held up by a rash of spontaneous suppliers' strikes. Then, as the GM walkout was followed in 1946 by wave after wave of strikes from Montauk Point to Malibu Beach, paralyzing the oil, lumber, textile, and electrical industries, newspapers began talking about the workers' "revolt" and labor's "rebellion." It was hard to believe that so widespread an upheaval wasn't planned, that it was a spontaneous backfire to the end of wartime austerity. This much was certain: the cumulative effect of the disruptions was threatening reconversion. If strikes against the public interest loomed, the President might feel it his duty to take a longer step than the appointment of impotent commissions. That is precisely what happened, and in the process Truman reached the low point of his Presidency.

His anger was understandable. No sooner had the GM strike been settled than 750,000 steelworkers banked their fires and hit the bricks. After eighty days they returned, but before the country could take a deep breath the 400,000 soft coal miners in twenty-one states left their pits. On April 18, with the miners still out, the railroads' two key brotherhoods announced that they would withdraw all their men in thirty days. The nation's transportation grid would stop functioning. The leaders of the two unions had long been allies of the Democratic party, and when Truman called them to the White House three days before the strike deadline and offered generous arbitration awards, he expected them to accept. Instead they shook their heads stubbornly.

"If you think I'm going to sit here and let you tie up this whole country," he said, "you're crazy as hell."

"We've got to go through with it, Mr. President," one of them replied. "Our men are demanding it."

Truman rose. "All right," he said. "I'm going to give you the gun. You've got just forty-eight hours—until Friday at this time—to reach a settlement. If you don't, I'm going to take over the railroads in the name of the government."

The forty-eight hours passed, the deadlock remained unbroken, and so, on that Friday, May 17, 1946, he signed an executive order seizing the railroads. He was now the brotherhoods' new employer. In that role he gave them another five days of reprieve. Nothing happened. The best he could get in exchange for his leniency was a curt note from them ending: "Your offer is unacceptable." By now it was Friday of the following week. The effect of the soft coal strike was beginning to reach the cities; to conserve the little they had, some were already cutting electricity during certain hours. A railroad strike at this juncture would have the effect of a national strike. He couldn't allow it. At issue was less what he would do than how he did it. The method he chose was deplorable.

Summoning his cabinet, he informed it that he would appear before a joint session of Congress Saturday and ask for authority to draft all railroad men, regardless of age or situation, into the Army. His attorney general said, "Unconstitutional." The President snapped, "We'll draft 'em first and think about the law later." He told his press secretary, Charles G. Ross, to clear all networks for a coast-to-coast fireside chat that same evening, and he handed him a dozen-page holograph on ruled tablet paper. "Here's what I'm going to say," he said tautly. "Get it typed up. I'm going to take the hide right off those sons of bitches."

Back in his own office, Ross couldn't believe what he was reading. It was probably the most splenetic outburst ever set down in the White House. It was also inaccurate, slanderous, and, toward the end, a dangerous incitement. He planned to tell the country that while America's young men had "faced bullets, bombs and disease to win the victory," the leaders of the coal and railroad unions had as much as fired "bullets in the backs of our soldiers" by holding "a gun at the head of the government." They were all liars, he said, and he singled out John L. Lewis and "Mr. Murray and his communist friends" for intimidating "a weak-kneed Congress." Next came the extraordinary statement:

> Every single one of the strikers and their demigog [sic] leaders have been living in luxury, working when they pleased and drawing from four to forty times the pay of a fighting soldier.

The coda read:

> Let's give the country back to the people. Let's put transportation and production back to work, *hang a few traitors,* and make our own country safe for democracy.* Come on, boys, let's do the job!

It might as well have ended, "Right on!" Here was a President who proposed to demand power for the people and save democracy by stringing up labor leaders. The expletives uttered in the elegant Grosse Pointe mansions of automobile executives in darkest 1937 had scarcely been worse. Ross didn't think Truman really

---
* Author's italics.

wanted to encourage necktie parties, certainly not that explicitly, and Clark Clifford concurred. Together they persuaded the President to accept a different draft. Even so, it was scathing. "The crisis at Pearl Harbor was the result of action by a foreign enemy," he began. "The crisis tonight is caused by a group of men within our own country who place their private interests above the welfare of the nation." He announced that he was calling Congress in session Sunday afternoon at four o'clock. If the engineers and trainmen weren't on the job then, he would turn them over to General Hershey.

It was a strange way to run railroads, his advisers privately thought, but their chief was going through with it. Sunday afternoon arrived with no capitulation from the brotherhoods. Their leaders were locked in a Statler Hotel room at Sixteenth and K streets, slowly giving ground to a jawboning administration negotiator, when the President rode down Pennsylvania Avenue, entered the House chamber through the Speaker's office, and mounted the podium to ask for authority permitting him, as commander in chief, "to draft into the Armed Forces of the United States all workers who are on strike against their own government." In Rayburn's office Clark Clifford kept vigil over the telephone. Five minutes after Truman had begun his speech, it rang. The negotiator said, "It's signed!" Clifford scribbled frantically on a scrap of paper, "Mr. President, agreement signed, strike over," and sent it to the lectern. Truman glanced at it. He looked up from his text, and smiled at the packed chamber. He said, "Gentlemen, the strike has been settled."

They gave him an ovation, and when he went on anyhow to ask for the legislation permitting him to draft future strikers jeopardizing the public welfare, the House whooped it through on the spot. Still, this was far from his finest hour. At a stroke he had alienated the labor movement, the American Civil Liberties Union, the liberal community, and every thoughtful conservative who had read the constitution the President had sworn to uphold. In the Senate Robert A. Taft, no champion of the unions, used his influence to table the bill; the proposal, he declared, "offends not only the constitution, but every basic principle for which the American Republic was established. Strikes cannot be prohibited without interfering with the basic freedom essential to our form of government." The embittered president of the railroad trainmen announced that every penny in his brotherhood's 47-million-dollar treasury would be spent defeating Truman in 1948. In New York the CIO stigmatized the President as the country's "number one strikebreaker," and from his aerie in the hills of West Virginia, John L. Lewis cried, "You can't mine coal with bayonets."

Maybe not, but the aroused vigilante in the White House was going to try. Lewis was courting disaster. Truman could survive the strikebreaker brand; he would later win labor back with his vetoes of the anti-union Case and Taft-Hartley bills. What he could not tolerate was the mine leader's arrogance and growing irresponsibility. The President came close to the truth when he said Lewis had "called two strikes in wartime to satisfy his ego." He had marched his 400,000 men in and out of the mines with no thought for the GIs overseas, and they knew it; in 1943 an editorial in the Middle Eastern edition of *Stars and Stripes* had ended, "Speaking for the American soldier—John L. Lewis, damn your coal-black soul." The Democratic party owed the old thespian nothing. He hadn't supported the ticket for ten years. The way was clear, therefore, for a confrontation between two bristling leaders. The very nature of the strike invited federal intervention. The American economy was still based on coal. It provided 62 percent of the country's electricity and 55 percent of its industrial power. Putting the railroad men back to work would have been useless if the miners didn't go too; nineteen out of every twenty locomotives in the United States burned coal.

Truman was so determined to stare down Lewis that he hadn't waited until the brotherhoods were tamed. Five days before they yielded at the Statler he had signed an executive order taking over the mines. Lewis's strike was then in its sixth week, and at first it appeared that this effort to intimidate him would be as ill-starred as all the others. "Truman doubts the legality of our demands?" he bellowed at a newspaperman. "What does Truman know about the legality of anything?" The President knew enough to be cagier this time. Putting his Secretary of the Interior in management's seat, he approved a compromise giving the United Mine Workers most of their demands. (The employers, who would have to pay, raged helplessly; in this struggle, reason was as irrelevant as constitutionality.) Then the President waited for the UMW chief to make his next move. Lewis's swaggering and blustering were sure signs that he was looking for an opening. When he found none, he created one. Raising a trivial point over vacation pay, he repudiated the contract in October and declared that he was reopening negotiations on all its clauses. He wanted "portal-to-portal" pay for his men (payment for travel time from the mine gate to the pithead). Truman told the Interior Department to stand fast while he, like Lewis, found a pretext for action. To their consternation, his New Deal lawyers discovered that there was nothing except the despised antiunion court injunction, which had been outlawed in the Norris-La Guardia and Wagner acts.

Truman wasn't disconcerted. He decreed that the law covered *private* employers, not the government. It was a novel interpretation, but now that the duel was in the open neither man could retire without loss of face. Even as the court papers were being served on Lewis in his UMW headquarters at Fifteenth and I streets, his lieutenants were passing the watchword in the mines: "No contract, no work." While he holed up in his Alexandria mansion, the mines were shut down one by one. In ten days cities were again cutting back electric power, industrial plants were shutting down, and locomotives and empty coal cars were being stranded on sidings. By then the struggle was approaching its climax. UMW lawyers had exhausted their repertoire of stratagems. On Thursday, November 21, Federal District Judge T. Alan Goldsborough cited Lewis for contempt of court, and on Tuesday, November 26, Goldsborough ruled that "The defendants, John L. Lewis and the United Mine Workers of America, have beyond a reasonable doubt committed and continue to commit a civil and criminal contempt of this Court." The fine was $3,510,000.

Lewis sat down, flabbergasted. It was the heaviest fine in labor history, and he saw himself facing a limited number of options. He couldn't choose jail, as Debs and Gompers had, because the government had dropped the charge of criminal contempt. He could include the judge among his enemies, and he seemed to be pondering that when he croaked, "Sir, I have already been adjudged in contempt of your court—" but he broke off there. His lawyers were dragging him back to his seat. A judge who would hand down multimillion-dollar fines was dangerous. Appeal was inevitable, but that would only delay the decision. Meanwhile the defendant had become entangled in court orders, writs, citations, briefs, and restraining orders. He had lost sight of his adversary. Where was Harry Truman?

The President had wisely withheld comment from the moment Lewis had knocked his own chip off his own shoulder. Yet a presidential triumph was far from a certainty. The initiative was still with Lewis, and there was only one sure way to wrench it from him. His power base must be eliminated or threatened. If both men remained mute while his lawyers threw up a new screen of legal motions, the national crisis would pass from the inconceivable to the unendurable. The miners might dislike Lewis, and some of them hated him, but they were convinced, almost to a man, that they needed his protection. The pits and tunnels would remain vacant until the men were told to return by him or by an equally persuasive voice. Perhaps the President's voice was strong enough. Harry Truman decided to try. That Saturday morning, the fifth anniversary of Pearl Harbor, Charlie Ross told the press that the President would broadcast a direct appeal to the miners in the evening, asking them to save their country by ignoring their chief and going back to work at once.

It was a breathtaking gamble, with presidential prestige at hazard, but it succeeded. Lewis had been stared down. At four o'clock he called a press conference at Fifteenth and I. Declaring that the Supreme Court deliberations "should be free from public pressure superinduced by the hysteria of an economic crisis," he said, "all mines in all districts will resume production of coal immediately. . . . Each member is directed to return to work immediately under the wages and conditions of employment on or before November, 1946." With those lines he tottered off the stage and into oblivion. He would never again hold the country in ransom, and his defeat, in becoming Truman's victory, made the President feel like a President, possibly for the first time. "I can tell you, there was a big difference in the Old Man from then on," Clark Clifford later told Cabell Phillips of the *New York Times*. "He was his own boss at last." Another presidential aide put it more succinctly. "When Harry walked back to the mansion," he said, "you could hear his balls clank."

Emil Mazey, Walter Reuther's right-hand man, was not available to the automobile workers' union that winter. He didn't even know what was happening in Detroit. As a draftee and leader of demobilization riots in Manila, Sergeant Mazey was deprived of mail and visitors and kept under constant watch. The surveillance didn't stop the rioting. Demonstrations intensified and spread to Tokyo, Guam,

China, Calcutta, Hawaii, London, and Vienna; to Le Havre, Paris, and Frankfort. By spring the disturbances had weakened U.S. military morale, damaged American prestige abroad, and dealt the Army a heavy blow.

Morale was already at its lowest since Pearl Harbor. That was why soldiers were so susceptible to skillful agitators. On V-J Day demobilization points had been frozen; service after that date won no credits toward an early discharge. Some inequities were unavoidable under the point system anyway, and the unexpectedly early end of the Pacific war increased them. Instead of transporting high-point outfits home in the summer of 1945, the Army had found it convenient to discharge low-point troops who had never seen a ship. The most abrasive issue, however, had nothing to do with mustering out. It was a universal grievance of enlisted men who felt that they were being systematically mistreated by their superiors.

Military precedence lay athwart the thrust of egalitarianism, twentieth-century America's most powerful social force. Under the best of circumstances enlisted men were anti-authoritarian, and with the coming of peace and the return to barracks life, gaps between the haves and have-nots had widened. Hanson W. Baldwin, military editor of the *New York Times* and no enemy of privilege, concluded afterward that there had been "solid grounds for real discontent." Generals, he noted, were literally feasting on caviar and champagne while the troops were fed C rations. Junior officers laid claim to the plushest quarters, the prettiest Red Cross girls, the most comfortable seats at the finest movies. The best buildings were reserved for their clubs, where GI bartenders served them choice liquors until their GI chauffeurs put them to bed. Some commanding officers retained unneeded men merely to defer relinquishment of their own temporary wartime ranks, and the accumulation of legitimate complaints was heightened by inexcusable ignorance and sensitivity at the highest levels, notably on the part of Secretary of War Robert P. Patterson.

Nevertheless there was something disgraceful about the Army's near-mutiny of 1946. Since the previous September officers had been discharging nearly a million men a month while cutting a soldier's point requirement to 50 and then to 38. The Navy suffered fewer embarrassing episodes despite greater grievances, and the Marine Corps avoided demonstrations by simply issuing an order forbidding them. The Army riots would have been less shameful if the rioters had been the combat veterans who had won the war, but they weren't. By Christmas of 1945 most of Bill Mauldin's Willies and Joes were home and out of uniform.

The first man to cast doubt on the Army's demobilization policy was, of all people, General MacArthur. On September 17, 1945, without consulting anyone in Washington, he called a press conference to announce that the occupation force in Japan would be cut from 400,000 to 200,000 within six months. Questioned by reporters, President Truman said feebly that though he hadn't been told, he was glad the general didn't need as many troops as he had thought. Dean Acheson commented that the size of MacArthur's force would be determined by policy makers, not the general, and instantly ran afoul of MacArthur's champions in Congress. (Had the administration been able to see into the future, Acheson later wrote, "we might have recognized this skirmish as the beginning of a struggle leading to relief of General MacArthur from his command on April 11, 1951.") If a five-star general could cut his garrison in half, restless soldiers reasoned, generals with fewer stars could, too.

The exact opposite happened. On January 6, 1946, the *Daily Pacifican,* a soldier's newspaper, reported that Army demobilization schedules had been cut from 800,000 men a month to 300,000 because of the difficulty in obtaining replacements. The replacement shortage, the *Pacifican* charged in a front-page appeal to President Truman, was of the Army's own making; General Hershey had cut his monthly draft quota from 88,000 to 21,000. Maintenance of large contingents in Manila was particularly vexing. As the *Pacifican* saw it, the only legitimate use of citizen soldiers in peacetime was to occupy conquered countries, and Filipinos weren't enemies: they were to become independent on July 1. Combat training for GIs, which had been resumed to take their minds off worries, had increased them; rumor had it that they would be used to hunt down Communist guerrillas in the Philippines or on the Chinese mainland. To cap it all, Secretary Patterson told an interviewer on Guam that he was "surprised" to hear of the V-J Day five-month-old point freeze.

With Mazey were hundreds of other CIO workers who had been blooded on Detroit picket lines in the late 1930s. In a matter of hours they had mimeographed leaflets, distributed them, and formed a cavalcade of fifteen trucks and jeeps. Honking horns and flourishing such signs as WHEN DO WE GO HOME? and WE DON'T LIKE

THIS DEAL, they paused at each camp to pick up volunteers. Altogether there were perhaps 150 of them in that first procession. After hearing a few speeches and passing the hat for a protest ad in the *New York Times,* they broke up, their fire apparently spent. But the incident had attracted the attention of the press, which served as a megaphone for grievances. Almost overnight, posts on Luzon were transformed into rebellious communes. The crowd that began to form the following evening in front of Manila city hall grew to 2,500, and its mood was ugly. This time the hat was returned to the speakers with a surplus, and supplementary cables were sent to Drew Pearson and Walter Winchell. The word was passed all over the island—write your congressman. With time on their hands and nothing better to do, 18,000 soldiers did it. Lieutenant General W. D. Styer, commander of the armed forces in the Western Pacific, then committed a major strategic error. The best way to calm the mob, he concluded, was to let it hear the soothing sound of his voice over a public address system in Manila's huge Rizal Stadium. All he achieved was a tenfold increase in the crowd's size. The *Times* put the story on page one: 20,000 MANILA GI'S BOO GENERAL; URGE CONGRESS TO SPEED SAILINGS.

A chain reaction had begun. As radio broadcasts and newspapers described the behavior of Styer's men, sympathetic demonstrations were staged on bases around the world. In Calcutta instigators demanded the liquidation of the China-Burma-India war theater. Secretary Patterson tried to explain the situation to occupation troops in Yokohama and was heckled. In Tokyo men paraded under signs reading, SERVICE, YEA, BUT SERFDOM NEVER and JAPS GO HOME, WHY NOT US? Calling "Eleanor! Eleanor! Eleanor!" thousands of London-based soldiers gathered beneath Mrs. Roosevelt's window in Claridge's Hotel and asked her to find out why transport room was found for GI brides and not them. (She appeared briefly, smiled, and told them she would try to find out.) The Paris reaction began early one afternoon when soldiers tacked up crudely lettered red-crayoned signs on the bulletin boards of both the Columbia and Rainbow Corner Red Cross Clubs: BACK UP YOUR MANILA BUDDIES. MEETING TONITE 8:30 ARC DE TRIOMPHE. At the Place d'Etoile polite gendarmes explained that because the arch was a French shrine, the rally must be held elsewhere. One group headed for the Trocadéro, across the Seine from the Eiffel Tower, yelling "Scabs!" at soldiers who refused to join them. The other column marched four abreast down the Champs Elysées to the Place de la Concorde, brandishing magnesium flares and chanting: "We wanna go home! We wanna go home! We wanna go home! We wanna go home. . . ."

The most offensive of the Wanna-Go-Home riots, as they were thereafter known, was in Germany. The Paris demonstrators at least knew how to keep step. In Frankfort four thousand GIs turned into a mindless, howling rabble. Agitators shinnied up lampposts and waved the horde on toward the I. G. Farben Building with flashlights. Turned back there by the points of MP bayonets, the protesters shouted derisively that General Joseph T. McNarney was too cowardly to confront them. McNarney was in Berlin at the time. On his return he became one of the few commanding officers to call ringleaders in and talk to them plainly. Eisenhower had referred all inquiries to his theater commanders, vaguely telling the press that he was in favor of sending home any soldiers "for whom there is no military need," and Wedemeyer all but apologized to China-Burma-India men for red tape that delayed their discharges. McNarney explained American commitments in Europe. Then he said, "We will get you home as quickly as we possibly can, but if your congressman gets the impression from his mailbag that what the public wants is 'to get the boys home and to hell with international commitments,' then you'll go home regardless of what happens to . . . chores in Europe that the nation accepted."

The general was sarcastic. In reality he had hit upon the key to the worldwide campaign. Already Capitol Hill was being swamped with complaints bearing APO return addresses. And that was only the beginning. In the second wave, parents, wives, and sweethearts joined the din with what Undersecretary of War Kenneth C. Royall called "that philosophy of 'me and my son John' that's flooding our congressmen with a deluge of criticism of demobilization." One senator received over two hundred pairs of baby bootees with "I miss my daddy" notes. The campaign was a test of congressional courage, and Congress flunked. "Every father, every mother, every child want their loved one to be with them at home," Robert F. Rich of Pennsylvania said. He added: "Remember, there is no place like home." John Rankin introduced a measure which would release every soldier who had been in uniform eighteen months, had dependents, or wanted to go to school—in other words, every draftee. Representative Mike Mansfield of Montana told reporters that he saw "no reason why the men overseas cannot be sent home and discharged as quickly as possible." Senators Tom Connally (Democrat) and Arthur Vandenberg (Republican) issued a bipartisan statement pledging support of the rebels, and a Senate subcommittee flew to the Philippines to take testimony from Sergeant Mazey and other instigators.

The *New York Times*, horrified, expressed dismay at the impact of the "breakdown of Army discipline" on foreign spectators. It pointed out that the demonstrators "are not yet civilians; they are still soldiers. What they have done," the editorial said bluntly, "is indefensible, and they must be made to understand this." In the *Times* view, Congress was guilty of abetting "a bring-the-boys-home campaign which disregards our international responsibilities and encourages such exhibitions as those in Manila and Le Havre."

From the administration's standpoint, the timing of the disturbances could scarcely have been worse. President Truman was trying to rally congressional approval for his plan to integrate all three armed forces into a single Department of Defense. Senior officers were touchy enough as it was. The brass already distrusted the White House. If the administration let them down in this new matter, the entire reorganization plan might be jeopardized. Therefore the President announced that after reviewing Army and Navy procedures he was "convinced that the services are carrying out demobilization with commendable efficiency and with justice to all concerned." All he achieved was a switch in congressional targets, from the War and Navy departments to himself.

Like Roosevelt before him, Truman had strongly endorsed universal military training. Now hope for it evaporated overnight. Instead there was grave doubt that the military establishment could maintain a skeletal force abroad. Armed strength was already down 80 percent. What had been the mightiest air force in the world had dwindled from 2,385,000 men to 165,000. The Navy was discharging 245,000 sailors each month; Nimitz warned that not a single squadron was fit for combat. With the draft due to expire on May 15, the Joint Chiefs were contemplating a withdrawal of all occupation troops from Korea. Already five million trained soldiers were back in mufti. Generals were contemplating grim arithmetic. At the very least they needed 350,000 troops in Germany, 375,000 in the Pacific, and between 725,000 (Eisenhower's estimate) and 1,375,000 (Truman's) elsewhere. But only 400,000 soldiers were volunteers.

With reenlistments declining, General Eisenhower told congressional leaders, there was very real danger that the United States would "run out of Army."

The general met the leadership in an unused room in the rear of the Congressional Library. Open testimony was out of the question. The political fires were too high. He had approached the Hill by side streets, uncomfortably aware that GIs chanting "We like Ike!" in new disturbances were endorsing his hazy comment as an endorsement of their insurgency. He told the congressmen that he had to have 1,550,000 men, and he quoted the Eighth Army chief of staff in Japan: "If any Japanese decided the time was ripe for revolt they would certainly pick a time when they believed there was dissatisfaction in the American Army. It appears that subversive forces are deliberately at work, for obscure reasons, to undermine the morale of our Army." Eisenhower added that in his opinion it might become necessary to let U.S. influence in Europe "go by default" to "some other country."

The other country was unnamed. In those months after the Japanese surrender it was unfashionable to speak of any nation as a potential enemy, but only one adversary was strong enough to challenge the United States. At the end of the war there had been ten million men in the Red Army, and ten million were still there. Russian soldiers stationed outside the Soviet Union staged no Wanna-Go-Home riots. Stalin could move at will through eastern Europe. Because Congress listened to its constituents instead of Eisenhower and Truman, by the summer of 1946 American military power had dwindled to two and a half divisions, largely replacements, with a combat efficiency at about 50 percent of the Army's wartime peak. After Churchill had called attention to the Iron Curtain running from Stettin in the Baltic to Trieste in the Adriatic, a large block of public opinion turned savagely on Truman. The ex-soldiers who had demonstrated, and the wives who had sent congressmen bootees, blamed the President, the State Department, intellectuals, and fellow travelers for the situation abroad. So far as is known, none of them looked in a mirror.

Sir William Hayter once compared negotiations with the Kremlin to a confrontation with an old-fashioned slot machine: you rarely got what you wanted, but you usually got something; you could "sometimes expedite the process by shaking the machine," but it was "useless to talk to it." Roosevelt had talked to it at Yalta, and he had hardly told Congress about Soviet promises before the Russians were openly flouting them. Stalin thought it magnanimous of him to treat with the western allies at all. Britain had provided time for the victory over Hitler, he said, and the United States contributed supplies, but Russia, with six million battle deaths, had "paid in blood." From Moscow Truman looked like a weakling and the United States like a disintegrating nation; Soviet economists had assured their leader that America was about to collapse into depression and chaos. Therefore Stalin demanded control of the Dardanelles, a slice of Turkish territory, a fixed share of Middle East oil, Caspian territory to shield his Baku oil fields, a Titoist Trieste, an Austrian Carinthia, a role in the occupation of Japan, and a physical presence in the Ruhr.

Truman's tongue-lashing of Molotov on April 23, 1945, had been the first intimation that the new President wasn't going to yield on any of them. The Russian, shaken, extended a formal invitation to Potsdam. As originally conceived, the conference there was to have implemented the decisions made at Yalta. Truman had misgivings about going, but there were many reasons he should, "the most urgent to my mind," as he wrote, being "to get from Stalin a personal reaffirmation of Russia's entry into the war against Japan, a matter our military chiefs were most anxious to clinch." The only part he really looked forward to was the ocean voyage aboard the U.S.S. *Augusta*. It was his first trip abroad since World War I, and his gossipy letters to Dear Mama and Mary convey a delightful picture of Harry, wearing a sport shirt and white sailor hat, running all over the ship to inspect every corner of it, finding a distant cousin in the crew, and snubbing the officers to eat with the enlisted men. After that: Potsdam. The meeting was instructive but depressing. He now knew beyond doubt that "Force is the only thing the Russians understand" and the Russians were "planning world conquest." Afterward he was "glad to be on my way home."

Potsdam left the future of the former Axis satellites unchanged; that is, papered over with ambiguities and occupied by Russians. The conference had been as pointless as Truman had thought it would be. He was so disheartened during it that at one moment—one of those fascinating moments which tempt the historian to speculate—he offered General Eisenhower the White House. The two of them were touring bombed Berlin, looking at rubble, when the President suddenly turned and said, "General, there is nothing you may want that I won't try to help you get. That definitely and specifically includes the Presidency in 1948." Eisenhower didn't know what to do, so he decided to treat the offer as a splendid joke. "Mr. President, I don't know who your opponent will be," he said, "but it will not be I."

As the months passed, Russian manners deteriorated. American scientists led by Oppenheimer toiled to perfect a sensible plan for the control of atomic armaments; when they had finished, Andrei Gromyko curtly rejected it out of hand. The behavior of the many Soviet front groups was, if possible, worse. Undersecretary of State Dean Acheson left a desk groaning with work to address the National Council of Soviet-American Friendship in Madison Square Garden. He expressed the hope that nations could reconcile their differences short of the point when "a knock on the door at night strikes terror into men and women." For this he was driven from the hall with boos and catcalls. "I have often wondered," he said, "who convinced the foreign offices of Communist countries that bad manners were a basic requirement for the conduct of international relations. Marx or Engels? Whoever did so, it was a great pity."[*]

The only member of the administration who retained his illusions about the Soviet Union was Secretary of Commerce Wallace. A visionary and a dreamer, Henry Wallace had long been suspicious of U.S. chauvinists; when Henry Luce hailed the coming century as the "American Century," Wallace had retorted that the postwar years "can and must be the century of the common man." Now, sitting in cabinet meetings and watching Harry Truman with hooded eyes, Secretary Wallace reached the conclusion that the President was an out-and-out warmonger. Something must be done about him, he decided. The people must be warned. He would warn them.

In retrospect, Wallace's defiant challenge of American foreign policy is less surprising than the fact that he had remained a member of the government that long. With Byrnes at State and Wallace at Commerce, there were two members of Truman's cabinet who thought they should be sitting in his chair. If Truman had possessed the charm of Franklin Roosevelt, he might have overridden the differences between personalities. Utterly lacking in wiles, he was

---

[*] Acheson's presence in Madison Square Garden was later cited by his critics as evidence of sympathy for Communism.

fated instead to cross one New Dealer after another. Byrnes had run afoul of him early. Leaving a Moscow conference, he had cabled the White House that he expected to broadcast a complete report to the people with a fireside chat as soon as he returned. Truman had reminded him that it was his first duty to report to the President, who would then make the chat, if any. Soon afterward Truman became embroiled with Harold Ickes in a struggle over patronage. On February 12, 1946, Ickes submitted his resignation, suggesting that it become effective March 31. Truman tartly made it February 15; Ickes then publicly charged him with collecting "a nondescript band of political Lilliputians" in the White House, and reporters observed that seldom had Washington seen such a sharp exchange between a cabinet member and his President.

It was repeated before the year was out. On March 5 Churchill, as a token of esteem for Truman, delivered his Iron Curtain speech on the campus of little Westminster College in Fulton, Missouri. His criticism of Soviet foreign policy was not well received; he was, as so often before, ahead of his time. The angriest sounds in Washington came from the Secretary of Commerce. Wallace resolved to put all Russophobes in their place when the moment came. It came in September, when Byrnes was in Paris for a crucial meeting of foreign ministers. On September 10 Wallace brought the President the final draft of a speech he meant to deliver before a U.S.-Soviet friendship rally. Truman didn't have time to read it; he thumbed through the manuscript while Wallace gave him the gist of it—he would, he said, take a more critical view of the Russians than he had in the past. Preoccupied, the President nodded casually and said he hoped the address would boost the prospects of liberal and left-wing congressional candidates and the Democratic state ticket in New York. In the lobby outside, reporters asked Wallace what he and the President had discussed. He suggested they listen to his speech.

Wallace kept his word in one respect. He rapped the Kremlin's knuckles. He rapped Whitehall's just as hard, however, and then delivered a powerful blow to the Truman-Byrnes foreign policy. Washington had no business interfering with the Russian presence in eastern Europe, he said; that was Stalin's sphere of influence. Next he argued that the administration should distribute atomic bomb plans to all governments, regardless of political persuasion. After that, he wanted the United States to disarm—whatever the other countries were doing. He felt that the mere thought of collective security treaties with Britain and western European countries was, on the face of it, wicked. "To make Britain the key to our foreign policy would, in my judgment, be the height of folly," he said. "Make no mistake about it: the British imperialist policy in the Near East alone, combined with Russian retaliation, would lead the United States straight to war." Then came these two sentences, written in since he had left 1600 Pennsylvania Avenue: "I am neither anti-British nor pro-British; neither anti-Russian nor pro-Russian. And just two days ago, when President Truman read these words, he said they represented the policy of his administration."

Reporters who had read advance copies massed at a 4 P.M. presidential press conference, three hours before the speech was to be delivered. Truman was asked whether he had approved the Secretary of Commerce's address, and he nodded. Did it accurately reflect administration policy? He replied that it did. Then, under the impression that Wallace would endorse established policy, he attended a stag party at Clark Clifford's house. He was there when lightning struck. The first rumble of thunder came at 6 P.M. At that time one of the advance copies reached the State Department desk of Will Clayton, who was Acting Secretary in Byrnes's absence. Calling Charlie Ross on the White House direct line, Clayton protested that "This will cut the ground right out from under Jimmy at Paris." He wanted a presidential repudiation, but Ross said it was too late; Truman had already approved Wallace's remarks. Next morning's newspapers heralded the "about-face" of American policy in end-of-the-world type. In Paris Senator Vandenberg told a newspaperman, "I can cooperate with only one Secretary of State at a time." Byrnes learned of the catastrophe from a British correspondent. After stewing for four days he cabled the President: "If it is not possible for you for any reason to keep Mr. Wallace, a member of your Cabinet, from speaking on foreign affairs . . . I must ask you to accept my resignation immediately."

Dean Acheson felt that "President Truman was naive. This is not a serious indictment. In the first place he was still learning the awesome responsibilities of the President of the United States. It did not occur to him that Henry Wallace, a responsible and experienced high officer of government, should not make a speech he had carefully prepared." If Truman had said that, he would have been understood. Instead he attempted to stamp out the fire with what *Time* called "a clumsy lie." He called a press conference to "clarify" what he called "a natural misunderstanding." He hadn't endorsed the speech at all, he explained; he had merely wished to defend Wallace's right to speak out. Above all, he had not approved the speech as "a statement of the foreign policy of this country." In the edgy question and answer period that followed, Truman was reminded that Wallace had in fact told his audience that his own refusal to choose between London and Moscow had been commended by the President as "the policy of this administration." This disastrous exchange followed:

> THE PRESIDENT: That is correct.
>
> Q: My question is, does that apply just to that paragraph, or to the whole speech?
>
> THE PRESIDENT: I approved the whole speech. . . .
>
> Q: Mr. President, do you regard Wallace's speech a departure from Byrnes' policy—
>
> THE PRESIDENT: I do not.
>
> Q:—toward Russia?
>
> THE PRESIDENT: They are exactly in line.

James Reston wrote scathingly in next morning's *Times,* "Mr. Truman seems to be the only person in the capital who thinks that Mr. Wallace's proposals are 'in line' with Mr. Truman's or Mr. Byrnes'." While mollifying the British, the President had nettled the reporters. To make a bad situation worse, Wallace refused to climb down. Calling his own press conference on the White House lawn, he declared: "I stand on my New York speech. Feeling as I do that most Americans are concerned about and willing to work for peace . . . I shall within the near future speak on this subject again."

That was too much. Confronted by the Secretary of State's ultimatum and the Secretary of Commerce's intransigence, Truman decided to dismiss Wallace. First he wrote him a longhand note laced with every profanity and blasphemy he could summon. Then he dispatched it to the Department of Commerce by hand. Wallace, stunned, telephoned Ross and said he thought the letter was not only unfit for publication; in his opinion it was too raw even to be filed in the National Archives as a presidential paper. After Wallace had read it over the phone, Ross agreed. The former secretary, as he had just become, sent it back to the White House, where Ross promptly burned it. That evening the President, purged of bitterness, wrote:

> Dear Mama and Mary:
> Well, I had to fire Henry today, and of course I hated to do it. ... If Henry had stayed Sec. of Agri. in 1940 as he should have, there'd never have been all this controversy, and I would not be here, and wouldn't that be nice? ... Henry is the most peculiar fellow I ever came in contact with. I spent two hours and a half with him Wednesday afternoon arguing with him to make no more speeches on foreign policy—or to agree to the policy for which I am responsible—but he wouldn't. ... Well, now he's out and the crackpots are having conniption fits. I'm glad they are. It convinces me I'm right. ...

He had been wrong, of course; he had handled things badly. Coming on top of the strikes, shortages, rising prices, the black market, and the general frustrations of reconversion, the Wallace incident contributed heavily to the erosion of Truman popularity. On the eve of his voyage to Potsdam in July 1945, Gallup had reported that 87 percent of the American people had approved of the way he was doing his job—an extraordinary vote of confidence in light of the fact that FDR's wartime high, just after Pearl Harbor, had been 84 percent. Then came a shift. "Washington has begun to turn against him," John Chamberlain wrote in the November 26, 1945, issue of *Life*. While Chamberlain's wish may have fathered that thought, a turning point was clearly reached sometime in 1946.

It was evident in little ways. On the right came a roar from the President of the NAM: "The President lets the public freeze while his guts quiver." On the left the liberal columnist Samuel Grafton called Truman "an object for pity." Even mainstream Democrats told one another, "You just sort of forget about Harry until he makes another mistake." Ickes called upon him to unite the country by announcing that he would not be a candidate in 1948. Truman's first eighteen months had been so inept, said Democratic freshman Congressman J. W. Fulbright of Arkansas, that in the national interest the President ought to step aside for a Republican successor. In California, Nixon was drawing heavy applause with such bromides as "I promise to preserve our sacred heritage in the name of my buddies and your loved ones, who died that these might endure." The people were restless, fed up with the Ins and receptive to the banishments of the Outs, whose two-word slogan, provided by the Harry M. Frost advertising agency in Boston and written large on billboards from coast-to-coast, was, "Had enough?"

The people said yes. For the first time in eighteen years the Republicans captured both houses of Congress—the 80th Congress, as Truman would later memorialize it, the most ultra-conservative since the Fighting 69th of the 1920s. Richard Nixon and Joe McCarthy were swept into office. The *Los Angeles Times* saw Stassen's star rising, and Nixon's with it: "Mr. Nixon is a friend of Governor Stassen, and his political philosophy is along the lines advocated by Stassen." *Life* jubilantly hailed the victory as a "significant shift in the government's center of gravity." Congress, which for years had been a "rubber stamp and whipping boy for the White House" would now, *Life* predicted, determine the direction of public life. A conference of Republican leaders proposed a slash of ten billion dollars from the budget, lower taxes, "abandonment of the philosophy of government interference with business and labor," and repeal of all social and welfare legislation passed since 1932, including social security and the Wagner Act. Senator Styles Bridges of New Hampshire crowed that "The United States is now a Republican country."

It wasn't. The returns of any political contest reflect, at most, the persuasion of those people who voted. As Theodore H. White has pointed out, mid-century America was always Republican until 5 P.M. on election day, when working men and women, on their way home, decided whether or not to stop at the polls. If they did, and only if they did, the country would go Democratic. In 1946 they didn't. A low vote—34 million—meant that Democrats in large numbers, discontented with the times and missing White House leadership, had stayed away. But Republicans misinterpreted the returns. They thought the people were disillusioned with the New Deal and wanted a swift return to the simplistic, pre-Crash, golden 1920s. That being true, they reasoned, they need only bait Truman during the next two years. Then the mansion at 1600 Pennsylvania would be returned to them.

Postwar Montage

A Walk in the Sun

Brief Encounter

B'WAY BIZ DROPS 50 PERCENT AS WORLD SERIES TELECAST

Moppin' up soda pop rickeys
To our hearts' delight
Dancin' to swingeroo quickies
Juke box Saturday night

JOLSON SINGS AGAIN!

Mammy, Mammy,
I'd walk a million miles
for one of your smiles,
My Mam-a-a-ammy!

Introducing: POLAROID!

The girl that I marry
Will have to be
As soft and as pink
As a nursery

Give me five minutes more
Only five minutes more
Let me stay, let me stay
In your arms

AMERICANS ATE 714 MILLION GALLONS OF ICE CREAM IN 1946

LYNCH 6 IN SOUTH IN '46

Senator Theodore Bilbo (D., Miss.) called on "every red-blooded white man to use any means to keep the niggers away from the polls."

FTC REVEALS: BOTH TONI TWINS WENT TO HAIRDRESSER

MORON'S ECSTASY $1.00

8 FLAVORS OF ICE CREAM, APPROXIMATELY A QUART
8 FRUIT AND NUT TOPPINGS, WHICH INCLUDE:
BANANAS — 2 HALVES MELBA PEACH — RASPBERRIES — MIXED NUTS — MARASCHINO CHERRIES — TUTTI-FRUTTI — PINEAPPLE — WHIPPED CREAM

NOTICE: THE MANAGEMENT ASSUMES NO RESPONSIBILITY OF ANY KIND, SHAPE, OR MANNER. Any person moron enough to finish a Moron's Ecstasy is eligible for membership in the Royal Order of Morons.

SINATRA PAYS OUT $9,000 FOR SLUGGING NY DAILY MIRROR MAN IN HOLLYWOOD

LUCKY STRIKE MEANS FINE TOBACCO!

NEW SURVEY SHOWS NUREMBERG TRIALS BORE U.S. PUBLIC

BEST SELLERS: Fiction
Try and Stop Me by Bennett Cerf
Black Boy by Richard Wright
The Egg and I by Betty MacDonald
Top Secret by Ralph Ingersoll
Pleasant Valley by Louis Bromfield

═══ M U Z A K ═══

BEST SELLERS: Fiction
Arch of Triumph by Erich Maria Remarque
Brideshead Revisited by Evelyn Waugh
The Snake Pit by Mary Jane Ward
The Foxes of Harrow by Frank Yerby
Cass Timberlane by Sinclair Lewis

The word canasta means basket in Spanish and most likely was suggested by the tray placed on the table to hold the stock and discards — according to Hoyle

FORTUNE POLL SHOWS 8.8 PERCENT OF U.S. STRONGLY ANTI-SEMITIC

THE ICEMAN COMETH

STRAPLESS, WIRED BRA KEY TO BARE-SHOULDERED LOOK

For Men of Discernment ... **LORD CALVERT**

Best actress of 1947: Loretta Young in *The Farmer's Daughter*

Gentlemen's Agreement   Crossfire   Miracle on 34th Street

Monsieur Verdoux   Great Expectations

That's just Elmer's tune

— **BIKINI BANG NO. 2 ROCKS RUSS** —

Fourteen

LIFE WITH HARRY

IN WARTIME the streams of history merge. Each of the republic's constituencies sees the struggle as a whole because everyone shares it and even participates in it, if only vicariously. Afterward the currents divide again. Insularity returns. The week remembered at the State Department for a reciprocal trade agreement recalls a merger in Wall Street, a fire sale on Main Street, a beauty contest in Pine Bluff, the installation of an Oriental rug for a young matron, and the World Series to fifty million baseball fans.

For President watchers, the four years, ten months, and ten days between V-J Day and Korea were one long succession of crises. In Washington the kitchen was always hot, and Harry Truman was always in it. Once he slipped away to visit Mexico, whose president showed him an erupting volcano. Harry said, "That's nothing compared to what I have back home." But of course there was more to the era than that. Truman saw events in a special light. He was the President, and men in high places have always been preoccupied with national destiny.

The hiatus between the two wars was certainly a time of tremendous flux. But it *was* peaceful. The guns were mute, the bombers grounded, the warships at anchor, the marines off doing pushups. It was a lacuna, a breathing space for the children of the Depression who had come of age overseas, and in this gentle nexus the college graduates of the swing generation—those likeliest to emerge as America's leaders in the 1960s and 1970s—returned to the arms of their girls, now young women. "Do you know what you are?"

Elspeth Rostow would ask her husband early one morning in 1961 during the Bay of Pigs crisis. "You are all the junior officers of the Second World War, come to responsibility."

Later, in the Johnson years, a Washington wit described the capital as "a city inhabited by powerful men and the women they married when they were young." That was unkind, and in its implication that postwar weddings had been casual detours from the highway of ambition it was also inaccurate. To the young veterans and their brides the late 1940s were exquisite years of easy laughter and lovers' vows, whose promises lingered like the fragrance of incense burning in little golden vessels on the altars of the heart. To be young and uncrippled was to be unbelievably lucky; to marry was to give of oneself, an exchange of gifts that multiplied in joy. It was a kind of fragile kaleidoscopic montage, held together by youthful passion, of a million disjointed sounds, colors, scents, tastes and snatches of quite ordinary Tin Pan Alley music; of an advertisement half glimpsed over a stranger's upturned collar on a Fifth Avenue double-decker bus; of the oleomargarine that came white in plastic bags with a yellow dye pill and had to be squeezed; of Kemtone that came in a powder that you mixed; of knowing what it was like to lie in bed together chain-smoking in that last decade before they took the fun out of cigarettes.

And it was playing charades with other young couples. And Alec Guinness's punting scene in *Kind Hearts and Coronets*. And that six-month wait for the first postwar Ford or Chevy, and shopping for the first crackly wash-and-wear shirts, and joking about the mad money she still kept pinned in her dirndl skirt; the shared jubilance of that cafeteria luncheon after you picked her up at the doctor's office and she said yes, it was true; the wonder at the supple touch of her breasts in that first pregnancy, and, all in the same mélange, the weekends of reading *The Death of a Salesman* to her in bed and choking up, of reading *1984* and sweating bullets, of watching Mary Martin wash her hair, hating Captain Queeg, and listening to Edith Piaf and Paul Robeson on the old Magnavox covering the place where the Kemtone had run out; of Sunday afternoons spent taking instant pictures of each other when the first black-and-white Polaroids came out in 1948, and playing Columbia's first ten- and twelve-inch 33⅓ LP Microgroove records in the summer of that same year and RCA Victor's 45 rpm the following January and then feeling the sudden hunger for the old 78s, and playing *them*, and afterward haunting Nick's and Eddie Condon's after hours in the

Village and walking the dead pavements of Fifty-second Street where Petrillo had killed swing and made way for bop, the tungsten-edged "progressive" jazz of Charlie Parker and Dizzy Gillespie. Outside Jimmy Ryan's darkened bar you bowed your head.

It was a time of emerging social distinctions, of an awareness of taste, when the men you didn't know wore clocks on their socks, called money "moola," yelled "Hubba! Hubba!" at passing girls, bowled Mondays, sent singing telegrams to each other at 3 A.M., tied tiny bells to the bedsprings of newly married couples and listened outside, did imitations of Franklin Roosevelt saying, "I hate wah, Eleanor hates wah," wore Robert Hall suits Sundays, tied foxtails to radio antennas, suspended baby boots from their rear-view mirrors, devoted Saturday mornings to ritualistic car washes, said "Long time no see" when they met, married wives who went to market with curlers in their hair and were always chewing gum, took their families to movies like *Four Jills in a Jeep* and *Sands of Iwo Jima*, but boycotted *Monsieur Verdoux* because *Parade* had exposed Charlie Chaplin as a Red.

Youngsters were now teen-agers (the word, which had come into general use, joined the language as "teen age" in the January 7, 1945, issue of the *New York Times Magazine*) and they were increasingly visible. Some inner-directed households kept them in their place. In her memoirs, *Souvenir* (1956), Margaret Truman wrote that she "was still called 'the little Truman girl'—a designation for which I had the usual teen-age distaste." Beyond the White House, however, Youth Power was reshaping social behavior, usually, older Americans grumbled, with excessive noise or bad taste. The younger ones were enthusiastic riders of scooters made from orange crates and roller-skate wheels.

With the number of popular songs up tenfold over the 1930s, there were now a half-million jukeboxes in the country, earning their owners 250 million dollars a year, all of it in nickels. The tunes were unmemorable, the words forgettable, but the jukeboxes were loved for themselves. They became so cherished an icon for the young that in 1947 the seniors of a Hudson Valley high school—Scarborough's—presented one to the school as a class gift while beaming parents and teachers looked on.

It was during the Truman years that America irrevocably joined the community of nations. The phrase "United Nations" had come to FDR in the middle of one night during the bleak Christmas of

1941, when Churchill was his White House guest. In its January 10, 1942, issue, *Time* reported that "a new phrase, the United Nations," had "slipped into the world's vocabulary. The year before, a *Fortune* survey had found that barely 13 percent of the electorate wanted to see America in any international organization. By March 1944, 68 percent did. A cross-section of college students that same year endorsed the proposal to send a U.S. delegation to a permanent U.N., fifty to one. Sumner Welles favored the idea and had written an eloquent plea for world government, *The Time for Decision*. It was the August 1944 selection of the Book-of-the-Month Club and sold almost a half-million copies. On the motion of Arkansas's Congressman Fulbright, the House of Representatives resolved 360 to 20 to support "the creation of appropriate international machinery with power adequate to establish and maintain a just and lasting peace among the nations of the world, and . . . participation by the United States therein." In the Senate the measure also had bipartisan support.

Philadelphia, Atlantic City, Chicago, San Francisco, and the Black Hills of South Dakota were competing vigorously with New York for the honor of providing the United Nations with a tax-free enclave. One small Connecticut city—Greenwich—had testily voted *not* to receive the new world organization, but that was put down to anti-Willkie, anti-*One World* spite. These were the months in which Senator Arthur Vandenberg was brooding in his Wardman Park* apartment, making his historic pivot toward faith in the viability of international interdependence. Crouched in a London air raid shelter as German robot bombs rocked the ground overhead, he had asked his escort, "How can there be immunity or isolation when man can devise weapons like that?" Vandenberg broke the power of his party's go-it-alone faction when he told a hushed Senate, "I have always been frankly one of those who believed in our own self-reliance. I still believe that we can never again—regardless of collaborations—allow our national defense to deteriorate to anything like a point of impotence. But I do not believe that any nation hereafter can immunize itself by its own exclusive action. . . . I want maximum American cooperation. . . . I want a new dignity and a new authority for international law. I think self-interest requires it."

---

* Now the Sheraton-Park. It still stands at the corner of Connecticut Avenue and Woodley Road N.W. and is still a rookery for eminent legislators.

Senators from both parties gave Vandenberg a rising ovation. The press hailed him for delivering a speech "of unquestioned greatness," "the most important address to come from the Senate in the last eighty years," "a courageous pledge to meet all aggression with force," "a promise that there will be no more Munichs," and "a shot heard round the world." In the excitement Washington turned a deaf ear toward a shot fired on the other side of the world. Returning from Paris in a barely controlled rage, Ho Chi Minh declared the independence of Vietnam, proclaimed himself president, and took to the hills. The State Department's Far Eastern desk issued no special directives to its men on the spot. After all, the rebels were only natives. Their insurgency was nothing a few companies of U.S. Marines couldn't break up, if it came to that. But, of course, it wouldn't. Vietnam was a French colony: the French Foreign Legion was on hand ready to suppress any serious uprising.

There was an elusive semantic problem here, and some grasp of it is important to an understanding of postwar weltpolitik. A quarter-century ago "the world," "the free world," and even "the United Nations," were not global concepts. As late as 1950, when Secretary of State George C. Marshall delivered his celebrated speech at Harvard launching the plan which would bear his name, it was clear from the text of the address that Marshall's "world" was confined to North America, western Europe, and their allies and dependencies. There was no "Third World" then, or anything like it. It is startling to note that the United Nations declaration of New Year's Day 1942 had been signed by just twenty-six countries: the United States, the United Kingdom, the USSR, and Nationalist China; five British dominions; eight European states, all of them then Nazi thralls; and nine South American republics. A united nation, in short, was one pledged to Hitler's defeat. In 1945 there were only four independent African countries: Egypt, where British influence was still paramount; Liberia, a peculiar kind of puppet of the United States; Ethiopia, which had just been freed from Italian Fascists; and South Africa, then as now ruled by a white oligarchy. On V-J Day U.N. membership had risen to 51 by the addition of liberated European states, the Scandinavian countries, and scattered small countries, but it was still largely a gentleman's club where one might clap his hands and call "Boy!" or assert independence by saying "I'm free, white, and twenty-one" without offending other members, including those whose skin happened to be black. The neighborhood, in other words, hadn't started to go.

At postwar dinner parties in Manhattan's opulent lower East Seventies, one of the smartest neighborhoods on that glittering island, the usual opening moves were to call for a drink—"Seabreezes," gin and citrus, were in vogue—while making it quite clear that (A) you never watched television and (B) you thought Christian Dior had taken leave of his senses. In the first instance you may or may not have been on the level, but in the second you were dead wrong. Christian Dior was at least as sane as you were. An obscure, middle-aged Parisian designer at the war's end, he had shrewdly guessed that women in the United States were still servile to fashions decreed in Paris and were ready to celebrate the end of Washington's hated Government Regulation L-85, which had limited them to two inches of hem, one patch pocket per blouse, no coat cuffs, no belts wider than two inches, no attached hoods or shawls, and no skirt more than 72 inches around. In the five years since Paris had fallen, a great many American girls had become accustomed to unpocketed and ruffleless blouses, spartan suits, and short skirts, the last of which had also brought enjoyment to men. But Dior said no. In late 1945, the orphic couturier sketched abundant skirts barely twelve inches from the floor, with unpadded shoulders but stuffed brassieres (or "falsies," as they were known), and shoes and hats that made men gasp. What Dior had going for him was that if women adopted his styles they would have to invest in entire new wardrobes. That brought the three-billion-dollar garment industry and the women's magazines down on his side with a thump. The ecstasy of *Harper's Bazaar* and *Vogue* and *Glamour* was unbounded. "Your bosoms, your shoulders and hips are round," one writer sang out. "Your waist is tiny, your skirt's bulk suggests fragile feminine legs. You are *you!*" Down with the barren, the harsh, and the sterile, they trumpeted on their slick pages, and up with Dior's full, luxurious, abundant (and expensive) New Look.

The New Look: that became fashion's war cry of '46. For American husbands, apart from their dismay over Dior's hidden leg, there was the prospect of bills running anywhere from $17.95 for a taffeta afternoon dress in Arkansas to $450 for a Paris original. In the case of their wives the stakes were more complicated. Most of them didn't like the costs, either. To many the V-plunge necklines, curving waists, sloping shoulders, midi-lengths, and the frothy organdy blouses erupting from peg-top skirts were downright ugly. But there was more to it than that. The promotional drive was an insult to their intelligence. The very prose in the slicks was crackers: "In this issue," *Vogue* giggled, "the merits of the cautious discard." What did that mean? It wasn't even a sentence. If women bought these absurd new outfits they would be conceding that they were dupes, the weaker sex, dithering little fools who couldn't be trusted with the family budget and were a menace on the roads.

The difficulty was that women lacked options, because society was still tightly sheathed in taboos—or, if you like, self-discipline. Their mothers had taught them to be modest and gentle in all ways, so they glowed in their wrath and did what, within the context of the time, could be done. In Kentucky 676 working women signed an anti-New Look manifesto. The loudest complaints were over skirt lengths, because girls were accustomed to showing more leg, and this was one alteration Singer couldn't make; it was impossible to let a short skirt down. "LBK" ("Little Below the Knee") clubs sprang up in several cities; 1,300 Dallas LBK members marched through the shopping distance with hems just below their kneecaps and LBK placards demanding freedom from French tyrants. In Paris Dior cried, "My God, what have I done?"—as though he didn't know.

The crisis came in 1946–47. It had to be resolved quickly; millions of yards of full-flowered chiffon and lace were piling up in the garment warehouses of Manhattan awaiting decisions from Little Rock, Denver, and Seattle. Customers were under pressure, too. Every time one girl passed another on a sidewalk, each was frantically deliberating which way to go. Some found brief refuge in what might have been called the third world of postwar fashion: new looks that weren't the New Look. Austere Britain, for example, was still rationing materials. Heels could be no higher than two inches, and clever Portobello Road modistes had designed "wedgies" with solid insteps that were cheap and looked smart. America's own dressmakers had revived the bare midriff and introduced the strapless wired brassiere in 1946. As Easter approached—it came on April 6 in 1947—the strugglers seemed locked neck-and-neck. And then feminine resistance suddenly vanished. Pushovers and dunces they might be, but no middle-class woman with cash or credit was willing to look like a frump that Sunday. Parading up the aisles, they clearly demonstrated to the rest of the country—that is, to their groaning husbands—that in matters of haut monde, a phrase which was not French by accident, they still danced to the music of a foreign piper.

In the aftermath of the struggle, the women guests not only struck their colors, they managed to forget that they had ever raised them. Women went about wearing, among other things, espadrilles, clogs, backless linen boots, spike-heeled "naked sandals," and fezzes garnished with veils, feathers, and even birdcages. The excesses of the shoemakers followed a certain logic; limited in the length of leg they could show, women with trim ones were trying to attract attention with odd footwear, varicolored nylons, and multiple ankle straps. But the hats made no sense whatever. Neither did impractical matching gloves nor the bizarre handbags. If they were making any social statement at all, it was an assertion of feminine intuition and a woman's right to be wrong, trivial, and fickle.

Over Seabreezes or Martinis at the typical Manhattan dinner party the general discussion of the gathering guests might touch upon Larry McPhail's coup in picking up the Yankees for three million dollars; Nicholas Murray Butler's retirement from Columbia University; the Pope's creation of four new American cardinals; and, on a gloomier note, a report from the University of Denver's National Opinion Research Center: 36 percent of Americans expected the country to be at war again within twenty-five years and another 23 percent within fifty years. Only 20 percent thought World War II was the last global struggle. And the poll had been conducted late in 1945, before the public knew how shaky relations with Stalin had become.

Buffet dinners were not acceptable in the lower East Seventies during these years, nor was dress optional. Wearing black tie and evening gowns, the guests found their places at a linened table, the guest of honor at the host's right, and all flanked by members of the opposite sex to whom they were not married. You were expected to divide your conversational time between them until, with the last wineglass empty and the candles burning low, the sexes took leave of one another. The men gathered around their host for brandy and Havana cigars, while the women went upstairs to do whatever women did on such occasions. It seems likely that at least part of the time they discussed prevalent topics of special interest. Yale pediatrician Arnold Gesell's *The First Five Years of*

Life was still selling briskly and usually sparked interest in powder rooms. (*The Robe* and *Peace of Mind* were better sellers, but to mention them in this company would have been social suicide). There was a current rage for matched purses and hats, adhesive black silk "beauty patches" for the face, and new dress fabrics featuring huge portraits of the wearer. Women were very much aware of the technological revolution, and like their sisters out on the farm they were grateful for it. Synthetic fabrics were changing their lives in Manhattan as well as in Iowa. Servants had almost vanished, but so had many of the reasons for hiring them. Electric clothes dryers had appeared in appliance stores less than a year after V-J Day, and during each year in the late 1940s women were buying 225,000 automatic dishwashers and 750,000 garbage disposal units. Frozen orange juice had come in 1947. Of course, some of the new devices were absurd. A young Chicago industrial designer named Jean Otis Reinecke was taking out a patent on an electric guitar which could be tuned up to such a pitch that it challenged the endurance of the human eardrum. Well, people said, it was a free country, and everybody knew it took all kinds, but some people were the absolute limit.

Advertising was about to enter a kind of Golden Age. A Navy veteran's best-selling roman à clef (Frederic Wakeman's *The Hucksters*, 1946) was making Madison Avenue a household word. Yet the very heralds of advertising's prosperity—the mass circulation magazines—would later become the communications industry's most prodigious failures. During the war periodical publishers had been as busy as foremen at Willow Run. Between Pearl Harbor and V-J Day each of them had gained, on the average, a quarter-million subscribers. Before the war they had sold at most a few thousand copies abroad; now that America was the acknowledged leader of the West, their readers included hundreds of thousands of Europeans. In one two-year period alone they increased their advertising income by a hundred million dollars. Even in the full flush of this prosperity, however, there were warnings of trouble ahead. Surveys by advertisers, John Fischer reported in *Harper's*, had disclosed that literate Americans were turning more and more to periodicals aiming at specific clienteles—*Yachting, Holiday, The New Yorker*. As for the mass audience, it was restless. Diverting it was no longer enough; it wanted to be captivated, enthralled, carried away. The days of the newsstand giants would be numbered, once the public discovered TV.

Television made stimulating conversation in the early Truman years, but it didn't make much else, certainly not money. The early Dumont sets were tiny, expensive, and limited in number, and there usually wasn't much to see. Two sports telecasts hinted at its great potential: TV's coverage of the Louis-Conn fight on June 19, 1946, and of the 1947 World Series. In each case the spectator who stayed home by his set saw more than men who had paid fifty dollars for a ringside or Yankee Stadium seat. But advertising sponsors were waiting before committing themselves. There were still far too few sets in living rooms to justify big budgets for the tube—only 172,000 of them as late as January 1, 1948, with fewer than twenty television stations. So radio remained smug. Hollywood didn't. The movie moguls came hat in hand to the great Madison Avenue advertising agencies, where brisk account executives mounted a nationwide offensive, suggesting to readers of hoardings and subway and trolley ads, "Why Not Go to a Movie Tonight?" and reassuring them that "Movies Are Better Than Ever." It wasn't true, and it didn't work; as word spread that nearly a quarter-million television sets a month were going into American homes, it couldn't. But that didn't seem to matter. The admen and their half-brothers the P.R. men were the alchemists and sorcerers of postwar society, the wizards whose florid wartime institutional advertising had softened up the market for the new fabrics and appliances, the new canned beer, and cigarettes double-wrapped in cellophane. When they cleared their throats at a Manhattan party, in Detroit's auto styling suites, or among oilmen and lobbyists, others fell silent. The image makers were known to have special insight. Attention must be paid. Everyone understood that polling skills and manipulative techniques were the experimental stage, like Newton watching the apple fall or Fleming finding the penicillin mold in his laboratory, but give it time, give it time; its possibilities knew no horizon, and some visionaries, remembering the rout of Upton Sinclair's EPIC in 1934, thought that one day its refined techniques might even be used in a presidential campaign.

Determining the communications industry's precise role in the boom was impossible, but media influence had clearly grown during the war, and it wasn't confined to the marketplace. Already ads and magazine articles were trying to form internalized profiles of what an individual was, or ought to be. Thus GIs had been bombarded with the puerile assurances that they were fighting for blueberry pie, while the girl next door—or the young bride left in the trailer camp at the point of embarkation—was wondering how much Joe had changed and what he was like now. She had his letters, of course, but censorship was crude and most soldiers were inarticulate about the things that really mattered. So she stopped at the newsstand or corner drugstore and turned to articles whose authors were only too eager to help her understand her faraway loved one, now about to return.

They told her that a "readjustment" problem lay ahead, and that she had better be ready to solve it. "Has Your Husband Come Home to the Right Woman?" the *Ladies' Home Journal* asked. Psychiatrists, sociologists, and writers explained over and over that Joe couldn't be the same. *Good Housekeeping* counseled patience: "After two or three weeks he should be finished with talking, with oppressive remembering. If he still goes over the same stories, reveals the same emotions, you had best consult a psychiatrist." To *House Beautiful* the solution was obvious. "Home must be the greatest rehabilitation center of them all!" it trumpeted, displaying the living room decor for a shell-shocked general. There were even primers on taking the bends out of WACs and WAVEs. Surprise her, her parents were urged, by redecorating her bedroom: "GI Jane will retool with ruffles." Irresponsible newspapers dwelt on the threat of deranged ex-servicemen at large. CRAZED VET RUNS AMOK, ran one headline.

Through Bill Mauldin and others, rumors of this sort of thing had reached the troops overseas. Anger flared when they heard embroidered versions of home front advice or outright lies; in 1944 the story made the rounds that Eleanor Roosevelt had recommended that combat divisions be quarantined in a Panama detention camp before their homecomings, to be taught how to behave among civilized people, and that even after discharge they should be required to wear conspicuous armbands warning decent girls that a potential rapist was in the vicinity. They weren't that way at all, the guys on the line said indignantly. It wasn't true that they were preoccupied with sex.

But they were.

After the Battle of El Alamein a Reuters correspondent reportedly asked an Eighth Army Tommy, "What's the first thing you're going to do after the war?"

"Hump my wife," was the soldier's instant reply.

"And the second thing?"

"Take off these goddamned hobnail boots."

It was much the same in all armies, and has been true of troops since the beginning of military history. Once the Betty Grable pinups came down and skirts were hoisted in bedrooms and parks, talk of readjustment disappeared; "the veteran question," noted William L. O'Neill, "never materialized. . . . Of all the surprising developments in the postwar years, the easy accommodation of this mass of men was perhaps the most astonishing."

In the 1940s, love American style was marked by three distinct features. The first was the speed with which wartime marriage contracts had been drawn, the second the frequency with which they were dissolved after the gunfire died down, and the third the swiftness with which nurseries became overpopulated. Before Hiroshima quick weddings were chic. The communications industry encouraged them; in a memorable film, *The Clock*, Robert Walker went to the altar with a girl exactly twenty-four hours after he had encountered her in Pennsylvania Station, despite the fact that they came from different backgrounds, didn't know each other's families, and had nothing in common except physical attraction. On some military bases near cities teeming with girls, nuptials were encouraged by the construction of special chapels. The press made much of celebrity weddings: Artie Shaw to Ava Gardner, Oona O'Neill to Charlie Chaplin, Judy Garland (after divorcing David Rose) to Vincente Minnelli, Gloria Vanderbilt (twenty-one) to Leopold Antoni Stokowski (fifty-eight), and, after starring in twenty-four Westerns together without exchanging a kiss, Roy Rogers to Dale Evans. Then the boys came home, and romances began to disintegrate. One of the chief reasons was limned in *The Best Years of Our Lives*, a movie about middle-class homecomings. Dana Andrews played a young flier who had married on impulse just before sailing. During his absence his bride, a shallow blonde, dreamed of him as he had been then, silver wings, smashed-down pilot's cap, and all. Mustered out, he couldn't wait to get back in civvies, and when she took one look at him in them she was as good as on the train to Reno, which in 1946 granted eleven thousand divorces, still an all-time high.

In those years, these matters—among them the engaging case of Loveless v. Loveless—attracted the interest of the young veterans' wives, who might have been found attending any one of several thousand kaffeeklatsches in, among other communities, Los Angeles. They were all a winning lot; unless they had suffered from prolonged malnutrition in the Depression, they showed no outward sign of those desperate years. (When they smiled the effect may have been different. Orthodontists and braces had been a luxury when they were young. Some would be wearing dentures before they were thirty.) According to a study of fifteen thousand girls completed in 1945 by New York's American Museum of American History, the average young American woman that year had longer legs, fractionally heavier hips, and a slightly thicker waist than her grandmother in 1890, but was slimmer-hipped and less voluptuous than Aphrodite of Cyrene. On her wedding day she stood about 5 feet 3½ inches (slightly taller if she had been born in California) and measured 33.9–26.4–37.4. By the time she had become eligible for L.A.'s morning kaffeeklatsches, motherhood had scored a few local gains in the battle of inches, but she continued to be trim, pert, and celebrated by European journalists of the time for her readiness to laugh at almost anything, including, self-deprecatingly, herself and her friends—"We're such a bunch of cows here," she would say, "just a yard of cackling hens." Her hair was brown, her eyes blue, and "dear," the most popular term of endearment in her parents' generation, had been succeeded by "honey." Unless she was a college graduate or a member of the League of Women Voters, her interest in public affairs was nil. She took pride in belonging to "the uncommitted generation." She and her husband seldom scanned a newspaper. All she expected of him was that he hold a steady job, and as a child of the Depression himself, that was what he expected of himself. The name of the game was security.

Except for patios and their tiny subtropical gardens, these young women could have been found anywhere in the country. They were in California because it was growing faster than any other state, was especially attractive to veterans ready to settle down, and had become known as the birthplace of postwar America's life-style. In these years the number of American supermarkets was tripling and would soon pass the twenty-thousand mark, but San Francisco's Crystal Palace Market, their prototype, had opened in 1922. Before Pearl Harbor, California had pioneered in the development of drive-in theaters, restaurants, banks, churches, and machines which would wash and wax a car with the driver in it; after it they popularized backyard barbecue pits and kidney-shaped swimming pools. California engineers laid out the first eight-lane superhighways, designed the first cloverleaf interchanges, and developed the exact-change toll booth. The first guest to arrive at a dinner party in a sport shirt was a Californian; so was the first wearer of an electric blue tuxedo jacket. On their beaches California women pioneered bathing suit seminudity and then nudity, and elsewhere they introduced the nation to street slacks, illuminated shrubbery, split-level living, and the custom of women smoking in public. In a word, they were imaginative; in another, casual. The coffee, unsurprisingly, was instant.

Typically, kaffeeklatsch conversation was about their children. They had become the beaming creators of a population explosion which was wholly unexpected. The government had unwittingly encouraged mushrooming births. "Instead of dating many girls until college and profession were achieved," Betty Friedan has noted, the veteran "could marry on the GI bill." Demographers hadn't expected the new couples to lie in bed and just neck, but they had thought they would exercise some restraint, like their older brothers and sisters in the 1930s. Parental moods had changed, however. "The veterans and their wives grabbed for the good things as if there were no tomorrow," Caroline Bird wrote. "They wanted everything at once—house, car, washing machine, children. . . . They had babies without worrying about how much it would cost to straighten their teeth or send them to college." It was easy to do, and lots of fun; if the figures Dr. Alfred Kinsey of Indiana University published in the third year after the war are set beside census data of the late 1940s, a few simple calculations reveal that America's 55,311,617 married men were reaching 136,666,060 sexual climaxes a week, or one emission every .0048 seconds. During those years a wife was being impregnated once every seven seconds, and the U.S. Bureau of the Census was blushing.

For the bureau this was a debacle. Every pre-Pearl Harbor population estimate went out the window. The war years had not been barren. "Goodbye babies" were being born throughout it, with the annual birth rate just below three million. But in 1946, the year after the troop transports began unloading, a half-million more infants were born than the year before. And that wasn't the end, or anything like it. The next year's crop passed 1946's record-breaker by over 400,000. By the mid-Sixties there would be between 20 and 30 million more Americans than long-range planners had counted on, with the greatest expansion in the teen-age population: the student generation which was destined to make so much news. Even in the Johnson-Goldwater election of 1964, before the bulk of the war babies reached their majority, fewer than one voter in four had been a Depression adult. It was then, in Johnson's second term, that certain generational differences began to emerge. Thus the conceptions of the Truman years would begin to exert a conspicuous influence upon society just as the parents were settling into middle age, and alter it in ways which would not always arouse their enthusiasm.

It was in these years that Dr. Spock's manual of baby care became the greatest best seller since best seller lists began in 1895. Spock devoted a section to what he called "permissiveness." He wrote: "It's basic human nature to tend to bring up your children about as you were brought up." Nevertheless, they should bear in mind that "Doctors who used to conscientiously warn young parents against spoiling are now encouraging them to meet their baby's needs, not only for food, but for comforting and loving." The Age of Spock had begun.

At the outset it was in many ways a marvelous age. One of Bill Mauldin's cartoons in *Back Home,* his sequel to *Up Front,* shows a father clutching groceries and wheeling a stroller while a uniformed sergeant heckles: "How's it feel to be a free man, Willie?" Veterans without number thought it felt great. Women's magazines began to note a phenomenon: the new fathers were volunteering to mix the baby's formula, take the 2 A.M. feeding, and even cope with the diaper service. (Disposable diapers wouldn't be available for another fifteen years.) As new gadgets and conveniences came on the market, parental chores became easier. (There were no electric knives, but electric knife sharpeners took the butchery out of carving; no central vacuuming systems, but vacuum cleaners became lighter and more efficient.) And if a couple wanted to dine out and take in a movie, older girls in the neighborhood were glad to sit for a price. (A quarter an hour was considered generous.) Emerging households, in fine, had been freed of their worst drudgery and most backbreaking tasks. The only difficulty was finding a home.

The postwar housing shortage was a direct consequence of the baby boom and the rapid Wanna-Go-Home demobilization. With the Army discharging nearly a million men a month by December 1945, and the Navy another quarter-million, there was almost no place to put them. America needed at least five million homes, and it needed them now. Clearly it wasn't going to get them from the housing industry. Once wartime controls were removed, labor and materials went into industrial construction; between V-J Day and Christmas ground had been broken for only 37,000 houses. President Truman asked Congress for price ceilings on housing and authority to channel half the country's building materials into low-cost ($10,000 or less) houses. The powerful housing lobby blocked him. The Senate did approve turning 75,000 temporary wartime buildings over to veterans and their families; government dormitories were remodeled for another 11,000 married GIs, and with winter blowing colder every day, 14,000 families were crowded into empty Army barracks. It was a dent, no more. Over a million families were doubling up. In arctic Minneapolis a husband, wife, and their little war baby spent seven nights in their car. In Atlanta two thousand people answered an ad for one apartment. Atlanta's distressed city fathers bought a hundred trailers for veterans' families. Trailer camps were springing up around every community of any size, especially those with campuses. The University of Missouri conducted a house-to-house canvass, reserving every foot of available space for children of Missouri parents, and then wrote out-of-state applicants that despite their qualifications, there was no room. North Dakota veterans converted grain bins into housing, and Benny Goodman and his band played for a Cleveland benefit at which citizens pledged rooms for rent. There wasn't anywhere near enough of this, though. Landlords were famous for their cold shoulders. Mauldin was bitter—his wrath continued to be a guide to the temper of his generation—and he expressed his anger in a savage drawing showing a GI and his wife and daughter confronting a fat, arrogant landlady. A sign by the door reads: "ROOMS/No Children or Dogs." The landlady is saying, "You soldiers just don't seem to understand our problems."

At the height of the crisis, every encampment of married GIs had its repertoire of gruesome stories. Their most striking advocate was an improbable U.S. Senator named Glen Taylor, a cowboy singer sent to the capital by the people of Idaho on the strength of his skill with a banjo. Standing on the Capitol steps with his wife and children, he wailed:

> Oh, give me a home near the Capitol dome,
> With a yard where little children can play;
> Just one room or two, any old thing will do,
> Oh, we cain't find a pla-ace to stay.

The country desperately needed a ten-year program to erect 1,500,000 homes a year, and for a while it looked as though the only answer would be tents. The housing industry's lobby had enough muscle to block a huge government effort, but the industry was too expensive and too slow, with its brick-by-brick methods, to do the job itself. Somehow the vacuum had to be filled, and by early 1949 it had become evident that assembly-line prefab developers —the peacetime equivalent of those who had wrought wartime production miracles—were going to do the job. The Henry J. Kaiser of housing was to be the emerging firm of Levitt & Sons. In shaping postwar society, William J. Levitt's purchase of a 1,500-acre potato field in Long Island's Nassau County ranks with DuMont's seven-inch TV screen and Howard Aiken's construction of the first U.S. computer at Harvard. The origins of suburbia as it is today can be traced to the staking out of that field, and those who scorn Levitt's first Levittown cannot know how grateful its first inhabitants were. Levitt made no announcement and bought no advertising. Word of mouth was enough; when he opened his modest sales office on the cold, blustery morning of March 7, 1949, over a thousand couples were waiting. Some of them had been there four days and nights living on coffee and doughnuts. When the doors opened it was like the Oklahoma Land Rush of 1889, with the Young Marrieds, as they were now beginning to be called, rushing around, resolved to be among the first to buy the basic four-room house for $6,990 or, with closing fees, landscaping, and kitchen appliances included, well under $10,000.

Levitt built homes as Kaiser had ships, on beltlines—17,500 houses in that first eruption, each like the other. On signal his bulldozers moved across the landscape in echelon, pivoting at red flags. Street pavers followed, then electricians with light poles and men bearing stamped street signs. Next, house lots were marked off. Convoys of trucks moved over the hardened pavements, tossing out prefabricated sidings at 8 A.M., toilets at 9:30, sinks and tubs at ten, sheetrock at 10:45, flooring at eleven. And so it went. Levitt's carpenters used only power tools; there wasn't a handsaw in town. Paint came from spray guns, and at first in just one two-toned "color scheme." Calculating that two thousand families could swim in a pool occupying the same amount of space as a tennis court, Levitt decreed eight pools and no courts. Everything was uniform. On Mondays wash was hung in 17,500 backyards; under no circumstances could it flap on Sundays. Picket fences were prohibited. Lawns had to be cut regularly. It was all in the deed. Even pleasant innovations conformed to Levitt's game plans. Trees were introduced at the rate of one every 28 feet (2.5 for each house), and the distance from trunk to trunk was precise to the inch. Curbstones curved gently, but always at the same angle. Families struggling to assert their identity were limited to interior decorating and the pitch of the door chime. (It had to be a chime, though; buzzers and bellpulls were out.) Architects and sociologists were aghast. To them this was the entrepreneur as a totalitarian. Yet the Levittowners didn't mind. To ex-GIs who remembered military regimentation, and their wives from Quonset huts and trailer camps, the hearths were no less warm for having been built according to standard specifications.

Bill Levitt became an instant legend, a checkout counter Paul Bunyan unscarred by the outraged aesthetes. As his imitators sprang up across the country he assembled his men, crossed the Pennsylvania state line, and targeted on eight square miles on the Delaware River which until then had been used to grow spinach. Levitt's draftsmen had plans for 1,100 streets accompanied by schools, churches, baseball diamonds, a town hall, factory sidings, parking lots, offices for doctors and dentists, a reservoir, a shopping center, a railroad station, newspaper presses, garden clubs—enough, in short, to support a densely populated city of 70,000, the tenth largest in Pennsylvania. Levitt called Levittown II "the most perfectly planned community in America," and when he spoke of it his voice grew husky. "Sure, there's a thrill in meeting a demand with a product no one else could meet," he said. "But I'm not here just to build and sell houses. To be perfectly frank, I'm looking for a little glory, too. It's only human. I want to build a town to be proud of." After a pause he added, "You have to have nerve. You have to think big."

Curiously, his own home was everything a Levittown house

wasn't—a lovely old Bucks County farmhouse with thick stone walls, hand-hewn rafters, stout beams, expansive rooms, and a stunning view of thick, uninhabited woods. He liked it, he admitted. But, he quickly added, most Americans, especially women, would not. "It isn't fair," he told a visitor, "to ask the public to pay for things they don't need and can't afford." Pointing to the old building's ornate moldings and other dust catchers, he said, "Imagine asking a modern housewife to clean this place. Imagine sticking your own wife way off in the country like this. People like people." They'd better, his tone suggested. They weren't going to get much choice.

Fifteen

A LITTLE TOUCH OF HARRY IN THE NIGHT

IT IS POSSIBLE to fix the time and place when the flag of world leadership began to pass from the dying British Empire to the United States. Late in the morning of Friday, February 21, 1947, Lord Inverchapel, the British ambassador in Washington, telephoned the State Department to request an emergency appointment with General George C. Marshall, who had just replaced Byrnes as Secretary of State. His lordship explained that he had been instructed to deliver "a blue piece of paper"—diplomatic cant for a formal and important message—from Whitehall. Dean Acheson replied that Marshall was away, speaking at the Princeton bicentennial. Could the matter wait until Monday?

Actually it couldn't, Inverchapel replied. He would ask his First Secretary, H. M. Sichell, to make the delivery now. Here a bit of stage business intruded. As Undersecretary, Acheson couldn't receive a First Secretary without violating protocol. Someone of lower rank was needed; therefore he designated as his representative Loy Henderson, director of the Office of Far Eastern and African Affairs. Thus it happened that two low-level diplomats, meeting in a dismal office in the Executive Office Building late that afternoon, took the first step in transferring world power westward.

Sichell had in fact brought two documents, both of them, as Acheson later recalled, "shockers." Acheson knew Greece was troubled. The Communists were reported ready to take over the country, there were rumors of British troop withdrawals, and Henderson had submitted a memorandum entitled "Crisis and Imminent Possibility of Collapse," urging massive aid to a coalition government as Greece's only hope of salvation. But nothing heretofore had signified the extent of Hellenic despair. If the Greeks didn't receive a first installment of over two hundred million dollars in the immediate future, he now read, they would succumb to a new barbaric invasion from Russia. Turkey was also in straits—that was the second piece of blue paper. The Turks were somewhat stronger, but lacking aid they, too, would be overwhelmed. Britain couldn't give either country anything more. The English were exhausted and depleted by their six-year struggle with Nazi Germany. Indeed, they, too, were in urgent need of fresh dollar transfusions; presently Lord Inverchapel would be approaching the Americans again, this time holding out his own silk hat.

Apprised of all this, Truman was startled. He had no idea the situation was that bad. To be sure, Churchill had warned that Europe had become "a rubble heap, a charnel house, a breeding ground of pestilence and hate," but that had been largely discounted as a peal of Churchillian thunder. The press had either ignored the extent of Europe's agony or underplayed it; *Time,* ever fortunate in its search for the epigrammatic bystander, had quoted the anonymous widow of a Czech partisan as saying, "We don't need much, but we need it quickly." That had made sense in Washington, where the premise had been that after a short period of turmoil and adjustment the continent, like the United States, would rebuild its peacetime economy. The week after V-J Day the President had reviewed Allied appeals for extensions of lend-lease and turned them down. Forty billion lend-lease dollars, he had said, was enough. The program must be liquidated as soon as possible; he was dead set against America's playing the role of a global Santa Claus after September 1945.

De Gaulle had protested, so had Chiang Kai-shek, and Churchill had cried: "I cannot believe that this is the last word of the United States. I cannot believe that so great a nation would proceed in such a rough and harsh manner." It didn't. One loaning device was merely discarded to be replaced by others, notably the United Nations Relief and Rehabilitation Administration (UNRRA). Yet despite the loans, credits, and outright gifts of eleven billion dollars, deprivation and want continued to stalk the Low Countries, France, Italy, Western Germany and the Balkans. In each of the two postwar autumns methodical Berliners had dug thousands of graves before the ground froze to accommodate neighbors whom they knew would never see another spring; UNRRA's gifts to Greece had barely sufficed to replace the rusted pipes and pumps of Athens's ruined water system. From the Aegean to the North Sea, Nazi tyranny had been succeeded not by freedom, but by hunger and disorder. Looted by the Germans, pounded by bombs, and gutted by resistance fighters, the blackened factories stood cold and mute. There were no raw materials for them anyway, and even if raw materials had magically appeared, the shattered railroad grid could not have brought them to the plants. Political leadership seemed about to pass to the Soviet Union, if only because there was no viable alternative.

The State Department, upon learning of the need for a massive rescue operation, had at first counted on Britain and her far-flung empire to provide it. In July 1946 Truman had signed a bill authorizing a fifty-year loan of $3,750,000,000 to His Majesty's government, and that, he had thought, should liquidate American obligations to Europe. But now the money was gone, with little to show for it. Some 17,000 homes, a quarter of London, still lay in ruins; the erection of 10,000 Nissen huts as emergency shelters had met the housing needs of only a fraction of the supplicants. While American women argued about the New Look, their English sisters were limited each year to one dress, four ounces of knitting wool, two yards of material, one-third of a petticoat, one-fourth of a suit, and one-fifth of a nightgown. Victory had brought America's great ally survival, but not much else.

Even that was menaced by the terrible winter which began in January 1947. Throughout that month and the next, temperatures remained below zero while blizzards piled layer upon layer of record-breaking snow accumulations. It paralyzed England. Agricultural production dropped below nineteenth-century levels. Industry shut down. Electricity was limited to a few hours each morning, unemployment rose to over six million, and rations were tighter than in wartime. On that bitter Friday when Sichell rode to Pennsylvania Avenue with the two blue pieces of paper, one for Greece and one for Turkey, Whitehall predicted "even worse things to come in the year ahead." The *Times* of London called the forecast "the most disturbing statement ever made by a British government." Any doubts about the magnitude of Europe's plight vanished when

Herbert Hoover returned from touring twenty-four countries at the President's request to report that their populations—and especially their children, the flotsam of war—were on the verge of starvation and could be saved only by American largess on an unprecedented scale.

Hoover's fellow Republicans in Congress weren't so sure. There was much talk about Uncle Sam being played for a sucker, of pouring money down a rathole or into a global WPA, of the American dream ending in bankruptcy. Europeans, in turn, were stung by such callous appraisals.

Anti-Americanism had spread. An Army chaplain noted that in continental eyes U.S. soldiers were pathetic young men who had no idea why they had fought or what victory meant, and who were interested in finding only three things: women to sleep with, brandy to steal, and the next boat home. "There he stands in his bulging clothes," the Reverend Renwick C. Kennedy wrote of the typical U.S. occupation soldier, "fat, overfed, lonely, a bit wistful, seeing little, understanding less—the Conqueror, with a chocolate bar in one pocket and a package of cigarettes in the other. . . . The chocolate bar and the cigarettes are about all that he, the Conqueror, has to give the conquered."

The transmittal of this mood to Capitol Hill raised congressional hackles, and for the first time since the 1930s legislators began muttering about Europe's failure to repay its debts. But there was more to the Greco-Turk issue. Communists were a genuine threat there. Since the British could no longer disperse them with a whiff of grapeshot, Washington had to face a hard choice. An enslaved Europe under the hammer and sickle seemed unthinkable. The Soviet Union would double its steel capacity, shipbuilding facilities, skilled labor, electrical and chemical output, scientific and technical knowledge, and industrial plant. That way, and only that way, Russia could match American power. "I believe that if we lose Western Europe," Admiral Forrest Sherman testified before a congressional committee, ". . . we would have an increasingly difficult time in holding our own. Whereas if we lost all of the Asiatic mainland, we could still survive and build up and possibly get it back again."

That was logical, although in 1947 it was less than compelling. The Russians were still remembered as a brave ally. Disillusion had just begun to sink in, and thus far its effect had been confined to depressed morale; savage as World War II had been, the conflict between good and evil had been plain, and the prospect of more strife on new issues was disheartening. In 1946 Herbert Bayard Swope had introduced the phrase "cold war" in a Bernard Baruch speech. Baruch had thought it too strong then and struck it out. On April 13, 1947, after another year of Soviet crudity, Baruch did use it in Columbia, South Carolina, but even then it was limited to what was called "the war of ideas," and as late as May 1950—just before Korea—Paul Hoffman could argue that "The cold war is a good war. It is the only war where the question of destruction doesn't enter into it at all."

Even in 1947, however, it was clear that General Markos and his 20,000 Communist (EAM) guerrillas could not be driven from Greek hills by better ideas. The legitimate government needed what the State Department's Policy Planning Staff called "massive non-ideological aid"—in a word, guns. Guns were better than butter in attracting congressional votes from anti-Communist Republicans. Truman and his advisers were determined to send both. Yet their experience in piecemeal commitments had been discouraging. Europe required reconstruction, not relief. America needed a genuine foreign policy. Casting about for a philosophy to fit its deeds, the administration found one in a current issue of the prestigious quarterly *Foreign Affairs*. The article was titled "The Sources of Soviet Conduct"; its author was identified only as "X."

"X" was George F. Kennan, then a brilliant if obscure student of the Russian mind. He had first written his treatise in America's Moscow embassy, where he had served as counselor. He had been motivated by a careful study of Stalin's hard-line 1946 speech to a gigantic rally of Communist party functionaries, in which the dictator denounced coexistence with democracies and pledged himself to a world revolution of the proletariat. In Kennan's view Soviet leaders were frightened Marxist evangelists who had been unbalanced by a quarter-century of western distrust. Communism was their pseudoreligion, the opiate for their insecurity. Seen as theology rather than politics, it emerged in Kennan's analysis as one of the world's great faiths, complete with dogma, rituals, and historic mission. It was as indestructible as, say, Mohammedanism, and like Islam it would take hold wherever weakened societies had made men yearn for change. Once embraced it could never be wholly eliminated. It could, however, be *contained*—limited to the frontiers of nations already under its spell.

In the context of the 1940s, containment was realistic. It made excellent sense to Harry Truman; as the largest and richest of the free nations, he declared, America must meet her obligations to "the free world." The President became so staunch an advocate of Kennan's views that they became known as "the Truman Doctrine." On his order they were incorporated in Policy Paper Number 68 of the National Security Council, and in Dean Acheson's opinion, NSC-68 became "one of the great doctrines in our history." In fact, even before Kennan's article became America's cold war strategy, Acheson, in the President's presence, outlined its principles to a meeting with the congressional leadership. At stake was the future of Turkey and Greece; "never," he wrote later, "have I spoken under such a pressing sense that the issue was up to me alone." When he had finished, there was a long pause. Then Arthur Vandenberg turned to Truman and said, "Mr. President, if you will say that to the Congress and the country, I will support you, and I believe that most of its members will do the same."

He did, and they did. On March 12 Truman asked a joint session to appropriate 400 million dollars—250 million for Greece and 120 million for Turkey. Then he, Marshall, Acheson and Vandenberg hit the sawdust trail to preach the gospel of containment before every influential group in the country, until, on May 22, the President signed the Greco-Turk aid bill into law in his temporary office in Kansas City's Muehlebach Hotel.

At the time, the Truman Doctrine looked like a master stroke. Its loudest critics then were right-wing mastodons who wanted to "roll" the Communists "back" to their prewar frontiers. Yet there were other dissenters whose questions, raised mildly at the time, remained unanswered a quarter-century later. Senator Taft, pointing out that the two governments were to receive American arms, suggested that Capitol Hill should be exceedingly careful about delegating its war-making powers to any chief executive, whatever the issue. General Albert C. Wedemeyer thought containment was an invitation to military folly, because the Russians could bleed America white by provoking aggression on the boundaries of its satellites, where the conflict would be "their third team opposing our first team." Most haunting of all, Walter Lippmann adopted Wedemeyer's arguments and added others of his own in a brilliant riposte to Kennan's reasoning.

Lippmann's slim volume was called *The Cold War: A Study in U.S. Foreign Policy* (1947). In it he was polite—Kennan was called "Mr. X" throughout—and devastating. Quoting the article in *Foreign Affairs*, he noted Kennan's view that it demanded "unalterable counterforce" to the Communists "at every point where they show signs of encroaching." If the Soviet Union were an island like Japan, he wrote, it could be blockaded by American air and sea power. Unfortunately, it was a land power, and as such it could only be contained by trench warfare or the endless hemorrhages of guerrilla warfare. "The Eurasian continent is a big place," he wryly commented, "and the military power of the United States has certain limitations." Already, in Greece, partisans had carried the struggle to the hills, where sophisticated weapons were useless and infantry skills were everything. Under containment, Lippmann continued, the outcome would depend upon draftees or satellite troops. Despair lay either way. America must "disown our puppets, which would be tantamount to appeasement and defeat and the loss of face," or must support them at an incalculable cost "on an unintended, unforeseen and perhaps undesirable issue." Repeatedly Lippmann returned to Asia and its traps for containment-minded diplomats. To accept a challenge there would permit the Communists to choose the battlefield, the weapons, and even the nationality of the Red battalions. "I find it hard," he concluded, "to understand how Mr. X could have recommended such a strategic monstrosity."

In eighteen months Greece was pacified, Turkey was invulnerable, and George Kennan was a hero. Washingtonians reminded one another that Lippmann wasn't infallible: after all, he had misjudged Roosevelt. But this time his instincts were right. While the triumph of the center in Greece would have been unlikely without American assistance, it would have been inconceivable if Tito hadn't quarreled with the Cominform and closed the border between Yugoslavia and Greece, depriving General Markos of his sanctuary. Superficial resemblances between Greece and Korea later strengthened advocates of containment and limited war without solving this problem of asylum, thereby contributing to Vietnam. It is worth noting that professional soldiers as far apart in other ways as MacArthur and Bradley agreed that the kind of conflict Lippmann had foreseen would be a strategic nightmare.

That was one side of the containment coin. The brighter side was the Marshall Plan, which grew out of the Truman Doctrine and became its great sequel. If the Greek and Turkish debt to Kennan's vision is less than had been supposed, western Europe's obligation is beyond price. Eventually the Marshall Plan—formally known as the European Recovery Program (ERP)—became as noncontroversial as social security.

If ERP began with any one man, it was Undersecretary of State Will Clayton. Flying home from a six-week canvass of Europe, Clayton put it on paper as the only alternative to war in the coming decade. In every country he had visited, subversive campaigns were destroying national integrity and independence. "Feeding on hunger, economic misery, and frustration," he wrote, "these attacks have already been successful in some of the liberated countries." He proposed that the President and the State Department shock the American people into action. After his plane from Zurich reached Washington, Clayton handed his memorandum to Acheson, who took it to the President. Acheson reminded Truman that the President had asked him to speak for him at a small southern function on May 8. If shock was the right prescription, perhaps he should strike a few sparks there.

Truman concurred, and so it happened that the ERP concept was first presented to an American audience on the campus of the Delta State Teachers College in remote Cleveland, Mississippi. Abroad, Acheson told his listeners, the margins of survival were so narrow that the cruel winter just passed had threatened the people of northern Europe with extinction. He said: "It is one of the principal aims of foreign policy today to use our economic and financial resources to widen these margins. It is necessary if we are to preserve our own freedoms and our own democratic institutions. It is necessary for our national security. And it is our duty and privilege as human beings."

That, in sum, was the Marshall Plan. It wasn't Marshall's yet, however. The Mississippians liked it, and the *New York Times,* forewarned, put it on page one with an analysis by James Reston, but the wire services were indifferent; economic stories were considered almost as dull as public addresses by long-winded bureaucrats. The press would listen to General Marshall, though, and so a second trial balloon was readied, to be launched by him. It is a measure of the speed with which the European economy was deteriorating that delivery of his speech was moved up from the Amherst College commencement on June 16 to Harvard's on June 5, while Dean Acheson was drumming up support among reporters. Acheson was particularly active with British correspondents. To Leonard Miall of the British Broadcasting System, Malcolm Muggeridge of the *Daily Telegraph*, and René MacColl of the *Daily Express* he said, "Don't waste time writing about it. As soon as you get your hands on a copy telephone the whole thing to London. And one of you must ask your editor to see that Ernie Bevin gets a full copy of the text at once. It will not matter what hour of the night it is; wake Ernie up and put a copy in his hand."

General Marshall spoke for fifteen minutes in Harvard Yard. He first described the torn "fabric of the European economy." The remedy lay in "breaking the vicious circle and restoring the confidence of the European people in the economic future of their own countries and of Europe as a whole." Aid must be continued. He was now thinking in terms of seventeen billion dollars. But UNRRA's random spending must be replaced by a program in which there was "some agreement among the countries of Europe as to the requirements of the situation and the part those countries themselves will take to give proper effect to whatever action might be undertaken by this government." America had made its move. Now it was Europe's turn.

Thanks to Muggeridge, that next move was made almost at once. In England the small hours of the following day had arrived, yet a boy from the *Daily Telegraph* bicycled to the home of sleeping Foreign Minister Ernest Bevin with a carbon of Muggeridge's story, dictated over a transatlantic phone, as Acheson had suggested. Almost at once Bevin and France's Georges Bidault called an all-European conference in Paris, after which applications for economic aid reached Washington from Britain, France, Italy, Greece, Turkey, Belgium, Holland, Denmark, Norway, Austria, Ireland, Iceland, Portugal, Sweden, Switzerland, Luxembourg, and, later, West Germany. After six weeks of debate and the rejection of a Taft amendment which would have slashed a billion dollars from the program, Congress passed it and then voted 597 million dollars to tide over the "Marshall gap"—the months that would pass before long-term aid could take hold.

On April 14, 1948, eleven days after President Truman had signed ERP into law, the appropriately named freighter *John H. Quick* left Galveston harbor with nine thousand long tons of wheat for

Bordeaux. It was the first in a six-vessel fleet carrying emergency food cargoes for France. All told, the Marshall Plan was to give Europe 12.5 billion dollars, less than Marshall had thought necessary. In addition, there were such tangential programs as the Displaced Persons Plan, under which 339,000 DPs became American citizens. It was a proud page in history. The Russians were furious, of course. They announced the imminence of something called "the Molotov Plan," which was never heard from again. Henry Wallace, now sidestepping rapidly to the left, called ERP "the Martial Plan." In the lower house of Congress seventy-five representatives had fought it, and in the upper house freshman Senator Joseph R. McCarthy had demanded that for every dollar spent the United States should receive the equivalent of a dollar in strategic materials or foreign bases.

McCarthy notwithstanding, European leaders were both moved and exultant. This was especially true in Britain. Churchill hailed ERP as "the most unsordid act in history." The London *Economist* described it as "the most straight-forward, generous thing that any country has ever done for others." Thirty months later, when England was back on its feet, the *Manchester Guardian* said, "Ordinary thanks are inadequate. Here is one of the most brilliant successes in the history of international relations," and Hugh Gaitskell, then chancellor of the exchequer, added: "We are not an emotional people . . . and not very articulate, but these characteristics should not . . . hide the real and profound sense of gratitude toward the American people."

Across the Channel from England, the continent was transformed. Malnutrition vanished, people could dress warmly in winter, raw materials moved swiftly, pulled by new diesel locomotives on new railroad tracks; the Saar and the Ruhr sprang to life, and factories were busier than they had been before the war. In 1951 the Marshall Plan would lead directly to Jean Monnet's Coal and Steel Community. Six years after that the Coal and Steel Community would lead to the Treaty of Rome and the European Economic Community, or Common Market, which in turn would grow in power until it could compete with the United States and the Soviet Union as an equal. But in the late 1940s America glittered on a solitary peak. No other nation could even come close to it. It could only lose its lead by some extraordinary misfortune, such as a President or Presidents who would squander its wealth and youth on a distant, Orwellian war. At that time the possibility was too remote to be raised. Not to worry, as the English say, was the American mood. The United States was, and would continue to be, rich, chivalrous, peaceful, and Number One.

Number Two was becoming more and more difficult. Mutilated and ravaged by the full force of the Nazi war machine, unable or unwilling to understand why their western allies had delayed the second front until 1944, the Russians were hypersensitive to any sign of life in prostrate Germany. This national apprehension, fortified by the paranoia of Joseph Stalin, had become a wretched cross borne by western soldiers and statesmen. It grew heavier as signs of European health—and, as a concomitant, German vigor—began to return. In 1948 it peaked. During those spring weeks when Congress was winding up its Marshall Plan debate, Soviet conduct became increasingly aggressive. In February Stalin had seized Czechoslovakia, and on June 24 he imposed a blockade on Berlin.

The immediate issue was currency control. To thwart German recovery, the Russians had been flooding the western zone with paper money printed with plates that had been in use since the beginning of the occupation. To suppress this inflation, the western authorities issued new money, and at the same time they signed the Brussels Defense Pact and agreed upon a constitution for awakening West Germany. Russians fought these reforms step by step. They walked out of conferences. They issued their own currency. They stopped rail traffic between Berlin and West Germany for two days, stopped traffic on a highway bridge for "repairs," and then, by ordering a full blockade, invited a complete rupture.

The western allies decided against retaliation. If possible, Truman wanted to avoid face-to-face confrontations. The only glimmer of hope was in the sky. Air traffic was moving in and out of West Berlin's two airports, Tempelhof in the American sector and Gatow in the British. No blockade could be built in the air. Soviet aircraft might challenge western planes, but the responsibility for an incident could easily be evaded with no loss of prestige on either side.

Still, an airlift of these dimensions brought perils of its own. West Berlin was home to two and a half million people, more than Los Angeles, Philadelphia, Detroit, or Cleveland. No one had ever tried to supply a community that large, or anything like it, by air.

Just keeping Berliners alive would require 4,000 tons a day—the takeoff or landing of one C-47 every three minutes and 36 seconds around the clock. Furthermore, every eastward plane would have to be overloaded, ten tons to the flight. That was enough for bare essentials. It was a possibility, a mathematical possibility, though it would mean danger for the fliers and hardship for Berlin. Enough coal could be brought in to keep the lights on, but there would be no fuel for warmth. To function normally, the city needed 8,000 tons a day, a takeoff or landing every minute and 48 seconds. It couldn't be done—yet.

The Germans promised a disciplined civilian response. The U.S. Air Force and the RAF worked out a carefully planned, split-second operation. To train new pilots, a duplicate of Berlin's air corridor approach paths and navigational aids was built in Montana. They learned to fly four-engine transports blindfolded with the new GCA (Ground Control Approach) radar. Crews had to go up with very little sleep. Maintenance men, hosing out fuselages black with coal dust, developed ugly skin diseases. And the schedule didn't always work. Twenty-eight Americans lost their lives in the Berlin airlift of 1948–49.

The fliers called it "Operation Vittles." In the beginning it didn't begin to bring enough victuals. During June and July 1948 the airlift averaged just 1,147 tons a day, and it looked as though the siege would succeed. The first break came on June 30, when squadrons of C-54s began arriving from Panama, Hawaii, and Alaska. These were larger ships; they could carry heavier loads and permit longer periods between landings and takeoffs. Clay flew back to Washington to request more of them and was given 160. As winter approached the airlift began to hit 4,000 daily tons with some consistency. West Berlin would survive and might do better, depending upon the young American, British and, now, French fliers.

They needed more room to land in Berlin, and now they were getting it. Two new airstrips were built at Tempelhof and a third on the British field. What they really needed was a third airdrome. In September the French offered a site at Tegel, in their occupational zone. They doubted that it would prove useful. The number of laborers needed would probably be prohibitive. Furthermore, they lacked rock crushers and other heavy equipment. The western allies were about to receive a useful lesson in what German tenacity could do when harnessed to American ingenuity. Over

20,000 Berliners, of both sexes and all ages, volunteered to work three shifts a day. Meanwhile C-54s began landing the necessary equipment. At the first planning session, Clay dryly recalls in his memoirs, his engineers advised him that the new airport would be ready in March, whereupon "I found it necessary to tell them that it would be completed in December." They met his timetable with the help of a little audacity on the part of General Jean Ganeval, the French commander. Getting into the spirit of the project, he removed a radio transmitting tower that obstructed the new runway. The tower was in the Soviet zone. He asked the Russians to remove it, and when they refused he marched in with a demolition team and blew it up.

That third field in the French sector put Operation Vittles over the top. In December the airlift's daily average reached 4,500 tons; in January and February, 5,500 tons. It was clear now that Berlin would make it and then some; coal rations could be doled out for homes and some industry. Clay's C-54 fleet had grown to 224. By early spring the airlift was landing 8,050 tons a day, and one day it put down 13,000 tons. Besieged Berlin was fast becoming one of the most affluent cities in Europe, with warehouses crammed, just in case the Russians didn't know they were beaten.

They knew. On May 12 the barricades came down. The airlift was now history. The impossible had been achieved. Counting the first weeks of a partial "little blockade" in early 1948, the siege had lasted fifteen months, and in it Americans and their allies had logged 277,264 flights, hauling 2,343,315 tons of food, fuel, medicine, and clothing—nearly one ton for every citizen of Berlin. Its feats had become legend, and the miracles wrought by its pilots did much to balance the loutish behavior of immature U.S. soldiers on leave. "America has saved the world," Churchill said grandly. Not the world, surely; but certainly a vital part of central Europe. If the airlift was not typically American, it was America at its best, living up to the Seabee-Air Force boast, "The difficult we do immediately; the impossible takes a little longer," and carrying it off with grace and generosity.

The country was generous and so were the men who drove its planes. American pride was divided almost equally between Operation Vittles and Operation Little Vittles, the inspiration of a first lieutenant named Carl S. Halverson. On his way in and out of Tempelhof, Halverson parachuted bags of candy to Berlin children watching below. The idea caught on; soon all the fliers were doing it. In December 1948 they mounted Operation Santa Claus. Day and night thousands of tiny parachutes floated down bearing gifts from the unseen *"amis"* soaring overhead to Berliners too young to understand the blockade. Every toy, every doll, every piece of candy was bought by the crews with their own money.

In this as in all ways, the continent was becoming curious about the American national character, with its faith in solutions, its technological know-how, its pragmatism, its interest in things rather than ideas, and, less fortunately, its philistinism. General MacArthur spoke for legions of his countrymen when he condescendingly told a visitor, "It is fascinating to go back and read Plato's vision of Utopia and see how far we have progressed . . . What a remarkable vision—what intellectual flashes—those old fellows had, living under their backward conditions!" To the MacArthurs of America, and they probably constituted a majority, good plumbing and get-up-and-go outweighed the exquisite winding of Socratic reasoning.

Europeans could often identify Americans in civilian clothes before they opened their mouths. In part this was attributable to table manners, tailoring, informality, and the 35-mm cameras that seemed to dangle from every American's shoulder. There was also something about the way they carried themselves. "Conquerors?" Eric Sevareid had said of the GIs. "They had no sense of conquering a country; they were just after the Germans and had to walk over this particular piece of the earth's surface to get at them." Even before the war, when living in Munich, Sevareid had noticed that whenever he or his countrymen went for a stroll, Germans turned to watch. He had concluded, "Nobody on earth walks as easily as the American. His body is neither rigid like an Englishman's nor compact and crowded like a Frenchman's, and his head turns very easily upon his neck." Some called it insolence, others called it self-confidence; conceivably it was indefinable, but it was real. Someone else said, "The British walk the earth as if they owned it; the Americans walk the earth as if they don't give a damn who owned it."

In the past, Hollywood had given Europeans a distorted view of Americans, like figures in a carnival fun house mirror. Now their impressions were based upon the homesick soldier, or, more and more, the American traveling abroad. It wasn't much of an improvement. Tourists from other countries represented its privileged classes; well-educated, well-read, and frequently multilingual. Because of the extraordinary standard of living in the United States citizens from all levels were crossing the ocean, often with loud wives and louder children in tow. It spoke well of their country that second-generation Americans could return to the lands of their fathers, but it played hob with the national reputation.

It was U.S. popular culture on this level—somewhere below what Orwell called "the lower-upper-middle class"—which gave rise to continental concern over the Americanization of the world. Arriving in large numbers from the Atlantic seaboard, a small army of tourists, technicians, exchange scholars, diplomats, journalists, USIS librarians, Red Cross girls, ECA administrators, Point Four agronomists, Stage Door Canteen hostesses, and American businessmen —five thousand of them in Paris alone—were carving out beachheads at customs offices and deploying inland in swelling numbers. Meanwhile the Fulbright and Smith-Mundt programs would soon bring forty thousand foreign students each year to study in America. Europeans asked one another what were these people bringing to Europe? And what were Pierre and Gretchen learning across the water?

To the disgust of French traditionalists, a beloved guillotine had been replaced in 1945 by a shiny new U.S. electric chair. It was somehow symbolic. (Americans agreed, though for other reasons.) In public places once brightened by colorful native dancers at Christmas, Europeans were captives of what had become the most widely heard voice in the history of man—Bing Crosby crooning "White Christmas" (1,700,000 records sold by V-J Day), "Silent Night" (1,500,000 records) or "Don't Fence Me In" (1,250,000). Peasants who for generations had been proud of their vital role in European society now learned that their countrymen were being fed by "The American Middle West—Breadbasket of the World," and palates once soothed by the finest wines from the choicest grapes were being washed by a cheap brown fluid called Coca-Cola—the notorious "Coke," now in the late 1940s selling 50 million bottles a day, enough to float a light cruiser. Frenchmen struck back. The continent had hardly recovered from the airlift when the National Assembly in Paris voted 366 to 202 "to prohibit the import, manufacture and sale of Coca-Cola in France, Algeria, and the French colonial empire."

Resentment of what had come to be called "Americanization" was as widespread as the unpopularity of John Bull in the long century of British domination, and as inevitable. In Europe's view, the colossus from across the sea was smothering its pride with a new economic imperialism even more demeaning than the old. One didn't need to be a Marxist to sympathize. What were the Oxford don's feelings when he read in the *Times* that the British Marketing Council was sending fifty executives each year to the Harvard Business School, with the Crown footing the bill? Or a Roman who learned that once more the lira was being devalued because of a "technical readjustment" on the New York Stock Exchange? Or the independent little Belgian service station owner upon discovering that Esso sold more gas on the continent than in the United States? Or any European when told that to the U.S. Department of Commerce Lausanne was known only as the capital of Union Carbide Overseas, Zurich as the home of the Corn Products Company abroad, and Paris, Brussels, and London, respectively, as the European headquarters of IBM, the Celanese Corporation, and Standard Oil of New Jersey?

Yet apart from the heavy-handed campaigns of these commercial Caesars, it did appear that the country's best men and best efforts were often badly abused. It seemed hard that the embassies of a country which had given over a hundred billion dollars in foreign aid should have to weigh the advantages of installing shatterproof window glass because they were so frequently the target of hostile demonstrations. The gifts had been taken quickly enough, and within a month, sometimes less, those who received them had publicly displayed their contempt for the dollar. It was in these Truman years that Louis Kronenberger, an American intellectual with a following in Europe, and certainly no chauvinist, wrote in exasperation:

> Americans have every right to be proud of a pioneer heritage that, first conquering and subduing the land, has gone on harnessing and commandeering the air waves. Americans have a right to exalt a national ideal and a native *modus operandi* that, beginning with maximum hardship, has ended in maximum comfort. Why shouldn't we be proud of how openhanded and hospitable we are, how alive and alert, of how the American way has conferred unimaginable opportunity on the poor and the elsewhere rejected?

Others struck back at European critics; *Time*, in a memorable issue, called France a prostitute. (Another riotous scene in the National Assembly.) Doubtless cutting all foreign aid from the budget would have enhanced presidential popularity, but it was never seriously considered. Even Senator Taft knew a return to isolationism was impossible, and conceded that an American President could no longer concern himself solely with domestic pressures. In an age of thermonuclear weapons, on a globe shrunk to a fraction of its prewar size, understanding the hopes and aspirations of other countries had become a matter of national security. It was precisely in this area that Harry Truman defied all the form sheets drawn up in the early weeks of his Presidency. Lacking brilliance in statecraft, he compensated for it with courage and native shrewdness. "When the Truman government found its feet," Dean Acheson later wrote, "its policies showed a sweep, a breadth of conception and boldness both new in this country's history and obviously centrally planned and directed." And at the time, quoting Shakespeare's *Henry V*, Acheson said that America's allies had been reassured, and her enemies discomfited, by the realization that in the darkest hour of any international crisis, the President would be a formidable adversary, providing "a little touch of Harry in the night."

Throughout the spring before the Berlin airlift, Republicans were watching the calendar with a mounting sense of pleasure. Sixteen years had passed since Franklin Delano Roosevelt had first cast them into outer darkness. They continued to despise everything about That Man, and in a sense thousands of them were still running against him, but his sorcery, they believed, had died with him; nevermore would the Grand Old Party be daunted by that wicked grin, that maniacal laughter, that tilted cigarette holder and flashing pince-nez.

In his place stood a humbler politician, who looked very much like a man of straw. HST could hardly have resembled FDR less. Truman's height was average, he wore ordinary spectacles, and his flat, high-pitched voice carried no echo of the cultivated, prep-school accent which had identified his predecessor as a patrician. Since it was assumed that Roosevelt alone had infused his programs with dynamic appeal, the obvious corollary was that all of them could be repealed, like the Eighteenth Amendment, after the American people had spoken in the next quadrennial referendum. That would come on November 2. They could hardly wait.

It was going to be so easy. "Truman is a gone goose," said Congresswoman Clare Boothe Luce, the lovely blonde lawmaker from Connecticut, and although Democrats flinched, no one contradicted her. Since the Republican sweep of the off-year elections in November 1946, every public opinion poll, every survey of political experts had spoken with one voice: if Harry Truman ran for the Presidency, he would be doomed. Gallup reported that between October 1947 and March 1948 the percentage of Americans who thought the President was doing a good job had dropped sharply—to 36 percent —and that if he ran then he would lose to Dewey, Stassen, MacArthur, or Vandenberg.

"If Truman is nominated," Joseph and Stewart Alsop told their readers, "he will be forced to wage the loneliest campaign in recent history." Even he had misgivings. His approach to Eisenhower at Potsdam was repeated in the autumn of 1947; he asked Secretary of the Army Kenneth C. Royall to tell the general that if Ike would run for President on the Democratic ticket, Truman would be proud to be his running mate. Eisenhower asked Royall to convey his heartfelt gratitude to the President, but with it his regrets. Possibly he thought that with Truman as his vice-presidential nominee he would lose.

In the middle of November 1947 presidential Special Counsel Clark Clifford handed his chief a thirty-five-page reelection scenario. In it Clifford pointed out that Truman had achieved far more than most people realized. He had been good to the farmer. He was the man who had faced down John L. Lewis. Jews were happy because he was an enthusiastic Zionist, blacks because he had ordered the commissioning of Negro officers. He had unified the armed forces and vetoed antilabor bills, and it was the Republican reactionaries on Capitol Hill—Taft, Wherry, Milliken, Bridges, Joe Martin and Charlie Halleck—who had turned back his proposals for a massive housing program and a social security base for medical care for the elderly. Clifford wanted the President to run as an underdog, and against the Eightieth Congress.

Truman's overtures to Eisenhower are unmentioned in his memoirs; he gives the impression that he never considered standing aside. In reality, he appears to have been hesitant as late as March 1, 1948, when he told a Key West press conference that he had been "so darned busy with foreign affairs and other situations that have developed that I haven't had any time to think about any presidential campaign." During the following week the CIO took a firm stand against Henry Wallace's third party candidacy. Apparently that persuaded him that he could make it. On March 9 he called in Chairman J. Howard McGrath of the Democratic National Committee and said, "Well, Howard, if you think so, let's do it." McGrath was puzzled (he hadn't asked the President to run, only to make up his mind), but in the lobby outside he gamely faced the White House press and announced: "The President has authorized me to say that if nominated by the Democratic National Committee, he will accept and run." Truman's stetson was in the ring.

Immediately most of the party's leaders demanded that he withdraw it. Ed Flynn, boss of the Bronx and a former Democratic national chairman, refused to appear on the same platform with the President in New York; a husky presidential aide literally had to drag him from his car. Senator Olin Johnson of South Carolina publicly snubbed Truman. Fulbright of Arkansas proposed that he resign so that a Republican could take over at once and restore national confidence. A six-man delegation of southern governors led by Strom Thurmond, alienated by the administration efforts at racial integration, prepared to secede from the party and back a southern candidate—thus guaranteeing a *four*-party race, two of them formed from Democratic splinters. In Manhattan McGrath had to cancel a meeting of wealthy Democratic contributors—only three men would come—and when he mentioned Truman's name at a Los Angeles rally he was drowned out by boos. The hecklers were led by James Roosevelt and other apostles of the New Deal. They were in good company. Among those vowing to dump Truman were James's brother Elliott, Leon Henderson, Claude Pepper of Florida, Chester Bowles, Walter Reuther, Wilson Wyatt, and young Mayor Hubert Humphrey of Minneapolis. Boss Jake Arvey of Illinois announced that he would no longer support Truman, and the ADA hierarchy came up with what *Time* called "an extraordinary idea." It was breathtaking. Why hadn't it been discovered before? They would draft General Eisenhower!

There is a strain of high comedy in the Democrats-for-Eisenhower movement of 1948. Unaware that he had twice turned down such a proposal from the President, or that he regarded himself as a conservative Republican—even Truman didn't know that—the prospect of Ike as the leader of their party swept up all the dumpers cited above, plus Frank Hague of Jersey City, John Bailey of Connecticut, Happy Chandler of Kentucky, Richard Russell of Georgia,

Mayor Edward J. Kelley of Chicago, and Senators Lister Hill and John Sparkman of Alabama. The final antic touch—it was also an unforgivable insolence—was a telegram to the White House from Hugh Mitchell, Democratic leader in the state of Washington, asking the President to serve as chairman of the Draft Eisenhower Committee.

So appealing was the Ike-or-die movement that as long as there was a glimmer of hope that the general might change his mind, it was quite clear that Truman couldn't be nominated by his own party. On the eve of the conventions Eisenhower slammed the door shut by announcing that "I would refuse to accept the nomination under any conditions, terms, or premises." With that, the party rank and file abandoned hope. A pall fell over Democratic delegates. Convinced that they would lose in November, and trying to cut their losses wherever possible, they asked the Republicans, who would be the first to convene in Philadelphia's Convention Hall, to leave their flags and bunting in place. *Noblesse oblige;* the GOP charitably agreed. Democratic gratitude was almost pathetic. They were already saving for a head start in 1952. Maybe Eisenhower would be willing to lead them then.

Meantime, Truman's staff was busily refurbishing what Clifford called his "portrait." ("Image" still hadn't come into general use.) The President was disdainful of the public relations approach—he called it "gimmickry"—but the idea of attacking the Republican Congress aroused his militant instincts. The first tactic in the grand strategy was to hit the Hill every Monday with a popular proposal that Taft and his colleagues were sure to table. In swift succession Truman proposed a St. Lawrence Seaway, broader civil rights legislation, federal housing, aid to China, extension of wartime controls, highway construction, and extension of the Reciprocal Trade Act—all destined to become issues in November.

If the polls are to be believed, Truman's prospects looked dimmest in April. It was then that the greatest inspiration of the campaign struck his staff, and it was perhaps indicative of the general confusion there that afterward none of three men—Clifford, George M. Elsey, and Charles S. Murphy—could remember whose idea it had been. All of them knew that the President had never learned to read a speech. He hung his head over the manuscript, had no sense of pace or emphasis, and usually killed his applause. In extemporaneous remarks, on the other hand, he was lively and effective. The question therefore arose, why not talk him into delivering an off-the-cuff speech before a sizable audience? He liked the idea, and on April 17, after reading a prepared text before the American Society of Newspaper Editors, he improvised for a half-hour on American-Soviet relations. The difference was startling and heartening; the editors cheered him at the end and remarked to one another on how well he had spoken. Four more extemporaneous addresses followed, climaxing in a political chalk-talk before a thousand young Democrats at the Mayflower Hotel on May 14. At the end of it he brought them all to their feet with: "I want to say to you that for the next four years there will be a Democrat in the White House—and you're looking at him!" Next morning's *New York Times* called it a "fighting" speech, delivered "in the new Truman manner." Satisfied that he had found the right campaign style, he and his staff now proposed to submit it to a coast-to-coast trial run.

Here they encountered a financial obstacle. It looked immovable. The party war chest was almost empty. Poverty was destined to haunt the Democrats throughout the campaign; few men of means had any confidence in the candidate's chances. Even in April suggestions for cutting costs were valued, and after the Mayflower dinner the staff came up with a big idea. Why shouldn't Truman dip into his $30,000-a-year presidential travel allowance to make a nationwide railroad journey to educate the people about his achievements at home and abroad, and, while he was at it, to say a few choice words about his problems with Congress?

This was the politics of desperation, a sign of how long the odds looked to Truman. To be sure, Presidents seeking reelection had frequently advertised themselves by finding it necessary to ride around dedicating monuments or opening bridges. Such jaunts were considered a legitimate use of taxpayers' money, justifiable because their purposes were ostensibly nonpartisan. This junket was something else. From the first, Truman served notice that he intended to spend every minute strafing the Republican Congress, and that, as Chairman Carroll Reece of the Republican National Committee observed, made it as "nonpolitical as the Pendergast machine." Doubtless Reece would have made more of the issue if Truman's cause hadn't seemed so hopeless, and if the tour itself, seen from a distance, hadn't looked like a debacle.

At 11:05 P.M. on June 3, over two weeks before the adjournment of Congress for the conventions, the sixteen-car "Presidential Special" glided out of Washington's Union Station and headed westward; although Truman usually flew from city to city, people then expected Presidents and presidential candidates to travel by rail. The last car in the caravan was the luxurious, armor-plated "Ferdinand Magellan," built by the Association of American Railroads for FDR. Walnut-paneled, in continuous radio contact with Washington, its most conspicuous feature was an outsize platform in the rear, protected by a striped canopy and equipped with a public address system. Unlikely as it seemed at the time, that platform was to become the stage for a campaign drama as stirring, in its way, as anything in the history of presidential politics.

Often it seemed likelier to be remembered for its small disasters. Democrats under the impression that he had in fact agreed to draft Eisenhower turned out with homemade signs reading: IKE FOR PRESIDENT! HARRY FOR VP! One state chairman—William Ritchie of Nebraska—tried to board the "Ferdinand Magellan" and was ejected; he angrily told reporters, "I'm convinced that he cannot be elected. He has muffed the ball badly. He seems to prefer his so-called buddies to the persons who have done the work and put up the money for the party." Elsewhere one of these so-called buddies, a 1918 veteran who had been asked to make speaking arrangements, thought it was to be a reunion of the 35th Division. Others were turned away, with the consequence that the President spoke to fewer than a thousand people in an auditorium with a capacity for ten thousand. Photographers had a marvelous time standing high in the rear and taking shots that showed him addressing acres of empty seats. Literally nobody, the pictures implied, was interested in what the President had to say, though *Time* commended his "growing entertainment value."

At least twice he appeared on the train platform in pajamas and a bathrobe. "I understand it was announced that I would speak here," he told one gaping crowd. "I'm sorry that I had gone to bed, but I thought you would like to see what I look like, even if I didn't have on any clothes." In Barstow, California, a girl eyed his blue dressing gown and asked him if he had a cold. He shook his head. She persisted, "You sound like it." He twinkled and said, "That's because I ride around in the wind with my mouth open." It was the truth. In Eugene, Oregon, after his usual introduction of

Bess ("my boss") and Margaret ("who bosses my boss"), he launched into an off-the-cuff discussion of Potsdam and, forgetting that reporters were present, said, "I like old Joe! He's a decent fellow. But Joe is a prisoner of the Politburo. He can't do what he wants to." Back East Mrs. Luce gave him both barrels. She was glad the Democrats had got round to admitting it, she said poisonously: "Good old Joe! Of course they like him. Didn't they give him all Eastern Europe, Manchuria, the Kuriles, North China, coalitions in Poland, Yugoslavia, and Czechoslovakia?"

From Washington, Halleck told reporters that Truman would be remembered as America's worst President, and Congressman Cliff Clevenger of Ohio said he was a "Missouri jackass." Then Taft slipped. It was a little thing. Speaking before the Union League Club in Philadelphia, he deplored Truman's "blackguarding Congress at whistle-stops all over the country." He had coined a word, and from the Republican viewpoint it was an unfortunate one. Democratic headquarters telegraphed the mayors of all the little towns and cities through which Truman's train had passed. They were indignant at the slur, and he happily distributed their replies to the press. In Los Angeles, where an enormous throng awaited the President, he grinned and cried, "This is the biggest whistle-stop!"

On June 18 he returned to Washington. He had been away two weeks, had covered 9,504 miles, and had delivered seventy-three speeches in sixteen states. For the most part he had followed Clifford's suggestion that he be "controversial as hell," and toward the end he had felt an intangible meshing of the crowd's mood and his own. After a new Congress was chosen in November, he had said in Illinois, "Maybe we'll get one that will work in the interests of the people and not the interests of men who have all the money." A murmur of agreement had risen from the upturned faces. In Bremerton, Washington, the strong voice of a lumberjack had rung out: "Pour it on, Harry!" and he had shot back, "I'm going to—I'm going to!" In Spokane a man said, "What about throwing eggs at Taft?" Truman replied, "I wouldn't throw *fresh* eggs at Taft!" "You've got the worst Congress you've ever had!" he had cried, and, "If you send another Republican Congress to Washington, you're a bigger bunch of suckers than I think you are!" The crowds had roared approval: "Pour it on!" and "Give 'em hell, Harry!" And he had flung back savagely, "That's what I'm doing! That's what I'm doing!"

Taft was right, of course. It was demeaning, it was in ghastly taste, its precedents had ugly implications for future campaigns, and it was unfair to Republicans like Vandenberg, without whom there would be no Truman Doctrine in the Balkans, no Marshall Plan, no Berlin airlift. But as the spectacle of one man fighting against all odds it was stirring. The White House correspondents thought so. Now and then, they told their wives back in the capital, the President had almost made them forget that he didn't have a chance.

In Philadelphia the city fathers had spent $650,000 sprucing up for the Republican, Democratic, and Progressive conventions, in that order; the "Dixiecrats," so named by a copyreader on the Charlotte, North Carolina, *News*, would convene on the hallowed ground of the old Confederacy. An eastern city was preferable because the Atlantic seaboard was the farthest reach of the coaxial cable bringing live transmission; the speakers knew that while Edward R. Murrow and the other famous commentators stubbornly clung to radio, the podium in Philadelphia's Convention Hall could be seen on some 400,000 little TV screens in the East. In those days that was something.

In 1948 newspapermen paid as much as $12 for a room and bath and muttered about inflation; in 1948 they assumed that a hotel's menial tasks would all be done cheaply by Negroes. Truman had been trying to do something about the plight of colored people, but the Republican platform committee, after weighing a civil rights plank, discarded it without qualms. The issue hadn't yet caught the imagination of the intellectual community; they were still half persuaded by the plea for more time in William Faulkner's 1948 novel *Intruder in the Dust*. Southern filibusters continued to kill every measure prohibiting poll taxes, and southern blacks, like their fathers before them, lived in terror of the rope; there had been a lynching in 1947, there would be two more in this convention year.

The big names in the Republican party were Thomas E. Dewey, Harold Stassen ("Man the oars and ride the crest,/Harold Stassen, he's the best"), General Douglas MacArthur, Halleck, Vandenberg, Taft ("To do the job, name our Bob," and "To steer our craft, let's have Taft"), Earl Warren, and Joseph W. Martin Jr. Joe McCarthy of Wisconsin and Richard Nixon were present, but were very small potatoes; McCarthy had been a Stassen delegate in the Wisconsin primary, and Nixon, also for Stassen, was up in the galleries—too insignificant to be seated in the California delegation. Their big issue was there, however. Voters in the Oregon primary had found Stassen's advocacy of a measure to outlaw Communists absurd, but the convention keynoter was declaring, "We shall ferret out and drive out every Red and pink on Federal payrolls."

Dewey was the Republican front runner, though he had taken a few nasty falls since announcing his candidacy on January 15—or, rather, telling young Jim Hagerty to make the announcement *for* him. He was always leaving such vulgar details to other men, explaining that he preferred to concentrate on issues. Actually he spent a lot of time worrying about his appearance. With his toothbrush moustache and his stiff manner, he reminded people of a Keystone cop, or the man on the wedding cake. During the primaries photographers had persuaded him to wear a ten-gallon hat and an Indian headdress which had been worn by Queen Marie of Romania on her visit to the United States in the 1920s. He never forgave himself; in the pictures he looked preposterous. Of his tepid manner, wicked gossips said—unjustly—"You have to know Tom Dewey well to dislike him."

It was a cruel mischance that had made Stassen Dewey's principal challenger that spring. Dewey's height was five feet eight inches, Stassen was six feet three inches, and when they posed together in primary lulls, the effect was that of a man and his son. By convention time Dewey had acquired elevator shoes. Still, the damage was done. It was particularly annoying because Stassen hadn't been expected to do as well as he had in the primaries. In Wisconsin, it had been thought, MacArthur's slate would carry all before it. The general's partisans were well financed, and the state had been flooded with instant biographies: *MacArthur: Hero of Destiny, MacArthur: Fighter for Freedom,* and *MacArthur the Magnificent.* On March 29 a *New York Times* headline guessed, MACARTHUR VICTORY DUE IN WISCONSIN. The next day delegates representing the general won only eight convention votes. Senator McGrath told reporters, "This leads me to the conclusion that to insure the election of the Democratic ticket in November we need only have the commentators united in predicting defeat." They had chuckled politely; national chairmen have their little jokes.

Despite Dewey's convention eve come-from-behind triumph in Oregon, he could hardly be called the choice of the party's rank and file. Gallup now reported that the country's registered Republicans preferred the Minnesota giant, 37 percent to Dewey's 24 percent. Figures like that deserved more study than Dewey gave them. The summer before, every other Republican voter had wanted the dapper New Yorker. Such an erosion of strength ought to have alarmed him, especially since the Democrats, under Roosevelt, had become the country's majority party. After his nomination he should have come on slugging. Instead his acceptance speech lulled the delegates to sleep: "The unity we seek is more than material. It is more than a matter of things and measures. It is most of all spiritual. Our problems are not outside ourselves, our problems are within ourselves."

After photographers had taken pictures of him and Earl Warren, his vice-presidential candidate, Dewey went home to rest. He would not leave Albany until September 19, six weeks before the election, which, as the *New York Times* noted, would make his campaign "the shortest undertaken in recent years by the presidential candidate of the major party out of power." He seemed to regard it almost as a formality. And the rest of the Republican leadership agreed. Several powerful Republicans, knowing that they would be members of the new administration, had traveled home from Philadelphia via Washington, stealing a march on their colleagues by picking up good houses at bargain prices.

"The Democrats act as though they have accepted an invitation to a funeral," the Associated Press observed on July 12, as delegates of the party in power trudged into Convention Hall through the soggy sauna of a Philadelphia heat wave. The bunting, gay three weeks ago, was stained and flyblown. KEEP AMERICA HUMAN WITH TRUMAN, said a high banner. Hardly anyone looked up at it. Truman "Victory Kits" were distributed, each with a notebook, pencil, and whistle—"For the Democratic graveyard," someone said. On the marquee of the Bellevue-Stratford a huge mechanical donkey flashed electric blue eyes at passersby, but that was just about the extent of the gaiety. Democratic delegates had a grim, hammered look. There were a few feeble signs of animation in rebel delegations which had recovered from the collapse of the Draft Eisenhower movement and were now reaching frantically, groping for any straw before they went down for the third time. Nineteen state chairmen held an election eve caucus. They approached Justice

Douglas. He declined and they gave up. Then Truman phoned Douglas and asked him to run for the Vice-Presidency. He said he wouldn't do that, either. For a while it looked as though the President might have to run alone. At last Alben Barkley, faithful old Alben, said he'd be glad to run the race.

In his humiliation Truman was spared nothing. He knew that a majority of the delegates didn't want him, that if he freed them now they would give him a standing ovation—and quickly choose someone else. It seemed inevitable that Henry Wallace would poll several million votes—enough, at any rate, to cost him New York. Now the Solid South was about to break up. Young (thirty-seven) Mayor Humphrey of Minneapolis, and Paul Douglas and Adlai Stevenson, the party's senatorial and gubernatorial candidates in Illinois, were leading the fight for a strong civil rights plank. Truman would have preferred to avoid heroics on this point. But North and South were groping for one another's throats; the Dixiecrats lost the key roll call 651½ to 582½. "We bid you goodbye!" cried Alabama's Handy Ellis, leading the way to the door.

It was Wednesday evening, July 14, when the Confederates left. The President almost ran into them when he arrived. His special train had left Union Station just as the evening session had been gaveled to order in Convention Hall. Seated in the "Ferdinand Magellan" between Clark Clifford and Sam Rosenman, Truman read through the notes for the speech. He was under the impression that he would go straight to the podium upon arriving. He didn't; he couldn't; the nominating speeches were just getting under way. He would have to wait four hours sweltering offstage. It is somehow appropriate that at that low point—the lowest point in his career—he was led to a small bleak room under the platform with a little balcony overlooking a littered alley. It was near the railroad tracks; he could hear the locomotives thundering by, feel them in the tremors of his straight chair. Talking now with Barkley, now with Homer Cummings, he squinted out at the grime and trash, mopping his forehead, rewriting the outline of his talk, glancing at the outline, brooding alone, and waiting.

At 12:42 A.M. on Thursday the President was finally nominated, 947½ votes to 362 for Georgia's Richard Russell and half a vote for Paul McNutt, former governor of Indiana. Despite the hour, the weariness, and clinging heat, Cabell Phillips wrote, the demonstration for Truman had "developed a sudden spontaneity; the whoops and rebel yells sounded real; delegates who had listlessly kept their seats while others paraded up and down the aisles picked up their banners and noisemakers and joined the aimless snake dance. Reporters standing on their benches in the press bank looked at one another in disbelief and said, 'This looks like it is for real.'"

Barkley was nominated by acclamation—underscoring the convention's failure to thus honor its presidential candidate—and at 1:45 A.M. he and Truman mounted the dais to the strains of "Hail to the Chief." At any other convention it would have been a sublime moment: the two leaders raising one another's arms high, the glaring lights, the tempo of the organ, the men standing on the collapsible chairs, and the excited women crying into handkerchiefs. There was all that, to be sure, but there was something else, too—a note of burlesque that seemed in keeping with the rest of it. Chairman Rayburn had just begun his introduction of Barkley when a stout, overdressed woman interrupted him. All evening a floral Liberty Bell had stood by the podium awaiting the emergence of the President. Now she presented it to him, or tried to; there was a sudden swishing under it—she just had time to stammer "doves of peace"— and abruptly flock after flock of white pigeons emerged from beneath the floral display and sailed back and forth and back and forth over the assembled delegates bearing their own tributes. Anyone familiar with pigeons, as the planners of this bit of stage business clearly were not, knew what came next. "Watch your clothes!" farmers in the crowd shouted. It was too late. People had been muttering it all through the long session, and here was the real thing, ruining their shirts and dresses. Luckily for the party's public image, or portrait, the press in 1948 considered such matters too indelicate for readers of family newspapers. Sam Rayburn saved the moment at the rostrum. He captured a passing bird and hurled it high overhead. The delegates cheered, and to their surprise and pleasure discovered that in that moment of slapstick their tensions had fled. They were relaxing, chuckling as they put away their pocket handkerchiefs and telling one another that whatever Harry had in store for them, it couldn't be fouler than that.

It was another, greater surprise. After Barkley's brief remarks, "the weary crowd," Irwin Ross tells us, "steeled itself for a dose of presidential oratory." Instead, the President spoke from the outline of his address, jotted down while waiting in the cheerless window over the alley near the coughing locomotives. Using his extemporaneous new style, he delivered a lashing, vibrant, give-'em-hell speech, and in Ross's words, "his strident, high-pitched tones electrified the audience." Stabbing the air with quick, awkward gestures, he cried, "Senator Barkley and I will win this election and make the Republicans like it—don't you forget it!" He shouted: "If the voters don't do their duty by the Democratic party, they are the most ungrateful people in the world!"

He then turned to the Republicans, reviewing the list of programs he had proposed, and the Hill had rejected, for medical care, housing, price controls, aid to education. They had killed such measures, he said—and then, in an unparalleled display of cynicism and hypocrisy, they had approved a presidential platform calling for all of them. Very well. He would test their sincerity.

He delivered his haymaker: "On the twenty-sixth day of July, which out in Missouri we call 'Turnip Day,' I am going to call that Congress back in session, and I am going to ask them to pass some of these laws they say they are for in their platform. Now, my friends, if there is any reality behind that Republican platform, we ought to get some action from a short session of the Eightieth Congress. They can do this job in fifteen days if they want to do it, and they will still have time to go out and run for office."

This, the *New York Times* reported, "set the convention on fire." The weather, the hour, the bitter internal strife and the impending defeat in November were for the moment forgotten. Truman waited till the din abated a bit, and then he drove it all home: "They are going to try to dodge this responsibility," he called, "but what that 'worst' Eightieth Congress does in this special session will be the test of whether they mean what they say!"

They were on their feet, giving him a standing ovation. He was hewing to the plan, keeping himself "controversial as hell," and the reaction outside Convention Hall confirmed it. Editorial writers were all but speechless; using federal funds for a campaign swing was bad enough, but calling a special congressional session to score partisan points was almost grounds for impeachment. Vandenberg told a reporter, "This sounds like a last hysterical gasp from an expiring administration." Congressman Hugh D. Scott Jr. of Pennsylvania deplored "the act of a desperate man who is willing to destroy the unity and dignity of his country and his government for partisan advantage after he himself has lost the confidence of the people"; and Walter George of Georgia, in a splendid Catherine wheel of mixed metaphors, cried, "The South is not only over a barrel—it is pilloried! We are in the stocks!"

Yet here and there men gave Truman grudging admiration. "There was no doubt that he had lifted the delegates out of their doldrums," said *Time*. "He had roused admiration for his political courage."

July was dominated by the two splinter parties and what everyone was calling "the Turnip session." Dixiecrat morale was high. The southern strategy was to throw the election into the House of Representatives. They believed they would win as many votes as Truman, and on July 14 they met in Birmingham. In one day they zipped through the entire convention ritual. Their nominees were Strom Thurmond for President and Governor Fielding L. Wright of Mississippi for Vice President. Here and there were omens that Dixie's thin white line might break. Russell and Harry Byrd of Virginia stayed away from Birmingham, not out of love for equal rights but because they thought their seniority on the Hill might be in jeopardy. Still, the Dixiecrat loss was a blow to the Democrats, particularly to Clifford, whose campaign scenario had assumed the continuing solidarity of the Democratic South.

Ten days later Wallace's Progressive Citizens of America (PCA) arrived in Philadelphia to form the Progressive Party of America (PPA). On December 29, when their leader had launched the movement by announcing his candidacy, the PCA future had looked very bright. "We have assembled a Gideon's army," he had said then. Progressives hadn't expected to win the Presidency in 1948, but they believed it might be theirs in 1952. The average delegate was about thirty years old, some twenty years younger than those at major party conventions. American campuses were heavily represented—more Ivy than Big Ten—and so were unions whose leaders had moved into deep left field. Boys with crew cuts, then part of the student life-style, wore open-necked sport shirts; girls were in bobby socks and dirndls; Negroes were heavily represented; there were many guitars and much singing of folk songs in the manner of Pete Seeger and vice-presidential candidate Glen Taylor. Everyone seemed to be having a lot of fun. To the casual eye Progressivism appeared to be flourishing.

In reality it was racked by internal strains. Rexford Guy Tugwell was the only New Deal recruit Wallace had managed to enlist, and he was in constant conflict with Lee Pressman, the Communist CIO general counsel who would later be ousted by Walter Reuther. One does not lightly affix Communist labels, particularly to public figures in the first postwar decade, and there was much confusion at the time among voters, who were under the impression that the Progressives were merely providing a liberal alternative to Truman. The confusion was deliberate, fomented by Communist party (CP) members who could hardly believe their luck in capturing a former Vice President of the United States. PCA was the mirror image of the Americans for Democratic Action (ADA), which had been formed in January 1947 to combat it. Three years after the 1948 election Michael Quill, who had broken with the CP, described their role in the Progressive movement to a CIO committee taking testimony about it. Quill was president of the Transport Workers Union and no red-baiter. In the autumn of 1947, he said, when his own sympathies were with the CP, Eugene Dennis, general secretary of the Communist party, told him and other labor leaders that the party hierarchy had "decided to form a third party led by Henry Wallace" and that Wallace "would come out in the next few weeks and announce his candidacy."

Wallace seems to have embarked on this extraordinary adventure wearing blinders. Late in the campaign, as he later told friends, he realized that he was being used, that nearly everyone around him was an avowed Communist. He must have been among the last to find out. The *New Republic* had tried to warn him; the *Nation* tried; so did *PM*. The *New York Post* had begged Wallace to join ADA, in vain. His candidacy had been supported by only two newspapers in the country, the *Daily Worker* and Pennsylvania's *York Gazette and Daily*. Reporters invited him to repudiate Red support, as FDR had in the 1930s. He refused.

The consequence was shattering publicity. Despite the vigor and enthusiasm of 3,200 attractive PPA delegates in Philadelphia—more than at either of the major party conventions—Wallace's Communist aides undid him at every turn. Potentially, his acceptance speech in Philadelphia's Shibe Park had the makings of one of the most memorable events in American politics. With tickets selling for $2.60 to 65¢—the proletariat in the bleachers—more than thirty thousand wildly cheering admirers attested to his continuing popularity. Given a reasonably fair press, which he might easily have had, he could have won over the Walter Reuthers and Jimmy Roosevelts, who needed very little persuading that July. He had only to disassociate himself from the Lee Pressmans. He declined; he wouldn't "repudiate any support that comes to me on the basis of interest in peace." A *Time* reporter called his attention to the resemblance between the PPA's platform and the CP's. "I'd say that they have a good platform," Wallace said of the Communists. He added gratuitously, "I would say that the Communists are the closest things to the early Christian martyrs."

With that, the wave of the Wallace movement broke. He would go on to the end doggedly, undeterred by hecklers who could see little resemblance between Communists and early Christian martyrs, his hand out, his brow damp, the familiar Wallace lick of hair in his eye. Invading the South, he was pelted with eggs, tomatoes, and firecrackers in three North Carolina towns. To the press, Truman regretted this "violation of the American concept of fair play." With that exception, the President ignored the PPA threat, trusting that it would shrink as Wallace's novelty appeal wore off. It did. With each passing week of the campaign, the Progressive effort lost momentum. Tugwell quietly withdrew his support, the left-leaning United Electrical Workers refused to endorse Wallace, and Progressive congressional candidates withdrew from local races. In the spring political analysts had conceded Wallace 3,500,000 votes at the least, eclipsing Debs's 1912 high of 901,000 for a third-party race. Gallup had given him 7 percent of the total vote then. By the third week in October, Gallup's forecast was down to 4 percent, and on November 2 the actual Wallace turnout would be less than that—1,157,172 votes. Democratic defections to the PPA undoubtedly cost Truman New York, but a careful reading of the returns strongly suggests that for every vote he lost to Wallace elsewhere, he picked up two or three sympathetic votes from the independent center.

Thurmond's popular vote was to be 1,169,021. His concentration in the old Confederacy did bring him 39 electoral votes (Alabama, Louisiana, Mississippi, South Carolina, and one Tennessee elector), but it can be argued that this was worse than nothing. The discovery that the party could win without the Solid South freed Democrats from the need to compromise with it; in attempting to thwart advocates of civil rights for Negroes, Thurmond had hastened their victories.

On July 26 Truman appeared before a hostile joint session on the Hill to present what he called his "shopping list" of needed legislation. During the thirty-minute speech he was interrupted only six times by applause, all of it from Democrats. The Republican members sat on their hands. Dewey, wary as always, refusing to "get in the gutter with Truman," as he called it, evaded reporters' questions about the Turnip session. He turned the whole thing over to Herbert Brownell and disappeared into his Albany study. Brownell was uneasy. He suggested to Taft that the party's congressional leadership might give the green light to a few noncontroversial bills, thereby crippling Truman's charge that it was obstructive. Why not amend the Displaced Persons Act, eliminating discriminatory clauses against Jews and some Catholics? Everyone agreed that the revision was needed, he argued, and Republican initiative now would cut the big Democratic pluralities in eastern metropolitan areas. Taft shook his head. It was a matter of principle, he said. In calling this session, the President had abused his powers. The shopping list must be ignored. Brownell having failed, Taft's GOP colleagues on the Hill tried to reason with him. Vandenberg said, "Bob, I think we ought to do something. We ought to do whatever we can to show that we are trying to use the two weeks as best we can. Then we have a better case to take before the public." According to Hugh Scott, who was there, "Bob Taft would have none of it. 'No,' he said, 'we're not going to give that fellow anything.' Anyone familiar with Bob Taft's method of ending a conversation will know that was the end of it."

Truman was delighted. In his message he had asked for legislation to control inflation, expand civil rights, increase minimum wages, extend social security coverage, and support housing programs—most of which had been vaguely endorsed in Dewey's platform. In agreeing to the hazy wording in Philadelphia, the Republican congressional leadership had never dreamed that they would be held accountable for it before the election. Taft's principle was sound, but there was also something to be said for keeping promises to the public. By sulking, the GOP seemed to be confirming the President's judgment of it.

On August 12 the White House issued a detailed report contrasting presidential proposals with inactivity on the Hill. At that day's press conference Truman deplored the "do-nothing" session and its "do-nothing Congress." Every name he had called it had been justified, he said; it had proved itself to be the "worst" Congress in history.

Before leaving, one Washington correspondent, pursuing a different story, reminded the President that it was nearly two weeks now since a plain, stocky woman in her mid-thirties named Elizabeth Bentley had begun testifying before the Senate Committee on Expenditures in the Executive Departments. Since then she and a House Committee on Un-American Activities witness, *Time* editor Whittaker Chambers, had charged that a number of government employees had spied for the Soviet Union. The accused included Alger Hiss, William T. Remington, and Lauchlin Currie. Did the President wish to say something about these espionage hearings?

"They are simply a red herring," Truman snapped. His thoughts still on the Eightieth Congress, he said: "They are using this as a red herring, as an excuse to keep from doing what they ought to do. Yes, you can quote me."

At 3:40 P.M. on Sunday, September 5, the engineer in the cab of the "Truman Special" blew his steam whistle twice and left Union Station in pursuit of six million enfranchised spectators. A Democratic campaign, financed from party coffers, was finally in business. There would be two major transcontinental tours of ten days each, a tour of the northeastern United States, and shorter trips into the states around the District of Columbia. In this first thrust the President would ride 32,000 miles and deliver over 250 speeches, then a record in campaigning. From each rural dawn to the day's last whistle-stop eighteen hours later, with the wide-eyed citizens of a small town gathered around the back of the "Ferdinand Magellan," holding torches high to see the scrappy little fellow on the platform, Truman was unfailingly full of fight—and always quotable.

Following the script of June's dress rehearsal, he was good-humored most of the time, admiring the local band, introducing Bess and Margaret, and ending his informal little talks with a plea to "Go to the polls on the second of November and cast your ballot for the Democratic ticket—and then I can stay in the White House for four more years," or "Do the right thing that will keep me from suffering a housing shortage on January 20, 1949." At the end of each stop the engineer would give a warning toot, and the medicine show would be on its way.

In the cities, crowds grew larger: 50,000 in Indianapolis; 50,000 in Denver; 250,000 in Boston; 250,000 in Detroit. "Nobody stomps, shouts, or whistles for Truman," Richard H. Rovere wrote in the October 9, 1948, *New Yorker*. "Everybody claps. I should say that the decibel count would be about the same as it would be for a missionary who had just delivered a mildly encouraging report on the inroads being made against heathenism in Northern Rhodesia. This does not necessarily mean that the people who come out to hear him intend to vote against him—though my personal feeling is that most of them intend to do exactly that."

Much that Truman said was absurd or irresponsible, and some of it mischievous. Harried and forlorn, supported by only 15 percent of the nation's newspapers, told on every side that he was wasting his time and everyone else's, he was capable of delivering demagogic lines. "The Republicans," he said, "have begun to nail the American consumer to the wall with spikes of greed." He called them "gluttons of privilege," called Dewey a "fascist" and compared him to Hitler, and to over 80,000 listeners at the National Plowing Contest in Dexter, Iowa, he charged that "This Republican Congress has already stuck a pitchfork in the farmer's back."

September became October, the days grew shorter, the nights deepened, cider appeared in the supermarkets, children scooped out pumpkins for jack-o'-lanterns, geese honked on their way southward at the first frost, bobwhites and barn swallows fled after them, squirrels hoarded white oak acorns, and still the Truman train crossed and recrossed the great fields of hayshocks, brown now but in trim straight rows, the locomotive meandering gracefully through the forests where maple tops were turning gold and staghorn sumac scarlet, where the long lonely whistle called those who could hear it to listen to the spry man introduce his wife and daughter, state his case, make his jokes, and then wave his hand and depart.

The low point for that train, according to Clifford, came toward the middle of October. As they paused in a small Midwest town, a member of the staff jumped off and bought the October 11 issue of *Newsweek*. The big black type read: FIFTY POLITICAL EXPERTS UNANIMOUSLY PREDICT A DEWEY VICTORY. "Unanimously," someone said hollowly, and there was a long silence. One of them trudged back and showed it to Truman. He blinked, grinned, and said lightly, "Oh, those damned fellows; they're always wrong anyway. Forget it, boys, and let's get on with the job." At that point, Clifford believes, neither Bess nor Margaret believed that the President had a chance. He himself did, however, and afterward he could prove it. On the afternoon of October 13, while riding from Duluth to St. Paul, he wrote out his state-by-state analysis of the coming vote on the back of a mimeographed copy of his Duluth speech and handed it to George Elsey, who sealed it and put it away until the day after the election. It then developed that Truman had predicted 340 electoral votes for himself, 108 for Dewey, 42 for Thurmond, with 37 marked "doubtful." It wasn't on the nose, and it omitted four electoral votes, but a great many men whose job was forecasting elections would have given almost anything to have written it.

Meanwhile the man who was following Harry around continued his triumphant tour of the nation. Superbly organized, rigorously on schedule, always met by liaison men, with facilities for distributing advance speech texts to the ninety-eight reporters aboard and a high-fidelity public address system which could carry the candidate's deep baritone tones from the rear platform to the press's bar car, Thomas E. Dewey's "Victory Special" provided the very latest thing in media equipment, designed to carry, spread, and disseminate whatever he wished to say.

He wished to say nothing. "Governor Dewey," Leo Egan reported in the *New York Times* late in September, "is acting like a man who has already been elected and is merely marking time, waiting to take office. In his speeches and in his manner there is an attitude that the election will . . . confirm a decision already made. . . . Governor Dewey is deliberately avoiding any sharp controversy with the Democratic incumbent."

Once in a while, in the Middle West and again in California, the two campaign trains would be only a day or two apart. Truman always noted the fact and reeled off a list of prickly questions for his opponent. Dewey declined the bait. He preferred to dwell upon the "incredible beauty" of the Rocky Mountains, the "soft, rolling, wooded country" through which he had been passing, the "teeming cities" and "fertile plains"—in sum, "the sheer majesty" of the United States.

Truman discussed housing, minimum wages, medical care for the elderly, crops. Dewey took his stand in behalf of water: "By adequate soil conservation," he said resonantly in Denver, "we can do much to preserve our own future. We must also use the water we have wisely and well. We need the water from our rivers for power as well as agriculture. . . . The mighty rivers of the west should be developed with a view to the widest possible use for conservation, power, navigation, flood control, reclamation, and irrigation."

In Des Moines, two days after Truman's "pitchfork in the back" speech, with the country waiting for the Republican standard-bearer's reply, Dewey said, "On January 20 we will enter into a new era. We propose to install in Washington an administration which has faith in the American people, a warm understanding of their needs, and the competence to meet them. We will rediscover the essential unity of our people and the spiritual strength that makes our country great. We will begin to move forward again shoulder to shoulder toward an even greater America and a better life for every American, in a nation working effectively for the peace of the world."

So thin was the meat in Dewey's formal addresses that resourceful newspapermen began looking for some anecdote, some light feature to relieve the gray paragraphs. On October 12, at Beaucoup, Illinois, the train abruptly moved backward, toward the crowd. It halted again after a few feet, and there were no casualties, but the governor was upset and angry. Depending upon which version you heard, he said either, "That's the first idiot I've ever had for an engineer" or "That's the first lunatic I've had for an engineer. He probably ought to be shot at sunrise but I guess we can let him off because no one was hurt." Possibly because it was one of the rare times that he had said anything real, the remark was passed on and on until it became an anti-Dewey slogan in union halls and railroad roundhouses all over the country.

Other Republicans were on the war path. Hugh Scott, now national chairman, had seized upon the Bentley-Chambers testimony, judging it as an issue with too many implications to be dismissed as a "red herring." Dewey made one tame reference to it and then soared off toward his most elegant generalities: "We have sometimes failed in our faith and often fallen short of it. But in our hearts we believe and know that every man has some of the Divine in him, that every individual is of priceless importance." To be fair, it must be set down that in the closing weeks of the campaign Dewey began to doubt his strategy. His crowds were dwindling and Truman's, the newspapers told him, were growing. His strategy board—Brownell, Scott, Elliott Bell and Russell Sprague—had decided to aim the final thrust at the industrial northwest; midwestern farmers were Republican by birth and would take care of themselves. Stung by Truman's hooks and jabs, he wanted to strike back, and in four communities he let loose. Truman's message vetoing the Taft-Hartley Law, for example, he said was "the wrongest, most incompetent, most inaccurate document ever put out of the White House in a hundred and sixty years." The crowds enjoyed it, and so did he, but his advisers were alarmed. Hagerty polled the newsmen and reported that all of them believed a slugfest would be a mistake, that it would be a confession of weakness. To be sure Dewey was getting the best counsel, Brownell set up a series of conference calls around the nation tying the candidate into round robin conversations with ninety of the ninety-six Republican state committeemen and committeewomen. All save one urged the governor to press forward on the high road and let Truman totter down the low road into oblivion. The exception, Harry Darby of Kansas, warned that the farm belt was in a mutinous mood. He was dismissed as a Cassandra, and Dewey resumed his crusade for unity, cleanliness, better water, and faith.

Down to the wire, the Truman train was bombarded with bills from managers of service industries terrified of being left unpaid. But after the disheartening *Newsweek* issue spirits began to lift a little. In bull sessions late on the train the younger staff members argued back and forth about the President's chances, though whenever they grew optimistic one of them would remind the others that every poll in the country contradicted them. In the last days Clifford thought there was something in the air, that Truman was picking up strength; when he rose to speak at the traditional Friday night before election rally in the Brooklyn Academy of Music, some of whose backers had been leaders of the "Dump Truman" movement before Philadelphia, the crowd gave him a twelve-minute standing ovation. Clifford reflected that if only the campaign could last two weeks more, they might have a chance.

In Chicago Adlai Stevenson and Paul Douglas stood side by side in an open car on their way to a Truman rally at the stadium. The silent crowds were four or five deep on the sidewalk. Fifteen years ago these had been the forgotten men and women at the bottom of the economic pyramid, the starving teachers and threadbare workers Insull had betrayed and Roosevelt had saved. Stevenson marveled at the size of the turnout. All Chicago seemed to be there, yet there was almost no cheering, hardly any sound at all. Douglas said, "They've come out today to see the death of the dream that they cherish."

In Baltimore, editor in chief Hamilton Owens of the *Sun* stopped by a young reporter's desk. "I've finished my editorial congratulating the new President," he said. "It's in type and on the stone." He paused and added with a twinkle, "If Truman won, I'd have to write another one, wouldn't I?" The little sally delighted him; he strode off chuckling.

Subscribers to *Life* that last weekend in October saw on page 37 of the new issue, dated November 1, a full-page photograph of Governor and Mrs. Dewey over the caption: THE NEXT PRESIDENT TRAVELS BY FERRY BOAT OVER THE BROAD WATERS OF SAN FRANCISCO BAY. Accompanying it was an eight-page windup on the campaign, in which the editors concluded that the U.S. was "about to ditch Truman and take Dewey" for reasons that involved "the brain as well as the emotions." The cover of Willard Kiplinger's weekly *Changing Times* for November 1 carried a 72-point type head announcing disclosures inside on WHAT DEWEY WILL DO. On Sunday, October 31, the *New York Times* reported the results of a month-long survey during which its sizable national staff had studied voter sentiment in every state. Its conclusion: Dewey would carry 29 states with 345 electoral votes (266 needed to win); Truman 11 states with 105 electoral votes; Thurmond 4 states with 38 electoral votes; in doubt, 43 electoral votes. The survey also found that the Republicans would retain control of both houses of Congress. To make sure it was right, the *Times* polled the forty-seven shrewdest journalists covering Dewey. In a secret ballot, they unanimously agreed that the governor would win handily.

In an editorial which would appear on November 3, the morning after the election, the *Detroit Free Press* would call upon Secretary of State Marshall to resign and urge Truman to appoint John Foster Dulles, Dewey's adviser on foreign affairs, in his place. "That," its editors argued, "would restore confidence in our foreign policy abroad and at home." (That same Truman Doctrine was pacifying Greece, the Marshall Plan was in full swing, and the Berlin airlift had entered its fifth month.) "True," the *Free Press* conceded, "that is asking a great deal of Mr. Truman. Yet these are times which, with all our unity and patriotism, will ask a great deal more of millions of other Americans." The editors generously described

America's "lame duck" President as "a game little fellow, who never sought the Presidency and was lost in it, but who went down fighting with all he had." *Free Press* readers were assured that Harry Truman would still make a living: "There's first the prospect of a $25,000 pension as a former President. Then there are all the radio contracts and the magazine articles and books which he can look forward to and which will net him a handsome income—close, they say, to a million. The path for him doesn't lead from the White House to the poorhouse."

Not everyone in the fourth estate wrote about the crushed President with such benevolence; one syndicated columnist wondered "how long Dewey is going to let Truman interfere with the running of this country." Like the *Free Press*, some writers had to complete their Wednesday columns on Monday for setting on Tuesday, while the voters made their choice. Thus Drew Pearson would astonish his millions of readers the day after the returns had been counted by disclosing, in his opening paragraph, "I surveyed the close-knit group around Tom Dewey, who will take over in the White House 86 days from now." He then triumphantly named the new President's entire cabinet. That same Wednesday Joseph and Stewart Alsop revealed that "The first post-election question is how the government can get through the next ten weeks. . . . Events will not wait patiently until Thomas E. Dewey officially replaces Harry S. Truman. Particularly in the fields of foreign and defense policy, somebody somewhere in Washington must have authority to give answers that will still be valid after January 20." The Alsops proposed that Dewey's cabinet nominees for the State and Defense posts immediately move in as "special assistants," guiding their lame-duck predecessors until Dewey's inaugural.

How did this happen? How could so many seasoned observers have climbed out so far on so shaky a limb? The answer is that they didn't think of it as a limb, let alone a shaky one. They had been telling one another that Truman's cause was hopeless for so long, and reading each other's analyses of why Dewey would easily defeat him, that they believed no other outcome was possible. Truman's campaign claim that "Everybody's against me but the people" had this seed of truth: unlike the pundits, he and the voters thought of the election as a contest, not a coronation. To those who had devoted their careers to the study of electoral trends, all the signposts pointed one way. When the party out of power captured control of Congress, as the Democrats had in 1930, it was virtually certain to win the Presidency two years later, as FDR had then. Besides, the Republicans were long overdue. Roosevelt's four straight victories could be attributed only to his charming personality, the Alsops and Pearsons told one another, and if there was one thing Truman lacked, it was charm. The Republican ticket had the money, the overwhelming support of the press—newspapermen naturally thought that this counted heavily—and, most important of all, the blessing of the public opinion polls.

It was twelve years since the *Literary Digest* fiasco. In the aftermath of the Democratic landslide of 1936, embittered Republicans had sworn that they would never again trust a straw vote. Afterward, however, they learned that George Gallup and Elmo Roper, then lesser known than the *Digest*'s pollsters, had spurned its direct mail for statistical samplings, which had forecast a big Roosevelt triumph. Since then these pollsters had been vindicated in every election. Metropolitan newspapers subscribed to their services—the *New York Times* was thought quaint for spending so much money on its own survey—and any pundit who contradicted them would have been considered a fool. Thus the beginning of the cycle: polls foresaw a Republican sweep, and columnists and editorial writers took it for gospel. It is even possible that men and women who planned to vote Democratic misled the pollsters because they wanted to keep up with the Joneses. Error was feeding upon error, and this chain was strengthened by poll takers who had become smug and, in at least one instance, arrogant.

Elmo Roper was arrogant. In a column dated September 9, nearly eight weeks before the election, he announced that he had surveyed the electorate for the last time. "Thomas E. Dewey," he wrote, "is almost as good as elected. . . . That being so, I can think of nothing duller or more intellectually barren than acting like a sports announcer who feels he must pretend he is witnessing a neck-and-neck race." Like so many professional election watchers, Roper believed in what some had come to call Farley's Law. After his sensational prediction in 1936, Farley had said that in his opinion, voters made up their minds during conventions; the campaigns, he implied, were ineffective carnivals. In laying his reputation on the line that first week in September, Roper was using figures gathered by his staff in August. Ironically, he did take another poll in the last week of the election showing a slight shift to Truman; it still gave

Dewey a heavy lead, however, so he decided not to hedge his bet.

All three of the national polls—Roper, Gallup, and Crossley—erred in failing to ask interviewees whether they actually intended to vote and in excluding from their samples most voters with grade school educations, who were likely to be Truman partisans. The pollsters' greatest blunder, however, was their indifference to the last-minute impact of Truman's great effort. Roper had closed his books before the Truman Special could pull out of Union Station. Crossley's last report (predicting 49.9 percent for Dewey and 44.8 for Truman, the rest going to Thurmond and Wallace) was a reflection of mixed state samplings taken in mid-August, mid-September, and mid-October. Gallup, the most industrious of the three, should have sensed what was happening in the country. His September 24 report foresaw 46.5 percent of the vote for Dewey to 38 percent for Truman. His last column, appearing in Sunday papers two days before the election, showed Truman gaining sharply —to 44 percent—and the interviews on which it was based had been conducted two weeks earlier. Clifford was right. The national mood was shifting daily, almost hourly.

In the memories of Americans now over forty, four events stand apart: Pearl Harbor, the death of Roosevelt, the election of 1948, and the assassination of John Kennedy. A man may have forgotten what happened on his twenty-first birthday, or a woman how she lost her virginity, but each can recall where he was when he heard about these four. They became milestones in the lives of people; even as their parents had said, "We met after the Armistice," or "We moved just before the Crash," so the swing generation came to date incidents in their private lives from the moment news reached them of the shots in Dallas, the attack on Hawaii, the stroke in Warm Springs, and the Truman miracle.

Everyone expected an early night. In the ballroom of New York's Roosevelt Hotel, Jim Hagerty told reporters, "We may be out of the trenches by midnight"; Governor Dewey, after voting in an East Fifty-first Street school ("Good luck, Mr. President!" a clerk called from an office window overhead), predicted that Truman's telegram of concession would arrive while he and Mrs. Dewey were dining at the home of his good friend Roger Straus at 6 East Ninety-third Street. In Washington the Statler Hotel, Republican by tradition as the Mayflower is Democratic, had redecorated its ballroom and set aside a corsage for each Republican lady, to be presented to her as she arrived. The Mayflower, on the other hand, was quiet as a stone. The Democratic National Committee was so sure of defeat that it hadn't bothered to reserve the hotel's ballroom. Putting the money aside for '52, the committeemen retired to their office suite, took the phone off the hook, broke out a couple of bottles of whiskey, and settled in for a wake. None of them had brought a radio; this was one evening when they could do without the news. (In the 1960s or 1970s one of them might have brought a transistor in his pocket, but in 1948 "portable" radios were comparatively heavy and bulky, and had to be plugged into wall outlets.) This was going to be one night when the committeemen would be far behind the swiftly developing political picture. Cabell Phillips of the *New York Times* was also out of touch. Back in Manhattan after Truman's campaign, he had boosted his spirits by buying a $47.50 topcoat—a real investment in those days—and a ticket to Lynn Fontanne and Alfred Lunt's latest play. As the first scattered returns came in from New Hampshire, Phillips entered the theater's Forty-seventh Street door and sat through two acts, unaware of the greater drama outside.

Those early figures from New Hampshire surprised Dewey; though he was leading, his margin was less than in 1944, less than any Republican candidate would expect from so staunch a party stronghold. Hurrying back to his hotel suite, he sat by a radio with his family and a few intimate friends, listening, reading wire service returns as they were brought to him, and jotting figures on a scratch pad.

Out in Missouri, President Truman had eluded the press several hours earlier with the help of Secret Service agents Henry Nicholson and Jim Rowley.[*] At 4:30 P.M. they had driven to Excelsior Springs, a resort thirty miles northeast from Independence, and checked into the Elms Hotel. The President took a Turkish bath and retired to his room at 6:30 with a ham sandwich and a glass of milk. He turned on the bedside radio. An announcer reported that he had taken an early lead of a few thousand votes. He went to bed and fell asleep almost instantly.

[*] Who would be chief of the Secret Service on November 22, 1963.

At 7:45 P.M. a Chicago *Tribune* editor faced an agonizing decision. The paper's bulldog edition was going to press, to reach the streets in time for the late theater crowd. The editor had to compose a headline. He couldn't just report that a national election had been held; they knew *that;* he needed a piece of hard news. Truman was now leading, but those first returns from New England were meaningless unless you knew where they came from. The Republican ticket might sweep Connecticut, for example, but if Hartford reported before the rest of the state, as it usually did, the figures would suggest a Democratic victory. Even the commentator in Connecticut couldn't tell you where the figures were from. He didn't know himself. In the race to be first on the air, he read scrawled notes the moment they were handed to him.

So the editor in the Tribune Building had to write his headline before he knew what was happening. He fell back on the one certainty in this election and blocked out the banner head: DEWEY DEFEATS TRUMAN.

By now the running totals made no sense. Truman had taken an early lead, as expected; Democratic strength lay in the cities, whose returns came in first because so many of them had voting machines and superior communications facilities. Correcting for this bias, Dewey seemed to be taking New York and New Jersey (but only because of a heavy Wallace vote in each). He was winning throughout the industrial East, with the exception of Massachusetts and Rhode Island. This reassured him; traditionally it was Democratic ground. Furthermore, Thurmond was depriving Truman of Mississippi, Louisiana, Alabama, and South Carolina. However, the Dewey margins were incredibly thin. Some counties that were GOP bastions were going Republican by a handful of votes. And Truman, outpolling Roosevelt in some places, was holding the popular vote lead in key cities.

The real shocks came from the other side of the Appalachian Range. The Democratic ticket had seized a strong lead in Wisconsin, Iowa, and Colorado, all three Republican fiefs; and as early reports came in from the eleven western states, only Oregon seemed to be going to Dewey.

At 10:30 in New York the curtain came down on the Lunts' second act. Cabell Phillips was thirsty. He had remained seated during the first intermission, but he decided to spend this one in a nearby bar. As he ordered scotch he became aware of a voice coming from the bar's radio, reciting the names of states, the number of wards and precincts, and a jumble of bewildering figures. Phillips had paid the bartender, and the first swallow of whisky was halfway down his throat when the clear voice of a commentator said, "Truman's lead now looks almost unassailable. If he can hold his lead in Ohio . . ."

Phillips gagged. Coughing scotch, he ran out the door and headed for Times Square. Midway in his sprint he remembered his new topcoat, paused, decided to forget it, and raced on.

Every fifteen or twenty minutes Dr. George Gallup was interviewed by a network announcer asking for his interpretation of the running tabulation. Gallup explained that the present Democratic plurality would be wiped out by the farm vote. By eleven o'clock the farm vote began to come in, and it was Democratic. Out on the plains they had remembered which party had given them parity and grain storage.

At 11 P.M. Herbert Brownell entered the Roosevelt Hotel ballroom and claimed a Dewey victory. Party workers cheered, but before they could ask details he hurried upstairs again. It seemed that Hagerty had overestimated the size of the landslide; they weren't going to be out of the trenches at midnight after all.

At midnight Harry Truman woke up. It took him a moment to adjust to the unfamiliar hotel room. Then he turned the radio on again. The voice was that of H. V. Kaltenborn, explaining that although Truman was 1,200,000 votes ahead in the count he was "still undoubtedly beaten." The President turned him off and went back to sleep.

In the Washington headquarters of the Democratic National Committee a latecomer who had passed a radio brought word that the President wasn't being overwhelmed after all; in some states he was even leading, though of course "the farmers haven't been heard from yet." One of the staff suggested they send out for a radio. They shrugged, then nodded. Might as well have a few laughs before it was all over.

"Meanwhile," Richard H. Rovere wrote, "the solid Statler walls were crumbling. Republican matrons were eating their corsages, Republican gentlemen were wilting their collars with nervous perspiration."

Shortly after midnight the party mood in the Roosevelt ballroom began to be replaced by anxiety and then consternation. Only now, at this late hour, had they been assured that Dewey had carried his home state—and by a mere 60,000 votes at that; if Wallace hadn't been on the ballot, Truman would have trounced him here.

It now appeared that the outcome hung on Ohio, Illinois, and California. Unbelievable as it was, any one of them could give Truman a winning combination. He would take a slight lead in one, then Dewey would pass him; all three were seesawing. At 1:45 A.M. Brownell, for reasons known only to him, returned to the ballroom and issued a second victory statement. He roused a few faint cheers. The others just stared at him.

At 4 A.M. Agent Rowley awoke the President and suggested he switch the radio on again. His lead was now a stunning two million votes, though H. V. Kaltenborn—whose voice Truman would gleefully mimic for friends to the end of his life—said he couldn't see how the President could be elected.

Dressing, the President told the agents to drive him back to the Muehlebach Hotel in Kansas City, because "It looks as if we're in for another four years." They arrived there at 6 A.M. Wan reporters wondered where he had been and how he managed to look as though he had had some sleep.

At 4:30 A.M., as the President's car pulled away from the Elms Hotel in Excelsior Springs, Hagerty had assembled the reporters at the Roosevelt and told them he had just been conferring with Dewey. He said: "We're in there fighting. The returns are still coming in, but it looks as if we won't know definitely until morning." Thirty-five minutes later he was back again. "We are not making any predictions or claims," he said.

Sometime after dawn, still unable to grasp that he was being beaten, the exhausted governor went to bed, and as he dozed the last hope slipped away from his haggard aides. Truman took Ohio at 9:30 A.M.—by 7,000 votes—putting him over the top with 270 electoral votes. An hour later, when Dewey awoke, he learned that he had also lost Illinois and California. At 11:14 A.M. he conceded. President Truman had not only won the race; he had forged a smashing victory in the electoral college—304* to 189, with 38 going to the Dixiecrat ticket. Moreover, he had carried Congress in with him. In the 80th Congress the Republicans had controlled the Senate 51 to 45, and the House 246 to 188. Now the Democrats held the whip hand in the Senate, 54 to 42 (a gain of 9 seats), and the House, 263 to 171 (a gain of 75). Paul Douglas, Hubert Humphrey, Lyndon Johnson, and Estes Kefauver were Senators-elect; G. Mennen Williams was governor of Michigan, Chester Bowles governor of Connecticut, and Adlai Stevenson governor of Illinois.

Taft was fit to be tied. "I don't care how the thing is explained," he said. "It defies all common sense to send that roughneck ward politician back to the White House." Elsewhere the character of Truman's achievement overrode rancor. "You just have to take off your hat to a beaten man who refuses to stay licked!" said the archconservative New York *Sun*. "Mr. Truman won because this is still a land which loves a scrapper, in which intestinal fortitude is still respected." The triumph was more than a personal victory, though. Two days after the election Walter Lippmann wrote, "Mr. Truman's own victory, the Democratic majorities in both houses of Congress, the Democratic victories in so many states, attest the enormous vitality of the Democratic party as Roosevelt led it and developed it from 1932 to 1944 . . . the party that Roosevelt formed has survived his death and is without question the dominant force in American politics."

In newsrooms and editorial chambers men avoided one another's eyes the morning after the election. The fourth estate and its sources were the laughingstock of the country and knew it. The Alsop brothers wrote: "There is only one question on which professional politicians, polltakers, political reporters and other wiseacres and prognosticators can any longer speak with much authority. This is how they want their crow cooked." When the President and his Vice-President-elect returned to Washington (Truman holding aloft the *Chicago Tribune*'s "Dewey Defeats Truman" headline) they were greeted by 750,000 cheerers and a huge sign across the front of the Washington *Post* Building: "Mr. President, we are ready to eat crow whenever you are ready to serve it." In a letter to his

---

* One Truman elector in Tennessee later defected to Thurmond.

own paper, Reston of the *Times* wrote that "we were too isolated with other reporters; and we, too, were far too impressed by the tidy statistics of the poll." *Time* said the press had "delegated its journalist's job to the polls." Several angry publishers canceled their subscriptions to the polls. The pollsters themselves were prostrate. Gallup said simply, "I don't know what happened." One *New York Times* reporter thought to call Wilfred J. Funk, the last editor of the *Literary Digest*, and ask for his comment. "I don't want to seem malicious," Funk replied, "but I can't help but get a good chuckle out of this."

Afterward the Survey Research Center of the University of Michigan conducted a poll on the polls, while Gallup and Roper scrupulously investigated themselves. The results of the studies are startlingly alike. The Michigan group found that of the 24,105,000 Truman voters, 14 percent, or 3,374,800, decided to vote for him in the last fortnight of the campaign. Gallup and Roper, taking a different approach, learned that one voter in every seven (6,927,000) made up his mind in the last two weeks of the election. Of these, 75 percent (5,195,000) picked Truman; 25 percent (1,732,000) chose Dewey, a difference of 3,463,000. Inasmuch as Truman's plurality over Dewey on November 2 had been 2,135,000, the inference is inescapable. Using either the Michigan figures or Gallup-Roper's, one finds that some 3,300,000 fence-sitters determined the outcome of the race in its closing days—when Dewey's instincts were urging him to adopt Truman's hell-for-leather style and slug it out with him, and when he didn't because all the experts told him he shouldn't.

Late Forties Montage

GALLAGHER: Some fuggin mornings like this I wish I'd catch a bullet.
WILSON: Only goddam trouble with that is you can't pick the spot.
STANLEY: You know if you could, the Army wouldn't be keeping me long.
GALLAGHER: Aaah, there ain't a goddam place you can get a million-dollar wound that it don't hurt.

Now is the hour
For me to say good-bye
Soon I'll be sailing
Far across the sea
While I'm away
Oh, please remember me

PYRAMID CRAZE SWEEPS U.S.

Paisan The Search Treasure of Sierra Madre Snake Pit
Best actor of 1949: Broderick Crawford in All the King's Men
Battleground Sands of Iwo Jima The Bicycle Thief Quartet
Home of the Brave Letter to Three Wives

We've a date in '48
Watch us roll up the vote in every state...
For the U.S.A. and the G.O.P.
On the great day of victory

Dear Seventeen:
I think you should have more articles on dates and shyness and put in some more about movie stars, too. Stories like those on atomic energy are very boring.

Nobody dast blame this man. You don't understand: Willy was a salesman. And for a salesman, there is no rock bottom to the life. He don't put a bolt to a nut, he don't tell you the law or give you medicine. He's a man way out there in the blue, riding on a smile and a shoeshine. And when they start not smiling back — that's an earthquake. And then you get yourself a couple of spots on your hat, and you're finished. Nobody dast blame this man. A salesman is got to dream, boy. It comes with the territory.

So in love with you am I

BEST SELLERS: Fiction
Came a Cavalier by Frances Parkinson Keyes
Raintree County by Ross Lockridge, Jr.
Parris Mitchell of King's Row by Henry and Katherine Bellamann
The Naked and the Dead by Norman Mailer
The Young Lions by Irwin Shaw

GM'S 1949 INCOME TAX PUT AT $444,377,889

BEST SELLERS: Nonfiction
The Gathering Storm by Winston Churchill
Crusade in Europe by Dwight D. Eisenhower
Peace of Mind by Joshua L. Liebman
Cheaper by the Dozen by Frank B. Gilbreth and Ernestine G. Carey
The Seven Storey Mountain by Thomas Merton

BIRTH RATE ZOOMS

Highbrow, lowbrow, upper middlebrow, and lower middlebrow... gradually they are finding their own levels and confining themselves more and more to the company of their own kind. You will not find a highbrow willingly attending a Simon & Schuster cocktail party any more than you will find an upper middlebrow at a Rotary Club luncheon or an Elks' picnic.

Now the reason this club hasn't made a deal is why should we? When you got players good enough to win a pennant on the road and a World Series on the road which is where they win the majority of their games and against a tremendous club like this one which you know is a great ball club because why have they played us more games in the World Series than anybody, then why would you want to change?... And whenever I make a deal I get swindled.

INDIA FREE

Goodnight, sweetheart
Though I'm not beside you
Goodnight, sweetheart
Still my love will guide you
Dreams enfold you
In each one I hold you
Goodnight, sweetheart
Goodnight

I'm just wild about Harry
And Harry's wild about me.
The fates decreed it, we concede it,
Harry made history

... Friendly Henry Wallace is O.K.
He'll end Jim Crow
Warmongers will all know
That with Henry peace will have its day.

Kiss Me Kate

RED-BLOODED AMERICANS!
Fight progressive education, mental health, fluoridation, vivisectionists, Freudianism, planned parenthood!

Sixteen

THE AGE OF SUSPICION

BEFORE CHECKING OUT of the Muehlebach and returning to Washington, President Truman was advised that he could not enter the White House. No coup; it just wasn't safe. The most famous home in America was in imminent danger of collapse. Its householder wasn't altogether surprised. According to the National Archives, "President Truman became concerned because of a noticeable vibration in the floors in his study." There had been more to it than that. The great chandeliers in the East Room had been tinkling when there was no breeze, and when the President held his physician's stethoscope against the walls, he could hear them creaking.

He had appointed a commission to look into the matter—just in time, as it turned out. In the last week of the campaign horrified engineers had discovered that blackened beams, burned by the British in 1814 and never replaced, were about to give way; frescoed ceilings weighing seventy pounds to the square foot were sagging six inches. While the First Family had been walking out one door en route to Independence, frantic construction men had rushed in another with props and scaffolding. The reconstruction would cost $5,400,000. It might have been cheaper to erect a new building, but tearing down the White House was unthinkable. The next tenant would have air-conditioning, fireproofing, and multiple outlets for television cables. Meanwhile the Trumans would pig it in Blair House, diagonally across the street at 1648 Pennsylvania Avenue.

The Fair Deal was christened in Blair House. During the first three years of his Presidency Truman had regarded himself as the executor of FDR's political will. But a third of the nation was no longer in want. The altered economy called for a new liberalism, "focused," as Cabell Phillips put it, "on the creation and equitable distribution of abundance, which now loomed as an attainable reality." Even before the miracle at the polls, a group of key Truman aides had conceived a program during a series of Monday evening seminars in the Wardman Park apartment of Oscar Ewing, director of the Federal Security Agency, whose advocacy of a national medical plan would soon make him the bugbear of the American Medical Association.* In embryonic form their list of proposals had first appeared on the Hill in the President's Turnip session proposals. Fully developed now, it included new measures for civil rights, housing, unemployment benefits, agricultural aid, and inflation control; a 3.2-billion-dollar tax cut for poor wage earners, federal aid to schools, and Taft-Hartley repeal. Together with Ewing's Medicare, they would later form the nucleus of Kennedy's New Frontier and Johnson's Great Society.

After a week of postelection convalescence at Key West, Truman put his back into his forthcoming State of the Union message. In time it would indeed alter history, but of the innovations which emerged from those last weeks in 1948, the one that would be most closely identified with Truman's name was to appear not in the January 5 State of the Union address, but at his inauguration two weeks later. As Clark Clifford recollects, "We were having a real problem during late December putting the inaugural speech together. Our man had won a smashing and surprising victory at the polls, and he and all of us felt that when he stood up to take the oath of office on January 20, he should have something big and new and challenging to present to the country." The message to Congress dwelt upon domestic issues; the inaugural would look abroad. The difficulty was that the great links of Truman's foreign policy had already been forged in Greece, Turkey, Berlin, and the European Recovery Plan. Then Clifford remembered "a State Department memorandum that had crossed my desk a few weeks or a few months earlier. A technical assistance program had been tried on a very modest scale in Latin America, and this memo raised the ques-

---

* In addition to Ewing the planners were Clifford, Charles S. Murphy, C. Girard Davidson, David A. Morse, and Leon Keyserling.

tion—not very hopefully as I recall—whether it might not be adapted to the Far East as a sort of substitute for the ERP." Clifford suggested it to the President, who said after a moment's reflection, "This looks good. We'll use it. We can work out the operating details later." Truman had already decided to tell the inauguration crowd that in dealing with other nations the United States would be sustained by faith in the United Nations, the Marshall Plan, and a new North Atlantic alliance. In addition to these three points he now had another, technical aid to backward countries. In the final draft it appeared as:

> Fourth. We must embark on a bold new program for making the benefits of our scientific advances and industrial progress available for the improvement and growth of underdeveloped areas. . . .

Point Four stirred the world. Endorsed by the U.N.'s Economic and Social Council on March 4, 1949, it roused the hope that American technical skills might revolutionize primitive agricultural techniques, raise the standard of living in Asia and Africa, and tame their rivers with new TVAs. "While there is some criticism of the President for having shot first and questioned later," James Reston wrote from Washington, "there is general approval of his colonial development program here." The *Christian Science Monitor* reported that "President Truman's dedication of United States technological resources to improve the lot of the globe's less fortunate people has kindled the imagination of thinking people throughout Britain and Western Europe." Predictably, there were rumbles of dissent on Capitol Hill from "the primitives," as Dean Acheson called them. Senator Kenneth Wherry and Joe Martin groaned, Senator Jenner of Indiana said the whole thing had been invented by Earl Browder, and Senator Taft wanted to know where the money was coming from.

Taft knew. It had to come from Congress. But many Democratic candidates who had ridden in on the President's coattails were turning out to be ungrateful; once again the Republican and southern Democratic coalition was bucking the administration. The chairmen of eighteen powerful Senate committees were from the South, and the President pro tempore of the Senate, the Speaker of the House, and the two party whips were all coalition members. Point Four, with a humble allotment of 45 million dollars, did not reach Truman's desk until June 5, 1950. Even then it was hedged with multiple restrictions which, as Cabell Phillips wrote, largely vitiated "the great propaganda value it had when President Truman first proposed it."

In the aftermath of his election, problems abroad bore upon Truman with special urgency. General Marshall was in Walter Reed Hospital having a kidney removed; he would continue as Secretary of State until the inaugural but step down then. Truman gave hard thought to the choice of a successor. He couldn't pick a crony, a faceless bureaucrat, or a free-spending campaign contributor like Louis Johnson, who would succeed James Forrestal as Secretary of Defense in March. Marshall's successor must be esteemed in friendly chancelleries, respected in Moscow, and known on the Hill.

Three weeks after the election he sent for Dean Acheson, who had retired to the private practice of law. As Acheson remembers it, he passed the Executive Mansion, of which only the outside wall had been left standing "for sentimental reasons," and was escorted to the President's "minute office" in Blair House. The President asked him to sit down, then grinned.

"You had better be sitting down when you hear what I have to say to you," he began. Without pausing he continued, "I want you to come back and be Secretary of State. Will you?"

Acheson recalls that he was "utterly speechless." The President suggested that he talk it over with his wife. Mrs. Acheson being agreeable, her husband accepted. He would take oath on January 21 and become the fifty-second and, with the possible exception of Seward, the most controversial of U.S. Secretaries of State.

As one crew of workmen rebuilt the White House, others were encircling the country's inner cities with America's new suburbs—the Hillendales, Gardenvilles, Northwoods, Parkvilles, Stoneleighs, Baynesvilles, Drumcastles, Anneslies, Wiltondales, Dunbartons, and Cedarcrofts. Levittown had become an American institution, with thousands of imitators, and outside Chicago a group of businessmen broke ground for another pilot development, Park Forest. Recognizing the housing needs of veteran families with small nest eggs but stable jobs, Park Forest's founders first erected rental "garden apartments" around a central shopping plaza. Then, as their tenants' savings accumulated, they added split-level ranch houses financed by themselves. The end result was a constantly recycling population of 30,000 whose predictable wants were supplied by stores in the shopping center—owned, again, by the businessmen. The inhabitants knew they were being exploited and loved it, and the envious hardhats who built Park Forest could hardly wait to reach the new suburbia themselves.

Baltimore spawned no fewer than sixteen developments, and it is worth noting that the president of the PTA in one of them, Loch Raven Village, was a 10th Armored veteran named Spiro T. Agnew. Agnew was in many ways representative of homeowners in the packaged communities. Although he had held a commission he was a zealous egalitarian ("Call me Ted"). He was active in the VFW and Kiwanis. As a licensed though not practicing lawyer, he was naturally interested in public office, but his style was the new politics. Thomas D'Alesandro Jr., Baltimore's incumbent mayor, advertised his background by remaining in his Little Italy home; Agnew, also a product of a downtown ethnic neighborhood, was doing his best to forget it. He attended the Episcopalian church. His favorite musician was Lawrence Welk. His leisure interests were all midcult: watching the Baltimore Colts on television, listening to Mantovani, and reading the sort of prose the *Reader's Digest* liked to condense. He was a lover of order and an almost compulsive conformist. Saturday mornings he happily joined other Loch Raven men in washing and waxing their '48 Fleetline Chevvies, '49 Buick Specials, and Oldsmobile 88s. Mondays he donned his double-breasted—later three-button—suit, set his snap-brim squarely on his head, and arrived in his Schreiber Food Stores office at 8:45 on the dot. Anyone who came in after nine o'clock heard about it. Agnew, the manager, believed firmly in punctuality, a stitch in time, and plenty of elbow grease.

Had they met, he would have aroused the professional interest of William H. Whyte Jr., a former Marine Corps officer only a year older than Agnew. As a staff writer for *Fortune,* Whyte had begun to type the Agnews as Organization Men. They might call their work a treadmill or a rat race, but they belonged to the firm—or whatever lay at the other end of their occupational umbilical cord, since junior executives were only one of the many species found in the developments. They included the young physician completing his residency in internal medicine and destined for group practice, the dental intern, the FBI agent, the salaried young attorney working for a prestigious law partnership, the promising young major attending staff school, the physicist in corporate shop, the Ph.D. in a pharmaceutical laboratory, the apprentice engineer at Pratt &

Whitney; even the vicar who would wind up a member of the church hierarchy. Most were well aware of the bond that joined them; as some frequently put it, they were "all in the same boat." They had few doubts about the boat's destination. Within a quarter-century, when their turn came, they and others like them would set the national tone, becoming what *Time* would later call the "command generation." Then they would have their hands full. For the present, they enjoyed their families while they could, met their peers at mixers, and enjoyed the communal sports of the development: canasta, ping-pong, Chinese checkers—and, in that presidential election year when their man lost, hushed conversations about an Indiana University research investigation which was becoming known to the whole world as the Kinsey Report.

In a Peter Arno cartoon of the time, a shocked woman looked up from the report (*Sexual Behavior in the Human Male*, 804 pages, $6.50, over 275,000 copies sold in 1948) and asked her husband, "Is there a *Mrs.* Kinsey?" There was, and there were also three Kinsey children, all conceived before he embarked upon his major work. Not that he had been idle before; his passion for taxonomy could be traced back to his school days in South Orange, New Jersey, when he submitted an account of the behavior of birds in the rain to a nature journal, which accepted it. Then, and thereafter, he was a stickler for explicit detail. Until he became interested in certain extracurricular activities of his Indiana students, his fellow zoologists thought he would be remembered for his prodigious study of the gall wasp, a harmless species found in eastern Central America. Kinsey traveled 80,000 miles collecting examples, and he measured, catalogued, and preserved 3,500,000 of them, to demonstrate their individual variations. Peering through his microscope, he recorded twenty-eight different measurements of each specimen. *PM* called it "a landmark in the history of entomology." As a scientist he had naturally played no favorites; every gall wasp was just as good as the next one to him; he rendered no judgment on their behavior. It was an attitude which would subsequently prove even more useful to him. It would also amaze the country.

Until the late 1930s the career of Alfred C. Kinsey had varied scarcely a jot from those of thousands of his colleagues: Harvard, graduate study, years of junior faculty teaching, tenure, and all those gall wasps. In Bloomington he had become a familiar campus figure, tall, heavyset, with sandy hair and a preoccupied manner. His students admired his patience and forbearance. He had all the right professorial hobbies: gardening, hiking, pottery, classical music. No scandal had touched him or even come within whispering distance of him. He was, in short, just the sort of educator a cautious dean would choose to teach a course on marriage problems. Certainly Indiana's dean never suspected that he would *create* problems—and, to boot, make the university a mecca for collectors of erotica.

Before he could reach even a tentative view of matrimonial difficulties, Kinsey reasoned, he must steep himself in facts about biological transactions between *Homo sapiens* mates. He went to the university library and received the jolt of his life. There were no facts worth mentioning, in Indiana or elsewhere. The staggering truth was that men and women knew more about gall wasps than each other. Human beings were even uninformed about the erotic behavior of members of their own sex, and therefore had no way of knowing whether or not they were normal. To a disciple of truth, this was unacceptable. He was seized with a determination to right the wrong which would glow within him until the end of his life, sustaining him through long periods of exhausting research. It was at about this time that Mrs. Kinsey said, "I hardly see him at night since he took up sex."

His friends saw him, though not informally. While on the job he no longer thought of them as friends. As an objective investigator he regarded them as just so many specimens, to be measured and catalogued in all their variations. Working with them, he developed his basic two-and-a-half-hour, 300-to-500-question interview. It covered the whole sexual spectrum—masturbation, nocturnal emissions, lewd fantasies, petting, intercourse before and after marriage, adultery, inversion, frequency of ejaculations, oral sex, anal sex, relations with animals, exotic pleasures. Whether his friendships survived this test is unknown, but in Bloomington and elsewhere word got around that he was turning over rocks no one had come near before. Nothing was beyond his scope. Babies, measured in the nursery with special instruments, were found to experience orgasms at the age of four or five months. Elderly spinsters confided that restrictive clothing brought them to climax. One preadolescent child had 26 orgasms in 24 hours; a scholarly and skilled attorney had averaged over 30 ejaculations a week for over 30 years.

Bankers, tramps, criminals, writers, diplomats, poets, pimps, editors, cowboys, teachers, cab drivers, literary agents, hospital orderlies, idle patricians—the responses of all of them were transcribed in code, filed, and later fed into IBM computers. As the completed interviews mounted into the thousands, Kinsey acquired a staff; university funding was supplemented by grants from the National Research Council and the Rockefeller Foundation. By the time the first volume on the human male reached the manuscript stage, Kinsey and his three chief interviewers had devoted forty man-years to the compilation of over 12,000 case histories. Now they were breaking down data on the human female. The first volume was scheduled to reach book counters in January 1948.

Americans since grown jaded by literature on mate swapping and the St. Louis laboratories of Masters and Johnson—where nurses and doctors' wives volunteered, in the name of science, for intercourse with total strangers—may find it hard to recapture the innocence of sex before Kinsey. Youths in their early teens held sotto voce discussions with other youths, spreading ignorance. Adults talked of it only to their spouses, and here too the blind were leading the blind. Kinsey interviewed thousands of married couples who said they had never experienced intercourse; gynecological examinations of the women confirmed them. One Kinsey investigator found 1,000 wives who were virgins and had no idea why their marriages had been childless. (Their husbands were equally perplexed.) For millions like them, the facts of life were mysteries as obscure as the interior of unexplored Brazil.

Apart from the dubious studies of Havelock Ellis—over a third of Ellis's patients reported that they had been seduced in their parents' homes by servants of the opposite sex, which suggests the narrowness of his social base—educated Americans lacked qualified guides. The rest of the population had no guides at all. Marriage manuals going back to Ovid's, in the first century of the Christian epoch, were flawed by error. In the absence of knowledge, superstition flourished. Boys believed that masturbation was a practice of degenerates; girls were told that "deep" or "French" kissing led to pregnancy and venereal disease. Because the sex drive is stronger than fear, onanism and mutual exploration by boys and girls continued—to be followed by paroxysms of remorse. What is perhaps hardest to grasp is the conviction of powerful social institutions that they had a sacred obligation to propagate these private terrors. Both church and secular leaders believed that only children scared stiff could be counted on to approach the altar as virgins. (How they would conquer their irrational fright in bed that first night was unmentioned and, like the rest of it, unmentionable.) Except for hurried and inept father/son, mother/daughter sessions, mature society went along with the incubi and the bogeys. The general feeling was rather like that of lodge brothers toward an initiate. They had been hazed; so must their offspring.

All this was predicated upon the assumption that the system worked—that boys who had been properly reared "saved themselves" for well-bred girls who had remained "pure"—hence white for brides—and that after marriage and until death they remained faithful to one another. Male homosexuals, usually called fairies or perverts, were considered indistinguishable from the criminally insane. Even among sophisticates such practices as pederasty, fellatio, cunnilingus, and sodomy with barnyard quadrupeds were presumed to exist only in fantasy and locker room jokes.

Then Kinsey told Americans this about themselves:

> Eighty-five percent of all married men had engaged in sexual intercourse before marriage.
>
> The average groom had experienced 1,500 orgasms before his wedding day.
>
> Fifty percent of American husbands had committed adultery.
>
> Fifty percent of American females "were nonvirgins, if single, or had been nonvirgins before marriage."
>
> Two out of every three single women had engaged in premarital sex of some kind.
>
> Ninety-five percent of all males were sexually active before their fifteenth birthday, and maximum activity occurred at sixteen or seventeen.
>
> The average unmarried male had three or four orgasms a week.
>
> One girl in every six had experienced orgasm before adolescence, and one in four by the age of fifteen.
>
> By the age of forty, more than one wife in every four (26 percent, or over seven million) had committed adultery at least once. (In view of the tendency to conceal infidelity, Kinsey believed that the actual figures were much higher.) Adultery tended to increase as a marriage lengthened.
>
> One male in every three, and one female in every seven, had some adolescent homosexual experience.
>
> Ten percent of the male population was "more or less exclusively

homosexual" for at least three years between the ages of sixteen and fifty-five.

Four percent (2,600,000) of American men were "exclusively homosexual throughout their lives, after the onset of adolescence."

Women who weren't virgins on their wedding day were twice as likely to commit adultery.

One in every six American farm boys had copulated with farm animals.

Nearly 70 percent of men had had relations with prostitutes by the age of thirty-five.

Among the thousands of interviewees were 2,094 single women who reported a total of 460,000 acts of sexual intercourse; 476 of them had become pregnant. To Kinsey's surprise, four out of five of the unmarried mothers expressed no regret.

Among American females, three out of every four nonvirgins did not regret their sexual experiences. The least regretful were those who had been the most promiscuous, the most regretful those who had had the least sex activity. Asked why they remained chaste, 22 percent of the virgins "frankly conceded lack of opportunity."

Nobody was neutral about the Kinsey Report. Sacks of mail descended upon the professor's office on the second floor of Bloomington's old Zoology Building. Kinsey became one of the first instant celebrities. His face, or something resembling it, appeared on the cover of *Time*, and to his horror strangers sought him out to reveal closely guarded secrets of their estral lives—secret to them, but to him repetitive accounts of acts practiced by millions. Late in the 1940s a teen-age sex club craze swept the country; girls were admitted to membership after coupling with a boy in the presence of the group and promising to engage in sexual congress at least once a week thereafter. When the wave reached Indiana, a reporter asked Kinsey to comment. In his matter-of-fact way—it was this, as much as anything, which offended those who held sex to be sacred —the zoologist pointed out that according to his studies there were 450,000 acts of fornication in Indiana every week. "And that," he said, "is why I don't get excited when the newspapers report three or four teen-agers having such experiences." On December 31, 1948, the *New York Times* reported that fake telephone calls from spurious Kinsey interviewers were harassing respectable matrons. After a year of Kinsey statistics people were beginning to wonder just what respectability was, and the issue was further clouded when the *Times* switchboard was jammed by female New Yorkers eager to be put in touch with *real* interviewers.

There was something peculiarly American about both the Kinsey project and its reception. "No other people has been so curious about itself," Clyde Kluckhohn observed, "nor so willing to subject itself to scientific analysis, nor so avid to read even the most sneering and superficial criticisms of outsiders. . . . More than anything else, the Kinsey studies testify to the continued vitality of a childlike trust in knowledge, particularly scientific knowledge, as an instrument for individual and social improvement." Within a generation it appeared that the country had come to regard the statistics as a challenge; if the new thing was to have bigger and better orgasms, the U.S. intended to be first. In 1970 the two best-selling titles on U.S. nonfiction lists told readers how to make themselves more sensual by extrapolating from Kinsey data. Indeed, by the late 1960s and early 1970s the children of Americans who had felt guilty about strong sex drives were becoming anxious if they weren't lusty enough. "America had no sooner got rid of being ashamed about sex," wrote Louis Kronenberger, "than it grew ashamed about the lack of it." In the Nixon years advocates of a vigorous new feminism waged a running battle with their critics over whether careers for women masculinized them or increased their sexual gratification. Both sides accepted Kinsey's figures as valid and, more significantly, both agreed that satisfied desire was important to the individual and even to society.

There, as elsewhere, the Truman and Nixon eras seem more than a generation apart. In 1972 the concept of chaperones, say, or the sight of men tipping their hats to approaching young women would seem as anachronistic as microskirts or four-letter words on the screen of your neighborhood theater would have been in 1948. It is singular to recall that when Norman Mailer published *The Naked and the Dead* that year, he could convey soldiers' profanity only by coining a new verb, to fug (fugging, fugger, motherfugger etc.). In 1949 Joseph W. Gannon, the arbiter of what the *New York Times* saw fit to print in its advertising columns, revised, bowdlerized, or rejected 1,456 submissions, mostly because he considered them prurient. Gannon had a genius for the right word. He always cut it out. An ad publicizing lingerie as "naughty but nice" was altered to read "Paris-inspired—but so nice." A night club ad featuring "50 of the hottest girls this side of hell" emerged from Gannon's laundromat as

"50 of the most alluring maidens this side of paradise." Curves were painted out of models in girdle displays, giving them an eerie, unisex appearance and raising the question of why they needed foundation garments at all, and the *Times* airbrushes dressed photographs of Sally Rand from clavicle to femur.

Those were desperate days for Sally. Bumping and grinding in Milwaukee, she was arrested for the nth time by a policewoman, Geraldine Sampson. Officer Sampson testified that the defendant had been appearing in a carnival sideshow without panties—"nude as could be." Indignantly Sally protested that she was stone broke; she didn't *have* any pants. Lacking a civil liberties lawyer to rescue her, she was convicted and shown to a cell. The cops took everything she had, including her woman's right to conceal her age. "I'm sorry, I just don't tell that," she demurred, but the bulls wangled it out of her anyhow, and then it was in all the papers. She was forty-six, a prophet before her time. On the West Coast a younger exhibitionist, who in 1946 had changed her name from Norma Jean Baker to Marilyn Monroe, was fired by Columbia Pictures in September 1948 after playing her first part. (Studio comments included "Can't act," "Voice like a tight squeak," "Utterly unsure of herself," and "Unable even to take refuge in her own insignificance.") But Norma Jean at liberty under the new name of Marilyn Monroe could make both ends meet by posing naked for girlie photographs, the most provocative of which was reproduced in vivid color on the tip of a best-selling condom.* That door was closed to Sally; in the world of commercial sex she was over the geriatric hill. Kinsey characteristically saw no difference between Sally and Marilyn, however. To him they were just two more digits to be fed into Bloomington's computers.

"All the standards are harum-scarum," Mark Sullivan complained after reading the Kinsey Report. "Children running the homes or the President of the United States barnstorming up and down the country—it's all the same dissolution of traditional, dependable ways." A Harvard graduate of '00, Sullivan didn't accept the New Deal, let alone Truman's Fair Deal. For men like him the postwar years were especially rough; it was a time of sharp breaks with the past and of accelerating change, that cruel solvent of custom.

---

* It was not advertised in the *New York Times*.

The White House wasn't all that was falling down. The reputation of Brink's, banker to banks, was set back when a mob wearing Halloween masks heisted it for a million dollars in Boston. In a Jersey election, Frank Hague's once mighty machine was stripped of its gears by a reform slate. The medical profession was embarrassed when a New Hampshire physician was charged with the "mercy killing" of a doomed and suffering patient. (He was acquitted.) White supremacists were beginning to suspect that the road ahead would be bumpy for them. When the limousine bearing Governor Strom Thurmond approached the reviewing stand in Truman's inaugural parade, the President found it necessary to turn his back and speak to someone behind him. Washington hotels trying to hang on to Jim Crow during the inauguration were bluntly told to integrate or face condemnation by the District's Commissioner of Housing. They integrated. In Oklahoma a court order—the first of thousands to come—directed the state university to admit a Negro woman student, and the Nobel Prize was awarded to an American diplomat named Ralph Bunche for negotiating an Arab-Israeli truce. When rednecks and wool-hats heard Bunche was black, they reached for their bottle of Hadacol.

Around the cracker barrels of northern New England, their Yankee counterparts grumbled about progress and its value, or lack of it. New York was building the largest airport in the world at Idlewild. Who for? California's Mount Palomar was completing the world's biggest telescope. To look at the moon? Everybody knew there was no future in that. The prevailing winds of style were setting weathervanes spinning. In Europe the guns had hardly cooled and already the Germans were exporting their first snub-nosed little Volkswagens, selling in the United States for $1,280. American women were reading *Flair*, a magazine with holes in it, and buying Tide, the first detergent, which began appearing on shelves in 1948. A lot of old-timers around a lot of country store barrels would have approved of anything that could scrub a youth named Eden Ahbez. Ahbez was the first hippie—or prehippie, if you like—and he surfaced in 1948: a shy, gentle vegetarian with shoulder-length hair and a full beard. He encapsulated his philosophy in a song, "Nature Boy." Nat King Cole made it the hit of the year:

> *There was a boy, a very strange, enchanted boy . . .*
> *A little sad and shy of eye.*

> *But very wise was he . . . This he said to me:*
> *"The greatest thing you'll ever learn*
> *Is just to love and be loved in return."*

In 1948 Allen Ginsberg was expelled by Columbia University for scribbling obscene anti-Semitic phrases on his dormitory window. The proud National Football League surprised everyone in the world of sport by merging with the All-America Football Conference. Frankie Sinatra suffered a massive throat hemorrhage; bobby-soxers drifted away to Perry Como and Frankie Laine. In *Down Beat* Stan Kenton nosed out Woody Herman as the country's number one jazz band, though some critics were beginning to wonder whether musical improvisation, like the swing generation itself, wasn't déjà vu; after touring Greenwich Village, Mary McCarthy gave the back of her tongue to "middle-aged jazz musicians in double-breasted suits trumpeting in a whisky transfiguration for middle-aged jazz aficionados, also in double-breasted suits."

Looking back over the first half of the twentieth century, Bruce Bliven was struck by "the alteration in the moral climate from one of overwhelming optimism to one which comes pretty close to despair." He noted that "during the first forty years of the century" there had been "a steady drift away from a sense of identification with the faiths for which the churches stood." Bliven was looking in the wrong places. God, or someone like Him, had leaped over the altar rail and hit the sawdust trail. In 1949 His presence was identified in the vicinity of a mammoth tent erected in Los Angeles by a thirty-year-old North Carolina evangelist named William Franklin Graham—"Billy" to the chosen. That year Billy Graham drew over 300,000 Californians to his canvas shrine and converted 6,000 of them, including a crooner, a cowboy, a racketeer, and a professional athlete.

On July 4, 1946, the Philippines had become a sovereign nation. The British raj had then withdrawn from India and Burma, and in 1949 the Dutch reluctantly granted independence to Indonesia. Colonialism, another prewar institution, was withering away. The United States approved of the demise; in the light of its own origins, it could hardly have done otherwise. But older Americans who found comfort in the familiar were losing one more well-worn bench mark, and they felt uneasy. Apart from the tension crackling between Blair House and the Kremlin—which was unsettling enough

—lesser stories on foreign affairs were puzzling or disturbing. Most stories about Nazi crimes had become boring. Closer to home, a cabal of Puerto Rican fanatics tried to assassinate the President in Blair House. The plot failed in spite of Harry Truman, who kept running around trying to get a better view of what was going on. Then the country relaxed; men remembered that with the incomparable Secret Service in charge, no one could kill a President.

Most Americans learned of such events from radio. The number of people who had seen a television screen was still smaller than those who had heard about it, though some popular radio programs, such as *Major Bowes Amateur Hour* and *Town Meeting of the Air*, had gone over to the tube. TV certainly needed them. Its seven-inch peepholes had been succeeded by twelve-inch and even fourteen-inch screens, and there was less of what was called "snow" in the pictures, but what the audiences were looking at was hardly worth watching. First there were the wrestlers, notably Gorgeous George, whose appearance in the ring was usually preceded by that of his valet, a small man wearing a tailcoat and bearing on a silver tray a monogrammed "GG" towel, a prayer rug, and various spray guns and atomizers, to spare his employer the stench of his competitor's sweat. At the outset there was always a bit of contrived suspense over which outfit George would wear. ("He's going to be in chartreuse tonight, folks! Correction, it'll be cherry red!") GG had 88 satin costumes and a weakness for ermine jockstraps. Describing a Georgeous George entrance for *Sport* in 1949, Hannibal Coons wrote:

> Knotted loosely at his throat is a scarf of salmon-colored silk. His hair, a mass of golden ringlets, looks as though he has just spent four hours in a beauty parlor. George makes the grand entrance, sneering at the peons. Slowly and calmly he removes his Georgie pins—gold-plated and sequined bobby pins—and casts them to the crowd. And shakes his hair like a lordly spaniel.

After the wrestlers came the lady wrestlers. They were worse, if that is possible—great hulking earth bitches with breasts like half-loaded gunny-sacks and pubic hair dangling down their thighs. They always seemed to have cut themselves shaving. One of their pet tricks was to pin the referee beneath them until he shrieked for mercy; their fans loved that. After the network producers had more than even they could stomach, the girls were sent back to wherever they had come from, and the gaps between baseball games and prizefights were filled with Leo Selzer's Roller Derby. The Derby was almost indescribable. Shapely hoydens were outfitted in hockey uniforms, crash helmets and roller skates and sent spinning around an old marathon dance ring, crashing into one another, clawing at each other, swearing, bleeding, crying, and, yes, pinioning the ref beneath and belting him with their steel rollers. It was thought to be merry. Families gathered round their sets couldn't get enough of it. One of the skaters, Gerry Murray, had almost as many followers as Georgeous George. Sportswriters were too squeamish to approve either of them. In 1949, when GG was at his peak and earning $70,000 a year, Red Smith raged in the New York *Herald Tribune:* "Groucho Marx is prettier, Sonny Tufts a more gifted actor, Connie Mack a better rassler, and the Princeton Triangle Club has far better female impersonators." After watching Gerry and her fellow gamines mix it up, John Lardner wrote, "The Roller Derby is a sport. Defenestration is also a sport, for those who like it."

Along the Atlantic seaboard television viewers, or "gawks," as Mencken called them, were fewest per thousand inhabitants in the District of Columbia, probably because there was so much else going on there. Washington society had by now acquired a style appropriate to the seat of a great power. Georgetown was being restored; Cleveland Park had a new elegance. Chefs from benighted Europe were establishing their reputations in the huge embassies on or just off Massachusetts Avenue. In the Virginia and Maryland suburbs of Alexandria, Arlington, Bethesda, and Chevy Chase, Friday cocktail parties were the chief adult sport. Republicans were rarely seen. In the grander affairs liberal Democrats set the tone, as they had for sixteen years.

Aside from shoptalk, cocktail and dinner party conversations in Greater Washington didn't vary much from those on the outer rims of other American metropolitan areas. In Pawling or Chestnut Hill more of the guests would know the finer points of expense account living; more would be aware that the Dow had broken through the 225 barrier and that General Motors would pay $444,377,889 in taxes this year. Here on Washington's Macomb Street, say, or Kalorama Circle, men would have a more detailed knowledge of the status of bills in committee, and women would be likelier to rhapsodize about the marvelous job young Telford Taylor was doing in Nuremberg. But until the end of the decade had all but arrived, the enthusiasms of other well-to-do communities in the 1940s were shared by educated Washingtonians. Everyone was amused, for example, by Russell Lynes's clever stratification of Americans into highbrows, lowbrows and middlebrows in the February 1949 *Harper's*—the beginning of a whimsical parlor game that sociologists would later take up with high seriousness. Adventure stirred in the blood of male Martini drinkers marveling over the exploit of a Norwegian anthropologist who had crossed the Pacific in 101 days on a raft. Women, wearing the same mid-calf skirts to be seen in Sutton Place or Dallas's Highland Park, might tick off the latest list of eligible bachelors, with multimillionaire Congressman John F. Kennedy near the top. (Jacqueline Bouvier was a temporary expatriate; she had dropped out of Vassar the year before to study at the Sorbonne.)

The cinema continued to be the most widely discussed form of entertainment. In its Indian summer the silver screen was showing some of its finest films: Joseph L. Mankiewicz's *All About Eve* (Bette Davis, George Sanders, Anne Baxter); Harry Cohn's *Born Yesterday* (Judy Holliday, Broderick Crawford); Carol Reed's *The Third Man* (Orson Welles, Joseph Cotten, Trevor Howard); *Twelve O'Clock High* (Gregory Peck); *Sunset Boulevard* (Gloria Swanson); *Father of the Bride* (Spencer Tracy, Elizabeth Taylor); MGM's $3,200,000 musical *Annie Get Your Gun* (Betty Hutton), and Roberto Rossellini's *Stromboli*, which would be picketed by Catholic groups because Ingrid Bergman, Rossellini's star, had proudly borne his illegitimate son.

To put coming events in greater perspective: *South Pacific* was just beginning its four-year run (1,694 performances) in those last months of the 1940s. In New Haven, Ethel Merman was learning to bellow *Call Me Madam*. T. S. Eliot's *The Cocktail Party*, Carson McCullers's *The Member of the Wedding*, and William Inge's *Come Back, Little Sheba* were running well. The best musical play of the year was Gian-Carlo Menotti's *The Consul*. Critics were panning Ernest Hemingway's *Across the River and Into the Trees*—one wag called it "Across the Ribs and Between the Knees." Hemingway himself was about to become the victim of a vicious Lillian Ross profile in the *New Yorker*. In London, George Orwell lay desperately ill. His reputation had finally been established the year before with *1984;* now admirers were discovering his earlier achievements: *Down and Out in Paris and London, Burmese Days,* and *Coming Up for Air.* Orwell, supremely a figure of the 1940s, would breathe his last in the first month of the new decade.

It is of some interest that two memorable hits then in rehearsal were about witches—Christopher Fry's *The Lady's Not for Burning* and John Van Druten's *Bell, Book and Candle*—for the United States was about to enter upon the greatest witch-hunt in its history. And ironies were not confined to Broadway. It was in 1949 that Tin Pan Alley churned out a catchy tune called "I'd Like to Getcha on a Slow Boat to China." No sooner had it displaced Huddie Ledbetter's "Goodnight, Irene" on *Your Hit Parade* than the blow fell. Owing to certain events on the mainland of Asia, the country learned, no Americans were going to China for a long time. Not to put too fine a point on it, the United States had suffered the worst diplomatic defeat in its two centuries. Like the rest of the capital, Washington hostesses had known that the debacle was imminent. Not even they could have guessed the savagery of the coming recriminations, but there was a distinctly brittle quality to social functions in that first full year of Truman's second administration. Something big was coming, it was in the air; there was no place for men to hide; soon the pall of the great suspicion would fall across the city.

On April 4, 1949, the day the NATO alliance was signed in the new State Department auditorium under the approving eye of Dean Acheson, a Communist general named Chu Teh began massing a million of Mao Tse-tung's seasoned troops on the north bank of the Yangtze, the last natural barrier between Mao and the few southern provinces still loyal to Chiang Kai-shek's Nationalist Chinese, or Kuomintang (KMT). Chu Teh's veterans stormed across the Yangtze on April 24, meeting only token resistance; Chiang had withdrawn 300,000 of his most reliable soldiers to form a rear-guard perimeter around Shanghai. In the first week of May Chu Teh was hammering at the gates of Shanghai, and Chiang fled across the Formosa Strait to Taiwan, taking as many Nationalist Chinese as he could. By now China was as good as lost to him. A few formalities remained: on June 26 KMT gunboats began blockading the ports of mainland China; Mao proclaimed Red China's sovereignty on September 21—the same day as West Germany's proclamation of sovereignty—and on December 8 Chiang announced the formation of his new government in Taipei. The world now had two Chinas. Sun Yat-sen's fifty-year-old vision of a democratic China was dead, and Franklin Roosevelt's expectation that Chiang would provide the non-Communist world's eastern anchor had died with it.

The American response was slow. Troops had been fighting in China under one flag or another since September of 1931. U.S. newspapers had carried regular accounts of Chinese Communist offenses and the progressive disintegration of Chiang's KMT since V-J Day. But China was so vast, its geography so unfamiliar, and the movements of its unmechanized armies so slow, that Americans had lost interest in the distant battles. They knew of Chiang, of course, and from time to time newspapers had carried photographs of Mao, sleek and guileful, stripped to the waist for summer marches and always chain-smoking or chewing melon seeds. But the conflict had been too complicated and too far away for the general reader. If developments became important, he had reasoned, his government would tell him about them.

It did. With the collapse of the Kuomintang, Acheson decided to lay the whole story before the people. On August 5, 1949, the State Department issued a 1,054-page White Paper conceding that the world's largest nation had fallen into Communist hands, announcing the cessation of aid to Nationalist China, and setting forth the chain of events which had led to this tragic end. Three American generals —Stilwell, Hurley, and Marshall—had tried in vain to persuade Chiang to break the power of his KMT warlords and rid the Nationalist Army of corruption and defeatism. Over two billion dollars of U.S. aid had come to Chiang since V-J Day. Virtually all of it had been a waste of powder and shot; 75 percent of the American arms shipped to the KMT had wound up in Mao's hands. In his introduction to the White Paper, Acheson bluntly called Chiang's regime incompetent, corrupt, and insensitive to the needs of its people. He added:

> The unfortunate but inescapable fact is that the ominous result of the civil war in China was beyond the control of the government of the United States. Nothing that this country did or could have done within the reasonable limits of its capabilities could have changed that result. . . . It was the product of internal Chinese forces, forces which this country tried to influence but could not.

To knowledgeable Washingtonians this was apparent, even superfluous. But the U.S. public was bewildered. All this talk of KMT inefficiency was a switch. The China it knew—Pearl Buck's peasants, rejoicing in the good earth—had been dependable, democratic, warm, and above all pro-American. Throughout the great war the United Nations Big Four had been Churchill, Roosevelt, Stalin, and Chiang. Stalin's later treachery had been deplorable but unsurprising. But Chiang Kai-shek! Acheson's strategy to contain Red aggression seemed to have burst wide open. His own White Paper admitted that Mao's regime might "lend itself to the aims of Soviet Russian imperialism." Everything American diplomats had achieved in Europe—the Truman Doctrine, the Marshall Plan, NATO—momentarily seemed annulled by this disaster in Asia.

Nor was that all. In late August, while editorial writers were still digesting the White Paper and the last daring Chinese Nationalists were sailing in junks from mainland ports to Taiwan, a B-29 flying laboratory returned from an Asian flight with dismaying photographs. The B-29's mission had been to gather stress routine. Its pictures were expected to interest only low-level technicians. When developed, however, they revealed clear traces of radioactive material. There could be but one explanation: an atomic explosion somewhere in Russia. This was a massive jolt; Americans had been told that the Soviet Union could not develop a nuclear weapon before the late 1950s, if ever. Told the news, President Truman shook his head again and again, asking, "Are you sure? Are you *sure?*" Then, convinced, he said heavily, "This means we have no time left."

He waited three weeks before telling the public. On September 23 he authorized the release of a terse statement: "We have evidence an atomic explosion occurred in the USSR." When they were handed copies of it, White House correspondents raced to their phones. After they had gone, the President lay low, anticipating an angry public reaction. His cabinet also made itself scarce, with one notable exception. Acheson was beginning to suspect that Secretary of Defense Louis Johnson was afflicted by mental illness, and Johnson's behavior that Friday seemed probative. He made himself available to the press, discussed troop dispositions, and said lightly of the Russian bomb, "Now, let's keep calm about this. Don't overplay the story." Most responsible editors, worried about the possibility of mass hysteria, were already trying to understate the announcement, but there was no way to soften the blow. In Chicago physicist Harold C. Urey told reporters he felt "flattened." He said:

"There is only one thing worse than one nation having the atomic bomb—that's two nations having it."

Now the administration began to pay for the President's campaign excesses the year before. Then the Republicans had nominated a gentleman who had been beaten by a slugger. Studying campaign stories from small newspapers through whose towns Truman had passed, they had discovered after November 2 how savage he had really been. They were going to flay this administration any way they could, and the Asian crisis and the loss of America's nuclear monopoly were gut issues. Increasingly one heard from the Republican side of the Senate floor that the administration had "lost" China —that the responsibility for Chiang's defeat lay in Washington, among traitors who had cunningly worked with other Communists abroad to bring Mao to power. It was all a Red conspiracy, the litany ran, and it all began when Roosevelt went to Yalta.

For hard-core anti-Communist vigilantes, the conspiracy went back even farther. The issue of Communists in the government predated the war and had a faithful constituency; the House Committee on Un-American Activities had been consistently high in Gallup polls since its inception. To be sure, there was considerable disagreement over what a Communist was. To some it meant Soviet spies, to others it signified dues-paying members of the Communist Party of America, and to countless implacable adversaries of Franklin Roosevelt and everything he represented, Communism was a vague term embracing all advocates of social change.

No one quarreled over the first definition. Russian espionage would clearly constitute a threat to national security. On that point Americans were united, and any fuzzing of the definition served only to fragment that unity. Yet hazier interpretations of Communism had become the meat upon which ultraconservatives fed.* To them, anyone who had altered the world they had known in their youth was suspect. If they could pin a Red label on one New Dealer and make it stick, they felt, they would discredit everything left of center in one stroke.

The rise of the loyalty issue began in the last months of the war. Like almost everything else the Committee on Un-American Activi-

---

* In postwar America the terms "ultraconservatism" and "the right" have become as irrelevant to traditional conservatism as the New Left is to prewar liberalism and radicalism. All are in revolt against the world as it is. Any attempt to rechristen them here would merely compound the confusion. Therefore here, as elsewhere, the author has reluctantly adopted the usage of the time.

ties tackled, the case of *Amerasia*, a reputable scholarly journal, turned into a hopeless muddle. Early in 1945 a research analyst for the Office of Strategic Services (OSS), while riffling through the January 26 issue of the magazine, discovered that one article contained information from a restricted OSS report, some of it quoted verbatim. There was nothing sinister in that. Like so many governmental agencies, the OSS routinely stamped "Confidential" on virtually every document, including, in this case, an innocuous briefing which the State Department had earlier made available to American foreign correspondents in China. Despite this, a heavy-handed OSS officer raided *Amerasia*'s office and found other "confidential" information: reports on rice yields in selected provinces, water tables, livestock populations. The Justice Department's prosecution fell apart when a grand jury refused to indict anyone. But the *Amerasia* case would never be forgotten by those who had pressed it. The charge of treason had been raised, and the fact that the topic of the classified data had been China would later seem portentous.

The "do-nothing" 80th Congress had hurt the Democrats more than anyone realized at the time. After capturing control of the Hill, the Republican leadership had projected no fewer than thirty-five major loyalty investigations. Uneasy over the *Amerasia* uproar, Truman named a commission in late 1946 to study possible threats to internal security, and on March 21, 1947, acting upon its recommendation, he issued Executive Order 9835 establishing a Federal Employee Loyalty Program. Nevertheless the din continued. Reluctantly, and ill-advisedly, the State Department permitted a team of congressional investigators, led by a Republican and an anti-Communist vigilante with the engaging name of Robert E. Lee, to examine its loyalty files. Lee left carrying information on 108 past, present, and prospective State Department employees. The files were completely unscreened. They included allegations, unconfirmed statements, malicious gossip, and data which had later been proved to be false. Some sources weren't even identified. Other material reflected the biases of Lee's team; the American Civil Liberties Union was listed as a Communist front, and a labor leader was identified as a Communist on the strength of a charge from a manufacturer whose plant he had struck. After a long lull another congressional team asked State to bring the Lee list up to date. The department replied that of the original 108, only 57 were still employed. With that, the list and its accompanying folders went back on a shelf to collect dust. But the figure 57 would be heard again.

Early in 1948 yet another House committee demanded the federal record of Dr. Edward U. Condon, the director of the National Bureau of Standards. Learning that Condon had become the victim of a whispering campaign, Truman declared that he was fed up with Republican fishing expeditions. On March 13 he directed all government offices to keep personnel files in strictest confidence; any congressional requests or subpoenas for them were to be rejected. The President's position had become intolerable—isolated passages in the files, wrenched from context, were implicating the administration as a helpless accomplice in slander—but his directive solved nothing. Freed from the hazard that official records might contradict them, the vigilantes merely stepped up their recklessness; Nixon of California, for example, flatly stated that Democrats were responsible for "the unimpeded growth of the Communist conspiracy in the United States." The Democratic leadership heatedly denied it, though some of their back-benchers chimed in with the opposition. On February 21 Congressman John F. Kennedy of Massachusetts said that at Yalta a "sick" Roosevelt, on the advice of General Marshall and other chiefs of staff, "gave" the Kuriles and other strategic places to the USSR. The administration had tried to force Chiang into a coalition with Mao, he said. President Truman had even treated Madame Chiang with "indifference," if not "contempt." The State Department had squandered America's wartime gains by listening to such advisers as Owen Lattimore of Johns Hopkins University. "This," Kennedy concluded, "is the tragic story of China, whose freedom we once fought to preserve. What our young men saved, our diplomats and our President have frittered away."

The fact that Kennedy briefly found common cause with the vigilantes has long been forgotten, possibly because of his later career. Others in the China debate had become more inflammatory. As early as October 1947 William C. Bullitt, ex-ambassador to France and a zealous vigilante, had published a "Report on China" in *Life* charging that Washington bureaucrats were shackling Chiang by withholding arms from him. The Luce publications were vehement on the issue; Henry Luce had been born in China's Shantung province, the son of a missionary, and he had become a key figure in what was beginning to be called the "China Lobby"—men whose commitment to the Kuomintang was so great that it seemed to preclude all else, including their allegiance to the United States. The

September 6, 1948, issue of *Life* declared that Yalta had been the "high tide" of appeasement. After that the level of rhetoric descended rapidly. Republicans began referring to their congressional adversaries as members of "the party of treason"—a slur that Rayburn attributed to Nixon, and never forgave. Mundt of South Dakota demanded that the President "ferret out" those on the federal payroll "whose Soviet leanings have contributed so greatly to the deplorable mess of our foreign policy."* Congressman Harold Velde of Illinois announced that Soviet spies were "infesting the entire country," like gypsy moths; Congressman Robert Rich of Pennsylvania charged that Dean Acheson was on Joseph Stalin's payroll. To Jenner of Indiana, every American whose advice to Chiang Kai-shek had failed to stanch the Red tide was, almost by definition, a criminal. Jenner called General Marshall "a front man for traitors," a "living lie" who had joined hands "with this criminal crowd of traitors and Communist appeasers who, under the continuing influence of Mr. Truman and Mr. Acheson, are still selling America down the river."

Each excess seemed to surpass the last. Democrats on the Hill thought the opposition touched bottom in December 1949, when Republicans in both houses of Congress overwhelmingly resolved that the Secretary of State had lost the confidence of the country, could not regain it, and should be fired by the President. Eventually this singular resolution reached the desk of Harry Truman, who promptly ripped it in half. But that wasn't the bottom. They hadn't even begun to see the bottom.

The liberal community regarded Republican vigilantes as stage heavies. Certainly some of them were behaving as though they had not only been cast as villains but were enjoying every minute of it. On a typical afternoon spectators might enter the Senate visitors' gallery to hear the administration denounced as one of "egg-sucking phony liberals" whose "pitiful squealing" would "hold sacrosanct those Communists and queers" who had "sold China into atheistic slavery." The ripest phrases were reserved for those "prancing

---

* The Communist issue was acquiring an idiom all its own. "Enemies of the Free World" were to be "ferreted out" despite "commiecrats" who "coddled" security risks and were "soft" on "fellow travelers." As Robert Griffith of the University of Georgia has pointed out, long before the rise of McCarthy, Congressman Eugene Cox of Georgia—among others—had begun a speech on subversion with the solemn declaration, "I hold in my hand . . ."

mimics of the Moscow party line in the State Department" who were "spewing the Kremlin's malignant smear" while "the Red Dean" (Acheson) "whined" and "whimpered" and "cringed" as he "slobbered over the shoes of his Muscovite masters." There were times when correspondents wondered whether anti-American polemics in the Soviet Politburo could possibly be as scathing as those heard under the Capitol dome.

Occasionally the voice of reason was heard on the Hill, most memorably when a Joint Congressional Committee was pondering the nomination of David E. Lilienthal, a distinguished public servant, for the chairmanship of the Atomic Energy Commission. Senator Kenneth D. McKellar of Tennessee, a Democratic vigilante, insisted that Lilienthal had harbored Communists in the TVA. Did he, McKellar asked Lilienthal, carry in his head a blueprint for Soviet revolution? The witness replied in part:

> This I *do* carry in my head, Senator. . . . One of the tenets of democracy . . . is a . . . repugnance to anyone who would steal from a human being that which is most precious to him—his good name—either by imputing things to him by innuendo or by insinuation. And it is especially an unhappy circumstance that occasionally that is done in the name of democracy. This, I think, can tear our country apart and destroy it if we carry it further. . . . This I deeply believe.

Such moments were rare, and apart from heartening men of good will, they achieved almost nothing. The Lilienthals of America erred in assuming that fear of internal subversion could be resolved by evidence and reason. It couldn't; otherwise there would have been no crisis in the first place. The anti-Communist terror was pathological. It would have to run its course before the delirium could end. In the meantime it would be a savage force in the hands of men who had fathomed how to use it. Senator Taft understood it. He knew precisely what he and his fellow Republicans were doing, and he knew why. After a vigilante exercise in verbal overkill ("The greatest Kremlin asset in our history has been the pro-Communist group in the State Department who promoted at every opportunity the Communist cause in China") Taft cut close to the bone when he told reporters: "The only way to get rid of Communists in the State Department is to change the head of government." In other words, he was warming up for 1952, when the people would have an opportunity to choose a new President, hopefully Robert A. Taft.

Tom Coleman, the Republican boss in Wisconsin and a Taft supporter, was more explicit. "It all comes down to this," he said. "Are we going to try to win an election or aren't we?"

But Democrats liked to win, too. Harry Truman was well aware that the stain of suspicion was spreading. Moreover, other issues were at stake for him. The Republicans were hunting witches, but the NKVD had been running real agents from Moscow, and the country's chief executive was responsible for its internal security. Truman's first inkling that the NKVD was at large in North America had come shortly after that evening in September 1945 when a Russian cipher clerk named Igor Gouzenko, stationed in the Soviet embassy at Ottawa on the staff of the military attaché, snatched up an armful of incriminating documents—all he could carry—and staggered out into the night and political asylum. The Canadians established a commission to investigate the Gouzenko papers. It uncovered a widespread apparatus of English and Canadian citizens whose trail ultimately led to two British physicists with Most Secret clearance: Dr. Alan Nunn May and Dr. Klaus Fuchs. The net comprised dedicated Communists and participants in a scheme, which had been largely successful, to pry loose atomic and other defense secrets Washington had shared with its Canadian allies.

At first the President appears to have been slow in grasping the implications of the Ottawa ring. The following February J. Edgar Hoover sent Truman confessions from Communist agents Elizabeth Bentley, a former employee in the Italian Library of Information in New York, and Whittaker Chambers. The Bentley and Chambers cases hardly qualified as FBI exploits. It was now seven years since Chambers had first tried to find someone in the government who would take him seriously, and when Miss Bentley first tried to turn herself in at the FBI's New Haven office, she had been ignored; agents believed her only after seeing a Soviet operative slip her two thousand dollars in a sidewalk stakeout. She and Chambers were strangers to one another, but they had this in common: their statements were sufficiently fantastic to raise questions about their sanity. Miss Bentley, a middle-aged Vassar graduate, declared that for five years she had served as a Soviet courier, picking up highly classified documents in Washington and turning them over to her Russian contact in New York. Among thirty-odd former government employees she accused of treachery were Lauchlin Currie, who had served as special assistant to President Roosevelt from 1939 to 1945, headed two missions to China, and now headed a Park Avenue import-export firm; Harry Dexter White, a former Assistant Secretary of the Treasury and the current executive director of the International Monetary Fund; and William W. Remington, a handsome young Dartmouth graduate who had become a rising star in the Department of Commerce. Chambers identified nine of the brighter lights in the Roosevelt administration as Communist party members, notably Alger Hiss, who was about to leave the State Department to become president of the Carnegie Endowment for International Peace.

Like others who had heard them out, Truman was skeptical. The Canadian ring had shaken him, however, and in that autumn's off-year election several GOP congressional candidates had used fallout from the *Amerasia* case to raise doubts about the administration. In response, on December 4 Attorney General Tom C. Clark made public a list of ninety organizations which in the opinion of the Justice Department were Communist fronts. Throughout the following year the list was repeatedly expanded—on one day, May 27, 1948, thirty-two additions were made. Suspicion fell upon everyone who had ever belonged to, say, the Anti-Fascist Refugee Committee, even though its original purpose had been confined to contributing food and medicine to America's Russian ally. Civil servants who had thus "followed the party line" were dismissed. In the vernacular of the time, they had been found to be "bad security risks."

At the time, the Truman administration's most spectacular contribution to vigilantism seemed to be its invocation of the Smith Act of 1940 to try eleven leaders of the Communist Party of America. The real terror seldom reached newsprint, however, because it was so ordinary, like being jobless in 1932. Apart from its other outrages, Executive Order 9835 encouraged Americans to snoop on colleagues, friends, neighbors, and even relatives. Furthermore, the loyalty program was an administrative monstrosity. On May 22, 1947, the FBI began stalking "disloyal and subversive persons" by conducting a "name check" of the two million people on federal payrolls, from mailmen to cabinet members. In addition, the bureau was answerable for disloyalty among the five hundred thousand annual applicants for government jobs. "Derogatory information" about an individual brought a "full field investigation" into his past, sometimes all the way back to childhood, with agents interrogating those who remembered him, or thought they remembered him, about his habits, associates, and convictions. Accumulated data were weighed by a regional loyalty board which could either dismiss charges or hold a hearing and reach a verdict. Adverse decisions could be appealed to a National Loyalty Review Board in Washington, whose rulings were final.

On what grounds could a good and faithful letter carrier, say, be fired? Pink slips went to those who had committed treason, engaged in espionage, advocated violent overthrow of the government (already forbidden by the Hatch Act), disclosed official confidences, or belonged to an association which the attorney general defined as subversive. Proof that a man had engaged in any of these activities need not be absolute; "reasonable grounds for belief" of subversion was enough. The ground rules for hearings were Kafkaesque. Charges were to be stated "specifically and completely" only if, in the judgment of the employing department, "security considerations permit." If not, the accused wasn't even told how or where he was said to have slipped. He might have learned of it if he had been granted the time-honored right to confront his accuser, but this, too, was denied him. FBI policy held that identification of informants would hamper future investigations, thus jeopardizing national security. Similarly, the attorney general's list of proscribed organizations, which had been drawn up by the FBI, was above challenge. The groups on it were not allowed to argue their innocence. If a civil servant had held membership in one of them—or, in many cases, if he merely *knew* someone who belonged—he was given notice. Guilt was, quite literally, by association.

Those victims who were privileged to know why they were being fired received a form which began, "The evidence indicates that," and continued with such accusations as these, taken from files of the time:

> Since 1943 you have been a close associate of ———, an individual who, evidence in our files indicates, has displayed an active, sympathetic interest in the principles and policies of the Communist Party.
>
> Your name appeared in an article in the 4 April 1946 edition of the *York Gazette and Daily* as a sponsor of a Philadelphia, Pa. mass meeting . . . sponsored by the National Committee to Win the Peace. The National Committee to Win the Peace has been cited by the Attorney General as Communist.

During your period of employment by Williams College, in Williamstown, Mass., you made statements to the effect that you believed "the House Committee on Un-American Activities hearings in Washington, D.C. are a greater threat to civil liberties than the Communist Party because they infringe upon free speech. . . ."

Your name appeared among the signers of an open letter . . . of the National Federation for Constitutional Liberties dated 28 December 1941 and urging speedier shipments of arms to the Union of Soviet Socialist Republics. The National Federation for Constitutional Liberties has been cited by the Attorney General as Communist.

The form would conclude with a formal notice of dismissal: "The foregoing information indicates that you have been and are a member, close affiliate, or sympathetic associate of the Communist Party." The luckless ex-employee had been cashiered by a court which "could proceed on mere rumor"—Webster's definition of a star chamber. The mere opening of the full field investigation was often enough to humiliate a man and shame his family. Guilty in the eyes of many until innocence had been proven, he became suspect the day his loyalty check began. Neighbors questioned by security officers cut him on the street, ignored invitations from his wife, and forbade their children to play with his. His sons might be barred from the Cub Scouts. He couldn't even call upon civil service friends without putting them, too, in the shadow of the ax. In the end he had to fall back upon his savings, if any, and his family.

In June of 1949 former Attorney General Clark, now a member of the Supreme Court, remarked that "never before" had the morale of federal officials been so high, "thanks to the Loyalty Order." It is hard to imagine what had made him think so. Nearly every other lawyer in the country knew that the program had made a sham of due process. Tom Paine's proud boast that the New World had become "the asylum for the persecuted lovers of civil and religious liberty from every part of Europe" mocked his memory. The most popular book in Washington was Bert Andrews's *Washington Witch Hunt*, a recital, by the respected chief of the New York *Herald*'s Washington Bureau, of the loyalty program's more flagrant injustices. John Lord O'Brian, writing in the *Harvard Law Review* of April 1948, had pointed out that the effect of an assertion of guilt by association was "analogous to that of a criminal conviction—loss of occupation, lasting disgrace, and a continued impairment of . . . ability to earn a livelihood." Already the program had cost twelve million dollars, and among the more diverting cases awaiting appeal was that of a man who had been dismissed for deserting the Army during World War I, when he was nine years old.

Those who trusted the National Loyalty Review Board to set things straight were grasping at a frail reed. In President Truman's memoirs he identifies Seth Richardson, the board's chairman, as "a prominent conservative Republican" who "worked in close contact with the Department of Justice." Doubtless the Richardson appointment was good politics—he had been a protégé of Harding and Coolidge—but it led to wretched equity. In his late sixties, the appeals chairman was best known in the capital as counsel for the American Medical Association and the Pullman Corporation. He was an American Legionnaire, an Elk, and a member of the Metropolitan, Burning Tree, and Chevy Chase clubs—exactly the sort of establishmentarian who defined loyalty negatively, as something which was not un-American, and who confused patriotism with orthodoxy.

Sometimes a single incident may illumine an entire era. The appeal of Dorothy Bailey sheds considerable light on this one. A graduate of Bryn Mawr and the University of Minnesota, Miss Bailey was forty-one in the spring of 1948. She had worked at the United States Employment Service for fourteen years and was regarded as an exemplary employee; her only public activity was in the United Public Workers of America, an organization not cited by the attorney general. Miss Bailey was president of her UPWA local, which may have inspired jealous gossip, though she had no known enemies. On the strength of unsupported charges that she was, or had been, a Communist and had "associated with known Communist Party members," she had been haled before the District of Columbia's regional loyalty board. The prosecution presented no evidence. No witnesses testified against her. She categorically denied the reports, presented several character witnesses—and was sacked anyway.

During Miss Bailey's appearance before Seth Richardson's review board, Paul Porter, her attorney, suggested that she may have been prey for hidden spite. The chairman answered that "five or six of the reports came from informants certified to us by the Federal Bureau of Investigation as experienced and entirely reliable." Pressed by Porter, Richardson refused to identify the sources. He then added that he couldn't if he wished to, because "I haven't the slightest knowledge as to who they are or how active they have been in anything." One of Richardson's fellow board members noted a damning phrase in the dossier, and this exchange followed:

BOARD MEMBER: Then another one says it first came to the informant's attention about 1936, at which time [you were] a known member of the so-called "closed group" of the Communist Party operating in the District of Columbia.

MISS BAILEY: First of all, I didn't know, or don't know, that there is a "closed group." The terminology is unfamiliar to me. I can say under oath and with the strongest conviction that I was not then and have never been a member of the Communist Party.

BOARD MEMBER: Here is another that says you were a member of the Communist Party, and he bases his statement on his knowledge of your association with known Communists for the past seven or eight years. That is part of the evidence that was submitted to us.

MR. PORTER: It is part of the allegations. I don't think that can be considered evidence.

CHAIRMAN RICHARDSON: It is evidence.

MR. PORTER: We renew our request, although we recognize the futility of it, that some identification of this malicious gossip be given this respondent or her counsel.

CHAIRMAN RICHARDSON: Of course, that doesn't help us a bit. If this testimony is true, it is neither gossip or [sic] malicious. We are under the difficulty of not being able to disclose this.

MR. PORTER: Is it under oath?

CHAIRMAN RICHARDSON: I don't think so.

BOARD MEMBER: It is a person of known responsibility who had proffered information concerning Communist activity in the District of Columbia.

MISS BAILEY: You see, that point in it worries me, because if I am convicted here that will make this person who has made these charges considered a reliable witness; and they are not, because the charges are not true, and whatever is said here should not add to their reliability.

Her appeal was denied. Reminded that the board's procedures were in flagrant contempt of constitutional guarantees, Richardson took refuge in the meaningless cliché that government service is "a privilege, not a right." He then glanced at his agenda, pored over the next batch of unsigned accusations, and began conferring with his colleagues. That was justice under the vigilantes.

Seldom in the long history of bureaucracy has there been such a waste of time and paper. Even in Richardson's kangaroo court, with every conceivable card stacked against the pleader, such a conviction as Miss Bailey's was rare. During the loyalty program's five years the FBI screened over 3,000,000 Americans and conducted 10,000 full field investigations. Preliminary indictments were filed against 9,077, of whom 2,961 were arraigned before regional boards and 378 were given notice. Asked to sum up his findings for a congressional committee, Richardson said: "Not one single case or evidence directing toward a case of espionage has been disclosed in the record. Not one single syllable of evidence has been found by the FBI indicating that a particular case involves a question of espionage."

"A specter is haunting Europe," Marx and Engels had written in 1848—"the specter of Communism." Now in the centennial of their Communist Manifesto the shadow of the same apparition had fallen across the United States. It seldom made sense. Richardson, for example, had been boasting to the congressmen: no spies had been found; therefore the searchers must have driven them out. This inverted logic was not confined to federal employees. Irène Curie, arriving in New York for a scientific meeting, was interned overnight on Ellis Island; anonymous telephone calls had warned that she might be an enemy agent. After the publication in *Liberty* magazine of "Reds in Our Atomic Bomb Plants," an article by J. Parnell Thomas insinuating that all scientists were security risks, the government for a time found it almost impossible to recruit young nuclear physicists.* Physicians subscribing to the *American Review of Soviet Medicine,* a professional journal issued by the American-Soviet Medical Society, asked that issues be mailed to them in plain paper wrappers.

Firms active in defense work were jittery—one spent $3,000,000 on new safes and strongboxes for classified documents entrusted to it—and colleges and universities were torn by a double allegiance, to the flag and to academic freedom. Legislature after legislature

---

* J. Parnell Thomas was chairman of the House Committee on Un-American Activities when the article appeared. He was convicted of fraud on December 3, 1949, fined $10,000, and sent to prison.

was requiring loyalty oaths from teachers, 11,000 of them at the University of California alone; UCLA fired 157 professors who balked. On the local level teacher oaths were administered by school board chairmen, PTA presidents, and police chiefs. In many communities Legion or VFW officers also studied classroom texts for subversive material.

If any occupation had to endure more than the teaching profession, it was show business. In New York three aggressive ex-FBI agents, egged on by vigilantes in the American Federation of Radio Artists, published *Counter-Attack,* a pamphlet listing 151 actors, directors, and writers whose names had appeared in the files of various congressional committees. *Counter-Attack* was circulated among communications executives, who were urged to fire anyone in it and to check it before hiring new people. Next the three issued *Red Channels,* a thicker directory of entertainers and announcers whose friends or "affiliations" were dubious. The industry trembled —*Counter-Attack* had described CBS as "the most satisfying network for the Communists"—and vice presidents kept copies of *Red Channels* in their bottom desk drawers. On Madison Avenue and throughout Hollywood it was rechristened "the blacklist."

Blacklisting was to be a feature of the entertainment industry for over a decade. It was a blunt instrument of blackmail, used to cow administrators whose livelihood depended upon public opinion. Time has blurred many sharp contours of the Age of Suspicion, but no brief can be held for those company heads who permitted themselves to be intimidated. Often they knew that a star had been blacklisted by a jealous competitor, and at the other end of the wage scale they summarily dismissed stagehands and deodorant demonstrators on preposterous charges that they were "disloyal" or "security risks." If one executive had stiffened his backbone the counterattackers' house of cards might have collapsed. None did.

The experience of Jean Muir was typical. One day she was the leading actress in *The Aldrich Family,* NBC's most popular radio serial. The next day her name was added to *Red Channels.* By afternoon the network had torn up her contract and put her on the street. NBC's explanation to the press set a new low in what had already become a low era, and established a precedent its competitors soon followed. Of course Miss Muir wasn't a Communist, the network spokesman said blandly. She was loyal to her country and always had been. Unfortunately, she had become controversial.

Controversy alarmed sponsors, stirred up the public, and hurt the product. In short, she had been fired because someone had lied about her. From then on, "controversial" was almost a synonym for "disloyal"—and just as likely to ruin a career. Eventually most people stopped trying to justify the blacklist. If questions were raised about its iniquities, there always seemed to be someone around who would shake his head and say maddeningly, "Where there's smoke, there's fire."

The worst of it was that he was right, there *was* a flame beneath all that smog. Not that Dorothy Bailey and Jean Muir had anything to do with it. They were martyrs, sacrificed to ignorance and fear as surely as any Salem "witch" in 1692. But it was a chilling fact that real agents had made off with real secrets. Once Stalin had the Bomb, few gave peace more than an even chance—Lloyd's of London didn't—and the swiftness with which Russian scientists built their first nuclear weapon owed almost everything to the ingenious espionage web Soviet Vice Consul Anatoli A. Yakovlev had spun between New York and Los Alamos during the war.

Yakovlev's apparatus would never have been discovered without the defection of Gouzenko in Ottawa. Even so, it took four years and the combined efforts of the Canadian Mounties, Scotland Yard, and the FBI to unravel the snarl. Fuchs was the key to it. His confession to a Yard inspector in Harwell and London led to Harry Gold in New York. Gold broke down when FBI agents found a New Mexico map in his apartment showing the routes he followed in his rendezvous with Fuchs and Greenglass. When Julius Rosenberg read of Gold's arrest in the *New York Herald Tribune* he took the paper to Ruth Greenglass. She and David would have to leave the country, he said; David could implicate all of them, including Ethel Rosenberg, his own sister. Ruth said, "We can't go anywhere. We have a ten-day-old infant." Rosenberg said, "Your baby won't die. Babies are born on the ocean and in trains every day. My doctor says that if you take enough canned milk and boil the water the baby will be all right."

Julius gave the Greenglasses a thousand dollars and mapped out a complex journey from Mexico City to Sweden to Czechoslovakia to Moscow. Local Communists would meet them and guide them on each leg of the trip, he said. They had passport photos taken and then hesitated again. Ruth was ill. Julius, climbing walls, gave them four thousand dollars more, but they told him they were going to stay and face punishment. Eleven days later the FBI picked David up. He then had to choose between his wife and his sister. He chose Ruth. Early one summer evening while the Rosenbergs were listening to *The Lone Ranger* the FBI knock came. Only Julius was taken then; Ethel was left to care for their two sons. Then she had to make other arrangements. She too was jailed. They had betrayed the country in wartime, and Sing Sing and electrocution lay ahead for both of them.

That was real treason, not the paranoid fantasies of superpatriots demanding loyalty oaths of kindergarten teachers and movie extras. Beyond doubt the Rosenberg-Greenglass-Gold-Fuchs-Nunn-May ring was one of the most successful in the history of international espionage. In Moscow it disgorged charts, formulae, and hundreds of pages of closely written data describing in detail everything from Oak Ridge's gaseous diffusion process for separating U-235 and U-238 to blueprints of the missile itself. The Russians could scarcely have learned more about nuclear weapons had they been full partners in the undertaking. At the cost of two billion dollars America had assembled the best scientific minds in western Europe and the United States, mobilized American industry, and united the two in a three-and-a-half-year search that culminated in success at Alamogordo and terror over Japan. By then the Soviet director of intelligence had a full account of the making of the bomb and even an eyewitness account, from Fuchs, of that first blast in the New Mexico desert. The information was beyond price. USSR physicists could not have duplicated it then. They grasped the theoretical physics involved, but in the late 1940s Russia simply did not have adequate industrial resources for so huge a venture. Treachery permitted them to close the nuclear gap. The Anglo-American traitors had hastened the onset of the Cold War by at least eighteen months.

So enormous were their crimes, and so leaky the British and American counterespionage nets through which they slipped, that public opinion might well have demanded new governments at 10 Downing Street and 1600 Pennsylvania Avenue. Nothing of the sort happened. As far as the electorate was concerned, the whole thing might have been an act of God. The security failures were lamented, of course, but in neither country was there any sustained search for scapegoats in the laboratories. The man in the street lacked sufficient scientific sophistication to appreciate what had happened. Gaseous diffusion processes would have made poor campaign issues. Furthermore, none of the guilty persons could be identified with any party except the Communist party. What the Republicans needed was a ring of full-fledged New Dealers, or at least one of them, who had turned U.S. secrets over to the USSR.

It is a central fact of mid-century American politics that they found what they wanted. Not the real thing, perhaps, but close enough to it to divide the country and make heads roll. If their Communists-in-government had not betrayed atom bomb plans, it was only because they didn't know any. All were cut from the same cloth as the spies in the labs—intelligent, sensitive and idealistic men who had been born shortly after the turn of the century and retained grim memories of the First World War. They had witnessed the collapse of the economy after the Crash, the unchecked aggression which had followed in Spain, Ethiopia, China, and central Europe, and the shame of Munich. Despairing of the western democracies, they had embraced Communism as the faith that would remake the world. Like religious fanatics they would do anything for the cause. Most of them were denied the golden opportunity of the physicists, but everyone could do something. Those in the administration could filch state secrets. If in the sub-cabinet, one might recommend Soviet solutions, such as the plowing under of Germany's Ruhr. Even ordinary people could serve as couriers. Harry Gold was a courier. Whittaker Chambers was another.

This is very complicated, and even today it cuts across beliefs so deeply held that confessions and overwhelming evidence are denied; Dean Acheson went to his grave believing Harry Dexter White innocent and the Hiss affair a "mystery." To comprehend the enormity of what began happening in the summer of 1948, one may imagine a large household whose children insist that they are pursued by a bogeyman. Others in the family repeatedly assure them that there is no such thing as a bogeyman. The house is searched over and over. Nothing is found, and although the children persist in their preposterous stories, everyone else in the home ignores them. Then one evening when the family is gathered together one child notices that a closet door is ajar. He flings it open —and out steps a real bogeyman, ten feet tall and all teeth. Igor Gouzenko in Canada had been such a child. Three years afterward American defectors began giving other evidence in Washington.

The difference was that their door didn't open on a closet. It led to the master bedroom.

Early in the Age of Suspicion liberals and intellectuals tried to drown the Red bogey in laughter. For ten years the House Committee on Un-American Activities had been trying to discredit Roosevelt reforms by frightening the country. It seemed inconceivable that anything of consequence could turn up now. When Elizabeth Bentley began testifying before a subcommittee of the Senate Committee on Expenditures in the Executive Department, the *New Yorker* turned the pitiless wit of A. J. Liebling on her. "Behind Schrafft's saccharine facade," he wrote, "Miss Bentley had handed Al* the secret formula for making synthetic rubber out of garbage, which has not yet been discovered, or a redundant tip on the approximate date of D Day, which the Allied Chiefs of Staff had communicated to their Russian colleagues as soon as it was decided upon. I forget where she passed on the information that she had received from a man who, she testified, told her he got it from Lauchlin Currie, former administrative assistant to President Roosevelt, on a subject that Currie has since sworn he knew nothing about —the breaking of a Russian code."

There was no end to the fun Liebling had with Miss Bentley that August. To him she was "the Nutmeg Mata Hari," and after the *New York World-Telegram* stopped calling her a "Red Spy Queen" and began referring to her as "striking" and "a blonde" (she was neither) the *New Yorker*'s press critic gaily rechristened her "the Red blonde Spy Queen." Then his comments became sharper. A joke was a joke, but this woman was damaging the reputations of decent men. The hearings, he wrote, "were reminiscent of a group of retarded children playing deteckative." Liebling thought that "An editor who couldn't smell an odor of burning synthetic rubber about Miss Bentley's inside-policy data has an extremely insensitive nose for news." To have suggested the suppression of testimony would have been entirely out of character for him, a violation of his most deeply held convictions; still, when South Dakota's bumbling Karl Mundt said, "Evidence is clouding up, but it isn't clear enough

---

* Her lover and chief contact. His real name was Jacob Golos. Before his death in 1944 Golos was a link in the chain whose other links included Harry Gold and Klaus Fuchs.

yet," Liebling remarked, "I feel that the press has been slighting the low-comedy aspects of the hearings."

As the summer wore on, they became less amusing. In sworn testimony Miss Bentley and Whittaker Chambers accused thirty-seven former government employees of participation in Soviet espionage. Of these, seventeen refused under oath to say whether they were Communists or spies. The names of those who took the Fifth Amendment are faintly evocative today, like a scratchy old Paul Robeson recording of "The Peat-Bog Soldiers" or "The Four Insurgent Generals." None of them had been known to the public before 1948, but all had been close to the seats of power and decision. Six others were not called to testify. Of those remaining, Harold Ware had died in 1935; Lee Pressman and John Abt admitted they were Communists but denied espionage; Laurence Duggan, a fourteen-year veteran of the State Department, either jumped or fell to his death from a sixteenth-floor Manhattan window after two witnesses had identified him as a Communist; former Assistant Secretary of State Harry Dexter White, against whom the evidence was formidable, died of a heart attack; and the other twelve swore that the charges against them were false. Two of these were then accused of perjury. The first, William Remington, was found guilty and later murdered in prison. The other was Alger Hiss.

His biographical sketch in the 1948–1949 edition of *Who's Who in America* read:

HISS, Alger, lawyer, B. Baltimore, Md. Nov. 11, 1904; s. Charles Alger and Mary L. (Hughes) H.; A.B., Johns Hopkins, 1926; LL.B., Harvard, 1929; m. Priscilla Fansler Hobson, Dec. 11, 1929; children—Timothy Hobson (stepson), Anthony. Mem. bars of Mass., N.Y. and U.S. Supreme Court; sec. and law clerk to Supreme Court Justice, 1929–30; asst. to gen. counsel and asst. gen. counsel, Agrl. Adjustment Administrn., Washington, D.C. 1933–35; legal asst., special Senate com. investigating munitions industry, 1934–35; special atty. U.S. Dept. Justice, 1935–36 . . . pres. Carnegie Endowment for Internat. Peace since Feb. 1, 1947; exec. sec. Dumbarton Oaks Conf., 1944; accompanied Pres. Roosevelt to Crimea Conf., Feb. 1945; sec. gen. United Nations Conf. on Internat. Organization, San Francisco, 1945; principal advisor, U.S. Del. to U.S. Gen. Assembly, Jan.–Feb. 1946. Mem. Phi Beta Kappa, Alpha Delta Phi. Club: Metropolitan (Washington). Home: 3210 P Street N.W., Washington 7, D.C. Office: 522 Fifth Avenue, New York 18, N.Y.

It would have been difficult to find a more attractive Rooseveltian figure. In the word of the man who became his prosecutor, he was "a prototype." Lean, tanned, elegantly tailored, he was every inch the patrician-as-idealist—the public servant who was also a member of a law firm with the name Choate in it, the reform Democrat who was listed in the Washington *Social Register*. At Johns Hopkins he had been a debater, a track star, and the "best hand-shaker" in his class. His reputation was flawless: Governor Adlai Stevenson of Illinois was prepared to testify to that; so were two U.S. Supreme Court justices, a former solicitor general of the United States, John W. Davis (a former presidential candidate) and John Foster Dulles. Hiss's presence was imposing. His well-modulated voice carried just the right trace of a Harvard accent. He smiled easily and broadly, like FDR at his most charming, and moved with a casual grace suggestive of Baltimore Cotillions or Gibson Island tennis matches, at both of which he was a familiar figure. Attending his own trials, he would seem less the defendant than a distinguished spectator. To call such a man a Communist was as unthinkable as calling him a liar.

Whittaker Chambers, who accused him of being both, was by his own admission a scoundrel and a blackguard. Before breaking with the party to join *Time* he had perjured himself a thousand times over. As a boy he had formed a suicide pact with his brother Dick; Dick had killed himself but Whittaker had backed out. Aged seventeen, he had set up housekeeping in a New Orleans flophouse with a prostitute named One-Eyed Annie. Later he brought another female tramp to live with him in his mother's Long Island home—she let him do it, he said, "because she had lost one son and did not want to lose another." He had been expelled from Columbia for writing a sacrilegious play. He had been a thief. Confronted with an oath he had taken upon going to work for the WPA, he readily conceded, in his phlegmatic way, that he had broken it in every particular. Now in 1948 he was a fat, rumpled, middle-aged, sad-looking man with a sickly complexion and heavily lidded eyes.

Yet it was Chambers who saw one aspect of the issue between the two men most clearly: "No feature of the Hiss case is more obvious, or more troubling as history," he wrote afterward, "than the jagged fissure, which it did not so much open as reveal, between the plain men and women of the nation, and those who affected to act, think and speak for them. It was not invariably, but in general, the 'best people' who were for Alger Hiss and who were prepared to go to almost any length to protect and defend him." That was certainly part of it. The other part was that to partisans on both sides Alger Hiss quickly became a symbol. Liberal Democrats saw him as representative of the New Deal achievements now under attack. To conservative Republicans he stood for the hated eastern elite. The liberals made the first commitment in the case. Hiss's innocence was so obvious to them that they staked everything on it and invited the opposition to do the same. Conservatives were slower on the field. In the beginning Chambers seemed an unlikely champion for them. But Congressman Richard M. Nixon showed them the way, and long before the true import of the Chambers-Hiss uproar was known—that is, before the charge of treason had been lodged—both sides had closed ranks and raised their banners. Thereafter the role of reason steadily diminished; the case incited blind, violent emotions in every quarter. It was the tragedy of the liberals that they were wrong. It was the triumph of Richard Nixon and his party that Chambers was not only right; he could prove it.

He didn't look right at first. Hiss played his part superbly. Others had taken refuge in the Fifth Amendment or in transparent evasions. Not he. On August 4, 1948, upon learning that Chambers had identified him as a Communist the day before in testimony before the House Committee on Un-American Activities, he telegraphed the committee from New York demanding that he be given the right to deny the charge under oath. Next day he faced the committee, the very picture of righteous indignation. He answered every question and denied each of Chambers's specifications. At the end Chairman Mundt thanked Hiss for his "very cooperative attitude" and "forthright statements." John Rankin walked round to shake Hiss's hand. Everyone was smiling except Nixon, who hadn't taken his eyes off Hiss's face. Before the month was out the young California congressman would appear to have had second sight. In fact he was blessed by an excellent source. The FBI had begun checking Hiss. An agent named Ed Hummer was phoning the results of each day's investigation to a priest named John Cronin, and Father Cronin was relaying it to Nixon. Still, there was little to go on in that first week in August, and Nixon deserves full marks for persistence and perspicacity. He said he wanted to see Chambers and Hiss face to face.

The rest of the committee decided to hear Chambers again; they thought Hiss might be the victim of mistaken identity. It was during this second session, which was closed to the public (and to Hiss), that the accuser began to reveal his encyclopedic knowledge of Hiss, Hiss's wife, and the Hiss household. The couple called one another "Hilly" and "Pross," he remembered. They had been devoted to their cocker spaniel. Their Volta Place house had been furnished with Hitchcock chairs stenciled in gilt, a gold mirror with an eagle on top, walls papered halfway with a mulberry pattern and the lower half paneled. Chambers knew much more about them than that, but for the moment he said just enough to establish his bona fides—little details about children, servants, food, books, furniture, and hobbies. One of Hiss's hobbies was bird-watching. Chambers told of how excited Hiss had become upon seeing a prothonotary warbler on the Potomac. By chance one of the congressmen, John McDowell, was himself an amateur ornithologist, and when Hiss was recalled before the committee McDowell asked him whether he had ever seen a prothonotary warbler. Hiss's eyes lit up. He replied brightly, "I have, right here on the Potomac. Do you know that place?" A moment later he said, "They come back and nest in those swamps. Beautiful head, a gorgeous bird." It had been a small feat. It impressed the committee more than he knew.

Clearly Chambers's knowledge of the Hisses was the sort that comes from only the closest friendship. Nixon therefore got his confrontation, on August 25, in suite 400 of the Commodore Hotel in New York. It was a critical point in the case. Hiss, rattled by Nixon's questioning and Chambers's evident knowledge of him, identified his accuser as one George Crosley, a free-lance writer and deadbeat he had met in the 1930s. Now Nixon began to close in. Hiss was asked to produce three people who would also testify that they knew Chambers as Crosley. Visibly upset, he replied, "I will if it is possible. Why is that a question to ask me? I will see what is possible. This occurred in 1935. The only people that I can think of who would have known him as George Crosley with certainty would have been the people who were associated with me in the Nye [munitions investigation] committee." After another sharp Nixon-Hiss exchange this colloquy followed, between the two principals, Congressmen Nixon, McDowell, and Louis Russell, a committee investigator:

Mr. McDowell: Then your identification of George Crosley is complete?

Mr. Hiss: Yes, as far as I am concerned, on his own testimony.

Mr. McDowell: Mr. Chambers, is this the man, Alger Hiss, who was also a member of the Communist Party at whose home you stayed?

Mr. Nixon: According to your testimony.

Mr. McDowell: You make identification positive?

Mr. Chambers: Positive identification.

(*At this point Mr. Hiss arose and walked in the direction of Mr. Chambers.*)

Mr. Hiss: May I say for the record at this point, that I would like to invite Mr. Whittaker Chambers to make those same statements out of the presence of this committee without their being privileged for suit for libel. I challenge you to do it, and I hope you will do it damned quickly. I am not going to touch him (*addressing Mr. Russell*). You are touching me.

Mr. Russell: Please sit down, Mr. Hiss.

Mr. Hiss: I will sit down when the chairman asks me, Mr. Russell, when the chairman asks me to sit down—

Mr. Russell: I want no disturbance.

Mr. Hiss: I don't—

Mr. McDowell: Sit down, please.

Mr. Hiss: You know who started this.

Mr. McDowell: We will suspend testimony here for a minute or two, until I return.

But it was too late. Hiss had blundered. Until this moment his gamble had made sense. He was right, 1935 *had* been a long time ago. It was his word against Chambers's, and given the differences between their reputations there could be small doubt about the outcome. Having been a Communist wasn't a crime anyhow, and the statute of limitations had expired on the felony of stealing government secrets. The committee had just about given up hope of making any case out of the Bentley-Chambers testimony. By daring Chambers to shed the privilege of congressional immunity, however, and by promising to sue for libel, Hiss had created a new situation. Now Chambers would be forced to produce his evidence. The whole wretched business would be moved into a court of law, which would determine which of them was lying. The loser would be found guilty of perjury and imprisoned.

Eight days later there was another Hiss-Chambers confrontation in Washington, for the public, under lights. Here Hiss's assurance had plainly ebbed. He had brought his lawyer, and he prefaced his answers with such circumlocutions as, "To the best of my recollection." Even when asked whether he came to the hearing in response to a subpoena he replied, "To the extent that my coming here quite voluntarily after having received the subpoena is in response to it —I would accept that statement." Chambers had told the congressmen that Hiss had given him a 1929 Model A Ford, to be used as the Communist party saw fit. This was something that could be checked in motor vehicle records. Hiss responded weakly; it had been an old car, just deteriorating on the street, of "practically no financial value, so he had let Crosley have it." Or thought he had: "I gave Crosley, to the best of my recollection," he began, whereupon Nixon broke in to say, "Well, now, just a minute on that point, I don't want to interrupt you on that 'to the best of my recollection,' but you certainly can testify 'Yes' or 'No' as to whether you gave Crosley a car. How many cars have you given away in your life, Mr. Hiss?" The laughter was unfriendly, and when Hiss clung to the periphrasis, insisting that it was only his "best recollection" that he had given Crosley the car, "as I was able to give him the use of my apartment," the laughter gave way to a heavy silence. Every member of the committee had the same thought: you do not turn your home and your automobile over to someone known to you only as a deadbeat. The three names Hiss had given them were useless. One man had died, a second couldn't be found, and the third had no memory of anyone named Crosley.

Two nights later Chambers appeared on *Meet the Press,* then a radio program, to accept Hiss's challenge. Hiss "was a Communist and may be one now," he said. The country waited for Hiss to take him to court. And waited. And waited. Finally, on September 27, Hiss sued for defamation in Baltimore. Before anything else could happen the national election intervened. This would have been a good time for Hiss to quit, and as things turned out, it was his last chance to do so. The Republicans were stunned by Truman's victory. They had lost control of the House of Representatives and with it control of the House Committee on Un-American Activities. In addition, two Republicans on the committee had been defeated for reelection. But events were about to move far beyond the scope of congressmen. On Wednesday, November 17, Chambers was scheduled to appear at a pretrial hearing in Baltimore as a defendant. Then he would have to show Hiss's lawyers his proof, if he had any, of an earlier association with the plaintiff. Thus cornered, he proceeded to establish beyond any reasonable doubt a fact that stunned the country: ten years earlier Alger Hiss, his wife Priscilla, and Whittaker Chambers had been members of a Soviet espionage apparatus passing state secrets to the Russians.

Between May or June of 1937 and April 1938, when Chambers broke with the party, Alger Hiss had given him every classified document, cable, report, and dispatch he could lay his hands on. They had been transmitted in three forms. Some had been originals which Chambers had microfilmed and then returned to Hiss. Hiss had summarized others in his own handwriting. Priscilla Hiss had copied the rest at home on her Woodstock typewriter; her husband had then slipped them back into State Department files. He hadn't been the only one doing this. Henry Julian Wadleigh, director of State's trade agreements section and another descendant of fine old American stock, had been another Chambers source. Wadleigh now admitted it. The statute of limitations protected him. But Hiss had denied it. He had gone too far. He had perjured himself, and now he was trapped.

Before dropping out of sight in 1938 Chambers had put three strips of microfilm and 84 papers—43 documents copied on Priscilla's typewriter and 41 memoranda in Alger's hand—in a large brown paper envelope. He had taken the envelope to Nathan Levine, a Brooklyn attorney and his wife's nephew, and had asked him to put it in a safe place. Now, ten years later, on November 14, 1948, he came to Levine and asked him for it. Covered with grime, it lay in a dumbwaiter shaft; Levine had to stand on his bathtub to fetch it. Chambers dusted it off in the kitchen and took the typewritten copies and longhand memoranda to the pretrial hearing in Baltimore. Their appearance there must have been shattering for Hiss, but he kept his head; he directed his attorneys to put the documents before the Justice Department at once. It was a clever move. If the Truman administration announced that the material was secret, Chambers just might be prevented from talking about it. There was another danger for Chambers: by producing the documents he had revealed himself to be the receiver of classified material. Nixon was at his wits' end, afraid the wrong man might be arrested. But Hiss wasn't the only clever one. Chambers hadn't brought everything to the pretrial hearing. He had hidden the microfilm in a hollowed-out pumpkin on his Maryland farm. On the night of December 2, when House investigators asked him if he had anything else, he led them there. The House Committee on Un-American Activities ordered that a twenty-four-hour watch be mounted over the pumpkin's contents, and two days later the newspapers had the story.

Democrats howled. The "pumpkin papers" seemed to be the last absurd act in the Chambers melodrama. The nature of the papers which had been released to the press made the twenty-four-hour watch seem ridiculous. As A. J. Liebling wrote in the *New Yorker*, they constituted "a mixed bag of trivia." None of it had been of much significance in 1938, let alone 1948. One paper had reported that the Japanese were trying to buy manganese from a Costa Rican island which had no manganese. Another solemnly noted that Hitler and Mussolini were exchanging staff officers. A third had been written at a time when the whole world knew the Nazi seizure of Austria was imminent. It recorded an opinion of the American consul general in Vienna: "it seems possible Hitler is seeking a foreign political triumph at the expense of Austria."

That was good for a chuckle, but it was the last laugh liberal Democrats were going to have from this business. As other papers were declassified it became evident that some of them had been enormously helpful in Moscow, and others were being withheld from newspapermen because the State Department had ruled that they were too secret, even in 1948, to be published without risking the national security. Moreover, the content of the documents was really beside the point. Had they been confined to weather reports or traffic accidents, their appearance in the hands of a former Communist courier would still have been shocking, and an occasion for a broad federal inquiry, because all of them had been transmitted in Code D, the department's most secret cipher. That meant the code had been broken and American diplomacy compromised on a very high level; agents of another government had been able to eavesdrop at will, picking up information on exchanges with foreign secretaries of friendly powers, names of confidential informers, troop transfers, presidential directives—the lot. And indeed, when former Undersecretary of State Sumner Welles examined enlargements of the pumpkin papers he declared that their acquisition by another government in 1938, and especially the loss of Code D, had been "most perilous to the interests of the United States."

Now the administration had no choice. In his press conferences

President Truman continued to maintain that talk of spies had been nothing more than a campaign red herring, but already his Justice Department was moving to preempt ground hitherto held by the House Committee on Un-American Activities. In New York the government recalled a grand jury and showed it some of the enlargements. Subpoenas were issued for Hiss, Chambers, and Mrs. Hiss. On December 15 Hiss was indicted on two counts of perjury. His first trial began on May 31, 1949, and ended on July 8 with the jury hung, eight for conviction and four not. There was a great deal of unpleasantness about the judge. He had been solicitous of the Hiss cause throughout, overruling the prosecution, sustaining the defense, and excluding witnesses who, had they been permitted to testify, would have clarified several points that baffled the jury. Those who had expected a guilty verdict were chagrined.

It was at this point that Richard Nixon first came to the attention of the country's liberal constituency and offended it deeply. Democrats had followed the trial numbly, hoping that the mountain of circumstantial evidence would somehow be explained away. The deadlock disappointed them, too. It was a blow to learn that eight jurors had believed Chambers, and they were in no mood to be jarred by a contentious young Republican congressman. He did go far. It was doubtless true that "the Truman administration," as he charged, was "extremely anxious that nothing bad happen to Mr. Hiss," and even fair to add that the court's "prejudice against the prosecution" had been "obvious and apparent." But it was unwise to demand an investigation of the judge, and unwiser still to raise the hackles of those who believed in simple justice by saying that "the average American wants all technicalities waived in this case." A trial without technicalities is a lynching bee. A. J. Liebling, stuck with Hiss and not much liking it, observed that apparently "it is un-American not to convict anybody Congressman Nixon doesn't like," and, in another thrust, that Nixon was "in the plight of a young bank teller who has bet his life savings on a horse that looks like faltering."

Chambers wasn't faltering. He was surer of himself when the second trial opened November 17 under an impartial judge and with a new attorney, less histrionic than the first, representing Hiss. Another consideration was working against the defense. Great political trials must be seen in the context of their times, and throughout 1949 and January 1950, when the second trial ended, the temperature of the cold war was dropping steadily. During every day of both trials Chiang Kai-shek was giving ground to the Chinese Communists until, on the day the second verdict came in, he had lost all of it. In eastern Europe the Red Army was suppressing one democratic government after another. NATO was coalescing to protect western Europe from it. Between the two trials Russia exploded its first atomic bomb. At home the attorney general's list of subversive organizations grew by the month. Accusations of spying were losing their novelty, and with it their incredibility. The FBI had arrested Judith Coplon on charges of espionage. The Smith Act defendants were being tried in the same building as Hiss; during quiet moments in his trial you could hear Communists demonstrating outside in Foley Square. In August 1948, when Chambers and Hiss had faced one another for the first time in a decade in that Commodore Hotel room, it had been possible to argue that Henry Wallace might be right. Seventeen months later, when Hiss's second jury retired to deliberate, opinion against Russia and its American admirers had hardened. The jurors found Hiss guilty on both counts.

That does not mean that Alger Hiss was a victim of world politics, except in the sense that it was world politics which had got him in trouble in the first place. Reading through transcripts of the two trials, one can only wonder that four people had voted to acquit him at the end of the first one, despite the biased judge. The documents alone should have been enough to condemn him. He admitted that the handwriting in the memoranda was his. He said that it had been his practice to summarize long documents for his chief, Francis B. Sayre. Sayre denied it, his secretary denied it; nobody in the State Department had heard of such a custom. In the trials Hiss was asked how Chambers had acquired these digests. He didn't know; he supposed someone had gone through his wastebaskets in the 1930s and saved them. Then, the relentless prosecutor asked, why had they been folded and not crumpled? Hiss agreed that it was a mystery.

U.S.A. v. Alger Hiss was a puzzle fashioned with such pieces: the Woodstock typewriter, the prothonotary warbler, the Hitchcock chairs stenciled in gilt, the Volta Place walls papered with a mulberry pattern, "Hilly" and "Pross," the handwritten notes—and the $400 "loan." The loan was in some ways the most convincing fragment of all. In the autumn of 1937 Chambers had needed a new automobile. After his trade-in he was short $400. He went to the Hisses and they gave it to him.

Here the records were very precise. On November 17, 1937, Mrs. Hiss had withdrawn $400 from their savings account. Four days later Chambers bought his auto. The bankbook and the car dealer's bill of sale were submitted as evidence. Mrs. Hiss testified that she had taken the money out to furnish their new home. She had no receipts, and the withdrawal had just about wiped out their savings. It left them a balance of $14.69—so little that Hiss had to borrow $300 from the bank to meet the monthly installments on his own car. In the depressed 1930s families didn't make such a sacrifice for a slight acquaintance who was known to be a poor credit risk. As for Mrs. Hiss's story, the prosecutor asked the jury, "Is that the way you do it when you have a checking account and a charge account, and you're not moved in? Do you take the $400 out in one lump? Do you go out and buy items for the house to be delivered later and pay for them in cash?" Two lady jurors smiled. Of course they didn't. Neither had Priscilla Hiss.

On that blustery Saturday in January 1950 when the jury reached its verdict, Congressman Nixon was flooded with congratulatory messages, including one from Herbert Hoover: "The conviction of Alger Hiss was due to your patience and persistence alone. At last the stream of treason that existed in our government has been exposed in a fashion that all may believe." Hoover had rarely displayed warmth, but the elation in those lines is unmistakable. It is easy to imagine his feelings that weekend. He had taken the measure of that New Deal crowd from the very beginning and now at last, at last, the country could see how right he had been.

At the other end of the emotional spectrum stood Dean Acheson. The Secretary of State had known Hiss since the younger man's graduation from Harvard Law School. In his United Nations liaison work Hiss had worked under Acheson's supervision, and when Acheson had resigned as Undersecretary of State in 1947, briefly to resume his private practice, his closest associates had presented him with a thermos carafe for ice water on a silver tray. Their names, inscribed around it, included Chip Bohlen, Loy Henderson, Dean Rusk, and Alger Hiss. On the Wednesday after the conviction, the same day that Hiss was sentenced to five years in the Lewisburg Federal Penitentiary, Acheson held a press conference. Homer

Bigart of the *New York Herald Tribune* asked the inevitable question: "Mr. Secretary, do you have any comment on the Alger Hiss case?" The response is remembered where other aspects of the trials have faded: "I should like to make it clear to you that whatever the outcome of any appeal which Mr. Hiss or his lawyers may take in this case, I do not intend to turn my back on Alger Hiss." Everyone must act according to his principles, he explained, and there could be no doubt about his: "I think they were stated for us a very long time ago. They were stated on the Mount of Olives, and if you are interested in seeing them you will find them in the 25th Chapter of the Gospel according to St. Matthew beginning with verse 34."*

That night Acheson wrote his daughter Mary:†

> . . . today I had my press conference. Alger's case has been on my mind incessantly. As I have written you, here is stark tragedy—whatever the reasonable probable facts are. I knew I would be asked about it and the answer was a hard one—not in the ordinary sense of do I run or do I stand. That presented no problem. But to say what one really meant—forgetting the yelping pack at one's heels—saying no more and no less than one truly believed. This was not easy.

The pack at his heels included Nixon, who told reporters he thought the secretary's comment "disgusting," and Congressman Walter Judd of Minnesota, who said Truman ought to turn his back on Acheson. The Hill was not interested in the Mount of Olives that month. It wanted scalps. Here it was less than five years after the war and the world had begun to disintegrate. China was gone, Stalin had the bomb, the State Department had been harboring spies—and there was worse to come. Six days after Acheson's press conference the President announced that work had begun on the deadly hydrogen bomb. Albert Einstein chilled the country by appearing on television to warn that "radioactive poisoning of the atmosphere and, hence, annihilation of any life on earth has been brought within the range of possibilities. . . . General annihilation beckons," and four days after *that* Scotland Yard arrested Fuchs

---

* "Naked, and ye clothed me: I was sick, and ye visited me: I was in prison, and ye came unto me. . . . Inasmuch as ye have done it unto one of the least of these my brethren, ye have done it unto me."

† Wife of William P. Bundy, who in the 1960s became one of the chief architects of the government's Vietnam policies.

for betraying America's atom bomb to the Russians. "How much more are we going to take?" Homer Capehart cried in the Senate. "Fuchs and Acheson and Hiss and hydrogen bombs threatening outside and New Dealism eating away the vitals of the nation. In the name of heaven, is this the best America can do?"

On January 7 the junior senator from Wisconsin dined at Washington's Colony Restaurant on Connecticut Avenue, halfway between the White House and Dupont Circle, with a Catholic priest, a professor of political science, and a Washington lawyer. He was, he told them, in desperate need of advice.

The past year had brought nothing but bad news to Joseph R. McCarthy. He had angered prestigious senators in both parties, and he had problems at home. Among other things, Wisconsin's State Board of Bar Commissioners had nearly disbarred him in 1949 over a breach of ethics: he had run for the Senate while holding judicial office. The commissioners had let McCarthy off with a warning. As he himself paraphrased the ruling, "It was illegal—Joe was naughty—but we don't think he'll do it again."

They didn't know their man. In a crisis he would do anything, and he had reached such a turning point now. In Washington he had attracted public attention chiefly by his defense of some Nazi war criminals. A poll of Washington correspondents had chosen him America's worst senator. In two years, he reminded his dinner guests at the Colony, he would be up for reelection.

He needed a campaign issue. Did they have any ideas?

Portrait of an American

EDWARD ROSCOE MURROW

SOMETIMES, when the wind is right and the London night plays tricks with the memory, one can almost hear the flak, the Luftwaffe armada droning overhead, and the din below. With a little imagination you can see the searchlights springing up. It is then, in fancy, that you can picture the lone figure of a gallant young American defying annihilation to tell his countrymen, through the static and the sputter of shortwave, what he felt they must know:

This—is London. . . .
I'm standing on a rooftop looking out over London. . . . I think probably in a minute we shall have the sound of guns in the immediate vicinity. The lights are swinging over in this general direction now. You'll hear two explosions. There they are! . . . I should think in a few minutes there may be a bit of shrapnel around here. Coming in, moving a little closer all the while.
The plane's still very high. Earlier this evening we could hear occasional—again, those were explosions overhead. Earlier this evening we heard a number of bombs go sliding and slithering across, to fall several blocks away. Just overhead now the burst of the antiaircraft fire. Still the nearby guns are not working. The searchlights now are feeling almost directly overhead. Now you'll hear two bursts a little nearer in a moment. There they are! That hard stony sound.

He was on top of the BBC building, a major German target, a place so dangerous that Winston Churchill's personal intervention was required before broadcasts from it could be permitted. Night after night Murrow went up there and elsewhere to describe the havoc around St. Paul's, the Abbey, Trafalgar Square. Buildings collapsed around him, his CBS office was destroyed three times, yet his measured, authoritative tones continued to bring the war ever closer to American homes. His effectiveness owed much to understatement. There were never any heroics in his newscasts. At the end he would simply sign off with the current London phrase: "So long—and good luck."

Though few realized it—particularly during his later duel with Joe McCarthy—Murrow was essentially a conservative. He believed in patriotism, personal honor, and the values of western civilization. At Washington State College, where he worked his way through in the traditional manner of ambitious poor boys, he was the cadet colonel of the ROTC unit. He had chosen Washington State because it offered the country's first collegiate course in radio broadcasting; in his steady, level-headed way he already knew what he wanted to be. He liked to describe himself as an accurate, objective old-time newsman ("I try to be a reporter; a commentator is a kind of oracle, and I am never so sure I'm right"), but in practice he was closer to an old-time missionary. In a revealing letter to his parents from London he wrote: "I remember you once wanted me to be a preacher, but I had no faith, except in myself. But now I am preaching from a powerful pulpit. Often I am wrong but I am trying to talk as I would have talked were I a preacher. One need not wear a reversed collar to be honest."

He had joined CBS in 1935 after five years with student and educational organizations, and in 1937, at the age of twenty-nine, he sailed for England to take over the CBS European bureau. It wasn't much of a job then. Most of his work was boring: scheduling speeches, concerts, cultural broadcasts. He was traveling to Poland in 1938 to set up a CBS School of the Air program when Hitler entered Austria. Chartering a plane, he reached Vienna in time to describe the arrival of the Nazi troops. Then he hired William L. Shirer, built a staff, and went on to cover Munich, the fall of Czechoslovakia, the London blitz, and the major European battles of World War II.

In 1945 CBS made him a vice president, but he quit after two years; he didn't understand budgets and couldn't bring himself to fire anybody. He returned to the air with a nightly 7:45 newscast which opened with the letters N-E-W-S in Morse code. London having made him, he retained the well-remembered phrases of those years in altered form, beginning each broadcast with "This—is the news," and signing off, "Goodnight—and good luck." In 1948 he and Fred W. Friendly produced their first *I Can Hear It Now* album, preserving voices which had made history in their time, and soon Murrow's annual year-end news roundups with CBS correspondents became as much a part of the Christmas holidays as Lionel Barrymore playing Scrooge.

He was reluctant to leave radio for television, but the switch was inevitable; he had become the country's most celebrated newscaster, and as *Cue* noted, he was "handsome enough to play a movie war correspondent." Millions who had never seen him had read of his "Doomsday look," or read Ernie Pyle's description of Murrow at his mike during the war: gesticulating, nodding, perspiring, glancing at the clock—and fumbling, always, for another cigarette. Beginning in 1951, with the debut of *See It Now* on CBS-TV, Americans could see Murrow at work on their living room screens. Because he was now at the height of his powers and insisted on complete independence from the network, they also saw some of the greatest broadcasts in the history of mass communications.

On December 28, 1952, Murrow took his cameras into the Korean front line to show the country what Christmas was like in foxholes. Nothing was too difficult, or too controversial, for *See It Now* and a companion program, *CBS Reports*. He interviewed Truman on MacArthur, MacArthur on Truman, and Khrushchev in the Kremlin. He investigated the cases of Harry Dexter White, Annie Lee Moss, J. Robert Oppenheimer, Irving Peress, and Lieutenant Milo Radulovich. *See It Now* was the first television program to discuss the relationship between cigarettes and lung cancer—a subject which Murrow, more than any other commentator, would have preferred not to think about. Most memorably, on the evening of March 9, 1954, *See It Now* tackled Senator McCarthy when he was his most powerful and exposed him as a fraud.

He said at the end: "This is no time for men who oppose Senator McCarthy's methods to keep silent. We can deny our heritage and our history, but we cannot escape responsibility for the result. There is no way for a citizen of a republic to abdicate his responsibilities."

It would be difficult to exaggerate the courage Murrow displayed on this program, or the malice it aroused. Merely by saying at the end of it, "I want to associate myself with every word just spoken by Ed Murrow," Don Hollenbeck, the network's regular 11 P.M. newscaster, touched off a Hearst crusade against himself which ended in his suicide. CBS—which was administering loyalty oaths to its own employees and hiring ex-FBI agents to investigate them—was appalled. (Murrow, now a director of the network, described the reaction of his colleagues at their next meeting as, "Good show. Sorry you did it.") McCarthy himself said scornfully that he hadn't seen it: "I never listen to the extreme left-wing, bleeding heart elements of radio and TV." He wouldn't deign to reply on the air, so CBS gave the time to Vice President Nixon, who spent it begging McCarthy to follow the Republican party line.

If Murrow's zeal as a cold-warrior was not fully appreciated then, it was only because it was shared by virtually everyone in the country, in public life and out. Like his countrymen he was an ardent advocate of NATO, the Truman Doctrine in Greece and Turkey, more spending on U.S. armaments, a stronger U.S. military presence in Europe, and the right of a President to send American troops abroad without congressional approval. He backed the Korean War

—"We have drawn a line," he said approvingly, "not across the peninsula but across the world"—and he predicted that "some form of intervention" in Vietnam "may prove inescapable."

But he also shared the liberal vision of Wilsonian self-determination. After Pearl Harbor he had said that the State Department had "misjudged the nature of this war. It is a worldwide revolution, as well as a war." That in itself was enough to recommend him to John Kennedy when the new President was looking for a United States Information Agency (USIA) director in 1960.

Murrow accepted, partly because he reciprocated Kennedy's admiration but also because he was discouraged by what was happening to mass communications in the United States. With situation comedies, quiz shows, and mindless Westerns, television was grossing a billion dollars a year. Murrow spoke out bitterly against TV's "decadence, escapism, and insulation from the realities of the world in which we live," but the titans of the industry weren't listening. Already CBS had killed *See It Now* as a weekly program and replaced it with occasional specials. Admen called the new broadcasts *See It Now and Then*.

His last years were sad. Uncomfortable as a bureaucrat, he saw USIA's reputation for integrity fall, a casualty of the Johnson administration's decision to use the agency for the dissemination of propaganda about the Vietnam War. One of the grimmest of his Doomsday predictions was coming true; demonstrations were being staged for TV, and cameramen, by their very presence, were encouraging urban rioting. The networks were becoming increasingly shameless in their pursuit of the advertising dollar. "Station breaks" were lengthened from 32 to 42 seconds, to cram in more commercials. *CBS Reports*, the last of Murrow's great news programs, was replaced by a show about a talking horse. On the day he died in the spring of 1965, CBS announced his death—and followed the bulletin with a cigarette commercial.

His ashes were scattered over his farm in Pawling, New York. But that wasn't the end of Ed Murrow. Buried six feet below the farm's soil lay a new television cable. As long as it lies there, as long as the social function of communications retains its great potential, the spirit of the man will live.

That—was Murrow.

Seventeen

INTO THE ABYSS

ILL HEALTH had forced Mary Acheson Bundy to leave her small son with her parents and enter a sanatorium in Saranac, New York. There, in that month of the Hiss verdict, she received a letter from her father noting that soon:

> . . . in a public speech I shall do my best to carry some sense of the problem in the Far East, the limitation of our power, the direction of our purpose. So much that is foolish, disloyal, and generally contemptible has been going on that it is good that we are—as I hope—free to go ahead on a clear and sensible course.

It was, in Acheson's words, "a supercharged moment to be speaking on Asian matters." The Chiang Kai-shek tragedy was now complete. He had been the generalissimo of a vast and superbly equipped army on V-J Day, and he had staggered from one setback to another until his forces melted away and he himself was a refugee on an island off the Chinese coast. Chiang's ineptness had been evident to nearly everyone who had been watching the disintegration of his strength. Even Colonel Robert R. McCormick of the *Chicago Tribune* had told the Associated Press, "The Chiang Kai-shek government cannot put down an insurrection which is falsely called a Communist insurrection." The colonel would soon change his mind, recognizing in the loss of China the most effective political issue since Roosevelt had wrested control of the White House from Hoover.

As Acheson posted the letter to his daughter, the Red Chinese regime was in its fourth month. Mao Tse-tung was in Moscow negotiating a Sino-Soviet friendship treaty with Joseph Stalin. Having just exploded his first atomic bomb, the Russian dictator had become a very useful friend to have. The American people knew that, and they were in no mood for gradations in guilt. Republicans on the attack encouraged the confusion in which Chiang, Fuchs, Hiss, Mao, the Rosenbergs, Yalta, and Acheson were all being wrapped up in one scarlet bundle. Senator Taft was being widely quoted as charging in the Senate that the State Department had "been guided by a left-wing group who obviously have wanted to get rid of Chiang and were willing at least to turn China over to the Communists for that purpose."

That was politics. Military strategy was something else. In 1947 the Joint Chiefs of Staff had unanimously agreed that South Korea was not worth fighting for, and on March 1, 1949, General MacArthur had told a *New York Times* correspondent in Tokyo:

> Our defense dispositions against Asiatic aggression used to be based on the west coast of the American continent. The Pacific was looked upon as the avenue of possible enemy approach. Now the Pacific has become an Anglo-Saxon lake, and our line of defense runs through the chain of islands fringing the coast of Asia. It starts from the Philippines and continues through the Ryukyu Archipelago, which starts in its main bastion, Okinawa. Then it bends back through Japan and the Aleutian Island chain to Alaska.*

A glance at that bend on a map shows that strategically, at least, MacArthur felt that he could live with hostile forces controlling Formosa or the Korean peninsula. But the general was a better politician than the Secretary of State. By the end of 1949 he was beginning to realize that American public opinion, shocked by the red star rising over mainland China, would interpret any further expansion by Communist arms as a stinging U.S. defeat. Acheson, for his part, remained resigned to a Maoist Taiwan. On December 18, 1949, he advised U.S. Asian missions that the importance of Formosa should be minimized since "its fall is widely anticipated." Two weeks later MacArthur leaked his copy of that memorandum to the press. In the general uproar Taft and Herbert Hoover demanded a naval defense of Formosa, but Truman vetoed it, and it was against this background that Acheson delivered the

---

* The general said substantially the same thing to G. Ward Price, the British journalist, that same month and to William R. Mathews of the *Arizona Daily Star* later in the year.

speech, first mentioned in the letter to his daughter, before the National Press Club on January 12, 1950.

Clearly it was no time for a Secretary of State to speak extemporaneously. His staff had therefore given him a thick folder of marked-up drafts. "But in the end," he writes in his memoirs, without further explanation, "I put the drafts aside and made the speech from a page or two of notes." For his audience he retraced the same defensive perimeter MacArthur had drawn ten months earlier, before the fall of China had altered the political picture in Washington: from the Aleutians to Japan, to the Ryukyus, to the Philippines. "So far as the military security of other areas in the Pacific is concerned," he added—and here he obviously had Formosa and South Korea in mind—"it must be clear that no person can guarantee these areas against military attack. Should such an attack occur," he declared, "the initial resistance" must come from "the people attacked." If they proved to be resolute fighters, he vaguely concluded, they were entitled to an appeal under the charter of the United Nations.

To the end of his life Acheson would bitterly deny that he had given the green light for aggression in South Korea by excluding it from the defensive perimeter. But when he told the Press Club that the United States was waiting "for the dust to settle" in China and added that America's line of resistance ran "along the Aleutians to Japan and then goes to the Ryukyus," the Communists could only conclude, as they did, that the United States was leaving people northwest of the Korea Strait to fend for themselves.

It was not like Acheson to misinterpret American policy, and in fact he had not done so. Like MacArthur the previous March, he had ruled out U.S. participation in an Asian land war. American intentions change, however. Hitler had failed to appreciate that, and as a consequence he had been destroyed. Now Stalin was repeating the error. The Soviet leader was dictating North Korean war plans (at this point Mao wasn't even advised of them) and he took Acheson at his word. The day after the secretary's Press Club speech Jacob Malik, the Russian representative at the United Nations, walked out on the Security Council because it had refused to reject the Chinese Nationalists and welcome emissaries from the new mainland regime. Stalin was putting the Americans on notice. From his point of view, the timing was perfect. The United States was drafting a Japanese peace treaty without consulting Moscow.

Since V-J Day the Russians had been hoping that Washington would give them a free hand in Korea. In George Kennan's opinion, "When they saw it wasn't going to work out that way, they concluded: 'If this is all we are going to get out of a Japanese settlement, we had better get our hands on Korea fast before the Americans let the Japanese back in there.'"

Meanwhile Truman's global strategy had begun to pivot. In April the President, presiding over a meeting of the National Security Council, abandoned defense perimeters and moved toward a new strategy under which the country could meet any threat to non-Communist governments. It was at that session that the council adopted NSC 68, the paper which, among other things, determined that 20 percent of the country's future income would be set aside for military use. Wise or not, the decision should never have been kept secret. Stalin, unaware of it, assumed that South Korea was as ripe for plucking as Czechoslovakia had been in 1938. Later, congressional critics taxed Acheson for calling poor signals, though they were in no position to throw stones. A week after the secretary's Press Club speech the economy-minded lower house defeated 193 to 192 a small appropriation which would have provided five hundred U.S. Army officers to supervise the equipping of South Korean troops. That night Acheson wrote Mary:

> This has been a tough day, not so much by way of work, but by way of troubles. We took a defeat in the House on Korea, which seems to me to have been our own fault. One should not lose by one vote. We were complaisant and inactive. We have now a long road back.

The first intersection on that road lay dead ahead.

In January 1950 Joseph R. McCarthy was forty-one years old, and in more ways than one he was a man on the skids. Elected four years earlier in the Republican sweep of 1946, he was in a fair way to becoming a disgrace to the United States Senate—a cheap politician who had sunk to taking $10,000 from the Lustron Corporation, a manufacturer of prefabricated housing, and an unsecured $20,000 from the Washington lobbyist for Pepsi-Cola. He had spent it recklessly in speculation in soybean futures and long phone conversations with bookies. A few men on the Hill knew that McCarthy's battered tan briefcase always carried a bottle of whiskey. He was in fact a borderline alcoholic, boastful among friends of his ability to "belt a fifth" every day. But at the rate he was going, he had six, maybe seven years left.

He was a rogue, and he looked the part. His eyes were shifty. When he laughed, he snickered. His voice was a high-pitched taunt. On the Senate floor he could be quickly identified by his heavy beard. He was in fact a prime specimen of what has been called the Black Irish: the thickset, bull-shouldered, beetle-browed type found on Boston's Pier Eight and in the tenements of South Chicago. He lacked the genius of Huey Long and the faith in himself. What he had going for him was a phenomenal ability to lie and an intuitive grasp of the American communications industry. That and ruthlessness. If he had a creed it was nihilism, a belief in nothing, or next to nothing. He enjoyed reading his name in the newspapers, and he wanted to remain a senator.

Sometime after the Colony dinner, which had not been particularly helpful to him, McCarthy telephoned the Republican National Committee to say that he would be available on the Lincoln's birthday weekend, five weeks hence, for speeches about Communists in the government. If the committee staff was elated, they concealed it. Certainly they weren't surprised. This, after all, was the party line. Richard Nixon, the anti-Communist hero of the hour, was warning that the Hiss case was just "a small part of the shocking story of Communist espionage in the United States." Nixon was much in demand, but to the best of the Republican National Committee's knowledge, McCarthy knew nothing about Communism. The only Lincoln Day booking the staff could find for him was a spot before the Ohio County Women's Club in Wheeling, West Virginia, followed by dates in Salt Lake City and Reno. En route to Wheeling, the dutiful airline hostess, observing a U.S. Senator on her passenger list, said, "Good afternoon, Senator McCarthy." He looked startled. "Why, good afternoon," he said. "I'm glad somebody recognizes me."

Before enplaning he had done a little—a very little—homework. It would be too much to call it research. For the most part his "rough draft," as he later described it to reporters, was a scissors-and-paste job made up of passages from other Republican addresses, only slightly altered. According to the *Wheeling Intel-*

ligencer, he had hacked out a paragraph from a speech Nixon had delivered in the House of Representatives on January 26:

NIXON IN CONGRESS	MCCARTHY IN WHEELING
The great lesson which should be learned from the Hiss case is that we are not just dealing with espionage agents who get 30 pieces of silver to obtain the blueprint of a new weapon . . . but this is a far more sinister type of activity, because it permits the enemy to guide and shape our policy.	One thing to remember in discussing the Communists is that we are not dealing with spies who get 30 pieces of silver to steal the blueprint of a new weapon. We are dealing with a far more sinister type of activity because it permits the enemy to guide and shape our policy.

So far as is known, his own investigation of subversion was limited to a single telephone call. He phoned Willard Edwards of the *Chicago Tribune* Washington staff and told him he needed help for his speech. From Edwards he learned of two inquiries, both brief and largely forgotten, into the loyalty of State Department workers. The first could be found in files of the *Congressional Record.* On July 26, 1946, James F. Byrnes, then Secretary of State, had written Congressman Adolph J. Sabath of Illinois explaining that during a preliminary screening of some 3,000 employees who had been transferred to the State Department from wartime agencies, the screeners had recommended against the permanent employment of 284. Of these, 79 had been discharged. By subtracting 79 from 284, McCarthy acquired the magical figure of 205—205 people whose dismissal had been suggested but who had still been on the rolls at the time of Byrnes's letter.* The senator's other source was known to anti-Communist vigilantes as "the Lee list." Robert E. Lee was the investigator for a House appropriations subcommittee who had been permitted to examine 108 State Department personnel files in connection with the *Amerasia* case. In 1948 the department had sent the committee a statistical summary reporting that of the 108, those still in departmental employ numbered 57—the "Heinz Varieties figure," as Richard H. Rovere would soon call it in the *New Yorker.*

* The implication is that by the time of McCarthy's Wheeling speech the figure may have become out of date. It was. In the August 1950 *Harper's* Alfred Friendly reported that as of February 1950 just 65 of the 205 were still in the State Department's employ. Of course Friendly had made more than one phone call. That kind of digging was beyond McCarthy's comprehension.

Thus Senator McCarthy had two numbers, 205 and 57. But that was *all* he had. To grasp the dimensions of his fraud, one must remember that at this point he had no dossiers, no raw data, and no specifications, however vague. He knew of the two outdated lists, but he had neither. If pressed, he was incapable of producing a single name, and was embarking on a speaking tour which would take him to West Virginia, to Utah after a change of planes in Colorado, and then to Reno, Nevada. On the other hand, it is highly unlikely that he anticipated a challenge. He expected to deliver a few time-honored homilies before small audiences of Republican women and return to find that Wisconsin papers had carried accounts of his trip, reminding Republican functionaries and contributors back home of his existence. Of course, he would make two or three wild charges, but they would be no wilder than those of other GOP speakers that weekend. Later he realized that he had stumbled upon a brilliant demagogic technique. Others deplored treachery. McCarthy would speak of *traitors*.

Wheeling's radio station WWVA recorded his remarks there and put them on the air that night. Unfortunately for history, the tape was erased immediately after the broadcast. All that survives, beyond the recollections of others present, are the notes of a *Wheeling Intelligencer* reporter named Frank Desmond. According to Desmond, the famous passage was:

> While I cannot take the time to name all the men in the State Department who have been named as members of the Communist Party and members of a spy ring, I have here in my hand a list of 205 that were known to the Secretary of State as being members of the Communist Party and are still working and shaping the policy of the State Department.

He may have been holding a laundry list, a shopping list, or an old Christmas card list. Whatever it was, it cannot have been important, because afterward he threw it away. Back in Washington the following week, with half the capital demanding that he prove his charges, he would try desperately—without success—to find out exactly what he had said. He even tried appealing to ham radio operators in the area who might have made a recording of the speech. He found none.

Desmond's story appeared in the *Intelligencer* and was reprinted inside the *Chicago Tribune* and on the front page of the *Denver Post*. Three days were to pass before the *New York Times* published the senator's charges. The Associated Press put two paragraphs of Desmond's account on its B wire, however, and someone in the State Department read them, for when the senator changed planes in Denver a newspaperman told him the department wanted the names of those accused so that investigations could begin at once. McCarthy said he had been misquoted; he had spoken not of 205 Communists but of 205 "bad security risks." The reporter asked if he might see the list. Of course, said the senator. Then he said he had left it in his baggage on the plane. The *Denver Post* has preserved a photograph showing McCarthy peering forlornly into his battered briefcase, searching for the fugitive list.

Late in the afternoon of February 20 a three-bell quorum call sounded in the Senate, and Joe McCarthy strode out on the floor carrying the tan briefcase, now bulging. The Democrats had demanded evidence, and twice since his return to the capital he had assured newspapermen that if he couldn't come up with it, he would resign. Now he was going to give the Senate one of the wildest evening sessions in its history. He had more than figures this time, though not much more. Lee had provided him with photostated copies of the 108 two-year-old dossiers prepared from State Department files for the House appropriations subcommittee. Of their subjects, only 40 still worked for the department. All had been subjected to a full field FBI investigation and cleared. Nevertheless, McCarthy stacked 81 obsolete dossiers on his desk and those of nearby senators and grandly announced that he had penetrated "Truman's iron curtain of secrecy."

The next few minutes were awful. Shuffling the first folders, he said that he would identify them by number only. That in itself was suspicious—after all, anything said on the floor was privileged—but what followed was shocking. Spectators realized that McCarthy was looking at these dossiers *for the first time*. He had to pause before each, riffling through papers to see what it contained. Another man would have been embarrassed beyond endurance. Not McCarthy. He stood there almost six hours, carrying the absurd farce forward, shrugging heavily when the files baffled him but never yielding the floor.

Some of his cases had nothing to do with the State Department.

Numbers 1 and 2 were employed by the United Nations. Numbers 21 through 26 worked for the Voice of America. Number 12 had once been employed by the Department of Commerce; McCarthy blandly conceded that he had no idea "where he is today. I frankly do not know." Number 62 was "not important insofar as Communistic activities are concerned." Of number 40 he said, "I do not have much information on this except that there is nothing in the files to disprove his Communist connections." Number 72 had the senator stumped. It was significant, he lamely said, "in that it is the direct opposite of the cases I have been reading. . . . I do not confuse this man as being a Communist. This individual was very highly recommended by several witnesses as a high type of man, a democratic American who . . . opposed Communism." (In addition, 72 had never worked for the State Department.) Astounded, Richard Rovere asked, "Could anything but sheer lunacy lead a man discussing 81 Communists to say that one of the Communists was an important example because he was not a Communist?"

But McCarthy plodded on doggedly. Number 9 was the same as number 77. Numbers 15, 27, 37, and 59 did not exist—they were just empty folders. Numbers 13 and 78 had only applied for jobs. Number 14, who was "primarily a morals case," appeared in the dossier of number 41. Number 52 was of note only because he worked for number 16—"who," McCarthy said, with the tone of a man finding gold at last, was "one of the most dangerous espionage agents in the Department."

He wasn't, of course. There wasn't a spy in the lot. But by inserting a phrase in a file here, deleting another there, and embellishing the whole performance with spurious investigative paraphernalia, he created an impression of subversion among those who read their newspapers by studying the comics first, the sports page next, and then glancing carelessly through the headlines. Sometimes McCarthy's alterations of truth in that February 20 performance were small. Three people "with Russian names" became "three Russians." Words like "reportedly" and "allegedly" vanished; "may have been" and "may be" were replaced by "was" and "is"; "considerable derogatory information" was translated into "conclusive evidence of Communist activity." Other changes were startling. Notations of FBI clearance were omitted or turned into FBI findings of guilt. If a "good American" had been turned away by State Department recruiting agents it was because they hired only Communists; the fact that the applicant may have been nearly seventy years old was unmentioned. The Republicans were aghast. Kenneth Wherry, the party's floor leader, did what he could for McCarthy with parliamentary motions, but avoided identification with him. Taft, who hardly knew McCarthy, told reporters afterward, "It was a perfectly reckless performance."

By the following morning the obsolescence of the folders was known and revealed on front pages. Jubilant Senate Democrats caucused and instructed their majority leader, Scott Lucas of Illinois, to call for "a full and complete" inquiry into "whether persons who are disloyal to the United States are or have been employed by the Department of State." Since the other Republicans were keeping their distance from McCarthy, and since he had insisted that he would welcome an investigation, Lucas's Senate Resolution 231 passed unanimously. Wherry did try to refer it to the Appropriations Committee, whose right-wing chairman, Kenneth McKellar of Tennessee, would have seen to it that liberal Democrats were given the least possible aid and comfort. That move failed on a straight party vote, and the matter went to Foreign Relations. There Tom Connally of Texas appointed a tough committee chaired by Millard E. Tydings, the aggressive patrician who had dominated Maryland politics for a quarter-century. Even before the naming of his fellow members (Brien McMahon of Connecticut and Theodore Francis Green of Rhode Island, Democrats; Henry Cabot Lodge of Massachusetts and Bourke B. Hickenlooper of Iowa, Republicans), McCarthy was calling it a kangaroo court. Tydings promised "neither a witch hunt, nor a whitewash." In private, however, he spoke patronizingly of Wisconsin's junior senator as "that boy." He had no way of knowing that this would be the first of five senatorial attempts to investigate McCarthy's charges, none of which would find anyone at the bottom of it all except McCarthy himself.

Of course, he had *some* help. Nobody, not even Joe McCarthy, could build that big a bonfire all alone. No congressional endeavor can get very far without lobbyists of some sort, and the fact that McCarthy had phoned a *Chicago Tribune* correspondent before flying to Wheeling is an indication that he knew where help lay. The role of investigator Lee is another sign. From the moment McCarthy's star began to rise over West Virginia, these men and their allies mounted a massive rescue operation, amassing names and data which would be available to him whenever he needed help. They hadn't chosen him, but he had chosen their issue. No alliance formed to influence legislation lands a U.S. Senator every day; when one does, the last thing it wants is to see him discredited.

This was the pressure group known as the China Lobby. For the most part it consisted of men employed by right-wing newspaper publishers: Willard Edwards and Walter Trohan of Colonel McCormick's *Tribune;* George Waters of the McCormick-owned *Washington Times-Herald;* Fulton Lewis Jr., whose broadcasts were heard over McCormick's Mutual radio network; Lawrence Kerley of William Randolph Hearst's *New York Journal-American;* Hearst reporters Howard Rushmore, Ken Hunter, and Ray Richards; and two Hearst columnists, George Sokolsky and J. B. Matthews. Matthews owned a copy of "Appendix Nine," the vigilante equivalent of anti-Semitism's Protocols of the Elders of Zion. Put together in 1944 by investigators for the House Committee on Un-American Activities, Appendix Nine comprised seven volumes containing 22,000 names gathered indiscriminately from letterheads and programs of organizations whose patriotism had been challenged, from informers, and from ultraconservative pamphlets published in the 1930s. Even the House Committee on Un-American Activities had thought it outrageous. The full membership had called it back and suppressed it, but Matthews had kept a pirated copy. Armed with it, McCarthy could talk endlessly, and anything missing from it could usually be acquired from Alfred Kohlberg, founder of the China Policy Association and chief patron of the China Lobby. For thirty years Kohlberg had profitably imported Oriental textiles from the mainland; with the collapse of Chiang Kai-shek he had been cut off, and now he funneled contributions from his considerable fortune into such publications as *Counter-Attack*, the *Freeman,* and Isaac Don Levine's *Plain Talk.*

These forces had been wandering around Washington looking for a leader. Now they were McCarthy's, and for the most part they served him well. His adversaries were formidable: the Democratic leadership on the Hill, President Truman (who said of him off the record that "the son of a bitch ought to be impeached"), and virtually every journalist to the left of McCormick and Hearst. In that first onrush of McCarthy, Joseph and Stewart Alsop were particularly effective, ridiculing the M.I.5 theatrics in McCarthy's office—how during phone conversations he would strike the mouthpiece with a pencil "to jar the needle of any listening device," and how toward the end of a telephone conversation obviously staged for the benefit of his interviewers, he gripped the receiver and muttered: "Yeah, yeah, I can listen, but I can't talk. Get me? You really got the goods on the guy? Yeah? Well, I tell you. Just mention this sort of casual to Number One, and get his reaction. Okay? Okay, I'll contact you later."

Walter Lippmann reported the impact of the senator's pyrotechnics on the Secretary of State: "No American official who has represented this government abroad in great affairs, not even Wilson in 1918, has ever been so gravely injured at home." Many old liberal publications such as the *Baltimore Sun* were strangely reticent in McCarthy's first year, but the *Washington Post* fought him every inch of the way; so did the *New York Times* and the *St. Louis Post-Dispatch;* and *Time* climbed on his back and stayed there. Probably the greatest stroke on either side of the battle was the work of Herbert Block ("Herblock"), the *Post*'s cartoonist. Block created an eponym by crudely lettering "McCarthyism" on a barrel of mud shakily supported by ten mud-bespattered buckets.

Yet the senator and his gamy henchmen always seemed to be gaining. Lippmann's stately prose was a pale thing beside McCarthy's description of the country's majority party: "The Democratic label is now the property of men and women who have . . . bent to the whispered pleas from the lips of traitors . . . men and women who wear the political label stitched with the idiocy of a Truman, rotted by the deceit of an Acheson, corrupted by the red slime of a [Harry Dexter] White." Even Herblock's contribution was turned around when Fulton Lewis told his listeners, "To many Americans, McCarthyism is Americanism," and the senator, addressing a Wisconsin audience, said, "McCarthyism is Americanism with its sleeves rolled."*

None of his sloganeering and billingsgate would have mattered much had it not been for one painful fact: McCarthy had kindled a fire in America's grass roots. Even as his facade was torn asunder, as his fellow senators took his accusations apart one by one and exposed his lies two by two, till he sat exposed (and grinning) before them, his support grew and stiffened across the land. The evidence was unmistakable. Gallup consistently found that 50 per-

---

* "Communism is twentieth-century Americanism"—Earl Browder, 1936 (see page 116).

cent of the public had a "favorable opinion" of the senator and thought he was helping the country; only 29 percent disapproved of him and 21 percent had no opinion at all. Reporters who accompanied McCarthy on post-Wheeling campaign trips were shocked by the tributes to him, and those on the Hill who discounted their stories were confronted by the most convincing attestation of all: the pyramids of rumpled dollar bills and change which arrived in McCarthy's mail each morning.

McCarthy invested the money in soybean futures while his fellow Republicans began having second and then third thoughts. Wherry began throwing an arm around Joe's husky shoulders. William F. Jenner asked to be photographed with him. Homer Ferguson exchanged subversive lists with him. Owen Brewster and Karl E. Mundt offered the services of their staffs. Hickenlooper, sitting on the Tydings committee, began coming down hard on the side of his embattled colleague from Wisconsin. Over in the House, a District of Columbia subcommittee took testimony on one of McCarthy's most preposterous claims, "links between homosexuality and Communism," notably a Soviet plot to ensnare "women employees of the State Department by enticing them into a life of lesbianism." Finally the last GOP pillar fell. The possibility of unearthing another bona-fide Democratic traitor who would do to the administration's China policy what Hiss had done to the New Deal was too much for Robert A. Taft, and that monument of integrity announced that "the pro-Communist policies of the State Department fully justify Joe McCarthy in his demand for an investigation." He then said to McCarthy, "If one case doesn't work, try another." As though Joe needed to be told.

On March 21 the conjurer's bag of tricks was empty, or so it appeared. Then McCarthy concocted the greatest prank of all. He told the Tydings committee that he was about to name the "top Russian espionage agent" in the United States. The committee assembled for an emergency session. There McCarthy blandly admitted that he had nothing new. "There's nothing mysterious about this one," he said. "This has all been put in the record already, plus some exhibits." And so it had. Owen Lattimore, a professor at Johns Hopkins and specialist in Asian studies—he was at that moment in the interior of Afghanistan—was neither a Communist nor an employee of the State Department. He had advised the government in Far Eastern matters, and the cold realism of his reports on Chiang Kai-shek had aroused the wrath of the China lobbyists, particularly Kohlberg. Everything there was to know about the man was known on the Hill. All the same, McCarthy informed the incredulous Tydings that Lattimore was "definitely an espionage agent," that his file was "explosive." He added: "If you crack this case, it will be the biggest espionage case in the history of this country." The following morning he laid all this before the press, withholding only Lattimore's name. He said, "I am willing to stand or fall on this one. If I am wrong on this, I think the subcommittee would be justified in not taking my other cases too seriously." The man whose name was in his pocket, he said, was that of the superspy who had been "Alger Hiss's boss in the espionage ring in the State Department."

That was on a Tuesday. By the end of the week Lattimore was being mentioned with increasing frequency in the Senate press gallery, and on Sunday, March 26, Drew Pearson broke the story. McCarthy, meantime, was going into one of his disappearing acts, vanishing only to return with an entirely different charge. Summoned from Afghanistan, Lattimore had sent word that he really wasn't the top Russian espionage agent in the United States, and he was flying back to clear up any misunderstandings on that score. But McCarthy had begun to say that he, too, had been misunderstood. "I fear in the case of Lattimore," he said on the Senate floor the following Thursday, "I have perhaps placed too much stress on the question of whether or not he has been an espionage agent." What he had really meant to say was that the professor was "the chief architect of our Far Eastern policy." The man was a "policy risk," McCarthy said, and then he said, "I believe you can ask almost any schoolchild who the architect of our Far Eastern policy is, and he will say, 'Owen Lattimore.'" The press gallery, where men were still trying to get information about the obscure professor, rocked with laughter.

Lattimore testified before the committee under klieg lights on April 6. The crowd in the marble-columned Senate caucus room, the largest since Wendell Willkie's appearance there to endorse lend-lease nine years earlier, heard the witness deny every allegation. He produced personal letters from Chiang Kai-shek and Madame Chiang expressing profound gratitude for his services. Tydings then revealed that four members of the committee had studied his loyalty file and found no evidence of subversion in it. Lattimore received an ovation and departed. Four days later McCarthy produced Louis Budenz, a former managing editor of the *Daily Worker*, who swore that in 1944 his superiors in the party had told him "to consider Owen Lattimore as a Communist."

The right-wing senators crowed. There, they said triumphantly; Joe had proved it; Budenz had been Lattimore's Whittaker Chambers. Two conservative newspapermen were briefly gulled. William S. White reported that Budenz had been "officially informed" that Lattimore was a traitor, and Arthur Krock observed that "many fair-minded persons" were changing their minds about McCarthy. They didn't keep them changed long. Abe Fortas and Paul Porter, Lattimore's lawyers, led Budenz through a devastating cross-examination. Yes, he conceded, in four years of FBI interviews he had told everything he knew about the Communist party. No, he had never mentioned Owen Lattimore. Yes, in 1947 he had advised a State Department security officer that Lattimore was not a Communist. Yes, in early 1949 he had written an article for *Collier's* magazine denying that Lattimore was a Communist. Yes, it was true that Owen Lattimore's name had appeared in none of Budenz's books about American Communists. How did he reconcile all this with his present testimony? He replied weakly that "in another book which I am writing Mr. Lattimore is very prominent." He stepped down and was succeeded by two other ex-Communists, Bella V. Dodd and Freda Utley. Miss Dodd ridiculed the notion that Lattimore was a Communist. Miss Utley was hazier, but she was certain he hadn't been a spy—and when it came to that, even Budenz found the allegation of espionage startling. McCarthy was unrepentant. He set his sights on another old China hand who, he averred, had written "a book which sets forth his pro-Communist answer to the problems of Asia as clearly as Hitler's *Mein Kampf* set forth his solutions for the problems of Europe." Questioned after reporters had left, he admitted that he hadn't read the book. In fact, he didn't even know the title. He promised to look it up. Once more he had been confuted; once more his name was in all the headlines.

Tydings's confidence was ebbing. He was being outfoxed and outbludgeoned, and he was too skillful a politician not to sense it. While he was shaping the report—which would be read only by Americans already aware of McCarthy's infamy—public support for McCarthy continued to grow. Even as Republican Margaret Chase Smith of Maine promulgated her anti-McCarthy "Declaration of

Conscience," signed by her and five other liberal Republican senators, Majority Leader Lucas, counting noses, discovered that just twelve Senate Democrats had spoken out against McCarthy. Tydings had won all the battles of reason and decency, but McCarthy had never tried to be reasonable or decent; he was a political charlatan, and his brand of quackery was sweeping the spring primaries. While the committee which had investigated him debated whether to use this adjective or that adverb, Willis Smith was ousting North Carolina Senator Frank P. Graham with a McCarthyite campaign; Congressman George A. Smathers was defeating Florida's liberal Senator Claude Pepper with a second McCarthyite campaign; and the senatorial candidacy of California's Helen Gahagan Douglas was being smeared by Manchester Boddy in a third McCarthyite primary—with Richard Nixon preparing yet a fourth McCarthyite campaign which would defeat her in the general election.

Thus the report was discredited before it had been written. In the end it ran pretty much as expected, accusing McCarthy of perpetrating "a fraud and a hoax" and engaging in deliberate, willful falsehoods. Knowing what it would be like, McCarthy had already branded it "a disgrace to the Senate" and "a green light to the Red fifth column in the United States." Taft had called the proceedings a "farce," a "whitewash," and an insult to "a fighting Irish Marine." Owen Brewster of Maine echoed him, Wherry assailed Acheson, and Republican National Chairman Guy Gabrielson maintained that the GOP was uncovering "spies, emissaries, agents and members of the Communist party" who "infest the government of the United States."

By summer optimists thought they saw signs that McCarthy had run his course. The wire services were reducing his news conferences to an inch or two of type, and most papers weren't printing that. Events in the struggle with Reds abroad had overwhelmed his sideshow; when he took the floor to brandish an "FBI report" exposing "three Communist agents" in the State Department, J. Edgar Hoover's repudiation of the performance surprised no one. For the moment, at least, McCarthyism seemed to be finished.

It was an illusion. Against all logic, Americans by the tens of millions had come to regard Wisconsin's junior senator as the symbol of anti-Communism, and as long as Communism remained an issue, he would be a hero to them. His arrogance continued to grow. Reminded that he had not replied to the committee's indictment, he said, "I don't answer charges, I make them." A reporter asked, "Wasn't that a classified document you were reading?" The senator snapped, "It *was*. I declassified it." At a cocktail party a girl inquired, "Senator McCarthy, when did you discover Communism?" Leering, he shot back: "Two and a half months ago."

While the government of the United States was engrossed in the question of how many Communists, if any, had worked in the State Department (205? 57? 108? 40? 66? 25? 1? 0?), the government of North Korea was deploying nine superbly equipped divisions to invade the almost defenseless Republic of Korea. Led by 20,000 Korean Communists who had been blooded in the great Russo-German battles of World War II, including Stalingrad, the 120,000-man North Korea Peoples Army (NKPA) was an elite force by any military standard. Supporting its troops were 122-mm howitzers, 76-mm divisional howitzers, 76-mm self-propelled guns, 120-mm mortars, the whole family of Soviet antiaircraft guns, and every imaginable infantry weapon from antitank rifles to burp guns. Sharpening the tip of the assault spear were 150 T-34 Soviet tanks—the steel giants that had shattered Krupp's Tigerpanzers in the Kursk salient—and clouds of Yak and Stormovik fighter planes. In the expert opinion of Colonel Robert D. Heinl Jr., USMC, the NKPA "was, among the Armed Forces of the Far East, probably better trained and equipped for its intended work than any other Army but Russia's."

Against it South Korean President Syngman Rhee could field little more than a constabulary. Ironically, the Pentagon had deliberately weakened Rhee's 65,000-man Army of the Republic of Korea (ROK). Each of the two Koreas had repeatedly announced its intention to invade the other and unite the peninsula in blood, but although the NKPA had regularly crossed the 38th Parallel with patrols—some of them as large as 1,500 men—Washington's main worry was seventy-five-year-old Rhee. To thwart his aggressive instincts, his ROK units were armed with ancient Japanese model 99 Mausers, short-range M-3 105-mm howitzers, obsolete 2.36-inch bazookas, no mortars larger than 81 mm, no recoilless rifles, no tanks, no offensive artillery, and no warplanes. The administration in Washington was the chief culprit in this negligence, but Capitol Hill was an accessory. Truman had earmarked sixty million dollars for South Korea in his 1950–51 budget, and Congress had cut it out.

American hope for South Korean defense was vested in a U.S. Military Advisory Group. It was a frail hope; in Seoul, Rhee's capital, the advisory officers were training ROK troops as MPs. Beyond that, the Americans provided only bombast. As late as June 13, 1950, the administration's William C. Foster testified before a congressional committee that "the rigorous training program [in South Korea] has built up a well-disciplined Army of 100,000 soldiers, one that is prepared to meet any challenge by the North Korean forces and one that has cleaned out the guerrilla bands in South Korea in one area after another"; and in a *Time* interview on the very eve of hostilities, homeward-bound Brigadier General William L. Roberts, the group's CO, called his protégés "the best damn Army outside the United States."

It wasn't true, and it wasn't saying much. The greatest shock awaiting the American people was the feeble state of their own military establishment. Its decline had begun with the Wanna-Go-Home riots, which had turned postwar demobilization into a rout; the United States had "fought the war like a football game," said General Albert C. Wedemeyer, "after which the winner leaves the field and celebrates." Then the unification controversy had torn service morale asunder. Secretary of Defense Louis Johnson announced his intention to "trim the fat out of the Armed Forces" and slashed away a lot of muscle by cutting their budgets from 30 billion dollars to 14.2 billions. The Pentagon abandoned defensive radar screens and protective devices to counter the new Russian submarines. By 1950 Russia had as many combat airplanes as the United States, four times as many troops, and thirty tank divisions to America's one. Only one U.S. infantry division approached top combat efficiency; altogether the Army had just 592,000 men in uniform, less than half its strength on Pearl Harbor Sunday. Lastly, the four divisions of U.S. occupation troops in Japan had been allowed to deteriorate until, in the later words of General William F. Dean, they had become a flabby force accustomed to "Japanese girlfriends, plenty of beer, and servants to shine their boots."

Their commanders could not plead ignorance of enemy intentions. Korea had an unhappy history of partitions reaching back to 108 B.C., and since V-J Day the 38th Parallel had become increasingly troubled. Apart from the patrolling back and forth and the saber-rattling of Rhee and Kim Il Sung, Rhee's counterpart in the North Korean capital of Pyongyang, the Central Intelligence Agency had alerted Washington to the probability of coming violence. CIA reports describing the immense NKPA buildup along the frontier warned that it could be justified only by plans for a large-scale offensive. If no one else read CIA briefs, the Secretary of State did; in testifying before congressional committees he had read several intelligence cables into the record, including one dated March 10, 1950, predicting that the "PA [NKPA] will attack South Korea in June 1950." To be sure, thirty months earlier the Joint Chiefs had told the White House that "from the standpoint of military security" the United States had "little strategic interest" in Korea. It hadn't had it then, perhaps, but any President who refused to confront fresh Communist aggression now would risk impeachment. Afterward the administration pointed out that Korea had been but one of many danger spots. Berlin had been threatening to erupt, the French had faced disaster in Indochina, and Romanian and Bulgarian troops were massing on Yugoslavia's frontiers. Administration defenders argued that it couldn't be on its toes everywhere. Precisely. That was the trouble with containment.

Entering the last weekend in June 1950, the United States stirred feebly in the hundred-degree temperatures of that summer's first heat wave. Those who could do it left their little television screens for air-conditioned theaters. Children were watching Robert Newton as Long John Silver in Walt Disney's *Treasure Island.* Joyce Cary's *The Horse's Mouth* offered literate escape in hammocks. On Morningside Heights Dwight Eisenhower, president of Columbia University, holed up with *The Maverick Queen,* Zane Grey's fifty-first novel, published posthumously. Dean Acheson spent the afternoon gardening on Harewood Farm, his Maryland home, and read himself to sleep after dinner. Outside, stealthy shadows flicked back and forth; since the rise of McCarthy the secretary's hate mail had become so great that he needed bodyguards around the clock.

Secretary of Defense Louis Johnson and Omar Bradley, chairman of the Joint Chiefs of Staff, were somewhere over the Pacific, flying home from Tokyo. President Truman was also airborne early that afternoon; at 2 P.M. Saturday his aircraft *Independence* darted down through a bank of storm clouds and entered its glide pattern above the Kansas City municipal airfield. Two hours before, the President had dedicated Baltimore's new Friendship International Airport ("to the cause of peace in the world"); now he expected to spend the rest of the weekend going over some family business with his brother Vivian and enjoying the company of old friends. White House correspondents had been told that the lid was on; no presidential activities were expected before Monday.

As usual, the higher echelons of the government were celebrating the President's absence from Washington by relaxing. Dean Rusk, the Assistant Secretary of State for Asian Affairs, was uncoiling at the home of Joseph Alsop. W. Bradley Connors, the department's public affairs officer for the Far East, was playing with his children in his Washington apartment. The last place any of them might have expected new developments was the United Nations; the U.N. had been deadlocked since January, when Jacob Malik of the USSR had begun boycotting the Security Council. The U.S. Representative on the Council was Warren Austin. He was pruning his apple orchard in Vermont. His deputy, Ernest Gross, was also away from the office, supervising a teen-age party in his Manhasset home on Long Island. Trygve Lie, secretary general of the United Nations, was loafing in nearby Forest Hills.

It was noon in New York, late morning in the Middle West, and 4 A.M. on the faraway 38th Parallel when, as MacArthur later put it, "North Korea struck like a cobra."

The summer monsoon had just begun there. Heavy rains were falling on the green rice paddies and the barren brown and gray mountain slopes when the North Korean artillery—forty miles of big guns, standing side by side—opened fire. The shelling was sporadic at first, as smaller batteries awaited flare signals from the 122-mm NKPA howitzers, but presently all artillery pieces were erupting flame, sheet after sheet of it, while officers studied the crumps to the south and corrected their ranges. Overhead, Yaks and Stormoviks winged through the warm moist air toward Seoul, less than fifty miles away. Like the Chinese, the North Koreans still used the bugle to herald charges, and with its first notes infantrymen lunged across the border toward their first objectives. Despite the rain and inevitable confusion in the darkness, NKPA General Chai Ung Jun put 90,000 men into South Korea without any traffic jams. Junks and sampans were landing amphibious troops ashore behind ROK lines to the south. Awakening to the din, South Koreans fumbled for their clothes. In a few hours they would be on the roads, hurrying away from the roar over the horizon. Some would be refugees for the rest of their lives.

Seven hours later, at 8 P.M. Eastern Daylight Saving Time, Bradley Connors became the first U.S. official in Washington to hear the news. Donald Gonzales of the United Press phoned to tell him that the UP correspondent in Korea was cabling fragmentary bulletins reporting heavy North Korean attacks all along the 38th Parallel. Did State know anything about it? Not to the best of his knowledge, Connors replied, but he would find out for certain right away. Hanging up, he tried to place a call to the U.S. embassy in Seoul. It was impossible, the operator told him; Sunday morning had arrived there, and all overseas circuits were closed. Connors hurried to the C Street entrance of the New State Department Building, but before an emergency circuit could be put together the department's communication center received a cable from John J. Muccio, the American ambassador in Seoul. Stamped in at 9:26 A.M., it read:

> North Korean forces invaded Republic of Korea at several places this morning. . . . It would appear from the nature of the attack and the manner in which it was launched that it constitutes an all-out offensive against the Republic of Korea.

Dean Rusk and John Hickerson, the department's assistant secretary for United Nations affairs, were quickly summoned, and at 10 P.M. Hickerson awoke Dean Acheson. Hickerson proposed a special meeting of the U.N. Security Council in the morning to call for a cease-fire. Since Warren Austin was in Vermont, he added, Ernest Gross should take the initiative in New York. Acheson agreed, instructed him to summon the Security Council through Trygve Lie, and picked up the white telephone that tied him in to the White House switchboard.

In Independence the Trumans had finished their evening meal. In the library of their home on North Delaware Street, the householder had begun to yawn; it was nearly his bedtime. Nevertheless, after Acheson's opening words—"Mr. President, I have very serious news. The North Koreans have invaded South Korea"—he said he would fly back at once. Better get a good night's sleep, Acheson advised him. Apart from putting the U.N. wheels in motion, nothing could be done now; they had to wait for more information. He would call again in the morning. The President asked if he could do anything now, and Acheson said yes, as a matter of fact, he could;

Louis Johnson had imposed absurd restrictions on communications between the State and Defense departments. He would like to deal directly with Secretary of the Army Frank Pace. Done, said Truman; he hung up, and the secretary began gathering in his hands the reins of American initiative. As he saw it, the chief theater of action now, even more important than the battlefield, was at Lake Success, New York.

"My God, Jack," said Trygve Lie when Hickerson called him, "this is war against the United Nations!" And so it was. The two Koreas were wards of the U.N. The United States merely represented it in the south. At Potsdam the Big Three had agreed that the peninsula's future would be determined in supervised elections; then the Russians had changed their minds and refused to allow U.N. commissioners above the 38th Parallel. At Acheson's direction, his staff drafted a Security Council resolution determining that the "armed attack on the Republic of Korea by forces from North Korea" constituted "a breach of the peace" and should be terminated at once in a cease-fire. Since the Soviet boycott of the council continued to be in effect, the measure passed 9 to 0.

Sunday morning the news from Muccio was all bad. A strong NKPA tank column was driving toward Seoul and Kimpo airport, apparently advancing at will; "South Korean arms," Acheson concluded, were "clearly outclassed." At 12:35 P.M. he phoned Independence and asked the President to return. Before boarding his aircraft Truman had a few words for reporters: "Don't make it alarmist. It could be a dangerous situation, but I hope it isn't. I can't answer any questions until I get all the facts." Back at 1628 Pennsylvania Avenue, he ordered an immediate conference of all his diplomatic and military advisers around Blair House's large mahogany dining table. There he made three decisions: MacArthur would be told to use all the planes and ships necessary for the evacuation of American civilians from Korea, going above the 38th Parallel if necessary; the general was to provide the ROK troops with ammunition; and the U.S. Seventh Fleet would patrol Formosa Strait, against the possibility that the Korean thrust was a feint masking a leap to Taiwan. Had Mao pursued Chiang there a year earlier, the Americans would have stood aside. Now domestic politics made U.S. neutrality impossible.

Monday, the fifth anniversary of the United Nations, was a dark day, "a day," said Acheson, "of steadily worsening reports from

Korea." Ignoring the U.N. appeal for a cease-fire, NKPA troops were enveloping Rhee's Seoul in a six-pronged drive. Already Rhee's government was moving south. The roads were solid with terrified people. ROK soldiers were still running; a desperate stand at Chunchon had disintegrated with the arrival of the first T-34 tank. Dr. John Myun Chang, the Korean ambassador to the U.S., called at the White House. Spinning the big globe in his office and putting his hand on Korea, the President said, "This is the Greece of the Far East. If we are tough enough now, there won't have to be any next step." Unconsoled, Dr. Chang left in tears. At 9 P.M. Truman convened another emergency session in Blair House. The "war cabinet," as he now called it, heard Chip Bohlen and George Kennan say that Russia's absence from the Security Council offered a great opportunity for the United States; they needn't worry about a Russian veto. With this in mind, the President approved a new Council resolution calling upon all U.N. members to lend a hand in throwing the North Koreans back. Obviously the most help would be expected from the Americans, and Truman was prepared to provide it. With the approval of his advisers, he directed naval and Air Force units in MacArthur's command to give direct tactical support to ROK defenders south of the 38th Parallel. At Acheson's urging, he also increased support of French troops fighting in Indochina.

Seoul fell Wednesday, and the ROK defenders retreated to the Han River. In Long Island's Stockholm Restaurant that noon, three unlikely diplomats—Trygve Lie, Jacob Malik, and Ernest Gross—met to keep a long-standing luncheon date. Naturally they talked about the war; there was nothing else to talk about. Malik held that Sunday's Security Council resolution was "illegal" because no Russian delegate had been present and Red China had not been admitted. While Gross waited tensely, Lie met his responsibilities as a scrupulous Secretary General. Forget about Sunday, he advised Malik; come to this afternoon's Council meeting and hear the new American resolution. "Won't you join us?" he asked. "The interests of your country would seem to me to call for your presence." But the Russian shook his head. He said vehemently, "No, I will not go there." Outside, Gross mopped his brow. He said to Lie, "Think what would have happened if he had accepted your invitation." What would have happened would have been a Soviet veto of the new U.S. move and then, in all probability, American intervention in Korea unsupported by the U.N.—in short, an earlier Vietnam.

Tuesday evening Americans with TV sets watched their first U.N. session, oddly interspersed between commercials and the performances of two children's puppets named Foodini and Pinhead. Malik's seat remained vacant, and the strong U.S. resolution carried. For the first time in history, an international organization had decided to resist aggression with force. That was how editorial writers put it the following morning, for Truman's decision to provide the ROK troops with naval support and air cover was enormously popular. When it was announced on the Hill, Congress rose in a standing ovation. The White House press received it with broad smiles. As titular head of the Republican party, Governor Dewey enthusiastically supported U.S. intervention. Even the *Chicago Tribune* congratulated the President, noting that approval of his stand was unanimous.

It wasn't quite. One man stood against the tide. All day Tuesday, while the Senate debated the new course of foreign policy, Robert Taft had sat apart, his head resting in his hand, thoughtful and silent. Now on Wednesday he took the floor. He charged that the administration had "invited" the NKPA attack by declaring that Korea lay beyond the American defensive perimeter. No wonder the North Koreans felt they could strike south with impunity, he said; "If the United States was not prepared to use its troops and give military assistance to Nationalist China against Chinese Communists, why should it use its troops to defend Nationalist Korea against Korean Communists?" Make no mistake, Taft said; he approved using U.S. might to throw the invaders back across the 38th Parallel, and if the administration had brought the issue before the Senate, he would have voted for it. But it hadn't. Instead it had "usurped the power of Congress," creating dangerous precedents for the future. The Constitution extended the right to declare war to Congress alone, and the President's action "unquestionably has brought about a de facto war." Taft concluded: "So far as I can see, and so far I have studied the matter, I would say there is no authority to use Armed Forces in support of the United Nations in the absence of some previous action by Congress dealing with the subject."

He sat down. The right-wing Republican senators gave him token applause, and, when the moment arose, expressed other views. On the question of whether the President "arrogates to himself the power to declare war," said William Knowland of California, "I believe that in the very important steps the President of the United States has taken to uphold . . . the United Nations and the free peoples of the world, he should have the overwhelming support of all Americans regardless of their party affiliation." The rest of the Taft bloc broke into loud, sustained applause. What with the prospect of a ROK stand on the Han, a Chiang Kai-shek offer of 33,000 Kuomintang veterans to fight the North Korean aggressors, and news that all British warships in the Pacific had been placed under the command of the U.S. Navy, the country was in no mood to weigh fine points of constitutional law. Yet Harry Truman agreed with Taft. He wanted a congressional resolution of support. Acheson argued against it. In his opinion Taft's speech, though "basically honest," was "bitterly partisan and ungracious." He insisted that the President "should not ask for a resolution of approval, but rest on his constitutional authority as Commander in Chief of the Armed Forces."

Among historical ironies, few are sharper than this: Dean Acheson, excoriated during his years of power as a tool of international Communism, was so implacable in his hostility toward it that he believed the President could commit America's armed might to an anti-Communist conflict without consulting anyone, acting on the strength of his position as commander in chief. Acheson never changed his mind. During the missile crisis of 1962, he wanted President Kennedy to invade Cuba. In his last years he became one of the most zealous of Vietnam hawks, wearing a red, white, and blue armband and lecturing Washington high school students on the need to stand up to the Reds. By then, of course, presidential authority to intervene in foreign wars had become much greater —largely because of precedents established, at Acheson's urging, in June 1950.

Between communiqués from Washington, Lake Success, Tokyo, and Seoul, the public was thoroughly muddled, and in a presidential press conference Thursday afternoon, the first since the outbreak of hostilities, Truman was urged to clarify matters:

Q. Mr. President, everyone is asking in this country, are we or are we not at war?

A. We are not at war.

Q. Mr. President, could you elaborate on that statement, "We are not at war," and could we use that in quotes?

A. Yes, I will allow you to use that in quotes. The Republic of Korea was set up with United Nations help. It was unlawfully attacked by a bunch of bandits who are neighbors, in North Korea. The United Nations held a meeting and asked the members to go to the relief of the Korean Republic, and the members of the United Nations are going to the relief of the Korean Republic to suppress a bandit raid on the Republic of Korea. That is all there is to it.

Q. Would it be correct to call it a police action under the United Nations?

A. Yes, that is exactly what it amounts to.

It amounted to more than one hundred thousand American casualties over the next three years, and the Republicans, who after their initial enthusiasm found less and less to like in the war, never let Harry Truman forget that he had once thought of it as a "police action." Homely phrases work only if the policies they epitomize work; had lend-lease failed, FDR's comparison of it with "a length of garden hose" would be less charitably remembered. The difference, unappreciated in June 1950, was that Roosevelt's goal had been total victory. The purpose in Korea was not unconditional surrender; it was a cease-fire, an end to aggression, a negative aim.

Thursday morning's communiqué from Tokyo reported that of South Korea's 65,000 defenders, nearly half had been killed, wounded, or taken prisoner. Plainly this mounting sacrifice could not go on much longer. Equally obvious, tactical support from U.S. naval and air units would not be enough to turn the war around. Hourly, now, the momentum of events was tugging Truman toward a stronger commitment. From the Dai Ichi Building in Tokyo came news that MacArthur had flown into Korea for a firsthand look at the struggle. Disregarding his Air Force weathermen, who had grounded all other aircraft at Haneda Airfield, the seventy-year-old general had boarded his old C-54, the *Bataan*, and told his pilot, "We go." Upon landing—Syngman Rhee met him at the airstrip—MacArthur said, "Let's go to the front and look at the troops. The only way to judge a war is to see the troops in action." He then drove northward under shellfire and reached the Han just in time to see the last, hopeless attempt to hold the bridges. For twenty minutes the general stood on a little mound just off the road watching the demoralized retreat, the screaming refugees, and the continual bombardment from the north. As a member of his staff noted, he had "encountered all the dreadful backwash of a defeated and dispersed Army." Back at his Japanese headquarters, he cabled the Pentagon: "The only assurance for holding the present line and the ability to regain later the lost ground is through the introduction of United States ground combat forces into the Korean battle area."

There it was. They had known all week that it was coming, and now it came chattering from a Pentagon telecom machine at 3 A.M. Friday, while most of the capital lay asleep. General J. Lawton Collins, in MacArthur's old role as the Army's chief of staff, answered that before taking such a momentous step the President would doubtless want to consult his advisers. Couldn't the war wait a few hours? Absolutely not, MacArthur replied. Every minute was crucial now. If the Republic of Korea was to be saved, American troops must be sent into the breach at once.

General Collins phoned Secretary of the Army Frank C. Pace Jr., and Pace called Blair House. It was just before 5 A.M. in Washington, but Truman was already up and shaved. Taking the call at his bedside table, he hesitated briefly and then authorized the commitment of one regiment to combat. He would assemble the members of his war cabinet at once, he said, to propose an expansion of this expeditionary force. Their approval was unanimous. Orders were cut that morning, and at 1:22 P.M. that June 30, the seventh day of the crisis, the calling up of reserve units was under way. The United States was at war all the way—with warships, warplanes, tanks, artillery, and ground troops—and Congress hadn't even been asked for an opinion.

Six weeks of agony followed. Americans assumed that the moment the U.S. 24th and 25th divisions left Japan and arrived in Korea, the fighting would take on a new cast. If the North Koreans didn't panic and flee, it was thought, they would at least lose their momentum. In fact, the U.S. divisions began crumbling as quickly as their new ROK allies. Out of condition and outnumbered by as much as twenty to one, the first detachments to arrive were for the most part green troops; fewer than 20 percent of them had seen action in World War II. Their only antitank weapons were ten-year-old bazookas, hopelessly ineffective against the mighty Soviet T-34s. Isolated and cut off from one another, in the first weeks many surrendered, including the major general commanding the 24th, before learning that the North Koreans took few prisoners. More often the NKPA tied the hands of captives behind their backs and bayoneted them. U.S. infantrymen then became afflicted by "bugout fever"—a yearning to return to their soft billets in Japan. MacArthur did what he could, skillfully maneuvering U.S. and ROK battalions so as to delay the enemy as much as possible while building a defensive perimeter around the Pusan bridgehead, but defeatism crept into the high command.

Osan, Yongdok, Hadong, Chindong'mi, the Nakton Bulge—the strange names appeared in headlines as a succession of front-page maps depicted the Pusan perimeter, smaller each morning. Ferocious NKPA attacks threw the 24th Division out of Taejon on July 20 and then began hammering the 25th at Taegu, the main U.S. supply base and communications hub. In the tough phrase of the hour, war correspondents wrote that MacArthur might "run out of real estate," and be driven into the sea. Then, on August 6, the long retreat ended. Infantrymen of the 27th Regiment and their ROK allies dug in their heels and stopped the Red tide at the walls of Taegu. Late in August the North Koreans staged one last massive attack in an attempt to capture Pusan, but by now the defenders had tanks and heavy artillery. The lines held on a 120-mile arc from the Sea of Japan on the east to the Korea Strait on the south. There, as summer waned, the line of opposing trenches grew stronger every week. It was a stalemate, and commentators wondered how it could become anything else. The mood of the men on the line was fatalistic. Their favorite expression was, "That's the way the ball bounces," and they sang:

*The Dhow, the Gizee, and Rhee
What do they want from me?*

But Douglas MacArthur was too gifted a strategist to be bottled up by an unimaginative siege, and the military force now arriving from an aroused America was too great to be contained within so narrow an enclave. At home selected National Guard units were being called up. Recruiting drives had been intensified and draft quotas increased to put 600,000 men in uniform as soon as possible. To be sure, the replacements were often neither enthusiastic nor cheerful. No one called them gung ho; Kilroy wasn't there; and a Corporal Stephen Zeg of Chicago doubtless spoke for thousands of others in Pusan when he told a reporter, "I'll fight for my country, but I'll be damned if I see why I'm fighting to save this hellhole."

Yet there were few organized protests against the war and fewer demonstrations in the States. The new infantrymen were the younger brothers of the men who had fought in World War II. Patriotism was still strong, and that early rout of American infantry by North Koreans had stung the country's pride.

Each day the stockpiles of men and steel behind the Pusan front grew larger. The 1st Cavalry Division arrived from Japan and the 2nd Infantry from home; then came 2,000 Tommies from the 27th British Brigade in Hong Kong and French, Turkish, Australian, Dutch, and Philippine troops—the van of supporting units from fifteen other U.N. members.

While the North Koreans worried about their long supply lines, their heavy casualties, and the inferior quality of teen-age replacements who were being drafted in the north at bayonet point, MacArthur was preparing the most brilliant stroke of his career. Against all advice, he proposed to divide his force, holding part of it here and staging an intricate amphibious attack with the other part, landing at the port of Inchon, twenty-four miles west of Seoul and one hundred and fifty miles from the present NKPA rear.

Two days before D-day, ten warships swept the harbor of mines and bombarded shore batteries. At 6:30 A.M. on September 15, the appointed day, as the first pink streaks of dawn broke in the east, the commanding admiral broke out the traditional amphibious signal "Land the landing force"—whereupon waves of small boats darted for the shore bearing the 1st Marine Division, which had sailed secretly from San Francisco two weeks earlier. It took the marines exactly forty minutes to seize Wohli Island, the key to Inchon's defense. Racing down a thousand-foot causeway, they then headed for Seoul while MacArthur announced to the world: "The Navy and Marines have never shone more brightly." By October 1 the North Korean army was all but destroyed. Half its men were in prisoner of war pens; the rest were divided into small detachments that moved furtively at night, trying to reach home. U.N. troops held everything in the peninsula south of the 38th Parallel. MacArthur appealed to the NKPA to lay down its arms, and at Lake Success a resolution backed by eight nations asked the U.N. General Assembly to "take all appropriate measures to ensure a stable situation in the whole of Korea"—thus approving a crossing into North Korea. But the Joint Chiefs were again urging caution upon MacArthur, and ominous rumbles were heard in Peking. U.S. intelligence reported that Chinese divisions were massing in Manchuria, just across the Yalu River from North Korea. President Truman decided that it was time he and General MacArthur had a little talk.

It was long overdue. As early as June, John Foster Dulles, the chief Republican foreign affairs adviser, had called on Truman to recommend that the general be "hauled back to the United States." Dulles had just returned from Tokyo. At the outbreak of the war, he said indignantly, MacArthur's headquarters had been caught unprepared. No one in the Dai Ichi Building would rouse the general —"they were afraid to disturb him"—so Dulles had to do it himself.

Late in July the general's dabbling in affairs which were none of his concern had prompted a second glance from the White House. At a time when diplomatic maneuvering in the U.N. required that Chiang Kai-shek be kept under wraps, MacArthur had flown to Formosa to call on the generalissimo and tell reporters that the U.S. ships patrolling Formosa Strait were "leashing" Chiang and should be withdrawn. The President, disturbed, had dispatched Averell Harriman to the Dai Ichi Building for a consultation with MacArthur. Harriman had returned gloomy. He felt that the general hadn't understood him, that he seemed to have "a strange idea that we should back anybody who will fight communism."

The next Truman knew, AP, UP, and INS were carrying the text of a special message MacArthur had sent to the annual convention of the Veterans of Foreign Wars. In it the general had proposed nothing less than a new foreign policy in the Pacific, with American arms holding a defensive line from Vladivostok to Singapore. Obviously this would commit the United States to an alliance with Chiang. The general thought that a sound idea. Those who believed such a move might provoke the Chinese Communists were appeasers, he said, guilty of offering a "fallacious and threadbare argument," while what was needed was "aggressive, resolute and dynamic leadership." The President, furious, demanded that the statement be withdrawn. MacArthur obeyed, but that accomplished nothing; it was already in the papers. Now, with the threat of a wider war, the White House arranged a face-to-face conference between the President and his most colorful general on lonely Wake Island.

They met on October 15 in an ugly cinder block outpost of the Civil Aeronautics Authority. In the crucial session, both men assumed that they were alone, but a zealous diplomat—Philip Jessup

—had stationed a secretary with a shorthand pad in the shadow of the door, which was ajar. Though MacArthur later challenged the accuracy of her stenographic transcript, there is no other reason to doubt it. If it is correct, MacArthur apologized handsomely for his message to the VFW. He also predicted that the war would be over by Thanksgiving. Then the Japanese peace treaty could be signed with or without Soviet cooperation, he said, and Korea could be reconstructed for as little as a half-billion dollars. Truman asked about the chance of either Russian or Chinese intervention in the war. The general replied that it was:

> Very little. Had they interfered in the first or second months it would have been decisive. We are no longer fearful of their intervention. We no longer stand hat in hand. The Chinese have 300,000 men in Manchuria. Of these probably not more than 100,000 to 125,000 are distributed along the Yalu River. Only 50,000 to 60,000 could be gotten across the Yalu River. They have no air force. Now that we have bases for our Air Force in Korea, if the Chinese tried to get down to Pyongyang, there would be the greatest slaughter.

There certainly would, though it would not be the kind of slaughter MacArthur had in mind. His intelligence was defective. Mao had assembled 850,000 soldiers in Manchuria. Already 120,000 men, the vanguard of his veteran Fourth Field Army, were south of the Yalu. They had been slipping over every night, bringing their armor and heavy guns with them and hiding before daybreak in the rugged hills of North Korea. The discovery of this momentous ruse was subsequently used to discredit MacArthur. That was unjust. He was not blameless in his autumn conduct of the war—his failure to issue winter clothing to his men against the possibility of a wider conflict is inexplicable—but his major oversights and aberrances, including his insubordination, came later. At Wake he was a loyal commander, telling his commander in chief what he believed to be the truth. In the six weeks which followed, his behavior was flawless. No blueprints for a new foreign policy issued from the Dai Ichi Building, and although technically he needed no authorization to cross the 38th Parallel in force, he waited until the U.N. General Assembly, recalling that the essential objective of his expedition was "the establishment of a unified, independent, and democratic Korea," directed him to move north.

He now led a splendid army built around seven U.S. divisions, the most recent of which was the magnificent old Third. By their side marched six seasoned ROK divisions and contingents from England, Australia, New Zealand, Thailand, and Turkey. Pyongyang fell on October 20. There, in the enemy capital, six years to the day after he had waded ashore at Leyte, MacArthur struck an antic pose and called out, "Any celebrities here to meet me? Where's Kim Buck Too?"

The general was convinced that his foes had lost heart. In this he was tragically mistaken—so wrong, in fact, that from this point forward there were two wars, one in Korea and the other in MacArthur's mind. The real battlefield was a bleak tract of towering heights and plunging chasms, a region so dismal that until now it had been largely uninhabited. There were no reliable maps of it. Here and there faint trails in the dirt hinted at earlier visitors, but they led nowhere. Passes between the windswept precipices were unexplored, and the spines of the mountain ranges ran north to south, so that any force moving northward on a broad front would have to be split into detachments inaccessible to one another in an emergency. It would be hard to imagine terrain better suited to guerrilla warfare. Tanks were useless in it, heavy artillery had to be left behind, and its deep gorges and canyons provided superb concealment for ambushers or troops hiding from aerial observation. So adaptable was it to the enemy's purpose that by October he had successfully tucked away in it 250,000 well-disciplined, sturdy-legged peasant riflemen who awaited only the signal to charge, sounded by their buglers and cymbal-swinging bandsmen, before throwing themselves on the flanks of the unsuspecting United Nations armies. Behind the ambushers, in the vastness of Manchuria, another 600,000 blue-uniformed Chinese soldiers stood ready to reinforce them. It was one of the greatest natural traps in the history of warfare.

MacArthur was euphoric. To his quartermasters in Japan he sent word to prepare billets for the Eighth U.N. Army, his left wing. He informed Omar Bradley that he expected to have the U.S. 2nd Division ready for reassignment to Europe in January, and he promised the country that he would "have the boys home by Christmas." It was all over but the mopping up, he told correspondents. On October 24 he advised the Joint Chiefs that he had drawn up his forces on a line between Pyongyang and Wonsan, a seaport forty-five miles to the east. Then he announced—actually *announced*—his battle plan. It was to be a giant pincer, with the Eighth Army driving north from Pyongyang while the rest of his troops, designated X Corps, moved out from Wonsan. The Eighth Army would be the western claw of the pincer, X Corps the eastern claw, and the high ground between them would be lightly held by ROK units. To the astonishment of officers who fought by the book, the general blandly notified them that he had decided to violate a basic military axiom. He had deliberately split his command between two ground commanders, giving the left wing to Lieutenant General Walton H. Walker and the right to his Dai Ichi GHQ. Intoxicated by his success at Inchon, he seemed to be increasing the difficulties already inherent in the terrain by assuring that neither hand would know what the other was doing.

In the last week of October a dozen U.N. spearheads began this northward sweep, striking out toward the Chongchon River on the left and the Changjin Reservoir on the right. Almost at once they ran into trouble. Major General Charles A. Willoughby, MacArthur's G2, had told them that the NKPA was completely demoralized, but a sharp North Korean counterattack isolated the 7th ROK Division and cut it up. Then, on October 26, an Eighth Army patrol picked up a Chinese soldier fully ninety miles south of where he should have been. Eyebrows went up as far back as 1600 Pennsylvania Avenue; presidential approval of MacArthur's drive had been based on his virtual guarantee that there would be, indeed could be, no effective Chinese intervention. The U.N. general replied that there was nothing to worry about, that Peking, like Moscow, made a practice of sending idealistic "volunteers" to fight under other Communist flags, and had in fact advertised its intention to do it in Korea.

Four days later sixteen soldiers from no known NKPA unit were taken north of Hamhung, in northeastern Korea. Interrogated by a Nisei officer who had grown up in Honolulu's Chinatown, they too were found to be Chinese. The following day a whole regiment of MacArthur's presumed volunteers was reported near the Changjin and Pujon reservoirs; prisoners from it said that they had crossed the Yalu on an ammunition train two weeks earlier. On November 1 a group of Soviet MIG-15 jets challenged U.S. fighters, briefly scrimmaged with them, and then returned to the Chinese side of the Yalu. By this time Chinese foot soldiers had been identified on every divisional front. On November 2 the 1st Cavalry sent back word that while reconnoitering the north bank of the Chongchon one of its battalions had been decimated by machine gun fire and screaming soldiers in blue Mao jackets. "We don't know whether they represent the Chinese government," the report said, but the battle had been "a massacre, Indian-style, like the one that hit Custer at Little Big Horn."

Inevitably, American officers were becoming preoccupied with the yellow peril. They were fighting in forbidden country, with long and vulnerable supply lines, and they weren't equipped for an extensive campaign. They knew little about China, but what they had heard was disturbing: its new regime regarded America as its natural enemy, and it held life cheap. The prospect of a confrontation with endless waves of charging Orientals was frightening. On November 3 the 24th Infantry actually disregarded an instruction from MacArthur. Informed that "the order of the day is full speed ahead to the Yalu River," the 24th turned about-face and retreated fourteen miles. Before anyone in GHQ could deal with this insubordination, the situation reports for November 4 had come in. The 1st Marine Division had identified three Chinese divisions in its sector; the 1st Cavalry had found five.

Reaction in the Dai Ichi Building was mixed. At first MacArthur told the Pentagon that while Chinese Communist intervention was "a distinct possibility," he did not have "sufficient evidence at hand to warrant immediate acceptance." After sleeping on it, he decided that the presence of eight hostile divisions was pretty good evidence. He advised the Joint Chiefs that his left wing had eluded "a possible trap . . . surreptitiously laid" and that there had not been "any possibility of a great military reverse." Still, he was upset. Having destroyed the North Koreans, the U.N. force had found that "a new, fresh army now faces us, backed up by a possibility of large alien reserves and adequate supply within easy reach to the enemy but beyond the limits of our present sphere of military action." These newcomers were operating from a "privileged sanctuary" across the Yalu. "Whether and to what extent these reserves will be moved forward to reinforce units now committed remains to be seen and is a matter of the gravest significance," he said. Already he was "in hostile contact with Chinese military units deployed for action against the forces of the Unified Command," and the Chinese were capable of massing in such numbers as "to threaten the ultimate destruction of my command."

Until this point the Joint Chiefs had interdicted bombing within five miles of the Yalu. MacArthur now asked for authority to destroy the Yalu bridges. He was still unconvinced that the Chinese intended to come in all the way, but as a lifelong student of the Asian mind, he said, he knew that "it is the pattern of the Oriental psychology to respect and follow aggressive, resolute, and dynamic leadership." Taking out those bridges would be aggressive, resolute and dynamic, and it would also serve the purpose of discouraging replacements. Permission to bomb was granted. The Joint Chiefs were disturbed, too. They didn't like the deployment of his forces, and they were beginning to wonder about Willoughby. Still, MacArthur was the senior soldier in the U.S. Army ("Senior," said one junior officer, "to everyone but God"). He was also seven thousand miles away, the commander on the spot, and to overrule him would break a standing U.S. military policy going back to 1864. They were unwilling to give him a blank check, however. He was reminded that "extreme care must be taken to avoid violation of Manchurian territory and airspace." His pilots must avoid targets inside Manchuria and, above all, the Yalu dam and power installations.

As the teletypes in the Dai Ichi Building rattled off these instructions, the Korean front fell silent. Patrols couldn't flush a single Chinese soldier. Apparently they had all vanished. General Willoughby was sure of it, had known it all along, and was in a mood to crow. As an old China hand he had spotted Peking's bluff. It had been called, and now the war was over. In Korea the ground commanders weren't so sure. The Chinese could have broken off action because they had had enough, as MacArthur and Willoughby now believed, or conversely because they were regrouping for a full-fledged attack. Altogether, they agreed, it was a mystery.

The fact that they were mystified is itself mysterious. For over two months Chou En-lai, foreign minster of the Central People's Government, had been trying every way he could think of to tell these Occidental intruders to go home. On August 25, when MacArthur was still boxed in at Pusan, Chou had notified the U.N. that Washington's support of Chiang Kai-shek's right to remain on Formosa was in itself a "criminal act" of "armed aggression," and he had pledged himself to "liberate from the tentacles of the United

States aggressors" all Oriental territories which didn't belong to them. Asia for the Asians, Chou was saying, and while Korea wasn't his either, his argument was no weaker than, and in many ways resembled, the Monroe Doctrine.

Since the Americans hadn't heard him the first time, Chou had tried again after Inchon. China, he had warned, would not "supinely tolerate their North Korean neighbors being savagely invaded by imperialists." Then, on October 3, he had summoned Sirdar K. M. Panikkar, the Indian ambassador to Peking. Chou solemnly informed him that the Chinese People's Republic would ally itself with North Korea and enter the war against the United Nations if U.N. troops crossed the 38th Parallel south to north. This message was transmitted to the State Department through New Delhi, Moscow, and Stockholm. It was published in all the great newspapers in the world, and just in case Washington had overlooked it, Chou repeated it over Peking's official government radio station a week later. MacArthur and Willoughby dismissed it as "diplomatic blackmail." They were wrong, though the administration could hardly reproach them for that. Remarking that Panikkar had in the past "played the game of the Chinese Communists fairly regularly," Truman concluded that Chou's message was probably "a bald attempt to blackmail the United Nations by threats of intervention in Korea."

In all probability, MacArthur was no more responsible for the approaching catastrophe than Eisenhower for the Battle of the Bulge—the analogy is Truman's—but his handling of the events leading up to it was another matter. Afterward he would say of himself that "no more subordinate soldier ever wore the uniform," yet on at least one sensitive issue he had treated Joint Chiefs' directive with something less than respect. In their view, the deployment of Caucasian troops near Korea's northern frontiers was needlessly provocative. On September 27 they had informed him that "as a matter of policy, no non-Korean ground forces will be used in the northeast provinces bordering the Soviet Union or in the area along the Manchurian border." He not only ignored this order; on October 24 he told his lieutenants in the field to "use any and all ground forces at their commands, as necessary, in order to capture all of North Korea." To the Chiefs he sent word that the Chinese despised weakness, while a show of strength "would effectively appeal to the reason in the Chinese mind."

MacArthur's racial chauvinism—for that is what it was—led him into a snare of his own making. By Thanksgiving nearly three weeks had passed since the last sign of Chinese activity at the front, and he concluded that his militance had scared them off. The CIA warned him that "at a minimum" Red China would increase its presence in Korea, try to tie up U.N. forces in battles of attrition, and "maintain the semblance of a North Korean state in being." Ignoring this, MacArthur went over to the attack for the second time that month, and again he provided the press with a preview of his strategy.

This, he told the correspondents, would be a "general offensive" to "win the war." He repeated his October promise to the men, directing Major General John B. Coulter to tell the troops that "They will eat Christmas dinner at home." The drive would open early on the morning of November 24, and he would fly over from Tokyo for the occasion. It was inconceivable that this final drive might fail. In a special communiqué to the U.N. he reported that the Air Force had "completely interdicted the rear areas." His left wing, he said, would advance against "failing resistance," while his right wing, "gallantly supported by naval air and surface action," continued to exploit its "commanding position." The juncture of the two "should for all practical purposes end the war." A reporter asked him if he knew how many Chinese soldiers were in Korea. "About thirty thousand regulars," the general fired back, "and thirty thousand volunteers." Losses would be "extraordinarily light."

In Washington the President was bemused. Earlier in the month the general had sounded an alarm in his messages that had seemed, in Truman's opinion, to portend impending disaster. Now, apparently, the grave danger did not exist, since the same commander was announcing victory even before the first men started marching. Indeed, the troops were celebrating it in advance; the day before the offensive was Thanksgiving, and American ingenuity saw to it that every man received a hot turkey dinner with buttered squash, Waldorf salad, cranberry sauce, mince pie, and after-dinner mints.

That was on Thursday. On Friday the attack went in, and on Sunday the Chinese struck with thirty-three divisions—300,000 men.

At 6:15 A.M. General Bradley phoned the White House. "A terrible message has come from General MacArthur," he told the President. "The Chinese have come in with both feet."

They had ruptured the entire U.N. front. The center, held by

ROK divisions, simply caved in, and in those central mountain ranges the ROK II Corps disintegrated. Turks, British units, and the 1st Cavalry rushed up to replace them. They were driven back thirty miles to Tokchon, lost Tokchon, and took off for the south in two-and-a-half-ton trucks, firing back at their tormentors as they fled. The Turks chose to make a stand. They ran out of bullets, went after the enemy with scimitars, and were wiped out. The 24th Division was driven back across the Chongchon River. Altogether the Chinese had slashed off forty miles of front. Pausing on the hilly ground between the Eighth Army on their right and X Corps on their left, they then swung east and west to envelop them. General Walker had to choose between retreat and annihilation. He sensibly withdrew. X Corps received the same order, but there the outcome was different.

Despite appalling casualties, Walker's command had remained intact. To be sure, every night seemed worse than the last. Heralded by the bugles and cymbals—and sometimes police whistles—masses of screaming Chinese would swoop down under flares. There was no end to them. In MacArthur's phrase, the enemy had a "bottomless well" of manpower. Still, Walker eventually stopped running and was able to re-form down by the 38th Parallel. X Corps, on the other hand, came apart. There the key force was the 1st Marine Division. As usual, the marines had been out in front of every other U.N. unit—about forty miles ahead. They had been way up on the Chosin Reservoir when the first bugles blew, and being alert, they decided that this would be a good time to wheel around, come down behind the Chinese assaulting the Eighth Army, and pounce on their rear. But the enemy had anticipated them. The next thing MacArthur knew, the marines had been cut off and surrounded. They were forty miles away from the nearest help, at Hungnam.

Their breakout was one of the great stories of the Korean War. "Retreat, hell!" the Marine general snapped at a war correspondent. "We're only attacking in a different direction." And Colonel Lewis B. "Chesty" Puller told his regiment, "The enemy is in front of us, behind us, to the left of us, and to the right of us. They won't escape *this* time." Joined by men from the 3rd and 8th divisions and the ROK Capital Division, they formed a column and hacked their way through walls of Chinese, moving ever eastward over a corkscrew trail of icy dirt for fourteen days of sub-zero cold, blizzards, and thousand-foot chasms. At one point they seemed utterly lost, confronted by an impassable gorge; then the pilots of the Combat Cargo Command arrived overhead with a huge suspension bridge dangling from their flying boxcars and parked it in the canyon. Once the column had to bury 117 marines in one frozen grave. Another time it took 2,651 casualties in four days of fighting and, lacking a hospital, had to carry every one of them. At last it reached the port of Hungnam and was evacuated.

The valor of individuals and units could not obscure the central fact: MacArthur's men had been dealt a stunning defeat, "the worst," *Time* said, "the United States has ever suffered." Correspondent Homer Bigart declared that "Unsound deployment of United Nations forces and a momentous blunder by General MacArthur helped insure the success of the enemy's strategy." An editorial in the *New York Herald Tribune*, a Republican paper, described the rout as a "colossal military blunder" which had demonstrated that MacArthur "can no longer be accepted as the final authority on military matters."

MacArthur took a different view. Although he was deeply depressed—"near panic," Acheson thought, reading his telecom messages—he couldn't see that he could be held responsible. On the fourth day of the Chinese blitz his communiqué recognized that "We face an entirely new war," and he seemed to be attributing it to bad faith in Peking. The enemy drive, he declared, had "shattered the high hopes we had entertained that the intervention of the Chinese was only of a token nature on a volunteer and individual basis as publicly announced."

At the end of the first week in December, while the Eighth Army was still in disarray and the 1st Marine Division was pinned in around the Chosin Reservoir, he told the Joint Chiefs that his men were reaching the end of their strength. He could see no alternative to "steady attrition leading to final destruction" unless the terms of the U.N. commitment were changed. The new situation, he said, "calls for political decisions and strategic plans in implementation thereof adequate fully to meet the realities involved." Translated from MacArthurese, this meant that he wanted the one thing no one in Washington or Lake Success could give him—freedom to invade Manchuria. To Acheson, in Washington, the communiqués from Tokyo "depicted MacArthur in a blue funk, sorry for himself, complaining of the restrictions against expanding the war, and sending to press and Pentagon what Lovett called 'posterity papers.'" No doubt. The general never forgot that he would be a figure in history. In the Dai Ichi Building, however, his request for authority to cross the Yalu made sense. There was no other way to win the war.

Unfortunately, winning it was out of the question. The nature of hostilities had changed since 1945. Hiroshima and Nagasaki had changed it. In a world with weapons capable of inflicting megadeaths, war was no longer the last argument of kings and presidents; if it spread and became global, it would mean the end of the human race. To be sure, MacArthur's enemies in Korea had no U-235 bombs, but their ally in Moscow did, and that in itself was enough to put a checkrein on him. There were other reasons, equally persuasive. The other fifteen members of the United Nations with men in his command wanted no part of a wider war. And even if the United States was prepared to discard the mantle of U.N. approval and go it alone, the logic of its global strategy argued against further Asian entanglement. A Manchurian campaign would have brought a sharp increase of anti-Americanism among nations in the emerging Third World and a virtual halt to American aid in the rebuilding of Europe.

If MacArthur couldn't win without crossing the Yalu—and clearly he now could not—new dilemmas arose. A United Nations defeat was unthinkable. At the same time, the two great adversaries could not, in the present circumstances, walk away. The mad solution, then, was war with neither triumph nor subjugation—a long, bloody stalemate which would end only when the exhausted participants agreed to a truce. That, in effect, is what ultimately happened, and in light of the later experience in Vietnam it seems bearable. At the time it was infuriating, especially to MacArthur, a proud officer steeped in nineteenth-century concepts of honor, who with every fiber of his being believed, as he would soon tell his countrymen, that "In war there is no substitute for victory."

Christmas was unreal that December. If you belonged to the swing generation and weren't a "two-time loser"—a World War II veteran trapped by reserve status into fighting the new war, too— your children were just becoming old enough to give the season a special charm and poignancy. The threat of the mushroom cloud hung over them, too. The number one tune on the hit parade was a lugubrious ballad called "The Tennessee Waltz." While you shopped for gifts among the agitated but strangely silent crowds and wondered whether there would even be a Christmas in 1951, loudspeakers moaned:

*I was waltzing with my darlin' to the Tennessee Waltz
When an old friend I happened to see
I introduced him to my loved one, and while they were waltzing,
My friend stole my sweetheart from me. . . .*

The headlines in kiosks were odd, even grotesque. While Chinese soldiers and young Americans were killing one another on the far side of the Pacific, a Chinese Communist delegation arrived in Lake Success to state their case. Between the U.N. sessions, one read, General Hu Hsiu-chuan and his thirteen aides bought Mixmasters and nylons for their wives and books on atomic bombs, presumably for themselves. A Montana draft board refused to allow the induction of any more boys until MacArthur was given nuclear weapons and the right to use them. Word reached Washington that a Soviet diplomat had assured Peking that Russia would enter the war if Manchuria were bombed. In a subsequent press conference the President hinted that atomic bombs might be used in Korea, and that MacArthur might be the man to decide when. That brought Prime Minister Clement Attlee over on the next plane from London. Truman told him to forget it, he hadn't said anything like that, it was all a rhubarb. Nevertheless, Attlee returned home looking grim. He had learned something else. Both Truman and Acheson had confided that the Korean situation looked hopeless. The President had just instructed MacArthur: "We consider that the preservation of your forces is now the primary consideration. Consolidation of forces into beachheads is concurred in."

Administration figures in the White House, the Pentagon, and the New State Building were quietly frantic. The President presided over a council of war every morning, as soon as that day's communiqués were in. Telecom circuits to the Dai Ichi Building were in use twenty-four hours a day. The National Security Council was in almost constant session. And all of it appeared to be in vain. Truman covered memorandum pages with his random thoughts. On one surviving page from that Christmas he scrawled: ". . . conference after conference on the jittery situation facing the country. Attlee, Formosa, Communist China, Chiang Kai-shek, Japan, Germany,

France, India, etc. I have worked for peace for five years and six months and it looks like World War III is near."

It was the worst year's end since the Bulge in 1944. The Communists recrossed the 38th Parallel the day after Christmas. Three days later the Joint Chiefs told MacArthur that while "a successful resistance [to aggression] would be of great importance to our national interest," it wasn't worth "serious losses." If he was forced back to the Kum River, they told him, they would order him "to commence a withdrawal to Japan." Replying on December 30, he called upon the administration to "recognize the state of war imposed by the Chinese authorities." It was his recommendation to follow this up by "dropping from 30 to 50 atomic bombs on air bases and other sensitive points" in Manchuria, and landing an amphibious force of 500,000 Chinese Nationalist troops from Formosa, supported by two divisions of U.S. Marines, at either end of the border between Korea and China. He added that further Communist incursions into Korea should be precluded "by laying down, after the defeat of the Chinese," a belt of radioactive cobalt all along the Yalu.*

That same Saturday South Koreans abandoned Seoul for the second time since spring. Temperatures along the Parallel fell below zero and stayed there. The Communists attacked every night. MacArthur's lines bent and began to buckle, and on New Year's Eve, at the very hour of "Auld Lang Syne," the greatest onslaught of all came billowing down through the dense snow and sailed into the U.N. lines.

* This from two mutually supporting interviews granted by the general during his retirement and withheld until his death.

Early Fifties Montage

CONGRESS REPEALS OLEO TAX

BATTLESHIP MISSOURI RUNS AGROUND

Best actress of 1950: Judy Holliday in **Born Yesterday**
Best supporting actor of 1950: George Sanders in **All About Eve**

Sunset Boulevard   The Asphalt Jungle   Twelve O'Clock High
Tight Little Island   The Third Man

FRANKIE SEEN SWOONING INTO OBSCURITY

It doesn't quite jell with me, T.J. When you glim the over-all picture you savvy that there are certain rock-bottom slants which have got to be considered before the final wrap-up if you're going to housebreak it for the top brass — If it's going to grab them where they live

Queeg looked up in horror. A vast dark bulk was bearing down on the Caine. Queeg opened and closed his mouth three times without uttering a sound, then he choked out, "All engines back full — bah — bah — belay that — All stop."

The bag of groceries that cost a city housewife $5 in 1935-1939 now costs her $9.83, the Bureau of Labor Statistics reported today

Only you can prevent forest fires.

When the sun in the morning creeps over the hill
And kisses the roses round my windowsill
Then my heart fills with laughter when I hear the trill
Of the birds in the treetops on Mocking Biird Hill

WOMEN'S SKIRTS RISE TO MID-CALF

What'll you have? PABST!

Chinese checkers — an ingenious new marble game

an odd-looking, snub-nosed little car drew some mildly curious stares. Few of the onlookers realized that it was a postwar model of the Volkswagen, the car which Hitler once promised to put in every German garage. With an air-cooled rear engine, and a luggage compartment under the hood, it was the first of 600 which Germany is shipping to the U.S. to sell at $1,280 to $1,977.

To at least one observer, it seemed that the men who sadly watched the humiliation of Joe Louis last week in Yankee Stadium were really feeling sorry for themselves. So many, in the uncomfortable long span of Louis's greatness, had themselves picked up fortyish weight and lost twentyish confidence.

I keep picturing all these little kids playing some game in this big field of rye and all. Thousands of little kids, and nobody's around — nobody big, I mean — except me. And I'm standing on the edge of some crazy cliff. What I have to do, I have to catch everybody if they start to go over the cliff . . . I'd just be the catcher in the rye and all. I know it's crazy but that's the only thing I'd really like to be. I know it's crazy.

BEST SELLERS: Fiction
The Cardinal by Henry Morton Robinson
From Here to Eternity by James Jones
Melville Goodwin, U.S.A. by John P. Marquand
Dinner at Antoine's by Frances Parkinson Keyes
A Rage to Live by John O'Hara

Best actor of 1951: Humphrey Bogart in **The African Queen**
Best actress of 1951: Vivien Leigh in **A Streetcar Named Desire**

An American in Paris   The Red Badge of Courage   Detective Story
The Lavender Hill Mob   Strangers on a Train   Quo Vadis   The River

BEST SELLERS: Nonfiction
Betty Crocker's Picture Cook Book
Look Younger, Live Longer by Gaylord Hauser
A King's Story by the Duke of Windsor
The Greatest Story Ever Told by Fulton Oursler
The Far Side of Paradise by Arthur Mizener

HEARST DEAD AT 88

Irene, goodnight, Irene, goodnight,
Goodnight, Irene, goodnight, Irene,
I'll kiss you in my dreams

III

SOWING THE WIND
1951–1960

Eighteen

A HOUSE DIVIDED

SEOUL FELL AGAIN on January 4, 1951. Once more the Communists achieved a major breakthrough, cutting off the U.S. 2nd Division at Wonju in the center of the Korean peninsula and rupturing the entire U.N. front. Lieutenant General Matthew B. Ridgway, MacArthur's new Eighth Army commander, had 200,000 men—half of them Koreans—to match the enemy's 400,000. In Washington Acheson was depressed by "the stench of spiritless defeat."

The U.N. lines held. Ridgway plugged the Wonju gap, throwing in his reserves, exploiting his superiority in the air, and adroitly moving in troops from his flanks. By the middle of January the fury of the enemy's New Year's Eve drive had been spent, and in the last week of the month the U.N. went over to the counteroffensive. The end of February found the Eighth Army back in the outskirts of Seoul. Ridgway recaptured the city on the night of March 14–15, and two weeks later the two great armies again squatted opposite one another on the 38th Parallel, almost exactly where they had been three months earlier—or, for that matter, nine months earlier, at the outbreak of the war.

A generation still flushed by the mighty triumphs of World War II and dazzled more recently by the miracle at Inchon could not accept the stalemate gracefully. To many Americans, the language of containment—the advocacy of limited objectives as an alternative to unlimited warfare—sounded sour and heretical. A *Life* editorial rejected "the pap" and the "pernicious fallacy" of "'coexistence' with Soviet communism." China lobbyists scorned administration reluctance to invade Manchuria as "appeasement," and ultraconservative Republicans found Dean Acheson's calls for restraint just short of treason.

Prewar isolationism was now passing through an extraordinary transformation. In December, as thirty-three divisions of Chinese began pouring through the sieve of MacArthur's defenses, two isolationists had publicly washed their hands of the Korean expedition. Speaking in Charlottesville, Virginia, on December 12, Joseph P. Kennedy had called upon his countrymen to "mind our own business and interfere only when someone threatens . . . our homes." Herbert Hoover had then joined Kennedy on December 17. American arms, he reasoned, could never triumph in a global conflict with Communist armies, but U.S. air and sea power *could* dominate the oceans and defend North and South America. He recommended that they resign themselves to that, meantime feeding "the hungry of the world" and—Hoover's perennial solution to national crises—balancing the budget.

Alert isolationologists noted something new, however. Hoover's go-it-alone hypothesis wasn't as lonely as it at first seemed and was not, indeed, confined to the western hemisphere. He wanted to hold the Atlantic and Pacific "with one frontier on Britain and the other on Japan, Formosa, and the Philippines." On the Senate floor Robert A. Taft, Hoover's successor as leader of the Republican right, made the same concession. Taft accepted the need to protect "the island democracies" if they were attacked and if a successful defense was possible. The Hoover-Taft doctrine, variously called the principle of Fortress America or Continentalism, was being set forth by New Year's Day as a viable alternative to NATO. The argument over which was best came to dominate all other news from Capitol Hill. Newspapermen called it the Great Debate.

The immediate issue before the country was an appropriation for four U.S. divisions which Truman had pledged to NATO. On January 5, 1951, Taft told the Senate, "The commitment of a land army to Europe is a program never approved by Congress into which we should not drift." Three days later Senator Wherry introduced Senate Resolution 8, opposing the assignment of U.S. ground forces to Europe pending the adoption of congressional policy, and on February 15 a majority of House Republicans signed a manifesto endorsing Hoover's Continentalism. Taft's adversaries were determined to depict him as an obstructionist, but what they failed to understand,

and he neglected to clarify, was the prop behind his whole position: the fact that the Constitution assigned war-making powers to Capitol Hill, not the White House. He did not mean to hobble the executive branch. On January 15 he declared that he was "quite prepared to sit down with the President . . . or anyone on the majority side, and try to work out a program which could command the unanimous and consistent support of the people of the United States." But Truman now had no intention of sharing the growing powers of the modern Presidency, accumulated through precedents dating back to Roosevelt's Hundred Days.

From the perspective of the 1970s, one of the most remarkable aspects of the debate was the tacit agreement on both sides to accept certain postulates which, twenty years later, were far from being accepted as eternal truths. "The free world" was a phrase favored by administration rhetoricians as well as those on the Hill, and by unanimous consent it included Chiang's Formosa, Rhee's South Korea, Bao Dai's Vietnam, Salazar's Portugal, Farouk's Egypt, Franco's Spain, Batista's Cuba, Perón's Argentina, French Algeria, the military dictatorship ruling Haiti, and all European colonies in Africa and Asia. Continentalists and internationalists alike assumed that any application of U.S. military power would be benign, and that no matter who won the debate, the American people would accept the result without demonstrations, protests, or even discussion. All debaters took it for granted that Communism was monolithic—that a central intelligence guided all Red activities, from Shanghai to the Elbe, so that any move, anywhere, by any Marxist, was presumed to have been made after calculating its effect on all of the free world. So closely held was this extraordinary belief that afterward President Truman would write in his memoirs:

> We were seeing a pattern in Indo-China and Tibet timed to coincide with the attack in Korea as a challenge to the Western world. It was a challenge by the Communists alone, aimed at intensifying the smoldering anti-foreign feeling among most Asian peoples. Our British allies and many statesmen of Europe saw in the Chinese moves a ruse to bring to a halt American aid in the rebuilding of Europe.

The debate arose over substantive disagreements between Hoover-Taft Republicans and Truman-Acheson Democrats, but it was far from being a party issue. Joseph Kennedy was still a Democrat; so were Senators George and Douglas, both of whom held that a President could not send soldiers abroad without congressional approval. Republican Senators Lodge and Knowland, on the other hand, believed that since the Senate had already approved of NATO in principle, Truman could provide the troops to implement it. Thomas E. Dewey, Earl Warren, Harold Stassen, and John Foster Dulles also threw their weight behind NATO, and in the end it was testimony by a future Republican President which determined the outcome of the Debate.

The witness was Eisenhower. General Marshall had spoken eloquently of the need for what was being called "collective security," but Marshall had been identified with Roosevelt-Truman policies too long to be considered above the battle. This was not true of Eisenhower, who had left Columbia to become supreme commander of the western European defense force only the week before Christmas. There was, he told Congress, no acceptable alternative to "the rearmament and defense of western Europe." He reported that the will to resist Stalin was strong among Europeans, recommended that the United States assume leadership of the North Atlantic alliance, and urged a larger U.S. military presence in Europe, with no congressional strings attached to future increases.

Taft protested that this would make the matter "more hazy and indefinite and uncertain in outline," but the debate was over, and he had lost it. As James Reston observed in the *New York Times*, Eisenhower had what Acheson lacked, "political support in the country." Moreover, he had "Republican support, a commodity that has been in short supply at the State Department ever since Senator McCarthy, Republican of Wisconsin, invaded West Virginia last spring." Wherry's resolution was withdrawn, and on April 4 Congress accepted a substitute measure approving the dispatch of the four divisions to Europe. The President was admonished not to send more without "further congressional approval," but there was nothing to stop his doing it.

It had been a hard winter for Republicans. Out of office for eighteen years, and unaware of the political strength gathering behind General Eisenhower, they looked toward more bleak seasons ahead. McCarthy was now the most famous figure in the party. In November he had gone into Maryland to purge Millard Tydings. It had been a disgraceful campaign. Tydings had been opposed by John Marshall Butler, a Republican nonentity. Backing Butler, McCarthy and the *Washington Times-Herald* pooled their talents to produce a one-issue tabloid called *From the Record*. It appeared on every Maryland doorstep the night before the election. In it was every shabby lie McCarthy had used against the Democratic senator, the whole topped off by a fake photograph doctored to make it appear that Tydings was shaking hands with Earl Browder. Tydings lost by 40,000 votes. He had been considered invincible. If he could be eliminated, no one was safe. Looking around at his senatorial colleagues on the morning after the election, a senior Democrat asked, "For whom does the bell toll?" He answered dryly, "It tolls for thee."

The following month an incident at Washington's Sulgrave Club offered a sign of how far Lincoln's party had fallen. Leaving a dinner there on the eve of Drew Pearson's fifty-third birthday, Senator Nixon found a drunken Senator McCarthy in the men's room, beating up Pearson. "This one's for you, Dick," McCarthy jeered, belting the columnist in the face. He added, "I'm going to prove a theory. If you knee a man in the balls hard enough, blood'll come out of his eyeballs." Nixon stepped in and said, "Let a Quaker stop this fight." He took McCarthy's arm. "Come on, Joe," he said, "it's time for you to go home." McCarthy said, "No, not till he goes first. I'm not going to turn my back on that son of a bitch." After Pearson had gone, McCarthy confessed to Nixon that he couldn't remember where he had left his car. For a half-hour the two of them searched the area, the California senator reading license plates while the Wisconsin senator lurched after him in the dark. Nixon found it and McCarthy roared off. It would have been better for Joe to sleep it off before driving, just as it would have been better for party morale if some other Republican had won the allegiance of millions, but the party had little choice; it had run out of idols some time ago.

Then came spring, and all that changed. On April 11 Harry Truman presented them with a martyred hero. He fired Douglas MacArthur, turned the Great Debate into a greater debate, and touched off the country's greatest emotional convulsion between V-J Day and Dallas twelve years later.

Unlike Eisenhower, MacArthur was not widely admired by fighting men. But generals are not measured by popularity. On any rating of performance, MacArthur eclipses other U.S. military leaders of his generation, and he may have been the most brilliant commander in the country's history. In 1918 he was named commander of the Rainbow Division in France, thereby becoming, at thirty-eight, the youngest general in the Army. Coming out of retirement to lead U.S. land troops against the Japanese, and then ruling postwar Japan as a kind of presidential viceroy, Douglas MacArthur had, by 1951, become a deity for many Americans. In forty-eight years as an officer, he had learned and practiced every soldierly virtue, with one exception: he made a poor second in command.

We shall never know what was in his mind that terrible winter after the Chinese came into the war. This much seems certain: he had lost his fighting spirit. According to Major General Chester V. Clifton, then aide to General Bradley and later military aide to Presidents Kennedy and Johnson, the Joint Chiefs of Staff decided as early as January that the general would have to be recalled on military, not political grounds: "What really counted was that MacArthur had lost confidence in himself and was beginning to lose the confidence of his field officers and troops. . . . And when he committed the final error of insubordination to the Commander-in-Chief —and there's absolutely no question about that—they had no trouble at all deciding what had to be done." Most Washingtonians doubted that the President had the nerve to tell him off, however. The *Washington Post* headline on the morning of April 11 read: MACARTHUR RECALL RULED OUT BY PRESIDENT, HILL HEARS; REPRIMAND IS STILL SEEN POSSIBLE.

By then the entire country knew of the dispute between the two men. The spirit of Wake had been long forgotten. As early as December the general had begun sniping at the President in the press, sending sharply worded letters to *U.S. News and World Report* and the president of the United Press. "I should have fired MacArthur then and there," Truman later said. Instead he had the Joint Chiefs tell the general that "no speech, press release, or public statement" on policy was to be released without prior clearance in Washington. After Christmas the President wrote MacArthur, praising his talents while gently reminding him that it was a presidential responsibility to "act with great prudence as far as extending the area of hostilities is concerned." To make certain that MacArthur understood the directive, two of the Chiefs—Collins and Hoyt S. Vandenberg—flew to Tokyo on January 12, delivered the letter to him in the Dai Ichi Building, and told him they were prepared to provide any additional clarification he might require. He said he needed none. During the next two months he was inaccessible to reporters. Then, in Dean Acheson's words, he perpetrated "a major act of sabotage of a Government operation . . . sabotage of an operation of which he had been informed, and insubordination of the grossest sort to his commander in chief."

The President had felt it was time for a cease-fire and peace negotiations. On March 20 he drafted a statement saying so, and copies were sent to each of the U.N. allies for comment. The Joint Chiefs dispatched the text to Tokyo in confidence, whereupon, to their amazement and horror, MacArthur called in the press and announced that he was prepared to negotiate with the enemy on his own terms. This torpedoed the Truman plan while achieving nothing. The general offered Peking annihilation, and as Walter Lippmann dryly noted, "Regimes do not negotiate about their survival." The Red Chinese merely reaffirmed their faith in victory. The peace offensive had failed before it could get started, leaving the President in a thin-lipped rage. He later wrote, "MacArthur left me no choice. I could no longer tolerate his insubordination." Then, before he could act, he was confronted by the last straw: a letter from the general to Congressman Joe Martin.

Martin, the Republican leader in the House, was one of several men on the Hill who had been treating MacArthur as a friendly foreign prince. Another of them, Republican Senator Homer Ferguson of Michigan, actually proposed that a congressional committee go to Tokyo so they could learn, from the general's own lips, what the goals of American policy should be and how to reach them. Since Martin was known to be one of Truman's more ferocious critics, MacArthur must have known that the only result of a letter to him would be mischief. On April 5 Martin rose in the House, declaring, "I owe it to the American people to tell the information I have from a great and reliable source." The information was a full-fledged assault on the administration by the general and a demand for the deploying of Nationalist Chinese troops on the Korean front. Later that day word came from London that MacArthur had made the same statements, for publication, in an interview with Lieutenant General H. G. Martin of the British Army. That evening Acheson received word that the President wanted to confer with him and General Marshall the next morning, immediately after the cabinet meeting. "I was," Acheson said in his memoirs, "in little doubt what the subject of our discussion would be."

The next day was April 7, a Friday. None of those close to him now doubted what Truman's response to MacArthur's latest insubordinations should be, but Acheson suggested that he wait until after the weekend for an opinion from the Joint Chiefs. On Monday Marshall reported that the Chiefs unanimously recommended that MacArthur be stripped of all his commands and replaced by Lieutenant General Matthew B. Ridgway, and that he and Bradley concurred in the recommendation. The next step was notifying MacArthur, and it cannot be said that this was handled well. Learning that the *Chicago Tribune* had the story, Truman snapped, "He's not going to be allowed to quit on me. He's going to be fired!" He ordered Bradley to push the thing through as quickly as possible. From the Pentagon Bradley sent word to Secretary of the Army Frank Pace, who was in Korea, advising him of the change of command and telling him to fly to Japan at once to inform MacArthur. Unfortunately for those who wished to soften the blow to the general's pride, Pace was cut off by a power failure, trapped in a tent during a hailstorm. Meanwhile the White House press secretary announced the news to a hastily called 1 A.M. press conference, releasing the text of the message which, Truman mistakenly thought, had just been delivered in Tokyo:

To General MacArthur from the President.

> I deeply regret that it becomes my duty as President and Commander-in-Chief of the United States military forces to replace you as Supreme Commander, Allied Powers; Commander-in-Chief, United Nations Command; Commander-in-Chief, Far East; and Commanding General, U.S. Army, Far East.
>
> You will turn over your commands, effective at once, to Lieutenant General Matthew B. Ridgway. You are authorized to have issued such orders as are necessary to complete desired travel to such place as you select.
>
> My reasons for your replacement will be made public concurrently with the delivery to you of the foregoing message.

But it wasn't concurrent; the hailstorm fixed that. As Pace waited for it to abate, reporters at the White House hastily copied the presidential statement—"With deep regret I have concluded that General of the Army Douglas MacArthur is unable to give his wholehearted support to the policies of the United States and of the United Nations . . ."—and sent it flashing around the world. In Tokyo, where the time was 3 P.M., an aide who happened to be listening to a news broadcast told Mrs. MacArthur and then the general, who was lunching with Senator Warren Magnuson of Washington.

MAC IS SACKED, the London *Evening Standard* announced, and Murray Schumach of the *New York Times* cabled from Seoul, "The widespread feeling among officers of field rank is that the relationship between General Headquarters in Tokyo and the Eighth Army in Korea will become more pleasant." But that was not the reaction in the United States. There a large part of the public, frustrated by the war no one could win, registered its displeasure with Harry Truman in every way short of actual violence. Flags were flown upside down or at half-mast from Eastham, Massachusetts, to Oakland, California. In San Gabriel, California, and Worcester, Massachusetts, Truman was burned in effigy; Ponca City, Oklahoma, burned an effigy of Acheson. Petitions were circulated. Clergymen fulminated in their pulpits. New anti-Truman jokes were heard: "This wouldn't have happened if Truman were alive," and "I'm going to have a Truman beer—just like any other beer except that it hasn't got a head." The *Los Angeles Herald-Examiner* suggested that the President was befuddled by drugs, and the *Daily Oklahoman* called the dismissal "a crime carried out in the dead of night," overlooking the fact that the dead of night in Oklahoma was broad daylight in Tokyo.

The Los Angeles City Council adjourned "in sorrowful contemplation of the political assassination" of MacArthur. The California, Florida, and Michigan legislatures passed resolutions censuring Truman. In Charlestown, Maryland, a woman was told she couldn't send a telegram to the White House calling the President a moron; she and the clerk rummaged through a *Roget's Thesaurus* until they found the acceptable "witling." Other Western Union offices were more permissive. Among the wires from constituents inserted in the *Congressional Record* by proud representatives on the Hill were IMPEACH THE IMBECILE; WE WISH TO PROTEST THE LATEST OUTRAGE ON THE PART OF THE PIG IN THE WHITE HOUSE; IMPEACH THE JUDAS IN THE WHITE HOUSE WHO SOLD US DOWN THE RIVER TO THE LEFT WINGERS AND THE UN; SUGGEST YOU LOOK FOR ANOTHER HISS IN BLAIR HOUSE; WHEN AN EX-NATIONAL GUARD CAPTAIN FIRES A FIVE-STAR GENERAL IMPEACHMENT OF THE NATIONAL GUARD CAPTAIN IS IN ORDER; IMPEACH THE B WHO CALLS HIMSELF PRESIDENT; IMPEACH THE LITTLE WARD POLITICIAN STU-

PIDITY FROM KANSAS CITY; and IMPEACH THE RED HERRING FROM THE PRESIDENTIAL CHAIR.

The White House mail room was swamped. The President's press office ruefully acknowledged that in the first 27,363 letters and telegrams counted, critics of the dismissal outnumbered those who supported it twenty to one. George Gallup found that 69 percent of the voters backed MacArthur, and only 29 percent Truman. Truman was booed at Griffith Stadium—the first public booing of a President since Hoover in 1932. Senator Jenner said, "This country today is in the hands of a secret coterie which is directed by agents of the Soviet Union." Senator McCarthy told a Milwaukee meeting that the President was "a son of a bitch" surrounded by henchmen drunk on "bourbon and benedictine," and Congressman Martin, in whose office the first GOP caucus was held the morning after the dismissal, told reporters that "the question of impeachments was discussed," implying that not just Truman but his entire administration might be tried.

After that caucus Martin invited MacArthur to address a joint session of Congress. The general accepted immediately; for an orator of his gifts, this was the chance of a lifetime. He was accepting his ouster philosophically, even serenely. "I have just left him," Major General Courtney Whitney told the press. "He received the word of the President's dismissal from command magnificently. He never turned a hair. His soldierly qualities were never more pronounced. This has been his finest hour." On April 17 the *Bataan* put down at the San Francisco airport and he set foot on his native soil for the first time since his first retirement from the Army fourteen years earlier. As he appeared at the head of the gangway, his gold-encrusted hat and his dramatic trench coat bathed in spotlights, the elated crowd surged toward him. Two hours were required for his motorcade to crawl through fourteen miles of cheering people to the St. Francis Hotel, where the city's police force linked arms to save him, his wife, and thirteen-year-old Arthur MacArthur II from being trampled to death. Next day one hundred thousand Californians hurrahed again when he stood on the steps of San Francisco's City Hall and declared, "The only politics I have is contained in a single phrase known well by all of you—God Bless America!"

At Washington National Airport MacArthur was greeted by a seventeen-gun salute and the Joint Chiefs, who presented him with a silver tea service. There was an awkward moment then. He was cordial to the Chiefs, unaware of their role in his martyrdom, but frosty toward the President's representative, an old National Guard crony of Truman's. Harry Vaughan slipped away muttering, and the way was clear for the hero's triumphant ride through three hundred thousand rooting Washingtonians. The hour's most memorable moment came at 12:30 P.M., April 19, when the listening country heard the radio networks pick up the House doorkeeper's announcement: "Mr. Speaker, General of the Army Douglas MacArthur."

The general strode to the rostrum and stood erect and impassive as the senators and congressmen cheered until they were hoarse. "I address you," he said at last, "with neither rancor or bitterness in the fading twilight of life, with but one purpose in mind: To serve my country." They went wild again. And again. And again. Altogether his thirty-four-minute address was interrupted by thirty ovations. Of those who argued that America could not fight a two-front war he said, "I can think of no greater expression of defeatism. If a potential enemy can divide his strength on two fronts, it is for us to counter his effort. You cannot appease or otherwise surrender to Communism in Asia without simultaneously undermining our efforts to halt its advance in Europe." His voice dropped a register: "Why, my soldiers asked of me, surrender military advantages to an enemy in the field?" After a pause he almost whispered, "I could not answer."

In tears, he said at the end: "I am closing out my fifty-two years of military service. When I joined the Army, even before the turn of the century, it was the fulfillment of all my boyish hopes and dreams. Since I took the oath at West Point, the hopes and dreams have all vanished. But I still remember the refrain of one of the most popular barracks ballads of that day, which proclaimed most proudly that old soldiers never die, they just fade away. And like the old soldier of that ballad, I now close my military career and just fade away, an old soldier who tried to do his duty as God gave him the right to see that duty. Good-bye."

Sperry Rand had announced that MacArthur had joined its board of directors, but obviously he was not going to fade away there or elsewhere. His peroration had struck so deep a chord in the hearts of his admirers that some of them thought of him as divine. "We heard God speak here today," cried Representative Dewey Short of Missouri, "God in the flesh, the voice of God." Herbert Hoover, another President whom the general had crossed, now spoke of him as "a reincarnation of St. Paul into a great General of the Army who came out of the East." One senator said, "It's disloyal not to agree with General MacArthur," and six thousand Daughters of the American Revolution, whom he addressed later in the afternoon, agreed. It was the DAR's Sixtieth Continental Congress in Constitution Hall. The ladies had voted to remove their hats so they wouldn't obscure one another's view of the general. He didn't disappoint them. "In this hour of crisis, all patriots look to you," he said, and "I have long sought personally to pay you the tribute that is in my heart."

Reading her minutes the next day, the DAR recording secretary general, Mrs. Warren Shattuck Currier, observed that the general's speech was "probably the most important event" in the history of the hall. Instantly Mrs. Thomas B. Throckmorton was on her feet. She moved, and the convention agreed with one voice, to strike the word "probably." By then MacArthur was in New York, the center of a historic demonstration. Over 2,859 tons of litter were being dumped on him, four times the previous record (for Eisenhower). Police put the number of spectators at 7,500,000, which was absurd, but it was certainly the largest crowd Manhattan had ever seen. Forty thousand longshoremen walked off their jobs to be there. Schools were closed. People crossed themselves as the general's limousine passed. Women sobbed into handkerchiefs. Eighteen victims of hysteria were hospitalized. Enterprising notion vendors with MacArthur buttons, pennants, and corncob pipes from the 1948 MacArthur-for-President campaign were sold out, and the only other business in business was Tin Pan Alley, whose tunesmiths were turning out five recordings of:

> *Old soldiers never die, never die, never die,*
> *Old soldiers never die,*
> *They just fade away.*[*]

"The country," said Senator James Duff of Pennsylvania, "is on a great emotional binge." Florists were offering a Douglas MacArthur tea rose ("needing no coddling or favor") and MacArthur orchids, cacti, gladioli, geraniums, peonies, and irises. At the Waldorf Astoria, where the MacArthurs checked into a $130-a-day suite, the switchboard began receiving three thousand calls a day from people

---

[*] A British army ballad, it was based on an American gospel hymn, "Kind Words Can Never Die."

who wanted to speak to the general. There he paid his respects to Hoover and was himself visited by Cardinal Spellman and a parade of powerful Republicans: Senator Taft, Senator Styles Bridges, Colonel McCormick, Henry Luce, and William Randolph Hearst. It was evident that politics was very much on the general's mind. In a series of speeches before state legislatures, beginning in Massachusetts, he attacked Truman's "appeasement on the battlefield" and his "timidity" in domestic and foreign policy. The President let these criticisms pass until MacArthur, speaking to an American Legion convention, claimed that his March offer to negotiate with the enemy had wrecked a "secret plan" by U.S. leaders to abandon Formosa to the Chinese Communists and give Peking a U.N. seat in exchange for peace in Korea. Truman said that was a lie, and that the general knew it. But by then the emotional binge was over. MacArthur was in politics up to his pipe and braided cap, and everybody knew it now, for he had been chosen to deliver the keynote address at the 1952 Republican National Convention.

Ten days after MacArthur's dismissal public opinion polls noted the first signs of a decline in his popularity. Simultaneously, another Communist offensive burst upon the U.N. line in Korea. It came as no surprise to Ridgway. Observing the ominous buildup behind the enemy's earthworks, he had ordered a salient thrust forward into the middle of them. The salient fell to the Chinese in the first phase of their new push, and over the next two weeks, as one ROK unit after another broke and ran, the Eighth Army once more reeled backward across the 38th Parallel. But the Reds again failed to break through. After a month they paused, exhausted, whereupon General James A. Van Fleet reversed the momentum of battle with a skillful counterattack. No sooner had he straightened the line than the Chinese bent it southward. Ridgway bent it right back. By the end of May 1951, he had cleared South Korea of Communist troops, and the jagged front stretched across the waist of the Korean peninsula, from the Sea of Japan on the east to the Yellow Sea on the west. The western anchor for both armies lay near the obscure village of Panmunjom.

The fighting was grim, colorless, and depressing. To enliven it, Ridgway's staff gave geographical features homely American names —"the Kansas-Wyoming Line," "the Utah Line," "Porkchop Hill," "the Punch Bowl"—a practice which would ultimately lead to Vietnam's grotesque "Operation Cedar Rapids" and "Operation Attleboro." Gone were World War II's crisp code words: Torch, Husky, Overlord, Anvil, Dragoon, Iceberg. If the horrors of war could not be liquidated, it seemed, military public relations men would wrap them in euphemisms until they had been thoroughly Americanized. Like the ubiquitous comic books and the turkey dinners served in foxholes on Thanksgiving, battlefield nomenclature would remind the men of home.

People at home stopped following news about the war. Suspecting that literally no one was reading about it any more, the editors of an Oregon newspaper ran one war story two days in a row—the same text, same byline, same head, and even the same position, halfway down column two on page one. Their hunch was confirmed; not a single subscriber noticed the repetition. In the Nebraska town of Hastings, Eric Goldman reported, an Army corporal named William Jensen, who had been shot in the thigh during the first Chinese attack, limped downtown, stared at the prosperous stores on Second Street, and said, "Man, I never saw anything like it. This town is just one big boom."

It was; all America was. Although at war abroad, the country had been neither invaded nor attacked, and nothing cherished was in peril. Unlike Kipling's nineteenth-century Tommy Atkins, who also fought in distant lands, the American soldier did not even have the feeling that he was contributing to the glory of empire. He was fighting battles whose sole objective was peace in another land, participating in a police action whose felons were not going to be punished, and it wasn't good enough. In James A. Michener's later view, "starting with the Korean War in 1950 our nation developed a seductive and immoral doctrine which I questioned at the time and about which I have become increasingly dubious. The mistaken doctrine was this: that we could wage with our left hand a war in which a few men chosen at random sacrificed their lives, while with our right hand we maintained an undisturbed economy in which the fortunate stay-at-homes could frolic and make a lot of money."

Seen in this light, the acclaim for MacArthur appears to have been an escape valve for a thwarted people. In addition it may have goaded administration peace efforts, which badly needed the energies of dedicated men. Arranging an armistice was a delicate business. Officially, the United States government had not even conceded the existence of North Korea and Communist China. The Chinese continued to insist that all its troops along the 38th Parallel were volunteers and therefore not subject to its discipline. Russia disclaimed any responsibility for the conflict. The State Department was wary of discussing peripheral issues—Formosa, Indochina, and diplomatic recognition of Peking and Pyongyang. The very fact that negotiations were under consideration would increase casualties as field commanders sparred to improve their positions. Lastly, there was no reliable go-between for peace feelers. Discretion was essential. Experience had demonstrated the impossibility of keeping a secret at the United Nations. Neutral nations, notably India, were also leaky; indeed, Krishna Menon, India's ambassador to the U.N., was an Americophobe who seemed bent upon terms which would humiliate the United States.

George Kennan found a way out. On leave from the State Department, he called Jacob Malik from Princeton and suggested they meet for unofficial conversations in Russian. These began on May 31 at Malik's Long Island summer home. After an awkward beginning they settled into a series of talkathons, interrupted only when Malik felt the need to "consider matters"; that is, to check with Moscow. Eventually he suggested initiatives between commanders in the field, and these were taken, although early results were discouraging. The Chinese remained suspicious. Ridgway, more tactful and less haughty than his predecessor, did persuade them to sit down in the ancient city of Kaesong, between the lines, on July 10, but quarrels about the agenda followed. In early autumn the talks were moved to Panmunjom. While they were better than nothing, communications kept breaking down. Korean hostilities dragged on through a second year of battle and into a third. American enthusiasm for the war, in Acheson's tart phrase, had "reached an irreducible minimum."

By now cold war temperatures had sunk to arctic levels. Tension between the Communist and free worlds dominated world affairs. It was a kind of pollution which was found everywhere: in novels, plays, movies, magazine articles; in newspaper serials (Herbert Philbrick's *I Led Three Lives*, the account of an FBI informer who had been a Communist party member for nine years, ran in more than five hundred papers throughout the 1950s); and on radio and television. The Cincinnati Reds changed their name for a time. Social studies teachers either came down hard on the evils of "Communist slavery" or risked dismissal. The highest lecture fees went to anti-Communist zealots and the biggest Americanism awards to contestants whose reasons for loathing Communists and fellow travelers, or pinkos, were most persuasive.

Even Miss America aspirants had to state their opinions of Karl Marx, and the most popular writer of the new decade was a former Brooklyn lifeguard whose hymns to sex and anti-Communist sadism had, by the end of 1951, sold over thirteen million copies. Wiry, with a crew cut, loudly contemptuous of "longhairs," thirty-three-year-old Mickey Spillane had published his first Mike Hammer novel, *I, the Jury* in 1947. As he grew more prolific, turning out *My Gun Is Quick, Vengeance Is Mine, One Lonely Night,* and *The Big Kill,* he was recognized as the latest expression of the vigilante streak of violence in the American national character. Mike Hammer was more than just another tough private eye. He brought his creator $50,000 a book by killing for justice and democracy. A typical scene in *One Lonely Night,* which appeared in 1951 and sold three million copies, ended with the gloat:

> "I killed more people tonight than I have fingers on my hands. I shot them in cold blood and enjoyed every minute of it. . . . They were Commies, Lee. They were Red sons-of-bitches who should have died long ago. . . . They never thought that there were people like me in this country. They figured us all to be soft as horse manure and just as stupid."

The nebulous figures behind Mike were variously described as "a new McCarthy," "another McCarthy," or a nameless reformer who had the courage to expose Commies in government, thereby winning the hatred of disloyal Ivy League graduates. To be consistent, Mike ought to have been a Jacobin hunting aristocrats, but much of the time Spillane wasn't coherent. Some of his passages were so dense that even the non sequitur was buried. In *The Girl Hunters,* while mourning for a McCarthy type named Leo Knapp, Mike reflects that "Reds just aren't the kind who can stand a big push. Like it or not, they are still a lousy bunch of peasants who killed to control but who can be knocked into line by the likes of us. They're shouting slobs who'll run like hell when class shows and they know this inside their feeble little heads." Class shows elsewhere when the author, pondering the gulf between Mike and Communist peasants, muses:

> Damn their stinking hides anyway. Damn them and their philosophies! Death and destruction were the only thing the Kremlin

crowd was capable of. They knew the value of violence and death and used it over and over in a wild scheme to smash everything flat but their own kind.

Then, presumably to distinguish between these apostles of death and destruction, whose currency is violence and death, and the clean, decent, American way, Mike tells a female captive what will happen if she tries to kill him with a shotgun whose barrels have been plugged with heavy clay.

"The barrel would unpeel like a tangerine and you'd get that whole charge right down your lovely throat and if you ever want to give a police medical examiner a job to gag a maggot, that's the way to do it. They'd have to go in and scrape your brains up with a silent butler and pick pieces of your skull out of the woodwork with needle-nosed pliers."

She vomits, and he continues:

"The worst of all is the neck because the head is gone and the neck spurts blood for a little bit while the heart doesn't know its vital nerve center is gone—and do you know how high the blood can spurt? No? Then let me tell you."

After throwing up again she says, "Man, are you mean." He wasn't as mean as comic books of the time, however. As a sop to reformers and child psychologists they ran pious credos. "This magazine is dedicated to the prevention of crime and subversion," appeared on the cover of one 1951 issue. "We hope that within its pages the youth of America will learn to know crime and treason for what they really are: sad, black, dead-end roads of fools and tears." But its pages taught American youth a lot more than that. Graphic drawings showed Negro corpses strung up by their wrists, boys driving white-hot pokers between thighs of disloyal girls, and girls, not to be outdone, stabbing Communist criminals in the eyes with icepicks ("P-put that down!!! NO! AG, AG, AG, UGG . . .").

These were recurring themes, together with rape, murder, stamping on children's faces, and drinking the blood of the opposite sex ("As she bites into his neck he feels a burning poisonous venom seeping through his veins paralizing [sic] his every muscle . . . He realizes the answer to it all!"). Phantom Lady's specialty was tying up victims and whipping them to death. How to hurt people was another common motif. Anatomical diagrams showed everything from "Eyes—finger jab or thumb gouge" to "Arch heel stamp," while the accompanying text explained, "There are certain spots in the body more sensitive than the rest. . . . The charts made for the use of government agents in training show just where those spots are and what to use against them." Some of the tableaux offered Mike Hammerism to the illiterate, as in the illustrations accompanying this message:

> So NOW YOU KNOW, fiends. Now you know WHY there is a ball game being played in the moonlight at midnight in the deserted Central City ball park. Look CLOSELY. SEE this STRANGE BASEBALL GAME! See the long strings of pulpy intestines that mark the base lines. See the two lungs and the liver that indicate the bases . . . the heart that is home plate. See Doc White bend and whisk the heart with the mangy scalp, yelling . . . "PLAY BALL . . . Batter up!" See the batter come to the plate swinging the legs, the arms, then throwing all but one away and standing in the box waiting for the pitcher to hurl the head in to him. See the catcher with the torso strapped on as a chest-protector, the infielders with their hand-mits [*sic*], the stomach-rosin bag, and all the other pieces of equipment that was once Central City's star pitcher, Herbie Satten.

Seasoned readers of the comics were not surprised to learn that villainous old Doc White, who had carved Herbie up, was an enemy agent. In that episode evil had won. More often Reds were depicted dangling from lynch ropes, pistol-whipped, buried alive, fed to sharks, or dangling from the bumpers of loyal Americans' jalopies— "These travel roads are tough on tires!" "But ya gotta admit, there's nothing like 'em for erasing faces!" "Yeah, even Stalin couldn't identify this meat!" The lesson was plain. Because organized society was helpless against the free world's enemies, the only hope lay with brutal men who weren't afraid to take the law into their own hands, men who were undeniably uncouth but obviously necessary. This was what people meant when they said, "I don't approve of McCarthy's methods, but he's got the right idea."

The right idea was to thumb your nose at authority, kick over the traces, take Commies down behind the gas works and break their necks. Ordinary men believed it because, like MacArthur, they were fed up with national policy. It was at loggerheads with everything they had learned as children, inimical to their traditions. Korea's war without victory was but one example. America, they had been taught, avoided entangling alliances. Now they were expected to forget all that. U.S. troops were the backbone of a NATO force which would comprise fifty divisions and 4,000 warplanes by the end of 1952. To support military bases around the globe, an unprecedented proportion of the national income was being poured into military hardware. In Washington the federal bureaucracy grew larger each month. Nor was that all; having suffered through its own Depression just a few years earlier, the United States now seemed to be doling out its new wealth to poor countries all over the world. The bill for all this was being passed along to U.S. taxpayers, who grew increasingly resentful.

Where could they turn? Their only seasoned allies were in the thinning ranks of prewar isolationism. The old America Firsters shared their dismay over America's new directions. "It's almost unbelievable in its grant of unlimited power to the Chief Executive," Vandenberg had written to his wife when he read the first Military Assistance Program. ". . . It would virtually make him the number one war lord of the earth." Taft had voted against it because it carried "an obligation to assist in arming, at our expense, the nations of Western Europe. With that obligation, I believe it will promote war in the world rather than peace"; and Senator Forrest Donnell of Missouri had condemned the concept of collective security as a "moral commitment" that would draw the United States into other peoples' wars.

Twenty years later those words would sound prophetic, but they did not seem so then. The right appeared to be the province of the discredited fossils who had applauded Munich. It occurred to almost no one in public life that the whole structure of international politics had become obsolescent on August 6, 1945, that the dropping of the first atomic bomb then had been a revolutionary act, and that all the panoply of diplomatic relations and military alliances—indeed, the very concept of the nation state—might now be as quaint and irrelevant as a senseless little barrack tune running through the mind of a seventy-year-old general. Armies and navies were useful only if threats to use them were believable. If a course of action has become incredible, all the assumptions based on it have lost their justification. In the atomic age, military solutions were still possible in disputes between little countries, or between little and big countries. Between great countries they meant nothing. One British military analyst saw this. Sir John Slessor said, "We have at last arrived at the point when war—in the sense of total world war as we have known it in our generation—has abolished itself as a practical instrument of policy." The flight of the *Enola Gay* over Hiroshima and of the *Great Artiste* over Nagasaki had demonstrated that warfare between superpowers would be a thousandfold more ghastly than the bloodiest Spillane fiction or the most revolting comic, and nothing since then had scattered this awful cloud. On the contrary, bombs had been growing much bigger.

After Japan's surrender, Los Alamos had gone into a temporary eclipse. Its celebrities left for college campuses, and key technicians moved to Albuquerque, where a new factory was about to begin assembly line production of nuclear weapons. Laboratories in the old Tech Area were stripped of equipment. Road repair was discontinued. Buildings decayed. After an inspection David Lilienthal reported to Washington that "We found a great many health hazards and fire hazards that were very damaging to morale." Nothing seemed likely to prevent the decay of Los Alamos into a ghost town —and then in the early 1950s something did. Overnight streets were paved. A hospital went up, then schools, and then a library. Stores, a theater, and a community center were built around a central mall; ground was broken for a stadium; athletes were recruited for a sports club called the "Los Alamos Atomic Bombers."

These signs of prosperity in the death business owed much to the dark, bushy-browed Hungarian named Edward Teller. His enthusiasm for ever greater explosions overcame moral qualms in the scientific community, the Pentagon, and the federal government. It is not too much to call him, as he was called, "the chief architect of the hydrogen bomb."

The H-bomb is the ultimate in deathmanship, a missile which may be anywhere from twenty-five to a thousand times more destructive than the weapons dropped in 1945. The energy for the A-bomb comes from fission, the splitting of uranium atoms; the H-bomb's power comes from fusion, the uniting of hydrogen atoms—the very process by which the sun gives light. Fusion can occur only at very high temperatures; therefore H-bombs are called thermonuclear weapons. Their theoretical possibilities had long been known, but after the horrors of Hiroshima conversations about them among atomic physicists were awed and guarded. The hypothetical new bomb was called the "Super." From time to time cryptic references to it appeared in the *Bulletin of the Atomic Scientists,* but the editors never defined it. In their opinion, the less the world knew about the Super, the better.

Teller disagreed. At Berkeley in the summer of 1942 he had been one of seven physicists who had mulled over the feasibility of man-made fusion, and he never forgot what he later called the thrilling "spirit of spontaneous expression, adventure and surprise." To his disappointment, the consideration of thermonuclear possibilities was discontinued in 1943. Since the temperatures required were so high that only a fission bomb could produce them, the fission riddle had to be solved first, anyhow, and once that happened, it was thought, they ought to stop. At about this time Teller began speaking of the mythic Super as "my baby." His colleagues were glad to leave it to him.

After V-J Day he said he would stay on at Los Alamos if he could start thermonuclear experiments. When the response was negative, he accepted an appointment at the University of Chicago's Institute for Nuclear Studies. The following year he returned for a conference on the Super, where he argued that the bigger bomb could be perfected in two years. He was in a minority. The leader of anti-Super physicists was Albert Einstein. Einstein thought it wrong even to consider construction of an H-bomb. Teller couldn't see why. The Hiroshima bomb, he pointed out, had been built because Nazi scientists were thought to be on the track of it. Now Soviet physicists were believed to be working on a thermonuclear device. Was Stalin any safer or saner than Hitler?

The turning point for the development of a new U.S. nuclear arsenal was the announcement, on September 23, 1949, that the Russians had exploded an atomic bomb. From this point on, the rise of the fusion bomb owed much to a series of stimuli which served to break down objections to it. First there was the discovery that Leningrad physicists had been investigating the possibility of fusing light nuclei as early as 1932. That convinced Alvarez and Ernest O. Lawrence; they came down hard on Teller's side, and the three of them became known in the scientific community as "the Supermen." The Supermen's chief adversaries were Einstein, Oppenheimer, and President James B. Conant of Harvard, the three biggest names in American science. All other things being equal, the opposition should have won easily, and in the beginning it did. On October 25, 1949, the Atomic Energy Commission met in Washington to weigh arguments in favor of a weapon which, if dropped on a major city, would instantly kill somewhere between 80 and 90 percent of the inhabitants. They rejected it. Apart from moral objections, the H-bomb project was thought to be so expensive and complex that it would slow down the mass production of A-bombs in Albuquerque, and even if it proved feasible, the only Russian targets large enough to justify its use were Moscow and Leningrad, both of which could be annihilated with fissionable materials.

That was a triumph for common sense, but it was only the beginning of the struggle. The Supermen had picked up an ally in Rear Admiral Lewis A. Strauss, USNR, one of AEC's five directors (the other four were then opposed), and they were gaining other converts in Secretary of Defense Louis Johnson, the Joint Chiefs, the Joint Congressional Committee on Atomic Energy, and Paul Nitze, director of the State Department's Policy Planning Staff. The prestige of the United States, the Supermen insisted, owed much to the dominance of American technology; if the Russians built the first fusion bomb, the U.S. would lose face. On January 13, 1950, Omar Bradley decided to approve the Super on the ground that as chairman of the JCS he could endorse no move which might lead to any Russian advantage, however temporary, in the accelerating arms race. Hiss had been convicted that month, setting the stage of McCarthyism, and four days after Bradley made his commitment word of the second stimulus favoring the H-bomb partisans came from London; Fuchs had been charged with treason. It was impossible to say with any certainty how much Fuchs had known, but he had sat in the highest councils of Anglo-American science, and official Washington was in a mood to overreact. Meeting in the Executive Office Building on January 31, a three-man *ad hoc* special committee—Secretaries Acheson and Johnson, AEC chairman Lilienthal—again pondered the advisability of a thermonuclear crash program. Lilienthal was outvoted. That afternoon President Truman announced that he had directed the AEC to develop "the 'hydrogen' or super bomb."

The consciences of many scientists were outraged. Speaking for them Oppenheimer said, "In some crude sense, which no vulgarity, no humor, no overstatement can quite extinguish, the physicists have known sin and this is a knowledge they cannot lose." The cover of the *Bulletin of Atomic Scientists* in each issue had carried a clock registering eight minutes to twelve; now it was moved up to three minutes before twelve. Under the leadership of Hans Bethe of

Cornell, twelve U.S. senior physicists issued a statement deploring Truman's decision. They declared: "We believe that no nation has the right to use such a bomb, no matter how righteous its cause. The bomb is no longer a weapon of war but a means of extermination of whole populations. Its use would be a betrayal of all standards of morality and of Christian civilization itself." Their sincerity was beyond question, but Bethe's indignation proved evanescent. In less than five months the resolution of the protestors was tested by the outbreak of the Korean War and the challenge of the new project to their scientific curiosity. The first was his undoing; he decided that patriotism required him to drop his objections to the H-bomb and plunge into the search for its early perfection—which he did with such vigor that his contribution to it became a major factor in its success. Curiosity was the greater goal for most, however. In June of 1951, on the first anniversary of North Korea's rupture of the 38th Parallel, Teller spoke before several distinguished associates at the Institute for Advanced Study at Princeton. Gordon Gray, the new chairman of the AEC, made notes of the discussion. They read in part:

> Out of the meeting came something which Edward Teller brought into the meeting with his own head, which was an entirely new way of approaching a thermonuclear weapon. . . . Calculations were made, Dr. Bethe, Dr. Teller, Dr. Fermi participating the most in this. Oppy [sic] very actively as well. . . . everyone around that table without exception, and this included Dr. Oppenheimer, was enthusiastic now that you had something foreseeable.

That same week Gray committed the AEC to the financing of America's first H-bomb plant. Thirteen years were to pass before the savage parody of Teller in the film *Dr. Strangelove*. By then the monsters of which he had dreamed at Berkeley would lie in underground silos, available at the touch of a button.

The first riddle to be solved was a math problem, or a series of them. Equations for the A-bomb had been complicated enough; the new ones went right off the blackboard. Each step in the completed device required a staggering number of precise calculations to gauge its impact on millions of tiny parts in the bomb, and since the steps succeeded one another in tiny fractions of a second—for all practical purposes they were instantaneous—the human mind could not cope with them. Nor were the calculating machines of 1951 much help. Despite its 500 miles of wire and 3,000,000 electrical connections, the instrument IBM had built for Harvard was nowhere near fast enough. Improved models were coming along, but the best of them, the new ENIAC, could recall only twenty-seven words. They were maddeningly temperamental. Storms put them out of commission. Tubes went out. Circuits went wrong. Repair crews couldn't find the trouble. Technicians would sit up night after night with a sick computer, spending months on one problem while other specialists in their design teams awaited an answer. Los Alamos added a day to the work week and round-the-clock shifts for computer crews. The Tech Area still marked time until one of the scientists, John von Neumann, decided to tackle the bottleneck. Neumann reflected the ambivalence of the Supermen; he called their goal "the hell weapon" and drove himself mercilessly in the search for it. In the 1930s he had acquired an international reputation in mathematics. His hobby was the construction of robots and mechanical toys, and now his most enduring contribution to the Superhunt became a kind of Supertoy. It could retain and remember 40,000 bits of "software"—computerspeak for data—and complete three months of equations in a day; he called it a "Mathematical Analyzer, Numerical Integrator and Computer." Only after the device was patented, and its name irretrievably registered with the AEC, did his colleagues realize that the acronym for it was MANIAC.

With maniacal help, then, the Supermen completed a sixty-five-ton H-bomb in the last year of the Truman Presidency. In that era of the Kansas-Wyoming Line and the Punch Bowl, it is perhaps unsurprising that they christened it "Mike." Mike was towed to Eniwetok atoll in the Marshalls and housed in a shed on the tiny island of Elugelab with various ion chambers, high-speed cameras, beta ray spectrographs, containers of uranium and heavy hydrogen, and other nuclear paraphernalia. There the ritual worked out seven years earlier on the semidesert near Alamogordo, New Mexico, was repeated. On the night of October 31–November 1, 1952, all ships withdrew forty miles while a team of volunteers made last-minute preparations. After they, too, had left, the countdown began on the boats over public address systems. At dawn the counters reached zero and Mike was immediately transformed into the first man-made star. Dumbfounded sailors saw a ball of fire rise five miles into the sky followed by a gigantic cauliflower-shaped cloud, all mauve and blue and gray-green, that rose twenty-five miles into the stratosphere while beneath it Elugelab burned, broke in two, and sank.

Divers found a mile-long, 175-foot-deep canyon in the ocean floor. The scientific observers calculated that the bomb's four-mile-wide fireball would have vaporized all of downtown Spokane or San Francisco, most of St. Louis or Pittsburgh, or everything in Manhattan from Central Park to Washington Square. Navy security was slack; descriptive letters were passed by censors. They were chilling; one witness wrote that "It would take at least ten suns" to equal the light of the explosion. Some of the letters found their way into local newspapers, and presently the whole world knew of the test and its awesome results. Nine months later Georgi Malenkov triumphantly announced in Moscow that "the United States no longer has a monopoly of the hydrogen bomb." Radioactive traces found in the skies over Asia by B-29 flying laboratories confirmed him. The British had meanwhile exploded their first atomic device, distinguished by a macabre Z-shaped cloud. The nuclear club was growing. The nightmare envisioned by Einstein, Oppenheimer, and Conant had come true, and the imbalance of terror had begun. "General annihilation," Einstein told reporters, "beckons."

Absolute weapons, it now developed, were to be provided with absolute transportation. In the early 1950s automation had not yet eliminated the human factor from bombing. Responsibility for America's nuclear arsenal was vested in the Strategic Air Command, which employed 270,000 men in a ceaseless B-29 shuffle around the globe, making certain that even if the United States ceased to exist, posthumous vengeance would be wreaked. SAC can hardly be called attractive. Each of its pilots was riding with more explosives than all the Allied air raids in World War II. Its generals put up billboards proclaiming PEACE IS OUR BUSINESS. They called sonic booms "the sound of freedom," and their annual maneuvers, in which who-hit-what-target was recorded in railroad boxcars stuffed with radar, were "the World Series of Bombing." Still, the generals and their pilots were people. As such, they were about to become obsolete.

Their replacements were to come from, of all places, the smoking ruins of the Third Reich's laboratories. Alone among World War II's belligerents, the Germans had foreseen the martial possibilities of rocket propulsion. The scientists who had hatched the V-1 and V-2 weapons were now the men of the hour, and SAC strategists were beating paths to their doors. With the thrust of rocket engines, a nuclear explosive could cross the Atlantic or the North Pole in less than a half-hour. SAC had considered rockets before and rejected them as too inaccurate. Their margin of error could not be honed below two-tenths of one percent. At a range of 5,000 miles this meant a deviation of ten miles, too much for an A-bomb. But it wasn't too much for an H-bomb. The sinking of Elugelab had cast matters in a new and brutal light. In the chilling words of *Fortune*, "Because of the quantum jump in the destructive power of the thermonuclear warhead, not to mention the still greater area of lethal fallout, delivery within eight or ten miles of the center of the target became militarily acceptable."

The admittance of the sinister word "fallout" into the language, and the expansion it implied in a bomb's circle of death, signaled a change in the whole concept of war. Another significant new term was "overdestroying." With the refinement of the H-bomb into a "fission-fusion-fusion" or FFF bomb—to the A-bomb trigger, and the fusion of the fuel, it added fusion of the bomb casing—the area of lethal fallout could be increased to 300 square miles.

It was at this point that people started digging. World War II's civil defense program had been something of a joke; the oceans had been too wide for Axis bombers to constitute a real menace, and the air-raid wardens in their flat white tin hats had been a little shamefaced about the whole thing. Now their long vigils made some sense. Reactivated, they supervised drills in schools. Elsewhere there was a brisk trade in amulets and quackery. Medicasters advertised lead-foil brassieres, lead girdles, aluminum pajamas, and drawstring bags to be pulled over the head in time of danger. One crank hawked a "U-235 Atomic Shock Cure" until the U.S. Public Health Service found its active ingredients to be bicarbonate of soda, table salt, and water. Another advocated shaving all pets so their hair wouldn't become radioactive. The SPCA protested, and nothing came of it.

Still, there was something unreal about *all* civil defense campaigns. The most determined, with the greatest potential for enterprising entrepreneurs, was the shelter program. In an attempt to encourage excavations, a construction company in Los Angeles staged a ground-breaking ceremony for one of the first family shelters in January 1951. A Mrs. Ruth Colhoun, a mother of three, ceremoniously turned over the first spadeful for television cameramen. She had contracted to pay $1,995 for an underground refuge with brightly painted concrete walls, shamrock green plastic carpeting, storage space concealed by clever sliding doors, and a lightweight Geiger counter. "I do a lot of canning and bottling in the summer," she cheerfully told the television audience, "and it will make a good storehouse." As an afterthought she added, "It will make a wonderful place for the children to play in, too."

For $3,000 you could have the "Mark I Kidde Kokoon." That included a three-way portable radio, air blower, wind-up clock, first aid kit, Sterno stove, radiation charts, protective apparel suits, chemical toilet, gasoline-driven generator, pick-and-shovel combination ("for digging out after blast"), and everything else needed for a family of five to spend three to five days underground.

For most people the sticking point was the problem of what to do on D-day about improvident neighbors who had neglected to build refuges of their own. After retreating to your own dugout you would have no room for them. It would be necessary to lock them out, and you might have to use force. Some kits began including pistols with this in mind, but the public wasn't prepared to be *that* realistic. In time the backyard cavities became curiosities. Some were converted to barbecue pits. Others were used to stow garden tools, snow tires, and children's bikes.

After a while stories of the horrors which would accompany a nuclear holocaust became familiar to Pentagon strategists, and they moved almost effortlessly from the consideration of megatons to megadeaths—each megadeath being the killing of one million persons, with ten or fifteen possible in a single day. The threat of a thermonuclear holocaust which could envelop the world in flame remained very real for some thoughtful people outside the military establishment, but they felt impotent. Cold-warriors had become deaf to warnings of doomsday, men in public life seemed paralyzed by McCarthyism, and intellectuals who had been in the grip of one international crisis or another since Munich could not summon the wit or strength to break the hold of this one.

Meanwhile, the passage of time had brought a new generation of Americans to maturity. Surely, sensitive men thought, the air-raid drills in public schools, with their apocalyptic implications, must have aroused the children. Their elders looked hopefully toward them and suffered a cruel disappointment.

In the twilight months of the Truman administration, college teachers gradually became aware of a slow, creeping rot in the country's intellectual life, which, it turned out, was the younger generation. It is curious to recall that in those years students were chastised for their apathy, but they were, and with justice; never had American youth been so withdrawn, cautious, unimaginative, indifferent, unadventurous—and silent.

The silent generation was a phenomenon of the 1950s, as characteristic of it as tailfins and white bucks. A vast hush had settled over the universities. Liberalism had become tired and dull. There seemed to be no indignant young men on campuses, no burning causes, and no militancy, except among a reactionary handful on the far right. Protest was confined to a few "beats," who like their peers were in full retreat from idealism and contention. For the majority, acts of social significance were replaced by the panty raid or something called "stuffing," in which the largest possible number of undergraduates would squash themselves into some small space —forty of them in a Volkswagen, say, or a dozen in an outdoor phone booth. At Fresno State in California, students lowered a booth into the deep end of the college swimming pool; seven volunteers then held their breaths long enough to cram themselves in it.

A few zealous sociologists tried to find significance in this—arguing that the stuffers were dramatizing interdependence—but the students themselves had no illusions. It was all meaningless, and they knew it; after the fun was over they could be found waiting in queues for interviews with recruiters from the nation's largest corporations. They waited so patiently for everything that visitors to campuses began commenting on their docility. Cartoonists depicted students as empty Brooks Brothers suits. Robert Frost said he was troubled by their "lack of decisiveness." A CCNY alumna returned for a social function and left shocked; the coeds could talk only of their future homes in suburbia, the very sort of trivial chatter which CCNY girls of other years had scorned as being typical of expensive women's colleges. Debaters from Oxford, touring American campuses, were startled to find free enterprise regarded not merely as an economic system, but as a way of life. "What is there to crusade about?" a bespectacled Princeton junior asked Professor Otto Butz. At Harvard David Riesman wrote of undergraduate complaints: "When I ask such students what they have done about these things, they are surprised at the very thought they could do anything. They think I am joking when I suggest that, if things came to the worst, they could picket!"

"Few young people," Murray Ross wrote in 1950, "share deeply in the life of a group dedicated, and actively devoted, to the highest goals of mankind." To find out what did stir youth, *Life* that year asked it for its heroes and heroines. Back like a straight arrow came the answers: Lincoln, Franklin Roosevelt, Joe DiMaggio, MacArthur, Babe Ruth, and Roy Rogers; Clara Barton, Vera-Ellen, Florence Nightingale, Doris Day, and Sister Elizabeth Kenny. Parental opinions could scarcely have been much different. Indeed, one of the most remarkable features of the new decade was the degree to which young Americans adopted the values of the older generation. The "dedication of bourgeois America to personal security," wrote William O'Neill of the University of Wisconsin, had produced "a generation with strongly middle-aged values." In the past it had been a safe assumption that a young man's politics would crystallize on the left and then move slowly to the right as he grew older. No more; college youth in the 1950s started in dead center and stayed there.

Of course, a majority in any student generation is silent; it is the articulate minority which win it its label. Not many undergraduates in the 1920s wore raccoon coats and only a few drove Stutz Bearcats; a handful in the 1930s joined the Young Communist League or struck for peace. But in the 1950s it was hard to find *any* who were articulate, *any* who could be called leaders. Typically, varsity football teams elected cocaptains, or revolving captains, and Phi Beta Kappa keys were quietly pocketed. Undergraduates seemed to spurn the very concept of leadership, preferring someone they called "the well-rounded man" who under close scrutiny resembled a faceless blob. Of this apotheosis William H. Whyte Jr. wrote in *The Organization Man* that it was "obtrusive in no particular, excessive in no zeal." Believing that leadership came from the group, that progress lay in something called problem-solving meetings, the well-rounded campus men had no use for drive and imagination. Above all, they distrusted individualism. The individual sought prestige and achievement at the expense of others. He was abrasive; he rocked the boat; he threatened the corporate One, and they wanted no part of him.

In their mystique the deadliest sin was to be controversial. The silent generation shunned commitments of any sort, and it was above all politically illiterate. Its members could not be disillusioned because they had no illusions. They kept their mouths shut, avoided serious discussions, and eschewed reformers as "bleeding hearts." In the conflict between independence and the system, they came down hard on the side of the system. They sought not fame, but the approval of others. Eager to collaborate in group actions, they deliberately suppressed traits which might set them apart. It was in these years that wealthy students began to cultivate shabby appearances, wearing denim to discourage any suggestion that they were different from others. Riesman was approached by a varsity swimmer who said, "I get sore at the guys I'm competing against. Something's wrong with me. I wish I could be like ———, who really cooperates with the other fellows. He doesn't care so much about winning." Whyte observed that students no longer dreamed of going into business for themselves. They wanted to work for someone else, and the bigger the firm, the more they trusted it. They were not much interested in becoming salesmen, however, or in rising to be key executives. Salesmen were contenders; executives sometimes had to be tough. Seniors more frequently told company recruiters that they wanted to be in personnel, because they liked people, or in public relations, where, Whyte dryly noted, they could "be nice to everybody on company time."

Protest was clearly alien to such an outlook. For professors, hostility to McCarthyism was the great passion of the time, but students weren't much interested. The senator won few recruits on campuses, but he didn't stir up much resentment, either; most undergraduates found the issue boring. This indifference was noticeable in all fields—including theology, journalism, and law—although it is significant that the occupational preferences of students had sharply changed. The great thing now was business administration. Between 1940 and 1950 the primacy of the humanities had declined, until fewer than three undergraduates in ten were majoring in a fundamental discipline. Vocational training had the allegiance of the young, and business was the most popular vocation because it offered the highest return on their investment of choice. At the end of the 1940s business majors had accounted for 19.4 percent of all college students in the United States. By 1955 they had come to constitute the largest undergraduate group.

If they had a paradigm, he was Tom Rath, Sloan Wilson's *Man in a Gray Flannel Suit*. At the beginning of the novel, Wilson's hero has a wife named Betsy, three children, a six-room house in Westport, a 1939 Ford, $10,000 in GI life insurance, and a $7,000-a-year job at a charitable foundation, where his duties are negligible. Life is pleasant, but rather austere; he needs a new car, the kitchen linoleum is starting to go, etc. Then Tom gets what looks like a break. He is offered a public relations job paying $9,000. He takes it and finds there is a hitch. In his new career he is expected to work. No more three-hour lunches, no long coffee breaks, being nice on company time; he has to produce now, and sometimes he has to stay at his desk after five o'clock or even come in on Saturdays, cutting into his time with Betsy and the kids. That incenses him. He tells the boss where to get off. Tom doesn't mind getting rich, but if in exchange he has to curtail his roles as husband, father, and all-around good fellow, he wants no part of it. This is the climax of the story, and the denouement is extraordinary. The boss backs down.

> "Of course," Hopkins said kindly, getting up and pouring himself another drink. "There are plenty of good positions where it's not necessary to put in an unusual amount of work. Now it's just a matter of finding the right spot for you."

The silent generation really believed that. Beneath its ersatz camaraderie lay an essential innocence, a Hans Christian Andersen belief that clock watchers, for some supernatural reason, would be rewarded with what was variously called "the good life," the "good, sensible life," and "the right, full life." Hopkins says defensively, "*Somebody* has to do the work," and Tom replies sympathetically, "I know." Somebody, but not him. No driven neurotic he:

> "I don't want to give up the time. I'm trying to be honest about this. I want the money. Nobody likes money better than I do. But I'm just the kind of guy who can't work evenings and weekends and all the rest of it forever. I guess there's even more to it than that. I'm not the kind of person who can get all wrapped up in a job —I can't get myself convinced that my work is the most important thing in the world."

Convinced that all great discoveries had been made, all great dreams realized, and all great fortunes amassed, the Toms of the 1950s were content to tinker with techniques and technicalities from nine to five, five days a week, while devoting the bulk of their energies to nonvocational interests—the church, civic activities, "getting to know" the kids, golf, Little Leagues, leading a rewarding life with Betsy and laying pipe with her. All this was to be theirs once they had signed up with the right recruiters before commencement, entered their names in the rat race, and roistered away down the superhighways of consumption. It was significant, as one social critic pointed out, that college students no longer spoke of "playing the game." Instead they "knew the score." They were aware that the score would change from time to time, but when that happened, they felt sure, somebody would tell them what to do.

There was no longer much talk of selling out. It was unnecessary. They were in bondage from the outset, as committed to the American way as any medieval youth off for the monastery. To them the world that awaited them after commencement was neither cold nor cruel, and certainly not hostile. Writing in *Daedalus*, the journal of the American Academy of the Arts and Sciences, one academician reported, "A dominant characteristic of students in the current generation is that they are gloriously contented both in regard to their present day-to-day activity and their outlook for the future. Few of them are worried—about their health, their prospective careers, their family relations, the state of national or international society or the likelihood of their enjoying secure and happy lives." Graduating seniors were prepared to embrace—and if need be, to defend—the status quo; they would obey the law, pay taxes, fulfill their military obligations, and vote, though thereafter politics would be none of their concern. They would conform to the dictates of society in their dress, speech, worship, choice of friends, length of hair, and above all, in their thought. In exchange they would receive all the rights and privileges of the good life; *viz.*, economic security.

That was the deal, and it shocked their teachers. Having survived the challenges of poverty and fascism, it seemed, the national legacy was to be betrayed by puerile hobbledehoys who preferred mink-handled beer can openers and fourteen-karat gold charge plates to ideals, and who accepted General Eisenhower's definition of an intellectual: "a man who takes more words than is necessary to say more than he knows."

In New York's Temple Rodeph Sholom, Rabbi Lewis I. Newman blamed panty expeditions on McCarthyism. By making "serious discussion and dissent on major issues dangerous," he argued, the Wisconsin senator had made it necessary for students to "find an expression for their bottled-up energies in foolish and unseemly 'raids' upon dormitories." This was stretching things; yet there was a seed of truth in it. If thoughtful discussion was not downright risky, it was certainly being discouraged on almost every level of organized society. A jet propulsion engineer was arrested, apparently on no other ground than that he had been a friend of the Rosenbergs. Owen Lattimore was indicted on seven counts of perjury before a congressional investigating committee.* The State Department banned travel in Communist countries. The dismissal of American employees at the U.N. as "security risks" had begun, and passage of the McCarran-Walter Immigration Act all but guaranteed the public humiliation of European scholars arriving to lecture on American campuses.

Now that McCarthy was at his height, nearly every week brought news of some fresh outrage against free thought, and pensive students could hardly avoid the conclusion that conformists were rewarded and heretics punished. Washington was the great battleground for the senator and his foes, but colorful skirmishes were being fought in almost every community of any size. San Antonio, Texas, for example, was going through agonies over a proposal that the public library brand books whose authors had been called Communists or were suspected of Communist sympathies with a red stamp. The advocates were led by Myrtle Glasscock Hance, a local housewife. Mrs. Hance, the *New York Times* reported, "has never made any pretense to literary attainments or wide acquaintance with books." But that didn't mean that she didn't have a pretty good idea of the hanky-panky inside. She produced a list of suspected authors and said she wanted something done about their books. She didn't demand that the books be actually burned. The stamp would satisfy her, provided it was bright red and "large enough to be seen immediately." Affixed to the inside front cover, it would specify the writer's Communist affiliations and sympathies, together with the number of his "citations." "The reader," Mrs. Hance said, "will then realize that in many instances he is reading Communist propaganda." San Antonio's mayor, whose own wife was a member of the Minute Women, thought Mrs. Hance's suggestion an excellent one. Then it developed that there was more to it than met the eye. Watchers were to take note of people who consulted the branded books. Their names were then to be turned over to the

---

* Lattimore was indicted twice, in 1952 and 1954. The last of the charges was dismissed in 1955.

FBI or, alternately, published in the *San Antonio News*. That aroused the city's powerful Maverick family, civil libertarians to the man. Before the clamor ended in the triumph of the antibranders, households had been divided and friendships torn asunder.

In Indiana another housewife, Mrs. Thomas J. White, a member of the Indiana State Textbook Commission, offered a novel interpretation of Anglo-Saxon folklore. She declared: "There is a Communist directive in education now to stress the story of Robin Hood. They want to stress it because he robbed the rich and gave to the poor. That's the Communist line. It's just a smearing of law and order." The Republican governor declined to take a stand, for Robin Hood or against him. In England William Cox, sheriff of Nottingham, told a reporter that in his opinion Hood (1160–?) had not been a Communist, but Wilbur Young, Indiana's superintendent of education, called a press conference to announce that he was rereading the tales of Robin Hood just the same. Nothing was above suspicion in the early 1950s, and in some quarters to be suspect was tantamount to guilt. As though blacklisting was not enough, Samuel French, the country's leading publisher of drama, announced a playwriting contest in which it reserved "the right to declare ineligible any author who is, or becomes publicly involved, in a scholastic, literary, political, or moral controversy."

With FBI agents openly conducting security checks on campuses and trustee demands for loyalty oaths, it would have been surprising if undergraduates had not held their tongues. Almost everyone else did. Paul G. Hoffman, chairman of the board at Studebaker-Packard and a liberal Republican, was an exception. His views on freedom would scarcely have seemed daring in any other era, but holding any opinion strongly was unusual then. After he had spoken at a large southwestern university a student asked, "Do you think there ought to be any study of Communism in a school such as this?" Hoffman answered, "Yes, I think we ought to teach what Communism is, so that the new and most important generation of Americans can know exactly why it is such a menace to our way of life." The student said, "I think so, too, but it's dangerous to say that around here now." In fact it wasn't entirely safe for Hoffman to say it. He was being watched, and when he sought to speak in Indianapolis again under the auspices of the American Civil Liberties Union, the American Legion saw to it that he was denied the use of the city's War Memorial. His topic this time was to have been free enterprise.

Vigilante persecution, horror of the new thermonuclear weapons, and parental tales of the Depression were all formative forces in the making of the silent generation. It was not without defenders. Writing in the *New York Times Magazine*, Princeton's Otto Butz held that its elders misjudged it. His own students, he wrote, were merely prudent. He thought it wrong to condemn them for their lack of political militance: "The future, indeed, may show that they are precisely the kind of realistic idealists which this country, in both its domestic and international life, has long been badly in need of." It was faint praise, found no echo, and has not been justified by the passage of time. A more eminent educator, Philip E. Jacob of the University of Pennsylvania, held that the values of the silent generation represented a departure from American tradition. Although students spoke well of sincerity, honesty, and loyalty, he wrote, their own standards were "generally low in regard to academic honesty, systematic cheating being a common practice rather than the exception at many major institutions." Their hedonism and anti-intellectualism seemed to him to represent an abandonment of their Puritan heritage, and he suggested that "Perhaps these students are the forerunners of a major cultural and ethical revolution," the "unconscious ushers of an essentially secular (though nominally religious), self-oriented (though group-forming) society."

If others saw the specter of revolution in the wings, they were keeping it to themselves. But Dr. Jacob had sketched an outline, and in time others would flesh it out. It is fascinating to speculate on how they felt about the voluntary gags worn then, for although they were too young to assess it, the mystique of the silent generation must have had an impact upon them in some dark place of the mind back beyond memory and below the level of speech. In the high summer of 1951, when the decade was just getting under way, Mark Rudd was a three-year-old in Maplewood, New Jersey; Mario Savio was eight and Kathy Boudin seven in Manhattan; Huey Newton ten in Oakland, California; Linda Sue Evans eight in Fort Dodge, Iowa; Cathlyn Platt Wilkerson six in New York; and Diana Oughton nine in Dwight, Illinois.

Early in the 1960s, when the silent generation had passed into history, a group of undergraduates at Wesleyan University, feeling a pang of nostalgia between periods in a basketball game, spontaneously burst into lyrics all had retained in their collective memory. They sang:

> *Winky Dink and you,*
> *Winky Dink and you,*
> *Always have a lot of fun*
> *To-geth-er!*

Then:

> *It's Howdy Doody time,*
> *It's Howdy Doody time,*
> *Bob Smith and Howdy too*
> *Say Howdy-Do to you!**

And then:

> *Mickey Mouse! Mickey Mouse!*
> *Forever let us raise our banners high!*
>
> *M-I-C*
> *—See you real soon!*
> *K-E-Y*
> *—Why? Because we like you!*
>
> *M-O-U-S-E!*

The chanting students shared bonds which had been unknown to their parents. They were members of the first television generation, reared in a time when public relations men had begun speaking of "images" and psychologists of "roles"—when "the public" in advertising jargon was being superseded by "the mass audience." In the 1930s the radio children's hour had been forty-five minutes. At other idle times its young admirers had either listened to adult programs or, if they were small and belonged to the great middle class, to parents reading fragments from a juvenile literature unchanged since their own childhoods: Mother Goose, Grimms' fairy tales, *A Child's Garden of Verses, Treasure Island, Peter Pan, Little Women, The Wizard of Oz*. All that began to recede in the late Truman years. Unless enshrined by Disney (Pinocchio, Sleeping Beauty) or a popular entertainer (Peter Pan, Oz), tales once told

---
* © Children's Songs, Inc. 1948.

at mothers' knees were to become progressively less familiar, until allusions to them were lost upon all but a select few from homes where children who read and were read to were not thought peculiar.

Winky, Howdy, Mickey, *Lucky Pup*, and *Life with Snarky Parker* were among the less objectionable survivors in the new medium. The general level was much lower. Really clever programs were given short shrift by sponsors. *Magic Cottage* and *Mr. I. Magination*, preferred by parents in a *TV Guide* survey, were swiftly cut down by the A. C. Nielsen and C. E. Hooper ratings. *Kukla, Fran, and Ollie,* Burr Tillstrom's charming puppet show, lasted longer, but eventually it, too, was trodden under by the prophets of violence: *Captain Video, Sky King, Space Cadet, Captain Midnight,* and *Superman,* whose young fans continued to cherish illusions of his indestructibility even after George Reeves, the actor who played him, drove his Jaguar into a stone wall in California, cut his forehead, and fainted at the sight of his own blood.

Roughly one-third of the new programs for children were devoted to crime and violence. The number of American firms manufacturing toy guns jumped from ten to nearly three hundred, and two-fisted, gunslinging William Boyd, who had been foresighted enough to buy up rights to his discarded celluloid horse operas, built one of television's first fortunes, grossing forty million dollars by 1950 in the sale of Hopalong Cassidy clothing alone. Hopalong's six-gun casualties contributed to the general television toll, which by 1954 actually exceeded the death rate in Korea. Some murders on the screen were quite horrible. Jack Gould of the *New York Times* campaigned against close-ups of young girls being strangled, but the predominant view in the network hierarchy was that TV was no gorier than, say, "Jack the Giant Killer," and that ferocity on the tube might even be doing some good by helping little watchers work out their aggression in fantasy. Anyway, violent programs were popular; kids wanted them. Therefore decisions to increase the homicidal level were reached in the sixty square blocks around Madison Avenue known as "the industry." It happened to be a short ride from the apartment where an eleven-year-old truant named Lee Harvey Oswald was watching all the TV mayhem he could get.

Almost everything about the new medium was debatable except its significance. Clearly that was immense. The Age of Television was dawning more rapidly than the Age of Radio. At the peak of radio's expansion, Americans had bought about 165,000 receivers a month. During every month of 1948 and 1949, more than 200,000 TV sets were sold, and that was only the beginning. On January 1, 1950, there were three million television owners in the United States. In that swing year—the year of McCarthy and Korea—another seven million sets were installed in American homes. Radio still dominated the airwaves, broadcasting to forty million receivers, but that was only because the majority hadn't yet bowed to salesmanship ("Is *your* little girl left out . . . ?") and social pressure. In metropolitan communities those forces were often augmented by newspaper campaigns. Misjudging the appeal of radio, newspapers had allowed station franchises to go to others, leaving them in the cold. This time they were in at the start. Baltimore provided an excellent illustration of how effective skillful merchandising, backed by journalistic indoctrination, can be. In the spring of 1949 Hooper's figures showed that 82 percent of the city's inhabitants listened to radio, while only 18 percent watched television. Then the *Baltimore Sun, Evening Sun,* and *Sunday Sun* began urging subscribers to enjoy programs on WMAR-TV, which was owned by them. As a consequence, in May 1950 the city became the first in which television's evening audience (50.2 percent) was larger than radio's.

It was not as satisfied, though. Once the novelty had worn off, WMAR-TV's delivery was found to be snowy and its programming so shabby at times as to constitute almost a new form of air pollution. "What happens to old, broken-down wrestlers?" Baltimoreans asked one another on street corners, and the answer was, "Nothing. They're still wrestling." *Time* declared, "Television became a major industry and cultural force in 1950," but during the first part of the year its performance level remained poor. Bright spots were appearing here and there: *Duffy's Tavern,* Jack Webb's *Dragnet,* and an elfin Amazon from West Virginia named Dagmar. Still, even the best of it was mostly second-bill vaudeville, and in fact the man of the hour, acclaimed as "Mr. Television," was Milton Berle, a mugging, vaudevillian joke stealer. Most of the big entertainers were veteran radio personalities. Two years earlier the Goldbergs had moved to the screen ("Enter, whoever"; "If it's nobody, I'll call back"), but for most the pendulum had not yet swung. Those who wanted the news from Ed Murrow or the latest ballad from Bing Crosby had to listen, not see, and Arthur Godfrey continued to keep in touch with his forty-million flock by radio, caressing them with what Fred Allen called Godfrey's "barefoot voice."

Part of TV's problems were technical. Cameramen were still feeling their way, installers put antennas up wrong, the first mass-produced sets kept breaking down, and repairmen were incompetent. Chicago's Hallicrafters Company didn't develop the first rectangular picture tube until January 1950. That permitted use of the whole tube face and saved 50 percent in cabinet space. The great obstacle to national television remained: curvature of the earth's surface. AM radio waves bend; FM and television beams do not. In those pioneer years TV receivers over the horizon could not pick up a station's picture, so program directors were limited to local talent. During the 1948 Republican National Convention engineers had tinkered with something called Stratovision, putting an antenna in a B-29 and sending it up to circle 25,000 feet above Pittsburgh. It was a good stunt—signals flickered on screens within a 250-mile radius—but something more substantial was required. The solution lay in coaxial cable and microwave relays. Within another three years a significant grid of cable was in the ground and working. Its first coast-to-coast television broadcast was President Truman's address at the Japanese Peace Treaty Conference in San Francisco on September 4, 1951, beamed to forty million viewers by 94 stations. With that, the networks began signing up local channels and the massive shift from radio to television began.

On the eve of it, *Radio Daily* announced its awards for 1950, and in them the standoff between the two giants then was evident:

RADIO	TELEVISION
Man of the Year: Jack Benny	*Man of the Year:* Sid Caesar
Woman of the Year: Eve Arden	*Woman of the Year:* Faye Emerson
Drama Show: Lux Radio Theater	*Drama Show:* Studio One
Comedy Show: Jack Benny	*Comedy Show:* Milton Berle

Over the next five years, dealer sales averaged five million TV sets a year, and they continued high until 88 percent of American families—forty million homes—had tubes, with 13 percent owning two or more and some with as many as six. For every farmer watching the screen in 1949, there were 27 ten years later. As early as 1950 one study had found that some junior high school students were spending an average of nearly thirty hours a week in front of tubes. Surveys were predicting, accurately, that the average American youth on the day of his high school graduation would have spent 11,000 hours in classrooms and 15,000 hours watching television, and a Westinghouse study later discovered that Americans were spending more man-hours in front of the screen than in working for pay.

Those who weren't watching—and in the 1950s few self-respecting intellectuals would admit to owning a set—were fascinated by those who were. Norman Cousins reported to his appalled readers that "the standardized television formula for an evening's entertainment is a poisoning, a variety show, a wrestling show"; Max Lerner held that TV was "the poor man's luxury because it is his psychological necessity"; and judges held that it was indeed a necessity, not subject to seizure by creditors. In 1954 the TV dinner appeared, obviating the need for people to tear themselves away from the screen to bolt supper, and that same year the water commissioner of Toledo made a remarkable discovery. Baffled by why water consumption surged upward during certain three-minute periods, he conducted a discreet little survey and found that all over Toledo, during television commercials, viewers were simultaneously dashing into bathrooms, voiding, and flushing their toilets in unison.

By then the average American family was watching TV between four and five hours a day; Louis Kronenberger commented that television was returning people to the home, whence the auto had lured them, but destroying the home in the process:

> Where Mother and Father, Jane and John on their treks and travels exchanged pleasantries and ideas, they sit now for hours, side by side, often shoulder to shoulder, scarcely exchanging a glance. Or if they do address one another, they do so crossly, campaigning for this program or that.

What were their choices? Some early network presentations were quite good. In 1950 the March of Time's *Crusade in Europe,* telecast by ABC, became the first documentary to win a Peabody Award. Murrow's *See It Now* began the following year, and the year after that Alistair Cooke started bringing an hour and a half of *Omnibus* into living rooms on Sunday afternoons, courtesy of the Ford Foundation. On other channels Jimmy Durante was funny, if broad; Victor Borge, the happy Dane, was charming, if *manqué;* Bishop Fulton J. Sheen, literate, if glib; NBC's televised operas outstanding by any standard. Sunday evenings NBC's *Philco-Goodyear Playhouse* and CBS's *Studio One* introduced live dramas by fine new playwrights, beginning with Paddy Chayefsky's *Marty*. Among commentators, CBS's Murrow was still supreme, but viewers could also switch to ABC's John Charles Daly or NBC's John Cameron ("Now hopscotch in the world for headlines") Swayze. David Brinkley was also at NBC, and in 1955 Chet Huntley joined him to form the famous newscasting team which would move to the top when Murrow retired.

Had these programs been typical, the quality of American life might have risen. Instead it sank. Those interested enough to monitor television fare and perceptive enough to judge it waged bitter disputes over who was responsible for its tasteless sludge. No one was, really; there simply wasn't enough talent to fill all those empty hours, and the very size of the waiting audience meant that concepts comprehensible to the majority had to be banal. Families were really amused by:

OZZIE: Er . . . uh . . . oh, dear . . . have you . . . seen the . . . the paper?
HARRIET: Gee, dear, Ricky may have seen it.
OZZIE: Uh . . . oh . . . well, gee . . . I . . .
RICKY (*bursting in*): Hi, Pop. I gave the paper to Dave to give to Thorny. (*Leaves*)
OZZIE: Oh, well . . . gee, dear, I . . . I wanted to read the . . . the paper.

Young viewers—and not only the young—caught their breaths at:

BOYD: Lucky, round up a posse. Bart Slime's kidnapped the judge's daughter.
GABBY HAYES: Wh-h-h-y, them dirty, no good—c'mon, Hoppy, let's go git them varmints.

And four million housewives hunched over their irons and ovens were actually moved when 203 stations broadcasted:

HELEN: Oh, Paul! The operation was a success!
PAUL: You mean that little guy will live to play shortstop again?
HELEN: Yes! Oh, I prayed for this so hard last night!
PAUL (*gently*): And your prayer was answered.
HELEN (*after a long pause*): Yes, Paul—my prayer—was answered.

Space Cadet was just as trite as *Hopalong Cassidy*, *My Favorite Husband* as inane as *Ozzie and Harriet* and *As the World Turns* or *The Edge of Night* as florid as *Helen Trent*. On TV the pot competed with the kettle. The real Sunday evening contest was not between *Studio One* and *Philco-Goodyear;* it was the 8 P.M. duel between CBS's Ed Sullivan and NBC's Steve Allen, and Sullivan won it going away by signing up the most expensive guest star of the time, young Elvis Presley, a former Memphis truck driver whose most memorable line was, "Goan . . . git . . . luhhv." For the privilege of presenting Presley on three Sullivan shows, CBS paid $50,000, which would have bought a lot of serious drama or documentary film.

TV morality made no more sense than Hollywood's. Presley's pelvis and Faye Emerson's plunging necklines were acceptable, but the chairman of the Federal Communications Commission called Godfrey's double-entendres "livery stable humor," and when Noel Coward retained the hells and damns in *Blithe Spirit* for CBS's Ford Star Jubilee, *Time* commented, "Viewers last week were treated to the raciest—and most profane—language that has ever been heard on TV." Groucho Marx was also in and out of trouble with network watchdogs, while the antics of Jerry ("I'm a bean bag") Lester, offensive to some, were passed over in silence. In part censorship seemed to be a matter of whose ox was being gored. Almost any vulgarity was tolerated on the giveaway shows. Yet when anti-Communist blacklisters formed an organization called AWARE, Inc., and smeared John Henry Faulk, a wit in the Will Rogers tradition, CBS quickly let him go. Faulk had to sue to be reinstated. After six years in the courts he won, but no action was taken against the vigilantes, among them Clayton (Bud) Collyer of *Break the Bank*.

Trendex ratings that February offer some insight into American mass taste in the 1950s. The top ten programs were *Ed Sullivan, The $64,000 Question, Perry Como, I Love Lucy, December Bride, Talent Scouts, You Bet Your Life, Red Skelton, What's My Line?,* and *Walt Disney*. On the whole they were bland and slick, and the dominant theme was slapstick, which may say something about television as a new medium, the national character, or the times. Allen Tate thought the tragedy of the 1950s lay in the mass media's destruction of ways to communicate through love. Louis Kronenberger believed it significant that with the advent of TV's square eye, all walls guarding privacy were crumbling. We had, he said, become a nation of peeping Toms.

But all words spoken in the United States were not for microphones, and millions of words were not being spoken at all. They were in print, in Braille, on tape, on newsprint, in phonographs, on celluloid, on plastic, on canvas, and even in architecture. Communications was having its revolution, as economics did in the 1930s and sex would in the 1960s. Never had there been so much information to transmit, or so many ways to transmit it. The volume was breathtaking. Beginning in 1950 the paperback industry alone sold over a quarter-billion books each year in drugstores and newsstands for twenty-five cents, thirty-five cents, and (for giants then) fifty cents. Already the industry had 81,000 titles in print, including seventeen editions of Jane Austen's *Pride and Prejudice.* "There is," D. W. Brogan argued, "abundant evidence that popular taste in the United States is improving." A random glance at paperback sales in January 1952 shows 400,000 for Ruth Benedict's *Patterns of Culture,* 1,250,000 for *The Naked and the Dead,* 750,000 for *Nineteen Eighty-four,* 500,000 for *A Streetcar Named Desire,* and—for a translation of the Odyssey with an abstract cover design—350,000. The broad rivers coming down from Canada were choked with logs waiting to sacrifice their pulp at mills so that America might be educated as well as entertained, inspired as well as amused, aroused as well as inflamed, and their thousands of square miles of paper went to *U.S. News* and the *New York Times, Commentary* and *Playboy, Holiday* and Grove Press, the *Encyclopaedia Britannica* and *Peyton Place, Mad* and the *American Scholar,* the books of Harold Robbins and John Crowe Ransom, and the works of Norman Cousins, Max Lerner, Allen Tate, and Louis Kronenberger.

Across America five thousand motion picture theater marquees had been darkened in the great box office recession which had accompanied the rise of television. Ernie Kovacs and *Queen for a Day* had stolen hearts once pledged to Clark Gable and Ginger Rogers. The tarnish of time clouded the stars' names embedded in Hollywood Boulevard's sidewalks. Bitter signs there read, "Buy Christmas Seals and Stamp Out TV," and studios would have had to close down without revenue from abroad, which now, for the first time, was providing 50 percent of the movie industry's gross. President Eric Johnston of the Motion Picture Association of America said,

"We will simply have to face the fact that we are in for a leveling off in the future because of the public's driving habits and television." In vast tracts of countryside films had become a summer business; since V-J Day the number of drive-in theaters had grown from 351 to 7,000. Meanwhile the gaudy old movie palaces on Main Street, the Paramounts and Capitals and Bijous and Foxes and Hippodromes—once the pride of the only big business to flourish throughout the Depression—went into eclipse.

Nationwide weekly attendance figures showed that about forty-five million people had stopped going to the pictures. Things perked up briefly with the Cinerama vogue and then dropped off again. Owners shut off their balconies. They let help go and took over the popcorn concessions themselves. After a while they took to showing films only on weekends, and finally many of them closed down altogether. Some became bowling alleys, supermarkets, banks, apartment houses, or even churches; in Manhattan, ironically, they were converted to television studios. In metropolitan neighborhoods and little cities, where they were abandoned to dust and mice, they turned into fire hazards and eyesores. Because the old exit doors were easily forced, some became trysting places for tramps and lovers. Beneath screens on which Paul Muni had defended Alfred Dreyfus and Gary Cooper had submitted to torture rather than divulge the cavalry's location, empty whiskey bottles accumulated, and where Charles Boyer had begged Hedy Lamarr to run away from the Casbah with him, and Jennifer Jones as Bernadette had been visited by the Virgin Mary, aisles became cluttered with cigarette butts, sanitary napkins, and used contraceptives.

Movies were still a social force. On certain occasions they brought the community together again, as for a reunion. Mike Todd's *Around the World in Eighty Days* did it with its 29 stars, 68,894 extras, and 7,959 animals, including four ostriches, six skunks, fifteen elephants, seventeen bulls, 512 monkeys, 800 horses, 950 donkeys, 2,448 bison, 3,800 sheep, and a scared cow. There were others: *Strangers on a Train, Moby Dick, Twelve O'Clock High, The Third Man, The Man with the Golden Arm, Guys and Dolls, The Desperate Hours,* and *The Bridge on the River Kwai.* Of the new stars, Judy Holliday, Kirk Douglas, Marilyn Monroe, William Holden, and Shirley MacLaine were at least as good as those in prewar constellations.

The chief problem was that the box office dollar was now much smaller, but there were other factors. Foreign films had become increasingly popular. Before the war most moviegoers had never seen a European picture; the few to come over were mostly British, tedious, and dull. J. Arthur Rank changed that. Alec Guinness, Jack Hawkins, and Michael Redgrave became as familiar to American audiences as American actors. The Italians sent Anna Magnani and Gina Lollobrigida, the Austrians Maria and Maximilian Schell, the French Brigitte Bardot and Yves Montand, the Japanese Toshiro Mifune, and the Swedes whole troupes whose performances suggested that Paris really wasn't the sexiest place in the world. In the late 1940s Hollywood pressure had kept these actors off neighborhood screens; to see them one had to seek out what were called "art theaters" in large cities.

Then, in February 1950, a federal court in New York dissolved corporate articles binding producers and distributors of films to local exhibitors. Exhibitors no longer showed what they were sent, sight unseen. They bought features one by one, and they could buy from anyone. All America was an open market for enterprising Europeans. The ruling had broad ramifications. Hollywood had been built on the assurance that every picture would have its chance with the public. To get Shirley Temple or Robert Taylor, exhibitors had had to buy a quota of B movies and experimental films. The result had been the double feature and "selected short subjects"; the unknown was shown with the known, and if it caught on, a star was born. No more. Improvisation was too risky after 1950. Exhibitors were free to turn down the obscure picture, making it a dead loss. As a result, the moguls on the Coast began sinking everything into superspectacles which, if they failed, entailed losses in the millions.

Altogether, it was to be a wretched decade for Hollywood. Month by month the film industry's once massive role in the national economy declined. Grimly refusing to open their treasure of old movies to the television networks, and as yet unable to interest them in using movie lots for TV production, the moguls watched the film capital decline until it had become all but a ghost town.

The film makers were caught in a wrenching transition. The nation's mores still proscribed the showing of sexual acts, or even nudity; of the harmless *Baby Doll*, *Time* said that it was "just about the dirtiest American-made motion picture that has ever been legally exhibited." Producers continued to be attuned to generalized entertainment. The notion that a film might appeal to one group in society was yet to come. Its first success was to be *Rock Around the Clock* (1954), and even then American youth was largely indifferent to it. The movie's breakthrough—and the emergence of rock-'n'-roll as a worldwide phenomenon—came first in Britain, where upheavals dating from World War II had first created an autonomous teen-age class. After the film had triggered rioting by three thousand Teddy boys that September, councils in a dozen English towns met in special session to discuss banning it, and police cordons were thrown around theaters where it was still being shown. The Teds' hair was of special interest. At a time when adolescent males in the United States remained faithful to the crew cut, the Teds wore theirs long, combing it in the back in a style which can be traced to wartime Los Angeles. It was called—not in mixed company, of course—the DA, or Duck's Ass. The Teds did not let it hang loose on their shoulders, to be sure; that would come later.

Before the transition, motion pictures had served as a social unifier. Appealing as they did to all ages and slighting no class—except blacks, who remained unnoticed even by themselves—films had strengthened familial ties and reminded moviegoers of values they shared. Wartime films warmed the melting pot by showing WASPs, ethnics, and minority Americans working together. In addition, Hollywood served as a social mentor. Consciously and unconsciously, fans modeled their behavior after that of the stars. By ruling that couples in films must not be shown sleeping in double beds, for example, the Hays Office, later the Breen Office, had altered styles in the entire bedding industry, and by excluding even the mildest profanity it helped keep the language, as was then said, clean. Moreover, to an extent unappreciated at the time, the generalized pretransition movies provided the country with a common lore. Even in the 1970s middle-aged strangers could relate to one another and find a meeting ground by references to *The Philadelphia Story, Mutiny on the Bounty,* or any other of a hundred films remembered and cherished, over thirty years later, by virtually an entire generation. Their children lacked that; no motion picture of the early Nixon years knitted itself into the American experience.

Of course, none of this had anything to do with art. Judged by that yardstick, the best movies of the 1960s and 1970s outshone almost everything before them. By then the transition was complete and it was possible to explore emotions and relationships which had been freed from the old taboos. Films had attained maturity; high seriousness on the screen had become possible; brilliant directors were using celluloid in ways undreamed of before. Still, something had been lost. Pictures had become divisive. Small children went to weekend matinees, teen-agers to movies made for them by stars their own age, and adults to films rated for them alone. Hollywood's old unifying force was gone.

The signposts, too, were different, and the possibilities for misunderstanding greatly increased. One misleading word was "nonconformity." In the 1950s some teen-agers began warning parents that they had decided to stop conforming to the rest of society. But within their subculture, conformity was absolute—"How," Irving Howe asked pointedly, "can a bobby-soxer admit to not enjoying Vaughn Monroe?"—and some examples of it were unconsciously entertaining: "Join the beat generation" cried an ad in an early issue of *Playboy*. "Buy a beat generation tieclasp! A beat generation sweatshirt! A beat generation ring!" That subcult was swiftly forming in the early 1950s. Money had become more plentiful for it in the prosperity accompanying the Korean War, and in 1955 it acquired its first martyr with the flaming death of James Dean, who had just starred in *Rebel Without a Cause*.*

The social sciences were rising in prestige. There was an immense curiosity about all the media—what they were doing, their influence, their meaning, their potential. David Riesman at Harvard and Reuel Denney in Chicago were investigating their role in the shaping and socialization of people, instilling in them a sense of what it meant to be an American man or woman, boy or girl, mature or old. At the University of Toronto Marshall McLuhan was defining "the visual, linear, older generation" and "the aural, tactile, and suffusing younger generation," and in Baltimore H. L. Mencken had completed his documentation of the growth of a national speech, "standard American," and the accompanying decline in regional speech.†

---

* Dean is as important in American legend as Jean Harlow and Marilyn Monroe. Nearly twenty years afterward, he would still be receiving fan mail. Excluding microfilm, the New York Public Library finds it impossible to keep Dean material. His worshipers steal it. The Lincoln Center Library for the Performing Arts has just one book about him. It is in French, and all the pictures in it have been cut out.
† One of the last, charming manifestations of which came ten years later, just after Lyndon Johnson moved into the White House, when a woman in Houston remarked, "Isn't it nice to have a President without an accent?"

In these same years the publicity business grew from a cloud no larger than a handout to the vastness of Marlboro Country. In 1948, when the Public Relations Society of America was founded, there were about a hundred PR firms in the country, many of them operating out of hole-in-the-wall offices, and fewer than fifty PR departments in industry. The number of public relations companies in Manhattan alone swiftly expanded to a thousand, and it was a rare business—or an impoverished governmental bureau—without its complement of mimeograph machines and amiable men eager to plant plugs and puffs. Very soon ranking PR advisers rose to the vice-presidential level in industry and, in Washington, became members of the subcabinet. With their arrival, images often came to supersede truth. They wrote commencement speeches for heads of corporations, cajoled newspapermen with free rides on company planes, subsidized the new call girl business, and, with Robert Montgomery's coaching of Eisenhower, made PR skills indispensable to political campaigns.

Meantime advertising had begun to move in subtler patterns. During the 1940s it had continued with straightforward appeals to vanity, sentiment, ambition, greed, and fear—Listerine's "Always a Bridesmaid, Never a Bride," "I Was a 98-lb. Weakling," "Your Best Friends Won't Tell You," and "They Laughed When I Sat Down at the Piano." Service of patriotism, the 1944 classic: Hyperbole had made superlatives so ordinary that the advertising department of R. H. Macy & Co. bought a six-column ad in the *New York Times* to taunt the rest of the industry with a glossary of "Unfamiliar Words & Phrases—As Used by Advertising Writers to Describe Female Apparel and Appurtenances." Included in it were "*gossamer:* the nearest thing to nothing—and better in black"; "*lush:* anything softer than stone"; "*glamorous:* anything plus a sequin"; and "*fabulous:* we haven't seen anything like it for an hour." By the time the 1950s were well under way, Madison Avenue's hacks had been shouldered aside by brighter account executives. The bark of the television auctioneer and the specter of B.O. had been replaced by "Cloud Nine, Calling Earth," "Bendix Starter Drive Puts 20 Million Women in the Driver's Seat," "A Bacardi Daiquiri Has Less Calories Than a Glass of Skim Milk," and "Steel Is As Big As All Outdoors!" Motivational advertising research had arrived in all its Day-Glo splendor. For a while there was even scary talk of something called subliminal advertising—slogans flashed on TV screens so rapidly that they eluded the conscious eye and embedded themselves in the subconscious, whence, presumably, they would emerge at the crucial shopping moment.

Beginning with the postwar vogue of Frederic Wakeman's *The Hucksters,* sophisticated Americans had been giving Madison Avenue and its works the sort of spellbound attention once invoked by Emile Coué and Howard Scott. By the end of the Truman era almost everyone in Winnetka or Bel Air could describe the difference between the hard sell and the soft sell; the significance of Roper, Nielsen, and Hooper; and what it meant to say, "Let's run this one up the flagpole," or "Put this on the train and see if it gets off at Westport."

The most beloved creatures of the soft sell were probably the Piel Brothers, though serious students of modern advertising honor above all others the name of Henry Morgan. An eccentric figure during the last of radio's great days, Morgan was capable of doing almost anything on the air. Once he auctioned off his entire staff for $83. He frequently interviewed himself, and on the assumption that Hollywood's Coming Attractions were more exciting than the features they were hawking, he would devote a full half hour to running off their sound tracks. Advertising a breakfast cereal—"Snap! Crackle! Pop!"—Morgan would put on earmuffs to muffle the deafening racket. One infuriated sponsor after another fired Morgan. Eventually he wound up in a dull, unimaginative hard-selling job, a talented casualty in the endless war for the consumer dollar.

Advertisers were spending ten billion dollars a year—2.2 percent of the Gross National Product—to manipulate the public, creating ever larger wants for ever more ingenious products. By stimulating the economy, the theory went, commercials were striking blows for the American way. Thus the glib adman came to occupy roughly the same place in the firmament which, in Coolidge's New Era, had been reserved for the financier. Nearly everyone believed in them; even Joseph Stalin bought two thousand transmitters to jam Free World electronic spiels before they could corrupt his people. Sports fans accepted without protest TV's fake rest periods, fake injuries, and "two-minute warnings" in the last period of football games, knowing that all of them were merely excuses for commercials. The Billy Graham Crusade invested in a special survey on the habits of subway straphangers to ascertain the best strategic location for Crusade ads; God, too, believed in motivational research.

Less than a quarter-century had passed since the Roaring Twenties collapsed in 1929, and the country was off on another binge in another bull market. The Fat Fifties, some were calling it. The New York Stock Exchange reported that one out of every nine Americans owned stocks, but most of the rest seemed to be debtors; Eric Goldman wrote that department stores were advertising plans under which customers could spend the rest of their lives owing a specified balance—$500, for instance—and for a fee "debt counselors" would give you a living allowance in exchange for your pay envelope, which they would then distribute among your creditors.

Automobiles were growing wider, longer, and lower. Each autumn's new models were hooked up with more junk, more chrome, and bigger tailfins. The dashboard on Cadillac's $13,074 Eldorado Brougham included lipstick, a Kleenex box, and four tumblers finished in gold. Outside Detroit the market offered those who had everything solid gold toothpicks, whiskey-flavored toothpaste, and His and Her submarines. The *Wall Street Journal* discovered a thriving mail-order business which offered life-size plastic replicas of famous models equipped with real hair, real fingernails, and real toenails; bachelors bought them and took them to bed, and some had invested thousands of dollars in wardrobes for them. Living women, meanwhile, were emerging from hairdressers with coiffures tinted Champagne Beige, Autumn Apricot, Fire Silver, Golden Cinnamon, Apple Green, Peacock Blue, and Sparkling Sherry. On weekends their husbands were exploring the possibilities of new radar-equipped fishing rods which sent out an electric impulse, found fish, and reported their bearings. At parties businessmen were showing curious friends little rectangles of plastic issued by the Diners Club. Ahead, for middle-class America, lay the wonders of credit card living.

All these were part of the tenor of the time. Throughout the decade tastelessness and vulgarity shrieked out from billboards and TV screens—wherever the peddler opened his pack and hawked his wares. If there was one moment which summed up the rest, it came on CBS-TV at the climax of *Judgment at Nuremberg*, a brilliant piece of theater produced by the network's *Playhouse 90*. The theme was the injustice of justice in Nazi Germany. Claude Rains, the American judge, confronted Paul Lukas, a German jurist. "How in the name of God," Rains asked, "can you ask me to understand the extermination of men, women, and children in—?" His lips moved soundlessly. The missing phrase was "gas ovens." It had been cut at the insistence of *Playhouse 90*'s sponsor, the American Gas Association.

It was the age of Lawrence Welk and of Suzy Parker, of Lavrenti P. Beria and of Albert Schweitzer, of the Superbomb and the Salk vaccine, of Orwellian despair and Reutherian hope. In the Kremlin sat a victor of World War II with a stubborn jaw and little sense of the comic; in the White House sat a victor of World War II with an equally stubborn jaw and just as small a sense of the comic. To the inhabitants of each country it was clearer than crystal that the rulers of the other must be humbled soon, probably by armed might. Both believed that the state of their own internal affairs had, in general, been fixed forever, and would be little changed by the passage of time. Neither trusted their own intellectuals, each worried about its children. Washington smiled on technology; so did Moscow. Fundamentalist preachers of state-approved faith were enjoying a vogue in the U.S.A. and in the USSR also.

Dr. Herman N. Sander, forty-one, of Candia, New Hampshire, was acquitted of first-degree murder in Manchester; he had been charged with the "mercy killing" of Mrs. Abbie Borroto, fifty-nine, an incurable cancer patient, by injecting air in her veins. The year of Our Lord one thousand nine hundred and fifty-one was succeeded by the year one thousand nine hundred and fifty-two. In Akron a convention of sheriffs deplored the lack of law and order. Officials of the 1950 census reported that the new population center of the United States was just outside Olney, Illinois. Puerto Rico became the first commonwealth of the United States, and William Randolph Hearst, dead at eighty-eight, was mourned in a requiem service at the Orphans of the Storm Shelter for Homeless Pets in Chicago.

Greek-born shipping tycoon Aristotle Socrates Onassis, forty-eight, was indicted on charges of conspiring to defraud the United States while buying surplus ships. Dore Schary told the Harvard Club of Los Angeles, "America is a happy-ending nation." Tornadoes in Arkansas, Tennessee, Missouri, Mississippi, Kentucky, and Alabama killed 236. Deploring the country's lackluster youth, a social critic in New York declared, "I am old-fashioned enough to think that the young should break ground, heave rocks, smash idols, even create a perceptible amount of damage." He concluded that if undergraduates "don't revolt in the name of sense, they ought to do it in the name of style."

Uranium mining began at Beaver Lodge Lake in Saskatchewan, Canada, reportedly the largest deposit of the metal in North America. Visiting Lincoln's tomb in Illinois, President Sukarno of newly independent Indonesia was heard saying to himself over and over again, "I love Americans!" Newark Airport was closed following three fatal crashes in two months, but Britain's De Havilland Comet flew the 6,724 miles from London to Johannesburg in less than 24 hours, opening the world's first jetliner passenger service. Secretary of State Dean Acheson, remaining faithful to propeller-driven aircraft, crossed the Atlantic in fourteen hours aboard the *Sacred Cow* and called it "a magnificent aircraft." Acting on CIA reports that Russians planned to spike the cocktails of American diplomats with the compound lysergic acid diethylamide, which was said to cause strange behavior, Dr. Louis Lasagna administered the drug to several Boston volunteers in 1952 and confirmed accounts of its remarkable properties. The more unstable an individual's personality, he found, the greater his sensitivity to LSD. Captured in Brooklyn after a clothing salesman spotted him, Willie Sutton was asked why he robbed banks. He said, "Because that's where the money is."

In Cairo a junta of army officers led by General Mohammed Naguib and Colonel Gamal Abdel Nasser deposed King Farouk and proclaimed Egypt a republic. The Dionne quintuplets, living near Callender, Ontario, turned sixteen. Connie Mack turned ninety-two. In the Soviet zone of Austria copies of Dwight D. Eisenhower's *Crusade in Europe* were confiscated as "fascist literature." A House subcommittee headed by Representative Ezekiel Gathings of Arkansas opened an investigation of obscene literature and was inundated with letters and packages containing pornography. Fleet Admiral Chester Nimitz confessed to Tex McCrary and Jinx Falkenburg that aboard boats "I always get seasick."

In a Maryland referendum voters approved by a four-to-one margin the state's controversial new Ober Anti-Subversive Act, whose provisions included periodic investigations of Communist activity. Actor John Barrymore Jr., twenty-two, was arrested in Las Vegas for driving recklessly while whooping it up on his second wedding anniversary. General Fulgencio Batista ousted the government of Carlos Piros in Havana and seized control of Cuba. The

California Supreme Court voided the University of California's loyalty oath but upheld the state loyalty oath. The U.S. Supreme Court approved New York's released time program in schools but threw out the state's ban of the motion picture *The Miracle*, thereby extending to films for the first time constitutional guarantees of free speech and a free press.

Joe Adonis was sentenced to prison for conspiring to violate New Jersey's gambling laws. The Missouri, Mississippi, and Red rivers rose over their banks, leaving three dead, 100,000 homeless, and damage estimated at $300,000,000. A House committee investigating the Katyn forest massacre of 10,000 Polish army officers in World War II declared that the Soviet NKVD was responsible. The junta which had ruled Bolivia was overthrown during riots in which two hundred were killed, and the Argentine government seized the independent newspaper *La Prensa*. The South African Supreme Court invalided a law putting colored voters on separate lists, but Prime Minister Daniel F. Malan declared the Supreme Court itself illegal. In Paris Arthur Koestler finished the manuscript of *The Age of Longing*, got drunk and then, "conditioned by my past experiences with policemen," as he later said, punched a gendarme. An Indiana parole board paroled David C. Stephenson, onetime Grand Dragon of the state's Ku Klux Klan and a sadistic murderer of the 1920s. The Dow Jones industrial average moved in the range between 206 and 236. Since Pearl Harbor, the Census Bureau reported, the number of air conditioners in the U.S. had tripled.

Five atomic explosions set off near Las Vegas, Nevada, included a small-scale bomb detonated in mid-air and the first atomic bomb maneuvers, in which five thousand troops took part. The U.S. Supreme Court upheld the convictions of eleven Communist leaders tried in 1949 for intent to overthrow the government, and the Massachusetts legislature banned the Communist party from the ballot. President Truman signed legislation extending the draft on June 19, 1951. The U.S. closed the Hungarian consulate in New York and banned American travel in Hungary.

The White House announced on October 3, 1951, that a second atomic explosion had taken place in the Soviet Union. A third was reported on October 22. West Germany swept Chancellor Konrad Adenauer into office and ratified the European Defense Community Pact. In Prague, Rudolf Slansky and nine other purged Communists were hanged for espionage and treason. Tariff concessions by the

United States to the Soviet Union and Red China were suspended. Radio Free Europe opened a transmitter in Munich to broadcast anti-Communist propaganda to Czechoslovakia, while the Russians restricted travel by foreign diplomats to within twenty-five miles of Moscow and, in New York, forced U.N. Secretary General Trygve Lie to step aside for Dag Hammarskjöld of Sweden.

All these things, and a thousand like them, passed as the falling calendar pages accumulated in the early 1950s. The snows yielded to greenery, summers passed in their heavily handsome way, leaves turned and snow returned as the seasons moved in sequence; the decade settled in; the Cold War deepened; politics grew uglier at the approach of another national election; and among the swing generation, now entering its thirties as the parents of learning children, a nagging feeling grew that the nation was in trouble.

Nineteen

RIGHT TURN

SOMETHING WAS IN A DECLINE, that was certain; if not the country's well-being, then its morals, its pride, its self-respect. Since the beginning of the Korean War cartoonists in Communist countries had been depicting Uncle Sam as an evil, leering old man, and accumulating headlines suggested that they might have a case. In both public life and private, a dismaying number of Americans in key positions were turning out to be thieves or worse. Their crimes seemed particularly outrageous when the criminals were in the federal government. The miscreants were called "influence peddlers" and "five-percenters" responsible for "the mess in Washington," and the issue grew into a severe handicap to Democratic hopes of extending the party's twenty-year hegemony for four more years.

That was precisely what Republicans meant it to be. Every shady implication was pushed to the very threshold of the White House until, by the spring of 1952, it was possible to infer that in one way or another the administration was responsible for most of the corruption in the country. No responsible Republican suggested that Harry Truman's hand had been in any till, of course, and as it happened, the first eminent crook of the 1950s—and TV's first superstar—had never been on the public payroll. He had contributed to Democratic war chests, however, and had become a figure in New York politics, and that was enough to attract the attention of an ambitious Tennessee senator investigating nationwide crime.

Frank Costello, alias Francisco Castaglia, alias Frank Severio, was a man of the period, an organization man of organized crime. He had been arrested only once, long ago, for assault and robbery. Thereafter he let others carry the guns. Moving up the rungs of his trade, he had become in turn a small-time henchman, bootlegger, slot machine operator, owner of gambling houses, and ultimately a friend and sponsor of New York politicians. By then he was trying to cover his tracks. He invested in real estate and oil wells and assured reporters that whatever he had been in the past, he was now a legitimate businessman. But he wasn't. He had been Lucky Luciano's chief lieutenant, and when Lucky was deported, Costello became his legatee, the biggest racketeer. His underworld connections crisscrossed the country. Carmine De Sapio of Tammany was Costello's creature. So, some said, was New York's Mayor William O'Dwyer.

Had Estes Kefauver's senatorial road show toured the country in the late 1940s or the mid-1950s, it would have attracted minimal attention—in the first period because not enough television stations had been established, and in the second because network programs had come to fill the hours of daytime TV. But the committee opened its hearings in May 1950. Lacking anything better to put on the air, local television directors in outlying cities covered the proceedings as a public service, and when the investigators pitched their tents in New York's Foley Square Courthouse on March 12, 1951, cameramen for WPIX-TV were prepared to do the same thing. Here the situation was somewhat different. The incidence of set ownership in New York was extremely high; the mass audience was already assembled. And here in the capital of the communications industry the facilities for relaying transmissions elsewhere had already been developed.

Costello's lawyer tried to circumvent the tube. He asked that the cameras be turned away from his client, explaining that "Mr. Costello doesn't care to submit himself as a spectacle." The senators agreed, but one of the technicians craftily suggested that they concentrate on Costello's hands. The result was superb theater: tense dialogue accompanied by clenched hands, fingers drumming the table top, gestures with papers and water glasses, nervous hands ripping sheets of paper to shreds. Yes, Costello conceded, he kept "a little cash" at home in a "little strongbox." No, he couldn't remember how much. Senator Charles Tobey threatened a search of his mansion, and the gangman suddenly recalled that he had $50,000 there. How had he acquired it? He muttered that he had generous friends. One friend, a fellow golfer who administered Roosevelt Raceway, had admitted that he paid Costello $15,000 a year for four years to see to it that the New York State Harness Racing Commission did not revoke the track's license because of bookie operations there. Rudolph Halley, the committee counsel, asked Costello if that was true. Not at all, said Costello, making fists; there had been some sort of misunderstanding, and he had "spread the propaganda around" that his friend was "a nice fellow" who didn't deserve mean treatment.

Costello's hands began to sweat. He had taken about all he could. Was this, he asked aggrievedly, any way to treat a hardworking businessman? His throat was sore. The television lights bothered him. He wanted to go home. Kefauver bluntly told him to continue answering questions, but Costello shook his head. Then:

KEFAUVER: You refuse to testify further? . . .

COSTELLO: Mr. Senator, I want to think of my health first. When I testify, I want to testify truthfully, and my mind don't function.

KEFAUVER: Your mind seems to be functioning pretty well.

COSTELLO: With all due respect to the senators . . . I have a lot of respect for them, I am not going to answer another question. . . . I am going to walk out.

He then did, thereby winning an eighteen-month stretch in Lewisburg Federal Penitentiary for contempt. His departure was witnessed by thirty million televiewers. According to Videodex figures, nearly 70 percent of New York's sets were tuned to the Kefauver hearings, giving it twice as large an audience as the previous autumn's World Series.

After eight days in Foley Square, the Kefauver committee returned to Washington. Its chairman was now a candidate for the Presidency, and thirty million households had been left with the distinct impression that something was rotten in U.S. cities. Ed Murrow said that "the television performance has been fascinating, the audience fantastic—perhaps because the midgets in the box have been real," and the advertising firm of Young & Rubicam, summing up the general impression, placed ads in New York newspapers to deplore sin and ask: *"Is there anything we can do about it?"*

One thing that could be done was to teach children the difference between right and wrong. Presumably that had already been accomplished, but while the Kefauver committee was still in session newspapers were documenting charges of corruption in the last place to be suspected, among college youth. For several winters the City College of New York had fielded one of the best basketball teams in the country. It now developed that three of its five starters had been taking money—as much as $1,500 each—to throw games in Madison Square Garden. And no sooner had they been indicted than similar confessions were signed by basketball players at New York University, Toledo University, Bradley University, and the University of Kentucky.

The Fagin of the Garden, one Salvatore T. Sollazo, went to prison for eight years; the others received lesser terms. Sollazo was a convenient scapegoat, and given an exciting sports season that fall, the stain on collegiate copybooks would have been quickly forgotten. Unfortunately another scandal emerged that August. West Point announced that ninety cadets had been expelled for cheating on examinations.

Shaving basketball points and cribbing in exams were symptomatic. The country was going through one of its periodic romps with vice—the first since the 1920s—and as always in such scarlet eras people were more tolerant of sin than they would admit. Grasping what was happening required a lot of reading between the lines. A spade was rarely called a spade; newspaper accounts of dissolution were larded with euphemisms. Typically, prostitutes were described as "call girls" or "party girls"; sometimes they were also "fun girls." In bed with a man they invariably "partied." ("After partying with this John, what did you do?" "I went into the bathroom for a towel.") The cumulative effect was to make the oldest profession sound glamorous.

In their furs and jewels, the whores of the 1950s practiced a harlotry far removed from the dime-a-hump "wild girls" who had ridden the rails in the early 1930s or the six-bit "victory girls" of World War II. Call girls never haunted pavements or bus terminals; they lounged around between silk sheets and made appointments by phone, like doctors. Many were beauty contest winners and/or college graduates. Some had majored in economics, and in court they almost seemed to regard themselves as generous contributors to the Gross National Product. In point of fact, the services they provided did play a certain role in business. Firms provided girls for out-of-town buyers as a matter of course, with the burgeoning public relations departments acting as procurers. Accounting stratagems saw to it that the fees were deductible. Only girls known for their discretion were recruited for this sort of work, but the payoffs were big, as much as five hundred dollars a trick. One wry madam marked her dossier for them "VIP"—for "Very Important Pieces."

In a way it made sense. Amateur entanglements were risky for star entertainers and executive vice presidents. The girl picked up under a streetlamp or at a big cocktail party came without references. She might be diseased, or a spy for a competitor, or the wife of a man with blackmail on his mind. She could show up a month later at the office or even at home, determined to parlay a casual encounter into a permanent liaison. Putting everything on a business basis removed those possibilities. It did the job and left no aftertaste. The bigger a man's name, the greater was the likelihood that he would be in the market for professional lust; the bit actors who played the star's ranch hands could prowl for lonesome waitresses, but the star himself needed a pro. And this was true of distinguished men in any occupation requiring a great deal of travel, including politicians of national distinction. The voters didn't know that then. Not that they had any illusions about men in high office. Far from it. They merely thought public figures were too busy stealing the country blind.

Major General Harry H. Vaughan was a big, genial Missourian with a vague resemblance to Hermann Göring and a natural talent for draw poker. He was not conspicuously talented otherwise, or even particularly shrewd. As military aide to Harry S. Truman he might have been expected to know that he would often be on display, yet he continued to be the sloppiest general officer ever in uniform. He simply couldn't remember to put on a blouse or cinch up his necktie on historic occasions, and was always making deals. Nothing shady, to be sure; just borderline things. In his first speech after Truman's ascension to the Presidency in 1945, for instance, he had told the Women's Auxiliary of the Alexandria Westminster Presbyterian Church about the terrible black market prices in occupied Germany, and as an example he revealed that he had sold his own fifty-five-dollar American watch to a Russian officer for five hundred dollars.

In the White House, Vaughan became celebrated for his gregariousness and his affability. His social energy seemed inexhaustible. He was always ready to grace a cocktail party or a dinner party.

Making new friends there, he would be ready, in the morning, to grease the machinery of government with a letter or a well-placed phone call. In almost any other line of endeavor this would have been unexceptionable. In his it was dangerous business.

The general's undoing was a sleazy ex-colonel in the Quartermaster Corps named James V. Hunt. There were others of Hunt's stripe around, but he was typical of them and, for that matter, representative of the influence peddlers of the time. For a fee—in Truman's Washington it was 5 percent of profits—the man with influence who "knew the ropes" and had "pull" saw to it that a difficult deal went through. At Hunt's request, Vaughan put outrageous pressure on regulatory agencies, procurement officers at the Pentagon, the State Department's passport office, and the Department of Agriculture. In occupied Europe a businessman with a to-whom-it-may-concern letter from the White House bought up essential oils for a perfume manufacturer. Federal trade regulations were bent for one Hunt client, surplus property disposal procedures for a second, public housing schedules for a third. In the readjustment to a peacetime economy scarce structural steel went to a California racetrack, scarce commercial sugar to a soft drink manufacturer. Vaughan let himself be the channel for campaign contributions from the beneficiaries. Worst of all, he accepted from one of them a personal gift which would become famous. It was a $520 Deepfreeze.

Three other Missouri cronies of the President were Donald Dawson, E. Merle Young, and William M. Boyle Jr. Their turf was the Reconstruction Finance Corporation. The RFC, established by Herbert Hoover to shore up firms facing ruin, had financed defense industries in the early 1940s and eased the pangs of adjustment after the war. Lately there hadn't been much need for it, but suddenly business over there began humming. A senatorial subcommittee under J. William Fulbright of Arkansas went to take a look and stumbled into a cesspool. Government appropriations were being used to plunge in all sorts of speculative ventures, including gambling hotels in Las Vegas and Miami. Some records were missing. Others showed out-and-out favoritism. After being turned down three times in its application for $565,000 in RFC funds, the American Lithfold Company had paid an $8,000 retainer to Boyle, who among other things was vice chairman of the Democratic National Committee. The loan was then approved. Dawson, a special assistant to the President, had repeatedly secured RFC money for political protégés who lacked collateral. Young was an RFC loan examiner. For ten years he had been supplementing his salary with "retainers" from firms whose loans he put through. After getting one for $150,000, a company showed its gratitude by sending Mrs. Young a present. It was a $9,540 mink coat.

That gift was disastrous. If there was one thing most American housewives wanted more than anything else, and never expected to get, it was a coat of mink. And here was a woman who had been given one because her husband had been defrauding the government. Fueled by Republicans—who overlooked the fact that their own national chairman had intervened to get a big RFC loan for the Carthage Hydrocol Company, of which he was president— rumors grew until there were those who thought everybody in the administration had a Deepfreeze in the basement and a mink on his wife's back. The wife of Senator Blair Moody wore on her new fur coat a receipt showing that it was mink-dyed muskrat, $381.25 with taxes. Harold W. Reed of the Mink Ranchers' Association found it necessary to issue a statement saying that all women with mink coats weren't married to crooks, that many were in fact "highly respectable people of discriminating taste."

Harry Truman said Fulbright's RFC investigation was "asinine." It wasn't, and Fulbright proved it wasn't. Under klieg lights and amplifying equipment in the Senate Caucus Room, he paraded before the press evidence that Dawson, while sitting at the President's right hand, had in effect headed a ring of conspirators who had been lining their pockets at the expense of the public. One memorable exhibit was the office diary of Walter Dunham, director of the RFC. In it were carefully logged scores of phone calls from Dawson and others putting in the fix for disreputable and discredited speculators who had found the door to politicians of easy virtue. Washington had seen nothing like it since Teapot Dome, but Truman continued to wear blinders. Young was indicted by a grand jury for perjury; the White House had no comment. Boyle was allowed to resign "for reasons of health" after the President had staunchly defended him for three months. Dawson, like Vaughan, continued to sit on presidential councils and make final decisions on personnel matters. It was literally wicked.

And there was more to come. As then organized, the Bureau of Internal Revenue was a standing invitation to malefaction. Its sixty-four regional offices were each headed by a collector of internal revenue. They, their deputy collectors, and the hierarchy in Washington were all political appointees. The jobs went to Democrats who had done the best job of shepherding voters to the polls in the last national election. Secretary of the Treasury Snyder, an honest Missourian, had felt scandal coming for some time and had been trying to nail down hearsay about bribery. He had gone so far as to demand the resignation of James P. Finnegan, the St. Louis collector, but Finnegan's ties to Truman were strong, and he hung on.

Now all that changed. With circumstantial evidence from a congressional committee, Finnegan was indicted by a grand jury; he quit then, and was later convicted of failing to report $103,000 on his own tax returns. Next Snyder suspended collector James G. Smyth of San Francisco and eight members of his staff; indictments for conspiracy to defraud the government followed. Dennis Delaney, the Boston collector, resigned and was indicted for accepting bribes. Collector Joseph Marcelle of Brooklyn was found to have omitted $32,000 in taxable income from his returns; he and Mordecai Miller, a sidekick, were sacked for refusing to identify the sources of their outside income for the King committee. George J. Schoenman, the Commissioner of Internal Revenue and a former White House aide, handed in his resignation, pleading ill health. Altogether, nine Democrats were on their way to prison, including Matthew H. Connelly, who had been President Truman's appointments secretary.

The sheer weight of evidence finally provoked Truman into reacting. Dismissing Caudle, he declared that he had been "sold down the river" by men he had trusted.* He then sent Congress plans for reorganization of the RFC and the Bureau of Internal Revenue. In the future the bureau would be known as the Internal Revenue Service; its personnel would all be under the civil service. But that was no longer enough to appease administration critics. The next presidential election was now less than a year away. The "mess in Washington" had become a vigorous campaign issue. Something had to be done to steal the Republican thunder, and therefore he announced the establishment of a presidential commission to investigate charges of corruption in the federal government.

Republicans wondered aloud whether there was a Democrat upright enough to head the commission. That was no joke to Truman.

---

* President Kennedy pardoned Connelly in 1962; President Johnson pardoned Caudle in 1965.

He first appointed Thomas F. Murphy, the prosecutor of Alger Hiss and now a federal district court judge. After accepting, Murphy changed his mind at the last minute without giving a reason—a stinging blow to presidential prestige. Next Truman announced that the housecleaning would be conducted by his Attorney General, J. Howard McGrath. The critics said that would be worse than nothing. The scandals had touched his department, too, and as a former chairman of the Democratic National Committee, McGrath had brought the very men now being indicted into the government. The GOP cried whitewash; so did the ADA; so did the House Judiciary Committee, which voted its own investigation of McGrath and Justice.

The farce now approached its climax. The desperate President named Newbold Morris, a liberal New York Republican lawyer, as chief commissioner. In rapid succession Morris appeared on *Meet the Press* to divulge unsupported suspicions of the Justice Department, rejected McGrath's offer of office space and had quarters opened in a downtown Washington office building instead, asked Congress for subpoena power and was turned down, and finally was subpoenaed himself—as a witness before a Senate committee which wanted to question him about the role of his own law firm in the illegal sale of surplus oil tankers to a foreign government. Morris then offended everyone in the government by mailing long questionnaires to all U.S. employees, including cabinet members, instructing them to list their net worth and their sources of income. When McGrath's questionnaire arrived, he blew up. Under the mistaken impression that Morris was answerable to him, he sent him a five-word memorandum: "Your employment is hereby terminated." Truman learned about it from an AP teletype. Then *he* blew up—and dismissed McGrath.

In those last months before the political conventions of 1952, Truman's grip seemed less and less firm. His handling of the steel strike that year was a parody of his resourceful disciplining of John L. Lewis six years earlier. When the steel companies refused to abide by a Wage Mediation Board award of March 20, offering higher wages to workers without any rise in steel prices, Truman directed Secretary of Commerce Charles Sawyer to seize the mills and run them as government property. He thought his emergency powers allowed him to do that, and he believed the Supreme Court would agree. It didn't; on June 2 it ruled that the seizure was illegal. The United Steel Workers then struck anyway, and to get the union's 600,000 men back on the job with a 16-cent increase, the President had to accept a $5.20 per ton rise in the cost of steel—the very thing he had been trying to avert.

Accompanying this stumbling performance in the White House was a dismaying rise in Republican irresponsibility. Too long out of power, losing faith in an electorate which had rejected it in five straight presidential elections, the minority party was determined to discredit the Democrats at all costs. Exposing the pilferers hiding under Truman's umbrella was its prerogative and even its duty. Hammering away at administrative incompetence was an additional service to the country; that is how the democratic system is supposed to work. But the GOP's extraordinarily savage attacks on Dean Acheson and General George C. Marshall were another matter. Neither had any connection with crooks like Caudle and Finnegan. As America's spokesmen abroad they represented the entire country. They deserved, at the very least, an acknowledgment that they were decent men in pursuit of honorable objectives.

Acheson was a patrician, with a distant, even arrogant manner toward his adversaries. General Marshall was altogether different. He was a military hero, like Eisenhower, identified with neither party. His service as presidential envoy to China had been as nonpartisan as Eisenhower's invasion of Europe. In the cabinet he had avoided all political winds. His only controversial position had been taken in the uproar which followed the dismissal of MacArthur. He had argued eloquently then for the concept of limited war. Doubtless that had angered MacArthur's admirers on the Hill, but the same position had been warmly defended by Omar Bradley and the Joint Chiefs. Besides, Republican antagonism toward Marshall had been marked before MacArthur's recall. In September 1950 twenty Republican senators had gone on record against his appointment as Secretary of Defense. Congressman Dewey Short of Missouri had called him "a cat's-paw and a pawn" for Truman; Joe Martin had characterized him as "an appeaser" responsible for Mao's takeover of China.* What had aroused them? Why were

* On the eve of World War II Martin had led the successful fights which rejected legislation to fortify Guam and Wake. Arming them, he had said then, might provoke Japanese warlords.

they stalking a distinguished officer who had been called the "greatest living American"?

The answer lay right there: Marshall was above the battle, a national symbol, and in the ruthless struggle for power any man who was above criticism was a threat to them. If he was not with them now, he might be ranged against them one day. That being so, they needed to spike his guns now, discrediting him so thoroughly that any future opinion from him would be discounted in advance. The last stage of the job went to McCarthy. In midafternoon on June 14, 1951, he began his longest and most famous Senate speech, charging Marshall with "a conspiracy so immense and an infamy so black as to dwarf any previous such venture in the history of man."

Liberal Republicans were trying to establish an intelligent, responsible opposition to the Truman administration. Margaret Chase Smith had declared that she did not want to see her party ride to victory on "the Four Horsemen of Calumny—Fear, Ignorance, Bigotry and Smear." Emmet John Hughes shunned the phrase "mess in Washington" as "petty, self-righteous, and extravagant." Hughes also thought it dangerous to challenge the patriotism of Democrats, but by early 1952 such advice had been rejected by the party's dominant Old Guard. Throughout that year Republican polemicists even persisted in calling the opposition "the Democrat party," insisting that it was grammatically correct, when in fact it was meant as a slight.

Speeches from the Republican right divided all Democrats into five categories: the criminals, the traitors, the cowards, the incompetents who always blundered into war, and the effete, who lacked sufficient vigor to invade China and conquer it. Differing politicians are usually tolerant of one another, but the consequence of this sort of oratorical thrust was to drive a deep schism between the parties.

The GOP line was popular. Most Americans had come to disapprove of Truman's Presidency, and no amount of whistle-stopping could have restored him to their good graces now. According to recurring Gallup samplings, his first-term low in public support had come in 1946, when just 32 percent of his constituents had been for him. Throughout 1950 the figure had varied between 37 and 46 percent. Thereafter—during his last two years in office—approval of him never rose above 32 percent. At times it dipped to 23 percent, which meant that fewer than one American in four stood behind him. He had never displayed the charm and magnetism of personal leadership. At best he had seemed to be a plucky fellow who had overcome his lack of talent by sheer determination. He saw himself that way. At his three hundredth press conference in April 1952 he told reporters: "I have tried my best to give the nation everything I have in me. There are a great many people—I suppose a million in this country—who could have done the job better than I did it. But I had the job and I had to do it. I always quote an epitaph which is in the cemetery at Tombstone, Arizona. It says: 'Here lies Jack Williams. He done his damnedest.'"

Nevertheless, to a Democrat of his convictions the prospect of a Republican administration was something to be regarded with horror. Who besides Truman could head the Democratic ticket? Estes Kefauver's name was heard everywhere. He had entered his name in all the primaries; his following was immense. Truman was unimpressed. A machine politician and proud of it, the President had no use for reformers who blackened the names of fellow Democrats. Yet most of the other possible candidates carried one handicap or another. Alben Barkley was seventy-two, too old. Russell of Georgia was anathema to the liberal wing. Harriman had never run for office. In the autumn of 1951 Truman thought he had found the best of all possible successors. Inviting Chief Justice Fred M. Vinson to the presidential retreat on Key West, he proposed that he step down from the bench and become the standard-bearer. Vinson hemmed and hawed, argued that the Supreme Court should not be a stepping-stone to the White House, and finally agreed to talk it over with his wife. She liked the idea even less; the chief judge, Truman regretfully noted in his papers, "firmly declined." With that, the President turned to Illinois. In the election of November 1948 the head of the state ticket there had forged a remarkable personal triumph, winning by the historic margin of 572,067 votes. Truman's own margin in Illinois had been 33,612. Alone, he doubtless would have lost the state. To David Lloyd, one of his presidential assistants, he said that he wanted to be notified of the next Washington visit of Governor Adlai E. Stevenson.

In that same month a Republican governor, Sherman Adams of New Hampshire, became chairman of the state's Eisenhower for President committee. At once he encountered a problem. To enter a name in New Hampshire's approaching presidential primary, he was required by law to offer evidence that his candidate was a member of the Republican party. Adams sent an inquiry to Eisenhower's county seat in Kansas. Back came this reply from County Clerk C. F. Moore:

> Mr. Eisenhower has never voted in this county as far as I know, the Primary laws were first put into operation in the year 1928 and he has never voted since then, I have been county clerk since January 14th, 1927, Dwight has never been in the city as far as I know of until after war No. 2 at least he has never voted or I would have known it as the party filiation books are still here ever since the primary or branding law was passed in the spring of 1927 and never went into effect until the Primary Election of 1928.
> Dwights father was a republican and always voted the republican ticket up until his death, however that has nothing to do with the son as many differ from their fathers of which I am sorry to see, the multitude beleives in going into debt and see how much they can spend, it has become a habit & will sink this nation into bankrupsy.
> I don't think he has any politics.

Not only had Eisenhower no politics; he had no religion, no conspicuous guiding principles, and few known views on most of the great issues of his time. For the second time in four years he was being offered the most powerful office in the world, yet the men making the proposal had no idea what he would do with it if he got it. To be sure, as president of Columbia University he had made such conservative remarks as "If all that Americans want is security, they can go to prison." At the same time, he had used his prestige to rally public opinion behind the Roosevelt-Truman foreign policy, and his accomplishments, including his present post as commander of NATO in Europe, had been achieved while representing Democratic administrations. All his fellow countrymen could be sure of was that he was a man of strength, decency, and tolerance; that he had won the respect of European statesmen; and that he displayed many of the ordinary characteristics which a democratic people like to find in their leaders—a fondness for dialect jokes, for example, and a bent for informal dress best expressed in the Eisenhower jacket.

He turned out to be a Republican, though the question remained unsettled for several agonizing weeks. Returning from France on January 6, 1952, Senator Henry Cabot Lodge Jr. of Massachusetts told reporters that the general would accept the Republican nomination if it were offered, and that he would not disown this statement by Lodge. He came close to it, though. In Paris next day he refused to identify his party affiliation for reporters; he merely said that the senator had given "an accurate account of the general tenor of my political convictions and of my Republican voting record." He dodged the question of accepting a draft. Persons working in his behalf, he warned, did so at his displeasure. While there could be "no question of the right of American citizens to organize in pursuit of their common convictions," their convictions in this case were not shared by the man they were meant to honor. He added: "Under no circumstances will I ask for relief from this assignment in order to seek nomination to political office, and I shall not participate in the preconvention activities of others who have an intention with respect to me."

Apparently the door was closed. In the next breath, however, he reopened it a crack. If he had no choice he would, of course, answer a call to "duty that would transcend my present responsibility." That was enough for Adams and Lodge, and they were off running for him. Among those now convinced that Eisenhower would be the Republican choice—and that he would soon forget his pledge to remain in Paris—was Harry S. Truman.

On January 20 Governor Stevenson spoke before the annual banquet of the Urban League in New York. He arrived in Washington at four o'clock the following afternoon for a conference on mine inspection and found that the Metropolitan Club had no room for him. A room had been reserved for him at the Roger Smith Hotel. Checking in, he was handed a message from Blair House; the President wanted to see him that very evening. At 11:15 P.M. Stevenson was back in his hotel room, feeling dazed. Calling a friend, he said, "This is Adlai, and I've just had the most incredible experience. Would you mind terribly coming down to the hotel for a little talk?" The friend found him in his shirtsleeves. Stevenson said, "I've just come from Blair House, and the President wants me to save the world from Dwight Eisenhower."

In Truman's memoirs he wrote that he had told the governor:

> . . . that I would not run for President again and that it was my opinion that he was best-fitted for the place. . . . I told him what I thought the Presidency is, how it has grown into the most powerful

and greatest office in the history of the world. I asked him to take it and told him that if he would agree he could be nominated. . . . But he said: No! He apparently was flabbergasted.

Stevenson had reminded Truman that he was an announced candidate for gubernatorial reelection, and "One does not treat the highest office within the gift of the people of Illinois as a consolation prize." He had obligations toward his two younger sons, who had been virtually abandoned by their socialite mother; blinding publicity could warp their lives. In addition, he doubted that he was ready for the Presidency. After another term in Springfield he might be equipped for it, but not now. Stevenson did not, of course, suggest that this would be a difficult year for the Democratic nominee, but it must have crossed his mind; unlike Truman, he knew how much the administration had been hurt by the recent scandals.

Ironically, Eisenhower briefly thought—while watching a telecast of the Democratic convention the following summer—that had he known that the other party would nominate a man of Stevenson's caliber, he would have stayed in Paris. Like millions of others, in America and around the world, Dwight Eisenhower had been touched by the magic of Adlai Stevenson. Physically the governor was unprepossessing: short, bald, broad of beam. Yet he came close to political genius. His integrity and devotion to public service were sensed at once; his intellect and wit delighted admirers in both parties. No twentieth-century politician, including Franklin Roosevelt and John Kennedy, won so loyal a following among liberal intellectuals. When he spoke, he evoked a lyrical sense of America's past and what she might be in the future. Stevenson dreamed Lincoln's dream; vast audiences sat hushed as he swept them up in it; for the young and the idealists in his party he became a kind of religion that year. Like Wendell Willkie twelve years earlier, he made his countrymen better just for pausing to reflect upon what he represented, and eight years later the lamp he had held so high for so long would show the way upward to another, younger Democratic nominee.

Truman refused to accept his withdrawal. Shortly after the President had breakfasted with Senator Paul Douglas of Illinois the next morning, January 22, the news of Stevenson's call at Blair House was on front pages across the country. The dismayed governor found himself accompanied by swarms of reporters. His name appeared in speculative accounts by all syndicated columnists, and he was featured in a *Time* cover story which said, "Whatever the truth behind the rumors, this much is evident: in a cold season for the Democrats, Adlai Stevenson is politically hot, and Harry Truman feels the need of a little warmth." Asked by the press whether he would accept a draft, Stevenson grappled with his conscience. How, he asked those close to him, could anyone in good health and already in public life refuse the greatest honor and greatest responsibility in American politics? His reply to reporters was as negative as he could make it; "No one," he said, could be "drafted by a modern convention against his oft-expressed wish." In fact it had not happened in seventy-two years. In January Stevenson thought a repetition of that inconceivable.

Six weeks later he wasn't so sure. On March 4 he and the President met again—at his request, according to Truman in his memoirs; at Truman's, according to Stevenson's papers. To avoid encouragement of the rising presidential boom, the governor flew to Washington under the name of an aide, William McCormick Blair Jr. During a refueling stop at Louisville, Barry Bingham, publisher of the *Louisville Courier-Journal* and an old friend, urged him to let the people "judge for themselves on the basis of the public record." Laughing, Stevenson said, "Well, you certainly haven't been much help to me!" At Blair House he reaffirmed to Truman that reelection in Illinois was the full measure of his ambition. But the President wasn't much help, either. "I felt," he later wrote, "that in Stevenson I had found the man to whom I could safely turn over the responsibilities of party leadership. . . . I felt certain that he would see it as his duty to seek the nomination."

On March 29, 1952, the governor was one of 5,300 Democrats gathered in Washington's National Guard Armory for the party's annual Jefferson-Jackson Day Dinner. Other guests included the Achesons, and on the way there Alice Acheson asked her husband whether he thought the President might disclose his political plans during his after-dinner remarks. Out of the question, the Secretary of State said briskly; this was too early for him to announce that he would run again, and if he had decided not to, he wouldn't reveal it before this audience, so many of whom would be disappointed. As it happened, Alice Acheson was the first person outside the Truman family to learn what was coming. She was seated beside the President, and as the time for speeches approached he showed her the last page of his. On it he had written in his own hand his decision not to seek another term. "You, Bess, and I," he said, "are the only ones here who know that." Distressed, she wanted to bring her husband over to argue with him, but he shook his head. "A little later," Acheson wrote, "we were stunned by the announcement. The party was quite unprepared to find a new leader and the material from which to choose seemed thin."

That was a Saturday evening. On Sunday Stevenson appeared on *Meet the Press,* now a television program, before a large number of studio spectators. The most heavily freighted question centered on his deposition in the Hiss case. The key testimony had been brief:

Q. Have you known other persons who have known Mr. Alger Hiss?
A. Yes.
Q. From the speech of those persons, can you state what the reputation of Alger Hiss is for integrity, loyalty, and veracity?
A. Yes.
Q. Specify whether his reputation for integrity is good or bad?
A. Good.
Q. Specify whether his reputation for loyalty is good or bad?
A. Good.
Q. Specify whether his reputation for veracity is good or bad?
A. Good.

In the cross-interrogation in behalf of the government, the following testimony had been taken:

Q. Were you ever a guest in the home of defendant Alger Hiss at any time in 1935, to and including 1938?
A. No, I have never been a guest in Mr. Hiss's home.
Q. Did you, prior to 1948, hear that the defendant Alger Hiss during the years 1937 and 1938 removed confidential and secret documents from the State Department and made such documents available to persons not authorized to see or receive them?
A. No.
Q. Did you, prior to 1948, hear reports that the defendant Alger Hiss was a Communist?
A. No.

After two years of McCarthyism, however, bland material like this was being transformed into political poison. Richard Nixon, California's new senator, was saying that Stevenson had "testified as a

character witness for Alger Hiss" and "in defense of Alger Hiss."*
Everett Dirksen, the Republican senatorial candidate in Illinois, was taking the same line ("What would Dirksen have said?" asked Stevenson. "Would he have told a lie?") and the *Chicago Tribune* had argued editorially that the governor should have avoided testifying because by giving evidence he had "arrayed himself willingly beside Alger Hiss."

Now on *Meet the Press* Stevenson said: "I am a lawyer, and I think it is the duty of all citizens and particularly of lawyers—it is the most fundamental responsibility of lawyers—to give testimony in a court of law, honestly and willingly. And I think it will be a very unhappy day for Anglo-Saxon justice when a man in public life is too timid to state what he knows or has heard about a defendant in a criminal case for fear that a defendant would be ultimately convicted. That is the ultimate timidity."

In response to other questions he said once more, "I must run for governor. I want to run for governor. I seek no other office. I have no other ambition." Lawrence Spivak asked, "Governor, doesn't this large studio audience give you any indication of how some people in the country feel about that?" Stevenson smiled. "It's very flattering indeed," he said, "and I suppose flattery hurts no one—that is, if he doesn't inhale."

What he had avoided saying was that among the members of the Carnegie Endowment's board of trustees, which had voted in favor of making Alger Hiss president of the foundation and against accepting his resignation during his trials, was Dwight D. Eisenhower.

On March 11 Eisenhower had won the New Hampshire primary, 44,497 to Taft's 35,820; eight days later Stassen won the Minnesota primary with 128,605 votes, but Ike was right behind him with 106,946 write-ins. From Paris came word that his showing in these two races had persuaded the general to "reexamine" his "political position." In short, he was packing.

Kefauver was winning Democratic delegates, humiliating the President in state after state, but the Republican primaries, after that first burst of enthusiasm for Eisenhower, were not a runaway for anyone. Taft beat the general in Nebraska, beat Warren in Wis-

---

* At the time of Nixon's first speech on this subject, the governor had been virtually unknown outside Illinois, and in the version which went into the *Congressional Record* his name was misspelled "Stephenson."

consin, and trounced Stassen in Illinois by over 700,000 votes; write-ins for Eisenhower put him third. On April 15, the general took New Jersey away from Taft. He won in Pennsylvania, and Governor Dewey's support guaranteed him the lion's share of New York's delegates. He picked up 20 delegates in Kansas, but only one in Kentucky, which gave the other 19 to Taft. Indiana went to Taft. On June 3, in the last two primaries, Warren won in California and Taft beat Ike in South Dakota. Nationally, Taft's lieutenants counted 588 convention votes—with 604 needed for the nomination.

Early in April Eisenhower had announced that his "surprising development as a political figure" was interfering with his military duties; he asked to be relieved, and the White House granted the request at once, naming General Matthew Ridgway as his successor in Paris. Ike's campaign opened on June 2 in his home town of Abilene, Kansas, where twenty thousand stood in a driving rain to hear him speak in the local ball park. As he saw it, the most pressing issue before the country was "liberty versus socialism." He wanted the Senate to have a stronger role in determining foreign policy, and he called for lower taxes, an improved Taft-Hartley law, "a decent armistice" in Korea, abolition of needless federal agencies, continuing membership in NATO, and the "rooting out" of "subversive elements." He was against controls to fight inflation and against "socialized medicine," and he thought protection of civil rights should be left to the states.

There didn't seem to be much there that Taft could quarrel with. On June 19, in an "Answer to Abilene," he criticized the general for misunderstanding Taft-Hartley, lacking an agricultural policy, failure to name "the persons responsible for the loss of China," and refusal to condemn the administration's handling of the Korean War. That was quibbling, and everybody who could read a newspaper knew it. Someone pointed out that the only real issue upon which it was easy to differentiate between the two candidates was General MacArthur. Taft had promised to give MacArthur a government job. Eisenhower promised to listen to anything MacArthur had to say.

On July 7, when the Republican National Convention opened in Chicago's International Amphitheater, hard by the stockyards, those present included Betty Furness, a thirty-six-year-old former actress who had contracted to appear on television commercials with the message, "You can be sure if it's Westinghouse." Before Betty had finished opening and closing refrigerator doors she would entrance seventy million viewers, including one GOP delegate who would try to put her name in nomination.

The three major networks had shipped thirty tons of equipment and over a thousand workers to the amphitheater, but the Taft forces who controlled the convention had made few concessions to the new medium. Apart from agreeing to the installation of a Tele-PrompTer, or "idiot board," at the lectern, they had spurned requests from the TV networks. Later in the week, as word spread among those in the hall that they were on television, repeated motions would be made to "poll the delegation," so that everybody could be sure he was seen by the folks back home. Viewers found it maddening. In the beginning, however, there was none of this, and when Delegate Cecil B. De Mille told reporters that this was the greatest show on earth, he meant the proceedings, not their transmission on television, which he as a movie mogul had sworn to stamp out.

Since conservatives had written the scenario, events bore an unmistakable rightist tinge. The keynote address was delivered by Douglas MacArthur. It was a great chance for a dark horse, but to the disappointment of his supporters he bungled it. Ike in mufti retained his appeal; MacArthur was merely another retired executive with a hairpiece. Whenever he mentioned God, which was often, his voice had a disconcerting way of rising a register and breaking, and he had developed a peculiar way of jumping up and down for emphasis. Toward the end of MacArthur's speech the delegates were babbling so much among themselves that the general could scarcely be heard. This time he did fade away. After speaking he returned to the Waldorf in New York to await the decision of the convention. For three days the *Bataan* stood on the tarmac at La Guardia Field, its motor warm and its tanks full, ready to fly him back if the party should turn to him. On Friday the plane went back to its hangar.

The most popular speech was Joe McCarthy's. Here Taft's program committee had correctly judged the temper of the audience. When Chairman Walter Hallanan said he would give the delegates "Wisconsin's fighting Marine," a man who had suffered much for his dedication to "exposing the traitors in our government," and the band struck up "The Marines' Hymn," a wild demonstration swept up half the men in the hall. Placards advertised his victims: "Hiss,"

"Acheson," "Lattimore." Joe grinned satanically. After a tribute to MacArthur ("the greatest American that was ever born") he launched into his text on a note of high drama: "We are at war tonight." Solemnly he recited statistics of the conflict—the number of square miles which the "Commie-loving" Democrats had handed over to the beasts in the Kremlin, the millions of souls they had plunged into torment, the perfidy of the "slimy traitors" who slithered even now in "the Red Dean's State Department." He said he had documents to prove all this. Huge graphs and charts were wheeled to the lectern. The data were meaningless, the scales unreadable, but that didn't matter; Joe explained it all while waving a pointer like a cattle prod.

That was the real keynote, and subsequent performances adjusted to Joe's level. Apart from the Westinghouse commercials and the attractive wives and daughters of candidates—most memorably "Honeybear" Warren and her sisters—the fare was grim. Young Senator Richard Nixon cried that "the American people have had enough of the whining, whimpering, groveling attitude of our diplomatic representatives, who talk of America's weaknesses and of America's fears, rather than of America's strengths and of America's courage." The platform was hewn from the same lumber. In writing the foreign policy plank, John Foster Dulles excoriated every aspect of the Democratic record abroad, from Roosevelt's failure to defend the Baltic republics in 1939 to Korea. A reporter reminded him that at the time of the Baltic seizure Dulles himself, an America Firster, was urging FDR to stay out of the "senseless, cyclical struggle" to maintain national sovereignties, and that as recently as last May 19 Dulles had written in *Life* that Truman's decision to defend South Korea had been "courageous, righteous, and in the national interest." How could he say otherwise now? He replied that if he were speaking as an individual, he couldn't. As a platform writer, however, he was merely setting forth the Republican case against the Democrats. It was, he agreed, a nice point.

Combative as the words at the podium were, the struggle for the nomination was fiercer. Its ferocity is suggested by an appeal from David S. Ingalls, Taft's cousin and campaign manager. Circulated among delegates that week, it began:

SINK DEWEY!!

TOM DEWEY IS THE MOST COLD-BLOODED, RUTHLESS, SELFISH POLITICAL BOSS IN THE UNITED STATES TODAY. He stops at nothing to enforce his will. His promises are worthless. He is the greatest menace that the Republican Party has. Twice he has led us down the road to defeat, and now he is trying the same trick again hidden behind the front of another man.

But how could Dewey do it? Taft seemed to have the nomination sewed up before the first gavel had fallen. On Sunday, July 6, when party functionaries were still arriving, the senator had walked briskly into a press meeting in the basement of Chicago's Conrad Hilton Hotel carrying a large, neat bundle of telegrams—530 of them —from delegates who had banded together in their determination to stick with him to the end. By Monday morning Taft had 607 such assurances—three more than needed. Both the temporary and the permanent chairman were pledged to him. He had a majority in the Platform Committee, the Credentials Committee, and the National Committee. His aides had even picked the music to be played and the singers who would sing it. There was, it seemed, no way he could be turned back.

The Eisenhower forces' only hope lay in challenging accredited delegates. Ever since the Civil War the Republican faith had been defended in southern states by skeletal organizations of loyal party workers. They had but two tasks: to serve as postmasters when a Republican President was in the White House, and to vote in the quadrennial conventions. As regulars, they were now backing Taft to a man.

Eisenhower men questioned their right to sit on the convention floor. The first contest arose in Texas, and it was typical. Only five voters had attended the Republican party's 1950 Fort Worth caucus, so Henry Zweifel, the national committeeman for Texas, had decided to hold the May 3, 1952, caucus in his own home. To his dismay his garden had been trampled by a hundred strangers wearing Ike buttons. On the ground that Democrats without standing in the Republican party had no right to choose the Republican nominee, Zweifel had ordered them out of the yard. Three weeks later, at the state convention in Mineral Wells, regular Republicans had chosen the delegates they would send to Chicago: 30 Taft men, 4 for Eisenhower, and 4 for MacArthur. The Eisenhower people had convened in a separate hall, picking 33 Ike delegates and 5 for Taft. Thus there were two slates of Texans at the national convention.

The party officials who would choose between them were, of course, Taft men. But Eisenhower spokesmen were denouncing what they called "the Texas Steal" and demanding that Taft himself denounce such tactics. The senator replied with some heat that he had never stolen anything in his life. GOP slates in the South had been chosen according to procedures which had been followed for eighty-four years, he said, and only those with larceny in their own hearts were saying otherwise. He was right. The issue was bogus. The Eisenhower delegations from the South were no more representative than the Taft southerners, and the Taftites were at least lifelong Republicans. Unfortunately for the senator, he was not the idol of a grateful nation. Shielded by Ike's five-star mantle, his floor managers had expanded operations; they were now challenging the slates from Georgia and Louisiana, too. Even more important, they had coaxed their leader into the ring.

Eisenhower had been against going to Chicago. He thought it unseemly. Instead, he would spend the week with his wife's family in Denver. On July 1 he and Mamie had celebrated their thirty-sixth wedding anniversary at the Dowds' eight-room gray brick house at 750 Lafayette Street, the closest thing to a home he had known in a tumbleweed marriage that had been spent on military posts. In an evening discussion his supporters now persuaded him that he must move on to Chicago. The next morning he told reporters that he was ready "to roar clear across the country for clean decent operations." He would fight "to keep our party clean and fit to lead the nation." The battle being waged in the Credentials Committee was a "straight-out issue of right and wrong." He deplored "smoke-filled rooms," "star chamber methods," and "chicanery," and he was "shocked" at the National Committee's decision temporarily seating pro-Taft delegations from the South. He demanded "fair play."

Fair play: that became the rallying cry of his followers. Lodge said Taftite southerners must be banished as "stains on the integrity of our party." There was a good deal of this sort of talk, some of it in the form of out-and-out charges that Taft was a thief, and the impact of it on the conservatives was galvanic. During two decades in the political Sahara they had learned much about bitterness, but their anger in the amphitheater transcended everything they had felt toward the Democrats. This convention wanted to nominate Taft. New Englanders excepted, if its members had felt free to follow their convictions they would have chosen him by acclamation and campaigned for him around the clock. Even the New York delegation eyed him longingly; only Dewey's whip kept it in line. One by one the men whose telegrams the senator had held were drifting toward Eisenhower's floor managers, doing it sneakily and hating themselves for it. Emotionally the high point of the week was reached Wednesday evening, at the climax of the debate over the Georgia slate, when Dirksen, his hair carefully mussed, mounted the podium in Taft's behalf, pointed at the New York standard, and intoned, "Reexamine your hearts before you take this action. We followed you before and you took us down the path to defeat." Crooking his finger at Dewey, he cried, "And don't take us down that road again!"

They roared their approval—and then reached for Ike buttons. It was the polls that did it. Loving Taft as they did, they loved victory more, and they believed that the general, unlike the senator, would lead them to 1600 Pennsylvania Avenue. A majority were looking for an honorable way into the Eisenhower camp. Unwittingly the Taft forces gave them one. By banning cameras and reporters from the credentials hearings, they created the impression that they were trying to steamroller their men through. "Fair play" had acquired a convincing ring. The issue was joined when an Eisenhower leader, Governor Arthur B. Langlie of Washington, put a motion before the convention asking that the contested delegates from Georgia, Texas, and Louisiana remain unseated until their qualifications had been approved by a majority of all the delegates. At that the senator's strategists skidded again. Ohio congressman Clarence J. Brown, a Taft manager, offered an amendment to the Langlie resolution which would have given Ike's people just about everything they wanted while keeping control of the proceedings in Taftite hands. Brown seemed to be conceding that play in fact had been less than fair. It gave his amendment the semblance of a deal—which is precisely what the Eisenhower floor managers called it. The roll call which followed determined the outcome of the entire convention. Brown's amendment was defeated, 658 to 548. By that margin control of the Republican party had passed into the hands of Dwight Eisenhower. His nomination followed, a few minutes before noon on Friday, the fifth day of the GOP marathon, when at the end of the first ballot the count stood: Eisenhower 595, Taft 500, Warren 81, Stassen 20, MacArthur 10, Senator Edward J. Thye waved the Minnesota standard and yelled above the roar, "Minnesota wishes to change its vote to Eisenhower!" Senators Bricker, for Taft, and Knowland, for Warren, then moved that the choice be made unanimous. Ike had it.

He had watched it on television in his suite at the Blackstone Hotel, standing with his four brothers and nervously fingering two good luck charms, a Salvation Army coin and a Boy Scout souvenir. As Minnesota switched, Herbert Brownell rushed up and embraced him. The general's eyes filled. Too moved to speak, he sought out Mamie for a private moment. Then he picked up a phone and asked to speak to Taft. It was precisely the right thing to do, and he, the presumed amateur in politics, was the one who had thought of it. He asked the senator if he could pay his respects. Fighting crowds all the way, he made his way to Taft's lair in the Conrad Hilton. Both men were exhausted, stunned, and dazed. Photographers begged them to smile. They complied, though Taft was clearly in agony. He was going through this for the sake of the party, and his devotion to it had never made a greater demand. Though his eyes were bleak with pain, he managed to keep on grinning. He said huskily, "I want to congratulate General Eisenhower. I shall do everything possible in the campaign to secure his election and to cooperate with him in his administration."

Eisenhower expressed surprise when Brownell told him that it was customary for presidential candidates to name their running mates. This would be the nominee's first decision as Republican standard-bearer, and it was characteristic of him that he turned instinctively toward a procedure of the army's staff system. He wanted "a man who had a special talent and an ability to ferret out any kind of subversive influence," but he would withhold his decision until Brownell could get "the collective wisdom of the leaders of the party."

It was too soon to invite conservatives to the conference; those summoned were all Ike men. They gathered in a room, which quickly became smoke-filled, in the Conrad Hilton. According to Paul Hoffman, the first name discussed was Taft. It was knocked down; they wanted a younger man, preferably a westerner. Dewey waited until all but one of the other possibilities had been considered and rejected. "Then," he said later, "I named Nixon as the logical nominee." The senator met all qualifications. He was thirty-nine, popular with conservatives, a hard campaigner, and had never been accused of being a security risk. After a brief discussion everyone agreed to the recommendation. Brownell phoned Eisenhower and asked the operator to find Nixon. The senator had loaned his car to Earl Behrens of the *San Francisco Chronicle* and had then gone off, no one knew where, with Murray Chotiner. He was one of the last men at the convention to learn he had been picked. By the time he could call his sister-in-law in Whittier, she knew it; it had been on television, too.

In one sense the freshman senator was a natural choice for the second spot on a presidential ticket: he was everything his leader was not. An extrovert and a genius at compromise, Eisenhower was a natural master of social situations. Shy, taciturn, and introverted, Nixon was a perfectionist. He couldn't stand cocktail parties. Humorless but earnest, a loner, proud of being the fastest dresser in the capital—eight minutes for formal clothes, two and a half for regular wear—he always carried in his inside pocket a list of things to do. Ike let others carry lists; that was what they were for. He was a backslapper; Nixon was a brooder. In economics and political ethics the general was a fundamentalist. The senator was a relativist, an opportunist, and a fatalist. The older man's strength lay in his appeal for independent voters, while Gallup traced the popularity of the younger man to registered Republicans, most of them his senior.

Of course, there was more to Richard Nixon than that. Twenty years later, after everything in his life had been subjected to minute analysis, aspects of his life would intrigue his countrymen. Somewhere in his impoverished Yorba Linda childhood lay the secret of the immense drive which brought him fame in Chicago only five years after a Washington newspaper story had featured him as the "Greenest Congressman in Town." Nixon's eye for detail had been Alger Hiss's nemesis, and in a way his own behavior was a pattern of odd little details. His sales executive manner, his indifference to what most men would call matters of principle, his extraordinary way of wolfing down lunches of cottage cheese and ketchup, his loathing of psychiatrists, the need always to wear a vest—hundreds of such Nixonian traits, each insignificant in itself, formed a fascinating mosaic. At the time of his elevation to the GOP's national ticket, however, he was still a one-dimensional politician, important only to the extent that he added or subtracted to Eisenhower's appeal. It seemed reasonable to believe that he would add something. As the man who had brought Hiss to justice Nixon commanded respect. It was not enough to say, as Democrats did, that he was a clean-shaven McCarthy, and that he had won his Senate seat by crucifying his opponent, Helen Gahagan Douglas. Mrs. Douglas had been crucified, all right, but the worst spikes had been driven into her by fellow Democrats. It was a conservative Democrat who had first called her the Communist candidate, making her primary triumph a pyrrhic victory and assuring her defeat before the Republicans had chosen their nominee.

Nixon was the first Californian to run for national office since Hoover, and the state's Republicans were eager to give him tangible evidence of their confidence in him. To those who asked how they could do it, Chotiner and Bernard Brennan replied that the best proof was cash. A vigorous campaigner needed a reservoir of it. The apparatus to receive it was already set up. Two years earlier Nixon and his staff had established a pipeline for contributions. Money was conveyed to what had become, in essence, an $18,000 contingency fund maintained for him by friends and admirers.

During the week between the departure of the Republicans and the arrival of the Democrats, Chicago was as serene as a hurricane's eye. Conventions are the lifeblood of hotels, and the Loop's hostelers had booked several small ones for the hiatus. The corridors where Ike had prevailed and Adlai would soon charm were momentarily swarming with safe driving instructors, life insurance salesmen, and the Ralston Purina sales force. It was a curious fact that memories of Taft seemed more viable than those of the general who had beaten him. For days after the Ohio senator had departed for his father's old summer place in Murray Bay, Quebec, his ghost haunted the scenes of his last great struggle to follow the elder Taft into the White House.

In that midsummer of 1952 it was by no means certain that the vanquished Taft conservatives would remain loyal to the Grand Old Party. Colonel McCormick's *Chicago Tribune* was describing Eisenhower as the candidate of Wall Street, Europe, Harry Truman, and Tom Dewey. Asked by a *Sun-Times* reporter what he thought of Republican chances in November, Colonel McCormick said, "Zero." A bitter *Tribune* editorial described the governor of New York as "the most unpopular figure in the Republican party today," and a reader in Racine, Wisconsin, wrote in that although he had been voting Republican since 1916, "I will not vote for Eisenhewey. Phewey on Eisenhewey!" Clearly the GOP house was badly divided.

Obviously much hinged on the outcome of what was already being called the second Betty Furness Show. Democratic hopes had been broaching and yawing since April 16, when Governor Stevenson had to all intents and purposes taken himself out of the race. En route to a fund-raising dinner at the Waldorf—where his presence, he felt, might be misconstrued—he had issued a firm statement saying that in view of his decision to run for reelection in Illinois, "I could not accept the nomination for any other office this summer." That, it appeared, had been that. Stevenson, the *New York Times* had observed, "seems effectively to have closed the door to his nomination."

Had any other state been chosen for the convention, he might have kept it closed, but as governor he would have to welcome the delegates. Those who knew how well he spoke believed the convention would be smitten by him, and his admirers set up a national Stevenson for President Committee headquarters on the fifteenth floor of the Conrad Hilton. Unlike the outposts of other candidates, this one had no contact, direct or indirect, with its man. The governor continued to do everything in his power to shut it down. At his request, friends reluctantly promised not to put his name in nomination, and on Sunday, July 20, the day before proceedings opened, he made an extraordinary appeal to a closed caucus of the Illinois delegation begging it not to join in a draft. Reporters outside, lying on the floor and putting their ears to a crack beneath a sliding partition, heard him say of the Presidency that "I do not dream myself fit for the job—temperamentally, mentally, or physically. And I ask therefore that you all abide by my wishes not to nominate me, nor to vote for me if I should be nominated."

No successful candidate in history had gone that far, but next day two events conspired against him. The first was a breakfast bid by Alben Barkley for the support of sixteen labor union leaders. Lacking a Stevenson commitment, the Vice President had a fair claim on Truman's support, and had the leaders backed him, Truman wrote in his memoirs, Barkley would have become the party's choice. They didn't, thereby taking him out of the race. The second event was, as predicted, the governor's stirring salute to the convention. He said: "Here, my friends, on the prairies of Illinois and of the Middle West we can see a long way in all directions. . . .

Here there are no barriers . . . to ideas and to aspirations. We want none; we want no shackles on the mind or the spirit, no rigid patterns of thought, and no iron conformity. We want only the faith and the conviction that triumph in free and fair contest."

He reviewed the years since Franklin Roosevelt's first nomination to the Presidency in Chicago twenty years before, and spoke movingly of the proud achievements since. Then his eyes sparkled mischievously. "But our Republican friends," he continued, "have said it was all a miserable failure. For almost a week pompous phrases marched over this landscape in search of an idea, and the only idea they found was that the two great decades of progress" were "the misbegotten spawn of bungling, of corruption, of socialism, of mismanagement, of waste and of worse. They captured, they tied and they dragged that ragged idea into this hall and they furiously beat it to death for a solid week." Indeed: "After listening to this everlasting procession of epithets about our misdeeds I was even surprised the next morning when the mail was delivered on time. . . . But we Democrats were by no means the only victims here. First they slaughtered each other, and then they went after us. And the same vocabulary was good for both exercises, which was a great convenience. Perhaps the proximity of the stockyards accounts for the carnage."

It was at that point that Eisenhower, watching in a Colorado fishing lodge, had misgivings. Simultaneously, the Democratic delegates took heart. "In one day," Anne O'Hare McCormick wrote in next morning's *New York Times*, "all the confused and unchanneled currents seemed to converge upon the shrinking figure of Governor Adlai Stevenson as the one and only, the almost automatic choice of the convention. Nothing but action by the President could alter the picture, and the general feeling here is that even that would now be too late."

Late Thursday afternoon Governor Henry F. Schricker of Indiana took the lectern and said: "Ninety-two years ago, the nation called from the prairies of Illinois the greatest of Illinois citizens, Abraham Lincoln. Lincoln, too, was reluctant. But there are times when a man is not permitted to say no. I place before you the man we cannot permit to say no, Adlai E. Stevenson of Illinois."

Fifteen minutes earlier, as Schricker made his way to the podium, Stevenson had bowed to the inevitable. In a call to the White House he had asked whether the President would be embarrassed if Stevenson allowed his name to be put in nomination. Truman said, "I have been trying since January to get you to say that. Why should it embarrass me?"

The balloting proceeded while Stevenson, sitting in a second-floor bedroom at 1416 North Astor Street, the home of William McCormick Blair Jr.'s father, wrote out his acceptance speech in longhand on a yellow ruled tablet. Kefauver led on the first two ballots. After the third Stevenson was two and a half votes short of a majority. Utah then switched its twelve votes, and early in the morning of Saturday, July 26, the reluctant governor became the Democratic choice of 1952.

The first moments of his candidacy were inauspicious. Over and over the organ bleated out the campaign song "Don't Let Them Take It Away," a crude appeal to mass cupidity, and the nominee was then introduced to the delegates by Harry Truman. Four years earlier, the President had ridden an underdog role to victory. Since then his political stock had depreciated, however, and Stevenson's smile seemed wan when the President cried, "You have nominated a winner, and I am going to take off my coat and do everything I can to help him win." To seventy million television watchers the scene was a reminder of Truman's least attractive side, his fondness for Pendergast politics. The new man accordingly looked like a Pendergast protégé, and moments later the governor dealt his own chances a blow. In a rare lapse of taste, he told them: "I have asked the merciful Father, the Father of us all, to let this cup pass from me. But from such dread responsibility one does not shrink in fear, in self-interest or in false humility. So, 'If this cup may not pass from me, except I drink it, Thy will be done.'"

To the devout, repeating Christ's prayer at Gethsemane was sacrilege. Ike switched off his television set, saying to his fishing companions, "After hearing that, fellows, I think he's a bigger faker than all the rest of them."

He missed a remarkable speech. When memories of the conventions had faded, Stevenson said, there would remain: "the stark reality of responsibility in an hour of history haunted with those gaunt, grim specters of strife, dissension and materialism at home, and ruthless, inscrutable, and hostile power abroad. The ordeal of the twentieth century—the bloodiest, most turbulent era of the Christian age—is far from over. Sacrifice, patience, understanding, and implacable purpose may be our lot for years to come. Let's face it—let's talk sense to the American people. Let's tell them the truth, that there are no gains without pains, that we are now on the eve of great decisions—not easy decisions, like resistance when you're attacked, but a long, patient, costly struggle which alone can assure triumph over the great enemies of man—war, poverty, and tyranny—and the assaults upon human dignity which are the most grievous consequences of each. . . .

"Better we lose the election than mislead the people," Stevenson said; "and better we lose the election than misgovern the people."

After posing on the rostrum with John Sparkman of Alabama, his vice-presidential nominee, Stevenson took the train to Springfield. There he resolved to disassociate himself from Truman and fashion his own identity. His headquarters would be here, not in Washington or even in New York. National Chairman Frank McKinney, a Truman man, would be replaced by Stephen A. Mitchell, a Chicago lawyer and Stevenson friend.

In declaring his political independence, he went so far as to tell an Oregon reporter that one of his major goals, if elected, would be to clean up "the mess in Washington." Referring to this in his memoirs, Truman dryly noted, "How Stevenson hoped he could persuade the American voters to maintain the Democratic party in power while seeming to disown powerful elements of it, I do not know."

In fact, political legacies meant little to either candidate. Eisenhower and Stevenson were each too strong and too genuine to be called anyone's foil. For all that, on the eve of their great match they were very different. As John Mason Brown pointed out, the center of Ike's celebrated smile was his mouth, while Stevenson's was in his eyes. The general's waves to crowds were sweeping, with his arms straight out, and while speaking he would frequently say, "I am told," or "someone told me." The governor would say instead, "It strikes me," or "I am reminded by." He gestured tentatively, keeping his elbows at his sides. He worried about the country's smug materialism, its "spiritual unemployment." Eisenhower would have been embarrassed by such phrases. Even "status quo" bothered him; if he had to say it in a speech, he would follow it with an apologetic, "'Course, I'm not supposed to be the educated candidate." And material prosperity did not alarm him; he saw it as a blessing, and as an American he was proud of it.

He was not a born speaker like his adversary. He needed time to find the natural rhythm of his campaign—so much time, in fact, that along the way some of his aides despaired of his ever getting it. Winding up his fishing trip, he said, "The great problem of America today is to take that straight and narrow road down the middle." It wasn't an arresting phrase to begin with, and when he used it the next day, and then the day after that, there was talk among the correspondents of crossing the 38th platitude. He was drawing large crowds, Richard H. Rovere reported on September 6, but "those that show up to lend an ear when he pleads for their assistance in unhorsing the Democrats are often rather thin."

During that first month almost the only bright note for the Republicans was their newspaper support. Just 201 daily papers were backing Stevenson, and their daily circulation was 4.4 million readers. Eisenhower, by contrast, was supported by 993 dailies with 40.1 million subscribers. But even here the news columns tended to undermine the pro-Ike editorials just by carrying quotations from the Democratic candidate. The governor's sense of timing was superb. Picking up Ike's concession that he would retain some Democratic programs, the governor remarked that he would be proud to stand on much of his party's record "if only . . . the general would move over and make room for me." The Republicans had lacked fresh ideas since the turn of the century, he charged, and "As to their platform, well, nobody can stand on a bushel of eels." Ending a 6,500-mile tour of the West on September 12, he learned that Taft had brought a conservative manifesto to the general's New York home, and that after a two-hour conference Eisenhower had agreed to it in every particular. Stevenson called it "the Surrender of Morningside Heights." He said, "Taft lost the nomination but won the nominee," and when an anguished Ike protested that the Presidency was no laughing matter, the governor jabbed him again: "My opponent is worried about my funnybone, but I'm worried about his backbone."

Television critic John Crosby wrote in the *New York Herald Tribune* that "To both the Republicans and the Democrats it's now fairly clear that Governor Adlai E. Stevenson is a television personality the like of which has not been seen ever before. The man is setting a pace that will not only be almost impossible for succeeding candidates to follow but one that will be pretty hard for Stevenson himself to maintain." To discouraged Republicans the race looked like

1948 all over again, with the other man lengthening his lead. After six weeks of it, the pro-Eisenhower Scripps-Howard chain ran a desperate editorial on the front page of all nineteen of its papers. "Ike," it said, was "running like a dry creek" because he was not "coming out swinging." He had said that he didn't know whether General Marshall had made mistakes. "If Ike doesn't know," the editorial continued, "he had better find out. For that's one of the big issues of this campaign. Ask any mother, father, or wife of a soldier now in Korea." It concluded, "We still cling to the hope that . . . he will hit hard. If he doesn't, he might as well concede defeat."

That was one of the turning points in the election. It led to a general decline in the level of the campaign, which was deplorable, but it also stiffened Eisenhower's resolve and made him a more militant competitor, which, from the Republican standpoint, was a good switch. At about the same time, Stevenson's wit began to generate a backlash. Louis Kronenberger has suggested that in an important context Americans "tend to fear and fight off humor." Some voters began saying that the general was right, that the struggle for the White House wasn't funny. Another September surprise was the realization that the Democratic candidate's intellect might not be an unqualified asset, that there were voters who would distrust it. A broad streak of anti-intellectualism had always been part of the American national character, and the fall of Hiss and the rise of McCarthy had been accompanied by a marked rise in the political use of anti-intellectual pejoratives—"longhairs," "do-gooders," "highbrows," "double-domes," "bleeding hearts." Now the 1952 campaign gave birth to another, a kind of watchword for Philistinism whose popularity was destined to remain high for the next five years.

Its coiner was John Alsop, the younger brother of two columnists, an insurance executive who was chairman of Connecticut's Republican speakers' bureau. In mid-September, when Stewart Alsop called to ask him how things stood, John said fine; it looked like a big GOP year in New England. He in turn asked how everything looked elsewhere. Stewart observed that while most intellectual celebrities had championed Eisenhower against Taft, many of them were now rooting for Stevenson. John thought a minute. As he later explained, he reflected that "while Stevenson was appealing and appealed strongly to people's minds, Eisenhower, as a man and as a figure, was appealing far more strongly to far more people's emotions." As his brother awaited his comment, John's mind's eye pictured the countenance of a typical intellectual in politics—a smooth, faceless, haughty, and very oval head. "Sure," he said, "all the eggheads are for Stevenson, but how many eggheads are there?"

Stewart put it in his column. Neither Alsop thought of the word as disparaging, but they quickly lost control of it. It answered a need and became a coast-to-coast sneer overnight. Louis Bromfield, an anti-intellectual intellectual, was one who seized upon it. Not knowing its origin, he wrote that "It seems to have arisen spontaneously from the people themselves." To him it stood for "a person of intellectual pretensions, often a professor or the protégé of a professor," who was "superficial in approach to any problem," and who was in addition "feminine," "supercilious," "surfeited with conceit," a "doctrinaire supporter of middle-European socialism," a "self-conscious prig" and, yes, "a bleeding heart." If Stevenson were elected, Bromfield prophesied, "the eggheads will come back into power and off again we will go on the scenic railway of muddled economics, Socialism, Communism, crookedness and psychopathic instability."

Suddenly the campaign became a pitched battle. Descending from the high plane established by the principals, partisans of both parties let fly wild charges, innuendos, absurd hyperbole—all the excesses that offend decency but stigmatize important elections all the same. Afterward there was some bewilderment over who had said what, understandable in the heat of the conflict and the confusion, in some quarters, over who was running. Harry Truman acted as though he was, and Henry Luce appeared to agree with him. Whistle-stopping all the way to the Pacific Northwest and back through the Middle West, the President spent two weeks questioning both Eisenhower's acumen and his character. Anthony Leviero of the *New York Times* said Truman had engaged the general in "an epic political conflict," and Arthur Krock described the tour as "a protracted assault on the personal integrity of General Eisenhower that is without parallel for a man in Mr. Truman's position." You could read all about it in *Time* and *Life*. You could not, however, find much there about the Democratic candidate for President. One issue of *Life* was devoted to pictures of the President and the general—there were none at all of Governor Stevenson.

Ike himself wasn't responsible for that. By and large his campaigning was as irreproachable as Stevenson's, and it is hard to fault his speeches. Doubtless he later wished that he could reword some of them. (On September 3 he said in Little Rock: "Thank goodness for a Supreme Court.") Others were naive, most memorably his egg lecture, in which he would hold aloft an egg and express outrage that a hundred different taxes might be levied on this little product of nature, to which the government had, he would say, made no contribution whatsoever. (As Taft had pointed out, the general didn't know much about agricultural policy.) Yet this was hardly demagogy, or even flamboyance. Emmet John Hughes was running a vigilant blue pencil over Ike's major speeches before they were delivered, crossing out such words as "crusade" in domestic affairs and "liberation" in foreign policy. Most of what was left was honest Eisenhower wrath. He may not always have had his facts quite right, but like his audiences he knew something had gone wrong for America, and it had put his dander up.

The crowds were with him now. The chant "We like Ike" was less a political call to arms than a hymn of praise. As John Alsop had noted, Stevenson sought to persuade men, but Eisenhower wanted to move them. And he was succeeding. The public, wrote James Reston, "likes his angry little outbursts against corruption, and his essays on America." Afterward Marquis Childs wrote that Ike had represented "strength, triumph, unswerving confidence. Millions were happy to take him on faith, on his face, on his smile, on the image of American manhood, on the happy virtue of his family life."

This was on a far higher level than Karl Mundt's formula for a Republican victory: K_1C_3 (Korea, Crime, Communism, Corruption). There were a lot of Mundts in the GOP, and by becoming the Republican nominee Ike had inherited them. He would have pleased their critics if he had repudiated them outright, but that wasn't his way. (It is fair to add that it wasn't FDR's way with Frank Hague or Stevenson's with Pat McCarran.) We know how the general felt about the Republican ultraconservatives. When Jenner tried to embrace him on a public platform in Indianapolis, Eisenhower recoiled. "I felt dirty," he told Hughes afterward, "from the touch of the man." In Green Bay, Wisconsin, on October 3, he refused to pose for photographers with Joe McCarthy, telling an audience that "The differences between me and Senator McCarthy are well known to him and to me, and we have discussed them." McCarthy stalked off, furious, though the incident was soon forgotten in the candidate's failure to break openly with the senator later that day in Milwaukee. Feeling belligerent when the Milwaukee speech was being planned, Ike had said to Hughes, "Listen, couldn't we make this an occasion for me to pay a personal tribute to Marshall—right in McCarthy's backyard?" It was so decided, and a Marshall encomium was included in the advance copies of the speech distributed to the press. Then Governor Walter J. Kohler Jr. boarded the train in Peoria. He convinced Adams and General Wilton B. "Jerry" Persons, Eisenhower's military aide, that the tribute might split Republican strength in the state. When they approached Ike, he said, "Are you trying to suggest that I take out that paragraph on Marshall?" Adams said, "That's right, General." Ike said, "Well, take it out. I covered that subject thoroughly in Colorado a few weeks ago."

He hadn't, though. Praising his old superior in Colorado wasn't the same as going after Tailgunner Joe in Wisconsin. As he himself had been the first to see, Milwaukee would have been a superb place to strike a blow for decency. He had forfeited it, and the press had let the country know why. That was not the first time the general had taken a bold stand and changed his mind. He had said he would remain in Paris and then asked to be relieved, had said he would not go to Chicago and then did. It was to become a disconcerting habit of his political years, giving his adversaries the impression that he was weak and giving his staff apoplectic moments, but it did not mean that he was afraid of McCarthy—he would later prove that he was not—or that he himself was any readier to campaign in the gutter.

Some Democrats said he was. That was probably inevitable. Any election with McCarthy in it was going to be the occasion for squalor. McCarthy himself was seeing to that. There is no way of determining his impact on the November outcome. While he was picking up votes from people who believed him or thought Eisenhower in the White House could handle him better than Stevenson, others, affronted by his tactics, were being driven into the Democratic camp. Election results were inconclusive. Four Democratic senators against whom he campaigned, Tydings among them, went down in defeat. At the same time, however, his own showing at the polls was unimpressive. Eisenhower carried Wisconsin 979,744 to 622,175. McCarthy won 870,444 to 731,402, which was not only smaller than the general's plurality; it made him low man on the winning state ticket.

Still, he was a force. His most striking performance was his televised attempt to pin a Communist tag on Stevenson. "Alger," he began, smirking as he corrected himself, "—I mean Adlai." No one else plumbed the political depths so thoroughly as McCarthy, but plenty of others were knee—or hip—deep. Either it was impossible to be elected without suggesting that Democrats were treasonous, or Republicans thought it impossible. Even in Green Bay, where Eisenhower had drawn the line between himself and Joe, he had felt obliged to add: "I want to make one thing very clear. The purposes that he and I have of ridding this government of the incompetents, the dishonest, and above all the subversives and the disloyal are one and the same. Our differences, therefore, have nothing to do with the end result we are seeking. The differences apply to method."

His running mate was more direct. Nixon repeatedly charged that a Democratic victory in November would mean "more Alger Hisses, more atomic spies, more crises." He was still flagellating Hiss, now in stir, and in a major address, televised nationally from New York on October 13, he once more took up the trial deposition which had been given then by the Democratic candidate. After declaring that the Russians had acquired hundreds of secret documents "from Hiss and other members of the ring" which meant "that the lives of American boys were endangered and probably lost because of the activities of a spy ring," he added: "Mr. Stevenson was a character witness, or should I say a witness for the reputation, and the good reputation, of Alger Hiss. He testified that the reputation of Alger Hiss for veracity, and for loyalty was good. . . . This testimony . . . was given after all these facts, this confrontation in which Hiss had to look into Chambers' mouth to identify him, after these papers came out of the pumpkin, after all of those facts were known . . . it was voluntary on Mr. Stevenson's part."

Democratic speakers were now charging that while Eisenhower was taking a high road to November, his running mate was on a low one. It was working out that way, though not because anyone had planned it. That was the kind of men they were. Ike was cautious and, for a general, remarkably unaggressive. That was part of his appeal. He was no readier to climb into a ring with Stevenson than with McCarthy. Nixon was by contrast a lunger, a street fighter with a long shiv and a jugular instinct. If he wounded good men that autumn, it is fair to add that there were Democrats with knives, too.

"Secret Nixon Fund!" cried the page one headline in the *New York Post*. A two-line banner on page two read:

> SECRET RICH MEN'S TRUST FUND KEEPS
> NIXON IN STYLE FAR BEYOND HIS SALARY
> By Leo Katcher
> Los Angeles—The existence of a "millionaire's club" devoted exclusively to the financial comfort of Senator Nixon, GOP vice presidential candidate, was revealed today. . . .

Katcher, a Hollywood movie writer, had managed to get most of the facts wrong, including the amount of money in the fund and the legality of it. The special bank account was well within both the letter and the spirit of the law. Men in public life seldom have enough money to meet their obligations. Some men put their wives on the payroll, or accepted extravagant legal fees, or spoke at $100-a-plate dinners. Stevenson had established a fund to backstop men who had left high-salaried jobs to serve Illinois. Other businessmen contributed to it, and as Stevenson said, there was "no question of improper influence, because there was no connection between the contributors and the beneficiaries."

There wasn't any in the Nixon fund, either. Contributions, none of which could exceed $500 in one year, were sent to Dana C. Smith, a Pasadena lawyer who acted as trustee and manager of the fund. Over a two-year period, 76 contributors had given an average of $240 each; the $18,235 had paid for recordings of speeches, travel vouchers, postage, and Christmas cards sent to former campaign workers. All of it had been accounted for. None had gone to Nixon or his wife. In addition, it had never been "secret." The account and Smith's administration of it had been a matter of public knowledge from its inception. In a way, Nixon was being hoist by his own petard. In his anti-Communist evangelism he had become a master of irrelevant minutiae. What had been in Chambers's mouth, or in the pumpkin, had nothing to do with Hiss's reputation. Indeed, the more spotless a spy's reputation, the more damaging the case against him, since he has been exploiting the trust of others. This was what had made Hiss's treachery so shocking. In that sense, by testifying to the faith men had had in him, Stevenson's deposition had made the verdict more damning. But Nixon had made it look the other way round. His syllogism had been: Hiss was a spy; Stevenson had known him; therefore Stevenson was under a cloud. The syllogism slandering him was: Some politicians take bribes; Nixon had taken money; Nixon was thus corrupt. The impact of the *Post* accusation was increased by the sanctimoniousness of his own campaign. His first reaction to the *Post* was in character. The Nixon train was about to pull out of Sacramento when a heckler yelled, "Tell 'em about the $16,000!" "Hold the train!" he shouted. "Hold the train!" It stopped, and he gave the crowd not the reasonable facts, but a muddled version of them. "You folks know the work I did investigating Communists for the United States," he said. "Ever since I have done that work, the Communists, the leftwingers, have been fighting me with every smear that they have been able to. Even when I received the nomination for the Vice Presidency, I want you folks to know—and I'm going to reveal it today for the first time—I was warned that if I continued to attack the Communists and crooks in this government they would try to smear me. . . ."

The country was not so easily diverted. The CIO was charging that Nixon had been bought by capital-gains Republicans who "knew a good investment when they saw one." California's franchise tax board had announced that it would investigate the fund. The Democratic National Committee was mailing a reminder to newspaper editors of criminal law provisions on "bribery and graft . . . by members of Congress," and Chairman Mitchell was wondering when Eisenhower would "cast away" his running mate. Mitchell's speculations were of no consequence to Nixon; Stevenson refused to make a judgment until all the facts were in. Eisenhower's opinion was another matter, though. If the standard-bearer thought a case could be made against his vice-presidential candidate, the result would be havoc. The general hadn't said he believed that, but he hadn't called it absurd, either, and as the long hours passed the silence aboard Ike's train, the Look Ahead, Neighbor Special, grew deafening.

Ike was getting conflicting advice. Taft approved of the fund. Hoover was issuing a statement to the effect that "If everyone in the city of Washington possessed the high level of courage, probity, and patriotism of Senator Nixon, this would be a far better nation."

Chairman Arthur Summerfield made a few calculations on what the party's printing bill would be if Ike switched running mates and said it was out of the question.

The general himself was undecided. He had Brownell summon Senator Knowland from Hawaii as a possible replacement for Nixon, and Paul Hoffman was instructed to supervise a thorough investigation of the fund. On Hoffman's orders, fifty lawyers and accountants began a round-the-clock audit of it. They found it aboveboard in every respect. By now the reporters on Ike's train were begging him for a comment. For the record he said he had faith in Nixon's honesty and felt sure that the senator would vindicate him by putting "all the facts before the people, fairly and squarely." That wasn't quite what the vice-presidential candidate had been expecting. It sounded as though he would have to prove his innocence. The general had just that in mind. When he joined the reporters covering his tour for a glass of beer and was asked, "Do you consider the Nixon thing a closed incident?" he frowned and replied, "By no means." He really didn't know Nixon very well, he said—he had only met him a couple of times—and he wanted evidence of the senator's probity—facts, figures, names, dates. "What was the use," he asked rhetorically, "of campaigning against this business of what has been going on in Washington if we ourselves aren't as clean as a hound's tooth?"

The general's comment reached Nixon in Portland, Oregon. According to Earl Mazo of the *Herald Tribune*, if the ballot had been cast there that night "Eisenhower would not have gotten a single vote from the Nixon staff." With the embattled vice-presidential candidate were Chotiner and William P. Rogers.* "We had calls from everybody, all offering advice," Rogers said later. "There were only a few of us that day who were reasonably sure it would work out all right."

At about this time pressure began to build for a radio-television report to the people. Dewey suggested to Nixon that he make it as soon as possible. Nixon agreed, but he thought he was entitled to a word with Eisenhower first. The call went through to the Look Ahead, Neighbor Special. After pleasantries, the senator described Dewey's proposal. "I'm at your disposal," he said. Then he said, "I want you to know that if you reach a conclusion either now or

* Who served as Nixon's Secretary of State from 1969 to 1973.

any time later that I should get off the ticket, you can be sure that I will immediately respect your judgment and do so." Ike said he didn't think that decision ought to be up to him, and Nixon bridled. He was being pilloried for nothing; he was offering to sacrifice himself for the cause; certainly the standard-bearer could do *something*. In earthy language he told the five-star general either to make a decision or get off the seat of power.

Two hours later Nixon received word that the Republican National Committee and Senatorial Congressional Campaign Committee had pledged $75,000 for a half-hour nationwide explanation of the fund. Batten, Barton, Durstine, and Osborn, the party's advertising agency, had put together a hookup of 64 NBC television stations, 194 CBS radio stations, and the 560-station Mutual Radio Network. They asked how soon the senator could be ready—there was a choice spot open the following night, right after *I Love Lucy*. Impossible, said Nixon; he had to return to California and marshal his thoughts. He could make it the night after that, however, and so it was decided that he would go on the air then, immediately after Milton Berle. Reserving a seat on the next United Airlines flight to Los Angeles, the senator made arrangements to go into seclusion there at the Ambassador Hotel.

En route, he pulled a sheaf of United's souvenir postcards from the seat in front of him and made sketchy notes:

> Checkers . . .
> Pat's cloth coat—
> Lincoln ref. to common people (?)

He later explained that he had thought of Checkers, the Nixon family dog, because FDR had used Fala so cleverly in the 1944 campaign. In Eugene, Oregon, a placard had read "No mink coats for Nixon," and sure enough, he thought, his wife didn't have one. The Lincoln reference was more complex. Mitchell had said, "If a fellow can't afford to be a senator, he shouldn't seek the office." It was a stupid remark. If it meant anything, it was that only wealthy men should go to Washington. Hadn't Lincoln said something about God loving the common people because he made so many of them?* At the Ambassador Hotel, after acknowledging the airport crowd—it was disappointingly small—Nixon put through a

* In fact Lincoln had said "common-looking people."

call to Paul Smith, his old Whittier history professor, asking him to pin down the quotation.

Meanwhile, something extraordinary had happened to the campaign. It was stalled. The public had forgotten about the presidential candidates. All eyes were on the GOP candidate for Vice President. TV programs were being interrupted for rumors that he had suffered a nervous breakdown and interrupted again to reveal that he was in good health, and speculation over what he was going to say was building. Even Eisenhower was becoming curious about it. At his direction Adams called Chotiner and asked what it would be. Chotiner said he didn't have the foggiest idea.

"Oh, come now, Murray, you must know," Adams said. "He has a script, doesn't he?" Chotiner said he didn't, and Adams asked, "What about the press?"

"We've set up television sets in the hotel for them," Chotiner replied, "and we have shorthand reporters to take it down, page by page."

"Look," said Adams, "we have to know what is going to be said."

"Sherm," Chotiner said, "if you want to know what's going to be said, you do what I'm going to do. You sit in front of the television and listen."

It was true. Nixon had a general idea of his theme, but there was no text, and he hadn't decided how to end it. Dewey had suggested that he ask voters to write to the Republican National Committee. It seemed to be a good idea, but what should they write? He didn't know. The pressure, he knew, was growing hourly, and press comment continued to be hostile to him. The Los Angeles *Daily News* was reporting that "Anything short of an enthusiastic burst of public support . . . will be interpreted in favor of what Eisenhower and his staff have already decided—that corruption cannot remain a campaign issue as long as one of their candidates is tainted with the slightest suspicion. Thus, Nixon will probably be asked to resign." Eisenhower and his staff had decided no such thing, though the general was certainly preoccupied with the issue. It seemed crucial. "There is one thing I believe," the general said to Adams; "if Nixon has to go, we cannot win." That evening Ike was interested only in a seat in front of a television set. The manager of the Cleveland Public Auditorium, where he was scheduled to speak afterward, led him up three flights of stairs to one. Mamie and William Robinson, publisher of the anti-fund *Herald Tribune*, sat with him; Summerfield and Jim Hagerty stood against the wall.

Nixon, meantime, was preparing to leave the Ambassador Hotel for NBC's El Capitan Theater in Hollywood. The cameramen, the electricians, and the men in the control room had been rehearsing there all day; everyone was ready except the star, who still hadn't decided how to wind up his talk. He was talking to Chotiner and Rogers, debating the best way for the audience to express its opinion of him—by writing to him, to Eisenhower, or to the National Committee—when the phone rang. The operator said it was long distance; a Mr. Chapman was calling. "Mr. Chapman" was Dewey's code name. Chotiner was told that the senator was unavailable, but the governor was adamant. Nixon reluctantly picked up the receiver.

Dewey said to him, "There has just been a meeting of all of Eisenhower's top advisers. They've asked me to tell you that in their opinion at the conclusion of the broadcast you should submit your resignation to Eisenhower. As you know, I haven't shared this point of view, but it's my responsibility to pass this recommendation to you."

Nixon was too shocked to speak. Dewey jiggled the receiver. He said, "Hello? Can you hear me?"

Nixon asked, "What does Eisenhower want me to do?" Dewey didn't know; he hadn't spoken directly to the general. Nixon said, "It's kind of late to pass on this kind of recommendation to me now."

"What shall I tell them you're going to do?" Dewey persisted.

Nixon exploded, "Just tell them that I haven't the slightest idea what I'm going to do, and if they want to find out they'd better listen to the broadcast! And tell them I know something about politics, too!"

It was 6 P.M. in Los Angeles, 9 P.M. in the East—a half-hour till broadcast time. After shaving, showering, and dressing, Nixon found he was too wrought up from Dewey's call to memorize his notes; he would have to go on holding them. At the theater the program director led him and Pat in and asked him what movements he would be making. Nixon said, "I don't have the slightest idea. Just keep the camera on me." With three minutes to go, he thought wildly of backing out. To Pat he said, "I just don't think I can go through with this one." She said of course he could, and it was too late to do anything else; already the camera was showing his calling card. It switched to him. He said: "My fellow Americans, I come before you tonight as a candidate for the Vice-Presidency and as a man whose honesty and integrity has been questioned."

He described the purpose of the fund and how it worked. The money had been used solely for campaign expenses, he said. Since he had never even seen it, none of it had been taxable or even reportable under federal law. He continued: "There are some that will say, 'Well, maybe you were able, Senator, to fake this thing. How can we believe what you say—after all, is there a possibility that maybe you got some sums in cash? Is there a possibility that you might have feathered your own nest?' And so now what I am going to do—and incidentally, this is unprecedented in the history of American politics—I am going at this time to give to this television and radio audience a complete financial history, everything I have earned, everything I have spent, everything I own."

Going back to his youth, he led up to the present and said he now owned:

A 1950 Oldsmobile.
A $3,000 equity in his California house, where his parents were living.
A $20,000 equity in his Washington house.
$4,000 in life insurance, plus a GI term policy.
No stocks, no bonds, nothing else.

He owed:

$10,000 on the California house.
$20,000 on the Washington house.
$ 4,500 to the Riggs National Bank in Washington.
$ 3,500 to his parents.
$ 500 on his life insurance.

"Well, that's about it," he said. "That's what we have and that's what we owe. It isn't very much, but Pat and I have the satisfaction that every dime that we have got is honestly ours."

By then he had doubtless won his audience. After running against FDR's forgotten man in five straight presidential elections, the Republicans had finally nominated a man with whom millions could identify. Nixon was carefully presenting himself as an ordinary man. Although he had been around "when the bombs were falling" during the war and was probably entitled to a star or two, he claimed no heroics. The key to the speech, however, was the detailed discussion of finances. This was, after all, a talk about money, and in laying every penny he had, or had had, on the line, he was telling a tale familiar to his listeners—the two-year-old car, the mortgages, the inadequate life insurance. Here, clearly, was a man who knew what it was to worry about getting the kids' teeth straightened, or replacing the furnace, or making the next payment on the very set now tuned to him. Of course, he said adroitly, it was fine that a man like Governor Stevenson, "who inherited a fortune from his father," could run for President. But it was equally fine that "a man of modest means" could also make the race, because they would all remember what Lincoln had said about the common man. . . .

Overeager Democrats had slandered him, panicky Republicans had talked of jettisoning him, and now he had exonerated himself. But Nixon, with his immense drive, was unwilling to settle for that. This was an opportunity to leave an indelible impression on the national memory—to do what Bryan had done with the cross of gold and Coolidge with the Boston police strike—and he meant to exploit it every way he could.

He told the audience: "I should say this—that Pat doesn't have a mink coat. But she does have a respectable Republican cloth coat. And I always tell her that she would look good in anything.

"One other thing I should probably tell you, because if I don't they'll be saying this about me, too. We did get something, a gift, after the nomination. A man down in Texas heard Pat on the radio mention the fact that our two youngsters would like to have a dog and, believe it or not, the day before we left on this campaign trip we got a message from Union Station in Baltimore, saying they had a package for us. We went down to get it. You know what it was?

"It was a little cocker spaniel dog in a crate that he had sent all the way from Texas—black and white, spotted, and our little girl Tricia, the six-year-old, named it Checkers. And you know, the kids, like all kids, love that dog, and I just want to say this, right now, that regardless of what they say about it, we're going to keep it."

It wasn't easy to appear on a nationwide hookup and "bare your life, as I have done," he said; he was doing it because his country was in danger, and the only man who could save it was Dwight Eisenhower. ("You say, why do I think it is in danger? And I say, look at the record. Seven years of the Truman-Acheson administration, and what's happened? Six hundred million people lost to the Communists.") He was approaching the peak. The clock told him that he was also running slow.

"I know that you wonder whether or not I am going to stay on the Republican ticket or resign. Let me say this: I don't believe that I ought to quit, because I am not a quitter. And, incidentally, Pat is not a quitter. After all, her name was Patricia Ryan and she was born on Saint Patrick's Day—and you know the Irish never quit."*

But the decision, he went on, was not his to make. He had decided—at this moment, while talking—to turn the whole thing over to the Republican National Committee "through this television broadcast." And he was going to ask his listeners to help the Committee decide: "Write and wire the Republican National Committee whether you think I should stay on or whether I should get off. And whatever their decision is, I will abide by it."

A director slipped into the studio and signaled vigorously that his time was almost up. Nixon didn't appear to see him. His eyes glassy, he kept talking to the camera: ". . . just let me say this last word. Regardless of what happens, I am going to continue this fight. I am going to campaign up and down America until we drive the crooks and those that defend them out of Washington. And remember, folks, Eisenhower is a great man. Folks, he is a great man, and a vote for Eisenhower is a vote for what is good for America—"

It was over. In Cleveland Eisenhower turned to Summerfield. He said, "Well, Arthur, you certainly got your seventy-five thousand dollars' worth."

In the El Capitan Theater Nixon was saying to the director, "I'm terribly sorry I ran over. I loused it up, and I'm sorry." Thanking the technicians, he gathered up his notes, stacked them neatly—and then, in a spasm of rage, flung them to the floor. Chotiner came in beaming and tried to congratulate him, but Nixon was inconsolable. "No, it was a flop," he said. "I couldn't get off in time." In the dressing room he wheeled away from his friends and burst into tears.

Later he was to have another memory of this moment. In his book, *Six Crises*, he would recall that the tears had been in the eyes of

* Actually she was born on March 16, 1912, the day before Saint Patrick's Day, and christened Thelma Catherine Ryan. Her father gave her the nickname Pat. Her mother was a native of Germany.

cameramen who had been moved by his eloquence. The makeup man, in his recollection, growled, "That ought to fix them. There has never been a broadcast like it before," while well-wishers jammed the studio switchboard and "everyone at the station agreed that the broadcast had been successful beyond expectations."

That came later. In the immediate aftermath of the speech he was haunted by the realization that the red camera light had blinked off just as he had been about to begin his most important sentence, giving his audience the address of the Republican National Committee. His faulty timing meant they didn't have it. Lacking it, he reasoned, they would be unable to respond, and the committee would receive no messages at all. As he approached his car outside, a huge Irish setter bounded up, wagging its tail. He said gloomily to Pat, "Well, we made a hit in the dog world, anyhow."

At the Ambassador Hotel he discovered that the impact of the broadcast had, in fact, been immense. The lobby cheered as he entered. He took a call there from Darryl Zanuck, who told him it had been "the most tremendous performance I've ever seen." Within the hour word arrived that people were appearing at Western Union offices all over the country. Bit by bit his staff began putting together the story of the nationwide reaction. According to Nielsen figures, half of the TV receivers in the country had been tuned to the broadcast. Counting radio, the audience had been 60,000,000. Of these, roughly 1,000,000 called, wired, or wrote. The mails brought $60,000 in small contributions, almost enough to pay for the broadcast. It was a remarkable personal triumph, and although he was at first unaware of its scale, by the end of the evening he knew that he had received messages of praise from virtually every outstanding member of the Republican party, with one exception. There had been nothing from Dwight Eisenhower.

This imagined slight—Ike had wired his congratulations, but the telegram had been lost in the avalanche of incoming messages—was to leave permanent scars on the relationship between Nixon and the general's advisers. The first word from Cleveland to reach the Ambassador Hotel was that the half-hour presentation hadn't been enough for Eisenhower; he wanted a face-to-face confrontation. That was partly true. Eisenhower did feel that the half-hour had been inadequate. For the sake of appearances he felt that the two of them ought to have a private word together the following evening, in Wheeling, before putting the fund behind them. However, he had expected that Nixon would receive the suggestion in the context of his admiration for the television performance. Coming this way, after the days of excruciating tension, it was a cruel disappointment, and Nixon blew up. "What more can he possibly want of me?" he shouted, and calling in Rose Mary Woods, his secretary, he dictated a telegram to Summerfield resigning as vice-presidential candidate pending the selection of a successor. Chotiner destroyed it before it could be sent, and Nixon himself had second thoughts, but both of them decided it was best to ignore the invitation to Wheeling. Instead, Nixon would pick up his own campaign train in Missoula, Montana. An insubordinate wire went to Ike: "Will be in Washington Sunday and will be delighted to confer with you at your convenience any time thereafter."

While that message was on its way, a call came in from Summerfield. He asked Chotiner, "Well, Murray, how are things out there?"

Chotiner replied, "Not so good."

"What in hell do you mean, 'Not so good'?"

"Dick just sent a telegram of resignation to the general."

"What! My God, Murray, you tore it up, didn't you?"

"Yes, I tore it up, but I'm not so sure how long it's going to stay torn."

"Well, Dick is flying to Wheeling to see the general, isn't he?"

"No, we're flying tonight to Missoula."

"What? My God, Murray, you've got to persuade him to come to Wheeling."

"Arthur, we trust you. If you can give us your personal assurance direct from the general that Dick will stay on the ticket with the general's blessing, I think I can persuade him. I know I can't otherwise."

Before Summerfield could call back the Nixon party was off for Montana, but a phone call from Bert Andrews in Cleveland reached Nixon at the airport. Andrews reminded him that he could hardly expect Eisenhower, a five-star general and the leader of the party, to fly to him. It was time to forget the fund. The press critics had turned around. The *Herald Tribune* was saying, "The air is cleared."* The Republican National Committee had been polled

---

* There were dissenters. Walter Lippmann said the response had been "with all the magnification of modern electronics, simply mob law," and to *Variety* the telecast had been "a slick production . . . parlaying all the schmaltz and human interest of the 'Just Plain Bill'—'Our Gal Sunday' genre of weepers."

and had voted to keep the ticket intact, 107 to 31. To underscore this, in Montana word at last reached Nixon from Ike: "Your presentation was magnificent. . . . My personal decision is to be based on personal conclusions. I would most appreciate it if you can fly to see me at once. Tomorrow I will be at Wheeling, W. Va. Whatever personal affection and admiration I had for you—and they are very great—are undiminished."

After a few token appearances in Missoula and a two-hour nap, Nixon flew to West Virginia. On the field in Wheeling he was still on the plane, helping Pat into her Republican cloth coat, when a solitary figure detached itself from the crowd below and darted up the ramp. It was Eisenhower. Surprised, Nixon blurted out, "What are you doing here, General? You didn't have to come up here to meet us." Putting his arm around his running mate's shoulders, Ike said, "Why not? You're my boy." As they posed for pictures in the terminal, Nixon's eyes began to fill.

He had lots of sympathizers now. Well-wishers had sent Checkers a vast assortment of dog collars, hand-woven dog blankets, a kennel, and a year's supply of dog food. The little spaniel had become the most famous pet in the country. Even those who had deplored the speech used it as a standard for measuring Nixon's later performances. "This mawkish ooze ill became a man who might become the President of the United States," said the Montgomery, Alabama, *Advertiser;* then, finding something in him to praise, the *Advertiser*'s editorial writer added a phrase to the language: "We have found ourselves dissolving our previous conception . . . the New Nixon rejoices us."

The first of Eisenhower's two most important campaign speeches was delivered on the evening of October 16 at the Alfred E. Smith Memorial Foundation dinner in Detroit; its statesmanlike approach to foreign policy won an endorsement of his candidacy from the *New York Times,* which had been leaning toward Stevenson. In the second speech, on October 24 in Detroit, the general promised that if elected, "I shall go to Korea." Truman called the pledge a stunt, and Stevenson delighted his followers by saying, "If elected, I shall go to the White House," but Eisenhower had struck a deep chord. The war continued to be America's most vexing issue; surely, people felt, progress would follow a visit to the front by the nation's greatest military hero. "For all practical purposes," Jack Bell of the Associated Press later wrote, "the contest ended that night."

But the wild swirls of accusations and countercharges continued right down to the wire. Outrageous stories were circulated over that first November weekend: Stevenson was a homosexual, Mamie was an alcoholic, "Adlai" was a Jewish name, Ike was dead but his aides wouldn't admit it. The campaign had been the ugliest since the Roosevelt-Landon donnybrook of 1936. That Sunday, November 2, an automobile with a Stevenson bumper sticker was forced off the Pennsylvania Turnpike and its driver beaten senseless. In Joplin, Missouri, one Raymond Nixon, no relation to the senator, received three threatening phone calls, and the New Orleans Police Department reported eleven brawls, all of them over politics. Sherman and Rachel Adams spent election day in New York. That evening Sinclair Weeks asked where they had been. At the Bronx Zoo, they said, watching the wild animals.

"Quite a change from a political campaign," he said.

"No," said Rachel, "not much."

In Libertyville, Illinois, on election day Stevenson visited a school which was also a polling place. "I would like to ask all of you children to indicate, by holding up your hands, how many of you would like to be governor of Illinois, the way I am," he said. Nearly every hand went up. "Well, that is almost unanimous," he said. "Now I would like to ask all the governors if they would like to be one of you kids." He raised his own hand. He was in good spirits, and confident. His staff formed a betting pool, each man contributing five dollars to it and writing his guess of the electoral vote on a slip of paper. His own slip predicted he would win 381 electoral votes, a landslide. The others were less optimistic, though none thought he would be defeated.

The front-page headline in the *New York Times* the previous morning had been: ELECTION OUTCOME HIGHLY UNCERTAIN, SURVEY INDICATES. "Neither Gen. Dwight D. Eisenhower, Republican, nor Gov. Adlai E. Stevenson, Democrat, can be regarded as now certain of election," the story began, summing up the last of seven exhaustive surveys conducted by *Times* reporters. Those burned four years earlier were making cautious forecasts. The public opinion polls warily noted unusually high numbers of undecided voters and suggested that this floating vote would be divided rather evenly between the two candidates. Nearly all of it went to Eisenhower. What the pollsters had overlooked, or ignored, was that the vast majority of this central group were new registrants. When previously indifferent voters register they usually augur a protest vote, and so it was this time. In the first great swing since 1932, the country went Republican.

Eisenhower won, 33,936,234 to 27,314,992. Republican editorial writers interpreted the victory as an endorsement for free enterprise, predicting that at the stroke of noon on inaugural day an efficient businessman's administration would turn the Pendergast politicians out. The *Chicago Tribune*, examining returns from the new suburbs, chortled that fresh air had done wonders for the judgment of those who had moved out from urban wards. It had certainly changed their politics. Coming from neighborhoods which had given lopsided majorities to Roosevelt and Truman, the young couples in the new developments had been converted to Ike's cause. The winning ticket had carried Levittown, Long Island, by 66 percent and Park Forest, Illinois, by 69.4 percent.

Adlai Stevenson could hardly be called discredited. He had polled more votes than any losing presidential candidate in the country's history—more, indeed, than any *winning* candidate except FDR in 1936 and Ike this time. Though Eisenhower wound up with 442 of the 531 electoral votes, his triumph was less impressive than those of the last three Republican Presidents. His plurality was below 11 percent. Theirs had been 28 percent (Harding), 30 percent (Coolidge), and 18 percent (Hoover). Moreover, despite his margin of six million votes, he had just barely managed to pull in a Republican Congress. The GOP majority in the new House was ten votes; in the Senate, merely one.

Nevertheless, 1952, like 1932, was a pivotal election. The Democrats remained the larger party, with a 5 to 3 ratio in registered voters, but registration meant less; the number of staunch Democrats—"knee-jerk liberals," Republicans were calling them—had diminished. It had become fashionable to say that you voted "for the man, not the party," as though those who had cast their ballots for FDR had done anything else. Independent registrations had now increased to more than 20 percent of the electorate. On Capitol Hill control was securely anchored in the Republican-Southern Democratic coalition first formed to fight Roosevelt's court reform bill fifteen years earlier. Its skepticism toward legislative innovation suited the country's new mood, which was conservative, content, and above all wary of nonconformity.

Adlai Stevenson spent election day evening in his basement office in Springfield, working on state business and listening to returns on a small portable radio. He had written out two statements, an acknowledgment of victory and a concession of defeat, and when Blair came in at nine o'clock he asked blandly, "Well, Bill, which is it to be—'A' or 'B'?" Blair replied, "I'm afraid it's 'B,' Governor." "O.K.," said Stevenson.

He reached the Leland Hotel lobby at 1:43. Smiling cheerfully at downcast volunteers, he stepped to a battery of microphones and said, "General Eisenhower has been a great leader in war. He has been a vigorous and valiant opponent in the campaign. These qualities will now be dedicated to leading us all through the next four years. . . ." After reading his telegram of concession, he looked out across the crowd. It was the end of an age, and they all felt it. Democrats of the swing generation had grown up under administrations of their own party. Now, with the age of reform over, they could not see the way ahead. Neither could he, but as their leader he wanted to say another word. After a pause he said: "Someone asked me, as I came down the street, how I felt, and I was reminded of a story that a fellow townsman of ours used to tell—Abraham Lincoln. He said he felt like a little boy who had stubbed his toe in the dark. He said that he was too old to cry, but it hurt too much to laugh."

He left, and millions discovered that tonight, at least, they were not too old for tears. In that broken moment of time they felt the first pangs of the barren loneliness Republicans had known for two decades—the frustrations of men accustomed to power but relegated to impotence.

Democrats slept late in the White House and at the Leland that Wednesday, November 5. Not so General Eisenhower; up early, he flew to Augusta. The day was still crisp and golden when the President-elect teed up for the first hole. The first ball he hit soared nearly 250 yards straight down the fairway. Two well-built young men congratulated him on his powerful drive, and he introduced them to the rest of his party as members of the Secret Service.

Montage: The Early Eisenhower Years

EAST BERLINERS RISE, BATTLE RUSSIAN TANKS

BARDAHL does it again!

BEST SELLERS: Fiction
The Silver Chalice by Thomas B. Costain
Lord Vanity by Samuel Shellabarger
East of Eden by John Steinbeck
The Old Man and the Sea by Ernest Hemingway
Too Late the Phalarope by Alan Paton

How much is that doggie in the window
The one with the waggly tail
How much is that doggie in the window
I do hope that doggie's for sale

I like Ike
I'll shout it over a mike
Or a phone,
Or from the highest steeple
I like Ike
And Ike is easy to like
Stands alone, the choice
Of we the people

STATE DEPT. BANS TRAVEL TO RUSSIA

CAIRO JUNTA SEIZES HELM

"OMNIBUS" SEEN LURING HIGHBROWS TO TELEVISION

GEORGE VI DIES — LIZ IS QUEEN

He was an old man who had fished alone in a skiff in the Gulf Stream and he had gone eighty-four days now without taking a fish.

GAMMA GLOBULIN CUTS POLIO FEAR

Best actor of 1953: William Holden in *Stalag 17*
Best supporting actress of 1953: Donna Reed in *From Here to Eternity*
Lila   *Moulin Rouge*   *Shane*   *Roman Holiday*

BEST SELLERS: Nonfiction
The Holy Bible Revised Standard Edition
Witness by Whittaker Chambers
Anne Frank: The Diary of a Young Girl
The Power of Positive Thinking by Norman Vincent Peale
A Man Called Peter by Catherine Marshall

"I like Ike, too," said Governor Stevenson:

MAU MAU LEADERS SENTENCED: KENYATTA GIVEN SEVEN YEARS

PUERTO RICO BECOMES 1st U.S. COMMONWEALTH

IKE CHRISTENS ATOMS-FOR-PEACE PROGRAM "OPERATION WHEATIES"

ARREST WILLIE SUTTON IN BROOKLYN

Alka-Seltzer is speedy!

LINK CIGARETTES TO LUNG CANCER, HEART DISEASE

The Great Inspirational Best Seller of Our Time

THE POWER OF POSITIVE THINKING

NORMAN VINCENT PEALE

A Practical Guide to Mastering The Problems of Everyday Living

Best actor of 1952: Gary Cooper in *High Noon*
Best actress of 1952: Shirley Booth in *Come Back, Little Sheba*
The Member of the Wedding   *The Man in the White Suit*   *Singing' in the Rain*
Viva Zapata!   *Limelight*

Twenty

WHAT WAS GOOD FOR GENERAL MOTORS

Late that autumn, while Washington awaited instructions from the first President-elect since FDR, the rest of the country turned, so to speak, from the bomb shelter to the barbecue pit, moving in rhythm to the tempos of the time. In the early 1950s that was easy. Rock 'n' roll lay in the future. Record stores had not yet been overwhelmed by teen-agers. Their typical customer was in his early twenties. His favorite songs were about love, not lust, and they were rendered tenderly by such mellow vocalists as Mario Lanza, Julie London, and Tony Bennett. Harry Belafonte, a U.S. Navy veteran, was earning $750,000 a year in the early 1950s —his album *Calypso* became the first LP to sell a million copies— and straight-arrow customers were buying 100,000 Mitch Miller albums every month. Miller was not only a performer; he was also the director of the Columbia Records popular music division, which meant that he profited twice from each sale. Yet it was all so relaxed that the public forgot that it was big business. On his Saturday evening television show Perry Como, one of Miller's fellow entrepreneurs, said he wouldn't mind going back to cutting hair for a living, and nobody in the studio audience laughed.

After seventeen years *Your Lucky Strike Hit Parade* was still going strong Saturday evenings on NBC, advertising a product still thought to be harmless. The number one hit in 1952 was Johnnie Ray's "Cry." It would be replaced in 1953 by Percy Faith's "Where Is Your Heart." Other melodies oozing from jukeboxes were "April in Portugal," "On Top of Old Smoky," Vera Lynn's "Auf Wiedersehn, Sweetheart," Rosemary Clooney's "Come on-a My House," and Tex Ritter's "High Noon." "High Noon" was the first big movie "theme." It was from the Gary Cooper picture of the same name. The tune was billed as "an original folk song by Dimitri Tiomkin," and it was so catchy that General Eisenhower couldn't get it out of his mind; he went around whistling it for months. In none of the lively arts was there anything startling or jumpy, anything that rocked the boat. This was a seedtime, a breathing spell, a space to stretch and regroup. Sensible Democrats knew it: "I agree that it is a time for catching our breath," said Adlai Stevenson; "I agree that moderation is the spirit of the times"; and Dean Acheson advised friends to "Do what nature requires, that is to have a fallow period."

In the hiatus between the Truman and Eisenhower administrations a Pueblo, Colorado, businessman and amateur named Morey Bernstein was preparing to make psychic history by mesmerizing an attractive thirty-three-year-old woman named Virginia Tighe. Until Bernstein fixed her with his eye she had been an ordinary Colorado housewife. Under his spell she spoke with a soft brogue, danced a jig, and identified herself as an Irishwoman named Bridey Murphy. Careful inquiries in Ireland disclosed that there had been such a person; she had been born in Cork in 1758 and was buried there. It then developed that Virginia, while speaking as Bridey, possessed an encyclopedic knowledge of early nineteenth-century Cork—its people, its places, and its customs. After a newspaper series about her appeared in the Denver *Post*, Virginia became a nationwide sensation. Bernstein's book about her, *The Search for Bridey Murphy*, went through eight printings; 30,000 long-playing records of her voice, speaking as Bridey, were sold at $5.95.

Psychiatrists, though stumped, suggested that Virginia could have woven together fragments of memory that lay in her subconscious. Sure enough, the *Chicago American* found that a Mrs. Anthony Corkell, née Murphy, had lived just across the street during Virginia's impressionable childhood. Mrs. Corkell had come from Cork. At the child's urging, she had repeatedly described her early life in Ireland and stories about it she had heard from her mother.

Receipts for motion picture theaters continued to be low. The storm that greeted Brigitte Bardot's performance in *And God Created Woman* says much about the 1950s. "There lies Brigitte," *Time* gasped, "stretched from end to end of the Cinemascope screen, bottoms up and bare as a censor's eyeball." The bowdlerizers did their duty. France's most famous piece of baggage could be seen only in the art theaters of very large cities, and not always there; Providence, Fort Worth, Memphis, and Philadelphia banned her outright. For a while, in the month of the Eisenhower landslide, movie exhibitors thought they might have something new in the deepies. Deepies were being hailed by their developers as the sequel to talkies. They were in 3-D photography; you put on a pair of glasses with cardboard rims, and you were on a roller coaster run amok, hurtling downward at 150 mph, or watching a spear sail right out of the screen headed for your throat. The first feature-length deepie, *Bwana Devil*, opened in Los Angeles on November 26, 1952. In one week it earned $95,000, and a Paramount executive, scoffing at the suggestion that the need to wear spectacles would ultimately mean poor box office, said, "They'll wear toilet seats around their necks if you give them what they want to see!" Then the novelty wore off, and sure enough, the deepies were as dead as Vitaphone.

The Ike-Stevenson campaign had been accompanied by two other fads: flying saucers and painting by the numbers. The first sighting of an airborne saucer is believed to have occurred in 1947, when a pilot in the state of Washington reported nine unidentified flying objects (UFOs) resembling shallow dishes and moving at about 1,200 mph in the skies above Yakima Indian Reservation. By the time of Ike's election the baffled Air Force was investigating fifty UFO reports a month; at the end of the decade $500,000 would have been spent on them, and the mystery would be as great as ever.

There was nothing unfathomable about enumerated art. It was a kind of crib for the inartistic, allowing them to pass themselves off as painters without creating anything. In a decade remarkable for its high incidence of sham, it served as a cultural weathercock. The idea of providing color-coded canvases is attributed to the Palmer Paint Company of Detroit. Customers bought an intricate outline of a still life, say, or a portrait—Milton Berle was a favorite. With it came as many as fifty oils or watercolors, each numbered. Matching numbers were stamped on the canvas, or paper. If sepia was 14, you covered every 14 area with it, and so on. Using the Palmer method, you could reproduce Leonardo da Vinci's *The Last*

Supper for $11.50 plus tax, with a "beautiful antique gold frame" thrown in. The frame was plastic.

At 5:30 in the starlit morning of Saturday, November 29, 1952, two men in heavy overcoats, their collars turned up against the cold, emerged from 60 Morningside Drive in Manhattan and entered a black limousine waiting at the curb. One of them was Secret Service agent Edward Green; the other was the President-elect of the United States. At that hour there was no traffic in the city. The car moved swiftly down the deserted streets toward the East River, crossed the Triborough Bridge, and swung across Long Island to a back road paralleling Mitchel Field. There two Constellations were waiting, the fastest aircraft in that pre-jet age. One was for the general, who hurriedly mounted the ramp, buffeted by a sharp, chill wind.

The other plane would carry Ike's staff. All over metropolitan New York, Secret Service automobiles had been coming and going through the small hours of that Saturday morning, their movements synchronized with those of the President-elect's limousine. Extraordinary measures had been taken to make certain that no outsider's curiosity was aroused. Eminent men awaiting transport had left home and dawdled at unfamiliar street corner rendezvous; Defense Secretary-designate Charles E. Wilson, the president of General Motors, had awaited his driver by hanging around Grand Central Station pretending to be a stranded passenger. Press Secretary Jim Hagerty had prepared a simulated Eisenhower agenda crowded with fake appointments. These would be released to the press, which would be told that the general was working busily at home. Reporters conscientiously standing watch at 60 Morningside Drive would see a steady procession of distinguished statesmen arriving and departing, for Hagerty had left nothing to chance. It was thought unlikely that Communists would make an attempt on Eisenhower's life, but with international tension as taut as it was, nobody was taking any chances.

The two planes landed outside Seoul Tuesday at 8 P.M. Generals Mark Clark and James A. Van Fleet met them. Their former commanding officer and next commander in chief spent three days in Korea, studying situation maps, listening to artillery fire, and visiting infantrymen. The American people first learned of the journey on Saturday, December 6. In a statement released by Hagerty they were warned that their next President had "no panaceas, no solutions," but assured that "much can be done and much will be done" to back the embattled U.N. forces along the 38th Parallel. Ike, meantime, was bound for Honolulu aboard the U.S. Navy cruiser *Helena* with his advisers. Caustic Democrats assumed that his only reason for flying the Pacific had been to fulfill his campaign pledge. It is true that he had achieved little in his seventy-two hours there, but there was more to the trip than that. Word that he had gone to the front was a sorely needed boost to U.S. morale, and the sight of the ice-rimmed foxholes had reminded him, as nothing else could, of the desperate need for a truce. Finally, there was the cruise on the *Helena*. During it he received and pondered advice from Douglas MacArthur, met and chose the next chairman of the Joint Chiefs, Admiral Arthur W. Radford, and became better acquainted with the man he had designated Secretary of State, John Foster Dulles. Since each of these last three believed that America's adversaries understood nothing but naked force, the trip was a fateful one.

The general had never before met the admiral, who came on board at Iwo Jima in his role as Commander in Chief, Pacific. Omar Bradley's second term as JCS chairman would expire in August, and Eisenhower had come to the conclusion that Bradley's successor must be a man who believed, as Charles E. Wilson did, that Asia would be the pivot of the cold war in the 1950s. Radford more than met that test; he was so ardent a champion of the Pacific theater that he wouldn't even hear of closing down Sands Point Naval Station in Seattle. He also agreed with their choice of a new strategic concept. Ike believed that huge defense budgets played into Stalin's hands; if the new administration tried to meet every Communist threat around the globe, he argued, it would spend the country into oblivion. More sensible, in his view, was a policy of discouraging aggression by building up a large stockpile of nuclear weapons. If the Soviet Union knew that a hopeless confrontation could end in bombs being unloaded on the Kremlin, the chances for world peace would be greater, or so the theory went. Dulles liked it. Later he would call it "massive retaliation."

It was dangerous, of course, and the subsequent debate over it became one of the great political issues of the 1950s. Some Democrats blamed it on George Humphrey, who would be Ike's Secretary of the Treasury. Humphrey was a passionate advocate of balanced budgets, and the Pentagon was the biggest spender of federal money. But Humphrey was only one of many converts to massive retaliation. Another was MacArthur. While aboard the *Helena* Eisenhower read that his old chief had told an NAM convention that he had "a clear and definite solution to the Korean conflict," involving "no increased danger of provoking universal conflict." He refused to disclose it publicly, but said he would give it to the President-elect. Most of the notables on the *Helena* no longer took MacArthur seriously. Ike disagreed. He wired the Waldorf that he looked forward to a meeting where "I may obtain the full benefit of your thinking and experience." MacArthur replied that he was pleased, "especially so because, despite my intimate personal and professional concern therewith, this is the first time that the slightest official interest in my counsel has been evidenced since my return."

On December 9 Hagerty released the exchange to the press. Harry Truman read it next morning while returning to Washington from his mother-in-law's funeral, and he all but went through the roof. If General MacArthur knew of a sensible way to end the fighting, he said, it was his duty to lay it before the President of the United States. At a press conference the following day he said he doubted that MacArthur had a workable plan. While still seething, he fired a salvo at the *Helena*. Ike's pledge to visit Korea, he said, had been an irresponsible piece of campaign demagogy. Everybody was angry now. MacArthur's thoughts were scarcely worth the price—calling at the Waldorf when he reached New York, Ike learned that his idea was to threaten Peking with extermination—and all hope was now gone for a smooth transition between incoming and outgoing administrations.

Prospects for it had never been great. Before flying to Seoul Eisenhower and his aides had called at the White House in an attempt to mesh the two foreign policies. Truman had introduced Acheson, who had reviewed world trouble spots. He dwelt at length on Vietnam, where the big question, he said, was whether the French had the will to carry on the fight against the Communists.

Ike wanted a good start, but he had his own way of preparing for it. His concept of leadership reflected his faith in experts and the delegation of authority. Sherman Adams was to be his chief of staff, with the title "the Assistant to the President." Beneath Adams would be the cabinet. Selecting it was the President-elect's first crucial task. Most Presidents have found the cabinet too unwieldy to be of much use as a deliberative body; they have preferred to work with the White House staff, leaving the secretaries to administer the departments. Eisenhower intended to treat his cabinet as a national council, laying all important matters before it; so instead of working in tandem with Truman and Acheson in the weeks before his inauguration, he would put his designated secretaries through two rehearsals at the Commodore Hotel in New York on January 12 and 13.

His appointees reflected his admiration for the American business community. Ike wanted his stewardship to be remembered as a business administration, and said so frequently. In his opinion, businessmen were abler than military men, and both more competent than politicians. To him, politicians were men of very small caliber. At the pinnacle of his value scale were the great captains of industry. His designated cabinet was so heavily weighted with them that Stevenson called it "the Big Deal," and TRB, writing in the *New Republic*, said it comprised "eight millionaires and a plumber." The plumber was Martin P. Durkin, a union leader. He was chosen to lead the Labor Department.

Humphrey at the Treasury, Wilson in the Pentagon, Attorney General Brownell, Postmaster General Summerfield, Secretary of Agriculture Ezra Taft Benson, Douglas McKay at Interior, Secretary of Commerce Sinclair Weeks, Oveta Culp Hobby, who would become the first Secretary of Health, Education and Welfare when the department was created April 11—the change from the Democratic appointees was breathtaking. Three of the newcomers would be General Motors men: Wilson and Summerfield and McKay, who were Chevrolet dealers. (During one stormy session of the new cabinet, Jerry Persons passed a note to Emmet John Hughes: "From now on, I'm buying nothing but Plymouths.") Since GM accounted for 7.8 percent of all Pentagon business, Wilson had to sell his stock in it. Then Ike insisted that all his nominees do the same.

Like Eisenhower himself, his designated secretaries were farther to the right on some issues than Republican politicians—Taft confided to friends that he had misgivings over the number of industrialists high in the government—and their rhetoric was more conservative still. In the coming months the country would be provided with some striking examples of it. The most voluble member of the new administration was Wilson, nicknamed "Engine Charlie" (the president of General Electric was named Charles E. Wilson, too).

Engine Charlie sometimes claimed that he was misquoted, and he was sometimes right. He never said, "What's good for General Motors is good for the country." What he said, in testifying before a Senate committee weighing his confirmation, was, "What was good for our country was good for General Motors, and vice versa"—a very different remark, one that was turned round by liberal reporters unsympathetic to the new regime. Wilson was capable of gaffes of his own, however. In dismissing complaints of excessive Pentagon spending he said, "I didn't come down here to run a grocery store."

Hughes has left a memorable description of Eisenhower's slow burn whenever he learned of a feisty Wilson remark; first came an "audible grinding of teeth," then a "strained tightening of the mouth," and lastly a "slow, pained rolling of the bright blue eyes heavenward." Engine Charlie's colleagues were sometimes stricken by foot-in-mouth attacks, too. George Humphrey said of Ernest Hemingway's 1952 novel, *The Old Man and the Sea*, "Why should anyone be interested in some old man who was a failure and never amounted to anything, anyway?" Weeks admitted that he didn't really believe in government regulation of trade, his job under Ike. Benson liked to talk about the "spiritual side" of farm prices. Confronted by a proposal to provide the country's children with free Salk vaccine, Mrs. Hobby denounced it as "socialized medicine" by "the back door." Another member of the administration, Howard Pyle, who as a deputy assistant to the President was privy to cabinet confidences, permitted himself to be quoted as saying that "the right to suffer is one of the joys of a free economy."

Seen in retrospect, the incoming cabinet was more impressive than any of those remarks would indicate. As a group it was characterized by dedication, industry, sobriety, and patriotism. Week after week the secretaries punctually took their places at their long coffin-shaped table in the West Wing of the White House, sitting erect on their high-backed black leather chairs, solemnly fingering the little white notebooks before them and nodding gravely whenever the chief executive spoke. Luckily they were not easily daunted, for their new burdens were immense. None of them, not even Wilson, had been asked to cope with anything anywhere near as large as the U.S. government of January 1953. The last time a Republican had occupied the White House there had been 630,000 civilian employees on the federal payroll. Now there were 2,561,000, a fourfold increase, and the budget, having risen from $3,863,000,000 to $85,400,000,000, was more than twenty times as large.

In some ways the most interesting figure in the new administration was the youngest and most partisan Republican at the cabinet table. Hughes saw Vice President Nixon as "crisp and practical and logical: never proposing major objectives, but quick and shrewd in suggesting or refining methods—rather like an effective trial lawyer, I kept thinking, with an oddly slack interest in the law." Like the others, Nixon sometimes made Ike wince. In discussing early Eisenhower decisions on television he said, "Incidentally, in mentioning Secretary Dulles, isn't it wonderful, finally, to have a Secretary of State who isn't taken in by the Communists, who stands up to them?" When Earl Warren was appointed to replace Fred Vinson, the Vice President incensed Ike by calling Warren "a great Republican Chief Justice,"* and he was photographed smiling over the rim of a wineglass at the Dominican Republic's Rafael Trujillo Molina while proposing "A toast to this great country and its illustrious ruler."

Those preinaugural cabinet meetings in the Commodore foreshadowed much that would follow in the Eisenhower years. From the very beginning they were devout. Each meeting opened with a silent prayer or a few prayerful words from Benson, who was one of the Council of Twelve Apostles of the Mormon Church. If Eisenhower forgot it, Dulles would clear his throat and murmur a reminder, and Ike would blurt out, "Oh my gosh! And I really need all the help we can get up there this morning. Ezra, please . . ." There was also a tremendous amount of talk. At that time the chief topic was the coming ceremony in Washington. Despite Democratic grumbling Ike had decided to replace the traditional toppers with homburgs—an illustration of his preference for the informal, one reason for his popularity in the new suburbs. He also read to the group the remarks he would make after taking the oath and, when they applauded, modestly protested that he had presented it "more for your blue pencils than your applause." Wilson said, "You flew the flag! It was wonderful!" Engine Charlie, it quickly developed, relished having the first word on any subject. When the President-elect spoke of one of his most cherished beliefs—the need for free trade with all nations, including the Communists—Wilson snapped, "Well, I'm a little old-fashioned. I don't like selling firearms to the

---

* Afterward he said he had meant to insert a comma between "Republican" and "Chief." Ike was unpropitiated.

Indians." That secretly pleased the anti-Communist vigilantes, but he could shock them, too; in a discussion of the possibilities for a cease-fire in Korea he asked, "Is there any possibility for a package deal? Maybe we could recognize Red China and get the Far East issues settled."

Eisenhower's preparations having gone well in New York, he left there on Sunday, January 18, 1953, and rode to Washington with his family on the Pennsylvania Railroad's Business Car No. 90, the same one he had used on his return from Europe in 1945. The capital's quadrennial upheaval had already begun. Every hotel room was occupied. The *New York Times* reported that hairdressers were offering a "Mamie bang" for $2 a coiffure if the customer wanted her own hair curled and anywhere up to $17.50 for "store hair." The President-elect was too busy to notice such trivia. His train had left Manhattan an hour late because he had been revising his inaugural address at the Commodore, and he and his staff continued to hone it Monday in the Statler's twelfth-floor presidential suite, three blocks from the White House. Unfortunately, too many advisers had a hand in it. As delivered Tuesday noon, it was prosy and tedious. The prayer preceding it, on the other hand, was entirely his own, and it gave that day its one really unforgettable moment. It reminded the country of the new President's most prized attribute, that of a unifier and healer. During the parade down Pennsylvania Avenue that followed, a button vendor checked his stock and made an interesting discovery. Two of his novelty pins read "I like everybody" and "I hate everybody." His supply of the first was exhausted; that of the second was almost untouched. To a bystander he remarked, "Most people like everybody today. We're not moving the 'hate' ones, except to kids."

Democrats had little reason to feel cheerful, though. Still smarting from Truman's brickbats, Ike had declined the outgoing President's invitation to share his last White House breakfast. Dulles had already twice called on Acheson, who rather wished he hadn't. Though both men were cold war hard-liners, they agreed on little else. Acheson suspected—correctly, it later developed—that his successor would bow to McCarthy pressure and dismiss John Carter Vincent, an able foreign service officer who had drawn the senator's fire.

McCarthy became a Republican problem at the stroke of noon on January 20. The GOP had been dishing out criticism for twenty years—the tenure of only one Republican senator reached back to the last Republican President—and now they would be taking it. Departing Democrats felt a surge of relief. Riding from 1600 Pennsylvania Avenue to Acheson's Georgetown home, Margaret Truman turned to her father and said jubilantly, "Hi, *Mister* Truman!" He looked astonished for an instant; then he laughed. There had been no advance word of his plans, yet the pavement outside Acheson's P Street home was crowded with five hundred well-wishers, and at Union Station five thousand had gathered to see the last departure of the "Ferdinand Magellan" for Independence. From the platform Truman told them that he would never forget this gesture "if I live to be a hundred"; chopping air in a parody of his awkward campaign gesture, he added with mock stridency, "And that's just what I expect to do!" The engineer gave a warning toot, the train lurched forward. A lone voice sang the first few bars of "Auld Lang Syne"; then, as the crowd joined in a thundering chorus, Truman receded into history.

The Executive Mansion, early Wednesday, January 21, 1953:
Although visits to two inaugural balls kept him up until nearly 2 A.M., the new President rises as usual at 7:30 and breakfasts alone in his bedroom with his customary half-grapefruit and coffee. Washington is a city of late risers, but West Point taught Ike that an early start is a virtue, and he still believes it; despite anguished protests he will schedule his weekly breakfast meetings with the National Security Council and the legislative leadership at 8 A.M., and his daily calendar will start no later than 8:30. Now, slipping into a dark brown suit and knotting a figured tie, he descends to the first floor and strides vigorously to the oval office in the West Wing, where Sherman Adams, also a lifelong early bird, awaits him. Squatting on a table behind the President's red leather desk chair is an ornate green marble clock-barometer, bought during the Grant administration for $400. Ike sets it. He is a methodical man; he will do it every morning.

His first appointment, at 8:02 A.M., is with Brownell. They discuss a few procedural matters; the cabinet will be sworn in at 5:30 P.M. in the East Room, and Wilson won't be able to make it because he is still selling his $2,500,000 of GM stock. (Republican Wayne Morse of Oregon will take the Senate floor today to urge that Wilson's name be withdrawn. Morse will be a liberal thorn in the administration's side throughout the decade, and eventually he will switch to the other party.) Brownell leaves for the Justice Department and is succeeded by Mr. and Mrs. James Bradshaw Mintener of Minneapolis. Mintener is general counsel for Pillsbury Mills. This is a social visit. Last spring he organized the Eisenhower write-in campaign in the Minnesota primary, and this is his reward.

The morning fills up with routine presidential business. Twenty-nine horsemen wearing red jackets and white caps swarm in; they are members of the Palomino Mounted Patrol of Colorado, which rode in yesterday's parade, and each gets an Eisenhower handshake. They are followed by the Junior Police Band of Denver, shepherded by Police Chief Herbert E. Forsyth. The mail room sends up good news: yesterday's events have inspired 1,500 congratulatory telegrams. Two Republican governors arrive for a fried chicken lunch. It is afternoon before Ike, preparing for a conference over his first State of the Union address, discovers that he doesn't have a key to his desk.

The key is provided by Adams, who also deals with most of the paperwork which, under Ike's predecessors, had been handled by the chief executive. With Persons and Hagerty, Adams is one of the three aides closest to the President. Except for Dulles, who can talk to Eisenhower at any time, everyone in the administration must approach the President through the former New Hampshire governor. On most matters his scrawled "OK, SA" is as good as a presidential signature. On a typical day he will handle 250 calls. Adams runs a trim ship; White House workers are warned against gossip sessions, smoking in corridors, putting their feet on desks, or other "eccentric habits" in "deportment."

While his executive officer toils, the commander ponders larger issues and keeps himself fit. At sixty-two the thirty-fourth President of the United States is a bald, handsome, energetic, ruddy, square-shouldered man standing five feet ten inches tall and weighing 178 pounds, just six pounds over his cadet weight forty years earlier. He holds his head high, his jaw set, and his strong mouth taut. In anger he will sock his right fist into his left palm and squeeze it; in repose his expression is stern, and if he chooses to be aloof his manner can be arctic. His most striking feature, however, is his famous grin.

Hoover kept fit with a medicine ball, FDR swam, Truman walked; Ike golfs. Outside, by the White House rose garden, the United States Golf Association is installing a putting green for him, and in good weather he will make iron shots across the Mansion's south grounds. On wet days he can swing clubs in his high-ceilinged bedroom. Directly across the hall from it he will soon convert a spare bedroom into a studio. The new First Lady gave him his first oils for Christmas after the war, and painting has become a serious hobby for him. At present he is working on portraits of his chief advisers. Democratic critics will tell how Adams, trying to handle a half-dozen crises at once, received a call from his chief asking, "Are your eyes blue?" They will remind the country that no President since Coolidge has relaxed more. An Eisenhower agenda, they will gibe, is a list of steps he will refrain from taking, and TRB will write in the *New Republic:* "The public loves Ike. The less he does the more they love him. That, probably, is the secret. Here is a man who doesn't rock the boat."*

Like most men in public life, Eisenhower dislikes wearing spectacles. Ann Whitman, his secretary, copies manuscripts of his speeches on a special machine with outsize type. Rather than carry his bifocals in his pocket, he leaves a dozen pairs lying around the Mansion; when thoughtful he will pick one up and chew at the earpiece. Paperback westerns are still his favorite light reading. His favorite author is Luke Short, though he has also read the first two books of Bruce Catton's Civil War trilogy, *Mr. Lincoln's Army* and *Glory Road,* and soon he will tackle the third, *A Stillness at Appomattox.* At his direction the collected works of Jefferson and Lincoln have been put on his office shelves. He will dip into them when he has time. One passage from Lincoln—Volume II, 1848–1858—describes his own approach to the Presidency. He likes to quote it:

> The legitimate object of government, is to do for a community of people, whatever they need to have done, but can not do at all, or can not, so well do, for themselves—in their separate, and individual capacities.
>
> In all that the people can individually do as well for themselves, government ought not to interfere.

Beginning at 10:30 A.M. next Wednesday, he will meet White House correspondents regularly in the Indian Treaty Room of the

---

* Some of the moves Ike did not make are worth noting. He did not invade Manchuria, send American troops to Indochina, wage preventive war, replace containment with a policy of "liberation," or end American participation in NATO —all measures that were urged on him by powerful advocates in his own party and administration.

Executive Office Building next door. In those sessions he will often seem unaware of major events. To the embarrassment of his aides, he will admit it is true: "You're telling me something about my own administration I never heard of," he will say. He will dismay them with awkward straggling sentences that wander over the landscape in defiance of all grammatical and syntactic rules. Clever reporters will write an Eisenhower version of the Gettysburg address:

> I haven't checked these figures, but 87 years ago, I think it was, a number of individuals organized a governmental set-up here in this country, I believe it covered certain Eastern areas, with this idea they were following up based on a sort of national independence arrangement and the program that every individual is just as good as every other individual. . . .

It is true that the only newspaper he usually reads is the Republican *Herald Tribune*. It is not true that his press conference manner is wholly inept (when Adams worries about a delicate subject before a press conference Ike will say with a wicked grin, "I'll just confuse 'em!") or that he spends most of his evenings watching television. His only regular TV program is the *Fred Waring Show*, Sunday evenings from nine to nine-thirty. He will attend the movies shown in the White House basement theater but rarely. His idea of pleasant diversion is a dinner with eight or ten congenial men in the solarium on the White House roof, with himself broiling steaks on a portable charcoal grill. Those invited to such an evening receive a note on monogrammed "DDE" stationery, usually addressed to them by their first names:

> I wonder if it would be convenient for you to come to an informal stag dinner on the evening of Tuesday, May twenty-eighth. I hope to gather together a small group, and I should like very much for you to attend if it is possible for you to do so. . . . Because of the informality of the occasion, I suggest that we meet at the White House about seven-fifteen, have a reasonably early dinner, and devote the evening to a general chat . . . I shall probably wear a dinner jacket, but a business suit will be entirely appropriate.
> With warm regard,
>
> Sincerely,
> DE

Who will be invited? Not politicians; in his opinion his responsibilities require him to see too much of them as it is. Not his administrators; once he has found a competent manager for a department or a bureau he assumes that he has done his duty and promptly forgets him and it. If Ike wants the evening to end in a bridge game, he taps one of his favorite partners—General Alfred M. Gruenther of NATO; William E. Robinson, president of Coca-Cola; or Clifford Roberts, an investment banker. For general conversation the President casts a wider net, but the guest list is drawn from the same group. A *U.S. News & World Report* survey of "presidential playtime companions" finds only one man associated even remotely with public life, an ex-governor of Colorado. Among the others are two cattlemen, two oilmen, two distillers, two golf champions, two realtors, and three bank presidents. Businessmen prevail—executives from hotel, soft drink, publishing, insurance, home appliance, and tire enterprises—and those not in industry are established conservatives: Herbert Hoover, Douglas MacArthur, Francis Cardinal Spellman, Bernard Baruch.

What will they discuss? If this is to be their first visit, some time must be spent admiring mementos presented to the general by grateful Allied governments. There is no way to avoid them; Ike has filled the presidential apartment's white oval study with cases displaying the awards and called it his "trophy room."* But in an hour the banter may run from rock gardens to modern architecture, Pat and Mike jokes, French cooking, good bourbon, Turkish baths, automobile styling, vegetable farming, Jewish humor, and poker. As a conversationalist, he prefers the specific to the general; mention McCarthy's flouting of constitutional rights and his attention wanders, but describe a victim of witch hunts and he is with you all the way, provided, that is, you are not bitter. The venomous and meanspirited are unwelcome here. Ike is generous, and expects his friends to be the same. Only gentlemen are admitted to these rooms. The rest must deal with Sherman Adams.

Robert A. Taft's political skills had never been more masterful, or his energy so inexhaustible. He was swarming all over the Hill, organizing the 83rd Congress, outwitting his adversaries, rewarding his allies, deciding who should have which office—doing everything, in short, but painting the Capitol dome, and some days he seemed

---

* To allay confusion: there are two oval rooms in the White House. The oval *office* is in the West Wing. The oval *study*, on the second floor of the Mansion, is in the First Family's living quarters.

capable of that. Taft made himself majority leader and put all key committee chairmanships in the hands of his ultraconservative friends: Eugene Millikin, Styles Bridges, William Langer, Hugh Butler, Homer Ferguson, and William Knowland. The Ike-before-Chicago senators—Carlson of Kansas, Ives of New York, Duff of Pennsylvania—found themselves consigned to unpopular, insignificant duties. In cutting up the senatorial pie Taft made but one slip. He thought he had outmaneuvered Joe McCarthy into the Government Operations Committee. There, it was expected, he would spend his time poring over figures from the General Services Administration. Taft said, "We've got McCarthy where he can't do any harm."

The first gavel had hardly fallen before Joe began looking for trouble. He found it in the list of administration nominees up for senatorial confirmation. At first glance the names seemed flawless, but McCarthy could find sin anywhere. James B. Conant was Ike's choice for high commissioner in Germany. The senator declared that as president of Harvard Conant held opinions "contrary to the prevailing philosophy of the American people." Eisenhower wanted General Walter Bedell Smith as Undersecretary of State. Smith was a formidable figure; he had been Eisenhower's chief of staff in World War II, and since then he had served as director of the CIA and as U.S. ambassador to the Soviet Union. Joe countered that Smith had testified at a pretrial hearing in a libel suit against McCarthy, and was known to have defended diplomat John Paton Davies despite charges made against him by McCarthy and Pat McCarran. The Senate wasn't ready to defy a popular President on such dubious grounds. Conant and Smith were approved. But McCarthy had staked his claim. The White House had been put on notice; he meant to be reckoned with.

The serious reckoning was over the appointment of Charles E. Bohlen to the Moscow embassy. Bohlen was important to Eisenhower and Dulles. He was the State Department's authority on the Soviet Union. In that role he had served as FDR's interpreter at Yalta, and anyone associated with that hated name was anathema to the Republican Right. In hearings before the Foreign Relations Committee Bohlen steadfastly refused to condemn the Yalta Conference. He even defended it against its senatorial critics as having been in the best interests of the United States at that time. With that, the gauntlet was down. Power was at stake; somebody had to lose.

The ultraconservatives subjected the Bohlen nomination to a rising stream of abuse. Bridges told the Senate that the Moscow appointment should go to "a deserving Republican." On March 20 McCarran charged that R. W. Scott McLeod, a McCarthy man who had been appointed the State Department's security chief, had been "unable to clear" Bohlen on the basis of "information received by the FBI"; McLeod had been "summarily overridden" by Dulles. The secretary immediately denied it. Later in the day McCarthy called Dulles a liar and demanded that he testify under oath. He said he knew what was in Bohlen's file, and that calling him a security risk was "putting it too weak." By now McLeod was distraught. Trapped between warring giants, he sought refuge in the White House. It was all a grotesque mistake, he told Adams and Persons. He had merely called Dulles's attention to certain "derogatory material" in Bohlen's FBI file. McLeod offered to resign, but Adams told him that if he did, the already unpleasant situation would only seem worse.

Dulles assured the Foreign Relations Committee that FBI investigators had "no doubt" of Bohlen's loyalty, but to the Senate ultraconservatives even a conservative Secretary of State was suspect. The only solution was for Taft and Sparkman of Alabama, who had been Stevenson's running mate, to form a two-man commission and study the FBI's Bohlen file together. On March 25 Taft reported their findings to the Senate:

> There was no suggestion anywhere by anyone reflecting on the loyalty of Mr. Bohlen in any way or any association by him with Communism or support of Communism or even tolerance of Communism . . . There was not any suggestion that would in my opinion create even a *prima facie* case or a *prima facie* charge of any ill doing on the part of Mr. Bohlen.

Nevertheless, McCarthy still wanted Bohlen's scalp. Eisenhower told White House correspondents that the diplomat's name would remain before the Senate. America's best interests would be served by the appointment, and that, said the President, was that. Responsible Republicans were left with little choice. Taft's personal opinion of Bohlen was low, but as majority leader he could hardly lead a revolt against Ike, especially since the evidence all ran the other way. With his great strength in the Senate he put the nomination through, 74 votes to 13.

At a glance McCarthy seemed to have sustained a defeat. Actually it was the other way round. The issue had divided Taft's forces; he didn't want to see another like it, and he sent Ike the price of his support: "No more Bohlens!" The President's aides had come to the same conclusion on their own. Meanwhile, the Wisconsin senator planned fresh outrages. In all Washington, it seemed, there was not one Republican prepared to defy Joseph R. McCarthy.

Forming battle lines against him, the new administration was weakened by several unwise campaign promises. The party platform adopted in Chicago had been a hodgepodge reflecting two decades of broken hopes, myths nursed in defeat, and promissory notes for heavy Republican contributors. One of them pledged Eisenhower to return rich submerged coastal lands to the states. The President redeemed it in full, despite a Wayne Morse filibuster, but his prestige suffered; he had entered politics as a crusader, and the quarrel over tidelands oil was no crusade. At George Humphrey's urging he met another campaign commitment on February 6, ordering an immediate end to wage controls and removing from controls a vast range of consumer goods, including meat, furniture, clothing, meals in restaurants, and almost all articles sold in retail stores. Then Humphrey also demanded tighter federal credit and a deep cut in defense appropriations. Here, too, Ike acceded, disappointing consumer advocates and paving the way, it later developed, for recession in late 1953 and the first half of 1954.

Republican myths were wildest in foreign affairs. Taiwan was the subject of one. In sending ships and planes to Korea on June 27, 1950, Truman had also declared:

> The occupation of Formosa by Communist forces would be a direct threat to the security of the Pacific area and to the United States forces pursuing their lawful and necessary functions. Accordingly, I have ordered the Seventh Fleet to prevent any attack on Formosa. As a corollary of this action, I am calling upon the Chinese government on Formosa to cease all air and sea operations against the mainland. The Seventh Fleet will see that this is done.

Acheson had called this "neutralizing" Formosa. The Republican ultraconservatives disapproved of it. In their view measures to neutralize Chiang Kai-shek were neither sensible nor loyal to the United States. Against all evidence, they were convinced that Chiang could easily defeat Mao Tse-tung's armies now, and that keeping him bottled up on the island was part of a sinister conspiracy. As a demonstration of their faith in Kuomintang arms, McCarthy, Knowland, and Bridges attended a formal dinner in the Chinese embassy and joined in the shouted Nationalist pledge, "Back to the mainland!" They stood up to do it, and the Chinese ambassador applauded vigorously.

They had vowed to "unleash Chiang Kai-shek." Eisenhower never used the phrase, but it was in the platform, and at his order the Joint Chiefs cabled the Seventh Fleet:

2 FEB 53

OPERATIONAL IMMEDIATE
TO: CINCPAC PEARL HARBOR TH
INFO: CINCFE TOKYO JAPAN

THAT PORTION UR CURRENT DIRECTIVE WHICH REQUIRES YOU INSURE THAT FORMOSA AND PESCADORES WILL NOT RPT NOT BE USED AS BASES OPNS AGAINST CHI MAINLAND BY CHI NATS IS RESCINDED.

But how could Chiang reconquer the mainland? Lacking ships, how could he even reach it? Still, Eisenhower went along with the fantasy. In drafting his State of the Union message he wrote that as a consequence of Truman's order, "the United States Navy was required to serve as a defensive arm of Communist China." Lewis Carroll could not have turned things round more. Furthermore, talk of reopening China's civil war was provocative; when word of it leaked through the press Anthony Eden warned the President that it might have "very unfortunate political repercussions without compensating military advantages." Disturbed, Ike decided on the way to Capitol Hill to end the passage on a peaceful note: "Permit me to make it crystal clear this order implies no aggressive intent on our part." What really became crystal clear was that Chiang, having been unleashed, possessed no teeth. Unhampered by Seventh Fleet patrols, Communist Chinese made a few exploratory amphibious moves and found that the Nationalists lacked strength to dominate or even make a showing in Formosa Strait. As the months passed Chiang came to miss American warships more and more, and on the first anniversary of Eisenhower's order to the Joint Chiefs the *New York Times* reported the results: eleven coastal islands had been lost to the Communists. The administration had by no means heard the last of Formosa. Because of possible political ramifications in the United States, or just to ward off Democratic horse laughs, the

Seventh Fleet was recalled. The term for that was "releashing Chiang."

The Chicago platform had further vowed to "repudiate all commitments contained in secret understandings such as those of Yalta which aid Communist enslavements." In writing that plank Dulles, like the rest of his party's leaders, had believed some things about the American State Department which simply were not true. They were convinced that the Communist empire had been built by Communists and Democrats at Teheran, Yalta, and Potsdam. They had resolved to set this wrong right. In his first speech as Secretary of State Dulles advised eastern Europe that it could "count on us," and he wrote this passage in the President's State of the Union address: "I shall ask the Congress at a later date to join in an appropriate resolution making clear that this government recognizes no kind of commitment contained in secret understandings of the past which permit . . . enslavement." The reference to Yalta, Potsdam, and Teheran was clear. When Eisenhower read it, the Republicans leaped to their feet cheering. The secret agreements did exist, then, they told one another; they had known it all along. Dulles at the time was still sure he would find the incriminating documents in some obscure vault at the State Department. But they weren't there. They weren't anywhere. They didn't exist. As the truth emerged, both the President and his Secretary of State began to revise their expectations. But the Republican mastodons of the Senate were already preparing a Yalta resolution. As worded by them, it would renounce all wartime agreements. If it went through, Eisenhower realized, the position of Americans in Berlin and Vienna would be extremely awkward.

The upshot was the first serious rift between the White House and the GOP leadership on the Hill. At his February 16 weekly meeting with the Republican legislative leaders Ike presented a waffled draft prepared by him and Dulles. It was virtually meaningless; the United States would express regret over the plight of eastern Europeans and assure them that "all peaceful means" would be used to help them. Taft bridled. That wasn't at all what he had in mind. Ike pointed out that stronger wording would, among other things, offend congressional Democrats, who would look upon it as an insult to the memory of FDR. But Taft had precisely that in mind. At the next weekly meeting between the President and the legislative leadership, on February 23, Ike and the majority leader squared off again. Taft would settle for nothing less than an outright repudiation of all agreements between Roosevelt and the Russians.

At this point an outside force intruded upon the intraparty row. It was Lyndon Johnson of Texas, the Senate's new minority leader. Johnson advised the White House that Democrats were just as unhappy about the situation in eastern Europe as Republicans, and would be glad to join them in lamenting it. However, they had no intention of pleading guilty to something neither they nor their Presidents had done. Emmet Hughes and Assistant Secretary of State Thruston Morton sympathized, and the administration resolution went to the Hill without teeth. Bitter ultras there trotted out all their old clichés about the "betrayals" of Roosevelt and Truman. Taft joined other members of the Foreign Relations Committee in adding an amendment asserting that the measure "does not constitute any determination by Congress as to the validity or invalidity of any provisions" of agreements between the United States and the Soviet Union. The Senate Democratic Policy Committee took this as a reflection upon Roosevelt. They rejected the amendment, and the issue was deadlocked.

Thus a central political fact of the 1950s emerged in the fifth week of the Eisenhower Presidency: Ike's foreign policy would be backed by Democratic senators and opposed by diehards in his own party. The President, resolved to forget the past, was baffled by the ultras' determination to hold an eternal inquest into the iniquities of Yalta. For their part, they came to believe that all their misgivings at Chicago had been justified. They saw Ike as the puppet of men like Dewey and Lodge, about whose patriotism they had grave doubts. They weren't quite sure where Dulles stood (neither, at times, was Eisenhower), and they were vigilant for any State Department attempt to succor what Knowland called "the Trojan horse of containment."

In 1953 Lyndon Johnson and his Democrats saved administration measures no fewer than fifty-eight times. The "enslaved peoples" resolution was not among them, however. The question would continue to bedevil Washington until 1955, when Dulles authorized the publication of all Yalta papers and chagrined Senate ultras found no campaign ammunition in them. All this had almost come to a head two years earlier. The administration draft of the resolution had again headed the agenda for the March 9, 1953, meeting between Eisenhower and the congressional leadership, but before they could meet, fate intervened and tabled it. Stalin would be giving no more orders to anyone. On March 4 he had been mortally stricken in Moscow.

The President was dining with Mrs. Eisenhower when the bulletin came in from Moscow Radio: "The heart of the inspired continuer of Lenin's will, the wise leader and teacher of the Communist Party and Soviet people—Joseph Vissarionovich Stalin—has stopped beating." The President sent formal condolences to Moscow. To the cabinet he remarked acidly the following morning, "Ever since 1946, I know all the so-called experts have been yapping about what would happen when Stalin dies and what we, as a nation, should do about it. Well, he's dead. And you can turn the files of our government inside out—in vain—looking for any plans laid. We have no plan. We are not even sure what difference his death makes."

Alone in his office with Emmet Hughes, he paced the oval room in a wide arc. Hughes's notes of that hour offer an exceptional glimpse of Ike in action. He said:

> Look, I am tired—and I think everyone is tired—of just plain indictments of the Soviet regime. I think it would be wrong—in fact, asinine—for me to get up before the world now to make another one of those indictments. Instead, just one thing matters: what have we got to offer the world? What are we ready to do, to improve the chances of peace? . . .
> Here is what I would like to say.
> The jet plane that roars over your head costs three-quarters of a million dollars. That is more money than a man earning ten thousand dollars a year is going to make in his lifetime. What world can afford this sort of thing for long? We are in an armaments race. Where will it lead us? At worse, to atomic warfare. At best, to robbing every people and nation on earth of the fruits of their own toil.

But there could be "another road before us," he said, "the road of disarmament." If taken it would give everyone "bread, butter, clothes, homes, hospitals, schools." How could it be reached?

> Let us talk straight: no double talk, no sophisticated political formulas, no slick propaganda devices. Let us spell it out, whatever we really offer . . . withdrawal of troops here or there by both sides . . . United Nations-supervised free elections in another place . . . free and uncensored air-time for us to talk to the Russian people and for their leaders to talk to us . . . and concretely all that we would hope to do for the economic well-being of other countries.

What do we say about the Soviet government? I'd like to get up and say: I am not going to make an indictment of them. The past speaks for itself. I am interested in the future. Both their government and ours now have new men in them. The slate is clean. Now let us begin talking to each other. And let us say what we've got to say so that every person on earth can understand it. Here is what we propose. If you—the Soviet Union—can improve on it, we want to hear it.

This is what I want to say. And if we don't really have anything to offer, I'm not going to make a speech about it.

Sherman Adams believed that "The Chance for Peace," Ike's April 16 speech to the American Society of Newspaper Editors, was the greatest in his career. Writing in the *New Yorker*, Richard H. Rovere called it "an immense triumph," one which "firmly established his leadership in America and re-established American leadership in the world." The *New York Times* found it "magnificent and deeply moving," and even the opposition *New York Post* agreed that it was "America's voice at its best." Long afterward in the 1960s, Hughes would chiefly remember the struggle to bring it off. Dulles fought it through every draft. Once Hughes asked him whether he thought American interests would be served by any armistice in Korea. Dulles shook his head. He said, "We'd be sorry. I don't think we can get much out of a Korean settlement until we have shown —before all Asia—our clear superiority by giving the Chinese one hell of a licking." Hughes passed this along to Eisenhower, who snapped, "If Mr. Dulles and his sophisticated advisers really mean that they cannot talk peace seriously, then I am in the wrong pew." Later he said, "Sometimes Foster is just too worried about being accused of sounding like Truman and Acheson." It was a difficult speech all the way; even delivering it was agony. That day Eisenhower was suffering from a vicious stomach upset. He could hardly hold up his head and nearly collapsed at the end.

Unlike hundreds of other such addresses in the 1950s, this one launched an effective peace offensive. The Chinese were tired of fighting, too. Dulles's rigid diplomacy had given Asia the impression that the new administration was immovable; that the Americans, as an Indian newspaper put it, were "hunting peace with a gun." Now their President said they weren't. A new spirit quickened at Panmunjom. More than peaceful intentions were needed to cut the knot there, of course; the negotiators were held fast in a vise of accumulated fears, hatreds and recriminations which had reached a climax in Peking's accusations that the Americans had resorted to bacteriological warfare.* Stalin's death undoubtedly contributed to a solution by removing the hardest of all the hard-liners. Dulles subsequently became convinced that Peking was cowed by blunt warnings, relayed by Nehru, that the United States was planning to issue tactical nuclear weapons to U.N. field commanders. Threats that the war would soon spread to Manchuria were certainly made; Eisenhower later told Adams about them. However, Adams doubted Dulles's dramatic assertion that the United States went "to the brink of total war" three times—in the Korean truce crisis of 1953, the Indochinese crisis of 1954, and the grave situation which arose from Mao's threat to invade Formosa in late 1954 and early 1955. Adams wrote: "Whether the Dulles policy was actually put to three crucial tests, as the Secretary believed it was, is a matter that is open to question. I doubt that Eisenhower was as close to the brink of war in any of these three crises as Dulles made him out to be."

In any event, Ike's appeal to reason was at the very least one clear note in an orchestration of events which roused the men on the other side and brought them back to the bargaining table. In the first sessions of the new beginning, progress was slow. The bottleneck was the fate of 132,000 North Korean soldiers in U.S. hands. The U.S. was determined to give them the right to decide whether or not they would go home. In 1945 the Allies had delivered Russian POW's, freed from the Germans, to Soviet commanders; many had then been sent to Siberia, and in some cases executed, for having allowed themselves to be captured. On May 7, 1952, Truman had declared: "We will not buy an armistice by turning over human beings for slaughter or slavery." Eisenhower was equally determined. More and more it became evident that the destiny of the POW's would determine the outcome of the talks.

The negotiations, resumed eleven days after the President's peace speech, dragged all through May. Holding the U.N. coalition together was becoming increasingly difficult. Some leaders of the

---

* This propaganda campaign enjoyed an astonishing success in neutral nations, despite the fact that American appeals for an investigation by the International Red Cross, accepted by the Red Cross, were rejected by Peking. At the time Chinese motives were obscure. Later it was learned that their leaders used the occasion to rid China of billions of insects and rats—for centuries the source of devastating Chinese epidemics—by telling the population that they had been put there by an unscrupulous enemy.

European left thought there might be something to Mao's bacteriological warfare charges. At the other end of the political spectrum, ultraconservatives were urging the U.S. to ignore its timid allies and answer MacArthur's call for total victory. Ike declined. "If you go it alone in one place," he told them, "you have to go it alone everywhere." The most chauvinistic hawk in the U.S. camp was Syngman Rhee. The seventy-eight-year-old South Korean President refused to consider any agreement which would leave Korea divided. Rather than accept as a border the 38th Parallel or the front line, he was prepared to face certain annihilation by driving toward the Yalu without the U.N. Later Adams observed: "The endless efforts to appeal to Rhee's sense of reason and to make him understand that the United States could not hazard a possible world war for a unified Korea left Eisenhower and Dulles limp and baffled." The dispute with Rhee, he added, was "more nerve-racking and frustrating than the haggling with the Communists."

The old man almost sabotaged the peace. On June 4 the Chinese and North Koreans consented to an arrangement under which prisoners who declared before a neutral Repatriation Commission that they did not wish to go home would, after a 120-day waiting period, be freed and demobilized. On June 8 a protocol was initiated, and everything seemed set when, on June 18 at two o'clock in the morning in Washington, Dulles was awakened by a call from a State Department watch officer. On Rhee's orders guards had opened stockyard gates and released 25,000 anti-Communist North Koreans. The operation had been painstakingly prepared; South Korean police had provided the refugees with food, shelter, and civilian clothing. Dulles called the President—the only time Eisenhower was awakened during his eight years in the White House. Ike was shocked. As expected, the Communists that morning accused the U.N. of "deliberately conniving" with Rhee and demanded that the POW's be recaptured "immediately"—an impossibility. They broke off negotiations on June 20 and launched a major offensive.

Dulles was undiscouraged. Convinced that the enemy would be receptive to new overtures, he told Ike that if the other side was as anxious for a cease-fire as he thought, "They will overlook Rhee's impetuosity and will be content to sign an agreement, provided they are given proper assurances." Peking confirmed him, through New Delhi. That left the assurances, which required further pressure on the intractable Rhee. Ike cabled the South Korean president that he had put the U.N. command in "an impossible situation." He sent Walter S. Robertson, Assistant Secretary of State for Far Eastern Affairs, to talk to him. Robertson sat down with Rhee in Seoul and listened hour after hour, and then day after day, while the angry old man poured out his pent-up feelings. After Rhee had run out of steam Robertson explained the U.S. dilemma. After two weeks Rhee gave in.

The armistice terms, announced two weeks before the signing ceremony, satisfied no one. After 37 months of bloodshed and 2,000,000 dead, 80 percent of them civilians and 54,000 of them Americans, Korea would be returned to its *status quo ante*. Rhee had gained 2,350 square miles as against Kim Il Sung's 850, but in all other respects the settlement was a draw. No principles had been vindicated. The U.N. had not even succeeded in putting through a reliable inspection system to prevent Kim from launching another attack. The end had come as a result of negotiations begun by President Truman, yet his terms for a truce had been harsher; as Paul Douglas pointed out, Truman "would have been flayed from one end of Washington to the other if he had accepted the present agreement."

When a photographer asked Eisenhower how he felt, he said simply, "The war is over, and I hope my son is coming home soon." The White House had no other comment on the coming truce. In official Washington only the Secretary of State spoke of it with satisfaction: "For the first time in history, an international organization has stood against an aggressor . . . All free nations, large or small, are safer today because the ideal of collective security has been implemented."

This was also the interpretation of the liberal community. Liberals then were faithful to the Roosevelt-Truman concept of world government and were determined to put the best possible face on its first effort to keep the peace. Richard H. Rovere summed up their conviction that Korea had been a blazing success:

> In Korea, the United States proved that its word was as good as its bond—and even better, since no bond had been given. History will cite Korea as the proving ground of collective security, up to this time no more than a plausible theory. It will cite it as the turning point of the world struggle against Communism.

Conservatives were not so easily hoodwinked. Walter Lippmann wrote in the *Herald Tribune*, "What has really happened is that both sides and all concerned have been held within a condition of mutual deterrent." The Old Guard was another matter. As Hanson W. Baldwin explained in the *New York Times*, ultraconservatives had taken it as an article of faith that Korea was "the right war in the right place at the right time if we wished to stop the spread of Asiatic Communism." They had not forgotten that the GOP platform had charged that under Truman the war had been waged by men "without will to victory" who "by their hampering orders" had "produced stalemates and ignominious bartering with our enemies." Now Korea, like Germany, was to be cut in twain. "Truman's war," as they saw it, was to become "Eisenhower's appeasement."

Jenner of Indiana and Malone of Nevada saw the approaching ceasefire as a Chinese victory. On the Senate floor Malone asked: "Does the distinguished Senator remember any change in State Department policy . . . by Mr. Dulles since he has taken office?" And Jenner responded: "I have noticed no change."

Knowland of California was asked in a broadcast interview, "Is this a truce with honor that we are about to get?" He replied, "I don't believe so," and predicted that under its terms, "Inevitably we will lose the balance of Asia." In Korea General Mark Clark said, "I cannot find it in me to exult in this hour," and General James A. Van Fleet, to whom U.N. copies of the convention would be brought for safekeeping after the ceremonies, turned away from correspondents who asked his opinion of it. "I don't know," he said tightly. "The answer must come from higher authority." The makings of an Old Guard revolt were present. All that was necessary was a signal from Robert A. Taft.

None came. The Senator from Ohio had been passing through a conversion much like that of Arthur Vandenberg seven years earlier. A gadfly and obstructionist under Roosevelt and Truman, Taft was now becoming a tower of administration strength. The crisis had come on April 30, 1953, in the Cabinet Room. Eisenhower had summoned the legislative leadership to break bad news; contrary to expectations, he would be unable to balance his first budget. Originally drawn up by Truman, it had anticipated a 9.9 billion-dollar deficit. Ike could cut that to 5.5 billion, he said, but he could slice no more without jeopardizing national security. Supportive presentations followed from Secretary Humphrey; Joseph M. Dodge, director of the budget, and Undersecretary of Defense Robert M. Keyes. The gist of them was that the cost of changing the country's static defense posture to a fluid stance, while anticipating an attack against the United States at any time, would be too expensive to permit further reductions.

Taft exploded. He lost control of himself, hammering the cabinet table with his fist and shouting in his hard, metallic voice that this Republican administration was turning out to be no different than those of the Democrats. The Pentagon was as greedy as ever. The budget would exceed 30 percent of the national income, and that was too much. Unless the government raised taxes—which at this point was inconceivable—the deficit would be outrageous. He yelled, "The one primary thing we promised the American people was reduction of expenditures! With a program like this, we'll never elect a Republican Congress in 1954! You're taking us down the same road Truman traveled! It's a repudiation of everything we promised in the campaign!" Addressing Taft at last, and speaking deliberately, Eisenhower began, "There are certain essential elements in the global strategy of the United States. They are not difficult to grasp. . . ." A concise review of cold war strategy followed.

It was a critical moment. Had Taft stalked out of the meeting, denounced the President's budget to the press, and set up a shadow cabinet on the Hill to battle the administration's foreign policy, Eisenhower's legislative program would have collapsed. Old Guard sentiment was hostile to Ike anyhow; one word from the powerful majority leader would have been enough. But Taft stayed. In possession of himself once more, he merely expressed the hope for substantial reductions in next year's budget—hopes which Eisenhower assured him were justified.

The storm had passed. Taft from that moment forward was the President's most important champion. Privately he gagged on the terms of the Korean cease-fire, but he suppressed his feelings; in speaking to the press he was more cautious than the Knowlands, Jenners, and Malones. To be sure, he could be as blunt as ever. (He once said, "It isn't honest to be tactful.") He conceded that he found the prospect of a divided Korea "extremely distasteful" because it left "a condition likely to bring war at any moment" and gave the Chinese freedom to attack Vietnam. But he refused to sow discontent or counsel despair.

At about this time reporters began to notice the change in him.

For six months the majority leader had served his party's President with distinction. His one goal since the inaugural, they wrote, had been to make this Republican administration a success. It had been a lonely struggle. Other senators on the Right were puzzled by his sense of loyalty, and to Democrats he was, as he always had been, an implacable adversary. Moreover, though none of them knew it yet, he was carrying another new burden. Over the past several weeks he had become increasingly aware that he was in ill health.

It mystified him. Before launching his campaign for the GOP presidential nomination the year before, he had submitted to a thorough physical checkup. Doctors assured him that he had never been fitter. In the first three months of the 83rd Congress he had been a legislative whirlwind. Then, in mid-April while golfing with Eisenhower in Augusta, he suffered a sharp, excruciating hip pain. During the next week he couldn't sleep. Massive doses of aspirin were ineffective; so was a rest at White Sulphur Springs, Montana, in May. On June 12 he checked into New York Hospital for a battery of tests. He used the name "Howard Roberts."

Physicians there prescribed deep X-rays and cortisone, put him on crutches, told him to keep his weight off his hipbone, and insisted that he relinquish the routine chores which went with being majority leader. On June 10 he delegated day-to-day decisions to Knowland. The appointment was to be considered temporary; Taft would continue to handle policy matters and attend White House meetings insofar as his treatments would permit. Before the next congressional session he expected to be back on the floor, heartier than ever. Minority Leader Lyndon Johnson was the last man to see him on the Hill. Taft waved at him and called twice, "I'll be back in January! I'll be back in January!"

There was something heroic about Robert Taft that June. Though in almost unbelievable pain, he dragged himself to Washington garden parties with his wife Martha, herself a cripple and almost wholly dependent upon him, rather than reveal his condition to her. Like many formidable men in public life he had always removed his stern mask when crossing his own threshold. Martha knew him as a devoted husband, and to their four sons he was "Gop," a delightful companion on camping trips who loved to play hearts, chew nickel candy, and entertain them hours on end with his encyclopedic memory of Gilbert and Sullivan.

He reentered New York Hospital in early July. His condition then was reported to be "good." The doctors expected him to be back at his desk by the end of the year and able to vote in close contests before then. He was to be discharged July 23. Then they suddenly announced that he needed more therapy. Signs of leukemia had appeared in blood tests. His return to Washington was postponed indefinitely.

Progress at Panmunjom continued to be smooth. The Chinese had just erected a new pagoda there, and on a freshly lacquered table eighteen copies of the armistice agreement were executed at 10:01 A.M. July 27 (8:01 P.M. July 26 in Washington). The signers were General William K. Harrison for the U.N., tieless and without decorations, and North Korea's General Nam Il, sagging in a baggy tunic weighed down with medals. No words were spoken, no hands shaken, and on Rhee's order no South Korean participated.

President Eisenhower was on television within the hour. He said, "With special feelings of sorrow and with special gratitude, we think of those who were called to lay down their lives in that far-off land to prove once again that only courage and sacrifice can keep freedom alive on the earth." He warned that the United States had "won an armistice on a single battlefield, not peace in the world," and said he hoped it would convince people of the wisdom of negotiating differences instead of resorting to "futile battle."

It was a time to review American foreign policy and strengthen the legislative role in it, but the man who would have recognized it as such, and explained it to American conservatives, lay stricken at New York Hospital that Sunday evening. At 10:30 P.M. Thursday Taft went into a coma. Thirteen hours later he was dead.

His departure at that juncture was a catastrophe. William S. White wrote in next morning's *New York Times*, "The death of Senator Robert A. Taft of Ohio has shaken the Republican party as it has not been shaken in half a lifetime. It has removed the one real bridge between the East and Midwest in the Eisenhower administration. The loss to the administration . . . is beyond calculation."

It was in fact a national tragedy. The only American statesman who really understood the role of congressional prerogative and the danger of an omnipotent Presidency—the one man who could have foreseen the end of the long road running from Pusan to My Lai—was mourned on the Hill by politicians who by their very expressions of grief revealed how little they had understood him. The eulogy was delivered by John Bricker, Ohio's junior senator. After thirty-five thousand mourners had passed through the Capitol rotunda, where the coffin lay on the black catafalque which had been used for Taft's father and Lincoln before him, the muffled brasses of the Marine Band struck up "America the Beautiful." Bricker said: "Senator Taft never hesitated to recommend the coercion of the law. . . . During life our departed leader created to himself an everlasting memorial. His services to his government, and through government to his fellow man, go on."

That was the best Bricker could do: Taft acclaimed as a law and order man. It was an ominous sign for Eisenhower. In the months ahead the snowy-haired Ohioan would distress the administration by his advocacy of a constitutional amendment which would have sharply limited the scope of treaties to which the U.S. could be a party and the President's authority to negotiate executive agreements. After Vietnam the measure would take on a somewhat different look, but at the time Ike believed it unwise. To Knowland he wrote:

> Adoption of the Bricker Amendment . . . by the Senate would be notice to our friends as well as our enemies abroad that our country intends to withdraw from its leadership in world affairs. The inevitable reaction would be of major proportions. It would impair our hopes and plans for peace and for the successful achievement of the important international matters now under discussion.

Knowland didn't see it that way. He rarely saw things Ike's way. Over the next five years he would make the President's weekly meetings with the legislative leadership a torment from which Ike would emerge livid, exhausted, and at times almost incoherent. Ironically, Eisenhower himself was responsible for Knowland's succession to the role as majority leader. Once Taft was dead, custom dictated that the President, as head of the majority party, select the new Senate leader. But here Eisenhower's concept of his office, so very different from FDR's and Truman's, disserved him. He firmly maintained that the Executive Department was but one of the government's three equal branches, and that presidential attempts to manipulate the men on the Hill were in contempt of the Founding Fathers. This was what he meant when he called himself a "constitutional President." Because of his respect for Congress, he stood aside in the days after Taft's death. On the day of the obsequies he pointedly told the cabinet, "I want to say with all the emphasis at my command that this administration has absolutely no personal choice for new majority leader. We are not going to get into their business."

They, however, were determined to get into his. During their long struggles against programs of the last five administrations the ultras had become skillful legislative guerrillas adept at penetrating executive agencies and making the lives of civil servants unlivable. Their chief weapon was the congressional investigation. Ike had assumed that inquiries on the Hill would be held in abeyance during his first year in the White House. In his opinion, he told the cabinet, Americans had been living too long on too high a level of tension; the endless hearings under klieg lights were unnecessary now; his administration should be allowed a period of grace to clean house. Only if it failed would Congress be justified in stepping in.

Brownell wryly observed that the 83rd was already in with both feet. These were ten separate investigations of the State Department alone; State men scarcely had time to read their mail. Ike replied that the administration must cooperate with the Hill: probably they were just checking up on Truman's people anyway. In fact they were turning over every stone in sight, including many which weren't in the government and some which had always been regarded as out of bounds for politicians. McCarthy was in pursuit of the Voice of America. Jenner's Internal Security subcommittee was looking for Communists in high schools, and the House Committee on Un-American Activities, now piloted by Republican Harold R. Velde of Illinois, was preparing to invade places of worship. On a radio program Velde explained that the committee had just about finished sweeping out subversives in show business. Now it was ready for a searching investigation of Christianity. The hunt, he said, would focus on "individual members of the cloth, including some who seem to have devoted more time to politics than . . . to the ministry."

To the end of Ike's life he never wavered in his belief that "our long-term good requires that leadership on the Hill be exercised through the party organization there," but there were times when even a constitutional President must rap knuckles. "Are you in favor of the federal government, through the Congress of the United States, investigating Communism in the churches?" Eisenhower was asked at his next press conference. No, he said; houses of God were the last places to look for disloyalty; he could see no possible good in questioning their patriotism. Maybe in this instance the investigators should be investigated, he said—hard words from a chief executive who believed in leaving the legislators alone.

But Republicans were running Congress, and Republicans of a very special breed at that. At times their ultraconservatism went beyond reaction. Judgment Day was approaching for Joe McCarthy; the Senate had begun to form ranks against him. Soon every member of the chamber would be asked to choose between him and Eisenhower, and the men of the right would be revealed as enemies of the President. With the single exception of Leverett Saltonstall of Massachusetts, every senior Republican Senate leader—Knowland, Dirksen, Styles Bridges, and Eugene Millikin—would vote for the demagogue.

George Sokolsky, McCarthy's muezzin, charged that under Eisenhower the Republican party "has gone so modern that it is indistinguishable from the New Deal," and Colonel McCormick had tried to read Ike out of the party in the *Washington Times-Herald* the morning after his inaugural. Most publicists were on the President's side, however. Seven months after Taft's funeral the *Times-Herald* was absorbed by the *Washington Post*, a very different kind of newspaper, which observed sharply that "Senator Knowland does not seem able to separate administration objectives from his own pet phobias." *Business Week* commented that "it is only natural for people to ask themselves whether Republicans are equal to the responsibilities of power," and Roscoe Drummond wrote in the *New York Herald Tribune* of a new sort of "mess in Washington."

> What is to be the consequence, what is to be the political harvest of this heedless divisiveness, this feuding, this name-calling, this miasmic preoccupation with bitter negative controversy within the Republican Administration? . . . The effect of this new kind of "mess" is to exhibit the Republican Government as quarrelsome, unproductive and legislatively nearly impotent."

There were days then when capital correspondents wondered in print whether the federal government was becoming an exercise in self-parody. Here was William Knowland, the helmsman of the Senate, pounding away at the President on the urgent need to institute a full naval blockade of the Chinese coast and vetoing Paul Nitze,

Wilson's choice to be his Assistant Secretary of State for Foreign Affairs, on the ground that as a member of the State Department Nitze had been one of "Acheson's architects of disaster." Here was Everett McKinley Dirksen triumphantly tacking a rider on an appropriations bill to provide that should Peking be admitted to the United Nations, all U.S. contributions to the U.N. should be terminated instantly. Five drafts of the rider passed the Senate, five times the President took up his pen, five times he put the pen down saying he couldn't live with this and still conduct foreign affairs. The impasse was broken by Styles Bridges's resolution asserting it to be the "sense of Congress" that Red China should forever be barred from U.N. membership. It passed both houses unanimously—the unanimity in the Senate being recorded approvingly by Vice President Richard M. Nixon. The height of these follies was reached when Hubert Humphrey drew up a bill making membership in the Communist party a felony. This had to be changed—it would have destroyed the McCarran Act, which required Communists to register, by making registration self-incriminating and thus evadable under the Fifth Amendment—but CP membership was nevertheless outlawed. Attorney General Brownell was horrified. The bill was still unconstitutional on at least six counts, and it canceled out several existing anti-Communist laws. Nevertheless, no one on Capitol Hill in the early 1950s was prepared to explain a no vote to his constituents. Humphrey's absurdity passed the Senate 79-0 and the House 265-2.

Apart from the coming struggle with McCarthy, that first year of the Eisenhower Presidency was his worst in Washington. Foster Dulles, prompted by Scott McLeod, was sacking seasoned forest service officers on the flimsiest of pretexts. State's passport office, now headed by Frances G. Knight—like McLeod a McCarthy appointee—was looking into the loyalty of Edward R. Murrow. Murrow's unpopularity in ultra circles arose from his October 20, 1953, *See It Now* CBS-TV program broadcast, in which Murrow described the plight of a University of Michigan senior named Milo Radulovich. After eight years of active duty in the Air Force Reserve, Radulovich had suddenly been classified as a security risk. He was accused of violating Air Force Regulation 36-52 by close association with "Communists or Communist sympathizers." Stripped of his lieutenant's rank, he was dismissed from the service, making him, in the political climate of the time, virtually unemployable. His case had been heard by a board of three colonels. The Air Force had produced no witnesses, specified no charges, had refused to identify the lieutenant's accuser, and had kept the evidence it said it had in an envelope which had remained sealed during the hearing. Murrow found out what was in it. The persons with whom Radulovich had been in close association were his father and his sister. Their questionable activity was reading a Serbian-language newspaper. The newspaper was published in Yugoslavia. Yugoslavia had broken with Moscow five years earlier, but the Air Force was taking no chances; it wanted no officers whose relatives read a journal using a foreign language which might be spoken by people who had once admired the late Joseph Stalin.

Five weeks after the Radulovich broadcast Secretary of the Air Force Harold E. Talbott appeared on *See It Now* to announce that he had decided, on second thought, that Lieutenant Radulovich's commission would be returned on the ground that he wasn't a threat to the nation's safety after all. It was a humiliating experience for Talbott, and it wasn't his last; in the summer of 1955 he was accused of shady dealings with firms holding Air Force contracts, and resigned under a cloud. In 1953 the administration felt protective toward him, however, and blamed Murrow. The credibility of the press was becoming a major problem. There were other Murrows, because there were other Radulovichs.

Abraham Chasanow, a civil servant who had worked in the Navy Hydrographic Office for twenty-three years, always to the satisfaction of his superiors, was one of them. Chasanow was suspended without pay on July 29, 1953. The personnel director informed him that he had been called a security risk. Two months later a naval board examined the evidence, found it worthless, and unanimously recommended that he be reinstated. Months passed; nothing happened. By now Chasanow, having exhausted his savings, was living on loans from his wife's relatives. On April 7, 1954, despite the lack of proof, Assistant Secretary of the Navy James H. Smith Jr. ordered Chasanow's dismissal. The messenger who laid this news before the public—together with the background details—was Anthony Lewis of the *Washington Daily News*. His stories about the case won a Pulitzer Prize, vindication for Chasanow, and further alienation of Republican conservatives and the press.

The trouble, said the reporters, was that in loyalty cases the administration's right hand sometimes didn't know what the left hand was doing, or, if it did, didn't care. They cited the unseemly row over the patriotism of Wolf I. Ladejinsky. The Ladejinsky incident was especially ridiculous because of his demonstrable patriotism. A militant anti-Communist and an expert on land reform, his work under MacArthur in Japan was regarded as a textbook example of how to outwit agrarian Communists. Ladejinsky's politics had in fact been commended by Scott McLeod. All the same, Ezra Taft Benson didn't want him in the Department of Agriculture. Benson discharged him as a security risk—whereupon Stassen cleared him, hired him with the President's approval, and sent him off to match wits with agrarian Communists in Asia.

For Ike, the pursuit of Communists was what he called, in a favorite expression, "a can of worms." The difficulties here, as elsewhere, went back to his campaign for the Presidency. The Republicans had said that the Democrats weren't doing enough about spies, yet it was hard to devise a harsher internal security program than the one Truman had established in 1947. Eisenhower tried it, on April 27, 1953, with his Executive Order 10450. Under it the mere suspicion of treachery brought termination of employment. So did suspicion of a great many other deviations from the accepted norm —drunkenness, drug addiction, participation in unusual sexual practices, conviction of a felony, mental illness, membership in a nudist colony, unsanitary habits, a reputation for lying—anything, in fact, deemed "inconsistent with the national security."

The regulation certainly thinned employee rolls. On October 23 the White House announced that in 10450's first four months 1,456 persons had left federal service, only five of whom had been hired since Eisenhower took office. To give further evidence of progress in the struggle against world Communism the White House issued a statement pointing to the conviction of 41 U.S. Communist party leaders under the Smith Act, verdicts against two other party members for spying and one for treason, the banishment of 84 alien subversives from American soil, and the addition of 62 new organizations to the attorney general's already bloated list of subversive organizations. In his second State of the Union message Eisenhower announced a new score. The number of "security risks" dismissed from government service, he said, had risen to 2,200. Later Nixon, declaring that "thousands of Communists, fellow travelers, and security risks have been thrown out" of government jobs, reported that 6,926 had been dropped from the payroll.

There, said delighted Republicans; it was true after all; the government had been infested with reds and pinks, and Ike had found them and booted them out. But the Democrats weren't having any of that. They went through civil service records and found that of the workers on the first list, only 863 had been discharged. The rest had resigned or retired; they would have left anyhow. As for Nixon's figures, only 1,743 of those dropped had been accused of disloyalty —and 41.2 percent of them had been hired by the Eisenhower administration. Stevenson guyed the Republican loyalty program as a "numbers game." So, in private, did the President. Dulles complained to the cabinet that he found himself wasting whole evenings reading files sent to him because someone in a worker's family—or even in his neighborhood—was reported to be a pacifist, a member of the United World Federalists, or an advocate of fluoridation.

The unkindest cut of all for 10450 came in a broadside from Harry P. Cain. Cain was a former Republican senator from Washington; defeated in the 1952 election, he had been appointed to the Subversive Activities Control Board as a favor to his old sidekicks on the Hill. Since they had included Jenner, McCarthy, and Dirksen, and since his own outlook had been ultraconservative, no one had dreamed that he might become a civil libertarian. Yet he did. In an emotional speech he flayed the White House for having "swung too far on the side of injustice." The President called Cain an ingrate; Adams reminded him that he belonged to a team and should not let the side down.

But the team had not yet learned to play together. McCarthy was raising hob with the Mutual Security Administration. Secretary of the Interior McKay had drummed out the distinguished director of the Fish and Wildlife Service and replaced him with a public relations flack. Secretary of Commerce Weeks continued to play politics with the National Bureau of Standards, a sanctuary that Harry Vaughan and Donald Dawson had not dared enter, and Dr. Clarence E. Manion, a former Notre Dame law school dean and extreme right-winger who had been appointed chairman of the President's Commission on Intergovernmental Relations, threw the White House into a turmoil by endorsing the Bricker amendment.*

The Bricker amendment had conservative chic. Some of its most ardent supporters didn't know what was in it; they had put their names and their money behind it because in certain boardrooms

---

* As a result, Adams forced him to resign.

and clubrooms it was the thing to do, just as backing the Liberty League had been stylish in those same places in 1936. It *must* be right, they felt; why else would those lobbying for it include the Daughters of the American Revolution, the American Medical Association, the Committee for Constitutional Government, the *Chicago Tribune,* and the Vigilant Women for the Bricker Amendment —"a volunteer organization of housewives and mothers of boys overseas"—which had brought to the Hill petitions signed by over a half-million Americans?

Similarly, those opposing it must be wrong; why else would *they* include the League of Women Voters, the Americans for Democratic Action, the *New York Times,* the *Washington Post,* the American Bar Association's Section on International and Comparative Law, the Association of the Bar of the City of New York, the American Association for the United Nations, and Eleanor Roosevelt?

Capital correspondents called the Bricker sortie "our greatest debate about the constitutional ordering of our foreign relations since 1788." It probably was. Had it not been obscured by the even graver struggle between Joseph R. McCarthy and the United States government, it would have been remembered as the greatest ultraconservative travail of the decade. When introduced in the Senate on January 7, 1953, the amendment had sixty-four senatorial cosponsors —the two-thirds of the Senate needed for a constitutional amendment. Dulles's plea that it was "dangerous to our peace and security" was ignored; after six months of begging Senate Republicans not to mortify their own President, Nixon had to tell the cabinet, "Well, there's just no doubt there's a lot of public support for this amendment."

Offering amendments to the U.S. Constitution had become an ultraconservative fashion of the early 1950s. Herblock depicted it as a kind of Scrabble. No fewer than 107 such proposals had been introduced in the 83rd Congress and referred to committees, among them one which would have interpreted treason not only as advocacy of the overthrow of the government but also of "weakening" it, "whether or not by force or violence." Others would have put the soil of any foreign country off limits to draftees unless Congress had declared war against it; prohibited the spending of taxpayers' money on welfare; limited new states to one senator; enjoined the federal government from meddling in any state's right to regulate the "health, morals, education, marriage, and good order" of its inhabitants; and affirmed that "this nation devoutly recognizes the authority and law of Jesus Christ, Saviour and Ruler of Nations through Whom are bestowed the blessings of Almighty God."

Six of the measures had reached the Senate floor, where each of them had been approved by majority vote, and four had received the two-thirds majority needed to send a proposed amendment on to the House of Representatives. From there, provided it was supported by two-thirds of those voting, it would go on to the state legislatures. This was senatorial irresponsibility. The prevailing sophistry was expressed by Dirksen: "If the legislatures say 'No,' that will be all right with the junior senator from Illinois; if they say 'Yes,' it will also be all right with me." Knowland took the same line. What, he asked, were the opponents of the Bricker amendment afraid of? Didn't they trust the people's judgment? The answer, of course, was that the founding fathers never meant Congress to be a transom through which schemes to alter the Constitution were to be passed, and that the state legislatures, lopsided with representatives of special interests and vulnerable to special pleaders, were no tribunes of the people. That reply was seldom made. Freshman Senator John Kennedy of Massachusetts argued that "reluctance to amend the Constitution is one of our most valuable safeguards and bulwarks of stability," but his colleagues were not listening to him yet.

Yalta was what the Bricker amendment was all about. The ghost refused to be exorcised. By now every informed citizen should have known what had happened in the Crimea during the first half of February 1945, but hallucinations of "secret agreements" continued to haunt Washington, kept alive by such bogeymen as William Jenner, who revealed in hushed tones that anti-Bricker forces were being masterminded by a "secret revolutionary corps" that included Owen Lattimore, Henry Wallace, Alger Hiss (who was in prison), and Harry Hopkins and Harry Dexter White (both of whom had died in the 1940s). Manion was not the only administration figure infected by the Bricker fever. In a January 29, 1954, cabinet meeting, after having listened to discussions of the amendment for over a year, Charlie Wilson volunteered that he shared the feelings of its backers that treaties should not be able to deprive people of their rights, and that conventions like Yalta and Potsdam ought to be outlawed. The President patiently explained once again that the

Bricker amendment could not have prevented Yalta and Potsdam, because they had been political accords, not treaties or executive agreements.

Back in his office Ike raged, "I'm so sick of this I could scream! The whole damn thing is senseless and plain damaging to the prestige of the United States. We talk about the French not being able to govern themselves—and we sit here wrestling with a Bricker Amendment." He had been going to the mat with it ever since his pre-inaugural cabinet rehearsals in the Commodore Hotel. At that time the idea had appealed to him. He had been caught up in the indignation at stories of FDR and Stalin carving up the world (somehow Churchill's presence was always forgotten), and he believed—as Bricker said he did—that resentment of the treaty-making process might be turned against the United Nations. The amendment sounded plausible; the United States would be insured against the possibility that an inept chief executive and a slumbering Senate might usurp the constitutional rights of the people and the individual states.

Then Dulles studied it. The more he thought about it, the more alarmed he became. Bricker's real hostility seemed to be toward *all* treaties and executive agreements. One of his remedies was to transfer the power to make them from the White House to the Hill. As Dulles saw it, this would mean that other governments would doubt the sanctity of treaties with the United States; what one Congress could do, another Congress could undo.* Eisenhower began to change his mind about the proposal. His complete conversion to the anti-Bricker camp was the byproduct of a tangential dispute over the so-called Status of Forces agreements. Under them, foreign governments were given legal jurisdiction in cases of offenses committed by American servicemen who were not acting in the line of duty. (The classic example was that of a U.S. soldier in Japan who fired an empty mortar shell at a group of women and killed one of them.) Ultraconservatives felt strongly that the armed forces should have complete jurisdiction over all American troops overseas. As it happened, Eisenhower knew more about Status of Forces treaties than anyone else in Washington, because as commander of NATO he had drafted some of them, negotiated them, and then kept watch over those administering them. He tried to explain their theory and

---

* Other advocates of a strong Presidency trotted this out. But by the same reasoning, administrations could repudiate treaties made by their predecessors.

practice to Knowland, but the majority leader flared up. Pounding the table he roared, "A young man drafted in peacetime, sent overseas against his will, assigned to a duty—by God, I don't think he ought to be turned over for trial! He's wearing the uniform of our country. I wouldn't want *my* son treated that way!"

Bricker felt the same way. His real motives were unmasked in an emotional attack on two State Department men. They opposed his amendment, but that was not why he went after them; they had testified for the NATO Status of Forces agreement, and he chastised them on that. It was a tactical error. The President was listening. Ike had already set the best constitutional lawyers he could find to work on the amendment. To his dismay they now reported that under it the United States could not have entered NATO. It specified that unless the Constitution assigned a specific matter to Congress, the Senate was powerless to act upon it. Such a treaty could become law under Bricker only if it was approved by legislation in each of the states. This, said Eisenhower, would permit state legislatures to renounce American treaties.* The President and his Secretary of State would, Ike said, be faced with the "impossible task of representing forty-eight governments."

The Bricker showdown came on February 26, 1954, at the end of a stunning sequence of parliamentary maneuvers. Bricker was defeated in the Status of Forces fight. To save his face, Ike proposed a mild procedural measure; when treaties came up votes would have to be recorded; they could not be shouted through. Bricker rejected the gesture. On February 25 his amendment fell short of the two-thirds vote; 50 senators were for it and 42 opposed.

Here, in the last desperate hour of the struggle, was a tragic incident. Chairman Walter George of the Senate Foreign Relations Committee drafted an amendment similar to Bricker's. It deserved serious attention. Not all Bricker supporters were irresponsible. One of them was Frank E. Holman, a former president of the American Bar Association. The ABA Committee on Peace and Law Through the United Nations had been behind Bricker, too, and so had some constitutional scholars. That did not make it good legislation, but it did suggest that amid all the clamor there were a few voices worth listening to. Since FDR's arrival in Washington the powers of the Presidency *had* grown to dismaying size. A chief exec-

* Bricker denied this interpretation.

utive with Eisenhower's scruples would not abuse them, but as subsequent events were to demonstrate, later inhabitants of the White House were not so circumspect. Furthermore, George was not just offering a restylized, Simonized Bricker amendment. His language was carefully drawn. It was more temperate than Bricker's, and he had omitted Bricker's notorious "which" clause, proscribing congressional action in matters beyond its delegated powers. That had been the sticking point for Ike, the provision that would have required that certain treaties be approved by the states. Without it, the heart of the administration's case against Bricker was gone. George's measure was farsighted in many ways, but because it, too, would have restricted presidential freedom in foreign policy, the White House decided to resist it.*

By the late 1960s and early 1970s senators who remembered the George amendment were having long second thoughts about it, and in the general mutiny against presidential behavior in Vietnam some of them could hear the voice of Knowland, by then long since defeated at the polls and retired to private life in California.† Knowland had endorsed the George proposal because, he said, he could not ignore "a dangerous tendency toward executive encroachment on legislative powers." Had Taft stood in Knowland's place that day he might have clothed the debate in dignity, but as it was all hope for rational contemplation was lost in the fog of emotion. A senator was either an Eisenhower man or he wasn't; that was all there was to it, and so Bricker dragged George down with him. Even so, the administration just squeaked through. There were 60 yeas and 31 nays on the George amendment—a margin of one vote, since it required a two-thirds margin. Had that thirty-first senator been ill, or in the men's room, and had affirmative action followed in the House and the legislatures, the history of American foreign policy over the next two decades would have been very different; to cite but one example, the notorious Tonkin Gulf resolution, authorizing U.S. intervention in Vietnam on a grand scale, would have been rejected as unconstitutional.

* The key clause in the George proposal provided that any provision of a treaty or other international agreement that conflicted with the Constitution—e.g., one which did not recognize that the war-making power is vested in Congress—should not be effective. In addition, international nontreaty agreements could not be effective as internal law except by act of Congress.
† He committed suicide in February 1974.

John Foster Dulles celebrated his sixty-sixth birthday the very day Bricker's amendment was defeated. He was an elder statesman and looked it. Everything about him emanated distinction: his leonine head and craggy face; his membership in the Metropolitan, Piping Rock, Down Town, and Century clubs; his chairmanships of the Carnegie Foundation and the Federal Council of Churches Commission on a Just and Lasting Peace; his Phi Beta Kappa key; and his degrees from Princeton, the Sorbonne, and George Washington Law School.

The most important fact in Dulles's life was his membership in the Presbyterian church. He regarded his religiosity as a great strength. In fact it was an encumbrance. In him anti-Communism was an extension of Presbyterianism—just as Communism itself, in George Kennan's view, was a gospel in the minds of Soviet leaders—and as a result his diplomacy, like theirs, was rigid and dogmatic. Eisenhower believed in compromise and conciliation, but the man he had chosen to conduct his foreign policy deeply distrusted both. Dulles skillfully sabotaged Stassen's disarmament plans on the ground that America's NATO partners would look upon them as a sign of slackening U.S. resolve. To him flexibility was worse than frailty; it was downright immoral. Dissent from his hard doctrines carried with it the stigma of sin. On one of his first trips abroad in 1953 he presented President Mohammed Naguib of Egypt, as a present from President Eisenhower, a nickel-plated automatic pistol. It was a reminder to statesmen in all uncommitted nations that militant vigilance against designing Communists was the price of American friendship. To neutral leaders like India's Nehru the world was not that simple. Nehru was trying to stake out a position between the two great rival blocs. He believed it important to be anti-colonialist as well as anti-Communist. Dulles saw neutralism as wicked; he virtuously shipped arms to Pakistan and lost India's friendship.

Despite Dulles's rhetoric, the only pro-Soviet government to be unseated in the 1950s was in Guatemala, a little country in America's back yard. Even that success was questionable; it sowed the seeds of later defeats in Latin America. The most disturbing aspect of Dulles evangelism, however, was its deliberate appeal to the populations of eastern Europe—his promises of a "rollback" of Russian tyranny there. In a cabinet meeting on July 17, 1953, he reported with immense satisfaction that Georges Bidault of France and Britain's Marquess of Salisbury had joined him three days earlier in an expression of concern over "true liberty" for East Europeans. This, he said, was "the first time to my knowledge that London and Paris have been willing to embrace this principle."

In his notes on that meeting Hughes wrote furiously, "Does he really believe that *words* are going to free anyone, any people?" But what Dulles believed was less important than the credulity of his listeners from Stettin to Trieste. There his failure to explain that America's determination to hasten their liberation must be confined to "every peaceful means"—a qualification Eisenhower was always careful to include—was to have tragic consequences. East German cities erupted in strikes, arson, and rioting. After Soviet tanks had suppressed an uprising by thirty thousand East Berliners, Ike emphasized to the press that the United States planned no physical intervention in eastern Europe, but by late November Dulles was inciting unrest in Lithuania, Latvia, and Estonia by declaring that the United States would not recognize Russia's incorporation of them and thereby "confirm their captivity."

To the relief of those who preferred diplomacy in a lower key, Dulles was frequently absent from the capital. In effect he was traveling round offering alliances as insurance policies against aggression, knitting the non-Communist world together with the steel thread of American military might. To NATO were added a rejuvenated Organization of American States (OAS), the Southeast Asia Treaty Organization (SEATO), and, in the Middle East, the Baghdad Pact, later to become the Central Treaty Organization (CENTO), which the United States did not join but backed heavily. Year by year new clauses were added to the covenants encircling the Communist countries, until America was committed by eight security treaties to the defense of forty-two nations. "Dulles," Walter Lippmann wrote in the *New York Herald Tribune*, "has shown himself to be not a prudent and calculating diplomat but a gambler who is more lavish than any other secretary of state has ever dreamed of being with promissory notes engaging the blood, the treasure, and the honor of this country."

Although none of the notes was called in Dulles's lifetime, there was considerable anxiety among those who would be called to account if they were. A parade of alarmed witnesses marched into congressional committee rooms to protest that while the administration was expanding U.S. military obligations, it was reducing the country's strength. For a general, Eisenhower was showing scant regard for the Pentagon. In one maneuver he cut five billion dollars from an Air Force budget, thereby estranging General Hoyt Vandenberg; another directive, issued while Formosa was approaching one of its periodic boiling points, reduced the size of the armed services from 3,200,000 men to 2,850,000. Only a President who had worn five stars could have accomplished that. He rejected all the strategic arguments that were raised as inapplicable in the nuclear age. "If you want to be coldly logical about it," he said at one White House meeting called to discuss further reductions in Army force levels, "the money being spent for ground forces could be used to better advantage on new highways to facilitate the evacuation of large cities in case of an enemy attack."

The President knew what he wanted, and George Humphrey, who had become the strong man of the cabinet, was behind him. Their goal was relief for the taxpayer, and they believed that this was the right way to go about getting it. "The New Look, with its planning predicated on nuclear retaliation," Sherman Adams wrote, obviously "led to an order from Eisenhower to reduce the number of army ground troops." Ike was commander in chief; the responsibility was his. To dispel any further confusion he instructed the Pentagon to assume that the United States would fight any future war with nuclear weapons. Democrats on the Hill complained that America was being lulled into a false sense of security, that the President's motives were political. They were, partly. One of the tinnier administration promises was "a bigger bang for a buck." Strategic monism also appealed to searchers for simplistic solutions. Clearly the United States planned no wars of conquest. Therefore, they said, the Department of Defense should be concerned, literally, with just defense. They only wanted America left alone, and the threat of massive retaliation was designed to guarantee that it would be.

Of course, their doctrine did no such thing, and with the Secretary of State marching to a different drum there was no way it could. It is amazing that so few observers spotted the discrepancies between the largesse of the administration's foreign policy and the relative parsimony of its military policy. Retaliation might have been an effective deterrent between the two world wars, when Presidents were sedulously avoiding entanglements abroad, but America was no longer that kind of country. The Pax Britannica had been replaced by a Pax Americana; where the British had once sent gunboats the United States now sent John Foster Dulles and his ballpoint pen. Superpowers need a wide range of deterrents to keep the peace, and it was precisely here that phrasemongering about a bigger bang for a buck—as though global politics were an old-fashioned Fourth of July celebration—became so irrelevant.

Young Henry Kissinger saw it. After taking his Ph.D. in 1954 and becoming a junior member of Harvard's government department, Kissinger wrote *Nuclear Weapons and Foreign Policy*, a closely reasoned examination of America's world posture. Massive retaliation, he concluded, was a fallacy: with the government's capacities for fighting a limited war sharply reduced, and with nothing left but the bomb, national survival became a stake in every diplomatic disagreement that verged on the use of force. Dean Acheson also saw the inconsistency. In a magazine article he examined administration claims that massive retaliation gave the United States "initiative" and rejected them as absurd; retaliation, he pointed out, is a response to somebody else's initiative. Richard Rovere saw the anomaly vividly; in a "Letter from Washington" dated April 8, 1954, he predicted that "if the worst happens in Indochina, where atomic bombs would be about as useless as crossbows, the ground forces will have to be restored to their former strength—and then some."

Washington and Indochina are exactly twelve hours apart—midnight in one is noon in the other—and so evening darkness had already enveloped the Maison de France, French army headquarters in Hanoi, when, at 10:30 on the morning of February 10, 1954, President Eisenhower entered the Indian Treaty Room for his regular Wednesday press conference. He was asked about the critical military situation half a world away. He said, "No one could be more bitterly opposed to ever getting the United States involved in a hot war in that region than I am. Consequently, every move that I authorize is calculated, so far as humans can do it, to make certain that that does not happen."

"Mr. President," the next reporter asked, "should your remarks be construed as meaning that you are determined not to become involved or, perhaps, more deeply involved in the war in Indochina regardless of how that war may go?"

Eisenhower replied that he could not forecast the future. However, he added: "I say that I cannot conceive of a greater tragedy for America than to get heavily involved now in an all-out war in any of those regions, particularly with large units."

Compared to what would come later, the American presence in Indochina at that time was slight. It dated from the previous administration. Until the late 1940s the three states of Indochina—Vietnam, Cambodia, and Laos—had been French colonies. On December 30, 1949, their status had changed somewhat; Paris had recognized them as "independent states" within "the French Union." That was mostly show, a token gesture of anti-colonialism designed to counter Russia's support of Ho Chi Minh's insurgent Viet Minh. On February 7, 1950, Washington and London had recognized the three states, Acheson stressing America's "fundamental policy of giving support to the peaceful and democratic evolution of dependent peoples toward self-government and independence." He had hoped that recognition from some Asian nations would follow, but they hung back, repelled by France's puppet ruler of Vietnam, Prince Bao Dai, an absentee chief of state who preferred to lie in the Riviera sun. Undeterred by the widespread contempt for Bao Dai, Acheson had doggedly continued to risk American prestige in Indochina. Later he would ruefully recall that one State Department colleague, John Ohly, had warned him that the U.S. was moving into a position in which "our responsibilities tend to supplant rather than complement those of the French." America could become a scapegoat for the French and be sucked into direct intervention, said Ohly, noting that "These situations have a way of snowballing." In his memoirs Acheson commented: "I decided . . . that having put our hand to the plow, we would not look back."

By the time of Eisenhower's inaugural the United States was paying a third of French costs, shipping arms to Indochina, and providing two hundred U.S. Air Force technicians. Ike continued the aid, but it was no longer enough. The Vietnam crisis deepened. On the morning of that February press conference it had come to center around one battle, a classic engagement which would alter world history and affect the United States more profoundly than Shiloh or the Argonne. For seven years now, the French army had been kept off balance by Ho Chi Minh's brilliant generalissimo, General Vo Nguyen Giap. Baffled by Giap's guerrilla tactics, so unfamiliar to officers trained at Saint-Cyr-l' École, the French had vowed to lure the Viet Minh into a pitched battle. On November 20, 1953, they had dropped 15,000 parachute troops on a strategic point almost two hundred miles west of Hanoi. The position covered lines of communications linking China, Tonkin, and Laos. This was Thai country, and the name of the place was a combination of three Thai words: *dien* (big), *bien* (frontier) and *phu* (administrative center). Dienbienphu: a big administrative center on the frontier. No name could have been more ordinary.

Geographically, that part of Southeast Asia is mostly chaos: cliffs, jagged peaks, unfathomable jungle, impenetrable canyons, impassable rivers. Here and there, however, the face of the land is dimpled by relatively smooth hollows, the larger of which may be cleared and used for airstrips. Dienbienphu was such a basin. Shaped like a long oak leaf in which brooks represent the ribs of the leaf and a central stream the median line, it was eleven miles long and three miles wide. Hills darkened by forests surrounded Dienbienphu. The French paratroopers built an airfield and then a series of *porc-épics* (porcupines)—strongholds to protect the field and harass the enemy. Military strategists since the time of Machiavelli have urged commanders to seize high ground, pointing out that should one side become entrenched on it, it can crush the other side with its artillery. The French, however, failed to seize the crests overlooking Dienbienphu. Holding them against guerrillas would have been difficult, and the high command in Hanoi decided that it was unnecessary. In the Maison de France war correspondents were told that French artillery was superior to anything Giap could mount, and besides, the Viet Minh couldn't possibly drag cannon through the mountains studding the countryside all around.

The Maison de France was wrong. Since November, 90,000 Vietnamese peasants had been hauling batteries of 105-mm field guns across the savage land to Dienbienphu. By January the greater part of Giap's artillery was in position overlooking the plain of gray and yellow clay below, and on February 10 in Washington, as Eisenhower was answering questions about Indochina in the Indian Treaty Room, Viet Minh soldiers of the 57th Regiment, resting from their backbreaking toil, were looking down the moonlit slopes to the blockhouses shielding twelve sleeping French battalions. Later the guerrillas' commanding officer, Captain Hien, would tell how the flickering torches around the airstrip that night had reminded him of the flames of the little sticks of firewood traditionally left on the thresholds of huts in his village to honor the dead.

Giap opened the siege of Dienbienphu with a dawn bombardment on March 13. A smoke screen which the French laid down to hide the airfield was unsuccessful, and pilots began to call the shallow basin *"un pot de chambre."* Three days earlier, at another Wednesday press conference, a correspondent had reminded the President of an observation by Senator John Stennis of Mississippi. Stennis had warned that the presence of the Air Force technicians already in Vietnam might be enough to bring the United States into the war. Not so, said Ike; there would be no U.S. intervention in Indochina unless Congress exercised its constitutional right to declare war.

Historians may wonder why the question of American involvement was even being discussed. The United Nations had no commitments in Indochina, and until the recent past the United States had had nothing to do with it; the only President who had expressed a genuine interest in the place was Franklin Roosevelt, and he had wanted to see it freed from French colonial rule. Eisenhower had refused to widen one Asian war against Communists only a year before. He had pointed out that even an air strike at Dienbienphu would be hazardous; it might pit U.S. airmen against the Chinese air force. Chances of a decisive blow were slight anyhow. French military strength in Indochina was much smaller than the U.N. force in Korea.

With the exception of Eisenhower, however, most administration leaders did not see it that way. In their view, the United States, as the strongest power in the free world, was the leader of a global struggle against world Communism. Since the Korean armistice Indochina had been the scene of the only active conflict in it. If the Communists were victorious on one front, interventionists reasoned, the security of all fronts would be endangered. That was also the reasoning of the intellectual community; writing in *Daedalus*, Walt W. Rostow, professor of economic history at the Massachusetts Institute of Technology, argued:

> The balance of power in Eurasia could be lost to the United States by the movement of Soviet or Chinese ground forces. And, equally, it could be lost if, in hope or despair, men and women in the decisive regions of Eurasia should turn to Communism. . . . the survival of the United States . . . would be in jeopardy if we were to become a democratic island in a totalitarian sea.

The consensus was that as long as American troops had been engaged in Korea, sending the French money, guns, and advice had been enough. Now more was needed, the argument went; failure to provide it would endanger the free world.

Eisenhower had authorized larger payments to the French the previous September—$385,000,000 before the end of 1954. At that time Dulles had defined America's goal in Indochina as success for the Navarre Plan, named for the French commander there. This, Dulles had explained, would defeat "the organized body of Communist aggression by the end of the 1955 fighting season," leaving only mopping-up operations, "which could in 1956 be met for the most part" by Vietnamese troops. The Navarre Plan failed, but as late as January 4, 1954, when the President reviewed his forthcoming State of the Union message with the congressional leadership, no consideration had been given to the possibility of shipping U.S. troops to Indochina. Ike planned to ask congressional approval of continued military aid to France. A Republican senator asked whether this meant sending American boys to Vietnam. "No," the startled President replied. He said, "I can write in 'material assistance,'" and he did.

By the end of the third week in March the situation in Indochina had deteriorated. Dulles's faith in the French continued to be strong —on March 23 he predicted that they would win—but the Pentagon was not so sure. The news from Dienbienphu was bleak. Giap's guns on the rim of the basin had rendered the airfield virtually inoperable. Attempts to parachute supplies to the twelve surrounded battalions from C-54s were only partly successful. If the drops were made from 6,000 to 8,000 feet, half the material landed in the Viet lines, and at 4,000 feet Viet antiaircraft batteries hit most of the planes. On all sides enemy trenches nibbled toward the French strongpoints, splitting up here and there to allow the installation of automatic weapons. Diplomatic channels brought Washington an appeal from Paris for an American air strike to take the pressure off the isolated garrison, and on March 22 General Paul Ely, the French chief of staff, flew over to ask for it.

Ridgway was vehemently opposed. Once the use of American air power was approved, he said, dispatching infantry would only be a matter of time. He knew something of the terrain: rice paddies, jungle, an impossible road net, wretched communications. Even the harbors were poor. U.S. intervention would be a "tragic adventure." He sent this opinion to Eisenhower, he later wrote in *Soldier*, his memoirs, explaining that "to a man of his military experience its implications were immediately clear." But Radford, also a man of military experience, thought sending U.S. bombers was a good idea. And any doubts over where the Secretary of State stood were removed in a speech he delivered before the Overseas Press Club on Monday, March 29. Its tone says as much about cold war rhetoric as its text:

> Under the conditions of today, the imposition on Southeast Asia of the political system of Communist Russia and its Chinese Communist ally, by whatever means, would be a grave threat to the whole free community. The United States feels that the possibility should not be passively accepted, but should be met by united action. This might have serious risks, but these risks are far less than would face us a few years from now if we dare not be resolute today.

On Saturday Dulles conferred with the congressional leaders of both parties at the State Department to explain the need for collective defense of the French position—expeditions from Britain, Australia, and New Zealand, as well as the United States. He felt confident that he could frighten the Chinese Communists into forsaking Ho Chi Minh. That failing, he said, the Viet Minh must be wiped out. No compromise was possible, even in theory. One observer was left with the impression that the Secretary of State had "grave doubts whether the United States could survive the establishment of Communist power in Indochina."

Sunday evening Dulles joined Eisenhower and Radford in the President's oval study. The immediate issue before them was whether intervention was justified, and if so on what terms. In Paris Bidault was pressing Ambassador Dillon hard. It was a measure of French despair that they were asking for atomic bombs. Two aircraft carriers with nuclear weapons aboard were cruising in the Gulf of Tonkin with the Seventh Fleet, but virtually no one in Washington seriously considered using them.* In fact, Eisenhower forbade any air strike. He was willing to consider Dulles's "united action"—an allied effort—under certain circumstances. The French must agree to see the war through. They must grant complete independence to Vietnam, Cambodia, and Laos. Both the French and the Indochinese states must ask the allies—the U.S. and Britain—to come in. Lastly, the decisive step must be taken by Congress,

---

* The French had a different impression. See Jules Roy *La Bataille de Dien Bien Phu*, Paris 1963, 270 ff.

which had the power to declare war, rather than by the President, who did not. Dulles was to do what he could within that context, and after an exploratory exchange of cables between Eisenhower and Churchill (whose reservations were later to become even greater than Ike's), the Secretary of State took off to see whether he could put an alliance together in London and Paris.

Three days later the President added a metaphor to the language. Although reluctant to make any U.S. commitment in Vietnam, he remained a firm believer in cold war catechisms. He had read and approved Dulles's Overseas Press Club speech before its delivery. Much more than French prestige was at stake in Indochina, he told the correspondents at that week's press conference. A Communist triumph there would enlarge the Red empire and deprive the United States of vital raw materials. It could mean the loss to the free world of all Southeast Asia, followed by threats to the U.S. defense perimeter in the Pacific: Australia, New Zealand, the Philippines, Formosa, and Japan. He said: "You have a row of dominoes set up, and you knock over the first one, and what will happen to the last one is the certainty that it will go over very quickly. So you have a beginning of a disintegration that would have the most profound influences."

Dulles, back from Europe, felt the chances for swift intervention were bright. Whitehall and the Quai d'Orsay had seemed receptive to suggestions for united action. If there was any moment during the crisis in which substantial allied aid for the beleaguered Maison de France was a possibility, this was it. Churchill had not yet thrown his great weight against the idea. To get it, the French were ready to give up almost anything except the Arc de Triomphe (where noisy demonstrators were protesting the course of the war). Eisenhower seemed immovable, but he might have changed his mind; if he didn't, Congress could act.

It was precisely at this point in the drama that Richard Nixon moved to stage center. His motives were obscure then, and he has never clarified them. At the time he appeared to be the fiercest hawk in Washington, but there is a large body of opinion in the capital which held then, and holds now, that the Vice President was merely floating a trial balloon for the administration. The occasion for its launching was the annual convention of the American Society of Newspaper Editors in Washington on Friday, April 16. His remarks were supposedly made off the record, but they were too sensational to remain there. What should the United States do, he was asked, if the French withdrew their troops and abandoned Vietnam? Should U.S. soldiers take their place? Nixon answered that they should. The plight of the free world was desperate, he said; any further retreat in Asia was unthinkable. He prayed that the French would dig in and win. "But under the circumstances, if in order to avoid further Communist expansion in Asia and particularly in Indochina—if in order to avoid it we must take the risk now by putting American boys in, I believe that the Executive Branch has to take the politically unpopular position of facing up to it and doing it, and I personally would support such a decision."

Reaction was immediate. Some members of the administration may have been ready for a new war, but the newspapers weren't; editorials called on Ike to repudiate his Vice President. Congress wasn't ready; Nixon was accused of irresponsible chauvinism. Abroad, garbled reports of imminent U.S. troop movements triggered nervous reactions which shattered all possibilities of an allied expeditionary force. London decided to see what could be accomplished at a nineteen-nation conference on Asia due to open in Geneva later in the month. On Monday Dulles returned from Augusta, where Eisenhower was golfing, to tell the press that American intervention in Vietnam was "unlikely."

Late in April the French made their third and last appeal for help. Dulles and Radford were in Paris on NATO business. Bidault begged the secretary for an American air strike. Otherwise, he said, Dienbienphu would fall. Dulles said he would sleep on it, but he was just being polite. Eisenhower had told him once more that only an act of Congress could put American servicemen in Indochina. Besides, Dulles could read the Paris newspapers. All hope for the beleaguered French garrison had been abandoned.

By now the agony of Dienbienphu had captured the imagination of the world: editors were playing the most fragmentary dispatches from Vietnam on their front pages. The French code name for the operation, one learned, was Vautour (Vulture). Page one maps depicted the strongpoints within the surrounded fortress—little hills named Anne-Marie, Gabrielle, Dominique, Isabelle, Huguette, Françoise, Claudine, Béatrice, and the twin hillocks of Eliane One and Eliane Four—"the Lollobrigidas." Christian de Castries, the senior French officer, had been promoted from colonel to brigadier on the theory that a hero ought to be a general. Geneviève de Galard-

Terraube, a French nurse, had refused to board the last plane back to Hanoi; she became "the Angel of Dienbienphu." Several stories told how de Castries, discovering that his part of the post was doomed, had called down artillery fire upon himself.

Many accounts of the siege were apocryphal. De Castries sent no orders to his artillery because he had no artillery left. The Beau Geste stories being featured in American newspapers had no connection with actual conditions in the entrenched camp. War correspondents were not to blame, for the French high command was also uninformed. By Easter Sunday, April 18, when beribboned officers from the Maison de France sang their annual hallelujahs in Hanoi Cathedral, they no longer knew much about their Vautour. Observation planes arriving overhead to see what was happening to the post were either destroyed by Giap's flak or driven away. The whole of the airstrip was being raked by Viet machine guns. A final attempt by C-54s to parachute supplies—together with de Castries's brigadier's stars, brandy to celebrate his promotion, and boxes of Croix de Guerre and Légion d'Honneur awards—failed completely. Recoilless guns on blockhouses, now in Viet hands, picked off Frenchmen pursuing the parachutes, and next morning the Viet Minh radio triumphantly announced the capture of everything dropped, including the brandy.

The men of Dienbienphu were now wretched beyond imagining. Half of them had already fallen. Alternately baked by the pitiless tropical sun and wrapped in sheets of rain, they lay burrowed under mounds of excrement and decaying corpses. Futile counterattacks on the lost emplacements left them in despair. Giap's barrages of 105s never slackened. Zagging Viet trenches continued to inch toward the French, bringing enemy infantry closer. For a while hopeful rumors had predicted a relief column from Hanoi, then an American air armada. The reports were believed by the men, by their officers, and even by de Castries, who found it hard to accept the fact that Navarre had sent him here to die. Now in April he knew: Hanoi ordered him to destroy all arms and supplies before they could fall into enemy hands. His men, he was told, were to be rallied for a last stand by the knowledge that they were holding up a Viet battle corps and defending the honor of France.

On May 7, the fifty-sixth day of siege, the tricolor over Dienbienphu was replaced by a white flag and then by the Viet Minh colors, red with a star of gold. The honor of France would never be the same again. In Geneva the multination conference on Asia had already begun. There was still talk of a U.S. expeditionary force. "No decision has been made to send American troops to Indochina," said Ed Murrow in a broadcast on the conference, "but neither has a decision been made not to send troops under any circumstances. And the second statement may prove to be more important than the first. If it comes down to the bare choice of losing Indochina to the Communists or saving it, some form of intervention may prove inescapable."

Then Dulles informed the conferring powers that although Indochina was important, it was not essential to the salvation of Southeast Asia from Communist domination. That cleared the way for a compromise. Vietnam was to be temporarily divided at the 17th Parallel, with the understanding that free elections in both halves of the country would reunite it on July 20, 1956. It was the best of a bad bargain, wrote Robert J. Donovan of the *New York Herald Tribune;* the domino had been kept "from going all the way over with a crash."

Meanwhile the Secretary of State's attempts to put together an Asian alliance continued, spurred by Eisenhower's declaration that "the free world" knew that "aggression in Korea and Southeast Asia" were "threats to the whole free community to be met only through united action." In September Dulles's mission ended successfully in Manila, where delegates from Australia, Britain, France, New Zealand, Pakistan, Thailand, the Philippines, and the United States pledged a joint defense against aggression. Article Four of their pact, creating the Southeast Asia Treaty Organization, committed them to act together if any one of them was attacked; provision was made to counter not only external threats but also internal subversion. A separate protocol extended the treaty's protection to Vietnam, Cambodia, and Laos.

American diplomacy seemed to be riding high. Few thought it important that the Geneva agreement had not been signed by representatives from either South Vietnam or the United States—Dulles's official role at the conference had been that of an observer—and that neither, therefore, was bound by the pledge to hold elections in Vietnam two years hence. Thus was set a historic trap. Failure to hold elections would lead to a renewal of hostilities. The difference would be that this time the Viet insurgency would be branded "aggression"—and thus a direct challenge to every member of the alliance forged in Manila. John Ohly's "snowballing" had begun.

In October the Secretary of State, speaking with great deliberation, told the cabinet: "The United States has never been so respected nor had such good relations as now."

In a private conversation afterward he said of Vietnam: "We have a clean base there, without the taint of colonialism. Dienbienphu was a blessing in disguise."

Portrait of an American

NORMA JEAN BAKER

SHE WAS THE BASTARD DAUGHTER of a paranoid schizophrenic—Gladys Pearl Baker, a film cutter for MGM, Paramount, and Columbia studios who was in and out of asylums all her life. Madness also claimed both Gladys's parents and her brother, who killed himself. She named her unwanted baby after Norma Talmadge, a silent star of that year: 1926. Years later, when the infant was grown, the casting director at Twentieth Century-Fox rechristened her Marilyn Monroe. Once, before she became famous, Marilyn tried to telephone the man who had fathered her. A secretary said, "He doesn't want to see you. He suggests you see his lawyer in Los Angeles if you have some complaint."

She hung up without replying, but if ever a girl emerging from childhood had reason to complain, she did. At one time or another she had lived with twelve sets of foster parents. Their standards varied wildly. In one home she was given empty whiskey bottles as toys; two others were ruled by religious fanatics. In one of them she was taught to sing "Jesus Loves Me" in time of trial, punished with a razor strop for thinking impure thoughts, and, when she undressed with a little boy to compare the differences in their bodies, called a slut. She loved a dog; a neighbor killed it. On a visit, her grandmother tried to smother her with a pillow. She spent twenty-one months in an orphanage, and when she became sixteen she married an older man she didn't love to escape her wretched situation as a ward of the state. Already she was a stammerer, a chronic insomniac—and a girl with a desperate, insatiable yearning to be wanted.

Her first husband taught her sexual ecstasy on a Murphy bed. She gloried in it and would pursue it for the rest of her life, but it wasn't enough; she craved the adoration of millions. As a child she had spent Saturday afternoons in Grauman's Egyptian Theatre, watching Bette Davis in *Jezebel* and Norma Shearer in *Marie Antoinette* and wishing she were up there on the screen. Outside, she would try to fit her feet into the concrete prints of Clara Bow, Janet Gaynor, and Gloria Swanson. After *Yank* ran a picture of her in an article on women in war work, she was given a screen test. In it she entered a room, sat down, and lit a cigarette. The first man to see the rushes said: "I got a cold chill. This girl had something I hadn't seen since silent pictures. This is the first girl who looked like one of those lush stars of the silent era. Every frame of the test radiated sex."

Billy Wilder, who later directed her in *Some Like It Hot*, called it "flesh impact," and said the only other stars who had it were Clara Bow, Jean Harlow, and Rita Hayworth. Audiences first saw it in a Marx Brothers comedy, *Love Happy*. Playing a bit part, Marilyn came swaying into the office of a private detective played by Groucho and said anxiously, "Some men are following me." Suddenly everyone was tremendously interested in her problem. After *The Asphalt Jungle* and *All About Eve* had made her a celebrity, that provocative walk was heavily insured by Lloyd's of London.

She was worth it. Her twenty-three films between 1950 and 1961 grossed 200 million dollars. Only Brigitte Bardot of France approached her in popularity. Each week on an average Marilyn received five thousand letters, a score of them proposals of marriage. In Turkey a distraught admirer slashed his wrists when she didn't accept him. *Pravda* and the Vatican's *L'Osservatore Romano* agreed that she symbolized a sinful society. Nunnally Johnson called her "a phenomenon of nature, like Niagara Falls and the Grand Canyon." To *Life* she was "a busty Bernhardt," and her voluptuous dimensions—37.5-23-36—were familiar to millions of men who didn't know those of their own wives. At various times her immense appeal was attributed to her breathless voice, her incandescence, her ash-blonde hair, her moist-lipped open mouth, her dreamy blue eyes, and that tremulous gait.

It was more elusive than that—and more earthy. Marilyn's need to be desired was so great that she could make love to a camera. Because of this, her lust aroused lust in audiences, sometimes even among women. There was nothing subtle about it. She was no tease. She was prepared, and even eager, to give what she offered. By the time she was fourteen the fathers of her friends had pawed her, and one summer an off-duty policeman had cut through a screen door to get at her. She never pretended to be shocked or even resentful.

She became the mistress of a theatrical agent. He lost weight; his physician told him he had a weak heart and must avoid strenuous exercise; but Marilyn's demands increased until he collapsed while with her in Palm Springs and died. Once, when she was married to Joe DiMaggio and he was away, she slipped on moccasins and prowled the foggy streets of San Francisco looking for a companion. Costarring with Yves Montand in *Let's Make Love* while she was Mrs. Arthur Miller, she seduced Montand on the set—and Miller knew it.

She exulted in her carnality. As a rising star she posed naked for a calendar. She didn't need the fifty dollars; she just liked the idea. ("You mean you didn't have anything on?" a scandalized woman reporter asked. "Oh yes," said Marilyn, "I had the radio on.") Acquiring from the photographer transparencies which showed her pubic hair, she gave them to DiMaggio as a wedding present. "Slugger," as she called him, was rather prim about sex, and she offended him deeply by straddling a New York sidewalk grating, during the filming of *The Seven-Year Itch*, until a gathering of cheering fans saw a blast of air toss her skirt above her hips. To her it had been one of the most exciting moments of her life.

In the last days of her life she was poring over *Playboy* prints of her taken in the nude. It was her ambition to have these pictures appear simultaneously on the covers of girlie magazines all over the world. She anticipated the coming of X-rated movies and yearned for it. When John Huston cut a shot of her exposed breasts from *The Misfits*, she was crushed. "Let's get the people away from the television sets," she said. "I love to do things the censors won't pass. After all, what are we all here for, just to stand and let it pass us by? Gradually they'll let down the censorship—sadly, probably not in my lifetime."

She became as big a star as Chaplin and Garbo, she gave a command performance for the Queen of England—and yet a feeling of achievement eluded her. Her three marriages ended disastrously; she suffered two miscarriages and couldn't have a child. Hollywood kept casting her in dumb blonde roles. She fled eastward and studied serious acting with the Strasbergs, but after two years she returned to California, still searching for the unattainable.

The release of *Some Like It Hot* in January 1959 was a personal triumph for her, but under the glitter there was a dark side the public had not yet seen. She was drinking heavily and had become addicted to barbiturates. Never prompt, she had become so unpunctual that she had alienated her fellow actors; Jack Lemmon and Tony Curtis, playing a pair of merry transvestites, had had to stand around all day waiting for her to appear. Attempts to wake her would begin at 6:30 A.M. with vats of black coffee and masseurs. Her snoring body would be rolled back and forth as attendants made her up horizontally. Sometimes shooting wouldn't begin until 4 P.M.; sometimes it would be postponed until the next morning, when the ritual would begin again.

She wouldn't learn her lines. In one scene she was supposed to say, "It's me, Sugar" at a certain moment. That required forty-seven takes. She seemed to be wholly indifferent to the inconvenience and the expense, which would add as much as a million dollars to the production costs of a movie. Once an assistant director knocked on the door of her dressing room and told her that the other actors were waiting. Marilyn replied, "Go fuck yourself."

Finally Fox fired her for being absent for all but five days during seven weeks of shooting *Something's Got to Give*. It was the summer of 1962, she was thirty-six years old, and she seemed to have lost her zest for life. To a *Life* reporter she said: "It might be kind of a relief to be finished. It's sort of like, I don't know what kind of a yard dash you're running, but then you're at the finish line, and you sort of sigh—you've made it! But you never have—you have to start all over again."

Her last affair was with a Washingtonian, a lawyer and a public man. She was afraid of destroying his political career, afraid that she was pregnant by him—and, finally, furious at him because he wanted her to join him for an evening with some friends and two prostitutes. She put a stack of Sinatra records on a spindle, swallowed all the Nembutals in her medicine cabinet, and sank into a lethal coma.

Her corpse, Coroner's Case No. 81128, lay unclaimed at the Los Angeles County Morgue until Joe DiMaggio arrived to arrange the funeral. Marilyn had given no thought to the disposal of her coffin, but it would be incorrect to say that she had not anticipated her last act. She had, and she had left exact instructions for it. As she had requested, her makeup was by Allan Snyder, her costume by Margie Plecher, and her hair style by Agnes Flanagan.

Chronology

1932	The Bonus Riot in Washington
	15,000,000 jobless
	Election of FDR
	Rumors of revolution
1933	Collapse of the nation's banks
	FDR's Hundred Days
	Back from the brink
1934	J. Edgar Hoover and *Famous Funnies*
	Black blizzards
	Dr. Townsend, Father Coughlin, and Huey Long
1935	The Second Hundred Days
	The birth of swing music
	The rise of John L. Lewis
	The Supreme Court challenges FDR
1936	The Liberty League: "Save the Constitution!"
	Gone With the Wind
	FDR routs Landon and the *Literary Digest*
1937	The Supreme Court "pack" plan
	Birth of Congress's conservative coalition
	Sit-down strikes in Detroit
	Japanese sink the U.S.S. *Panay*
	Isolationism at its peak
1938	Munich and H. V. Kaltenborn
	New England hurricane
	Orson Welles's Martian broadcast
1939	New York World's Fair
	World War II starts. Lindbergh: "Keep out!"
1940	The Fall of France
	America First; "God Bless America"
	Einstein writes FDR a letter
	Willkie vs. the Champ
1941	House Bill 1776: Lend-Lease
	Nazi sub torpedoes the *Reuben James*
	CCNY dismisses Bertrand Russell
	Marian Anderson sings at the Lincoln Memorial
	Pearl Harbor: "This is no drill"
1942	Retreat in the Pacific; Midway; Guadalcanal
	GIs invade North Africa
	At home: "I'll Walk Alone"
	The ordeal of the Issei and Nisei
1943	Salerno, Cassino, and Tarawa
	At home: Frank Sinatra and Henry J. Kaiser
1944	Anzio, Normandy, the Bulge
	Saipan and Leyte Gulf
1945	Iwo Jima and Okinawa
	The U.N. Charter
	FDR dies; Truman is President
	V-E Day
	Hiroshima and Nagasaki
	V-J Day
1946	Postwar inflation and strikes
	"Wanna-go-home" riots
	Churchill uses "Iron Curtain" in Missouri
1947	The Truman Doctrine and the Marshall Plan
	A New Look in fashions
1948	The Kinsey Report
	The Berlin airlift
	Dixiecrats and Henry Wallace's Progressives
	Truman beats Dewey
1949	William J. Levitt's first Levittown
	First report of flying saucers
	TV: Gorgeous George and skating derbies
	China becomes Red China
	Russia has the Bomb
1950	The conviction of Alger Hiss
	The rise of Joe McCarthy
	War in Korea; Inchon; Red China attacks
1951	Direct Distance Dialing starts
	The Great Debate
	MacArthur is relieved
	The age of Mickey Spillane
	The silent generation emerges
	TV replaces radio as popular entertainment
	Kefauver crime hearings
1952	The hydrogen bomb
	Scandals shake Truman administration
	Nixon's "Checkers" speech
	Ike beats Stevenson, who is "too c to cry"
1953	Massive retaliation; bigger bang a buck
	Stalin dies; peace in Korea
	The death of Taft
1954	*McCall's* coins "togetherness"
	The Bricker amendment
	The Army-McCarthy hearings